# University Casebook Series

May, 1993

---

**ACCOUNTING AND THE LAW, Fourth Edition (1978), with Problems Pamphlet (Successor to Dohr, Phillips, Thompson & Warren)**

George C. Thompson, Professor, Columbia University Graduate School of Business.
Robert Whitman, Professor of Law, University of Connecticut.
Ellis L. Phillips, Jr., Member of the New York Bar.
William C. Warren, Professor of Law Emeritus, Columbia University.

**ACCOUNTING FOR LAWYERS, MATERIALS ON (1980)**

David R. Herwitz, Professor of Law, Harvard University.

**ADMINISTRATIVE LAW, Eighth Edition (1987), with 1993 Case Supplement and 1983 Problems Supplement (Supplement edited in association with Paul R. Verkuil, Dean and Professor of Law, Tulane University)**

Walter Gellhorn, University Professor Emeritus, Columbia University.
Clark Byse, Professor of Law, Harvard University.
Peter L. Strauss, Professor of Law, Columbia University.
Todd D. Rakoff, Professor of Law, Harvard University.
Roy A. Schotland, Professor of Law, Georgetown University.

**ADMIRALTY, Third Edition (1987), with 1991 Statute and Rule Supplement**

Jo Desha Lucas, Professor of Law, University of Chicago.

**ADVOCACY, see also Lawyering Process**

**AGENCY, see also Enterprise Organization**

**AGENCY—PARTNERSHIPS, Fourth Edition (1987)**

Abridgement from Conard, Knauss & Siegel's Enterprise Organization, Fourth Edition.

**AGENCY AND PARTNERSHIPS (1987)**

Melvin A. Eisenberg, Professor of Law, University of California, Berkeley.

**ANTITRUST: FREE ENTERPRISE AND ECONOMIC ORGANIZATION, Sixth Edition (1983), with 1983 Problems in Antitrust Supplement and 1992 Case Supplement**

Louis B. Schwartz, Professor of Law, University of Pennsylvania.
John J. Flynn, Professor of Law, University of Utah.
Harry First, Professor of Law, New York University.

**BANKRUPTCY, Third Edition (1993)**

Robert L. Jordan, Professor of Law, University of California, Los Angeles.
William D. Warren, Professor of Law, University of California, Los Angeles.

**BANKRUPTCY AND DEBTOR–CREDITOR LAW, Second Edition (1988)**

Theodore Eisenberg, Professor of Law, Cornell University.

**BUSINESS ASSOCIATIONS, AGENCY, PARTNERSHIPS, AND CORPORATIONS (1991), with 1993 Supplement**

William A. Klein, Professor of Law, University of California, Los Angeles.
Mark Ramseyer, Professor of Law, University of California, Los Angeles.

**BUSINESS CRIME (1990), with 1992 Case Supplement**

Harry First, Professor of Law, New York University.

**BUSINESS ORGANIZATION, see also Enterprise Organization**

**BUSINESS PLANNING (1991)**

Franklin Gevurtz, Professor of Law, McGeorge School of Law.

**BUSINESS PLANNING, Temporary Second Edition (1984)**

David R. Herwitz, Professor of Law, Harvard University.

**BUSINESS TORTS (1972)**

Milton Handler, Professor of Law Emeritus, Columbia University.

**CHILDREN IN THE LEGAL SYSTEM (1983), with 1990 Supplement (Supplement edited in association with Elizabeth S. Scott, Professor of Law, University of Virginia)**

Walter Wadlington, Professor of Law, University of Virginia.
Charles H. Whitebread, Professor of Law, University of Southern California.
Samuel Davis, Professor of Law, University of Georgia.

**CIVIL PROCEDURE, see Procedure**

**CIVIL RIGHTS ACTIONS (1988), with 1992 Supplement**

Peter W. Low, Professor of Law, University of Virginia.
John C. Jeffries, Jr., Professor of Law, University of Virginia.

**CLINIC, see also Lawyering Process**

**COMMERCIAL AND DEBTOR–CREDITOR LAW: SELECTED STATUTES, 1992 EDITION**

**COMMERCIAL LAW, Third Edition (1992)**

Robert L. Jordan, Professor of Law, University of California, Los Angeles.
William D. Warren, Professor of Law, University of California, Los Angeles.

**COMMERCIAL LAW, Fifth Edition (1993)**

E. Allan Farnsworth, Professor of Law, Columbia University.
John O. Honnold, Professor of Law Emeritus, University of Pennsylvania.
Curtis R. Reitz, Professor of Law, University of Pennsylvania.
Steven L. Harris, Professor of Law, University of Illinois.
Charles Mooney, Jr., Professor of Law, University of Pennsylvania.

**COMMERCIAL PAPER, see also Negotiable Instruments**

**COMMERCIAL PAPER AND BANK DEPOSITS AND COLLECTIONS (1967), with Statutory Supplement**

William D. Hawkland, Professor of Law, University of Illinois.

**COMMERCIAL TRANSACTIONS—Principles and Policies, Second Edition (1991)**

Alan Schwartz, Professor of Law, Yale University.
Robert E. Scott, Professor of Law, University of Virginia.

**COMPARATIVE LAW, Fifth Edition (1988)**

Rudolf B. Schlesinger, Professor of Law, Hastings College of the Law.
Hans W. Baade, Professor of Law, University of Texas.
Mirjan P. Damaska, Professor of Law, Yale Law School.
Peter E. Herzog, Professor of Law, Syracuse University.

**COMPETITIVE PROCESS, LEGAL REGULATION OF THE, Revised Fourth Edition (1991), with 1991 Selected Statutes Supplement**

Edmund W. Kitch, Professor of Law, University of Virginia.
Harvey S. Perlman, Dean of the Law School, University of Nebraska.

**CONFLICT OF LAWS, Ninth Edition (1990), with 1992 Supplement**

Willis L. M. Reese, Professor of Law, Columbia University.
Maurice Rosenberg, Professor of Law, Columbia University.
Peter Hay, Professor of Law, University of Illinois.

**CONSTITUTIONAL LAW, CIVIL LIBERTY AND INDIVIDUAL RIGHTS, Second Edition (1982), with 1992 Supplement**

William Cohen, Professor of Law, Stanford University.
John Kaplan, Professor of Law, Stanford University.

**CONSTITUTIONAL LAW, Ninth Edition (1993), with 1993 Supplement**

William Cohen, Professor of Law, Stanford University.
Jonathan D. Varat, Professor of Law, University of California, Los Angeles.

**CONSTITUTIONAL LAW, Twelfth Edition (1991), with 1993 Supplement (Supplement edited in association with Frederick F. Schauer, Professor, Harvard University)**

Gerald Gunther, Professor of Law, Stanford University.

**CONSTITUTIONAL LAW, INDIVIDUAL RIGHTS IN, Fifth Edition (1992) (Reprinted from CONSTITUTIONAL LAW, Twelfth Edition), with 1993 Supplement (Supplement edited in association with Frederick F. Schauer, Professor, Harvard University)**

Gerald Gunther, Professor of Law, Stanford University.

**CONSUMER TRANSACTIONS, Second Edition (1991), with Selected Statutes and Regulations Supplement**

Michael M. Greenfield, Professor of Law, Washington University.

**CONTRACT LAW AND ITS APPLICATION, Fourth Edition (1988)**

Arthur Rosett, Professor of Law, University of California, Los Angeles.

**CONTRACT LAW, STUDIES IN, Fourth Edition (1991)**

Edward J. Murphy, Professor of Law, University of Notre Dame.
Richard E. Speidel, Professor of Law, Northwestern University.

# UNIVERSITY CASEBOOK SERIES—Continued

**CONTRACTS, Sixth Edition (1993)**

John P. Dawson, late Professor of Law, Harvard University.
William Burnett Harvey, Professor of Law and Political Science, Boston University.
Stanley D. Henderson, Professor of Law, University of Virginia.

**CONTRACTS, Fourth Edition (1988)**

E. Allan Farnsworth, Professor of Law, Columbia University.
William F. Young, Professor of Law, Columbia University.

**CONTRACTS, Selections on (statutory materials) (1992)**

**CONTRACTS, Second Edition (1978), with Statutory and Administrative Law Supplement (1978)**

Ian R. Macneil, Professor of Law, Cornell University.

**COPYRIGHT, PATENTS AND TRADEMARKS, see also Competitive Process; see also Selected Statutes and International Agreements**

**COPYRIGHT, PATENT, TRADEMARK AND RELATED STATE DOCTRINES, Revised Third Edition (1993), with 1991 Selected Statutes Supplement and 1981 Problem Supplement**

Paul Goldstein, Professor of Law, Stanford University.

**COPYRIGHT, Unfair Competition, and Other Topics Bearing on the Protection of Literary, Musical, and Artistic Works, Fifth Edition (1990), with 1993 Statutory and Case Supplement**

Ralph S. Brown, Jr., Professor of Law, Yale University.
Robert C. Denicola, Professor of Law, University of Nebraska.

**CORPORATE ACQUISITIONS, The Law and Finance of (1986), with 1992 Supplement**

Ronald J. Gilson, Professor of Law, Stanford University.

**CORPORATE FINANCE, Brudney and Chirelstein's Fourth Edition (1993)**

Victor Brudney, Professor of Law, Harvard University.
William W. Bratton, Jr., Professor of Law, Rutgers University, Newark.

**CORPORATION LAW, BASIC, Third Edition (1989), with Documentary Supplement**

Detlev F. Vagts, Professor of Law, Harvard University.

**CORPORATIONS, see also Enterprise Organization and Business Organization**

**CORPORATIONS, Sixth Edition—Concise (1988), with 1993 Case Supplement and 1992 Statutory Supplement**

William L. Cary, late Professor of Law, Columbia University.
Melvin Aron Eisenberg, Professor of Law, University of California, Berkeley.

**CORPORATIONS, Sixth Edition—Unabridged (1988), with 1993 Case Supplement and 1992 Statutory Supplement**

William L. Cary, late Professor of Law, Columbia University.
Melvin Aron Eisenberg, Professor of Law, University of California, Berkeley.

**CORPORATIONS AND BUSINESS ASSOCIATIONS—STATUTES, RULES, AND FORMS, 1993 Edition**

**CORRECTIONS, see Sentencing**

**CREDITORS' RIGHTS, see also Debtor–Creditor Law**

**CRIMINAL JUSTICE ADMINISTRATION, Fourth Edition (1991), with 1993 Supplement**

Frank W. Miller, Professor of Law, Washington University.
Robert O. Dawson, Professor of Law, University of Texas.
George E. Dix, Professor of Law, University of Texas.
Raymond I. Parnas, Professor of Law, University of California, Davis.

**CRIMINAL LAW, Fifth Edition (1992)**

Andre A. Moenssens, Professor of Law, University of Richmond.
Fred E. Inbau, Professor of Law Emeritus, Northwestern University.
Ronald J. Bacigal, Professor of Law, University of Richmond.

**CRIMINAL LAW AND APPROACHES TO THE STUDY OF LAW, Second Edition (1991)**

John M. Brumbaugh, Professor of Law, University of Maryland.

**CRIMINAL LAW, Second Edition (1986)**

Peter W. Low, Professor of Law, University of Virginia.
John C. Jeffries, Jr., Professor of Law, University of Virginia.
Richard C. Bonnie, Professor of Law, University of Virginia.

**CRIMINAL LAW, Fifth Edition (1993)**

Lloyd L. Weinreb, Professor of Law, Harvard University.

**CRIMINAL LAW AND PROCEDURE, Seventh Edition (1989)**

Ronald N. Boyce, Professor of Law, University of Utah.
Rollin M. Perkins, Professor of Law Emeritus, University of California, Hastings College of the Law.

**CRIMINAL PROCEDURE, Fourth Edition (1992), with 1993 Supplement**

James B. Haddad, late Professor of Law, Northwestern University.
James B. Zagel, Chief, Criminal Justice Division, Office of Attorney General of Illinois.
Gary L. Starkman, Assistant U.S. Attorney, Northern District of Illinois.
William J. Bauer, Chief Judge of the U.S. Court of Appeals, Seventh Circuit.

**CRIMINAL PROCESS, Fifth Edition (1993), with 1992 Supplement**

Lloyd L. Weinreb, Professor of Law, Harvard University.

**CRIMINAL PROCESS, PART ONE—INVESTIGATION (1993) (Reprint of Chapters 1–6 of Weinreb's CRIMINAL PROCESS, Fifth Edition)**

**CRIMINAL PROCESS, PART TWO—PROSECUTION (1993) (Reprint of Chapters 7–18 of Weinreb's CRIMINAL PROCESS, Fifth Edition)**

**DAMAGES, Second Edition (1952)**

Charles T. McCormick, late Professor of Law, University of Texas.
William F. Fritz, late Professor of Law, University of Texas.

**DECEDENTS' ESTATES AND TRUSTS, see also Family Property Law**

**DECEDENTS' ESTATES AND TRUSTS, Eighth Edition (1993)**

John Ritchie, late Professor of Law, University of Virginia.
Neill H. Alford, Jr., Professor of Law, University of Virginia.
Richard W. Effland, late Professor of Law, Arizona State University.
Joel C. Dobris, Professor of Law, University of California, Davis.

**DISPUTE RESOLUTION, Processes of (1989)**

John S. Murray, President and Executive Director of The Conflict Clinic, Inc., George Mason University.
Alan Scott Rau, Professor of Law, University of Texas.
Edward F. Sherman, Professor of Law, University of Texas.

**DOMESTIC RELATIONS, see also Family Law**

**DOMESTIC RELATIONS, Second Edition (1990), with 1993 Supplement**

Walter Wadlington, Professor of Law, University of Virginia.

**EMPLOYMENT DISCRIMINATION, Third Edition (1993)**

Joel W. Friedman, Professor of Law, Tulane University.
George M. Strickler, Professor of Law, Tulane University.

**EMPLOYMENT LAW, Second Edition (1991), with 1992 Statutory Supplement and 1992 Case Supplement**

Mark A. Rothstein, Professor of Law, University of Houston.
Andria S. Knapp, Visiting Professor of Law, Golden Gate University.
Lance Liebman, Professor of Law, Harvard University.

**ENERGY LAW (1983), with 1991 Case Supplement**

Donald N. Zillman, Professor of Law, University of Utah.
Laurence Lattman, Dean of Mines and Engineering, University of Utah.

**ENTERPRISE ORGANIZATION, Fourth Edition (1987), with 1987 Corporation and Partnership Statutes, Rules and Forms Supplement**

Alfred F. Conard, Professor of Law, University of Michigan.
Robert L. Knauss, Dean of the Law School, University of Houston.
Stanley Siegel, Professor of Law, University of California, Los Angeles.

**ENVIRONMENTAL POLICY LAW, Second Edition (1991)**

Thomas J. Schoenbaum, Professor of Law, University of Georgia.
Ronald H. Rosenberg, Professor of Law, College of William and Mary.

**EQUITY, see also Remedies**

**EQUITY, RESTITUTION AND DAMAGES, Second Edition (1974)**

Robert Childres, late Professor of Law, Northwestern University.
William F. Johnson, Jr., Professor of Law, New York University.

**ESTATE PLANNING, Second Edition (1982), with 1985 Case, Text and Documentary Supplement**

David Westfall, Professor of Law, Harvard University.

**ETHICS, see Legal Ethics, Legal Profession, Professional Responsibility, and Social Responsibilities**

**ETHICS OF LAWYERING, THE LAW AND (1990)**

Geoffrey C. Hazard, Jr., Professor of Law, Yale University.
Susan P. Koniak, Professor of Law, University of Pittsburgh.

**INTERNATIONAL LAW, see also Transnational Legal Problems, Transnational Business Problems, and United Nations Law**

**INTERNATIONAL LAW IN CONTEMPORARY PERSPECTIVE (1981), with Essay Supplement**

Myres S. McDougal, Professor of Law, Yale University.
W. Michael Reisman, Professor of Law, Yale University.

**INTERNATIONAL LEGAL SYSTEM, Third Edition (1988), with Documentary Supplement**

Joseph Modeste Sweeney, Professor of Law, University of California, Hastings.
Covey T. Oliver, Professor of Law, University of Pennsylvania.
Noyes E. Leech, Professor of Law Emeritus, University of Pennsylvania.

**INTRODUCTION TO LAW, see also Legal Method, On Law in Courts, and Dynamics of American Law**

**INTRODUCTION TO THE STUDY OF LAW (1970)**

E. Wayne Thode, late Professor of Law, University of Utah.
Leon Lebowitz, Professor of Law, University of Texas.
Lester J. Mazor, Professor of Law, University of Utah.

**JUDICIAL CODE and Rules of Procedure in the Federal Courts, Students' Edition, 1993 Revision**

Daniel J. Meltzer, Professor of Law, Harvard University.
David L. Shapiro, Professor of Law, Harvard University.

**JURISPRUDENCE (Temporary Edition Hardbound) (1949)**

Lon L. Fuller, late Professor of Law, Harvard University.

**JUVENILE, see also Children**

**JUVENILE JUSTICE PROCESS, Third Edition (1985)**

Frank W. Miller, Professor of Law, Washington University.
Robert O. Dawson, Professor of Law, University of Texas.
George E. Dix, Professor of Law, University of Texas.
Raymond I. Parnas, Professor of Law, University of California, Davis.

**LABOR LAW, Eleventh Edition (1991), with 1993 Statutory Supplement and 1992 Case Supplement**

Archibald Cox, Professor of Law, Harvard University.
Derek C. Bok, President, Harvard University.
Robert A. Gorman, Professor of Law, University of Pennsylvania.
Matthew W. Finkin, Professor of Law, University of Illinois.

**LABOR LAW, Second Edition (1982), with Statutory Supplement**

Clyde W. Summers, Professor of Law, University of Pennsylvania.
Harry H. Wellington, Dean of the Law School, Yale University.
Alan Hyde, Professor of Law, Rutgers University.

**LAND FINANCING, Third Edition (1985)**

Norman Penney, late Professor of Law, Cornell University.
Richard F. Broude, Member of the California Bar.
Roger Cunningham, Professor of Law, University of Michigan.

### LAW AND MEDICINE (1980)

Walter Wadlington, Professor of Law and Professor of Legal Medicine, University of Virginia.

Jon R. Waltz, Professor of Law, Northwestern University.

Roger B. Dworkin, Professor of Law, Indiana University, and Professor of Biomedical History, University of Washington.

### LAW, LANGUAGE AND ETHICS (1972)

William R. Bishin, Professor of Law, University of Southern California.

Christopher D. Stone, Professor of Law, University of Southern California.

### LAW, SCIENCE AND MEDICINE (1984), with 1989 Supplement

Judith C. Areen, Professor of Law, Georgetown University.

Patricia A. King, Professor of Law, Georgetown University.

Steven P. Goldberg, Professor of Law, Georgetown University.

Alexander M. Capron, Professor of Law, University of Southern California.

### LAWYERING PROCESS (1978), with Civil Problem Supplement and Criminal Problem Supplement

Gary Bellow, Professor of Law, Harvard University.

Bea Moulton, Professor of Law, Arizona State University.

### LEGAL ETHICS (1992)

Deborah Rhode, Professor of Law, Stanford University.

David Luban, Professor of Law, University of Maryland.

### LEGAL METHOD (1980)

Harry W. Jones, Professor of Law Emeritus, Columbia University.

John M. Kernochan, Professor of Law, Columbia University.

Arthur W. Murphy, Professor of Law, Columbia University.

### LEGAL METHODS (1969)

Robert N. Covington, Professor of Law, Vanderbilt University.

E. Blythe Stason, late Professor of Law, Vanderbilt University.

John W. Wade, Professor of Law, Vanderbilt University.

Elliott E. Cheatham, late Professor of Law, Vanderbilt University.

Theodore A. Smedley, Professor of Law, Vanderbilt University.

### LEGAL PROFESSION, THE, Responsibility and Regulation, Second Edition (1988)

Geoffrey C. Hazard, Jr., Professor of Law, Yale University.

Deborah L. Rhode, Professor of Law, Stanford University.

### LEGISLATION (1993)

William D. Popkin, Professor of Law, Indiana University at Bloomington.

### LEGISLATION, Fourth Edition (1982) (by Fordham)

Horace E. Read, late Vice President, Dalhousie University.

John W. MacDonald, Professor of Law Emeritus, Cornell Law School.

Jefferson B. Fordham, Professor of Law, University of Utah.

William J. Pierce, Professor of Law, University of Michigan.

**LEGISLATIVE AND ADMINISTRATIVE PROCESSES, Second Edition (1981)**

Hans A. Linde, Judge, Supreme Court of Oregon.
George Bunn, Professor of Law, University of Wisconsin.
Fredericka Paff, Professor of Law, University of Wisconsin.
W. Lawrence Church, Professor of Law, University of Wisconsin.

**LOCAL GOVERNMENT LAW, Second Revised Edition (1986)**

Jefferson B. Fordham, Professor of Law, University of Utah.

**MASS MEDIA LAW, Fourth Edition (1990), with 1993 Supplement**

Marc A. Franklin, Professor of Law, Stanford University.
David A. Anderson, Professor of Law, University of Texas.

**MUNICIPAL CORPORATIONS, see Local Government Law**

**NEGOTIABLE INSTRUMENTS, see Commercial Paper**

**NEGOTIABLE INSTRUMENTS, Fourth Edition (1993)**

E. Allan Farnsworth, Professor of Law, Columbia University.

**NEGOTIABLE INSTRUMENTS AND LETTERS OF CREDIT (1992) (Reprinted from Commercial Law), Third Edition (1992)**

Robert L. Jordan, Professor of Law, University of California, Los Angeles.
William D. Warren, Professor of Law, University of California, Los Angeles.

**NEGOTIATION (1981) (Reprinted from THE LAWYERING PROCESS)**

Gary Bellow, Professor of Law, Harvard Law School.
Bea Moulton, Legal Services Corporation.

**NEW YORK PRACTICE, Fourth Edition (1978)**

Herbert Peterfreund, Professor of Law, New York University.
Joseph M. McLaughlin, Dean of the Law School, Fordham University.

**OIL AND GAS, Sixth Edition (1992)**

Richard C. Maxwell, Professor of Law, Duke University.
Stephen F. Williams, Judge of the United States Court of Appeals.
Patrick Henry Martin, Professor of Law, Louisiana State University.
Bruce M. Kramer, Professor of Law, Texas Tech University.

**ON LAW IN COURTS (1965)**

Paul J. Mishkin, Professor of Law, University of California, Berkeley.
Clarence Morris, Professor of Law Emeritus, University of Pennsylvania.

**PENSION AND EMPLOYEE BENEFIT LAW (1990), with 1993 Supplement**

John H. Langbein, Professor of Law, University of Chicago.
Bruce A. Wolk, Professor of Law, University of California, Davis.

**PLEADING AND PROCEDURE, see Procedure, Civil**

**POLICE FUNCTION, Fifth Edition (1991), with 1993 Supplement**

Reprint of Chapters 1–10 of Miller, Dawson, Dix and Parnas's CRIMINAL JUSTICE ADMINISTRATION, Fourth Edition.

**PREPARING AND PRESENTING THE CASE (1981) (Reprinted from THE LAWYERING PROCESS)**

Gary Bellow, Professor of Law, Harvard Law School.
Bea Moulton, Legal Services Corporation.

**PROPERTY—INTRODUCTION, TO REAL PROPERTY, Third Edition (1954)**

Everett Fraser, late Dean of the Law School Emeritus, University of Minnesota.

**PROPERTY—FUNDAMENTALS OF MODERN REAL PROPERTY, Third Edition (1992)**

Edward H. Rabin, Professor of Law, University of California, Davis.
Roberta Rosenthal Kwall, Professor of Law, DePaul University.

**PROPERTY, REAL (1984), with 1988 Supplement**

Paul Goldstein, Professor of Law, Stanford University.

**PROSECUTION AND ADJUDICATION, Fourth Edition (1991), with 1993 Supplement**

Reprint of Chapters 11–26 of Miller, Dawson, Dix and Parnas's CRIMINAL JUSTICE ADMINISTRATION, Fourth Edition.

**PSYCHIATRY AND LAW, see Mental Health, see also Hinckley, Trial of**

**PUBLIC UTILITY LAW, see Free Enterprise, also Regulated Industries**

**REAL ESTATE PLANNING, Third Edition (1989), with Revised Problem and Statutory Supplement (1991)**

Norton L. Steuben, Professor of Law, University of Colorado.

**REAL ESTATE TRANSACTIONS, Third Edition (1993), with Statute, Form and Problem Supplement (1993)**

Paul Goldstein, Professor of Law, Stanford University.
Gerald Korngold, Professor of Law, Case Western Reserve University.

**RECEIVERSHIP AND CORPORATE REORGANIZATION, see Creditors' Rights**

**REGULATED INDUSTRIES, Second Edition (1976)**

William K. Jones, Professor of Law, Columbia University.

**REMEDIES, Third Edition (1992)**

Edward D. Re, Professor of Law, St. John's University.
Stanton D. Krauss, Professor of Law, University of Bridgeport.

**REMEDIES (1989)**

Elaine W. Shoben, Professor of Law, University of Illinois.
Wm. Murray Tabb, Professor of Law, Baylor University.

**SALES, Third Edition (1992)**

Marion W. Benfield, Jr., Professor of Law, Wake Forest University.
William D. Hawkland, Professor of Law, Louisiana State Law Center.

**SALES (1992) (Reprinted from Commercial Law) Third Edition (1992)**

Robert L. Jordan, Professor of Law, University of California, Los Angeles.
William D. Warren, Professor of Law, University of California, Los Angeles.

**SALES AND SECURED FINANCING, Sixth Edition (1993)**

John Honnold, Professor of Law Emeritus, University of Pennsylvania.
Steven L. Harris, Professor of Law, University of Illinois.
Charles Mooney, Jr., Professor of Law, University of Pennsylvania.
Curtis R. Reitz, Professor of Law, University of Pennsylvania.

# UNIVERSITY CASEBOOK SERIES—Continued

**SALES LAW AND THE CONTRACTING PROCESS, Second Edition (1991) (Reprinted from Commercial Transactions) Second Edition (1991)**

Alan Schwartz, Professor of Law, Yale University.
Robert E. Scott, Professor of Law, University of Virginia.

**SALES TRANSACTIONS: DOMESTIC AND INTERNATIONAL LAW (1992)**

John Honnold, Professor of Law Emeritus, University of Pennsylvania.
Curtis R. Reitz, Professor of Law, University of Pennsylvania.

**SECURED TRANSACTIONS IN PERSONAL PROPERTY, Third Edition (1992) (Reprinted from COMMERCIAL LAW, Third Edition (1992))**

Robert L. Jordan, Professor of Law, University of California, Los Angeles.
William D. Warren, Professor of Law, University of California, Los Angeles.

**SECURITIES REGULATION, Seventh Edition (1992), with 1993 Selected Statutes, Rules and Forms Supplement, and 1993 Cases and Releases Supplement**

Richard W. Jennings, Professor of Law, University of California, Berkeley.
Harold Marsh, Jr., Member of California Bar.
John C. Coffee, Jr., Professor of Law, Columbia University.

**SECURITIES REGULATION, Second Edition (1988), with Statute, Rule and Form Supplement (1991)**

Larry D. Soderquist, Professor of Law, Vanderbilt University.

**SECURITY-INTERESTS IN PERSONAL PROPERTY, Second Edition (1987)**

Douglas G. Baird, Professor of Law, University of Chicago.
Thomas H. Jackson, Dean of the Law School, University of Virginia.

**SECURITY INTERESTS IN PERSONAL PROPERTY, Second Edition (1992)**

John Honnold, Professor of Law Emeritus, University of Pennsylvania.
Steven L. Harris, Professor of Law, University of Illinois.
Charles W. Mooney, Jr., Professor of Law, University of Pennsylvania.

**SELECTED STANDARDS ON PROFESSIONAL RESPONSIBILITY, 1993 Edition**

**SELECTED STATUTES AND INTERNATIONAL AGREEMENTS ON UNFAIR COMPETITION, TRADEMARK, COPYRIGHT AND PATENT, 1991 Edition**

**SELECTED STATUTES ON TRUSTS AND ESTATES, 1992 Edition**

**SOCIAL RESPONSIBILITIES OF LAWYERS, Case Studies (1988)**

Philip B. Heymann, Professor of Law, Harvard University.
Lance Liebman, Professor of Law, Harvard University.

**SOCIAL SCIENCE IN LAW, Second Edition (1990)**

John Monahan, Professor of Law, University of Virginia.
Laurens Walker, Professor of Law, University of Virginia.

**TAXATION, FEDERAL INCOME (1989)**

Stephen B. Cohen, Professor of Law, Georgetown University.

**TAXATION, FEDERAL INCOME, Second Edition (1988), with 1993 Supplement (Supplement edited in association with Deborah H. Schenk, Professor of Law, New York University)**

Michael J. Graetz, Professor of Law, Yale University.

**TAXATION, FEDERAL INCOME, Seventh Edition (1991)**

James J. Freeland, Professor of Law, University of Florida.
Stephen A. Lind, Professor of Law, University of Florida and University of California, Hastings.
Richard B. Stephens, late Professor of Law Emeritus, University of Florida.

**TAXATION, FEDERAL INCOME, Successor Edition (1986), with 1993 Legislative Supplement**

Stanley S. Surrey, late Professor of Law, Harvard University.
Paul R. McDaniel, Professor of Law, Boston College.
Hugh J. Ault, Professor of Law, Boston College.
Stanley A. Koppelman, Professor of Law, Boston University.

**TAXATION, FEDERAL INCOME, OF BUSINESS ORGANIZATIONS (1991), with 1993 Supplement**

Paul R. McDaniel, Professor of Law, Boston College.
Hugh J. Ault, Professor of Law, Boston College.
Martin J. McMahon, Jr., Professor of Law, University of Kentucky.
Daniel L. Simmons, Professor of Law, University of California, Davis.

**TAXATION, FEDERAL INCOME, OF PARTNERSHIPS AND S CORPORATIONS (1991), with 1993 Supplement**

Paul R. McDaniel, Professor of Law, Boston College.
Hugh J. Ault, Professor of Law, Boston College.
Martin J. McMahon, Jr., Professor of Law, University of Kentucky.
Daniel L. Simmons, Professor of Law, University of California, Davis.

**TAXATION, FEDERAL INCOME, OIL AND GAS, NATURAL RESOURCES TRANSACTIONS (1990)**

Peter C. Maxfield, Professor of Law, University of Wyoming.
James L. Houghton, CPA, Partner, Ernst and Young.
James R. Gaar, CPA, Partner, Ernst and Young.

**TAXATION, FEDERAL WEALTH TRANSFER, Successor Edition (1987)**

Stanley S. Surrey, late Professor of Law, Harvard University.
Paul R. McDaniel, Professor of Law, Boston College.
Harry L. Gutman, Professor of Law, University of Pennsylvania.

**TAXATION, FUNDAMENTALS OF CORPORATE, Third Edition (1991)**

Stephen A. Lind, Professor of Law, University of Florida and University of California, Hastings.
Stephen Schwarz, Professor of Law, University of California, Hastings.
Daniel J. Lathrope, Professor of Law, University of California, Hastings.
Joshua Rosenberg, Professor of Law, University of San Francisco.

**TAXATION, FUNDAMENTALS OF PARTNERSHIP, Third Edition (1992)**

Stephen A. Lind, Professor of Law, University of Florida and University of California, Hastings.
Stephen Schwarz, Professor of Law, University of California, Hastings.
Daniel J. Lathrope, Professor of Law, University of California, Hastings.
Joshua Rosenberg, Professor of Law, University of San Francisco.

**TAXATION OF CORPORATIONS AND THEIR SHAREHOLDERS (1991)**

David J. Shakow, Professor of Law, University of Pennsylvania.

# UNIVERSITY CASEBOOK SERIES—Continued

**WATER RESOURCE MANAGEMENT, Fourth Edition (1993)**

A. Dan Tarlock, Professor of Law, IIT Chicago–Kent College of Law.

James N. Corbridge, Jr., Chancellor, University of Colorado at Boulder, and Professor of Law, University of Colorado.

David H. Getches, Professor of Law, University of Colorado.

**WOMEN AND THE LAW (1992)**

Mary Joe Frug, late Professor of Law, New England School of Law.

**WILLS AND ADMINISTRATION, Fifth Edition (1961)**

Philip Mechem, late Professor of Law, University of Pennsylvania.

Thomas E. Atkinson, late Professor of Law, New York University.

**WRITING AND ANALYSIS IN THE LAW, Second Edition (1991)**

Helene S. Shapo, Professor of Law, Northwestern University.

Marilyn R. Walter, Professor of Law, Brooklyn Law School.

Elizabeth Fajans, Writing Specialist, Brooklyn Law School.

# University Casebook Series

---

# LAW, LANGUAGE, AND ETHICS

## AN INTRODUCTION TO LAW AND LEGAL METHOD

WILLIAM R. BISHIN
CHRISTOPHER D. STONE

*University of Southern California*

Mineola, New York
THE FOUNDATION PRESS, INC.
1972

Bishin & Stone Law, Language & Ethics UCB
9th Reprint—1993

PRINTED ON 10% POST
CONSUMER RECYCLED PAPER

*To Sharlee, Susannah*
*and Benjamin*

*To Ann and Jessica*

Law, Language, and Ethics is born of the belief that every legal problem—whether it concern the "great issues" of civil disobedience or the hum-drum matters of Offer and Acceptance and Last Clear Chance—has its roots and perhaps its analog in traditionally "philosophical" realms. Strip away the technical legal terms, plumb the debate's assumptions, and a host of implicit philosophical positions will be found. Some of these will be inarticulate conclusions about the nature of reality, of knowledge, and of language. Others will be about the requisites of morality, the meaning of "the good life," the ends of social organization, the nature of man. What is more, although the lawyer may not always be aware of it, in his day-to-day tasks of counselling, planning and contending, he is engaged in activities that philosophy—as well as such related disciplines as psychology and sociology—has long sought to analyze and illuminate. These include stating problems, clarifying questions, determining "facts", interpreting language, formulating and analyzing theories.

In view of this, it is curious that those concerned with law have not more fully exploited the wealth of available philosophical—and related theoretical—literature. To be sure, there is a Philosophy of Law; there are courses in Jurisprudence. Yet these offerings have been especially concerned with their own compartmentalized subject matter: what is law? what is justice? what is the nature of the judicial function? And, strange to say, even these courses fail to use much of traditional philosophical works. When Aristotle, Plato, Aquinas, or Kant are considered, it is usually in their jurisprudential aspect. Otherwise, an indigenous group of thinkers is drawn upon— Austin, Holmes, Cardozo, Hohfeld, Kelsen, Llewellyn, Frank, Fuller, H. L. A. Hart—all concerned with "Law": as institution, process, idea or system of power relationships. All of these have, of course, contributed enormously to the study of law. But we believe that there are many other sources that need to be explored and more pervasive lessons to be learned.

It is our faith that the student who has learned these lessons— who has studied law as a special but not unique effort of the human mind to make "reality" comprehendable and manageable—will be able to see beyond the categories postulated by common sense and everyday life. He will consequently be more free, more responsible, and better able fully to exploit his intellectual resources in the solution of his, and the society's, problems.

\* \* \*

This book is in no small measure the result of the encouragement and intellectual stimulation of the faculty of the U.S.C. Law Center. Law, Language, and Ethics would not have gotten beyond its embryonic stage without the early support of George Lefcoe, Martin Levine, Francis Jones, Leonard Ratner and the late Harold Solomon. Professor Lefcoe was, indeed, the original proponent of a philosophically oriented introduction to legal thought and his strong and successful support of such a course in the early 1960s places us forever in his debt.

Since that time, Law, Language, and Ethics has profited from the suggestions and criticisms of many other of our colleagues. These include Gary Bellow, Scott Bice, Richard Epstein, Michael Levine, and Joel Shor.

During our work here, the administrations of the Law Center and of the University have been willing to encourage—even when they were being forced to defend—the sorts of innovation in education which Law, Language, and Ethics represents. For their time, energy, and commitment of Law Center resources we are especially grateful to Orrin B. Evans, Dorothy W. Nelson and John Jerry Wiley.

\* \* \*

The actual production of the volume drew upon the patience, energy, good nature and intellectual acumen of a number of persons.

For a host of administrative, editorial and clerical services, we are indebted to Sharlee Bishin and Ann Stone.

The enormous task of typing the manuscript and related correspondence, keeping track of hundreds of copyright permissions, and generally seeing that the intellectual spirit came to rest in a tangible body owes to our matchless Linda Bloxham, and to Shirley Gold, Mrs. Burt Gordon, Lupe Hartline, Anna Lew, Diane Lloyd, Barbara Markham, Gladys McHugh, Pat Sales, and Jan Sumek.

\* \* \*

We are further indebted, as much as to anyone, to the students of the U.S.C. Law Center who during the past seven years lived through the series of drafts and redrafts from which the present volume emerged. From them we received countless suggestions, criticisms, and recommendations as to pieces that might be included; more importantly, it was their tolerance and even enthusiasm—so much as can be mustered for heavy loads of poorly bound and not consistently legible mimeographed volumes—that inspired us to see the work through. Not being able to remember all those who made concrete and isolable contributions to Law, Language, and Ethics, we should like to single out those we can recall and beg forgiveness of those we cannot. In the former category are Ed Arnett, Barry Currier, Tom Dobson, Christine Duckworth, John Edmunds, Chuck Elsesser, Larry Flax, Jim Foster, Robert Harter, Stephen Herzberg, Paul Horton, Richard Jacobson, Charles Plotkin, Paul Rasmussen and Land Wayland.

Finally, the number and variety of readings can only barely suggest the debt we owe to the libraries and librarians on the U.S.C. campus. For their sleuthing and their forbearance we especially thank R. Paul Burton, our omniscient and generous law librarian, and Francis Gates, Emergy Baldi-Becht, Mrs. Janet Casebier and Laurence Jackson, all of the law library. Wallace Nethery, head of the Hoose Library of Philosophy, extended his services unstintingly.

W. R. Bishin
C. D. Stone

February 1, 1972

*

# SUMMARY OF CONTENTS

## INTRODUCTION
### CHOICE AND AUTHORITY

## PART ONE

### THE DILEMMAS OF ROLE, RULE AND REASON

## PART TWO

### THE QUEST FOR AUTHORITY: ITS LIMITS AND ILLUSIONS

*

# TABLE OF CONTENTS

## INTRODUCTION

## Choice and Authority

## *PART ONE*

## The Dilemmas of Role, Rule and Reason

### CHAPTER ONE. STICKING TO FIRM GROUND(?)

### CHAPTER TWO. THE MORAL DILEMMA

### CHAPTER THREE. THE EPISTEMOLOGICAL DILEMMA

## PART TWO

### The Quest for Authority: Its Limits and Illusions

## CHAPTER FOUR. THE AUTHORITY OF PERCEPTION

## CHAPTER FIVE. THE AUTHORITY OF CONCEPTS

## TABLE OF CONTENTS

# TABLE OF CONTENTS

*PART THREE*

# Skepticism and the Nature of Knowledge

## CHAPTER NINE. SKEPTICISM AND THE "FACT–MINDED" AND LANGUAGE–BOUND CONCEPTIONS OF REALITY

# TABLE OF CONTENTS

## CHAPTER THIRTEEN. THE RULE OF ROLE

## CHAPTER FOURTEEN. SELF–KNOWLEDGE
## AND SELF–DECEPTION

## CHAPTER FIFTEEN. THE LANGUAGE OF MEANING

## PART FIVE

## A Meaningful Life and the Social Order

### CHAPTER SIXTEEN. ONE'S OBLIGATION TO ONE'S SELF—AND OTHERS

### CHAPTER SEVENTEEN. OBLIGATIONS TO THE SYMBOLS OF THE SOCIAL GROUPING: COHESION AND INDIVIDUALISM

## CHAPTER EIGHTEEN. OBLIGATIONS TO INSTITUTIONAL PROCESSES OF DECISION: THE PROBLEM OF "CIVIL DISOBEDIENCE"

## CHAPTER NINETEEN. THE FUTURE OF TRUST

## TABLE OF CONTENTS

†

*INTRODUCTION*

# CHOICE AND AUTHORITY

*MAX BROD*

**POSTSCRIPT TO THE FIRST EDITION (1925)**
**OF FRANZ KAFKA'S "THE TRIAL"** *

All Franz Kafka's utterances about life were profound and original, and so too was his attitude toward his own work and to the question of publication altogether. It would be impossible to overrate the gravity of the problems with which he wrestled in this connection, and which for that reason must serve as a guide for any publication of his posthumous works. The following indications may help to give at least an approximate idea of his attitude.

I wrested from Kafka nearly everything he published either by persuasion or by guile. This is not inconsistent with the fact that he frequently during long periods of his life experienced great happiness in writing, although he never dignified it by any other name than "scribbling." Anyone who was ever privileged to hear him read his own prose out loud to a small circle of intimates with an intoxicating fervor and a rhythmic verve beyond any actor's power, was made directly aware of the genuine irrepressible joy in creation and of the passion behind his work. If he nevertheless repudiated it, this was firstly because certain unhappy experiences had driven him in the direction of a kind of self-sabotage and therefore also toward nihilism as far as his own work was concerned; but also independently of that because, admittedly without ever saying so, he applied the highest religious standard to his art; and since this was wrung from manifold doubts and difficulties, that standard was too high. It was probably immaterial to him that his work might nevertheless greatly help many others who were striving after faith, nature, and wholeness of soul; for in his inexorable search for his own salvation, his first need was to counsel, not others, but himself.

* From The Trial 326–335 (Modern Library ed. 1956). With the permission of Alfred A. Knopf, Inc.

That is how I personally interpret Kafka's negative attitude toward his own work. He often spoke of "false hands" beckoning to him while he was writing; and he also maintained that what he had already written, let alone published, interfered with his further work. There were many obstacles to be overcome before a volume of his saw the light of day. All the same, the sight of the books in print gave him real pleasure, and occasionally, too, the impression they made. In fact there were times when he surveyed both himself and his works with a more benevolent eye, never quite without irony, but with friendly irony; with an irony which concealed the infinite pathos of a man who admitted of no compromise in his striving for perfection.

No will was found among Kafka's literary remains. In his desk among a mass of papers lay a folded note written in ink and addressed to me. This is how it runs:

> DEAREST MAX, my last request: Everything I leave behind me (in my bookcase, linen-cupboard, and my desk both at home and in the office, or anywhere else where anything may have got to and meets your eye), in the way of diaries, manuscripts, letters (my own and others'), sketches, and so on, to be burned unread; also all writings and sketches which you or others may possess; and ask those others for them in my name. Letters which they do not want to hand over to you, they should at least promise faithfully to burn themselves.
>
> Yours,
>
> FRANZ KAFKA

A closer search produced an obviously earlier note written in pencil on yellowed paper, which said:

> DEAR MAX, perhaps this time I shan't recover after all. Pneumonia after a whole month's pulmonary fever is all too likely; and not even writing this down can avert it, although there is a certain power in that.
>
> For this eventuality therefore, here is my last will concerning everything I have written:
>
> Of all my writings the only books that can stand are these: *The Judgment, The Stoker, Metamorphosis, Penal Colony, Country Doctor* and the short story: *Hunger-Artist*. (The few copies of *Meditation* can remain. I do not want to give anyone the trouble of pulping them; but nothing in that volume must be printed again.) When I say that those five books and the short story can stand, I do not mean that I wish them to be reprinted and handed down to posterity. On the contrary, should they disappear altogether that would please me best. Only, since they do exist, I do not wish to hinder anyone who may want to, from keeping them.
>
> But everything else of mine which is extant (whether in journals, in manuscript, or letters), everything without exception in so far as it is discoverable or obtainable from the addressees by request (you know most of them yourself;

it is chiefly  .  .  .  and whatever happens don't forget the couple of notebooks in  .  .  .  's possession)—all these things, without exception and preferably unread (I won't absolutely forbid you to look at them, though I'd far rather you didn't and in any case no one else is to do so)—all these things without exception are to be burned, and I beg you to do this as soon as possible.

FRANZ

If, in spite of these categorical instructions, I nevertheless refuse to perform the holocaust demanded of me by my friend, I have good and sufficient reasons for that.

Some of them do not admit of public discussion; but in my opinion those which I can communicate are themselves amply sufficient to explain my decision.

The chief reason is this: when in 1921 I embarked on a new profession, I told Kafka that I had made my will in which I had asked him to destroy this and that, to look through some other things, and so forth. Kafka thereupon showed me the outside of the note written in ink which was later found in his desk, and said: "My last testament will be quite simple—a request to you to burn everything." I can still remember the exact wording of the answer I gave him: "If you seriously think me capable of such a thing, let me tell you here and now that I shall not carry out your wishes." The whole conversation was conducted in the jesting tone we generally used together, but with the underlying seriousness which each of us always took for granted in the other. Convinced as he was that I meant what I said, Franz should have appointed another executor if he had been absolutely and finally determined that his instructions should stand.

I am far from grateful to him for having precipitated me into this difficult conflict of conscience, which he must have foreseen, for he knew with what fanatical veneration I listened to his every word. Among other things, this was the reason why, during the whole twenty-two years of our unclouded friendship, I never once threw away the smallest scrap of paper that came from him, no, not even a post card. Nor would I wish the words "I am far from grateful" to be misunderstood. What does a conflict of conscience, be it never so acute, signify when weighed in the balance against the inestimable blessing I owe to his friendship which has been the mainstay of my whole existence!

Other reasons are: the instructions in the penciled note were not followed by Franz himself; for later he gave the explicit permission to reprint parts of *Meditation* in a journal; and he also agreed to the publication of three further short stories which he himself brought out, together with *Hunger-Artist*, with the firm Die Schmiede. Besides, both sets of instructions to me were the product of a period when Kafka's self-critical tendency was at its height. But during the last year of his life his whole existence took an unforeseen turn for the better, a new, happy, and positive turn which did away with his self-hatred and nihilism. Then, too, my decision to publish his posthumous work is made easier by the memory of all the embittered struggles preceding every single publication of Kafka's which I extorted from him by force and often by begging. And yet afterwards he was reconciled with these publications and relatively satisfied with them. Finally in a posthumous publication a whole series of objections no longer applies; as, for instance, that present publication might hinder future work and recall the dark shadows of personal grief and pain. How closely non-publication was bound up for Kafka with the problem of how to conduct his life (a problem which, to our immeasurable grief, no longer obtains) could be gathered from many of his conversations and can be seen in this letter to me:

> . . . I am not enclosing the novels. Why rake up old efforts? Only because I have not burned them yet? . . . Next time I come I hope to do so. Where is the sense in keeping such work which is "even" bungled from the aesthetic point of view? Surely not in the hope of piecing a whole together from all these fragments, some kind of justification for my existence, something to cling to in an hour of need? But that, I know, is impossible; there is no help for me there. So what shall I do with the things? Since they can't help me, am I to let them harm me, as must be the case, given my knowledge about them?

I am well aware that something remains which would prohibit publication to those of outstandingly delicate feelings. But I believe it to be my duty to resist the very insidious lure of such scruples. My decision does not rest on any of the reasons given above but simply and solely on the fact that Kafka's unpublished work contains the most wonderful treasures, and, measured against his own work, the best things he was written. In all honesty I must confess that this one fact of the literary and ethical value of what I am publishing would have been enough to decide me to do so, definitely, finally, and irresistibly, even if I had had no single objection to raise against the validity of Kafka's last wishes.

Unhappily Kafka performed the function of his own executor on part of his literary estate. In his lodgings I found ten large quarto notebooks—only the covers remained; their contents had been completely destroyed. In addition to this he had, according to reliable testimony, burned several writing pads. I only found one file in his lodgings (about a hundred aphorisms on religious subjects), an autobiographical sketch which must remain unpublished for the moment, and a pile of papers which I am now putting in order. . . .

. . . .

I took the manuscript of *The Trial* into my keeping in June 1920 and immediately put it in order. The manuscript has no title; but Kafka always called it *The Trial* in conversation. The division into chapters as well as the chapter headings are his work; but I had to rely on my own judgment for the order of the chapters. However, as my friend had read a great part of the novel to me, memory came to the aid of judgment. Franz regarded the novel as unfinished. Before the final chapter given here a few more stages of the mysterious trial were to have been described. But as the trial, according to the author's own statement made by word of mouth, was never to get as far as the highest Court, in a certain sense the novel could never be terminated—that is to say, it could be prolonged into infinity. At all events, the completed chapters taken in conjunction with the final chapter which rounds them off, reveal both the meaning and the form with the most convincing clarity; and anyone ignorant of the fact that the author himself intended to go on working at it (he omitted to do so because his life entered another phase) would hardly be aware of gaps. My work on the great bundle of papers which at that time represented this novel was confined to separating the finished from the unfinished chapters. I am reserving the latter for the final volume of the posthumous edition; they contain nothing essential to the development of the action.

## NOTES AND QUESTIONS

1. *Brod's Dilemma.* Why should this "case" appear in a law school casebook? Does Brod's problem have anything in common with the problems that confront a lawyer or judge? Or are there different "sorts" of problems in the world, each with its special technique for handling, so that there is something called "thinking like a lawyer" and something else called "thinking like a scientist" or "thinking like a friend"?

If so, how is Brod's methodology different from that of a judge deciding a law-suit? In what ways was Brod apparently more, and in what ways less, constrained in reaching his decision than would be a court in the interpretation of a Constitutional or statutory provision, a contract or a will?

2. *Stating the Problem.* Does Brod ever state or define his problem in so many words? If not, should he have? What purposes, if any, are served by statements of the form, "The issue in this case is _____"?

How does one confronted with a problem know what *is* the issue that the problem presents? Consider the array that may have occurred to Brod. Suppose he had seen "the issue" as "whether I, Max Brod, should burn all the manuscripts my friend Franz Kafka left on his death pursuant to his written instructions?" Would this have been an adequate statement of the issue? Would it have been more or less useful than a judicial declaration that "the issue in this case is whether plaintiff or defendant should win"? In what ways would such a statement of the issue have been improved upon by:

(1) "What did Kafka want me to do?";

(2) "What would Kafka want me to do?";

(3) "What does the public interest require me to do?";

(4) "Ought people (*i. e.*, in general) to carry out other persons' wishes?";

(5) "Ought people to carry out wishes expressed by people of dubious competence?"

What other statements of "the issue" can you think of? How did Brod decide which to select?

**3.** *Responsibility: The Decision to Decide.* Given the anguish (the "conflict of conscience") that the dilemma posed for Brod, why did he take it upon *himself* to decide whether the manuscripts should be destroyed? Had Kafka not already made that decision? If Kafka were to be "overruled" at all, why by Brod alone? What alternatives were there, in terms of sharing that decision with others? If Brod regarded the literary value of the works as critical, why should he not have called in a panel of literary experts? If Kafka's mental state were at issue, shouldn't Brod have sounded out other of Kafka's friends on their views as to his mental condition?

Further, does it not appear that Kafka intended the instructions to constitute, as he says, his "last will"? And if so, could Brod be certain that the notes did not amount to valid holographic (handwritten) wills?[1] Were there not important matters for the courts to determine—whether the "notes" were wills, how they ought to be interpreted, whether they were void as against public policy, whether Kafka had been competent?

How did Brod decide whether and to what extent *he* should decide these things? Are the objections that one makes of dictators applicable to Brod? Were there, on the other hand, some things that Brod— alone—*had to* decide?

**4.** *Brod's Method of Interpretation.* How did Brod *know*, from reading Kafka's instructions, what they *meant*? Is the entire meaning contained in the words themselves? Consider, for example, the letter written in ink. "Dearest Max", writes Kafka, "my last request: Everything I leave behind me . . . to be burned unread." Does this mean that the letter itself should have been "burned unread" and that Brod was disobedient at the very start? If not, what theory of interpretation would give Brod support? On the extension of such a theory, might Brod be reasoning that he was not disobeying Kafka, but rather following Kafka's *real* meaning? Can you construct such an argument?

Are the ways in which Brod must go about interpreting Kafka's language related to the ways in which he must go about interpreting Kafka's (other) acts? On what evidence, for example, did Brod decide that the earlier oral request to destroy his papers was not meant seriously? In what ways is the process of recreating the intent of Kafka related to the process of interpreting the meaning of his words and acts? How does the task that faced Brod compare with the task of a court in determining "legislative intent"?

**5.** *Rules, Reasons and the Theory of Decision.* Brod sets forth (pp. 3–4) a number of what he calls "good and sufficient reasons,") for his decision not to burn the manuscripts. What is a reason? How is it different from a fact? or a rule? Is there a difference

---

1.  Section 578 of the Austrian General Civil Law (*Osterreichische Allgemeine Burgerliche Recht*) (Vienna 1926) provided at the time,
    Whoever desires to make a will unattested must write the will with his own hand, and sign it. The date and place is not essential on handwritten wills, though it is advisable to do so in order to avoid possible lawsuits.

between a reason and a "good reason"? What make a reason a "good" one? What makes it a "sufficient" one?

Consider what Brod finally gives as the ultimate justification of his decision:

My decision does not rest on any of the reasons given above but simply and solely on the fact that Kafka's unpublished work contains the most wonderful treasures. . . . In all honesty, I must confess that this one fact of the literary and ethical value of what I am publishing would have been enough to decide me to do so, definitely, finally, and irresistibly.

What is the "fact" on which Brod's argument, as he says, "rests"? What makes it a "fact"? Is it incumbent on Brod to demonstrate in some way that it *is* a fact? Or are "facts" the sort of statements that are obvious "on their face"? Consider the following from V. W. GRANT, GREAT ABNORMALS, 36–37 (1968).

Edmund Wilson, a literary analyst of high stature, thinks that the religious meaning of Kafka's writings is "practically nil" and concludes: "I do not see how one can possibly take him for either a great artist or a moral guide." . . . D. S. Savage, in a thoughtful study, feels that Kafka failed as a religious philosopher because he offers no solution for the problems he explored. He merely raised issues; he resolved nothing. . . .

Charles Neider, a prominent Kafka student, has concluded that the writer was not, in reality, a "thinker" at all; that the complexities of his constructions have been exaggerated, and that "it is possible that Kafka would not have achieved such stature if his meaning had been transparent." In the same vein the view has been frequently expressed that those who manage to find profundities in Kafka's writings are no more than cultists who find in the many obscurities in his work an opportunity to enhance their reputations as interpreters, and to assure the baffled reader there are great truths here despite his own failure to find understandable meanings.

In what sense of "facts" does anyone ever make a decision "simply and solely on the fact" of $X$? Can you find express or implied in Brod's argument something like a rule or rules which makes the dictate of the "facts" more "irresistible" to Brod?

6. *Obligations.* In solving problems like Brod's, of how much use is it to consider one's obligations to others? How many different —and perhaps conflicting—obligations might Brod have been "under"? How could he weigh his obligations to the dead with his obligations to the living and unborn—and with those he may have owed to himself? Was Brod under less of an obligation if we construe Kafka's request as unilaterally imposed on Brod, rather than as a product of a prior agreement between the two? Why? What is there about a promise that gives rise to more of an obligation than a wish? How do obligations "arise" and what accounts for their strength? Why shouldn't a friend's wishes impose the obligations in our thinking of

a command of law? And, conversely, why shouldn't a command of law have the authority of a friend's wishes, and nothing more? And when all this talk about obligations is said and done—when all the obligations are defined and weighed—how far has one advanced towards the solution of a concrete problem?

7. *A Man's Role.* Consider that Brod was not only Kafka's friend, he was a lawyer as well. Does this additional consideration influence your assessment of the propriety of Brod's actions? Why? In what ways do people's obligations seem to depend upon their "role" in society? Would you say that Brod, as lawyer, should have taken different considerations into account? That he should have decided differently? Can you make a case for different analyses depending upon whether the recipient of the notes was Kafka's wife, or the trash man, or the bank that kept the safety deposit box in which some of the manuscripts were situated?

How did Brod decide whether he was to think about the problem as friend or as lawyer? How did he *know* which role to adopt?

Would "knowing his role" really have made a difference? Suppose that Brod, with "his" views of the situation as disclosed in the "postscript", were sitting as a judge in a Czech probate court, and some other lawyer had brought before him the instruments, requesting that Judge Brod give him directions on whether to burn the manuscripts or not. Would Brod reason differently, *qua* judge, than he did, *qua* friend? *Qua* lawyer? Or would he, as judge, simply reach—and "rationalize"—the same decision that he had made as friend or as lawyer, etc.?

8. *The Decision to Write an Opinion*: Why did Brod undertake to write the "postscript"? Why did he not simply burn the notes and never mention the matter to anyone?

9. *The Decision: Did Brod Decide "What He Wanted to Decide"?* In the last analysis, when Brod concluded that he was going to have Kafka's manuscripts published, was he just "deciding what he wanted to decide"? This is a charge that is often made about decision-makers—perhaps more about judges than any others. Why? What are people who make it trying to assert?

The problem of "deciding what one wants to decide" is more complex than might first appear. Take the case of a captured seaman who is forced by buccaneers, at sword's point, to "walk the plank". If he decides to walk off into the ocean, is he not "deciding what he wants to decide"? But if this is the sense in which Brod—or a judge—decided what he wanted to decide, is it not a trivial sense? Surely, something more must be meant. But what?

Is it always clear what it is that one wants? Was it clear to Brod? To what extent do "conflicts of conscience" like his stem from doubts as to what one wants? How does one go about determining "his" wants? Did Brod ever do so? Could he be satisfied with his decision without having done so?

10. *Did Brod Do the "Right" Thing?* Is it possible for someone with a problem like Brod's to be fully satisfied, whichever way he

chooses? Is it easier for a judge, with a "legal framework" behind him, to feel confident that he has done "right"?

What does it mean to say a decision was "right" or "wrong"? If you say Brod was "right" are you saying anything more than that you agree with what he did (or would have done the same thing yourself)? What facts do concepts like "right" and "wrong", "moral" and "immoral", refer to, if they refer to facts at all? Is it possible to have a meaningful argument about whether Brod was "right" or "wrong", or is it a matter of *de gustibus non disputandum* (there's no disputing taste)? If the latter, how can we criticize our—and others'— actions?

## THOMAS HASLEM v. WILLIAM A. LOCKWOOD

37 Conn. 500 (1871)

Trover, for a quantity of manure; brought before a justice of the peace and appealed by the defendant to the Court of Common Pleas for the county of Fairfield, and tried in that court, on the general issue closed to the court, before BREWSTER, J.

On the trial it was proved that the plaintiff employed two men to gather into heaps, on the evening of April 6th, 1869, some manure that lay scattered along the side of a public highway, for several rods, in the borough of Stamford, intending to remove the same to his own land the next evening. The men began to scrape the manure into heaps at six o'clock in the evening, and after gathering eighteen heaps, or about six cart-loads, left the same at eight o'clock in the evening in the street. The heaps consisted chiefly of manure made by horses hitched to the railing of the public park in, and belonging to, the borough of Stamford, and was all gathered between the center of the highway and the park; the rest of the heaps consisting of dirt, straw and the ordinary scrapings of highways. The defendant on the next morning, seeing the heaps, endeavored without success to ascertain who had made them, and inquired of the warden of the borough if he had given permission to any one to remove them, and ascertained from him that he had not. He thereupon, before noon on that day, removed the heaps and also the rest of the manure scattered along the side of the highway adjacent to the park, to his own land.

The plaintiff and defendant both claimed to have received authority from the warden to remove the manure before the 6th of April, but in fact neither had any legal authority from the warden, or from any officer of the borough or of the town. The borough of Stamford was the sole adjoining proprietor of the land on which the manure lay scattered before it was gathered by the plaintiff. No notice was left on the heaps or near by, by the plaintiff or his workmen, to indicate who had gathered them, nor had the plaintiff or his workmen any actual possession of the heaps after eight o'clock in the evening on the 6th of April.

Neither the plaintiff while gathering, nor the defendant while removing the heaps, was interfered with or opposed by any one. The removal of the manure and scrapings was calculated to improve the appearance and health of the borough. The six loads were worth one dollar per load. The plaintiff, on ascertaining that the defendant had removed the manure, demanded payment for the same, which the defendant refused. Neither the plaintiff nor defendant owned any land adjacent to the place where the manure lay. The highway was kept in repair by the town of Stamford.

On the above facts the plaintiff claimed, and prayed the court to rule, that the manure was personal property which had been abandoned by its owners and became by such abandonment the property of the first person who should take possession of the same, which the plaintiff had done by gathering it into heaps, and that it was not and never had been a part of the real estate of the borough or of any one else who might be regarded as owning the fee of the soil. He further claimed that if it was a part of the real estate, it was taken without committing a trespass, and with the tacit consent of the owners of such real estate, and that thereby it became his personal property of which he was lawfully possessed, and at least that he had acquired such an interest in it as would enable him to hold it against any person except the owner of the land or some person claiming under the owner.

The defendant claimed, upon the above facts, that the manure being dropped upon and spread out over the surface of the earth was a part of the real estate, and belonged to the owner of the fee, subject to the public easement; that the fee was either in the borough of Stamford or the town of Stamford, or in the parties who owned the lands adjacent; that therefore the scraping up of the manure, mixed with the soil, if real estate, did not change its nature to that of personal estate, unless it was removed, whether the plaintiff had the consent of the owner of the fee or not; and that, unless the heaps became personal property, the plaintiff could not maintain his action. The defendant further claimed, as matter of law, that if the manure was always personal estate, or became personal estate after being scraped up into heaps, the plaintiff, by leaving it from eight o'clock in the evening until noon the next day, abandoned all right of possession which he might have had, and could not, therefore, maintain his action.

The court ruled adversely to the claims of the plaintiff and held that on the facts proved the plaintiff had not made out a sufficient interest in, or right of possession to, the subject matter in dispute, to authorize a recovery in the suit, and rendered judgment for the defendant.

The plaintiff moved for a new trial for error in this ruling of the court.

Curtis and Hoyt [Counsel for the plaintiff-appellant], in support of the motion.

1. The manure in question was personal property abandoned by its owners. 2 Bla.Com., 387, 402; 2 Kent Com., 356.

2. It never became a part of the real estate on which it was abandoned. 2 Smith Lead.Cas., 252, 258; 1 Washb.R.Prop., bk. 1,

ch. 10, sec. 11, § 6.  Parsons v. Camp, 11 Conn., 525; Needham v. Allison, 4 Fost., 355; Plumer v. Plumer, 10 id., 558.

3.  It being personal property abandoned by its owners, and lying upon the highway, and neither the owners of the fee nor the proper authorities of the town and borough having by any act of theirs shown any intention to appropriate the same, it became lawful for the plaintiff to gather it up and remove it from the highway, providing he did not commit a trespass, and removed it without objection from the owners of the land.  Church v. Meeker, 34 Conn., 421. And no trespass was in fact committed.  No person interfered with the plaintiff or made any objection.  This court cannot presume a trespass to have been committed.  1 Greenl.Ev., § 34; 1 Swift Dig., 173.

4.  But if the manure had become a part of the real estate, yet when it was gathered into heaps by the plaintiff it was severed from the realty and became personal estate.  1 Swift Dig., 534; Bouvier Law Dict., "Real Property."  And being gathered without molestation from any person owning or claiming to own the land, it is to be considered as having been taken by the tacit consent of such owner.  Martin v. Houghton, 45 Barb., 258.

5.  The plaintiff therefore acquired not only a valid legal possession, but a title by occupancy, and by having expended labor and money upon the property.  Such a title is a good legal title against every person but the true owner.

6.  If the plaintiff had a legal title then he had the constructive possession.  If he had legal possession, and only left the property for a short time intending to return and take it away, then he might maintain an action against a wrong doer for taking it away.  1 Swift Dig., 530; 1 Smith Lead.Cas., 473; Bird v. Clark, 3 Day, 272; Williams v. Dolbeare, id., 498; Bulkeley v. Dolbeare, 7 Conn., 232; Heath v. Milward, 2 Bing., N.C., 98.  The leaving of property for a short time, intending to return, does not constitute an abandonment. The property is still to be considered as in the possession of the plaintiff.

Olmstead [Counsel for the defendant-respondent], contra.

1.  The manure mixed with the dirt and ordinary scrapings of the highway, being spread out over the surface of the highway, was a part of the *real estate*, and belonged to the owner of the fee, subject to the public easement.  1 Swift Dig., 107; Emans v. Turnbull, 2 Johns., 322; Fay v. Muzzey, 13 Gray, 53; Goodrich v. Jones, 2 Hill, 142; Daniels v. Pond, 2 Pick., 367; Parsons v. Camp, 11 Conn., 525; 1 Wms.Exrs., 615.

2.  The scraping up of the manure and dirt into piles, if the same was a part of the real estate, did not change its nature to that of *personal property*, unless there was a severance of it from the realty by removal, (which there was not), whether the plaintiff had the consent of the owner of the fee or not, which consent it is conceded the plaintiff did not have.

3.  Unless the scraping up of the heaps made their substance *personal property*, the plaintiff could not maintain his action either for trespass or trespass on the case.

4.  In trespass *de bonis asportatis*, or trover, the plaintiff must have had the *actual possession*, or a right to the immediate possession, in order to recover.  1 Hilliard on Torts, ch. 18, § 8.

5.  If the manure was always personal estate, it being spread upon the surface of the earth, it was in possession of the owner of the fee, who was not the plaintiff.  Church v. Meeker, 34 Conn., 432; 1 Swift Dig., 107.  The scraping of it into heaps, unless it was removed, would not change the *possession* from the owner of the fee to the plaintiff.  The plaintiff therefore never had the *possession*.

6.  If the heaps were personal property the plaintiff never had any right in the property, but only *mere possession*, if anything, which he abandoned by leaving the same upon the public highway from 8 o'clock in the evening until 12 o'clock the next day, without leaving any notice on or about the property, or any one to exercise control over the same in his behalf.  2 Hilliard on Torts, ch. 18, § 19, note *c*; id., ch. 18, § 14; Church v. Meeker, supra.

PARK, Judge.  We think the manure scattered upon the ground, under the circumstances of this case, was personal property.  The cases referred to by the defendant to show that it was real estate are not in point.  The principle of those cases is, that manure made in the usual course of husbandry upon a farm is so attached to and connected with the realty that, in the absence of any express stipulation to the contrary, it becomes appurtenant to it.  The principle was established for the benefit of agriculture.  It found its origin in the fact that it is essential to the successful cultivation of a farm that the manure, produced from the droppings of cattle and swine fed upon the products of the farm, and composted with earth and vegetable matter taken from the land, should be used to supply the drain made upon the soil in the production of crops, which otherwise would become impoverished and barren; and in the fact that manure so produced is generally regarded by farmers in this country as a part of the realty and has been so treated by landlords and tenants from time immemorial.  Daniels v. Pond, 21 Pick., 367; Lewis v. Lyman, 22 Pick., 437 Kittredge v. Woods, 3 N.Hamp., 503; Lassell v. Reed, 6 Greenl., 222; Parsons v. Camp, 11 Conn., 525; Fay v. Muzzy, 13 Gray, 53; Goodrich v. Jones, 2 Hill, 142; 1 Washb. on Real Prop., 5, 6.

But this principle does not apply to the droppings of animals driven by travelers upon the highway.  The highway is not used, and cannot be used, for the purpose of agriculture.  The manure is of no benefit whatsoever to it, but on the contrary is a detriment; and in cities and large villages it becomes a nuisance, and is removed by public officers at public expense.  The finding in this case is, "that the removal of the manure and scrapings was calculated to improve the appearance and health of the borough."  It is therefore evident that the cases relied upon by the defendant have no application to the case.

But it is said that if the manure was personal property, it was in the possession of the owner of the fee, and the scraping it into heaps by the plaintiff did not change the possession, but it continued as before, and that therefore the plaintiff cannot recover, for he neither had the possession nor the right to the immediate possession.

The manure originally belonged to the travelers whose animals dropped it, but it being worthless to them was immediately abandoned; and whether it then became the property of the borough of Stamford which owned the fee of the land on which the manure lay, it is unnecessary to determine; for, if it did, the case finds that the removal of the filth would be an improvement to the borough, and no objection was made by any one to the use that the plaintiff attempted to make of it. Considering the character of such accumulations upon highways in cities and villages, and the light in which they are everywhere regarded in closely settled communities, we cannot believe that the borough in this instance would have had any objection to the act of the plaintiff in removing a nuisance that affected the public health and the appearance of the streets. At all events, we think the facts of the case show a sufficient right in the plaintiff to the immediate possession of the property as against a mere wrong doer.

The defendant appears before the court in no enviable light. He does not pretend that he had a right to the manure, even when scattered upon the highway, superior to that of the plaintiff; but after the plaintiff had changed its original condition and greatly enhanced its value by his labor, he seized and appropriated to his own use the fruits of the plaintiff's outlay, and now seeks immunity from responsibility on the ground that the plaintiff was a wrong doer as well as himself. The conduct of the defendant is in keeping with his claim, and neither commends itself to the favorable consideration of the court. The plaintiff had the peaceable and quiet possession of the property; and we deem this sufficient until the borough of Stamford shall make complaint.

It is further claimed that if the plaintiff had a right to the property by virtue of occupancy, he lost the right when he ceased to retain the actual possession of the manure after scraping it into heaps.

We do not question the general doctrine, that where the right by occupancy exists, it exists no longer than the party retains the actual possession of the property, or till he appropriates it to his own use by removing it to some other place. If he leaves the property at the place where it was discovered, and does nothing whatsoever to enhance its value or change its nature, his right by occupancy is unquestionably gone. But the question is, if a party finds property comparatively worthless, as the plaintiff found the property in question, owing to its scattered condition upon the highway, and greatly increases its value by his labor and expense, does he lose his right if he leaves it a reasonable time to procure the means to take it away, when such means are necessary for its removal?

Suppose a teamster with a load of grain, while traveling the highway, discovers a rent in one of his bags, and finds that his grain is scattered upon the road for the distance of a mile. He considers the labor of collecting his corn of more value than the property itself, and he therefore abandons it, and pursues his way. *A* afterwards finds the grain in this condition and gathers it kernel by kernel into heaps by the side of the road, and leaves it a reasonable time to procure the means necessary for its removal. While he is gone for his bag, *B* discovers the grain thus conveniently collected in heaps and appropriates it to his own use. Has *A* any remedy? If he has not, the law in this instance is open to just reproach. We think under such circumstances *A* would have a reasonable time to remove the property, and during such reasonable time his right to it would be protected. If this is so, then the principle applies to the case under consideration.

A reasonable time for the removal of this manure had not elapsed when the defendant seized and converted it to his own use. The statute regulating the rights of parties in the gathering of sea-weed, gives the party who heaps it upon a public beach twenty-four hours in which to remove it, and that length of time for the removal of the property we think would not be unreasonable in most cases like the present one.

We therefore advise the Court of Common Pleas to grant a new trial.

In this opinion the other judges concurred.

NOTES AND QUESTIONS

1. *The Language of Haslem v. Lockwood.* Why was it necessary for court and counsel to turn a prosaic case concerning eighteen heaps of manure into a controversy over the meaning of "real" and "personal property," "possession," "abandonment," "legal title," and "reasonable time"? How does the use of such terms, and the need to bring "what happened" under those headings, influence the way the lawyers and judge conceived and thought about the problem? Could they not have framed their problem in more ordinary terms, weighed the equities, and resolved it in a more common-sensical way? Is it likely the outcome would have been any different? What are the arguments for and against such a special language of the law?

2. *The Lawyers' Arguments.* Why were the lawyers concerned with whether the manure was real or personal property? What significance did the categorization of the manure as "real property" or "personal property" have in the broader framework of their arguments? Who wanted the manure designated "real property"? Why? Does the fact that the action was brought in trover provide a clue?

Similarly, what were the lawyers trying to achieve by their arguments over whether the plaintiff had obtained "possession"? Or whether and when there had been "abandonment"? Whose "abandonment" were Curtis and Hoyt arguing for, and why? Whose "abandonment" was Olmstead arguing for, and why? Is "abandonment" the same notion in each of these two arguments? Does it play the same role in each of its two uses? Is its determination, in each case, based upon an appeal to the same "facts", or sorts of facts? Could you state a single "rule" which would tell you whether the manure had been abandoned by the owners of the horses *and* whether it had been abandoned by Plaintiff?

What does, or should, any of this have to do with whether **Mr.** Haslem or Mr. Lockwood should be permitted to have the value of the manure?

3. *The Dispute.* Why were the parties *really* in dispute? Does the total amount in controversy give you some clue? How do you suppose the value of the manure compared with the total legal fees the parties had to pay to perfect this case to the highest court of Connecticut?

For what purposes is it appropriate for courts to lend their energies (read: "the society to lend its energies through courts")? What would have happened, had the courts decided not to decide this one?

4. *The Law.* What was "the law" at the time this case came before the Supreme Court of Connecticut? Does the decision in *Haslem* support Holmes's observation that the law is "the prophecies of what the courts will do in fact, and nothing more pretentious"? Is it meaningless to ask whether the judge "followed the law"? Does Holmes's position mean there is no "law" until the case comes down? If so, how is "law" being used? Suppose that Plaintiff had walked into your office and told you his problem. How would you have known what questions to ask him? How, and to what extent, could you have found out what the courts would do?

5. *The Application of Legal Terms.* How was the judge supposed to decide whether the manure was real property or personal property? Can one tell by sensory evidence, *i. e.*, by looking, smelling, listening to, tasting, or feeling it?

6. As far as can be told, did court or counsel in *Haslem* ever state a definition of "personal" or "real property"? Of "possession"? Of "abandonment," "title," or "reasonable time"? Could the controversy over these terms have been resolved simply by referring to a standard dictionary of the English language? A law dictionary?

Do you suppose the court had something like a definition of each of the terms "in mind" as it analyzed the case? Why? When you apply terms in your day-to-day experience, do you find it necessary to have a definition "in mind"?

7. Where other than in dictionaries might lawyers and judges find definitions of dispositive legal terms? In statutes? In the imaginations of judges and lawyers? In judicial opinions? Did the cases and other authorities cited by counsel in *Haslem* tell Judge Park whether the manure was real or personal property? How do prior cases "tell" their readers whether something *in the case before them* is (ought to be?) real or personal property? How many authorities can you find that are used both by Olmstead and by Curtis and Hoyt? How do you explain this?

8. What arguments does Defendant's counsel Olmstead advance in favor of categorizing the manure as real property?

How is the judge to decide whether Olmstead's point #1 is correct or not, that "the manure mixed with the dirt . . . was a part of the real estate"? What ever makes something a "part of" something else? The facility of severing? Or the necessity? Is a sliver in one's finger or a bandage on one's hand a part of one's person?

How "mixed with" the dirt does something have to be before it becomes "a part of" the real estate? Could lawyers agree to a single definition of "a part of" that might run throughout the law? Suppose a rule were fashioned in quantitative terms, so that if some personal property is mixed, say, 5 p.p.m. (or 100 p.p.m.) with certain real estate it would become "a part of" the real estate? Would a rule stated in such terms be adequate to satisfy the ends of the law of property? Would it resolve the disputes people are trying to resolve in cases like *Haslem*?

In answering these questions, does it matter whether to say (a) "the manure was part of the real estate" (referring to the physical substance, the land) is a different type of statement than (b) "the manure was part of the real estate" (in the sense of "real property", the legal categorization)? What is the problem? Are the procedures for determining the truth or falsity of the two statements, (a) and (b) the same? Can they each be "true" or "false" in the same way?

9.    Consider the question of possession. In the ordinary sense of the term, did the plaintiff *ever* possess the manure? If so, did he ever possess all of it at one time? Did he, for example, possess the third heap while he was working on the fifteenth? And even if he did possess all of it when on the premises, does it comport with ordinary usage to say that he retained possession when he departed and left the heaps on someone else's property?

What does the legal term make it *sound as though* the law is looking to? How much more complicated must the actual legal inquiry be? Why is there this disparity?

10.    In support of his position that Plaintiff had abandoned possession, Olmstead argues (point #6) that Plaintiff left the manure without leaving any "notice". How should the judge go about deciding whether this is true or not? If he thinks only of the picture that comes to mind when the word "notice" is uttered, Olmstead is certainly right. Suppose the judge looks, however, not for a *picture* that comes to mind, but to a *function*: what function would a notice have performed, if a notice had been left? Can you make an argument that a notice *was* left?

What is it to *be* an X other than to fulfill the function of X?

11.    *Judge Park's Opinion.* Did the task of having to write an opinion influence the way in which the Court conceived and solved the problem? Why might this be so? How do the reasons for having courts write opinions compare with the reasons Brod may have had for writing his "opinion" in the matter of Kafka's posthumous instructions?

12.    Note Judge Park's explanation of the cases holding manure to be "real estate." Is it proper—is it "legal"—to define a juridical concept "for the benefit of agriculture"? Must not a fair and impartial legal system define its concepts in a way which favors no particular interest or group? Is it possible to have a legal system at all

if this requirement is not met? How, for example, *could* a court authoritatively choose between the social and equitable factors implicated in the dispute between Haslem and Lockwood if the definition of legal concepts required such choices? Consider, for example,

—the interest in removing manure from a highway before it emits too noxious an odor;

—the interest of the neighborhood in peace and quiet after 8 p.m.;

—the importance of agriculture to the economy of Nineteenth Century Connecticut;

—the purchasing power of six dollars;

—the time and expense to the public of trial and appellate court proceedings;

—the prevailing conceptions of "fairness" within the community;

—the reasonable expectations of persons in the positions of Plaintiff and Defendant;

—the comparative wealth of Plaintiff and Defendant;

Is there an argument that the benefits which a legal system brings to a society are lost when such interests become a part of legal calculations? Once such considerations are introduced, can one distinguish the mode of solving the problem of Messrs. Haslem and Lockwood from the mode of solving the problem that Max Brod faced?

Yet, was it possible for Judge Park to resolve the dispute *without* considering such factors? Why?

13. On what grounds did Judge Park overturn the lower court's decision? Were they authoritative legal grounds? Can you state a "rule of the case" to your satisfaction?

What reason did the judge give for holding that the manure was not real property; that the owners of the horses had abandoned the manure; that the "plaintiff had the peaceable and quiet possession of the property"; that the appropriate time limit was that to be found in the seaweed statute? Does his analogy to the scattered grain establish the proposition for which it is presented? What is required for an analogy to provide support for an argument? Does Judge Park offer it?

Does Judge Park's opinion come down to the view that the defendant was morally a wrongdoer and that the law, *i. e. Judge Park*, would not protect immoral behavior? Is this an oversimplified—or overly cynical—view of what he did?

14. To the extent the decision did rest on Judge Park's assessment of the relative morality of the parties' actions, how did he go about making that judgment? What specifically made defendant a "wrongdoer", who appeared before the court "in no enviable light"?

Is there any authoritative way to determine what is morally right and wrong? How does a lawyer, facing a judge who may take these notions into account, know how to argue to him? What facts can he point to? How does he know what rules to invoke? Did Judge Park suppose that "right" was what the majority of people in the community considered "right"? Or what was "best" for the majority of people in the community, irrespective of what they thought? Or did he feel that notions of "right" and "fairness" could be deduced from biblical authority? Did Judge Park hold the same moral views as Max Brod? Could a lawyer reading the opinions tell?

If the decision comes down to matters like these, can it satisfy our notions of what the law is supposed to do, and how it is supposed to work?

15. What should a lawyer's education consist in? In what respects are the demands of a good legal education similar to those of a good education in, say, chemistry? Consider, in this regard, the observations of a non-scientist in an article about science:

> A chemistry textbook . . . is written to train a chemist. It offers, as the subject matter of chemistry, the current body of chemical doctrines. But a body of doctrines exists to explain something that is not itself a doctrine . . . .. In a typical chemistry textbook (good textbooks, do, of course, exist), what this something is gets three pages of vague discussion in the preface. "Chemistry," says the textbook in front of me, "deals with the substances of the universe." It is a useless definition that never reappears. The reader plunges immediately into the laws of combining weights and volumes. He is on his way to becoming a chemist, the very person least likely even to comprehend what you mean when you ask what chemistry is about, (or so it would seem. When I recently asked a young chemistry professor this question, the first words he uttered were "spectroscopic analysis.") [2]

In what respects do you think a poor chemistry education would resemble a poor legal education? Considering the problems in preparing and deciding a case like *Haslem* (any case?) what characteristics and subject matter might the education of the lawyers and judges have included?

In answering these questions, consider the observations of the same author that what is involved in the development of scientific theories, (*e. g.*, the abandonment of the ether description of light propagation in favor of new theories) "is less a description of the real world than a real shift in interest. . . ."

What putative "descriptions of the real world" does Judge Park discern as "interests" the realization of which he is prepared to achieve by shifting descriptions? When ought a scientist to make such shifts? When ought lawyers and judges to be so engaged?

16. What benefit was this case to the advancement or improvement of social order, other than its resolution of the immediate difficulties between Haslem and Lockwood? What guidance do you suppose it gave to others in the community? Of what use might it be

2. Karp, Searching for Science, 8 Colum.Univ.Forum 12, 13 (1965).

to subsequent judges? Consider, in this last regard, Sharkiewicz v. Lepone, which follows, and its use of Haslem v. Lockwood.

## SHARKIEWICZ V. LEPONE

139 Conn. 706 (1953)

Frank Sharkiewicz pro se, the appellant (plaintiff).

No appearance for the appellees (defendants).

JENNINGS, J. The complaint alleged that the defendants unlawfully converted a car owned by the plaintiff to their own use.

The finding as corrected in one particular may be summarized as follows: The plaintiff was the owner of a 1936 Oldsmobile coupe. It was worth less than $20. It had been parked on property of the defendant Mary Lepone for several years prior to November 27, 1944, at an agreed rental of $1 a month. On several occasions (the dates are not stated) Mrs. Lepone ordered the plaintiff to remove the car from her premises. It was not removed. On or about December 4, 1944, Mrs. Lepone sold the car to the other defendants, doing business as Steinman Auto Parts, for the sum of $1 and other valuables, for junk. On these facts the trial court concluded that the plaintiff had abandoned the car and that there was no illegal conversion thereof.

Title 17 of the General Statutes is concerned with motor vehicles and related matters. It covers over 100 pages and contains 224 sections. This indicates that motor vehicles are a very special kind of property and require special treatment. Section 2475 deals with abandoned motor vehicles. The plaintiff claims that its rather elaborate provisions for conducting a sale of an abandoned vehicle make the sale by the named defendant illegal as a matter of law. This is not so. All of the provisions relate to the sale of a car placed in storage by an officer.

The plaintiff also claims that the car was not abandoned and that its sale was an illegal conversion. The validity of this claim depends on the correctness of the court's conclusion that the car was abandoned. "Abandonment in its general sense is the intentional relinquishment of a known right." Glotzer v. Keyes, 125 Conn. 227, 232, 5 A.2d 1. It is ordinarily a question of fact. Id., 235. "To constitute an abandonment there must be an intention to abandon or relinquish accompanied by some act or omission to act by which such an intention is manifested." Id., 233. Most of the cases, including that cited, concern the abandonment of property rights, but personal property may also be abandoned. Haslem v. Lockwood, 37 Conn. 500, 507. This is so when its possession is voluntarily forsaken by the owner. Crosson v. Lion Oil & Refining Co., 169 Ark. 561, 566, 275 S.W. 899.

The only fact to support the conclusion that the car was abandoned by the plaintiff was his failure to remove it in accordance with Mrs. Lepone's order. The only reasonable interpretation of the finding is that the plaintiff was a tenant of Mrs. Lepone at least until November 27, 1944. The car was sold December 4, 1944. In the absence of the date when the order to remove was given, the interval between November 27 and December 4 is insufficient to show, as a matter of law, an intent by the plaintiff to abandon the car. The subordinate facts do not support the conclusion that the car was abandoned. In the absence of abandonment, the plaintiff was constructively in possession of the car. See State v. Courtsol, 89 Conn. 564, 568, 94 A. 973.

The defendants are unrepresented, there was no attachment and this litigation should be terminated. The finding that the car was not worth more than $20 was not attacked. None of the parties can have any legitimate ground of complaint if judgement is directed for that amount. See Patalano v. Chabot, 139 Conn. 356, 362, 94 A.2d 15.

There is error, the judgement is set aside and the case is remanded with direction to render judgement for the plaintiff against all defendants in the amount of $20.

In this opinion BROWN, C.J., BALDWIN and INGLIS, Js., concurred.

O'SULLIVAN, J. (dissenting). I dissent on the following ground: On September 20, 1944, a marshal of the Hartford fire department notified Mrs. Lepone that a dilapidated coupe which had been standing in her yard for several months was a fire hazard and would have to be removed. The automobile belonged to the plaintiff and its general condition is fully disclosed by the fact that it was eventually sold for $1. Between September 20, 1944, and the following December 4, Mrs. Lepone called the plaintiff on the telephone several times and also sent word to him through his brother to get the car off her premises. In spite of these repeated orders, the plaintiff did nothing to carry them out. On December 4 she sold the car to the other defendants and they removed it.

The court found that "[t]his car was abandoned by the plaintiff when . . . he failed to remove the property from the premises as required by the defendant Lepone." No assignment of error has been directed to this finding. It still remains unchallenged, and even if it were attacked it would still be amply supported as an ultimate fact by the other subordinate facts found.

## Notes and Questions

1. How far did the Connecticut courts progress toward constructing a rule defining "abandonment" in the near seventy-five years between *Haslem* and *Sharkiewicz*? If twenty-four hours was enough to constitute an abandonment of property worth six 1871 dollars, why were not seven days enough for an abandonment of property worth no more than twenty 1944 dollars? Is this a question Judge Jennings answers? Is it a question a judge *ought* to feel called upon to answer?

Should *Sharkiewicz* be taken as overruling Haslem v. Lockwood? As distinguishing it? As ignoring it? Why do the answers to these questions matter?

2. Does the court attempt to explain why both the lower court and the dissenting judge mistakenly thought that plaintiff *had* aban-

doned his property? How do Jennings' explanations compare with the ones offered by Judge Park in *Haslem*?

Can you account for the different findings of fact in the lower and appellate court opinions? Can you account for the different findings of fact in the majority and dissenting opinions of the appellate court?

3. If the *Haslem* opinion had gotten into the hands of Mr. Sharkiewicz or Mrs. Lepone early in their dispute, would it have made any difference? Would it have enabled them to know what "the law" was, and thus settle their dispute themselves, without a court order? If not, would the difficulty have been that their case was just different from *Haslem*? Are not, however, all cases "different"? Do the difficulties of using *Haslem* as a precedent owe to there being something especially peculiar about "abandonment" relative to other legal terms? Do you suppose that "corporation", "possession", "domicile" are any less troublesome?

4. Law, it is often said, helps make social life predictable, uniform, systematic, manageable: all of which tend to make people's lives both secure and free. Do *Haslem*, or *Sharkiewicz*, or the two of them read together, make it clear what society gains when it attempts to organize the relations of people by means of law? Or does it give us reason to doubt the superiority of legal institutions over the apparently less structured, less word-conditioned form of problem resolution employed, for example, by Max Brod? Indeed, under the surface, is there really any difference? Was the court in *Haslem* or *Sharkiewicz* confined to a special set of "legal" principles and methods that can be distinguished from the principles and methods Max Brod used in resolving his dilemma? Is it likely that the lawsuits would have been decided any differently had they been submitted to a panel of dentists or clergymen rather than to a panel of judges?

5. Was there a legal system in existence in Connecticut in 1944?

What do people mean when they speak of a legal system? The Random House Dictionary of the English Language (Unab. ed.) defines "system" as "1. an assemblage or combination of things or parts forming a complex or unitary whole: *a mountain system; a railroad system.* . . . 3. an ordered and comprehensive assemblage of facts, principles, doctrines, or the like, in a particular field of knowledge or thought . . . ." What system is evidenced by the decisions in *Haslem* and *Sharkiewicz*? What "unitary whole" or "order and comprehensive assemblage"? What is it that people want when they say they want a legal system? Is it within their reach?

## PART ONE

# THE DILEMMAS OF ROLE, RULE AND REASON

### INTRODUTORY NOTE

Social order can be achieved only through some restrictions on individual choice. Which choices are to be constrained, the panoply of sanctions relied upon (legal penalties, social shame, internalized guilt), as well as the method by which these decisions are reached are much of what give each society its special character.

Of these limits on discretion, the most familiar are probably those that apply generally to all persons living in the society, *e. g.*, the law of crimes, or the less formal sanctions against lying. But some of the most fundamental limits on discretion are those that are applied *systemically*—not to everyone in the same way, or even to persons per se, but to persons only indirectly as the performers of certain roles or the holders of certain offices.

Restrictions of the latter sort are expressed in admonitions like, "as a scientist, it is your responsibility to pursue knowledge, and not concern yourself with how the government may put that knowledge to use"; or, "as a trustee, you are held to 'something stricter than the morals of the marketplace' "; or, "as a prosecutor, it is your duty to put your kindness to one side, and seek conviction."

These and similar appeals are part of a process in which societies try to structure themselves through a division of functions. Such a division ordinarily calls for (a) a class of rules that prescribe which problems are to be channeled to which offices, (b) a class of rules to guide the procedures for each office, and (c) a class of rules for each office to execute. These rules direct the officeholder to decide the problems channeled to him in accordance with the policies they embody, and not in accordance with his personal interests, or even with his estimate of what would be best for society "on the whole".

Courts of law provide an example. The judge "applies" or "follows" the law: For example, where legislation is involved, he should not rethink and make anew the judgments of fact and value that a legislator or voter would—and presumably did—take into account.

> The duty of the judge is to pronounce verdict and sentence in accordance with the law; and the question 'What verdict and sentence ought he to pronounce?' turns solely on the question 'What verdict and sentence are laid down in the law for this crime'. As judge, he is not concerned with the consequences, beneficial or harmful, of what he pronounces. Similarly, the question 'Was that a just sentence?' is one that cannot be settled by reference to its consequences, but solely by reference to the law. . . .

23

In assessing the justice of a punishment in a particular case, therefore, we are concerned only with . . . two points. The punishment is just if and only if the accused committed the crime and the punishment is that laid down by the law for that crime. The question of the probable effects on the accused or on others (the reform and deterrence so greatly emphasized by utilitarians) is relevant only in so far as judges are allowed considerable latitude within which they may be guided by considerations other than what the law prescribes. In practice, both in civil and in criminal cases, judges often express regret at being in duty bound to give the verdicts they do and recommend the alteration of the law.

But the duty of the legislator is quite different. It is not to decide whether a particular application of the law is just or not, but to decide what laws ought to be adopted and what penalties are to be laid down for the breach of each law.[1]

This sort of division is not peculiar to the relationship of the courts to the legislatures. As indicated, the entire social order consists of a vast network of such correlative functions, the design of which is, in large measure, to circumscribe the ambit of consideration appropriate for each person in his particular job.

Thus the soldier is under an obligation to follow "superior orders" without thinking whether to do so is the best way to go about winning the war; or whether it was best to fight the war to begin with. The lawyer is, again within certain limits, to make the most effective case he can for those who come to him for aid. The rules of his role do not give him title to consider and apply all the values he may hold as a human being, from wondering whether it wouldn't be better for the society "on the whole" if he "threw" the case and his client were convicted. He is—we are all in at least some of our offices and roles—to think of "the law", but not of "justice", to think of making boxcars run on time for "the Fatherland", but not to think that they are bringing innocent people to the gas chambers.

By such arrangements, people are able to know where it is that they should send which problems; and to have a sense of what sort of treatment the problems will receive when they get there. They will thus know what standards will be invoked and what arguments they will have to make.

The office holder, in turn, may be the better able to organize his thinking about the problems before him: he need not consider every fact that might conceivably be relevant or track out every consequence that his actions might entail; or reconsider every social value that, by adequate stretch of the imagination, his decision could conceivably involve. He can pose his problem in a special, limited, and manageable way, trusting that many of the considerations have already been disposed of by others, and trusting to others to reconsider it

1. P. M. Nowell-Smith, Ethics 236–37 (1954). By kind permission of Penguin Books Limited and Professor Nowell-Smith.

in their special, limited and manageable ways if the rules of the larger system should make such review appropriate.

This process of parcelling out social responsibility involves the society and the individual in a number of serious problems. Some of these are, broadly speaking, "moral" (section 2); still others are epistemological and semantical (section 3).

### Moral Dilemmas

The moral dilemma that this system presents is one that has been made acute for us by such men as Nietzsche, Thoreau and Sartre. How, they ask, can one justify the commission of acts not because *he* believes them best, according to his values, but because *others* expect them of him; because *others* want them; because *others* think them best? Why should he place his fellows before himself; and why should he think that his fellows' judgment, even as to their common interests, is superior to his own? Even in a democratic society—a society of consent—mightn't one believe, firmly, that the majority is *wrong*, practically or morally? How, then, can a citizen obey a law he believes to be unjust? How can a judge maintain his sense of integrity and self-respect when his decisions—because "the law says so"—leave unremedied social practices which he believes to be immoral? If each man does not think every matter through, as best he can—if he does not assume the full measure of his responsibility—is he not renouncing his reason and resigning himself to a life something less than human?

The short answer to these questions is, of course, that enormous problems would exist both for the society and for the individual if each of us regarded himself as a wholly independent atom. But the answer is too short. The other extreme—slavish obedience to rules—has its own special problems, as the history of Nazi Germany testifies. Thus, some intermediate position must be found, and, indeed, there has always been broad sentiment in our society that there are occasions when an individual ought to disregard the rules of his office in favor of some over-riding moral ideal.

The individual's moral dilemma can be framed, then, as one of determining *when* he ought to satisfy obligations other than those set down for him by the society's institutions. To answer this question, the rules which define his role cannot provide the final answer. Yet if the answer is not to be found there, how effectively can the organizing function of a system of roles and offices be fulfilled? And if the roles and rules do not *always* provide the right answers, where, ultimately, are the right answers to be found?

### The Epistemological and Semantical Dilemmas

The second group of problems might be gathered under the heading "Is law knowable?" Even where an individual has decided he ought to perform those acts his office commands, how can he know, objectively, what it is he is supposed to do?

The rules the office holder is to "carry out" (*e. g.*, the law, if the office holder is a judge) must somehow be communicated to him. In some situations, as in a sergeant's orders to his men, the "rule" may be communicated orally; in more elaborate institutional structures, there is greater reliance on writings, *e. g.*, statutes, administrative regulations, printed opinions from past cases. In either case, there are symbols to be interpreted, and the interpretation involves the office holder in a number of seemingly complex and overlapping inquiries. First, it would appear, he must determine what his authority *is, i. e.*, what cases, if any, he is authorized to decide; second, in any concrete case in which he takes jurisdiction, he must ascertain (a) what rule he is authorized to apply, (b) what the rule he is to apply *means*; and, (c) *what the facts are*, specifically, whether they are such as to make the rule applicable.

It might seem that these inquiries do not pose an insuperable problem, for we are constantly encountering systems of offices and of rules which—though less than perfectly—seem to work. Judges seem to be carrying out "the will of the legislature"; lawyers seem to be able to plan their clients' actions on the basis of precedent. Obviously, they could not do so if they did not know to some extent the rules which defined and directed discretion. Yet it is possible to argue—and it has been argued—that the apparent successes of such systems are illusory. In law, for example, one can point to case after case in which there is heated disagreement about the existence and applicability of a controlling legal rule. Not only do the lawyers find grounds on which to differ but the judges as well frequently find themselves in open, vocal debates with each other—and still many more judicial disagreements may be left undisclosed to preserve public respect for law and for courts. Cases are decided, it is therefore contended, not "solely by reference to law", but according to other factors hidden from view—values that are peculiarly the decision-maker's "own" values, and not necessarily those he is directed to invoke. If the hidden and overt controversies could be attributed solely to the stupidity, carelessness or dishonesty of lawyers, judges and legislators this phenomenon could be viewed simply as a problem of education and of morals. But people of conceded good faith and of acknowledged intellectual competence are continually being drawn into these legal controversies. Among themselves they apparently see different facts, different rules, and different meanings, even when looking at the same words. It is this phenomenon which stirs doubt as to whether law is really knowable and whether in a meaningful way we do have—or can have—a government of laws and not of men.

## CHAPTER ONE

# Sticking to Firm Ground(?)

## UNION PACIFIC RY. v. CAPPIER

72 Pac. 281 (Kansas 1903)

SMITH, J.  This was an action brought by Adeline Cappier, the mother of Irvin Ezelle, to recover damages resulting to her by reason of the loss of her son, who was run over by a car of plaintiff in error, and died from the injuries received.  The trial court, at the close of the evidence introduced to support a recovery by plaintiff below, held that no careless act of the railway company's servants in the operation of the car was shown, and refused to permit the case to be considered by the jury on the allegations and attempted proof of such negligence.  The petition, however, contained an averment that the injured person had one leg and an arm cut off by the car wheels, and that the servants of the railway company failed to call a surgeon, or to render him any assistance after the accident, but permitted him to remain by the side of the tracks and bleed to death.  Under this charge of negligence a recovery was had.

While attempting to cross the railway tracks, Ezelle was struck by a moving freight car pushed by an engine.  A yardmaster in charge of the switching operations was riding on the end of the car nearest to the deceased, and gave warning by shouting to him.  The warning was either too late, or no heed was given to it.  The engine was stopped.  After the injured man was clear of the track, the yardmaster signaled the engineer to move ahead, fearing, as he testified, that a passenger train then about due would come upon them.  The locomotive and car went forward over a bridge, where the general yardmaster was informed of the accident, and an ambulance was telephoned for.  The yardmaster then went back where the injured man was lying, and found three Union Pacific switchmen binding up the wounded limbs and doing what they could to stop the flow of blood.  The ambulance arrived about 30 minutes later, and Ezelle was taken to a hospital, where he died a few hours afterwards.

In answer to particular questions of fact, the jury found that the accident occurred at 5:35 p. m.; that immediately one of the railway employees telephoned to police headquarters for help for the injured man; that the ambulance started at 6:05 p. m., and reached the nearest hospital with Ezelle at 6:20 p. m., where he received proper medical and surgical treatment.  Judgment against the railway company was based on the following question and answer:  "Q.  Did not defendant's employees bind up Ezelle's wounds, and try to stop the flow of blood, as soon as they could after the accident happened?  A.  No."  The lack of diligence in the respect stated was intended, no doubt, to apply to the yardmaster, engineer, and fireman in charge of the car and engine.  These facts bring us to a consideration of their legal duty toward the injured man after his condition became known.  Counsel for defendant in error quote the language found in Beach on

27

Contributory Negligence (3d Ed.) § 215, as follows: "Under certain circumstances, the railroad may owe a duty to a trespasser after the injury. When a trespasser has been run down, it is the plain duty of the railway company to render whatever service is possible to mitigate the severity of the injury. The train that has occasioned the harm must be stopped, and the injured person looked after, and, when it seems necessary, removed to a place of safety, and carefully nursed, until other relief can be brought to the disabled person." The principal authority cited in support of this doctrine is Northern Central Railway Co. v. State, 29 Md. 420, 96 Am.Dec. 545. The court in that case first held that there was evidence enough to justify the jury in finding that the operatives of the train were negligent in running it too fast over a road crossing without sounding the whistle, and that the number of brakemen was insufficient to check its speed. Such negligence was held sufficient to uphold the verdict, and would seem to be all that was necessary to be said. The court, however, proceeded to state that, from whatever cause the collision occurred, it was the duty of the servants of the company, when the man was found on the pilot of the engine in a helpless and insensible condition, to remove him, and to do it with proper regard to his safety and the laws of humanity. In that case the injured person was taken in charge by the servants of the railway company, and, being apparently dead, without notice to his family, or sending for a physician to ascertain his condition, he was moved to defendant's warehouse, laid on a plank, and locked up for the night. The next morning, when the warehouse was opened, it was found that during the night the man had revived from his stunned condition, and moved some paces from the spot where he had been laid, and was found in a stooping posture, dead, but still warm, having died from hemorrhage of the arteries of one leg which was crushed at and above the knee. It had been proposed to place him in the defendant's station house, which was a comfortable building, but the telegraph operator objected, and directed him to be taken into the warehouse, a place used for the deposit of old barrels and other rubbish. The Maryland case does not support what is so broadly stated in Beach on Contributory Negligence. It is cited by Judge Cooley, in his work on Torts, in a note to a chapter devoted to the negligence of bailees (chapter 20), indicating that the learned author understood the reasoning of the decision to apply where the duty began after the railway employees had taken charge of the injured person. After the trespasser on the track of a railway company has been injured in collision with a train, and the servants of the company have assumed to take charge of him, the duty, no doubt, arises to exercise such care in his treatment as the circumstances will allow. We are unable, however, to approve the doctrine that when the acts of a trespasser himself result in his injury, where his own negligent conduct is alone the cause, those in charge of the instrument which inflicted the hurt, being innocent of wrongdoing, are nevertheless blamable in law if they neglect to administer to the sufferings of him whose wounds we might say were self-imposed.

With the humane side of the question courts are not concerned. It is the omission or negligent discharge of legal duties only which

come within the sphere of judicial cognizance. For withholding relief from the suffering, for failure to respond to the calls of worthy
charity, or for faltering in the bestowment of brotherly love on the
unfortunate, penalties are found not in the laws of men, but in that
higher law, the violation of which is condemned by the voice of conscience, whose sentence of punishment for the recreant act is swift
and sure. In the law of contracts it is now well understood that a
promise founded on a moral obligation will not be enforced in the
courts. Bishop states that some of the older authorities recognize a
moral obligation as valid, and says: "Such a doctrine, carried to its
legitimate results, would release the tribunals from the duty to administer the law of the land, and put in the place of law the varying
ideas of morals which the changing incumbents of the bench might
from time to time entertain." Bishop on Contracts, § 44. Ezelle's
injuries were inflicted, as the court below held, without the fault of
the yardmaster, engineer, or fireman in charge of the car and locomotive. The railway company was no more responsible than it would
have been had the deceased been run down by the cars of another
railroad company on a track parallel with that of plaintiff in error.
If no duty was imposed on the servants of defendant below to take
charge of and care for the wounded man in such a case, how could a
duty arise under the circumstances of the case at bar? In Barrows
on Negligence, p. 4, it is said: "The duty must be owing from the
defendant to the plaintiff, otherwise there can be no negligence, so
far as the plaintiff is concerned. . . . And the duty must be owing to plaintiff in an individual capacity, and not merely as one of
the general public. This excludes from actionable negligence all failures to observe the obligations imposed by charity, gratitude, generosity, and the kindred virtues. The moral law would obligate an
attempt to rescue a person in a perilous position—as a drowning
child—but the law of the land does not require it, no matter how little
personal risk it might involve, provided that the person who declines
to act is not responsible for the peril." See Kenney v. The Hannibal
& St. Joseph Railroad Company, 70 Mo. 252–257. In the several
cases cited in the brief of counsel for defendant in error to sustain
the judgment of the trial court it will be found that the negligence
on which recoveries were based occurred after the time when the person injured was in the custody and care of those who were at fault
in failing to give him proper treatment.

The judgment of the court below will be reversed, with directions
to enter judgment on the findings of the jury in favor of the railway
company. All the Justices concurring.

## QUESTIONS

1. What is the specific error that the Supreme Court of Kansas
found the lower court to have made? At what point in the trial did
it occur and what were its procedural consequences?

2. What is the likely effect of the Supreme Court's rule on the
readiness of people to aid others in distress? What risk do they
assume if they do nothing? What risk do they assume if they begin
to render aid? Why did the court come to such a result? Did it do

so because it was *bound*—*i. e.*, is it possible that the judges' own sentiments were to the contrary, but controlling authoritative sources compelled them to ignore their own ideas of a "just" result? If so, what were the *sources*; and why did they feel *compelled* by them?

3. By what sorts of authority is the highest court of a state "bound" in cases which do not involve the U. S. Constitution or federal treaties or laws? Was the *Cappier* court presented with any Kansas statute absolving the railroad from liability? Does Judge Smith cite any Kansas common law precedent?

4. Why did the counsel and court concern themselves with the *Northern Central* case, a Maryland decision? In the absence of contrary Kansas authority, was it not good evidence of the general common law rule? Why did Judge Smith refuse to follow it? Could the principle for which *Northern Central* was cited by plaintiff properly be dismissed as mere dictum? Even though the Maryland court had concluded that "there was sufficient evidence of negligence to be submitted to the jury" regarding the operation of the train, could it have been certain that the jury's verdict was based on a finding of negligence in the *operation of the train* rather than a finding of negligence in the *ministering of aid*? On the ministering of aid the Maryland court had said,

> We are next brought to the question, whether the defendant be liable for the negligence of its agents in their treatment and disposition of the deceased, subsequent to the collision. This, we think, free from doubt or difficulty. From whatever cause the collision occurred, after the train was stopped, the injured man was found upon the pilot of the defendant's engine, in a helpless and insensible condition, and it thereupon at once became the duty of the agents, in charge of the train, to remove him, and to do it with a proper regard to his safety and the laws of humanity. And if in removing and locking up the unfortunate man, though apparently dead, negligence was committed, whereby the death was caused, there is no principle of reason or justice upon which the defendant can be exonerated from responsibility. To contend that the agents were not acting in the course of their employment in so removing and disposing of the party, is to contend that the duty of the defendant extended no farther than to have cast off by the wayside the helpless and apparently dead man, without taking care to ascertain whether he was dead or alive, or if alive, whether his life could be saved by reasonable assistance, timely rendered. For such a rule of restricted responsibility no authority has been produced, and we apprehend none can be found. On the contrary, it is the settled policy of the law, "to give such agents and servants a large and liberal discretion, and hold the companies liable for all their acts, within the most extensive range of their charter powers." 1. Read. on Railw., 510; Derby v. Phila. and Read. Railway Co., 14 How., 468, 483.

Why did Judge Smith not reason the problem out the same way the Maryland court had done? Is the Maryland court's analysis less "legal" than Smith's?

5. How had Beach read the *Northern Central* case? How had Cooley read it? How can we be certain, simply on the evidence we have, viz., that Cooley footnoted the case in a chapter on bailments? Are the two "readings" necessarily inconsistent? And, even if so, why does Smith follow his reading of Cooley's reading, rather than his reading of Beach's reading? Was Cooley more "the law" than Beach? By reference to what authority was *that* choice made?

6. What is the strongest case that Judge Smith marshals in support of his position? Why does he cite the *Hannibal & St. Joseph* case with a "see" reference? In that case, a fire had broken out on the defendant railroad's right-of-way through the railroad's negligence, and spread to plaintiff's ground. The Court expressly said, 70 Mo. at 256,

> The record did not present the question of the liability of the company for the neglect of its section hands to extinguish the fire, and, therefore, the remarks on that subject [in an earlier disposition] are no[t] authoritative, but only entitled to that consideration which is due to any observation on legal questions falling from the able and learned judge who delivered the opinion of the court.

7. Judge Smith suggests that Ezelle's "own negligent conduct was alone the cause" and refers to the wounds as "self-imposed". Does the use of the term "cause," with its scientific connotations, help create an impression that Judge Smith was basing his decision on hard, objective facts—not moral sentiments?

In what sense was Ezelle's negligent conduct "alone the cause"? If cause is meant in a scientific, or non-legal conclusory sense, why were Ezelle's acts more "the cause" than the railroad's? On the other hand, if cause in the legal sense is meant, is the court fairly confronting plaintiff's position? Is she not maintaining that even if Ezelle caused (negligently or otherwise) the accident, the railroad caused the death; and is it not the death for which she is suing?

8. Even if under the law of Kansas the railroad had no duty to Ezelle *unless* and *until* it took him into its "custody and care", is it clear that the case ought not to have gone to the jury?

9. Judge Smith cites Bishop to the effect that courts' enforcing moral obligations "would release the tribunals from the duty to administer the law of the land, and put in the place of law the varying ideas of morals which the changing incumbents of the bench might from time to time entertain." Do the changing incumbents have varying ideas of what the *law* is? (Did the trial court Judge have the same idea as Judge Smith; did Beach, in his treatise on Contributory Negligence, agree with Cooley, in his work on Torts)?

10. Could it be argued that Judge Smith *was* acting according to his notions of morality, but that these expressed themselves in a concern for the rightness of imposing *legal* liability on the railroad? Consider these remarks of John Stuart Mill:

.  .  .  The only purpose for which power can rightfully
be exercised over any member of a civilized community
against his will is to prevent harm to others  .  .  .  He
cannot rightfully be compelled to do or forbear because it will
be better for him to do so  .  .  .  because in the opinions
of others, to do so would be wise or even right.

ON LIBERTY 13 (1956).  If a starving man is refused food by a
passerby, would it comport with Anglo-American notions of liberty to
legally penalize the passerby, even assuming the refusal to have been
immoral?  How distinguishable is that case from *Cappier*?

Could it thus be argued that Judge Smith, notwithstanding his
protestations that he had to stick to "legal duties" *was* acting on moral
grounds, but for him the moral concern was that evidenced by Mill?
Is it important to know how Mill is using the word "harm" in order
to answer this question?

In either event, what was it, after all, that made appeal to "the
law" more certain, or in any other way preferable to a direct appeal
to morality?

11.  Why did Judge Smith play down his own autonomy and
freedom in each of the numerous choices he made?  Was he concealing
his discretion from the litigants and the public in the interests of
reassuring them that the decision was "the law's", not "his"?  Or
might he himself have been unaware of how much freedom he had
within "the law"?  Is it possible that people want to repress the awareness of how many choices they truly have—that they want to (in Erich
Fromm's phrase) "escape from freedom"?  Why?

12.  Yet, is this a case in which we can say that the judge "decided what he wanted to decide", or "just invoked his 'gut reaction' "?
Is the opinion and its appeal to "law" pure sham?  Can we really
suppose that Judge Smith's "gut reaction" was in favor of promulgat-
ing a rule that allowed—even encouraged—letting little boys who have
been struck by railroad cars bleed to death?  Is it any more likely
that the sole explanation for his decision is that he simply and instinctively felt that it was immoral to enforce morality in circumstances like *Cappier*?  May there not be something to Judge Smith's
professed belief that "the law"—something, somehow—put special
restraints upon him as judge?

*FELIX S. COHEN*

## THE ETHICAL BASIS OF LEGAL CRITICISM *

An ethics, like a metaphysics, is no more certain and no less dangerous because it is unconsciously held.  There are few judges, psychoanalysts, or economists today who do not begin a consideration of
their typical problems with some formula designed to cause all moral
ideals to disappear and to produce an issue purified for the procedure
of positive empirical science.  But the ideals have generally retired to

* From  3–7,  33–36  (Cornell  U.  Press
1959).

hats from which later wonders will magically arise.  A historical school of law disclaims concern with ethics and repeatedly invokes a *Zeitgeist* or a *Volksgeist* to decide what the law ought to be.  An analytical school of jurisprudence again dismisses questions of morality, and again decides what the law ought to be by reference to a so-called logical ideal, which is not an ideal of logic at all, but an aesthetic ideal of symmetrical analogical development.  Those who derive the law from the will of the sovereign usually introduce without further justification the premise that it is good to obey that will.  And those who define law in terms of actually prevailing social demands or interests make frequent use of the undisclosed principle that these demands *ought* to be satisfied.

The objection, then, is not that jurists have renounced ethical judgment but that they have renounced ethical science.  Ethical science involves an analysis of ethical judgments, a clarification of ethical premises.  Among the current legal crypto-idealisms there can be no edifying controversy, since there is no recognition of the moral issues to which their differences reduce.  One looks in vain in legal treatises and law-review articles for legal criticism conscious of its moral presuppositions.  The vocabularies of logic and aesthetics are freely drawn upon in the attempt to avoid the disagreeable assertion that something or other is intrinsically better than something else.  Particular decisions or legal rules are "anomalous" or "illogical," "incorrect" or "impractical," "reactionary" or "liberal," and unarguable ethical innuendo takes the place of critical analysis.

. . . .

But the relevance of ethics to the philosophy of law would be clear even if it were not unconsciously assumed by those who appear to deny or to ignore the connection.  For ethics is the study of the meaning and application of judgments of *good, bad, right, wrong,* etc., and every final valuation of law involves an ethical judgment. When we say, for instance, that a given law is bad, that one judicial decision is better than another, that the American constitution ought to be revised, or that laws ought to be obeyed, we are passing judgments whose truth or falsity cannot be established without a consideration of ethics.  That portion of jurisprudence which is not concerned merely with the positive nature of law or with its technical relation to assumed ends is, accordingly, a part of the domain of ethics.

There is no way of avoiding this ultimate responsibility of law to ethics.  Every final determination of the general end of law, the standard of legal criticism, (whether this be labeled "justice," "natural law," "the protection of natural rights," or "the organization of social interests"), must reduce to the general form, "The law ought to bring about as much good as it can."

. . . .

The ethical responsibilities of the judge have so often been obscured by the supposed duty to be logically consistent in the decision of different cases that it may be pertinent to ask whether any legal decision can ever be logically inconsistent with any other decision.

In order to find such an inconsistency we must have two judgments, one for the plaintiff and one for the defendant. But this means that we must have two cases, since a second judgment in the same case would supersede the first judgment. And between the facts of any two cases there must be some difference, so that it will always be logically possible to frame a single legal rule requiring both decisions, given the facts of the two cases. Of course such a rule will seem absurd if the differences between the two cases are unimportant (*e. g.* in the names or heights of the two defendants). But whether the difference is important or unimportant is a problem not of logic but of ethics, and one to which the opposing counsel in the later case may propose contradictory answers without becoming involved in self-contradiction.

The confusion arises when we think of a judicial decision as implying a rule from which, given the facts of the case, the decision may be derived (the logical fallacy of affirming the consequence). That logically startling derivation of the "law of precedents" from judicial precedents, Black's *Handbook of the Law of Judicial Precedents*, thus sums up the matter:

> Even if the opinion of the court should be concerned with unnecessary considerations, or should state the proposition of law imperfectly or incorrectly, yet there is a proposition necessarily involved in the decision and without which the judgment in the case could not have been given; and it is this proposition which is established by the decision (so far as it goes) and for which alone the case may be cited as an authority.

But elementary logic teaches us that every legal decision and every finite set of decisions can be subsumed under an infinite number of different general rules, just as an infinite number of different curves may be traced through any point or finite collection of points. Every decision is a choice between different rules which logically fit all past decisions but logically dictate conflicting results in the instant case. Logic provides the springboard but it does not guarantee the success of any particular dive.

If the doctrine of *stare decisis* means anything, and one can hardly maintain the contrary, despite the infelicitous formulations which have been given to the doctrine, the consistency which it demands cannot be a logical consistency. The consistency in question is more akin to that quality of dough which is necessary for the fixing of a durable shape. Decisions are fluid until they are given "morals." It is often important to conserve with new obeisance the morals which lawyers and laymen have read into past decisions and in reliance upon which they have acted. We do not deny that importance when we recognize that with equal logical justification lawyers and laymen might have attached other morals to the old cases had their habits of legal classification or their general social premises been different. But we do shift the focus of our vision from a stage where social and professional prejudices wear the terrible armor of Pure Reason to an arena where human hopes and expectations wrestle naked for supremacy.

### NOTES AND QUESTIONS

1. What does Cohen mean, "an ethics, like a metaphysics, is no more certain and no less dangerous because it is unconsciously held"? Is this criticism applicable to the opinion of Judge Smith in the *Cappier* case? Could you make an argument that an ethics that is unconsciously held is *more* dangerous than one that is systematically articulated?

Consider in this regard the observations of Cardozo:

> . . . There are times when precedents seem to lead to harsh or bizarre conclusions, at war with social needs. The law assumes the aspect of a scholastic exercise, divorced from the realities of life. In such junctures, judges would do well to keep before them as a living faith that a choice of methods is theirs in the shaping of their judgments. I do not mean to say that any one method has ever been consistently pursued in a whole department of the law to the exclusion of the others. Interaction has been inevitable, even when unconscious. I mean that particular causes have been determined and particular rules established or extended in submission to a technique which was supposed to coerce when it was intended to advise. We have not yet been able to orient ourselves with all our opportunities for experiment in centuries of experience. We do not know where we should face. Judges march at times to pitiless conclusions under the prod of a remorseless logic which is supposed to leave them no alternative. They deplore the sacrificial rite. They perform it, none the less, with averted gaze, convinced as they plunge the knife that they obey the bidding of their office. The victim is offered up to the gods of jurisprudence on the altar of regularity. . . . We seek to find peace of mind in the word, the formula, the ritual. . . .[2]

2. What evidence is there in favor of Cohen's assertion that in large areas of intellectual endeavor—and not merely in the law—there is an inclination "to cause all moral ideals to disappear and to produce an issue purified for the procedure of positive empirical science"? Why should this be so? Are there fundamental differences between the methods and subject matters of "positive empirical science" and ethics?

3. Is it possible to reason about ethics—about what is "good" and "bad", "moral" and "immoral"? Or are such judgments all "just a matter of opinion"? Consider in this regard the maxim, *de gustibus non disputandum,* and Cohen's remark that certain problems are problems "not of logic but of ethics". Are ethical judgments simply a matter of taste? Is there no "logic" to them? Is this part of the reason why the law seeks to play down its involvement in ethics and its (tautological?) insistence that it enforces only "legal duties" and not "moral duties"?

---

2. The Growth of The Law in Selected      214–15 (1947). Reprinted with Permission of Yale University Press.
Writings of Benjamin Nathan Cardozo

4.   Does Cohen's reference to an "ethical science" suggest that we can reason about ethics?  Can we?  Suppose two people disagree whether it was "immoral" for the railroad's agents not to have rendered aid to Ezelle?  How can they resolve their differences other than by force or coin-flipping?  In what way are the procedures open to them like—and unlike—the procedures a scientist may invoke in determining the freezing temperature of water?  In what way are the procedures like, and unlike, the procedures of a court in determining the constitutionality of a statute?  Do the differences, such as there may be, warrant a court's removing itself from a position of having to make moral judgments?  Do they warrant a court's maintaining a posture—for public consumption—that it is staying clear of moral judgments?  See *e. g.*, Hare, Freedom and Reason (1963); Edwards, The Logic of Moral Discourse (1955); Toulmin, Reason in Ethics (1950).

5.   How are the dilemmas posed in the questions above reflected in the excerpt from Holmes, which follows?

OLIVER WENDELL HOLMES, JR.

THE PATH OF THE LAW *

When we study law we are not studying a mystery but a well known profession.  We are studying what we shall want in order to appear before judges, or to advise people in such a way as to keep them out of court.  The reason why it is a profession, why people will pay lawyers to argue for them or to advise them, is that in societies like ours the command of the public force is intrusted to the judges in certain cases, and the whole power of the state will be put forth, if necessary, to carry out their judgments and decrees.  People want to know under what circumstances and how far they will run the risk of coming against what is so much stronger than themselves, and hence it becomes a business to find out when this danger is to be feared.  The object of our study, then, is prediction, the prediction of the incidence of the public force through the instrumentality of the courts.

The means of the study are a body of reports, of treatises, and of statutes, in this country and in England, extending back for six hundred years, and now increasing annually by hundreds. . . . It is to make the prophecies easier to be remembered and to be understood that the teachings of the decisions of the past are put into general propositions and gathered into text-books, or that statutes are passed in a general form.  The primary rights and duties with which jurisprudence busies itself again are nothing but prophecies.  One of the many evil effects of the confusion between legal and moral ideas, about which I shall have something to say in a moment, is that theory is apt to get the cart before the horse, and to consider the right or the duty as something existing apart from and independent of the consequences of its breach, to which certain sanctions are added afterward.

* From 10 Harv.L.Rev. 457, 457–58, 459, 460–61, 464 (1897).

But, as I shall try to show, a legal duty so called is nothing but a prediction that if a man does or omits certain things he will be made to suffer in this or that way by judgment of the court;—and so of a legal right.

. . . .

The first thing for a business-like understanding of the matter is to understand its limits, and therefore I think it desirable at once to point out and dispel a confusion between morality and law, which sometimes rises to the height of conscious theory, and more often and indeed constantly is making trouble in detail without reaching the point of consciousness. You can see very plainly that a bad man has as much reason as a good one for wishing to avoid an encounter with the public force, and therefore you can see the practical importance of the distinction between morality and law. A man who cares nothing for an ethical rule which is believed and practised by his neighbors is likely nevertheless to care a good deal to avoid being made to pay money, and will want to keep out of jail if he can.

I take it for granted that no hearer of mine will misinterpret what I have to say as the language of cynicism. The law is the witness and external deposit of our moral life. Its history is the history of the moral development of the race. The practice of it, in spite of popular jests, tends to make good citizens and good men. When I emphasize the difference between law and morals I do so with reference to a single end, that of learning and understanding the law. For that purpose you must definitely master its specific marks, and it is for that that I ask you for the moment to imagine yourselves indifferent to other and greater things.

I do not say that there is not a wider point of view from which the distinction between law and morals becomes of secondary or no importance, as all mathematical distinctions vanish in presence of the infinite. But I do say that that distinction is of the first importance for the object which we are here to consider,—a right study and mastery of the law as a business with well understood limits, a body of dogma enclosed within definite lines. . . .

. . . . The prophecies of what the courts will do in fact, and nothing more pretentious, are what I mean by the law.

. . . .

. . . For my own part, I often doubt whether it would not be a gain if every word of moral significance could be banished from the law altogether, and other words adopted which should convey legal ideas uncolored by anything outside the law. We should lose the fossil records of a good deal of history and the majesty got from ethical associations, but by ridding ourselves of an unnecessary confusion we should gain very much in the clearness of our thought.

## QUESTIONS

1. What does Justice Holmes mean by "the law"? In what sense does his position rest on the assumption that the law is "a business with well understood limits, a body of dogma enclosed within definite lines"? To what extent can Holmes predict what his client's

legal rights will be without also predicting the moral judgments of witnesses, magistrates, grand juries, prosecutors, judges, parole boards, etc.?

2.   Evaluate Holmes's suggestion that words with moral significance be banished from the law.  Can any word in the law not—by virtue of its being in the law—have moral overtones?  Suppose the word "crime" were replaced with "emirc."  What difference would it make?

3.   What judgments—about the "rationality" of ethics; about that portion of human affairs any given institution can manageably handle; about what the aspirations of a legal system ought to be— underlie Holmes's position?

*HANS KELSEN*

THE PURE THEORY OF LAW *

1.   The Pure Theory of Law is a theory of the positive law.  As a theory it is exclusively concerned with the accurate definition of its subject-matter.  It endeavours to answer the question, What is the law? but not the question, What ought it to be?  It is a science and not a politics of law.

That all this is described as a "pure" theory of law means that it is concerned solely with that part of knowledge which deals with law, excluding from such knowledge everything which does not strictly belong to the subject-matter law.  That is, it endeavours to free the science of law from all foreign elements.  This is its fundamental methodological principle.  It would seem a self-evident one.  Yet a glance at the traditional science of law in its nineteenth and twentieth century developments shows plainly how far removed from the requirement of purity that science was.  Jurisprudence, in a wholly uncritical fashion, was mixed up with psychology and biology, with ethics and theology.  There is to-day hardly a single social science into whose province jurisprudence feels itself unfitted to enter, even thinking, indeed, to enhance its scientific status by such conjunction with other disciplines.  The real science of law, of course, is lost in such a process.

2.   The Pure Theory of Law seeks to define clearly its objects of knowledge in these two directions in which its autonomy has been most endangered by the prevailing syncretism of methods.  .  .  .

    .  .  .  .

    .   .   .   In its proper meaning, as distinct from that which it has in law, "justice" connotes an absolute value.  Its content cannot be ascertained by the Pure Theory of Law.  Indeed it is not ascertainable by rational knowledge at all.  The history of human speculation for centuries has been the history of a vain striving after a solution of the problem.  That striving has hitherto led only to the emptiest

* From  50  Law.Q.Rev.  474, 477, 482,
491, 497–98 (1934).  With the permission of Stevens & Sons.

of tautologies, such as the formula *suum cuique* or the categoric imperative. From the standpoint of rational knowledge there are only interests and conflicts of interests, the solution of which is arrived at by an arrangement which may either satisfy the one interest at the expense of the other, or institute an equivalence or compromise between them. To determine, however, whether this or that order has an absolute value, that is, is "just," is not possible by the methods of rational knowledge. Justice is an irrational ideal. However indispensable it may be for the willing and acting of human beings it is not viable by reason. Only positive law is known, or more correctly revealed, to reason.

. . . The Pure Theory of Law retains its anti-ideological tendency by its attempt to insulate the positive law from every kind of natural law-justice ideology. The possibility of a valid order superior to positive law it considers outside its sphere of discussion. It confines its attention to the positive law, and prevents the science of law giving itself out as a higher order or from deriving a justification from such an order; or it prevents the discrepancy between such a presupposed ideal of justice and the positive law from being misused as a juristic argument against the validity of the latter. The Pure Theory of Law is the theory of legal positivism.

. . . .

. . . This is the legal relationship: the connexion between two conditions of fact, of which the one is a human behavior characterized as a legal duty, the other a human behavior characterized as a right. The Pure Theory of Law, by rejecting so-called subjective law in all its appearances—legal right, legal duty, legal subject— as an entity different in kind from the objective law, and by showing it to be only a special form of figurative exposition of the objective law, has made way for the overthrow of that subjectivistic attitude which produced the concept of subjective right, that attitude of special pleading which regards the law only from a party interest point of view, considering how it may benefit the individual and his interests. It is the specific attitude of Roman jurisprudence which, in essentials the product of the advisory practice of the jurisconsults, was received along with Roman Law. The attitude of the Pure Theory of law is on the contrary wholly objective and universalistic. It is concerned fundamentally with the law as a whole, seeing every single phenomenon only in its systematic relation to all others, seeing in every part of the law the function of the whole. In this sense it is a truly organic view of law. But in calling law an organism the theory does not mean any supra-individual and supra-empirical, metaphysical entity of a biological nature, a conception which in general hides ethico-political postulates, but solely that the law is a system, and that all legal problems are problems of system. Legal theory thus becomes a structural analysis, as exact as possible, of the positive law, an analysis free of all ethical or political judgments of value.

NOTES AND QUESTIONS

1. How closely does our own legal system approximate that which Kelsen advocates? Was any such system available to Judge Smith? To the judges in *Haslem* and *Sharkiewicz*? Why?

2. Why do you suppose that Kelsen wants a system of law "free of all ethical or political judgments of value"? Why might he have been concerned over the involvement of the legal system in such questions? What are the risks for the courts in getting so involved? Consider in addition to the problems adverted to by Judge Smith, the dissent of Justice Frankfurter in Baker v. Carr, 369 U.S. 186 (1962), in which the majority of the Supreme Court held that federal courts have jurisdiction to review the apportionment of state legislatures:

> . . . Disregard of inherent limits in the effective exercise of the Court's "judicial Power" not only presages the futility of judicial intervention in the essentially political conflict of forces by which the relation between population and representation has time out of mind been and now is determined. It may well impair the Court's position as the ultimate organ of "the supreme Law of the Land" in that vast range of legal problems, often strongly entangled in popular feeling, on which this Court must pronounce. The Court's authority—possessed of neither the purse nor the sword—ultimately rests on sustained public confidence in its moral sanction. Such feeling must be nourished by the Court's complete detachment, in fact and in appearance, from political entanglements and by abstention from injecting itself into the clash of political forces in political settlements.

369 U.S. at 267

3. If judging could feasibly be made "structural analysis" of the sort Kelsen recommends, would the "public confidence" with which Frankfurter was so concerned be increased? How would the nature of the judge's intellectual and moral task change from what is?

4. What is the relationship between Kelsen's desire for a Pure Theory of Law and his view that the idea of justice "is not ascertainable by rational knowledge at all. . . . From the standpoint of rational knowledge there are only interests and conflicts of interest. . . ." If you cannot *reason* about justice, the way you can reason about, say a mathematical problem, is there any use in submitting arguments on justice to a judge or to anyone else? How and where are sheer "conflicts of interest" resolved? On the battlefield? In the legislature, by a show of hands? On the view that "justice is an irrational ideal", are each of these forums better suited than courts for bringing about the requisite "arrangements" and "compromises"?

The position that ethical statements are "irrational" goes back at least as far as the Sophists with whom Socrates argued. But the immediate tradition with which Kelsen's views—at least in this excerpt—is associated is that of the logical positivists, whose approach is exemplified by the selections from Rudolf Carnap reprinted below.

In these passages, Carnap argues that metaphysical, aesthetic and ethical statements are essentially meaningless. A meaningful statement, Carnap would say, is one like "the temperature outside this room is 90°". That statement *conveys* information; it tells us, for example, that if we let a thermometer (defined as glass hollowed out to such and such a bore, filled with so much mercury of such and such a purity, calibrated at such and such intervals) stand outside, the mercury will rise until its surface line is even with the marking "90". On the other hand, the statement "killing is wrong" (when what is meant is something other than "you will get in trouble with the law if you kill") though it may look, in form, like the sentence "the temperature is 90°," actually conveys no information—or at least no information other than of what the utterer subjectively feels. It would be equivalent, in other words, to an exclamation such as "killing, ugh".

Carnap's project, at the time this piece was written, was to "eliminate metaphysics" through "logical analysis of language". This is a strange sounding program, and a foreword may help to explain it.

Carnap's position is exemplified by his reaction to the following passage from Heidegger's *Was ist Metaphysik?* (1929)

> "What is to be investigated is being only and—*nothing* else; being alone and further—*nothing*; solely being, and beyond being—*nothing*. *What about this Nothing?* . . . *Does the Nothing exist only because the Not, i. e. the Negation, exists?* Or is it the other way around? *Does Negation and the Not exist only because the Nothing exists?* . . . We assert: *the Nothing is prior to the Not and the Negation.* . . . Where do we seek the Nothing? How do we find the Nothing. . . . We know the Nothing. . . . *Anxiety reveals the Nothing.* That for which and because of which we were anxious, was 'really'—nothing. Indeed: the Nothing itself—as such—was present. . . . *What about this Nothing?—The Nothing itself nothings.*" [3]

To Carnap, this smacked of pure gibberish.[4] What is more, he thought he could demonstrate that in a logically constructed language, such phrases would not even be *speakable*. In an ordinary, spoken language, the word "nothing" can stand in the place of a substantive, as in "nothing is outside", which *sounds and looks like* "a boy is outside", and so we are are not struck by the peculiarity of the construc-

3. Quoted from and criticized in Carnap, "The Elimination of Metaphysics Through Logical Analysis of Language", *infra*.

4. A nineteenth century logician had made the point in another medium.
    "The King: 'I haven't sent the two Messengers . . . Just look along the road and tell me if you can see either of them.'
    'I see nobody on the road,' said Alice.
    'I only wish *I* had such eyes,' the King remarked in a fretful tone. 'To be able to see Nobody! And at that distance too.' "
    L. Carroll, *Through the Looking Glass,* in *The Annotated Alice* 279 (Gardner ed. 1963).

tion. But a logical language heads off this confusion by representing nothing with a negation sign, –, and the sentence "there is nothing outside" would be represented by preceding the representation of "there is something, X, such that X is outside", (∃X.OuX), with a negation sign, –. Thus the representation of "there is nothing outside" would be, "– 'there is some thing X such that X is outside' ", –(∃X.OuX), and the mysterious word "nothing" disappears—as do many of Heidegger's statements, e. g., "the Nothing itself nothings."

In the selection that follows, Carnap indicates how he would apply a comparable analysis to rid language of all metaphysics, and make clear that discussion of such matters as "what ought to be"— in a moral sense—is not possible, or, as he says, is "meaningless."

*Rudolf Carnap*

## The Elimination of Metaphysics Through Logical Analysis of Language *

## 1.  Introduction

There have been many *opponents of metaphysics* from the Greek skeptics to the empiricists of the 19th century. Criticisms of very diverse kinds have been set forth. Many have declared that the doctrine of metaphysics is *false*, since it contradicts our empirical knowledge. Others have believed it to be *uncertain*, on the ground that its problems transcend the limits of human knowledge. Many antimetaphysicians have declared that occupation with metaphysical questions is *sterile*. Whether or not these questions can be answered, it is at any rate unnecessary to worry about them; let us devote ourselves entirely to the practical tasks which confront active men every day of their lives!

The development of *modern logic* has made it possible to give a new and sharper answer to the question of the validity and justification of metaphysics. The researches of applied logic or the theory of knowledge, which aim at clarifying the cognitive content of scientific statements and thereby the meanings of the terms that occur in the statements, by means of logical analysis, lead to a positive and to a negative result. The positive result is worked out in the domain of empirical science; the various concepts of the various branches of science are clarified; their formal-logical and epistemological connections are made explicit. In the domain of *metaphysics*, including all philosophy of value and normative theory, logical analysis yields the negative result *that the alleged statements in this domain are entirely meaningless*. Therewith a radical elimination of metaphysics is attained, which was not yet possible from the earlier antimetaphysical standpoints. It is true that related ideas may be found already in several earlier trains of thought, e. g. those of a nominalistic kind; but it is only now when the development of logic during recent decades

* From Logical Positivism 60–68, 76– 77 (A. J. Ayer ed. The Free Press of Glencoe 1959). With permission of the MacMillan Company and Professor Carnap. Copyright by The Free Press, a Corporation, 1959.

provides us with a sufficiently sharp tool that the decisive step can be taken.

In saying that the so-called statements of metaphysics are *meaningless*, we intend this word in its strictest sense. In a loose sense of the word a statement or a question is at times called meaningless if it is entirely sterile to assert or ask it. We might say this for instance about the question "what is the average weight of those inhabitants of Vienna whose telephone number ends with '3'?" or about a statement which is quite obviously false like "in 1910 Vienna had 6 inhabitants" or about a statement which is not just empirically, but logically false, a contradictory statement such as "persons $A$ and $B$ are each a year older than the other." Such sentences are really meaningful, though they are pointless or false; for it is only meaningful sentences that are even divisible into (theoretically) fruitful and sterile, true and false. In the strict sense, however, a sequence of words is *meaningless* if it does not, within a specified language, constitute a statement. It may happen that such a sequence of words looks like a statement at first glance; in that case we call it a *pseudostatement*. Our thesis, now, is that logical analysis reveals the alleged statements of metaphysics to be pseudo-statements.

A language consists of a vocabulary and a syntax, i. e. a set of words which have meanings and rules of sentence formation. These rules indicate how sentences may be formed out of the various sorts of words. Accordingly, there are two kinds of pseudo-statements: either they contain a word which is erroneously believed to have meaning, or the constituent words are meaningful, yet are put together in a counter-syntactical way, so that they do not yield a meaningful statement. We shall show in terms of examples that pseudo-statements of both kinds occur in metaphysics. Later we shall have to inquire into the reasons that support our contention that metaphysics in its entirety consists of such pseudo-statements.

## 2. The Significance of a Word

A word which (within a definite language) has a meaning, is usually also said to designate a concept; if it only seems to have a meaning while it really does not, we speak of a "pseudo-concept."

. . . . . .

What, now, is *the meaning of a word*? What stipulations concerning a word must be made in order for it to be significant? (It does not matter for our investigation whether these stipulations are explicitly laid down, as in the case of some words and symbols of modern science, or whether they have been tacitly agreed upon, as is the case for most words of traditional language.) First, the *syntax* of the word must be fixed, i. e. the mode of its occurrence in the simplest sentence form in which it is capable of occurring; we call this sentence form its *elementary sentence*. The elementary sentence form for the word "stone" e. g. is "x is a stone"; in sentences of this form some designation from the category of things occupies the place of "x," e. g. "this diamond," "this apple." Secondly, for an elementary sentence $S$ containing the word an answer must be given to the following question, which can be formulated in various ways:

(1.) What sentences is $S$ *deducible* from, and what sentences are deducible from $S$?

(2.) Under what conditions is $S$ supposed to be true, and under what conditions false?

(3.) How is $S$ to be *verified*?

(4.) What is the *meaning* of S?

(1) is the correct formulation; formulation (2) accords with the phraseology of logic, (3) with the phraseology of the theory of knowledge, (4) with that of philosophy (phenomenology). Wittgenstein has asserted that (2) expresses what philosophers mean by (4): the meaning of a sentence consists in its truth-condition. ((1) is the "metalogical" formulation; it is planned to give elsewhere a detailed exposition of metalogic as the theory of syntax and meaning, i. e. relations of deducibility.)

In the case of many words, specifically in the case of the overwhelming majority of scientific words, it is possible to specify their meaning by reduction to other words ("constitution," definition). E. g. " 'arthropodes' are animals with segmented bodies and jointed legs." Thereby the above-mentioned question for the elementary sentence form of the word "arthropode," that is for the sentence form "the thing $x$ is an arthropode," is answered: it has been stipulated that a sentence of this form is deducible from premises of the form "$x$ is an animal," "$x$ has a segmented body," "$x$ has jointed legs," and that conversely each of these sentences is deducible from the former sentence. By means of these stipulations about deducibility (in other words: about the truth-condition, about the method of verification, about the meaning) of the elementary sentence about "arthropode" the meaning of the word "arthropode" is fixed. In this way every word of the language is reduced to other words and finally to the words which occur in the so-called "observation sentences" or "protocol sentences." It is through this reduction that the word acquires its meaning.

For our purposes we may ignore entirely the question concerning the content and form of the primary sentences (protocol sentences) which has not yet been definitely settled. In the theory of knowledge it is customary to say that the primary sentences refer to "the given"; but there is no unanimity on the question what it is that is given. At times the position is taken that sentences about the given speak of the simplest qualities of sense and feeling (e. g. "warm," "blue," "joy" and so forth); others incline to the view that basic sentences refer to total experiences and similarities between them; a still different view has it that even the basic sentences speak of things. Regardless of this diversity of opinion it is certain that a sequence of words has a meaning only if its relations of deducibility to the protocol sentences are fixed, whatever the characteristics of the protocol sentences may be; and similarly, that a word is significant only if the sentences in which it may occur are reducible to protocol sentences.

Since the meaning of a word is determined by its criterion of application (in other words: by the relations of deducibility entered into by its elementary sentence-form, by its truth-conditions, by the method of its verification), the stipulation of the criterion takes away one's freedom to decide what one wishes to "mean" by the word. If the word is to receive an exact meaning, nothing less than the criterion of application must be given; but one cannot, on the other hand, give more than the criterion of application, for the latter is a sufficient determination of meaning. The meaning is implicitly contained in the criterion; all that remains to be done is to make the meaning explicit.

Let us suppose, by way of illustration, that someone invented the new word "teavy" and maintained that there are things which are teavy and things which are not teavy. In order to learn the meaning of this word, we ask him about its criterion of application: how is one to ascertain in a concrete case whether a given thing is teavy or not? Let us suppose to begin with that we get no answer from him: there are no empirical signs of teavyness, he says. In that case we would deny the legitimacy of using this word. If the person who uses the word says that all the same there are things which are teavy and there are things which are not teavy, only it remains for the weak, finite intellect of man in eternal secret which things are teavy and which are not, we shall regard this as empty verbiage. But perhaps he will assure us that he means, after all, something by the word "teavy." But from this we only learn the psychological fact that he associates some kind of images and feelings with the word. The word does not acquire a meaning through such associations. If no criterion of application for the word is stipulated, then nothing is asserted by the sentences in which it occurs, they are but pseudo-statements.

.   .   .   .

Let us briefly summarize the result of our analysis. Let "a" be any word and "$S(a)$" the elementary sentence in which it occurs. Then the sufficient and necessary condition for "a" being meaningful may be given by each of the following formulations, which ultimately say the same thing:

1.   The *empirical criteria* for a are known.

2.   It has been stipulated from what protocol sentences "$S(a)$" is *deducible*.

3.   The *truth-conditions* for "$S(a)$" are fixed.

4.   The method of *verification* of "$S(a)$" is known.

## 3.   Metaphysical Words Without Meaning

Many words of metaphysics, now, can be shown not to fulfill the above requirement, and therefore to be devoid of meaning.

.   .   .   .

[Take] the word "God." .   .   .   . In its *metaphysical* use .   .   .   . the word "God" refers to something beyond experience. The word is deliberately divested of its reference to a physical being or to a spiritual being that is immanent in the physical. And as it is not given a new meaning, it becomes meaningless. To be sure, it often looks as though the word "God" had a meaning even in metaphysics.

But the definitions which are set up prove on closer inspection to be pseudo-definitions. They lead either to logically illegitimate combinations of words (of which we shall treat later) or to other metaphysical words (e. g. "primordial basis," "the absolute," "the unconditioned," "the autonomous," "the self-dependent" and so forth), but in no case to the truth-conditions of its elementary sentences. In the case of this word not even the first requirement of logic is met, that is the requirement to specify its syntax, i. e. the form of its occurrence in elementary sentences. An elementary sentence would here have to be of the form "$x$ is a God"; yet, the metaphysician either rejects this form entirely without substituting another, or if he accepts it he neglects to indicate the syntactical category of the variable $x$. (Categories are, for example, material things, properties of things, relations between things, numbers etc.).

. . . . .

Just like the examined examples "principle" and "God," most of the other *specifically metaphysical terms are devoid of meaning*, e. g. "the Idea," "the Absolute," "the Unconditioned," "the Infinite," "the being of being," "non-being," "thing in itself," "absolute spirit," "objective spirit," "essence," "being-in-itself," "being-in-and-for-itself," "emanation," "manifestation," "articulation," "the Ego," "the non-Ego," etc. These expressions are in the same boat with "teavy," our previously fabricated example. The metaphysician tells us that empirical truth-conditions cannot be specified; if he adds that nevertheless he "means" something, we know that this is merely an allusion to associated images and feelings which, however, do not bestow a meaning on the word. The alleged statements of metaphysics which contain such words have no sense, assert nothing, are mere pseudo-statements. Into the explanation of their historical origin we shall inquire later.

### 4. The Significance of a Sentence

So far we have considered only those pseudo-statements which contain a meaningless word. But there is a second kind of pseudo-statement. They consist of meaningful words, but the words are put together in such a way that nevertheless no meaning results. The syntax of a language specifies which combinations of words are admissible and which inadmissible. The grammatical syntax of natural languages, however, does not fulfill the task of elimination of senseless combinations of words in all cases. Let us take as examples the following sequences of words:

1. "Caesar is and"

2. "Caesar is a prime number"

The word sequence (1) is formed countersyntactically; the rules of syntax require that the third position be occupied, not by a conjunction, but by a predicate, hence by a noun (with article) or by an adjective. The word sequence "Caesar is a general," e. g., is formed in accordance with the rules of syntax. It is a meaningful word sequence, a genuine sentence. But, now, word sequence (2) is likewise syntactically correct, for it has the same grammatical form as the sentence just mentioned. Nevertheless (2) is meaningless. "Prime number" is a predicate of numbers; it can be neither affirmed nor denied of a person. Since (2) looks like a statement yet is not a statement, does not assert anything, expresses neither a true nor a false proposition, we call this word sequence a "pseudo-statement." The fact that the rules of grammatical syntax are not violated easily seduces one at first glance into the erroneous opinion that one still has to do with a statement, albeit a false one. But "*a* is a prime number" is false if and only if *a* is divisible by a natural number different from *a* and from 1; evidently it is illicit to put here "Caesar" for "*a*". This example has been so chosen that the nonsense is easily detectable. Many so-called statements of metaphysics are not so easily recognized to be pseudo-statements. The fact that natural languages allow the formation of meaningless sequences of words without violating the rules of grammar, indicates that grammatical syntax is, from a logical point of view, inadequate. If grammatical syntax corresponded exactly to logical syntax, pseudo-statements could not arise. . . . . It follow that if our thesis that the statements of metaphysics are pseudo-statements is justifiable, then metaphysics could not even be expressed in a logically constructed language. This is the great philosophical importance of the task, which at present occupies the logicians, of building a logical syntax.

. . . . .

We have seen earlier that the meaning of a statement lies in the method of its verification. A statement asserts only so much as is verifiable with respect to it. Therefore a sentence can be used only to assert an empirical proposition, if indeed it is used to assert anything at all. If something were to lie, in principle, beyond possible experience, it could be neither said nor thought nor asked.

(Meaningful) statements are divided into the following kinds. First there are statements which are true solely by virtue of their form ("tautologies" according to Wittgenstein; they correspond approximately to Kant's "analytic judgments"). They say nothing about reality. The formulae of logic and mathematics are of this kind. They are not themselves factual statements, but serve for the transformation of such statements. Secondly, there are the negations of such statements (*"contradictions"*). They are self-contradictory, hence false by virtue of their form. With respect to all other statements the decision about truth or falsehood lies in the protocol sentences. They are therefore (true or false) *empirical statements* and belong to the domain of empirical science. Any statement one desires to construct which does not fall within these categories becomes automatically meaningless. Since metaphysics does not want to assert analytic propositions, nor to fall within the domain of empirical science, it is compelled to employ words for which no criteria of application are specified and which are therefore devoid of sense, or else to combine meaningful words in such a way that neither an analytic (or contradictory) statement nor an empirical statement is produced. In either case pseudo-statements are the inevitable product.

Logical analysis, then, pronounces the verdict of meaninglessness on any alleged knowledge that pretends to reach above or behind experience. This verdict hits, in the first place, any speculative metaphysics, any alleged knowledge by *pure thinking* or by *pure intuition* that pretends to be able to do without experience. But the verdict equally applies to the kind of metaphysics which, starting from experience, wants to acquire knowledge about that which *transcends experience* by means of special *inferences* (e. g. the neo-vitalist thesis of the directive presence of an "entelechy" in organic processes, which supposedly cannot be understood in terms of physics; the question concerning the "essence of causality," transcending the ascertainment of certain regularities of succession; the talk about the "thing in itself"). Further, the same judgment must be passed on all *philosophy of norms*, or *philosophy of value*, on any ethics or esthetics as a normative discipline. For the objective validity of a value or norm is (even on the view of the philosophers of value) not empirically verifiable nor deducible from empirical statements; hence it cannot be asserted (in a meaningful statement) at all. In other words: Either empirical criteria are indicated for the use of "good" and "beautiful" and the rest of the predicates that are employed in the normative sciences, or they are not. In the first case, a statement containing such a predicate turns into a factual judgment, but not a value judgment; in the second case, it becomes a pseudo-statement. It is altogether impossible to make a statement that expresses a value judgment.

### NOTES AND QUESTIONS

1. In how many ways is Kelsen's program for a Pure Theory of Law related to Carnap's program for ridding language of meaningless statements? If legislators could express themselves in terms which were reducible to "protocol sentences", would this make it easier for them more exactly to communicate their will to the law-appliers? Would a legal system built on a language that eliminates intersubjective differences (such as personal value judgments) be desirable? Would it be feasible?

2. If Carnap and Kelsen are right that ethical judgments are "meaningless," *i. e.*, there is no rational procedure for resolving their truth, what support do they give for Judge Smith's reluctance to get involved in "morals" in the *Cappier* case? Query: do terms like "intent" *"mens rea"*, "negligence", "contract", "abandonment", etc., stand in any better stead with respect to the positivist's criteria? If not, should they be eliminated?

3. In what sense is the sentence "Brod's decision was immoral" "meaningless"? Are there empirical criteria for validating the sentence? Does it convey no information at all? How is it different, in this regard, from the sentence, "Brod read Kafka's notes"? Does the second appeal to "facts", but not the first? Or is Carnap saying that the relationship of the first sentence to the facts it appeals to is one of deduction, but no such deduction is possible from the "facts" to an ethical judgment?

Compare the statement "to say that a man acted rightly, or that he acted wrongly, is not to say what he did." A. J. Ayer, "On the

Analysis of Moral Judgments," in Chapter 9, *infra*. Is to say that "John killed $X$ with a knife" simply to say what John did? Or is the utterer inevitably adding something like a personal, subjective judgment?

4.  How central a role do "protocol sentences" play in Carnap's position? What does Carnap tell us of the nature of protocol sentences? Why do you suppose that as of the time of writing this piece (1932), their nature had "not yet been definitely settled"? (See the selections on the Correspondence Theory of Truth in Chapter 6, *infra*).

5.  Consider the following criticism of Carnap.

"Many linguistic utterances," says Carnap, "are analogous to laughing in that they have only an expressive function, no representative function. Examples of this are cries like 'Oh, Oh,' or, on a higher level, lyrical verses. The aim of a lyrical poem in which occur the words 'sunshine' and 'clouds,' is not to inform us of certain meteorological facts, but to express certain feelings of the poet and to excite similar feelings in us. . . . Metaphysical propositions— like lyrical verses—have only an expressive function, but no representative function. Metaphysical propositions are neither true nor false, because they assert nothing. . . . But they are, like laughing, lyrics and music, expressive. They express not so much temporary feelings as permanent emotional and volitional dispositions."

. . . .

In their criticism of metaphysical propositions, namely that such propositions are usually psuedo-answers to psuedo-questions, these logicians have my full assent

. . . .

. . . .

. . . [H]ere is the point of my radical divergence from them. Where Carnap speaks of "cries like 'Oh, Oh,' or, on a higher level, lyrical verses," I can see only a complete failure to apprehend a fundamental distinction. Why should we cry our feelings at such high levels that anyone would think we were *talking*? Clearly, poetry means more than a cry; it has reason for being articulate; and metaphysics is more than the croon with which we might cuddle up to the world in a comfortable attitude. We are dealing with symbolisms here, and what they express is often highly intellectual. . . .

. . . .

[I]f we consider how difficult it is to construct a meaningful language that shall meet neo-positivistic standards, it is quite incredible that people should ever *say* anything at all, or understand each other's propositions. At best, human thought is but a tiny grammar-bound island, in the midst of a sea of feeling expressed by "Oh-oh" and sheer babble. The island has a periphery, perhaps, of mud—factual and hypothetical concepts broken down by the emotional tides into the "material mode," a mixture of meaning and nonsense. Most of us live the better part of our lives on this mudflat; but in artistic moods we take to the deep, where we flounder about with symptomatic cries that sound like propositions about life and death, good and evil, substance, beauty, and other non-existent topics.

S. K. Langer, Philosophy in a New Key 83–88 (3d ed. 1957).[5]

At what point is Langer taking exception to Carnap? What does she suggest about the possibility of resolving *e. g.*, moral and aesthetic debates by reason? What are the implications for law and lawyering if, as Felix Cohen argues, legal judgments and criticism inevitably involve value judgments *and*, if as Carnap argues, dispute over value judgments is worthless? What would be the implications if Cohen is right and Langer is right?

---

**5.** Reprinted with permission of the President and Fellows of Harvard College.

## CHAPTER TWO

# The Moral Dilemma

*HERMAN MELVILLE*

## BILLY BUDD *

[When the saintly Billy Budd, an impressed seaman, was falsely charged with mutinous intent by the Master-at-Arms Claggart, Captain Vere summoned the accused to his cabin. There he required Claggart to make his charge to the sailor's face. When Billy did not at first respond, the Captain demanded that he defend himself. The shock of the accusation and a latent speech defect, however, reduced the seaman to a "strange dumb gesturing and gurgling." Even after the Captain realized the cause of Billy's silence and adopted "words so fatherly in tone" as to reassure him, he could not utter a recognizable sound. Instead, the Captain's words "prompted yet more violent efforts at utterance—efforts soon ending for the time in confirming the paralysis, and bringing to his face an expression which was a crucifixion to behold." Then, "quick as the flame from a discharged cannon at night, his right arm shot out," and Claggart fell dead to the deck. "I never bore malice against the master-at-arms," Billy later testified at his court martial. "Could I have used my tongue I would not have struck him. But he foully lied to my face and in presence of my captain, and I had to say something, and I could only say it with a blow, God help me!"

The following is from the speech given at the court martial by Captain Vere, who, standing over Claggart's body soon after the blow, had "vehemently exclaimed—'Struck dead by an angel of God! Yet the angel must hang.' "]

"Hitherto I have been but the witness, little more; and I should hardly think now to take another tone, that of your coadjutor, for the time, did I not perceive in you—at the crisis too—a troubled hesitancy, proceeding, I doubt not, from the clash of military duty with moral scruple—scruple vitalized by compassion. For the compassion, how can I otherwise than share it? But, mindful of paramount obligations, I strive against scruples that may tend to enervate decision. Not, gentlemen, that I hide from myself that the case is an exceptional one. Speculatively regarded, it well might be referred to a jury of casuists. But for us here acting not as casuists or moralists, it is a case practical, and under martial law practically to be dealt with

"But your scruples: do they move as in a dusk? Challenge them. Make them advance and declare themselves. Come now: do they import something like this: If, mindless of palliating circumstances, we are bound to regard the death of the master-at-arms as the prisoner's deed, then does that deed constitute a capital crime whereof

* From 68–69 (Signet ed. 1961).

51

the penalty is a mortal one? But in natural justice is nothing but the prisoner's overt act to be considered? How can we adjudge to summary and shameful death a fellow creature innocent before God, and whom we feel to be so?—Does that state it aright? You sign sad assent. Well, I too feel that, the full force of that. It is Nature. But do these buttons that we wear attest that our allegiance is to Nature? No, to the King. Though the ocean, which is inviolate Nature primeval, though this be the element where we move and have our being as sailors, yet as the King's officers lies our duty in a sphere correspondingly natural? So little is that true that, in receiving our commissions, we in the most important regards ceased to be natural free agents. When war is declared are we, the commissioned fighters, previously consulted? We fight at command. If our judgments approve the war, that is but coincidence. So in other particulars. So now. For suppose condemnation to follow these present proceedings. Would it be so much we ourselves that would condemn as it would be martial law operating through us? For that law and the rigor of it, we are not responsible. Our vowed responsibility is in this: That however pitilessly that law may operate, we nevertheless adhere to it and administer it.

"But the exceptional in the matter moves the hearts within you. Even so too is mine moved. But let not warm hearts betray heads that should be cool. Ashore in a criminal case will an upright judge allow himself off the bench to be waylaid by some tender kinswoman of the accused seeking to touch him with her tearful plea? Well the heart here denotes the feminine in man, is as that piteous woman and, hard though it be, she must here be ruled out."

He paused, earnestly studying them for a moment, then resumed.

"But something in your aspect seems to urge that it is not solely the heart that moves in you, but also the conscience, the private conscience. But tell me whether or not, occupying the position we do, private conscience should not yield to that imperial one formulated in the code under which alone we officially proceed?"

## NOTES AND QUESTIONS

1. Why, and to what extent, do people feel that what they ought to do depends, not upon whether they are *people*, merely, but upon whether they are judges or lawyers, soldiers or seamen? Why shouldn't the members of the court martial just vote as they believed? Do you think, in fact, the people trying Budd would be able to prevent "warm hearts [from] betray[ing] heads that should be cool"? How can people disregard their feelings and beliefs? How much of the social order depends upon it? Compare the everyday judicial injunctions to juries to disregard testimony or improper remarks.

In Dunn v. United States, 307 F.2d 883 (5th Cir. 1962), the Fifth Circuit reversed a conviction on the basis of opening statements by the United States Attorney—to the effect that "This case is replete with fraud and is one of the most flagrant cases we have ever tried in the Southern District of Georgia"—as well as an improper remark about kickbacks in his summation. 307 F.2d at 885. Judge Gewin wrote that the instructions to the jury to "disabuse your minds of that statement" "cannot remove the prejudice", observing, "if you throw a skunk into the jury box, you can't instruct the jury not to smell it".

> .  .  .  Trials are rarely, if ever, perfect, but gross imper-
> fections should not go unnoticed.  In every case involving
> improper argument of counsel, we are confronted with rela-
> tivity and the degree to which such conduct may have af-
> fected the substantial rights of the defendant.  It is better to
> follow the rules than to try to undo what has been done.
> Otherwise stated, one "cannot unring a bell"; "after the
> thrust of the saber it is difficult to say forget the wound".
> .  .  .

307 F.2d at 886.

2.  What standards of conduct is Captain Vere appealing to? What is the significance of his calling attention to the buttons the men wear?  Of the assertion that the heart "denotes the feminine in man"?

What does Captain Vere mean, that for the martial law "and the rigor of it, we are not responsible"?  If the men choose to invoke it, how could they not be responsible for it?  What does "responsible" mean?

What is the relationship between Captain Vere's argument (a) that the men decide according to their *role*, and (b) that they decide Billy Budd's fate, not by looking to Budd as an individual, but according to general rule?

What arguments can you make for and against the men's adopting the role distinction that Captain Vere advocates?  What sorts of human being is such a division of the self apt to produce?  And what sort of a society?

HENRY DAVID THOREAU

CIVIL DISOBEDIENCE *
A common and natural result of an undue respect for law is, that you may see a file of soldiers, colonel, captain, corporal, privates, powder-monkeys, and all, marching in admirable order over hill and dale to the wars, against their wills, ay, against their common sense and consciences, which makes it very steep marching indeed, and produces a palpitation of the heart.  They have no doubt that it is a damnable business in which they are concerned; they are all peaceably inclined.  Now, what are they?  Men at all? or small movable forts and magazines, at the service of some unscrupulous man in power? Visit the Navy Yard, and behold a marine, such a man as an American government can make, or such as it can make a man with its black arts—a mere shadow and reminiscence of humanity, a man laid out

* From  The  Portable  Thoreau  111–12
(C. Bode ed. Viking Press 1947).

alive and standing, and already, as one may say, buried under arms with funeral accompaniments, though it may be,

> "Not a drum was heard, not a funeral note,
>     As his corse to the rampart we hurried;
> Not a soldier discharged his farewell shot
>     O'er the grave where our hero we buried."

The mass of men serve the state thus, not as men mainly, but as machines, with their bodies. They are the standing army, and the militia, jailers, constables, *posse comitatus*, etc. In most cases there is no free exercise whatever of the judgment or of the moral sense; but they put themselves on a level with wood and earth and stones; and wooden men can perhaps be manufactured that will serve the purpose as well. Such command no more respect than men of straw or a lump of dirt. They have the same sort of worth only as horses and dogs. Yet such as these even are commonly esteemed good citizens.

## QUESTIONS

How does a person who wants to maximize individual realization agree to any social bonds at all? What if he wants, in fathoming his capacities for anger or for aimlessness, to kill a man, like Mersault in Camus' THE STRANGER? How is Thoreau different from such a man? Could there be a *society* of Thoreaus?

*FRIEDRICH NIETZSCHE*

## BEYOND GOOD AND EVIL *

One must subject oneself to one's own tests that one is destined for independence and command, and do so at the right time. One must not avoid one's tests, although they constitute perhaps the most dangerous game one can play, and are in the end tests made only before ourselves and before no other judge. Not to cleave to any person, be it even the dearest—every person is a prison and also a recess. Not to cleave to a fatherland, be it even the most suffering and necessitous —it is even less difficult to detach one's heart from a victorious fatherland. Not to leave to a sympathy, be it even for higher men, into whose peculiar torture and helplessness chance has given us an insight.

.   .   .

.   .   .   .

The extraordinary limitation of human development, the hesitation, protractedness, frequent retrogression, and turning thereof, is attributable to the fact that the herd-instinct of obedience is transmitted best, and at the cost of the art of command. If one imagine this instinct increasing to its greatest extent, commanders and independent individuals will finally be lacking altogether; or they will suffer inwardly from a bad conscience, and will have to impose a deception on themselves in the first place in order to be able to command: just as if they also were only obeying. This condition of things actually exists in Europe at present—I call it the moral hypocrisy of

---

* From 56, 120–21 (H. Zimmern transl. MacMillan 1907).

the commanding class. They know no other way of protecting themselves from their bad conscience than by playing the role of executors of older and higher orders (of predecessors, of the constitution, of justice, of the law, or of God himself), or they even justify themselves by maxims from the current opinions of the herd, as "first servants of their people," or "instruments of the public weal."

NORMAN O. BROWN

## APOLLO AND DIONYSUS *

If there is a "way out" from the dialectic of cumulative repression, guilt, and aggression, it must lie not in sublimation but in an alternative to sublimation. To understand our present predicament we have to go back to its origins, to the beginning of Western civilization and to the Greeks, who taught and still teach us how to sublimate, and who worshipped the god of sublimation, Apollo. Apollo is the god of form—of plastic form in art, of rational form in thought, of civilized form in life. But the Apollonian form is form as the negation of instinct. "Nothing too much," says the Delphic wisdom; "Observe the limit, fear authority, bow before the devine." Hence Apollonian form is form negating matter, immortal form; that is to say, by the irony that overtakes all flight from death, deathly form. Thus Plato, as well as his shamanistic predecessors Abaris and Aristeas, is a son of Apollo. Apollo is masculine; but, as Bachofen saw, his masculinity is the symbolical (or negative) masculinity of spirituality. Hence he is also the god who sustains "displacement from below upward," who gave man a head sublime and told him to look at the stars. Hence his is the world of sunlight, not as nature symbol but as a sexual symbol of sublimation and of that sunlike eye which perceives but does not taste, which always keeps a distance, like Apollo himself, the Far-Darter. And, as Nietzsche divined, the stuff of which the Apollonian world is made is the dream. Apollo rules over the fair world of appearance as a projection of the inner world of fantasy; and the limit which he must observe, "that delicate boundary which the dream-picture must not overstep," is the boundary of repression separating the dream from instinctual reality.

But the Greeks, who gave us Apollo, also gave us the alternative, Nietzsche's Dionysus. Dionysus is not dream but drunkenness; not life kept at a distance and seen through a veil but life complete and immediate. Hence, says Nietzsche, "The entire symbolism of the body is called into play, not the mere symbolism of the lips, face, and speech, but the whole pantomime of dancing, forcing every member into rhythmic movement" (Rilke's "natural speech by means of the body"). The Dionysian "is no longer an artist, he has become a work of art." Hence Dionysus does not observe the limit, but overflows; for him the road of excess leads to the palace of wisdom; Nietzsche says that those who suffer from an overfullness of life want a Dionysian art. Hence *he does not negate any more.* This, says Nietzsche, is the essence of the Dionysian faith. Instead of negating, he affirms the dialectical unity of the great instinctual opposities: Dionysus reunifies male and female, Self and Other, life and death. Dionysus is the image of the instinctual reality which psychoanalysis will find the other side of the veil. Freud saw that in the id there is no negation, only affirmation and eternity. In an earlier chapter we saw that the reality from which the neurotic animal flees in vain is the unity of life and death. In this chapter we have seen the dreams of infantile sexuality and of Apollonian sublimation are not, are negations of, the instinctual reality. The instinctual reality is Dionysian drunkenness; in Freud's words, "We can come nearer to the id with images, and call it a chaos, a cauldron of seething excitement."

The human ego must face the Dionysian reality, and therefore a great work of self-transformation lies ahead of it. For Nietzsche was right in saying that the Apollonian preserves, the Dionysian destroys, self-consciousness. As long as the structure of the ego is Apollonian, Dionysian experience can only be bought at the price of ego-dissolution. Nor can the issue be resolved by a "synthesis" of the Apollonian and the Dionysian; the problem is the construction of a Dionysian ego. Hence the later Nietzsche preaches Dionysus, and to see in this Dionysus a synthesis of Apollo and Dionysus is to sacrifice insight for peace of mind. Not only does Dionysus without the Dionysian ego threaten us with dissolution of consciousness; he also threatens us with that "genuine witches' brew," "that horrible mixture of sensuality and cruelty" (Nietzsche again), which is the revolt of the Dionysian against the Apollonian, and an ambivalent mixture, but no fusion, between the instinctual opposites.

Since we are dealing with bodily realities, not abstract intellectual principles, it is well to listen to one who knew not only the life of the mind, but also the life of the body and the art of the body as we do not—Isadora Duncan, who tells how she experienced the Dionysian ecstasy as "the defeat of the intelligence," "the final convulsion and sinking down into nothingness that often leads to the gravest disasters —for the intelligence and the spirit." But her Dionysian ecstasy is the orgasm—that one moment, she says, worth more and more desirable than all else in the universe. The Dionysian ego would be freed from genital organization and of that necessity of "ridding the organism of sexual cravings and concentrating these in the genital" (Ferenczi). While the Apollonian ego is the ego of genital organization, the Dionysian ego would be once more a body-ego and would not have to be dissolved in body-rapture.

The work of constructing a Dionysian ego is immense; but there are signs that it is already under way. If we can discern the Dionysian witches' brew in the upheavals of modern history—in the sexology of de Sade and the politics of Hitler—we can also discern in the romantic reaction the entry of Dionysus into consciousness. It was Blake who said that the road of excess leads to the palace of wisdom; Hegel was able to see the dialectic of reality as "the bacchanalian revel, in which no member is not drunk." And the heirs of the romantics are Nietzsche and Freud. The only alternative to the witches' brew is psychoanalytical consciousness, which is not the Apollonian scholasticism of orthodox psychoanalysis, but consciousness embracing and affirming instinctual reality—Dionysian consciousness.

## UNITED STATES V. KINDER

14 C.M.R. 742 (ACM 7321 (1954)

> Sentence adjudged 16 July 1953 by General Court-Martial convened at Headquarters, Fifth Air Force (Rear), APO 970. Approved sentence: Dishonorable discharge (suspended), total forfeitures and confinement at hard labor for two (2) years.

Upon trial, the accused pleaded not guilty to the premeditated murder, on or about 27 September 1952, at or near K–9 Air Base, APO 970, of an oriental male human being who has been referred to by the name of Bang Soon Kil, by means of shooting him with a rifle, in violation of the Uniform Code of Military Justice, Article 118 (Charge I and its Specification) but during the trial changed the plea to not guilty to premeditated murder . . . but guilty to involuntary manslaughter by culpable negligence, in violation of the Uniform Code of Military Justice, Article 119. He also pleaded not guilty to conspiring with Second Lieutenant George C. Schreiber and Airman First Class Robert W. Toth, on or about 27 September 1952 at or near K–9 Air Base, APO 970, to commit the substantive offense of premeditated murder alleged in the Specification of Charge I, in violation of the Uniform Code of Military Justice, Article 81 (Charge II and its Specification). He was found guilty as charged and sentenced to be dishonorably discharged from the service, to forfeit all pay and allowances, and to be confined at hard labor for the term of his natural life. No evidence of previous convictions was considered. The convening authority approved only so much of the sentence as provides for dishonorable discharge, forfeiture of all pay and allowances, and confinement at hard labor for two years, suspended the execution of that portion of the sentence adjudging dishonorable discharge for the period of confinement and six months thereafter with a provision for automatic remission of the suspended portion of the sentence unless the suspension is sooner vacated, designated the Fifth Air Force Correction Center, APO 970, as the place of confinement pending completion of appellate review, and forwarded the record of trial to The Judge Advocate General of the United States Air Force for review by a Board of Review.

. . . .

On the evening of 26 September 1952, shortly before midnight, the accused while posted as a guard on Post 13 in the bomb dump (R 42, 70), apprehended a Korean in the bomb dump (R 43, 46, 47). At approximately 2400 hours on that date Airman First Class Robert W. Toth, the Sergeant of the Guard, Airman Second Class Willard E. Carpenter, and another airman, while on patrol in a jeep, went to the accused's post (R 42, 203). Airman Carpenter observed the Korean at this time and noticed no evidence that he had been beaten or suffered injuries; however, he did smell alcohol on the Korean and observed that the Korean appeared to be a little bit drunk (R 43–47). Leaving the accused on post, Toth and Carpenter, with the Korean in the back seat of the jeep, proceeded to the Air Police Operations office (R 43, 44). En route to that office, Toth got out of the jeep, walked around it, reached in, and pistol whipped the Korean about the head with a .45 pistol (R 43, 44, 47, 203) by striking him with the butt end of the pistol three or four times on [the] back of the head and a few times with the side of the pistol on the right side of the head. The Korean slipped between the seats of the jeep and his head was bloody (R 43, 44, 47, 48, 203). At the Air Police Operations office the Korean "more or less" staggered and Airman Toth with a hand on the Korean's shoulder "more or less" carried him into the office where he laid him on the floor face up (R 43–45, 69, 70).

. . . . .

The accused's testimonial version was that when he arrived at the Air Police Operations office Lieutenant Schreiber asked him to describe in detail what happened when he apprehended the Korean (R 179, 187, 245). During his explanation Lieutenant Schreiber, Toth, and he were standing within the area of a four foot circle (R 179, 187, 245). Addleman and Lieutenant Penabaker were present in the office talking (R 245). Mullins came into the office once (R 246). He doesn't remember that anyone else was in the office (R 245–248). After his explanation he proceeded into the gun room adjoining the office where he cleaned his carbine (R 178, 187, 246). While cleaning his carbine he heard parts of a conversation between Lieutenant Schreiber and Toth in which they discussed the disposition of the Korean (R 178, 179, 188, 189). Lieutenant Schreiber asked Toth where would be a good place to take the Korean to shoot him (R 178, 179). Toth replied that B–14 would be the most conspicuous place that a sentry would shoot a Korean (R 178). Lieutenant Schreiber replied that he guessed that was as good a place as could be found (R 178). After spending seven to ten minutes cleaning his carbine he [Kinder] reentered the office to put his carbine away (R 187, 246). Lieutenant Schreiber and Toth were still talking (R 187, 246). Lieutenant Schreiber called him and said "Red come here." (R 187, 246). He walked over to where Lieutenant Schreiber and Toth were standing and Lieutenant Schreiber said "Why, Red, don't you think it would be a good idea, if the Korean were shot—if one of my guards shot a Korean?" (R 187, 195). He replied, "Yes, sir, I suppose it would" (R 195). He made that reply because Lieutenant Schreiber suggested it and he "figured" that was what he wanted him to say (R 195). Lieutenant Schreiber then said, "Do you think you can take this Korean out and shoot him." (R 187, 195, 246). He replied "No, sir, I don't think I could. I would rather not" (R 178, 188, 194, 246). Lieutenant Schreiber then said "Get (take) your carbine and clip and go with Toth" (R 178, 188, 189, 190, 196, 246). Lieutenant Schreiber did not use the words "Kill the Korean." (R 189, 190, 196). He understood from the conversation he had heard between Lieutenant Schreiber and Toth that Lieutenant Schreiber meant for him to shoot the Korean (R 188, 189, 190, 196). He said "Is that an order?", and

Lieutenant Schreiber replied, "Yes, that is an order." (R 178, 181, 188, 189, 190, 196, 246). In his opinion he had received an order to shoot the Korean (R 188, 195). He was about two feet from Lieutenant Schreiber at this time and doesn't remember how far away Toth was (R 179). Lieutenant Schreiber told Toth to get the Korean out to the truck (R 178). Just before the Korean was taken out of the office, Lieutenant Schreiber said "I would ask Toth to do it but Toth was Sergeant of the Guard." (R 190, 191, 194).

Leaving the office with his rifle and clip he went outside to the truck (R 179). Toth came out and said "Kinder, you drive, and go to B–14" (R 179, 246). Lieutenant Schreiber came outside and told Mullins to go along (R 179). He testified that when he first came out of the office, it was not his intention to kill the Korean, but to take him out and turn him loose, but in later testimony unequivocally stated that when he left the office he intended to kill the Korean although he did not want to (R 182, 183, 190). He drove the truck to revetment B–14 in the bomb dump which was where Toth had told him to drive (R 179, 180). Toth rode in the back of the truck and either Mullins or Borchardt, or possibly both, rode in the front of the truck with him (R 180, 191). In the truck on the way to the bomb dump he told Mullins "this was a hell of a thing to have to do to stay in the Air Force and get along." (R 186, 191). The only thing Toth said to him between the office and revetment B–14 was when Airman Toth tapped on the window of the truck and said "Stop here!" (R 196). At the revetment he got out of the truck and Toth helped the Korean out the back of the truck (R 179, 180, 196). Toth then said, "Kinder, when I hear the shots, I will turn around and come back" (R 197). The arrangement was that Toth would return after a signal of three shots in the air (R 194). Up until the time he got into the truck Lieutenant Schreiber was directing the incident (R 195), but thereafter Toth directed the incident (R 195).

He doesn't distinctly remember firing his weapon. (R 180). He was between ten and fifteen yards from the Korean (R 181, 193). It was very dark and he could see an outline or silhouette of the Korean but could not tell whether the Korean was facing him or not (R 180, 181, 193). The Korean just stood there and made no move to run (R 181, 193, 245; Court Exhibit 7). Holding the carbine in one hand like a pistol, he did not aim but pointed in the general direction of the Korean, and shot him (R 180, 190, 192, 245). He did not try to fire more than one shot as the carbine would not fire on automatic (R 183). The Korean "more or less sat down like any normal person would" (R 246). After firing the one shot he fired three shots into the air to signal the Sergeant of the Guard (R 194).

A few seconds after he fired the carbine the truck returned (R 180, 192, 194). Toth, Mullins and Borchardt got out of the truck (R 192, 246) and Airman Toth asked if he shot the Korean (R 179, 180, 246, 247). He replied, "No, I don't think so. I only fired one shot and heard the Korean groan a couple of times." (R 180, 193, 246). He believes Borchardt walked over to the Korean (R 247). Thereafter, Rumpff, Lieutenant Schreiber, an ambulance and Renteria arrived (R 192, 247; Court Exhibit 7). Renteria asked him what happened and he told him he would tell him tomorrow (R 192, 247). He did not make the remark "Die you son of a bitch." (R 196, 197). He admitted that the statement he made to the 17th Air Police Investigation Section at K–9 Air Base was not the truth but was what Lieutenant Schreiber told him to tell (R 183, 194).

. . . .

When Lieutenant Schreiber came into the organization he called a meeting of the Air Policemen and stated that any orders that he gave were definitely not to be questioned in any way (R 180). Lieutenant Schreiber had "chewed him out" several times, once threatened to demote him, and once removed him as Sergeant of the Guard and placed him under a man with less time in the service and in grade than he (R 180). He fully understood he was to obey the orders of Lieutenant Schreiber no matter what they were (R 181, 196). He knew it would have been wrong to shoot the Korean without an order (R 188, 190). He thought Lieutenant Schreiber had the authority to order the Korean shot (R 188). At the time he did not know the difference between a legal and an illegal order (R 185) and thought that any order Lieutenant Schreiber gave him was legal (R 185). He thought the order to shoot the Korean was legal (R 192, 194). While he was at the office there were present five or six persons senior in rank or duty assignment to him and none told him he did not have to obey the order (R 180, 181). He first found out that the order was illegal on 10 March 1953, when questioned by the Office of Special Investigations (R 184). He would not have thought an order to kill another American was illegal but he would not have obeyed it (R 185). Though he had been an air policeman and worked in stockades "quite a bit" and knew that persons are court-martialed for offenses, he thought that Lieutenant Schreiber could order him shot under certain circumstances such as if he were deserting the Air Force in time of danger (R 188, 189, 194). He did not know what Lieutenant Schreiber would have done to him if he had not obeyed but he does not believe he would have had him shot (R 184). He had not heard of anyone being shot for an offense without getting a trial (R 191). He has seen men serving life sentences for disobeying orders in front line positions "involving the enemy" but six months was the "worst" sentence he has heard of a man serving for disobeying an order not "involving the enemy" (R 197).

. . .

. . . The evidence of the instant case clearly demonstrates not only that the order of the accused's superior officer to shoot the victim was unlawful, but in addition that the superior officer issuing the order was fully aware of its illegality and resorted to subterfuge in arranging the circumstances of the execution of the order and falsification in reporting the circumstances under which the homicide of the victim was brought about to conceal the illegal circumstances of the homicide. The evidence clearly establishes that the superior officer of the accused subverted lawful authority and maliciously and corruptly issued the unlawful order to shoot the victim that resulted in the homicide.

The Manual for Courts-Martial, United States, 1951, in paragraph 197b, contains the following provisions pertinent to the defense of justification for a homicide:

"b. *Justification*—A homicide committed in the proper performance of a legal duty is justifiable. Thus executing a person pursuant to a legal sentence of death, killing in suppression of a mutiny or riot, killing to prevent the escape of a prisoner if no other reasonable apparent means are adequate, killing an enemy in battle, and killing to prevent the commission of an offense attempted by force or surprise such as burglary, robbery, or aggravated arson, are cases of justifiable homicide.

"The general rule is that the acts of a subordinate, done in good faith in compliance with his supposed duty or orders, are justifiable. *This justification does not exist, however, when* those acts are manifestly beyond the scope of his authority, or *the order is such that a man of ordinary sense and understanding would know it to be illegal,* or the subordinate willfully or through negligence does acts endangering the lives of innocent parties in the discharge of his duty to prevent escape or effect an arrest." (Page 351; italics supplied.) (Substantially similar provisions appeared in the MCM USA, 1928, par. 148a and MCM, USAF, 1949, par. 179a).

In Winthrop's Military Law and Precedents, Second Edition, Reprint 1920, the defense of justification for a criminal act by a soldier based on obedience to the order of a military superior is treated as follows:

"OBEDIENCE TO ORDERS. That the act charged as an offence was done in obedience to the order—verbal or written—of a military superior, is, in general, a good defence at military law.

. . . . .

"Further the order, to constitute a defence, must be a legal one. It must emanate from a proper officer—a superior authorized to give it—and it must command a thing not in itself unlawful or prohibited by law. In other words, it must be an order which the inferior is bound to obey. While obedience by inferiors is the fundamental principle of the military service, it is yet required to be rendered only to a lawful order. It is 'the lawful orders of the superiors appointed over them' that 'all inferiors' are, by par. 1 of the Army Regulations, 'required to obey strictly and to execute promptly;' and it is the 'lawful command of his superior officer' which by the 21st Article of War, 'any officer or soldier' may be punished even with death for disobeying. But for the inferior to assume to determine the question of the lawfulness of an order given him by a superior would of itself, as a general rule, amount to insubordination, and such an assumption carried into practice would subvert military discipline. Where the order is apparently regular and lawful on its face, he is not to go behind it to satisfy himself that his superior has proceeded with authority, but is to obey it according to its terms, the only exception recognized to the rule of obedience being cases of orders so manifestly beyond the legal power or discretion of the commander as to admit of no rational doubt of their unlawfulness. Such would be a command to violate a specific law of the land or an established custom or written law of the military service, or an arbitrary command imposing an obligation not justified by law or usage, or a command to do a thing wholly irregular and improper given by a superior when incapacitated by intoxication or otherwise to perform his duty. Except in such instances of palpable illegality, which must be of rare occurrence, the inferior should presume that the order was lawful and authorized and obey it accordingly, and in obeying it he can scarcely fail to be held justified by a military court.

"It may be added that an order which might not be regarded as legal in time of peace, may furnish to the inferior obeying it a complete defence in time of war, as being warranted by the laws and usages of war." (pp. 296–97).

.  .  .  .  .

Of controlling significance in the instant case is the manifest an unmistakable illegality of the order not only from the words of the order but under the circumstances in which it was given and executed. Human life being regarded as sacred, moral, religious and civil law proscriptions against its taking existing throughout our society, we view the order as commanding an act so obviously beyond the scope of authority of the superior officer and so palpably illegal on its face as to admit of no doubt of its unlawfulness to a man of ordinary sense and understanding. The distance from the battle line and other circumstances of the instant case cannot be reasonably considered as furnishing any basis to a man of ordinary sense and understanding to assume that the laws and usages of war, which justify the killing of an enemy in battle, would justify the killing in the instant case. In our view no rational being of the accused's age, formal education, and military experience could have, under the circumstances, considered the order lawful. Where one obeys an order to kill a severely injured, defenseless human being who is not resorting to violence, for the apparent reason of making his death an example to others, the evidence must be strong, indeed, to raise a doubt that the slayer was not aware of the illegality of the order. Particularly is this so where the circumstances are similar to those of the instant case and the slayer is aware that subterfuge will be resorted to in arranging the circumstances of the killing so as to justify the killing in the view of constituted military authority and after the killing the slayer joins in making a false report of the circumstances of the killing. The inference of fact is compelling from the circumstances of the instant case that the accused complied with the palpably unlawful order fully aware of its unlawful character. In view of the state of the evidence, the court properly rejected the testimony of the accused that he believed the order to be legal (U. S. v. Strong (No. 244), 1 USCMA 627, 5 CMR 55; U. S. v. Peterson (No. 199), 1 USCMA 317, 3 CMR 51; AMC 5560, Affronte, 7 CMR 815). As the evidence establishes that the accused was aware that Lieutenant Schreiber's order to shoot the victim was unlawful, the accused's act of shooting the victim which resulted in the homicide was not justifiable as an act committed in compliance with the order of a superior officer.

. . . .

An aspect of the case relating to the element of intent to commit murder arises from the argument by the defense counsel that the accused airman in complying with the order of his superior officer was an "automaton" and "was so deprived of his will, that he was without intent, and obedience of an order then constituted the carrying out of the intent of another." It is elementary that if the argument of the defense were a correct exposition of legal principle, then the accused could not be guilty of any criminal offense because of the lack of criminal intent, not only specific but general. It has been well and correctly stated:

> "The obedience of a soldier is not the obedience of an automaton. A soldier is a reasoning agent. He does not respond, and is not expected to respond, like a piece of machinery. It is a fallacy of wide-spread consumption that a soldier is required to do everything his superior officer orders him to do. A very simple illustration will show to what absurd extreme such a theory could be carried. If every military person were required, regardless of the nature of the command, to obey unconditionally, a sergeant could order the corporal to shoot the lieutenant, the lieutenant could order the sergeant to shoot the captain, the captain could order the lieutenant to shoot the colonel, and in each instance the executioner would be absolved of blame . . . ."

. . . .

For the foregoing reasons, the Board of Review finds the findings of guilty and the approved sentence correct in law and fact. Article 66(c) having been complied with, the findings of guilty and the sentence are

Affirmed.

Kandel, Butt and Swigert, Judge Advocates. 1 February 1954.

## NOTES AND QUESTIONS

1. Why did Kinder shoot the "oriental male human being"? Did Kinder want to shoot him? How much did he exercise or suspend his own powers of reason? (How does anyone ever "suspend" reason?) What—or "where"—were his own emotions? What do you gather from the language in which he characterizes the killing?

2. In what sense did Kinder *follow* an order, and in what sense was he a part of making it? How did he know that the words "don't you think it would be a good idea if the Korean were shot . . . ." were instructions (a) to him (b) to shoot (and kill) the Korean?

What else, other than the "mere words", did he rely on? How much was the judgment "his" and how much was the judgment that "of others"?

3.  How much do people *want* "freedom," and how much does their behavior reflect a readiness to escape its burdens? What happened to Kinder's sense of "self"? Why? What were the pressures under which he lived? How do they compare with the pressures of everyday civilian life?

4.  In what sense was Kinder "responsible" for killing the "oriental male human being"? Given the strength of the social forces that influence any individual's behavior, does assigning individual "responsibility" make any sense? Why do we talk *as though* the individual were a free and independent atom?

5.  Were Schreiber and Toth responsible?[1] More or less so than Kinder? What about those who trained Kinder? Those who sent him to Korea? The President, as Commander-in-Chief?

How is Kinder's case different from that of Lieutenant Calley?

6.  What are the social "needs" for producing men who follow orders? What, for example, would be the consequences if law enforcement officers decided to review judicial decrees and orders on the theory that, after all, they are *responsible* for carrying them out? Why and when should the law counteract—rather than reinforce— these tendencies to blind obedience? Was Kinder's behavior any less defensible than that of a lawyer who defends and saves the life of a man he believes to be a murderer, because "it is the calling of his profession"?

7.  Why does the Board of Review assume that the choice presented to Kinder was either to follow or not to follow the order as he understood it? What else might Kinder have done?

8.  Why does the Board of Review state that "human life being regarded as sacred, moral, religious and civil law proscriptions against its taking exist throughout society"? How was Kinder's training and day-to-day existence apt to influence his interpretation of the sacredness of human life?

9.  Why does the Board of Review believe that "no rational being could have considered" the order lawful? Do you think that Kinder ever even considered whether the order was "lawful" or not? Why?

10.  Does it matter whether Kinder knew that his actions were illegal? Would it have made any difference to those who heard his case if they were convinced of his ignorance of the law? Might it be that Kinder was convicted not for the commission of a knowingly

---

1.  Toth was honorably discharged, left Korea and returned to the United States. Subsequently he was charged with murder and conspiracy to commit murder, and taken back to Korea to stand trial. The United States Supreme Court held, on petition for habeas corpus, that his civilian status deprived the military courts of jurisdiction and he was ordered released. United States *ex rel.* Toth v. Quarles, 350 U.S. 1 (1955). Schreiber was convicted and given 5 years confinement. See United States v. Schreiber, 5 U.S. C.M.A. 602 (1955).

*illegal* act, but rather for the commission of a knowingly *immoral* act?

11. The Board of Review observes that a soldier is "not an automaton, but a 'reasoning agent'". Is being a "reasoning agent" consistent with war? Is it consistent with obediently carrying out any orders, in any circumstances? How was Judge Smith, in the *Cappier* case, more or less a "reasoning agent" than Kinder?

12. Why did the convening authority (the first reviewer of the original court martial) reduce the sentence to two years?

NOTE

In 1969, six American Special Forces officers were charged by the army with the pistol murder of a Vietnamese they had employed for intelligence purposes, but whom they apparently came to suspect of being a double agent. According to the N. Y. Times, Sept. 27, 1969, § 1 at 11, the mother of one of the accused argued, "I don't care if my son or any other mother's son shot this double agent, our enemy."

> The boys were acting under orders at all times. This is war. What are we playing, a game of hide and seek?

> What would the Army do if this double agent shot our son?" she continued, in a statement read over the telephone from her home. "They would just call to say, 'Your son was killed in the line of duty. We are sorry.' "

> Mrs. Marasco, whose husband Frank is a real estate and insurance agent, was also critical of reporters and announcers who refer to her son as "the triggerman, instead of calling them heroes—because that is what they all are, heroes defending our country.

The charges were subsequently dismissed. See the N. Y. Times, Oct. 5, 1969, § 4, at 4.


NOTE: UNITED STATES MANUAL FOR COURTS-MARTIAL (1951)

169. ARTICLE 90—ASSAULTING OR WILLFULLY DISOBEYING OFFICER

∙ ∙ ∙ ∙

b. DISOBEYING SUPERIOR OFFICER

*Discussion.*—The willful disobedience contemplated is such as shows an intentional defiance of authority, as when an enlisted person is given a lawful command by an officer to do or cease doing a particular thing at once and refuses or deliberately omits to do what is ordered.

∙ ∙ ∙ ∙

The order must relate to military duty and be one which the superior officer is authorized under the circumstances to give the accused. Disobedience of an order which has for its sole object the attainment of some private end, or which is given for the sole purpose of increasing the penalty for an offense which it is expected the accused may commit, is not punishable under this article.

A person cannot be convicted under this article if the order was illegal; but an order requiring the performance of a military duty or act is presumed to be lawful and is disobeyed at the peril of the subordinate. Acts involved in the disobedience of an illegal order might under some circumstances be charged as insubordination under Article 134.

That obedience to a command involved a violation of the religious scruples of the accused is not a defense.

The order must be directed to the subordinate personally. Failure to comply with the general or standing orders of a command, or with the regulations of an armed force, is not an offense under this article, . . .

As long as it is understandable, the form of an order is immaterial, as is the method by which it is transmitted to the accused, but the communication must amount to an order, and the accused must know that it is from his superior officer, that is, a commissioned officer who is authorized to give the order whether he is superior in rank to the accused or not.

*Proof.*—(a) That the accused received a certain command from a certain officer, as alleged; (b) that such officer was the superior officer of the accused; and (c) that the accused willfully disobeyed the command.

A command of a superior officer is presumed to be a lawful command.

*Jean–Paul Sartre*

## Existentialism and Humanism *

Man is nothing else but that which he makes of himself. That is the first principle of existentialism. And this is what people call its "subjectivity," using the word as a reproach against us. But what do we mean to say by this, but that man is of a greater dignity than a stone or a table? For we mean to say that man primarily exists— that man is, before all else, something which propels itself towards a future and is aware that it is doing so. Man is, indeed, a project which possesses a subjective life, instead of being a kind of moss, or a fungus or a cauliflower. Before that projection of the self nothing exists; not even in the heaven of intelligence: man will only attain existence when he is what he purposes to be. Not, however, what he may wish to be. For what we usually understand by wishing or willing is a conscious decision taken—much more often than not— after we have made ourselves what we are. I may wish to join a party, to write a book or to marry—but in such a case what is usually called my will is probably a manifestation of a prior and more spon-

* From 28–32 (P. Mairet transl., Methuen 1948). With the permission of Editions Nagel.

taneous decision. If, however, it is true that existence is prior to essence, man is responsible for what he is. Thus, the first effect of existentialism is that it puts every man in possession of himself as he is, and places the entire responsibility for his existence squarely upon his own shoulders. And, when we say that man is responsible for himself, we do not mean that he is responsible only for his own individuality, but that he is responsible for all men. The word "subjectivism" is to be understood in two senses, and our adversaries play upon only one of them. Subjectivism means, on the one hand, the freedom of the individual subject and, on the other, that man cannot pass beyond human subjectivity. It is the latter which is the deeper meaning of existentialism. When we say that man chooses himself, we do mean that every one of us must choose himself; but by that we also mean that in choosing for himself he chooses for all men. For in effect, of all the actions a man may take in order to create himself as he wills to be, there is not one which is not creative, at the same time, of an image of man such as he believes he ought to be. To choose between this or that is at the same time to affirm the value of that which is chosen; for we are unable ever to choose the worse. What we choose is always the better; and nothing can be better for us unless it is better for all. If, moreover, existence precedes essence and we will to exist at the same time as we fashion our image, that image is valid for all and for the entire epoch in which we find ourselves. Our responsibility is thus much greater than we had supposed, for it concerns mankind as a whole. If I am a worker, for instance, I may choose to join a Christian rather than a Communist trade union. And, if, by that membership, I choose to signify that resignation is, after all, the attitude that best becomes a man, that man's kingdom is not upon this earth, I do not commit myself alone to that view. Resignation is my will for everyone, and my action is, in consequence, a commitment on behalf of all mankind. Or if, to take a more personal case, I decide to marry and to have children, even though this decision proceeds simply from my situation, from my passion or my desire, I am thereby committing not only myself, but humanity as a whole, to the practice of monogamy. I am thus responsible for myself and for all men, and I am creating a certain image of man as I would have him to be. In fashioning myself I fashion man.

This may enable us to understand what is meant by such terms—perhaps a little grandiloquent—as anguish, abandonment and despair. As you will soon see, it is very simple. First, what we do mean by anguish? The existentialist frankly states that man is in anguish. His meaning is as follows—When a man commits himself to anything, fully realising that he is not only choosing what he will be, but is thereby at the same time a legislator deciding for the whole of mankind—in such a moment a man cannot escape from the sense of complete and profound responsibility. There are many, indeed, who show no such anxiety. But we affirm that they are merely disguising their anguish or are in flight from it. Certainly, many people think that in what they are doing they commit no one but themselves to anything: and if you ask them, "What would happen if everyone did so?"

they shrug their shoulders and reply, "Everyone does not do so," But in truth, one ought always to ask oneself what would happen if everyone did as one is doing; nor can one escape from that disturbing thought except by a kind of self-deception. The man who lies in self-excuse, by saying "everyone will not do it" must be ill at ease in his conscience, for the act of lying implies the universal value which it denies. By its very disguise his anguish reveals itself. This is the anguish that Kierkegaard called "the anguish of Abraham." You know the story: An angel commanded Abraham to sacrifice his son: and obedience was obligatory, if it really was an angel who had appeared and said, "Thou, Abraham, shalt sacrifice thy son." [2] But anyone in such a case would wonder, first, whether it was indeed an angel and secondly, whether I am really Abraham. Where are the proofs? A certain mad woman who suffered from hallucinations said that people were telephoning to her, and giving her orders. The doctor asked, "But who is it that speaks to you?" She replied: "He says it is God." And what, indeed, could prove to her that it was God? If an angel appears to me, what is the proof that it is an angel; or, if I hear voices, who can prove that they proceed from heaven and not from hell, or from my own subconsciousness or some pathological condition? Who can prove that they are really addressed to me?

Who, then, can prove that I am the proper person to impose, by my own choice, my conception of man upon mankind? I shall never find any proof whatever; there will be no sign to convince me of it. If a voice speaks to me, it is still I myself who must decide whether the voice is or is not that of an angel. If I regard a certain course of action as good, it is only I who choose to say that it is good and not bad. There is nothing to show that I am Abraham: nevertheless I also am obliged at every instant to perform actions which are examples. Everything happens to every man as though the whole human race had its eyes fixed upon what he is doing and regulated its conduct accordingly. So every man ought to say, "Am I really a man who has the right to act in such a manner that humanity regulates it-

---

**2.** Genesis 22 reads "And it came to pass after these things, that God did prove Abraham, and said unto him, Abraham; and he said, Here am I. 2 And he said, Take now thy son, thine only son, whom thou lovest, even Isaac, and get thee into the land of Moriah; and offer him there for a burnt-offering upon one of the mountains which I will tell thee of. 3 And Abraham rose early in the morning, and saddled his ass, and took two of his young men with him, and Isaac his son; and he clave the wood for the burnt-offering, and rose up, and went unto the place of which God had told him. 4 On the third day Abraham lifted up his eyes, and saw the place afar off. 5 And Abraham said unto his young men, Abide ye here with the ass, and I and the lad will go yonder; and we will worship, and come again to you. 6 And Abraham took the wood of the burnt-offering, and laid it upon Isaac his son; and he took in his hand the fire and the knife; and they went both of them together. 7 And Isaac spake unto Abraham and his father, and said, My Father: and he said, Here am I, my son. And he said, Behold, the fire and the wood: but where is the lamb for a burnt-offering? 8 And Abraham said, God will provide himself the lamb for a burnt offering, my son: so they went both of them together. 9 And they came to the place which God had told him of; and Abraham built the altar there, and laid the wood in order, and bound Isaac his son, and laid him on the altar, upon the wood. 10 And Abraham stretched forth his hand, and took the knife to slay his son. . . ."

self by what I do." If a man does not say that, he is dissembling his anguish. Clearly, the anguish with which we are concerned here is not one that could lead to quietism or inaction. It is anguish pure and simple, of the kind well known to all those who have borne responsibilities. When, for instance, a military leader takes upon himself the responsibility for an attack and sends a number of men to their death, he chooses to do it and at bottom he alone chooses. No doubt he acts under a higher command, but its orders, which are more general, require interpretation by him and upon that interpretation depends the life of ten, fourteen or twenty men. In making the decision, he cannot but feel a certain anguish. All leaders know that anguish. It does not prevent their acting, on the contrary it is the very condition of their action, for the action presupposes that there is a plurality of possibilities, and in choosing one of these, they realise that it has value only because it is chosen. Now it is anguish of that kind which existentialism describes, and moreover, as we shall see, makes explicit through direct responsibility towards other men who are concerned. Far from being a screen which could separate us from action, it is a condition of action itself.

## QUESTIONS

1. What is Sartre pointing out in his treatment of the Abraham example? Even if one were prepared to submit to some authority, can one ever be certain *what his orders are*? How, for example, could Kinder have been certain that he had heard Schreiber correctly? (See U. S. v. Schreiber, 5 U.S.C.M.A. 602, 607 (1955) for two other versions of what Schreiber had said to Kinder—both from the same witness.) And even if he had *heard* correctly, how could he be certain *what the words meant*? And even if he could have known what the words meant, how could he be certain *of the credentials*—the authority—of the person issuing them? How does one decide when to stop taking evidence on these matters?

How do these problems influence your estimate of whether Kinder was *following* an order? In what sense is any man ever simply "following orders"?

2. Is the thrust clear of Sartre's statement that when each man decides "he chooses for all men"? Is this the same as to say (as Sartre later says) that "our responsibility is . . . much greater than we had supposed for it *concerns* all men" (emphasis added)? Could Judge Smith, in the *Cappier* case, have maintained that in deciding as he did, *qua* judge and according "to law", he *was* deciding for all mankind, and the particular example he wanted to set was that of a person acting according to his assigned office? Could Kinder say that he was choosing for all men, in the sense that in time of war, the orders of one's superior ought never to be questioned by anyone (perhaps even if the law provided a "loophole")? What rejoinder, if any, could Sartre make?

3. Why should we assume that "When a man commits himself to anything . . . he is at the same time a legislator deciding for the whole of mankind"? What are the grounds for and against such

an assumption? Consider Kinder's decision whether to shoot this particular Korean: in what way is his decision legislation "for all humanity"?

4. What is Sartre's view of the limits of reason? Elsewhere he says, "what is usually called my will is probably a manifestation of a prior and more spontaneous decision" and "in the end, it is the feeling that counts"? Does this mean that discussion and dialogue over basic choices is futile?

## DEFENSE ARGUMENT

### NUREMBERG TRIALS *

27 August 1946

Dr. Laternser [Defense Counsel]: My Lord, Gentlemen of the Tribunal:

. . . .

If one thing stands out clearly from the collection of evidence—and I shall have to deal with this in detail later on—it is the fact that the German military leaders did not dominate their country and did not drive it into the war, that they were not politicians, but exclusively, and perhaps even too exclusively, soldiers—which is the tragic part. Had they been politicians, Germany would not have fallen into this abyss. If we keep this clearly in our minds, it is obvious that these men are in fact facing trial before this Court only because they served their country as soldiers.

If the Prosecutor, Colonel [Telford] Taylor, argues that Hitler could not have waged his wars without the assistance of the Armed Forces, that argument cannot be invalidated. Nobody has ever been able to wage a war without soldiers. However, what Carlyle says is true for the German military leaders as for all soldiers:

> "If a man becomes a soldier, his soul and his body thereby become the property of his commanding officer. He is not allowed to decide for himself whether the cause for which he fights is good or bad. His enemies are selected for him, and not by him. It is his duty to obey and to ask no questions."

If the German military leaders are today indicted before this Court as an alleged "criminal organization," this indictment does not only apply to them, but is in fact directed—however strongly it may be desired to deny this publicly—at the soldiers in general, or at least at the military leaders as a class.

By indicting the military leader—who, obeying the orders of his government, has fulfilled his military duties—because the Prosecution declares the action of his government to be illegal and represents him as a partner to such action of the government, the Prosecu-

* From XXII Trial of the Major War Criminals Before the International Tribunal Nuremberg 44, 45–46 (1948).

tion places upon him the obligation to examine the legality of his country's policy, and raises him to the position of a judge called upon to give a verdict on the policy of his state.

It cannot be my task to present the consequences of such a mental revolution for the soldiers of the world.

PROSECUTION ARGUMENT

NUREMBERG TRIALS *

29 August 1946

SIR DAVID MAXWELL-FYFE: . . . .

All decent men find it difficult to blame others for absence of moral courage—they are only too conscious of their own failings in that direction. But there comes a point when, faced with crimes which are obvious murder or barbarity, there is a higher duty. Even Dr. Laternser admitted this was so. His suggestion to the witness Schreiber that he ought to have protested at the Army Staff's proposals for bacteriological warfare came strangely on behalf of these men whose very defense has been to declare the impossibility and uselessness of protest. What nonsense—what utter nonsense—is this which you have been asked to listen to by these defendants and their generals when their own counsel, to discredit a witness, must ask the very question which the Prosecution have been asking of themselves since the day this Trial began. In fairness to all military tradition it should not go forth that soldiers have sheltered behind the letter of a command from facing moral problems—and deciding them, rightly or wrongly, as moral problems. Great captains are not automata to be weighed against a rubber stamp. I need not traverse the history of our military figures—the philosophy of Montrose, the brooding thoughts of Marshal Ney, the troubled heart of Robert E. Lee in 1861—to find examples. Two of the greatest names in German military history spring to one's mind: Von Clausewitz leaving the Prussian Army to serve in that of Russia; Yorck von Wartenburg making his decision of neutrality—both put what they deemed the needs of Europe and humanity above the orders of the moment. How much more clear and obvious was the duty when the work of drafting, issuing, and carrying out the Nacht und Nebel Decree, the Commando Order, the Commissar Order, Hitler's order to murder our 50 Air Force officers, meant the defiling of every idea which every soldier cherishes and holds dear; when—as all of them who ever served upon the Eastern Front could see with their own eyes—they were asked to support and co-operate in a calculated system of mass-extermination and utter brutality.

These men, of all men, knew their leader to be a callous murderer, yet for years they had met in conference after conference to sit at his feet and listen to his words. They fed his lust for power and enslavement with the best of their professional skill. While the de-

* From *Id.* at 221, 236-37.

fenseless peoples of the East, the men, women and children of Poland, of the Soviet Union, and of the Baltic states, were being deliberately slaughtered and deported into slavery to allow for German "Lebensraum," these men talked of the necessities of war. When their own cities were bombed and Germans killed, they called it murder. Only in July 1944, when Hitler's star was dimmed, did three Field Marshals and five Colonel Generals recognize that he was murdering also their own country and took action. When that star was rising in victory they had hailed it and ignored the blood-red colour of the clouds from which it rose.

*JUDGMENT*

NUREMBERG TRIALS *

30 September 1946

MR. FRANCIS BIDDLE [Member of the Tribunal for the United States, reading the Judgment]

. . . .

It was also submitted on behalf of most of these defendants that in doing what they did they were acting under the orders of Hitler, and therefore cannot be held responsible for the acts committed by them in carrying out these orders. The Charter specifically provides in Article 8:

"The fact that the defendant acted pursuant to order of his Government or of a superior shall not free him from responsibility, but may be considered in mitigation of punishment."

The provisions of this article are in conformity with the law of all nations. That a soldier was ordered to kill or torture in violation of the international law of war has never been recognized as a defense to such acts of brutality, though, as the Charter here provides, the order may be urged in mitigation of the punishment. The true test, which is found in varying degrees in the criminal law of most nations, is not the existence of the order, but whether moral choice was in fact possible.

*STANLEY MILGRAM*

SOME CONDITIONS OF OBEDIENCE AND DISOBEDIENCE TO AUTHORITY **

The situation in which one agent commands another to hurt a third turns up time and again as a significant theme in human relations. It is powerfully expressed in the story of Abraham, who is commanded by God to kill his son. It is no accident that Kierkegaard,

* From *Id.* at 456–466.

** From 6 Int. Journ. Psychiatry 259, 259–62, 268–295, 273, 275–76 (1968).

With the permission of the International Journal of Psychiatry and Professor Milgram.

seeking to orient his thought to the central themes of human experience, chose Abraham's conflict as the springboard to his philosophy.

War too moves forward on the triad of an authority which commands a person to destroy the enemy, and perhaps all organized hostility may be viewed as a theme and variation on the three elements of authority, executant, and victim. We describe an experimental program, recently concluded at Yale University, in which a particular expression of this conflict is studied by experimental means.

In its most general form the problem may be defined thus: if X tells Y to hurt Z, under what conditions will Y carry out the command of X and under what conditions will he refuse. In the more limited form possible in laboratory research, the question becomes: if an experimenter tells a subject to hurt another person, under what conditions will the subject go along with this instruction, and under what conditions will he refuse to obey. The laboratory problem is not so much a dilution of the general statement as one concrete expression of the many particular forms this question may assume.

. . . .

*Subject Population.* The subjects used in all experimental conditions were male adults, residing in the greater New Haven and Bridgeport areas, aged 20 to 50 years, and engaged in a wide variety of occupations. . . .

*The General Laboratory Procedure.* The focus of the study concerns the amount of electric shock a subject is willing to administer to another person when ordered by an experimenter to give the "victim" increasingly more severe punishment. The act of administering shock is set in the context of a learning experiment, ostensibly designed to study the effect of punishment on memory. Aside from the experimenter, one naive subject and one accomplice perform in each session. On arrival each subject is paid $4.50. After a general talk by the experimenter, telling how little scientists know about the effect of punishment on memory, subjects are informed that one member of the pair will serve as teacher and one as learner. A rigged drawing is held so that the naive subject is always the teacher, and the accomplice becomes the learner. The learner is taken to an adjacent room and strapped into an "electric chair."

The naive subject is told that it is his task to teach the learner a list of paired associates, to test him on the list, and to administer punishment whenever the learner errs in the test. Punishment takes the form of electric shock, delivered to the learner by means of a shock generator controlled by the naive subject. The teacher is instructed to increase the intensity of electric shock one step on the generator on each error. The learner, according to plan, provides many wrong answers, so that before long the naive subject must give him the strongest shock on the generator. Increases in shock level are met by increasingly insistent demands from the learner that the experiment be stopped because of the growing discomfort to him. However, in clear terms the experimenter orders the teacher to continue with the procedure in disregard of the learner's protests. *Thus, the naive subject must resolve a conflict between two mutually incom-*

*patible* demands from the social field. *He may continue to follow
the orders of the experimenter and shock the learner with increasing
severity, or he may refuse to follow the orders of the experimenter
and heed the learner's pleas. The experimenter's authority operates
not in a free field, but against ever-mounting countervailing pressures from the person being punished.*

A few technical points need to be considered before the findings
of the study are described. For the purpose of delivering shock, a
simulated shock generator is used, with 30 clearly marked voltage levels that range from 15 to 450 volts (and each activated by one of 30
individual lever switches set in a horizontal line). The naive subject
is given a sample shock of 45 volts to convince him of the authenticity
of the instrument. The generator bears verbal designations that
range from "Slight Shock" to "Danger: Severe Shock."

The responses of the victim are standardized on tape, and each
protest is coordinated to a particular voltage level on the shock generator. Starting with 75 volts the learner begins to grunt and moan.
At 150 volts he demands to be let out of the experiment. At 180 volts
he cries out that he can no longer stand the pain. At 300 volts he
refuses to provide any more answers to the memory test, insisting
that he is no longer a participant in the experiment and must be
freed. In response to this last tactic, the experimenter instructs the
naive subject to treat the absence of an answer as equivalent to a
wrong answer, and to follow the usual shock procedure. The experimenter reinforces his demand with the statement: "You have no
other choice, you must go on!" (This imperative is used whenever
the naive subject tries to break off the experiment.) If the subject
refuses to give the next higher level of shock, the experiment is considered at an end.     .    .    .

.    .    .    .    .

Experiments in this series show that the physical *presence* of
an authority is an important force contributing to the subject's obedience or defiance. Taken together with the first experimental series
on the proximity of the victim, it would appear that something akin
to fields of force, diminishing in effectiveness with increasing psychological distance from their source, have a controlling effect on
the subject's performance. As the victim is brought closer, the subject finds it harder to administer shocks to him. When the victim's
position is held constant relative to the subject, and the authority is
made more remote, the subject finds it easier to break off the experiment. This effect is substantial in both cases, but manipulation
of the experimenter's position wielded the more powerful results.
Obedience to destructive commands is highly dependent on the proxi-
mal relations between authority and subject.

*Tensions.* The description of final scores does not fully convey
the character of the subjects' performance, and it would be useful
to interrupt our reporting of quantitative relationships to remark on
the subjects' general reaction to the situation.

One might suppose that a subject would simply break off or
continue as his conscience and temperament dictated. Yet this is

very far from what happened. There were powerful reactions of tension and emotional strain in a substantial proportion of the participants. Persons were observed to sweat, tremble, stutter, bite their lips, and groan as they found themselves increasingly implicated in the experimental conflict. Some sense of the subjects' mood can be gotten from a transcript of their remarks at break-off point. Here are the remarks of [a] defiant subject:

. . . .

> The man is banging. He wants to get out . . . I'm sorry. If the man wants to get out I'd just as soon stop . . . I don't want to administer any more [extremely excited] . . . I will gladly refund the check, but I will not harm this man . . . I'm sorry, I will not give him any more if he obviously wants to get out. There is no money in the world that will make me hurt another individual. [Subject 010X]

And here is a transcript from an obedient subject. He began the experiment calmly, but became increasingly tense as the experiment proceeded. After administering the 150-volt shock, he began to address the experimenter in agitated tones:

*150 volts delivered.* You want me to keep going?

*165 volts delivered.* That guy is hollering in there. There's a lot of them here. He's liable to have a heart condition. You want me to go?

*180 volts delivered.* He can't stand it! I'm not going to kill that man in there! You hear him hollering? He's hollering. He can't stand it. What if something happens to him? . . . I'm not going to get that man sick in there. He's hollering in there. You know what I mean? I mean I refuse to take responsibility. He's getting hurt in there. He's in there hollering. Too many left here. Geez, if he gets them wrong. There's too many of them left. I mean who is going to take responsibility if anything happens to that gentleman?

[The experimenter accepts responsibility.]

All right.

*195 volts delivered.* You see he's hollering. Hear that. Gee, I don't know. [The experimenter says: "The experiment requires that you go on."]—I know it does, sir, but I mean—hugh—he don't know what he's in for. He's up to 195 volts.

*210 volts delivered.*

*225 volts delivered.*

*240 volts delivered.* Aw, no. You mean I've got to keep going up with the scale? No sir, I'm not going to kill that man! I'm not going to give him 450 volts! [The experimenter says: "The experiment requires that you go on."] —I know it does, but that man is hollering in there, sir

. . . .

Despite his numerous, agitated objections, which were constant accompaniments to his actions, the subject unfailingly obeyed the experimenter, proceeding to the highest shock level on the generator. He displayed a curious dissociation between word and action. Although at the verbal level he had resolved not to go on, his actions were fully in accord with the experimenter's commands. This subject did not want to shock the victim, and he found it an extremely disagreeable task, but he was unable to invent a response that would free him from E's authority. Many subjects cannot find the specific verbal formula that would enable them to reject the role assigned to them by the experimenter. Perhaps our culture does not provide adequate models for disobedience.

. . . . .

*Levels of Obedience and Defiance.* One general finding that merits attention is the high level of obedience manifested in the experimental situation. Subjects often expressed deep disapproval of shocking a man in the face of his objections, and others denounced it as senseless and stupid. Yet many subjects complied even while they protested. The proportion of obedient subjects greatly exceeded the expectations of the experimenter and his colleagues. At the outset, we had conjectured that subjects would not, in general, go above the level of 'Strong Shock.' In practice, many subjects were willing to administer the most extreme shocks available when commanded by the experimenter. For some subjects the experiment provides an occasion for aggressive release. And for others it demonstrates the extent to which obedient dispositions are deeply ingrained, and are engaged irrespective of their consequences for others. Yet this is not the whole story. Somehow the subject becomes implicated in a situation from which he cannot disengage himself.

. . . .

*Postscript.* . . .

There are now some other generalizations I should like to make, which do not derive in any strictly logical fashion from the experiments as carried out, but which, I feel, ought to be made. They are formulations of an intuitive sort that have been forced on me by observation of many subjects responding to the pressures of authority. The assertions represent a painful alteration in my own thinking; and since they were acquired only under the repeated impact of direct observation, I have no illusion that they will be generally accepted by persons who have not had the same experience.

With numbing regularity good people were seen to knuckle under the demands of authority and to perform actions that were callous and severe. Men who are in everyday life responsible and decent were seduced by the trappings of authority, by the control of their perceptions, and by the uncritical acceptance of the experimenter's definition of the situation, into performing harsh acts.

What is the limit of such obedience? At many points we attempted to establish a boundary. Cries from the victim were inserted; not good enough. The victim claimed heart trouble; subjects still shocked him on command. The victim pleaded that he be let free, and his answers no longer registered on the signal box; subjects continued to shock him. At the outset we had not conceived that such drastic procedures would be needed to generate disobedience, and each step was added only as the ineffectiveness of the earlier techniques became clear. . . .

The results, as seen and felt in the laboratory, are to this author disturbing. They raise the possibility that human nature, or—more specifically—the kind of character produced in American democratic society, cannot be counted on to insulate its citizens from brutality and inhumane treatment at the direction of malevolent authority. A substantial proportion of people do what they are told to do, irrespective of the content of the act and without limitations of conscience, so long as they perceive that the command comes from a legitimate authority. If in this study an anonymous experimenter could successfully command adults to subdue a fifty-year-old man, and force on him painful electric shocks against his protests, one can only wonder what government, with its vastly greater authority and prestige, can command of its subjects. There is, of course, the extremely important question of whether malevolent political institutions could or would arise in American society. The present research contributes nothing to this issue.

In an article entitled "The Dangers of Obedience," Harold J. Laski wrote:

> . . . civilization means, above all, an unwillingness to inflict unnecessary pain. Within the ambit of that definition, those of us who heedlessly accept the commands of authority cannot yet claim to be civilized men.

> . . . Our business, if we desire to live a life not utterly devoid of meaning and significance, is to accept nothing which contradicts our basic experience merely because it comes to us from tradition or convention or authority. It may well be that we shall be wrong; but our self-expression is thwarted at the root unless the certainties we are asked to accept coincide with the certainties we experience. That is why the condition of freedom in any state is always a widespread and consistent skepticism of the canons upon which power insists.

## QUESTIONS

1. What does Milgram contribute to an understanding of moral decision making? In the light of his experimental findings, how "free" is an individual to choose from among "the plurality of possibilities" of which Sartre speaks? To what extent, and through what processes, are choices constrained by the systems in which people —like judges—find themselves?

Consider, in this regard, C. Wright Mills's observations that "caught in the limited milieux of their everyday lives, ordinary men often cannot reason about the great structures—rational and irrational—of which their milieux are subordinate parts."

Accordingly, they often carry out series of apparently rational actions without any ideas of the ends they serve, and there is the increasing suspicion that those at the top as well—like Tolstoy's generals—only pretend they know. The growth of such organizations, within an increasing division of labor, sets up more and more spheres of life, work, and leisure, in which reasoning is difficult or impossible. The soldier, for example, 'carries out an entire series of functionally rational actions accurately without having any idea as to the ultimate end of this action' or the function of each act within the whole. Even men of technically supreme intelligence may efficiently perform their assigned work and yet not know that it is to result in the first atom bomb.

The Sociological Imagination 167–8 (1959).

2. How did the context in which the experiments were conducted —the institutional setting, the announced purposes, etc.—influence the behavior of the subjects? How did it influence the *meaning* of their actions? Suppose the subjects had been called upon by friends to explain what they had spent the day doing: would they be apt to describe their actions as "hurting people"?

3. What is the relationship between language and responsibility implied by Milgram's remarks? He observes that "Many subjects cannot find the specific verbal formula that would enable them to reject the role assigned to them by the experimenter." How much help would having the "right" verbal formula have been? Consider Milgram's discovery of the "curious dissociation between words and actions" in the subject who kept insisting he would not go on—but did.

4. Note the effect of the experimenter's telling the subject that he—the experimenter—"accepts responsibility"? How can you account for the uttering of words such as "I accept responsibility" having such an effect on human behavior?

5. In view of your answers to questions 3 and 4, how may the "plurality of possibilities" confronting any individual be influenced by the language available to him? How may language make it possible for us to be more responsible? How may it be used to relieve us of our responsibility?

6. Consider Milgram's summary observations that "with numbing regularity good people were seen to knuckle under to authority and to perform actions that were callous and severe." Might someone not argue that there was, perhaps, something "callous and severe" in Dr. Milgram's own regard for the emotional well-being of his "subjects"? How do you account for this? How might Milgram justify his procedures? Does the autonomous pursuit of truth lead to more moral results than the subordination to authority? What comments might Mills offer? See Baumrind, *Some Thoughts on Ethics of Research: After Reading Milgram's "Behavioral Study of Obedience"*, 19 Am. Psychologist 421 (1959).

NOTE

How is the position of a judge in following the "superior orders" of "the law" different from the dilemma of the soldier? How is Kinder less—or otherwise—justified than Judge Smith in the *Cappier* case? Consider in this regard the remarks of Cardozo, Growth of the Law, *supra* p. 35. Is Cardozo saying that judges ought never to follow the law, as law, or only that they ought to follow it sometimes, but not others? If the latter, by reference to what principles would one make the necessary distinctions?

How, indeed, does the position of the lawyer in regard the demands of his client compare with the position of the soldier and judge, respectively? Why, and to what extent, do people assume that a lawyer should fashion his actions by what his client thinks best? What sort of image does this give the lawyer in the society? Is it a deserved one?

Consider in this regard the selection from Aristotle which follows: how could the author of the Nichomachean Ethics ("we become just by doing just acts, temperate by doing temperate acts") *also* have been the author or this? What is his conception of justice in the lawyer? Have civilized societies, from at least as early as the fourth century B.C., simply come to assume that lawyers are a special case of human being?

*ARISTOTLE*

RHETORIC *

[L]et us take laws and see how they are to be used in persuasion and dissuasion, in accusation and defence. If the written law tells against our case, clearly we must appeal to the universal law, and insist on its greater equity and justice. We must argue that the juror's oath "I will give my verdict according to my honest opinion" means that one will not simply follow the letter of the written law. We must urge that the principles of equity are permanent and changeless, and that the universal law does not change either, for it is the law of nature, whereas written laws often do change. This is the bearing of the lines in Sophocles' *Antigone*, where Antigone pleads that in burying her brother she had broken Creon's law but not the unwritten law:

> Not of to-day or yesterday they are,
> But live eternal: (none can date their birth.)
> Not I would fear the wrath of any man,
> (And brave Gods' vengeance) for defying these.

We shall argue that justice indeed is true and profitable, but that sham justice is not, and that consequently the written law is not, because it does not fulfil the true purpose of law. Or that justice is like

---

* From The Basic Works of Aristotle 1374–75 (R. McKeon ed. Random House 1941), derived from XI The Oxford Translation of Aristotle (W. R. Roberts, transl. 1924). With the permission of Random House and the Clarendon Press, Oxford.

silver, and must be assayed by the judges, if the genuine is to be distinguished from the counterfeit.  Or that the better a man is, the more he will follow and abide by the unwritten law in preference to the written.  Or perhaps that the law in question contradicts some other highly-esteemed law, or even contradicts itself.  Thus it may be that one law will enact that all contracts must be held binding, while another forbids us ever to make illegal contracts.  Or if a law is ambiguous, we shall turn it about and consider which construction best fits the interests of justice or utility, and then follow that way of looking at it.  Or if, though the law still exists, the situation to meet which it was passed exists no longer, we must do our best to prove this and to combat the law thereby.  If however the written law supports our case, we must urge that the oath "to give my verdict according to my honest opinion" is not meant to make the judges give a verdict that is contrary to the law, but to save them from the guilt of perjury if they misunderstand what the law really means.  Or that no one chooses what is absolutely good, but every one what is good for himself.  Or that not to use the laws is as bad as to have no laws at all.  Or that, as in the other arts, it does not pay to try to be cleverer than the doctor: for less harm comes from the doctor's mistakes than from the growing habit of disobeying authority.  Or that trying to be cleverer than the laws is just what is forbidden by those codes of law that are accounted best.—So far as the laws are concerned, the above discussion is probably sufficient.

CHARLES P. CURTIS

## THE ETHICS OF ADVOCACY *

I want first of all to put advocacy in its proper setting.  It is a special case of vicarious conduct.  A lawyer devotes his life and career to acting for other people.  So too does the priest, and in another way the banker.  The banker handles other people's money.  The priest handles other people's spiritual aspirations.  A lawyer handles other people's troubles.

But there is a difference.  The loyalty of a priest or clergyman runs, not to the particular parishioner whose joys or troubles he is busy with, but to his church; and the banker looks to his bank.  It is the church or the bank, not he, but he on its behalf, who serves the communicant or the borrower.  Their loyalties run in a different direction than a lawyer's.

.    .    .    .

.    .    .    .    His loyalty runs to his client.  He has no other master.  Not the court? you ask.  Does not the court take the same position as the church or the bank?  Is not the lawyer an officer of the court?  Why doesn't the court have first claim on his loyalty?  No, in a paradoxical way.  The lawyer's official duty, required of him indeed

* From  4  Stan.L.Rev.  3, 3–8, 18–23     of Trustees of the Leland Stanford
(1951).  Copyright 1951 by the Board     Jr. University.

by the court, is to devote himself to the client. The court comes second by the court's, that is the law's, own command.

Lord Brougham, in his defense of Queen Caroline, in her divorce case, told the House of Lords: "I once before took occasion to remind your Lordships, which was unnecessary, but there are many whom it may be needful to remind, that an advocate, by the sacred duty which he owes his client, knows in the discharge of that office but one person in the world—that client and no other. . . . Nay, separating even the duties of a patriot from those of an advocate, and casting them if need be to the wind, he must go on reckless of the consequences, if his fate it should unhappily be to involve his country in confusion for his client's protection."

Lord Brougham was a great advocate, and when he made this statement he was arguing a great case, the divorce of Queen Caroline from George IV before the House of Lords. Plainly he was exerting more than his learning and more than his legal ability. Years later he explained to William Forsythe, the author of a book on lawyers called *Hortensius*, who had asked him what he meant. Before you read Brougham's reply, let me remind you that the king, George IV, was the one who was pressing the divorce, which Brougham was defending, and that George had contracted a secret marriage, while he was heir apparent, with Mrs. Fitzherbert, a Roman Catholic. Brougham knew this, and knew too that it was enough to deprive the king of his crown under the Act of Settlement. Brougham wrote:

> The real truth is, that the statement was anything rather than a deliberate and well-considered opinion. It was a menace, and it was addressed chiefly to George IV, but also to wiser men, such as Castlereagh and Wellington. I was prepared, *in case of necessity*, that is, in case the Bill passed the Lords, to do two things—first, to resist it in the Commons *with the country at my back*; but next, if need be, to dispute the King's title, to show he had forfeited the crown by marrying a Catholic, in the words of the Act, "as if he were naturally dead." What I said was fully understood by Geo. IV; perhaps by the Duke and Castlereagh, and I am confident it would have prevented them from pressing the Bill beyond a certain point.

Lord Brougham's menace has become the classic statement of the loyalty which a lawyer owes to his client, perhaps because being a menace it is so extreme. And yet the Canons of Ethics is scarcely more moderate, " . . . entire devotion to the interest of the client, warm zeal in the maintenance and defense of his rights and the exertion of his utmost learning and ability. . . ."

. . . . .

I cannot forget what one of the very best Boston trustees once told me. He had, of course, in his many trusts large real estate holdings in Boston. He was a citizen of Boston. He told me once that he either refused to contribute to the campaigns of candidates for mayor or else he contributed to both of them, because, he said, "The assessments on the real estate I hold in trust, things being as they are in Boston, would be put in hazard if I were to come out definitely for a candidate and he lost." The better trustee, and he was a good trustee, the worse a citizen.

The person for whom you are acting very reasonably expects you to treat him better than you do other people, which is just another way of saying that you owe him a higher standard of conduct than you owe to others. This goes back a long way. It is the pre-platonic ethics which Socrates had disposed of at the very outset of the *Republic*; that is that justice consists of doing good to your friends and harm to your enemies. A lawyer, therefore, insensibly finds himself treating his client better than others; and therefore others worse than his client. A lawyer, or a trustee, or anyone acting for another, has lower standards of conduct toward outsiders than he has toward his clients or his beneficiaries or his patrons against the outsiders. He is required to treat outsiders as if they were barbarians and enemies. The more good faith and devotion the lawyer owes to his client, the less he owes to others when he is acting for his client. It is as if a man had only so much virtue, and the more he gives to one, the less he has available for anyone else. The upshot is that a man whose business it is to act for others finds himself, in his dealings on his client's behalf with outsiders, acting on a lower standard than he would if he were acting for himself, and lower, too, than any standard his client himself would be willing to act on, lower, in fact, than anyone on his own.

You devote yourself to the interests of another at the peril of yourself. Vicarious action tempts a man too far from himself. Men will do for others what they are not willing to do for themselves— nobler as well as ignoble things. What I want to do now is to illustrate this in the practice of law by a number of perplexing situations. They raise ethical problems, but none of them, I think, has a simple right or wrong answer, and I know of no canons of ethics or morals which lead to any answer. How could there be when the cause of the perplexity is the difference between acting for another and acting for yourself?

I will start with the story of Sam the Lookout.

A distinguished New York lawyer was once called over to sit in a conference of admiralty lawyers with the crew of a ship which had been in a collision. The lawyers were going over the testimony which the members of the crew would give at the approaching trial. Finally they came to the lookout, and the Captain, who was asking the questions, turned to him and said, "You, of course, were up in the eyes on the forecastle keeping a sharp lookout." The seaman squirmed in his chair, twisted his cap, and said, "The truth is, Captain, I was in the head having a smoke." The lawyers leaned forward, but the Captain turned to reassure them. "That's all right, gentlemen, he'll testify that he was keeping a sharp lookout. Won't you Sam?" "No," said Sam, "I guess I can't do that."

And then, this lawyer said, such a storm of indignation burst over Sam as he had never seen. The Captain and the rest of the crew cursed him for betraying his ship. Let him go to the head if he had to. Let him even have his smoke if he must. But when he did let him also take the consequences. The collision was not his fault, they agreed. The fog was too thick for him to have seen the other vessel in time, but was he now going to let his own ship down? If he left his post on his own affairs, he had no right to make the ship pay the penalty. What if it was perjury? He'd taken that risk. Not the ship, but he had taken the risk of perjury.

The admiralty lawyers sat back and listened. They seemed to recognize that there were peculiarities in the ethics of the sea which they could not but respect, though distinctly they were not a part of admiralty law. The meeting broke up with Sam still obstinately refusing to do what, the Captain insisted, any good seaman ought to know he was in honor bound to do.

Then I tried to find a situation in which a lawyer may be in duty bound to lie for his client. I asked an eminent and very practical judge. He told me he hoped I was joking. I went to two leaders of the bar, both ex-presidents of bar associations. One said, "No, I don't believe there is such a situation." The other said, "Why, of course, there are." But he has not yet given me one.

Finally I thought I had one. It was the case of a lawyer who, I felt very sure, had lied to me when he told me that he did not represent a certain man. I was secretary of the Grievance Committee of the Bar Association at the time, and I was trying to find out whether this man had been blackmailed by some other lawyers. I went to this lawyer and asked him. If he had even admitted to me that he had represented this man, I should have been pretty sure that the man had indeed been blackmailed, for I knew that he had not gone to his regular counsel, but to a different lawyer, in order to keep the whole affair secret. The lawyer told me he did not even know the man.

I recall thinking then that this lawyer was doing just right by lying to me, but I don't know who else agreed with me. My lawyer had gone on to make the same denial to the Grievance Committee, and later, when the Bar Association brought proceedings for his disbarment, in the course of those proceedings, persisted in his denial before the court itself. He was not disbarred, but he was subsequently reprimanded and suspended.

I take it that it is inadmissible to lie to the court. A lawyer's duty to his client cannot rise higher than its source, which is the court. Perhaps my lawyer did wrong to lie to the Grievance Committee, but I am not so sure. I know he did right to lie to me, and I am inclined to hope that in his place I should have lied to the Grievance Committee as well.

It may be that it all depends on whether you are asked the question by someone who has a right to ask it. If he has no right to ask and if simple silence would, or even might, lead him to the truth, then, I believe your lawyer is in duty bound to lie. For the truth is not his, but yours. It belongs to you and he is bound to keep it for you, even more vigorously than if it were only his own. He must lie, then, beyond the point where he could permissibly lie for himself. But this only illuminates the problem from a different angle, the right to ask instead of the duty to answer. Let me give you a situation in which a lawyer must lie to someone who does have the right to ask him the question.

A lawyer is called on the telephone by a former client who is unfortunately at the time a fugitive from justice. The police want him and he wants advice. The lawyer goes to where his client is, hears the whole story, and advises him to surrender. Finally he succeeds in persuading him that this is the best thing to do and they make an appointment to go to police headquarters. Meanwhile the client is to have two days to wind up his affairs and make his farewells. When the lawyer gets back to his office, a police inspector is waiting for him, and asks him whether his client is in town and where he is. Here are questions which the police have every right to ask of anybody, and even a little hesitation in this unfortunate lawyer's denials will reveal enough to betray his client. Of course he lies.

And why not? The relation between a lawyer and his client is one of the intimate relations. You would lie for your wife. You would lie for your child. There are others with whom you are intimate enough, close enough, to lie for them when you would not lie for yourself. At what point do you stop lying for them? I don't know and you are not sure.

. . . .

Let us now go back and reconsider, and perhaps reconstruct, in the light of my examples and our discussion, this "entire devotion" which a lawyer owes to his client.

The fact is, the "entire devotion" is not entire. The full discharge of a lawyer's duty to his client requires him to withhold something. If a lawyer is entirely devoted to his client, his client receives something less than he has a right to expect. For, if a man devotes the whole of himself to another, he mutilates or diminishes himself, and the other receives the devotion of so much the less. This is no paradox, but a simple calculus of the spirit.

. . . .

There is authority for such detachment. It is not Christian. Nor is the practice of law a characteristically Christian pursuit. The practice of law is vicarious, not altruistic, and the lawyer must go back of Christianity to Stoicism for the vicarious detachment which will permit him to serve his client.

E. R. Bevan, in his *Stoics and Sceptics*, summarized the Stoic faith as follows: "The Wise Man was not to concern himself with his brethren . . . he was only to serve them. Benevolence he was to have, as much of it as you can conceive; but there was one thing he must not have, and that was love . . . . He must do everything which it is possible for him to do, shrink from no extreme of physical pain, in order to help, to comfort, to guide his fellow men, but whether he succeeds or not must be a matter of pure indifference to him. If he has done his best to help you and failed, he will be perfectly satisfied with having done his best. The fact that you are no better off for his exertions will not matter to him at all. Pity, in the sense of a painful emotion caused by the sight of other men's suffering, is actually a

vice . . . .. In the service of his fellow men he must be prepared
to sacrifice his life; but there is one thing he must never sacrifice:
his own eternal calm."

But let the greatest modern Stoic of them all, because he outgrew
it, tell us about himself. "I have been able," Montaigne said, "to concern myself with public affairs without moving the length of my nail
from myself, and give myself to others without taking anything from
myself . . . .. We carry ill what possesses and carries us. Anyone who uses only his own judgment and address proceeds more gaily.
He feints, he ducks, he counters at his ease, and according to the needs
of the occasion. When he misses, it is without torment, without af-
fliction, ready and whole for a new enterprise. The bridle is in his
hand." And further on, "The mayor and Montaigne have always been
two people, clearly separated. There's no reason why a lawyer or a
banker should not recognize the knavery that is part of his vocation.
An honest man is not responsible for the vices or the stupidity of his
calling, and need not refuse to practice them. They are customs in his
country and there is profit in them. A man must live in the world and
avail himself of what he finds there."

The Stoics gave us a counsel of perfection, but it is none the less
valid. If a lawyer is to be the best lawyer he is capable of being, and
discharge his "entire duty" to his clients, here in the Stoic sage is
his exemplar. Here in Stoicism is his philosophy. Let him be a
Christian if he choose outside the practice of the law, but in his relations with his clients, let him be a Stoic, for the better Stoic, the better
lawyer.

A lawyer should treat his cases like a vivid novel, and identify
himself with his client as he does with the hero or the heroine in the
plot. Then he will work with "the zest that most people feel under
their concern when they assist as existing emergencies, not actually
their own; or join in facing crises that are grave, but for somebody
else." I can't put it more neatly than Cozzens. I can only add that
this zest may deepen into a peculiar and almost spiritual satisfaction,
as wide as it is deep. He will be taking T. S. Eliot's advice to readers
of Dante. "You are not called upon to believe what Dante believed,
for your belief will not give you a groat's worth more of understanding
and appreciation; but you are called upon more and more to understand it. If you read poetry as poetry, you will 'believe' in Dante's
theology exactly as you believe in the physical reality of his journey;
that is, you suspend both belief and disbelief. . . . What is necessary to appreciate the poetry of the Purgatorio is not belief, but suspension of belief."

How is a lawyer to secure this detachment? There are two ways
of doing it, two devices and all lawyers, almost all, are familiar with
one or the other of them.

One way is to treat the whole thing as a game. I am not talking
about the sporting theory of justice. I am talking about a lawyer's
personal relations with his client and the necessity of detaching himself from his client. Never blame a lawyer for treating litigation as
a game, however much you may blame the judge. The lawyer is de-

taching himself.  A man who has devoted his life to taking on other
people's troubles, would be swamped by them if he were to adopt them
as his own.  He must stay on the upland of his own personality, not
only to protect himself, but to give his client the very thing that his
client came for, as Brandeis and Fish and Cravath and Montaigne
so well understood.

I must refer again to the Stoics.  In Gilbert Murray's small book,
*The Stoic Philosophy*, he says, "Life becomes, as the Stoics more than
once tell us, like a play which is acted or a game played with counters.  Viewed from outside, the counters are valueless; but to those
engaged in the game their importance is paramount.  What really
and ultimately matters is that the game shall be played as it should
be played.  God, the eternal dramatist, has cast you for some part in
His drama, and hands you the role.  It may turn out that you are cast
for a triumphant king;  it may be for a slave who dies of torture.
What does that matter to the good actor?  He can play either part;
his only business is to accept the role given him, and to perform it
well.  Similarly, life is a game of counters.  Your business is to
play it in the right way.  He who set the board may have given you
many counters;  He may have given you few.  He may have arranged
that, at a particular point in the game, most of your men shall be
swept accidentally off the board.  You will lose the game;  but why
should you mind that?  It is your play that matters, not the score
that you happen to make.  He is not a fool to judge you by your
mere success or failure.  Success or failure is a thing He can determine without stirring a hand.  It hardly interests Him.  What interests Him is the one thing which He cannot determine—the action
of your free and conscious will."

But this is not a Stoic monopoly.  "I want you to understand,"
Yeats wrote, "that once one makes a thing subject to reason, as distinguished from impulse, one plays with it, even if it is a very serious
thing.  I am more ashamed because of the things I have played with
in life than of any other thing."  Yeats was no Stoic, as his shame
shows.

The other way is a sense of craftsmanship.  Perhaps it comes to
the same thing, but I think not quite.  There is a satisfaction in playing a game the best you can, as there is in doing anything else as
well as you can, which is quite distinct from making a good score.

> "Who can put life into  .  .  . ?"  Let us not
>     brawl—
> But—No joy in crafts-goal well won?
> No pleasure in pitching a neatly curved ball?
> No fun in the fact that good doing is fun,
> That races, in part, are just there to be run?

A lawyer may have to treat the practice of law as if it were a
game, but if he can rely on craftsmanship, it may become an art,
and "Art, being bartender, is never drunk;  and Magic that believes
itself, must die."  "Who sweeps a room as for Thy laws, Makes that
and th' action fine."  I wonder if there is anything more exalted

than the intense pleasure of doing a job as well as you can irrespective of its usefulness or even of its purpose. At least it's a comfort.

I have compared the lawyer to the banker who handles other people's money and to the priest who handles other people's spiritual aspirations. Let me go further. Compare the lawyer with the poet whose speech goes to the heart of things. "Yet he is that one especially who speaks civilly to Nature as a second person and in some sense is the patron of the world. Though more than any he stands in the midst of Nature, yet more than any he can stand aloof from her." (Thoreau).

## QUESTIONS

1. Curtis observes that "the court comes second by the court's, that is the law's, own command." Where does he find "the command" that the lawyer's "loyalty to his client" should extend even to lying?

2. Do you agree with Montaigne that "an honest man is not responsible for the vices or the stupidity of his calling, and need not refuse to practice them"? Is Montaigne implying that a dishonest man would be responsible? Was Adolf Eichman, charged with carrying out Hitler's orders to exterminate the Jews during World War II, not responsible? What about the admiralty lawyers in Curtis's example who "sat back and listened"? Does their responsibility, or lack of it, depend upon whether they were "honest men"?

3. What is "detachment"; what is being detached from what?

4. What do you suppose is the psychological effect of a lawyer's treating his cases "like a vivid novel", or like a game, or a play? Re-read Kinder's narration of the killing of the captured Korean. Is there an element of unreality in his description of the event? Does the likening of serious activities, *e. g.*, law and war, to games, make it easier on the participants? If so, why?

5. Compare Curtis's use of the game image to that of Nietzsche: "One must not avoid one's tests, although they constitute perhaps the most dangerous game one can play. . . ." What is the difference?

Further excerpts from Curtis's article appear in Chapter 6, *infra*.

*AMERICAN BAR ASSOCIATION*

CODE OF PROFESSIONAL RESPONSIBILITY (1970) *

### CANON 7

## A LAWYER SHOULD REPRESENT A CLIENT ZEALOUSLY WITHIN THE BOUNDS OF THE LAW

### Ethical Considerations

EC 7–1 The duty of a lawyer, both to his client and to the legal system, is to represent his client zealously within the bounds of the law, which includes Disciplinary Rules and enforceable professional regulations. The professional responsibility of a lawyer derives from his membership in a profession which has the duty of assisting members of the public to secure and protect available legal rights and benefits. In our government of laws and not of men, each member of our society is entitled to have his conduct judged and regulated in accordance with the law; to seek any lawful objective through legally permissible means; and to present for adjudication any lawful claim, issue, or defense.

EC 7–2  The bounds of the law in a given case are often difficult to ascertain. The language of legislative enactments and judicial opinions may be uncertain as applied to varying factual situations. The limits and specific meaning of apparently relevant law may be made doubtful by changing or developing constitutional interpretations, inadequately expressed statutes or judicial opinions, and changing public and judicial attitudes. Certainty of law ranges from well-settled rules through areas of conflicting authority to areas without precedent.

EC 7–3  Where the bounds of law are uncertain, the action of a lawyer may depend on whether he is serving as advocate or adviser. A lawyer may serve simultaneously as both advocate and adviser, but the two roles are essentially different. In asserting a position on behalf of his client, an advocate for the most part deals with past conduct and must take the facts as he finds them. By contrast, a lawyer serving as adviser primarily assists his client in determining the course of future conduct and relationships. While serving as advocate, a lawyer should resolve in favor of his client doubts as to the bounds of the law. In serving a client as adviser, a lawyer in appropriate circumstances should give his professional opinion as to what the ultimate decisions of the courts would likely be as to the applicable law.

*Duty of the Lawyer to a Client*

EC 7–4  The advocate may urge any permissible construction of the law favorable to his client, without regard to his professional opinion as to the likelihood that the construction will ultimately prevail. His conduct is within the bounds of the law, and therefore permissible, if the position taken is supported by the law or is supportable by a good faith argument for an extention, modification, or reversal of the law. However, a lawyer is not justified in asserting a position in litigation that is frivolous.

EC 7–5  A lawyer as adviser furthers the interest of his client by giving his professional opinion as to what he believes would likely be the ultimate decision of the courts on the matter at hand and by informing his client of the practical effect of such decision. He may continue in the representation of his client even though his client has elected to pursue a course of conduct contrary to the advice of the lawyer so long as he does not thereby knowingly assist the client to engage in illegal conduct or to take a frivolous legal position. A lawyer should never encourage or aid his client to commit criminal acts or counsel his client on how to violate the law and avoid punishment therefor.

EC 7-6  Whether the proposed action of a lawyer is within the bounds of the law may be a perplexing question when his client is contemplating a course of conduct having legal consequences that vary according to the client's intent, motive, or desires at the time of the action.  Often a lawyer is asked to assist his client in developing evidence relevant to the state of mind of the client at a particular time.  He may properly assist his client in the development and preservation of evidence of existing motive, intent, or desire; obviously, he may not do anything furthering the creation or preservation of false evidence.  In many cases a lawyer may not be certain as to the state of mind of his client, and in those situations he should resolve reasonable doubts in favor of his client.

EC 7-7  In certain areas of legal representation not affecting the merits of the cause or substantially prejudicing the rights of a client, a lawyer is entitled to make decisions on his own.  But otherwise the authority to make decisions is exclusively that of the client and, if made within the framework of the law, such decisions are binding on his lawyer.  As typical examples in civil cases, it is for the client to decide whether he will accept a settlement offer or whether he will waive his right to plead an affirmative defense.  A defense lawyer in a criminal case has the duty to advise his client fully on whether a particular plea to a charge appears to be desirable and as to the prospects of success on appeal, but it is for the client to decide what plea should be entered and whether an appeal should be taken.

## QUESTIONS

What is the Code of Professional Responsibility trying to accomplish?  How much effect on conduct can a written code have?  How much concrete guidance does it offer?  Are there reasons for a professional code other than to guide the behavior of the profession?

## LON L. FULLER

### FREEDOM—A SUGGESTED ANALYSIS *

. . . Our basic concern is not with the word "freedom" as a counter in a game of logic but with the ideal it expresses.  We want to know what that ideal demands of us when we are called upon to act formatively toward society, when we have the responsibility for establishing, changing, or taking steps to preserve particular forms of social order, meaning, by that phrase, laws, agreements, institutions, and every kind of social arrangement that may shape men's relations with one another.

### The "Essay On Liberty"

If in search of an answer to this question we turn to the most obvious place, that is, to the *Essay on Liberty*, we are bound, I think,

* From 68 Harv.L.Rev. 1305, 1310–15 (1955). With the permission of Harvard Law Review Association.

to be disappointed.  What Mill offers us is not so much a prescription for the realization of freedom as a perceptive analysis of its values when achieved.  Furthermore, there seems to run through the *Essay* a tacit assumption that what we have called "the forms of social order" are inherently inimical to freedom.  Mill seems to assume that the ideal condition would be one in which, unhampered by social arrangements of any kind, the individual would, in effect, choose everything for himself—his satisfactions, his mode of life, his relations with others.  Only the unfortunate circumstance that his actions may impinge harmfully on others makes it necessary to qualify this ideal.

### Is Unlimited Choice The Ideal Condition?

This analysis seems to me fundamentally defective.  In the first place, its conception of the ideal condition is false—false not merely because it is out of keeping with reality but false even as a utopia. If the individual had in fact to choose everything for himself, the burden of choice would become so overwhelming that choice itself would lose its meaning.

Some idea of what it would be like to have to choose everything can be conveyed through the example of language.  When we are intent on free self-expression, language often seems a kind of prison.  It bends our thoughts in unwanted directions; it errects blank walls before things we want desperately to put in words.  Yet our frustration is as nothing compared to that we would feel if by some miracle the whole of language were to vanish and we were set free to create a new language for ourselves, to construct our own grammar, to draw up our own vocabulary.

The complex network of institutional ways by which the bulk of our energies is directed and channeled is not an unfortunate limitation on freedom.  It is essential to freedom itself.  It preserves us from the suffocating vacuum of free choice into which we would be precipitated if we had to choose everything for ourselves.

This is not to say that the existing allocation of choice cannot be improved or that, if it were wholly satisfactory, it would automatically preserve itself without effort on our part.  But it does mean that we do not necessarily increase the effective choice of the individual by increasing the range of choice open to him.  Mill opposed as an infringement of liberty the requirement of a governmental license for the practice of any profession.  Yet I suspect that most of those needing medical care would regard the fact that physicians must be licensed, not as an impairment of the patient's choice of a physician, but as the welcome facilitation of a choice that still remains difficult even though the range of choice is narrowed and the patient is not compelled to make his selection from among all those who are willing to offer themselves as healers.  On the other hand, I am sure that most people would not see a similar facilitation of choice in the fact that photographers and hairdressers are in some states required to pass an examination before they can practice their callings.

### The Necessity For Forms Of Social Order To Make
### Individual Choice Effective

The second great defect in Mill's essay (closely related to the one I have just been discussing) lies in his assumption that all formal social arrangements—whether legal, customary, institutional, or contractual—are limitations on freedom, that is, restrictions on choice. Mill seemed strangely blind to the fact that in all significant areas of human action formal arrangements are required to make choice effective. The choices a man can make without requiring collaborative social effort for their realization are trivial. Our more important choices are meaningless if there is no way of carrying them over into the larger social order on which we are dependent for almost all our satisfactions. But, to give social effect to individual choice, some formal arrangement, some form of social order, is necessary.

The most obvious example is that of an election. If men are to be given some share in choosing their lawmakers, a machinery of election is required. This machinery will in turn carry with it its own compulsions, for instance, against voting twice. Not only that, but the forms through which choice is channeled by an election law will of necessity exclude other forms of choice. Thus, if the election is to be by the system known as proportional representation (PR) the electorate must necessarily forego the form of choice involved in election by a simple majority.

At the other extreme from the necessarily elaborate apparatus of an election stands the most elementary form of social order by which individual choice can receive social effect—the simple agreement of two parties. This form of order also carries both a facilitation and a restriction of choice with it. Through an agreement the individual makes his own choice effective, but he does it at the cost of binding himself to the other party. Here, reduced to its simplest terms, is a characteristic of all the forms of order by which individual choice is given social effect.

NOTE

In *Freedom as a Problem of Allocating Choice*, 112 PROC.AM. PHIL.SOC. 101, 103 (1968), Professor Fuller observes that:

> . . . [I]f society seriously left a man alone, and thrust none of its facilities on him, he would starve to death. It might also be observed that the original meaning of the words "liberty" and "freedom" was not absence of constraint, but enfranchisement. To be free, to enjoy liberty, was—in the original sense of the terms—to be admitted to effective participation in the affairs of the family, the tribe, or the nation. And meaningful participation in affairs requires that one accept, and act through, the forms of procedure that make possible a functioning whole.

## CHAPTER THREE

# The Epistemological Dilemma

JOHN M. ZANE

## GERMAN LEGAL PHILOSOPHY *

. . . Montesquieu pointed out with clearness the executive, the legislative and the judicial functions of government. Legislation establishes rules for the future. An *ex post facto* or retroactive law or a legislative judgment such as a bill of attainder or a decree of divorce, is not legislation whatever else it may be. The executive power cannot legislate nor can it adjudicate. The judicial power can only adjudicate. It can render a judgment upon a particular concrete state of facts. Every judicial act resulting in a judgment consists of a pure deduction. The figure of its reasoning is the stating of a rule applicable to certain facts, a finding that the facts of the particular case are those certain facts and the application of the rule is a logical necessity. The old syllogism, "All men are mortal, Socrates is a man, therefore he is mortal", states the exact form of a judicial judgment. The existing rule of law is: Every man who with malice aforethought kills another in the peace of the people is guilty of murder. The defendant with malice aforethought killed *A. B.* in the peace of the people, therefore the defendant is guilty of murder.

The rule of law and its application may be reached in a thousand different ways, but a judgment of a court is always this pure deduction. Now it must be perfectly apparent to any one who is willing to admit the rules governing rational mental action that unless the rule of the major premise exists as antecedent to the ascertainment of the fact or facts put into the minor premise, there is no judicial act in stating the judgment. The man who claims that under our system the courts make law is asserting that the courts habitually act unconstitutionally.

CHRISTOPHER D. STONE

## TOWARDS A THEORY OF CONSTITUTIONAL LAW CASEBOOKS *

The importance of laying bare the epistemological roots of how judges decide cases has more significance than merely to reveal how judges decide. It has consequences in dealing with the lasting controversies about the Court's institutional role. For example, I do not see how one can very fruitfully discuss separation of powers without laying a foundation in semantic analysis and epistemology: our estimate of the feasibility of separating the legislative and constitutional law drafting functions from the judicial function depends upon how

* From 16 Mich.L.Rev. 288, 337–38 (1918). With the permission of Michigan Law Review.

* From 41 S.Cal.L.Rev. 1, 7–8 (1968). With the permission of Southern California Law Review.

adequately we believe printed symbols can transmit from draftsman to judge the directions that the former wants the latter to be bound by.

A model "legal system" may serve to illustrate this. Consider a government that consists for simplicity only of a legislative and a judicial branch. The officials set up among themselves a language $L$ by agreeing on a set of symbols and on rules for manipulating them ("+" is "defined" by agreement that $2 + 2 = 4$). They further "agree" (and here not mere covenant but shared psychological conditioning would be required) on the set of perceptions that are to be associated with each of $L$'s symbols. Then, if the perception experienced on reading *Eros* were not one of the perceptions programmed to win *Eros* the "connotation" of the symbol "freedom of speech," *Eros* would not be accorded the benefits of $L$'s counterpart of our first amendment.

Now, let me put aside for a moment whether such a government would be desirable (or even whether we would be warranted in calling its "judicial" branch by that term). What I want to emphasize is the relevance to constitutional debate of the assumption that such a language system (including the implicit assumptions about how the mind categorizes) *could* be brought about. If we believe that a language could be designed which transmitted complete instructions for all the decisions with which the system was to be presented, then we could go on to debate the desirability of setting up a government in which all the utilitarian and moral considerations were to be vested exclusively in the legislative (and constitutional law making) branch. If such a language *could* exist, then we could have a political system in which there would be no excuse for judges to orient their decisions by reference to their own maps of what ought to be. But if we do not believe that a language system could operate so as to allow so pure a separation of functions, a fortiori, we cannot expect such a performance in our present system. We emerge from these considerations with altered expectations of the judicial methodology. Our perspective on the problem of "separation of powers" shifts, to be viewed only secondarily as a problem for political science, with its concern for, *e. g.*, life tenure and electoral base. Primarily—at its source—the question of how interpreters can be bound to a limited function is seen as a quandary of language and epistemology.

## UNITED STATES v. BUTLER

297 U.S. 1 (1936).

[Under the Agricultural Adjustment Act of 1933, the Secretary of Agriculture was authorized to enter into individual agreements with farmers to reduce acreage and production in return for government subsidies. Funds for these payments were to be collected through a tax on the processors of the particular commodity. A cotton processor refused to pay the tax on the ground that the AAA was unconstitutional. The trial court upheld the statute, but a federal court of appeals struck it down.]

Mr. Justice ROBERTS delivered the opinion of the Court.

In this case we must determine whether certain provisions of the Agricultural Adjustment Act, 1933, conflict with the Federal Constitution.

. . . .

*Second.* The Government asserts that even if the respondents may question the propriety of the appropriation embodied in the statute their attack must fail because Article I, § 8 of the Constitution authorizes the contemplated expenditure of the funds raised by the tax. This contention presents the great and the controlling question in the case.[1] We approach its decision with a sense of our grave responsibility to render judgment in accordance with the principles established for the governance of all three branches of the Government.

There should be no misunderstanding as to the function of this court in such a case. It is sometimes said that the court assumes a power to overrule or control the action of the people's representatives. This is a misconception. The Constitution is the supreme law of the land ordained and established by the people. All legislation must conform to the principles it lays down. When an act of Congress is appropriately challenged in the courts as not conforming to the constitutional mandate the judicial branch of the Government has only one duty,—to lay the article of the Constitution which is invoked beside the statute which is challenged and to decide whether the latter squares with the former. All the court does, or can do, is to announce its considered judgment upon the question. The only power it has, if such it may be called, is the power of judgment. This court neither approves nor condemns any legislative policy. Its delicate and difficult office is to ascertain and declare whether the legislation is in accordance with, or in contravention of, the provisions of the Constitution; and, having done that, its duty ends.

The question is not what power the federal Government ought to have but what powers in fact have been given by the people. It hardly seems necessary to reiterate that ours is a dual form of government; that in every state there are two governments,—the state and the United States. Each State has all governmental powers save such as the people, by their Constitution, have conferred upon the United States, denied to the States, or reserved to themselves. The federal union is a government of delegated powers. It has only such as are expressly conferred upon it and such as are reasonably to be implied from those granted. In this respect we differ radically from nations where all legislative power, without restriction or limitation, is vested

---

1. Other questions were presented and argued by counsel, but we do not consider or decide them. The respondents insist that the act in numerous respects delegates legislative power to the executive contrary to the principles announced in Panama Ref. Co. v. Ryan, 293 U.S. 388, and A. L. A. Schechter Poultry Corp. v. United States, 295 U.S. 495; that this unlawful delegation is not cured by the amending act of August 24, 1935; that the exaction is in violation of the due process clause of the Fifth Amendment since the legislation takes their property for a private use; that the floor tax is a direct tax and therefore void for lack of apportionment amongst the states, as required by Article I, § 9; and that the processing tax is wanting in uniformity and so violates Article I, § 8, clause one, of the Constitution. [Footnote by the Court.]

in a parliament or other legislative body subject to no restrictions except the discretion of its members.

Article I, § 8, of the Constitution vests sundry powers in the Congress. . . .

. . . .

The clause thought to authorize the legislation—the first,—confers upon the Congress power "to lay and collect Taxes, Duties, Imposts and Excises, to pay the Debts and provide for the common Defence and general Welfare of the United States. . . . ." It is not contended that this provision grants power to regulate agricultural production upon the theory that such legislation would promote the general welfare. The Government concedes that the phrase "to provide for the general welfare" qualifies the power "to lay and collect taxes." The view that the clause grants power to provide for the general welfare, independently of the taxing power, has never been authoritatively accepted. Mr. Justice Story points out that if it were adopted "it is obvious that under color of the generality of the words, to 'provide for the common defence and general welfare,' the government of the United States is, in reality, a government of general and unlimited powers, notwithstanding the subsequent enumeration of specific powers." The true construction undoubtedly is that the only thing granted is the power to tax for the purpose of providing funds for payment of the nation's debts and making provision for the general welfare.

Nevertheless the Government asserts that warrant is found in this clause for the adoption of the Agricultural Adjustment Act. The argument is that Congress may appropriate and authorize the spending of moneys for the "general welfare"; that the phrase should be liberally construed to cover anything conducive to national welfare; that decision as to what will promote such welfare rests with Congress alone, and the courts may not review its determination; and finally that the appropriation under attack was in fact for the general welfare of the United States.

The Congress is expressly empowered to lay taxes to provide for the general welfare. Funds in the Treasury as a result of taxation may be expended only through appropriation. (Art. I, § 9, cl. 7.) They can never accomplish the objects for which they were collected unless the power to appropriate is as broad as the power to tax. The necessary implication from the terms of the grant is that the public funds may be appropriated "to provide for the general welfare of the United States." These words cannot be meaningless, else they would not have been used. The conclusion must be that they were intended to limit and define the granted power to raise and to expend money. How shall they be construed to effectuate the intent of the instrument?

Since the foundation of the Nation sharp differences of opinion have persisted as to the true interpretation of the phrase. Madison asserted it amounted to no more than a reference to the other powers enumerated in the subsequent clauses of the same section; that, as the United States is a government of limited and enumerated powers, the grant of power to tax and spend for the general national welfare must be confined to the enumerated legislative fields committed to the Congress. In this view the phrase is mere tautology, for taxation and appropriation are or may be necessary incidents of the exercise of any of the enumerated legislative powers. Hamilton, on the other hand, maintained the clause confers a power separate and distinct from those later enumerated, is not restricted in meaning by the grant of them, and Congress consequently has a substantive power to tax and to appropriate, limited only by the requirement that it shall be exercised to provide for the general welfare of the United States. Each contention has had the support of those whose views are entitled to weight. This court has noticed the question, but has never found it necessary to decide which is the true construction. Mr. Justice Story, in his Commentaries, espouses the Hamiltonian position. We shall not review the writings of public men and commentators or discuss the legislative practice. Study of all these leads us to conclude that the reading advocated by Mr. Justice Story is the correct one. While, therefore, the power to tax is not unlimited, its confines are set in the clause which confers it, and not in those of § 8 which bestow and define the legislative powers of the Congress. It results that the power of Congress to authorize expenditure of public moneys for public purposes is not limited by the direct grants of legislative power found in the Constitution.

But the adoption of the broader construction leaves the power to spend subject to limitations.

As Story says:

. . . .

"A power to lay taxes for the common defense and general welfare of the United States is not in common sense a general power. It is limited to those objects. It cannot constitutionally transcend them."

That the qualifying phrase must be given effect all advocates of broad construction admit. Hamilton, in his well known Report on Manufactures, states that the purpose must be "general, and not local." Monroe, an advocate of Hamilton's doctrine, wrote: "Have Congress a right to raise and appropriate the money to any and to every purpose according to their will and pleasure? They certainly have not."

. . . .

As elsewhere throughout the Constitution the section in question lays down principles which control the use of the power, and does not attempt meticulous or detailed directions. Every presumption is to be indulged in favor of faithful compliance by Congress with the mandates of the fundamental law. Courts are reluctant to adjudge any statute in contravention of them. But, under our frame of government, no other place is provided where the citizen may be heard to urge that the law fails to conform to the limits set upon the use of a granted power. When such a contention comes here we naturally require a showing that by no reasonable possibility can the challenged legislation fall within the wide range of discretion permitted to the Congress. How great is the extent of that range, when the subject is the promotion of the general welfare of the United States, we need hardly remark. But, despite the breadth of the legislative discretion, our duty to hear and to render judgment remains. If the statute plainly violates the stated principle of the Constitution we must so declare.

We are not now required to ascertain the scope of the phrase "general welfare of the United States" or to determine whether an appropriation in aid of agriculture falls within it. Wholly apart from that question, another principle embedded in our Constitution prohibits the enforcement of the Agricultural Adjustment Act. The act invades the reserved rights of the states. It is a statutory plan to regulate and control agricultural production, a matter beyond the powers delegated to the federal government. The tax, the appropriation of the funds raised, and the direction for their disbursement, are but parts of the plan. They are but means to an unconstitutional end.

From the accepted doctrine that the United States is a government of delegated powers, it follows that those not expressly granted, or reasonably to be implied from such as are conferred, are reserved to the states or to the people. To forestall any suggestion to the contrary, the Tenth Amendment was adopted.[2] The same proposition, otherwise stated, is that powers not granted are prohibited. None to regulate agricultural production is given, and therefore legislation by Congress for that purpose is forbidden.

It is an established principle that the attainment of a prohibited end may not be accomplished under the pretext of the exertion of powers which are granted.

"Should Congress, in the execution of its powers, adopt measures which are prohibited by the constitution; or should Congress, under the pretext of executing its powers, pass laws for the accomplishment of objects not intrusted to the government; it would become the painful duty of this tribunal, should a case requiring such a decision come before it, to say that such an act was not the law of the land." M'Culloch v. Maryland, 4 Wheat. 316, 423, 4 L.Ed. 579, 605. . . .

. . . Said the court, in M'Culloch v. Maryland: . . .

"Let the end be legitimate, let it be within the scope of the constitution, and all means which are appropriate, which are plainly adapted to that end, which are not prohibited, but consist with the letter and spirit of the constitution, are constitutional."

The power of taxation, which is expressly granted, may, of course, be adopted as a means to carry into operation another power also expressly granted. But resort to the taxing power to effectuate an end which is not legitimate, not within the scope of the Constitution, is obviously inadmissible.

"Congress is not empowered to tax for those purposes which are within the exclusive province of the States." Gibbons v. Ogden, 9 Wheat. 1, 199, 6 L.Ed. 23, 70.

. . . .

2. The Tenth Amendment declares: "The powers not delegated to the United States by the Constitution, nor prohibited by it to the States, are reserved to the States respectively or to the people." [Footnote by the Court.]

Congress has no power to enforce its commands on the farmer to the ends sought by the Agricultural Adjustment Act. It must follow that it may not indirectly accomplish those ends by taxing and spending to purchase compliance. The Constitution and the entire plan of our government negative any such use of the power to tax and to spend as the act undertakes to authorize. It does not help to declare that local conditions throughout the nation have created a situation of national concern; for this is but to say that whenever there is a widespread similarity of local conditions, Congress may ignore constitutional limitations upon its own powers and usurp those reserved to the states. If, in lieu of compulsory regulation of subjects within the states' reserved jurisdiction, which is prohibited, the Congress could invoke the taxing and spending power as a means to accomplish the same end, clause 1 of § 8 of Article I would become the instrument for total subversion of the governmental powers reserved to the individual states.

If the act before us is a proper exercise of the federal taxing power, evidently the regulation of all industry throughout the United States may be accomplished by similar exercises of the same power.
.  .  .

.  .  .  .

Assume that too many shoes are being manufactured throughout the nation; that the market is saturated, the price depressed, the factories running half-time, the employees suffering. Upon the principle of the statute in question Congress might authorize the Secretary of Commerce to enter into contracts with shoe manufacturers providing that each shall reduce his output and that the United States will pay him a fixed sum proportioned to such reduction, the money to make the payments to be raised by a tax on all retail shoe dealers or their customers.

Suppose that there are too many garment workers in the large cities; that this results in dislocation of the economic balance. Upon the principle contended for an excise might be laid on the manufacture of all garments manufactured and the proceeds paid to those manufacturers who agree to remove their plants to cities having not more than a hundred thousand population. Thus, through the asserted power of taxation, the federal government against the will of individual states, might completely redistribute the industrial population.

A possible result of sustaining the claimed federal power would be that every business group which thought itself under-privileged might demand that a tax be laid on its vendors or vendees the proceeds to be appropriated to the redress of its deficiency of income.

These illustrations are given, not to suggest that any of the purposes mentioned are unworthy, but to demonstrate the scope of the principle for which the Government contends; to test the principle by its applications; to point out that, by the exercise of the asserted power, Congress would, in effect, under the pretext of exercising the taxing power, in reality accomplish prohibited ends. .  .  .

.  .  .  .

Hamilton himself, the leading advocate of broad interpretation of the power to tax and to appropriate for the general welfare, never suggested that any power granted by the Constitution could be used for the destruction of local self-government in the states. Story countenances no such doctrine. It seems never to have occurred to them, or to those who have agreed with them, that the general welfare of the United States, (which has aptly been termed "an indestructible Union, composed of indestructible States,") might be served by obliterating the constituent members of the Union. But to this fatal conclusion the doctrine contended for would inevitably lead. And its sole premise is that, though the makers of the Constitution, in erecting the federal government, intended sedulously to limit and define its powers, so as to reserve to the states and the people sovereign power, to be wielded by the states and their citizens and not to be invaded by the United States, they nevertheless by a single clause gave power to the Congress to tear down the barriers, to invade the states' jurisdiction, and to become a parliament of the whole people, subject to no restrictions save such as are self-imposed. The argument when seen in its true character and in the light of its inevitable results must be rejected.

. . .

The judgment is Affirmed.

Mr. Justice Stone, dissenting.

. . .

1.  The power of courts to declare a statute unconstitutional is subject to two guiding principles of decision which ought never to be absent from judicial consciousness. One is that courts are concerned only with the power to enact statutes, not with their wisdom. The other is that while unconstitutional exercise of power by the executive and legislative branches of the government is subject to judicial restraint, the only check upon our own exercise of power is our own sense of self-restraint. For the removal of unwise laws from the statute books appeal lies not to the courts but to the ballot and to the processes of democratic government.

. . . .

. . . While all federal taxes inevitably have some influence on the internal economy of the states, it is not contended that the levy of a processing tax upon manufacturers using agricultural products as raw material has any perceptible regulatory effect upon either their production or manufacture. . . . Here regulation, if any there be, is accomplished not by the tax but by the method by which its proceeds are expended, and would equally be accomplished by any like use of public funds, regardless of their source.

The method may be simply stated. Out of the available fund payments are made to such farmers as are willing to curtail their productive acreage, who in fact do so and who in advance have filed their written undertaking to do so with the Secretary of Agriculture. In saying that this method of spending public moneys is an invasion of the reserved powers of the states, the Court does not assert that the expenditure of public funds to promote the general welfare is not a substantive power specifically delegated to the national government, as Hamilton and Story pronounced it to be. It does not deny that the expenditure of funds for the benefit of farmers and in aid of a program of curtailment of production of agricultural products, and thus of a supposedly better ordered national economy, is within the specifically granted power. But it is declared that state power is nevertheless infringed by the expenditure of the proceeds of the tax to compensate farmers for the curtailment of their cotton acreage . . ..

. . . .

. . . It is insisted that, while the Constitution gives to Congress, in specific and unambiguous terms, the power to tax and spend, the power is subject to limitations which do not find their origin in any express provision of the Constitution and to which other expressly delegated powers are not subject.

The Constitution requires that public funds shall be spent for a defined purpose, the promotion of the general welfare. Their expenditure usually involves payment on terms which will insure use by the selected recipients within the limits of the constitutional purpose. Expenditures would fail of their purpose and thus lose their constitutional sanction if the terms of payment were not such that by their influence on the action of the recipients the permitted end would be attained. The power of Congress to spend is inseparable from persuasion to action over which Congress has no legislative control. Congress may not command that the science of agriculture be taught in state universities. But if it would aid the teaching of that science by grants to state institutions, it is appropriate, if not necessary, that the grant be on the condition, incorporated in the Morrill Act, [July 2, 1862], . . . . that it be used for the intended purpose. Similarly it would seem to be compliance with the Constitution, not violation of it, for the government to take and the university to give a contract that the grant would be so used. . . .

These effects upon individual action, which are but incidents of the authorized expenditure of government money, are pronounced to be themselves a limitation upon the granted power, and so the time-honored principle of constitutional interpretation that the granted power includes all those which are incident to it is reversed. "Let the end be legitimate," said the great Chief Justice, "let it be within the scope of the Constitution, and all means which are appropriate, which are plainly adapted to that end, which are not prohibited, but consist with the letter and spirit of the Constitution, are constitutional." M'Culloch v. Maryland, 4 Wheat. 316, 421, 4 L.Ed. 579, 605. This cardinal guide to constitutional exposition must now be re-phrased, so far as the spending power of the federal government is concerned. Let the expenditure be to promote the general welfare, still, if it is needful in order to insure its use for the intended purpose to influence any action which Congress cannot command because within the sphere of state government, the expenditure is unconstitutional. And taxes otherwise lawfully levied are likewise unconstitutional if they are appropriated to the expenditures whose incident is condemned.

Congress through the Interstate Commerce Commission has set aside intrastate railroad rates. It has made and destroyed intrastate industries by raising or lowering tariffs.  These results are said to be permissible because they are incidents of the commerce power and the power to levy duties on imports.  .  .  .  The only conclusion to be drawn is that results become lawful when they are incidents of those powers but unlawful when incident to the similarly granted power to tax and spend.

Such a limitation is contradictory and destructive of the power to appropriate for the public welfare, and is incapable of practical application.  The spending power of Congress is in addition to the legislative power and not subordinate to it.  This independent grant of the power of the purse, and its very nature, involving in its exercise the duty to insure expenditure within the granted power, presuppose freedom of selection among divers ends and aims, and the capacity to impose such conditions as will render the choice effective.  It is a contradiction in terms to say that there is power to spend for the national welfare, while rejecting any power to impose conditions reasonably adapted to the attainment of the end which alone would justify the expenditure.

The limitation now sanctioned must lead to absurd consequences. The government may give seeds to farmers, but may not condition the gift upon their being planted in places where they are most needed or even planted at all.  The government may give money to the unemployed, but may not ask that those who get it shall give labor in return, or even use it to support their families.  It may give money to sufferers from earthquake, fire, tornado, pestilence or flood, but may not impose conditions—health precautions designed to prevent the spread of disease, or induce the movement of population to safer or more sanitary areas.  .  .  .

That the governmental power of the purse is a great one is not now for the first time announced.  Every student of the history of government and economics is aware of its magnitude and of its existence in every civilized government.  .  .  .

The suggestion that it must now be curtailed by judicial fiat because it may be abused by unwise use hardly rises to the dignity of argument.  So may judicial power be abused.  "The power to tax is the power to destroy," but we do not, for that reason, doubt its existence, or hold that its efficacy is to be restricted by its incidental or collateral effects upon the states.  .  .  .  The power to tax and spend is not without constitutional restraints.  One restriction is that the purpose must be truly national.  Another is that it may not be used to coerce action left to state control.  .  .  .

.  .  .  .  [I]nterpretation of our great charter of government which proceeds on any assumption that the responsibility for the preservation of our institutions is the exclusive concern of any one of the three branches of government, or that it alone can save them from destruction is far more likely, in the long run, "to obliterate the constituent members" of "an indestructible union of indestructible states" than the frank recognition that language, even of a constitution, may mean what it says: that the power to tax and spend includes the power to relieve a nation-wide economic maladjustment by conditional gifts of money.

Mr. Justice BRANDEIS and Mr. Justice CARDOZO join in this opinion.

## QUESTIONS

1. Where a statute's constitutionality is drawn into question, says Justice Roberts, "the judicial branch has only one duty,—to lay the article of the Constitution which is invoked beside the statute and to decide whether the latter squares with the former." Why does he make this remark? Compare it with his statement, "the question is not what power the federal Government *ought* to have but what powers *in fact* have been given by the people." (Italics supplied). Are the two statements similar in their aim? Whose criticisms is Justice Roberts implicitly defending himself against?

2. How valid is the picture of the judicial process which is suggested by the statements quoted above? What assumptions about language and epistemology does it presuppose? What ideas about facts, for example, are implicit in the search for the powers which have "in fact" been given Congress by the people, as opposed to those it "ought" to have? Is the "fact" referred to the sort of "fact" that can be "known" without the influence of the knower's concepts of what ought to be, *e. g.*, his ideas of how basic governmental power in the society ought to be distributed? How does this relate to what Roberts is seeking to convey by the image of "squaring"? One definition of "squares" is "to test with measuring devices for deviation from a right angle, straight line or plane surface." RANDOM HOUSE. How adequately does this reflect the actual process by which Roberts decided that the Agricultural Adjustment Act was unconstitutional?

3. What was it that the Court had to "square" with what? Is Roberts suggesting that the *words* of the Constitution are to be squared with the *words* of the statute? Is this possible; can "general Welfare" be "squared with," *e. g.*,

> 9(a). To obtain revenue for extraordinary expenses, incurred by reason of the national economic emergency, there shall be levied processing taxes as hereinafter provided. . . . ?

Is this how we ordinarily go about determining meaning? How do we decide whether a "cat" is a "mammal"? Do we merely set one word next to the other the way we might set a swatch of cloth next to a color chart? What more is involved?

4. Why would Justice Stone have upheld the Act? Is his view of the Judge's obligation to the words of the Constitution different from that presented by Roberts? Consider Stone's call for "the frank recognition that language, even of a constitution, may mean what it says"? Can you make an argument that, of the two Justices, it is Stone who most closely approximates what Roberts was trying to suggest by his image of "squaring"? On the other hand, in what way does language even "mean what it says"? What does "general welfare", for example, *say*? If interpretation is as simple as suggested,

why should we have to—as Stone suggests—reflect upon the distinction between "power" and "wisdom"? How limited an inquiry is the Court pursuing when it sets out along those lines?

5. For what reason does Roberts conclude that he is "not now required to ascertain the scope of the phrase 'general welfare of the United States'"? If this is the case, why did he discuss the "general welfare" clause at all? Is it possible to apply the Tenth Amendment without first ascertaining "the scope of the phrase 'general welfare'"? And if that "scope" must be determined, can one do so without enlarging the judicial function beyond the limited model implied by the statements of Roberts quoted in question 1, above?

6. On what basis does Justice Roberts conclude that Congress was given no power to regulate "agriculture"? Is the reason that Article I does not contain the *word* "agriculture"? How compelling a reason is that?

Are the effects of Federal regulation ever wholly "general" or "national"? Is it possible for the Congress to enact laws which do not have "local" consequences? Can it be enough to establish unconstitutionality that a Federal law "regulates" a "local" activity? Does Justice Roberts think it is enough? Or does he, as Justice Stone insists, think it is enough when the authorizing Constitutional provision is the "general welfare" clause? To what extent do the answers to these questions demand an inquiry into the meaning of "regulate" and "local"? And where does this meaning come from?

7. Which of the opinions in *Butler*—the majority's or the dissent's—rests most heavily on the need for a "separation of powers"?

How, according to Justice Stone, did Justice Roberts violate his obligations of "judicial self-restraint"? Did Justice Roberts consider himself "unrestrained"? Does the conception of judicial review which he proposes permit courts to strike down legislation which displeases them? Does Roberts's conception permit courts to strike down legislation which "on balance" they consider contrary to the Constitution?

What standards, if any, do Justices Roberts and Stone propose by which to judge the propriety of particular instances of judicial review? Does Justice Stone's distinction between "power" and "wisdom" provide a standard? Does Justice Roberts' reference to statutes which "plainly" violate the Constitution? Does Justice Stone provide a rule by which one could determine whether a particular enactment is within the legislature's "power", whatever may be its "wisdom"? Does Justice Roberts indicate the conditions under which a Constitutional violation becomes "plain"? Are the justices called upon to provide rules of this sort? If so, is there an explanation for the failure to provide them? If not, in what sense are their positions legally justifiable?

JOHN RAWLS

## TWO CONCEPTS OF RULES *

In this paper I want to show the importance of the distinction between justifying a practice [3] and justifying a particular action falling under it, and I want to explain the logical basis of this distinction and how it is possible to miss its significance. While the distinction has frequently been made, and is now becoming commonplace, there remains the task of explaining the tendency either to overlook it altogether, or to fail to appreciate its importance.

To show the importance of the distinction I am going to defend utilitarianism against those objections which have traditionally been made against it in connection with punishment and the obligation to keep promises. I hope to show that if one uses the distinction in question then one can state utilitarianism in a way which makes it a much better explication of our considered moral judgments than these traditional objections would seem to admit. Thus the importance of the distinction is shown by the way it strengthens the utilitarian view regardless of whether that view is completely defensible or not.

To explain how the significance of the distinction may be overlooked, I am going to discuss two conceptions of rules. One of these conceptions conceals the importance of distinguishing between the justification of a rule or practice and the justification of a particular action falling under it. The other conception makes it clear why this distinction must be made and what is its logical basis.

### I

The subject of punishment, in the sense of attaching legal penalties to the violation of legal rules, has always been a troubling moral question. The trouble about it has not been that people disagree as to whether or not punishment is justifiable. Most people have held that, freed from certain abuses, it is an acceptable institution. Only a few have rejected punishment entirely, which is rather surprising when one considers all that can be said against it. The difficulty is with the justification of punishment; various arguments for it have been given by moral philosophers, but so far none of them has won any sort of general acceptance; no justification is without those who detest it. I hope to show that the use of the aforementioned distinction enables one to state the utilitarian view in a way which allows for the sound points of its critics.

For our purposes we may say that there are two justifications of punishment. What we may call the retributive view is that punish-

* From 64 Phil. Rev. 3, 3–7, 13, 14, 16–17, 18–19, 22, 23, 24–27 (1955). With the permission of Professor Rawls and the Philosophical Review.

3. I use the word "practice" throughout as a sort of technical term meaning any form of activity specified by a system of rules which defines offices, roles, moves, penalties, defenses, and so on, and which gives the activity its structure. As examples one may think of games and rituals, trials and parliaments. [Footnote from original.]

ment is justified on the grounds that wrongdoing merits punishment. It is morally fitting that a person who does wrong should suffer in proportion to his wrongdoing. That a criminal should be punished follows from his guilt, and the severity of the appropriate punishment depends on the depravity of his act. The state of affairs where a wrongdoer suffers punishment is morally better than the state of affairs where he does not; and it is better irrespective of any of the consequences of punishing him.

What we may call the utilitarian view holds that on the principle that bygones are bygones and that only future consequences are material to present decisions, punishment is justifiable only by reference to the probable consequences of maintaining it as one of the devices of the social order. Wrongs committed in the past are, as such, not relevant considerations for deciding what to do. If punishment can be shown to promote effectively the interest of society it is justifiable, otherwise it is not.

I have stated these two competing views very roughly to make one feel the conflict between them: one feels the force of *both* arguments and one wonders how they can be reconciled. From my introductory remarks it is obvious that the resolution which I am going to propose is that in this case one must distinguish between justifying a practice as a system of rules to be applied and enforced, and justifying a particular action which falls under these rules; utilitarian arguments are appropriate with regard to questions about practices, while retributive arguments fit the application of particular rules to particular cases.

We might try to get clear about this distinction by imagining how a father might answer the question of his son. Suppose the son asks, "Why was *J* put in jail yesterday?" The father answers, "Because he robbed the bank at *B*. He was duly tried and found guilty. That's why he was put in jail yesterday." But suppose the son had asked a different question, namely, "Why do people put other people in jail?" Then the father might answer, "To protect good people from bad people" or "to stop people from doing things that would make it uneasy for all of us; for otherwise we wouldn't be able to go to bed at night and sleep in peace." There are two very different questions here. One question emphasizes the proper name: it asks why *J* was punished rather than someone else, or it asks what he was punished for. The other question asks way we have the institution of punishment; why do people punish one another rather than, say, always forgiving one another?

Thus the father says in effect that a particular man is punished, rather than some other man, because he is guilty, and he is guilty because he broke the law (past tense). In his case the law looks back, the judge looks back, the jury looks back, and a penalty is visited upon him for something he did. That a man is to be punished, and what his punishment is to be, is settled by its being shown that he broke the law and that the law assigns that penalty for the violation of it.

On the other hand we have the institution of punishment itself, and recommend and accept various changes in it, because it is thought by the (ideal) legislator and by those to whom the law applies that, as a part of a system of law impartially applied from case to case arising under it, it will have the consequence, in the long run, of furthering the interests of society.

One can say, then, that the judge and the legislator stand in different positions and look in different directions: one to the past, the other to the future. The justification of what the judge does, *qua* judge, sounds like the retributive view; the justification of what the (ideal) legislator does, *qua* legislator, sounds like the utilitarian view. Thus both views have a point (this is as it should be since intelligent and sensitive persons have been on both sides of the argument); and one's initial confusion disappears once one sees that these views apply to persons holding different offices with different duties, and situated differently with respect to the system of rules that make up the criminal law.

One might say, however, that the utilitarian view is more fundamental since it applies to a more fundamental office, for the judge carries out the legislator's will so far as he can determine it. Once the legislator decides to have laws and to assign penalties for their violation (as things are there must be both the law and the penalty) an institution is set up which involves a retributive conception of particular cases. It is part of the concept of the criminal law as a system of rules that the application and enforcement of these rules in particular cases should be justifiable by arguments of a retributive character. The decision whether or not to use law rather than some other mechanism of social control, and the decision as to what laws to have and what penalties to assign, may be settled by utilitarian arguments; but if one decides to have laws then one has decided on something whose working in particular cases is retributive in form.

The answer, then, to the confusion engendered by the two views of punishment is quite simple: one distinguishes two offices, that of the judge and that of the legislator, and one distinguishes their different stations with respect to the system of rules which make up the law; and then one notes that the different sorts of considerations which would usually be offered as reasons for what is done under the cover of these offices can be paired off with the competing justifications of punishment. One reconciles the two views by the time-honored device of making them apply to different situations.

. . .

I shall now consider the question of promises. The objection to utilitarianism in connection with promises seems to be this: it is believed that on the utilitarian view when a person makes a promise the only ground upon which he should keep it, if he should keep it, is that by keeping it he will realize the most good on the whole. So that if one asks the question "Why should I keep *my* promise?" the utilitarian answer is understood to be that doing so in *this* case will have the best consequences. And this answer is said, quite rightly, to conflict with the way in which the obligation to keep promises is regarded.

. . .

Ross has [observed]:  however great the value of the practice of promising, on utilitarian grounds, there must be some value which is greater, and one can imagine it to be obtainable by breaking a promise.  Therefore there might be a case where the promisor could argue that breaking his promise was justified as leading to a better state of affairs on the whole.  And the promisor could argue in this way no matter how slight the advantage won by breaking the promise.  If one were to challenge the promisor his defense would be that what he did was best on the whole in view of all the utilitarian considerations, which in this case *include* the importance of the practice.  . . .

. . . .

From what I have said in connection with punishment, one can foresee what I am going to say about these arguments and counter-arguments.  They fail to make the distinction between the justification of a practice and the justification of a particular action falling under it, and therefore they fall into the mistake of taking it for granted that the promisor  . . .  is entitled without restriction to bring utilitarian considerations to bear in deciding whether to keep *his* promise.  But if one considers what the practice of promising is one will see, I think, that it is such as not to allow this sort of general discretion to the promisor.  Indeed, the point of the practice is to abdicate one's title to act in accordance with utilitarian and pruden-tial considerations in order that the future may be tied down and plans coordinated in advance.  There are obvious utilitarian advan-tages in having a practice which denies to the promisor, as a de-fense, any general appeal to the utilitarian principle in accordance with which the practice itself may be justified.  There is nothing contradictory, or surprising, in this:  utilitarian (or aesthetic) rea-sons might properly be given in arguing that the game of chess, or baseball, is satisfactory just as it is, or in arguing that it should be changed in various respects, but a player in a game cannot properly appeal to such considerations as reasons for his making one move rather than another.  It is a mistake to think that if the practice is justified on utilitarian grounds then the promisor must have com-plete liberty to use utilitarian arguments to decide whether or not to keep his promise.  The practice forbids this general defense; and it is a purpose of the practice to do this.  Therefore what the above ar-guments presuppose—the idea that if the utilitarian view is accepted then the promisor is bound, if, and only if, the application of the utilitarian principle to his own case shows that keeping it is best on the whole—is false.  The promisor is bound because he promised; weighing the case on its merits is not open to him.

Is this to say that in particular cases one cannot deliberate whether or not to keep one's promise?  Of course not.  But to do so is to deliberate whether the various excuses, exceptions and defenses, which are understood by, and which constitute an important part of, the practice, apply to one's own case.  Various defenses for not keeping one's promise are allowed, but among them there isn't the one that, on general utilitarian grounds, the promisor (truly) thought his action best on the whole, even though there may be the defense that the consequences of keeping one's promise would have been *extremely* severe. While there are too many complexities here to consider all the necessary details, one can see that the general defense isn't allowed if one asks the following question: what would one say of someone who, when asked why he broke his promise, replied simply that breaking it was best on the whole? Assuming that his reply is sincere, and that his belief was reasonable (i. e., one need not consider the possibility that he was mistaken), I think that one would question whether or not he knows what it means to say "I promise" (in the appropriate circumstances). It would be said of someone who used this excuse without further explanation that he didn't understand what defenses the practice, which defines a promise, allows him. If a child were to use this excuse one would correct him; for it is part of the way one is taught the concept of a promise to be corrected if one uses this excuse. The point of having the practice would be lost if the practice did allow this excuse.

. . .

### III

So far I have tried to show the importance of the distinction between the justification of a practice and the justification of a particular action falling under it by indicating how this distinction might be used to defend utilitarianism against two long-standing objections. One might be tempted to close the discussion at this point by saying that utilitarian considerations should be understood as applying to practices in the first instance and not to particular actions falling under them except insofar as the practices admit of it. One might say that in this modified form it is a better account of our considered moral opinions and let it go at that. But to stop here would be to neglect the interesting question as to how one can fail to appreciate the significance of this rather obvious distinction and can take it for granted that utilitarianism has the consequence that particular cases may always be decided on general utilitarian grounds. I want to argue that this mistake may be connected with misconceiving the logical status of the rules of practices; and to show this I am going to examine two conceptions of rules, two ways of placing them within the utilitarian theory.

The conception which conceals from us the significance of the distinction I am going to call the summary view. It regards rules in the following way: one supposes that each person decides what he shall do in particular cases by applying the utilitarian principle; one supposes further that different people will decide the same particular case in the same way and that there will be recurrences of cases similar to those previously decided. Thus it will happen that in cases of certain kinds the same decision will be made either by the same person at different times or by different persons at the same time. If a case occurs frequently enough one supposes that a rule is formulated to cover that sort of case. I have called this conception the summary view because rules are pictured as summaries of past decisions arrived at by the *direct* application of the utilitarian principle to particular cases. Rules are regarded as reports that cases of a certain sort have been found on *other* grounds to be properly decided in a certain way (although, of course, they do not *say* this).

There are several things to notice about this way of placing rules within the utilitarian theory.

1. The point of having rules derives from the fact that similar cases tend to recur and that one can decide cases more quickly if one records past decisions in the form of rules. If similar cases didn't recur, one would be required to apply the utilitarian principle directly, case by case, and rules reporting past decisions would be of no use.

2. The decisions made on particular cases are logically prior to rules. . . .
. . .

3. Each person is in principle always entitled to reconsider the correctness of a rule and to question whether or not it is proper to follow it in a particular case. As rules are guides and aids, one may ask whether in past decisions there might not have been a mistake in applying the utilitarian principle to get the rule in question, and wonder whether or not it is best in this case. The reason for rules is that people are not able to apply the utilitarian principle effortlessly and flawlessly; there is need to save time and to post a guide. On this view a society of rational utilitarians would be a society without rules in which each person applied the utilitarian principle directly and smoothly, and without error, case by case. On the other hand, ours is a society in which rules are formulated to serve as aids in reaching these ideally rational decisions on particular cases, guides which have been built up and tested by the experience of generations. If one applies this view to rules, one is interpreting them as maxims, as "rules of thumb"; and it is doubtful that anything to which the summary conception did apply would be called a *rule*. Arguing as if one regarded rules in this way is a mistake one makes while doing philosophy.

. . . .

The other conception of rules I will call the practice conception. On this view rules are pictured as defining a practice. Practices are set up for various reasons, but one of them is that in many areas of conduct each person's deciding what to do on utilitarian grounds case by case leads to confusion, and that the attempt to coordinate behavior by trying to foresee how others will act is bound to fail. As an alternative one realizes that what is required is the establishment of a practice, the specification of a new form of activity; and from this one sees that a practice necessarily involves the abdication of full liberty to act on utilitarian and prudential grounds. It is the mark of a practice that being taught how to engage in it involves being instructed in the rules which define it, and that appeal is made to those rules to correct the behavior of those engaged in it. Those engaged in a practice recognize the rules as defining it. The rules cannot be taken as simply describing how those engaged in the practice in fact behave; it is not simply that they act as if they were obeying the rules. Thus it is essential to the notion of a practice that the rules are publicly known and understood as definitive; and it is essential also that the rules of a practice can be taught and can be acted upon to yield a coherent practice. On this conception, then, rules are not generalizations from the decisions of individuals applying the utilitarian principle directly and independently to recurrent particular cases. On the contrary, rules define a practice and are themselves the subject of the utilitarian principle.

To show the important differences between this way of fitting rules into the utilitarian theory and the previous way, I shall consider the differences between the two conceptions on the points previously discussed.

1. In contrast with the summary view, the rules of practices are logically prior to particular cases. This is so because there cannot be a particular case of an action falling under a rule of a practice unless there is the practice. This can be made clearer as follows: in a practice there are rules setting up offices, specifying certain forms of action appropriate to various offices, establishing penalties for the breach of rules, and so on. We may think of the rules of a practice as defining offices, moves, and offenses. Now what is meant by saying that the practice is logically prior to particular cases is this: given any rule which specifies a form of action (a move), a particular action which would be taken as falling under this rule given that there is the practice would not be *described as* that sort of action unless there was the practice. In the case of actions specified by practices it is logically impossible to perform them outside the stage-setting provided by those practices, for unless there is the practice, and unless the requisite proprieties are fulfilled, whatever one does, whatever movements one makes, will fail to count as a form of action which the practice specifies. What one does will be described in some *other* way.

One may illustrate this point from the game of baseball. Many of the actions one performs in a game of baseball one can do by oneself or with others whether there is the game or not. For example, one can throw a ball, run, or swing a peculiarly shaped piece of wood. But one cannot steal base, or strike out, or draw a walk, or make an error, or balk; although one can do certain things which appear to resemble these actions such as sliding into a bag, missing a grounder and so on. Striking out, stealing a base, balking, etc., are all actions which can only happen in a game. No matter what a person did, what he did would not be described as stealing a base or striking out or drawing a walk unless he could also be described as playing baseball, and for him to be doing this presupposes the rule-like practice which constitutes the game. The practice is logically prior to particular cases; unless there is the practice the terms referring to actions specified by it lack a sense.

2. The practice view leads to an entirely different conception of the authority which each person has to decide on the propriety of following a rule in particular cases. To engage in a practice, to per-

form those actions specified by a practice, means to follow the appropriate rules. If one wants to do an action which a certain practice specifies then there is no way to do it except to follow the rules which define it. Therefore, it doesn't make sense for a person to raise the question whether or not a rule of a practice correctly applies to *his* case where the action he contemplates is a form of action defined by a practice. If someone were to raise such a question, he would simply show that he didn't understand the situation in which he was acting. If one wants to perform an action specified by a practice, the only legitimate question concerns the nature of the practice itself ("How do I go about making a will?").

This point is illustrated by the behavior expected of a player in games. If one wants to play a game, one doesn't treat the rules of the game as guides as to what is best in particular cases. In a game of baseball if a batter were to ask "Can I have four strikes?" it would be assumed that he was asking what the rule was; and if, when told what the rule was, he were to say that he meant that on this occasion he thought it would be best on the whole for him to have four strikes rather than three, this would be most kindly taken as a joke. One might contend that baseball would be a better game if four strikes were allowed instead of three; but one cannot picture the rules as guides to what is best on the whole in particular cases, and question their applicability to particular cases as particular cases.

3 and 4. To complete the four points of comparison with the summary conception, it is clear from what has been said that rules of practices are not guides to help one decide particular cases correctly as judged by some higher ethical principle. And neither the quasi-statistical notion of generality, nor the notion of a particular exception, can apply to the rules of practices. A more or less general rule of a practice must be a rule which according to the structure of the practice applies to more or fewer of the kinds of cases arising under it; or it must be a rule which is more or less basic to the understanding of the practice. Again, a particular case cannot be an exception to a rule of a practice. An exception is rather a qualification or a further specification of the rule.

It follows from what we have said about the practice conception of rules that if a person is engaged in a practice, and if he is asked why *he* does what *he* does, or if he is asked to defend what he does, then his explanation, or defense, lies in referring the questioner to the practice. He cannot say of *his* action, if it is an action specified by a practice, that he does it rather than some other because he thinks it is best on the whole. When a man engaged in a practice is queried about his action he must assume that the questioner either doesn't know that he is engaged in it ("Why are you in a hurry to pay him?" "I promised to pay him today") or doesn't know what the practice is. One doesn't so much justify one's particular action as explain, or show, that it is in accordance with the practice. The reason for this is that it is only against the stage-setting of the practice that one's particular action is described as it is. Only by reference to the practice can one *say* what one is doing. To explain or to defend one's own action, as a particular action, one fits it into the practice which defines it. If this is not accepted it's a sign that a different question is being raised as to whether one is justified in accepting the practice, or in tolerating it. When the challenge is to the practice, citing the rules (saying what the practice is) is naturally to no avail. But when the challenge is to the particular action defined by the practice, there is nothing one can do but refer to the rules. . . .

## NOTES AND QUESTIONS

1. As Rawls says, his "larger" objective in this piece is to try to defend utilitarianism from some traditional objections that have been made to it. One of these is that it seems to support punishment of innocent persons. If, for example, there has been a well-publicized murder that cannot be solved and thus threatens skepticism about the efficacy of the criminal law machinery, it is hard to see why, for the greatest good of the greatest number, the authorities should not pick an innocent man, tell the public he is the one who "did it", and punish him. Can you see how this causes a dilemma for the utilitarian? How is Rawls's distinction between the justifying of a rule and the justifying of a practice aimed at "rescuing" the utilitarian from the appearance of an "immoral" (in the popular conception) position?

2. Why does Rawls conceive the "practice" view of rules as leading "to an entirely different conception of the authority which each person has to decide on the propriety of following a rule in particular cases"? Can you give an example of (a) an argument defending one's act by reference to a practice, and (b) one defending the practice itself?

3. What does the "practice" view have in common with the views of Zane and Nowell-Smith, above? Compare it with the famous position of Austin:

> The existence of law is one thing; its merit or demerit is another. Whether it be or be not is one enquiry; whether it be or be not conformable to an assumed standard, is a different enquiry.[4]

4. Ultimately, can the summary-practice distinction relieve the decision-maker of moral responsibility for his decision?

Is there a distinction between *explaining* one's action (telling why someone *is* doing some action) and *justifying* one's action (explaining why someone *ought* to be doing some action)?

> One writer maintains that to say that "I promised to pay him today" functions as an explanation of the agent's hurrying to pay someone some money. It performs this function because, in the fact that one has made a promise to do Y, one has a reason for doing Y. It performs this function by creating the *presumption* that hurrying to pay the money is perfectly normal to be expected, since there is ordinarily nothing untoward or unusual about keeping

---

4. The Province of Jurisprudence Determined 184 (1954).

> promises. Most of the time there are good reasons (moral, prudential, etc.) for keeping a promise, and most of the time people do in fact keep them. But that there is nothing untoward or unusual about what one is doing does not imply that what one is doing is morally justified. This is a separate question. This question can be settled only from the point of view of a moral agent who has adopted a moral point of view.

Jones, *Making and Keeping Promises*, 76 ETHICS 287, 293 (1966). Jones maintains that "appealing to [the] practice cannot justify an action, where 'justify' means to show that one morally ought (on balance) to do it." (p. 294). To what extent is Rawls subject to this remonstration?

5. Even if the decision-maker feels obliged to decide on the basis of a "practice", how does he *know* what the practice *means* in the concrete case before him? In the *Butler* case, for example, are not Justices Roberts and Stone both appealing (as Professor Rawls would have them do) to the same "practice"? If so, how do you account for their different conclusions? Consider Rawls' analysis in light of the problems that are involved in interpreting promises and contracts, *e. g., whether* what one said and/or did amounted to a promise; if so, *what it was* that the promisor undertook to do; and whether the sort of thing promised *fell under* "the various excuses, exceptions and defenses, which are understood by, and which constitute an important part of, the practice . . ." of promise-keeping or contract enforcing? How do these excuses, etc., come to be "understood by" and to "constitute" part of "the practice"?

6. What, according to Rawls, are the reasons for having summary rules?—for having practice rules? Could it be argued that summary rules serve any of the purposes which Rawls attributes to practice rules? Is there an argument that practice rules serve purposes which Rawls attributes to summary rules? What is the significance of your answer?

7. In another, unexcerpted portion of his essay, Professor Rawls says:

> . . . I may have talked of the summary and practice conceptions of rules as if only one of them could be true of rules, and if true of any rules, then necessarily true of *all* rules. I do not, of course, mean this. Some rules will fit one conception, some rules the other; and so there are rules of practices (rules in the strict sense), and maxims and "rules of thumb."

At another place, Professor Rawls says that "it is not always easy to say where" the conception of a practice rule is "appropriate."

> Nor do I care to discuss at this point the general sorts of cases to which it does apply except to say that one should not take it for granted that it applies to many so-called "moral rules." It is my feeling that relatively few actions of the moral life are defined by practices and that the prac-

tice conception is more relevant to understanding legal and legal-like arguments than it is to the more complex sort of moral arguments.

How would one go about testing whether "legal" rules are of the practice or summary variety?

8. What accounts for the (perhaps growing) tendency to liken human and political activities—from court processes to war—to games and to cast the problems that arise from them in the terminology of games?

## NOTE

Consider in regard to the summary-practice distinction the case of Kondo v. Katzenbach, 356 F.2d 351 (D.C.Cir. 1966). Appellants had been depositors of the Yokohama Specie Bank, Ltd., a Japanese bank, the property of which in the United States was seized on Pearl Harbor Day and vested as enemy property under the Trading with the Enemy Act. After World War II, Congress enacted legislation authorizing the Alien Property Custodian to pay from the vested proceeds the claims of former owners, several thousand Americans of Japanese ancestry. Procedures for settlement were complex and lengthy and involved the circulation of letters to eligible claimants, instructing them as to what they would have to do to recover. Finally, at one point in 1961, a settlement was proposed, and claimants told by the Custodian that if they did not make complaint to review their proposed settlement within 60 days, their complaints would not be reviewable. Of an original approximately 7500 Yen certificate holders, including appellants, who had complied with the initial provision for setting the repayment machinery in motion, some 4100 "missed" the deadline and their claims were sought to be barred.

The Court, 2–1, turned down appellants' claims with the following statement:

> The unique and unfortunate circumstances which have deprived these appellants of their deposits in the Yokohama Specie Bank command sympathetic consideration of their problem. Arguments made to the court were broadly spiced with a strong emotional appeal. Appellants' sincere counsel valiantly attempted under the label of "equitable considerations" to lead the court to abandon established legal principles and upon purely humane grounds return to the appellants the funds which represented their savings on December 7, 1941. Benevolence is a noble virtue, but it cannot be a foundation for legal opinions, regardless of the need of the litigant or the strictly emotional appeal of his plight. It is not for the courts to turn their backs upon legal principles, precepts and established law in order to accomplish an end which is suggested by a desire to accomplish a humane objective. To do so would immediately constitute the creation of a program of judicial legislation in complete disregard of our constitutional limitations and separation of powers. Obviously, Congress, enacting into law the will of

the people, must write our country's laws. The dangers of wartime, the military and economic problems of the early 1940's are far behind us. Perhaps now the necessities that required the enactment of the Trading with the Enemy Act have so far passed into history that Congress may wish to reconsider the status of these appellants and another disposition of their claims. It is not for the court to suggest to Congress what it should or should not do. We suggest only that the relief sought by these appellants lies solely in legislative hands.

Affirmed.

356 F.2d at 359.

Can you describe the Court of Appeals' opinion in the terminology of Rawls' analysis?

The United States Supreme Court reversed, 8–0, *sub nom.* Honda v. Clark, 386 U.S. 484 (1967).

*JOHN AUSTIN*

## THE PROVINCE OF JURISPRUDENCE DETERMINED *

The existence of law is one thing; its merit or demerit is another. Whether it be or be not is one enquiry; whether it be or be not conformable to an assumed standard, is a different enquiry. A law, which actually exists, is a law, though we happen to dislike it, or though it vary from the text, by which we regulate our approbation and disapprobation. This truth, when formally announced as an abstract proposition, is so simple and glaring that it seems idle to insist upon it. But simple and glaring as it is, when enunciated in abstract expressions the enumeration of the instances in which it has been forgotten would fill a volume.

Sir William Blackstone, for example, says in his 'Commentaries,' that the laws of God are superior in obligation to all other laws; that no human laws should be suffered to contradict them; that human laws are of no validity if contrary to them; and that all valid laws derive their force from that Divine original.

Now, he *may* mean that all human laws ought to conform to the Divine laws. If this be his meaning, I assent to it without hesitation. The evils which we are exposed to suffer from the hands of God as a consequence of disobeying His commands are the greatest evils to which we are obnoxious; the obligations which they impose are consequently paramount to those imposed by any other laws, and if human commands conflict with the Divine law, we ought to disobey the command which is enforced by the less powerful sanction; this is implied in the term *ought*: the proposition is identical, and therefore perfectly indisputable—it is our interest to choose the smaller and more uncertain evil, in preference to the greater and surer. If this be Blackstone's meaning, I assent to his proposition, and have

* From 184–86 (Noonday Press ed. 1954).

only to object to it, that it tells us just nothing. Perhaps, again, he means that human lawgivers are themselves obliged by the Divine laws to fashion the laws which they impose by that ultimate standard, because if they do not, God will punish them. To this also I entirely assent: for if the index to the law of God be the principle of utility, that law embraces the whole of our voluntary actions in so far as motives applied from without are required to give them a direction conformable to the general happiness.

But the meaning of this passage of Blackstone, if it has a meaning, seems rather to be this: that no human law which conflicts with the Divine law is obligatory or binding; in other words, that no human law which conflicts with the Divine law *is a law*, for a law without an obligation is a contradiction in terms. I suppose this to be his meaning, because when we say of any transaction that it is invalid or void, we mean that it is not binding: as, for example, if it be a contract, we mean that the political law will not lend its sanction to enforce the contract.

Now, to say that human laws which conflict with the Divine law are not binding, that is to say, are not laws, is to talk stark nonsense. The most pernicious laws, and therefore those which are most opposed to the will of God, have been and are continually enforced as laws by judicial tribunals. Suppose an act innocuous, or positively beneficial, be prohibited by the sovereign under the penalty of death; if I commit this act, I shall be tried and condemned, and if I object to the sentence, that it is contrary to the law of God, who has commanded that human lawgivers shall not prohibit acts which have no evil consequences, the Court of Justice will demonstrate the inconclusiveness of my reasoning by hanging me up, in pursuance of the law of which I have impugned the validity. An exception, demurrer, or plea, founded on the law of God was never heard in a Court of Justice, from the creation of the world down to the present moment.

But this abuse of language is not merely puerile, it is mischievous. When it is said that a law ought to be disobeyed, what is meant is that we are urged to disobey it by motives more cogent and compulsory than those by which it is itself sanctioned. If the laws of God are certain, the motives which they hold out to disobey any human command which is at variance with them are paramount to all others. But the laws of God are not always certain. All divines, at least all reasonable divines, admit that no scheme of duties perfectly complete and unambiguous was ever imparted to us by revelation. As an index to the Divine will, utility is obviously insufficient. What appears pernicious to one person may appear beneficial to another. And as for the moral sense, innate practical principles, conscience, they are merely convenient cloaks for ignorance or sinister interest: they mean either that I hate the law to which I object and cannot tell why, or that I hate the law, and that the cause of my hatred is one which I find it incommodious to avow. If I say openly, I hate the law, *ergo*, it is not binding and ought to be disobeyed, no one will listen to me; but by calling my hate my conscience or my moral sense, I urge the same argument in another and more plausi-

ble form:  I seem to assign a reason for my dislike, when in truth
I have only given it a sounding and specious name.  In times of civil
discord the mischief of this detestable abuse of language is apparent.
In quiet times the dictates of utility are fortunately so obvious that
the anarchical doctrine sleeps, and men habitually admit the validity
of laws which they dislike.  To prove by pertinent reasons that a law
is pernicious is highly useful, because such process may lead to the
abrogation of the pernicious law.  To incite the public to resistance
by determinate views of *utility* may be useful, for resistance, grounded on clear and definite prospects of good, is sometimes beneficial.
But to proclaim generally that all laws which are pernicious or contrary to the will of God are void and not to be tolerated, is to preach
anarchy, hostile and perilous as much to wise and benign rule as to
stupid and galling tyranny.

INTERSTATE COMMERCE COMMISSION V. ALLEN E. KROBLIN, INC.

113 F.Supp. 599 (N.D.Iowa, E.D. 1953)

GRAVEN, District Judge.

The issue in this case is whether or not the interstate transportation by truck of New York dressed and eviscerated poultry is within the scope of the so-called "agricultural" exemption of the Interstate
Commerce Act. . . .

. . . [T]he defendant is engaged in transporting New York
dressed and eviscerated poultry in interstate commerce without a
certificate of public convenience and necessity.  The [Interstate
Commerce] Commission asks that the defendant be enjoined from
so doing until he obtains such certificate.  The defendant admits
that it is so engaged and that it does not have a certificate of public
convenience and necessity.  It claims that under the provisions of
Section 203(b) (6) it is not required to have such certificate. . . .

[That section] in its present form exempts from the certificate
provisions of the Act:

". . . (6) motor vehicles used in carrying property
consisting of ordinary livestock, fish (including shell fish),
or agricultural (including horticultural) commodities (not
including manufactured products thereof), if such motor
vehicles are not used in carrying any other property, or passengers, for compensation".

While Section 203(b) (6) includes fish as well as horticultural
commodities, it is commonly and generally referred to as the agricultural exemption.

This particular case is but one engagement of a much larger battle that has been raging for many years.  The battle commenced when
legislation was proposed granting regulatory powers to the Interstate
Commerce Commission as to interstate transportation by motor vehicles and has continued ever since  .  .  .. The battle has been,
and is being, waged as to what regulatory powers the Interstate Commerce Commission should have as to the interstate transportation by

motor vehicles of products generally referred to as agricultural commodities, and as to the exact scope of Section 203(b) (6). Those engaged in interstate transportation by motor vehicle who operate under certificates of public convenience and necessity issued by the Interstate Commerce Commission under the Act are generally referred to as regulated or certificated carriers. Those who are so engaged without being required to obtain such certificates are generally referred to as unregulated or uncertificated carriers. The battle referred to has been waged on the floors of the House and the Senate, before Congressional Committees, before the Interstate Commerce Commission, and in the Courts. In that battle the regulated motor vehicle carriers and the railroads have, in general, contended for very limited exemptions from the certificate provisions of the Act and for a strict construction of the provisions providing for exemptions. Farm groups, other groups interested in the scope of the coverage of Section 203(b) (6), the unregulated carriers, and the Department of Agriculture have in general advocated a broad statutory exemption from the certificate provisions of the Act and for a liberal construction of the exemption provision as enacted.

· · ·

[The determination that frozen eviscerated chickens *were* "manufactured products" had previously been made by the Commission in 1951 as part of a broad proceeding, selections from which appear below. Note that the I.C.C. Hearing Examiner had held, partly on testimony of scientists, that frozen eviscerated chickens were *not* "manufactured". Reviewing this decision, the Commission had reversed. It is this decision which the Commission is now seeking to enforce against Kroblin in U. S. District Court.]

## No. MC–C–968

### DETERMINATION OF EXEMPTED AGRICULTURAL COMMODITIES

(52 M.C.C. 511)
Submitted December 8, 1949. Decided April 13, 1951

### REPORT OF THE COMMISSION ON ORAL ARGUMENT

### BY THE COMMISSION:

Exceptions to the order recommended by the examiner were filed by the rail carriers and Railway Express Agency, Inc., and a number of motor carriers and motor-carrier associations, to which the Secretary of Agriculture, the State of Alabama, and numerous agricultural interests and others replied; and the parties were heard in oral argument. Our conclusions differ somewhat from those recommended.

· · ·

### POULTRY AND LIVESTOCK GROUPS

*Poultry group.*—The basic commodities comprising the poultry group are chickens, turkeys, ducks, geese, squabs, feathers, and eggs.

The various treatments accorded chickens preparatory to marketing are killing, scalding, picking, drying, waxing, pinning, singeing, washing, cooling, grading, eviscerating, cutting up, packing, freezing, and storing. The same treatments with the exception of drying and waxing apply to turkeys, and with the exception of scalding, drying, and waxing, ducks and geese undergo the same treatment as those applied to chickens. Squab are killed, picked, washed, cooled, graded, eviscerated, packed, frozen, and stored.

The killing of chickens and turkeys is accomplished in the main by wholesalers, but the practice of killing on the farm is said to be on the increase, particularly in commercial producing areas. In the larger plants, the fowls are killed by machinery. Scalding is usually effected by dipping the poultry into large tanks of hot water and dragging the fowls through the tank by means of an overhead chain; or it may be done by subjecting the poultry to a series of hot water sprays. Picking is done both by machinery and by hand. Some hand picking is usually necessary in order to remove pin feathers and hair, although this may be accomplished by the application of hot wax; when the wax method is used, it is necessary to dry the fowl before applying the wax. After removal of the wax the fowls are cooled by appropriate means, graded, and packed in barrels or crates and covered with ice for shipment. In some instances waterproof paper is placed in the barrels and always when crates are used. In many instances the various treatments described are rendered at plants owned and operated by farm cooperatives. Turkeys and chickens are sometimes wrapped in cellophane for marketing, thus preventing evaporation. The practice of cutting up poultry into different parts for the consumer trade is increasing and is done on the farm to some extent.

Producers of ducks on Long Island, N. Y., are organized and carry on all of the marketing operations including the freezing and storage of such fowl. The method of removing feathers from ducks and geese differs somewhat from that of chickens because the feathers of the former are saved for other uses. Accordingly, particular pains are taken to keep the feathers clean and dry.

The scientist testifying with respect to this group does not consider any of the above described treatments or practices, including freezing, to be manufacturing. He pointed out that the freezing of poultry by the quick-freeze method or otherwise does not change the nature of the poultry in any way except to harden it. When thawed out it remains a fresh fowl. Freezing merely enables the fowl to be kept for a long period. Such treatments as smoking, cooking, and canning, however, are said to cause the fowl to become a manufactured product. In the smoking process, some type of curing liquid is added, and the bird is actually cooked, and therefore, is a manufactured product.

. . .

Summarizing, the scientists conclude that the following items are unmanufactured agricultural commodities: Chickens and turkeys, New York dressed, drawn, eviscerated, cut up, or frozen; ducks and geese, New York dressed, eviscerated, cut up or frozen; . . .

. . .

The examiner concluded that the following are unmanufactured agricultural commodities: (1) Chickens, turkeys, ducks, geese, and squab, alive or killed, picked, drawn, cut up, frozen or unfrozen; . . .

A number of the exceptants assail the examiner's finding with respect to the items embraced in (1) above. They contend that this finding is contrary to previous decisions of division 5, and that the conversion of a "live inedible fowl" into "a dead edible fowl" satisfies the definition of the word "manufacture" as laid down by the courts. They argue that if dressed poultry is to be considered an unmanufactured agricultural commodity then fresh meat and meat products should be accorded a similar classification. Certain of the parties contend that the processing of poultry does not differ materially from the treatments accorded fresh vegetables in the freezing process, and that since the latter are deemed to be manufactured products, no distinction should be made in the case of dressed poultry. Repliants say that dressed poultry still has all of its original characteristics except those which have been removed in the dressing process, and that the classification of this commodity as an unmanufactured agricultural commodity is proper.

The words "agricultural commodities (not including manufactured products thereof)" do not include ordinary livestock as the latter are separately mentioned in section 203(b)(6). Section 20(11) of the act provides that "The term 'ordinary livestock' shall include all cattle, swine, sheep, goats, horses, and mules, except such as are chiefly valuable for breeding, racing, show purposes, or other special uses." It necessarily follows that the term as used in section 203(b)(6) has the same meaning. Livestock, such as race horses, show horses, and the like do not come under the classification of "ordinary livestock," and the transportation of animals of this type is subject to the certificate or permit requirements of the act. Owsley Common Carrier Application, 31 M.C.C. 778. Poultry, however, are included within the broader description "agricultural commodities." It is clear also that certain products of live animals, such as are embraced in the definition of ordinary livestock, are likewise included; and there is no dispute that wool, at least in the form sheared from the sheep, is an agricultural commodity. These products are in themselves basic agricultural commodities, separate and distinct from the livestock. But slaughtered animals are not embraced in the definition of ordinary livestock and we are impelled to conclude that the products thereof, such as fresh meat and meat products, do not fall within the description "agricultural commodities" as used in section 203(b)(6). It logically follows that neither killed poultry nor any products thereof come within the term under consideration. We conclude that poultry other than that alive is not an agricultural commodity within the meaning of section 203(b)(6). Further, we are of the opinion that birds of the air such as doves and pigeons are not agricultural commodities.

. . .

LEE, Commissioner, concurring in part:

On the whole I think this is a sound report. It has my approval to the full extent to which it finds that commodities named therein fall within the partial exemption provided in section 203(b)(6) of the act. I find it necessary separately to state my views because of the findings, with which I am unable to agree, that certain agricultural commodities do not fall within that exemption after having been subjected to commonly followed forms of processing. I believe these findings improperly narrow the scope of the exemption contrary to the intention of Congress.

. . .

. . . It appears that the House, in adopting the subcommittee's amendment, and the Senate, in concurring in that amendment, intended that the distinction between any particular "agricultural commodity," falling within the exemption, and "manufactured products thereof," excluded from the exemption, is not to be based upon whether such "agricultural commodity" has been subjected to processing, such as the simple processing of shelling an egg or even the elaborate processing of pasteurizing milk with the relatively complex and costly equipment of a modern, big city dairy, but is to be based upon whether, as the result of processing, such "agricultural commodity" has been so changed that a new and distinctive commodity or article is produced. To give recognition to this intention of the Congress in interpreting the words "manufactured products thereof" will accord to them their usual and popular meaning which, even in the absence of supporting legislative history, should here be attributed to them.

Chickens, turkeys, ducks, geese, and guineas alive and after having been killed are still known by the same names. The dressing and cutting into pieces of a chicken or a turkey does not result in the production of a distinctive article having any new characteristics or uses. It still is an agricultural commodity. Surely the Thanksgiving turkey which the farmer's wife so carefully stuffs and places in the oven is not a manufactured article.

---

INTERSTATE COMMERCE COMMISSION v. KROBLIN

113 F.Supp. 599 (The District Court's disposition), continues:

. . .

. . . The parties are in agreement that live poultry is an agricultural commodity. They are in disagreement as to whether New York dressed and eviscerated poultry is an "agricultural commodity" or a "manufactured product." While eviscerated poultry is somewhat more extensively processed than is New York dressed poultry, yet counsel in argument stated that no distinction is claimed as between the two so far as the agricultural exemption is concerned. Since the parties are in agreement that live fowls as they leave the farm are an "agricultural commodity," the real disagreement between the parties is as to when they become a "manufactured product." It is the claim of the Interstate Commerce Commission that they probably become such upon being killed and in all events after they have been New York dressed or eviscerated. It is the claim of the defendant and the Secretary of Agriculture that by such dressing or eviscerating the fowls have not as yet reached the point where they can be properly and legally classified as a "manufactured product" and that something further or other is required before they have that status.

In a number of the fields of law the question has arisen as to what steps, or processing, are necessary before a particular item can be classified as a "manufactured product." Much difficulty has been experienced in interpreting the word "manufactured" used in Section 203(b) (6). In the report under S.Res. 50, a witness stated (p. 802) that much of this difficulty was occasioned by the fact that the word "manufactured" has not been commonly used in statutes dealing with agriculture and that the word most commonly used is "processed." The same witness stated (p. 803) there were a number of jurisdictions in which it was held that slaughtering was not a manufacturing business. The parties have cited and discussed decisions in cases arising under Tariff Act and the Patent Act as what constituted a "manufactured" article within the purview of those Acts. Some of the decisions contain definitions of "manufacture," "manufactured," and "manufactured products." Some of the decisions set forth tests which the parties claim are applicable and determinative in the present case. The parties also presented a number of non-judicial definitions and tests which are claimed to be applicable and determinative. In that connection the defendant and the Secretary of Agriculture cite and rely upon the cases hereafter referred to. In the case of Frazee v. Moffitt, C.C.N.D.N.Y.1882, 20 Blatchf. 267, 18 F. 584, it was held that hay was not a manufactured product. That case arose under a federal statute which imposed an import duty at a certain rate upon unmanufactured articles and at another rate upon manufactured articles. In the case of Hartranft v. Wiegmann, 1887, 121 U.S. 609, 7 S.Ct. 1240, 30 L.Ed. 1012, it was held that sea shells which had been subjected to processing whereby two or three layers of each shell were removed and the inner shell polished on an emery wheel and mottoes etched on the polished inner shell were not manufactured articles under the Tariff Act. In the case of Anheuser-Busch Brewing Ass'n v. United States, 1908, 207 U.S. 556, 28 S.Ct. 204, 52 L.Ed. 336, it was held that corks which had been extensively processed were not manufactured articles under the Tariff Act. The defendant and the Secretary of Agriculture call attention to the following statement of the Court in the latter case, 207 U.S. at page 562, 28 S.Ct. at page 206:

> " . . . Manufacture implies a change, but every change is not manufacture, and yet every change in an article is the result of treatment, labor, and manipulation. But something more is necessary, as set forth and illustrated in Hartranft v. Wiegmann, 121 U.S. 609, 7 S.Ct. 1240, 30 L.Ed. 1012. There must be transformation; a new and different article must emerge, 'having a distinctive name, character, or use.' . . ."

The defendant and the Secretary of Agriculture particularly rely upon the definition of the word "manufacture" approved in the case of American Fruit Growers, Inc., v. Brogdex Co., 1931, 283 U.S. 1, 51 S.Ct. 328, 75 L.Ed. 801. In that case the Court held that an orange which had become impregnated with a borax solution through immersion in a solution and thereby rendered resistant to blue mold was

not a manufactured article within the meaning of the Patent Law.
Interestingly, the Interstate Commerce Commission, in the report in
a proceeding entitled "Determination of Exempted Agricultural Commodities," 52 M.C.C. 511, stated that the definition which was approved in the Fruit Growers case was the appropriate and applicable
definition to be used in connection with the determination of whether
a commodity is or is not a "manufactured product" under the agricultural exemption.   The definition referred to is as follows, at page
11 of 283  U.S., at page 330 of 51 S.Ct.:

> "Manufacture," as well defined by the Century Diction-
> ary, is 'the production of articles for use from raw or pre-
> pared materials by giving to these materials new forms, qual-
> ities, properties, or combinations, whether by hand-labor
> or by machinery'; also 'anything made for use from raw
> or prepared materials.' "

It is the claim of the defendant and the Secretary of Agriculture
that under the latter definition dressed poultry is not a manufactured
product.   The Interstate Commerce Commission making use of the
same definition concluded that dressed poultry is a manufactured
product.   The Interstate Commerce Commission presented a booklet
issued by the Executive Office of the President, Bureau of the Budget,
dated November, 1945, Part I, entitled Standard Industrial Classification Manual.   On page 7 thereof there is included as "manufacturing"
establishments "Establishments primarily engaged in killing, dressing,
packing, and canning poultry, rabbits, and other small game for the
trade  .  .  .."   At the trial the defendant presented evidence to the
effect that the Department of Agriculture in its statistical reports and
in general had classified dressed poultry as a non-manufactured product.   When the Secretary of Agriculture later appeared as amicus
curiae he contended similarly.

The definitions relied upon by the parties are broad, general definitions.   The relating of them to a particular article, product or commodity requires still further defining of the words used in the definition, i. e., a defining of the definition.   In the present case it has
been a case of "thrust and parry" (see 30 Vanderbilt L.Rev., pp. 401–
406) between the parties in the matter of relating definitive words to
the particular commodity involved.   This Court is of the view that
the tracing out of the meaning of "manufactured products" in the
agricultural exemption by means of general definitions and the attempted definition of those definitions would only lead into a semantic
wilderness.   All of the parties are agreed that the words "agricultural commodities" and "manufactured products thereof" used in the
agricultural exemption are ambiguous words.   They are not defined
in the Act.   Therefore, it is necessary that resort be made to decisions
construing the provisions of the agricultural exemption and to the extrinsic aids of legislative history and administrative interpretation.
See Jones, Extrinsic Aids in the Federal Courts, 25 Iowa Law Review
737 (1940).   It would seem desirable to first refer to decisions and
matters connected with administrative, interpretative, and legislative
history in a general chronological order.

.   .   .

The weight given by the courts to administrative interpretation is based in part at least upon the theory that a particular agency has "expertness" in a particular field in which it has been entrusted with responsibility by Congress. The Secretary of Agriculture claims that he has been charged with responsibility in the particular field here involved. His claim in that regard is set forth in the brief filed in his behalf as follows:

> "By section 203(j) of the Agricultural Marketing Act of 1946 (7 U.S.C. section 1622 (j) [7 U.S.C.A. § 1622(j)]), Congress has authorized and directed the Secretary of Agriculture to assist 'in improving transportation services and facilities *and in obtaining equitable and reasonable transportation rates and services and adequate transportation facilities for agricultural products* and farm supplies by making complaint or petition to the Interstate Commerce Commission . . . with respect to rates, charges, tariffs, practices, and services, or by working directly with individual carriers or groups of carriers' (emphasis supplied). . . .
>
> The Secretary of Agriculture is also authorized to participate in proceedings before the Commission relative to rates, charges, tariffs, and 'practices' relating to the transportation of farm products (7 U.S.C. section 1291(a) and (b), and in such cases the Secretary may take part in the subsequent judicial proceedings (7 U.S.C. section 1291(b)."

. . . .

It is the claim of the Secretary of Agriculture that his responsibility in the matter of the transportation of agricultural commodities is such that the administrative interpretation of the Department of Agriculture as to whether or not "dressed poultry" is a "manufactured product" is entitled to equal weight with that of the Interstate Commerce Commission. In oral argument counsel for the Secretary of Agriculture stated that so far as "expertness" in the matter of farm commodities was concerned the "expertness" of the Department of Agriculture in the matter of the classification of them was not only equal to but, if anything, greater than that of the Interstate Commerce Commission. He further stated that the Department of Agriculture has had more to do with poultry, including the classification thereof, for a much longer period of time than has the Interstate Commerce Commission. The defendant, as heretofore noted, presented evidence at the time of the trial to the effect that the Department of Agriculture classifies "dressed poultry" as an unmanufactured product.

The Interstate Commerce Commission states that it is the particular agency which is charged with the responsibility of enforcement of the provisions of Section 203(b)(6) and that such being the case its administrative interpretations are entitled to great weight and not the interpretations of the Department of Agriculture.

. . .

In the present case, the only relevancy of administrative construction or interpretation is to the matter of Congressional intent. The question is whether or not the agency making the particular contention or interpretation has correctly ascertained the intent of Congress. Administrative construction or interpretation is but one of several extrinsic aids in the interpretation of statutes. Another extrinsic aid is legislative history. Where the provisions of a statute are ambiguous, the legislative history may often be revealing on the matter of legislative intent and may be more satisfactory evidence of legislative intent than administrative construction or interpretation. In the present case the parties are in controversy as to whether the administrative constructions or interpretations advanced are in accord with the intent of Congress as revealed by the legislative history of the Act. All of the parties contend that the legislative history of the Act supports their respective claims as to the intent of Congress. It would then seem desirable to next give consideration to the legislative history of the Act before proceeding any further with the matter of administrative construction or interpretation.

In the present case, the matters of importance are what was the purpose of Congress in enacting Section 203(b)(6), and what commodities did it intend to include within its provisions? The parties are agreed that the purpose of Section 203(b)(6) was to benefit the farmers. The amendment was not necessary to relieve the farmers of the expense and trouble of complying with the regulations of the National Motor Carrier Act where they operated their own trucks to transport their produce or farm supplies. They were relieved of that trouble by Section 203(b)(4a) and Section 203(b)(9) of the Act. Section 203(b)(6) provided for exemption for commercial truckers transporting the commodities therein referred to. It is therefore clear that Congress concluded that the farmers would be benefited by having the commercial truckers engaged in hauling farm commodities exempted from the certificate provisions of the Act. In Congressional Committee hearings on proposed amendments to Section 203(b)(6), there are frequent references to the matter of the difference in the cost of transportation as between the certificated and uncertificated carriers. In Senate Hearing on S. 2357, an economist appearing in behalf of the National Grange stated, on p. 452 thereof, that the abolition of the exemption would mean an increase of transportation costs for farm products by 15 to 25 percent. On pages 502 and 503 of Senate Hearing S. 2357 a witness stated that when following the decision in the case of Interstate Commerce Commission v. Love, supra, trucks hauling fish were relieved of regulation the transportation rate on fish between Boston and Chicago dropped from $1.25 a hundred to $1.00 a hundred. On page 376 of Senate Hearing No. 2357 a witness stated that the certificated carriers were rapidly losing out to the uncertificated carriers in the transportation of farm commodities. On page 503 of Senate Hearing No. 50, a witness listed 17 items that made for higher costs on the part of the certificated carriers in comparison to the uncertificated carriers. They were as follows:

> "Principal among the expenses borne by the regulated carrier (even when transporting an exempt load) and not incurred by the average itinerant owner-operator are the following: (1) cost of preventive maintenance; (2) cost of su-

pervising transportation and maintaining safety program, including examining and training drivers and safety patrol work; (3) pay for union helper loading and unloading; (4) full union pay scale for driver; (5) extra pay for waiting time; (6) employee benefits of group insurance, etc.; (7) cost of branch terminals for checking equipment, serving shippers on tracers, claims, etc.; (8) cost of tariff publication and distribution; (9) cost of maintaining claim agent, processing claims and payment of uninsured claims; (10) cargo insurance; (11) public liability and property damage insurance in adequate limits; (12) workmen's compensation insurance; (13) general and administrative expense, including accounting department, communication expense and law expense; (14) State fuel taxes based on reporting mileages; (15) Federal and State unemployment charges; (16) social-security payments by employers or employees; (17) office rents. In addition, such owner-operators customarily do not collect, report and pay the 3-percent Federal transportation tax, which, when not collected from the shipper, becomes the carrier's obligation.

"These services and facilities, which the regulated carrier provides, all cost money and they all are provided in conformity with the requirements of law, the best interest of labor, the needs of the shippers, and protection for the public."

However, in Senate Hearing S. 2352, on page 441 thereof, a representative of the Department of Agriculture stated as follows:

"We believe that the principal reason why sections 203 (b) (4a) and (6) were incorporated in the original Motor Carrier Act, 1935, was that the Congress then recognized that the flexible transportation service needed to move farm and fishery commodities could not be performed by general merchandise haulers."

In the present case it was claimed in oral argument by counsel for the defendant and the Secretary of Agriculture that the biggest benefit to the farmers of exempting commercial truckers engaged in hauling farm commodities from the certificate provisions of the Act was the flexibility of operations permitted such carriers. It was stated by them that poultry is a commodity as to which the market is variable and shifting and that it is frequently necessary to be able to make shifts and changes in marketing arrangements on short notice and, in some cases, even when the commodities are enroute. It was also stated that the certificated carriers who operated over fixed routes between specified points were ill adapted for the marketing of poultry. . . . On the matter of Congressional intent, as indicated by the legislative history, all of the parties discussed in their briefs and oral arguments that part of the legislative history relating to the original enactment of the Act wherein the House amended the House Committee Amendment so as to strike out the words "unprocessed agricultural products" and inserted in lieu thereof "agricultural commodities not including manufactured products thereof," 79 C.R. 12,220. In connection with such change, the Interstate Commerce Commission points out that in the discussion relating to the change reference was made to the possibility that there might be some doubt as to whether "pasteurized milk" and "ginned cotton" might not be included within the term "unprocessed agricultural products." The Interstate Commerce Commission contends that the purpose and effect of the change in terms was to include ginned cotton and pasteurized milk within the scope of the exemption. The defendant and the Secretary of Agriculture claim that it was not the intent of Congress by the change in terms to limit the effect of the change to ginned cotton and pasteurized milk. It is the claim of the defendant and the Secretary of Agriculture that by the change in terms Congress manifested the intent that the mere fact that an agricultural commodity had been processed would not cause it to be outside of the scope of the exemption. It is their claim that Congress by the change manifested the intent that farm commodities could be processed without losing their status as an exempt commodity and that it was only when such commodities had achieved the status of manufactured articles that they lost their exempt status. Those contentions brought the discussion of the parties back to a discussion of the meaning of "manufactured" products which, as heretofore noted, ended in an exchange of definitions.

. . .

An unusually large number of amendments have been proposed to Section 203(b)(6) and there is an unusually large amount of legislative history material available in connection therewith. The action and attitude of Congress as to proposed amendments could be indicative of Congressional intent as to the scope and coverage of that subparagraph.

. . .

By the Act of June 29, 1938, c. 811, § 3, 52 Stat. 1237, Congress amended the subparagraph by striking out the word "exclusively" which appeared in the subparagraph as originally enacted relating to the use of motor vehicles which hauled exempt commodities. The effect of striking out the word "exclusively" was to greatly broaden the scope of the exemptions afforded by that subparagraph in that it made the load being hauled at the time the test of exemption.

Also in 1938 three bills were introduced: S. 3768, S. 3941, and H.R. 10508, 75th Congress, 3d Session. S. 3768 would have had the effect of limiting the exemptions of the subparagraph among other ways to "unmanufactured products obtained as a result of raising and keeping livestock, bees, or poultry." H.R. 10508 was identical with S. 3941. The effect of them would have been to eliminate the exemption for any vehicle which hauled non-exempt commodities at any time. Congress did not enact any of the bills. . . .

By Act of September 18, 1940, Congress inserted the word "ordinary" preceding the word "livestock" in the subparagraph. The effect of this change was to lead the Commission to change its interpretation of the status of poultry which it had first classed as livestock and therefore exempt only when alive. On May 28, 1943, Senator Lodge introduced a bill, S. 1148, 78th Congress, 1st Session, providing for the amendment of the subparagraph. The effect of the amendment would have been to limit the exemption to transportation by actual producers. Congress did not adopt it. On March 30, 1950, H.R. 7547, 81st Congress, 2d Session, was introduced by Mr. Kilday. It specifically provided that the exemption afforded by the subparagraph should in the case of poultry be limited to "live poultry" and in general provided for excluding from the exemption those commodities that were "slaughtered, frozen or processed." The Senate Committee on Interstate and Foreign Commerce, acting under S. 50, held the extensive Committee hearings heretofore referred to in connection with transportation problems. In connection therewith hearings were held on H.R. 7547, Senate Committee Report S. 50, pages 811 et seq. The purpose and intended effect of H.R. 7547 is set forth at pages 825 and 826 of that Report. The bill was not enacted. From March 3, 1952, to April 9, 1952, the Senate Committee on Interstate and Foreign Commerce held extensive hearings on S. 2357, 82d Congress, 2d Session. That bill was introduced by Senator Johnson of Colorado. That bill provided that the exemptions provided for in the subparagraph should not be applicable to the transportation of agricultural commodities which had been "processed to a greater extent than is customarily done by farmers prior to their marketing . . . ." Senator Johnson filed an amendment to S. 2357 to limit the exempt transportation to the point of "first off-the-farm processing." The bill and the amendment are entitled as bills to "restrict the application of the agricultural and fish exemption for motor carriers" under the Interstate Commerce Act. . . . The Senate Committee held extensive hearings on the matter of restricting the exemption for agricultural and other commodities as proposed by the bill as originally introduced by Senator Johnson and by the amendment to the bill proposed by the Legislative Committee of the Interstate Commerce Commission. There was a rather surprising outcome. The Senate Committee struck out all language in the bill and the amendment to it which would have had the effect of restricting the exemption of farm commodities under Section 203(b)(6) and instead recommended to the Senate that Section 203(b)(6) be liberalized in the matter of exemptions by inserting the words "including horticultural" after the word "agricultural" in that subparagraph. Congress followed that recommendation by the enactment of Public Law 472, 82d Congress, 2d Session, 66 Stat. 479, approved July 9, 1952.

The construction or interpretation of Section 203(b)(6) contended for by the Interstate Commerce Commission would be highly restrictive of the scope of Section 203(b)(6) so far as poultry is concerned.

There are two features that stand out most predominantly in the voluminous legislative history relating to amendments made or proposed to Section 203(b)(6). One feature is that every amendment that Congress has made to it has broadened and liberalized its provisions in favor of exemption and the other feature is that although often importuned to do so, Congress has uniformly and steadfastly refused or rejected amendments which would either directly or indirectly have denied the benefits of the exemptions contained therein to truckers who are engaged in operations similar to that of the defendant herein. It is believed that the actions and attitude of Congress as manifested in connection with amendments to Section 203(b) (6) are preponderantly indicative of an intent on the part of Congress that the words "manufactured products" used in that subparagraph are not to be given the restricted meaning contended for by the Interstate Commerce Commission herein.

It is the holding of the Court that New York dressed poultry or eviscerated poultry do not constitute "manufactured" products within the intent and meaning of Section 203(b)(6). It is the feeling of the Court that an opposite holding would in reality constitute an attempt to accomplish by means of judicial construction that which Congress has steadfastly refused to allow to be accomplished by legislation.

Judgment will be entered in accord with this opinion.

## QUESTIONS

1. In its opinion, the Commission had said that "the primary issue is the meaning of the . . . words" "Agriculture commodities (not including manufactured products thereof)". In what sense was the Commission right? Are the rail carriers, motor carriers, farmers organizations, shippers, and growers who appeared, the state of Alabama and the United States Department of Agriculture concerned about what words *mean*? What is the "primary issue" to each of them?

2. What is the relationship between determining whether eviscerated chickens are "manufactured products" and deciding—

(a) How ought revenue from chicken sales be allocated as between the chicken farmers and various types of transportation companies?[5]

(b) Should consumers have to pay, through increased prices for chicken, to support regulated truck carriage in the United States?

(c) Should the Interstate Commerce Commission be allowed to extend its jurisdiction and the growth of "federal bureaucracy"?

Must the Court be indifferent, in deciding whether eviscerated chickens are "manufactured products", to the interests which its decision will necessarily affect? *Can* it exclude such considerations from mind?

**5.** The United States Department of Agriculture undertook a study to compare the transportation rates on unfrozen and frozen poultry, both before and after the decisions which, like *Kroblin*, freed them from ICC stewardship. The results showed that in 1956–57, poultry firms were paying 33% *less* for the transport of unfrozen poultry than they had had to pay in 1952, the last full year of ICC control. In the same 1956–57 period, frozen poultry rates had settled 36% below the prices the commission had been supporting in 1955. "Interstate Trucking of Fresh and Frozen Poultry under Agricultural Exemption," Marketing Research Report No. 224 (Washington, D.C.: Dept. of Agriculture, 1958), p. 1. Certain objections to the survey methods the Department used are noted in Stone, The ICC: Some Reminiscences on the Future of American Transportation, 2 New Individualist Review 3, 12 (1963).

3.   Eleven scientists were called to testify as to whether the various products under investigation were "manufactured" or not. Why?  Is the inquiry a "scientific" one?  What sort of aura does having scientists testify lend to the Commission's investigations? What is it that makes a scientist competent to tell whether the eviscerating of chickens makes them "manufactured products"?  Is there anything in his training that makes him an expert on whether the power of unregulated motor carriers ought to be increased?

4.   What might the Commission have thought it would accomplish by the elaborate description of the processing of poultry, viz., "killing, scalding, picking, drying, waxing, pinning, singeing, washing, cooling, grading, eviscerating, cutting up, packing, freezing, and storing."  Can *picturing* what happens to the chickens in this detail tell us what we want to know?  Would we be getting closer to an answer if we took each of those terms, say, "killing", and depicted in finer detail what was involved, that is, step by step *how* the chickens are killed?

5.   Why, ultimately, does the Commission reverse its Examiner on the matter of the chickens?  How compelling are the reasons given? To what extent can its decision be called a mere carrying out of the will of Congress, as expressed in the Interstate Commerce Act?

6.   Comment on Commissioner Lee's analysis.  What force is there to his remark, "surely the Thanksgiving turkey which the farmer's wife so carefully stuffs and places in the oven is not a manufactured product."  When, as here, the term will have specially defined legal consequences, what force should there be to an inquiry into its ordinary, everyday uses?  Does Commissioner Lee's opinion indicate that he is insensitive to the broad political and economic ramifications of what the decision entails?  Or does he feel that in the absence of other clear considerations, recourse to ordinary usage is presumptively the most likely way to establish Congressional intent?

7.   Why did the U. S. District Court disagree with the Commission?

Of what guidance were the cases to which the Court referred? Take for example, Hartranft v. Weigemann.  What was involved in that case?  What was the Court there deciding when it was deciding whether the shells were "manufactured products" in the context of the tariff act?  Similarly, what was the Court deciding in Fruit Growers v. Brogdex, when it decided whether oranges were "manufactured products" in the context of the patent laws?

8.   How useful did the Court find appeals to dictionaries and administrative expertise?  Why?  How different are appeals to "legislative intent"?  What is a court trying to do, when it sets out to establish "legislative intent"?  Why should it do so?  How does the aim compare with the reconstruction of "intent" in analyzing and criticizing the behavior of a human being?  How did the evidence the court looked to in establishing legislative intent compare with the sort of evidence one considers in establishing human intent?  Given the nature of the "evidence" the court can muster, what constraints does the endeavor impose on the court's just "deciding what it wants

to decide"?  Does the endeavor go so far as to put the court under, in Rawls' terms, a "practice"?  See Bice, *Raoul Berger: Congress v. The Supreme Court,* 44 So. CAL. L.REV. 499 (1971).

9.  In reading the court's opinion, do you get a clear idea of the overall purposes of the Interstate Commerce Act?  How, without a sense of overall purpose, can it know what facts to look to?  What values to apply?  Whose interests to weigh most heavily?

Consider in this regard the "National Transportation Policy" which Congress enacted in 1940 as a guide to the administration of the Interstate Commerce Act.

> "It is hereby declared to be the national transportation policy of the Congress to provide for fair and impartial regulation of all modes of transportation subject to the provisions of this act (chapters 1, 8, 12, and 13 of this title), so administered as to recognize and preserve the inherent advantages of each; to promote safe, adequate, economical, and efficient service and foster sound economic conditions in transportation and among the several carriers; to encourage the establishment and maintenance of reasonable charges for transportation services, without unjust discriminations, undue preferences or advantages, or unfair or destructive competitive practices; to cooperate with the several States and the duly authorized officials thereof; and to encourage fair wages and equitable working conditions—all to the end of developing, coordinating, and preserving a national transportation system by water, highway, and rail, as well as other means, adequate to meet the needs of the commerce of the United States, of the Postal Service, and of the national defense.  All of the provisions of this act (chapters 1, 8, 12, and 13 of this title), shall be administered and enforced with a view to carrying out the above declaration of policy."

Act Sept. 18, 1940, ch. 722, title I, § 1, 54 Stat. 899.

Might the difficulties of applying the particular provisions found in *Kroblin* be traced to the vagaries of overall purpose?

In reading the Commission's opinion, do you get a clear idea of its own sense of purpose?  How may the effective operation of an agency —or of a human being—be hampered by a failure to communicate to it a sense of its proper role?  Why?

---

Given all the *difficulties* of establishing a system in which decision-makers are "bound" by their assigned roles and rules, are the *efforts* worth it?  Do the written rules really serve to give anyone guidance, or is all the legal jargon mere pretense and sham?  Would we be better off, as Sartre seems to suggest, to trust to our instincts— and openly acknowledge it?  If so, what sort of social order would ensue?  How would it be different from that which we now have? Consider, in this regard, the selection from Montaigne which follows. (You may wish to keep in mind that Montaigne was no mere armchair philosopher, but a government employee and, for a period, mayor of Bordeaux).

## MICHAEL DE MONTAIGNE

## OF EXPERIENCE *

Reason has so many shapes that we know not which to lay hold of; experience has no fewer. The inference that we try to draw from the resemblance of events is unsure, because events are always dissimilar . . . Both the Greeks and the Romans, and we ourselves, use eggs for the strongest example of similarity. However, there have been men, and notably one at Delphi, who recognized marks of difference between eggs, so that he never mistook one for another; and although there were many hens, he could tell which one any egg had come from. Dissimilarity necessarily intrudes itself into our works; no art can attain similarity. Neither Perrozet nor any other card-maker can smooth and whiten the backs of his cards so carefully that some players will not distinguish them simply by seeing them slip through another man's hands. Resemblance does not make things so much alike as difference makes them unlike. Nature has committed herself to make nothing separate that was not different.

Therefore I have little sympathy for the opinion of the man who thought by a multiplicity of laws to bridle the authority of judges . . . . He did not realize that there is as much freedom and latitude in the interpretation of laws as in their creation; just as they just fool themselves who think they can end disputes by citing us to the express words of the Bible. For the range of our creativity is no less trammelled when ostensibly "comprehending" the meaning of others than when setting forth the views that are frankly "our own". As if there were less animosity and bitterness in commentary than in invention!

We see how far he was deceived. For we have in France more laws than all the rest of the world together, and more than would be needed to govern all the worlds imagined by Epicurus. *As formerly we suffered from crimes, so now we suffer from laws* [Tacitus]. And yet we have given our judges so much room for opinion and decision that there never was so full a liberty or so full a license. What have our legislators gained by selecting a hundred thousand particular cases and actions, and applying a hundred thousand laws to them? This number bears no proportion to the infinite diversity of human actions. Multiplication of our imaginary cases will never be able to cope with the variety life presents. Add to them a hundred times as many more: and still no future event will be found to correspond so exactly to any one of all the many, many thousands of selected and recorded events that there will not remain some circumstance, some difference, that will require separate consideration in forming a judgment. There is little relation between our actions, which are in per-

---

* From Essais (Bk. III, Ch. 13) (Ville-
main ed. Paris 1825). Transl. C. D.
Stone and E. Arnett.

petual mutation, and fixed and immutable laws. The most desirable laws are those that are rarest, simplest, and most general and I even think that it would be better to have none whatsoever than to have them in so prodigious a number as we have.

Nature always gives us better laws than those we give ourselves. Witness the picture of the Golden Age of the poets, and the state in which we see nations live which have no other laws. Some employ, as the only judge in their quarrels, the first traveler passing through their mountains. Others on market day elect one of themselves who decides all their suits on the spot. What danger would there be in having our wisest men settle our disputes in this way, according to the circumstances and at sight, without being bound to precedents or consequences? For every foot its own shoe! King Ferdinand, when he sent colonists to the Indies, wisely provided that no students of the law should accompany them, for fear that lawsuits might breed in this new world, this being by nature a science generating altercation and division; and judging, with Plato, that lawyers and doctors are an ill provision for a country.

*PART TWO*

# THE QUEST FOR AUTHORITY:
# ITS LIMITS AND ILLUSIONS

### INTRODUCTORY NOTE

In Part I we saw how incredibly complex and overwhelming decision and action can be, and that, out of and in response to these difficulties, there emerges desire for *system*, system both in individual thought and in social organization. We encountered the position that the order such systemization requires can be advanced by the institution of rules and offices. But we saw, too, that the effectiveness of a system of rules and offices presupposes the efficacy of symbolic communication: not only must the person who is assigned to "carry out" his job be willing to do so, he must also know what the rules he is subject to mean for him to do.

How realistic is it to say that the rules and offices we now have—or could have—work in the systematic and authoritative way they are supposed to? In each of the cases we have studied so far, the person charged with carrying out his "orders" was able to find (or we were able to find for him) what appeared to be a large residue of discretion, notwithstanding the ostensible authority of the constitutional provisions, statutes, precedent, and so forth, with which he was supposedly "bound". Can we really say, with any degree of comfort, that Judge Park in *Haslem*, Smith in *Cappier*, Roberts and Stone in *Butler*, or Judge Graven in *Kroblin*, were doing nothing more than stating what was "laid down in the law"? Indeed, what is more disquieting, is there any reason to assume that the "authority" that those cases were claimed to involve had *any force and effect at all*? May we rightly argue, citing Montaigne and Sartre, perhaps, that the authorities by which we seek to bind our administrators become so much pretense, and that, in the end, the decisions are *all* discretion?

This latter assertion calls for a number of inquiries including, importantly, one into the nature of discretion, *e. g.*, is it true that one cannot have "a little bit of discretion", the way a girl cannot be "a little bit pregnant"; is to say that people have discretion the same as to say that they are merely deciding, in some way destructive of social order, the way "they want to decide"? These are problems, however, that will be dealt with in Parts III and IV. Before we get into them we have a prior inquiry that will occupy Part II: how widespread—how inevitable—is discretion? For looking back over the materials we have examined thus far, one might still say, "true, the judges in *those cases* obviously did a lot more than to carry out printed instructions, like programmed machines. But these cases were not typical; in all of them the law was (perhaps purposely) drafted loosely, or the situation was unique, or the precedent especially unclear. This doesn't mean that the law *could not be*—as perhaps in more typical cases it is—written in such a way as to make the judge's function relatively mechanical."

This is the position to which the next five chapters respond. Are there "typical" cases in which authority controls, in which a person making a decision has virtually no autonomy, his decision being simply dictated by the world "as it exists"—by its facts and rules? Or is *every decision* creative and formulative, loading on our shoulders the responsibility of freedom; and, if so, on what basis can any viable form of social order emerge?

To explore these questions in detail, this Part breaks down the decision process into the five "steps" to which common sense might suppose all legal judgments to be subject—the act of perceiving (Chapter 4), the invocation of concepts (Chapter 5), the establishment of what the facts are (Chapter 6), the framing of the issue (Chapter 7), and the application of linguistic rules (Chapter 8).

The purpose of the organization is to enable us to test, at every such "step" of the decision process, the validity of the view that it is possible to eliminate the influence of individual peculiarities, prejudices and values. How, and in what way, and at what stage of decision may each man's ultimate judgment be influenced by his beliefs, including his closely held values? At what stage, if any, is such an influence inevitable? And, indeed, how meaningful is it to suppose that our judgments are a product of a step by step process, in which first we perceive, *then* we decide what the facts are, *then* we apply rules, etc.?

The selections are designed not only to illuminate the problems of legal system. They serve as well to demonstrate the epistemological conceptions that judges and lawyers and human beings in general are acting upon every day—and to point up where our misconceptions may invite faulty analysis and error.

———

## CHAPTER FOUR

# The Authority of Perception

## INTRODUCTORY NOTE

To what extent can any human being make *any* judgment wholly pure of "value"—of his attitudes, expectations, ideas about what he and his group consider proper? When his judgment calls for invoking "higher" cognitive functions—employing memory, drawing inferences, balancing presumptions—it is not so difficult to argue that his "personal" views will put a strain on his judgment, making it hard to separate out his "own" attitudes from those of his role—those that he is assigned to have.

How pervasive in mental activity are the influences a "pure theory of law" wants to purge? If any stage of learning and thinking should prove "pure" we might expect it to be the most primitive level of experience: the knowledge that is seemingly presented to us through our immediate perceptions. But is even the knowledge given by our most direct perceptions so simple and indubitable that we can be certain it is a mere report of what objectively exists in the world, and is not influenced by individual and cultural differences, including, perhaps, those of a moral and political nature? The logical positivists seem to be making such a supposition in speaking of "protocol sentences" as a firm ground upon which can be built all "scientific" knowledge. And, presumably, on such knowledge could be built a 'pure' system of law under which judges were limited to applying preordained norms to objective "facts"—without further excursions into the weighing and treating of values. (See the selection from Carnap, supra, p. 42.) Is such knowledge possible? If two different judges —or jurors—are observing the same witness, long before they make a judgment on what he says, will they even *hear* the same things? Will they *see* the same things? If there are differences, does anything like "choice" go into bringing them about?

The "purity" of perceptual knowledge from the distortions of personal and group idiosyncrasies was long maintained, supported on the view (which one finds in Locke, *infra*), that in perception we do nothing but passively accept and fill up with knowledge of what is "out there". ("The bucket theory of the mind" is the way Karl Popper refers to the position). Long before, Pythagoras had maintained that what we saw was determined by particles continuously flying from the surface of bodies through our pupils to give us an exact report of objects "as they were". Empedocles and Plato took issue only insofar as to suggest that the cause of vision is something emitted from the eye, which meeting with something else that proceeds from the object, was reflected back into the eye.[1]  E. R. Jaensch, a psychologist prominent in Nazi Germany, explained that at least so far as Aryans were concerned "to the points of the retina correspond firmly and unequivocally determined locations in the visual space", a characteristic which

1.  See J. Priestley, The History and Present State of Discoveries Relating to Vision, Light and Colours 1-2 (London 1772).

gave the Aryan a firm tie with reality; perception had, for the Aryans, an unquestionable authority.    Others—Jews, "Parisians", Turks, Indians, etc.—showed a lack of clear-cut and rigid evaluation of stimuli.    According to Jaensch, this type (the S-type) demonstrated "no firm tie with reality.    In fact he has no ties at all.    He is the liberalist at large.    .   .   .    This social liberalism is paralleled by innumerable other forms of liberalism, all of them mentally rooted in the S-type; liberalism of knowledge, of perception, of art, etc."    To Jaensch, perception being authoritative, there was little reason to compromise it with "theory".    He saw the attempt among German physicists to discredit Einstein's physics as part of "the struggle for consideration of reality in natural science and against the S-type inclination to dissolve all reality into theory." [2]

Jaensch's theories may appear extreme.    But beneath the surface he may have been making, in part unwittingly, some important points. How authoritatively and how skeptically we regard "the given" is part and parcel of our most fundamental attitudes towards life.    Those who question the reliability of the common-sensical world of perception are destined to carry their skepticism through all the "facts" and judgments that are built upon it.    Conversely, those who are convinced that the raw data of their knowledge is authoritative, are apt to have less tolerance for theory, conjecture and fancy,—an emotional state that may be associated with a lessened inclination to question any of the authority that is exercised over them.    The assumptions cannot help but influence the ways in which we organize our personal, social and political lives, from what we are willing to allow witnesses to testify to in court to how much we will tolerate discussion as a way of correcting "error". [3]

--------

SMITH v. BOCKLITZ

  344 S.W.2d 97 (Mo. 1961)

A pedestrian brought an action against a motorist and against the owner of a bus for injuries sustained by the pedestrian when he was struck by motorist's automobile while he was crossing the street in front of the standing bus.    The Circuit Court for the County of St. Louis, Douglas L. C. Jones, J., rendered a judgment adverse to the pedestrian, and he appealed.    The Supreme Court, Hyde, J., held that the testimony of the pedestrian that the bus driver motioned for the pedestrian to cross the street was properly stricken because it stated the pedestrian's conclusion as to the bus driver's intention, and that the pedestrian was properly limited to a description of the bus driver's motion.    [Note by West].

  .   .   .   .   .

HYDE, Judge.

  .   .   .   .

2.  See E. Frankel-Brunswik, Further Explorations by a Contributor to the "The Authoritarian Personality", in Studies in the Scope and Method of "The Authoritarian Personality" 252–254 (Christie and Jahoda eds. 1954).

3.  See T. Adorno, The Authoritarian Personality (1950).

Plaintiff claims error in striking certain of his answers and an answer of one of his witnesses, on direct examination, and instructing the jury to disregard them.  Plaintiff (nine years old at the time) was struck by a car going north in the middle lane of three northbound lanes of Kingshighway in St. Louis.  Plaintiff and a companion had crossed the three southbound lanes on the west side of the street and were standing by defendant's bus which was stopped in the western northbound lane near the middle line of the street.  Cars were stopped in that lane for a traffic light ahead.  Plaintiff said he started east across the northbound lanes when defendant's bus driver, Puhse, made a motion in that direction with his hand.  The negligence submitted by plaintiff's verdict-directing instruction was as follows:

> "that said bus was stopped south of Arthur Lee Smith; that Puhse saw Smith there; that thereafter, Puhse made a motion with his hand; that the motion was seen by Arthur Lee Smith; that the motion was one made with said hand diagonally from west to east; that the motion was made with the hand moving more rapidly from west to east than in any other direction; that at the time Puhse made the said motion, an automobile being driven by Harry Edward Bocklitz was in motion northwardly on Kingshighway; that it was moving alongside the bus in the lane immediately adjacent to the east side of the bus; that Puhse knew that the said automobile was in motion in such position at the time he made the said motion with his hand; that such motion was of such nature that a child of Arthur Lee Smith's then age, experience, and understanding would ordinarily take and understand it to be a sign or signal from Puhse to proceed eastwardly across Kingshighway; that Puhse failed to exercise ordinary care in making the said motion with his hand under such circumstances; that he was thereby negligent; that Arthur Lee Smith took and understood the said motion of Puhse's hand to be a sign or signal that he should proceed eastwardly across the street; that he then and there so proceeded; that in so doing, he came into the second traffic lane west of the east curb; that he was then and there struck by the automobile operated by the said Bocklitz."

The rulings concerning the answers of plaintiff and his companion Charles Harbert and their accounts about Puhse's actions were as follows:

(Plaintiff's testimony) "Q.  Now was there any other traffic on Kingshighway going north on Kingshighway that was south of you at the time that you were in the center of the street?  A.  There was some passing cars but we stood there until they had gone past before we had started—before the bus driver had motioned for us to go on across.

"Mr. Green: Objection, your Honor.  We object to the statement and ask that it be stricken as not being responsive.  It's a conclusion on the part of this witness.

"The Court: It may be stricken.

"Mr. Green: And the jury instructed to disregard it.

"The Court: The jury is so instructed to disregard it.   .   .   .

"Q.   And did anything happen while you were standing in that particular area in front of the bus?   A.   We waited there awhile and the bus driver motioned for us to cross.

"Mr. Green: Objection, your Honor.   Again we ask that that be stricken, that the jury be instructed to disregard it and, if necessary, that the witness be instructed not to refer repeatedly in that manner. He can tell what the operator did but he cannot tell what conclusions he drew from the operator's action.

"The Court: Objection sustained.   You can tell us, Arthur, what the operator did.

"Q.   (By Mr. Susman): Tell us, Arthur, what did the operator do at that time?   A.   He moved his hand diagonally.

"Q.   In which direction?   A.   Towards the east curb.

"Q.   And was that a—can you describe it more fully?   Was it a rapid motion, a slow motion or what kind of a motion was it?

"Mr. Green: Objection to the leading and suggestive nature of the question.

"The Court: Overruled.

"Q.   (By Mr. Susman): Describe the motion that he used.   A. He were moving his hand diagonally faster to the east curb than he was to the west curb.   .   .   .

"Q.   And when he moved his hand in this rapid fashion to the east curb as you have described what did you do then, if anything? A.   I started across the street."

(Harbert's testimony)   "Q.   While you were standing there in front of the bus did you see the bus driver do anything at all?   A. Yes.   Q.   What did you see him do?   A.   I saw the bus driver motion the direction of us to go east to the east side of the curb.

"Mr. Green: We'll object to this as being a conclusion on the part of the witness, what the motion meant.   We don't object to his testifying as to what the operator's hands did but we do object to the interpretation of what the operator meant.   Object to that and ask the jury be so instructed.

"The Court: Jury is so instructed.

"Q.   (By Mr. Susman): Describe in detail what this bus operator did that you saw?   A.   He motioned to the east curb.

"Q.   He motioned his hand to the east curb, you say?   A.   Yes.

"Q.   Did you see him do that?   A.   Yes.

"Q.   Were you looking at him at that time?   A.   Yes.

"Q.   And when he did that what did you do?   A.   We proceeded across."

The bus driver denied that he waved to the boys or motioned to them in any way.   Plaintiff had made a separate settlement with Bocklitz before the trial.

While these rulings of the trial court may have been technical they were technically correct. The answers stricken did state the witnesses' conclusions as to the bus driver's intention. It is argued that these answers represented the state of mind of plaintiff, a nine year old boy, but instead these answers undertook to represent the state of mind of the bus driver. It is also argued that these answers expressed to plaintiff and his companion an instant idea which could only be stated by them as "he motioned for us to go across" and could not be precisely reproduced to the jury exactly as it appeared to plaintiff and his companion in any other language. This contention is refuted by their testimony hereinabove set out in which they clearly described the kind of hand motions the bus driver made, the circumstances under which they were made, and how they acted when they saw these motions. This gave the jury all the facts needed for them to determine what the bus driver's motions meant to plaintiff and whether or not he started across because of them.

## QUESTIONS

1. Can you think of any good reasons why the legal system might wish to exclude plaintiff's testimony that the driver "motioned for" him to cross? Consider in this regard defense counsel's position that the witness could "tell what the operator *did* but he cannot tell what *conclusions he drew* from the operator's actions"; and that he could "testify as to what the operator's hands did but we do object to the *interpretation* of what the operator meant" (emphasis added).

Why was defense counsel opposed to the introduction of "conclusions" and "interpretations"? What assumptions about mental activity underlie the distinctions he was seeking to make? Is it possible to utter a statement about what someone *did*, simpliciter? Suppose you were told to "describe what you now see." Could you see— and state—what simply *is* in the world about you? Or would you be influenced by your (own) expectations; by your prior learning; by the language available to you, etc.?

2. From a technical legal point of view, three related evidence rules (all highly controversial) might have been available to the court to support its ruling: (a) that the testimony was "mere opinion" as to which the plaintiff had no knowledge,[4] (b) that it was a

---

4. 7 Wigmore, Evidence, § 1917, at 1–2: . . . The so-called Opinion Rule is in its scope much narrower than the term "opinion"; it deals with opinion in a special sense only. And it is not the only rule which may serve to raise an objection to opinion-testimony. . . .

. . .

[The] principle of *personal observation* came early into play in emphasizing the impropriety of testimony by one who speaks only from hearsay. This was probably what Lord Coke had in mind in the passage attributed to him in Adams v. Canon, in 1622:

"It is no satisfaction for a witness to say that he 'thinketh' or 'persuadeth himself,' and this for two reasons; first, because the judge is to give an absolute sentence, and for this ought to have a more sure ground than 'thinking'; secondly, the witness cannot be sued for perjury."

It is the phrases resorted to for expressing this principle that are here of interest. Such a witness is told by the Court: "That is mere opinion; we want what you *know*, not what you *think* or *believe*." This is one phrase

conjecture as to the driver's state of mind, a "fact" as to which the plaintiff could have had no knowledge;[5] and (c) that it went to the "very issue" that the jury had to decide.[6]

Even if the plaintiff's statement is understood as going to the driver's intention, (as the appellate court seems to have interpreted it), does it fall under any of these rules? As for (c), above, in view of the fact that this was a negligence action, (as opposed, say, to an action in which the driver were being charged with homicide) can one maintain that the driver's intent was "the very issue" for the jury?

As for (a), and (b), in what sense is it true that another's intentions cannot be perceived? Are statements as to another's intentions wholly unrelated to what one perceives? Conversely, is a statement that someone "was moving his hand diagonally faster from the east curb to the west curb" wholly "pure" of one's "opinions"?

3. Suppose that instead of predicating a distinction between (i) what one perceives and (ii) inferences from and about that which one perceives, the judge had asked himself which of the two forms of statements, if introduced, would most effectively further the goals of a negligence trial and the integrity of the court system. Would he have come to the same result?

For example, in terms of getting before the jury how "an average reasonable man" would have reacted in the boy's position, is the statement the boy was allowed to give a better indicator than "he motioned us to cross"? In what sense did the boy actually and honestly *see* the driver "moving his hand diagonally faster to the east than to the west side of the curb"? Are people apt to "see" such details, when they have no special reason to attend to them? Is it more demanding intellectually to perceive "a table" than to perceive the complicated variegation of shades and shapes that make up a table?

4. Can you restate a rule of evidence for the Smith case based upon the materials that follow and their skepticism towards the

of contrast which the Court might use,—the contrast between knowing (*i.e.* personally observing) and opining (*i.e.* believing without sufficient observation).

But there is another phrase; the judge might say, "We want not your *opinion*; have you any *facts*? For we can guess and opine as well as you can; tell us facts if you have them." This demand for "facts" means, as before, some real or positive grounds of knowledge in the witness. The principle of objection which the judge has in mind is the same in both cases; he will have knowledge, not opinion—facts, not opinion.

5. *Id.* § 3661, at 773 (3d ed. 1940): . . . Testimony to Another Per-

son's State of Mind. The argument has been made that, because we cannot directly see, hear, or feel the state of another person's mind, therefore testimony to another person's state of mind is based on merely conjectural and therefore inadequate data.

6. *Id.* § 1921, at 18: . . . (3) OPINIONS ON THE VERY ISSUE BEFORE THE JURY. Another erroneous test, prevalent in some regions . . . is that an opinion can never be received when it touches "the very issue before the jury":

1883, ELLIOTT, J., in Yost v. Conroy, 92 Ind. 471: "It is a general rule that a witness cannot be allowed to express an opinion upon the exact question which the jury are required to decide."

naive realist view of perception?  Consider also what account should be given to the fact that counsel for the bus company can always bring out further details by cross-examination.

The revised draft of the Proposed Rules of Evidence for the United States Courts and Magistrates, 88, 91 S.Ct. 88 (No. 12 (pamphlet 1971)), provides at Rule 701:

## OPINION TESTIMONY BY LAY WITNESSES

If the witness is not testifying as an expert, his testimony in the form of opinions or inferences is limited to those opinions or inferences which are (a) rationally based on the perception of the witness and (b) helpful to a clear understanding of his testimony or the determination of a fact in issue.

### Advisory Committees' Note

The rule retains the traditional objective of putting the trier of fact in possession of an accurate reproduction of the event.

Limitation (a) is the familiar requirement of first-hand knowledge or observation.

Limitation (b) is phrased in terms of requiring testimony to be helpful in resolving issues.  Witnesses often find difficulty in expressing themselves in language which is not that of an opinion or conclusion.  While the courts have made concessions in certain recurring situations, necessity as a standard for permitting opinions and conclusions has proved too elusive and too unadaptable to particular situations for purposes of satisfactory judicial administration.  McCormick § 11.  Moreover, the practical impossibility of determining by rule what is a "fact," demonstrated by a century of litigation of the question of what is a fact for purposes of pleading under the Field Code, extends into evidence also.  7 Wigmore § 1919.  The rule assumes that the natural characteristics of the adversary system will generally lead to an acceptable result, since the detailed account carries more conviction than the broad assertion, and a lawyer can be expected to display his witness to the best advantage.

What problems do you foresee arising from the use of the term "rationally based"?  How far can the provisions of (b) go towards solving them?

## CHOICE v. THE STATE OF GEORGIA

31 Ga. 424 (1860)

LUMPKIN, J.

. . .

The next assignment is, that the Court erred in allowing Luther J. Glenn and J. A. Hayden to give their opinions as to the sanity or insanity of the prisoner; and in allowing them to give their statements, that "the prisoner was drinking," when such statements were made as conclusions, and not as facts.

. . . .

Before dismissing, finally, this fourth exception, upon which I am fully conscious of having occupied too much time already, I would suggest, that it does not fairly represent the testimony of Glenn and Hayden. Their testimony, when taken altogether, is wholly unexceptionable. Glenn, for instance, says "prisoner, *from his appearance*, had been drinking;" and Hayden, upon his cross-examination, swore, that, "although he did not see Choice drinking, yet he judged, *from his manner and appearance*, that he had been drinking; had seen him frequently in that condition before."

By reading the testimony, it will be seen that expressions similar to that excepted to, abound on every page of it. The witness, Gregory, says: "Saw prisoner a short time before he left Rome for Atlanta; had been drinking several days; does not know that he was drinking; *was acting like a man who had been drinking.*" Again, by the same: "thought, at the time he left Rome, the exciting cause of prisoner's insanity was liquor." Echols testified: "Prisoner appeared to be drinking; witness supposed him to be drunk." Bartlett, sworn: "Did seem like a drunken man."

After such expressions as these, selected almost at random from the answers of the prisoner's witnesses, it would seem rather captious to object to the statements of Glenn and Hayden, that prisoner "appeared to be drinking." Such expressions, both in ordinary life and in the Courts, convey to the mind, with sufficient certainty, the condition of a person, so as to enable one to pronounce a decision thereon, with reasonable assurance of its truth. Really, no other rule is practicable. If the witness must be confined to a simple narration of facts, how the person leered or grinned, how he winked his eyes or squinted, how he wagged his head, etc., all of which drunken men do, you shut out, not only the ordinary, but the best mode of obtaining truth.

QUESTIONS

How does the position of the judge in the *Choice* case differ from that of the Judge in *Smith*? What does the judge mean in suggesting that to prohibit a witness from describing someone as "drunken" will "shut out, not only the ordinary, but the best mode of obtaining truth"? Can you support his view from the materials that follow? Suppose that the witness, instead of using the word "drunken", had to break down his observations into "leered", "tottered", "staggered", etc. Are these ultimate perceptual categories, or do they, too, reflect intellectual synthesis? Could "leered" be further broken down into perceptual components? As the process progresses, are we getting closer to the sort of description that the legal system wants? In what sense of "reality" are we getting "closer to reality"? In what sense are we getting farther away? Are we getting closer to presenting what different observers would agree to having seen?

*JOHN LOCKE*

OF IDEAS *

CHAPTER I.

Of Ideas in General, and Their Original

SECT. 1. *Idea is the object of thinking.*—Every man being conscious to himself that he thinks, and that which his mind is applied about whilst thinking, being the ideas that are there, it is past doubt, that men have in their minds several ideas, such as are those expressed by the words whiteness, hardness, sweetness, thinking, motion, man, elephant, army, drunkenness, and others. It is in the first place then to be inquired, how he comes by them. . . .

SECT. 2. *All ideas come from sensation or reflection.*—Let us then suppose the mind to be, as we say, white paper, void of all characters, without any ideas; how comes it to be furnished? Whence comes it by that vast store which the busy and boundless fancy of man has painted on it, with an almost endless variety? Whence has it all the materials of reason and knowledge? To this I answer in one word, from experience; in that all our knowledge is founded, and from that it ultimately derives itself. Our observation employed either about external sensible objects, or about the internal operations of our minds, perceived and reflected on by ourselves, is that which supplies our understandings with all the materials of thinking. These two are the fountains of knowledge, from whence all the ideas we have, or can naturally have, do spring.

. . . . .

SECT. 25. *In the reception of simple ideas, the understanding is for the most part passive.*—In this part the understanding is merely passive; and whether or no it will have these beginnings, and, as it were, materials of knowledge, is not in its own power. For the objects of our senses do, many of them, obtrude their particular ideas upon our minds, whether we will or no; and the operations of our minds will not let us be without, at least, some obscure notions of them. No man can be wholly ignorant of what he does when he thinks. These simple ideas, when offered to the mind, the understanding can no more refuse to have, nor alter, when they are imprinted, nor blot them out, and make new ones itself, than a mirror can refuse, alter, or obliterate the images or ideas which the objects set before it do therein produce. As the bodies that surround us do diversely affect our organs, the mind is forced to receive the impressions, and cannot avoid the perception of those ideas that are annexed to them.

* From An Essay Concerning Human
Understanding (Bk. II, c. 1) 75–76, 83
(Hayes & Zell 1860).

BERTRAND RUSSELL

## APPEARANCE AND REALITY *

Is there any knowledge in the world which is so certain that no reasonable man could doubt it? This question, which at first sight might not seem difficult, is really one of the most difficult that can be asked. When we have realized the obstacles in the way of a straightforward and confident answer, we shall be well launched on the study of philosophy—for philosophy is merely the attempt to answer such ultimate questions, not carelessly and dogmatically, as we do in ordinary life and even in the sciences, but critically, after exploring all that makes such questions puzzling, and after realizing all the vagueness and confusion that underlie our ordinary ideas.

In daily life, we assume as certain many things which, on a closer scrutiny, are found to be so full of apparent contradictions that only a great amount of thought enables us to know what it is that we really may believe. In the search for certainty, it is natural to begin with our present experiences, and in some sense, no doubt, knowledge is to be derived from them. But any statement as to what it is that our immediate experiences make us know is very likely to be wrong. It seems to me that I am now sitting in a chair, at a table of a certain shape, on which I see sheets of paper with writing or print. By turning my head I see out of the window buildings and clouds and the sun. I believe that the sun is about ninety-three million miles from the earth; that it is a hot globe many times bigger than the earth; that, owing to the earth's rotation, it rises every morning, and will continue to do so for an indefinite time in the future. I believe that, if any other normal person comes into my room, he will see the same chairs and tables and books and papers as I see, and that the table which I see is the same as the table which I feel pressing against my arm. All this seems to be so evident as to be hardly worth stating, except in answer to a man who doubts whether I know anything. Yet all this may be reasonably doubted, and all of it requires much careful discussion before we can be sure that we have stated it in a form that is wholly true.

To make our difficulties plain, let us concentrate attention on the table. To the eye it is oblong, brown and shiny, to the touch it is smooth and cool and hard; when I tap it, it gives out a wooden sound. Any one else who sees and feels and hears the table will agree with this description, so that it might seem as if no difficulty would arise; but as soon as we try to be more precise our troubles begin. Although I believe that the table is "really" of the same colour all over, the parts that reflect the light look much brighter than the other parts, and some parts look white because of reflected light. I know that, if I move, the parts that reflect the light will be different, so that the apparent distribution of colours on the table

* From The Problems of Philosophy 7–12 (Galaxy Book ed. 1959).

will change.   It follows that if several people are looking at the table at the same moment, no two of them will see exactly the same distribution of colours, because no two can see it from exactly the same point of view, and any change in the point of view makes some change in the way the light is reflected.

For most practical purposes these differences are unimportant, but to the painter they are all-important: the painter has to unlearn the habit of thinking that things seem to have the colour which common sense says they "really" have, and to learn the habit of seeing things as they appear.   Here we have already the beginning of one of the distinctions that cause most trouble in philosophy—the distinction between "appearance" and "reality," between what things seem to be and what they are.   The painter wants to know what things seem to be, the practical man and the philosopher want to know what they are; but the philosopher's wish to know this is stronger than the practical man's, and is more troubled by knowledge as to the difficulties of answering the question.

To return to the table.   It is evident from what we have found, that there is no colour which preeminently appears to be *the* colour of the table, or even of any one particular part of the table—it appears to be of different colours from different points of view, and there is no reason for regarding some of these as more really its colour than others.   And we know that even from a given point of view the colour will seem different by artificial light, or to a colour-blind man, or to a man wearing blue spectacles, while in the dark there will be no colour at all, though to touch and hearing the table will be unchanged.   This colour is not something which is inherent in the table, but something depending upon the table and the spectator and the way the light falls on the table.   When, in ordinary life, we speak of *the* colour of the table, we only mean the sort of colour which it will seem to have to a normal spectator from an ordinary point of view under usual conditions of light.   But the other colours which appear under other conditions have just as good a right to be considered real; and therefore, to avoid favouritism, we are compelled to deny that, in itself, the table has any one particular colour.

The same thing applies to the texture.   With the naked eye one can see the grain, but otherwise the table looks smooth and even. If we looked at it through a microscope, we should see roughnesses and hills and valleys, and all sorts of differences that are imperceptible to the naked eye.   Which of these is the "real" table?   We are naturally tempted to say that what we see through the microscope is more real, but that in turn would be changed by a still more powerful microscope.   If, then, we cannot trust what we see with the naked eye, why should we trust what we see through a microscope?   Thus, again, the confidence in our senses with which we began deserts us.

The *shape* of the table is no better.   We are all in the habit of judging as to the "real" shapes of things, and we do this so unreflectingly that we come to think we actually see the real shapes. But, in fact, as we all have to learn if we try to draw, a given thing looks different in shape from every different point of view. If our table is "really" rectangular, it will look, from almost all points of view, as if it had two acute angles and two obtuse angles. If opposite sides are parallel, they will look as if they converged to a point away from the spectator; if they are of equal length, they will look as if the nearer side were longer. All these things are not commonly noticed in looking at a table, because experience has taught us to construct the "real" shape from the apparent shape, and the "real" shape is what interests us as practical men. But the "real" shape is not what we see; it is something inferred from what we see. And what we see is constantly changing in shape as we move about the room; so that here again the senses seem not to give us the truth about the table itself, but only about the appearance of the table.

Similar difficulties arise when we consider the sense of touch. It is true that the table always gives us a sensation of hardness, and we feel that it resists pressure. But the sensation we obtain depends upon how hard we press the table and also upon what part of the body we press with; thus the various sensations due to various pressures or various parts of the body cannot be supposed to reveal *directly* any definite property of the table, but at most to be *signs* of some property which perhaps *causes* all the sensations, but is not actually apparent in any of them. And the same applies still more obvious to the sounds which can be elicited by rapping the table.

Thus it becomes evident that the real table, if there is one, is not the same as what we immediately experience by sight or touch or hearing. The real table, if there is one, is not *immediately* known to us at all, but must be an inference from what is immediately known. Hence, two very difficult questions at once arise; namely, (1) Is there a real table at all? (2) If so, what sort of object can it be?

It will help us in considering these questions to have a few simple terms of which the meaning is definite and clear. Let us give the name of "sense-data" to ·the things that are immediately known in sensation: such things as colours, sounds, smells, hardnesses, roughnesses, and so on. We shall give the name "sensation" to the experience of being immediately aware of these things. Thus, whenever we see a colour, we have a sensation *of* the colour, but the colour itself is a sense-datum, not a sensation. The colour is that *of* which we are immediately aware, and the awareness itself is the sensation. It is plain that if we are to know anything about the table, it must be by means of the sense-data—brown colour, oblong shape, smoothness, etc.—which we associate with the table; but, for the reasons which have been given, we cannot say that the table *is* the sense-data, or even that the sense-data are directly properties of the table. Thus a problem arises as to the relation of the sense-data to the real table, supposing there is such a thing.

QUESTIONS

1. In Russell's view, to what extent is that which we claim to know through perception "what simply exists"—and to what extent does it bear the stamp of a highly complex mental operation?

Is it meaningful to say of perceiving what we say of mathematical calculations—that, for example, it can be done stupidly or intelligently? Can we be trained to perceive? How? What does your answer suggest as to how much our judgments about the world are objective reports—pure and simple—of sense data received by the brain?

2. What does Russell's position suggest with respect to the distinction suggested in *Smith* between "he was moving his hand diagonally faster to the east curb than to the west curb" and "he motioned us to cross"? Can we say that the one statement is simply a report of what the driver *did* but the other is an *interpretation?* Can you subject the perceptual basis for the former statement to the sort of analysis Russell makes of our perception of a table?


ALFRED NORTH WHITEHEAD

SYMBOLISM: ITS MEANING AND EFFECT *

There is still another symbolism more fundamental than any of the foregoing types. We look up and see a coloured shape in front of us, and we say,—there is a chair. But what we have seen is the mere coloured shape. Perhaps an artist might not have jumped to the notion of a chair. He might have stopped at the mere contemplation of a beautiful colour and a beautiful shape. But those of us who are not artists are very prone, especially if we are tired, to pass straight from the perception of the coloured shape to the enjoyment of the chair, in some way of use, or of emotion, or of thought. We can easily explain this passage by reference to a train of difficult logical inference, whereby, having regard to our previous experiences of various shapes and various colours, we draw the probable conclusion that we are in the presence of a chair. I am very sceptical as to the high-grade character of the mentality required to get from the coloured shape to the chair. One reason for this scepticism is that my friend the artist, who kept himself to the contemplation of colour, shape and position, was a very highly trained man, and had acquired this facility of ignoring the chair at the cost of great labour. We do not require elaborate training merely in order to refrain from embarking upon intricate trains of inference. Such abstinence is only too easy. Another reason for scepticism is that if we had been accompanied by a puppy dog, in addition to the artist, the dog would have acted immediately on the hypothesis of a chair and would have jumped onto it by way of using it as such. Again, if the dog had refrained from such action, it would have been because it was a well-trained dog. Therefore the transition from a coloured shape to the notion of an object which can be used for all sorts of purposes

which have nothing to do with colour, seems to be a very natural
one; and we—men and puppy dogs—require careful training if we
are to refrain from acting upon it.

## Questions

1. In what way does Whitehead's analysis represent a "caveat"
to Russell's? What bearing do Whitehead's observations have on the
problem of the *Smith* case? Is a "higher grade character of mentality" called for in the perception expressed by the statement, "he
motioned us to cross" than in the perception expressed by the statement, "he moved his hand diagonally faster from the east curb than
to the west curb"? Does your answer suggest arguments as to the
propriety of the court's ruling?

2. What, if anything, do the views of Whitehead have in common with those of James and Langer, which follow?


*WILLIAM JAMES*

### Reflex Action and Theism *

The world's contents are *given* to each of us in an order so foreign
to our subjective interest that we can hardly by an effort of the
imagination picture to ourselves what it is like. We have to break
that order altogether,—and by picking out from it the items which
concerns us, and connecting them with others far away, which we
say "belong" with them, we are able to make out definite threads of
sequence and tendency; to foresee particular liabilities and get ready
for them; and to enjoy simplicity and harmony in place of what was
chaos. Is not the sum of your actual experience taken at this moment
and impartially added together an utter chaos? The strains of my
voice, the lights and shades inside the room and out, the murmur of
the wind, the ticking of the clock, the various organic feelings you
may happen individually to possess, do these make a whole at all?
Is it not the only condition of your mental sanity in the midst of them
that most of them should become non-existent for you, and that a few
others—the sounds, I hope, which I am uttering—should evoke from
places in your memory that have nothing to do with this scene
associates fitted to combine with them in what we call a rational
train of thought,—rational, because it leads to a conclusion which
we have some organ to appreciate? We have no organ or faculty
to appreciate the simply given order. . . .

### Notes and Questions

In what ways do the views presented by James differ from those
of Locke? What additional considerations is James suggesting as a
determinant of what we perceive? What would happen to us if our
brains were allowed to receive every possible stimulus from the outside world?

* From The Will to Believe and Other
Essays 118 (Dover ed. 1956).

Aldous Huxley, in Doors of Perception 22–23 (1954) quotes with approval the position of C. D. Broad that

". . . we should do well to consider much more seriously than we have hitherto been inclined to do the type of theory which Bergson put forward in connection with memory and sense perception. The suggestion is that the function of the brain and nervous system and sense organs is in the main *eliminative* and not productive. Each person is at each moment capable of remembering all that has ever happened to him and of perceiving everything that is happening everywhere in the universe. The function of the brain and nervous system is to protect us from being overwhelmed and confused by this mass of largely useless and irrelevant knowledge, by shutting out most of what we should otherwise perceive or remember at any moment, and leaving only that very small and special selection which is likely to be practically useful."

Huxley observes that on this view, each human is potentially "Mind at Large". Biological survival demands that the potential of Mind at Large must be "funneled through the reducing valve of the brain and nervous system." Huxley viewed psychoactive drugs, such as the mescaline he experimented with, as in some way cancelling out the brain's filtering capacity. With the brain inoperative, thought was allowed to by-pass the constraints of symbol-systems such as language, which by their very nature delimit the categories of perception and thought. (For a discussion of this position, see the selection from Henle, *infra* at 159.)

In support of the position that the "increased awareness" of drug states owes to a chemically induced neutralizing of agents necessary for brain functioning, see D. X. Freedman, *Aspects of the Biochemical Pharmacology of Psychotropic Drugs* in Psychiatric Drugs (P. Solomon, Ed. 1966).

*Susanne K. Langer*

## Discursive and Presentational Forms *

Our merest sense-experience is a process of *formulation*. The world that actually meets our senses is not a world of "things," about which we are invited to discover facts as soon as we have codified the necessary logical language to do so; the world of pure sensation is so complex, so fluid and full, that sheer sensitivity to stimuli would only encounter what William James has called (in characteristic phrase) "a blooming, buzzing confusion." Out of this bedlam our sense-organs must select certain predominant forms, if they are to make report of *things* and not of mere dissolving sensa. The eye and the ear must have their logic—their "categories of understand-

* From Philosophy in a New Key 89–91 (3rd ed. Harvard U. Press 1957). Copyright 1942, 1951, 1957 by the President and Fellows of Harvard College. Reprinted by permission of Harvard University Press.

ing," if you like the Kantian idiom, or their "primary imagination," in Coleridge's version of the same concept. An object is not a datum, but a form construed by the sensitive and intelligent organ, a form which is at once an experienced individual thing and a symbol for the concept of it, for *this sort of thing.*

A tendency to organize the sensory field into groups and patterns of sense-data, to perceive forms rather than a flux of light-impressions, seems to be inherent in our receptor apparatus just as much as in the higher nervous centers with which we do arithmetic and logic. But this unconscious appreciation of forms is the primitive root of all abstraction, which in turn is the keynote of rationality; so it appears that the conditions for rationality lie deep in our pure animal experience—in our power of perceiving, in the elementary functions of our eyes and ears and fingers. Mental life begins with our mere physiological constitution. A little reflection shows us that, since no experience occurs more than once, so-called "repeated" experiences are really *analogous* occurrences, all fitting a form that was abstracted on the first occasion. *Familiarity* is nothing but the quality of fitting very neatly into the form of a previous experience. I believe our ingrained habit of hypostatizing impressions, of seeing *things* and not sense-data, rests on the fact that we promptly and unconsciously abstract a form from each sensory experience, and use this form to *conceive* the experience as a whole, as a "thing."

.    .    .    .

.    .    . In other words, the activity of our senses is "mental" not only when it reaches the brain, but in its very inception, whenever the alien world outside impinges on the furthest and smallest receptor. All sensitivity bears the stamp of mentality. "Seeing," for instance, is not a passive process, by which meaningless impressions are stored up for the use of an organizing mind, which construes forms out of these amorphous data to suit its own purposes. "Seeing" is itself a process of formulation; our understanding of the visible world begins in the eye.

This psychological insight, which we owe to the school of Wertheimer, Köhler, and Koffka, has far-reaching philosophical consequences, if we take it seriously; for it carries rationality into processes that are usually deemed pre-rational, and points to the existence of forms, i. e. of *possible symbolic material,* at a level where symbolic activity has certainly never been looked for any epistemologist. The eye and the ear make their own abstractions, and consequently dictate their own peculiar forms of conception.

NOTES AND QUESTIONS

1. In what ways is the view of perception discussed by Langer like, and unlike, those of James and Locke, respectively? In what ways is James more like Locke than Langer?

The capacity of the human eye to impress forms on "reality" is explored in R. L. GREGORY, THE INTELLIGENT EYE (1970.) According to Gregory, mechanical "eyes" such as those that operate elevator doors cannot be made with the capacity to process data; whereas the human eye is somehow capable of "seeing the present with stored objects from the past."

2. The gestaltist view (or views) may be illustrated by considering the diagram below.

```
                   .
                   .
                   .
       .   .   .   .   .   .   .
                   .
                   .
                   .
```

What do you "see"? K. Koffka points out that in our "behavioural field" there is a cross. He adds that "in reality in the geographical environment, there is no cross, there are just [thirteen] dots in a certain geometrical arrangement." PRINCIPLES OF GESTALT PSYCHOLOGY 76–77 (1936). You might consider how Koffka uses the term "in reality"; is he suggesting that the "geographical environment" defines "reality" more than our behavioural field? Does it make sense to use "reality" in this way?

3. Does the position that perception is active and formulative entail that something like "values" or even individual physiological differences are necessarily involved in any instance of seeing, hearing, smelling, etc.? Is it possible to accept the view that perception is in some sense formulative, without supposing that individuals formulate differently? What additional assumptions have to be made in order to sustain the position that "values" are involved?

4. How far do the materials that follow go towards establishing that our perceptions are not merely biologically "given", but subject to development and variations among societies and even, within the same society, between different individuals?

What is the significance for the law?

GARDNER MURPHY, LOIS MURPHY & THEODORE NEWCOMB

EXPERIMENTAL SOCIAL PSYCHOLOGY *

The world to which the child is introduced is a world of complex and multitudinous impressions, a world of sound, touch and pain, a world of stress and relaxation. Much that is sharp and clear to the adult is confused or undifferentiated to the child. There is probably always a figure and a ground, probably an endless *selection* from the whirl and welter of impressions. We know, however, neither the mechanism of selection nor the content selected, except in so far as behavior at the moment or thereafter reveals it.

* From 215–21 (rev. ed. 1937). Copyright 1931, 1937 by Harper & Row     Publishers, Inc. Reprinted by permission of the publishers.

This first world of the child is certainly not a social world in any true psychological sense. The mother's face is responded to just as a light is responded to. The mother's voice is responded to in about the same way as any other sound of equal volume. From the flux of impressions pouring in through the senses all the time, some aspects must be chosen and emphasized. The choice is largely in terms of aspects of experience which help or hinder the activity in progress; these are selected over all that is irrelevant to social activity. The mother's preparations for nursing are soon selected in this way; they lead to the cessation of crying and the appearance of a smile. The selection is not, as a rule, the selection of isolated elements but of related organized features of experience. One signal indicating specific satisfying experience about to be realized is, for example, a pattern including eyes, nose and mouth. The patterns of things as they are must in time be recognized as patterns because they function in this way. The social world, then, is given accent in terms of what it means for our own organic activity, and the accent usually falls upon patterns, clusters of experienced qualities which regularly recur together.

. . . .

Much of the process of learning to group and organize impressions is still easily observed in the adult. In a surface covered with scattered dots or in the panoply of the heavens one may see various and changing patterns or constellations. Patterns vary with the person and with the occasion, but they are all patterns limited by the material. Different persons and different cultures select and organize and give their own meanings to such material. The same stars which for the Egyptians were a Wagon, for the Romans Seven Oxen, for the Arabs the Great Bear, present material which in fact consists of a schema for each of these things. The social definition of reality is not the arbitrary imposing of subjective caprice; it is the fulfillment of one specific reality partly given in the material.

An experimental illustration from Calley will be helpful. On the surface of a piece of paper one observes with rigid fixation the development of a definite grain of vertical or horizontal lines or indeed of diagonals or curved lines. By changing the mental set one sees on the surface of the paper a flower or a death's head. These patterns are as objective as is the whole piece of paper itself. If the material is taken to the testing laboratory the physicist reports an extremely complex, mottled surface of tiny protuberances and hollows, thousands of high and low points. There are, then, in the "smooth surface" plenty of vertical, horizontal, oblique and curved lines. All that is necessary is to select and to reject, to see certain patterns and to remain blind to others. The individual sees what he wants to see, not in the sense that he manufactures out of whole cloth but in the sense that he appropriates to himself, from what is given, the pattern that he needs. So it is with social reality. The child learns, as he grows, to take what is meaningful to his culture and, in addition, what is specially meaningful to himself. He learns to see social reality not "as it is"; he learns to respond to it not "as it is." The adult works out an analysis of it in his study, not as it is, but as it impresses itself upon his own selective awareness, his own competence, his own interest in making sense out of it.

Not only do social factors participate prominently in the formation of early percepts, but they appear to give special weight to percepts of human situations. We learn to perceive things in a social world which stresses or values some patterns more than others. Response to the sight and sound of others is frequently a biologically dominant response; other factors may become important because of their association with the social. To use Holt's terminology, adience to the objects of the social world makes them pivotal features in the construction of the whole world of perception.

This is not merely suggested by the everyday activity of children and adults, but is experimentally supported by two lines of research. First, after controlling the size, shape, color and other features of postage stamps, it has been possible to show that sheer acceptance of the stamp as a stamp of one's own country gives it an apparent size greater than that of control stamps. It is actually bigger because it belongs to one's own nationality. This overvaluing tendency remains in the case of unfamiliar stamps which the subjects accept as American stamps on the basis of the experimenter's assertion. Control subjects in Canada give the same special weight to the stamps of their own nation. (Sheer degree of familiarity is an insufficient explanation of the results.) The valuing tendency alters the apparent size of objects in other ways. Three-cent stamps are judged bigger than two-cent stamps of exactly the same physical dimensions. Thus social habits participate in the determination of the percept, and the degree of their participation is measurable.

. . . .

Outstanding in the study of social factors in perception is the work of Sherif. Each percept in the social world is shown to depend upon a frame of reference, both its quality and its quantity being defined relative to this frame. The frame itself goes back genetically to earlier frames, and we might at times be lost in conjecture as to the earliest infantile patterns of perception. But at the time set for any experiment we must discover the frames of reference actively functioning. The Trobrianders, believing that sons resemble fathers but never the other sons of the same father, cannot see fraternal resemblances which to the ethnologist seem striking indeed. They protest against the bad taste and the lack of "common sense" of him who declares that brothers resemble one another. Data are organized to show that all social life involves arbitrary classification in terms of those resemblances and differences which are stylized within the group.

The next step is a systematic search through the literature of experimental psychology to show the role of frames of reference in controlling laboratory behavior. Here, again, objects are perceived with reference to a personal or social frame of reference which is found to involve the same interplay of outer and inner factors (structure of the stimulus world and structure of the organism) that are found elsewhere. The result is to show the applicability of quantitative concepts to all social frames of reference.

Third, a laboratory situation is set up in which social factors determine a reference frame which must be used by the subject in perceiving. A single point of light in a dark room may be located here or there, may move up and down or in circles or in any defined direction. The fact that the outer world now has no organization at all beyond the simple relation of figure and ground permits inner factors of expectation or suggestion to exercise an overwhelming influence. In one situation the experimenter himself, in another a second subject acting side by side with the first, in a third situation a larger group of subjects, define for the individual the nature and extent of the movement perceived. The relative effects of one and of several companions in the group situation, and the relative prestige value of various subjects for one another, are defined and carefully measured. Thus an advanced student of psychology, primed in advance as to the judgments of direction and extent which he should give, established the general range and central tendency followed by a more *naive* subject. When a single subject experienced this stimulus situation alone and was then transferred to the group situation, he usually abandoned his personal habit and assimilated a *norm* as defined by the behavior of other members of the group. After he had served in three experimental studies of one hour each, rendering judgments in the group situation, he retained, when alone, the habits of judgment acquired in the group situation. Here we have a well-defined clue as to the way in which social norms continue to function even when the individual is no longer in the presence of those from whom the norm was acquired.

Sherif shows in the light of Piaget's data that moral judgments conform to the same laws found in the study of judgments regarding extent of movement. Of special importance in the moral judgments, however, is the participation of value tendencies, each of which has arisen in a social situation and continues to have its effect in the situation calling for moral judgment. Value tendencies directed toward the ego are of special weight. The research on ego level and aspiration level . . . is shown to fit the same general picture as the Piaget material and Sherif's laboratory study.

. . . .

. . . . As language and the system of images develop, the child builds up an "inner world" in contrast to the "outer world." As the words and gestures which symbolize social reality are given less overt expression, he learns to maintain orientation to the world and to himself by an inner system of signaling. Whether this inner system is largely verbal or not is immaterial to the present issue. The essential point is that the social controls which in the very small child are external to the organism are, in the older individual, largely interiorized. Throughout his working hours the individual signals to himself as to the direction to be taken, the right vs. the wrong, the wise vs. the foolish. We do not, however, mean to imply that this process is carried out with full consciousness. In fact, what was said above regarding subliminal conditioning applies with a

vengeance to the complex process of maintaining a direction through
the day's work. The impulses to act are frequently touched off by
inner signals too faint to be noticed: "I don't know why I did that."
Subliminal cues, new outlooks on life, new insights into problems
come constantly out of an inner void which has long baffled investigation. Civilized man is, we think, to an extraordinary degree a
proprioceptive animal whose culture, once a part of his external
world, is now a part of his bodily make-up, functioning with equal
freedom at levels known and levels unknown to his personal awareness.

QUESTIONS

1. Compare the observations of Murphy *et al.* with the passage
from Langer, above. Note that Langer says "A tendency to organize
the sensory field into groups  .  .  .  seems to be inherent in our
receptor apparatus," while Murphy *et al.* speak of a "choice" which
"is largely in terms of aspects of experience which help or hinder the
activity in progress". Are these positions inconsistent? Are there
only two alternatives—that the forms with which we organize experience are inherent *or* that they are subject to a "choice" that is resolved
by the individual's appropriating "from what is given, the pattern
that he needs"? Is it ever possible that individuals—and societies—
develop percepts that they don't "need"—that are, indeed, self-
destructive?

2. What is the bearing on the *Smith* controversy of the suggestion that we learn to "see" those things which help or hinder our
engagement in social activities? What do you suppose Murphy would
testify as an expert witness on the point of whether, as a matter of
perception theory, the plaintiff actually and honestly "saw" (a) the
driver's hand move diagonally faster to the east curb than to the west
curb rather than (b) the driver motion for him to cross?

3. From a larger perspective, on Murphy's view, can we say that
we apply the law to what we see? Or is what we see a function, in
part, of the law?

4. What are Murphy *et al.* suggesting as to the effect on perception of our ideas of "the right vs. the wrong, the wise vs. the
foolish"? What arguments can be made for and against the proposition that our perceptions are not only judgments, but value judgments?
To the extent this view can be supported, how "value-free" can legal
inquiry be?

5. What is the suggested relationship between one's sense of
self—of how one defines who he is—and what he perceives? How does
one's "inner system of signalling" which Murphy *et al.* describe operate to "maintain orientation to the world and to himself"?

Consider in this regard the following from S. H. Hayakawa.

The Darwinism of the man in the street accepts as given
the notion that self-preservation is the first law of life.
However, the idea of self-preservation is a biological ideal
which cannot, without extension or refinement or some

sophistry, be extended to account for the complexities of human behavior. . . .

. . .

Once you grasp the fundamental semantic idea that man is a symbolic class of life—this is Korzybski's formulation—once you grasp that all human behavior is conditioned by, shaped by, mediated by symbols, then the idea of self-preservation as the first law of life can be modified quite simply to include human behavior, by a simple re-statement, as follows:
. . . The basic purpose of all human activity is the protection, the maintenance, and the enhancement, *not of the self, but of the self-concept, or symbolic self.*

Next, let me give you a definition of the self-concept. "The self-concept or self-structure may be thought of as an organized configuration of perceptions of the self which are admissible to awareness" (Rogers). Human beings are hopelessly addicted to the processes of abstraction, symbolization, and of talking to themselves, not only about the universe around them, but about themselves. Hence, human beings, in addition to abstracting from and symbolizing the data of their environment, abstract and symbolize about themselves. And each of us, therefore, possesses not only a self, but a concept of self.

. . .

. . . Our environment is not a given, obvious fact. When ten of us walk down the same street, we actually see ten different environments, because each of the ten men have different sets of values, different ideas and different interests and, therefore, we do not actually inhabit the same environment. The self-concept, in a sense, creates the environment to which we react.

I will give a very elementary illustration of this. In a shop window, let us say, there are 75 hats, every one of them a potential stimulus. It is conceivable for a man or woman to walk by that shop window without even looking. But, let us say that one woman walks by—and, as she sees one of the hats she thinks "I must have that—That's for me" and she stops dead, and busy as she is, she has to dash in and get it before she can go on. Now, why is it that that one item in a complex environment almost comes out of that environment to hit her in the eye? The point I am making is that the self-concept determines perception, because, since the purpose of the organism is to constantly enhance the self-concept, if there is something in the environment that would be enhancing to that self-concept, your perceptual processes almost reach out in the environment for those things that enhance the self-concept. She is going in to buy that hat, which is going to look real good on her self-concept, although it may look like hell on her! [7]

7. The Self-Concept—Why We Reject
Some Ideas and Accept Others 15
Jour. Dental Med. 3, (1960).

*PAUL HENLE*

## LANGUAGE, THOUGHT, AND CULTURE *

Ordinarily, language is taken for granted. Its fluent and easy use leads to the assumption that it is a transparent medium for the transmission of thought. Because it offers no apparent obstacle to our customary flow of ideas, one assumes that it is a vehicle equally fitted to convey any beliefs. Scientifically, it is assumed to be of interest to linguists and perhaps to psychologists interested in child development or aphasia, but that is all. Such a conception of language has been challenged by a number of linguists and anthropologists. Edward Sapir, more than twenty years ago, maintained that:

> The relation between language and experience is often misunderstood. Language is not merely a more or less systematic inventory of the various items of experience which seem relevant to the individual, as is so often naively assumed, but is also a self-contained, creative symbolic organization, which not only refers to experience largely acquired without its help but actually defines experience for us by reason of its formal completeness and because of our unconscious projection of its implicit expectations into the field of experience.

Sapir added that the force of this claim could be realized only when the relatively similar Indo-European languages were compared with widely differing languages such as those indigenous to Africa and America.

Benjamin Lee Whorf in a series of papers has developed Sapir's claim, maintaining that a language constitutes a sort of logic, a general frame of reference, and so molds the thought of its habitual users. He claimed also that, where a culture and a language have developed together, there are significant relationships between the general aspects of the grammar and the characteristics of the culture taken as a whole . . . .

. . . .

To claim a causal relation between language and culture is not, of course, to say which influences the other. Either may be the causal agent, both may be joint effects of a common cause, or there may be mutual causal action. Indeed this latter is to be expected with continuing factors such as language and culture. The connections which we shall investigate in the next section will be largely causal.

With this brief discussion of the factors involved, we may turn to the evidence for relationships. It will be convenient to begin with the evidence for a connection between language and thought and to open the discussion with a consideration of the relationship between vocabulary and perception. Languages differ notoriously in vocabulary, and this difference is generally correlated with a difference

* From 1–2, 5–10 (U. of Mich. Press 1958). With the permission of University of Michigan Press.

in environment. Thus, Whorf notices that Eskimo languages have a variety of words for different kinds of snow where we have only one. Aztec is even poorer than we in this respect, using the same word stem for cold, ice, and snow. Sapir gives detailed evidence over a broader field in claiming that the vocabulary of a language clearly reflects the physical and social environment of a people. Indeed, the complete vocabulary of a language would be "a complex inventory of all the ideas, interests, and occupations that take up the attention of the community . . . ." He notices that among the Nootka of the northwest coast, marine animals are defined and symbolized with precise detail. Some desert people reserve the detailed lexicon for berries and other edible food plants. Similarly, the Paiute, a desert people, speak a language which permits the most detailed description of topographical features, a necessity in a country where complex directions may be required for the location of water holes. Sapir points out that what holds for the physical environment, holds even more clearly for the social. Status systems in various cultures, however complex, and differentiations due to occupations are all mirrored in languages.

So far, the argument merely shows that vocabulary reflects the environment of a people. Since the culture is largely dependent on this environment, especially where technology is relatively undeveloped, we have an argument suggesting at least that vocabulary and general ways of acting are effects of a common cause, so one may be an index to the other.

All this still says nothing concerning perception and would have little to do with it, if perception were merely a matter of recording what is presented. This is not the case, however, and there is abundant evidence to show that perception is influenced by mental set. Such effects of mental set have been summarized by Bruner and Goodman in a now classical paper. They say:

> . . . subjects can be conditioned to see and hear things in much the same way as they can be conditioned to perform such overt acts as knee jerking, eye blinking, or salivating. Pair a sound and a faint image frequently enough, fail to present the image, and the subject sees it anyway when the sound is presented. Any student of suggestion, whether or not he has purused Bird's exhaustive bibliography of the literature on the subject, knows that. Not perception? Why not? The subject sees what he reports as vividly as he sees the phi-phenomenon.

In addition, they point out, reward and punishment, experience, and social factors may all be of influence. Their own research goes on to show that children overestimate the size of coins, that the amount of overestimation is, in general, dependent upon the value of the coin, that the error is greater with coins than with cardboard discs of the same size, and that it is greater with poor than with rich children. Clearly, as they say, it will not do to consider a perceiver as a "passive recording instrument of rather complex design."

The question then becomes one of whether knowing an item of vocabulary—at least one which has application to sense experience—

constitutes a set directed toward perceiving in terms of this word. The existence of such a set would mean noticing those aspects of the environment which pertained to the application of the term and tending to neglect others. Direct evidence on the point is not available, but it seems reasonable to conjecture that there is such a set. There is strong motivation to learn the language of a society on the part of children and newcomers, for only through knowing the language can wants be satisfied and communication be established. Ability to use the words of a language is thus prized, and this desire is reinforced by the discovery that the vocabulary is useful in dealing with the environment. Given the motivation to learn the language it is reasonable to infer a set favoring the application of it and so an influence on perception.

It would seem then to be consistent with what we know of mental set on other grounds to assume that the world appears different to a person using one vocabularly than it would to a person using another. The use of language would call attention to different aspects of the environment in the one case than it would in the other. Numerous illustrations of this sort may be given. The Navaho, for example, possess color terms corresponding roughly to our "white," "red," and "yellow" but none which are equivalent to our "black," "gray," "brown," "blue," and "green." They have two terms corresponding to "black," one denoting the black of darkness, the other the black of such objects as coal. Our "gray" and "brown," however, correspond to a single term in their language and likewise our "blue" and "green." As far as vocabulary is concerned, they divide the spectrum into segments different from ours. It would seem probable that on many occasions of casual perception they would not bother to notice whether an object were brown or gray, and that they would not merely avoid discussions as to whether a shade of color in a trying light was blue or green, but they would not even make the distinction.

This example must not be taken as showing that the Navahos are incapable of making color distinctions which are familiar to us. They do not suffer from a peculiar form of color-blindness any more than we do since we lack words for the two sorts of black which they distinguish. The point is rather that their vocabulary tends to let them leave other distinctions unnoticed which we habitually make.

If we are right in claiming an influence of vocabulary on perception, it might be expected that vocabulary would influence other aspects of thought as well. The divisions we make in our experience depend on how we perceive and so would be subject to the same linguistic influence as perception. Once again, one would expect the influence to run in both directions. If, in thinking about the world, one has occasion to use certain ideas, one would expect them to be added to the vocabulary, either directly or through metaphor; this is probably the primary influence. Once the term is in the vocabulary, however, it would constitute an influence both on perception and conception.

The observations which are forced differ in different languages. Thus Kluckhohn and Leighton comparing English with Navaho say:

> English stops with what from the Navaho point of view is a very vague statement—"I drop it." The Navaho must specify four particulars which the English leaves either unsettled or to inference from context:
>
> 1.   The form must make clear whether "it" is definite or just "something."
>
> 2.   The verb stem used will vary depending upon whether the object is round, or long, or fluid, or animate, etc., etc.
>
> 3.   Whether the act is in progress, or just about to start, or just about to stop, or habitually carried on, or repeatedly carried on, must be rigorously specified . . .
>
> 4.   The extent to which the agent controls the fall must be indicated . . .

Dorothy Lee has noticed that, in a similar fashion, Wintu requires the indication in suffixes of the evidence on which a statement is based thus forcing an observation. She says:

> He (the Wintu) cannot say simply *the salmon is good.* That part of *is good* which implies the tense (now) and the person (it) further has to contain one of the following implications: (the salmon is good) I see, I taste (or know through some sense other than sight), I infer, I judge, I am told.

Just as is the case with vocabulary, one may claim that the forced observations imposed by inflections constitute a mental set. Because it must be mentioned in speaking, the time of an action is more likely to receive the attention of a user of English than of a user of Wintu. Again, it is easy to make a statement in English without considering the evidence for it. A Wintu might be expected to be more perceptive in this respect. The influence here is similar to that exerted by vocabulary except that it is concentrated on relatively fewer items—those which form the basis of inflection—and so is stronger with regard to these.

Finally, under the heading of language comes the factor of sentence structure. While again one would expect that the primary influence runs from thought and social needs to sentence structure, there may be a reciprocal influence as well.

### NOTES AND QUESTIONS

1.   What is Henle suggesting as to the relationship between language and perception (and thought)? Take the analysis one step further: what does the language of any culture itself reflect? Is a language system—vocabulary and structure—neutral with respect to the values of the culture that employs it? Or is there embedded, deep within language's influence on the mind, the culture's view of the "right" and "wrong" ways to perceive and conceptualize? What effect is had on our perceptions and thought by our acquaintance with terms like "harm", "responsibility", "the individual", "free", "blame", etc.?

Suppose those terms were abolished from the language: would we perceive differently those things that were going on around us? How would our society be different?

2. Consider the influence of language on perception in the day-to-day work of the courts. Do the courts allow adequately for such influence? Do you suppose that "diagonally" was as much as part of the vocabulary of the boys in the Smith case as "motioned"? What significance might be attached to your answer by Henle's analysis?

State v. Ingram, 237 N.C. 197, 74 S.E.2d 532 (1953) involved a prosecution for assault upon a female. There was no physical touching, but the prosecution based its case on the theory of the defendant's actions having constituted such a "display of . . . menace of violence . . . as to cause the reasonable apprehension of immediate bodily harm." On the stand, the prosecutrix' testimony included the remark that the defendant had been "leering" at her. Asked, apparently on cross-examination, whether she had used the word "leer" in a prior proceeding in the Recorder's court, "she said she didn't think so, but that just before the first trial in November 1951 she looked up the word in the dictionary and as well as she remembered 'it was a curious look' ". On an appeal of his conviction, defendant won a reversal on the grounds that "we may not predicate an assault upon the fact of his approach across the field as related by the witness."

We do not know, of course, how much the appellate court was influenced by the collapse of the prosecutrix' "leer" testimony. But consider: suppose her education had been such that she *had* known the word "leer"; or "lascivious"; or "lewd"? Wouldn't she then have been able to make out a more convincing case that she was in "reasonable apprehension of immediate bodily harm"? Indeed, had she known those words, and if Henle is right, might she not have been more likely to have *seen* his look as "lewd" or "lascivious"; and would she not then, in truth, *have been* in more apprehension than if she had not known the words? Is it possible that the conviction or acquittal of the defendant depended not only on what he *did*, but also, in part, on the language the prosecutrix knew?

3. The "Whorfian hypothesis" discussed by Henle has been subjected to some empirical investigation; the case for language being *determinative* of what people "see" is not as uncontroversial as a reading of Henle alone might suggest. See J. H. Greenberg, *Concerning Inferences From Linguistic to Nonlinguistic Data*, *in* LANGUAGE AND CULTURE (H. Hoijer, ed. 1956) and R. W. Brown and E. H. Lennenberg, *A Study in Language and Cognition*, 49 JOURN. ABNORMAL PSYCH. 454 (1954). Both articles, and others in this area, are reprinted in PSYCHOLINGUISTICS (Sol Saporta, ed. 1961).

4. If the demands of a culture work their way into our perceptions, might we find different perceptual patterns among different groups in the society—different sub-cultures, as it were?

H. GROSS, CRIMINAL INVESTIGATIONS 62–65 (1924), suggests that "an intelligent boy is undoubtedly the best observer to be found." He goes on,

The world begins to take him by storm with its thousand matters of interest; what the school and his daily life furnish cannot satisfy his overflowing and generous heart. He lays hold of everything new, striking, strange, all his senses are on the stretch to assimilate such things as far as possible. A change in the house, a bird's nest, anything out of the way in the fields, remain unnoticed and unobserved; but nothing of that sort escapes the boy, everything which emerges above the monotonous level of daily life gives him a good opportunity for exercising his wits, for extending his knowledge, and for attracting the attention of his elders, to whom he communicates his discoveries. . . . [H]e has already got some principles; lying is distasteful to him, because he thinks it mean; he is no stranger to the sentiment of self-respect, and he never loses an opportunity of being right in what he affirms. Thus he is, as a rule, but little influenced by the suggestions of others, and he describes objects and occurrences as he has really seen them. We say again that an intelligent boy is as a rule the best witness in the world.

With a young girl of the same age, Gross says, "it is a different affair."

Her natural qualities and her education prevent her acquiring the necessary knowledge and the breadth of view which the boy soon achieves, and these are the conditions absolutely indispensable for accurate observation. The girl remains longer in the narrow family circle, at her mother's apron strings, while the boy is off with his playmates, picking up in the fields and the woods all sorts of knowledge of the ordinary aspect of common things; which is the best training for discovering, distinguishing, and observing anything extraordinary or out of the way when it turns up. With his father and his playmates the boy learns to know the great sum of practical things of which life is composed, and which one must know before being able to talk about them. The girl has no training of this sort; she goes out less, she has little to do with workmen, artisans, or tradesmen, who are in many ways the school-masters of the boy anxious to learn; she sees little of human life, and when anything extraordinary happens she is incapable, one might almost suggest, of seizing it with her senses, that is to say, of observing accurately. If beside her there be danger, noise, fear, all which attract the boy and serve to excite his curiosity, she gets out of the way in alarm, and either sees nothing or sees it indistinctly from a distance. . . .

But, to be just, we must recognise on the other hand that no one notices and knows certain things more cleverly than a young girl. If her imagination does not carry her away, she can furnish information more valuable than any grown-up person. The reason is the same as we have given for her exaggerations and inventions. Her school, her life, her daily tasks, do not afford sufficient nourishment for her imaginations and her dreams; the sexual instinct begins to awaken; she searches around her, almost unconsciously, for incidents touching, however remotely, this sphere. No one discovers more rapidly than a sprightly young girl approaching maturity the little carryings-on and intrigues of her neighbors; the delicacy of her sensibility enables her to seize the least shade of sympathy which the pair she is observing have for each other; and long before they have found it out themselves, she knows what their true feelings are for each other. She notes accurately the birth of the intimacy; she knows when they spoke for the first time. And she anticipates long before what the result will be, reconciliation or rupture; in short she knows everything earlier and better than anyone else in her circle.

Connected with this is the trick young girls have of spying on certain people. An interesting beauty or a young man acquaintance have no more vigilant watcher of all their goings on, than their neighbour—a little girl of twelve to fourteen. No one knows better than she, who they are, what they do, what company they keep, when they go out, and how they dress. She even notes the moral traits of those coming under her supervision—their joy, their grief, their disappointments, their hopes, and all their experiences. If one desires information on such subjects the best witnesses are school girls—always supposing that they are willing to tell the truth.

Do you suppose there really are such differences in observation and testimonial capacity between boys and girls? Is it possible that the differences Gross finds may be influenced by his own preconceptions about the proper "place" of boys and girls in societies? To the extent some such differences are real, do you suppose they are determined biologically? In what part might such traits be dictates of cultures that need to maintain the woman as a second-class citizen? See G. Greer, The Female Eunuch (1971); B. Friedan, The Feminine Mystique (1963); S. De Beauvoir, The Second Sex, (1953).

*Floyd H. Allport*

Theories of Perception and The Concept of Structure *

*Attitude, Set, and Determining Tendency*
.   .   .   Near the beginning of the present century it was recognized that there was something else, hitherto unnoticed, that lay behind association and behind the conscious contents or the overt reaction. We do not always have perception, then will, then action;

* From 84, 376–77, 409–10, 411–13 (John
Wiley & Sons 1955). Reprinted with
permission of John Wiley & Sons.

there may be a pre-established attitude that determines what is to be perceived and how one shall react. The volitional part of the experience may occur before the stimulus-object appears. When the stimulus does appear and the perception or overt reaction occurs the subject may be entirely unconscious of the steering effect of this preparatory attitude. Yet it was the attitude, or set, of the subject, not the stimuli nor the mechanical laws of association, that determined the reaction.

. . .

## Orientation to Hypothesis-Theory: Example from the Solution of an Overt Problem

This basic idea underlying the reformulation by Bruner and Postman was that all cognitive processes, whether they take the form of perceiving, thinking, or recalling, represent "hypotheses" which the organism sets up, or that are evoked by the particular situation. These hypotheses, in perception at least, are largely in the background and are usually unconscious. They require "answers" in the form of some *further* experience, answers that will either confirm or disprove them. Adjustment of the organism to the environment proceeds by this process of hypothesis-confirmation or rejection. The answer, if the hypothesis is confirmed, comes into consciousness as some kind of percept, image, idea, or memory that is suddenly attained and that fits into the expectancy-pattern, or supposition, of which the hypothesis is composed. If the added items, whose source is provided either by the environment or by "memory-traces," do not fit this pattern of the hypothesis, the percept is not clearly formed, the idea for solution of the problem is not yet gained, or the memory-item is not yet recalled. The process then continues. One tries again with a new hypothesis and with its testing by sensory or memory material that is being provided.

The forming or arousing of hypotheses in the situation concerned, together with the receiving of information related to them, their testing, and their ultimate confirmation or rejection through this information, constitute the processes of thinking, perceiving, and remembering. When we perceive, think, or remember we are evoking and testing organismic hypotheses. We have long been familiar with the term hypothesis and with its testing as employed in a purely logical sense in scientific or philosophical inquiry. Bruner and Postman propose that we use the same term as the name of a postulate to be used in describing the *actual psychological process* involved in all cognition. Hypothesis-confirmation is the process that invariably takes place, no matter whether the hypothesis to be confirmed is as complex as a principle of physics or as simple as the assumption or expectancy that the object one is looking at is an "apple." We have always the background or prior *hypothesis,* and we have some added *information;* and the cognitive process is an interrelating or matching of the two.

. . . . .

*Translation of Hypothesis-Theory Into Set Concepts:*
*Illustrative Cases*

So much for the general statement. Before proceeding with its application to directive-state experiments let us look at a few examples from familiar situations. Just as the runner is set on the mark, anticipating the pistol-shot that will raise the energies enough for the set to pass over into full overt action, so the perceiver in the perceptual experiment sits with his eyes fixated on the tachistoscope awaiting a stimulus, or perhaps one of a class of stimuli, that will raise the energies of the perceptual set above the threshold where a full and conscious percept will be attained. And just as the leaping forward at the firing of the pistol is exactly the act that the structural patterning of the nerves and muscles of the runner was prepared to accomplish (were incipiently accomplishing), and just as the pistol-shot was "congruous," i. e., capable of being intercalated into this setting, so the type of stimulus-object exposed in the tachistoscope is congruous with the perpetual set-structure of the subject. In hypothesis-theory we say that the stimulus-information in these cases is "appropriate or supporting to the hypothesis." "Hypothesis-supporting" really means that the stimulation-input "fits" the set-structure, and the energies of the whole aggregate are thereby raised.

Let us consider another example to illustrate further this feature of so-called "selectivity." We are set, let us say, to find a brooch we have lost. Suddenly our eyes fall upon it and we perceive it almost instantly. The "brooch hypothesis" (an expectancy of an object that has a certain glittering appearance) is "confirmed." In a parallel sense, as soon as the pistol is fired and the runner leaps forward we might say that his "hypothesis" ("I must spring forward at the pistol-shot") is confirmed. Hence, just as the set-structure of the runner is selective for the sound for which it is prepared and leads only to a certain kind of response when that stimulus occurs, so perceptual sets are selective of certain stimulus-inputs and prepare only a certain kind of response (i. e., a perceptual response).

But the runner sometimes leaps forward before the pistol is fired. "False starts" are sometimes made. Similarly, if we are very intent, we might "perceive" the brooch before there is any brooch to perceive. The set in this case, having high energies, is near the threshold point and the aggregate is somewhat unstable. Expressed in terms of hypothesis-theory this case would be an instance in which, in the absence of stimulus-information, a dominant hypothesis alone can sometimes "organize the perceptual situation." A related case would be one in which our gaze falls upon a shiny bit of broken glass and we "clearly perceive" it to be the brooch, only to be disappointed upon a longer or more careful examination. The hypothesis in this case was that an object which is about to appear will be the brooch, and it was non-veridical. The illusion of perceiving the brooch might be spoken of in hypothesis-theory as the work of the hypothesis in "transforming" the stimulus-input into "information consistent with the hypothesis." . . .

. . . . .

Let us take another example. We sometimes "perceive" an acquaintance a little distance away though our hypothesis so to perceive may be non-veridical. Still the hypothesis (set) may be very strong, and as we advance and get ready to speak to our acquaintance, this hypothesis may be said, temporarily at least, to have a "monopoly." Further stimulus-input is received, and the hypothesis that "the person is so and so" becomes infirmed. We may be called upon, however, in order to prevent our embarrassment, to attain a new percept, a more veridical one. So a new hypothesis (set) is quickly activated or aroused. Perhaps the individual before us, though someone other than we thought, is still someone we know; or at the very least would have the set-meaning "a human being" or "person," with reference to whom, as to all human beings, a certain consideration and a certain dignity of bearing are expected. In any case the added stimulus-input that proved negatively related to our first set leads to the arousal of some other set. It leads, in other words, to an "hypothesis-shift." Should it *continue* to do so, as when we struggle to recall the identity of a person we have not seen for some time, the process becomes one of repeated "trial and check" until a set happens to become available with which the details of the stimulus-input are fully compatible and the set-aggregate is thereby raised in energies to full perceptual recognition. In terms of structural theory we could say that the new set represents a broader structuring that brings into the total aggregate of the present situation, as a part or substructure, a structurization earlier set up with respect to the individual in question.

It would be well to note in all these instances how clearly motor elements enter as essential parts of the aggregate. We are set not merely to perceive but to react in appropriate ways to the expected object. The discrimination of the brooch is scarcely separable from what one is set to do with it. The person we mistakenly accost must, after all, be *dealt with* in some way. These considerations remind us that set was earlier discussed as involving patterns of muscle-tensions and proprioceptive backlash from those patterns (Freeman). They also support our earlier attempt to carry over the hypothesis-concept to sets within a *social* situation where overt behavior comes into play, and to the preparedness for what others expect us to do under our "hypothesis" of so acting as to appear worthy and acceptable within a collective aggregate. As soon as we begin to translate hypothesis-theory into the language of sets and motor adjustments we see that it must be broadened. Perception cannot be sharply limited to the use of stimulus-input merely as "information" by which to confirm or deny a purely "cognitive" proposition. Perhaps this is only saying that perception cannot be isolated from the total structural matrix of the individual's behavior. From this standpoint "hypotheses" must be regarded as parts of a broader design that sometimes renders the term itself inappropriate. We have "hypotheses" not merely to see or hear, but to do; sets for some kind of *action*, not merely sets for drawing conclusions. And all these processes are a part of the total aggregate and probably form an essential part of the perceiving activity through exactly the same logic of set-structure and its energic enhancement that has been used for perception in the narrower sense. The recognition of this fact makes the term hypothesis, as used in the experimental program, seem too narrow.

## QUESTIONS

1. What further perspectives on the *Smith* case does Allport suggest? What, for example, is suggested by Allport's theory about the role of *hypothesis* in perception? If we assume that perceiving involves the continual testing and disconfirming of hypotheses, what was likely to have been the dominant hypothesis of two young boys waiting—and wanting—to cross the street? What were they looking *for*?

## NOTE: PERCEPTION AND MEMORY

One ought not to leave this chapter without considering how the materials it includes, although most immediately concerned with perception, may also illuminate the workings of memory processes. What relationships do you suppose exist between the processes of perception and recall? May the same factors that guide the brain in selecting forms from the "buzzing, blooming, confusion" of the external world also guide us in recalling—and reconstructing—impressions stored away in the "buzzing, blooming confusion" of our internal worlds, *i. e.*, the mind?

An eminent law teacher, C. S. Morgan, once walked into another teacher's class, presenting to the lecturer a note. The lecturer, by pre-arrangement, read the note and said, "I will be there at two o'clock." Morgan said "thank you", and left. A week later, the professor in charge of the class presented to the class questions, prepared by Morgan, to test their perception and recall. What sorts of differences do you think might have been tested? What results would you expect? Would you think that Gross, supra, p. 163, would prove correct that the boys' responses were, as a class, different from those of the girls? How would the students' memory be altered by presenting them with specific questions (as in a courtroom situation), rather than having them narrate unguided by "clues"? See Morgan, *A Study in the Psychology of Testimony*, 8 J.AM.INST.CRIM. L. 222 (1917).

## CHAPTER FIVE

# The Authority of Concepts

## INTRODUCTORY NOTE

Obviously, perception is only one phase in the total process of making a judgment. When one decides that "plaintiff abandoned the manure" or "the chickens were manufactured products", one is doing more than reporting the raw interaction of nerve endings and reality; one is invoking a number of *concepts*—abandoned, manure, chicken, manufactured product.

The institution of concepts is part of the process of attempting to make the world manageable—to systematize ourselves free of the "buzzing blooming confusion" of which James wrote. Instead of trying to think about and speak about an infinite variety of perceptual experiences, we conceptualize *a person, X,* and speak of what *he* does "through time"; instead of trying to capture, in thought and communication, all the myriad differences among all the myriad different things we sit on, we generalize into a far smaller number of class concepts: *chairs, benches, pews,* etc.

In law, as in all human thought, we institute concepts which we hope will make systematic relationships possible, *i. e.,* relationships that are understandable, manageable, plannable and predictable. Consider, for example, the role that the concepts of *possession* and *abandonment* are called upon to play in situations like that in the *Haslem* case. People want to know what sorts of actions, with respect to what sorts of objects, will entitle them to, and disentitle them from, ownership (and all the legal consequences ownership entails). Since every human action, and every object, is distinguishable—and becomes the more distinguishable the more precisely we describe it—the systematizing of relationships demands the invocation of categories with a certain level of generality. If the categories—the concepts—had not some generality—if they did not overlook some potential distinctions—they could not be embodied in anything that could serve as a *rule.* But given the concepts, we are able to say that, while there are certain differences between *this* fact situation and *that,* they are equally cases in which someone has gained *possession*; and having gained possession, certain consequences of having gained possession attach, irrespective of the individual differences.

On the surface, then, a case could be made that concepts are the dominant device that rescues our thought—both everyday and legal—from disorder. But as we shall see, the more deeply we get involved in an analysis of concepts in operation, a number of questions arise that cast doubts on how far they can actually advance us towards making law objective and knowable, towards relieving judges of the burden of detailed inquiry and choice. Do we really have, for each supposed concept (abandonment, domicile, manufactured product, etc.) anything as simple as a "picture in the mind"? If so, do we really solve problems—or even begin to solve problems—by bringing them to bear on, and seeing whether they "correspond" to, aspects of the situation? If we are equipped—or can equip ourselves—with anything of that sort, can we be confident that different persons are equipped with the same concepts? If concepts have any authority in our thinking at all, can we avoid having to choose what is "within" and what is "without" each concept?

---

# Introduction

## A.L.I. Discussion of the Tentative Draft, Conflict of Laws, Restatement No. 1.*

JUDGE CARDOZO: I will call section [9].

> "Section [9]. *Domicil is the place with which a person has a settled connection for legal purposes; either because his home is there or because it is assigned to him by the law.*"

MR. LEWIS: As the reporter has said, this restatement of domicil is based—and I think when he said the majority of his advisers or the great majority believed that domicil was a single conception in the law, and not the multiple conception, one thing for inheritance, another thing for taxation, another thing for divorce—this restatement is based on the conception by the group working on the subject that there is a single conception of domicile.

Now, we have received criticisms that this is fundamentally a wrong point of view, and without making any invidious distinctions I think the person who impressed us as having in his criticism given more consideration to that subject than anyone else who took the opposite point of view is Professor Cook, and I am quite sure that the meeting here would be glad to hear from Professor Cook if he cares to say anything on the subject.

. . . .

MR. [WALTER WHEELER] COOK: Mr. President and members of the Institute, it is very difficult to put in a few words what I would like to say, but as I see it any concept such as domicil is a tool which lawyers use, judges use, in determining what ought to be done in a concrete situation. As I see it, the same word is used in dealing with a great variety of situations. The reporter has enumerated some of them: Divorce, taxation, jurisdiction to enter a personal judgment, what to do with a man's personal property when he dies intestate; and other purposes.

A judge or court deciding a case always has one of those concrete situations before him. In passing upon the exact scope of the concept as applicable to that case the Judge always has in mind that case and not all the other purposes. I believe that it is extraordinarily unlikely that the court would always draw the line, that it ought always to draw the line delimiting the boundary of the concept at exactly the same place for all these purposes. I do not believe that has happened or ever will happen. I do not believe you can determine the

* From 3 A. L. I. Proc. 222, 225–31    with the permission of the American (1925). Copyright 1925. Reprinted    Law Institute.

exact scope of any legal concept unless you know what you are trying to do with it, because, as I said at the beginning, it is a tool which we use in order to make up our mind what we ought to do under the circumstances. Now, obviously, I cannot in a few minutes go into the details of that proposition at all. But if I am right, we would need first of all, before making up our minds, as to the exact scope to be given to the concept, to get clearly in mind and to keep in mind all the purposes for which we are going to use this tool.

After we had done that and examined each situation we can decide whether it is true that exactly the same tool will answer all these different purposes equally well. There is no doubt that what you might call the core of the concept is the same in all these situations; but as you get out towards what I like to call the twilight zone of the subject, I don't believe the scope remains exactly the same for all purposes.

However, suppose we start out with the idea that you have a single concept. The attempt here in the restatement is to determine exactly what the scope of that concept is going to be. Assuming we are going to have a single concept for all purposes, we certainly cannot make up our mind in choosing between conflicting views without having in mind all those purposes, and I do not find in the restatement any attempt to set forth all the purposes, at least adequately, for which we are going to use this concept.

Later on there will be a chapter in the restatement on jurisdiction to enter a personal judgment on constructive personal service, and we are told that jurisdiction depends perhaps on domicile. We will already have a definition, already made, which was made without, it seems to me, having clearly in mind what we were going to use the definition for. At least, it does not appear in the restatement. I find nothing more than the casual enumeration of a few of the purposes. But, however, my fundamental point is—and it would apply to all fields of the law—that we can never make up our minds in a doubtful case, when we do not know just how far a concept goes, what is the best view as to the scope of the concept unless we know our problem. The court has a concrete problem to solve. It is trying to decide whether the courts of the state should grant a divorce on constructive service; whether the man is sufficiently connected with the State to make that a reasonable thing to do. It may be reasonable to do that, but not reasonable to apply the same concept in the case involving the validity of the provisions of a will. The court has a will to consider, or a divorce, or the administration of an estate, or whatever it may be, and the exact point at which it draws the line is undoubtedly drawn with the concrete problem that they have before them in mind.

WILLIAM BROWNE HALE (Illinois): Would it be your view that the differences in the definition of domicile are so great that it would be unwise to state a definition of domicile except in connection with each subject matter?

MR. COOK: I think it might be possible to collect all the definitions in one place. I do not think you necessarily would have to distribute them.  But I do not believe we can make up our minds as to the exact scope it ought to have for a particular purpose without having that purpose in mind, and we ought to address ourselves to the question of whether it ought to have the same exact scope for all purposes.  I do not believe it should.  I am not talking about a theoretical thing, but what the courts actually do.  What I think the courts should do and are actually doing is, that while they use the same word as if they had a single concept, actually you will find they have not.  . . .

.  .  .  .

MR. BEALE:  I am going to ask my associate, Mr. Scott, to speak on this question in reply.

AUSTIN W. SCOTT (Massachusetts):  The reporter has done me the honor of asking me to assist him as one of his advisers in preparing this draft, and I am somewhat familiar with what we have gone through in preparing it.  I think all the advisers agree with Mr. Cook, that this generalization should not be taken up without regard to the specific applications.  This conception of domicil comes up over and over again in different branches of law.  In framing the principles governing domicil we have constantly borne that in mind.  Of course, we are now presenting a generalization at the outset, but it is based upon conclusions we have drawn with great agony of spirit from a whole lot of specific cases and classes of cases, cases involving divorce and taxation and the rest.  You can only be assured whether this is really accurate when the whole thing is completed.  Of course, no action could be finally taken on this thing today.

But when Professor Cook suggests that this is a sort of *a priori* idea of ours which might or might not work when we come to apply it, that we had not thought yet whether it would work, why, then, I think he does not quite realize the way in which we have gone about preparing this generalization.

Indeed what he says I think goes pretty deep.  I do not quite see how you can have any restatement of any subject if you cannot draw generalizations.  Of course, you have at first presented these generalizations, and you may have to qualify them.  A tentative generalization at the outset may be too broad.  But it seems to me Professor Cooks' position is that you cannot draw any generalizations. The law, he says, is the prediction as to what the courts will do.  They will always act on an individual case, and therefore all you can do is to predict what they will do in that individual case.

I think it is true that the law, as I think Mr. Justice Holmes said, is a prophecy of what the courts will do.  But the courts have adopted certain principles, comparatively few in number, and those principles can be stated so they can be applied to particular cases, and presumably will be applied; and therefore a principle which presumably will be applied by the court can be stated as law, even though the prophecy may be conceivably in a particular case wrong.  Now, we are therefore justified in drawing certain conclusions about domicil, if there is any such conception running through the law.

After examining all these different branches in which the conception is employed, we reach the conclusion that it is a single conception, that wherever the courts feel that there has got to be only one place to which a man is attached for certain legal purposes, they employ this conception of domicil, and employ equally, no matter what the question is, whether it is one of jurisdiction or taxation or otherwise. Now, that is a question of law on which we may differ, but we have reached the conclusion that there is a dominant conception. Whether it is right or not will depend on the rest of the restatement, but if it is right it seems to me that these sections we have here stated represent as near as we can represent what the courts not only have said, but have actually decided when a question is raised in any one of these numerous classifications, in which it has been held that there may be one place with which he has a certain relation, with which he has a certain connection, either because his home is there, if he has a home, or for other sufficient legal reasons here enumerated, if he has not a home. . . .

## QUESTIONS

1. What is Cook suggesting by referring to concepts as "tools"? How much influence do concepts really have on the way in which we solve concrete problems?

Consider the case of Jones, who has a house in Florida in which he lives 10 months of the year. His wife, all of whose income derives from Jones, rents an apartment and lives in New York throughout the year. Jones lives with her two months a year. Can New York levy income taxes on all of Jones's earnings? Can the New York courts obtain personal jurisdiction over Jones by service posted on the door of the New York apartment during the period while he is in Florida? When he dies, does Florida or New York get the estate taxes?

Does Cook think the solution to these three problems is to be reached by reference to the same concept of domicil? Or even to three different concepts of domicil?

2. What is the relationship between having a concept and having a name for the concept? If we did not have a word, "domicil", might we still have the concept *domicil*? Do you suppose that, historically, the concept might have preceded the word? Do we have a concept of *person*, because we have the word, "person"—or is it the other way around, our having come up with the word "person" (or its etymological predecessors) because we had a concept, *person*, which needed a name? If the word "domicil"—or "abandoned", or "trespass"—were banished from the legal vocabulary, would it make any difference at all?

Do we have a concept for each word, or may the same word "bring to mind" a broad range of concepts, *i. e.*, is there one concept, *manufactured product*, for the words "manufactured product"? Or might there be different concepts for "manufactured product" depending upon whether one's concern was with the tariff law, the patent law, or the Interstate Commerce Act? If there are different concepts of *manufactured product* in each of the three contexts, how different may the three concepts be? Need there be any resemblance among them at all?

How do your answers to these questions relate to Cook's position?

3. Why were the Members of the A.L.I. setting out to define the concept of domicil? What is involved in *defining* a concept? Why—and when—do people try to do so? Would a concept be of any use if it were not defined? Consider redness: can you define it? Can you correctly identify red objects? How are defining and identifying related? Could we identify cases of people being domiciled in such and such a jurisdiction without a definition of domicil in mind?

Is the task of defining a concept based upon the view that concepts are pictures in the mind, and the definition will help us all to paint the same picture? If so, is the view sound? Do we have anything like a picture in the mind for each of the concepts we use? If so, what is the picture associated with the concept of *or*, or of *free speech*—or of *domicil?*

4. Is Cook's chariness of defining domicil based on the view that to define concepts is useless? Or that a single concept could not serve for all the purposes to which the word "domicile" is put? Or that a single concept could not adequately describe all the different past decisions involving "domicil"? Or that it would be better not to try to invoke one concept for all the different types of situations in which "domicil" arises? Can you defend each of these views?

5. What is the significance of Cook's saying that we cannot know "what is the best view as to the scope of the concept unless we know our problem"? In what sense can we know what the problem we are facing *is* without knowing what concepts we are to bring to bear on it? Might Cook just mean that problems of whether, *e. g.,* New York can tax Jones's earnings, should be framed and decided without invoking any concept of domicil? Could one do so? How? What criteria might one invoke?

6. Of what use is the definition that finally emerged? What does it mean to have a "home" somewhere; or "a settled connection for certain legal purposes"; or to be a place "assigned by the law"? What were the members of the Institute agreeing to, when they agreed to Section 9? In what sense have the tasks of judges and lawyers been simplified by the definition?

7. If there could be a useful definition of a concept, what would it have to include? Consider explicating the concept of chair.

ARTHUR KOESTLER

THE ACT OF CREATION *

. . . .

In one of his experiments, Carl Duncker—the psychologist . . . set his experimental subjects the task of making a pendulum. The subject was led to a table on which had been placed, among some miscellaneous objects, a cord with a pendulum-weight attached to its end, and a nail. All he had to do was to drive the nail into the wall and hang the cord with the pendulum-weight on the nail. But there was no hammer. Only fifty per cent of the experimental subjects (all students) found the solution: to use the pendulum-weight as a hammer.

Next, another series of students, of the same average age and intelligence, were given the same task under slightly altered conditions. In the first series the weight on the table was attached to the cord, and was expressly described to the students as a "pendulum-weight". In the second series, weight and cord were lying separately on the table, and the word "pendulum-weight" was *not* used. Result: *all* students in the second group found the solution without difficulty. They took in the situation with an unprejudiced mind, saw a nail and a weight, and hammered the nail in, then tied the cord to the nail and the weight to the cord. But in the minds of the first group the weight was firmly "embedded" into its role as a "pendulum-weight" and nothing else, because it had been verbally described as such *and* because visually it formed a unit with the cord to which it was attached. Thus only half of the subjects were able to wrench it out of that context—to perform the shift of emphasis which transformed a "pendulum-weight" into a "hammer". . . .

I have quoted only one among many experiments on similar lines. The fact that fifty per cent of Duncker's presumably bright students failed at this simple task is an illustration of the stubborn coherence of the perceptual frames and matrices of thought in our minds. The visual gestalt of weight-attached-to-cord, plus the verbal suggestion of their venerated teacher, made that pendulum-weight stick to its matrix like an insect caught in amber.

. . . .

. . . Woodworth's remark "often we have to get away from speech in order to think clearly" [applies] to a wide range of creative activities—from mathematics and physics to philosophy, and there is no need to labour the point further. What needs stressing once more is that words are symbols for perceptual and cognitive events, but they are not the events. They are vehicles of thought, but the vehicle should not be confused with the passengers.

Let me recapitulate. (1) The child has formed a variety of preverbal concepts of persons, objects, and recurrent events to which later verbal symbols become attached as labels; without the previously existing person-concept, the symbol "Mama" would have nothing to refer to; it would remain meaningless—an empty vehicle without passenger. (2) At a later stage, the word and the concept may be acquired simultaneously: "Mummy" what does SEDUCTRESS mean?" "A very bad woman who uses too much make-up." (3) The *concept* "seductress" will undergo drastic changes during adolescence and later years; the *word* SEDUCTRESS remains unchanged. It is a vehicle with a fixed, immutable structure; whereas the passengers are constantly changing, getting in and out of the bus. We may even distinguish between passengers of first and second class: trim denotations, furtive connotations, and stow-aways hidden under the seats. . . . (4) The word SEDUCTRESS refers to different concepts in different people. (5) The word which is attached to a concept may become detached from it, leaving the concept more or less unimpaired . . . .

## QUESTIONS

1. What does Koestler view as the role of concepts in thought? Are they inevitably useful? How might Cook have used the Duncker experiment to support the position he was taking before the A.L.I.?

2. What does Koestler's analysis of "seductress" suggest as to the possibility of limiting a word to a single fixed concept? What comparisons can you draw between the child's acquisition of a concept for the word "seductress" and the law's acquisition of a concept for "domicile"? Is it inevitable that, in each case, "the passengers will change"? Can we, as through definitions, affect the passenger turnover? Was the mother not doing so in Koestler's example?

*ERNST CASSIRER*

## LANGUAGE AND CONCEPTION *

. . . According to the traditional teachings of logic, the mind forms concepts by taking a certain number of objects which have common properties, *i. e.*, coincide in certain respects, together in thought and abstracting from their differences, so that only the similarities are retained and reflected upon, and in this way a general idea of such-and-such a class of objects is formed in consciousness. Thus the concept *(notio, conceptus)* is that idea which represents the totality of essential properties, *i. e.*, the *essence* of the objects in question. In this apparently simple and obvious explanation, everything depends on what one means by a "property," and how such properties are supposed to be originally determined. The formulation of a general concept presupposes *definite* properties; only if there are fixed characteristics by virtue of which things may be recognized as similar or dissimilar, coinciding or not coinciding, is it possible to collect objects which resemble each other into a class. But—we cannot help

* From Language and Myth 24–26 (S. Langer, transl. 1946). Reprinted with permission of Yale University Press.

asking at this point—how can such differentiae exist prior to language? Do we not, rather, *realize* them only by means of language, through the very act of naming them? And if the latter be the case, then by what rules and what criteria is this act carried out? What is it that leads or constrains language to collect just *these* ideas into a single whole and denote them by a word? What causes it to select, from the ever-flowing, ever-uniform stream of impressions which strike our senses or arise from the autonomous processes of the mind, certain pre-eminent forms, to dwell on them and endow them with a particular "significance"? As soon as we cast the problem in this mold, traditional logic offers no support to the student and philosopher of language; for its explanation of the origin of generic concepts presupposes the very thing we are seeking to understand and derive— the formulation of linguistic notions. The problem becomes even more difficult, as well as more urgent, if one considers that the form of that ideational synthesis which leads to the primary verbal concepts and denotations is not simply and unequivocally determined by the object itself, but allows scope for the free operation of language and for its specific mental stamp. . . .

. . . [A]ll the intellectual labor whereby the mind forms general concepts out of specific impressions is directed toward breaking the isolation of the datum, wresting it from the "here and now" of its actual occurrence, relating it to other things and gathering it and them into some inclusive order, into the unity of a "system." The logical form of conception, from the standpoint of theoretical knowledge, is nothing but a preparation for the logical form of judgment; all judgment, however, aims at overcoming the illusion of singularity which adheres to every particular content of consciousness. The apparently singular fact becomes known, understood and conceptually grasped only in so far as it is "subsumed" under a general idea, recognized as a "case" of a law or as a member of a manifold or a series. In this sense every genuine judgment is synthetic; for what it intends and strives for is just this synthesis of parts into a whole, this weaving of particulars into a system.

## WILLIAM JAMES

### THE SENTIMENT OF RATIONALITY *

The facts of the world in their sensible diversity are always before us, but our theoretic need is that they should be conceived in a way that reduces their manifoldness to simplicity. Our pleasure at finding that a chaos of facts is the expression of a single underlying fact is like the relief of the musician at resolving a confused mass of sound into melodic or harmonic order. The simplified result is handled with far less mental effort than the original data; and a philosophic conception of nature is thus in no metaphorical sense a labor-saving contrivance. The passion for parsimony, for economy of means in thought, is the philosophic passion *par excellence*; and any character

* From The Will to Believe and Other
Essays 65–66 (Dover 1956).

or aspect of the world's phenomena which gathers up their diversity into monotony will gratify that passion, and in the philosopher's mind stand for that essence of things compared with which all their other determinations may by him be overlooked.

More universality or extensiveness is, then, one mark which the philosopher's conceptions must possess. Unless they apply to an enormous number of cases they will not bring him relief. The knowledge of things by their causes, which is often given as a definition of rational knowledge, is useless to him unless the causes converge to a minimum number, while still producing the maximum number of effects. The more multiple then are the instances, the more flowingly does his mind rove from fact to fact. The phenomenal transitions are no real transitions; each item is the same old friend with a slightly altered dress.

Who does not feel the charm of thinking that the moon and the apple are, as far as their relation to the earth goes, identical; of knowing respiration and combustion to be one; of understanding that the balloon rises by the same law whereby the stone sinks; of feeling that the warmth in one's palm when one rubs one's sleeve is identical with the motion which the friction checks; of recognizing the difference between beast and fish to be only a higher degree of that between human father and son; of believing our strength when we climb the mountain or fell the tree to be no other than the strength of the sun's rays which made the corn grow out of which we got our morning meal?

## QUESTIONS

1. What are Cassirier and James suggesting is the role of concepts in making the world comprehendable? How do they help us gather our experiences "into some inclusive order, into the unity of a 'system'"? Is this not what the Members of the A.L.I. were trying to do with the concept of domicil? Is Cook's reluctance based on a belief that there are costs of "system"—and they may be too high? Are there not, for example, costs that we pay for concepts in the overlooking of differences among individual events?

Think of teaching a child the color yellow. The child brings to you a banana and asks what color it is; you say "yellow". She returns with a scarf of a slightly different color and asks, again, what color it is; again, you say "yellow". The child looks dubious; it does not look like the same color as the banana. Oh well, the world is a strange place. She returns with a daisy of another color still; you tell her that, too, is "yellow". How much of teaching concepts is instruction in ignoring differences? (After a period, is it possible that the child's capacity to *perceive* distinctions will become less discriminating?) Is this a peculiarity of learning colors?

On the other hand, how would our thought and communication processes be affected if we had no vehicles for thought which were capable of glossing over differences?

2. If the function of concepts is to make a *system* comprehendable, can we understand the individual concept without understanding

the larger system of which it is a part? Can we, for example, understand the concept of a king in chess, without understanding all the rules of the game of chess, of which the king is a part, *i. e.*, the nature of the board, the rules governing the king's powers, the rules relating to the other pieces? Or can we fully understand domicil without understanding the whole body of rules relating to, *e. g.*, personal jurisdiction?

If we need to know all these other things, of how much help are the concepts, themselves, in solving our problems?

## JOHN HOSPERS

### CONCEPTS *

Knowledge is expressed in propositions: "I know that I am now reading a book," "I know that 2 plus 2 equals 4," and so on. But before we can understand any propositions at all, even false ones, we must first have concepts. I cannot understand what is meant by the sentence "Ice melts" before I have the concept of ice and melting. We might well express this otherwise by saying that in order to understand what is meant by "Ice melts" we must understand the meanings of the *words* "ice" and "melt." But to understand the meanings of words, we must have concepts: to understand the meaning of a word already involves having a concept.

How do we acquire the concepts that we have? It was once thought that at least some of our concepts are innate—that they are, so to speak, "wired into us." Suppose that the concept of redness (or being red) were innate: then we would have it without having to experience any instances of it—that is, without ever having to see anything red. A person born blind could have the concept just as well as a man who could see. It seems so obvious that a person born blind does not possess the concept of redness, or of any other color, that no one has held that this concept, or the concept of any other sensory property, is innate. *Some* concepts, however, have been believed to be innate: for example, the concept of cause and the concept of God. If the concept of cause is innate, then we could know what the word means, and be in full possession of the concept, without ever having seen causes operating. This too seems implausible to us, but we shall examine the concept of cause in detail in Chapter 5. Perhaps the God example seems more plausible, since God, if one exists, is not seen or otherwise perceived, and yet we do seem to possess the concept (though this too has been denied). If we cannot perceive God and we nevertheless have the concept, how, it might be asked, do we come by it? May it not be innate? We shall try to answer this question when we consider the alternative theory, that concepts are derived from experience. Meanwhile, it is worth noting that the theory of innate concepts is no longer held. The rise of modern psychology has dealt it

* From An Introduction to Philosophical Analysis 101–102, 108–111, 112 (2d ed. 1967). Copyright 1967. Reprinted by permission of Prentice-Hall, Inc., Englewood Cliffs, New Jersey.

a death-blow. No evidence has ever arisen to show that any concept that people have is innate; perhaps they don't have certain concepts that they claim to have, but when they do have a concept, it is derived in some way from experience—that is to say, they would not be able to have the concept unless they first had certain experiences.

.   .   .   .

.   .   .   But what is a concept? How do we tell when we have one?

Let us try one possible answer to these questions: (1) We have a concept of X when we know the definition of the word "X." But this answer is far too narrow: we do know the meanings of countless words—"cat," "run," "above"—and use them every day without being able to state a definition for them.   .   .   .   Whatever having a concept involves, it does not require being able to state a definition—something that even the compilers of dictionaries often have a hard time doing. And in the case of words like "red" that are not verbally definable at all, we can never state a definition—from which we would have to conclude, according to this view, that we can never have a concept of red.

So let us try again: (2) We have a concept of X when we can apply the word "X" correctly; we have a concept of redness and orangeness when we can correctly apply the words "red" and "orange" in all cases. This criterion does not require us to give a definition but only to use the word with uniform correctness. It is also much more in line with our actual use of the term "concept": we do say, for example, "He must have some concept of what a cat is, for he always uses the word 'cat' in the right situations—he never applies the word 'cats' to dogs or anything else."

There is, however, one way in which this criterion is still too restrictive: it assumes that in order to have a concept we must first be acquainted with a *word*. Doubtless this is usually the case, but it is not *always* the case. A person may have something in mind for which no word yet exists, and he may then *invent* a word for it; or he may use an old word in a new sense, giving it a meaning it never had before. In either case, it seems plausible to say that he had the concept *prior* to the existence (or new usage) of the word. When the first physicists adapted the use of the common word "energy" for their own special purposes, they had in mind a highly abstract concept, and they presumably had this concept in mind before they had a word for it. Doubtless there are many concepts that one cannot have without much prior acquaintance with language, but this cannot be the case for all concepts, else how would language have got started? Using a word correctly seems to be a *consequence* of having the concept, but not a precondition of having it: that is if you have a concept, *and* know the word for it, you will then be able to use the word correctly; but having the concept is not the same thing as being able to use the word.

Let us, then, try once more, so as not to involve the acquaintance with a word in the having of a concept. (3) We have a concept of X (of X-ness) when we are able to distinguish X's from Y's and Z's and indeed from everything that is not an X. We might well do this whether we had a word for X or not, though of course it would be most convenient if we did have a word, and normally we would have. Thus if a child can distinguish cats from dogs and pigs and all other things, he has a concept of what is a cat, even though he cannot state a definition and even though he has never heard the word "cat" and connected the word with the thing by way of ostensive definition.

We have now specified what a concept is in such a way as to make it possible to have a concept without knowing any words. A dog that can distinguish cats from birds can be said to have these concepts, although it knows no words. Even this definition might be objected to, however, on the ground that being able to distinguish X's from Y's is, once again, a *consequence* of having the concept of X, but not what having the concept consists in. One is tempted to say that if you have a concept of X, you can, *as a result*, distinguish X's from other things; but you have to have the concept first. But what then would having the concept be? Moreover, we can devise machines that can effectively differentiate some things from others; do we wish to say that these machines have concepts?

In reply to such objections, we might say (4) that to have a concept of X is simply to have some *criterion-in-mind*. It would consist in some kind of "mental content" quite independent of words and quite independent of distinguishing X's from Y's and Z's. But it is not easy to state what such a criterion-in-mind would be like, or how one would know, through introspection alone, whether one possessed such a criterion. Surely the way one would know whether one had a criterion for X would be whether it would enable one to distinguish X's from Y's and Z's. A criterion for identifying X's would (it would seem) automatically be a criterion for distinguishing X's from non-X's. And so we would be back with our third criterion after all.

I can, of course, have a concept of X even though there are no X's in the world at all. I may have a concept of a sort of thing that is a reptile, larger than an elephant, and flies through the air. I could easily identify such a creature if it existed, and the fact that it does not exist does not prevent me from having the concept of such a creature. I have such a concept, then, although no such creature exists and there is no word to designate this peculiar combination of characteristics. (Let us take care to note that I can have the concept even if I cannot state any characteristics at all; for in the case of verbally indefinable words, no characteristics can be stated. I cannot state in words what distinguishes red from orange, though I know how to make the distinction in practice, and therefore I have a concept of these two colors.)

It is clear, then, that we can have a concept without having an image. . . .

*Are all concepts based on experience?* . . . We are not born with concepts, nor do we (as Plato thought) remember them from a state of existence prior to our birth; so how else could we acquire them except through experience?

The difficulty lies in showing in each case how the concept was actually derived from experience. With sensory concepts like redness, the case is relatively easy: as small children we had various red things pointed out to us, and by acts of successive abstraction . . . we came to recognize the characteristic, redness, that all the cases pointed to had in common. But how did we derive through experience the concept of liberty, of honesty, of marginal utility, of four, of logical implications? We do have these concepts, and, let us quickly note, we have them *without* any corresponding images. When we think of liberty, we may imagine the Statue of Liberty, and when we think of slavery, we may imagine African slaves being whipped; but neither of these images constitutes the meaning of the words "liberty" and "slavery"—others may imagine something very different when they think of liberty or slavery, and still others may have no images at all. There is no image *of* liberty or slavery the way there is an image of red or sweet. These are abstract concepts, to which there are no corresponding images. If we have images, they are not of liberty but of particular things or situations that may or may not exemplify liberty. We can all understand the same concept, liberty, even though we all have different images (or none at all) when we think about it. What we *think* of when we think of liberty is very different from what we *imagine* when we think of it; what we imagine, if anything, is only an incidental accompaniment.

This is not to say that we could have the concept of liberty if we had never had any sense-experiences at all: our having the concept is in some way or other dependent on experience; but it is far from easy to say how. Perhaps if we had always lived under a tyranny and never seen or heard of people who could express their opinions without fear of punishment, we would not be able to form the concept of liberty—though even this is doubtful, for as long as we were aware of restraints upon our behavior, we could conceive of a state-of-affairs in which these restraints were absent. It is, indeed, very difficult to know upon *what* experiences our concept of liberty is dependent. At any rate, the relation between the concept and sense-experience is very indirect: there is no particular sense-experience, or even any single kind of sense-experience, that we must have had had before we can have this concept. Whatever the connection is between the concept and experience, it is sufficiently indirect that no one has given a clear account of exactly what this connection is in every case.

. . . . . .

More puzzling still, there are words that we can use with systematic accuracy that do not seem to be connected with experience, even by way of abstraction: consider connective words like "and" and "about," which have a function in a sentence but do not correspond to any distinguishable items in the world . . . .

## Questions

1. Does the concept of concepts help us to understand our thinking process—or does it only obscure how we think? Why do you suppose people have such trouble stating what a concept is?

2.   Hospers maintains that to understand what is meant by "ice melts" we have to understand the concepts of ice and melting. Is this true? Does understanding communication consist in—or depend upon —a serial fitting of words to concepts? If a man says "freedom forever", do we picture a concept of (a) freedom and (b) forever? Do children learn the meaning of "ice melts" by learning the concept of something called "ice" and the concept of a process called "melts"? Are there such things as *the* concept of ice and *the* concept of melting? Do we not have ideas about ice and melting that are constantly subject to change, like (to use Koestler's example) our ideas about seductress? If there is a concept of *ice*, is not part of it the concept of *melting*—and vice-versa?

3.   What does one have to understand to understand "Jones is domiciled in New York"? How adequate an answer is it to say, "the concept of domicil (and of Jones and of New York)"?

4.   Does Hospers demonstrate to your satisfaction that "to understand the meaning of a word involves having a concept" or that "using a word correctly seems to be a consequence of having the concept"? Suppose that whenever Jones is asked, "is the ice melting" he answers correctly (to the satisfaction of everyone who undertakes to verify his answers), "yes" when it *is* melting and "no" when it is not. Might we say, in the face of this evidence, that Jones uses the language correctly, but he doesn't have the concepts? Or if he answered wrongly, might we yet say, he has the concept, but he doesn't understand the language? If one cannot defend an affirmative answer to the last two questions, of what use is the concept of "having a concept"; what does it add?

5.   In similar vein, why does Hospers insist that "having a concept" of X and Y is something more than being able to distinguish Xs from Ys? What does it add to say "but you have to have the concept first"? In what sense can we ever know whether the person who made the proper distinctions "had the concept first"?

6.   How accurately do you suppose the notion of "having a concept in mind" reflects the actual process of a judge deciding whether manure has been *abandoned*, as in the *Haslem* case, or whether eviscerated chickens are *manufactured products*, as in *Kroblin*? Did you yourself have anything like a picture—or criteria—in mind for each of these concepts as you began to read the case? If so, did your picture change as you considered the case? In deciding how each of those cases was to come out, how critical a role was played by any such pictures? In other words, if there is any mental experience corresponding to "having a concept", how important a function does it serve in making a judgment?

7.   What would be the consequences for a legal system if every person had, or could have, the same "picture in mind" for abandonment, due process of law, domicile, etc.? What is the significance in these terms, then, if Hospers is right that "modern psychology" has dealt a death blow to the belief in innate ideas, and all ideas—even that of red—are learned through experience? If so, can a legal system be made "pure" of the effects of individual differences attributable

to differences in education, normative outlook, etc., even when it is apparently invoking the most rudimentary concepts?

8. With regard to the claim that no concepts are innate, see N. CHOMSKY, ASPECTS OF THE THEORY OF SYNTAX (1965). After extensive research into the complex structure of languages, Chomsky decided that the explanation that we learned language simply "through experience" was far too pat; and, indeed, unbelievable. Chomsky takes the view that we are able to learn language as rapidly as we do owing to the way in which our brains have developed structurally, which may well be viewed as a case of innateness.

If, after millions of years of evolution, there is an innate structure to the human hand, why not, he asks, an innate structure to the organization of the brain, predisposing it to acquire knowledge along lines that it is "fitted out" to handle? Chomsky observes, *op. cit.*, at 59,

> [T]here is surely no reason today for taking seriously a position that attributes a complex human achievement entirely to months (or at most years) of experience, rather than to millions of years of evolution or to principles of neural organization that may be even more deeply grounded in physical law—a position that would, furthermore, yield the conclusion that man is, apparently, unique among animals in the way in which he acquires knowledge. Such a position is particularly implausible with regard to language, an aspect of the child's world that is a human creation and would naturally be expected to reflect intrinsic human capacity in its internal organization.
>
> In short, the structure of particular languages may very well be largely determined by factors over which the individual has no conscious control and concerning which society may have little choice or freedom. On the basis of the best information now available, it seems reasonable to suppose that a child cannot help constructing a particular sort of transformational grammar to account for the data presented to him, any more than he can control his perception of solid objects or his attention to line and angle. Thus it may well be that the general features of language structure reflect, not so much the course of one's experience, but rather the general character of one's capacity to acquire knowledge—in the traditional sense, one's innate ideas and innate principles.

If Chomsky is right, and the brain is fitted out with at least some innate concepts, might we not all have the same "picture in mind" for at least some rudimentary concepts?

---

## SECTION ONE: THE USES AND ABUSES OF LEGAL CONCEPTS: WHERE IS THE CORPORATION?

### INTRODUCTORY NOTE

The corporation is an obvious—and classic—example of an attempt to simplify analysis of enormously complex problems through the institution of a concept.  A thousand people, living in fifty different jurisdictions, want to put capital into a business.  They will have to establish comprehensible rights and duties among themselves—and in their relations with employees, creditors, debtors, governmental agencies, directors, officers and state courts.  Further, the creditors, debtors, etc. need comprehensible relations among themselves: when someone owes this phantasmagoria of human interchange $1000, who is he to pay—his pro rata share to each and every stockholder?  A pro rata share to each of the corporation's creditors?  One of the very purposes of the organization is to make the answer "no".  We say he is to pay "the corporation".  Just as we say today (although the common law was reluctant to do so) that "the corporation" is capable of *mens rea* and can commit a crime; and that "it" may intend to drive competitors out of business, and that "it" may be doing business in some states but not in others, and that "it" is a "person" within the intendment of the Fourteenth Amendment, and that "it" must pay taxes.

All of this conceptualization is to the end of bringing forth systematic, manageable relationships out of what would otherwise be a "buzzing, blooming confusion".  But while in theory the concept should improve the ordering of business affairs, in practice its operation is not so simple.

Many of the problems stem from the fact that while we can point to a real, tangible president of the corporation, or to the company name on the office door, there seems to be no entity *the corporation* we can point to when we need to locate the corporation; no separately identifiable corporate brain can be examined to discover "its" intent to commit a crime; no corporate hand can be found to sign a check, or to bind "it" to a contract.

These "peculiarities" about the concept of the corporation have long been recognized, giving rise to a body of puzzled literature about what it is that we are thinking about, when we think about a corporation.  "That invisible, intangible, and artificial being, that mere legal entity. . . ." was the way Chief Justice Marshall referred to the corporation in Bank of the United States v. Devaux, 9 U.S. (5 Cranch) 61, 86.  (1809)  In Trustees of Dartmouth College v. Woodward, he described it as "existing only in contemplation of law."  17 U.S. (4 Wheat.) 518, 636 (1819).  "Into its nostrils", Maitland wrote, "the State must breathe the breath of a fictitious life for otherwise it would be no animated body but individualistic dust".  Maitland, Introduction, $xxx$, to O. GIERKE, POLITICAL THEORIES OF THE MIDDLE AGES (1927).  See also Timberg, *Corporate Fictions: Logical, Social and International Implications*, 46 Col. L.Rev. 533 (1946).

This section examines what it is about the concept of the corporation that makes it so commonly thought of as a "fiction".  Is it any more of a "fiction" than other legal, relational concepts like ownership, right and duty?  How do any of them operate in thought and legal argument?  How far can they go towards simplifying analysis?  How much can they save the lawyer and judge from a painstaking—a lawyerlike—analysis of specific facts and specific rules?

And in such analysis, can one obviate the need to formulate—and to test one's progress against—normative judgments?

## TAUZA V. SUSQUEHANNA COAL COMPANY

220 N.Y. 259 (1917)

CARDOZO, J.  The plaintiff, a resident of this state, has brought suit against the Susquehanna Coal Company, a Pennsylvania corporation.  The defendant's principal office is in Philadelphia; but it has a branch office in New York, which is in charge of one Peterson.  Peterson's duties are described by the defendant as those of a sales agent.  He has eight salesmen under him, who are subject to his orders.  A suite of offices is maintained in the Equitable Building in the city of New York, and there the sales agent and his subordinates make their headquarters.  The sign on the door is "Susquehanna Coal Company, Walter Peterson, sales agent."  The offices contain eleven desks and other suitable equipment.  In addition to the salesmen there are other employees, presumably stenographers and clerks.  The salesmen meet daily and receive instructions from their superior.  All sales in New York are subject, however, to confirmation by the home office in Philadelphia.  The duty of Peterson and his subordinates is to procure orders which are not binding until approved.  All payments are made by customers to the treasurer in Philadelphia; the salesmen are without authority to receive or indorse checks.  A bank account in the name of the company is kept in New York, and is subject to Peterson's control, but the payments made from it are for the salaries of employees, and for petty cash disbursements incidental to the maintenance of the office.  The defendant's coal yards are in Pennsylvania, and from there its shipments are made.  They are made in response to orders transmitted from customers in New York.  They are made, not on isolated occasions, but as part of an established course of business.  In brief, the defendant maintains an office in this state under the direction of a sales agent, with eight salesmen, and with clerical assistants, and through these agencies systematically and regularly solicits and obtains orders which result in continuous shipments from Pennsylvania to New York.

To do these things is to do business within this state in such a sense and in such a degree as to subject the corporation doing them to the jurisdiction of our courts.  The decision of the Supreme Court in International Harvester Co. v. Kentucky (234 U.S. 579) is precisely applicable.  There sales agents in Kentucky solicited orders subject to approval of a general agent in the home state.  They did this, not casually and occasionally, but systematically and regularly.  Unlike the defendant's salesmen, they did not have an office to give to their activities a fixed and local habitation.  The finding was that travelers negotiating sales were not to have any headquarters or place of business in that state, though they were permitted to reside there (234 U.S. at p. 584).  Yet because their activities were systematic and regular, the corporation was held to have been brought within Kentucky, and, therefore, to be subject to the process of the

Kentucky courts. "Here," said the court (p. 585), "was a continuous course of business in the solicitation of orders which were sent to another State and in response to which the machines of the Harvester Company were delivered within the State of Kentucky. This was a course of business, not a single transaction." That case goes farther than we need to go to sustain the service here.  . . .

The defendant refers to cases in which corporations, whose situation was not unlike the defendant's, have been held not to be doing business in this state within the meaning of section 15 of the General Corporation Law and kindred statutes (citing cases). But activities insufficient to make out the transaction of business, within the meaning of those statutes, may yet be sufficient to bring the corporation within the state so as to render it amenable to process (International Text Book Co. v. Tone, decided herewith [220 N.Y. 313]). In construing statutes which license foreign corporations to do business within our borders we are to avoid unlawful interference by the state with interstate commerce. The question in such cases is not merely whether the corporation is here, but whether its activities are so related to interstate commerce that it may, by a denial of a license, be prevented from being here (International Text Book Co. v. Pigg, 217 U.S. 91). "A statute must be construed, if fairly possible, so as to avoid not only the conclusion that it is unconstitutional but also grave doubts upon that score" (U. S. v. Jin Fuey Moy, 241 U.S. 394, 401; Hovey v. DeLong H. & E. Co., *supra*, at p. 429). But the problem which now faces us is a different one. It is not a problem of statutory construction. It is one of jurisdiction, of private international law (Dicey, Conflict of Laws, pp. 38, 155). We are to say, not whether the business is such that the corporation may be prevented from being here, but whether its business is such that it *is* here. If in fact it is here, if it is here, not occasionally or casually, but with a fair measure of permanence and continuity, then, whether its business is interstate or local, it is within the jurisdiction of our courts (International Harvester Co. v. Kentucky, *supra*, at p. 587). To hold that a state cannot burden interstate commerce, or pass laws which regulate it, "is a long way from holding that the ordinary process of the courts may not reach corporations carrying on business within the state which is wholly of an interstate commerce character" (234 U.S. at p. 588). The nature and extent of business contemplated by licensing statutes is one thing. The nature and extent of business requisite to satisfy the rules of private international law may be quite another thing. In saying this we concede the binding force of the decision of the Supreme Court in Riverside & Dan River Cotton Mills v. Menefee (237 U.S. 189) and kindred cases (Bagdon v. Philadelphia & Reading Coal & Iron Co., 217 N.Y. 432, 438; Pomeroy v. Hocking Valley Ry. Co., 218 N.Y. 530). Unless a foreign corporation is engaged in business within the state, it is not brought within the state by the presence of its agents. But there is no precise test of the nature or extent of the business that must be done. All that is requisite is that enough be done to enable us to say that the corporation is here [citing cases]. If it is here it may be served (HALSBURY, L.C., in La Compagnie Generale Transatlantique v. Law, L.R. [1899 A.C.] 431).

We hold, then, that the defendant corporation is engaged in business within this state. We hold further that the jurisdiction does not fail because the cause of action sued upon has no relation in its origin to the business here transacted. That in principle was our ruling in Bagdon v. Philadelphia & Reading Coal & Iron Co. (217 N.Y. 432, 438). We applied it there to a case where service had been made on an agent designated by the corporation under section 16 of the General Corporation Law (Consol.Laws, ch. 23). It applies, however, with equal force to a case where service has been made upon an officer or managing agent (Barrow S. S. Co. v. Kane, 170 U.S. 100; Bagdon v. Phila. & Reading C. & I. Co., *supra*). The essential thing is that the corporation shall have come into the state. When once it is here, it may be served; and the validity of the service is independent of the origin of the cause of action. . . .

. . . . .

Order affirmed.

## QUESTIONS

1. What does Cardozo mean by saying that the question is "whether [the corporation's] business is such that it *is* here. If in fact it is here . . . then . . . it is within the jurisdiction of our courts." Can a corporation's being in New York be a fact? What sort of a fact?

In what sense can a corporation *be* anywhere? How is that question different from asking whether the corporation's president can be anywhere? What differences are there in the inquiries that are necessary to answer the two questions?

2. Consider the facts that Cardozo recites for us, *i.e.*, those about the corporation's salesmen, its office in the Equitable building, etc. Can any number of facts of this sort—of what things exist or happen in New York—amount to the *corporation's existence* in New York? Can these facts—in and of themselves—constitute an explanation or justification of Cardozo's opinion?

To know where the corporation *is*, don't we need to know, in addition to these sorts of facts, "facts" about what the rules of the legal system are? Why?

3. Cardozo indicates that defendant had cases to cite "in which corporations, whose situation was not unlike defendant's, have been held not to be doing business in this state within the meaning of" General Corporation Laws § 15. That section read,

> No foreign stock corporation . . . shall do business in this state without having first procured from the secretary of state a certificate that it has complied with all the requirements of law to authorize it to do business in this state. . . . No foreign stock corporation doing business in this state shall maintain any action in this state upon any contract made by it in this state, unless prior to the making of such contract it shall have procured such certificate.

What sorts of cases under this statute do you suppose the corporation was advancing, and with what arguments? How does Cardozo distinguish the cases? Is he leaving open the possibility that Susquehanna Coal Corp. might both be "doing business" and not "doing business" in New York? Could you explain such a result? What does this suggest one has to know in order to know where a corporation is "doing business"?

4. Can you find in the opinion anything like a general rule or theory which explains why, under the facts given, the corporation was "in" New York so as to be amenable to New York's processes? Without such a rule or theory, can Cardozo be convincing, for example, when he says that *International Harvester* "is precisely applicable"? Can you draw a line between business activities which are—in the language of International Harvester—"systematic and regular" and those that are "casual" and "occasional"? Does Cardozo spend much effort trying to do so? What would doing so have involved?

5. What was this case really about? How many economic and social consequences of Cardozo's decision can you think of? What would the consequences have been had he held the other way? What values are involved in the choice? Does Cardozo ever state and acknowledge them? What accounts for his failure to come to grips with the moral considerations involved? Might he have felt that to do so was not necessary because this was an "easy case" under the law as it stood? How much may his failure to do so have been made simpler —to the public's loss as well, perhaps, as to his own—by allowing himself to speak of where the corporation *is* "in fact"?

## HUTCHINSON v. CHASE & GILBERT

45 F.2d 139 (2d Cir. 1930)

L. HAND, Circuit Judge.

The plaintiffs sued the defendant, a Massachusetts corporation, in the state court; the defendant removed for diversity of citizenship, and moved to set aside the service, because it was not doing business within the state of New York. The judge so held, and dismissed the complaint. The plaintiffs do not complain because the judgment was not limited to setting aside the service, and for this reason we treat it as though it had gone no further.

The plaintiffs alleged that the defendant promised in New York to pay for their services in the purchase by it of certain shares of stock, and that they had performed in that state; they demand the contract price, and, by an alternative count, a quantum meruit. Process was served in New York upon the defendant's vice president, who chanced to be there, and the only question is whether the defendant was "present" in such sense that it could be reached in a cause of action arising upon a contract, made in the course of the same activities on which the defendant's supposed "presence" depends. For this reason we have not before us the question . . . whether without expressed consent a foreign corporation may be sued upon transactions arising outside the state of the forum.

The defendant's business is that of an "engineering manager" of public utility corporations, of whose shares it owns a controlling in-

terest, either directly, or through a holding company. These it super-
vises, looking after their property, and acting as engineer, so far as
may be necessary to keep them in operation, and to extend their service. Only one of these is a New York corporation, and this has never
been actually engaged in business; the defendant's control of it is
by the ownership of a majority of the shares of a company which in
turn owns its shares. The defendant leases an office in New York
at a small rental, keeps a small bank account there, on which it draws
from Boston, where all its work is done, and employs a stenographer.
It uses these facilities only upon occasional visits to New York, when
its officers wish to bargain for the purchase of company shares. These
negotiations never result in closing contracts, because all such are
referred to the home office, though at times the formal exchange of
papers takes place in New York. Its directors and shareholders have
always met in Boston, except that once on two successive days the directors met in New York, and on one of these, the shareholders. This
was necessary because of the negotiations for the purchase of shares
on that occasion. Its name appears in the telephone book, and of
course on the office door. On the other hand the contract in suit was
made in New York, and certain bonds of a subsidiary company were
once offered for sale here by an underwriter or selling agent, whose
prospectus was accompanied by a letter, dated at New York and signed
by the defendant. In general, the business is conducted in Boston,
where are all its records, and where all its officers and directors reside.

The theory of personal jurisdiction in an action in personam is,
ordinarily at any rate, derived from the power over the defendant,
consequent upon his presence within the state of the forum. McDonald
v. Mabee, 243 U.S. 90, 37 S.Ct. 343, 61 L.Ed. 608, L.R.A.1917F, 458.
The service of a capias subjects him de facto to such commands as its
courts may utter, though in its stead a notice will usually serve. Such
a theory is not really apposite to a corporation, however conceived,
and it is only by analogy that it can be used. So long as it was thought
of as a fictitious personality, created by the state of its origin, there
were logical difficulties—or at least there were thought to be,—in
treating it as existent outside the limits of that state. Bank of Au-
gusta v. Earle, 13 Pet. 519, 10 L.Ed. 274. As to jurisdiction, the express consent of a corporation to be sued elsewhere avoided its territorial limitations (Lafayette Ins. Co. v. French, 18 How. 404, 15 L.
Ed. 451 . . . and beginning with Lafayette Ins. Co. v. French,
supra, this has been extended to cases where the corporate activities
within the foreign state are such as empower that state to exact such
a consent. We are not here troubled by the question whether the foreign state had power to exclude the corporation from the activities relied upon. International Harvester Co. v. Kentucky, 234 U.S. 579,
34 S.Ct. 944, 58 L.Ed. 1479.

It scarcely advances the argument to say that a corporation must
be "present" in the foreign state, if we define that word as demanding such dealings as will subject it to jurisdiction, for then it does no
more than put the question to be answered. Indeed, it is doubtful
whether it helps much in any event. It is difficult, to us it seems im-

possible, to impute the idea of locality to a corporation, except by virtue of those acts which realize its purposes. The shareholders, officers and agents are not individually the corporation, and do not carry it with them in all their legal transactions. It is only when engaged upon its affairs that they can be said to represent it, and we
can see no qualitative distinction between one part of its doings and
another, so they carry out the common plan. If we are to attribute
locality to it at all, it must be equally present wherever any part of
its work goes on, as much in the little as in the great.

When we say, therefore, that a corporation may be sued only
where it is "present," we understand that the word is used, not literally, but as shorthand for something else. It might indeed be argued
that it must stand suit upon any controversy arising out of a legal
transaction entered into where the suit was brought, but that would
impose upon it too severe a burden. On the other hand, it is not plain
that it ought not, upon proper notice, to defend suits arising out of
foreign transactions, if it conducts a continuous business in the state
of the forum. At least, the Court of Appeals of New York seems still
to suppose this to be true, in spite of the language in Old Wayne Mut.
Life Ass'n v. McDonough, 204 U.S. 8, 27 S.Ct. 236, 51 L.Ed. 345, and
Simon v. Southern Ry., 236 U.S. 115, 35 S.Ct. 255, 59 L.Ed. 492,
Tauza v. Susquehanna Coal Co., 220 N.Y. 259 . . . But a single
transaction, is certainly not enough, whether a substantial business subjects the corporation to jurisdiction generally, or only as to local transactions. There must be some continuous dealings in the state of the
forum; enough to demand a trial away from its home.

This last appears to us to be really the controlling consideration,
expressed shortly by the word "presence," but involving an estimate
of the inconveniences which would result from requiring it to defend,
where it has been sued. We are to inquire whether the extent and continuity of what it has done in the state in question makes it reasonable
to bring it before one of its courts. Nor is it anomalous to make the
question of jurisdiction depend upon a practical test. This for example is avowedly the case as to corporations engaged in interstate
commerce. Davis v. Farmers' Co-operative Equity Co., 262 U.S. 312,
43 S.Ct. 556, 67 L.Ed. 996. No doubt there are governmental reasons
for protecting such corporations from local interference; yet, as mere
matter of municipal law, the loss and inconvenience to ordinary companies from being sued wherever they may chance to have any dealings whatever, cannot properly be ignored, and may constitute a test
of jurisdiction, just as they do of venue, really a kindred matter. If
so, it seems to us that nothing is gained by concealing what we do by
a word which suggests an inappropriate analogy, that is, the presence
of an individual who may be arrested and compelled to obey. This
does not indeed avoid the uncertainties, for it is as hard to judge what
dealings make it just to subject a foreign corporation to local suit,
as to say when it is "present," but at least it puts the real question, and
that is something. In its solution we can do no more than follow the
decided cases.

Possibly the maintenance of a regular agency for the solicitation
of business will serve without more. . . . In Tauza v. Susque-

hanna Coal Co., supra, there was no more, but the business was continuous and substantial. Purchases, though carried on regularly, are not enough . . . nor are the activities of subsidiary corporations . . . or of connecting carriers . . .. The maintenance of an office, though always a make-weight, and enough, when accompanied by continuous negotiation, to settle claims . . . is not of much significance . . .. It is quite impossible to establish any rule from the decided cases; we must step from tuft to tuft across the morass.

In the case at bar, the defendant has never done any continuous business in New York. It has come here on occasion, when it found likely opportunities to buy control in a company which would fit in with its general plans. Had its business been primarily in dealing in the shares of public utility companies, and had it had a local agent, whose duty it was to bargain for these, it may be that it could not escape, merely because he had no power to close purchases here, but must refer them to the home office. This was not the case. The acquisition of a new company whose business the defendant might supervise was of necessity sporadic; it was no part of its ordinary activity. While the chief holding company controlled by the defendant in turn controls indirectly nearly a hundred smaller companies, it by no means follows that to acquire all of these the officers had to go to New York. On the contrary, it is extremely likely that in case of most of them the shares were locally held. Only one of them was in New York and this had never done any business. So far as appears, the visits to New York were infrequent, and concerned only the holding units, which are few. There is no evidence that it ever borrowed money in New York, if that be material; the sale of certain bonds of a holding company, in the control of another company which the defendant in turn controlled, was immaterial, and no more was shown. None of this, and not all of it, seems to us a good reason for drawing the defendant into a suit away from its home state. In the end there is nothing more to be said than that all the defendant's local activities, taken together, do not make it reasonable to impose such a burden upon it. It is fairer that the plaintiffs should go to Boston than that the defendant should come here. Certainly such a standard is no less vague than any that the courts have hitherto set up; one may look from one end of the decisions to the other and find no vade mecum.

Judgment affirmed.

## QUESTIONS

1. Just from the facts as given, how many corporate acts and actors can you place in New York? Why did they not amount to the corporation's being "present" in New York?

2. Hand says, "if we are to attribute locality to it at all, it must be equally present wherever any part of its work goes on, as much in the little as the great." Does he follow this principle?

3. How does Hand distinguish the *Tauza* case? How much evidence is there in the *Tauza* opinion that the activities there were "continuous and substantial"? Does Hand ever give us the criteria by

which we can determine what "continuous" and "substantial" mean? Did Cardozo?

4. Is one of the valid criticisms of the *Tauza* opinion that by the way he treated the problem, Cardozo did not advance our understanding of the concepts of corporation, and presence, leaving Hand to "step from tuft to tuft across the morass"? Is Hand making the area any less of a morass for others? Could he have contributed to systematizing this area of law more than he did? How?

5. Hand recognizes that "present" is a "shorthand for something else", but does he ever replace it with concepts which do not themselves need defining? Why was it "fairer that the plaintiffs should go to Boston than that the defendant should come down here"? Would the defendant, *i.e.*, the corporation, really have had to "come down" to New York? *Could* the defendant have come down to New York?

Does Hand ever tell us what standard of "fairness" and "reasonableness" he is invoking, or explain what facts were relevant to which inquiries, and why? Is it self-evident how one would decide, for example, whether it was less "fair" or "reasonable" for the Susquehanna Coal company's lawyers to have had to travel to meet Tauza's lawyers in New York, rather than vice-versa; or for Chase and Gilbert's lawyers to have had to travel to New York to meet Hutchinson's lawyers, rather than the other way around? (Is the real question, who was to have the burden of retaining local counsel?)

6. Of what service in solving the problems of the *Tauza* and *Hutchinson* cases were the concepts of the *corporation,* and *presence*? Or the A.L.I.'s definition of *domicil*? How much did they succeed in simplifying and organizing the law? How much did they succeed in making it possible to exclude from consideration the personal values of the decider? Were the decisions a help at arriving at a sound decision, or a hindrance? Or did they make no difference at all?

GILBERT RYLE

THE CONCEPT OF MIND *

[A] category-mistake . . . represents the facts of mental life as if they belonged to one logical type or category (or range of types or categories), when they actually belong to another. . . .
. . . .

A foreigner visiting Oxford or Cambridge for the first time is shown a number of colleges, libraries, playing fields, museums, scientific departments and administrative offices. He then asks "But where is the University? I have seen where the members of the Colleges live, where the Registrar works, where the scientists experiment and the rest. But I have not yet seen the University in which reside and work the members of your University." It has then to be explained to him that the University is not another collateral institution, some ulterior counterpart to the colleges, laboratories and offices which he has seen. The University is just the way in which all that he has already seen is organized. When they are seen and when their co-ordination is understood, the University has been seen. His mistake lay in his innocent assumption that it was correct to speak of Christ Church, the Bodleian Library, the Ashmolean Museum *and* the University, to speak, that is, as if "the University" stood for an extra member of the class of which these other units are members. He was mistakenly allocating the University to the same category as that to which the other institutions belong.

The same mistake would be made by a child witnessing the march-past of a division, who, having had pointed out to him such and such battalions, batteries, squadrons, etc., asked when the division was going to appear. He would be supposing that a division was a counterpart to the units already seen, partly similar to them and partly unlike them.
.   .   .

One more illustration. A foreigner watching his first game of cricket learns what are the functions of the bowlers, the batsmen, the fielders, the umpires and the scorers. He then says "But there is no one left on the field to contribute the famous element of team-spirit. I see who does the bowling, the batting and the wicket-keeping; but I do not see whose role it is to exercise *esprit de corps*." Once more, it would have to be explained that he was looking for the wrong type of thing.   .   .   .

These illustrations of category-mistakes have a common feature which must be noticed. The mistakes were made by people who did not know how to wield the concepts *University, division* and *team-spirit*.

## QUESTIONS

1. What is a "category mistake"? Can you state the problem of the *Tauza* and *Hutchinson* cases in terms of different "types of things", *i.e.*, things that were capable of physical location in space and time and things that were not?

2. Does the structure of our language always keep us firmly aware of such differences among categories? Consider Cardozo's reference to the corporation being "here in fact." Suppose he had asked, "given the facts of the activities of Shenandoah's employees in New York, ought we, as judges, to regard the corporation as amenable to process served on Peterson in New York?" What different inquiries are encouraged when the primary question is restated in terms that make it impossible to forget that more is involved in the problem than locating where something exists?

Consider these questions in the light of the selection from Felix Cohen, which follows.

FELIX S. COHEN

## TRANSCENDENTAL NONSENSE AND THE FUNCTIONAL APPROACH *

### I.   The Heaven of Legal Concepts

Some fifty years ago a great German jurist had a curious dream. He dreamed that he died and was taken to a special heaven reserved for the theoreticians of the law.  In this heaven one met, face to face, the many concepts of jurisprudence in their absolute purity, freed from all entangling alliances with human life.  Here were the disembodied spirits of good faith and bad faith, property, possession, *laches,* and rights *in rem.*  Here were all the logical instruments needed to manipulate and transform these legal concepts and thus to create and to solve the most beautiful of legal problems.  .  .  .

.  .  .  The question is raised, "How much of contemporary legal thought moves in the pure ether of Von Jhering's heaven of legal concepts?"  One turns to our leading legal textbooks and to the opinions of our courts for answer.  May the Shade of Von Jhering be our guide.

### 1.   Where Is a Corporation?

Let us begin our survey by observing an exceptionally able court as it deals with a typical problem in legal procedure.  In the case of Tauza v. Susquehanna Coal Company, a corporation which had been chartered by the State of Pennsylvania was sued in New York.  Summons and complaint were served upon an officer of the corporation in New York in the manner prescribed by New York law.  The corporation raised the objection that it *could not* be sued in New York.  The New York Court of Appeals disagreed with this contention and held that the corporation could be sued in that State.   What is of interest for our purposes is not the particular decision of the court but the mode of reasoning by which this decision was reached.

The problem which the Court of Appeals faced was a thoroughly practical one.  If a competent legislature had considered the problem of when a corporation incorporated in another State should be subject to suit, it would probably have made some factual inquiry into the practice of modern corporations in choosing their sovereigns and into the actual significance of the relationship between a corporation and the state of its incorporation.  It might have considered the difficulties that injured plaintiffs may encounter if they have to bring suit against corporate defendants in the state of incorporation.  It might have balanced, against such difficulties, the possible hardship to corporations of having to defend actions in many states, considering the legal facilities available to corporate defendants.  On the basis of *facts* revealed by such an inquiry, and on the basis of certain political or ethical *value judgements* as to the propriety of putting financial burdens

* From  35  Colum.L.Rev.  809,  809–11,     of the Columbia Law Review Association, Inc.
812,  821,  829,  830,  838–841  (1935).
With the permission of the Directors

upon corporations, a competent legislature would have attempted to formulate some rule as to when a foreign corporation would be subject to suit.

The Court of Appeals reached its decision without avowedly considering any of these matters. It does not appear that scientific evidence on any of these issues was offered to the court. Instead of addressing itself to such economic, sociological, political, or ethical questions as a competent legislature might have faced, the court addressed itself to the question, "Where is a corporation?" Was this corporation *really* in Pennsylvania or in New York, or could it be in two places at once?

Clearly the question of *where a corporation is*, when it incorporates in one state and has agents transacting corporate business in another state, is not a question that can be answered by empirical observation. Nor is it a question that demands for its solution any analysis of political considerations or social ideals. It is, in fact, a question identical in metaphysical status with the question which scholastic theologians are supposed to have argued at great length, "How many angels can stand on the point of a needle?" Now it is extremely doubtful whether any of the scholastics ever actually discussed this question. Yet the question has become, for us, a symbol of an age in which thought without roots in reality was an object of high esteem.

Will future historians deal more charitably with such legal questions as "Where is a corporation?" Nobody has ever seen a corporation. What right have we to believe in corporations if we don't believe in angels? To be sure, some of us have seen corporate funds, corporate transactions, etc. (just as some of us have seen angelic deeds, angelic countenances, etc.). But this does not give us the right to hypostatize, to "thingify," the corporation, and to assume that it travels about from State to State as mortal men travel. Surely we are qualifying as inmates of Von Jhering's heaven of legal concepts when we approach a legal problem in these essentially supernatural terms.

Yet it is exactly in these terms of transcendental nonsense that the Court of Appeals approached the question of whether the Susquehanna Coal Company could be sued in New York State. "The essential thing," said Judge Cardozo, writing for a unanimous court, "is that the corporation shall have come into the State." Why this journey is *essential*, or how it is *possible*, we are not informed. The opinion notes that the corporation has an office in the State, with eight salesmen and eleven desks, and concludes that the corporation is really "in" New York State. From this inference it easily follows that since a person who is in New York can be sued here, and since a corporation is a person, the Susquehanna Coal Company is subject to suit in a New York court.

The same manner of reasoning can be used by the same court to show that the Dodge Bros. Motor Corporation "cannot" be sued in New York because the corporation (as distinguished from its corps of New York employees and dealers) is not "in" New York.[1]

.  .  .  .  .

1. Holzer v. Dodge Bros. Motor Co.,
233 N.Y. 216, 135 N.E. 268 (1938).

Of course, it would be captious to criticize courts for delivering their opinions in the language of transcendental nonsense. Logicians sometimes talk as if the only function of language were to convey ideas. But anthropologists know better and assure us that "language is primarily a pre-rational function." Certain words and phrases are useful for the purpose of releasing pent-up emotions, or putting babies to sleep, or inducing certain emotions and attitudes in a political or a judicial audience. The law is not a science but a practical activity, and myths may impress the imagination and memory where more exact discourse would leave minds cold.

Valuable as is the language of transcendental nonsense for many practical legal purposes, it is entirely useless when we come to study, describe, predict, and criticize legal phenomena. And although judges and lawyers need not be legal scientists, it is of some practical importance that they should recognize that the traditional language of argument and opinion neither explains nor justifies court decisions. When the vivid fictions and metaphors of traditional jurisprudence are thought of as reasons for decisions, rather than poetical or mnemonic devices for formulating decisions reached on other grounds, then the author, as well as the reader, of the opinion or argument, is apt to forget the social forces which mold the law and the social ideals by which the law is to be judged. Thus it is that the most intelligent judges in America can deal with a concrete practical problem of procedural law and corporate responsibility without any appreciation of the economic, social, and ethical issues which it involves.

. . . .

## II.  *The Functional Method*

. . . .

. . . [Functionalism] seeks to discover the *significance* of [a] fact through a determination of its implications or consequences in a given mathematical, physical or social context.

. . . [T]he functional method is not a recent invention. Plato's attempt to define "justice" by assessing the activities of a just state, and Aristotle's conception of the soul as the way a living body behaves are illustrious examples of functional analysis. So, too, Hume's analysis of causation in terms of uniformity of succession, and Berkeley's analysis of matter in terms of its appearances, are significant attempts to redefine supernatural concepts in natural terms, to wash ideas in cynical acid (borrowing Holmes' suggestive phrase).

If functional analysis seems novel in the law, this is perhaps traceable to the general backwardness of legal science, which is the product of social factors that cannot be exorcised by new slogans.

With these caveats against the notion that the functional approach is a new intellectual invention which will solve all the problems of law (or of anthropology, economics, or any other science), we may turn to the significant question: "What are the new directions which the functional method will give to our scientific research?"

. . . .

## 2. The Nature of Legal Rules and Concepts

If the functionalists are correct, the meaning of a definition is found in its consequences.  . . .

The consequence of defining law as a function of concrete judicial decisions is that we may proceed to define such concepts as "contract," "property," "title," "corporate personality," "right," and "duty," similarly as functions of concrete judicial decisions.

.  .  .  .  .

Consider the elementary legal question: "Is there a contract?"

When the realist asks this question, he is concerned with the actual behavior of courts.  For the realist, the contractual relationship, like law in general, is a function of legal decisions.  The question of what courts *ought* to do is irrelevant here.  Where there is a promise that will be legally enforced there is a contract.  So conceived, any answer to the question "Is there a contract" must be in the nature of a prophecy, based, like other prophecies, upon past and present facts.  So conceived, the question "Is there a contract?" or for that matter any other legal question, may be broken up into a number of subordinate questions, each of which refers to the actual behavior of courts: (1) What courts are likely to pass upon a given transaction and its consequences?  (2) What elements in this transaction will be viewed as relevant and important by these courts?  (3) How have these courts dealt with transactions in the past which are *similar* to the given transaction, that is, *identical in those respects which the court will regard as important?*  (4) What forces will tend to compel judicial conformity to the precedents that appear to be in point (*e.g.*, inertia, conservatism, knowledge of the past, or intelligence sufficient to acquire such knowledge, respect for predecessors, superiors or brothers on the bench, a habit of deference to the established expectations of the bar or the public) and how strong are these forces?  (5) What factors will tend to evoke new judicial treatment for the transaction in question (*e.g.* changing public opinion, judicial idiosyncrasies and prejudices, newly accepted theories of law, society or economics, or the changing social context of the case) and how powerful are these factors?

These are the questions which a successful practical lawyer faces and answers in any case.  The law, as the realistic lawyer uses the term, is the body of answers to such questions.  The task of prediction involves, in itself, no judgment of ethical value.  Of course, even the most cynical practitioner will recognize that the positively existing ethical beliefs of judges are material facts in any case because they determine what facts the judge will view as important and what past rules he will regard as reasonable or unreasonable and worthy of being extended or restricted.  But judicial beliefs about the values of life and the ideals of society are *facts*, just as the religious beliefs of the Andaman Islanders are facts, and the truth or falsity of such moral beliefs is a matter of complete unconcern to the practical lawyer, as to the scientific observer.

Washed in cynical acid, every legal problem can thus be interpreted as a question concerning the positive behavior of judges.

There is a second and radically different meaning which can be given to our type question, "Is there a contract?" When a judge puts this question, in the course of writing his opinion, he is not attempting to predict his own behavior. He is in effect raising the question, in an obscure way, of whether or not liability *should* be attached to certain acts. This is inescapably an ethical question. What a judge ought to do in a given case is quite as much a moral issue as any of the traditional problems of Sunday School morality.

It is difficult for those who still conceive of morality in other-worldly terms to recognize that every case presents a moral question to the court. But this notion has no terrors for those who think of morality in earthly terms. Morality, so conceived, is vitally concerned with such facts as human expectations based upon past decisions, the stability of economic transactions, and even the maintenance of order and simplicity in our legal system. If ethical values are inherent in all realms of human conduct, the ethical appraisal of a legal situation is not to be found in the spontaneous outpourings of a sensitive conscience unfamiliar with the social context, the background of precedent, and the practices and expectations, legal and extra-legal, which have grown up around a given type of transaction.

It is the great disservice of the classical conception of law that it hides from judicial eyes the ethical character of every judicial question, and thus serves to perpetuate class prejudices and uncritical moral assumptions which could not survive the sunlight of free ethical controversy.

.   .   .

Intellectual clarity requires that we carefully distinguish between the two problems of (1) objective description, and (2) critical judgment, which classical jurisprudence lumps under the same phrase. Such a distinction realistic jurisprudence offers with the double-barreled thesis: (1) that every legal rule or concept is simply a function of judicial decisions to which all questions of value are irrelevant, and (2) that the problem of the judge is not whether a legal rule or concept actually exists but whether it *ought* to exist. Clarity on two fronts is the result. Description of legal facts becomes more objective, and legal criticism become more critical.

## QUESTIONS

1. What is Cohen's objection to Cardozo's opinion in *Tauza*? Is his statement of the case, and of Cardozo's opinion, wholly fair? What might Cardozo respond to the charge that he was speaking "transcendental nonsense"?

2. What does Cohen mean by "the functional method"? What does it ask us to focus inquiry on, in the place of abstract concepts? Can you illustrate his point by distinguishing between the questions, (a) "what is 'length'?" and (b) "how do we measure?"; and (a) "what is 'truth'?" and (b) "by virtue of what criteria do we say that a statement, *S*, is 'true'?" What shifts of attention do the (b)s represent as compared with the (a)s?

3.   What such shifts in attention does Cohen say the legal realists would make with the question, "is there a contract?"

Consider the question, "is the $X$ corporation in New York?"   In Cohen's view, how should a lawyer rephrase that question so as to make clearer what inquiries his task involves?   How should a judge rephrase the question?

4.   Cohen says at one point that "if the functionalists are correct, the meaning of a [term?] is found in its consequences."   What does he mean, "is found in"?   Is the meaning of a term like contract *synonymous* with the consequences of a judge's saying, in any given case, "there is a contract"—for example, (a) Seller must make specific performance to Buyer or (b) Jones must pay Smith $10,000? When the judge says, "there is a contract", does he *mean* (a) or (b)?

5.   Suppose you were a judge and two lawyers came before you with a color sample, saying, "Judge, the issue in the case is, 'is this color red'?"   Would you be willing to decide the case with the issue so framed?   Or would you insist on the lawyers' answering, (a) "Are you asking me, is it red for purposes of a safety law which says all cars must be equipped with red tail lights (in which case if I, a judge, say it is not red, the person who drove a car with tail lights that color will be fined)" or, (b) "Are you asking me, is it red for purposes of a criminal syndicalism statute banning the waving of a red flag, (in which case if I, a judge, say it is red, the person who carried a flag that color will be imprisoned and public demonstrations impeded); or (c) "are you asking me, is it red for purposes of resolving a contract dispute in which Seller agreed to deliver to Buyer 100 gross of red shirts, (in which case if I, as judge, say *that* color is not red, Seller will be in breach of his contract)"?   Are the questions that you would want to explore further in contexts (a), (b) and (c) the same questions?   In what sense would the further questions be questions about the concept *red*?   In what sense would they be broader questions about the ideals of society regarding traffic control, free speech and commerce?

Is it legitimate for a judge to decide what is red on the basis of such broad-scale inquiries into a whole range of values which seem so unrelated to redness?   What limits are there on a judge who takes this "sophisticated" tack?   What do you think Cohen's position would be?

If you were inclined to take the "sophisticated" approach, could you justify your further questions on the ground that you do not have *a* concept *red*; nor do you organize your thinking about individual images, out of context?   How strong an argument could you make?

NOTE:   HYPOSTATIZATION

The shortcoming that Cohen accuses Cardozo of can be seen as arising from *hypostatization*: treating a conceptual, relational idea as though it were *a concrete thing* (and, hence, locatable in space and time).   This is an error that is often encouraged by the structure of our language, as pointed out by the selection from Carnap, Chapter

202 THE QUEST FOR AUTHORITY Ch. 5

1, *supra*, "The Elimination of Metaphysics Through Logical Analysis of Language." The phrase "what is 'justice'?", for example, puts justice in the same place as "a hammer" in the phrase "what is 'a hammer'?" Thus, a person who has learned that he can explain what a hammer is by pointing to a thing, a hammer, looks around for something to point to in answer to the question, "what is 'justice'?"; but in that case, as with the corporation, *there is no thing to point to*. Query: what must one do to explain what such concepts mean? What is Cohen's answer?

### ALF ROSS

### Tu-Tu *

On the Noisulli Islands in the South Pacific lives the Noit-cif tribe, generally regarded as one of the more primitive peoples to be found in the world today. Their civilization has recently been described by the Illyrian anthropologist Ydobon, from whose account the following is taken.

This tribe, according to Mr. Ydobon, holds the belief that in the case of an infringement of certain taboos—for example, if a man encounters his mother-in-law, or if a totem animal is killed, or if someone has eaten of the food prepared for the chief—there arises what is called *tû-tû*. The members of the tribe also say that the person who committed the infringement has become *tû-tû*. It is very difficult to explain what is meant by this. Perhaps the nearest one can get to an explanation is to say that *tû-tû* is conceived of as a kind of dangerous force or infection which attaches to the guilty person and threatens the whole community with disaster. For this reason a person who has become *tû-tû* must be subjected to a special ceremony of purification.

It is obvious that the Noit-cif tribe dwells in a state of darkest superstition. "*Tû-tû*" is of course nothing at all, a word devoid of any meaning whatever. To be sure, the above situations of infringement of taboo give rise to various natural effects, such as a feeling of dread and terror, but obviously it is not these, any more than any other demonstrable phenomena, which are designated as *tû-tû*. The talk about *tû-tû* is pure nonsense.

Nevertheless, and this is what is remarkable, from the accounts given by Mr. Ydobon it appears that this word, in spite of its lack of meaning, has a function to perform in the daily language of the people. The *tû-tû* pronouncements seem able to fulfill the two main functions of all language: to prescribe and to describe; or, to be more explicit, to express commands or rules, and to make assertions about facts.

If I say, in three different languages, "My father is dead," "Mein Vater ist gestorben," and "Mon pere est mort," we have three different sentences, but only one assertion. Despite their differing linguis-

* From 70 Harv.L.Rev. 812, 812–814,
816–820 (1957). With the permission
of Harvard Law Review Association.

tic forms, all three sentences refer to one and the same state of affairs (my father's being dead), and this state of affairs is asserted as existing in reality, as distinct from being merely imagined. The state of affairs to which a sentence refers is called its semantic reference. It can more precisely be defined as that state of affairs which is related to the assertion in such a way that if the state of affairs is assumed actually to exist then the assertion is assumed to be true. The semantic reference of a sentence will depend upon the linguistic usages prevailing in the community. According to these usages a certain definite state of affairs is the stimulus to saying "My father is dead." This state of affairs constitutes the semantic reference of the pronouncement and can be established quite independently of any ideas the speaker may possibly have concerning death—for example, that the soul at death departs from the body.

On the other hand, if I say to my son "Shut the door," this sentence is clearly not the expression of any assertion. True, it has reference to a state of affairs, but in a quite different way. This state of affairs (the door's being shut) is not indicated as actually existing, but is presented as a guide for my son's behavior. Such pronouncements are said to be the expression of a prescription.

According to Mr. Ydobon's account, within the community of the Noit-cif tribe there are in use, among others, the following two pronouncements:

(1) If a person has eaten of the chief's food he is *tû-tû*.

(2) If a person is *tû-tû* he shall be subjected to a ceremony of purification.

Now it is plain that quite apart from what "*tû-tû*" stands for, or even whether it stands for anything at all, these two pronouncements, when combined in accordance with the usual rules of logic, will amount to the same thing as the following pronouncement:

(3) If a person has eaten of the chief's food he shall be subjected to a ceremony of purification.

This statement obviously is a completely meaningful prescriptive pronouncement, without the slightest trace of mysticism. This result is not really surprising, for it is simply due to the fact that we are here using a technique of expression of the same kind as this: "When x = y and y = z, then x = z," a proposition which holds good whatever "y" stands for, or even if it stands for nothing at all.

Although the word "*tû-tû*" in itself has no meaning whatever, yet the pronouncements in which this word occurs are not made in a haphazard fashion. Like other pronouncements of assertion they are stimulated in conformity with the prevailing linguistic customs by quite definite states of affairs. This explains why the *tû-tû* pronouncements have semantic reference although the word is meaningless. The pronouncement of the assertion "N.N. is *tû-tû*" clearly occurs in definite semantic connection with a complex situation of which two parts can be distinguished:

(1) He who kills a totem animal becomes *tû-tû*;

chief's food or has killed a totem animal or has encountered his mother-in-law, etc.  .  .  .  .

(2) The state of affairs in which the valid norm which requires ceremonial purification is applicable to N.N., more precisely stated as the state of affairs in which if N.N. does not submit himself to the ceremony he will in all probability be exposed to a given reaction on the part of the community. . . . .

. . . .

Of course it would be possible to omit this meaningless word altogether, and instead of the circumlocution:

(1) He who kills a totem animal becomes tu-tu;

(2) He who is *tû-tû* shall undergo a ceremony of purification.

to use the straightforward statement:

(3) He who has killed a totem animal shall undergo a ceremony of purification.

One might therefore ask whether—when people have realized that *tû-tû* is nothing but an illusion—it would not be advantageous to follow this line. As I shall proceed to show later, however, this is not the case. On the contrary, sound reasons based on the technique of formulation may be adduced for continuing to make use of the "*tû-tû*" construction. But although the "*tû-tû*" formulation may have certain advantages from the point of view of technique, it must be admitted that it could in certain cases lead to irrational results if against all better judgment the idea that *tû-tû* is a reality is allowed to exert its influence. If this should be the case, it must be the task of criticism to demonstrate the error and to cleanse one's thinking of the dross of such imaginary ideas. But even so, there would be no grounds for giving up the *tû-tû* terminology.

But perhaps it is now time to drop all pretense and openly admit what the reader must by now have discovered, that the allegory concerns ourselves. It is the argument concerning the use of terms such as "right" and "duty" approached from a new angle. For our legal rules are in a wide measure couched in a *tû-tû* terminology. We find the following phrases, for example, in legal language:

(1) If a loan is granted, there comes into being a claim;

(2) If a claim exists, then payment shall be made on the day it falls due.

This is only a roundabout way of saying:

(3) If a loan is granted, then payment shall be made on the day it falls due.

The claim mentioned in (1) and (2), but not in (3), is obviously, like *tû-tû*, not a real thing; it is nothing at all, merely a word, an empty word devoid of all semantic reference. Similarly, our assertion to the effect that the borrower becomes pledged corresponds to the allegorical tribe's assertion that the person who kills a totem animal becomes *tû-tû*.

We too, then, express ourselves as though something had come into being between the conditioning fact (juristic fact) and the conditioned legal consequence, namely, a claim, a right, which like an intervening vehicle or causal connecting link promotes an effect or provides the basis for a legal consequence. Nor, really, can we wholly deny that this terminology is associated for us with more or less indefinite ideas that a right is a power of an incorporeal nature, a kind of inner, invisible dominion over the object of the right, a power manifested in, but nevertheless different from, the exercise of force (judgment and execution) by which the factual and apparent use and enjoyment of the right is effectuated.

In this way, it must be admitted, our terminology and our ideas bear a considerable structural resemblance to primitive magic thought concerning the invocation of supernatural powers which in turn are converted into factual effects. Nor can we deny the possibility that this resemblance is rooted in a tradition which, bound up with language and its power over thought, is an age-old legacy from the infancy of our civilization. But after these admissions have been made, there still remains the important question—whether sound, rational grounds may be adduced in favor of the retention of a *"tû-tû"* presentation of legal rules, a form of circumlocution in which between the juristic fact and the legal consequence there are inserted imaginary rights. If this question is to be answered in the affirmative, the ban on the mention of rights must be lifted. I believe that this question must be answered in the affirmative and shall take the concept of ownership as my point of departure.

The legal rules concerning ownership could, without doubt, be expressed without the use of this term. In that case a large number of rules would have to be formulated, directly linking the individual legal consequences to the individual legal facts. For example:

If a person has lawfully acquired a thing by purchase, judgment for recovery shall be given in favor of the purchaser against other persons retaining the thing in their possession.

If a person has inherited a thing, judgment for damages shall be given in favor of the heir against other persons who culpably damage the thing.

If a person by prescription has acquired a thing and raised a loan that is not repaid at the proper time, the creditor shall be given judgment for satisfaction out of the thing.

If a person has occupied a *res nullius* and by legacy bequeathed it to another person, judgment shall be given in favor of the legatee against the testator's estate for the surrender of the thing.

If a person has acquired a thing by means of execution as a creditor and the object is subsequently appropriated by another person, the latter shall be punished for theft.

An account along these lines would, however, be so unwieldy as to be practically worthless. It is the task of legal thinking to conceptualize the legal rules in such a way that they are reduced to systematic order and by this means to given an account of the law in force which is as plain and convenient as possible. This can be achieved with the aid of the following technique of presentation.

On looking at a large number of legal rules on the lines indicated, one will find that it is possible to select from among them a certain group that can be arranged in the following way:

$$F_1 - C_1 \quad F_2 - C_1 \quad F_3 - C_1 \ldots F_p - C_1$$
$$F_1 - C_2 \quad F_2 - C_2 \quad F_3 - C_2 \ldots F_p - C_2$$
$$F_1 - C_3 \quad F_2 - C_3 \quad F_3 - C_3 \ldots F_p - C_3$$
$$\vdots \qquad\qquad \vdots \qquad\qquad \vdots \qquad\qquad \vdots$$
$$F_1 - C_n \quad F_2 - C_n \quad F_3 - C_n \ldots F_p - C_n$$

The conditioning fact $F_1$ is connected with the legal consequence $C_1$, etc. This means that each single one of a certain totality of conditioning facts $(F_1-F_p)$ is connected with each single one of a certain group of legal consequences $(C_1-C_n)$; or, that it is true of each single F that it is connected with the same group of legal consequences $(C_1 + C_2 \ldots + C_n)$; or, that a cumulative plurality of legal consequences is connected to a disjunctive plurality of conditioning facts.

These $n \times p$ individual legal rules can be stated more simply and more manageably in the figure:

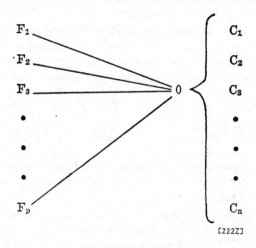

[2222]

"O" (ownership) merely stands for the systematic connection that $F_1$ as well as $F_2$, $F_3$ . . . $F_p$ entail the totality of legal consequences $C_1$, $C_2$, $C_3$ . . . $C_n$. As a technique of presentation this is expressed then by stating in one series of rules the facts that "create ownership" and in another series the legal consequences that "ownership" entails.

It will be clear from this that the "ownership" inserted between the conditioning facts and the conditioned consequences is in reality a meaningless word, a word without any semantic reference whatever, serving solely as a tool of presentation.

## QUESTIONS

1. What is Ross's conception of the criteria which render a word or concept *meaningless*? Does he view "ownership" as devoid of

meaning because it can be replaced by a series of "conditioning facts" and "legal consequences"? Or because there is no "semantic reference" in the sense of "no state of affairs" that we can point to? Or both? Are the complaints the same? Does either one make sense? Under his standards is liberty a *"tû-tû"*? How about red?

2. Under Ross's criteria, would he say that the number 4 "has no meaning whatever"? What "state of affairs" can we point to and say, "that is 4"? Cannot 4 be replaced by expressions of "conditioning facts" and "consequences", *i. e.*, instead of saying "$4 + 3 = 7$", could we not replace the 4 by $(2 + 2)$ and say "$(2 + 2) + 3 = 7$"? Indeed, can a concept like ownership be substituted for in this way as satisfactorily and thoroughly as can be done with the concept of 4?

3. What is Ross' conception of "a state of affairs"? He says that "My father is dead" and "Mein Vater ist gestorben" refer to a "state of affairs   .   .   .   asserted as existing in reality," the sort of affairs qualified to serve, presumably, as his "conditioning facts". Can such "states of affairs" be defined simply by reference to "what exists", independently of notions about law and ethics?

Take, for example, the "state of affairs" that "My father is dead" supposedly refers to. Is it wholly clear when someone is dead or not? *Can* "the semantic reference   .   .   .   be established quite independently of any ideas the speaker may have concerning death   .   .   ."? If our interest is in deciding a legal problem involving death, is it so clear we will be able to judge whether someone is dead or not, without knowing more about the law? And without, perhaps, getting involved in far-reaching ethical controversy? Is it inconceivable that X might be "dead" for purposes of allowing a heart transplant to go ahead without holding the surgeon liable, but not "dead" for purposes of prosecuting someone who, out to kill X, slipped into his hospital room and plunged a knife into him at the same moment? Can a series of "facts" expressed in terms of heart-beat, brain activity, etc., tell us, in and of themselves, whether someone is dead or not, if "dead" is then going to be used as a term in a legal rule?

4. What does Ross say is the relationship between the series of "conditioning facts" that go to making up a concept and the "legal consequences" that flow from invoking the concept? What does he mean in speaking of facts being "connected with" consequences? Is the "connection" always of the same quality? What problems does he gloss over by leaving "connected with" undefined?

5. Do each of the "conditioning facts" that (somehow) "connect with" the invocation of a concept entail the totality of legal consequences "connected with" that concept? Does Ross give us a clear and consistent answer? Consider the ownership example: Do the facts that create ownership (so as to invoke *some* of the consequences of ownership) entail the invocation of *all* the consequences of ownership? If, for example, the facts are adequate to show my "ownership" of Blackacre for one purpose (*e.g.*, my power to keep trespassers off it) does it necessarily follow that, on the same facts, I have all the consequences of ownership at my disposal (*e.g.*, I can sell it, I am liable for taxes on it, etc.)? If not—if there are different standards

and we don't know *which* facts are "connected with" *which* consequences, in what way has the concept given us "systematic order"?

Consider the problem in the area of corporation law: Do the
facts that make it appropriate to invoke *some of the consequences*
of being a corporation assure the propriety of invoking *all the consequences* that are "connected with" being a corporation? For example,
the assertion that the business of A, B and C "is a corporation"
(rather than the A-B-C partnership) *might* be made (i) by A, B and
C, as part of a claim that they should not be taxed pro rata on the
earnings of the business, but rather have the business taxed at the
corporate rate; (ii) by A, B and C to protect themselves from personal liability in a tort suit brought by P, who fell down the elevator
shaft in one of the business's properties; (iii) by A, B and C, to protect themselves from personal liability in a contract suit brought by
plaintiff, who delivered goods to their business, and has not been paid;
(iv) by Seller, who signed a contract with A to deliver goods to "the
A-B-C-Corp.", A, B and C refusing delivery on the grounds that they
are a partnership; (v) by the Attorney General of the state, who
wants the officers to file information regarding their business as required of all "corporations"; (vi) by A, B and C, who want to bring
a suit against Defendant in federal court, and cannot obtain diversity
jurisdiction unless they can sue in the corporate name; etc. The
*sorts* of facts that might be relevant in invoking the concept include:
(a) whether A, B and C duly filed papers with the Secretary of State;
(b) whether the Secretary of State approved them; (c) whether the
incorporators placed their seal on the appropriate papers; (d) whether the appropriate number of directors have been elected; (e) whether the directors have met; (f) whether the subscribed stock has been
issued; (g) whether the stock has been paid for, and whether statutory or charter minimum capital requirements have been met in other
respects; (h) whether the people involved represented themselves to
the public as a corporation; (i) whether the people dealing with them
had reason to believe the business was not duly incorporated; (j)
whether the capital that the promoters had put into the business was
"unreasonably thin" relative to the anticipated liabilities; etc.

Do you suppose these "facts", (a) through (j), go equally towards
deciding whether or not A-B-C is a corporation for each of the consequences, (i) through (vi)? Do the facts that would allow Seller
to recover in case (iii) preclude the Internal Revenue Service from
coming back the next day and urging that A, B and C are *not* operating as a corporation and are individually and directly liable for the
taxes?

Similarly, do you suppose the same "facts" go to prove that "two"
corporations, Parent Co. and Subsidiary Co. (97% owned) are
"really" *a* corporation (i) in a tort suit brought against them both
jointly by Plaintiff who was injured by a man driving one of Subsidiary's trucks; and (ii) in a hearing on the bankruptcy of Subsidiary, wherein Creditors of Subsidiary are seeking to subordinate
or disallow Parent's claim to collect on the so-called "loans" it had
made to Subsidiary? (See, *e.g.*, Berkey v. Third Avenue Ry. Co., 244
N.Y. 84 (1926), for a case of the (i) variety; and Taylor v. Standard

Gas & Electric Co., 306 U.S. 307, 59 S.Ct. 543, 83 L.Ed. 669 (1939), for a case of the (ii) variety.) Does the same evidence have the same relevance in each case? What relationship is/ought there to be? In what sense is "the connection" "systematic"? In what sense does the concept of the corporation save people from undertaking a full-fledged functional analysis?

7. How much is Ross's project (and Felix Cohen's, above) dependent upon the feasibility of Carnap's goal: to reduce all meaningful concepts to protocol statements that do nothing more than express "experience"? (See Carnap, "The Elimination of Metaphysics", *supra,* Chapter 1). If "ownership" is to be reduced to a fact expressed in terms of "possession", what facts will we reduce "possession" to? Where can we end without still relying on a *"tû-tû"* word? Ultimately, can Ross's analysis avoid facing the same objections that Carnap's must meet? See the criticisms of "reductionism" in the selections from W. V. O. Quine and Brand Blanshard, *infra,* Chapter 6, Sec. 3.

8. H. L. A. Hart argues the futility of a project such as Ross's because of what he calls the "defeasible" character of legal concepts: the existence of a network of defenses that can be raised to defeat the invocation of the concept after the "conditioning facts" (as Ross would say) have made out a prima facie case. For example, even if we could, in the first instance, reduce "there is a contract" to a complex set of facts, $F_1$ . . . $F_n$, the party asserting there is not a contract can still raise "negatives", *e.g.,* misrepresentation, duress, the agreement's being against public policy, impossibility of performance, etc. This "shows how wrong it would be to succumb to the temptation . . . to identify the meaning of a legal concept, say 'contract', with the statement of the conditions in which contracts are held to exist; since, owing to the defeasible character of the concept, such a statement, though it would express the necessary and sometimes sufficient conditions for the application of 'contract', could not express conditions which were always sufficient." Hart, *The Ascription of Responsibility and Rights,* 1937–8 PROC. ARIST. SOC., reprinted in LOGIC AND LANGUAGE 161. (A. Flew ed. 1965) Why could Ross not simply respond that negatives of this sort could be stated as "facts" (at least as well as affirmative "facts" can be so stated), e.g., "$F_{10}$: Plaintiff did not employ duress", etc., with the only difficulty being that the list of "facts" would be lengthened?

Professor Hart acknowledges the force of some criticisms of his views on defeasibility, and related matters, in the "Postscript," *Responsibility and Retribution,* Chapter IX of PUNISHMENT AND RESPONSIBILITY, (1968). See also Hart, *Scandinavian Realism,* 1959 Camb.L.J. L.J. 233 and Hart, *The Ascription of Responsibility and Rights, supra.*

*H. L. A. HART*

## DEFINITION AND THEORY IN JURISPRUDENCE *

### I

. . . The first efforts to define words like "corporation" "right" or "duty" reveal that these do not have the straightforward connection with counterparts in the world of fact which most ordinary words have and to which we appeal in our definition of ordinary words. There is nothing which simply "corresponds" to these legal words and when we try to define them we find that the expressions we tender in our definition specifying kinds of persons, things, qualities, events, and processes, material or psychological, are never precisely the equivalent of these legal words though often connected with them in some way. This is most obvious in the case of expressions for corporate bodies and is commonly put by saying that a corporation is not a series or aggregate of persons. But it is true of other legal words. Though one who has a right usually has some expectation or power the expression "a right" is not synonymous with words like "expectation" or "power" even if we add "based on law" or "guaranteed by law." And so too, though we speak of men having duties to do or abstain from certain actions the word "duty" does not stand for or describe anything as ordinary words do. It has an altogether different function which makes the stock form of definition, "a duty is a . . . .," seem quite inappropriate.

. . . . .

### II

Long ago Bentham issued a warning that legal words demanded a special method of elucidation and he enunciated a principle that is the beginning of wisdom in this matter though it is not the end. He said we must never take these words alone, but consider whole sentences in which they play their characteristic role. We must take not the *word* "right" but the sentence "You have a right" not the *word* "State" but the sentence "He is a member or an official of the State." . . . [I]n what follows I shall use as a simple analogy the rules of a game which at many vital points have the same puzzling logical structure as rules of law. And I shall describe four distinctive features which show, I think, the method of elucidation we should apply to the law and why the common mode of definition fails.

1. First, let us take words like "right" or "duty" or the names of corporations not alone but in examples of typical contexts where these words are at work. Consider them when used in statements made on a particular occasion by a judge or an ordinary lawyer. They will be statements such as "A has a right to be paid £10 by B." "A is under a duty to fence off his machinery." "A & Company, Ltd. have a contract with B." It is obvious that the use of these sentences silently assumes a special and very complicated setting, namely the

* From 70 L.Q.Rev. 37, 38–39, 41, 42–
43, 44–46, 47–48, 53–56 (1954). With      the permission of Oxford University
Press and Professor Hart.

existence of a legal system with all that this implies by way of general obedience, the operation of the sanctions of the system, and the general likelihood that this will continue. But though this complex situation is assumed in the use of these statements of rights or duties they do not *state* that it exists. There is a parallel situation in a game. "He is out" said in the course of a game of cricket has as its proper context the playing of the game with all that *this* implies by way of general compliance by both the players and the officials of the game in the past, present, and future. Yet one who says "He is out" does not *state* that a game is being played or that the players and officials will comply with the rules. "He is out" is an expression used to appeal to rules, to make claims, or give decisions under them; it is not a statement *about* the rules to the effect that they will be enforced or acted on in a given case nor any other kind of statement *about* them. The analysis of statements of rights and duties as predictions ignores this distinction, yet it is just as erroneous to say that "*A* has a right" is a prediction that a court or official will treat *A* in a certain way as to say that "He is out" is a prediction that the umpire is likely to order the batsman off the field or the scorer to mark him out. No doubt, when someone has a legal right a corresponding prediction will normally be justified, but this should not lead us to identify two quite different forms of statement.

2. If we take "*A* has a right to be paid £10 by *B*" as an example, we can see what the distinctive function of this form of statement is. For it is clear that as well as presupposing the existence of a legal system, the use of this statement has also a special connection with a particular rule of the system. This would be made explicit if we asked "Why has *A* this right"? For the appropriate answer could only consist of two things: first, the statement of some rule or rules of law (say those of Contract), under which given certain facts certain legal consequences follow; and secondly, a statement that these facts were here the case. But again it is important to see that one who says that "*A* has a right" does not *state* the relevant rule of law; and that though, given certain facts, it is correct to say "*A* has a right" one who says this does not state or describe those facts. He has done something different from either of these two things: he has drawn a conclusion from the relevant but unstated rule, and from the relevant but unstated facts of the case. "*A* has a right" like "He is out" is therefore the tail-end of a simple legal calculation: it records a result and may be well called a conclusion of law. It is not therefore used to predict the future as the American Realists say; it refers to the present as their opponents claim but unlike ordinary statements does not do this by describing present or continuing facts. . . .

3. A third peculiarity is this: the assertion "Smith has a right to be paid £10" said by a judge in deciding the case has a different status from the utterance of it out of court, where it may be used to make a claim, or an admission and in many other ways. The judge's utterance is official, authoritative and, let us assume, final; the other is none of these things, yet in spite of these differences the sentences are of the same sort: they are both conclusions of law. We can compare this difference in spite of similarity with "He is out" said by

the umpire in giving his decision and said by a player to make a claim.
. . .

4.  In any system, legal or not, rules may for excellent practical
reasons attach identical consequences to any one of a set of very different facts.  The rule of cricket attaches the same consequence to
the batsman's being bowled, stumped, or caught.  And the word "out"
is used in giving decisions or making claims under the rule and in
other verbal application of it.  . . .   In a game a rule may simply
attach a single consequence to the successive actions of a set of different men—as when a team is said to have won a game.  A more
complex rule may prescribe that what is to be done at one point in a
sequence shall depend on what was done or occurred earlier: and it
may be indifferent to the identity of the persons concerned in the sequence so long as they fall under certain defining conditions.  An
example of this is when a team permitted by the rules of a tournament
to have a varying membership is penalised only in the third round—
when the membership has changed—for what was done in the first
round.  In all such cases a sequence of action or states of affairs is
unified simply by falling under certain rules; they *may* be otherwise
as different as you please.  Here can be seen the essential elements
of the language of legal corporations.  For in law, the lives of ten men
that overlap but do not coincide may fall under separate rules under
which they have separate rights and duties and then they are a collection of individuals for the law; but their actions may fall under
rules of a different kind which make what is to be done by any one
or more of them depend in a complex way on what was done or occurred earlier.  And then we may speak in appropriately unified
ways of the sequence so unified, using a terminology like that of corporation law which will show that it is *this* sort of rule we are applying to the facts.  But here the unity of the rule may mislead us when
we come to define this terminology.  It may cast a shadow: we may
look for an identical continuing thing or person or quality *in* the sequence.  We may find it—in "corporate spirit."  This is real enough;
but it is a secret of success not a criterion of identity.

### III

These four general characteristics of legal language explain both
why definition of words like "right," "duty," and "corporation" is
baffled by the absence of some counterpart to "correspond" to these
words, and also why the unobvious counterparts which have been so
ingeniously contrived—the future facts, the complex facts or the psychological facts—turn out not to be something in terms of which we
can define these words although to be connected with them in complex
or indirect ways.  The fundamental point is that the primary function of these words is not to stand for or describe anything but a distinct function; this makes it vital to attend to Bentham's warning that
we should not, as does the traditional method of definitions, abstract
words like "right" and "duty," "State," or "corporation" from the sentences in which alone their full function can be seen, and then demand
of them so abstracted their genus and differentia.

Let us see what the use of this traditional method of definition presupposes and what the limits of its efficacy are, and why it may be misleading. It is of course the simplest form of definition, and also a peculiarly satisfying form because it gives us a set of words which can always be substituted for the word defined whenever it is used; it gives us a comprehensive synonym or translation for the word which puzzles us. It is peculiarly appropriate where the words have the straightforward function of standing for some kind of thing, or quality, person, process, or event, for here we are not mystified or puzzled about the general characteristics of our subject-matter, but we ask for a definition simply to locate within this familiar general kind or class some special subordinate kind or class. Thus since we are not puzzled about the general notions of furniture or animal we can take a word like "chair" or "cat" and give the principle of its use by first specifying the general class to which what it is used to describe belongs, and then going on to define the specific differences that mark it off from other species of the same general kind. And of course if we are *not* puzzled about the general notion of a corporate body but only wish to know how one species (say a college) differs from another (say a limited company) we can use this form of definition of single words perfectly well. But just because the method is appropriate at this level of inquiry, it cannot help us when our perplexities are deeper. For if our question arises, as it does with fundamental legal notions because we are puzzled about the general category to which something belongs and how some general type of expression relates to fact, and not merely about the place within that category, then until the puzzle is cleared up this form of definition is at the best unilluminating and at the worst profoundly misleading. . . .

How then shall we define such words? If definition is the provision of a synonym which will not equally puzzle us these words cannot be defined. But I think there is a method of elucidation of quite general application and which we can call definition, if we wish. Bentham and others practised it, though they did not preach it. But before applying it to the highly complex legal cases, I shall illustrate it from the simple case of a game. Take the notion of a trick in a game of cards. Somebody says "What is a trick?" and you reply "I will explain: when you have a game and among its rules is one providing that when each of our players has played a card then the player who has put down the highest card scores a point, in these circumstances that player is said to have 'taken a trick'." This natural explanation has not taken the form of a definition of the single word "trick": no synonym has been offered for it. Instead we have taken a sentence in which the word "trick" plays its characteristic role and explained it first by specifying the conditions under which the whole sentence is true, and secondly by showing how it is used in drawing a conclusion from the rules in a particular case. Suppose now that after such an explanation your questioner presses on: "That is all very well, that explains 'taking a trick'; but I still want to know what the word 'trick' means just by itself. I want a definition of 'trick'; I want something which can be substituted for it whenever it is used." If we yield to this demand for a single word definition we might reply: "The trick is just a collective name for the four cards." But someone may object: "The trick is not just a name for the four cards because these four cards will not always constitute a trick. It must therefore be some entity to which the four cards belong." A third might say: "No, the trick is a fictitious entity which the players pretend exists and to which by fiction which is part of the game they ascribe the cards." But in so simple a case we would not tolerate these theories, fraught as they are with mystery and empty of any guidance as to the use made of the word within the game: we would stand by the original two-fold explanation; for this surely gave us all we needed when it explained the conditions under which the statement "He has taken a trick" is true and showed us how it was used in drawing a conclusion from the rules in a particular case.

If we turn back to Bentham we shall find that when his explanation of legal notions is illuminating, as it very often is, it conforms to this method though only loosely. Yet curiously what he tells us to do is something different: it is to take a word like "right" or "duty" or "State": to embody it in a sentence such as "you have a right" where it plays a characteristic role and then to find a *translation* of it into what we should call factual terms. This he called the method of paraphrase—giving phrase for phrase not word for word. Now this method is applicable to many cases and has shed much light; but it distorts many legal words like "right" or "duty" whose characteristic role is not played in statements of fact but in conclusions of law. A paraphrase of these in factual terms is not possible and when Bentham proffers such a paraphrase it turns out not to be one at all.

. . . .

## V

If we look now at the type of theory so attractive to common sense which asserts that statements referring to corporations are "abbreviations" and so can be reduced or translated into statements referring only to individuals, we can see now in precisely what way they failed. Their mistake was that of seeking a paraphrase or translation into other terms of statements referring to corporations instead of specifying the conditions under which such statements are true and the manner in which they are used. But in assessing these common-sense theories it is important to notice one very general feature of the language involved in the application of legal rules which the attempt to paraphrase always obscures. If we take a very simple legal statement like "Smith has made a contract with Y" we must distinguish the meaning of this conclusion of law, from two things: from (1) a statement of the facts required for its truth, *e.g.*, that the parties have signed a written agreement, and also from (2) the statement of the legal consequences of it being true, *e.g.*, that Y is bound to do certain things under the agreement. There is here at first sight something puzzling; it seems as if there is something intermediate between the facts, which make the conclusion of law true, and the legal consequences. But if we refer to the simple case of a game we can see what this is. When "He is out" is said of a batsman (whether by a player, or by the umpire) this neither makes the factual statement that the ball has struck the wicket nor states that he is bound to leave the wicket: it is an utterance the function of which is to draw a conclusion from a specific rule under which in circumstances such as these, consequences of this sort arise, and we should obviously neglect something vital in its meaning if, in the attempt to give a paraphrase, we said it meant the facts alone or the consequences alone or even the combination of these two. The combined statement "The ball has struck the wicket and he must leave the wicket" fails to give the whole meaning of "He is out" because it does not reproduce the distinctive manner in which the original statement is used to draw a conclusion from a specific but unstated rule under which such a consequence follows on such conditions. And no paraphrase can both elucidate the original and reproduce this feature.

I dwell on this point because it is here that the common-sense theories of corporate personality fail. The theory that statements referring to corporations are disguised abbreviations for statements about the rights and duties of individuals was usually expounded with such crudity as not to deserve consideration. It is easy to see that a statement about the rights of a limited company is not equivalent to the statement that its members have those same rights. A conveyance by Smith & Co. Ltd. to the sole shareholder Smith is of course not a conveyance by Smith to Smith. But a few theorists, among them Hohfeld, have stated this type of theory with a requisite degree of subtlety. Hohfeld saw that to say that Smith & Co. Ltd. has a contract with $Y$ was, of course, not to say the same thing about the members of the company: he thought it was to say something different and very complicated about the way in which the capacities, rights, powers, privileges, and liabilities of the natural persons concerned in the company had been affected. Though more formidable in this guise, the theory fails because, although it gives us the legal consequences upon the individuals of the original statement, it does not give us the force and meaning of that statement itself. The alleged paraphrase is less than the original statement "Smith & Co. Ltd. has a contract with $Y$" because it gives no hint of what the original statement is used to do, namely, to draw a conclusion of law from special rules relating to companies and from rules extended by analogy from the case of individuals. So the paraphrase, complex and ingenious as it is, gives us too little; but it also give us too much. It dissipates the unity of the simple statement "Smith & Co. has a contract with $Y$" and substitutes a statement of the myriad legal rights, duties, powers, etc., of numerous individuals of whom we never have thought nor could have thought in making the original statement. Hence it is that those who are attracted to this common-sense form of analysis feel cheated when they look at it more closely. And they *are* cheated; only they should not in despair clutch at the Realist or Fiction theories. For the elements which they miss in the translation, the analogy with individuals, the unity of the original statement, and its direct application to fact cannot be given them in these theories nor in any translation of the original; it can only be given in a detailed description of the conditions under which a statement of this form is true and of the distinctive manner in which it is used to draw a conclusion from specific rules in a particular case.

I have of course dealt only with the *legal* personality of corporations. I have argued that if we characterise adequately the distinctive manner in which expressions for corporate bodies are used in a legal system then there is no residual question of the form "What is a corporation?" There only *seems* to be one if we insist on a form of definition or elucidation which is inappropriate. Theories of the traditional form can only give a distorted account of the meaning of expressions for corporate bodies because they all, in spite of their mutual hostility, make the common assumption that these expressions must stand for or describe something, and then give separate and incompatible accounts of its peculiarity as a complex or recondite or a fictitious entity; whereas the peculiarity lies not here but in the distinctive characteristics of expressions used in the enunciation and application of rules. . . .

## VI

If we put aside the question "What is a corporation?" and ask instead "Under what types of conditions does the law ascribe liabilities to corporations?" this is likely to clarify the actual working of a legal system and bring out the precise issues at stake when judges, who are supposed not to legislate, make some new extension to corporate bodies of rules worked out for individuals.

### Questions

1. How would Hart's explanation of the statement "the Susquehanna Coal Company is in New York" be like—and unlike— Ross's? Does Hart think that terms like corporation refer to concrete "states of affairs"? Does he think they are meaningless?

2. What is Hart pointing out in his explanation of the meaning of "taking a trick"? Can what is meant by "taking a trick" be fully explicated by reference to physical descriptions of card players, their actions and the cards? What else is needed? Consider the statement by a baseball umpire, "Ball four; you walk." What would you have to explain to someone, to explain what that means? How would your explanation be like the task of explaining the statement "the Susquehanna Coal Company is in New York"?

3. Does Hart's explanation of the role of legal concepts answer the question whether, and how, they can provide order and system for us?

Suppose we agree, for example, that the statement "the Susquehanna Coal Co. is in New York" can only be understood by understanding the "distinctive manner" in which it "is used to draw a conclusion from a specific but unstated rule under which such a consequence follows on such conditions". Do we know what this "distinctive manner" is? How "specific" is the unstated rule that make the utterance of that statement appropriate? Can you state it? Can you state the "conditions" that make the invocation of the rule appropriate? Can the concepts help us to answer these questions if the concepts can only be understood in terms of the answers to *them*?

Are there not, in fact, a number of rules, or even bodies of rules, that would make the statement, "the Susquehanna Coal Co. is in New York" appropriate, *e. g.*, (a) rules relating to whether the corporation was "in" New York for purposes of giving New York courts jurisdiction upon service in New York of an agent of the corporation, and (b) rules relating to whether New York can validly demand a license fee from the corporation? Does Hart's analysis help us to understand how the two sets of rules and conditions are related to one another, if at all? If there is any relationship, does the concept help us to make our understanding of it systematic?

4.  Further, how accurate is the position that the application of legal concepts is to be understood by analyzing their function in *legal rules* that spell out the conditions for and consequences of applying them? Can the "rules" for legal usage be prescribed in a fashion that splits off a "legal meaning" from ordinary meaning, so that the judge's use of the legal concept can be "pure" of the ordinary nuances? If one wants to know the meaning of the concept *corporation* "in law" can he find out by reading the rules of law that, completely and of themselves, tell us how to "move" the word in the game, "law"? Or is there an interplay between the "rules" (such as there may be) of the ordinary usage and the rules for the legal usage? If so, what effect must this have on our understanding how a legal system works?

Consider, for example, whether the application of the concept "abandoned" in the *Haslem* case (see the Introduction) could be fully understood by reference to legal rules alone. Let us even suppose (what could be questioned) that there is a concrete body of legal rules for the judge to apply, *e. g.*, "one cannot maintain an action for trover to recover property that he has 'abandoned' "; "someone who has left personal property for an unreasonable time shall be deemed to have 'abandoned' it"; "an intent to 'abandon' personal property shall be presumed where it has been out of the abandoner's possession an unreasonable time", etc. Are these rules adequate to tell the judge whether the manure was "abandoned"? In deciding the question, do you suppose he can be uninfluenced by ordinary non-legal "rules" for when we say something has been "abandoned"—or how we use "left", "intending to return", "unreasonable time", etc. As vague and uncertain as the "rules" of ordinary usage may be, are the "legal" rules so certain as to obviate the need to seek recourse to them? And conversely, don't legal decisions as to "abandonment", "rights", "duties", and so forth, feed back into the everyday usage?

Consider, in this regard, the remarks of O. W. Holmes, *The Path of the Law*, 10 Harv.L.Rev. 457, 459–60, 464 (1897):

> I do not say that there is not a wider point of view from which the distinction between law and morals becomes of secondary or no importance, as all mathematical distinctions vanish in presence of the infinite. But I do say that that distinction is of the first importance for the object which we are here to consider,—a right study and mastery of the law

as a business with well understood limits, a body of dogma enclosed within definite lines. . . . The law is full of phraseology drawn from morals, and by the mere force of language continually invites us to pass from one domain to the other without perceiving it, as we are sure to do unless we have the boundary constantly before our minds. The law talks about rights, and duties, and malice, and intent, and negligence, and so forth, and nothing is easier, or, I may say, more common in legal reasoning, than to take these words in their moral sense, at some stage of the argument, and so to drop into fallacy. For instance, when we speak of the rights of man in a moral sense, we mean to mark the limits of interference with individual freedom which we think are prescribed by conscience, or by our ideal, however reached. Yet it is certain that many laws have been enforced in the past, and it is likely that some are enforced now, which are condemned by the most enlightened opinion of the time, or which at all events pass the limit of interference as many consciences would draw it. Manifestly, therefore, nothing but confusion of thought can result from assuming that the rights of man in a moral sense are equally rights in the sense of the Constitution and the law. . . .

. . . . .

. . . For my own part, I often doubt whether it would not be a gain if every word of moral significance could be banished from the law altogether, and other words adopted which should convey legal ideas uncolored by anything outside the law. We should lose the fossil records of a good deal of history and the majesty got from ethical associations, but by ridding ourselves of an unnecessary confusion we should gain very much in the clearness of our thought.

. . . . .

How is Holmes' desire to banish from the law words of moral significance related to the view that the law is "a business with well understood limits, a body of dogma enclosed within definite lines"? Is it? Would it be of much avail to banish such words as "right" and "duties" in the interest of working "a wedge" between legal language and ordinary language?[2] If the courts replaced "duty" with a new word "ytud", would "ytud" not work its way back into the ordinary language; and would the ordinary language not work its understanding of "ytud" back into the law? Cannot a case be made that we *want* our judges to draw on words of moral significance, with, to some extent, their connotations in the ordinary language? Cannot the same case be made for the overlap between "legal" and "ordinary" uses of "abandoned," "reasonable time," etc. Why was Holmes concerned?

**2.** The image is from Simpson, The Analysis of Legal Concepts, 80 L.Q. Rev. 535 (1964). Professor Simpson's criticisms of Hart, Ross and W. N. Hohfeld are strongly recommended for those who would pursue further the problems raised in this chapter.

5.  What *is* the relationship between, say, "manufactured product" as it occurs (a) in a tariff act, where the rules for its application—such as they are—are rules relating to import duties, (b) in the Interstate Commerce Act, where the rules are rules of Interstate Commerce Commission jurisdiction, and (c) in ordinary usage(s)? Is the phrase, in each usage, associated with a different concept—so that there are three concepts of manufactured product for the one term "manufactured product"? If not, what is the relationship between them?

Consider, in this regard, the observations of WITTGENSTEIN, PHILOSOPHICAL INVESTIGATIONS §§ 66–67 (1963) in which he raises the question of what relationship, if any, obtains as among all the things we call "games", *e.g.*, board games, card games, ball games, Olympic games, etc.  If you look at the various sorts of "games", Wittgenstein pointed out, you will not see any feature common to *all* of them; on the contrary, as you pass from one sort of "game" to another, "you find many correspondences with the first group, but many common features drop out, and others appear".  The result of such an investigation shows "a complicated network of similarities overlapping and criss-crossing: sometimes overall similarities, sometimes similarities of detail".  Wittgenstein went on to call these similarities "family resemblances"; things in a family are called by the same name, say "number", because each

> "has a—direct—relationship with several things that have hitherto been called number; and this can be said to give it an indirect relationship to other things we call the same name.  And we extend our concept of number as in spinning a thread we twist fibre on fibre.  And the strength of the thread does not reside in the fact that some one fibre runs through its whole length, but in the overlapping of many fibres."

Do you agree with Wittgenstein?  Can you describe the relationship any more precisely than Wittgenstein did?  If not, why not? What are the implications for a legal system if a judge, in invoking a concept, is always involved in an analysis of overlapping fibres? What is the consequence for a "pure" legal system if the different threads of ordinary usage overlap with the different threads of legal usage?  Can we keep our "legal" concepts pure of the nuances of everyday, ordinary language?

---

## SECTION TWO: THE CONCEPT OF A THING: IS THE PERSON A FICTION?

To this point, our examination of legal concepts has focused on the concept of the corporation, along with some other legal concepts like ownership, right and duty.  With these terms it is fairly obvious, as Hart observes in the excerpt above, that they "do not have [a] straightforward connection with counterparts in the world of fact." But what about concepts that are not so patently "shorthands" for a complex of relationships? Consider the concept of *chair*, or *cat* (Hart's examples) or *person*. How "straightforward" is the relationship between *them* and the "world of facts"? Can these terms— any more than right and duty—be understood without understanding a complex structure of rules?

## KEELER v. SUPERIOR COURT FOR COUNTY OF AMADOR

80 Cal.Rptr. 865 (D.C.A.1969)

FRIEDMAN, Associate Justice.

Petitioner Robert Keeler is charged by information with aggravated assault upon his divorced wife, with wilfully conflicting corporal injury upon her and with the murder of the unborn child she was carrying at the time of the alleged assault. He seeks a writ of prohibition to stay his prosecution on the murder charge.

The California Penal Code (section 187) defines murder as "the unlawful killing of a human being, with malice aforethought." Manslaughter too is defined as the killing of a human being. (Pen.Code, § 192.) Petitioner contends that a fetus is not in law a human being, hence that no homicide is committed by one who puts it to death.

We summarize the evidence at the preliminary hearing: Mrs. Keeler had secured an interlocutory decree of divorce from petitioner in September 1968. On February 23, 1969, she was driving on a narrow mountain road in Amador County enroute to Stockton, where she was living with another man in a nonmarital relationship. She was pregnant by this man. As she drove along, petitioner drove his own car in front of her, blocking her passage. She stopped, and he walked over to her and said he had heard of her pregnancy. He opened the door of her car and drew her out by the arm. He looked at her abdomen and said: "You sure are. I'm going to stomp it out of you." He pushed her back against the car with his hands on her shoulders and kicked his knee into her abdomen. He then struck her in the face several times. She lost consciousness. After the attack he left.

Mrs. Keeler managed to get back into her car and continued to Stockton. The police and an ambulance were summoned to her home, and she was taken to a hospital. Doctors observed her injuries. She was bleeding extensively from the nose and mouth. She had lacerations on her face which required suturing. She had a fracture of the nasal bone and a tooth had been knocked out. There was extensive bruising on the exterior of her abdomen. On the abdomen were two or three crescent-shaped marks which appeared to be heel imprints.

A Caesarean section was performed. The doctor examined the baby *in utero*. He said that when he reached in to feel the baby's head, ". . . it was constricted like a bag of mush." The head of the fetus had been extensively and severely fractured. Its death had been immediate. Because there was no maceration of the skin of the fetus, the doctors believed the baby had been alive eight hours before its delivery. Mrs. Keeler testified that the baby had moved in her earlier that day, but not after she left the scene of the attack. Her obstetrician stated that the pregnancy had been progressing normally and he had been able to detect movement as well at fetal heart tones. The fetus had attained a weight of approximately five pounds. Medical estimates of the term of pregnancy varied from 31 weeks to 36 weeks.   There was medical testimony that the fetus had "definitely" reached the stage of viability, that is, "with reasonable medical certainty" premature separation from the mother at that point of pregnancy would not have ended the child's life.

There are many descriptions in legal literature of the English common law doctrine which refused to recognize feticide as homicide, demanding that a child be fully born and functionally independent of its mother in order to be treated as a homicide subject.  .  .  .

These descriptions are not quite accurate, or at any rate represent an incomplete statement of historic development.  The most thorough and scholarly inquiry on the subject (Means, *op. cit.*)[3] discloses the common law's heavy borrowings from theological and philosophic inquiries into the incipience of human quality.  Although theologians tended to attach human value to the embryo immediately after conception, the early common law required quickening, that is, animation. Bracton's, The Laws and Customs of England, quoted in Means, *op. cit.*, page 419, represents a 13th-century description of English law: "If there be anyone who strikes a pregnant woman or gives her a poison whereby he causes an abortion, if the foetus be already formed or animated, and especially if it be animated, he commits homicide." Bracton's declaration thus imparted human status to the embryo at some point during the second trimester of pregnancy, when quickening occurs.  (See Means, *op. cit.*, pp. 412, 420.)

Eventually the common law shifted to the "born alive" theory, as represented by Sir Edward Coke's description of English law in mid-17th century (quoted in Means, *op. cit.*, p. 420): "If a woman be quick with childe, and by a potion or otherwise killeth it in her wombe, or if a man beat her, whereby the childe dyeth in her body, and she is delivered of a dead childe, this is a great misprision, and no murder; but if the childe be born alive and dyeth of the potion, battery, or other cause, this is murder; for in law it is accounted a reasonable creature, in *rerum natura*, when it is born alive."

Such a rule tends to precipitate as the artificial formalism of an esoteric discipline, achieving increasing alienation from the religious, moral and scientific ponderings which attended its inception.  In juxtaposition to later-adopted abortion statutes, the common law rule left a no-man's land between the prohibitions against abortion and homicide.   In some states and in Great Britain itself, the gap was filled by statutes defining feticide as a crime.  (See 40 C.J.S. Homicide §§ 2, 38, pp. 825, 899–900; Williams, *op. cit.*, pp. 11–12.)  California has not enacted a feticide statute.

The question is one of law, not of morality, medicine or popular belief.  (Cf. Knutson, *When Does a Human Life Begin? Viewpoints*

---

**3.** The Law of New York Concerning Abortion and the Status of the Foetus, 1664–1968: A Case of Cessation of          Constitutionality 14 N.Y. Law Forum 411 (1968).

*of Public Health Professionals,* 57 Am. Journal of Public Health (Dec. 1967) p. 2163 et seq.) Inquiry into the rule's present status, nevertheless, should be grounded in the conditions of modern life, rather than those of past centuries in which the rule evolved. The common law did not congeal into immobility after its transportation to the American states. (See Katz v. Walkinshaw (1903) 141 Cal. 116, 122–124, 70 P. 663, 74 P. 766, 64 L.R.A. 236). The "born alive" rule of England never crystallized as acknowledged California law. In Scott v. McPheeters (1939) 33 Cal.App.2d 629, 635, 92 P.2d 678, 93 P.2d 562, the court observed that a "seven-months baby" has well developed organs and is capable of life outside the mother's womb. It posed the rhetorical question: "Who may say that such a viable child is not in fact a human being in actual existence?"

McPheeters was a civil damage case, but in People v. Chavez, supra, 77 Cal.App.2d 621, 176 P.2d 92, became an instrumentality in the evolutionary development of California homicide law. There a mother permitted her baby to die after it dropped from her womb. In a remarkable opinion the court held that evidence of life after complete separation from the mother's body was not needed, thus affirming her conviction of manslaughter. It observed (77 Cal.App.2d at p. 625, 176 P.2d 92, at p. 94) that neither birth nor removal by Caesarean section created a human being, rather, that the baby "has started an independent existence after it has reached a state of development where it is capable of living and where it will, in the normal course of nature and with ordinary care, continue to live and grow as a separate being." Citing McPheeters, the court stated (77 Cal.App. 2d at p. 626, 176 P.2d at p. 95) that the common law rule denying identity to a viable fetus is contrary not only to "common experience and the ordinary course of nature" but also to the law's presumption that "things happen according to the ordinary course of nature . . . ." (See Civ.Code, § 3546.)

Both McPheeters and Chavez are implicit with recognition of 20th-century advances in obstetrics and pediatrics. Today American medical men and hospitals are prepared with the learning, techniques and equipment to preserve the lives of premature infants. Given normal development through the first seven months of intrauterine life, a premature infant is expected to live.[4] To crystallize the "born alive" doctrine of 17th-century England as the law of 20th-century America would run counter to the traditions and spirit of the common law. " 'It is contrary to the spirit of the common law itself to apply

---

4. The Encyclopaedia Britannica (1968 ed., vol. 8, p. 327) states: "Infants born before 6¼ months (27 weeks) are rarely viable; from 6¼ to 7 months they may survive with good care, and after 7 months (30 weeks) they are generally viable."
A set of 1954 statistics displays an 80% survival rate for infants delivered during the 32d and 33d weeks of pregnancy and weighing 1500 to 1750 grams; an 88% rate when delivered after 33 to 34 weeks of pregnancy and weighing 1750 to 2000 grams; a 96% rate when delivered after 34 to 36 weeks and weighing 2000 to 2500 grams. (5 Lawyers' Medical Cyclopedia, § 37.17, p. 420.) A set of 1961 statistics exhibits a 98% survival rate for infants weighing 2000 to 2500 grams. (7 The Cyclopedia of Medicine, Surgery, Specialties, p. 275.) In the case at bar, the fetus had attained a weight of 2205 grams (approximately five pounds) at the time of its death. [Footnote by the Court.]

a rule founded on a particular reason to a case where that reason utterly fails.' " (Katz v. Walkinshaw, supra, 141 Cal. at p. 122, 70 P. 663, quoting from Crandall v. Woods (1857) 8 Cal. 136, 143. . . .

Except where the felony-murder doctrine applies, an essential element of murder is an intent to kill or an intent with conscious disregard for life to commit acts likely to kill. . . . Here the evidence would support a finding of murderous intent directed against the unborn infant. Uncertainty as to its viability presents no impediment to a rule endowing it with status as a human being when it reaches a viable state. An autopsy is a usual sequel and pathologists' findings will be available. Viability of the fetus may be made the subject of expert medical testimony and the question submitted to the jury in company with the other questions of fact. In passing upon that question, as others, the jury are bound by the law's demand for proof beyond a reasonable doubt. (Pen.Code, § 1096.) [5]

Nor is the offender's advance uncertainty as to the character of his offense a source of objection. This is not a case where *mens rea* swings on verbal uncertainties in a criminal statute. (Cf. People v. Belous, 71 Cal.2d 954, 80 Cal.Rptr. 354, filed 9/5/69.) Petitioner's actions evince a general intent to harm and destroy. Preceding his assault he investigated neither the law nor the precise stage of fetal development. "[T]he law is full of instances where a man's fate depends on his estimating rightly, that is, as the jury subsequently estimates it, some matter of degree. If his judgment is wrong, not only may he incur a fine or a short imprisonment . . . ; he may incur the penalty of death." (Nash v. United States (1913) 229 U.S. 373, 377, 33 S.Ct. 780, 781, 57 L.Ed. 1232, per Holmes, J.)

Even where, according to the evidence, the offender's malicious design is aimed at the mother alone, the infliction of death upon her viable fetus might yet be murder, although probably not of the first degree. A killing of the latter sort might be submitted to the jury as second degree felony-murder, a killing committed in the perpetration of a felony not enumerated in Penal Code, section 189, but nevertheless inherently dangerous to life. (People v. Williams (1965) 63 Cal.2d 452, 457, 47 Cal.Rptr. 7, 406 P.2d 647.)

A rule recognizing the slaying of a viable fetus as homicide engenders no practical conflict with the abortion laws. Abortions, legal

5. In applying the "born alive" rule, various courts have adopted auxiliary tests of "life," such as respiration and blood circulation. The isolation of these tests from medical fact is exemplified by the somewhat poetic utterance of an Iowa court: "Life means respiration. Not to have breathed is not to have lived." (State v. Winthrop (1876) 43 Iowa 519 [22 Am.Rep. 257].) It is now recognized that a fetus makes respiratory movements before birth; that the actual intake of air may commence during delivery; on the other hand, that some delay may ensue between complete extrusion from the mother's body and the intake of air. The notion of independent blood circulation is equally unrealistic, for there is no direct linkage between the blood of the mother and the blood of the fetus. (Williams, op. cit., pp. 6–9; Lear, His Momentary Ancestor, Saturday Review, Dec. 7, 1968, pp. 73–74.) Such judicial tests demonstrate the difficulty of applying artificial divisions to a continuous process. Proof beyond a reasonable doubt of capacity to live outside the womb provides a test more in keeping with the realities of continuous human development. [Footnote by the Court.]

or illegal, almost invariably occur during the early stage of pregnancy. California's Therapeutic Abortion Act does not sanction any termination of pregnancy after the twentieth week. (Health & Safety Code, § 25953.) A fetus reaches the stage of viability only during the third trimester of pregnancy. . . . .

. . . . .

## QUESTIONS

1. How does Judge Friedman decide that the foetus was a person —a human being the killing of which could support a charge of murder? Does there appear to have been a mental concept *person* which could simplify his task?

2. What does Judge Friedman mean, "the question is one of law, not of morality, medicine, or popular belief"? Does he mean he could "find" the answer to the case by appeal to authoritative legal rules and definitions?

3. How would you decide whether the foetus was a person or not? What role is played in your analysis by a concept *person*? If you have ideas in mind when you think of a person, what ideas are they? Is there a "straightforward connection" between any such ideas and the foetus that was in controversy here?

4. Would you deem it an adequate solution to the problem to reason, "If I say the foetus was a person, then its killer can be tried for murder. I think its killer is the sort of a person who ought to be tried for murder; therefore I judge the foetus a person." Do you think that is all Judge Friedman's opinion amounted to?

## NOTE

Judge Friedman's opinion was reversed by the Supreme Court of California, Keeler v. Superior Court of Amador County, 87 Cal.Rptr. 481 (1970). Justice Mosk, writing for the Court, took the position that the manslaughter statute had to be interpreted with reference to the intent of the legislature at the time of its earliest enactment—1850. Reviewing the common law as it would have been known to the original California legislators, the Court decided that the unlawful and malicious killing of a "human being" was not intended to include feticide. 87 Cal.Rptr. at 483, 486. In the view of the Court, then, the subsequent developments in the sciences of obstetrics and pediatrics were not deemed relevant. 87 Cal.Rptr. at 488. In addition, to interpret the law otherwise, the majority felt, would constitute a violation of due process of law. 87 Cal.Rptr. at 490 *ff*.

In his dissent, 87 Cal.Rptr. at 494 *ff.*, Acting Chief Justice Burke wrote:

> The majority hold that "Baby Girl" Vogt, who, according to medical testimony, had reached the 35th week of development, had a 96 percent chance of survival, and was "definitely" alive and viable at the time of her death, nevertheless was not a "human being" under California's homicide statutes. In my view, in so holding, the majority ignore signifi-

cant common law precedents, frustrate the express intent of the Legislature, and defy reason, logic and common sense.

Penal Code section 187 defines murder as "the unlawful killing of a human being with malice aforethought." Penal Code section 192 defines manslaughter as "the unlawful killing of a human being, without malice.". The majority pursue the meaning of the term "human being" down the ancient hallways of the common law, citing Coke, Blackstone and Hale to the effect that the slaying of a "quickened" (i.e. stirring in the womb) child constituted "a great misprision," but not murder. Although, as discussed below, I strongly disagree with the premise that the words of our penal statutes must be construed as of 1648 or 1765, nevertheless, there is much common law precedent which would support the view that a viable fetus such as Baby Girl Vogt is a human being under those statutes.

The majority cast a passing glance at the common law concept of quickening, but fail to explain the significance of that concept: At common law, the quickened fetus *was* considered to be a human being, a second life separate and apart from its mother. As stated by Blackstone, in the passage immediately preceding that portion quoted in the majority opinion (fn. 6), "Life is the immediate gift of God, a right inherent by nature in every individual; *and it begins in contemplation of law as soon as an infant is able to stir in the mother's womb*." . . .

          . . . . .

Of course, I do not suggest that we should interpret the term "human being" in our homicide statutes in terms of the common law concept of quickening. At one time, that concept had a value in differentiating, as accurately as was then scientifically possible, between life and nonlife. The analogous concept of viability is clearly more satisfactory, for it has a well defined and medically determinable meaning denoting the ability of the fetus to live or survive apart from its mother.

The majority opinion suggests that we are confined to common law concepts, and to the common law definition of murder or manslaughter. However, the Legislature, in Penal Code sections 187 and 192, has defined those offenses for us: homicide is the unlawful killing of a "human being." Those words need not be frozen in place as of any particular time, but must be fairly and reasonably interpreted by this court to promote justice and to carry out the evident purposes of the Legislature in adopting a homicide statute. . . .

          . . . . .

We commonly conceive of human existence as a spectrum stretching from birth to death. However, if this court properly might expand the definition of "human being" at one end of that spectrum, we may do so at the other end. Consider the following example: All would agree that "Shooting or otherwise damaging a corpse is not homicide. . . ." (Perkins, Criminal Law (2d ed. 1969) ch. 2, § 1, p. 31.) In other words, a corpse is not considered to be a "human being" and thus cannot be the subject of a "killing" as those terms are used in homicide statutes. However, it is readily apparent that our concepts of what constitutes a "corpse" have been and are being continually modified by advances in the field of medicine, including new techniques for life revival, restoration and resuscitation such as artificial respiration, open heart massage, transfusions, transplants and a variety of life-restoring stimulants, drugs and new surgical methods. Would this court ignore these developments and exonerate the killer of an apparently "drowned" child merely because that child would have been pronounced dead in 1648 or 1850? Obviously not. Whether a homicide occurred in that case would be determined by medical testimony regarding the capability of the child to have survived prior to the defendant's act. And that is precisely the test which this court should adopt in the instant case.

THOMAS R. McCOY

## LOGIC VS. VALUE JUDGMENT IN LEGAL AND ETHICAL THOUGHT *

Abortion law reform is usually debated in terms of: "Is the fetus a human life or isn't it?" "Is it murder or isn't it?" "When does human life begin?" "Is the fetus a person or isn't it?" The form of the questions implies that they can be answered by the discovery of an objective fact—the precise point in time when the collection of component cells "becomes" a "human life," a "person." The debate is hopeless. An answer is impossible because the mutual exclusivity of the terms "human life" and "nonhuman life" does not reflect any point of discontinuity in reality. The conception "human life" is a *choice* to group together a large number of real objects (*e.g.,* you and me) because they are sufficiently similar in certain respects.

We are like the child before seeing the sea anemone; we do not experience the sensation of choice in the application of the names "human life" and "nonhuman life" to the real objects in our ordinary experience. Because these real objects are either very similar or very dissimilar to other members of the class, we tend to assume that reality is neatly divisible according to our conceptions of human life and nonhuman life. We make assertions like, "The fetus is not a human life until it reaches viability," or "until the time of birth," or "until it is 'socialized,' many months after birth." These "factual" statements are made in the context of an unarticulated abstract judgment that the law should prohibit only the taking of a human life. In

* From 23 Vand.L.Rev. 1277, 1288–1290 (1971). With the permission of Vanderbilt Law Review.

other words, these assertions are alternative minor premises in a syllogism the conclusion of which is either that the law should or that the law should not prohibit abortion of a fetus at a particular stage of development. But the disagreement evidenced in these assertions is not, as the assertions lead one to believe, a factual disagreement. It is merely semantic. There is no existential sense in which any one of those points *is* the point which separates human life from non-human life. These assertions are, usually unbeknown to the speaker, the result of a choice—a choice to draw a conceptual line across what is in reality a continuum. Medical science can observe in great detail all of the characteristics of the fetus at any stage of development. Size and shape of the various organs and limbs, operation of the circulatory system, motor ability, and various reflexes can be observed and described in terms of low order abstractions. At any point in development the sum of those characteristics is what the fetus *is* in reality. These are the nonverbal facts of the problem, and in terms of these nonverbal facts the fetus possesses significant similarities and significant dissimilarities to you and me, the admitted members of the class "human life." And with each succeeding day, hour, minute, the similarity increases. To ask whether at any point it "is" a human life is not to ask about a fact. It is to ask: "How similar to you and me must it be before I call it a human life?" That is a value judgment, a choice of degree.

In the context of abortion law reform this value judgment is obviously not the type made by the scientist about the use of a class word for purposes of communication. It is the second type of value judgment: Should the consequences of inclusion in the class "human life" be imposed on this individual? Simply stated, then, the question of abortion law reform is: "How similar to you and me must a thing be before we prohibit its being killed?" Thus, the syllogism which most accurately reflects the nature of the question is:

> Only killing of objects which are similar enough to you and me should be prohibited.

> The fetus at *X* point of development is (or is not) similar enough to you and me.

> Killing of the fetus should (or should not) be prohibited.

When the question is accurately formulated, it is found to be precisely the same question presented by infanticide, euthanasia, and extermination of mental and physical defectives. *How similar?* The individuals who are the subject of infanticide, euthanasia, and extermination of mental and physical defectives are simply at different points on the continuum of similarity to you and me, part of which we choose to call human life.

Why not allow killing of the fetus after it is viable, why not one day after birth, why not two months after birth? This is not necessarily an argument against abortion law "reform." The ethical or legal choice can be made at any point on the continuum depending upon the reasons offered in justification of the point chosen. The point is simply that those who are resisting "reform" with this type of argument more accurately perceive the nature of the question. Both the moral and legal prohibitions of abortion are questions of degree. The two differ only in that different factors are relevant to the choice of the point where we attach the prohibition against killing the object in question.

## QUESTIONS

1.  Do you agree with McCoy that problems like that of the *Keeler* case can be resolved by inventorying similarities in the objects of the killing? If so, how do we decide what sort of similarities to look to—size, ability to reason, ability to sustain life without aid of others? Which of them are "enough"?

2.  If comparing similarities is involved in the choice to invoke the concept, should we be primarily concerned with whether the foetus is similar enough to "you and me" that we want to treat its death as murder; or whether the killer of the foetus has shown behaviour similar enough to people we want to treat as murderers? Are the analyses the two questions invite the same?

## STATE v. WINTHROP

43 Iowa 519 (1876)

ADAMS, J.—The defendant is a physician, and was employed by one Roxia Clayton to attend her in childbirth. The child died. The defendant is charged with having produced its death. Evidence was introduced by the State tending to show that the child, previous to its death, respired and had an independent circulation. Evidence was introduced by the defendant tending to disprove such facts.

The defendant asked the court to give the following instruction:

"To constitute a human being, in the view of the law, the child mentioned in the indictment must have been fully born, and born alive, having an independent circulation and existence separate from the mother, but it is immaterial whether the umbilical cord which connects it with its mother be severed or not."

The court refused to give this instruction, and gave the following:

"If the child is fully delivered from the body of the mother, while the after birth is not, and the two are connected by the umbilical cord, and the child has independent life, *no matter whether it has breathed or not, or an independent circulation has been established or not*, it is a human being, on which the crime of murder may be perpetrated."

The giving of this instruction, and the refusal to instruct as asked, are assigned as error.

The court below seems to have assumed that a child may have independent life, without respiration and independent circulation. The idea of the court seems to have been that the life which the child lives between the time of its birth and the time of the establishment of respiration and independent circulation is an independent life. Yet the position taken by the Attorney-General, in his argument in behalf of the State, is fundamentally different. He says: "It will probably not be contended that independent life can exist without independent circulation, and hence the existence of the former necessarily presumes the existence of the latter, and so other or further proof is unnecessary." He further says: "The instruction complained of amounts to nothing more than the statement that, if the child had an independent life, then it was not necessary to establish those facts upon which the existence of life necessarily depends." If such was the meaning of the court below, the language used to express it was very unfortunate. The court said that, if the child had independent life, it is no matter whether an independent circulation had been established or not. The Attorney-General says that if the child had independent life, it had independent circulation, of course. But whether we take the one view or the other, we think the instruction was wrong. We will consider first the view that independent life and independent circulation necessarily co-exist, and examine the instruction as if that were conceded.

It follows that where a child is born alive, and the umbilical cord is not severed, and independent circulation has not been established, independent life is impossible, and the instruction amounts to this, that if the jury should find independent life under such circumstances, although it would be impossible, they might find the killing of the child to be murder. Such an instruction could serve no valuable purpose, and would necessarily involve the jury in confusion. It would do worse than that; it would tell the jury in effect that they might find independence of life in utter disregard of the conditions in which alone it could exist. To show how the defendant was prejudiced, if the instruction is to be viewed in this light, we may say that there was evidence that the *ductus arteriosus* was not closed. This evidence tended to show, slightly at least, that independent circulation had not been established. The instruction told the jury, by implication, that they might disregard this evidence. But we feel compelled to say that we do not think that the Attorney-General's interpretation of the instruction ever occurred to the court below. It is plain to see that the court below meant that independent life is not conditioned upon independent circulation. The error, if there was one, consisted in assuming that it was not. The question presented for our determination is by no means free from difficulty. Can the child have an independent life, while its circulation is still dependent upon the mother? There are two senses in which the word independent may be used. There is actual independence, and there is potential independence. A child is actually independent of its father when it is earning its own living; it is potentially independent when it is capable of earning its own living. We think the court below used the word *independent* in the latter sense. While the blood of the child circulates through the *placenta*, it is renovated through the lungs of the mother. In such sense it breathes through the lungs of the mother. Wharton & Stille's Medical Jurisprudence, 2 Vol., Sec. 128. It has no occasion during that period to breath through its own lungs. But when the resource of its mother's lungs is denied it, then arises the exigency of establishing independent respiration and independent circulation. Children, it seems, oftentimes do not breath immediately upon being born, but if the umbilical cord is severed, they must then breathe or die. Cases are recorded, it is true, where a child has been wholly severed from the mother, and respiration has not apparently been established until after the lapse of several minutes of time. During that time it must have had circulation, and the circulation was independent. Whether it had inappreciable respiration, or was in the condition of a person holding his breath, is a question not necessary to be considered for the determination of this case. It is sufficient to say, that while the circulation of the child is still dependent, its connection with the mother may be suddenly severed by artificial means, and the child not necessarily die. This is proven by what is called the Caesarean operation. A live child is cut out of a dead mother and survives. Such a child has a potential independence antecedent to its actual independence. So a child which has been born, but has not breathed, and is connected with the mother by the umbilical cord, may have the power to establish a new life upon its own resources antecedent to its exercise. According to the opinion of the court below, the killing of the child at that time may be murder. It is true that after a child is born it can no longer be called a *foetus*, according to the ordinary meaning of that word. Beck says, however, in his Medical Juris., 1 Vol., 498: "It must be evident that when a child is born alive, but has not yet respired, its condition is precisely like that of the *foetus in utero*. It lives merely because the *foetal* circulation is still going on. In this case none of the organs undergo any change." Casper says, in his Forensic Medicine, 3 Vol., 33: "In *foro* the term 'life' must be regarded as perfectly synonymous with 'respiration.' Life means respiration. Not to have breathed is not to have lived."

While, as we have seen, life has been maintained independent of the mother without appreciable respiration, the quotations above made indicate how radical the difference is regarded between *foetal* life and the new life which succeeds upon the establishment of respiration and independent circulation.

If we turn from the treatises on Medical Jurisprudence to the reported decisions, we find this difference, which is so emphasized in the former, made in the latter the practical test for determining when a child becomes a human being in such a sense as to become the subject of homicide. In Rex v. Enoch, 5 C. & P., 539, Mr. Justice J. PARKE said: "The child might have breathed before it was born, but its having breathed is not sufficiently life to make the killing of the child murder. There must have been an independent circulation in the child, or the child cannot be considered as alive for this purpose."

In Regina v. Trilloe, 1 Carrington & Marshman, 650, ERSKINE, J., in charging the jury, said: "If you are satisfied that this child had been wholly produced from the body of the prisoner alive, and that the prisoner wilfully and of malice aforethought strangled the child, after it had been so produced, and while it was alive, and while it had an independent circulation of its own, I am of the opinion that the charge is made out against the prisoner." See also Greenleaf on Ev., 3 Vol., Sec. 136.

It may be asked why, if there is a possibility of independent life, the killing of such a child might not be murder.

The answer is, that there is no way of proving that such possibility existed if actual independence was never established. Any verdict based upon such finding would be the result of conjecture.

Reversed.

## TOWNSHEND ON LIBEL AND SLANDER (3d Ed., 1877)

§ 95. Every communication of language by one to another is a publication. But to constitute an *actionable publication*, that is, such a publication as may confer a remedy by civil action, it is essential that there be a publication to a *third person*, that is, to some person other than the author or publisher and he whom or whose affairs the language concerns (§ 107). No possible form of words can confer a right of action for slander or libel, unless there has been a publication to some third person. . . .

## WENNHAK v. MORGAN AND WIFE

20 Q.B.D. 635 (1888), [1886–90] All E.R. 572.

Motion by the plaintiff for a new trial on the ground of misdirection.

The action was against the defendant and his wife for libel, and for malicious damage to a document.

At the trial before Mathew, J., and a jury, it appeared from the opening speech of the plaintiff's counsel that the plaintiff, a domestic servant, had been in the employment of a lady who had since gone abroad, and who gave him a good character in writing. The plaintiff afterwards entered the service of the defendant on the faith of the character, which he handed to the defendant. Finding that the place did not suit him the plaintiff gave notice to leave. After the notice had been given, the defendant one morning summarily dismissed the plaintiff, charging him with having been absent from the house during the night without leave. The plaintiff asked for his character, which was delivered to him by the defendant's wife, when it was found that the defamatory words complained of had been written upon it by the defendant.

The words were to the effect that the plaintiff had been dismissed for staying out all night without leave.

On the opening the learned judge held that there was no publication. . . .

*Bassett Hopkins,* for the plaintiff. There was evidence of publication by the husband to the wife. The principle that husband and wife are one person in law is not applicable to the law of libel. An action would lie for defaming a man to his wife, or a wife to her husband: Wenman v. Ash; in that case Maule, J., said: "In the eye of the law, no doubt, man and wife are for many purposes one: but that is a strong figurative expression and cannot be so dealt with as that all the consequences must follow which would result from its being literally true. For many purposes, they are essentially distinct and different persons,—and, amongest others, for the purpose of having the honour and feelings of the husband assailed and injured by acts done or communications made to the wife." At any rate the Married Women's Property Act, 1882 (45 & 46 Vict. c. 75), s. 12, has the effect of destroying the identity of husband and wife.  .  .  .

*Roland V. Williams,* for the defendant. First, there was no evidence of publication of the libel. No case can be found in which it has been held that an action will lie for a defamatory statement made by the defendant to his wife only. In Wenman v. Ash the statement was not made by the defendant to his wife, but was made by the defendant to the wife of the plaintiff.  .  .  .

HUDDLESTON, B. Two questions arise in this case. First, whether there was a publication under the circumstances; and, secondly, whether the learned judge was right in taking upon himself the issue as to the amount of damages to which the plaintiff was entitled. [for a cause of action based on defendant's maliciously writing on the character reference—Ed.] With respect to the first of those points this is, as far as we know, the first time it has ever been alleged in cases of this kind that the handing over of a libel by the libeller to his wife is a publication. I think that the question can be decided on the common law principle that husband and wife are one. The uttering of a libel to the party libelled is clearly no publication for the purposes of a civil action. And if a libel is uttered on a privileged occasion to a husband when his wife is present, it has been held that her presence does not take away the privilege.

.  .  .  .

We think it our duty to hold that, according to a well recognised principle, husband and wife are in the same position, and therefore that the uttering of a libel by a husband to his wife is no publication, in cases apart from the Married Women's Property Act, and that on that ground the decision of the learned judge was right.  .  .  .

MANISTY, J. I come to the same conclusion. The case, although in one view a comparatively small one, involves a very important principle. On the first point the maxim and principle acted on for centuries is still in existence, viz., that as regards this case, husband and wife are in point of law one person. The earlier authorities on this point are collected in Montague Lush on Husband and Wife, at p. 3.

It would be enough to say that that is the law and the ground of the law. But what is the real foundation of it? It is, after all, a question of public policy, or, as it has been well called, social policy. No doubt that principle has been interfered with by judge-made law. Public opinion has altered in some circumstances, and no better illustration of that can be given than the change of view as to deeds of separation between husband and wife. But, if public policy is considered, what is there to shew any change in judicial opinion or public policy with respect to communications between husband and wife hitherto held sacred? It has been argued that in some cases it might be well that publication of slander by a man to his wife should be actionable. But look at the other side, would it be well for us to lay down now

that any defamation communicated by a husband to a wife was actionable? To do so might lead to results disastrous to social life, and I
for one would be no party to making new law to support such actions.

. . . .

NOTES AND QUESTIONS

1. In the *Wennhak* case, what sort of a "connection" was there
between the concept of person and "the world of fact"? What judgments were involved in deciding whether Morgan and his wife were
a person?

2. Is it clear what the outer boundaries of a person are? Can
this, too, not be a difficult decision involving choice? Suppose that
Morgan had met Wennhak walking on the street and, in anger, had
kicked Wennhak's cane. The tort of battery demands an intentional
and unpermitted contact with the plaintiff's person: would Wennhak
have been able to maintain a suit for battery? See Fisher v. Carrousel
Motor Hotel, 424 S.W.2d 627 (Texas 1967). There, plaintiff, a Negro
mathematician with NASA, was standing in a cafeteria line during
luncheon at a convention held at defendant hotel in Houston. Flynn,
an employee of the hotel, came up to plaintiff, "snatched the plate from
[his] hand and shouted that he, a Negro, could not be served in the
club." Plaintiff testified that only the plate had been touched. The
Court of Appeals reversed a jury verdict for plaintiff on the grounds
that there was "no physical contact and no evidence of fear or apprehension of physical contact." *Held*: reversed. The action could be
maintained

> . . . so long as there is contact with clothing or an object
> closely identified with the body. 1 Harper & James, The
> Law of Torts 216 (1956); Restatement of Torts 2d, §§ 18
> and 19. In Prosser, Law of Torts 32 (3d ed. 1964), it is said:

>> " . . . The protection extends to any part of the
>> body, or to anything which is attached to it and
>> practically identified with it. Thus contact with
>> the plaintiff's clothing, or with a cane, a paper, or
>> any other object held in his hand will be sufficient;
>> . . . The plaintiff's interest in the integrity of
>> his person includes all those things which are in
>> contact or connected with it."

> Under the facts of this case, we have no difficulty in
> holding that the intentional grabbing of plaintiff's plate
> constituted a battery. The intentional snatching of an object
> from one's hand is as clearly an offensive invasion of his
> person as would be an actual contact with the body. . . .

> . . . .

> The rationale for holding an offensive contact with
> such an object to be a battery is explained in 1 Restatement
> of Torts 2d § 18 (Comment p. 31) as follows:

>> "Since the essence of the plaintiff's grievance
>> consists in the offense to the dignity involved in the
>> unpermitted and intentional invasion of the invio-

lability of his person and not in any physical harm done to his body, it is not necessary that the plaintiff's actual body be disturbed. Unpermitted and intentional contacts with anything so connected with the body as to be customarily regarded as part of the other's person and therefore as partaking of its inviolability is actionable as an offensive contact with his person. There are some things such as clothing or a cane or, indeed, anything directly grasped by the hand which are so intimately connected with one's body as to be universally regarded as part of the person."

We hold, therefore, that the forceful dispossession of plaintiff Fisher's plate in an offensive manner was sufficient to constitute a battery, and the trial court erred in granting judgment notwithstanding the verdict on the issue of actual damages.

. . . .

Id. at 629–630.

3. What are those who call the corporation "a fiction" trying to point out? What dangers are they trying to warn us of? Considering how the concept of person is used in *Keeler*, *Wennhak* and *Fisher*, could it, too, be called "a fiction"?

Consider, in this regard, Holmes's remark that "it leads nowhere to call a corporation a fiction. If it is a fiction, it is a fiction created by law with intent that it should be acted on as true." Klein v. Board of Tax Supervisors, 282 U.S. 19, 24 (1930). What does Holmes mean by "true"? Can the same point be made of all our concepts—legal and otherwise—that they are the basic building blocks of thought that we act on *as if* they were "true"? See VAIHINGER, THE PHILOSOPHY OF "AS IF" (1924).


*DAVID HUME*

OF PERSONAL IDENTITY *

There are some philosophers, who imagine we are every moment intimately conscious of what we call our *self*; that we feel its existence and its continuance in existence; and are certain, beyond the evidence of a demonstration, both of its perfect identity and simplicity. The strongest sensation, the most violent passion, say they, instead of distracting us from this view, only fix it the more intensely, and make us consider their influence on *self* either by their pain or pleasure. To attempt a further proof of this were to weaken its evidence; since no proof can be derived from any fact of which we are so intimately conscious; nor is there any thing, of which we can be certain, if we doubt of this.

* From Treatise of Human Nature (Bk. 1, Pt. IV, Sec. VI) in The Complete          Works of David Hume 310–318, 324 (Little, Brown 1854).

Unluckily all these positive assertions are contrary to that very experience which is pleaded for them; nor have we any idea of self, after the manner it is here explained. For, from what impression could this idea be derived? This question it is impossible to answer without a manifest contradiction and absurdity; and yet it is a question which must necessarily be answered, if we would have the idea of self pass for clear and intelligible. It must be some one impression that gives rise to every real idea. But self or person is not any one impression, but that to which our several impressions and ideas are supposed to have a reference. If any impression gives rise to the idea of self, that impression must continue invariably the same, through the whole course of our lives; since self is supposed to exist after that manner. But there is no impression constant and invariable. Pain and pleasure, grief and joy, passions and sensations succeed each other, and never all exist at the same time. It cannot therefore be from any of these impressions, or from any other, that the idea of self is derived; and consequently there is no such idea.

But further, what must become of all our particular perceptions upon this hypothesis? All these are different, and distinguishable, and separable from each other, and may be separately considered, and may exist separately, and have no need of any thing to support their existence. After what manner therefore do they belong to self, and how are they connected with it? For my part, when I enter most intimately into what I call myself, I always stumble on some particular perception or other, of heat or cold, light or shade, love or hatred, pain or pleasure. I never can catch *myself* at any time without a perception, and never can observe any thing but the perception. . . .

. . . I may venture to affirm of the rest of mankind, that they are nothing but a bundle or collection of different perceptions, which succeed each other with an inconceivable rapidity, and are in a perpetual flux and movement. . . .

What then gives us so great a propension to ascribe an identity to these successive perceptions, and to suppose ourselves possessed of an invariable and uninterrupted existence through the whole course of our lives? . . .

We have a distinct idea of an object that remains invariable and uninterrupted through a supposed variation of time; and this idea we call that of *identity* or *sameness*. We have also a distinct idea of several different objects existing in succession, and connected together by a close relation; and this to an accurate view affords as perfect a notion of *diversity*, as if there was no manner of relation among the objects. But though these two ideas of identity, and a succession of related objects, be in themselves perfectly distinct, and even contrary, yet it is certain that, in our common way of thinking, they are generally confounded with each other. That action of the imagination, by which we consider the uninterrupted and invariable object, and that by which we reflect on the succession of related objects, are almost the same to the feeling; nor is there much more effort of thought required in the latter case than in the former. The relation facilitates the transition of the mind from one object to another; and renders its passage as smooth as if it contemplated one continued object. This resemblance is the cause of the confusion and mistake, and makes us substitute the notion of identity, instead of that of related objects. However at one instant we may consider the related succession as variable or interrupted, we are sure the next to ascribe to it a perfect identity, and regard it as invariable and uninterrupted. Our propensity to this mistake is so great from the resemblance above mentioned, that we fall into it before we are aware; and though we incessantly correct ourselves by reflection, and return to a more accurate method of thinking, yet we cannot long sustain our philosophy, or take off this bias from the imagination. Our last resource is to yield to it, and boldly assert that these different related objects are in effect the same, however interrupted and variable. In order to justify to ourselves this absurdity, we often feign some new and unintelligible principle, that connects the objects together, and prevents their interruption or variation. Thus, we feign the continued existence of the perceptions of our senses, to remove the interruption; and run into the notion of a *soul*, and *self*, and *substance*, to disguise the variation. . . .

. . . . 

. . . [S]uppose any mass of matter, of which the parts are contiguous and connected, to be placed before us; it is plain we must attribute a perfect identity to this mass, provided all the parts continue uninterruptedly and invariably the same, whatever motion or change of place we may observe either in the whole or in any of the parts. But supposing some very *small* or *inconsiderable* part to be added to the mass, or subtracted from it; though this absolutely destroys the identity of the whole, strictly speaking, yet as we seldom think so accurately, we scruple not to pronounce a mass of matter the same, where we find so trivial an alteration. The passage of the thought from the object before the change to the object after it, is so smooth and easy, that we scarce perceive the transition, and are apt to imagine, that it is nothing but a continued survey of the same object.

. . . . 

This may be confirmed by another phenomenon. A change in any considerable part of a body destroys its identity; but it is remarkable, that where the change is produced *gradually* and *insensibly*, we are less apt to ascribe to it the same effect. The reason can plainly be no other, than that the mind, in following the successive changes of the body, feels an easy passage from the surveying its condition in one moment, to the viewing of it in another, and in no particular time perceives any interruption in its actions. From which continued perception, it ascribes a continued existence and identity to the object.

But whatever precaution we may use in introducing the changes gradually, and making them proportionable to the whole, it is certain, that where the changes are at last observed to become considerable, we make a scruple of ascribing identity to such different objects. There is, however, another artifice, by which we may induce the imagination to advance a step further; and that is, by producing a reference of the parts to each other, and a combination to some *common end* or purpose. A ship, of which a considerable part has been changed by frequent reparations, is still considered as the same; nor does the difference of the materials hinder us from ascribing an identity to it. The common end, in which the parts conspire, is the same under all their variations, and affords an easy transition of the imagination from one situation of the body to another

. . . .

The whole of this doctrine leads us to a conclusion, which is of great importance in the present affair, viz. that all the nice and subtile questions concerning personal identity can never possibly be decided, and are to be regarded rather as grammatical than as philosophical difficulties. Identity depends on the relations of ideas; and these relations produce identity, by means of that easy transition they occasion. But as the relations, and the easiness of the transition may diminish by insensible degrees, we have no just standard by which we can decide any dispute concerning the time when they acquire or lose a title to the name of identity. All the disputes concerning the identity of connected objects are merely verbal, except so far as the relation of parts gives rise to some fiction or imaginary principle of union, as we have already observed.

What I have said concerning the first origin and uncertainty of our notion of identity, as applied to the human mind, may be extended with little or no variation to that of simplicity. An object, whose different coexistent parts are bound together by a close relation, operates upon the imagination after much the same manner as one perfectly simple and indivisible, and requires not a much greater stretch of thought in order to its conception. From this similarity of operation we attribute a simplicity to it, and feign a principle of union as the support of this simplicity, and the centre of all the different parts and qualities of the object.

## QUESTIONS

1. What point is Hume making with respect to whatever concept we may have of our own selves? Is it simply derived from experience? Or is it—as Holmes said of the corporation—a fiction we act on as if it were true? Why should we do so?

2. What leads us to believe that the world consists of objects—including persons—persisting through time? What "evidence" is there to the contrary? Is each person not a different phenomenon at every moment (are you not in some sense a different phenomenon, having read this sentence, than "you" were a moment ago)? With your cells constantly dying and renewing, what fraction of molecules now in your body do you suppose were there fifteen years ago? With regard—or disregard—to what criteria do we suppose there to be a thing, such as *you*, that is "the same" through changes, rather than a succession of entities? What suggestions does Hume make?

3. When one says—pointing to an object—"that is a 'chair' ", how "straightforward" is the relationship between the idea of "chair" and the object (the chair)—even when "chair" is being used in an ordinary (non-legal) way? Is all that one wants to convey about "chair" conveyed by what the listener *sees* when he looks at the object

pointed to? Does he see, for example, the *functions* of the chair—
that its primary use is to be sat on in such and such a way? Is not
this part of the meaning of "chair"? Is not the ordinary use of
"chair" entangled with rules for its own application? Does Hume
help explain how this comes about?

## T. R. V. MURTI

### THE CENTRAL PHILOSOPHY OF BUDDHISM *

The characteristic standpoint of the Ābhidharmika system can
be expounded as a polemic against substance, the permanent and the
universal conceived as real in the systems of the ātma tradition.
Though the arguments were formulated in strict logical form later
and belong rather to the Sautrāntika school, they are quite relevant
here too.

. . . .

. . . [T]he same logic is applied to refute the reality of
the Whole (avayavī). What constitutes *one* thing? We might hold
with common sense that the table is one entity, the tree is one, though
they may consist of parts. But the table is partly seen and partly
not, as it is impossible to see all the parts at once. Parts of the tree
move and some other parts do not; a part of it is in shade and a part
of it is sunlit. How can that be one entity to which two or more opposed characteristics (e.g. seen and unseen, moving and unmoving,
dark and sunlit) are ascribed? It is not possible to escape this logic
by stating that what is moving is one part and what is not moving is
different from it. For, both the parts belong to the *same* thing; the
characteristics of the parts belong to the thing—the whole—of which
they are parts. Therefore, there are as many things as there are
distinguishable "parts" or aspects. An entity has no extensity or
complexity of content. The oneness of many things ("parts" and
aspects) is illusory as the oneness of a heap of corn. Horizontally,
spatially, a thing has no expanse. It is not only an instant (kṣaṇika)
lacking duration, but a spatial point lacking all magnitude and diversity as well.

By the same logic we are led to the denial of the universal
(sāmānya) or identical aspect of things. Each entity is discrete and
unique (svalakṣaṇa). The existence of the universal, uniform and
identical, in all the particulars is beset with insuperable difficulties.
How can one entity exist in a number of particulars separated by distance of space and time, in entirety, untouched by what happens to
the particulars? Moreover, in cognising a thing, we do not certainly
cognise it (the particular) and its duplicate (the universal). The
polemic of the Buddhist against the universal is too well-known to
need any detailed statement. All existence, for the Buddhist, is particular; the universal is a thought-construct, a vikalpa.

* From 70–73 (1955). With the permission of George Allen & Unwin, Ltd.

The real is momentary; it is simple, unitary; it is particular, unique. This view militates against the conception of the real as permanent, as substance, as universal and identical. . . .

The rejection of substance, soul and all relations is Humean in character. Hume recognises two main principles of his philosophy: *"that all our distinct perceptions are distinct existences, and that the mind never perceives any real connexion among distinct existences. Did our perceptions either inhere in something simple and individual, or did the mind perceive some real connexion among them, there would be no difficulty in the case."*

But there is a very important difference which should not be lost sight of. Hume would account for the notion of substance, causality etc. through the operation of the empirical laws of association and habit. The Buddhist was alive, like Kant, to the fact that these notions are *a priori* and are not of empirical origin.

## NORMAN O. BROWN

### BOUNDARY *

Originally everything was body, ONE BODY (Novalis); or Freud: "Originally the ego includes everything, later it detaches from itself the external world. The ego-feeling we are aware of now is thus only a shrunken vestige of a far more extensive feeling—a feeling which embraced the universe and expressed an inseparable connection of the ego with the external world." . . .

The distinction between self and not-self is made by the childish decision to claim all that the ego likes as "mine," and to repudiate all that the ego dislikes as "not-mine." It is as simple as that; but here is Freud's more formal description: "The objects presenting themselves, in so far as they are sources of pleasure, are absorbed by the ego into itself, 'introjected' (according to an expression coined by Ferenczi); while, on the other hand, the ego thrusts forth upon the external world whatever within itself gives rise to pain (the mechanism of projection)." "Thus at the very beginning, the external world, objects, and that which was hated were one and the same thing. When later on an object manifests itself as a source of pleasure, it becomes loved, but also incorporated into the ego."

Here is the fall: the distinction between "good" and "bad," between "mine" and "thine," between "me" and "thee" (or "it"), come all together—boundaries between persons; boundaries between properties; and the polarity of love and hate.

The boundary line between self and external world bears no relation to reality; the distinction between ego and world is made by spitting out part of the inside, and swallowing in part of the outside. On this Freudian insight Melanie Klein and her followers have built. "Owing to these mechanisms [of introjection and projection] the infant's object can be defined as what is inside or outside his own body,

---

* From Love's Body 141–44, 146–47,          the permission of Random House and
  159–61 (Random House 1966). With          Professor Brown.

but even while outside, it is still part of himself and refers to himself, since 'outside' results from being ejected, 'spat out': thus the body boundaries are blurred.  This might also be put the other way round: because the object outside the body is 'spat out,' and still relates to the infant's body, there is no sharp distinction between his body and what is outside."

The net-effect of the establishment of the boundary between self and external world is inside-out and outside-in; confusion.  The erection of the boundary does not alter the fact that there is, in reality, no boundary.  The net-effect is illusion, self-deception; the big lie.  Or alienation.  "Le premier mythe du dehors et du dedans: l'alienation se fond sur ces deux termes."  Where Freud and Marx meet.

. . . .

The existence of the "let's pretend" boundary does not prevent the continuance of the real traffic across it.  Projection and introjection, the process whereby the self as distinct from the other is constituted, is not past history, an event in childhood, but a present process of continuous creation.  The dualism of self and external world is built up by a constant process of reciprocal exchange between the two.  The self as a stable substance enduring through time, an identity, is maintained by constantly absorbing good parts (or people) from the outside world and expelling bad parts from the inner world.  "There is a continual 'unconscious' wandering of other personalities into ourselves."

Every person, then, is many persons; a multitude made into one person; a corporate body; incorporated, a corporation.  A "corporation sole"; everyman a parson-person.  The unity of the person is as real, or unreal, as the unity of the corporation.

We tend to think of any one individual in isolation; it is a convenient fiction.  We may isolate him physically, as in the analytic room; in two minutes we find that he has brought his world in with him, and that even before he set eyes on the analyst, he had developed inside himself an elaborate relation with him.  There is no such thing as a single human being, pure and simple, unmixed with other human beings.  Each personality is a world in himself, a company of many.  That self, that life of one's own, which is in fact so precious though so casually taken for granted, is a composite structure which has been and is being formed and built up since the day of our birth out of countless never-ending influences and exchanges between ourselves and others. . . .  These other persons are in fact therefore parts of ourselves.  And we ourselves similarly have and have had effects and influences, intended or not, on all others who have an emotional relation to us, have loved or hated us.  We are members one of another.

Riviere, *"The Unconscious Phantasy of an Inner World,"* 358–359.

. . . .

It is not schizophrenia but normality that is split-minded; in schizophrenia the false boundaries are disintegrating.  "From pathol-

ogy we have come to know a large number of states in which the
boundary lines between ego and outside world become uncertain."
Schizophrenics are suffering from the truth. " 'Everyone knows' the
patient's thoughts: a regression to a stage before the first lie." Schizophrenia testifies to "experiences in which the discrimination between
the consciousness of self and the consciousness of the object was entirely suspended, the ego being no longer distinct from the object;
the subject no longer distinct from the object; the self and the world
were fused in an inseparable total complex." Schizophrenic thought
is "adualistic"; lack of ego-boundaries makes it impossible to set
limits to the process of identification with the environment. The
schizophrenic world is one of mystical participation; an "indescrib-
able extension of inner sense"; "uncanny feelings of reference"; occult psychosomatic influences and powers; currents of electricity, or
sexual attraction—action at a distance.

"The patient connects herself with everybody." "You and I, are
we not the same?  .  .  . Sometimes I cannot tell myself from other
people.  .  .  . It seemed to me as though I no longer existed in my
own person alone, as though I were one with the all." In a patient
called Julie, "all perception seemed to threaten confusion with the
object. 'That's the rain. I could be the rain.' 'That chair—that wall.
I could be that wall. It's a terrible thing for a girl to be a wall.' "

Definitions are boundaries; schizophrenics pass beyond the reality-principle into a world of symbolic connections: 'all things lost
their definite boundaries, became irridescent with many-colored significances." Schizophrenics pass beyond ordinary language (the language of the reality-principle) into a truer, more symbolic language:
"I'm thousands. I'm an in-divide-you-all. I'm a no-un (i.e., nun, noun, no one)." The language of *Finnegans Wake*. James Joyce and
his daughter, crazy Lucia, these two are one. The god is Dionysus,
the mad truth.

The mad truth: the boundary between sanity and insanity is a
false one. The proper outcome of psychoanalysis is the abolition of
the boundary, the healing of the split, the integration of the human
race. The proper posture is to listen to and learn from lunatics, as in
former times—"We cannot deny them a measure of that awe with
which madmen were regarded by people of ancient times." The
insane do not share "the normal prejudice in favor of external reality." The "normal prejudice in favor of external reality" can be sustained only by ejecting (projecting) these dissidents from the human
race; scotomizing them, keeping them out of sight, in asylums; in-
sulating the so-called reality-principle from all evidence to the contrary.

Dionysus, the mad god, breaks down the boundaries; releases the
prisoners; abolishes repression; and abolishes the *principium in-
dividuationis*, substituting for it the unity of man and the unity of
man with nature. In this age of schizophrenia, with the atom, the
individual self, the boundaries disintegrating, there is, for those who
would save our souls, the ego-psychologists, "the Problem of Identity."
But the breakdown is to be made into a breakthrough; as Conrad said,
in the destructive element immerse. The soul that we can call our

own is not a real one. The solution to the problem of identity is, get lost. Or as it says in the New Testament: "He that findeth his own psyche shall lose it, and he that loseth his psyche for my sake shall find it."

## QUESTIONS

1. Insofar as the law considers "the individual" to be the unit on which to place responsibility, is it doing nothing more than adopting a concept "given in reality"? Is there anything more unnatural about holding a corporate entity responsible for a crime than holding an individual responsible? If the most "natural" category is that which emerged earliest in civilization, are not "corporate" concepts— the kin and tribe—the most "natural"? What is suggested by the selection from Maine, which follows these questions?

2. Is it inevitable that people should have any concept of self or person at all? What does Brown mean "the boundary line between self and external world bears no relation to reality"? How does the boundary line—and the concept of person—come about? What does Brown see as the costs of what he calls "the 'let's pretend' boundary"?

3. On what grounds does Brown assert that "every person . . . is many persons; a multitude made into one person; a corporate body . . . the unity of the person is as real, or unreal, as the unity of the corporation"?

4. Do we ever overlook the "fiction" of the individual person? What about the widespread practice of cutting off a robber's hand? What about the defense of insanity: does this amount to saying that some *part* of the self was responsible for the crime, there was no agency, and the whole, corporate person ought not to be held responsible? What can one say of statutes of limitation in this regard?

*SIR HENRY MAINE*

### PRIMITIVE SOCIETY AND ANCIENT LAW *

. . . [S]ociety in primitive times was not what it is assumed to be at present, a collection of *individuals*. In fact, and in the view of the men who composed it, it was *an aggregation of families*. The contrast may be most forcibly expressed by saying that the *unit* of an ancient society was the Family, of a modern society the individual. We must be prepared to find in ancient law all the consequences of this difference. It is so framed as to be adjusted to a system of small independent corporations. It is therefore scanty, because it is supplemented by the despotic commands of the heads of households. It is ceremonious, because the transactions to which it pays regard resemble international concerns much more than the quick play of intercourse between individuals. Above all, it has a peculiarity of which the full importance cannot be shown at present. It takes a view of *life* wholly unlike any which appears in developed jurisprudence.

* From Ancient Law 142–43 (F. Pollock ed. 1930).

Corporations *never die,* and accordingly primitive law considers the entities with which it deals, *i.e.,* the patriarchal or family groups, as perpetual and inextinguishable. This view is closely allied to the peculiar aspect under which, in very ancient times, moral attributes present themselves. The moral elevation and moral debasement of the individual appear to be confounded with, or postponed to, the merits and offences of the group to which the individual belongs. If the community sins, its guilt is much more than the sum of the offences committed by its members; the crime is a corporate act, and extends in its consequences to many more persons than have shared in its actual perpetration. If, on the other hand, the individual is conspicuously guilty, it is his children, his kinsfolk, his tribesmen, or his fellow-citizens who suffer with him, and sometimes for him. It thus happens that the ideas of moral responsibility and retribution often seem to be more clearly realised at very ancient than at more advanced periods, for, as the family group is immortal, and its liability to punishment indefinite, the primitive mind is not perplexed by the questions which become troublesome as soon as the individual is conceived as altogether separate from the group.

QUESTIONS

1. How "primitive" is the notion that the corporate group, not the individual, is the proper locus for responsibility? How often, and on what occasions, do we still think in terms that blur the "boundary" between person and group? Hitler's speeches holding the Jews responsible for the world's problems are well known (See HEIDEN, DER FEUHRER 1944); less known is Albert Einstein's piece, "To the Heroes of the Warsaw Ghetto," in which he wrote:

> The Germans as an entire people are responsible for these mass murders and must be punished as a people if there is justice in the world and if the consciousness of collective responsibility in the nations is not to perish from the earth entirely. Behind the Nazi party stands the German people, who elected Hitler after he had in his book and in his speeches made his shameful intentions clear beyond the possibility of misunderstanding. The Germans are the only people who have not made any serious attempt of counteraction leading to the protection of the innocently persecuted. When they are entirely defeated and begin to lament over their fate, we must not let ourselves be deceived again, but keep in mind that they deliberately used the humanity of others to make preparation for their last and most grievous crime against humanity.[6]

2. How much does even a legal system like our own, largely predicated upon the responsibility of the individual person, stick to its assumptions? Is a jury, in considering the guilt of a defendant, immune from considerations of his race or religion (or cult)?—his

6. From Bulletin of the Society of Polish Jews, New York, 1944, reprint- ed in Ideas and Opinions 212–13 (1954).

early social environment? Do lawyers discourage juries from thinking in these terms?

3. In how many ways do you suppose there to be a relationship between the legal system and the culturally prevailing concept of one's self—one's boundaries—one's presumed capacities to be autonomous? What other influences are there on the concept? Consider what effect transplantability of organs will have; the population explosion; the advances in biology, with our greater understanding of gene pools. How will these affect the ways in which each of us thinks of his individual self-hood; his relation to the cosmos; his attitudes towards death and towards others; his "own" inner worth, dignity and importance?

CHAPTER SIX

# The Authority of the Facts

## INTRODUCTORY NOTE

Facts are commonly thought of as the unassailable components of the real world, upon which we must build if we are to reach true decisions. One court has said

> A "fact" is a statement of that which someone knows, an actuality, and not a generalized statement. . . .

> "Fact" is defined in Webster's New International Dictionary, Second Edition, as "The assertion or statement of a thing done or existing . . .. Law. Specif.: Usually in pl. Any of the circumstances or matters of a case as they are alleged to be; also, that which is of actual occurrence; reality as an event or events."

> "Fact" is defined in 35 C.J.S., pp. 384–385, with supporting cases, as follows: "an act or action which is the subject of testimony; action or deed; an actual happening in time or space; an actuality; . . .; an event; . . .; something fixed, unchangeable; a thing done; a thing done or said; . . .; what took place, as distinguished from what might or might not have happened; . . .."

> As stated in Churchill v. Meade, 92 Or. 626, . . . "Facts are actualities. They are what took place, not what might or might not have happened. Things that have in very truth occurred are usually capable of proof." [1]

This attitude towards fact supposes that, unlike "opinions" or "inferences", the fact is an item of existence independent of personal —and social—assumptions and prejudices. How accurate is this view? In making a decision, how much is the decision maker's autonomy—and responsibility—reduced by the existence of unchallengeable, objective truths that are simply "given" to him?

----

## INTRODUCTION

*JEROME FRANK*

### FACT SKEPTICISM *

> . . . [M]any "rule-skeptics" . . . maintain that legal uncertainty is restricted, for the most part, to the growing points in the rules, to the cases where the facts present novel situations or where, under the impact of newly emerging social needs or altered policy attitudes, the courts change the rules.

1. American Life Ins. Co. v. Powell, 65 So. 2d 516, 523 (Ala. 1953).    * From 316–321 (Princeton University Press 1949).

Professor Walter Wheeler Cook, a leading *rule-skeptic*, illuminated that subject. He differentiated between (1) "routine" cases and (2) those involving "new and unusual situations." He said that "many of the cases which present themselves to a trial judge are so much like other cases already passed upon that they are disposed of in a more or less routine way without much thought," and are decided "automatically" or by "habit." A "system of rules and principles . . . can be expected to provide 'certainty' and 'predictability' of decisions . . . in routine cases that fit into the existing pattern without any real thought." The legal generalizations "will give us the answer" in "the vast bulk of human transactions . . ."

But not so, said Cook, when "new and unusual situations" arise which do not fit into the existing legal rules. Then a judge must engage in "reflective thinking," must act creatively. He must then treat the rules as working tools. For, "whatever else they may be, generalizations are not fixed rules for deciding doubtful cases, but instrumentalities for their investigation, methods by which the net value of past experience is rendered available for present scrutiny of new perplexities . . .; they are hypotheses to be tested and revised for their further working. To call a generalization a tool is not to say it is useless; the contrary is patently the case. A tool is something to use. Hence it is something to be improved by noting how it works."

With this view of the function of legal rules I concur. But I think there is something naive in Cook's conception of "routine cases," for it blithely assumes that the facts in any such a case come before the judge at a trial in a manner requiring no "real thought" on his part. This attitude is the more surprising since Cook, elsewhere,[2] disclosed a singularly alert awareness of the protean nature of "facts" and of the way in which human purposes affect the very determination of what "facts" are. When, he wrote in 1937, we look at the "external world," it "presents itself to us as a shifting, varying series of changing patterns of color, sound, odor or what not," which may be called "brute, raw events . . . If we try to describe . . . these 'crude, raw events,' we discover . . . that there are an infinite number of aspects of any 'situation,' and that, in order to talk about it at all, we have to select from among these infinitely varied aspects, those which for some reason or other we are going to talk about. In the second place, we discover that in talking about the selected aspects, we have to relate them in such a way as to put them under some category, some class, for which we have (or perhaps create) a verbal symbol or name. . . . In other words, in making a 'statement of facts' about the 'given' situation . . ., so as to state 'what it is,' I have in every case necessarily selected certain aspects, thereby [bringing] all the selected 'data' . . . under some category. Then and then only can I say 'what it is'—that is, make a 'statement of fact.'" The "facts," Cook concludes, "are the product

2. See the excerpt from Cook, "Facts"
and "Statements of Fact", 4 U.Chi.
L.Rev. 233 (1937), *infra* at 277 ff.

first of 'abstraction' from the concreteness [of the] 'brute, raw event,'
[and] then of interpretation of the elements abstracted. . . ."

Strangely, Cook overlooks this analysis when he explains the
difference between "routine" cases and others.  There he writes as
if, for a court in all kinds of cases, the first step—the initial "selection" ("abstraction") from the "brute, raw events"—is "automatic,"
and as if, except in "unusual" cases, the court effortlessly puts the
facts, thus "automatically" selected, under some legal category (a
legal rule or principle).  Cook assumes that the court receives the
winnowed "data," that they are "given," and that the court engages
solely in their "interpretation."  As a result, Cook's description of
the decisional process is too simple.  In a law-suit, the "selections"
are more numerous and complicated.

Here I must revert to what I said in earlier chapters.  There are
three steps in the selection: (a) First the witnesses make their selections from the "brute, raw event" of the past about which they testify.  What they pick out depends not only on their individual capacities for seeing, hearing, touching or smelling, but also on each witness' individual emotional condition at the time when he "selects";
similar factors, plus bias or lying, affect the witnesses' "selections"
when asked to recollect what they originally observed, and again when
they testify.  (b) Second, when the testimony is oral and the witnesses tell differing stories, the trial court (omitting, for the moment, its
gestalt) makes a "selection": it chooses to believe some and to dis-
believe other testimony.  (c) Only after the completion of this second
step does there occur the kind of selection which Cook describes.  The
trial court must now, from the previously selected facts, cull out those
facts which are "relevant," i.e., those which fit into some well-settled
rule or some new rule the court contrives.

Cook's discussion of legal reasoning in the process of deciding a
lawsuit relates exclusively to this last step of "selection," i.e., to the
"interpretation" of the "data."  Cook says nothing of the difficulties
and uncertainties involved in the witnesses' "selection" and in the
trial court's first stage of "selection" from the witnesses' testimony.
More serious is Cook's disregard of the gestalt factor in the trial
court's decision, a factor which often means that the trial court (jury
or judge) made no real selection of facts to be fitted into a rule, but
reached the decision by way of an undifferentiated, unarticulated,
reaction to the oral testimony.  Accordingly, Cook leaves unexamined
the most baffling and disturbing aspects of the decisional process.
To phrase my criticism more sharply, he does not observe that there
is no knowing, before a suit is begun, whether the case will appear to
the trial court to be a "routine" case or one which is "unusual."

. . . . . .

That legal rules frequently intertwine with the "facts," that a
rule often gets its meaning in its "application" to "new" fact situations, is an idea, once unorthodox, but now increasingly accepted,
thanks largely to the efforts of the legal skeptics.  In a searching
study of "legal reasoning," recently published, Professor Edward Levi

goes beyond that idea.[3] Legal reasoning, he says, "has a logic of its own." He criticizes the much repeated "doctrine" that "the legal process" is a "method of applying general rules of law to diverse cases. . . . If this were the doctrine, it would be disturbing to find that the rules change from case to case and are made from case to case. Yet this change in the rules is the indispensable dynamic quality of law. . . . Not only do new situations arise, but in addition peoples' wants change. The categories used in the legal process must be left ambiguous in order to permit the infusion of new ideas. . . . In this manner the [rules] come to express the ideas of the community." We do have "a system of rules," but they are "discovered in the process of determining similarity or difference" in "fact situations." The "rules change as the rules are applied. More important, the rules arise out of a process which, while comparing fact situations, creates the rules and then applies them." The changes occur "because the scope of a rule of law, and therefore its meaning, depends upon a determination of what facts will be similar to those present when the rule is first announced. The finding of similarity or difference is the key step in the legal process. . . . The problem for the law is this: When will it be just to treat different cases as though they were the same? A working legal system must therefore be willing to pick out key similarities and to reason from them to the justice of applying a common classification."

Granted the "facts," Levi's exposition admirably answers many questions which have puzzled lawyers and nonlawyers concerning "legal logic." But, like Cook, Levi hurdles the chief difficulty to an understanding of the decisional process. He sees it as one of "comparing fact situations," of the "finding of similarity or difference" in facts, involving the ability to "pick out key similarities." One who reads Levi would think that the facts of a case appear in court ready-made, waiting only to be compared with those of some previous cases. Levi is debonnaire in his unconcern with all the pain and anguish of giving birth to the facts which are compared with those in earlier cases. Levi, although for a considerable time a successful practicing lawyer, is a "rule-skeptic," not a "fact-skeptic." He by-passes the chief work of trial courts.

## QUESTIONS

1. What does Frank mean by a "fact skeptic"? What reasons does he give for fact skepticism? Does he mean that witnesses and judges are unconstrained by "reality" to decide what the facts are? What is the bearing of fact skepticism in the ideal of an objective legal system, pure of the idiosyncrasies of individuals?

Compare Frank's picture of the role of facts in the legal system with that of Julius Stone:

> Every rule of law is predicated on the existence of the facts on which its operation proceeds, its function (or 'the lawmaker's intention') being to attach legal consequences to

3. Levi, An Introduction to Legal Reasoning, 15 U.Chi.L.Rev. 501 (1948).

these facts. Different rules attach different consequences to different facts; which rule we apply, then, with its consequences, depends on what facts are found.

SOCIAL DIMENSIONS OF LAW AND JUSTICE 734–5 (1966). Are the facts that "are found" independent of the system of rules that the lawmaker sets out to invoke? Do we first find "the" facts, and then apply rules?

2. What is the function of the lawyer in bringing before the court the facts that it will hear? How much of his efforts are in furtherance of a search for the truth?

CHARLES P. CURTIS

THE ETHICS OF ADVOCACY *

I will start with the story of Sam the Lookout.

A distinguished New York lawyer was once called over to sit in a conference of admiralty lawyers with the crew of a ship which had been in a collision. The lawyers were going over the testimony which the members of the crew would give at the approaching trial. Finally they came to the lookout, and the Captain, who was asking the questions, turned to him and said, "You, of course, were up in the eyes on the forecastle keeping a sharp lookout." The seaman squirmed in his chair, twisted his cap, and said, "The truth is, Captain, I was in the head having a smoke." The lawyers leaned forward, but the Captain turned to reassure them. "That's all right, gentlemen, he'll testify that he was keeping a sharp lookout. Won't you Sam?" "No," said Sam, "I guess I can't do that."

And then, this lawyer said, such a storm of indignation burst over Sam as he had never seen. The Captain and the rest of the crew cursed him for betraying his ship. Let him go to the head if he had to. Let him even have his smoke if he must. But when he did let him also take the consequences. The collision was not his fault, they agreed. The fog was too thick for him to have seen the other vessel in time, but was he now going to let his own ship down? If he left his post on his own affairs, he had no right to make the ship pay the penalty. What if it was perjury? He'd taken that risk. Not the ship, but he had taken the risk of perjury.

The admiralty lawyers sat back and listened. They seemed to recognize that there were peculiarities in the ethics of the sea which they could not but respect, though distinctly they were not a part of admiralty law. The meeting broke up with Sam still obstinately refusing to do what, the Captain insisted, any good seaman ought to know he was in honor bound to do.

Then I tried to find a situation in which a lawyer may be in duty bound to lie for his client. I asked an eminent and very practical judge. He told me he hoped I was joking. I went to two leaders of

* From 4 Stan.L.Rev. 3, 6–11 (1951). Copyright 1951 by the Board of Trustees of the Leland Stanford Jr. University.

the bar, both ex-presidents of bar associations.  One said, "No, I don't believe there is such a situation."  The other said, "Why, of course, there are."  But he has not yet given me one.

Finally I thought I had one.  It was the case of a lawyer who, I felt very sure, had lied to me when he told me that he did not represent a certain man.  I was secretary of the Grievance Committee of the Bar Association at the time, and I was trying to find out whether this man had been blackmailed by some other lawyers.  I went to this lawyer and asked him.  If he had even admitted to me that he had represented this man, I should have been pretty sure that the man had indeed been blackmailed, for I knew that he had not gone to his regular counsel, but to a different lawyer, in order to keep the whole affair secret.  The lawyer told me he did not even know the man.

I recall thinking then that this lawyer was doing just right by lying to me, but I don't know who else agreed with me.  My lawyer had gone on to make the same denial to the Grievance Committee, and later, when the Bar Association brought proceedings for his disbarment, in the course of those proceedings, persisted in his denial before the court itself.  He was not disbarred, but he was subsequently reprimanded and suspended.

I take it that it is inadmissible to lie to the court.  A lawyer's duty to his client cannot rise higher than its source, which is the court.  Perhaps my lawyer did wrong to lie to the Grievance Committee, but I am not so sure.  I know he did right to lie to me, and I am inclined to hope that in his place I should have lied to the Grievance Committee as well.

It may be that it all depends on whether you are asked the question by someone who has a right to ask it.  If he has no right to ask and if simple silence would, or even might, lead him to the truth, then, I believe your lawyer is in duty bound to lie.  For the truth is not his, but yours.  It belongs to you and he is bound to keep it for you, even more vigorously than if it were only his own.  He must lie, then, beyond the point where he could permissibly lie for himself.  But this only illuminates the problem from a different angle, the right to ask instead of the duty to answer.  Let me give you a situation in which a lawyer must lie to someone who does have the right to ask him the question.

A lawyer is called on the telephone by a former client who is unfortunately at the time a fugitive from justice.  The police want him and he wants advice.  The lawyer goes to where his client is, hears the whole story, and advises him to surrender.  Finally he succeeds in persuading him that this is the best thing to do and they make an appointment to go to police headquarters.  Meanwhile the client is to have two days to wind up his affairs and make his farewells.  When the lawyer gets back to his office, a police inspector is waiting for him, and asks him whether his client is in town and where he is.  Here are questions which the police have every right to ask of anybody, and even a little hesitation in this unfortunate lawyer's denials will reveal enough to betray his client.  Of course he lies.

And why not? The relation between a lawyer and his client is one of the intimate relations. You would lie for your wife. You would lie for your child. There are others with whom you are intimate enough, close enough, to lie for them when you would not lie for yourself. At what point do you stop lying for them? I don't know and you are not sure.

To every one of us come occasions when we don't want to tell the truth, not all of it, certainly not all of it at once, when we want to be something less than candid, a little disingenuous. Indeed, to be candid with ourselves, there are times when we deliberately and more or less justifiably undertake to tell something less or something different. Complete candor to anyone but ourselves is a virtue that belongs to the saints, to the secure, and to the very courageous. Even when we do want to tell the truth, all of it, ultimately, we see no reason why we should not take our own time, tell it as skillfully and as gracefully as we can, and most of us doubt our own ability to do this as well by ourselves and for ourselves as another could do it for us. So we go to a lawyer. He will make a better fist of it than we can.

I don't see why we should not come out roundly and say that one of the functions of a lawyer is to lie for his client; and on rare occasions, as I think I have shown, I believe it is. Happily they are few and far between, only when his duty gets him into a corner or puts him on the spot. Day in, day out, a lawyer can be as truthful as anyone. But not ingenuous.

A lawyer is required to be disingenuous. He is required to make statements as well as arguments which he does not believe in. But the further his statements descend toward the particular, the more truthful he may be, indeed must be, because no one appreciates the significance of the particular better than a lawyer. In the higher brackets of generality, he has to be freed from his own beliefs and prejudices, for they are irrelevant, unless they are pressed into service for the client. But his insincerity does not extend to the particular, except, of course, particulars which do not belong to him, but are his client's secrets. Barring these, when he is talking for his client, a lawyer is absolved from veracity down to a certain point of particularity. And he must never lose the reputation of lacking veracity, because of his freedom from the strict bonds of veracity and of the law are the two chief assets of the profession.

I have said that a lawyer may not lie to the court. But it may be a lawyer's duty not to speak. Let me give you a case from the autobiography of one of the most distinguished and most conscientious lawyers I or any other man has ever known, Samuel Williston. In his autobiography, *Life and Law*, he tells of one of his early cases. His client was sued in some financial matter. The details of the claim are not important. Williston, of course, at once got his client's letter file and went through it painstakingly, sorting, arranging, and collating it. The letters, we may well believe, told the whole story, as they usually do in such a case. Trial approached, but the plaintiff's lawyers did not either demand to see the correspondence, nor ask for their production. "They did not demand their production and we did not feel bound to disclose them." At the close of the trial, "In the course of his remarks the Chief Justice stated as one reason for his decision a supposed fact which I knew to be unfounded. I had in front of me a letter that showed his error. Though I have no doubt of the propriety of my behavior in keeping silent, I was somewhat uncomfortable at the time."

This was a letter, a piece of evidence, a fact. Suppose it had been a rule of law. Suppose the Chief Justice had equally mistakenly given as a reason for his decision some statute or regulation which Williston knew had been repealed or amended, and it was not a letter but a copy of the new statute which he had in front of him. Williston would have interrupted the Chief Justice and drawn his attention to it. This is sometimes debated, but it is beyond dispute that this would have been Williston's duty, and there is no doubt at all that he would have performed it as scrupulously as he respected his duty to his client.

In the House of Lords, Lord Birkenhead observed in the course of a hearing, "Their Lordships were therefore very much in the hands of counsel and those who instructed counsel in these matters, and the House expected, and indeed insisted, that authorities which bear one way or the other upon matters under debate should be brought to the attention of their Lordships by those who are aware of those authorities. That observation was irrespective of whether or not the particular authority assisted the party who was aware of it. It was an obligation of confidence between their Lordships and all those who assisted in the debates in this House in the capacity of counsel."

In that case Lord Birkenhead was referring to a statute. The Committee on Professional Ethics of the American Bar Association has said that a lawyer has the same duty to advise the court of judicial "decisions adverse to his client's contentions." Mr. Robert B. Tunstall of the Virginia bar has pointed out that Lord Birkenhead was referring to a statute which was indeed so controlling that the House of Lords ordered the case reargued when it was finally brought to their attention. Mr. Tunstall thinks the opinion of the Committee of the American Bar Association went too far. A lawyer surely has no duty to argue his opponent's case for him, nor should he be reproached for failure to suggest to the court an argument against him which his opponent has neglected.

But this distinction between statutes and precedents is not going to tell us how to reconcile a lawyer's obligations to the court with his obligations to his client. The Committee on Professional Ethics in its opinion said, "A lawyer is an officer of the court. His obligation to the public is no less significant than his obligation to his client. His oath binds him to the highest fidelity to the court as well as to his client. It is his duty to aid the court in the due administration of justice." And the Committee quoted one of the Canons of Ethics, "The conduct of the lawyer before the Court and with other lawyers should be characterized by candor and fairness."

This is all very well, but you can't say that Williston was showing the highest fidelity to the court when he sat there with the letter in front of him. He was being faithful to his client, and uncomfortable that he could not be candid with the court. At first sight, the reasons which the Committee gave are not very helpful. If I ask you which of these two girls you love most, you are in effect declining to answer when you say, "Both." The Committee should have gone on to distinguish a lawyer's loyalties. The court has priority over the client in matters of law and the client has a priority over the court in matters of fact.

## QUESTIONS

1. How important is getting at the truth in anyone's life?

2. In the anecdote of Sam the Lookout, why did the lawyers "sit back and listen"? Should they have? Did the lawyers' responsibility extend to the way in which "the facts" were apparently going to be presented to the admiralty court?

3. Does Curtis ever tell us what a lie *is?* If it is a statement that does not correspond with "the truth" or with "the facts", what do these terms mean? Suppose I tell someone who is about to drink a drink that I know to be poisoned, "that drink will be bad for you"; he drinks it and dies. Did I lie? Did my answer "correspond with 'the truth' or 'the facts' "? By what standards is any statement true or false?

4. Is it clear what is involved in believing or disbelieving what one is saying? If a lawyer says, "judge, my client is an honest man," what would he have to believe to believe that statement "true" or "false"?

5. On the issue of keeping silent, why should the court have "priority over the client in matters of law and the client . . . a priority over the court in matters of fact"? Does it make sense to try to make such a distinction in this context? Can you do so: what is a matter of fact as opposed to a matter of law?

7. Why should it be "inadmissible to lie to the court"? Is it really? What about a lawyer who pleads a defendant "not guilty", even though the client has told him he committed the crime? Consider in this regard, too, the following Opinion of the New York County Lawyer's Association. Is such behaviour as the Association is responding to atypical of the lawyer's practice? If not, why were the judge and "leaders of the bar" to whom Curtis spoke in disagreement with him?

## NEW YORK COUNTY LAWYERS' ASSOCIATION

## OPINION No. 206 (1922) *

*Question.* In the opinion of your Committee, is there any impropriety in interposing a general denial in an unverified answer in a divorce action in New York where the defendant informs his attorney that the allegations of adultery in the complaint are true but that he is not certain that the plaintiff will be able to prove them?

* From Opinions of the Committees on Professional Ethics of the Association of the Bar of the City of New York and the New York County Lawyers' Association 637–38 (Columbia University Press, 1956).

*Answer.* In the opinion of the Committee, in New York the privilege of interposing such answer is a statutory right of the client (probably in order to protect the defendant against an admission of adultery whether express or implied from a failure to answer [Civil Practice Act, Section 1148]). They are, therefore, of the opinion that it is not improper for the lawyer, if his client desires it, to interpose such an answer in his behalf, though the Committee fully appreciates that generally an attorney is not justified in interposing a pleading which he knows to be false in fact. Under the practice in New York such judgments are not granted by default or upon the admission of guilt by the answer, or without proof of the offense charged. The answer, therefore, has not the effect of the ordinary pleading, and its presence does not operate as a deception.

MONROE H. FREEDMAN

## PROFESSIONAL RESPONSIBILITY OF THE CRIMINAL DEFENSE LAWYER: THE THREE HARDEST QUESTIONS *

In almost any area of legal counseling and advocacy, the lawyer may be faced with the dilemma of either betraying the confidential communications of his client or participating to some extent in the purposeful deception of the court. This problem is nowhere more acute than in the practice of criminal law, particularly in the representation of the indigent accused. The purpose of this article is to analyze and attempt to resolve three of the most difficult issues in this general area:

1. Is it proper to cross-examine for the purpose of discrediting the reliability or credibility of an adverse witness whom you know to be telling the truth?

2. Is it proper to put a witness on the stand when you know he will commit perjury?

3. Is it proper to give your client legal advice when you have reason to believe that the knowledge you give him will tempt him to commit perjury?

These questions present serious difficulties with respect to a lawyer's ethical responsibilities.[4] Moreover, if one admits the possibility of an affirmative answer, it is difficult even to discuss them without appearing to some to be unethical. It is not surprising, therefore, that reasonable, rational discussion of these issues has been un-

---

* From 64 Mich.L.Rev. 1469, 1469–72, 1473, 1474–75, 1478–80, 1481–84 (1966). With the permission of Michigan Law Review Association.

**4.** The substance of this paper was recently presented to a Criminal Trial Institute attended by forty-five members of the District of Columbia Bar. As a consequence, several judges (none of whom had either heard the lecture or read it) complained to the Committee on Admissions and Grievances of the District Court for the District of Columbia, urging the author's disbarment or suspension. Only after four months of proceedings, including a hearing, two meetings, and a *de novo* review by eleven federal district court judges, did the Committee announce its decision to "proceed no further in the matter." [Footnote by Professor Freedman]

common and that the problems have for so long remained unresolved. In this regard it should be recognized that the Canons of Ethics, which were promulgated in 1908 "as a general guide," are both inadequate and self-contradictory.

## I.  THE ADVERSARY SYSTEM AND THE NECESSITY FOR CONFIDENTIALITY

At the outset, we should dispose of some common question-begging responses. The attorney is indeed an officer of the court, and he does participate in a search for truth. These two propositions, however, merely serve to state the problem in different words: As an officer of the court, participating in a search for truth, what is the attorney's special responsibility, and how does that responsibility affect his resolution of the questions posed above?

The attorney functions in an adversary system based upon the presupposition that the most effective means of determining truth is to present to a judge and jury a clash between proponents of conflicting views. It is essential to the effective functioning of the system that each adversary have, in the word of Canon 15, "entire devotion to the interest of the client, warm zeal in the maintenance and defense of his rights and the exertion of his utmost learning and ability." It is also essential to maintain the fullest uninhibited communication between the client and his attorney, so that the attorney can most effectively counsel his client and advocate the latter's cause. This policy is safeguarded by the requirement that the lawyer must, in the words of Canon 37, "preserve his client's confidences." Canon 15 does, of course, qualify these obligations by stating that "the office of attorney does not permit, much less does it demand of him for any client, violations of law or any manner of fraud or chicane." In addition, Canon 22 requires candor toward the court.

The problem presented by these salutary generalities of the Canons in the context of particular litigation is illustrated by the personal experience of Samuel Williston, which was related in his autobiography. Because of his examination of a client's correspondence file, Williston learned of a fact extremely damaging to his client's case. When the judge announced his decision, it was apparent that a critical factor in the favorable judgment for Williston's client was the judge's ignorance of this fact. Williston remained silent and did not thereafter inform the judge of what he knew. He was convinced, and Charles Curtis agrees with him, that it was his duty to remain silent.

In an opinion by the American Bar Association Committee on Professional Ethics and Grievances, an eminent panel headed by Henry Drinker held that a lawyer should remain silent when his client lies to the judge by saying that he has no prior record, despite the attorney's knowledge to the contrary. The majority of the panel distinguished the situation in which the attorney has learned of the client's prior record from a source other than the client himself. William B. Jones, a distinguished trial lawyer and now a judge in the United States District Court for the District of Columbia, wrote a separate opinion in which he asserted that in neither event should the lawyer expose his client's life. If these two cases do not constitute "fraud or chicane" or lack of candor within the meaning of the Canons (and I agree with the authorities cited that they do not), it is clear that the meaning of the Canons is ambiguous.

The adversary system has further ramifications in a criminal case. The defendant is presumed to be innocent. The burden is on the prosecution to prove beyond a reasonable doubt that the defendant is guilty. The plea of not guilty does not necessarily mean "not guilty in fact," for the defendant may mean "not legally guilty." Even the accused who knows that he committed the crime is entitled to put the government to its proof. Indeed, the accused who knows that he is guilty has an absolute constitutional right to remain silent. The moralist might quite reasonably understand this to mean that, under these circumstances, the defendant and his lawyer are privileged to "lie" to the court in pleading not guilty. In my judgment, the moralist is right. However, our adversary system and related notions of the proper administration of criminal justice sanction the lie.

Some derive solace from the sophistry of calling the lie a "legal fiction," but this is hardly an adequate answer to the moralist. Moreover, this answer has no particular appeal for the practicing attorney, who knows that the plea of not guilty commits him to the most effective advocacy of which he is capable. Criminal defense lawyers do not win their cases by arguing reasonable doubt. Effective trial advocacy requires that the attorney's every word, action, and attitude be consistent with the conclusion that his client is innocent. As every trial lawyer knows, the jury is certain that the defense attorney knows whether his client is guilty. The jury is therefore alert to, and will be enormously affected by, any indication by the attorney that he believes the defendant to be guilty. Thus, the plea of not guilty commits the advocate to a trial, including a closing argument, in which he must argue that "not guilty" means "not guilty in fact."

There is, of course, a simple way to evade the dilemma raised by the not guilty plea. Some attorneys rationalize the problem by insisting that a lawyer never knows for sure whether his client is guilty. The client who insists upon his guilt may in fact be protecting his wife, or may know that he pulled the trigger and that the victim was killed, but not that his gun was loaded with blanks and that the fatal shot was fired from across the street. For anyone who finds this reasoning satisfactory, there is, of course, no need to think further about the issue.

It is also argued that a defense attorney can remain selectively ignorant. He can insist in his first interview with his client that, if his client is guilty, he simply does not want to know. It is inconceivable, however, that an attorney could give adequate counsel under such circumstances. How is the client to know, for example, precisely which relevant circumstances his lawyer does not want to be told? The lawyer might ask whether his client has a prior record. The client, assuming that this is the kind of knowledge that might present ethical problems for his lawyer, might respond that he has no record. The lawyer would then put the defendant on the stand and, on cross-examination, be appalled to learn that his client has two prior convictions for offenses identical to that for which he is being tried.

. . . .

The problem is compounded by the practice of plea bargaining. It is considered improper for a defendant to plead guilty to a lesser offense unless he is in fact guilty. Nevertheless, it is common knowledge that plea bargaining frequently results in improper guilty pleas by innocent people. For example, a defendant falsely accused of robbery may plead guilty to simple assault, rather than risk a robbery conviction and a substantial prison term. If an attorney is to be scrupulous in bargaining pleas, however, he must know in advance that his client is guilty, since the guilty plea is improper if the defendant is innocent. Of course, if the attempt to bargain for a lesser offense should fail, the lawyer would know the truth and thereafter be unable to rationalize that he was uncertain of his client's guilt.

. . . .

## II.  THE SPECIFIC QUESTIONS

The first of the difficult problems posed above will now be considered: Is it proper to cross-examine for the purpose of discrediting the reliability or the credibility of a witness whom you know to be telling the truth? Assume the following situation. Your client has been falsely accused of a robbery committed at 16th and P Streets at 11:00 p. m. He tells you at first that at no time on the evening of the crime was he within six blocks of that location. However, you are able to persuade him that he must tell you the truth and that doing so will in no way prejudice him. He then reveals to you that he was at 15th and P Streets at 10:55 that evening, but that he was walking east, away from the scene of the crime, and that, by 11:00 p. m., he was six blocks away. At the trial, there are two prosecution witnesses. The first mistakenly, but with some degree of persuasion, identifies your client as the criminal. At that point, the prosecution's case depends on this single witness, who might or might not be believed. Since your client has a prior record, you do not want to put him on the stand, but you feel that there is at least a chance for acquittal. The second prosecution witness is an elderly woman who is somewhat nervous and who wears glasses. She testifies truthfully and accurately that she saw your client at 15th and P Streets at 10:55 p. m. She has corroborated the erroneous testimony of the first witness and made conviction virtually certain. However, if you destroy her reliability through cross-examination designed to show that she is easily confused and has poor eyesight, you may not only eliminate the corroboration, but also cast doubt in the jury's mind on the prosecution's entire case. On the other hand, if you should refuse to cross-examine her because she is telling the truth, your client may well feel betrayed, since you knew of the witness's veracity only because your client confided in you, under your assurance that his truthfulness would not prejudice him.

The client would be right. Viewed strictly, the attorney's failure to cross-examine would not be violative of the client's confidence because it would not constitute a disclosure. However, the same policy that supports the obligation of confidentiality precludes the attorney from prejudicing his client's interest in any other way because of knowledge gained in his professional capacity. When a lawyer fails to cross-examine only because his client, placing confidence in the lawyer, has been candid with him, the basis for such confidence and candor collapses. Our legal system cannot tolerate such a result.

.    .    .    .

The third question is whether it is proper to give your client legal advice when you have reason to believe that the knowledge you give him will tempt him to commit perjury. This may indeed be the most difficult problem of all, because giving such advice creates the appearance that the attorney is encouraging and condoning perjury.

If the lawyer is not certain what the facts are when he gives the advice, the problem is substantially minimized, if not eliminated. It is not the lawyer's function to prejudge his client as a perjurer. He cannot presume that the client will make unlawful use of his advice. Apart from this, there is a natural predisposition in most people to recollect facts, entirely honestly, in a way most favorable to their own interest. As Randolph Paul has observed, some witnesses are nervous, some are confused about their own interests, some try to be too smart for their own good, and some subconsciously do not want to understand what has happened to them. Before he begins to remember essential facts, the client is entitled to know what his own interests are.

The above argument does not apply merely to factual questions such as whether a particular event occurred at 10:15 or at 10:45. One of the most critical problems in a criminal case, as in many others, is intention. A German writer, considering the question of intention as a test of legal consequences, suggests the following situation. A young man and a young woman decide to get married. Each has a thousand dollars. They decide to begin a business with these funds, and the young lady gives her money to the young man for this purpose. Was the intention to form a joint venture or a partnership? Did they intend that the young man be an agent or a trustee? Was the transaction a gift or a loan? If the couple should subsequently visit a tax attorney and discover that it is in their interest that the transaction be viewed as a gift, it is submitted that they could, with complete honesty, so remember it. On the other hand, should their engagement be broken and the young woman consult an attorney for the purpose of recovering her money, she could with equal honesty remember that her intention was to make a loan.

Assume that your client, on trial for his life in a first-degree murder case, has killed another man with a penknife but insists that the killing was in self-defense. You ask him, "Do you customarily carry the penknife in your pocket, do you carry it frequently or infrequently, or did you take it with you only on this occasion?" He replies, "Why do you ask me a question like that?" It is entirely appropriate to inform him that his carrying the knife only on this occasion, or infrequently, supports an inference of premeditation, while if he carried the knife constantly, or frequently, the inference of premeditation would be negated. Thus, your client's life may depend upon his recollection as to whether he carried the knife frequently or infrequently. Despite the possibility that the client or a third party might infer that the lawyer was prompting the client to lie, the lawyer must apprise the defendant of the significance of his answer. There is no conceivable ethical requirement that the lawyer trap his client into a hasty and ill-considered answer before telling him the significance of the question.

A similar problem is created if the client has given the lawyer incriminating information before being fully aware of its significance. For example, assume that a man consults a tax lawyer and says, "I am fifty years old. Nobody in my immediate family has lived past fifty. Therefore, I would like to put my affairs in order. Specifically, I understand that I can avoid substantial estate taxes by setting up a trust. Can I do it?" The lawyer informs the client that he can successfully avoid the estate taxes only if he lives at least three years after establishing the trust or, should he die within three years, if the trust is found not to have been created in contemplation of death. The client then might ask who decides whether the trust is in contemplation of death. After learning that the determination is made by the court, the client might inquire about the factors on which such a decision would be based.

At this point, the lawyer can do one of two things. He can refuse to answer the question, or he can inform the client that the court will consider the wording of the trust instrument and will hear evidence about any conversations which he may have or any letters he may write expressing motives other than avoidance of estate taxes. It is likely that virtually every tax attorney in the country would answer the client's question, and that no one would consider the answer unethical. However, the lawyer might well appear to have prompted his client to deceive the Internal Revenue Service and the courts, and this appearance would remain regardless of the lawyer's explicit disclaimer to the client of any intent so to prompt him. Nevertheless, it should not be unethical for the lawyer to give the advice.

. . . . .

Essentially no different from the problem discussed above, but apparently more difficult, is the so-called *Anatomy of a Murder* situation. The lawyer, who has received from his client an incriminating story of murder in the first degree, says, "If the facts are as you have stated them so far, you have no defense, and you will probably be electrocuted. On the other hand, if you acted in a blind rage, there is a possibility of saving your life. Think it over, and we will talk about it tomorrow." As in the tax case, and as in the case of the plea of guilty to a lesser offense, the lawyer has given his client a legal opinion that might induce the client to lie. This is information which the lawyer himself would have, without advice, were he in the client's position. It is submitted that the client is entitled to have this information about the law and to make his own decision as to whether to act upon it. To decide otherwise would not only penalize the less well-educated defendant, but would also prejudice the client because of his initial truthfulness in telling his story in confidence to the attorney.

. . . .

### POSTSCRIPT

At the beginning of this article, some common question-begging responses were suggested. Professor John Noonan has added yet another: the role of the advocate is to promote a wise and informed judgment by the finder of fact.[5] This is the position of the 1958 Joint Conference on Professional Responsibility of the Association of American Law Schools and of the American Bar Association, and it is, of course, the primary basis of Professor Noonan's argument.

Professor Noonan graciously compliments me on "[making the] principles vital by showing how they would govern particular cases." He adds, "this scholarly explication of what is often taken for granted serves a very useful function." At the risk of appearing ungrateful, I am compelled to observe that Professor Noonan's own position fails in precisely that respect. His general proposition simply does not decide specific cases, nor does he make the effort to demonstrate how it might do so. Indeed, Professor Noonan occasionally appears to be struggling against confronting the particular cases.

For example, how would the Joint Conference principle resolve the situation where the prosecution witness testifies that the crime was committed at 10:15, and where the lawyer knows that his client has an honest alibi for 10:15, but that he actually committed the crime in question at 10:45? Can the lawyer refuse to present the honest alibi? Is he contributing to wise and informed judgment when he does so? If he should decide that he cannot present the alibi, how should he proceed in withdrawing from the case? Does it matter whether he has forewarned his client that he would withdraw if he discovers that his client is in fact guilty? Will it contribute to wise and informed judgment if the client obtains another lawyer and withholds from him the fact of his guilt? Similar questions might be asked regarding the problem of the guilty plea by the innocent defendant. One might ask, in addition, whether such a plea is really a lie to the court, in the moral sense, or whether it is just a convention, which is Professor Noonan's view of the not-guilty plea by the guilty defendant.

In the situation involving avoidance of estate taxes, the Joint Conference principle would probably require that the lawyer refuse to

---

**5.** Noonan, The Purposes of Advocacy and the Limits of Confidentiality, 64 Mich.L.Rev. 1485 (1966). Professor Noonan adds a further *petitio principii* when he argues, in the language of Canon 15, that the lawyer "must obey his own conscience." It may be that the wisest course is to make each lawyer's conscience his ultimate guide. It should be recognized, however, that this view is wholly inconsistent with the notion of professional ethics which, by definition, supersede personal ethics. In addition, it should be noted that personal ethics, in the context of acting in a professional capacity for another, can require a conclusion different from that which one might reach when acting for himself. For example, the fact that a lawyer would not commit perjury on his own behalf does not in any way preclude a decision to put on the witness stand a client who intends to perjure himself in his behalf. [Footnote by Professor Freedman]

answer his client's question. Such a result would be required because, in the assumed circumstances, an answer could be justified as contributing to wise and informed judgment only by what Professor Noonan characterizes as "brute rationalization." However, is it realistic to disregard as irrelevant the undoubted fact that virtually every tax lawyer in the country would answer the client?

Finally, Professor Noonan argues that it would be better to let the truthful (but misleading) witness remain unimpeached and to trust the trier of fact to draw the right conclusions. This is necessary, he contends, because "repeated acts of confidence in the rationality of the trial system are necessary if the decision-making process is to approach rationality." This means that the fortunes, liberty, and lives of today's clients can properly be jeopardized for the sake of creating a more rational system for tomorrow's litigants. It is hard to believe that Professor Noonan either wants or expects members of the bar to act on this advice.

Thus, Professor Noonan does not realistically face up to the lawyer's practical problems in attempting to act ethically. Unfortunately, it is precisely when one tries to act on abstract ethical advice that the practicalities intrude, often rendering unethical the well-intended act.

## QUESTIONS

1. The attorney, Freedman, observes, "functions in an adversary system based upon the presupposition that the most effective means of determining truth is to present to a judge and jury a clash between proponents of conflicting views." Is this supposition defensible? In any given case, might there not be better ways of getting at "the truth" than the adversary system as Curtis and Freedman describe it? Is a lawyer foreclosed, qua lawyer, from examining that presupposition as a general rule of conduct? Why should "effective functioning of the system" seem more important to the lawyer than seeing that the guilty are punished? What if the lawyer firmly believes his client is guilty and feels he is more capable of judging the matter than the judge or jury?

2. What is "the truth"? What attitudes towards "the truth" is the adversary system built upon?

3. What is the role of the lawyer in establishing what the facts are? Is his task adequately described as "gathering them"? To what extent do the facts the law system needs exist before the lawyer begins his job? Does a killer have, at the time of his killing, an intent *in fact*? How does—and how should—the lawyer function in *making* this fact? Under what state of affairs is a lawyer's statement that someone acted in "blind rage" or "with premeditation" a lie? Are statements about "blind rage" or "premeditation" statements about facts, capable of truth or falsity?

*F. S. Cohen*

## Field Theory and Judicial Logic *

### I.  *The Paradoxes of Judicial Logic*

*Are Lawyers Liars?*  Anyone who has read the statement of facts in a large number of briefs of appellants and appellees is likely to conclude that any resemblances between opposing accounts of the same facts are purely fortuitous and unintentional.  The impression that opposing lawyers seldom agree on the facts is strengthened if one listens to opposing counsel in almost any trial.  Now, as a matter of simple logic, two inconsistent statements cannot both be true.  At least *one* must be false.  And it is always possible that *both* are false, as, for example, when the plaintiff's attorney says the defendant speeded into the zone of the accident at sixty miles an hour and the defendant's counsel insists his client was jogging along at twenty miles an hour, while, in fact, he was moving at forty miles an hour.  Thus, a logician may conclude that either (1) at least half of our practicing lawyers utter falsehoods whenever they open their mouths or fountain pens, or (2) that a substantial majority of practicing lawyers utter falsehoods on a substantial number of such occasions.  If we define a liar as a person who frequently utters such falsehoods, it would seem to follow logically that most lawyers are liars.

How the edifice of justice can be supported by the efforts of liars at the bar and ex-liars on the bench is one of the paradoxes of legal logic which the man in the street has never solved.  The bitter sketch of "Two Lawyers" by Daumier still expresses the accepted public view of the legal profession.  So, too, does the oft-told story of Satan's refusal to mend the party wall between Heaven and Hell when it was his turn to do so, of St. Peter's fruitless protests and threats to bring suit, and of Satan's crushing comeback: "Where do you think you will find a lawyer?"

Of course, lawyers know that the popular opinion on these subjects is inaccurate.  Lawyers have ample opportunity to know how earnestly two litigants will swear to inconsistent accounts of a single event.  Lawyers thus have special opportunities to learn what many logicians have not yet recognized: that truth on earth is a matter of degree, and that, whatever may be the case in Heaven, a terrestrial major league batting average above .300 is nothing to be sneezed at.

The difference between the lawyer's and the logician's view of truth is worth more attention than it has had from either lawyers or logicians.

From the standpoint of rigorous logic, a proposition is either true or false.  There is no middle ground.  A statement such as "It is raining," which is true at one time and place and not at another,

* From 59 Yale L.J. 238, 238–42 (1950).   Law Journal Company and Fred B.
  Reprinted by permission of the Yale    Rothman & Co.

is ambiguous, and an ambiguous sentence is not a proposition, though each of its possible meanings may constitute a proposition. Indeed, the characteristic of being either true or false is commonly utilized in modern logic as the defining characteristic of propositions.

Life, unfortunately, is not so simple. Logicians may define propositions, but whether they can find or create propositions is another matter. Even if we convince ourselves that there *are* propositions, it does not necessarily follow that we can actually create them or find them; we may convince ourselves that there is, somewhere, an oldest man on earth, without ever being sure who he is.

One of the greatest modern logicians, Alfred North Whitehead, used to say: "We shall meet propositions in Heaven." By this he meant that the symbolism of terrestrial life is too fuzzy ever to reach absolute precision, so that unambiguousness is an ideal rather than an attainable fact. Every actual humanly constructed sentence has different shades of meaning to different readers. This is most likely to be the case in fields of controversy where different readers bring different examples, contexts and values to bear on any given word. In any such situation a sentence will embody not a single proposition but several propositions which are ideally distinguishable. Some of these propositions may be true. Some may be false. The relation of true meanings to false meanings that flow from a single sentence generally involves a complicated quantitative distribution pattern. The simple, traditional true-false dichotomy is often quite useless.

Take, for instance, a typical humanly constructed sentence, one which has been uttered, down through some 3000 years, by hundreds of millions of human beings of many races, many tongues, and many religions:

*The Lord is my shepherd; I shall not want.*

What sense does it make to ask whether this sentence is true or false?

Of course, there may be literal-minded readers of the Bible who will insist that the sentence has only one "correct" meaning, which is true, and that any variant interpretation is simply erroneous.

There are, no doubt, equally dogmatic individuals who will insist that the sentence is simply false. If they are dogmatic atheists, they will tell us: "There is no Lord and therefore He cannot possibly be a shepherd." If they are Montana cattlemen, they may add that nobody in the sheep business could possibly deserve to bear the name of the Lord. Others there are who have outgrown the effort to make God in man's image, but still recite these words with full sincerity. To some such, the words of the Psalmist mean that the forces of evil are somehow self-defeating, that ultimate victory rests with the forces of righteousness, that none of us is self-sufficient, that none of us is capable of protecting himself against all the dangers that surround us from cradle to grave, and that sanity requires a faith in an unseen power that will protect us and guide us as a faithful shepherd guides his sheep, seeing that their wants are fulfilled. But one who thus translates the words of an ancient poet into the context of his own beliefs has no right to assume that this is the only context in which those words have significance.  He will be content to say that they have truth for him.

This dependence of meaning upon a personal frame of reference is something that many of us take for granted when we refuse to argue over affirmations of religious faith.  May not the same dependence of meaning and truth upon varying contexts be found in non-religious fields as well, even in the mundane fields which concern lawyers and their clients?  May we not say, even, that law as, *par excellence*, the field of controversies, is the field in which the imposition of different meanings upon the same verbal formula is most characteristic and most significant?

If anybody asks us whether the first sentence of the Twenty-third Psalm is true or false, we may properly conclude that the interrogator is lacking in imagination and guilty of the fallacy of misplaced concreteness.  That is because we realize that a sentence of this sort (and perhaps every other humanly constructed sentence, in greater or lesser degree) means many things to many minds.  Perhaps, if we look closely enough, a sentence never means exactly the same thing to any two different people.  For no two minds bring the same apperceptive mass of understanding and background to bear on the external fact of a sound or a series of marks.  Indeed, I doubt whether any sentence means exactly the same thing to me the first time I hear it that it means the tenth time or the hundredth time.  Of course, for many practical purposes, we are disposed to overlook such variations of meaning.  Each of us is likely to try to fix on a particular segment of our thinking, at a particular time, as "the real meaning" of any sentence.  We may then consider all other interpretations as more or less serious aberrations.  Perhaps we may be justified in holding that our own specific understanding of the sentence at a particular time is a proposition, and either false or true.  But what, then, shall we say of the sentence as a social fact, a source of many interpretations, a matrix of many propositions?  Must we not say that the truth of any assertion is a matter of degree, that from certain angles the sentence may give light and that at other angles it may obscure more light than it gives?  The angle or perspective and the context are part of the meaning of any proposition, and therefore a part of whatever it is that is true or false.

The location of words in a context is essential to their meaning and truth.  The fallacy of simple location in physical space-time has finally been superseded in physics.  We now realize that the Copernican view that the earth moves around the sun and the older Ptolemaic view that the sun moves around the earth can both be true, and that for practical though not aesthetic or religious purposes the Ptolemaic and Copernican astronomics may be used interchangeably.[6]  We realize that Euclidean and non-Euclidean geometries can both be true.  What is a straight line in one system may be an ellipse in another system, just as a penny may be round in one perspective, oval in a second, and rectangular in a third.

---

6.  See *Note*, The Copernican Revolution, *infra* at 321 ff.

A prosecuting attorney who assumes that policemen are accurate and impartial observers of traffic speeds will arrive at one estimate of the speed of a defendant charged with reckless driving.  The defendant's attorney, if he assumes that his client is an honest man and that policemen on the witness stand generally exaggerate in order to build up an impressive record of convictions, will arrive at another estimate.  If each honestly gives his views the court will have the benefit of synoptic vision.  Appreciation of the importance of such synoptic vision is a distinguishing mark of liberal civilization.  To the anthropologist, the tolerance that is institutionalized in a judicial system geared to hear two sides in every case represents a major step in man's liberation from the tyranny of word-magic.  If we do not feel that we have to annihilate those who say things we do not believe or, what is generally more irritating, say things we do believe but say them in strange ways or in unfamiliar accents, we are able to conserve our energy for more useful purposes.  Energy so conserved may produce science, art, baseball, and various other substitutes for indiscriminate individualistic slaughter.

The disagreements of opposing lawyers on statements of simple fact, and the even wider disagreements that characterize their views on more complicated facts ("opinion" and "law"), call for a more humane and social view of truth and meaning than appears in most of the traditional logic books.  This is not to say that the traditional logic books are wrong.  It is only to say that so far the logicians, having concentrated their vision on the logical heavens where words continue at rest and mean the same thing forever, have not fully explored the imperfect efforts of human beings to communicate with each other.  But there are welcome indications today that logicians are beginning to pay more attention to the real world where people seldom say exactly what they mean or mean all they say, where no two people ever quite understand each other, where the accumulation of different views of the same event is the only remedy we have found for fanaticism, and where the logic of fiction has a more direct bearing upon every-day discourse than the logic of science.

In a certain sense, it is true that lawyers are liars.  In the same sense, poets, historians, and map-makers are also liars.  For it is the function of lawyers, poets, historians, and map-makers not to reproduce reality but to illumine some aspect of reality, and it always makes for deceit to pretend that what is thus illumined is the whole of reality.  None of us can ever possibly tell the whole truth, though we may conscientiously will to do so and ask divine help towards that end.  The ancient wisdom of our common law recognizes that men are bound to differ in their views of fact and law, not because some are honest and others dishonest, but because each of us operates in a value-charged field which gives shape and color to whatever we see.  The proposition that no man should be a judge of his own cause embodies the ancient wisdom that only a many-perspectived view of the world can relieve us of the endless anarchy of one-eyed vision.

QUESTIONS

1. *Are* lawyers liars? Do the observations of Cohen directly meet the problems raised by Curtis and Freedman? Is Cohen suggesting that the differences in lawyers' presentations of facts can be satisfactorily explained in terms of honestly held, different "illusions"? Is the "relativism" of truth—whatever this means—an adequate ethical justification for lawyers to say that whatever is in the interests of their clients is true? Do the difficulties of deciding what statements are true constitute a license to say that which one believes to be false?

2. What does Cohen mean to suggest by observing that "truth is a matter of degree"? Degree of what? Can one infer from this Cohen's belief that some statements are "more true" than others? What makes them so? With reference to what criteria can we distinguish which statement is more true than another?


LOUIS M. BROWN

PREVENTIVE LAW/CURATIVE LAW: FACTS
(COLD-HOT) MAKE DIFFERENCE *

In bold outline, there are two different kinds of facts which a client may bring to his lawyer. The problem presented to the lawyer for solution may have arisen out of past ("cold") facts which gave rise to a trouble case—the usual litigation problem. Or the client may seek help with respect to a contemplated future course of action—future facts: "hot" facts. Where the facts are "hot," the trouble, if any, has not occurred and, hopefully, may never occur.

In the typical litigation case, the client has already "signed on the dotted line" and either wants to get out of the deal; or wants the other fellow to do (or pay damages for) what he had previously agreed to do. The litigating lawyer is largely an historian. A goal of the trial lawyer is to recreate facts in the courtroom—to write history through witnesses and documents.

By contrast the planning lawyer is largely concerned with the development of the client's future facts. In the typical preventive-law lawyering situation, the client has not yet "signed on the dotted line." Should he sign? Are there alternative possibilities? How can he sign and still get the best protection?

One of the interesting features of the practice of preventive law is that, to some extent, by helping his client choose facts, a lawyer helps his client choose the most desirable legal result. His client gets a different legal (and practical) result, depending on whether or not he signs on the dotted line. And, if he signs, he may get differing legal results, depending on the language used (the "facts" chosen) in the document. Different facts lead to different legal consequences.

* From 40 Cal. B. J. 258 (1965).

The difference in the time-characteristic of facts lies at the bottom of much of the difference between the nature of the practice of the litigating and the preventive law lawyer.

QUESTIONS

What distinction is Professor Brown making between "hot" and "cold" facts? How "cold" are the past facts with which the litigating lawyer deals? What differences are there, in terms of their respective responsibility to—and for—"the facts", between the litigating lawyer and the planning lawyer?

———

SECTION ONE: FACTS/OPINIONS/INFERENCES

ARTHUR L. CORBIN

LEGAL ANALYSIS AND TERMINOLOGY *

.  .  .  The following definitions are offered, chiefly for the benefit of beginning students of the law, in order to assist in establishing an exact terminology and a definiteness and accuracy of mental concept. These definitions are in large part based upon the articles of Professor Wesley N. Hohfeld, referred to below.

I.   FACT: This is a world of *facts*. Physical existence and physical relations are facts. Our mental processes are facts. The existence of any legal relation is a fact. All changes and variations are facts. Facts include acts and events.

II.   ACT: An act is one of that class of facts manifest to the senses that consists of voluntary physical movements (muscular contractions that are willed) of human beings. A forbearance is a consciously willed absence of physical movement. Animals other than men can act or forbear, but they do not become parties to a legal relation.

III.   EVENT: Any change in the existing totality of facts, including the acts of human beings.

IV.   OPERATIVE FACT: Any fact the existence or occurrence of which will cause new legal relations between persons. A clear distinction should always be observed between the physical phenomena and the legal relations consequent thereon. The former are in the world of the senses, the latter are intellectual conceptions. Operative facts have also been described as "investitive," "constitutive," "causal," and "dispositive." The "extinguishment" of a legal relation is necessarily the creation of a new one.

* From 29 Yale L.J. 163, 163–64 (1919).     Law Journal Company and Fred B.
Reprinted by permission of the Yale     Rothman & Co.

V.  EVIDENTIAL FACT: Any fact the existence or occurrence of which tends to prove the existence of some other fact.  For example, a footprint on the sand is a fact from which we may infer the recent presence of a man.

*J. R. Lucas*

## On Not Worshipping Facts *

My sights in this paper are trained on facts.  Most people think that they know what facts are; that while their friends often, and themselves occasionally, are ignorant of the facts, at least they know what sort of things facts are—they can recognise a fact when they see it.  Facts, in the popular philosophy of today, are good, simple souls; there is no guile in them, nor any room for subjective bias, and once we have made ourselves acquainted with them, we have reached the beginning and summit of all wisdom.

This view is false; and not only false, but dangerously false.  Facts are not at all what people think they are; they are not the simple solid elements out of which the whole fabric of our knowledge is constructed, and the belief that they are is responsible for many of the obsessions which afflict academics, not least the historians.

.   .   .  We should be chary of making facts the cornerstone of our thinking, since at the higher levels of abstraction where philosophers talk about Acquaintance with Facts, and discuss the relations between True Propositions and Facts, too little context remains for any determinate meaning to survive.  There are other words better suited to be philosophical specimens, which can stand being isolated and examined *in vacuo*, without losing their sense: it is in terms of these that a philosopher, when tempted to say something about Facts, should rephrase what he has to say, since then he is less likely to be misled.

That the meaning of the word "fact" is not the same in all cases can be brought out by Aristotle's Method of Opposites.  We ask "What is it being contrasted with?  Is it a fact as opposed to a fiction?  Or as opposed to a theory?  Or as opposed to an interpretation?  Or a question of fact as opposed to a question of law?"  This in itself is enough to show that there is no one unitary concept of fact, but rather a whole sheaf of concepts, bound together indeed, but distinct.  More formal proofs can be produced: the fact/nonfact contrast may be used twice in the same sentence to make different distinctions; so that what are correctly described as facts according to one contrast are equally correctly not described as facts according to the other.  .   .   .

.   .   .   .   .

To explain my first crude version of [the] meaning [of "fact"], I shall need to set it in the context of a *dialogue*, a *discussion*, or a *dispute*.   .   .   .

* From 8 Phil.Q. 144, 144–48, 150, 152, 156 (1958).  Reprinted with permission of The Editor, The Philosophical Quarterly and Professor Lucas.

In a dispute there is always some point at issue: but in any discussion that is to continue, there must also be many points which are common ground. It is fruitless to argue if we do not disagree about something: it is fruitless, too, to argue if we disagree about everything. We must start with some points of agreement if our discussion is to get us anywhere, and only by taking them as agreed and unquestionably true can we hope to reach agreement over the point at issue. These points of agreement we call *the facts*. On the basis of these we argue and may succeed in reaching a conclusion. If we do reach a conclusion, then this point now agreed between us will be *a fact* in any further dispute the pair of us may have. That is to say, a fact is a fact relative to a given dispute, or relative to two or more persons at a given time arguing about a given point. The points that both sides accept as true, each side will describe by the word "fact": points whose truth one side would challenge should not be called facts, unless their truth can be established on the basis of other facts, premisses, that is, which are conceded as unquestionably true. The word "fact" is an incomplete symbol; the complete locution being "facts in respect of such and such a dispute." Before we can answer the question "What are the facts?" we need to know, either from the context or by being told explicitly, with respect to what dispute the question is being asked. This is the fundamental reason why we cannot talk of Facts with a big F: the word "fact" is an incomplete symbol, and as the issue in dispute varies, so also will the facts.

Let me take some examples. In a court of law there may be two sorts of issue in dispute: issues of fact and issues of law. In most criminal cases, it is a question only of determining what actually happened—a question of fact; while in many civil cases, the sole difficulty is to determine the correct interpretation of the law—a question of law; and there are yet other cases in which the court has to decide both a question of fact and a question of law. There will be rival accounts of what happened, but some things, different in each case, will not be contested by either party: both plaintiff and defendant, for example, might agree that plaintiff had chartered a ship from the defendants upon certain terms, and the ship had taken a cargo on board at Buenos Aires and discharged it at Pembroke Dock. They disagree on other points—the condition of the cargo before it was taken on board, whether it was properly examined in South America, when the deterioration took place, and what was the cause; but there are some points they do agree about; and on the basis of these and other facts, the court reaches a conclusion about what actually happened. This question having been settled, it is no longer a point in issue but becomes a *fact* with respect to the next question the court has to address itself to, namely what the legal consequences are; that is to say, how the law lays it down that cases like this are to be treated.

. . . . .

A similar variableness appears in value-judgments. Very seldom is the distinction between facts and values either as sharp as philosophers like to think, or drawn where they think it ought to be drawn.

Often the facts which we adduce to support an evaluative conclusion, are not absolutely non-evaluative themselves. In a dispute about a man's moral worth we claim, and it will be conceded to us, that at least *this* action was generous and that just, and it will be claimed against us, and we shall concede, that some other deed was inexcusable and yet another difficult to defend. Again, in discussing the morality of euthanasia, we do not begin from facts purely "descriptive"; our starting point will be a mixture of "factual" facts—that there are some painful diseases that are known to be incurable, some general moral principles—that it is wrong to kill and wrong not to alleviate unnecessary suffering, (these are sometimes called "moral facts"), and some more specific common moral judgments— that to kill a person in such and such circumstances would be to murder him, and all these are usually described by non-philosophers as facts. Only in the abstract examples invented by philosophers is the sense of the word "fact" fixed, and only there can it be equated to that which "descriptive" statements describe.

Even scientists determine what constitutes a fact by reference to the questions in dispute. The Theory of Evolution, the Theory of Special Relativity, and Quantum Mechanics, started by being spec- ulations, then became hypotheses, then were well-founded theories, and now can be described as facts. They are the starting point for further discussion. . . .

. . . .

I shall now go beyond my first approximation and alter my definition in two ways to make it more exact. First, I replace the reference to actual parties in actual disputes by ideal parties in actual or ideal disputes. A fact is what a disputant would concede as true if he were a reasonable man living at that time. Not what an *unquestioned* true statement states—some people will question any- thing—but what an *unquestionably* true statement states. This alteration weakens the dependence of the facts upon the issue in dispute, and substitutes an implicit reference to time. Many issues are dead. The reasonable man does not spend much time reassuring himself that the battle of Hastings was fought in 1066 A.D. or the battle of Marathon in 490 B.C. Although it is logically possible to impugn those dates, although indeed the date of Marathon has been impugned, yet the arguments in favour of the traditional dates are strong, and the consensus of opinion among those who have gone into the matter is so overwhelming that the reasonable man may feel fairly confident that he would not disagree with their findings.

. . . . . .

In most cases where the word "fact" is used of a definite type of statement, an epistemological distinction between the more and the less certain is being made, with the facts being those that are more certain and less disputable than statements of some other, less favoured, type . . . . .

. . . One weakness alone attaches to the method: as there are few facts, if any, that we cannot in our metaphysical moments be uncertain of, our concept of truth is *regressive*; our criterion grows progressively and indefinitely more stringent. At first we exclude those propositions of morals, theology and metaphysics, whose elimination is welcome to many of the enlightened; but the more we think, the more nice we become as to what are unquestionable truths; and so the truths of logic, mathematics, and natural science, of common sense and everyday life, join the procession to the guillotine.

For there are no basic facts: there are only facts relative to a dispute. Since there is nothing that cannot on some occasion be reasonably doubted, there can be no truths established beyond doubt to all comers, no elemental facts which we just have to accept and on which all else is based. Nothing is never doubtful, though this is not to say that everything is always doubtful. In every dispute we have to start somewhere, though there is nowhere that is the starting point for every dispute.

This is a little too strong: though there is nothing we *cannot* doubt, there are many things that, apart from our metaphysical moments, we *do not* doubt: there is a core of accepted truths that are unquestioned by all people living at a given time, and unquestionable by any reasonable man at that time, not engaged in philosophy; and on these established platitudes, accepted by the many though not by the philosophers, we can base all our reasonable and practical contentions. These facts, adequate for our non-philosophical constructions, prove, however, shifting sands when we try to build a theory of knowledge or theory of truth upon them: because then we try to have our facts as basic facts, neutral elemental atoms, facts not with regard to this or that specifiable issue, but with regard to any conceivable issue; facts not in the context of a dispute between two actual or likely disputants, but in the context of any argument between any possible disputants whatsoever, or rather, facts in no context at all. We think too much of facts as hard, brute facts, existing independently of us and ineluctable, as things that are what they are, and whose consequences will be what they will be, and about which we must not seek to be deceived. Having hypostatised them, we bow down to them, and prostrate ourselves before them. It is unnecessary. It is impossible. Facts are not sacred: they are not worth worshipping: they do not exist: they are not even things.

## QUESTIONS

1. What is Lucas trying to demonstrate about the meaning of the word "fact" in asking what it is being contrasted with, *e. g.*, a fiction, a theory, a question of law? Are his own definitions of "fact" sensitive to the thrust of this analysis; that is, is his own definition adequate to explain the uses of "fact" in every context in which we want to use the term? If *A* and *B* agree (for purposes of a dispute on another issue) that "proof of murder does not require a showing of criminal intent", or that "the empire state building is 100 feet high", is it meaningless for another to ask, "but is it a fact"? What would Lucas' response be? Is it adequate? Cannot people who agree be *wrong* on what they agree to? Is Lucas giving us the definition

of "assumption" or of "fact"? Or is he saying that they are the same (at least so long as the assumers are reasonable men)?

2. What is the effect of Lucas's altering his definition to take into account "what a disputant would concede as true if he were a reasonable man living at the time?" Is he saying that it was a "fact" in Nazi Germany that Aryans were racially superior to non-Aryans; or that the majority were "unreasonable"; or that the relevant community for determining "reasonableness" was the world? What dilemmas does this definition raise? Is not one of the functions of saying "this is a fact" to call attention to "the truth" of beliefs that reasonable men are overlooking or not questioning? Are there not propositions that are commonly considered "facts" that most men, much less reasonable men, know nothing about? Would Lucas's definition be improved by substituting "should concede" for "would concede"? What does he mean by "an unquestionably true statement"?

3. If, as Lucas maintains, facts are not "simple solid elements", what is the difference between a "statement of fact" and an "opinion", distinctions on which, in one form or other, many legal decisions seem to hinge? Is Lucas's analysis in terms of agreement relative to a dispute (and/or social grouping) adequate for a conceptually satisfactory handling of the problems the law wishes to resolve by reference to facts-opinion dichotomies?

Compare with Lucas's approach Oliphant's suggestion (following) that the distinction can be explicated in terms of numbers of stimuli and frequency of the inferences. How different is his suggested analysis from Lucas's? Is it any more satisfactory?

## HERMAN OLIPHANT

### FACTS, OPINIONS, AND VALUE-JUDGMENTS *

#### "Facts" versus "Opinion"

The merits of the common assumption that there is a hard and fast difference between *facts*, which can yield objective results, and *opinions or judgments*, which can yield only subjective ones, may now be considered. If the distinction be sound, the case for scientific methods in the study of the social sciences is indeed precarious, because it must be admitted that a very substantial part of the "significant" data of the social sciences consists of so-called opinions or judgments. But is there any such absolute distinction here or in any other science?

All would agree that the census enumerator collects "facts" not opinions, but, in the bare process of enumerating the number of people in a given area, he is reporting a number of generalized inferences. From a multitude of stimuli presented to his senses, he infers that what is before him is a man or a child and reports his inferences. Much more remote inferences, and inferences more open to the possi-

* From 10 Texas L.Rev. 127, 132–33          the Texas Law Review and Fred B.
  (1932). Reprinted by permission of       Rothman & Co.

bility of error, are found in his report of such so-called "facts" as a person's residence, age, sex, and occupation.  Thus the Census Bureau has had to struggle with such problems as whether one who grows and digs clams for a living is engaged in fishing, mining, or agriculture!

All would recognize the statement, "This is a table," as a statement of fact.  The statement, "This injury caused the plaintiff to lose his hearing," would be called an expression of opinion.  But the difference between these two statements is largely a matter of number of items of sense experience constituting the basis of the inference in each case and of the frequency with which the person involved is called upon to draw the inference.  On the basis of these two variables, we can arrange any homogeneous group of both so-called facts and so-called opinions into two reverse gradations.  At the lower end of one gradation, we should have inferences resting on a very few sense stimuli, and, at the lower end of the other, those very frequently made.  At the upper end of one, we should have inferences drawn from the maximum of sense stimuli, and, of the other, those made most infrequently.  Each gradation could be, and in life is, so uniformly populated that the point at which what we now call facts shades off into what we now call opinions could not be detected; and, more important from the standpoint of scientific methods, how far up that scale we can go in selecting data upon which to build statistical or other general inferences depends entirely upon the purposes we have in mind at the moment.  What frequency of an inference from what paucity of stimuli produces a "fact" and what infrequency of inference from what abundance of stimuli produces an "opinion"?  Thus doubly relative is the supposed distinction between "fact" and "opinion".

## Questions

1.  How adequately can the dichotomy between "facts" and "opinions" be reduced to terms of "items of sense experience" or "frequency with which the person is called upon to draw the inference"?  Take Oliphant's own examples of "this is a table" (which he calls "a statement of fact") and "this injury caused the plaintiff to lose his hearing" (which he calls "an expression of opinion").  Are there more "items of sense experience" in support of the former than of the latter?  How many "items" is the judgment "this is a table" based upon?  (Refer to the analyses of the perception of a table by Russell and Whitehead in Chapter 4).  Are not both judgments based upon "sense experience" (and prior judgments and beliefs) accumulated over the person's life-time?

2.  What assumptions is Oliphant making in supposing that the relative "factness" or "opinionness" of a statement is a function of the number of items in support?  Could the difficulty be removed if we weighed the preponderance of supportive "items" over and above the number of inconsistent "items"?  Does Oliphant's suggestion that we take into account the frequency of drawing the inference help resolve the problems?  Consider that only once is one likely to draw the inference that "On October 2, 1971, at 7:48 A.M., there was a fly on

the asterisk key of Professor Enots's typewriter"; how frequently have people drawn the inference that cauliflower tastes good? Yet, which would more likely be called the statement of fact (be it true or false) and which the statement of opinion?

3. How much does either Lucas's or Oliphant's analysis help us to apply the distinction between "statements of fact" and "statements of opinion" on which the A.L.I. *Restatement of Torts* provisions on Trade Disparagement are built?

*AMERICAN LAW INSTITUTE*

RESTATEMENT OF TORTS §§ 626, 627 (1938) *

DISPARAGEMENT OF QUALITY OF LAND, CHATTELS AND INTANGIBLE THINGS

(*Trade Libel*)

§ 626. DISPARAGING STATEMENT OF FACT.

One who without a privilege to do so publishes an untrue statement of fact which is disparaging to the quality of another's land, chattels or intangible things, under circumstances which would lead a reasonable man to foresee that the conduct of a third person as purchaser or lessee thereof would be determined thereby, is liable for pecuniary loss resulting to the other from the impairment of vendibility so caused.

*Comment:*

a. The phrase "a statement of fact" includes every form of conduct which asserts or implies the existence or non-existence of a fact. It includes not only a specific statement that a particular fact exists or has existed but also a statement which, though in form an expression of opinion, implies the existence of some fact or facts which have led its maker to hold the opinion in question. . . . It includes every statement except an expression of opinion upon facts or supposed facts which are disclosed to or otherwise known to or assumed by the recipient.

*Illustration:*

1. *A* says that the *X* automobile will not "stand up." This statement implies that *A* knows of certain facts relating to the construction or material of the *X* car which have led him to believe that such cars will not last as long as purchasers reasonably anticipate.

. . . .

§ 627. DISPARAGING STATEMENTS OF OPINION.

One who without a privilege to do so publishes an opinion which disparages the quality of another's land, chattels or intangible things under circumstances which make it foreseeable that its publication may influence the conduct of some third person as purchaser or lessee thereof is liable for pecuniary loss resulting to the other from the impairment of vendibility so caused if, but only if, the publisher does not hold the opinion which he expresses.

### QUESTIONS

1. What different legal consequences did the A.L.I. seek to attach to "statements of facts" and "statements of opinions"? Is a distinction based upon this dichotomy workable? How is a statement of fact different from a statement of opinion?

2. Consider the illustration under Sec. 626: "*A* says that the automobile will not 'stand up'." Does your judgment as to whether this is a statement of fact or an opinion depend upon the words that are uttered—or upon, in addition at least, circumstances that make up the context—for example, whether *A* is an auto mechanic or a passerby? Or whether, for example, the addressee of the remarks is an experienced automobile designer or an ordinary man? Or whether *A* is a friend of the addressee or a salesman for the *Y* automobile company (brand *X*'s arch competitor)?

3. Are there any "opinions"—in common parlance—that do not imply the "existence of some fact." Are no "facts" implied by the statement, "In my opinion, peanut butter tastes better than jam"?

4. What, indeed, is a "statement" within this purview? Suppose *A* and *B* are competitors in producing and selling outdoor equipment. *A*, in his catalogue, includes a picture of *B*'s power ventilator, except that *A* has caused lines to be drawn through the pictures of *B*'s product in the form of a large "X" and written the single word "old" in the margin. Is this a statement? If so, of "fact" or of "opinion" in the context of the Restatement? See Upton House Cooler v. Alldritt, 73 So.2d 848 (Fla.1954).

5. Does it do any good to say that the difference between "facts" and "opinions" is "a matter of degree"? Doesn't that leave one with the question, "degree of what?"

6. Is it possible to answer, "what is a 'fact'"? and "what is an 'opinion'?" without knowing the purposes sought to be achieved by the person making the distinction? Will the *function* of the distinction be the same in all cases? Could the goals of the A.L.I. authors have been achieved by reference to terminology other than that of the facts-opinion dichotomy? Might they do better by a draft that did not use either "facts" or "opinions"? Suppose you were one of the Restatement editors: what advice might you have given in 1938?

7. In the current redraft for the *Restatement (Second) of Torts* (Tent. Draft No. 12, 1966), Section 626 is to be reframed to read:

§ 626. DISPARAGEMENT OF QUALITY.

### (*Trade Libel*)

The rules as to liability for the publication of injurious falsehood stated in § 623A apply to the publication of matter disparaging the quality of another's land, chattels or intangible things, which the publisher should recognize as likely to affect the conduct of third persons in respect to interests in such property.

Section 627 (and other sections) are to be replaced with a new section, 623A.

§ 623A. LIABILITY FOR PUBLICATION OF INJURIOUS FALSEHOOD.

One who publishes an untrue statement of fact or opinion which he should recognize as likely to result in harm to interests of another having pecuniary value, through the action of third persons in reliance upon the statement, is subject to liability for pecuniary loss resulting to the other from such harm if, but only if

(a) The publisher is motivated by ill will toward the other, or

(b) He knows or has reason to know the matter to be otherwise than as stated, or that he has not the basis for knowledge or belief professed by his assertion, or

(c) He intends to interfere with the interests of the other in a manner which he has no privilege to do.

Why do you suppose that facts and opinions are lumped together in this way? One of the comments observes (p. 136), *"Fact and Opinion.* The general rule stated in this Section applies whether the injurious statement is one of fact or merely one of opinion. The fact that the statement is one of opinion only may, however, be important in determining whether there is a privilege to disparage the goods of a competitor. See § 649."

Does this mean that the A.L.I. is bailing itself out of the facts-opinions dichotomy? Section 649, CONDITIONAL PRIVILEGE OF COMPETITORS, (Tent. Draft No. 13, 1967) reads,

A vendor or lessor is conditionally privileged to make an unduly favorable comparison of the quality of his own land, chattels or other things, with the quality of the competing land, chattels or other things of his competitor, although he does not believe that his own things are superior to those of his competitor, if the comparison does not contain assertions of specific unfavorable facts.

What difficulties does the Restatement now face? What is a "specific unfavorable fact"? Consider in this regard the selection from Walter Wheeler Cook, which follows.

*WALTER WHEELER COOK*

## "FACTS" AND "STATEMENTS OF FACT" *

The Civil Practice Act recently adopted in Illinois contains one section which in its wording deliberately departs from the language commonly used in codes of civil procedure. This is section 33, which provides that

All pleadings shall contain a plain and concise statement of the pleader's cause of action, counterclaim, defense, or reply.

This language is similar to that of the corresponding section of the New York Civil Practice Act, but differs—and this is the interesting point—in that all reference to "facts" is omitted. To bring out the difference it will be helpful to quote the section of the New York Act, italicizing the part which refers to "facts". The New York provision reads:

SECTION 241. Every pleading shall contain a plain and concise statement of the *material facts*, without unnecessary repetition, on which the party pleading relies, but not the evidence.

Order 19, rule 4 of the English rules governing the matter contains similar language. It reads:

Every pleading shall contain, and contain only, a statement in summary form of the *material facts* upon which a party pleading relies for his claim or defense, as the case may be, but not the evidence by which they are proved.

For the purpose of simplifying our discussion let us concentrate our attention upon the complaint. The New York and the English law is that the plaintiff must state the "material facts"; the Illinois provision is merely that he must give a plain and concise "statement of the cause of action."

This departure from the traditional language of the codes, we are told by the late Professor Edward W. Hinton, who was in a position to know, was intentional and done for a purpose. The explanation which Professor Hinton gives is as follows:

The Committee . . . . decided to omit the word "facts" in order to minimize so far as possible the controversy that has arisen in so many code states where pleadings have been constantly attacked as setting out conclusions rather than facts.

In explanation of the action of the Committee Professor Hinton goes on to say:

All the earlier writers on Code Pleading emphasized that the new system was a fact system and that the pleader was to state facts, the whole facts, and nothing but the facts, and that has led to a great deal of useless controversy. No

* From 4 U.Chi.L.Rev. 233, 233–34, 235–39, 241–42, 246 (1936). Reprinted　with permission of The University of Chicago.

pleading was ever formulated that stated facts and nothing but facts. It is impracticable if not impossible to make a pure fact statement. The common-law system with which you are familiar made practically no attempt to require the statement of facts. Just consider for a moment. The common count in assumpsit alleged that the defendant was indebted to the plaintiff for goods, wares, and merchandise sold [and] delivered to him, and, being so indebted, in consideration thereof undertook and promised to pay—not a single fact. Absolutely not a single fact. What, in point of law, creates a debt? It is not stated. What, in point of law, constitutes a delivery? It is not stated. What, in point of law, constitutes a promise? It is not stated. The pleader simply states the legal result of unstated facts. Those are the common counts in assumpsit.

If we ask whether this omission of the words "material facts" from the Illinois Act has prevented the same doubts and difficulties from arising as arose under earlier codes, the answer seems to be that it has not done so.

. . . .

. . . Why is it that apparently the omission of the word "facts" from the Illinois Act has apparently had small effect in preventing the kind of controversies which have raged under the ordinary code provisions which retain that word? It is to the solution of this problem that the remainder of this paper will be directed. It is hoped to demonstrate what the source of the difficulty is and thereby to point the way which if followed by other drafting committees and legislative bodies will prevent a recurrence of the type of controversy under consideration. The aim of the present paper is therefore severely practical. Unfortunately, the problem can not be solved—or at least so the present writer believes—without making an excursion into a field of discussion which, it is feared, is anathema to the average member of the legal profession. That is to say, we shall have to consider certain matters usually relegated to that curious and supposedly useless study known as "philosophy." The reference is, however, not to philosophy in the sense of metaphysical discussion of the ultimate nature of the universe—in that we are not here interested. The reference is rather to an examination of such fundamental matters as the meaning of words and how words get their meaning, and similar problems. What, for example, is the meaning of the word "facts," and what of the words "statements of fact"? Our problem thus reduces itself to this: What do the words "facts" and "statements of fact" mean? Let us begin with "facts." "Facts," we are told, are just what they are, they exist. Here it will be useful to recall to mind a well-known statement found in a leading text-book on code pleading.

This writer tells us:

> The issuable facts [in an action or suit] should not only be stated to the complete exclusion of the law and the evidence, but they should be alleged as they *actually existed or*

*occurred.* . . . . The allegations must be of dry, naked, actual facts.

Note that underlying this passage are two assumptions: (a) the "facts" existed or occurred; (b) they can be "alleged," *i.e.*, "stated" in language which will describe them "as they actually existed or occurred." The eminent author of the passage quoted is not alone in this belief; it is shared by men in other walks of life, even by scientists of reputation. Thus we find a professor of chemistry in one of our large universities telling us that

> the fundamental facts of chemistry will still be valid at the end of the next half century. Of course that must be, for facts, defined as "the direct result of observation, unmodified by any act of reason," are eternal.

If we ask how much sense and how much non-sense such statements make, we shall discover first of all that all those who make such statements are assuming—as indeed do all scientists the present writer happens to know—that there is an external world of "fact," and that we must take due account of these external "facts" if we wish to continue to exist and be more or less comfortable. On this much all are agreed. It is in this sense of the word "fact" that we can say that "facts" are coercive; that they exist independently of our will; that they are "compelling elements of common-sense experience, a careful adjustment to which is the necessary condition of successful, or even continued living."

Suppose now that we wish to make some "statement" about these "facts": can we describe them as they "actually exist or occur," that is, as "dry, naked, actual facts"? The writers quoted, pleader and scientist alike, obviously assume that we can. And that, the present writer is convinced, is not only an erroneous assumption; it is philosophical and scientific non-sense which ignores the difficulties involved in the use of language and in the determination of what you are going to say the "facts" are. Upon another occasion, when discussing the problem orally before a bar association, I ventured to suggest that had the framers of the Code, had the judges who construed it, had the legal profession generally, realized this, much useless litigation might have been avoided and large sums of money saved both for clients and for the community.

Let us examine into the matter. When we look at this "external world" of coercive "facts", with what are we presented? Here it is difficult to talk at all without saying more, and also less, than one is justified in doing, and so one runs the risk of serious misinterpretation. Nevertheless the risk must be taken. Without attempting precise analysis—that is unnecessary for our present purposes—we can at least say that what is "out there" in the external world presents itself to us as a shifting, varying series of changing patterns of color, sound, odor, and what not. We may with C. I. Lewis call this the "given," meaning thereby the element in all experience which we are aware we do not create by thinking and can not in general displace and alter. Or, as the present writer expressed the matter upon another occasion, we may call this the "brute fact element" in experience, or perhaps "brute, raw events." If we try to describe this "given," these "brute, raw events," we discover first of all that there are an infinite number of aspects in any "situation," and that in order to talk about it at all we have to select from among these infinitely varied aspects those which for some reason or other we are going to talk about. In the second place we discover that in talking about the selected aspects we have to relate them in such a way as to put them under some category, some class, for which we have (or perhaps create) a verbal symbol or name. If for example I say that I have in my hand a fountain pen, I have selected from the variety of colors, shapes, etc. now presented to me a particular combination, and I have related these selected aspects so as to place them into the class of "objects" represented by the verbal symbol "fountain pen."

In other words, in making a "statement of fact" about the "given" situation (series of events), so as to state "what it is," I have in every case necessarily selected certain aspects, thereby neglecting all the other possible aspects which I might have observed, and then have interpreted the selected "data"—to use a scientific term—so as to bring them under some category. Then and only then can I say "what it is," that is, make a "statement of fact." Apparently all "statements of fact" are the result of a process of this sort, and are not the "direct result of observation, unmodified by any act of reason" as the professor of chemistry quoted above seemed to think. This will become clear if we examine any book on chemistry. We find that the "facts" described do not accord with the "given," the "brute, raw event" out there "as it is" in any absolute sense. They are the product first of "abstraction" from the concreteness of the "given," and then of interpretation of the elements abstracted: see the illustrations given at a later point in this discussion.

Next to be noted is that what our observer "abstracts" from the "given" will depend upon his past experience and education as well as upon the purpose he has in view at the time. As his fund of experience widens and also as his purpose changes he will select different combinations of aspects and relate them in different ways.

. . . .

Suppose I am looking out of the window of the room in which you and I are and you ask me: "What do you see?" Any reply I make, assuming I see "something" will be a "statement of fact." Suppose my reply is: "I see an object": this tells you something but not much; nevertheless it is a "statement of fact." Perhaps you ask for a more detailed statement. I reply: "I see an inorganic object." You now know more than before, but perhaps you are still not satisfied, and my next reply may be: "I see a vehicle." This is equally a "statement of fact," as will be a statement that "I see an automobile." I may under your urging go on to more and more detailed statements, such as: "I see a five passenger sedan;" "I see a 1935 Ford four-door sedan, with blue body and black wheels"; and so on. Each statement becomes more and more detailed, tells you more and more about what you could see if you were to look.

Suppose now the only directions you were to give me when you asked me to look out of the window and tell you what I saw were that I was to "state in plain and concise language the facts" of the situation outside the window, or at least of that part of it in which I was interested; or suppose, to adopt language like that of the Illinois Civil Practice Act, you told me to "state what you see in plain and concise language." Is it not clear that any one of the answers given above would prima facie comply with these directions, and that none of these answers would be an adequate guide to me as to what you wished to know? There seems only one answer to this, namely, that I would be completely at a loss as to how general or how specific you desired my statement to be.

In other words, a direction to "state the facts" of a situation or to "describe the situation" is an inadequate guide without more. The matter will, to be sure, be helped if I know for what purpose my answer is to be used, and of course that is the case in pleading: the pleader's statement is for the purpose of informing the court and the other party of the grounds upon which the pleader asks action in favor of his client. Even so our difficulties are not over. How much of the "concrete particularity" of the given situation shall the pleader tell the court and the other party? The language of the English order, of the New York Civil Practice Act, and of the Illinois Civil Practice Act are silent on the point. If we say by way of explanation: "Tell enough fairly to apprise the court and the other party of the issues," there is still plenty of opportunity for doubt as to what is required.

. . .

To sum up our argument: when ancient landmarks are swept away, they must obviously be replaced by other marks at least equally useful in guiding the wayfarer through the pleading wilderness. But, from the very nature of verbal symbols and of "facts," a direction to "state the facts constituting the cause of action" or to "state in plain and concise language the cause of action" can not possibly furnish adequate guidance. It can do little more than generate doubt and uncertainty and provoke controversy and litigation. That has been the uniform experience in the past. If such directions are accompanied by an adequate set of forms, which while not required are sufficient if used, the difficulty is solved and peace and good order reign in the pleader's world. It is to be hoped that the example now about to be set by the new federal rules will be followed by all committees which in the future may be set at the task of "simplifying pleading."

---

## Section Two: Knowing the Past, Present and Future

How different is our knowledge of facts about the past, present and future, *e. g.*, (a) John killed Mary, (b) John is killing Mary and (c) John will kill Mary? Is the one based on memory and records of "what happened", the other a report of direct sensations telling what is "out there", and the last on inferences from the first two?

It might seem as though the present was known "as it is", *i. e.*, as ultimate, brute fact. But as Chapter 4 indicated, even our perception is at best a blend of what exists in the world, theory about the world, language, and emotional attitudes. The problem of "facts" about the present is even further complicated for a reason suggested by Cook, above, that once we put our perceptions into language (either as a preparatory stage for communication or as part of private thought processes) we are thereby generalizing—and thereby talking about more than the isolated present "fact".

This position may be expressed by saying that the meaning of *no* synthetic proposition can be purely ostensive; that is, to use A. J. Ayer's example, even if I point to something (that is white) and say "this is white", I may be understood as saying (a) I am experiencing a sense-content which resembles strongly the sense-contents I have in my past experience been taught to classify as "white"; (b) I am committing myself in the future to classify as "white" sense contents that (strongly?) resemble the one I am now having; (c) if I should discover in the future that I had an abnormal color-sense, I would change my position that the experience I am now having made it appropriate for me to say "this is white".[7] In such fashion, even the most apparently rudimentary "facts" about the present are very much entangled with "facts" about the past and future. It is only in a limited way that we may be said to know facts about the world as *it is*.

What, then, about our knowledge of the past and of the future? How is each of them related to "the facts"?

It would seem as though our knowledge of the past and of the future were radically different; indeed, it may seem a bit odd to use the term "knowledge" with respect to the future at all. But the apparent distinction is not so easy to defend. If we want to "know" the alignment of Pluto, the Earth and Saturn 1000 years in the future, we are left to rely on extrapolations from records of past and present observations as to the planets' relative positions, masses, velocities, and so forth, and project—infer, we say—on the basis of our best theories about the significance of these facts. But how different is this process from the way we come to "know" the relative position of these planets 1000 years in the past? Are we not left to a sort of inference, here, too? Indeed, is one not inferring from basically the very same data, only reversing the processes?

Consider, in this regard, the selection that follows from Hans Reichenbach's posthumously published THE DIRECTION OF TIME. Reichenbach was concerned to differentiate past and future by reference to probable states of entropy (a measure of the organization of matter and energy). All information, Reichenbach maintained, is based upon the relative probability of things. A man flying over a desert island who sees a "random" distribution of coconuts strewn about the ground does not get the information he would get from

7. *Cf.* A. Ayer, Language, Truth and Logic 90–93 (Dover ed. undated).

piles of coconuts arranged into the form SOS. The latter is a highly improbable distribution of coconuts, and thus can tell us a "fact" about the past: that the odds are at least extremely high that some person is or was down below, and in trouble. The following passage elaborates on the relationship of past and future from the point of relative amounts and qualities of information that are necessary to achieve comparable degrees of probably good inferences.

## HANS REICHENBACH

## THE DIRECTION OF TIME *

We might be tempted to [say] that the future is unknown, whereas the past is known. Such a statement, however, would be obviously false. Some events of the future are well known, such as astronomical events, or the fact that there will be general elections in the fall. And many events of the past are unknown; if they were known, historians and geologists would have an easier task. The difference between the past and the future is not a difference between knowing and not knowing; it is to be formulated with respect to the way in which we acquire such knowledge.

Our knowledge of the past is based on *records*, whether they be documents written by a chronicler, or fossils included in geological strata, or traces of blood on a garment. In contrast, it appears absurd to speak of records of the future. Records are small by-products of comprehensive events, the total effects of which include many other and more important happenings. The chronicle is a by-product of a war that killed thousands of people; the fossils are by-products of extensive geological events; the traces of blood on the garment may be by-products of an act of murder. Such isolated data are not enough, if we wish to predict the future.

The happenings of the future can be foretold only on the basis of comprehensive information covering the total occurrence. If we wish to predict whether there will be a war, we have to know the state of armament of various countries, their political aspirations, and many other things. If we wish to predict whether a certain area of the ground will later be covered by water, we have to make measurements concerning changes of level over much wider areas. In order to predict an act of murder, we would have to have a detailed knowledge of a certain person's state of mind.

. . . .

. . . Even those who insist that such detailed predictions are possible in principle, though not in practice, will admit that these forecasts cannot be based on a few isolated indications. This difference concerning details springs from the peculiar difference between inferences regarding the future and inferences concerning the past. *Predictions* require a knowledge of the total cause; *postdictions*, or statements about past events, can be based on partial effects, on records.

* From 21–23, 150–51, 179 (University of California Press 1956). With the permission of the Regents of the University of California.

We formulate this result as follows:

*Statement 5.   We can have records of the past, but not of the future.*

.   .   .   .

Suppose we find in the sand traces of footprints, somewhat smoothed out by the wind, but still recognizable as impressions of human feet. We conclude from this "record" that at some earlier time a man walked over the sand, thus causing the footprints. What is the logical schema of this inference?

The different arrangements of grains of sand can be classified into states by the use of simple rules. One state is given by a smooth surface of the sand; another one by the condition described, in which the surface carries the imprints of human feet. When we wish to compute the probabilities of such states it would be incorrect to assume that all arrangements of grains of sand are equiprobable. While the sand is left alone, exposed only to the shuffling by the wind, its arrangements are slowly changed; but the wind exerts a discriminating influence, blowing away little mounds of sand and filling holes, with the effect that a smooth surface, or a surface showing wavelike patterns, is more probable than a state in which the sand shows distinct holes. This is the probability metric which observation teaches us to hold for the isolated sand system, when we understand by isolation the exclusion of all influences other than the agitation by the wind or the waves of the ocean.

In terms of this metric, the state given by the footprints is a highly ordered state, whereas a smooth surface is an unordered state; in fact, the latter is the state of equilibrium for the sand. We have here the case that a highly ordered state is preserved for some time; and we ask, how can we explain the presence of this ordered state?

This is the same type of question which was discussed above (§ 14) with respect to micro-processes. We observe a state which in the history of the isolated system is very improbable; how can we account for it? The answer is, as before, that we assume the observed state to be a product of interaction, that we prefer an interpretation in which the system was not isolated in the past.   .   .   .

For this reason, the footprints take over the function of a record. They allow us to infer that at some earlier time an interaction took place, that a person's steps caused the ordered state of the sand; because this state was not "shuffled away", it is a record of the interaction. Records are ordered macro-arrangements the order of which is preserved; they are frozen order so to speak.

.   .   .   .

.   .   .   We conclude that the occurrence of information requires past interaction, that is, that information can be supplied only by postinteraction states.

This can be concluded, at least, when information consists in a deviation of the frequency of occurrences from a chance distribution. In § 18 we studied natural records, such as footprints in the sand and fossils in the ground. They are all of this kind: chance would not produce those phenomena, which we interpret rightly as the product of past causes. It is not different with artificial records. When we write on paper, or record music on phonograph disks, or store information in the "memory" of an electronic computer, there result specific arrangements of elements, like ink marks on paper, grooves in wax disks, electric charges in little condenser elements, which are too highly ordered to be interpreted as a product of chance. For this very reason, they are records and supply information. All information is a record of the past. . . . .

To study a suitable example, let us investigate the logical mechanism of registering instruments. They are used to register observables which vary irregularly and cannot be predicted. For instance, a barograph registers measurements of atmospheric pressure, the values of which vary irregularly, on a rotating drum. The zigzag line drawn by the pen of the instrument on a sheet of paper contains the record of these irregular variations.

It would be impossible for us ever to predict the varying values of the atmospheric pressure, but it is easy to record them. We face here a striking difference between past and future, which was mentioned earlier, in § 2. For physical quantities of irregular variation, *prediction* is technically impossible, whereas *postdiction* is easily achieved by the use of registering instruments. . . . .

## QUESTIONS

1. What is Reichenbach's position on the differences between predicting and postdicting? What does it mean to say that we can have "records of the past, but not of the future"? Is this any more than a tautology, *i. e.*, that the evidence from which we postdict is, by definition, "records"? What is Reichenbach suggesting beyond this? How can we "know" the past on the basis of more isolated data than it takes to "know" the future? Consider his example of an act of murder: do we *know* from the bloody garment that there was a murder? Is he saying that the inference from the bloody garment to a murder in the past is a stronger inference than the inference from two people and a knife in a room to a murder in the future? Is Reichenbach's point about records that our knowledge of the past is not made more certain with the more we know of the present—that certain isolated items of knowledge are as valuable in postdicting as the sum of knowledge? Or only that there is a more strongly diminishing marginal utility of information when we are postdicting than when we are predicting?

2. What place does Reichenbach leave for *theory*? Are our postdictions achieved by simply applying unquestionable formulas to "records"? How do we know what "records" are relevant to our postdictions? How much of learning what happened in the past involves a "cutting and pasting" of records, and how much an active theorizing—a testing and revising of hypotheses? (In this regard, see the selection from Collingwood, *infra*, Chapter 15).

VOELKER v. COMBINED INS. CO. OF AMERICA

73 So.2d 403 (Fla.1954)

HOBSON, Justice.

.　.　.　.

Edward H. Voelker left West Palm Beach, Florida, at approximately 10:30 or 11:00 P. M., on the 13th day of February, 1952, for a trip to Dunedin, Florida. He was driving his own automobile when he departed from West Palm Beach and while on this trip he met his death at a point near Six Mile Bridge on State Road 80, in Palm Beach County. At about 1:20 A.M., on February 14, 1952, one C. S. Clements and his wife discovered the automobile driven by Voelker, which evidently had been involved in some type of accident, on the south side of the canal that borders State Road 80.

Since there were no eyewitnesses to the ostensible accident which either caused or immediately preceded Edward Voelker's death, the testimony is composed entirely of circumstantial evidence. According to the witnesses who observed the automobile as well as the scene of the tragedy, the physical facts indicated that Voelker's car, which was a 1941 black Pontiac, had proceeded to cross Six Mile Bridge, thereafter obviously had made a sharp curve to the left and had run down the bank before coming to rest on the edge of the canal and in the position heretofore outlined. The left front tire of the car contained about one half its normal air capacity. The front and rear fenders on the left side of the car were scraped and battered. The back fender which "looked like it had been sideswiped" was bent in slightly "with some of what looked like grey paint" on it. The door handle on the left front door was broken down, the lock was jammed, the left front headlight was broken and some glass which matched the glass of this headlight was found near the end of the bridge. The ignition switch was turned off, and the light switch, which was of the pull and push botton type, was also in the "off" position. The right front door of the automobile was open wide and the car was out of gear. About twenty feet from the end of the bridge the witness F. O. Cole found a headlight rim, with grey paint upon it, which had been run over and looked "like it came off a Model A Ford."

Mr. Clements, who, with his wife, discovered the wrecked car, reported the matter to the Highway Patrol. Patrolman Joseph P. Bertrand made an investigation and found Voelker's body floating in the canal about eight feet in front of the car. He caused the automobile to be towed into Belle Glade, Florida. Constable Whitlock also made an investigation at the scene of the accident and ordered the body released to the Berry Funeral Home, of Belle Glade and Pahokee, Florida. Voelker's body was immediately embalmed and later delivered to the Scobee-Vogel Funeral Home in West Palm Beach. No witness who examined or observed the body of Edward Voelker found or saw any marks or abrasions thereon, or, indeed, any other indications of external injury, and Voelker's eyeglasses were still in place.

These cases were tried before a jury which rendered verdicts in favor of the appellant. The appeal in each case is from the final judgment entered by the trial judge upon motion of counsel for appellee for a directed verdict after entry of the original final judgment rendered pursuant to the jury's verdict.

Each of the policies issued by the Combined Insurance Company of America insured Voelker "against loss caused by bodily injuries which are not caused or contributed to by disease, and are effected exclusively by accidental means". Section B of each policy provides: "If Such Injuries shall be sustained by the Insured, and shall within thirty days from the date of the accident causing Such Injuries be the *sole* cause of loss of life by the Insured, and provided Such Injuries to the Insured shall occur:  .  .  .  While actually driving or riding in any automobile,  .  .  .  the Company will pay the sum of $500.00. [sic]"  (Italics supplied.)

.  .  .  .  .

The fact that circumstantial evidence is relied upon in a civil action at law does not alter either the rule that it is solely within the province of the jury to evaluate or weigh the evidence or that the burden of establishing a right of recovery by a preponderance of the evidence is upon the plaintiff. Consequently, in such a case if the circumstances established by the evidence be susceptible of a reasonable inference or inferences which would authorize recovery and are also capable of an equally reasonable inference, or inferences, contra, a jury question is presented. We cannot overemphasize our use of the adjective "reasonable" as modifying the noun "inference". Of course if none of the inferences on the one hand accords with logic and reason or human experience, while on the other hand an inference which does square with logic and reason or human experience is deducible from the evidence, the question is not for the jury but is one of law for the court.

There are several reasonable inferences which we feel might have been drawn by the jury from the circumstantial evidence in this case. Edward Voelker might have suffered a heart attack [which we believe might properly be classified as an internal bodily injury] following the accident and might conceivably have died from such attack while standing on the edge of the canal and his dead body have fallen into the water. He could have received internal bodily injuries, such as a brain concussion, spinal cord injury or, indeed, even a broken neck, and after leaving his automobile could have walked around the front thereof to appraise the situation, and while standing at the bank of the canal might have dropped dead into the water. Such inferences pre-suppose that Voelker received bodily injuries "while actually driving or riding" in the car and they might permit the conclusion that his death was attributable solely to such bodily injuries. There is, however, another equally reasonable contrary inference that he received no bodily injuries either external or internal, alighted from his car, walked around to the front thereof to perform the very normal act of evaluating the predicament in which he found himself and without realizing his proximity to the waters of the canal may accidentally have stepped, or tripped and fallen, therein and have drowned as a consequence thereof.  Assuming that the latter inference explains the manner in which he met his death, the appellant could not have prevailed in this suit because such inference excludes the essential premise that Edward Voelker received bodily injuries which caused his death "while actually driving or riding" in his automobile.  Again the evidence was susceptible of another contrary inference, that Voelker was addled or semiconscious as a result of internal bodily injuries and while in such condition might have slipped or tripped and fallen into the canal and drowned. This inference does not exclude the theory that the decedent received bodily injuries "while actually driving or riding" in his automobile, but does negative the thought that bodily injuries were the "sole" cause of loss of his life.

It is obvious that from the fact the car showed it had been damaged, as hereinbefore outlined, the jury inferred that Voelker had met with an accident "while actually driving or riding" in his automobile.  It is also patent that the jury predicated upon such inference the further inference that he received bodily injuries in such accident.  Will this court under any circumstances sanction such action, which appears to violate the general rule that inference may not be founded upon inference any more readily than presumption may be predicated upon presumption?  In search of the proper answer to this query we have pursued the thought that perhaps there is or should be an exception to the rule which prohibits the pyramiding of inferences.

It is our considered judgment that when an inference, such as the inference that Voelker experienced an accident while driving his automobile across Six Mile Bridge, is inescapable, that is to say when no contrary *reasonable* inference may be indulged, such inference is elevated for the purpose of further inference to the dignity of an established fact.  We are also convinced that this principle creates an exception to which the often-stated rule against laying inference upon inference must yield, or perhaps it would be more accurate to say that the rule itself should never be applied without reference to its purpose, which is nothing more nor less than to protect litigants from verdicts or judgments based upon speculation.  We do not believe that the "inference upon inference" rule, whose common acceptance has been justly and appropriately criticized by Professor Wigmore  .  .  .   should be construed to mean that under no conceivable circumstances may one inference be deduced from another.  We think, however, that such method of establishing an ultimate fact should not ordinarily be indulged unless the first inference meets a test which may be analogized to the criminal rule concerning circumstantial evidence, i. e., in the ordinary case, only if the prior or basic inference is established to the exclusion of any other reasonable theory should another be drawn from it.  .  .  .

Although it has not always been admitted by the courts, it can no longer be doubted that cases may and do exist wherein circumstantial evidence is as convincing of an asseverated fact as is testimonial evidence.  This we believe to be such a case, and we hold that the jury would have been entirely justified to have inferred, from its prior inescapable inference that Voelker met with an accident, that he received bodily injuries "while actually driving or riding" in his automobile. The latter inference however, is not the last which must be drawn before appellant may be said to have proven her right to recover under the policies of insurance here involved.

Appellant is not entitled to a favorable decision unless the inference that Voelker received bodily injuries "while actually driving or riding" in his automobile is the *only* reasonable inference which may be drawn from the prior inference that Voelker met with an accident. In other words, this second inference must meet the test of the criminal rule, as did the first inference, if it is to be a proper predicate for the further inference that "bodily injuries" were the *sole* cause of loss of Voelker's life. Is this second inference one which may be said to exclude all other reasonable theories? We think not.

In view of the fact that no bruises or abrasions were found upon Voelker's body, it is equally reasonable to assume that he received no bodily injuries and that he, as aforementioned, walked around to the edge of the canal to appraise this situation, slipped or tripped into the waters of the canal and drowned, or that he and the person driving the other car involved in the accident had an altercation and that such person pushed or shoved Voelker, intentionally or unintentionally, into the canal, and fled the scene, whereupon Voelker met his death by drowning.

The theory that Voelker met his death by drowning cannot be excluded, for there is no evidence upon the question whether water was found in his lungs and none which even suggests that credence should be given to the supposition that the body of a person who meets death by drowning will not float until sufficient time has elapsed for decomposition to set in. If indeed this supposition be more than folklore, it is not an open and notorious fact of which this Court can take judicial notice. There may be other reasonable inferences, which we do not at the moment envisage, that may be drawn from the inescapable inference that Voelker had an accident with another motor vehicle. However, if there were but one reasonable inference other than that Voelker received bodily injuries in the accident the jury would not have been justified in inferring that Voelker's internal bodily injuries were the *sole* cause of his death.

Affirmed.

QUESTIONS

1. How different is the task the court faces in Voelker—discovering "a fact" about the past—from the task of predicting a "fact" about the future? What, if anything, gives our "postdictions" more certainty than our "predictions"? How do the mental operations involved in the one process compare with the other?

2. Is there any knowledge that is based upon *an* inference, rather than an inference upon an inference? Can it be maintained that all knowledge—even knowledge of the present—is based upon inferences upon inferences? Consider the statement, "what I am now

looking at is a table." Can you break down this statement into a series of inferences: "I am receiving certain impressions through my eyes"; "I infer from past experience that my eyes are reliable in regard to such images"; "I infer from the shapes, colors, etc., that there is an object in front of me of such and such design and shape"; "from past experience I infer that the function of such an object is for people to sit in"; "from the way people have responded in the past, I infer that calling that object a 'chair' would most adequately convey to others what I was seeing", etc. Similarly, is a prediction to the effect that "it will rain tomorrow" *a* prediction any more than it is a prediction as to, say, cloud formation, upon a prediction, as to, say, temperature?

3. How successful can we be in distinguishing past, present and future "facts" by reference to the *number of inferences* that must be pyramided one upon the other? Does it make sense for the court to speak of the number of inferences the jury went through in Voelker? Why does the court suppose that the jury's decision involved an inference (from an accident) to an inference (he received bodily injuries in the accident) to an inference (that the bodily injuries were the sole cause of death)? Is the court supposing that this is the way in which the jury *did* think or the way in which it *ought* to have thought? Could not the first inference—that Voelker had been in an accident—be itself reduced to a series of inferences? Conversely, is it impossible that the jury simply inferred from "the whole fact situation" that "Voelker was killed in the car and tumbled (or was thrown) into the water"?

4. What problems is the court getting into by stating a rule that limits pyramiding if there be "but one reasonable inference other than" an intermediate inference?

Suppose we assume that the jury did think in terms of the categories (a) Voelker was in an accident; (b) he sustained injuries in the accident; (c) the injuries were the sole cause of his death. If the jurors could "reasonably" calculate that the odds favoring the first were 9.9 in 10 (*i. e.*, supposing 9.9 in 10 to constitute "an inescapable inference")); of the second, 9 in 10 (*i. e.*, supposing the remaining 1 in 10 to constitute "at least one other reasonable inference"); and of the third 9 in 10, what would the total odds be in such a situation? Are they not even as high as the odds on which a man can be convicted of crime? Yet, would the chain of reasoning be allowable under the court's analysis? Why should a civil verdict be unobtainable on such odds?

Suppose that the jurors had made a special finding that they had judged "from all the evidence" that the odds of Voelker's having-been-in-an-accident-thereby-receiving-injuries-from-which-he-died were 7 in 10. Would that not represent their judgment as to what "the preponderance of the evidence" dictated? Would the court have allowed such a finding? If not, why?

5. Is not part of the problem the court faces that a rule inhibiting the pyramiding of inferences is fruitless unless there are associated rules detailing the categories in which "facts" may legitimately be described?

6. What is the court really concerned about in the *Voelker* case? What is it trying to do in terms of organizing and limiting the jury's function? What is the problem the court is seeking to prevent when it speaks in terms of limiting the jury's making an inference on an inference? Does the court's rule succeed in preventing verdicts "based upon speculation"? Does its rule necessarily distinguish between the more and the less "speculative" judgment? How does the rule it states,—like the rule of the A.L.I. on trade disparagement, above— rest upon an oversimplified view of epistemology—here, of how the mind goes about "knowing" the past? Can you restate a rule that achieves what the court may be wanting to achieve, without grounding itself in what may be mistaken assumptions?

*Clarence Morris*

## Duty, Negligence and Causation *

### III. Is The Defendant Liable for Unforeseeable Consequences?

. . . .

Once misconduct causes damage the specific accident has happened in a particular way and has resulted in a discrete harm. When, after the event, the question is asked—"were the particular accident and the resulting damages foreseeable?"—the cases fall into three classes:

(1) In some cases damages resulting from misconduct are so typical that it is impossible to convince judges and jurors that they were unforeseeable. If Mr. Builder negligently drops a brick on Mr. Pedestrian, who is passing the urban site of a house under construction, even though the dent in Pedestrian's skull is microscopically unique in pattern, Builder could not sensibly maintain that the bashed-in skull was an unforeseeable consequence.

(2) In some cases the freakishness of the facts refuses to be downed, and any description that minimizes it is viewed as misdescription. For example, in a recent Louisiana case the defendant-trucker negligently left his truck on the highway at night without setting out flares. A car crashed into the truck and caught fire. The plaintiff came to the rescue of the car occupants—a man and wife. After the rescuer got them out of the car he returned to the car to get a floor mat to pillow the injured wife's head. A pistol lay on the mat rescuer wanted to use. He picked it up and handed it to the husband. The accident had, unbeknownst to the rescuer, temporarily deranged the husband, and he shot rescuer in the leg. Such a consequence of negligently failing to guard a truck with flares is so unarguably unforeseeable that no judge or juror would be likely to hold otherwise. (Incidentally, the Louisiana court held the trucker liable to the rescuer on the ground that foreseeability is not a requisite of liability.)

* From 101 U.Pa.L.Rev. 189, 196–98 (1952). With permission of the University of Pennsylvania.

(3) Between these extremes are cases in which the consequences are neither typical nor wildly freakish. In these cases unusual details are arguably—but only arguably—significant. If they are held to be significant, then the consequences are unforeseeable; if they are held to be insignificant then the consequences are foreseeable. For example, in a Texas case two men were sent out on a service truck to tow a stalled car. One of them, the plaintiff, made the tow rope fast and tried to step from between the vehicles as the truck started. His artificial leg slipped into a mud hole in the road, which would not have been there had the defendant-railroad not disregarded its statutory duty to maintain this portion of the highway. He was unable to extricate his peg-leg, and was in danger of being run over by the stalled car. He grabbed the tail gate of the service truck to use its forward force to pull him out of the mud. A loop in the tow rope lassoed his good leg, tightened, and broke it. As long as these details are considered significant facts of the case the accident is unforeseeable. No doubt some judges would stress them and so hold. As a matter of fact the Texas courts have on occasion ruled that much less freakish injuries were unforeseeable. But in the peg-leg case the court quoted with approval the plaintiff's lawyer's "description" of the "facts" which was couched in these words: "The case stated in the briefest form, is simply this: Appellee was on the highway, using it in a lawful manner, and slipped into this hole, created by appellant's negligence, and was injured in undertaking to extricate himself." The court also adopted the injured man's answer to the railroad's attempt to stress unusual details:

> "Appellant contends: it could not reasonably have been foreseen that slipping into this hole would have caused the appellee to have become entangled in a rope, and the moving truck, with such dire results. The answer is plain: The exact consequences do not have to be foreseen."

In this third class of cases foreseeability can be determined only after the significant facts have been described. If the official description of facts adopted by the court is detailed, the accident is called unforeseeable; if it is general, the accident is called foreseeable. Since there is no authoritative guide to the proper way to describe facts, the process of holding a loss is—or is not—foreseeable is most fluid, beggaring attempts at accurate prediction.

This third class of cases includes most but not quite all, of the arguable cases on the scope of liability. . . . In these cases advocates and judges can and do state logical and acceptable analyses of either foreseeability or unforeseeability.

QUESTIONS

1. How are the problems a court faces in determining foreseeability like the problems of what Reichenbach might call "postseeability"? How are the problems different? What does Professor Morris see as the significance, in the peg-leg case, of the court having adopted the plaintiff's description of "the facts"? How else might "the facts" have been described, and with what effect on the apparent

probability of the accident? What does this say for the feasibility of casting legal rules in terms of probabilities without also having tandem rules delimiting proper categories of description? What are the consequences for a mechanical jurisprudence, if courts' decisions are so fundamentally dependent upon the characterization of the facts?

2. Professor Morris states that in his second class of cases, "the freakishness of the facts refuses to be downed, and any description that minimizes it is viewed as misdescription". Can you describe the Louisiana case so that it would not sound "freakish" to the person to whom you were describing it? How does one judge what is a description and what a misdescription? In what sense, in any of the three classes of cases, is it true that "advocates and judges can and do state logical and acceptable analyses of either foreseeability or unforeseeability"? How is "logical" being used here? With what effect is "logical" being used?

## ERIC D'ARCY

### ACT, CONSEQUENCES, AND CIRCUMSTANCES *

"In some circumstances", says Bentham, "even to kill a man may be a beneficial act; in others, to set food before him may be a pernicious one." The point is well taken. Asked whether one believes that it is wrong to do $X$, one often has to say that it depends on the circumstances; in some circumstances it would be wrong, in others it may be permissible, or even commendable; circumstances alter cases. But there is a prior point. Circumstances may affect not only one's final moral evaluation of an act, but also one's characterization of it; in some circumstances $X$ is $P$, in others it is $Q$. In performing "the very same act", one is tempted to say, a person may, in different circumstances, be doing different things: in signing his name, for example, he may be drawing a checque, entering a contract, or giving his autograph to an admirer. Indeed, he may even be doing opposite things: issuing a death-warrant, or granting a reprieve.

In examining an act with a view to its moral evaluation, then, we must study the role of Circumstances, and the way that 'act' and 'circumstances' are mutually related in the composition of a good or bad deed. Bentham does so in terms of their consequences; but he does not tell us what he means by 'act', nor how it is to be distinguished from 'consequences'. I shall begin, therefore, by investigating that distinction.

### § I. ACT AND CONSEQUENCES

The question with which our inquiry begins is this: In analysing the elements which constitute a given human performance, how are we to decide which of them belong to the act and which of them belong to the consequences of the act? We may illustrate the point at issue with two examples. First, $A$ tells a lie and $B$ is deceived; $A$ is thus

* From Human Acts 1–6, 8–12, 14–20, 38     With permission of Oxford University
(Oxford at the Clarendon Press 1963).     Press.

able to rob *B*.  Where are we to draw the line between 'act' and 'consequences'?  Are we to say that *A*'s *act* is simply "deceiving *B*", with the *consequence* of being in a position to rob him?  Or is *A*'s act "telling a lie", with the two consequences (1) *B* is deceived, and (2) *A* is thus in a position to rob him?  Second, Macbeth killed Duncan, and as a consequence of that act became King.  But could one not also say that Macbeth stabbed Duncan, and as a consequence of this act the King died?  Was his *act* "stabbing", which produced the *consequence* of the King's death; the further consequence of Macbeth's becoming King following from the circumstances of Duncan's being King and Macbeth's standing in (some sort of) line to the throne?  Or was his act "killing the King", with the consequence of succeeding to the throne?  The examples indicate one possible answer to our question.  Perhaps the line to be drawn between 'act' and 'consequences' is not a fixed line: perhaps it is possible to make several different but equally correct statements as to what is the act and what the consequences.  Let us first consider two other answers that stand at opposite extremes.

## (i) *Two extremes*

During the racial troubles in Arkansas in 1956, Professor J. J. C. Smart read a paper in defence of Extreme Utilitarianism.  In the discussion which followed, he considered a hypothetical case in which white people believed that some crime had been committed by a negro.  Since the criminal's identity was not established they proposed to lynch five negroes chosen at random.  The local sheriff knew this, and after investigation felt that the only alternative was to arrest some negro, "frame" a case against him, "pack" the jury, and have him found guilty, sentenced to death, and shot.  From premises of Extreme Utilitarianism Smart argued that, if this were indeed the only alternative to the lynching of the five, he would be a wicked man if he did not carry out the plan; and that the correct description of what he did would be, not "judicial murder", but "saving four lives."  There are, of course, two separate problems here: one, Was the sheriff justified, or even obliged, so to act? the other, What would be the correct characterization of such an act?  It is only with the latter that we are concerned.

Now suppose that the sheriff himself acted as executioner; consider the following possible descriptions of his last act in the drama:

1.  He tensed his forefinger.
2.  He pressed a piece of metal.
3.  He released a spring.
4.  He pulled the trigger of a gun.
5.  He fired a gun.
6.  He fired a bullet.
7.  He shot a bullet at a man.
8.  He shot a bullet towards a man.
9.  He shot a man.
10. He killed a man.

11. He committed judicial murder.

12. He saved four lives.

One possibility would be to say that the sheriff's act was to tense his finger, with the consequence that he pressed a piece of metal; another, that his act was to press a piece of metal, with the consequence that he released a spring; another, that his act was to kill a man, with the consequence that he saved five others; or simply, that his act was to save four lives. At one extreme, then, is Smart's suggestion that the last is the correct characterization.

At the opposite extreme is the theory of the nineteenth-century jurist Austin, which has passed into a good deal of modern legal theory, and with some modification into more purely philosophic writing: for instance, in Prichard. . . .

. . . [F]or Austin, the line between 'act' and 'consequences' is to be drawn at the point where muscular control ends. The term 'act' applies only to voluntary movements of the limbs, organs, or muscles; the term 'circumstances' to any relevant facts prior to or concomitant with the act; and the term 'consequences' to the events subsequent to, and caused by, that act in those circumstances. For Austin, then, the sheriff's *act* would be tensing his forefinger; the *circumstances* of the act, that his finger was on the trigger of a cocked and loaded gun which was pointing at a man whom he had framed; the *consequences* of his act, the movement of the trigger, the release of the hammer, the explosion of the cartridge, the expulsion of the bullet, its flight towards the victim, its entry into his body, his wound and death; plus, of course, whatever followed from that. In the litany, suggested above, of twelve possible answers to the question, "What was his act?", Austin would say that only the first is correct. Notice that it is not the fourth, "He pulled the trigger", but "the muscular motions by which" he pulled the trigger; hence, "He tensed his forefinger".

The argument that leads to this conclusion seems to take four steps. First, only a voluntary act is an act; second, only that which is immediately produced by the will is voluntary; third, only the movements of certain muscles, organs, and limbs can be immediately produced by the will; therefore, fourth, only those movements can be acts. Each of these steps presents difficulties. For instance, the first suggests that the phrase "voluntary act" is pleonastic, and the phrase "involuntary act" self-contradictory. But this is to deal rather high-handedly with English usage. If the act X is ascribed to A, it makes perfectly good sense to accept the ascription as correct, but the act was voluntary; whereas if murder is ascribed to him, it does not make sense to accept the ascription as correct and to inquire whether or not his victim died. If A is accused of having done X, and one pleads on his behalf that X was "not a voluntary act", it is the adjective that one is stressing, not the noun: one is saying that, though admittedly A did in some sense do X, he did not do it in the relevant sense, viz. "voluntarily".

.  .  .  .  .

Austin's theory carries the further implication that only a physiologist could tell us the name of our acts. When I speak, for instance, my *act*, what I *do*, is not "to speak", but to tighten certain muscles in and around and behind my mouth; the sounds produced as simply *consequences* of my act. I could not name or identify the muscles involved, and am not aware of the existence of most of them; yet on this theory it is my desire for their movement which causes them to move. . . . To find out what "I really do" I should have to consult a trained physiologist. Only he could tell me, too, with a precision and a certainty that the most skilful psychoanalyst might well envy, what I "really desire"—when I speak, or open a door, or press the self-starter button of my car: for he alone knows the muscular contractions which on Austin's theory are caused by my desire for them, and constitute my act.

. . . . .

## (ii) *Three theses*

As answers to our question, then, Smart's suggestion and Austin's theory stand at opposite extremes. In suggesting that the truth lies somewhere between them, I shall put forward three theses. The first is of rather general application; the second and third apply specifically to the problem of distinguishing between 'act' and 'consequence'.

*Thesis One: There is not necessarily one, and only one, correct description of a given act.* This tells against the implication of a theory such as Austin's, that it is only a trained physiologist who can give the correct description of an act; and it helps to reassure us about the connotation and denotation of the term 'act' in ordinary language. Three points may be made.

1.   The description of an act appropriate to a given occasion may vary with the specialized interest of the inquirer or narrator. In the list, given above, of twelve contemplated alternative descriptions of a given episode, there is none that can be rejected as simply false, but the first eight would in most contexts, and certainly in contexts where a moral evaluation or legal trial of the act was being made, be misleading in various degrees. Justice would not be done if, in a subsequent trial, the sheriff were exonerated because "All he did was to release a spring".

But there are contexts in which the first of those twelve descriptions ("He tensed his forefinger"), or the third ("He released a spring"), could be the most appropriate answer to the question "What did he do?" because of the special sort of answer required by the questioner, the particular aspect of the incident in which he was interested. For instance, a person who is being introduced to firearms for the first time, and learning to shoot, may have got as far as loading and cocking the gun, holding and aiming it, and crooking his right forefinger on the trigger. Later he happens to be watching a newsreel film of the execution, and sees the sheriff carry out the movements which he himself has learnt; then there is a report, and the negro falls; and he asks, "What did the sheriff do after he got his hands and fingers right?" The answer, "he tensed, or suddenly squeezed, his forefinger", would then be perfectly in place. Again, a student of elementary ballistics may know that the bullet is driven out of the barrel by the gases which are suddenly released when the cartridge explodes, and that the cartridge is exploded by the sudden impact of the hammer upon it; but why did the hammer make such an impact when the sheriff pulled the trigger? The answer will begin with an explanation of the way that trigger and hammer are connected by a spring-mechanism, and conclude with some such words as, "So you see, when he pulled the trigger he released the spring."

. . . .

2. A different factor is the presence of specialized efforts, interests, or intentions of the agent. . . . Hampshire has remarked that, although at a given moment there may be a set of possible true answers to the question "What are you doing now?", there is generally one that seems to the agent peculiarly appropriate to his present intentions. We might think of a test-pilot who could truthfully answer, "Holding the joy-stick"; "Looking through the windscreen"; "Listening to the control-tower"; "Smoking a cigarette"; or, "Flying over the North Sea". But the answer that seemed most appropriate to him might be, "Testing the new Vickers jet." Probably it was in these last terms that he would look forward to "what he would be doing" on this day, or apologize for being unable to accept some other commitment; and if he were later trying to "date" some other event, he might say, "It must have been Tuesday, because I remember it was the day before I was to test the new Vickers jet."

. . . .

3. A third point draws attention to the fact that makes the other two possible. One's description of a person's act may vary according to the special interest of the inquirer or the specialized intention of the agent because, as Hampshire says, at any moment of a man's waking life there is always a set of possible true answers to the question, "What is he doing now?" . . .

Thesis Two: The term which denotes the act, in the description of a given incident, may often be elided into the term which denotes a consequence of the act: "doing X with the consequence Y", may often be redescribed simply as "doing Y". For instance, if A stabbed B, and thus killed him, we may say simply that A killed B. The act of flicking a switch may produce the consequences that (1) contact is made between two points, so that (2) current flows from outside the room, through these points and the wire in the room, into the globe and through its filament, and thus (3) the globe is illuminated; but this may also be described simply as, "putting on the light", or "lighting the lamp". If a person sings a song and thus entertains a group of people, we may say either that he is singing a song, or entertaining them; and if as a result of the latter he raises money for the Red Cross, we may say that he is raising money for the Red Cross; and if as a result of that he boosts morale, or helps the war efforts, we may also say that he is boosting morale, or helping the war effort. We may therefore often elide one possible description, the term X, into another term Y, where (1) Y is the result or consequence of the agent A's doing X; (2) A is nevertheless said to be doing Y, e. g. entertaining people; (3) the elision is so complete that Y gives no hint of the specific nature of X.

.   .   .   .

.   .   .   .   Since the sheriff encompassed the one man's death in order to save the lives of four others, Smart suggested that it would be quite proper to re-describe his act as "saving four lives". Just as the description, "singing a song", may be elided into the description, "entertaining people", and the latter description shows no trace of the former, because the latter was a consequence of the former: so the description of the sheriff's act, "committing judicial murder", would be elided without trace into the description, "saving four lives", since that was the consequence of the murder.

In discussions of the moral evaluation of an act, the importance of such re-descriptions is considerable. An apologist for killing people who are suffering from incurable diseases may say that such an act is "really just putting an end to the unfortunate people's suffering"; Dr. Verwoerd said that he would "really describe *apartheid* as good neighbourliness". St. Paul said that one must not lie, even in order to promote the glory of God; but if an act may always be re-described in terms of its consequences, then the act of the person who told lies so high-mindedly could be re-described simply as "promoting the glory of God". Such suggestions have macabre possibilities. Imperious Caesar, dead and turned to clay, might stop a hole to keep the wind away; but if our formula holds for all values of *a*, killing him with that end in view might be re-described simply as "blocking a draught".

Hence the importance of the contention that there are [elisions that it is not proper to make]. Our third thesis takes up that contention.

*Thesis Three: Certain kinds of act are of such significance that the terms which denote them may not, special contexts apart, be elided into terms which (a) denote their consequences, and (b) conceal, or even fail to reveal, the nature of the act itself.* Typical examples are the acts of killing, maiming, slandering, torturing, deceiving, or seriously offending another person; betraying or deserting a friend or an ally; breaking a contract or a promise or a confidence; stealing or destroying or spoiling something which the owner, or the community, looks on as precious; sacrificing or endangering one's own life, happiness, good name, health, or property. For instance, "Macbeth stabbed Duncan and, as a consequence, killed him", may be re-described simply as, "Macbeth killed Duncan"; but, "Macbeth killed Duncan and, as a consequence, succeeded him," may not be re-described simply as, "Macbeth succeeded Duncan". To quote a more recent example, it was alleged during the Eichmann trial that a Nazi research institute asked a concentration-camp commandant to supply it with a number of infant bodies for use in some experiments, and that in order to comply with this request the commandant had the required number of babies of Jewish women prisoners gassed. Now to describe his act as "assisting medical research", or "promoting the advancement of science", simply would not do, even though research may have been assisted or scientific knowledge advanced as a result of his act. Taking human life, we feel, is an act of such significance that one cannot elide its description into a term which denotes its consequence, or an end to which it was a means, unless that term makes clear that this was the means used.  Had the commandant gassed the children in order to comply with Hitler's decree that the Jewish people were to be destroyed, it might not be altogether inaccurate to subsume his act under some such description as "genocide"; though perhaps the relation of particular murders to a policy of genocide is not that of act to consequence, or of means to end, but of part to whole.

This thesis, then, is supplementary to the theses that several alternative descriptions of a given act are possible, and that one may often, in analysing a given incident, draw the line between 'act' and 'consequences' now at one point, now at another.  It holds that in certain cases there is one point at least in which an 'act'/'consequences' line *must* be drawn.  The previous thesis is exemplified by the fact that "*A* told *B* an untruth with the consequence that B was deceived" may be re-described as simply, "A deceived B"; the present thesis is exemplified by the fact that "*A* deceived *B* with the consequence that he won his vote" may not be re-described simply as "*A* won *B*'s vote".  In the terms of the twelve contemplated descriptions of the sheriff's act, Number 1 ("He tensed his finger") usually *should* be elided into one of the latter descriptions, e. g. Number 9 ("He shot a man"); similarly, Number 9 may be elided into Number 10 ("He killed a man").  But Number 10 may not be elided into Number 12 ("He saved four lives"); an 'act'/'consequences' line must be drawn between Numbers 10 and 12.  Tensing one's finger is simply part of the act of shooting, or shooting a man; but killing a man is not simply part of the act of saving four lives.  It might be objected that each is a means to an end: tensing the forefinger a means, firing the gun the end; killing one man a means, saving four others the end.  But for one thing, this overlooks the fact that a means is often an act, and that an act is often a means.  Furthermore, even if killing a man is intended by the agent, and characterized by an observer, simply as a means to an end, it is a means whose nature must be clearly revealed in any normal account of what was done.

. . . .

To put forward this thesis is not necessarily to imply, with Aquinas and Kant, that there are certain kinds of acts which are always morally wrong, never permissible in any circumstances.  It is not to lay down some rigid rule for the moral evaluation of a given kind of act, but to say something about its characterization in moral discourse.  The point is not that these acts are so wicked that sound moral judgment must always condemn them, but that they are so significant for human existence and welfare and happiness that they must always be taken into account before sound moral judgment can be passed on them; and if they are to be taken into account, their presence must first be revealed. . . .

## SECTION THREE:  WHAT MAKES A PROPOSITION TRUE?

### INTRODUCTORY NOTE

So far, we have been examining various classes of statements, inquiring into the differences, such as they may be, between statements of fact, inferences, opinions, etc.  But what, it remains to be investigated, about the truth of any of them?  Putting aside for a moment whether the proposition "the driver motioned us to cross the street" ought to be classified for any given purpose as an opinion, an inference, or a statement of fact—was it *true*?  If so, on what basis?

That question immediately involves us in a number of others.  One might ask, for example, "what is *'truth'*?" but that is not the same as asking whether any particular statement is true.  Indeed, the question "what is 'truth'?" may be so difficult to answer, and have lingered unsatisfactorily resolved for so many centuries, for the very reason that it is not at all clear what those who ask it are asking, *i. e.*, what an answer satisfactory to them would look like.  If we ask, on the other hand, what do we mean, is it "true" that "the driver motioned us to cross the street?," one may start his investigation with a considerably better sense of direction.  Further, it is about the truth of specific propositions—not some abstract property, "truth"—that people—and courts—are interested.

But even when we come a step closer to earth by investigating not "truth", but what it is that makes specific propositions true, some distinctions between classes of propositions remain to complicate the inquiry.  Propositions can be so grouped as to suggest (though perhaps wrongly) that the analysis of their truth will take us along different paths.

One such fundamental distinction is that suggested by Hume and elaborated by Kant—a proposed dichotomy between analytic statements (what Hume called Relations of Ideas) and synthetic statements (what Hume called Matters of Fact).  An example of the former would be the statement that $2 + 2 = 4$, or that all bachelors are unmarried males.  These statements would be true (Hume and Kant felt) independently of any experience in the world: even in a world of less than four objects (if we could imagine such) four would be equal to the sum of two plus two; and even if all males of all ages were married, we could still, by examining the very concept of bachelor, come up with the truth that a bachelor was an unmarried male.  Synthetic statements, on the other hand, were said to depend for their truth upon what actually happens in the world.  For example, to know whether the statement "it is raining" is true, one has to investigate "facts" about the world to see whether it *is* raining.  There will be, indeed, threshold definitional problems (*Where* is it supposedly raining?  *How much* moisture in what period of time constitutes "rain"?) but no amount of refining and analyzing concepts will ultimately tell us whether the statement is true or false, without consulting experience.  (This hard-and-fast division between the analytic and synthetic is criticized by Brand Blanshard and W. V. O. Quine in this Section.)

Another traditional, basic distinction, stressed by logical positivism and related philosophies, is that between *meaningful* statements and *meaningless* statements, the latter being statements that are not capable of truth *or* falsity. For example, "the present population of New York City is 175 people," may be wrong, but it is at least meaningful because it can be disconfirmed by sensible experience; but, *e. g.*, "Johnny glass four salads" or "God is the first principle of all beneficence" are statements which no possible experience could contribute to disconfirm.

Even among statements that do not seem definitional or meaningless other differences in truth characteristics may be significant. Consider the propositions that "the defendant is guilty", "the writing exchanged between A and B was a contract", "the bus driver was not negligent". The significance of these statements is so interwoven with the web of ceremonies and consequences which the legal system attaches to them, and what they mean so varies with who is saying them (the lawyer in his summation, exhorting it; the judge in his decision, declaring it) that to speak of their truth or falsity may be misleading, and the problems they present will be dealt with more fully later.

What we wish to focus on here are propositions of the more ordinary, apparently synthetic variety. But what is ordinary? Consider the differences that are suggested by "the driver motioned the plaintiff to cross the street"; "the driver rotated his hand clockwise in the direction of the east curb"; "Plaintiff thought the driver motioned him to cross the street." Even if we decide each of them are capable of being true or false, why need all of them be "true" in the same sense of "true"? Are our beliefs as to the truth of each of them arrived at by fundamentally the same cognitive processes? Is the evidence to which one appeals in support of them fundamentally the same? Do they play fundamentally the same role in the usages to which they may appropriately be put? (Apparently not in Missouri, under *Smith v. Bocklitz, supra,* Chapter 4.)

Why do we believe some propositions to be true, and others false? What different sorts of tests determine whether a certain proposition is true? Take the proposition, "my client was not at 5th and Main at 10:45 P.M." If the proposition is true, is it true because it *corresponds* with the facts? But what are the facts—and how does a statement "correspond" with them? (Not, certainly, in the way in which skin from under the deceased's fingernails corresponds with skin from the defendant). Or is it true because the belief that the door is closed is *coherent* with other statements one believes—that the client is honest; that he says he was at 5th and Main at that time; that there is a photograph taken at 5th and Main at that time, which shows a man who looks like the client? Or is it true because the supposition that it is true *works*, that is, that a better state of affairs will come about if it is acted on *as though* it were true than if it were acted on as though it were false?

IN RE COLGATE-PALMOLIVE COMPANY

59 F.T.C. 1452 (1961)

## OPINION OF THE COMMISSION

By Commissioner ELMAN:

This is an appeal from the hearing examiner's initial decision dismissing a complaint charging respondents Colgate-Palmolive Company and Ted Bates & Company, Inc., with having violated Section 5 of the Federal Trade Commission Act by using false, misleading, and deceptive television commercials in advertising Colgate-Palmolive's shaving cream, "Rapid Shave."

We hold that the initial decision was erroneous; that the allegations of fact in the complaint have been fully substantiated; that respondents, by using these commercials, engaged in unfair and deceptive acts and practices, and unfair methods of competition, in interstate commerce, in violation of Section 5; and that, to protect the public against the recurrence of such unlawful conduct, an appropriate cease and desist order should be entered against both respondents.

### I.

Respondent Colgate-Palmolive Company makes and sells a shaving cream called "Rapid Shave."  Respondent Ted Bates & Company, Inc., is an advertising agency which prepared and placed for publication the three 60-second television commercials advertising "Rapid Shave" which are involved in this proceeding.  These commercials were presented on programs sponsored by Colgate-Palmolive that were broadcast on a national network in the latter part of 1959.  .  .  .

The first of these (Commission Exhibit 2, entitled "Sandpaper Mask—Gifford") opens by showing a football being place-kicked, with the ball zooming toward the viewer.  The picture then "cuts" to a football player whose face is hidden behind a mask that appears to be made of coarse, gritty sandpaper.  The voice of an unseen announcer asks: "Who is the man behind the sandpaper mask?"  The football player strips off the sandpaper mask, revealing a heavy growth of whiskers.  As the player rubs his cheek ruefully, the announcer says: "It's triple-threat man, Frank Gifford—backfield sensation of the New York Giants  .  .  .  a man with a problem just like yours  .  .  .  a beard as tough as sandpaper  .  .  .  a beard that needs  .  .  .  PALMOLIVE RAPID SHAVE  .  .  . super-moisturized for the fastest, smoothest shaves possible."

As the announcer says "a beard as tough as sandpaper," the picture shifts to the sandpaper mask, and a hand brings a can of "Rapid Shave" into view in front of the sandpaper, with the words "Super-Moisturized" and "Fastest Smoothest Shaves" appearing on the film under the shaving cream.  The announcer's voice continues: "To prove RAPID SHAVE'S super-moisturizing power, we put it right from the can  .  .  ."  As this is being said, we see one hand pressing the top of the "Rapid Shave" can so as to dispense a small amount of lather into the other hand.  The lather is then spread in one continuous motion upon the surface of the sandpaper, and the first hand reappears with a razor and shaves a clean path through the lather and the gritty surface of the sandpaper. While this is taking place, the voice of the announcer continues ". . . onto this tough, dry sandpaper. It was apply . . . soak . . . and off in a stroke." These words are spoken at a normal conversational pace, and there is no "fade," "dissolve," or other pictorial indication of any lapse of time between "apply," "soak," and "off in a stroke"; the intervals preceding and following the word "soak" last no more than a second.

The picture then shifts to Frank Gifford lathering his face as the announcer continues: "And super-moisturized PALMOLIVE RAPID SHAVE can do the same for you."

At this point the "split screen" technique is introduced. On one side of the screen a hand is seen applying "Rapid Shave" to sandpaper in an action that parallels Gifford's on the other side of the screen. As Gifford makes a razor stroke down his cheek, the hand makes a similar stroke down the lathered strip of sandpaper. Again the shaving, on both sides of the screen, is begun directly after the lather is applied. And, again, there is no "fade," "dissolve" or other visual indication of any lapse of time between the lathering and the shaving of the sandpaper, on one side of the screen, and Gifford's face, on the other. While this is being seen, the announcer says: "In this sandpaper test . . . or on your sandpaper beard, you just apply RAPID SHAVE . . . then . . . take your razor . . . and shave clean with a fast, smooth stroke."

We then see Gifford, stroking his clean-shaven face with a look of satisfied approval. The picture at this point shifts to cans of "Rapid Shave" surrounded by the words "Super-Moisturized" and "Fastest, Smoothest Shaves," while the announcer continues: "Try RAPID SHAVE . . . or cooling, soothing RAPID SHAVE-MENTHOL . . . both super-moisturized . . . for the fastest, smoothest shaves possible. They both outshave the tube . . . outshave the brush." In a concluding jingle, to a tune reminiscent of "Here we go 'round the mulberry bush," an unseen male chorus sings lustily: "RAPID SHAVE outshaves them all. Use RAPID SHAVE in the morning."

The sights and sounds we have described proceed in a rapid sequence, the whole commercial lasting 60 seconds.

. . . . .

## II.

In one basic respect, the case is free from factual controversy. Respondents concede that the televised "sandpaper" demonstrations were conducted not on real sandpaper but on what is known in the industry as a "mockup," or simulated prop. As the examiner found, "Actually no sandpaper was employed in the commercials. What was represented as sandpaper was in fact a mock-up made of plexiglass to which sand had been applied."

In dismissing the complaint, the examiner went on to explain, and to justify, respondents' use of a mock-up rather than actual sandpaper:

> There appear to be several reasons why it was not feasible to use sandpaper. One reason doubtless was that the length of the commercials—60-seconds—was not adequate for sandpaper to be soaked to the point where it could be shaved cleanly. Aside from this, however, there were technical difficulties peculiar to television. When placed under a television camera, sandpaper appears to be nothing more than plain, colored paper; the texture or grain of the sandpaper is not shown. Thus it is necessary to improvise—use a mock-up—if what is seen by the television audience is to have the appearance of sandpaper.

### III.

The examiner considered that the facts of the case raised only one question: "Has there been any material misrepresentation of the product?" To that question, the examiner answered:

> In the present case it seems clear that there has not. The shaving cream does possess at least adequate moistening or wetting properties, and sandpaper can be shaved through use of the product, provided adequate time for soaking is allowed.

> Essentially, what is presented here would appear to be little or nothing more than a case of harmless exaggeration or puffing. Obviously the sandpaper sequences were employed simply for the purpose of emphasizing and dramatizing the recognized moistening or wetting properties of the cream. It is difficult to believe that anyone could have been misled as to the properties or qualities of the product.

We believe the examiner erred, his answers being wrong essentially because he asked the wrong questions.

### IV.

.   .   .   .

.   .   .   Specifically, was it deceptive to the public and an unfair advertising practice for respondents to conduct a "sandpaper" test before the viewers' eyes to prove the product's "super-moisturizing power" on what was represented as sandpaper, and what the viewers had every reason to suppose was sandpaper, but was actually a plexiglass mock-up?

.   .   .   .

The heart of these commercials was the visual "sandpaper test" —a test that was, in reality, not taking place. This would be deceptive and unfair advertising even if "Rapid Shave" was as effective in shaving sandpaper as respondents represented. A likely result of such an illegal practice is that "purchasers are deceived into purchasing an article which they do not wish or intend to buy, and which they might or might not buy if correctly informed.   .   .   ." Federal Trade Commission v. Royal Milling Co., 288 U.S. 212, 217. "We are of opinion that the purchasing public is entitled to be protected against that species of deception, and that its interest in such protection is specific and substantial." *Ibid.*

Respondents urge, however, that if (assuming the fact to be true) their product will do to real sandpaper all that the mock-up demonstration claims for it, the consumer has not been induced to buy a product less valuable or meritorious than what he thought he was buying, and therefore he has not been hurt in any substantial way. But this has never been the test of what constitutes a material misrepresentation under the statute. "It is sufficient to find that the natural and probable result of the challenged practices is to cause one to do that which he would not otherwise do  .  .  .  and that the matter is of specific public interest." Bockenstette v. Federal Trade Commission, 134 F.2d 369, 371 (C.A. 10). "It is not necessary that the product so misrepresented be inferior or harmful to the public; it is sufficient that the sale of the product be other than as represented." L. & C. Mayers Co. v. Federal Trade Commission, 97 F.2d 365, 367 (C.A.2).

Respondent would have us hold that a television demonstration purporting to prove the qualities claimed for a product, where the public is told it is seeing one thing when it is actually seeing something different, is nonetheless lawful and not deceptive if in fact the product involved has the qualities claimed for it. This would flout the principle implicit in the multitude of cases which hold that one may not advertise so-called "phony" or dishonest testimonials; or imply an erroneous source or origin for a product; or fail to disclose that a product, although as good as a new one, has in fact, been reprocessed; or deceive the public into believing that one is in a certain line of business when this is not so. The vice assailed in these cases is the use of a falsification of fact, extrinsic to the objective value of the product, to sell that product, whether or not it may deserve to be bought on its own merits. "[T]he public is entitled to get what it chooses," and, "substitution would be unfair though equivalence were shown." Federal Trade Commission v. Algoma Lumber Co., 291 U.S. 67, 77–78.

QUESTIONS

1.  Although the language of Section 5 of the Federal Trade Commission Act is fairly broad ("unfair methods of competition in commerce, and unfair or deceptive acts or practices in commerce, are declared unlawful"), as Commissioner Elman indicates, the specific charge in the complaint was that the representations were "false, misleading and deceptive." (Complaint, para. 6, 59 F.T.C. at 1454.) "In truth and in fact," the complaint reads, "that which is represented to be sandpaper was a 'mock-up'  .  .  .  ." Was it necessary, under the terms of the Act, for the Commission to have gotten itself involved in "reality" and "falsification of facts"? Why did it not approach the problem directly as one of an "unfair" advertisement? Is it possible that an inquiry into "truth" and "fact" sounds more objective than one into "fairness"? In the final analysis,

how successful is Commissioner Elman in avoiding making a judgment based on moral considerations? Could he, by sticking to an analysis of "reality", have managed to do otherwise?

2. Notice the form of the complaint: "false, misleading *and* deceptive." What does this imply as to the relationship among the concepts? What *is* the relationship between a statement's being false and a statement's being deceptive? Is falsehood dependent on deceiving someone? If so, what does deceiving someone consist in? And if so, may the same statement be both true and false depending not upon "the facts" alone but upon the listener? Can a statement be deceptive and yet not false? Or false and yet not deceptive? Or true but deceptive? If falsity depends upon misleading someone, what must it mislead him to—a belief that does not correspond with reality?; an action that is not in his best interests? What do your answers tell you about the criteria that make a statement "true"?

3. To the extent that the Commission did, by the language of its complaint, set for itself the task of proving that something was false, what was it that was "false"? Can a visual experience, as such, be "false"? Or is what is "false" or "true" some proposition we must impute to the person having the experience? For example, if someone hallucinates a dragon, is it meaningful to say that the perception itself is "false", or is falsehood his belief (if he has it) that, say, "dragons exist," or "there is a dragon in the room"? If falsehood can only be a quality of a proposition, is it not necessary for the Commission to tell us which *proposition* the viewer falsely *believed* as a result of the perception? Is it at all obvious what the (average, reasonable?) viewer believed? In the Commission's Findings of Fact, it holds, "11. These commercials clearly convey the impression that very coarse pieces of sandpaper are actually being shaved. . . . " 59 F.T.C. at 1476. Does this mean that the Commission necessarily had to impute to the viewer something like, "I am presently seeing the proof of Rapid Shave's ability to shave sandpaper"? Why would not a viewer as likely think "Rapid Shave can shave sandpaper", or "Rapid Shave shaves very well"?

Notice that the voice accompanying the representation said, "to prove Rapid Shave's super-moisturizing power, we put it right from the can. . . . " What tense is the verb, "to put"? Can you make an argument for Respondent based on this ambiguity, in light of the comment, "It *was* apply . . . soak . . . and off in a stroke"? Is this an example of how important, and how difficult, it is to fix on the specific proposition whose truth or falsity is being put to the test?

Is this inquiry—putting together and imputing to the viewer some proposition—one that can be accomplished without at least covert invocation of principles and policies?

4. Commissioner Elman says of the sandpaper test that it "was, in reality, not taking place" and that what the viewer was seeing "was actually a plexiglass mock-up." What assumptions is he making about what reality *is*? Is it meaningful to speak of "reality" independent of a reference (even if only implicit) to some

particular perceiver of that reality? If the advertisement had shown real sandpaper, what would it have looked like to the people in the studio? What would it have looked like to the viewers at home? Does your answer suggest that there may be two different realities, rather than "a" reality? Or is one reality "more real" than the other? On what grounds? Or would it be best to leave "reality" out of the description altogether? What are the virtues of assuming that there is "a" reality? What effects does it generally have—on enabling people to communicate; on spurring inquiry? What effects did it have in this case?

Consider the case of an oar, part of which is under the water. Because of the refractive capacity of water, to all observers (except one looking directly along the oar's axis) the oar looks bent. What assumptions—about perception and "reality", if you like—are being made by a person who says (a) "the oar is straight"? What assumptions are being made by one who says (b) "The oar is bent"? Is the former or the latter statement "false"? Whose statement is more "misleading"? Is the statement of the former false or misleading unless he states it in the form (c) "the oar looks bent to me, but it is straight in fact"? Is that statement "more true" than either of the others? Is his answer (c) still false or misleading unless he says (d) "the oar appears to me to be bent X degrees, but because of my position in looking at the oar, and because I judge the water to be of such and such a composition, and because water of such and such a composition has a refractive index of Y, I judge the oar to be straight"? Where does one stop? Is the problem one that is adequately explicated in terms of "reality" and "falsification of facts"? To what considerations does one's analysis extend? How is the problem of the oar like the problem of the *Colgate* case?

FEDERAL TRADE COMMISSION v. COLGATE-PALMOLIVE CO.

380 U.S. 374, 85 S.Ct. 1035, 13 L.Ed.2d 904.

Mr. Chief Justice WARREN delivered the opinion of the Court.

. . .

. . . The Commission's order was as inclusive as its discussion. It ordered both re[s]pondents to cease and desist from:

"Representing, directly or by implication, *in describing, explaining*, or purporting to prove the quality or merits of any product, that pictures, depictions, or demonstrations . . . *are genuine or accurate representations* . . . *of*, or prove the *quality or merits of, any product*, when such pictures, depictions, or demonstrations are *not in fact genuine or accurate representations* . . . *of*, or do not prove the quality or merits of, *any such product*." (Emphasis added.)

The Court of Appeals understandably was concerned with the broad language in the Commission's opinion and order, especially since the Commission was not dealing with an established deceptive practice but was applying the flexible standards of § 5 to a hitherto unexplored area. The breadth of the Commission's order was potentially limitless, apparently establishing a per se rule prohibiting the use of simulated props in all television commercials, since commercials by definition describe "the qualities or merits" of products. The court's impression that the order was "quite ambiguous" was not alleviated when in oral argument counsel for the Commission stated that if a prominent person appeared on television saying "I love Lipsom's iced tea," while drinking something that appeared to be tea but in fact was not, the commercial would be a deceptive practice.

In light of the Commission's order and its oral argument, the court concluded that it was the Commission's intention to prohibit all simulated props in television commercials. The court could not agree with this position since it believed that "where the only untruth is that the substance [the viewer] sees on the screen is artificial, and the visual appearance is otherwise a correct and accurate representation of the product itself, he is not injured." But, in setting aside the Commission's order, the court gave little specific guidance for the drafting of a new one. It merely criticized the Commission for holding that mock-ups are "illegal per se," and indicated that the Commission's order "may" have been too broad in other respects as well.

Following the decision by the Court of Appeals, the Commission entered a new "proposed final order" on February 18, 1963. This order was accompanied by an explanatory opinion that admitted error in the original disposition of the case and expressed an intention to eliminate the errors found by the Court of Appeals. The Commission explained that its new order was not directed toward the broad prohibition of all undisclosed simulated props in commercials, but merely toward prohibiting respondents from misrepresenting to the public that it was seeing for itself a test, experiment or demonstration which purportedly proved a product claim. According to the Commission, the television commercial in question did not merely tell viewers that the experiment had been or could be performed, but instead told them that they were seeing it for themselves and did not have to take the seller's word for it. This, and not the mere use of a prop, was the misrepresentation found to be a deceptive practice. Over the vigorous objection of respondents, the Commission issued its final order on May 7, 1963. Both respondents were ordered to cease and desist from:

> "Unfairly or deceptively advertising any . . . product by presenting a test, experiment or demonstration that (1) is represented to the public as actual proof of a claim made for the product which is material to inducing its sale, and (2) is not in fact a genuine test, experiment or demonstration being conducted as represented and does not in fact constitute actual proof of the claim, because of the undisclosed use and substitution of a mock-up or prop instead of the product, article, or substance represented to be used therein."

Respondents again appealed to the Court of Appeals. Despite the urgings of respondents that it limit its review to a determination whether the Commission's order was consistent with the previous mandate, the court re-examined the Commission's new order on the merits. The court recognized that the new order no longer prohibited the use of all simulated props in commercials, but found that it would be impossible under it to distinguish between commercials which depicted a test, experiment or demonstration, and those which did not. The court held that so long as there is an accurate portrayal of a product's attributes or performance there is no deceit and instructed the Commission, "as we thought we had directed it before," to enter an order merely prohibiting respondents from using mock-ups to demonstrate something which in fact could not be accomplished.

We hold that the Commission's order of May 7, 1963, was not in disregard of the Court of Appeals' first mandate and was a good-faith attempt to incorporate the legal principles contained therein.

. . .

. . . .

We are not concerned in this case with the clear misrepresentation in the commercials concerning the speed with which Rapid Shave could shave sandpaper, since the Court of Appeals upheld the Commission's finding on that matter and the respondents have not challenged the finding here. We granted certiorari to consider the Commission's conclusion that even if an advertiser has himself conducted a test, experiment or demonstration which he honestly believes will prove a certain product claim, he may not convey to television viewers the false impression that they are seeing the test, experiment or demonstration for themselves, when they are not because of the undisclosed use of mock-ups.

We accept the Commission's determination that the commercials involved in this case contained three representations to the public: (1) that sandpaper could be shaved by Rapid Shave; (2) that an experiment had been conducted which verified this claim; and (3) that the viewer was seeing this experiment for himself. Respondents admit that the first two representations were made, but deny that the third was. The Commission, however, found to the contrary, and, since this is a matter of fact resting on an inference that could reasonably be drawn from the commercials themselves, the Commission's finding should be sustained. For the purposes of our review, we can assume that the first two representations were true; the focus of our consideration is on the third, which was clearly false. . . .

. . . .

. . . It is generally accepted that it is a deceptive practice to state falsely that a product has received a testimonial from a respected source. In addition, the Commission has consistently acted to prevent sellers from falsely stating that their product claims have been "certified." We find these situations to be indistinguishable from the present case. We can assume that in each the underlying product claim is true and in each the seller actually conducted an experiment sufficient to prove to himself the truth of the claim. But in each the seller has told the public that it could rely on something other than his word concerning both the truth of the claim and the validity of his experiment. We find it an immaterial difference that in one case the viewer is told to rely on the word of a celebrity or authority he respects, in another on the word of a testing agency, and in the present case on his own perception of an undisclosed simulation.

Respondents again insist that the present case is not like any of the above, but is more like a case in which a celebrity or independent testing agency has in fact submitted a written verification of an experiment actually observed, but, because of the inability of the camera to transmit accurately an impression of the paper on which the testimonial is written, the seller reproduces it on another substance so that it can be seen by the viewing audience. This analogy ignores the finding of the Commission that in the present case the seller misrepresented to the public that it was being given objective proof of a product claim. In respondents' hypothetical the objective proof of the product claim that is offered, the word of the celebrity or agency that the experiment was actually conducted, does exist; while in the case before us the objective proof offered, the viewer's own perception of an actual experiment, does not exist. Thus, in respondents' hypothetical, unlike the present case, the use of the undisclosed mock-up does not conflict with the seller's claim that there is objective proof.

We agree with the Commission, therefore, that the undisclosed use of plexiglass in the present commercials was a material deceptive practice, independent and separate from the other misrepresentation found. We find unpersuasive respondents' other objections to this conclusion. Respondents claim that it will be impractical to inform the viewing public that it is not seeing an actual test, experiment or demonstration, but we think it inconceivable that the ingenious advertising world will be unable, if it so desires, to conform to the Commission's insistence that the public be not misinformed. If, however, it becomes impossible or impractical to show simulated demonstrations on television in a truthful manner, this indicates that television is not a medium that lends itself to this type of commercial, not that the commercial must survive at all costs. Similarly unpersuasive is respondents' objection that the Commission's decision discriminates against sellers whose product claims cannot be "verified" on television without the use of simulations. All methods of advertising do not equally favor every seller. If the inherent limitations of a method do not permit its use in the way a seller desires, the seller cannot by material misrepresentation compensate for those limitations.

. . . .

The Court of Appeals . . . could find no difference between the Rapid Shave commercial and a commercial which extolled the goodness of ice cream while giving viewers a picture of a scoop of mashed potatoes appearing to be ice cream. We do not understand this difficulty. In the ice cream case the mashed potato prop is not being used for additional proof of the product claim, while

the purpose of the Rapid Shave commercial is to give the viewer
objective proof of the claims made. If in the ice cream hypothetical
the focus of the commercial becomes the undisclosed potato prop and
the viewer is invited, explicitly or by implication, to see for himself
the truth of the claims about the ice cream's rich texture and full
color, and perhaps compare it to a "rival product," then the commercial has become similar to the one now before us. Clearly, however, a commercial which depicts happy actors delightedly eating ice
cream that is in fact mashed potatoes or drinking a product appearing
to be coffee but which is in fact some other substance is not covered
by the present order.

. . . . .

REVERSED AND REMANDED

Mr. Justice HARLAN, whom Mr. Justice STEWART joins, dissenting in part.

. . . .

I do not agree that the use of "mock-ups" by the television advertiser is of itself a deceptive trade practice. Further, while there
was an independent deceptive element in this commercial, I do not
think this record justifies the broad remedial order issued by the
Commission. I would remand the case to the Commission for further
proceedings.

## I

### "MOCK-UPS" AS SUCH

The faulty prop in the court's reasoning is that it focuses entirely
on what is taking place in the studio rather than on what the viewer
is seeing on his screen. That which the viewer sees with his own eyes
is not, however, what is taking place in the studio, but an electronic
image. If the image he sees on the screen is an accurate reproduction
of what he would see with the naked eyes were the experiment performed before him with sandpaper in his home or in the studio, there
can hardly be a misrepresentation in any legally significant sense.
While the Commission undoubtedly possesses broad authority to give
content to the proscriptions of the Act, its discretion, as the Court
recognizes, is not unbridled, and "in the last analysis the words
'deceptive practices' set forth a legal standard and they must get their
final meaning from judicial construction". . . . In this case,
assuming that Rapid Shave could soften sandpaper as quickly as
it does sand-covered plexiglass, a viewer who wants to entertain his
friends by duplicating the actual experiment could do so by buying a
can of Rapid Shave and some sandpaper. If he wished to shave
himself, and his beard were really as tough as sandpaper, he could
perform this part of his morning ablutions with Rapid Shave in
the same way as he saw the plexiglass shaved on television.

I do not see how such a commercial can be said to be "deceptive"
in any legally acceptable use of that term. The Court attempts to
distinguish the case where a "celebrity" has written a testimonial

endorsing some product, but the original testimonial cannot be seen over television and a copy is shown over the air by the manufacturer. The Court states of his "hypothetical": "In respondents' hypothetical the objective proof of the product claim that is offered, the word of the celebrity or agency that the experiment was actually conducted, does exist; while in the case before us the objective proof offered, the viewer's own perception of an actual experiment, does not exist." . . . But in both cases the viewer is told to "see for himself," in the one case that the celebrity has endorsed the product; in the other, that the product can shave sandpaper; in neither case is the viewer actually seeing the proof; and in both cases the objective proof does exist, be it the original testimonial or the sandpaper test actually conducted by the manufacturer. In neither case, however, is there a material misrepresentation, because what the viewer sees *is* an accurate image of the objective proof.

Nor can I readily understand how the accurate portrayal of an experiment by means of a mock-up can be considered more deceptive than the use of mashed potatoes to convey the glamorous qualities of a particular ice cream (*ante*, pp. 392–393); indeed, to a potato-lover "the smile on the face of the tiger" might come more naturally than if he were actually being served ice cream.

It is commonly known that television presents certain distortions in transmissions for which the broadcasting industry must compensate. Thus, a white towel will look a dingy gray over television, but a blue towel will look a sparkling white. On the Court's analysis, an advertiser must achieve accuracy in the studio even though it results in an inaccurate image being projected on the home screen. This led the Court of Appeals to question whether it would be proper for an advertiser to show a product on television that somehow, because of the medium, looks better on the screen than it does in real life. 310 F.2d 89, 94; 326 F.2d 517, 523, n. 16.

A perhaps more commonplace example suggests itself: Would it be proper for respondent Colgate, in advertising a laundry detergent, to "demonstrate" the effectiveness of a major competitor's detergent in washing white sheets; and then "before the viewer's eyes," to wash a white (not a blue) sheet with the competitor's detergent? The studio test would accurately show the quality of the product, but the image on the screen would look as though the sheet had been washed with an ineffective detergent. All that has happened here is the converse: a demonstration has been altered in the studio to compensate for the distortions of the television medium, but in this instance in order to present an accurate picture to the television viewer.

In short, it seems to me that the proper legal test in cases of this kind concerns not what goes on in the broadcasting studio, but whether what is shown on the television screen is an accurate representation of the advertised product and of the claims made for it.

QUESTIONS

1.　What is the significance the Court attaches to a distinction between (1) claiming a product has a certain quality, and (2) claiming a product has the quality, while backing up the claim with the proffer of a test as "additional proof" of the product claim? What problems does the invocation of such a distinction raise? How adequately does the Court distinguish the ice cream-mashed potato hypothetical? Is not every meaningful statement on some level a claim about proof?

2.　What is the Court trying to say by its statement that "the viewer's own perception of the actual experiment does not exist"? Should not the Court be speaking in terms of, "the viewer's belief that X was the case, was false"? Does the Supreme Court—any more than the F.T.C.—adequately explain *what* statement it is assuming the viewer to have formed falsely?

3.　Note that, in its Opinion, the Court "accepts" the Commission's finding that the "representation to the public" was "that the viewer was seeing [the] experiment for himself." Why was this representation "clearly false"? Can we answer without knowing whether "representation" refers to the *intent* of the sponsor, *i. e.*, what it *wanted* the viewer to believe, or the *belief* the average viewer actually formed? Can a statement be false if no one believes it or is prepared to act on it? If your answer is no, does this commit you to saying that Chicken Little's claim that "the sky is falling" was neither true nor false because no one believed it?

If, on the other hand, your answer is yes, and you believe the truth of a statement is unrelated to its effects on people's beliefs or actions, does this commit you to saying that its truth or falsity depends upon its correspondence with "the facts"? If so, how does one judge (a) what "the facts" *are* and (b) what the statement *means* so as to be able to judge (c) whether the statement "corresponds" with the facts?

4.　How much was the legal process concerned in *Colgate*, with "truth" and "falsity" and how much with proper—according to some ethical standards—description? How much with the dignity of the viewing public? With the ethics of the market place? Why did the Commission's complaint turn the inquiry towards "truth" and "reality" rather than "unfairness"? What was it seeking to gain? How much do these references simplify the law's task, and how much do they obscure what the Commission and courts were really charged with looking into? To what extent can we relieve decision makers of ethical choice by instructing them to look at *the facts* and determine *the truth* of statements about them?

————

## A.  Correspondence

BERTRAND RUSSELL

### TRUTH AND FALSEHOOD *

We are now in a position to understand what it is that distinguishes a true judgment from a false one.  For this purpose we will adopt certain definitions.  In every act of judgment there is a mind which judges, and there are terms concerning which it judges.  We will call the mind the *subject* in the judgment, and the remaining terms the *objects*.  Thus, when Othello judges that Desdemona loves Cassio, Othello is the subject, while the objects are Desdemona and loving and Cassio.  The subject and the objects together are called the *constituents* of the judgment. . . .

. . . .

. . . [A] belief is *true* when it *corresponds* to a certain associated complex, and *false* when it does not.  Assuming, for the sake of definiteness, that the objects of the belief are two terms and a relation, the terms being put in a certain order by the "sense" of the believing, then if the two terms in that order are united by the relation into a complex, the belief is true; if not, it is false.  This constitutes the definition of truth and falsehood that we were in search of.  Judging or believing is a certain complex unity of which a mind is a constituent; if the remaining constituents, taken in the order which they have in the belief, form a complex unity, then the belief is true; if not, it is false.

Thus although truth and falsehood are properties of beliefs, yet they are in a sense extrinsic properties, for the condition of the truth of a belief is something not involving beliefs, or (in general) any mind at all, but only the *objects* of the belief.  A mind, which believes, believes truly when there is a *corresponding* complex not involving the mind, but only its objects.  This correspondence ensures truth, and its absence entails falsehood.  Hence we account simultaneously for the two facts that beliefs (a) depend on minds for their *existence*, (b) do not depend on minds for their *truth*.

We may restate our theory as follows:  If we take such a belief as "Othello believes that Desdemona loves Cassio", we will call Desdemona and Cassio the *object-terms*, and loving the *object-relation*.  If there is a complex unity "Desdemona's love for Cassio," consisting of the object-terms related by the object-relation in the same order as they have in the belief, then this complex unity is called the *fact corresponding to the belief*.  Thus a belief is true when there is a corresponding fact, and is false when there is no corresponding fact.

It will be seen that minds do not *create* truth or falsehood.  They create beliefs, but when once the beliefs are created, the mind cannot make them true or false, except in the special case where they concern future things which are within the power of the person be-

---

* From The Problems of Philosophy 126–
30 (Galaxy Book ed. 1959).

lieving, such as catching trains. What makes a belief true is a *fact*, and this fact does not (except in exceptional cases) in any way involve the mind of the person who has the belief.

QUESTIONS

1. In what way can a belief "correspond" to its "associated complex"? Consider Othello's belief that Desdemona loves Cassio. What is the "fact" that "corresponds" with this belief, making the belief true if the fact exists, and false if it does not? Can you describe the "fact"? Would you recognize it if you saw it? Could you say how your belief corresponded with it?

2. What is the range of inquiry involved in Othello's arriving at the judgment "Desdemona loves Cassio"? How adequately is it described as simply looking to discover whether "a complex unity, 'Desdemona's love for Cassio'" exists?

3. Is it valid to suppose that a statement is either true or false, depending upon the existence of a certain state of affairs? Consider the inquiry that is involved by, and what it means to say, "we are in a recession"; or "it is warm today". Do these statements always mean the same? Are the criteria that make them true or false always the same? If not, what is it that makes them "true" or "false"? Is it possible that a statement can be true in some contexts but not in others? If so, can the correspondence theory account for it?

4. Does it make sense to define truth in such a way as to depend upon a fact that does "not . . . in any way involve the mind of the person who has the belief"? Is there a simple real relationship in the world, Desdemona's love for Cassio, that can meaningfully be conceived independently of Othello's—or anyone else's—mind? Is the same state of affairs going to make Othello believe that Desdemona truly loves Cassio for purposes (a) of warning Desdemona to stop seeing Cassio; (b) of moving Desdemona to the other side of town; or (c) of killing Cassio? On the other hand, note that Russell is seeking to define what it *means* to say a statement is true, not how we go about (psychologically) *deciding* it true. What is Russell trying to do by defining truth this way; what is he trying to avoid? Yet, what is the function of defining truth in a way that ignores the processes by which any human mind can go about judging a statement true or false? Is not this attempt "metaphysical" in the most discredited sense?

5. Consider the statement, "There is a clock on the wall." Under the correspondence theory of truth, the statement is true if there is a clock on the wall, and false if there is not. The truth thus is seen to hinge on the relationship—correspondence—of that single statement with reality. What difficulties are presented for the procedures suggested by the uncertainties of what a "clock" (the word) *means* and what object on the wall *is*? Suppose the object on the wall "loses" one minute every day relative to the Bureau of Standards clock in Washington; suppose no one, in fact, refers to it in conducting their lives, *i. e.*, no one treats it as a "clock"; suppose it has stopped ten years ago, and no one has sought to rewind it; under these circumstances is the

object, or is it not, a "clock"?  To determine whether the object is a "clock", do we hold up to "reality" one statement, or a whole series of statements about adequacy to fulfill a function, common usage of language, etc.?

6.  How would Russell judge the cases put to us in Justice Harlan's opinion, such as where a television viewer seems to be seeing a white towel emerge from the wash, which in the studio is blue?  Would Russell say *if* the viewer believed that *if* he were in the studio, the towel would appear white, then the viewer's belief would be false?  Is the viewer apt to have such a specific and refined belief?  If an articulate statement "comes to mind" at all, is it not more likely to be, simply, "the towel is white"?  Can we say whether *this* belief corresponds with "the facts" or not?  What facts are we to correspond it with?

*Brand Blanshard*

## The Tests of Truth *

.   .   .

"Take the judgment, 'That bird is a cardinal'.  If you heard someone make that remark, how would you test it?  You would look and see. If there was a correspondence between what was asserted and what you saw, you would call the judgement true; if not, false.  This is the way we actually assure ourselves of the truth of all such judgements, and it is correspondence that assures us."

Now, plausible as this argument is, it goes to pieces on inspection. It assumes that, corresponding to our judgement, there is some solid chunk of fact, directly presented to sense and beyond all question, to which thought must adjust itself.  And this 'solid fact' is a fiction. What the theory takes as fact and actually uses as such is another judgement or set of judgements, and what provides the verification is the coherence between the initial judgement and these.

Consider the cardinal.  This is supposed to be fact, unadulterated brute fact, given directly to our senses and providing a solid reality to which our thought is to correspond.  But no bird is a mere sense datum, or even a collection of sense data.  Suppose that standing in our place were an animal with all our senses, each developed to the highest acuteness, but unable to attach meanings to sense data as we do, or note likenesses, implications, and differences.  Would such a creature perceive what we perceive?  Plainly not.  To recognize a cardinal is a considerable intellectual achievement, for to do it one must grasp, implicitly but none the less really, the *concept* of cardinal, and this can only be done by a leap far out of the given into ideal classification.  The most ignorant person among us who achieves such recognition could unpack from it a surprising wealth of contents.  The idea of living organisms, the thought of the bird kingdom and its outstanding characteristics, the notions of flight and a peculiar song and a deter-

* From 2 The Nature of Thought 228–      With permission of George Allen &
   30 (George Allen & Unwin Ltd. 1939).     Unwin Ltd.

minated colour—these and many other notions are so bound up with the identification that our thought would lose its character with the removal of any one of them. Not that they are logical implicates which later analysis might find to be entailed by our identification; they are parts or components of it, as truly as 'plane' is part of 'plane triangle'; they are part of what we mean when we use the word 'cardinal'. And these essential elements, at least at the time and for the most part, are not given in sense at all. They are elements in a theory, and a theory of no little complexity, which is based on sense data if you will, but could not possibly consist of them.

Indeed, that the brute-fact view of perception is untrue is proved by this alone, that perception may be mistaken; I may take the cardinal for a robin. If the object were mere given fact, such a mistake would be impossible. A fact is what it is, and cannot possibly be something else. If it appears to be something else, the seeming must be in our thought, and the perception that involves such seemings has advanced beyond the given into the region of judgement. What makes the error possible is a theory of ours.

It may be said that if perception is itself theory, that only means that we must look a little further for the verifying fact. Somewhere the bow of theory must come to earth; it cannot float loose in the clouds; a theory that rests on nothing but theory is a mere intellectual caprice. Very well; let us go on in our search for fact. By way of testing our perception, we stealthily approach the bird, observe it from new angles, and not fresh characteristics. Does *this* bring us our ultimate fact unmixed with theory? Obviously not. Suppose we proceed with this method to its farthest possible limit; suppose we shoot the bird, seize it, carry it off to a biological laboratory, and subject it to minute and exhaustive dissection; would *that* give us our solid facts? No again. For every notation of a new trait, or even remarking of an old one, would as truly go beyond brute fact and as truly involve an element of theory as would the original judgement. And so long as it contains this element of theory, it must of course be checked by further perceptions; but then these further perceptions once again are judgements; in no case are they brute facts. Thus the facts with which our judgements were to tally seem forever to elude us, and we find ourselves in a region where, on every side, there are only judgements and still more judgements.

QUESTIONS

1. How do the views of Blanshard differ from those of Russell? To what extent are they addressing themselves to the same question? What does Blanshard think of the worth of defining truth in a way that does not adequately take into account how judgments are made?

2. What is Blanshard's implicit criticism of Russell? What does Blanshard think of the worth of defining truth in a way that does not adequately take into account how judgments are made? (Blanshard supports a coherence theory of truth, both as to how we *test* truth, and as to how truth must be *defined*; see subsection c. *infra*.

## B.  Pragmatism

WILLIAM JAMES

PRAGMATISM'S CONCEPTION OF TRUTH *

Truth, as any dictionary will tell you, is a property of certain of our ideas. It means their "agreement," as falsity means their disagreement, with "reality." Pragmatists and intellectualists both accept this definition as a matter of course. They begin to quarrel only after the question is raised as to what may precisely be meant by the term "agreement," and what by the term "reality," when reality is taken as something for our ideas to agree with.

In answering these questions the pragmatists are more analytic and painstaking, the intellectualists more offhand and irreflective. The popular notion is that a true idea must copy its reality. Like other popular views, this one follows the analogy of the most usual experience. Our true ideas of sensible things do indeed copy them. Shut your eyes and think of yonder clock on the wall, and you get just such a true picture or copy of its dial. But your idea of its "works" (unless you are a clockmaker) is much less of a copy, yet it passes muster, for it in no way clashes with the reality. Even though it should shrink to the mere word "works," that word still serves you truly; and when you speak of the "time-keeping function" of the clock, or of its spring's "elasticity," it is hard to see exactly what your ideas can copy.

You perceive that there is a problem here. Where our ideas cannot copy definitely their object, what does agreement with that object mean? . . .

Pragmatism . . . asks . . . "Grant an idea or belief to be true, . . . what concrete difference will its being true make in any one's actual life? How will the truth be realized? What experiences will be different from those which would obtain if the belief were false? What, in short, is the truth's cash-value in experiential terms?"

The moment pragmatism asks this question, it sees the answer: *True ideas are those that we can assimilate, validate, corroborate and verify. False ideas are those that we can not.* That is the practical difference it makes to us to have true ideas; that, therefore, is the meaning of truth, for it is all that truth is known-as.

This thesis is what I have to defend. The truth of an idea is not a stagnant property inherent in it. Truth *happens* to an idea. It *becomes* true, is *made* true by events. Its verity *is* in fact an event, a process: the process namely of its verifying itself, its veri-*fication*. Its validity is the process of its valid-*ation*.

But what do the words verification and validation themselves pragmatically mean? They again signify certain practical consequences of the verified and validated idea. . . .

* From Pragmatism 198–213 (Longmans,
Green & Co. 1946).

Let me begin by reminding you of the fact that the possession of true thoughts means everywhere the possession of invaluable instruments of action; and that our duty to gain truth, so far from being a blank command from out of the blue, or a "stunt" self-imposed by our intellect, can account for itself by excellent practical reasons.

The importance to human life of having true beliefs about matters of fact is a thing too notorious. We live in a world of realities that can be infinitely useful or infinitely harmful. Ideas that tell us which of them to expect count as the true ideas in all this primary sphere of verification, and the pursuit of such ideas is a primary human duty. The possession of truth, so far from being here an end in itself, is only a preliminary means towards other vital satisfactions. If I am lost in the woods and starved, and find what looks like a cow-path, it is of the utmost importance that I should think of a human habitation at the end of it, for if I do so and follow it, I save myself. The true thought is useful here because the house which is its object is useful. The practical value of true ideas is thus primarily derived from the practical importance of their objects to us. . . .

.   .   .   .

Take, for instance, yonder object on the wall. You and I consider it to be a "clock," altho no one of us has seen the hidden works that make it one. We let our notion pass for true without attempting to verify. If truths mean verification-process essentially, ought we then to call such unverified truths as this abortive? No, for they form the overwhelmingly large number of the truths we live by. Indirect as well as direct verifications pass muster. Where circumstantial evidence is sufficient, we can go without eye-witnessing. Just as we here assume Japan to exist without ever having been there, because it *works* to do so, everything we know conspiring with the belief, and nothing interfering, so we assume that thing to be a clock. We *use* it as a clock, regulating the length of our lecture by it. The verification of the assumption here means its leading to no frustration or contradiction. Verifi*ability* of wheels and weights and pendulum is as good as verification. For one truth-process completed there are a million in our lives that function in this state of nascency. They turn us *towards* direct verification; lead us into the surroundings of the objects they envisage; and then, if everything runs on harmoniously, we are so sure that verification is possible that we omit it, and are usually justified by all that happens.

Truth lives, in fact, for the most part on a credit system. Our thoughts and beliefs "pass," so long as nothing challenges them, just as banknotes pass so long as nobody refuses them. . . .

.   .   .   .

. . . Primarily, no doubt, to agree means to copy, but we saw that the mere word "clock" would do instead of a mental picture of its works, and that of many realities our ideas can only be symbols and not copies. "Past time," "power," "spontaneity,"—how can our mind copy such realities?

To "agree" in the widest sense with a reality *can only mean to be guided either straight up to it or into its surroundings, or to be put into such working touch with it as to handle either it or something connected with it better than if we disagreed.* Better either intellectually or practically! And often agreement will only mean the negative fact that nothing contradictory from the quarter of that reality comes to interfere with the way in which our ideas guide us elsewhere. To copy a reality is, indeed, one very important way of agreeing with it, but it is far from being essential. The essential thing is the process of being guided. Any idea that helps us to *deal,* whether practically or intellectually, with either the reality or its belongings, that doesn't entangle our progress in frustrations, that *fits,* in fact, and adapts our life to the reality's whole setting, will agree sufficiently to meet the requirement. It will hold true of that reality.

QUESTIONS

1. To what extent when James speaks of "truth" is he describing the criteria for what the positivists would call "meaningfulness" (aside from truth or falsity)?

2. Whose position would James most strongly support in *Colgate*? Note Respondents' argument, set forth in the Commission's Opinion, "that if . . . their product will do to real sandpaper all that the mock-up demonstration claims for it, the consumer has not been induced to buy a product less valuable or meritorious than what he thought he was buying, and therefore he has not been hurt in any substantial way." Can you, using James, turn this argument into one that goes to the charge that the advertisement was "false"?

3. James says that an idea "is made true by events." What events—what character of events—make an idea true? Consider the idea that "I am witnessing Rapid Shave being used to shave sandpaper." Since the viewer cannot be in the studio at the time of witnessing the experiment itself, in what form is the statement amenable to validation, other than as something like "Rapid Shave can shave sandpaper"? As Justice Harlan points out, "a viewer who wants to entertain his friends by duplicating the actual experiment could do so by buying a can of Rapid Shave and some sandpaper. If he wished to shave himself, and his beard were really as tough as sandpaper," he could. Are you willing to say that this makes the original "idea"— that "I am witnessing Rapid Shave being used to shave sandpaper"— "true"? What alternative standards of truth are there? Does not James' strength lie in the difficulties of applying correspondence? But do the difficulties of applying the correspondence theory in any given case abandon us to the view that truth is merely what "guides" us "towards other vital satisfactions"?

4. Is it clear what is meant by a belief's "working", or, in the terms of the excerpt above, of its "leading to no frustration or contradiction"? Consider the example in Justice Harlan's dissent, of a detergent commercial "proving" the product's capabilities by reference to a towel that is (in the studio) blue but is (in the viewer's home) white. Does pragmatism entail that the belief, "the towel is

white", be true for the viewer and false for the man in the studio? What difficulties would this consequence present? Can James avoid it? If the viewer went to buy the detergent being advertised, and used it, presumably his belief—that the detergent was effective in making towels white—would lead "to no frustration or contradiction". Is it therefore true that, in terms of "cash value", his belief that the towel was white was true? Or is his belief "frustrated" if his purchase leads him to discover that white towels are more bother than towels that emerge from the wash dingy gray, and he therefore comes to wish that he had bought some other detergent? (And is his original belief therefore "false"?) Suppose the viewer went not to the store but to the studio: would he not there find his original belief contradicted, seeing the towel as blue? Does James' position thus entail that the truth of a statement depends solely on whether, in this case, one goes to the store or the studio? What if one did both, finding a practical truth in the assumption that the towel had been washed white, and frustrated to find that the towel was "actually" blue in the studio? Can a statement be both true and false for the same person? Do experiences always "frustrate" and "contradict" beliefs unambiguously? Do they *ever* do so unambiguously?

5. Consider the objections to pragmatism by A. C. Ewing.

(a) It is quite conceivable that a belief might work well and yet not be true or work badly and yet be true. There are very many drunkards who would be greatly benefited if they believed that next time they took alcohol it would kill them, but this does not make the belief true. (b) While true beliefs *usually* work, this is usually only because they are first true. It pays to believe that there is a motor car coming when this is true because if I do not believe it I may be run over, but it only pays because there really is a motor car, i.e. because the belief is first true. (c) What works for one man may not work for another, and what works for him at one time may not work for him at another. Does it follow that it has ceased to be true when it ceases to work, or that it is true for one man and not for another? The view that reality is a system in which everything is completely determined has worked for some men and the view that there was undetermined individual freedom for others, but both views cannot be true. God cannot both exist and not exist even if some men are helped by belief in his existence and others hindered.[8]

---

## C. *Coherence*

### Introductory Note: The Copernican Revolution

The coherence theory differs from the correspondence theory primarily in this regard: the correspondence theorists maintain that

---

8. From The Fundamental Questions of Philosophy (1951); reprinted in E. Nagel and R. Brandt, Meaning and Knowledge: Systematic Readings in Epistemology 126 (1965).

to say a statement $S$ is true *means* that that statement, in and of itself, corresponds to reality, *e.g.*, the statement, "there is a clock on the wall" is true if and only if there is a clock on the wall. The coherence theorists, by contrast, build on the view that we never *judge* the truth of any statement by reference to whether that statement, by itself, corresponds to reality. Our judgments always involve a complex relationship between a whole host of judgments—indeed, our entire body of beliefs. To the coherence theorist, our judgment as to the truth of the statement, "there is a clock on the wall" involves a complex of statements, most evidently, $S_1$, "I believe there are objects outside my brain"; $S_2$, "I am receiving impressions on my optic nerve that I associate with objects of such and such shape and character"; $S_3$, "I am not hallucinating"; $S_4$, "If I act as though that object is a clock, *i.e.*, tells time accurately to such and such a degree, I will not be disappointed in my dealings with reference to which time is critical"; $S_5$, "If I refer to that object as a 'clock' in my conversations with others, they will respond the way I want them to, *e.g.*, if I say, 'what time does the clock say', they will turn and look to *it*", etc. In various ways the coherence theorists take the position that since whenever we *judge* the truth of a statement we inevitably do so by reference to how adequately it coheres with a whole system of beliefs, to define the *meaning* of truth in any other way is unrealistic, or even inconsistent.

To understand how the coherence theorists come to their position, it may be useful to review the so-called Copernican revolution, the shift from viewing the earth as the center of the universe to viewing it as one of a number of planets spinning about the sun.

The major steps in the Copernican revolution are generally familiar.[9] From their inspections of the skies, early astronomers were confronted with a series of observations which, in relatively "raw," unelaborated form, present no understanding of the universe beyond that there are certain regular angular changes between celestial bodies and the horizon. That is, when one looks at the stars at night, as time passes he experiences a series of photochemical reactions across the back of his eye. The same photochemical reactions can be interpreted to mean at least (a) we are rotating one way and the stars the other; (b) we are rotating and the stars are stationary; or (c) the earth is stationary and the stars are rotating about it. All three of these interpretations (and others; can you think of them?) fit the experience one is having in the back of the eye. To pick any of the three *involves an intellectual construct.*

The earliest astronomers opted for (c); that is, they fitted their observations into a more comprehensive, articulate cosmology by positing the universe as essentially a two sphere affair, with an enormous outer sphere, on which the stars were marked, rotating about a stationary inner sphere, the earth. The sun and planets circled about the earth in concentric circles.

---

**9.** The author, in the passages that follow, is indebted to two books by Thomas S. Kuhn, The Structure of Scientific Revolutions (1962) and The Copernican Revolution (1957); and to Professors Gibson Reaves and John Russell of the U.S.C. Dept. of Astronomy, for their criticisms.

This conception was simple to grasp, and (or one may read for "and", "because") it comported with, or "cohered with", so many other beliefs. As for the stars spinning around us, rather than our spinning under the mantle of the stars, to have held otherwise would have been to discredit both common sense (why did people who jumped straight into the air come down in the same place?) and the capacity of our senses (most importantly, the inner ear) accurately to report when we are spinning. As for man's being in the center of the system, to have held otherwise would have been a blow to man's psyche, for geocentrism was homocentrism was egocentrism. As for the circles and spheres, to have held otherwise would have been blasphemy, for spheres were perfect, even morally perfect, and gods, as perfect, would author only perfect products. Thus, the belief that was formed as to the structure of the universe was not a simple and direct report of photochemical activity at the back of the eye; it was a judgment infused with a whole host of beliefs about common sense, gods, the reliability of the inner ear, geometry, self-respect and much more.

As centuries passed, however, increasingly accurate observations and instrumentation introduced complications for the easy maintenance of this system. They showed that celestial bodies were deviating from the positions they should have had, if they were all moving in simple concentric circles about the earth, even to the extent of apparent reversals in direction. Of course, today we explain the deviations those astronomers were discovering by saying that the earth is not stationary and in the center of the universe, but is spinning about an axis (that is itself not stationary to a plane) and is, with the other planets, travelling about the sun in a nearly elliptical orbit. Early astronomers could have explained the deviations this way (and a few heretics did, at least to the extent of positing heliocentric orbits). But a wholesale acceptance of such a model would have torn the elaborate fabric of beliefs that had been woven around the geocentric cosmology; it would, at the very least, have called to question the authority of common sense, of the ancients, and of the church. Indeed, to some extent the whole idea of social order was modeled on the orderliness of the planetary system.

"The heavens themselves, the planets and this centre" [*i.e.*,
    the earth]
Observe degree, priority and place,
Insisture, course, proportion, season, form.
.   .   .
.   .   .   But when the planets
In evil mixture to disorder wander,
What plagues and what portents! what mutiny!
What raging of the sea! shaking of earth!
Commotion in the winds! frights, changes, horrors,
Divert and crack, rend and deracinate
The unity and married calm of states
Quite from their fixture!

SHAKESPEARE, TROILUS AND CRESSIDA, Act I, Sc. III. To minds which viewed political and social events as linked to the heavens, or even dictated by the positions of heavenly bodies, a tampering with cosmological beliefs was a tampering with man's laws, both in the broadest and the narrowest senses of the term.[10]

There were thus high costs to abandoning the basic tenets of the early two sphere model, or even calling the system to question; too many other beliefs would have to be called in to question with it. For centuries, therefore, astronomers worked out a less "costly" explanation of the deviant observations. The universe was indeed earth-centered and built upon circular motions, but only in a more complex way than had theretofore been realized: the paths of the planets about the earth were fundamentally perfect circles, but sometimes the circle served not as the path of the planet itself, but was a "deferent"—the locus of the center of a lesser circular orbit ("epicycle") on which the planet was actually travelling. In other words, the planets were not moving along ellipses, but were travelling (to the greater glory of God's mathematical capacities) along circles upon circles! Before one condemns the ancients for their ignorance, it is important to note that by modifying the original simple circular hypothesis in this way, so as to substitute a complex of epicycles on deferents, the astronomers were perfectly able to predict the direction of any planet consonant with their capacity to observe, *i.e.*, at least in this sense, the new system *worked*. As new and more refined observations showed "errors" in the contemporary model, another epicycle could always be added to keep the predictive capacity of the system in line.

It was against this background that Copernicus's DE REVOLUTIONIBUS ORBIUM CAELESTIUM was published in 1543. Copernicus, as we know, challenged the need to fill the sky with so much conceptual gadgetry. (Had Copernicus been familiar with the term "legal fictions", he might have spoken of "astronomical fictions"). He said that, in reality, the sun was in the center of the solar system (as some ancients had long before maintained) and that all the planets were revolving about it. He thus fathered a "revolution" in cosmological thought that was to be accomplished only after centuries of ridicule, inquisition (see the Abjuration of Galileo in section 4, *infra*), and burning at the stake.

When we look back now on this revolution, what does it mean?

The history of the overthrow of geocentrism provided a number of important intellectual lessons. One of its contributions is the suspicion of common sense that it will hopefully engender for cen-

---

10. An excellent discussion of the relationship between laws of nature and human laws is to be found in 2 Needham, Science and Civilization in Ancient China, ch. 18 (1956). Needham makes the point that while the word "astronomy" (from the Greek and Latin words for "star" and "law") has ordinarily been assumed to refer to the law of the stars in the sense of laws the *stars* had to obey, "the significance might be rather that of the laws which the stars gave to every man in fixing his fate," Vol. 2 at 535.

turies to come, owing to our shock, in retrospect, that so many people could have been so wrong so long.

But the more philosophical thinking that must follow in the wake of the Copernican revolution goes a step beyond musing over how many had missed the truth; it sees that we have to reconsider both how we come to judge truth and what truth means.   In what way, indeed, had Ptolemaic earth-centered astronomy been "false"? The geocentrists seem to have wasted energy, perhaps, in filling the sky with epicycles, but their theorizing was able to predict the observed positions of the planets as accurately as Copernicus's.   The model enabled early astronomers to predict eclipses, to measure the earth's circumference, and to make, as early as the second century B.C., remarkably accurate estimates of the sizes and distances of the sun and moon.   If a model, to be "true", must do more than this, exactly what must it do?   Indeed, have we replaced it now because of brute, contrary facts—or because of a mixture of facts and ideas about simplicity of description as an aesthetic desideratum of scientific theories?   To say Ptolemaic astronomy had always been false, because it was subsequently disconfirmed (or could be replaced by a simpler model) seems to entail abdicating the hope of realizing any "true" theories, for we are sobered enough now to recognize that all our theories are subject to disconfirmation in our future.[11]

One possible response to this dilemma is not to use the concept "true" at all.   Another alternative is to retain the concept with most of its connotations, but strip away the aspiration that some propositions can be "true" eternally and independently of our other propositions about the world that we use to confirm or to disconfirm them. The latter alternative embraces various forms of pragmatism, including the coherence theory of truth.   Its proponents may agree with the positivists that statements are meaningful only if they can be confirmed or disconfirmed, at least in theory, by sensible experience.   But unlike the positivists, they do not believe that the validation of the statement consists in simply holding that statement, by itself, up against some corresponding experience.   As we learn from the history of astronomy, when one observes the heavens, one's experience, in terms of what is happening at the back of one's eyes, can confirm quite a range of statements.   What we inevitably do in validating a statement—the coherence theorists point out—is to test the statement under review against the body of statements we have come to believe in at the time of the validation.   So viewed, no statement is true because of *an independent experience* but each new experience puts to test the truth of *a whole system of mutually supportive statements.* An impressive exposition of such a theory is provided by the contemporary logician, W. V. O. Quine, *infra,* who is willing to follow out the implications of coherence theory thinking to their extreme consequences, viz., that even the most seemingly immutable and simply "analytic" logical relations, such as the proposition of identity, are "true" only with respect to their usefulness in maintaining the bal-

11.   On the subject of confirmation and disconfirmation, see K. Popper, Conjecture and Refutations (1965).

ance of our beliefs, and are not immune from revision in the light of some possible (though nigh impossible to imagine) experience.

WILLARD VAN ORMAN QUINE

TWO DOGMAS OF EMPIRICISM *

Modern empiricism has been conditioned in large part by two dogmas. One is a belief in some fundamental cleavage between truths which are *analytic*, or grounded in meanings independently of matters of fact, and truths which are *synthetic*, or grounded in fact. The other dogma is *reductionism*: the belief that each meaningful statement is equivalent to some logical construct upon terms which refer to immediate experience. Both dogmas, I shall argue, are ill-founded. One effect of abandoning them is, as we shall see, a blurring of the supposed boundary between speculative metaphysics and natural science. Another effect is a shift toward pragmatism.

### 1.　*Background for Analyticity*

Kant's cleavage between analytic and synthetic truths was foreshadowed in Hume's distinction between relations of ideas and matters of fact, and in Leibniz's distinction between truths of reason and truths of fact. Leibniz spoke of the truths of reason as true in all possible worlds. Picturesqueness aside, this is to say that the truths of reason are those which could not possibly be false. In the same vein we hear analytic statements defined as statements whose denials are self-contradictory. But this definition has small explanatory value; for the notion of self-contradictoriness, in the quite broad sense needed for this definition of analyticity, stands in exactly the same need of clarification as does the notion of analyticity itself. The two notions are the two sides of a single dubious coin.

Kant conceived of an analytic statement as one that attributes to its subject no more than is already conceptually contained in the subject. This formulation has two shortcomings: it limits itself to statements of subject-predicate form, and it appeals to a notion of containment which is left at a metaphorical level. But Kant's intent, evident more from the use he makes of the notion of analyticity than from his definition of it, can be restated thus: a statement is analytic when it is true by virtue of meanings and independently of fact.
.　.　.
.　.　.　.

The most naive view of the relation [between a statement and the experiences which contribute to or detract from its confirmation] is that it is one of direct report. This is *radical reductionism*. Every meaningful statement is held to be translatable into a statement (true or false) about immediate experience. Radical reductionism, in one form or another, well antedates the verification theory of meaning ex-

* From From a Logical Point of View 20–21, 38–39, 41–46, (2d ed. rev. Harper Torchbooks 1961). With the permission of Philosophical Review, the President and Fellows of Harvard College, and Professor Quine.

plicity so called. Thus Locke and Hume held that every idea must either originate directly in sense experience or else be compounded of ideas thus originating. . . . More reasonably, and without yet exceeding the limits of what I have called radical reductionism, we may take full statements as our significant units—thus demanding that our statements as wholes be translatable into sense-datum language, but not that they be translatable term by term.

. . . .

Radical reductionism, conceived now with statements as units, set itself the task of specifying a sense-datum language and showing how to translate the rest of significant discourse, statement by statement, into it. Carnap embarked on this project in the *Aufbau*. [See Chapter 1, *supra*—Ed.]

. . . .

Carnap . . . in his later writings . . . abandoned all notion of the translatability of statements about the physical world into statements about immediate experience. Reductionism in its radical form has long ceased to figure in Carnap's philosophy.

But the dogma of reductionism has, in a subtler and more tenuous form, continued to influence the thought of empiricists. The notion lingers that to each statement, or each synthetic statement, there is associated a unique range of possible sensory events such that the occurrence of any of them would add to the likelihood of truth of the statement, and that there is associated also another unique range of possible sensory events whose occurrence would detract from that likelihood. This notion is of course implicit in the verification theory of meaning.

The dogma of reductionism survives in the supposition that each statement, taken in isolation from its fellows, can admit of confirmation or infirmation at all. My countersuggestion . . . is that our statements about the external world face the tribunal of sense experience not individually but only as a corporate body.

. . . .

The idea of defining a symbol in use was, as remarked, an advance over the impossible term-by-term empiricism of Locke and Hume. The statement, rather than the term, came with Frege to be recognized as the unit accountable to an empiricist critique. But what I am now urging is that even in taking the statement as unit we have drawn our grid too finely. The unit of empirical significance is the whole of science.

## 6. *Empiricism without the Dogmas*

The totality of our so-called knowledge or beliefs, from the most casual matters of geography and history to the profoundest laws of atomic physics or even of pure mathematics and logic, is a man-made fabric which impinges on experience only along the edges. Or, to change the figure, total science is like a field of force whose boundary conditions are experience. A conflict with experience at the periphery occasions readjustments in the interior of the field. Truth values have to be redistributed over some of our statements. Reëvaluation of some statements entails reëvaluation of others, because of their logical interconnections—the logical laws being in turn simply certain further statements of the system, certain further elements of the field. Having reëvaluated one statement we must reëvaluate some others, which may be statements logically connected with the first or may be the statements of logical connections themselves. But the total field is so underdetermined by its boundary conditions, experience, that there is much latitude of choice as to what statements to reëvaluate in the light of any single contrary experience. No particular experiences are linked with any particular statements in the interior of the field, except indirectly through considerations of equilibrium affecting the field as a whole.

If this view is right, it is misleading to speak of the empirical content of an individual statement—especially if it is a statement at all remote from the experiential periphery of the field. Furthermore it becomes folly to seek a boundary between synthetic statements, which hold contingently on experience, and analytic statements, which hold come what may. Any statement can be held true come what may, if we make drastic enough adjustments elsewhere in the system. Even a statement very close to the periphery can be held true in the face of recalcitrant experience by pleading hallucination or by amending certain statements of the kind called logical laws. Conversely, by the same token, no statement is immune to revision. Revision even of the logical law of the excluded middle has been proposed as a means of simplifying quantum mechanics; and what difference is there in principle between such a shift and the shift whereby Kepler superseded Ptolemy, or Einstein Newton, or Darwin Aristotle?

For vividness I have been speaking in terms of varying distances from a sensory periphery. Let me try now to clarify this notion without metaphor. Certain statements, though *about* physical objects and not sense experience, seem peculiarly germane to sense experience —and in a selective way: some statements to some experiences, others to others. Such statements, especially germane to particular experiences, I picture as near the periphery. But in this relation of "germaneness" I envisage nothing more than a loose association reflecting the relative likelihood, in practice, of our choosing one statement rather than another for revision in the event of recalcitrant experience. For example, we can imagine recalcitrant experiences to which we would surely be inclined to accommodate our system by reëvaluating just the statement that there are brick houses on Elm Street, together with related statements on the same topic. We can imagine other recalcitrant experiences to which we would be inclined to accommodate our system by reëvaluating just the statement that there are no centaurs, along with kindred statements. A recalcitrant experience can, I have urged, be accommodated by any of various alternative reëvaluations in various alternative quarters of the total system; but, in the cases which we are now imagining, our natural tendency to disturb the total system as little as possible would lead us to focus our revisions upon these specific statements concerning brick houses or centaurs. These statements are felt, therefore, to have a sharper empirical reference than highly theoretical statements of physics or logic or ontology.

The latter statements may be thought of as relatively centrally located within the total network, meaning merely that little preferential connection with any particular sense data obtrudes itself.

As an empiricist I continue to think of the conceptual scheme of science as a tool, ultimately, for predicting future experience in the light of past experience. Physical objects are conceptually imported into the situation as convenient intermediaries—not by definition in terms of experience, but simply as irreducible posits comparable, epistemologically, to the gods of Homer. For my part I do, qua lay physicist, believe in physical objects and not in Homer's gods; and I consider it a scientific error to believe otherwise. But in point of epistemological footing the physical objects and the gods differ only in degree and not in kind. Both sorts of entities enter our conception only as cultural posits. The myth of physical objects is epistemologically superior to most in that it has proved more efficacious than other myths as a device for working a manageable structure into the flux of experience.

Positing does not stop with macroscopic physical objects. Objects at the atomic level are posited to make the laws of macroscopic objects, and ultimately the laws of experience, simpler and more manageable; and we need not expect or demand full definition of atomic and subatomic entities in terms of macroscopic ones, any more than definition of macroscopic things in terms of sense data. Science is a continuation of common sense, and it continues the common-sense expedient of swelling ontology to simplify theory.

Physical objects, small and large, are not the only posits. Forces are another example; and indeed we are told nowadays that the boundary between energy and matter is obsolete. Moreover, the abstract entities which are the substance of mathematics—ultimately classes and classes of classes and so on up—are another posit in the same spirit. Epistemologically these are myths on the same footing with physical objects and gods, neither better nor worse except for differences in the degree to which they expedite our dealings with sense experiences.

The over-all algebra of rational and irrational numbers is underdetermined by the algebra of rational numbers, but is smoother and more convenient; and it includes the algebra of rational numbers as a jagged or gerrymandered part. Total science, mathematical and natural and human, is similarly but more extremely underdetermined by experience. The edge of the system must be kept squared with experience; the rest, with all its elaborate myths or fictions, has as its objective the simplicity of laws.

Ontological questions, under this view, are on a par with questions of natural science. Consider the question whether to countenance classes as entities. This, as I have argued elsewhere, is the question whether to quantify with respect to variables which take classes as values. Now Carnap has maintained that this is a question not of matters of fact but of choosing a convenient language form, a convenient conceptual scheme or framework for science. With this I agree, but only on the proviso that the same be conceded regarding scientific hypotheses generally. Carnap has recognized that he is able to preserve a double standard for ontological questions and scientific hypotheses only by assuming an absolute distinction between the analytic and the synthetic; and I need not say again that this is a distinction which I reject.

The issue over there being classes seems more a question of convenient conceptual scheme; the issue over there being centaurs, or brick houses on Elm Street, seems more a question of fact. But I have been urging that this difference is only one of degree, and that it turns upon our vaguely pragmatic inclination to adjust one strand of the fabric of science rather than another in accommodating some particular recalcitrant experience. Conservatism figures in such choices, and so does the quest for simplicity.

Carnap, Lewis, and others take a pragmatic stand on the question of choosing between language forms, scientific frameworks; but their pragmatism leaves off at the imagined boundary between the analytic and the synthetic. In repudiating such a boundary I espouse a more thorough pragmatism. Each man is given a scientific heritage plus a continuing barrage of sensory stimulation; and the considerations which guide him in warping his scientific heritage to fit his continuing sensory promptings are, where rational, pragmatic.

## Questions

1. Quine speaks of our field of force as engaged in a continual "conflict with experience at the periphery". What does he mean by this? How is it related to his view that our knowledge is always "underdetermined by experience"? Can you illustrate his statement that our knowledge is "underdetermined by experience" by the Copernican revolution?

2. What assumptions about the inflexibility of experience itself does Quine risk in speaking of "conflicts with experience" and of experience as "the boundary conditions" of the field? Is experience itself a "given"; or are our very perceptions of what is happening— even before they are articulated into statements of belief—influenced by the same forces that organize the force field? Refer to the readings in Chapter 4.

3. What is the significance, in Quine's model, of a statement being placed near the center of the field of force? What is the significance of its being placed towards the periphery? What does he mean, "any statement can be held true come what may, if we make drastic enough adjustments elsewhere in the system"? Think of a statement—any statement—and work out what adjustments, *e.g.*, trade-offs in beliefs as to the truth of other statements, must be made to hold the first statement true. Could not someone even place the statement, "there are centaurs" near the center of his field of force? What would the "costs" be?

4. Quine observes that a "conflict with experience" occasions "readjustments in the interior of the field." What ways are there in which "readjustments" would be accomplished? Quine specifies only the redistribution of truth values over some of our statements,

*i.e.*, to say some statements that we formerly held true are false, and vice-versa. What other "readjustments" could be made?

5. Note that Quine is addressing himself to the organization of *statements*, and he seems to assume, as indicated in question 4, that each statement is held either true or false. How adequate a representation of mental functioning can be yielded on these assumptions? How much of one's world-view can be explained in terms of statements held true or false and how much in terms of probabilities, presumptions and unverbalized attitudes? (Are these attitudes part of what Quine refers to, in passing, as "conditions of equilibrium affecting the field as a whole"?) Is it possible that our minds are capable of entertaining a range of beliefs which we do not hold either true or false in any meaningful way, but entertain in a sort of limbo in between? See L. FESTINGER, A THEORY OF COGNITIVE DISSONANCE (1957). Is it clear when statements are contradicting one another, rather than cohering with one another?

6. Do human beings have one field of force which they bring to bear on all their judgments in life, irrespective of their role; or is it possible that each human being, as he shifts roles, somewhat shifts the organization of statements in his field as a function of the office that he is engaged in? For example, is it possible that a human being acting in the capacity of a judge can through conscious effort—or cultural conditioning—somewhat restructure the organization of beliefs he brings, *qua* citizen, to the polling booth? What would such a reorganization look like, in terms of which beliefs would a man, say, as judge, move closer to the center, and which beliefs closer to the periphery? Are there beliefs which could be held "true" in some roles, but neither true nor false in others?

7. Quine's position can be illustrated with an anecdote from the annals of the Los Angeles County Museum of Science and Industry. The Museum maintains an exhibit to illustrate the "law" of probability. The exhibit consists of a glass aquarium, the lower half divided by glass separators into nine equal-sized compartments. The upper half is a multi-layered grid of wires that form an intricate crisscrossing above the compartments. On top of all this, at the very center of the exhibit, is a hole through which small, rubber balls are dropped in rapid succession. As each ball drops, it falls directly on the top median cross-wire and bounces, either slightly to the right or slightly to the left. The path the ball then takes depends upon which cross-wires it proceeds to strike thereafter, and from what angle, as it works its ways down through the wires towards ultimate lodging in one of the glass subdivisions at the bottom. Now, if the "law" of probability is "working," the piles of balls that are being amassed at the bottom of the glass subdivisions should have the configuration of a bell curve. That is, more balls will fall into the central compartment, directly below the ejection hole, than in any other subdivision. The least number will fall in the two subdivisions at the extreme ends, since the bouncy path that a ball must take to find its way to the extremes is a less probable route than the paths relatively straight down into the more central compartments.

One day a year or so ago, one of the authors, on a trip through the Museum, discovered that the configuration that was developing was by only the broadest stretch of the imagination a facsimile of a bell curve. The compartment at one end had gathered considerably more balls than the compartment at the other end. The "law of probability" was being violated, at least in central Los Angeles, and the author, in the throes of civic responsibility, immediately reported the crisis to those in whose jurisdiction the transgression was occurring: the Museum police. He gratuitously ventured a few predictions, with illustrations, as to the dire consequences on civil government if his fears were correct. (As for some of the consequences of the law of probability breaking down, see Robert M. Coates, *The Law* The New Yorker (1947)). The reaction of the Museum police can fairly be described as uneasy, but more about the author's motives than about the possibility that instead of allocating itself "evenly" about the freeway system, that afternoon's rush hour traffic was as likely as not going to turn every bit of itself loose on the Harbor Freeway, South—as improbable as that configuration had theretofore seemed. The officers' response was a sentiment that may be as near the "center" of modern man's force field as the law of probability: go back to the exhibit and keep watching it, it will all work out right in the long run, just give it more time.[12] The author returned to the exhibit. No change: the east end of the exhibit was clearly losing out to the west end. The police, reassembled now at the scene by the insistent author, did not opt to condemn our joint eyesights, as they might have (it would have been too improbable that we should all lose our vision at once, and in the same manner—and think of how serious a trade-off that would be in terms of repercussions throughout the field). They hypothesized, with a confidence that could not be rippled, the following theories, as operating jointly and severally: the balls were not perfectly round; the wires were never installed quite perfectly; the wires had stretched; we had to give it more time, and it would eventually even out. All of these hypotheses would, if we follow the analysis of Quine, have occasioned less "readjustments" in the prevailing "force field" of knowledge than the abandonment of the law of probability. The author reported what he had observed to his students, who responded with the policemen's skepticism; but when a group was assembled at the Museum for an on-site inspection, it was discovered that the authorities had, in the interim, shut the exhibit down. If it wasn't proving the law of probability, it had to be wrong!

So much for the illustration. But it does not answer a question that Quine, as logician, does not deal with: of all the propositions that *could* be relatively impregnable to the assault of experience, how does one go about selecting some to dwell in the security of the center of his "field of force," banishing others to live a hand-to-mouth existence at the rim? How can we explain the mechanism that is passed over by the metaphor, "conditions of equilibrium"? At that point of inquiry, logical analysis must yield jurisdiction to psychology, psychoanalysis or some allied discipline. Can a comprehensive epistemology

12. See Sullivan, The End of the "Long Run," Centennial Review of Arts and Sciences (Summer 1960), Chapter 19 *infra.*

be built on logic alone?   (See the Note, *The Freudian Revolution, infra*, p. 342).

## BRAND BLANSHARD

### THE TESTS OF TRUTH *

.  .  .  When we are thinking about historical facts, or events reported in the newspapers, or things actually seen and heard, it seems to the plain man obvious that our thought could be tested only by correspondence with fact.  But if we were to take this same man by the hand, lead him off to another room in the gallery of knowledge, and set him down before a law of logic or a mathematical proof, he would probably desert his former standard without misgiving.  These insights do not need comparison with fact; they are self-evident as they stand.  If he had met these first, instead of judgements about things and events, he would probably have laid it down with confidence that the test was a certain clearness and convincingness apparent at once to anyone who could grasp the truth at all.  But then disillusionment would again have overtaken him when he began to move from one region to another.  For just as correspondence deserts us when we move from facts to abstractions, so self-evidence deserts us when we move back again from abstractions to facts.  Where is the self-evidence in the judgement that it rained yesterday in Guatemala?

On the face of it common sense is without any consistent standard. It keeps swinging back and forth between two different standards, correspondence for matters of fact and self-evidence for the abstract and formal.  But we hold that this oscillation and inconsistency are superficial only.  We hold that these two standards are not so far apart as they seem and that both resolve themselves on analysis into a single standard, coherence.  The way to establish this is to show that even in matters of fact it is coherence rather than correspondence that we actually use, and that even in regions of the abstractest formality it is once more coherence rather than self-evidence that is in the end our court of appeal.  We shall not argue that these types of judgment cover between them the whole of knowledge, though many philosophers would say they do.  It is enough to point out that they are the kinds traditionally placed at the poles of knowledge.  If types so far apart can be shown to depend on a single criterion, it is unlikely that any third type will come forward to challenge its universality. We shall open the case for coherence, then, by considering the two types of judgment that seem to demand most obviously another standard.

Take first the judgment of fact. "Burr killed Hamilton in a duel". "That is a cardinal on the branch yonder."  To the plain man it seems obvious that the test of such judgments is whether they correspond with fact.  But as regards the first of them, there is a simple distinction which, if perceived, would shake his confidence.  When he re-

* From 2 The Nature of Thought 225–28,        & Unwin Ltd. 1939).  With permission
237–38, 244–46, 292–93, 264–66, 260,        of George Allen & Unwin Ltd.
268–69 (in that order) (George Allen

flects on the judgment, "Burr killed Hamilton in a duel", he sees, or
thinks he sees, that its truth *means* correspondence; and it is natural
to say that if truth means this, then it must also be tested by this. But
the two questions are distinct, and in saying that the test here is correspondence, he is pretty clearly confusing the test of truth with its
meaning. For the slightest consideration will show that the use of
correspondence as a test is here out of the question; one of the terms
that are to correspond is irrecoverably gone. There is no person living who could have witnessed the famous duel; and even if there were,
he could not, through correspondence merely, validate his memories.
Our test in such cases must clearly be found elsewhere. And the
more we reflect, the plainer it becomes that this test is the way our
judgment is implicated with a host of further judgments that we are
compelled to make when we investigate. If this belief about Hamilton
is true, then a thousand references in newspapers, magazines, and
books, and almost endless facts about the fortunes of Hamilton's family, about the later life of Burr, and about American constitutional
history, fall into place in a consistent picture. If it is false, then the
most credible journalists, historians and statesmen, generation after
generation, may be so deluded about events that happen before the
eyes of a nation that no single historical fact is any longer above suspicion. If evidence of this weight is to be rejected, then in consistency
we must go on to reject almost every hint that takes us beyond immediate perception. And intellectually speaking, that would pull our
house about our heads. What really tests the judgement is the extent
of our accepted world that is implicated with it and would be carried
down with it if it fell. And that is the test of coherence.

"But in any such judgement", it may be replied, "the value of
correspondence is seen in a false light. *Of course* it cannot be used in
those special cases where one of the terms has vanished. But that
does not disqualify it where it *is* applicable nor does it show that any
other test can really supplant it where it is not. Indeed, in an instance
like this, where correspondence cannot be applied, we see that our
judgement is incapable of proof altogether, by coherence or anything
else; every judgement of historical fact must retain to the end a touch
of uncertainty. It must do so for the reason that it is beyond reach
of the one thing that could establish it, namely, that perception of the
event itself which would make appeal to correspondence possible. On
the other hand, when we turn to the judgements where appeal to correspondence *is* possible, we find that it is always resorted to, and that
in such cases uncertainty is banished. Take the judgment, 'That bird
is a cardinal.' . . ." [Blanshard's analysis of this statement appears above at pp. 316 *ff.*]

. . . .

We have been considering the correspondence test in the region
of its greatest strength, namely, in judgements where the natural appeal is to perception. If it fails here, it will hardly succeed where the
reference to sensible fact is remote or absent. A few judgements
of this kind have been given already; let us cite two or three more;
they will suggest how much easier our case would have been if we
had not discussed the matter on ground where correspondence is at

its strongest. "I ought to pay my just debts"; "between any two points on a line an intermediate point may be inserted"; "if I had served my God as diligently as I have done the king, He would not have given me over in my grey hairs". How would one go about it to apply correspondence in such cases? Even its initial plausibility has here vanished.

But it is time to turn to the second main rival of coherence. Just as it seems at first obvious that statements about perceivable things are to be verified by correspondence, so it seems obvious that such statements as "2 + 2 = 4" and "a proposition cannot at once be true and false" are to be tested by their self-evidence. To search for evidence outside them implies that they fall short of being clear and certain as they are, whereas they seem to possess already the greatest clearness and certainty of which any judgement is incapable [sic]. To try to prove a proposition when the proof is no more certain than the proposition itself and probably far less so, would appear to be idle or stupid.

An enormous number of such "truths" have at various times been taken as self-evident. Among these are propositions about conduct, such as "it is my duty to produce the greater good rather than the less"; propositions about existence, such as "I am"; propositions about quantity, such as "things equal to the same thing are equal to each other"; spatial propositions, such as "two straight lines cannot enclose a space"; temporal propositions, such as "what is before A is before all that is contemporary with A"; laws of logic, such as "$x$ must be either A or not-A". These and great numbers of others from the most diverse fields of knowledge have been put forward as absolutely certain "within their own four corners". But this very profusion of self-evident truths gives rise to a suspicion which many writers have thought enough in itself to annul their claims.

. . . . . .

. . . . Ask the plain man how he knows that a straight line is the shortest line between two points or, what seems to him equally axiomatic, that 2 + 2 = 4, and he will probably answer that such things wear their truth on their face. But if this were challenged, would he not naturally say something like this: "So you doubt, do you, that a straight line is the shortest line? But you can't really live up to such a doubt. If a straight line isn't shortest, why do you cut across a field? Why are roads built straight? For that matter, is there anything we have been taught to believe about space and motion that wouldn't have to be given up if we gave up belief in the axiom? As for the 2 + 2 example, it is really the same thing again. Try making the sum anything but four, and see where it takes you. If 2 + 2 were 5, 1 + 1 would not be 2, and then 1 would not be 1; in fact not a single number, or relation between numbers, would remain what it is; all arithmetic would go." This is the sort of defense, I think, that the plain man would offer; at any rate he would recognize it as reasonable if offered by someone else. And that means that his certainty does not rest on self-evidence merely. He is appealing to the coherence of his proposition with an enormous mass of others which he sees must stand or fall with it. Perhaps it will be replied that certainty may rest partly on self-evidence and partly on coherence also. But consider what this implies. If a proposition is fully self-evident, it is completely certain as it stands, and to say that such certainty can be added to is to contradict oneself. It follows that if a proposition is really self-evident to the plain man, then when he goes on to show that its untruth would destroy all our views about space and motion, this insight adds nothing whatever to the certainty he has already. Can we accept that? I do not think we can. The insight that a proposition has the support of an entire science, so that it cannot be rejected without rejecting the science with it, does surely increase its certainty. But if it were fully certain already, this would be impossible. Its certainty, therefore, does not rest on self-evidence alone.

Indeed it is clear on reflection not only that the certainty of these axiomatic propositions is bound up with a system which includes them but that the same is true of their meaning. " 'A straight line is the shortest distance between two points' is true of Euclidean space, i.e., within a system defining Euclidean geometry, but may be false of certain non-Euclidean spaces. *The very meaning of 'straight', 'line', 'short', and 'point', is a function of the system"*. . . .

We add only one more point about axioms. Their "self-evidence" varies from case to case, and it is instructive to consider whether this is really a variation in self-evidence or in something else on which the seeming self-evidence depends. Mr. Russell writes: "Self-evidence has degrees: it is not a quality which is simply present or absent, but a quality which may be more or less present, in gradations ranging from absolute certainty down to an almost imperceptible faintness". If we consider at random a number of propositions that have been accepted as self-evident, we do seem to find these gradations. "The sun is rising"; "the Venus de Milo is a more perfect work of art than the Laocöon"; "ex nihilo nihil fit"; "cruelty is wrong"; "two parallel lines cannot enclose a space"; "a proposition cannot be both true and false". These vary widely in certainty. The judgement about the sun, taken in earlier times as self-evident, is now rejected flatly; the judgement about the statues would be made, one suspects with great uncertainty; the other would probably all be accepted. But here again I do not think their certainty would be rated equal; it may be hazarded that most people would regard this as gradually increasing and as reaching a maximum at the end in the law of contradiction.

. . . .

## COHERENCE AS THE NATURE OF TRUTH

. . . .

Coherence means more than consistency. It means not only that the various constituents entering into the system of truth are compatible with each other, but also that they necessitate each other. The system assumed is a system ideally perfect, for nothing less than this would satisfy intelligence as stable beyond rectification. In such a system there would be no loose ends. Difference anywhere would be reflected in difference everywhere.

Now it has been held that this ideal is merely a cloud-castle, that it can never be made to embrace the facts of our actual disorderly

world. There are many who would freely admit that nothing exists
or occurs out of relation to *some* other things, but would regard the
view that everything is related by necessity to *everything* else as
demonstrably false. If the fact is that Bishop Stubbs died in his bed,
this surely might be false without everything else being false that is
now accepted as true.

Now it is obvious that we cannot show in *detail* that a difference
anywhere in the system of truth must be reflected everywhere; we do
not know enough, nor is it likely we ever shall. But we can do something else that is as near to this as can be reasonably asked. We can
show that in the system of truth, *so far as reflected in our knowledge,*
such interconnection holds, and that the denial of an apparently isolated judgement does in fact have implications for every other. The
argument is as follows: When I say that Bishop Stubbs died in his
bed, or indeed when I say anything, I always do so on evidence. This
evidence may be hard or easy to bring to light, but it is there invariably; I never simply discharge judgments into the air with no ground
or warrant at all. And by the rules of hypothetical argument, to admit
the falsity of a judgement is to throw doubt upon its ground. Indeed
it is to do more. It is to throw doubt, if I am consistent, upon *all* evidence of this kind and degree. Now the evidence on which it is believed that Bishop Stubbs died a natural death is of the kind and
degree that would be accepted without hesitation by any historian or
scientist. It is the sort of evidence on which science and history generally rest. Hence if I deny this proposition, and thus call in question
the value of this sort of evidence, I must in consistency call in question
most science and history also. And that would shatter my world of
knowledge. Thus the truth about Bishop Stubbs is anything but isolated. However unimportant practically, it is so entangled with my system of beliefs that its denial would send repercussions throughout the
whole.

.  .  .  .

.  .  . To be sure, no fully satisfactory definition [of coherence]
can be given; and as Dr. Ewing says, "it is wrong to tie down the advocates of the coherence theory to a precise definition. What they
are doing is to describe an ideal that has never yet been completely
clarified but is none the less immanent in all our thinking. Certainly
this ideal goes far beyond mere consistency. Fully coherent knowledge would be knowledge in which every judgement entailed, and was
entailed by, the rest of the system. Probably we never find in fact
a system where there is so much of interdependence. What it means
may be clearer if we take a number of familiar systems and arrange
them in a series tending to such coherence as a limit. At the bottom
would be a junk-heap, where we could know every item but one and
still be without any clue as to what that remaining item was. Above
this would come a stonepile, for here you could at least infer that what
you would find next would be a stone. A machine would be higher
again, since from the remaining parts one could deduce not only the
general character of a missing part, but also its special form and function. This is a high degree of coherence, but it is very far short of
the highest. You could remove the engine from a motor-car while

leaving the other parts intact, and replace it with any one of thousands
of other engines, but the thought of such an interchange among human
heads or hearts shows at once that the interdependence in a machine
is far below that of the body. Do we find then inorganic bodies the
highest conceivable coherence? Clearly not. Though a human hand,
as Aristotle said, would hardly be a hand when detached from the
body, still it would be something definite enough; and we can conceive systems in which even this something would be gone. Abstract
a number from the number series and it would be a mere unrecog-
nizable $x$; similarly, the very thought of a straight line involves the
thought of the Euclidean space in which it falls. It is perhaps in such
systems as Euclidean geometry that we get the most perfect examples
of coherence that have been constructed. If any proposition were lacking, it could be supplied from the rest; if any were altered, the repercussions would be felt through the length and breadth of the system.
Yet even such a system as this falls short of ideal system. Its postulates are unproved; they are independent of each other, in the sense
that none of them could be derived from any other or even from all the
others together; its clear necessity is bought by an abstractness so extreme as to have left out nearly everything that belongs to the character of actual things. A completely satisfactory system would have
none of these defects. No proposition would be arbitrary, every proposition would be entailed by the others jointly and even singly, no proposition would stand outside the system. The integration would be so
complete that no part could be seen for what it was without seeing its
relation to the whole, and the whole itself could be understood only
through the contribution of every part.

.  .  .  .

It [was] contended in the last chapter that coherence is in the
end our sole criterion of truth. We have now to face the question
whether it also gives us the nature of truth. We should be clear at
the beginning that these are different questions, and that one may reject coherence as the definition of truth while accepting it as the test.
It is conceivable that one thing should be an accurate index of another
and still be extremely different from it.  .  .  .

.  .  .  .

.  .  . [T]he adherents of correspondence sometimes insist that
correspondence shall be its own test. But  .  .  .  [i]f truth does
consist in correspondence, no test can be sufficient. For in order to
know that experience corresponds to fact, we must be able to get at
the fact, unadulterated with idea, and compare the two sides with each
other. And we have seen in the last chapter that such fact is not
accessible. When we try to lay hold of it, what we find in our hands
is a judgement which is obviously not itself the indubitable fact we are
seeking, and which must be checked by some fact beyond it. To this
process there is no end. And even if we did get at the fact directly,
rather than through the veil of our ideas, that would be no less fatal to
correspondence. This direct seizure of fact presumably gives us truth,
but since that truth no longer consists in correspondence of idea with
fact, the main theory has been abandoned. In short, if we can know
fact only through the medium of our own ideas, the original forever

eludes us; if we can get at the facts directly, we have knowledge whose truth is not correspondence. The theory is forced to choose between scepticism and self-contradiction.

Thus the attempt to combine coherence as the test of truth with correspondence as the nature of truth will not pass muster by its own test. The result is *in*coherence. We believe that an application of the test to other theories of truth would lead to a like result. The argument is: assume coherence as the test, and you will be driven by the incoherence of your alternatives to the conclusion that it is also the nature of truth.

## QUESTIONS

1. To the extent the coherence theorists' description of how we make judgments is correct, what does it say for the possibility of a "pure" theory of law? Under their analysis, is it possible to bring to bear on a decision only a certain set of beliefs ("the law") and exclude beliefs as to what ought to be?

2. Under the coherence theory, is it possible that different people will be able to construct different "fields" (in Quine's metaphor), so that the same statement deemed "true" by some people will be deemed "false" by others? If so, how will they be able to resolve their differences? Can this dilemma be resolved by saying that an individual statement is not the unit to be spoken of as "true" or "false", but rather the whole system of our beliefs? Cannot two different persons work up "coherent" but different systems of belief even on the same experience? Can a single person work up two or more different, but coherent systems?

3. Blanshard observes that "the denial of an apparently isolated judgment [has] implications for every other." Can we judge whether he is right or wrong in this unless we have a definition of "implications"? Would you agree with him if "implications" were equivalent to "affects each person's assessment of the probability of each statement to which he has assigned (or will thereafter assign) a probability"? In the *Voelker* case, above, does the belief that the car's ignition switch was off, shift, however infinitesimally, the probability of every other statement about the case? Does it shift the probability that $2 + 2 = 4$? Do not the coherence theorists have an obligation to explain "cohere" (or "implications" or "germaneness"), much as the pragmatists have an obligation difficulty to define "work" (or "frustrate")? Is not part of the difficulty the fact that these terms—like "germaneness" and "implications"—cannot be defined by reference to a vocabulary of abstract *logic* alone, but take us rather inevitably into the realm of *psycho*logic?

*FRANCIS BACON*

## NOVUM ORGANUM *

### xlv

The human understanding is of its own nature prone to suppose the existence of more order and regularity in the world than it finds. And though there be many things in nature which are singular and unmatched, yet it devises for them parallels and conjugates and relatives which do not exist. Hence the fiction that all celestial bodies move in perfect circles; spirals and dragons being (except in name) utterly rejected. . . .

### xlvi

The human understanding when it has once adopted an opinion (either as being the received opinion or as being agreeable to itself) draws all things else to support and agree with it. And though there be a greater number and weight of instances to be found on the other side, yet these it either neglects and despises, or else by some distinction sets aside and rejects; in order that by this great and pernicious predetermination the authority of its former conclusions may remain inviolate. And therefore it was a good answer that was made by one who when they showed him hanging in a temple a picture of those who had paid their vows as having escaped shipwreck, and would have him say whether he did not now acknowledge the power of the gods—"Aye," asked he again, "but where are they painted that were drowned after their vows?" And such is the way of all superstition, whether in astrology, dreams, omens, divine judgments, or the like; wherein men having a delight in such vanities, mark the events where they are fulfilled, but where they fail, though this happen much oftener, neglect and pass them by. But with far more subtlety does this mischief insinuate itself into philosophy and the sciences; in which the first conclusion colors and brings into conformity with itself all that come after, though far sounder and better. Besides, independently of that delight and vanity which I have described, it is the peculiar and perpetual error of the human intellect to be more moved and excited by affirmatives than by negatives; whereas it ought properly to hold itself indifferently disposed towards both alike. Indeed in the establishment of any true axiom, the negative instance is the more forcible of the two.

### xlvii

The human understanding is moved by those things most which strike and enter the mind simultaneously and suddenly, and so fill the imagination; and then it feigns and supposes all other things to be somehow, though it cannot see how, similar to those few things by which it is surrounded. But for that going to and fro to remote

---

* From Book I (1620), at 71–72, 73–74   (George Routledge & Sons, London
   of the Ellis and Spedding transl.   (undated)).

and heterogeneous instances, by which axioms are tried as in the fire, the intellect is altogether slow and unfit, unless it be forced thereto by severe laws and overruling authority.

## QUESTIONS

In what ways is Bacon a coherence theorist? What does be mean that, "the human understanding is of its own nature prone to suppose the existence of more order and regularity in the world than it finds"? How much does the human brain have a species-specific "nature" and how much are the mind's efforts subject to the molding force of social institutions? Is it obvious what sorts of organizations of ideas display "order and regularity"? Or are these notions subject to the forces that go into the making of the mind?

In what ways can Bacon be called a coherence theorist? What does he mean that, "the human understanding is of its own nature prone to suppose the existence of more order and regularity in the world than it finds"? How much does the human brain have a given "nature" that makes it so prone and how much are the mind's efforts a result of the molding force of social institutions?

Consider, in regard to the coherence theory, this passage from the beginning of Sherwood Anderson's WINESBURG, OHIO (1919)

> [I]n the beginning when the world was young there were a great many thoughts but no such things as a truth. Man made the truths himself and each truth was a composite of a great many vague thoughts. All about in the world were the truths and they were all beautiful.
>
>   .   .   .   .
>
> And then the people came along. Each as he appeared snatched up one of the truths and some who were quite strong snatched up a dozen of them.
>
> It was the truths that made the people grotesques. The old man had quite an elaborate theory concerning the matter. It was his notion that the moment one of the people took one of the truths to himself, called it his truth, and tried to live his life by it, he became a grotesque and the truth he embraced became a falsehood.

*GUY DE MAUPASSANT*

## OF "THE NOVEL" *

  .   .   .   I conclude that the higher order of Realists should rather call themselves Illusionists.

How childish it is, indeed, to believe in this reality, since to each of us the truth is in his own mind, his own organs! Our own eyes and ears, taste and smell, create as many different truths as there

---

\* From the Introduction to Pierre et Jean (Clara Dell, transl. P. F. Collier & Son 1902).

are human beings on earth.   And our brains, duly and differently
informed by those organs, apprehend, analyze, and decide as differently as if each of us were a being of an alien race.   Each of us, then,
has simply his own illusion of the world—poetical, sentimental, cheer-
ful, melancholy, foul, or gloomy, according to his nature.   And the
writer has no other mission than faithfully to reproduce this illusion,
with all the elaborations of art which he may have learned and have
at his command.   The illusion of beauty—which is merely a conventional term invented by man!   The illusion of ugliness—which is
a matter of varying opinion!   The illusion of truth—never immutable!   The illusion of depravity—which fascinates so many minds!
All the great artists are those who can make other men see their
own particular illusion.

## Questions

From which of the theories of "truth" does de Maupassant receive strongest support?   Does the belief that "there are as many
different truths as there are human beings on earth" relieve the individual of trying to determine which statements—or organization
of statements—are "more true" than (or in some other sense preferable to) others?   Or is de Maupassant suggesting that there are
no standards by reference to which one "illusion" can be deemed superior to any other?

## Note: The Freudian Revolution

The contours of the Freudian revolution are at least as hard
to define, its implications at least as hard to digest in the juices of
common sense, as were those of the Copernican revolution.   But the
present subject matter demands that at least the following remarks
be ventured.

As with Copernicus's revolution, Freud's work was set in motion
by an uneasy awareness of phenomena that contemporary models
explained, if at all, only in the most cumbersome ways.   In the case
of Copernicus's work, the anomalous phenomena included retrograde
motion of the planets;  in the case of Freud's, the analogous role
was played by dreams, "mistakes" (such as "slips of the tongue")
and the behavior of the insane.   Earlier scientific investigators had
been able to work these observations into models that presupposed
the devil, but these were no longer satisfactory as christianity and
science parted ways.   Through his analyses of many patients, as well
as of himself, Freud was able to fill the void by working these phenomena into a model of human nature that had shattering implications
for theretofore prevailing concepts of knowledge and of culture.   In
the fantasies of "madmen" and neurotics, Freud discovered recurrent
patterns too regular to dismiss as happenstance;  and these patterns,
moreover, incredibly, bore striking resemblance to patterns in the
dreams, the "Freudian slips," the inspirations of wit and art, of the
"sane."   The theory that Freud advanced was that these unassociated
mental phenomena were not chance, *i. e.*, meaningless, happenings.
We could assign to them a "cause" and fit them into a broader system
of understanding if we regarded them as emissary creatures somehow

sent to the surface of consciousness from the depths of a vast, turbulent, unmapped sea of our mental lives. The distinction between those we deemed sane and those we deemed insane was a distinction that could be made only at the surface, some of us being better able to oil down the turbulence more effectively than others; in the depths, we were all caught up in the same currents. And it was at the lowest levels that were flowing, unseen, the wishes and needs that had the greatest influences on our lives. How could we be so unaware of them? Could we ever bring them to the surface, to look at them and deal with them head on? Freud's answer, the key to understanding his science, is based upon the concept of repression.

As posits with which to construct a model that would explain the mechanics of repression and human behavior, Freud developed the concepts, *id, ego* and *super-ego*. This hypostatization of "parts" of the psyche sounds metaphysical, indeed (and much like the concepts one finds at the early stage of any science). But it is no more odd than to speak of a projectile's path as being the product of the "forces" of gravity, magnetic "fields" and the "energy" that was imparted to it on thrust.

Of the three "parts" of this model, the id was, in Freud's words, "the dark inaccessible part of the personality," basically a pool of energies of the most primary instinctual drives which strove unreservedly to bring about the immediate satisfaction of their needs according to the dictates of the "pleasure principle." Its jurisdiction contained no element of concern as to implications—"practical" or "moral." It was immune to modification in the face of time and experience, and was untouched by the laws of logic. The ego, which was usually said by Freud to have developed "out of" the id, in a manner that is explored more fully below, is primarily an agency of reconciliation. If unmediated, the uninhibited, anxietyless, uninformed drives of the id would send the body off on the first impulse of its whims into certain quick destruction: the id would not know about, sense, or be concerned with the dangerous consequences of steep cliff or freezing climate. As a remedy, a large part of the ego's function is in the service of adjusting the id to the "reality" of the world, and of adjusting the "reality" of the world to the adjusted aims of the id. In the former capacity, the id is conceived as having jurisdiction over the perceptual apparatus, gathering and collating, through the nervous system, information about the location, temperature, noises, etc. of the outer world. By development of the higher mental functions, this information is coordinated so that desires of the id that are unrealizable according to the ego's guiding principles are either sent back to the id (repression) and/or deflected towards other goals that are more "sensible" ("sublimation").[13] The desires for immediate satisfactions are transformed into desires for delayed, planned, "sensible" satisfactions; desires for play are transformed into desires for work; the tendency towards receptivity is programmed into a tendency toward productivity. With the id's functioning having

---

13. For a modification of this image, see H. Fingarette, The Self in Transformation (1963), especially at ch. 1.

been moderated in this way by the ego to the needs of reality, the ego then, in its capacity to command muscular activity, directs the body to do what it can to realize the moderated goals.

In the development of the species, the ego comes to be charged not only with staving off the twin dangers of external world and "senseless" id, but with mediating as well the severe demands of the third "part" of the psyche, the super-ego. In Freud's words,

> The part which is later taken on by the super-ego is played to begin with by an external power, by parental authority. Parental influence governs the child by offering proofs of love and by threatening punishments which are signs to the child of loss of love and are bound to be feared on their own account.

But Freud's investigations, especially observations of patients with delusions of being observed, led him to the theory that a more indirect mechanism was later brought into play in the interest of inducing anxiety in the child, and this "special agency," as he called it, was deemed the superego. The establishment of the superego was related by Freud to the strength of the Oedipus complex and the biological fact that the infant human's period of dependence on his parents is, in the total animal kingdom, peculiarly long relative to life span. Freud hypothesized that the combination of an extended period of repressing agressiveness within the family bonds, and a concomitant guilt, resulted in the child's introjecting the potential retaliation of the parent; that is, the child internalizes the anticipated punishment, directing it towards his own ego. Once this mechanism is established, the superego develops a separate existence from the ego, in the form of what is commonly called "conscience," and "the tensions between the harsh super-ego and the ego that is subjected to it, is called by us the sense of guilt." Once endowed with its separate existence, the superego becomes the agency to encrust upon the developing infant's mental processes the bulk of the ancient taboos and repressions of the culture, for in internalizing *his* parents' anxieties, to some extent he internalizes those of their parents, which had been, in turn, internalized in them.

What light does Freud throw on the problems of fact, reality and truth?

First, Freud changed dramatically the typical pre-Freudian picture of the relationship between the pursuit of knowledge and man's supposed "true essence." Philosophy's smug picture of man as the inherently contemplative animal, methodically leaving no stone unturned in the quest for knowledge, falls on both counts. Man is not inherently a reflective animal. And if there is a methodology to our quest for knowledge, it is one that systematically leaves certain stones unturned.

The second implication Freud's analysis holds for epistemology has to do with the views we associate with Kant. The pre-Kantian British empiricist tradition had viewed the mind as a passive receptor of knowledge. (See the selection from Locke in Chapter 4). Kant, by contrast, had asserted that our knowledge was limited by the categories of understanding which the mind was fitted out to handle; we could never know reality except *through* the mind, and thus we never could come to know pure reality, but only a mix of reality and mind. Kant thereby turned the focus of knowledge inwards, away from what was "out there" and towards mental processes—the forms of knowledge by which the mind was exercising its stamp on "the world as it really (?) is." The Freudians (and, indeed, all the schools of psychology and sociology which Freud influenced) can be viewed as carrying on this Kantian tradition of studying the active role of the mind in constituting knowledge. But while Kant had assumed that our knowledge of knowledge could not push beyond a set of relatively static "forms of understanding" that were "given" to the mind's structure, Freud's analysis of the psyche, with its maelstrom of dynamic interactions, with its belief in ontogenetic and phylogenetic development of our most basic ideas, held forth the promise of uncovering deeper insights into how we form beliefs than Kant could foresee. Where Kant felt he had to abandon to the realm of the *a priori* the tendency of the mind to posit objects and to connect events according to the "law" of causality, Freud showed that these tendencies might be explained in terms of the dynamics of ego and id. Even the "modes of representation" that Kant considered to be the most futile to try to analyze, those of space and time, might, to Freudians, be shown to be the scars of instinctual renunciation. Was there not a part of our minds—the id—that was wholly untouched by notions of time?

This brings us to a third consequence of Freud's work for the theory of knowledge: its reinforcement and its elaboration of the coherence theory of truth. Freud supports the view that, at its roots, knowledge is not the rude inventorying of things and relations that stock the world outside our minds. It is the assemblage of theories that can strongly influence the forces of the mind. Certain ideas the mind systematically screens from itself at the perceptual level. Others, admitted to the mind, are actively repressed. And organizing this whole phantasmagoria of thought is not, most centrally, propositions about logic, but propositions about self and self-image, about sexual desires and the fear of death. To revert to our illustration of Quine's position, to understand why someone will lodge more faith in the laws of probability than in the probability exhibit's carpenter (supra pp. 331 *ff.*) demands that we understand how we live—what is behind our dancing, crying, loving, praying, working, and playing. Under this analysis, the "equilibrium conditions" of each man's world view express the resolution of the clash between his desires and the social and personal forces that are working to manipulate them and bring them under control.

## Section Four: "Facts", "Law" and the Organization of Society

### Introductory Note

As Quine indicates (section 3, above) among the many beliefs that a human being holds "true", there are wide differences as to the amount and quality of evidence required to make him change his mind. Some statements that we presently hold "true", we will hold "false" (or considerably less probable) on scant evidence to the contrary. Other beliefs, closer to the center of one's field of force, become more and more immune to reevaluation in the face of "recalcitrant experience": rather than to trade away the beliefs on which the whole scaffolding has been built, there will be a preference for smoothing out incoherence by reevaluating the statements that are more peripheral. Indeed, could it be otherwise than that each human being should hold some beliefs relatively more immune from revision than others? Suppose each morning, on arising, each human were a tabula rasa, wholly uncommitted as to which beliefs were true and which were false, bringing to his day no presumptions of fact or custom. *Could he function at all?*

This section deals with the applicability of the force field metaphor not only to the individual mind, but to the entire society and its institutions. Consider for example how many devices the society has to "explain away" experiences that are potentially "incoherent" with the basic assumptions about which it has organized itself. Much as an individual can explain away a deviant perception on the grounds, *e. g.*, that he was hallucinating, so the society can explain away action inconsistent with its premises on the basis, say, that the deviant is "insane." Thomas Szasz, in Law, Liberty and Psychiatry (1968) tells of the attempt of a Negro woman to kill intergration leader Martin Luther King. At the time, 1958, it was probably a relatively "core" belief in the society that all Negroes wanted integration. The woman's act was, with respect to this belief, a "recalcitrant experience". The Associated Press' dispatch on the event is telling: "she never gave a coherent reason for the attack." (Can you reconstruct the dialogue on her examination?) Rather than to try her for attempted murder—which would have presupposed that a person could be (1) sane; (2) a Negro, and (all at the same time) (3) against integration—the state committed her to an institution for the criminally insane. Szasz comments (p. 194):

> Probably no one was surprised by this sequence of events. An unprovoked attack on an antisegregationist leader by a Negro woman must have seemed to the proverbial man on the street as "just about as crazy as you can get." Consequently, in the public eyes, Mrs. Curry was committable. Suppose, however, that the attack had been made on a segregationist leader. Would she still have been committable in the public eye or, would her act have been interpreted as a political crime based on revenge? Suppose Mr. King

had been assaulted by a member of the Ku Klux Klan. Would the public have labeled the attacker as mentally ill? Or would his act have been regarded as a political crime?

Is this response to a social event atypical? Could the society and its institutions function satisfactorily if every day, each and every one of the premises it was operating on was equally open to reconsideration? Is it not inevitable in each society there are some "facts" that are considerably less subject to empirical confirmation than others? Suppose we brought out towards the periphery of our social force field beliefs like "all men are created equal"; "individuals are responsible for their actions"; "free speech contributes to a good society", and took evidence and testimony on these beliefs in the same way we take evidence and testimony on pending appropriations bills. Could we not do so? How would the society be different?

In point of fact, how much of any society's activities are aimed at keeping certain beliefs relatively immune from review (consider, once more, the resistance to the Copernican revolution), and at regulating and adjusting the processes by which others can be revised in the light of "recalcitrant experiences"?

How does the legal system contribute to the regulation, presentation and formulation of this system of beliefs?

When courts divide statements into those of "fact" and those of "law", how much are they doing so from a belief that the two sorts of statements are inherently differently related to "reality"? How much are they doing so to maintain a social counterpart to Quine's "field of force", *making* certain statements relatively immune from challenge, and *specifying what* statements are challengeable only by *which* agencies (juries, regulatory commissions, etc.)—not on account of inherent differences in the ways in which the statements could be verified, but with an aim towards advancing certain express—or implicit—social policies and values?

## THE DECLARATION OF INDEPENDENCE IN CONGRESS, July 4, 1776

### The Unanimous Declaration of the Thirteen
### United States of America

. . . .

We hold these truths to be self-evident, that all men are created equal, that they are endowed by their Creator with certain unalienable Rights, that among these are Life, Liberty and the pursuit of Happiness. That to secure these rights, Governments are instituted among Men, deriving their just powers from the consent of the governed.—That whenever any Form of Government becomes destructive of these ends, it is the Right of the People to alter or to abolish it, and to institute new Government, laying its foundation on such principles and organizing its powers in such form, as to them shall seem most likely to effect their Safety and Happiness.

QUESTIONS

1. When the founding fathers stated that "all men are created equal" was "self-evident", what were they doing in Quine's terms? How is the statement "all men are created equal" different from the statement, "there is a bluebird on the window ledge outside every room" in terms of their respective bases in experience? Can that question be answered simply by *reading* the two statements, or does one have to know, in addition, something about the society we are speaking of, and the relative need it attaches to holding the statements true so as to give organization to other experiences?

2. It is clear what is *meant* by the statement "All men are created equal" without reference to other beliefs in the predominant force-field? What, *e. g.*, did "men" mean to them in that expression? How many of the signers, for example, owned slaves? See F. McKISSICK, ⅗ OF A MAN (1969). Did "men" in this context include in its meaning "women"? Could eighteen year olds vote?

3. Even when the range of meaning of "men" is established, is not our analysis of the statement still dependent on knowing more about the force field? Is our society ever presented with evidence "recalcitrant" to the statement that "all men are created equal"? Is it not always? How can we "explain" such evidence away? When do we do so? What are the advantages of explaining such evidence away? What are the disadvantages?

4. Can we imagine a society which placed the statement, "all men are created equal" (with respect to some specified capacities) at the periphery of its "force field"? What would the significance of so placing it be? Can we imagine a society that placed the statement, "there is a blue bird on every window ledge" at the center of its force field, holding it true "come what may"? What would a society that did these things have to "give up", in the sense of making other beliefs more open to question? With what results?

5. Thomas Emerson, in THE SYSTEM OF FREEDOM OF EXPRESSION (1970) states, after outlining the "case" for free expression, "the validity of the foregoing premises has never been proved or disproved, and probably could not be. Nevertheless, our society is based on the faith that they hold true and, in maintaining a system of freedom of expression, we act upon that faith." *op. cit.*, at 7–8. Can you translate this statement into the force-field metaphor? Could you make an argument for free expression that was provable or disprovable? By reference to what standards would you prove it? Would you not, in your process of putting the value of free speech to the test, be withdrawing from review some of the statements to which you appeal in your test of it? What is the significance of your answer?

GALILEO'S ABJURATION

I, Galileo Galilei, son of the late Vincenzio Galilei of Florence, aged seventy years, tried personally by this court, and kneeling before You, the most Eminent and Reverend Lords Cardinals, Inquisitors-General throughout the Christian Republic against heretical depravity, having before my eyes the Most Holy Gospels, and laying on them my own hands; I swear that I have always believed, I believe now, and with God's help I will in future believe all which the Holy Catholic and Apostolic Church doth hold, preach, and teach. But since I, after having been admonished by this Holy Office entirely to abandon the false opinion that the Sun was the centre of the universe and immovable, and that the Earth was not the centre of the same and that it moved, and that I was neither to hold, defend, nor teach in any manner whatever, either orally or in writing, the said false doctrine; and after having received a notification that the said doctrine is contrary to Holy Writ, I did write and cause to be printed a book in which I treat of the said already condemned doctrine, and bring forward arguments of much efficacy in its favor, without arriving at any solution: I have been judged vehemently suspected of heresy, that is, of having held and believed that the Sun is the centre of the universe and immovable, and that the Earth is not the centre of the same, and that it does move.

Nevertheless, wishing to remove from the minds of your Eminences and all faithful Christians this vehement suspicion reasonably conceived against me, I abjure with a sincere heart and unfeigned faith, I curse and detest the said errors and heresies, and generally all and every error and sect contrary to the Holy Catholic Church. And I swear that for the future I will neither say nor assert in speaking or writing such things as may bring upon me similar suspicion; and if I know any heretic, or one suspected of heresy, I will denounce him to this Holy Office, or to the Inquisitor and Ordinary of the place in which I may be. I also swear and promise to adopt and observe entirely all the penances which have been or may be by this Holy Office imposed on me. And if I contravene any of these said promises, protests, or oaths, (which God forbid!) I submit myself to all the pains and penalties which by the Sacred Canons and other Decrees general and particular are against such offenders imposed and promulgated. So help me God and the Holy Gospels, which I touch with my own hands. I, Galileo Galilei aforesaid, have abjured, sworn, and promised, and hold myself bound as above; and in token of the truth, with my own hand have subscribed the present schedule of my abjuration, and have recited it word by word. In Rome, at the Convent della Minerva, this 22d day of June, 1633.

> I, Galileo Galilei, have abjured as
> above, with my own hand.

## Notes and Questions

1. For some years prior to his development of the telescope (1610), Galileo had believed that the sun was in the center of a solar system, contrary to Holy Scripture. He had expected the telescope to convince others by affording necessary proof. Some of his contemporaries, however, refused to look through the telescope; others, who looked, saw—or professed to see—nothing significant. He was formally denounced in 1615 "for holding as true the false doctrine taught by some that the Sun is the center of the world and immovable

and that Earth moves also with a diurnal motion". He refused to desist, as a result of which he was tried and sentenced in 1633. See DE SANTILLANA, THE CRIME OF GALILEO (1955).

2. What arguments could the Papal authorities make for refusing to entertain evidence contrary to the belief that the earth was at the center of the universe? Does any society not hold some "truths" immune from review? What was so good about opening to question the organization of the solar system—moving statements about the solar system to the "periphery"? What associated beliefs were called into question in the process? Why should the statement "Science must be allowed an untrammeled range" be more immune from review than "the word of the Church should not be challenged"? Is it a relevant consideration that Science untrammeled has given us the knowledge to make the H-bomb?

3. What objections are there to trying Galileo for his heresy? Is not one of them that it is difficult *really* to believe that truth is nothing but coherence? What standards are there for judging which beliefs are "better" to hold immune from review than others? Is it an adequate defense of the relative unchallengeability of a statement that it grants social cohesion and limits strife? Why should the progress of "science" outweigh the stability of the social order? By what standards is the stability of the social order not so much a positive as a negative factor? See A. KOESTLER, DARKNESS AT NOON.


JOHN HONNOLD

REVIEW OF A. P. BLAUSTEIN AND C. C. FERGUSON,
DESEGREGATION AND THE LAW *

The crucial point in any analysis of the Brown v. Board of Education [14] decision is the Court's conclusion that racial segregation imposes special harmful effects upon Negro children. The opinion stated that separating the Negro children "from others of similar age and qualifications solely because of their race generates a feeling of inferiority as to their status in the community that may affect their hearts and minds in a way unlikely to be undone." The Court quoted from the finding of the Kansas court that segregation by force of law "is usually interpreted as denoting the inferiority of the Negro group" and produces a "sense of inferiority" which "affects the motivation of a child to learn." The Court then concluded: "Whatever may have been the extent of psychological knowledge at the time of Plessy v. Ferguson, this finding is amply supported by modern authority." At this point the Court dropped a footnote which referred to several sociological studies on the relationship between racial segregation and the development of Negro children.

* From 33 Ind.L.J. 612, 613–15 (1958).     14. The School Desegregation Case, 347
With permission of the Indiana Law        U.S. 483 (1954), Chapter 12 *infra.*
Journal.

This is the point in the Court's opinion which has drawn the strongest fire, aimed at establishing that the decision is not "law" but "sociology." And this is the crucial point in the opinion, for if it is now found that racial segregation has a special damaging effect upon Negroes, it is clear, contrary to the assumption of earlier decisions, that separation is *not* equal and that the Fourteenth Amendment's requirement of equality has been violated. Also reduced in significance are arguments that the framers of the Amendment did not anticipate integrated schools, for any such assumption would have reflected a judgment concerning the facts to which their basic constitutional standard would apply; under conventional legal traditions, as the facts change or become more clearly perceived, the results required by the basic standard also must change.

. . . .

The problem suffers from inherent difficulty which can easily blur analysis. As has already been noted, the essential issue is one of *fact*—whether segregation involves special harm for Negroes and therefore violates the constitutional standard of equality. But the basic factual issue can not be relitigated in each case which involves the question. Rather, the factual question seems to be merely a phase in the Court's development of constitutional wisdom, comparable to that involved in deciding the extent to which the constitutional ideal of a federal system permits states and nation to tax each other, or permits state taxation of interstate commerce.

Answering such questions calls for wisdom based on information which often is too diffuse for presentation in a trial; the most that can be done is to call the Court's attention in the briefs to responsible studies which have been made of the question. But there are times when some of the evidence of social or economic questions could well be submitted to the clash of cross-examination and rebuttal which is possible only at the trial. The social scientists supporting the plaintiffs submitted the results of specific experiments concerned with a specific question of fact: the psychological effect of segregation. These cases had representative counsel from both great camps in attendance. For this reason, it seems appropriate to have employed the trial as a laboratory for investigation of such data to help in the necessary education of the Court. The chief pity is that counsel for the states did not adequately use their opportunity for cross-examination and rebuttal, with the result that the reliability of some of the data can remain open to conjecture.

But the relevance of the issues on which the social scientists wrote and testified is inescapable, although it does not serve the usual narrow function of closing the record of a particular case but instead leads to a general constitutional ruling which will govern subsequent cases until the basic factual assumptions can be shown to be wrong. And there must be opportunity for such further proof. For example, representatives of southern states, in a case in which adequate warning is given to responsible representatives of the opposite camp, should have the opportunity to marshall evidence—including testimony by social scientists—in support of the proposition that a system of segregation does not handicap the Negro. If such a showing were made, the current constitutional rule that segregation violates the constitutional requirement of equality would have to be modified.

EDMOND CAHN

JURISPRUDENCE *

. . . In the months since the utterance of the *Brown* and *Bolling* opinions, the impression has grown that the outcome, either entirely or in major part, was caused by the testimony and opinions of the scientists, and a genuine danger has arisen that even lawyers and judges may begin to entertain this belief. The word "danger" is used advisedly, because I would not have the constitutional rights of Negroes—or of other Americans—rest on any such flimsy foundation as some of the scientific demonstrations in these records.

. . . .

. . . For at least twenty years, hardly any cultivated person has questioned that segregation is cruel to Negro school children. The cruelty is obvious and evident. Fortunately, it is so very obvious that the Justices of the Supreme Court could see it and act on it even after reading the labored attempts by plaintiffs' experts to demonstrate it "scientifically."

*Claims and Facts.*—When scientists set out to prove a fact that most of mankind already acknowledges, they may provide a rather bizarre spectacle. Fifty years ago, certain biologists who were engaged in just this sort of enterprise, provoked George Bernard Shaw to denounce their "solemnly offering us as epoch-making discoveries their demonstrations that dogs get weaker and die if you give them no food; that intense pain makes mice sweat; and that if you cut off a dog's leg the three-legged dog will have a four-legged puppy." Then Mr. Shaw called the scientists a number of fearful names (beginning with "dolts" and "blackguards"), none of which would be remotely applicable to the psychologists and psychiatrists who testified in the desegregation cases. So far as I can judge, all of these are fine, intelligent, dedicated scholars. Yet one can honor them as they deserve without swallowing their claims.

Professor Kenneth B. Clark of the psychology department of City College acted as general social science consultant to the NAACP legal staff and served as liaison between the lawyers and the scientists. His endeavors having been long and arduous, perhaps it was natural that he should exaggerate whatever the experts contributed to the case. In an article written while the country was waiting for the Supreme Court's decisions, he asserted, *"Proof* of the arguments that segregation itself is inequality and that state imposed racial segregation inflicts injuries upon the Negro *had to come from the social psychologists and other social scientists."* (Emphasis supplied.)

* From 30 N.Y.U.L.Rev. 150, 157, 159–60 (1955). With permission of New York University Law Review.

When Professor Clark wrote thus, he could not know that Chief Justice Warren's opinions would not mention either the testimony of the expert witnesses or the submitted statement of the thirty-two scientists. The Chief Justice cushioned the blow to some extent by citing certain professional publications of the psychological experts in a footnote, alluding to them graciously as "modern authority." In view of their devoted efforts to defeat segregation, this was the kind of gesture a magnanimous judge would feel impelled to make, and we are bound to take satisfaction in the accolade. Yet, once the courtesy had been paid, the Court was not disposed in the least to go farther or base its determination on the expert testimony.

## QUESTIONS

1. Compare the views of Professors Honnold and Cahn. What is the significance that they see, for the disposition of subsequent cases, of the "factual" social science evidence that the Supreme Court alluded to in *Brown*? If the Supreme Court based its decision in *Brown* on empirical evidence, why was not its finding—that segregated school systems were unconstitutional—one of fact, and thus a judgment (a) on the specific record before the Court in *Brown* (b) as to the specific school systems before the Court in *Brown*?

2. Are there any reasons why, as Honnold suggests, "representatives of southern states" should not have the opportunity "to marshall evidence—including testimony by social scientists—in support of the proposition that "a system of segregation does not handicap the Negro"? Does Cahn have an adequate answer?

See also the selection from Wechsler, *Toward Neutral Principles of Constitutional Law*, 73 Harv.L.Rev. 1 (1959), Chapter 12 *infra*.

## STELL v. SAVANNAH-CHATHAM COUNTY BOARD OF EDUCATION

220 F.Supp. 667 (S.D.Ga.1963)

SCARLETT, District Judge.

### THE ISSUES

This is a class action in the right of the minor Negro plaintiffs as students in public schools of Savannah-Chatham County to enjoin defendant Board of Education from operating a bi-racial school system. Alternately plaintiffs pray a mandatory injunction to compel defendants to submit a plan for the admission of Negro applicants to the white schools now maintained in Savannah-Chatham County.

It was alleged in the complaint that admission to the various public schools of Savannah-Chatham County is determined solely upon the basis of race and color and that plaintiffs are irreparably injured thereby.

The defendants formally denied these allegations but conceded the existence of a dual school system for white and Negro students in the City and County. Defendants further pleaded certain administrative difficulties which would ensue if the relief demanded in the complaint were to be granted.

A motion to intervene on behalf of themselves and their class was made by minor white school children alleging that the separation of Negro and white children in the public schools was not determined solely by race or color but rather upon racial traits of educational significance as to which racial identity was only a convenient index.

Among these significant factors for consideration in devising a rational program best suited to the peculiar educational needs of Negro and white school children in separate schools were:

(a) differences in specific capabilities, learning progress rates, mental maturity, and capacity for education in general;

(b) differences in physical, psychical and behavioral traits.

The differences were alleged to be of such magnitude as to make it impossible for Negro and white children of the same chronological age to be effectively educated in the same classrooms.

It was alleged that to congregate children of such diverse traits in schools in the proportion and under the conditions existing in Savannah would seriously impair the educational opportunities of both white and Negro and cause them grave psychological harm.

Plaintiffs objected to the motion for intervention, stating that the decision of the Supreme Court in Brown v. Board of Education of Topeka, 347 U.S. 483, 74 S.Ct. 686, 98 L.Ed. 873, created a conclusive presumption of injury to Negro students by reason of segregation such as to withdraw from white children or school authorities any right to show either an absence of injury from segregation in the area concerned or that compulsory integration of Negro and white school children rather than segregation would cause great and irreparable injury to both.

. . . .

The proofs closed, plaintiffs renewed their objection of irrelevancy [to the evidence of Negro inferiority and the harm, to both races, of educational integration—Ed.] and moved to strike the evidence submitted by intervenors. .. . .

In stating the basis for the objection to this evidence, counsel for plaintiffs said:

" . . . the law is settled by the Supreme Court in the Brown case that segregation itself injures negro children in the school system. That is what the Supreme Court's decision is all about, so we do not have to prove that."

A ruling on plaintiffs' objection therefore made it essential to consider the legal parameters of the Supreme Court's Brown decision.

. . . .

## I

The binding effect of any decision is legally a problem of privity of party or precedent, of prior adjudication or estoppel. Under the principles of *res judicata* and *stare decisis* fall most of the rules which govern these concepts.

As to parties and privies the final decision in Brown or in any court of final jurisdiction is *res judicata,* that is to say it is a conclusive adjudication as to all questions determined by the Court, whether of law or of fact. . . .

The general principles are set forth by Mr. Justice Stone in Hansberry v. Lee:

"It is a principle of general application in Anglo-American jurisprudence that one is not bound by a judgment in *personam* in a litigation in which he is not designated as a party or to which he has not been made a party by service of process. Pennoyer v. Neff, 95 U.S. 714 . . . and judicial action enforcing it against the person or property of the absent party is not that due process which the Fifth and Fourteenth Amendments requires. [sic.]" . . .

. . . . .

Since intervenors were not parties to nor members of any class represented by defendants in Brown, it follows that Brown does not bind them under the doctrine of *res judicata.*

While *res judicata* applies to decisions of both law and fact, *stare decisis* is applicable only on questions of law and relates generally to all causes subsequently arising in the same or an inferior court. It applies as well to strangers as to privies. 21 C.J.S. Courts §§ 188, 212, pp. 305, 386; 14 Am.Jur. 290. Under this principle therefore this Court is bound by the decision in Brown v. Board of Education to the extent that it states rules of law. It has no application to any determinations of fact in that case. . . .

In the case of Quon v. Niagara Fire Ins. Co. of New York, 190 F.2d 257, 260, the rule was stated by the Ninth Circuit Court of Appeals in this way:

". . . . the judgment of fact of one court on a particular record cannot bind another court, or even the same court, to make a similar finding on a different record. The imponderables such as credibility and inferences crowd upon one judging of facts."

In Partos v. Pacific Coast S.S. Co., 9 Cir., 95 F.2d 738, 742, the same court aptly illustrated the rule:

"Even if, on the identical complicated probative facts and contradictory testimony in another case . . . another court found seaworthiness as an ultimate fact, it would not prevent us from weighing the evidence and making the contrary finding."

## II

It is therefore apparent that the governance of the present issues by Brown is the question of whether the applicable portion of the determination in that case—the injury occurring through segregation as plaintiffs put it—is a finding of fact or a conclusion of law. For this let us look to the words and record in Brown.

Several courts which have previously considered this question have concluded that the decision in Brown is in large part based on questions of fact contained in four case records before the Supreme Court. . . .

In Brown the Supreme Court stated for itself the nature of its inquiry:

"We come then to the question presented: Does segregation of children in public schools solely on the basis of race, even though the physical facilities and other "tangible" factors may be equal, deprive the children of the minority group of equal educational opportunities?" (347 U.S. p. 493, 74 S.Ct. p. 691).

Although it would appear sufficiently clear on its face that this calls for a conclusion of fact rather than law, we are confirmed when we find that Court looking to the testimonial and other evidence in the records before it and to a submission of scientific opinion rather than seeking the answer to this question in the law books.

From the Kansas record, the Court read.

" . . . the policy of separating the races is usually interpreted as denoting the inferiority of the negro group. A sense of inferiority affects the motivation of a child to learn. Segregation with the sanction of law, therefore, has a tendency to [retard] the educational and mental development of Negro children and to deprive them of some of the benefits they would receive in a racial[ly] integrated school system."

These are facts, not law. To make these findings the Kansas District Judge considered evidence—not cases. Whether Negroes in Kansas believed that separate schooling denoted inferiority, whether a sense of inferiority affected their motivation to learn and whether motivation to learn was increased or diminished by segregation was a question requiring evidence for decision. That was as much a subject for scientific inquiry as the braking distance required to stop a two-ton truck moving at ten miles an hour on dry concrete.

Again, the Supreme Court quoted the record that Negro children in Delaware were "receiving educational opportunities which are substantially inferior to those available to white children otherwise similarly situated," (Ftn. 10, p. 494 of 347 U.S., p. 691 of 74 S.Ct.) a statement which could only be of factual rather than legal significance.

The Supreme Court put at rest any residual question on the nature of its inquiry when it indicated its reliance on scientific information:

"Whatever may have been the extent of psychological knowledge at the time of Plessy v. Ferguson, [163 U.S. 537, 16 S. Ct. 1138, 41 L.Ed. 256,] this finding is amply supported by modern authority." (347 U.S. 494, 74 S.Ct. 692).

The teachings of psychology in 1896, in 1954, or in 1963 are inquiries requiring evidence in the same sense as repeated determinations of "seaworthiness." Actually, the non-legal authority to which the Court referred was neither testimonial nor documentary in character but came from a "Brandeis" type brief filed directly in the Supreme Court by the National Association for the Advancement of Colored People. The possible significance of this authorship is considered in the next point.

It was only after marshalling these facts and considering the statements of "modern authority" that the Court came to the conclusion that the minor Negro plaintiffs in those cases were injured by segregation and thereby "deprived of the equal protection of the laws guaranteed by the Fourteenth Amendment." (347 U.S. p. 495, 74 S.Ct. p. 692).

The Court holds that the existence or non-existence of injury to white or black children from integrated or segregated schooling is a matter of fact for judicial inquiry and was so treated in Brown.

[The Injunction was denied and complaint dismissed. Reversed, 318 F.2d 425 (5th Cir. 1963) ; See Jackson Municipal Separate School District v. Evers, *infra*].

## JACKSON MUNICIPAL SCHOOL DISTRICT v. EVERS

357 F.2d 653 (5th Cir. 1966)

WISDOM, Circuit Judge:

These cases tax the patience of the Court.

More than ten years have passed since Brown v. Board of Education, 1954, 347 U.S. 483, 74 S.Ct. 686, 98 L.Ed. 873. Decisions too numerous to mention in this Court and in the Supreme Court show unyielding judicial approval of the legal principle that segregated schooling is inherently unequal. The principle extends beyond public schools. It is "no longer open to question that a State may not constitutionally require segregation of public facilities." Johnson v. State of Virginia, 1964, 373 U.S. 61, 83 S.Ct. 1053, 10 L.Ed.2d 195.

Yet at this late date, bewitched and bewildered by the popular myth that Brown was decided for sociological reasons untested in a trial, the defendants and intervenors attempt to overturn Brown on a factual showing. They assert that innate differences in the races in their aptitude for educability are a reasonable basis for classifying children by race, demonstrate that separate schools for Negro children are to the advantage of both races, and justify continued school segregation in Mississippi. We rejected this identical contention on an interlocutory appeal in Stell v. Savannah-Chatham County Board of Education, 5 Cir. 1963, 318 F.2d 425, less than two weeks after the court below had sustained the contention. Even before Stell, in St. Helena Parish School Board v. Hall, 5 Cir. 1961, 287 F.2d 376, we held that a trial judge abused his discretion in permitting an intervention by persons whose sole purpose was to introduce evidence tending to show that the Supreme Court's decision in Brown was wrong.

When Stell was before us a second time, we said, 333 F.2d 55 at 61:

"[T]he District Court was bound by the decision of the Supreme Court in Brown. We reiterate that no inferior federal court may refrain from acting as required by that decision even if such a court should conclude that the Supreme Court erred either as to its facts or as to the law. . . . Thus was the Savannah case ended then, and there it must end now. We do not read the major premise of the decision of the Supreme Court in the first Brown case as being limited to the facts of the cases there presented. We read it as proscribing segregation in the public education process on the stated ground that separate but equal schools for the races were inherently unequal. This being our interpretation of the teaching of that decision, it follows that it would be entirely inappropriate for it to be rejected or obviated by this court.

. . .

The intervenors in Stell sought review of this Court's decision by the Supreme Court and failed, even though their petition for a writ of certiorari (No. 512, October Term, 1964) was supported by Amicus Curiae Statements from the Attorneys General of Alabama, Arkansas, Louisiana, Mississippi, North Carolina, South Carolina and Virginia.

The trial judge wrote an elaborate opinion in which he made detailed findings in favor of the School Boards and the intervenors, but entered an order "contrary to the facts and the law applicable thereto" because he felt "bound by the decision of this court in Stell". We dismiss the appeal, and affirm the order of injunctive relief. . . .

QUESTIONS

1. Why was Judge Scarlett "wrong"? Why was not the holding in Brown a holding that, e. g., "segregated school systems are unconstitutional, where the effects include psychological harm to the children"? Since the Supreme Court had used the latest psychological evidence in deciding, in 1954, that Plessy v. Ferguson had been wrong in 1896, why was this not a sign to Judge Scarlett that he should hear testimony on the most authoritative psychological insights on the problem as of 1963? Is it an adequate answer to say that the Supreme Court in Brown had decided "a matter of law"? Had it? Or had it decided a "fact"—but a non-reviewable "fact"? Or is a non-reviewable fact what a matter of law decided by the U. S. Supreme Court is?

2. Are not all holdings based upon the facts in the record before the Court? When the Supreme Court has decided any case, how can lower courts (or the Supreme Court in a subsequent decision) ever know whether and to what extent a holding has laid down a general "rule of law" (or "constitutional fact"—see infra, p. 365) and to what extent the holding is to be limited to "its facts"? Why was the Fifth Circuit confident that Brown had done the former?

3. Judge Scarlett observes in the Stell case that the issues inquired into in Brown were "as much a subject for scientific inquiry as the braking distance required to stop a two-ton truck moving at ten miles an hour on dry concrete." How does the Fifth Circuit answer this contention? Can you express what the Fifth Circuit regards the Supreme Court as having done, in terms of "scientific inquiry" and the distribution of statements in a Quine-type social force field?

4. Do you suppose that the Supreme Court wants inquiry into the effects of desegregated schools to be treated on a par with inquiry into braking distance; or on a par with inquiry into the proposition that "all men are created equal"? Why?

How much can the different attitudes the Court takes towards these propositions be explained in epistemological terms, and how much in terms of the Court's concept of its role relative to the maintenance of certain values?

### NOTE: MATTERS OF FACT/MATTERS OF LAW

The matter of fact/matter of law dichotomy comes up in many contexts, the *Brown-Stell* situation being only one example. What are the differences; how does one distinguish a matter of fact from a matter of law? Is what people want to express by this dichotomy translatable into respectively different relationships the two classes of statement bear to "reality" and to "the law", so that the one is simply a report of what exists and the other a report of what a body of legal rules decrees?

Consider, for example, the two statements $S(a)$ "defendant had a gun in his possession," and $S(b)$ "defendant is guilty" (uttered by a duly appointed judge after a trial consistent with the authoritative procedures, etc.) The latter is, as clearly as can be, a statement of law, in the sense that its meaning cannot be understood independently of a body of rules and rituals; clearly $S(b)$ involves far more than a report of "reality". But is the meaning of $S(a)$ uninvolved in these same rules? Is the evidence on which a witness will utter $S(a)$ to a policeman the same evidence, and does it require the same state of mind on his part, as that on which he will utter $S(a)$ on the witness stand in a murder trial? Is it possible he might believe $S(a)$ "true" for the first purpose (where the "rules" say that what he is saying will amount to the policeman's investigating Defendant's involvement a little more deeply) but not "true" for the second purpose (where the "rules" say that what he is saying will amount to increasing the probability of the jury bringing back a verdict of "guilty"?) If so, does not the reason have to do with the fact that, in the second context, the meaning of $S(a)$ is involved, albeit in a very complex way, with a statement of law? That is, can any statement of "fact" (ostensibly a report of reality) ever be wholly dissociated from a statement of "law" (ostensibly a report of the legal rules) when the "fact" will have "legal" consequences?

If there is some such complex involvement, how can "fact" and "law" be distinguished? Will the distinction always be the same? Are people always trying to attach the same consequences to a fact-law dichotomy in each context in which the dichotomy is invoked? Can we ever make an adequate general distinction between fact and law in epistemological terms, or do we have to look at particular types of cases, and include reference to institutional aims and rules? Consider, for example, Lord Jessell's opinion in *Eaglesfield v. Marquis of Londonderry*, involving an action for misrepresentation and Judge Simmons' opinion in *Savannah, F. S. W. Ry. Co. v. Daniel*, involving what constitutes a "drawbridge" in a negligence action.

What different *function* is the fact/law dichotomy playing in the two cases? Does either opinion adequately explain its use of the distinction? What more might each opinion have added?

## EAGLESFIELD v. MARQUIS OF LONDONDERRY

(1876) 4 Ch. D. 693

[The Llanidloes Railroad Company had been authorized by Parliament to issue £100,000 of No. 1 Preference Stock (stock which is of a very choice sort, because, among other things, the holders of such shares are entitled to be paid dividends before the holders of any other class; if the company's income is low, there then may not be money available to pay any dividends to holders of less preferred shares). After £85,000 of such shares had been issued, the Llanidloes Company and a number of other railroads were consolidated into the Cambrian Railways Company by an act of Parliament, the Cambrian Railways Act, 1864. The Act had appeared to reserve to the new Company the power to issue all the stocks that the dissolved companies had been authorized to issue, but not gotten around to issuing prior to the consolidation. Relying on this provision, the directors of the new company were under the good faith impression, supported by an opinion of a solicitor, that they could still issue an additional £15,000 Preference Stock "Llanidloes No. 1" that would rank on an equal footing with the original £85,000 issue of the "Llanidloes No. 1". They issued the stock to a creditor of the company, one Savin, who turned around and sold £10,000 of the shares to Eaglesfield and the other plaintiffs. Nothing on the certificates indicated that these shares were in any way different from the original £85,000 issue.

Thereafter the new company found itself in "embarrassed circumstances". A plan was filed in Chancery for arranging its affairs (a type of bankruptcy proceeding). The Vice-Chancellor, construing the acts of Parliament, decided that the £10,000 issue bought by Eaglesfield from Savin was *not* on an equal footing with the original No. 1 Preference Stock, but ranked quite poorly—below both it and an issue of No. 2 Preference Stock. Eaglesfield's stock was thus probably next to worthless.

Plaintiffs then filed a bill alleging that they had been deceived by the form in which the stock had been issued and the certificates made, and praying that the company, the directors and secretary might be held liable for the misrepresentation.

Defendants maintained that the misrepresentation, if there had been any, was one of *law*, not of *fact*, and that, as everyone is taken to know the law equally, no liability attached. See generally, CHESHIRE AND FIFOOT, CONTRACTS, pp. 168 *ff.*]

JESSEL, M.R.: (4 Ch. D. at 702–703)

It was put to me that this was a misrepresentation of law and not of fact. It was said the company and the directors did not know their Acts of Parliament, and their solicitor had told them this, which they believed, that the new £15,000 Preference Stock would be and be treated as part of the Llanidloes No. 1 Preference Capital, and rank and stand upon the same footing in all respects as the £85,000 Llanidloes No. 1 Preference Stock.

Of course, solicitors can give wrong advice as well as other people, and I have no doubt he did think that this would rank as part of the Llanidloes No. 1 Preference Stock. But does that make it a misrepresentation of law? A misrepresentation of law is this: when you state the facts, and state a conclusion of law, so as to distinguish between facts and law. The man who knows the facts is taken to know the law; but when you state that as a fact which no doubt involves, as most facts do, a conclusion of law, that is still a statement of fact and not a statement of law. Suppose a man is asked by a tradesman whether he can give credit to a lady, and the answer is, "You may, she is a single woman of large fortune." It turns out that the man who gave that answer knew that the lady had gone through the ceremony of marriage with a man who was believed to be a married man, and that she had been advised that that marriage ceremony was null and void, though it had not been declared so by any Court, and it afterwards turned out they were all mistaken, that the first marriage of the man was void, so that the lady was married. He does not tell the tradesman all these facts, but states that she is single. That is a statement of fact. If he had told him the whole story, and all the facts, and said, "Now, you see, the lady is single," that would have been a misrepresentation of law. But the single fact he states, that the lady is unmarried, is a statement of fact, neither more nor less; and it is not the less a statement of fact, that in order to arrive at it you must know more or less of the law.

There is not a single fact connected with personal *status* that does not, more or less, involve a question of law. If you state that a man is the eldest son of a marriage, you state a question of law, because you must know that there has been a valid marriage, and that that man was the first-born son after the marriage, or, in some countries, before. Therefore, to state it is not a representation of fact seems to arise from a confusion of ideas.

It is not the less a fact because that fact involves some knowledge or relation of law. There is hardly any fact which does not involve it. If you state that a man is in possession of an estate of £10,000 a year, the notion of possession is a legal notion, and involves knowledge of law; nor can any other fact in connection with property be stated which does not involve such knowledge of law. To state that a man is entitled to £10,000 Consols involves all sorts of law. Therefore this is a statement of fact, and nothing more; and I hold the argument to be wholly unfounded which maintained that it was a statement of law.

## QUESTIONS

1. Does Lord Jessel take the position that a statement can be determined to be one of "fact" or of "law" by reference to the statement itself? Or is he saying that to determine whether the state-

ment is one of fact or of law depends upon the other statements offered by the utterer by way of context? Consider your answer in the light of the discussion of the A.L.I. Restatement of Torts (Trade Disparagement) §§ 626–627 in this chapter, section 1.

2. Consider Lord Jessel's remark that "To state that a man is entitled to £10,000 Consols involves all sorts of law. Therefore, this is a statement of fact, and nothing more. . . ." Granted Lord Jessel's analysis of the mutual involvement of "facts" and "law", how adequate is this statement as justification for calling Plaintiff's representation one of "fact"? How would you have decided the case? Can you justify your answer simply in terms of "fact" and "law" or do you find yourself involved in a broader excursion into the rules and purposes of the law of contracts and commercial dealings?

3. Given the rules of the legal system, when Lord Jessel declares defendants' representation to have been one of fact, what is he doing in terms of organizing social relationships? Where, for example, is he placing liability for failure to make careful—or just "the right"—examination of a document? What effects will his decision have on the obligations of solicitors to their clients? On the obligations of directors to stockholders and potential stockholders? What effect will the defining of these obligations have on the behavior of persons involved in stock, and similar transactions? In what ways can they avoid liability?

## SAVANNAH, F. & W. RY. v. DANIELS

17 S.E. 647 (Ga.1892)

SIMMONS, J. The plaintiff sued the railroad company for damages on account of the death of her son, which she claimed was caused by the negligence of the defendant while he was upon its bridge over the Ogeechee river, where he had a right to be. It was alleged that the defendant was negligent in not slowing down its train to a speed of not more than four miles an hour at the time; that the train should have been stopped before going on the bridge, unless signaled to proceed by the bridge tender or his substitute; but that, without either slowing up or stopping, it ran over and across the drawbridge so negligently, recklessly, and carelessly as to kill her son. The verdict was in favor of the plaintiff, for $2,000; and the defendant made a motion for a new trial, which was overruled, and it excepted.

A statute, conceded to be applicable in the present case, prescribes that "every train of passenger cars drawn by one or more locomotives . . . shall also slow down to a speed of not more than four miles an hour before running on, or crossing, any drawbridge over a stream which is regularly navigated by vessels." Acts 1880–81, p. 165. . . A rule of the defendant is in the language of the statute. It is complained that the court erred in refusing to give the following in charge to the jury, as requested in writing: "The rule of the company, and the statute of the state which has been put in evidence by the plaintiff, and which requires trains to be run at a speed of not more than four miles an hour across drawbridges, is applicable only to the drawbridge itself, and does not apply to the trestling, or approaches to the draw-bridge; for, if the engineer has his train sufficiently under control to go over the drawbridge at a speed of not more than four miles an hour, then the law and the rule of the company is complied with, no matter at what rate of speed he may have approached the bridge."

The following instructions are complained of: "As to what con-stitutes a drawbridge, I leave that for the jury to say.  There have been contentions on both sides as to what constitutes a drawbridge. The defendant contends that the part which turns on the pivot,—that directly over the channel,—and which opens, constitutes the draw-bridge, while the plaintiff contends that not only that part, but also the trestle, and every part across the river, constitutes the drawbridge. I think that is a question of fact for the jury to determine."  We think the court erred in leaving this question to the jury.  As a rule, ques-tions in regard to the interpretation and construction of statutes are for the court alone; and there is no reason for treating as an excep-tion to the rule the question of what constitutes a "drawbridge," within the meaning of this statute.  "Whether a structure is or is not a bridge may sometimes be a question of fact.  The structure may be of such a peculiar construction, or so peculiarly located, in the particular case, as to require its character to be determined by the jury, under the facts of the particular instance.  So it must sometimes be that what are parts of a bridge is a question to be determined as one of fact, and not of law.  Generally, however, the question of what is or is not a bridge is for the court, and not for the jury."  Elliott, Roads & S. 25.  Here the question is whether, in all cases to which the statute is applicable, the term "drawbridge," as used in the statute, includes the whole of the bridge structure, or only a certain part of it; that is to say, whether it includes, in all cases, the trestles and approaches from the embankments beyond the river, as well as the bridge proper, or is confined to the bridge proper or the "draw,"—a question which, it will be seen, is of a different character from that presented in the cases above referred to.  That the term "drawbridge," as stated in the opinion of the learned judge of the court below, may have, in addition to its general and ordinary meaning, a special and technical significa-tion, we do not think should control, as a reason for leaving the con-struction of the statute to the jury.  The importance of treating the question as one of law is manifest when it is considered that the object of the statute is to regulate the daily conduct of railroad com-panies in a matter of considerable risk to the safety of life and prop-erty.  The opinion of the court is supposed to be consistent in the construction of laws, and the interpretation adopted by the trial judge is subject to review by a court of last resort, whose construction is controlling in all similar cases; but the opinions of juries may vary, and there may be different verdicts on exactly the same state of facts. It is highly important to the public in general, as well as to the rail-road companies, that the duty imposed by this statute should be clearly defined and understood; but if the jury, in each case, could construe the law for itself, there would be no means of arriving at a construction which could be regarded as final, and the limits of the duty imposed must remain unsettled. Treating the question, then as one of law, we think the term "drawbridge," as used in this statute, should be construed to mean the bridge proper,—that is to say, that part of the structure which is directly over the river,—and as not including the trestles or approaches on either side of the river. Although the term "drawbridge" is often applied to the movable section of a bridge, it means also the whole bridge, of which the "draw" or movable section forms a part. The Century Dictionary defines the term as meaning "a bridge, one or more sections of which can be lifted or moved aside to permit the passage of boats," and the definition in Webster's Dictionary accords with this. We think the latter signification is the one which should be adopted in construing this statute. In arriving at the sense in which the term is here used, the object of the enactment ought to control, which is to reduce the speed before the movable part of the bridge is reached so that a stop would be easy in case the "draw" should not be properly adjusted for the train to run over it. Of course, if the train were running at the rate of four miles an hour on reaching the "draw," it could not be stopped in time. The danger could be obviated, however, if the speed were brought within this limit upon reaching the bridge proper; for then the persons operating the train could easily see the condition of the draw in time to stop the train before reaching it. But, to accomplish the object of the statute, there would be no occasion, before reaching the bridge proper, to reduce the speed to the limit stated. We think the court should have instructed the jury, as requested by counsel for the defendant, that the restriction to four miles an hour does not apply to the trestling or approaches to the drawbridge, and that, if the engineer has his train sufficiently under control to go over the drawbridge at a speed of not more than four miles an hour, the law and the rule of the company are complied with. In the present case there was a long trestle extending across a marsh, over which the train had to pass before the river or the bridge proper was reached. If the jury applied the statute to this trestle, over which the evidence shows that the train was running more than four miles an hour, this would result in fixing negligence upon the defendant, without regard to whether the speed was reduced to the prescribed limit before reaching the bridge proper, or not, and without regard to whether all ordinary care and diligence was used on the part of the defendant to avoid running into the deceased when it was discovered that he was on the track. There was evidence from which the jury could find that in this respect proper diligence was exercised; but if the rate of speed was in violation of the statute while running on the trestle, or approach to the bridge proper, as the jury may have found it was, the absence of fault in other respects might not avail to relieve the defendant from liability, an unlawful rate of speed being negligence per se. We cannot say, therefore, that the failure of the court to charge properly on this subject did not result in harm to the defendant, and the case being an exceedingly close one, under the evidence, we think the error was such as to call for a new trial. Judgment reversed.

QUESTIONS

1.  What different consequences attach to the fact/law dichotomy in *Savannah* as opposed to *Eaglesfield?* Does the distinction play the same role in both contexts? Yet, differences aside, in both situations is it not the role of the fact/law dichotomy to allocate responsibility —to determine who has to undertake an independent examination of the "truth" of some class of statements?

2.  When Judge Simmons decided that whether the bridge was a "drawbridge" was a question of law, what was he doing in terms of the distribution of functions between judges and juries? Why did he remove the question from the jury? Did he do so because he thought that all *interpretation* of statutes is to be done by judges, and *application* by juries? (Can such a distinction be maintained?) Or did he feel that *if* we treated this particular question about drawbridges as one of law, rather than fact, the effects would be superior in terms of the consequences it would have for social organization? Could you support such an argument?

But does the court go far enough in its reasoning to justify its decision? How successfully can a decision handed down in *this case* make "the duty imposed by this statute [be] clearly defined and understood"?

3.  On the reasoning of the court in *Savannah*, should the question of whether or not there was *negligence* not also have been decided by the trial court, rather than the jury? Could not Judge Simmons have argued that because "the opinions of juries may vary, and there may be different verdicts on exactly the same state of facts", negligence should be a question of law so that "the limits of the duty imposed" by the law will not "remain unsettled"? How can you distinguish the problem with the meaning of "drawbridge" from the problem with the meaning of "negligence"?

Consider these questions in conjunction with the problems of "constitutional fact" discussed in the following Note.

NOTE: CONSTITUTIONAL FACTS

The fact/law dichotomy sometimes serves to distribute responsibilities not simply as between sellers and purchasers (as in *Eaglesfield*) or as between judges and juries (as in *Savannah*) but as between courts (and other judicial bodies) at different levels. Since courts of review cannot—if only because of the demands on their time —review de novo every finding of a lower body, each reviewing agency finds itself faced with the problem of what sorts of prior determinations it should leave undisturbed and which it should undertake to review or re-review. And when it does undertake to review a prior finding, what presumptions of correctness—what deference—should it accord to the decision of the lower body? For example, how much scrutiny—how much re-reviewing of the evidence—should the Supreme Court of the United States make of a federal appeals court's review of an administrative agency's review of a hearing examiner's findings? See Universal Camera v. N. L. R. B., 340 U.S. 474 (1951).

The resolution of these sorts of issues is at the heart of many of the everyday problems that courts face.

Part of the solution depends upon making a distinction—again—between "fact" and "law". The reviewing agency may say that while its scope of review will be extremely narrow where findings of "fact" are involved, no such strong presumptions will be accorded rulings of "law".

This, however, raises as many questions as it answers. What sorts of findings are of "law"—reviewable de novo—and which—those of "fact"—are not? If the one class of statements simply involved interpreting legal documents and the other simply involved interpreting "reality," the dichotomy would not be hard to understand and apply. But in this context, as in the others, what is "fact" and what is "law" are not easily distinguished from each other. Is a determination that a film is "hard core pornography" a statement of fact about the film—or a statement of law interpreting the First Amendment, *i.e.*, whether its "protection" extends to this particular film? Regarded from the first perspective, the determination of whether the film is "hard core pornography" would not be reviewed by a higher court; regarded from the second perspective, it would be reviewed. How can a court of review, *e.g.*, the U. S. Supreme Court, determine which perspective is the "right" one? This is the problem that gives rise to the doctrine of "constitutional fact". See Strong, *The Persistent Doctrine of "Constitutional Fact"* 46 N.C.L.Rev. 223 (1968); Strong, *Dilemmic Aspects of the Doctrine of "Constitutional Fact"*, 47 N.C.L.Rev. 311 (1969); L. JAFFE, JUDICIAL CONTROL OF ADMINSTRATIVE ACTION (1965); Davis, *Judicial Control of Administrative Action: A Review*, 66 Colum.L.Rev. 635 (1966); cf. Karst, *Legislative Facts in Constitutional Litigation*, 1960 S.Ct.Rev. 75.

Under this "doctrine", even if a question is in some senses one of "fact", (*e. g.*, the initial determination is of the sort that might properly be made by a jury) if its determination is "decisive of constitutional rights" it may be carefully re-reviewed by the U. S. Supreme Court on the grounds that the question is one of "the very issues to review which" the Supreme Court sits. For example, in Watts v. Indiana, 338 U.S. 49 (1949) appellant had been convicted in an Indiana trial court of murder while attempting rape, and sentenced to death. At trial, his confession had been offered in evidence; he objected to its admission on the grounds that it had not been voluntarily given, and thus to admit it would violate Due Process. The trial court heard his evidence on threats and intimidation, but ruled that the confession had been, in fact (?), voluntarily given, thus admitting it. On appeal to the Indiana Supreme Court, Chief Justice Starr of Indiana wrote, "the evidence of admissibility being conflicting, the court's ruling adverse to appellant cannot be questioned in this appeal as we cannot weigh the evidence", Watts v. State, 82 N.E.2d 846 (Ind.1948); in other words, the Indiana court regarded the finding of voluntariness as one of "fact"—non-reviewable. On appeal to the United States Supreme Court, Justice Frankfurter, reversing, explained,

On review here of State convictions, all those matters which are usually termed issues of fact are for conclusive determination by the State courts and are not open for reconsideration by this Court. Observance of this restriction in our review of State courts calls for the utmost scruple. But "issue of fact" is a coat of many colors. It does not cover a conclusion drawn from uncontroverted happenings, when that conclusion incorporates standards of conduct or criteria for judgment which in themselves are decisive of constitutional rights. Such standards and criteria, measured against the requirements drawn from constitutional provisions, and their proper applications, are issues for this Court's adjudication. . . . Especially in cases arising under the Due Process Clause is it important to distinguish between issues of fact that are here foreclosed and issues which, though cast in the form of determinations of fact, are the very issues to review which this Court sits. . . .

358 U.S. at 50–51.

See also Norris v. Alabama, 294 U.S. 587, (1935). There, Negro defendants in a nationally publicized rape case a charge that their conviction had violated Due Process because of a practice of systematically excluding Negroes from jury service in the county of trial. The state trial court judge took evidence on the point, and concluded that even if it were assumed that there were no bona fide names of Negroes on the jury rolls "it was not established that race or color caused the omission. The [trial] court pointed out that the statute fixed a high standard of qualifications for jurors . . . and that the jury commission was vested with a wide discretion." The trial court also adverted to the fact that "more white citizens possessing age qualifications had been omitted from the jury roll than the entire negro population of the county." 294 U.S. at 593.

Speaking for a unanimous Court, Chief Justice Hughes wrote:

The question is of the application of [an] established [Constitutional] principle to the facts disclosed by the record. That the question is one of fact does not relieve us of the duty to determine whether in truth a federal right has been denied. When a federal right has been specially set up and claimed in a state court, it is our province to inquire not merely whether it was denied in express terms but also whether it was denied in substance and effect. If this requires an examination of evidence, that examination must be made. Otherwise, review by this Court would fail of its purpose in safeguarding constitutional rights. Thus, whenever a conclusion of law of a state court as to a federal right and findings of fact are so intermingled that the latter control the former, it is incumbent upon us to analyze the facts in order that the appropriate enforcement of the federal right may be assured.

249 U.S. at 589–90. The Supreme Court then made an elaborate independent examination of the record as reflected in the following passages:

The testimony showed the practice of the jury commission. One of the commissioners who made up the jury roll in question, and the clerk of that commission, testified as to the manner of its preparation. The other two commissioners of that period did not testify. It was shown that the clerk, under the direction of the commissioners, made up a preliminary list which was based on the registration list of voters, the polling list and the tax list, and apparently also upon the telephone directory. The clerk testified that he made up a list of all male citizens between the ages of twenty-one and sixty-five years without regard to their status or qualifications. The commissioner testified that the designation "col." was placed after the names of those who were colored. In preparing the final jury roll, the preliminary list was checked off as to qualified jurors with the aid of men whom the commissioners called in for that purpose from the different precincts. And the commissioner testified that in the selections for the jury roll no one was "automatically or systematically" excluded, or excluded on account of race or color; that he "did not inquire as to color, that was not discussed."

But, in appraising the action of the commissioners, these statements cannot be divorced from other testimony. As we have seen, there was testimony, not overborne or discredited, that there were in fact negroes in the county qualified for jury service. That testimony was direct and specific. After eliminating those persons as to whom there was some evidence of lack of qualifications, a considerable number of others remained. The fact that the testimony as to these persons, fully identified, was not challenged by evidence appropriately direct, cannot be brushed aside. There is no ground for an assumption that the names of these negroes were not on the preliminary list. The inference to be drawn from the testimony is that they were on that preliminary list, and were designated on that list as the names of negroes, and that they were not placed on the jury roll. There was thus presented a test of the practice of the commissioners. Something more than mere general asseverations was required. Why were these names excluded from the jury roll? Was it because of the lack of statutory qualifications? Were the qualifications of negroes actually and properly considered?

The testimony of the commissioner on this crucial question puts the case in a strong light. That testimony leads to the conclusion that these or other negroes were not excluded on account of age, or lack of esteem in the community for integrity and judgment, or because of disease or want of any other qualification. The commissioner's answer to specific inquiry upon this point was that negroes were "never discussed." . . .

We are of the opinion that the evidence required a different result from that reached in the state court. We think that the evidence that for a generation or longer no negro had been called for service on any jury in Jackson County, that there were negroes qualified for jury service, that according to the practice of the jury commission their names would normally appear on the preliminary list of male citizens of the requisite age but that no names of negroes were placed on the jury roll, and the testimony with respect to the lack of appropriate consideration of the qualifications of negroes, established the discrimination which the Constitution forbids. The motion to quash the indictment upon that ground should have been granted.

294 U.S. at 594–96.

What do *Watts* and *Norris* suggest as to how the Supreme Court's *function* changes relative to other institutions, depending upon whether it labels a "lower" finding one of "constitutional fact" or of ordinary fact? Yet, what criteria are available for the Court to determine whether a lower finding was one of fact or constitutional fact? How can fact and law *not* be "intermingled"? Thus: how can the Supreme Court, in any case in which the violation of a constitutional right is asserted, stop short of reviewing the entire record de novo? As a way of avoiding this flood, how useful is Justice Frankfurter's formula limiting review to conclusions that incorporate "standards of conduct or criteria for judgment which in themselves are decisive of constitutional rights"? In a state case where the voluntariness of a confession is in issue (and, hence, the "meaning" of the Fifth and Fourteenth Amendments) what sorts of "uncontroverted happenings" are *not* "decisive" of the defendant's constitutional rights? Suppose the interrogating officer wore two guns? Or the defendant, during interrogation, was served meat but no potatoes? Would these facts be "decisive"? Why—or why not?

From what point of view is the Supreme Court better able than lower bodies to make judgments on "constitutional facts"? How, for example, was Chief Justice Hughes better positioned than the trial court to make the determination required in *Norris*? Was not the inquiry required there of the very sort that is traditionally left to trial courts, which can personally view the witnesses and make that much better a judgment on their credibility?

Do the answers not have to do with the fact that the Supreme Court regarded the problems in *Watts* and *Norris* not merely as constitutional problems, but as involving a class of constitutional problems that were also very important social problems that needed special judicial attention and rule-formulations? (Query: is full-blown review by the Supreme Court a good way to encourage responsible handling of these problems by lower courts?) If so, though, why is the Supreme Court prepared to keep reviewing whether, in any given instance, a confession is voluntary but not whether, in any given instance, a desegregated school system is injurious (or unconstitutional)? Can you explain it simply in terms of what a fact is?

## CHAPTER SEVEN

# The Authority of the Issue

## Introductory Note

Judges often speak of (and teachers often ask for) "the issue" that a case presents. But is it clear in what sense each case has *an* issue (or even several issues)? What are people trying to do, when they seek to isolate some statement as the issue? What role does the issue play in the process of judgment?

Consider the shipwrecked seaman who, on board a sinking lifeboat, is told by the mate "men, go to work", apparently as a request to throw excess passengers overboard. See United States v. Holmes, 32 Fed.Cas. 360 No. 15, 383 (C.C.E.D.Pa.1842). Does he, before he acts, either consciously or unconsciously put to himself some issue that he must resolve? If so, what issue is posed for him: to ask the mate to explain more precisely what he means?; to ask the mate to justify his command, if it is to be interpreted as a command to throw persons overboard?; to ask the mate for further rules as to selecting persons to be thrown overboard? Even supposing that the seaman decides to perform the muscular series of actions that are being asked of him, think of how many different ways there are to characterize "the" issue the same bodily movements might present: "Ought I to obey my mate?"; "ought I to throw 14 people out of the boat?"; "ought I to kill 14 people?"; "ought I to save 27 people (the balance on board)?"; "ought I to diminish the public's confidence in the willingness of seamen to put the lives of passengers ahead of their own?" How does the seaman decide *which* of the issues is *the* issue which he confronts? (By reference to another, more comprehensive issue?) What differences does each of the different verbalizations invite or entail—in terms of the different inquiries and justifications that seem appropriate to his considerations; in terms of different weight to be given different sources of obligation; in terms of different emotional wells that are tapped within him? How much more "bound" to a single statement of "the issue" is an officer of the law—a prosecutor or judge—who not only has facts to deal with but a body of law "to apply"? How much, and with what consequences, are those operating within a legal system autonomous with respect to the issue that they put before themselves? What consequences attach to their selection of "the issue"? How closely does the verbalized "legal issue" correspond to the non-verbalized issues that may be guiding their thinking?

---

SECTION ONE: WHAT IS THE ISSUE IN A CONTROVERSY?

FRIGALIMENT IMPORTING Co. v. B. N. S.
INTERNATIONAL SALES CORP.

190 F.Supp. 116 (1960)

FRIENDLY, Circuit Judge.

The issue is, what is chicken? Plaintiff says "chicken" means a young chicken, suitable for broiling and frying. Defendant says "chicken" means any bird of that genus that meets contract specifications on weight and quality, including what it calls "stewing chicken" and plaintiff pejoratively terms "fowl". Dictionaries give both meanings, as well as some others not relevant here. To support its [position], plaintiff sends a number of volleys over the net; defendant essays to return them and adds a few serves of its own. Assuming that both parties were acting in good faith, the case nicely illustrates Holmes' remark "that the making of a contract depends not on the agreement of two minds in one intention, but on the agreement of two sets of external signs—not on the parties' having *meant* the same thing but on their having *said* the same thing." The Path of the Law, in Collected Legal Papers, p. 178. I have concluded that plaintiff has not sustained its burden of persuasion that the contract used "chicken" in the narrower sense.

The action is for breach of the warranty that goods sold shall correspond to the description, New York Personal Property Law, McKinney's Consol. Laws, c. 41, § 95. Two contracts are in suit. In the first, dated May 2, 1957, defendant, a New York sales corporation, confirmed the sale to plaintiff, a Swiss corporation, of

"US Fresh Frozen Chicken, Grade A, Government Inspected, Eviscerated

2½–3 lbs. and 1½–2 lbs. each

all chicken individually wrapped in cryovac, packed in secured fiber cartons or wooden boxes, suitable for export

75,000 lbs. 2½–3 lbs. .........................at $33.00

25,000 lbs. 1½–2 lbs. .........................at $36.50

per 100 lbs. FAS New York

scheduled May 10, 1957 pursuant to instructions from Penson & Co., New York."

The second contract, also dated May 2, 1957, was identical save that only 50,000 lbs. of the heavier "chicken" were called for, the price of the smaller birds was $37 per 100 lbs., and shipment was scheduled for May 30. The initial shipment under the first contract was short but the balance was shipped on May 17. When the initial shipment arrived in Switzerland, plaintiff found, on May 28, that the 2½–3 lbs. birds were not young chicken suitable for broiling and frying but stewing chicken or "fowl"; indeed, many of the cartons and bags plainly so indicated. Protests ensued. Nevertheless, shipment under the second contract was made on May 29, the 2½–3 lbs. birds again being stewing chicken. Defendant stopped the transportation of these at Rotterdam.

This action followed.  .  .  .

QHESTIONS

1. In what sense is "what is chicken?" the issue that Judge Friendly has to decide? Why? Does this adequately indicate the range of considerations that he must inquire into in order to decide this case? Is a different intellectual route suggested by, "What did this particular contract—not just the one word 'chicken'—mean"? or "what constitutes a breach of warranty that goods shall correspond to the description under New York law?" In what senses are these more, and in what senses less adequate indications of the intellectual route that the court must take? How about, "Ought courts to allow a seller to unethically defeat the expectations of a buyer?"; "Ought courts to refrain from seeking particular justice in an individual case in order to encourage contract negotiators to take such care in their draftsmanship as to enable courts to spend their limited time on other matters in the future?" What consequences does Judge Friendly's statement of the issue have: on further questions that are raised—and those that are not raised; on the facts that become relevant to the disposition of the case; on the values that are deemed relevant; on giving future litigants insight into his thinking? on giving guidance as to what the case shall "stand for" as precedent? Why did Judge Friendly select "what is chicken" as the issue, rather than one of these other possibilities?

2. Do you suppose Judge Friendly was "bound" by, say, the lawyers' pleadings, to adopt the "what is chicken" formulation of the issue rather than some of the others?

3. See United States v. Yazell, 382 U.S. 341 (1966). The case grew out of a disaster loan made by the Small Business Administration to a man named Yazell and his wife, following flood damage to their shop in Texas. The Yazells defaulted on the note. The Government brought suit, whereupon Mrs. Yazell moved for summary judgment on the ground that under the Texas law of coverture she had no capacity to bind herself personally, and hence the contract could not be enforced against her separate property. At the outset of his opinion, Mr. Justice Fortas observes, 382 U.S. at 342–343:

> .  .  . Specifically, the question presented is whether, in the circumstances of this case, the Federal Government, in its zealous pursuit of the balance due on a disaster loan made by the Small Business Administration, may obtain judgment against Ethel Mae Yazell of Lampasas, Texas.

Query: How do you suppose the case came out?

Seven pages later, Mr. Justice Fortas rephrases the issue in the following terms, 382 U.S. at 350–351:

> The issue is whether the Federal Government may voluntarily and deliberately make a negotiated contract with

knowledge of the limited capacity and liability of the persons with whom it contracts, and thereafter insist, in disregard of such limitation, upon collection (a) despite state law to the contrary relating to family property rights and liabilities, and (b) in the absence of federal statute, regulation or even any contract provision indicating that the state law would be disregarded.

In what sense are these two issues "the same"? In what respects are they different? How else might "the issue" have been phrased? What theories of law is each phrasing of the issue implicitly assuming? Consider these questions in the light of the selections from Fisher and Finkelstein.

ROGER FISHER

FRACTIONATING CONFLICT *

Issues between people and between governments do not have objective edges established by external events. These problems of life lie in a seamless web of interrelated facts and circumstances. People and governments can choose which congeries of events shall be considered as a unit for the purpose of working out relations with others. Related events may be joined together for some purposes and treated separately for other purposes. Ideological, national, racial, and religious differences may be "fundamental," but may nonetheless be treated either as relevant or as irrelevant to economic questions that come up daily for decision.

. . . .

In short, this paper is not concerned with debating whether major conflicts of interest exist between countries; it is concerned with dealing with them. It does not suggest that any one country has complete control over the formulation of international conflict issues, but that it has a measure of control. It does not suggest that it is always wise to fractionate conflict into little issues, but that it is often wise to do so. Actions affecting the size of an issue should be undertaken consciously, with the advantages and disadvantages in mind. The formulation of issues in dispute between our country and another should not be undertaken accidentally or emotionally. Defining an issue in big terms—for example, defining issues in South Vietnam or Berlin in terms of freedom versus communism—may satisfy the human desire for clear, simple black-and-white choices. But it may be as ineffective as arguing military policy in terms of whether one is for peace or for war.

. . . .

There are, perhaps, an infinite number of ways in which international issues might be sliced. For a first approximation, it may

* From 93 Daedalus 920, 922–933 (1964).
With permission of the American
Academy of Arts and Sciences.

be useful to consider five dimensions which measure the size of a conflict issue:

(1) The parties on each side of the issue;

(2) The immediate physical issue involved;

(3) The immediate issue of principle;

(4) The substantive precedent which settlement will establish;

(5) The procedural precedent which settlement will establish.

With respect to each of these, there is a certain amount of choice as to how big or small the issue is made. Although these variables are not wholly independent, they will serve as a basis for exploring different ways in which conflict issues may be increased or decreased in size.

## PARTIES ON EACH SIDE OF THE ISSUE

Objectively, there is no single correct definition of the parties on each side of a dispute. Each party is often free to define one or both sides in the way that best suits its interests. For example, if a Polish fishing vessel has damaged a transatlantic cable, the party on the "left-hand" side of the dispute might be taken as the helmsman of the ship, the captain of the ship, the department of the Polish government concerned with regulating fishing, the Polish government, the Soviet government, Krushchev, or "the Communists." The party on the "right-hand" side might be considered to be the private company owning the cable, the United States, or the West.

. . . .

There are advantages in downgrading a dispute and in treating it as one between individuals, or at least as one in which the other government is not involved. As long as disputes are considered in this way, there is little chance of war. Part of the strong emotional outburst by the Soviet Union over the U2 incident in 1960 was apparently due to President Eisenhower's insistence that the flights were official governmental action, not unauthorized conduct on the part of the Central Intelligence Agency.

. . . .

## IMMEDIATE PHYSICAL ISSUE INVOLVED

Any particular conflict can be thought of as having a certain minimum size in factual or physical terms. This is measured by the inconsistency between the physical events desired by the two adversaries. If two men want to sit at the same time on a particular chair that will only hold one, a conflict is defined which can hardly be further reduced.

. . . .

There are two ways of expanding the physical size of an issue: first, by defining more broadly the subject matter in dispute; second, by bringing in different subjects which are related only because the parties are the same.

By rational extension, almost anything can be related to anything else. The question for each party is whether it would prefer to deal with issues separately or together. Should it seek agreement on a portion of a problem and be willing to postpone consideration of other aspects, or should it insist that nothing will be agreed upon until all of a defined subject matter is settled? For example, countries can agree on co-operative development of weather satellites as a separate issue, or insist that the subject is intimately connected with military satellites and that a single agreement must cover both aspects of the problem. The question of releasing prisoners from the April, 1961 landing on Cuba could be treated as a special issue (in fact, each prisoner could be considered separately), or it could be treated as part of a single over-all political dispute between the United States and Cuba.

．　．　．　．

## THE TECHNIQUE OF COUPLING ISSUES

The immediate issue under discussion between two sides may be expanded by coupling one dispute with another. Here the connection is made not by broadening the definition of the subject matter but by recognizing that two matters involve the same parties. The considerations involved in coupling one dispute with another deserve more study. If the joining of problems is made as an offer, the process seems constructive, facilitating agreement: "I will let you have what you want in the X dispute if you will let me have what I want in the Y dispute." Without such bargaining, it may be difficult to settle either dispute. ．　．　．

．　．　．　．

## THE IMMEDIATE ISSUE OF PRINCIPLE

．　．　．　．

To be strong and effective, a country apparently needs principles and needs to adhere to them. Principles can be flexible, however, and the extent to which they are involved in a particular controversy can be limited in two ways. The first is by recognizing that we can be loyal to our principles without insisting that our opponents be disloyal to theirs. To arouse the maximum support of our own people, we often identify a dispute as a conflict of principle, in which one principle or the other must yield. We do this also as a form of committal strategy in which we strengthen our negotiating position by tying our own hands and making it harder to back down. ．　．　．

In many instances, an issue is defined differently for several different audiences. Each government may tell its own people that a particular issue is an important step in furthering its national goals and is an application of strongly-held national principles. At the same time, it may be explaining to its adversary that the particular matter can be settled pragmatically without regard to differences of principle. While explaining to the American people that the Antarctic Treaty was furthering the principle of complete inspection for any disarmament agreement, the United States government could point out to the Soviet Union that it could accept this practical solution without abandoning any matter of principle.

. . . .

## SUBSTANTIVE PRECEDENT WHICH SETTLEMENT WOULD ESTABLISH

In almost every conflict each side is thinking not only of how much it would lose immediately if it yielded a point, but of how much it would lose by way of precedent. Similarly, a country may press a position, not for the immediate consequences, but with the hope of establishing a precedent for the future.

. . . .

The scope of a precedent is always somewhat ambiguous. In political affairs, as in the legal system, ambiguity permits a nice accommodation between consistency and flexibility as new circumstances arise. . . . .

For several days in the fall of 1962, Russian guards for the war memorial were allowed to enter West Berlin in armored cars instead of buses. Later the United States told the Russian guards to revert to transportation by bus, which they did. The United States was not effectively tied up by the armored car precedent because it distinguished the circumstances. The armored cars were allowed during a period of rioting. Once the rioting had stopped, the cases were different.

*LAWRENCE S. FINKELSTEIN*

### COMMENTS ON "FRACTIONATING CONFLICT" *

. . . . Professor Fisher's operating assumption appears to be that what he describes as the "sizing" of disputes or conflicts is a matter which can often be determined by rational choice. Again, it is useful to be reminded that we should be alert to such choices when it is possible to make them. However, it seems reasonable to ask how often one should expect to be able to make such choices with respect to intense conflict situations. His assumption is that the components of a dispute—the parties, the immediate physical issues, the principles at stake and the way they are applied, and the precedential implications—although inherently connected, can be treated separately. It is far from clear that this is so in all cases. For example, the Fisher assumption does not seem to respond with sufficient candor to the difference which he recognizes between conflicts which consist of accumulated grievances over discrete issues which *are* separable, and conflicts which exist because of fundamental hostility arising out of ultimately conflicting objectives and principles. In the latter category, issues may be no more than the means by which conflict is conducted. If the relations between the parties resemble

* From *Id.* 942, 944–45 (1964). With permission of the American Academy of Arts and Sciences.

*ad hominem* arguments, it is because the parties' beliefs about their intentions toward each other lie at the heart of the matter.

Even in such conflicts one should, of course, be alert to the possibility that disputes over issues can be insulated or separated from the main source of overriding conflict. It was, after all, possible to reach agreement on an Austrian peace treaty, an Antarctic disarmament treaty, and, most recently, on a reduction in production of nuclear materials, even though these issues and others on which agreement has been possible were intimately related to the overall texture of relationships between the Soviet Union and the United States. With respect to even such successes, however, it may be an instructive rather than merely a semantic distinction to point out that the settlement of these issues did not take place apart from, but rather as part of, the conduct of conflict relationships between the parties.

. . . .

. . . How much have Indian-Pakistan relations been fundamentally altered by the Indus waters settlement and all the other agreements, desirable in themselves, between the two countries? Is the amelioration of relations with the Soviet Union which we welcome today a consequence of the test ban treaty or is the latter a reflection of a mutual will to improve relations, growing from more fundamental causes, rooted in changing perceptions of the relationship? One thing is clear: the role of the existing agreements between the Soviet Union and the United States as stepping stones on the path of improving relations is not separable from the larger context. The interaction between small issues and large conflicts is at the core of Professor Fisher's subject. It deserves thoughtful and intensive exploration.

All this brings me back to my starting point. Professor Fisher's argument is a valuable beginning, but one which needs and deserves fuller development, both from Professor Fisher and others who may be inspired to put his hypotheses to more elaborate tests than he has done in this article.

## QUESTIONS

1. What are the "five dimensions" which Fisher says "measure the size of a conflict issue"? How adequately can the five of them be distinguished from one another?

2. Consider Professor Fisher's example of the Polish fishing vessel which has damaged a transatlantic cable. What characterizations of the parties to "the issue" can you think of in addition to those given? What different consequences does each characterization invite—in terms, say, of the difficulty of resolving the dispute by getting reparations made? In terms of smoothing out differences of larger consequence?

3. What is the primary issue that Finkelstein takes with Fisher's thesis? In a legal dispute, how many of the rationally imaginable ways to slice up an issue are never thought of, or practically foreclosed from consideration, because of factors outside the issue-formulator's consciousness or control?

BARENBLATT v. UNITED STATES

360 U.S. 109 (1959)

Mr. Justice HARLAN delivered the opinion of the Court.

. . . . .

Pursuant to a subpoena, and accompanied by counsel, petitioner on June 28, 1954, appeared as a witness before this congressional Subcommittee. After answering a few preliminary questions and testifying that he had been a graduate student and teaching fellow at the University of Michigan from 1947 to 1950 and an instructor in psychology at Vassar College from 1950 to shortly before his appearance before the Subcommittee, petitioner objected generally to the right of the Subcommittee to inquire into his "political" and "religious" beliefs or any "other personal and private affairs" or "associational activities," upon grounds set forth in a previously prepared memorandum which he was allowed to file with the Subcommittee. Thereafter petitioner specifically declined to answer each of the following five questions:

"Are you now a member of the Communist Party? [Count One.]

"Have you ever been a member of the Communist Party? [Count Two.]

"Now, you have stated that you knew Francis Crowley. Did you know Francis Crowley as a member of the Communist Party? [Count Three.]

"Were you ever a member of the Haldane Club of the Communist Party while at the University of Michigan? [Count Four.]

"Were you a member while a student of the University of Michigan Council of Arts, Sciences, and Professions?" [Count Five.]

In each instance the grounds of refusal were those set forth in the prepared statement. Petitioner expressly disclaimed reliance upon "the Fifth Amendment."

. . . . .

## CONSTITUTIONAL CONTENTIONS

Our function, at this point, is purely one of constitutional adjudication in the particular case and upon the particular record before us, not to pass judgment upon the general wisdom or efficacy of the activities of this Committee in a vexing and complicated field.

The precise constitutional issue confronting us is whether the Subcommittee's inquiry into petitioner's past or present membership in the Communist Party transgressed the provisions of the First Amendment, which of course reach and limit congressional investigations. Watkins, supra, at 197.

The Court's past cases establish sure guides to decision. Undeniably, the First Amendment in some circumstances protects an individual from being compelled to disclose his associational relationships. However, the protections of the First Amendment, unlike a proper claim of the privilege against self-incrimination under the Fifth Amendment, do not afford a witness the right to resist inquiry in all circumstances. Where First Amendment rights are asserted to bar governmental interrogation resolution of the issue always involves a balancing by the courts of the competing private and public interests at stake in the particular circumstances shown. These principles were recognized in the *Watkins* case, where, in speaking of the First Amendment in relation to congressional inquiries, we said (at p. 198): "It is manifest that despite the adverse effects which follow upon compelled disclosure of private matters, not all such inquiries are barred. . . . The critical element is the existence of, and the weight to be ascribed to, the interest of the Congress in demanding disclosures from an unwilling witness."

. . . .

That Congress has wide power to legislate in the field of Communist activity in this Country, and to conduct appropriate investigations in aid thereof, is hardly debatable. The existence of such power has never been questioned by this Court, and it is sufficient to say, without particularization, that Congress has enacted or considered in this field a wide range of legislative measures, not a few of which have stemmed from recommendations of the very Committee whose actions have been drawn in question here. In the last analysis this power rests on the right of self-preservation, "the ultimate value of any society," Dennis v. United States, 341 U.S. 494, 509. Justification for its exercise in turn rests on the long and widely accepted view that the tenets of the Communist Party include the ultimate overthrow of the Government of the United States by force and violence, a view which has been given formal expression by the Congress.

. . . .

We conclude that the balance between the individual and the governmental interests here at stake must be struck in favor of the latter, and that therefore the provisions of the First Amendment have not been offended.

We hold that petitioner's conviction for contempt of Congress discloses no infirmity, and that the judgment of the Court of Appeals must be

Affirmed.

Mr. Justice BLACK, with whom THE CHIEF JUSTICE and Mr. Justice DOUGLAS concur, dissenting.

. . . .

But even assuming what I cannot assume, that some balancing is proper in this Case, I feel that the Court after stating the test ignores it completely. At most it balances the right of the Government to preserve itself, against Barenblatt's right to refrain from revealing Communist affiliations. Such a balance, however, mistakes the factors to be weighed. In the first place, it completely leaves out the real interest in Barenblatt's silence, the interest of the people as a whole in being able to join organizations, advocate causes and make political "mistakes" without later being subjected to governmental penalties for having dared to think for themselves.  It is this right, the right to err politically, which keeps us strong as a Nation.  For no number of laws against communism can have as much effect as the personal conviction which comes from having heard its arguments and rejected them, or from having once accepted its tenets and later recognized their worthlessness.  Instead, the obloquy which results from investigations such as this not only stifles "mistakes" but prevents all but the most courageous from hazarding any views which might at some later time become disfavored.  This result, whose importance cannot be overestimated, is doubly crucial when it affects the universities, on which we must largely rely for the experimentation and development of new ideas essential to our country's welfare.  It is these interests of society, rather than Barenblatt's own right to silence, which I think the Court should put on the balance against the demands of the Government, if any balancing process is to be tolerated.  Instead they are not mentioned, while on the other side the demands of the Government are vastly overstated and called "self preservation."  It is admitted that this Committee can only seek information for the purpose of suggesting laws, and that Congress' power to make laws in the realm of speech and association is quite limited, even on the Court's test.  Its interest in making such laws in the field of education, primarily a state function, is clearly narrower still.  Yet the Court styles this attenuated interest self-preservation and allows it to overcome the need our country has to let us all think, speak, and associate politically as we like and without fear of reprisal.  Such a result reduces "balancing" to a mere play on words and is completely inconsistent with the rules this Court has previously given for applying a "balancing test," where it is proper:  "[T]he courts should be *astute* to examine the *effect* of the challenged legislation.  Mere *legislative preferences or beliefs* . . . may well support regulation directed at other personal activities, but be insufficient to justify such as diminishes the exercise of rights so vital to the maintenance of democratic institutions."  Schneider v. Town of Irvington, 308 U.S. 147, 161.  (Italics supplied.)

(b) Moreover, I cannot agree with the Court's notion that First Amendment freedoms must be abridged in order to "preserve" our country.  That notion rests on the unarticulated premise that this Nation's security hangs upon its power to punish people because of what they think, speak or write about, or because of those with whom they associate for political purposes.  The Government, in its brief, virtually admits this position when it speaks of the "communication of unlawful ideas."  I challenge this premise, and deny that ideas can be proscribed under our Constitution.  I agree that despotic governments cannot exist without stifling the voice of opposition to their oppressive practices.  The First Amendment means to me, however, that the only constitutional way our Government can preserve itself is to leave its people the fullest possible freedom to praise, criticize or discuss, as they see fit, all governmental policies and to suggest, if they desire, that even its most fundamental postulates are bad and should be changed; "Therein lies the security of the Republic, the very foundation of constitutional government." On that premise this land was created, and on that premise it has grown to greatness. Our Constitution assumes that the common sense of the people and their attachment to our country will enable them, after free discussion, to withstand ideas that are wrong. To say that our patriotism must be protected against false ideas by means other than these is, I think, to make a baseless charge. Unless we can rely on these qualities—if, in short, we begin to punish speech—we cannot honestly proclaim ourselves to be a free Nation and we have lost what the Founders of this land risked their lives and their sacred honor to defend.

. . . .

The fact is that once we allow any group which has some political aims or ideas to be driven from the ballot and from the battle for men's minds because some of its members are bad and some of its tenets are illegal, no group is safe. Today we deal with Communists or suspected Communists. In 1920, instead, the New York Assembly suspended duly elected legislators on the ground that, being Socialists, they were disloyal to the country's principles. In the 1830's the Masons were hunted as outlaws and subversives, and abolitionists were considered revoluntionaries of the most dangerous kind in both North and South. Earlier still, at the time of the universally unlamented alien and sedition laws, Thomas Jefferson's party was attacked and its members were derisively called "Jacobins." Fisher Ames described the party as a "French faction" guilty of "subversion" and "officered, regimented and formed to subordination." Its members, he claimed, intended to "take arms against the laws as soon as they dare." History should teach us then, that in times of high emotional excitement minority parties and groups which advocate extremely unpopular social or governmental innovations will always be typed as criminal gangs and attempts will always be made to drive them out. It was knowledge of this fact, and of its great dangers, that caused the Founders of our land to enact the First Amendment as a guarantee that neither Congress nor the people would do anything to hinder or destroy the capacity of individuals and groups to seek converts and votes for any cause, however radical or unpalatable their principles might seem under the accepted notions of the time. Whatever the States were left free to do, the First Amendment sought to leave Congress devoid of any kind or quality of power to direct any type of national laws against the freedom of individuals to think what they please, advocate whatever policy they choose, and join with others to bring about the social, religious, political and governmental changes which seem best to them. . . .

## QUESTIONS

1. What *was* the issue in Barenblatt v. United States? Why?

2. What possible fractionations of "the issue" makes the balance appear most favorable to upholding the contempt conviction? What

fractionations put the same "facts" in a light most heavily weighted towards Barenblatt?

3. In what ways did the majority see the balance that was involved? What different balances did the dissenters see? What *made* the majority perceive the issue differently from the dissenters? What statement of the issue would Justice Black not even entertain? Why?

4. What do the different fractionations of the issues suggest about the priority of the values of the two groups? Can you reconstruct which beliefs are closer to the center of, in the terms of Quine's model (Chapter 6, Sec. 3, *supra*), the "force field" of each?

## UNITED STATES v. SISSON

294 F.Supp. 515 (D.C.Mass. 1968)

WYZANSKI, Chief Judge.

Defendant construes his motion to dismiss the indictment [1] as including a contention that he is entitled to have the indictment dismissed on the ground that he is being ordered to fight in a genocidal war.

The issue of defendant's standing to raise the genocidal question and the issue whether the question is a question not within this Court's jurisdiction resemble the issues already considered by this Court in denying defendant's motion to dismiss the indictment on the ground that defendant has been ordered to fight in a conflict as to which Congress has not declared war. However, there are differences between the problems which the earlier motion presented and the ones now raised.

For argument's sake one may assume that a conscript has a standing to object to induction in a war declared contrary to a binding international obligation in the form of a treaty, in the form of membership in an international organization, or otherwise. One may even assume that a conscript may similarly object to being inducted to fight in a war the openly declared purpose of which is to wipe out a nation and drive its people into the sea. Conceivably, in the two situations just described, the conscript would have a standing to raise the issue and the court would be faced with a problem which was not purely a political question, but indeed fell within judicial competence.

The issue now tendered by this defendant is unlike either of the two cases just mentioned. At its strongest, the defendant's case is that a survey of the military operations in Vietnam would lead a disinterested tribunal to conclude that the laws of war have been violated and that, contrary to international obligations, express and implied, in treaty and in custom, the United States has resorted to barbaric methods of war, including genocide.

1. Charging Sisson with wilfully refusing to perform a duty under the Selective Service Act of 1967. See also United States v. Sisson, 297 F. Supp. 902 (D.Mass.1969), Chapter 18 *infra*.

If the situation were as defendant contends, the facts would surely be difficult to ascertain so long as the conflict continues, so long as the United States government has reasons not to disclose all its military operations, and so long as a court was primarily dependent upon compliance by American military and civilian officials with its judicial orders. It should be remembered that the tribunal at Nuremberg, probably because it had a Russian judge, was unable to face up to the problems tendered by the Katyn massacres. Moreover, neither at Nuremberg nor at Tokyo, tribunals upon which an American judge sat, was there any attempt to resolve the problems raised by the nuclear bombing of Hiroshima and Nagasaki. It is inherent in a tribunal composed partly of judges drawn from the alleged offending nation that a wholly disinterested judgment is most unlikely to be achieved. With effort, self-discipline, and judicial training, men may transcend their personal bias, but few there are who in international disputes of magnitude are capable of entirely disregarding their political allegiance and acting solely with respect to legal considerations and ethical imperatives. If during hostilities a trustworthy, credible international judgment is to be rendered with respect to alleged national misconduct in war, representatives of the supposed offender must not sit in judgment upon the nation. An analogous path of reasoning must lead one to conclude that a domestic tribunal is entirely unfit to adjudicate the question whether there has been a violation of international law during a war by the very nation which created, manned, and compensated the tribunal seized of the case.

Because a domestic tribunal is incapable of eliciting the facts during a war, and because it is probably incapable of exercising a disinterested judgment which would command the confidence of sound judicial opinion, this Court holds that the defendant has tendered an issue which involves a so-called political question not within the jurisdiction of this court. . . .

The motion to dismiss the indictment is again denied.

### QUESTIONS

1. What does Judge Wyzanski construe as "the issue" tendered by Sisson? What effect does this construction have on Wyzanski's opinion? Why? How does his construal of the issue give shape to the inquiry—and outcome? How does it influence the facts that appear necessary to its resolution; and how do the facts necessary to its resolution, in turn, pose a problem in terms of the court's conception of its role?

2. Considering the fact that defendant had moved to dismiss on the grounds "that he is being ordered to fight in a genocidal war," was Wyzanski's statement of the issue the only statement possible? Does "a genocidal war", in that context, necessarily refer to a war that is having a genocidal *effect*? Note that Wyzanski was willing to assume "that a conscript may . . . object to being inducted to fight in a war the openly declared purpose of which is to wipe out a nation and drive its people into the sea." Why would that issue be

within "judicial competence" but not the issue that Wyzanski said
was posed by the motion to dismiss? How do the two different statements differ in terms of the inquiries they invite and the difficulties
they raise for, *e.g.*, judicial integrity? If openly declared genocidal
*purpose* was an issue that defendant might appropriately have tendered, what reasons might there be for Wyzanski's not construing *that*
as the issue defendant was raising?

## Section Two: What *Was* the Issue in a Controversy?

### Herman Oliphant

#### A Return to Stare Decisis *

. . . [A] court may make a statement broad enough to dispose of the case in hand as well as to cover also a few or many other
states of fact. Statements of this . . . sort may cover a number
of fact situations ranging from one other to legion. Such a statement
is sometimes called the *decision* of the case. Thereby the whole ambiguity of that word is introduced and the whole difficulty presented.

If a more careful usage limits the word *decision* to the *action*
taken by the court in the specific case before it, *i. e.*, to the naked
judgment or order entered, the difficulty is not met; it is merely
shifted. *Stare decisis* thus understood becomes useless for no decision
in that limited sense can ever be followed. No identical case can arise.
All other cases will differ in some circumstance,—in time, if in no
other, and most of them will have differences which are not trivial.
*Decision* in the sense meant in *stare decisis* must, therefore, refer to a
proposition of law covering a group of fact situations of a group as a
minimum, the fact situation of the instant case and at least one other.

To bring together into one class even this minimum of two fact
situations however similar they may be, always has required and always will require an abstraction. If Paul and Peter are to be thought
of together at all, they must both be apostles or be thought of as having
some other attribute in common. Classification is abstraction. An
element or elements common to the two fact situations put into one
class must be drawn out from each to become the content of the category and the subject of the proposition of law which is thus applied to
the two cases.

But such a grouping may include multitudes of fact situations so
long as a single attribute common to them all can be found. Between
these two extremes lies a gradation of groups of fact situations each
with its corresponding proposition of law, ranging from a grouping
subtending but two situations to these covering hosts of them. This
series of groupings of fact situations gives us a parallel series of corresponding propositions of law, each more and more generalized as we

* From 14 A.B.A.J. 72, 73–74 (1928).
With permission of the American Bar
Association.

recede farther and farther from the instant state of facts and include more and more fact situations in the successive groupings. It is a mounting and widening structure, each proposition including all that has gone before and becoming more general by embracing new states of fact. For example, $A$'s father induces her not to marry $B$ as she promised to do. On a holding that the father is not liable to $B$ for so doing, a gradation of widening propositions can be built, a very few of which are:

1. Fathers are privileged to induce daughters to break promises to marry.

2. Parents are so privileged.

3. Parents are so privileged as to both daughters and sons.

4. All persons are so privileged as to promise to marry.

5. Parents are so privileged as to all promises made by their children.

6. All persons are so privileged as to all promises made by anyone. There can be erected upon the action taken by a court in any case such a gradation of generalizations and this is commonly done in the opinion. Sometimes it is built up to dizzy heights by the court itself and at times, by law teacher and writers, it is reared to those lofty summits of the absolute and the infinite.

Where on that gradation of propositions are we to take our stand and say "This proposition is the decision of this case within the meaning of the doctrine of *stare decisis*?" Can a proposition of law of this third type ever become so broad that, as to any of the cases it would cover, it is mere dictum?

That would be difficult enough if it ended there. But just as one and the same apple can be thrown into any one of many groups of barrels according to its size, color, shape, etc., so also there stretches up and away from every single case in the books, not one possible gradation of widening generalizations, but many. Multitudes of radii shoot out from it each pair enclosing one of an indefinite number of these gradations of broader and broader generalizations. For example, a contract for wages contains a stipulation that it shall be non-assignable by the employee. A court holds that the laborer can assign any way and that his assignee can sue the employer for the wages regardless of the stipulation. This holding can serve as the apex of many triangles of generalizations. At the base of one will be a broad generalization treating the claim as property and asserting the alienability of property; at the base of another will be an equally broad generalization having to do with contractual stipulations opposed to public policy and the base of a third will be [a] similarly wide generalization concerning the liquidation of claims in the labor market. Others could be enumerated and other cases similarly analyzed. That is not needed, for we all know of at least one case appearing in the casebooks of more than one subject upon which securely rests more than one inverted pyramid of favorite theory.

A student is told to seek the "doctrine" or "principle" of a case, but which of its welter of stairs shall he ascend and how high up shall

he go? Is there some one step on some one stair which is *the* decision
of the case within the meaning of the mandate *stare decisis*? That is
the double difficulty. Each precedent considered by a judge and each
case studied by a student rests at the center of a vast and empty
stadium. The angle and distance from which that case is to be viewed
involves the choice of a seat. Which shall be chosen? Neither judge
nor student can escape the fact that he can and must choose. To
realize how wide the possibilities and significant the consequences of
that choice are is elementary to an understanding of *stare decisis*.
To ask whether there exists a coercion of some logic to make that
choice either inevitable or beneficent, searches the significance of
*stare decisis* in judicial government and the soundness of scholarship
in law. This question is real and insistent. It is one which should be
asked explicitly and faced squarely.

QUESTIONS

1. In looking back on a case to decide what it "stood for,"
what function is played by deciding what the prior issue was? What
is the relationship between the facts and the issue in invoking *stare
decisis*?

2. What would you say the *Barenblatt* case and the *Sisson* case
"stood for"? What are some of the possibilities? How much are one's
efforts limited by what one reads in the opinion and how much by what
one knows extrinsically? How adequately can you answer the question
without knowing more about the current case in which someone is
seeking to "apply" the rule of the previous case? Why? In what
sorts of situation might *Barenblatt* be invoked, by whom, and with
what end? For each concrete possibility, how might *Barenblatt* be
*distinguished*? Inasmuch as there will always be differences between
cases, with respect to what criteria is a distinction a significant distinction, in the sense that the "rule" of the prior case will not be
applicable to the new facts situation? Can the grounds for distinguishing cases be expressed adequately in terms of differing "facts"
and "issues"? If not, what more is needed?

---

SECTION THREE: LAWYERS, LEGAL PROCEDURE,
AND THE PRODUCTION OF AN ISSUE

From the moment he begins working on a case, one of the lawyer's
most important tasks is the narrowing of the issue for trial. Much of
the purpose behind pleading and other pre-trial activity has a similar
aim. But there have been, throughout the history of legal procedure,
different resolutions as to how much the parties should be compelled
to disclose before trial, and how much they should be bound to their
early commitments. Common law pleading, of which Stephen writes,
has given way to more liberal "notice" pleading such as manifested
in the Federal Rules of Civil Procedure, of which James writes. One
result of the modern development is that we no longer try to pin the
parties down to a simple issue before trial through the operation of
the pleadings themselves. But the various modern pre-trial discovery

techniques—bills of particulars, interrogatories, requests to admit, etc.—are used towards much the same ends. The considerations that are involved in deciding how these techniques are to be used are many and complex, and are treated more fully in courses in civil procedure. The excerpts that follow suggest discussion both of the feasibility and the desirability of different amounts of narrowing and defining the scope of trial issues in advance. How is James's attitude, and that of the Federal Rules, different from that of Stephen? Why?

HENRY JOHN STEPHEN

COMMON LAW PLEADING *

## CONCLUSION

To the view that has been taken in this work, of the principles of the system of pleading, it may be useful to subjoin a few remarks on the merits of that system, considered in reference to its effects in the administration of justice.

When compared with other styles of proceeding, it has been shown to possess this characteristic peculiarity—that it *produces an issue*; that is, it obliges the parties so to plead, as to develope [sic], by the effect of their own allegations, some particular question as the subject for decision in the cause. With respect to the *degree* of particularity with which such question, or issue is developed, we have seen in the first place, that it is always distinctly defined as consisting either of *fact* or *law*, because, in the former case it arises on a traverse,—in the latter it presents itself in the very different shape of a demurrer. But independently of this distinction, it will be remembered, that the issue produced is required to be *certain* or specific. It is true, that some issues are framed with much less certainty than others: but still it is the universal property of all, to define the question for decision, in a shape more or less specific.

That prior to the institution of any proceeding for the purpose of decision, the question to be decided should be, by some means, publicly adjusted, as consisting either of fact or law, and this too with some certainty or specification of circumstance, is evidently required, by the nature of the English common law system of jurisprudence. For, by the general principles of that system, questions of law are determinable exclusively by the judges; while questions of fact (some few instances excepted), can be decided only by a jury; and in those excepted cases are referred to other appropriate modes of trial. Unless therefore some public adjustment of the kind above described, took place between the parties, they would be unable, after the pleading had terminated, to pursue further their litigation. For they might disagree upon the very form of the proceeding, by which the decision was to be obtained; or, if they both took the same view of the general nature of the question, so that they both referred their controversy

* From A Treatise on the Principles of Pleading in Civil Actions 444–450 (3rd ed. 1837).

to the same method of determination,—for example, trial by jury—they might yet differ as to the shape of the question to be referred.

A public adjustment of the point for decision of the specific kind above described, being for this reason necessary, there are two ways in which it might conceivably be effected—either by a retrospective selection from the pleading, or by the mere operation of the pleading itself. The law of England, in producing an issue, pursues the latter method. For as has been shown, the alternate allegations are so managed, that by the natural result of that contention, the undisputed and immaterial matter is constantly thrown off, until the parties arrive at demurrer, or traverse;—upon which a tender of issue takes place, on the one hand, and an acceptance of it on the other; and the question involved in the demurrer or traverse, is thus mutually referred for decision.

The production of an issue, when thus defined and explained, apepars to be attended with considerable advantage in the administration of justice—for the better comprehension of which it will be useful to advert to those styles o[f] juridical proceeding, in which no issue is produced.

In almost every plan of judicature with which we are acquainted, except that of the common law of England, the course of proceeding is to make no public adjustment whatever of the precise question for decision. For as all matters, whether of law or fact, are decided by the judge, and by him alone, upon proofs adduced on either side by the parties, the necessity upon which that practice has been shown to be founded in the English common law system does not arise. Consequently the mutual allegations are allowed to be made *at large* as it may be called;—that is, with no view to the exposition of the particular question in the cause by the effect of the pleading itself. The litigants indeed, before they proceed to proof, must explore the particular subject in controversy, in order to ascertain whether any proof be required, and to guide them to the points to which their proof is to be directed. And upon the hearing of the cause, the judge must of course also ascertain for his own information, the precise point to be decided, and consider in what manner it is met by the evidence. But in these proceedings, neither the court nor the parties have any public exposition of the point in controversy to guide them; and they judge of it as a matter of private discretion, upon retrospective examination of the pleadings.

This, as already stated, is the almost universal method; but there is another, which also requires notice; viz. that which at present prevails in the Scottish judicature. Since the trial by jury in civil causes has been engrafted upon the juridical system of Scotland, it has, of course, been found necessary to adjust and settle publicly, between the parties, the particular question or questions on which the decision of the jury is to be taken. But, instead of eliciting such question (called by analogy to the law of England, the issue,) by the mere effect and operation of the pleading itself, according to the practice of the English courts, the course taken has been to adjust and settle the issue *retrospectively* from the allegations, by an act of court;

and these allegations have consequently continued to be taken *at large*, according to the definition of that term already given.

Now the English common law method, as compared with either of those that have been just described, possesses this advantage, that the undisputed or immaterial matter which every controversy more or less involves, is cleared away by the effect of the pleading itself; and therefore, when the allegations are finished, the essential matter for decision necessarily appears. But under the rival plans of proceeding, by which the statements are allowed to be made at large, it becomes necessary, when the pleading is over, to analyze the whole mass of allegation, and to effect for the first time the separation of the undisputed and immaterial matter, in order to arrive at the essential question. This operation will be attended with more or less difficulty, according to the degree of vagueness or prolixity in which the pleaders have been allowed to indulge; but where the allegations have not been conducted upon the principle of coming to issue, or, in other words, have been made at large, it follows from that very quality, that their closeness and precision can never have been such as to preclude the exercise of any discretion in extracting from them the true question in controversy; for this would amount to the production of an issue. Therefore it will always be in some measure doubtful, or a point for consideration, to what extent, and in what exact sense, the allegations on one side, are disputed on the other, and also to what extent the law relied upon by one of the parties, is controverted by his adversary. And this difficulty, while thus inherent in the mode of proceeding, will be often aggravated, and present itself in a more serious form, from the *natural tendency* of judicial statements, when made at large, to the faults of vagueness and prolixity. For where the pleaders state their cases in order to present the materials from which the mind of the Judge is afterwards to inform itself of the point in controversy, they will of course be led to indulge in such amplification on either side, as may put the case of the particular party in the fullest and most advantageous light, and to propound the facts in such form as may be thought most impressive or convenient, though at the expense of clearness or precision. On the other hand, it is evident, that upon the English common law method, the pleaders having no object but to produce the issue, are without the least inducement, either to an uncertain, or a too copious manner of statement; and, on the contrary, have a mutual interest to effect the result at which they aim, in the shortest and most direct manner.

*Fleming James, Jr.*

## The Revival of Bills of Particulars Under The Federal Rules *

Soon after the [Federal Rules of Civil Procedure] went into effect the question arose whether a party could be compelled by interrogatories (under rule 33) or requests for admission (under rule 36)

* From 71 Harv.L.Rev. 1473, 1473–77, 1479–80, 1481–84 (1958). With permission of Harvard Law Review Association.

to state the details of his claim or contention of fact. Most of the
early cases held he could not be; but there has been a recent tendency
on the part of courts and commentators to favor compelling such a
statement. Typical recent rulings require a party to specify the
particulars of a claim of negligence, contributory negligence, assumption
of the risk, and estoppel. In the case of Alaska v. The Arctic
Maid the plaintiff, seeking to recover back taxes, propounded the
following interrogatory to the defendant, who was alleging the invalidity
of the tax:

> Indicate by specific factual situations connected with
> any or all of your operations in waters north of Dixon Entrance
> between 1949 through 1954, how the tax  .  .  .
>
>      .   .   .   .
>
> (b) abridges, impairs, and/or denies your right to take
> or preserve fish in waters in which fishing is permitted by
> the Secretary of the Interior,
>
>      .   .   .   .
>
> (d) constitutes an attempted taking of your property
> and a denial of your right to fish and preserve fish.

The district judge, concluding that the defendant's answer would
"limit the subjects of controversy, or narrow and clarify the basic
issues between the parties  .  .  .  ." overruled the defendant's
objection to the interrogatory.

Let us compare such recent rulings with orders for bills of
particulars. The substance of what is sought is the same. These
rulings do not call for facts as a witness would give them, from observation
or knowledge, but for the contentions or claims of fact selected,
combined, and stated in terms of their legal consequences,
as a pleader would set them forth. Contentions need not rest on a
party's personal knowledge or observation, nor reflect the party's
own selection or judgment. Indeed they will often represent instead
the work product of his lawyer. Of just such stuff are bills of particulars
made.

Interrogatories or requests for admission which are directed to
the contentions set forth in a pleading may be filed at any time after
the pleading itself has been filed. These devices do not delay the
closing of the pleadings and will often be resorted to after the issues
are closed. In this respect these discovery devices do differ from the
bill of particulars provided for in rule 12(e) as it stood originally.
But they do not differ from the practice which prevails in some
states and which did prevail in the federal courts before the rules.
Under this practice requests for bills of particulars ordinarily come
after issue closed, and do not prolong the pleading stage.

      .   .   .   .

In all essentials, then, the practice of eliciting detailed contentions
of fact by discovery devices is the same as the practice of eliciting
such contentions by bills of particulars after the closing of issue.

Is such a practice consistent with the spirit and framework of
the rules?

One of the great battles of modern procedure has been over how much detail to require in pleadings. From the beginning the Federal Rules of Civil Procedure have been committed to the notion that pleadings should be short, plain, and general. . . .

. . . .

All this suggests that the deposition-discovery devices were intended to reach information and not claims or contentions.

It is true, of course, that a principal purpose of discovery procedure is to narrow the issues at trial. But it does not follow that discovery devices were meant to do everything which will narrow issues. Clearly, for example, discovery may not be used to compel an election of remedies. Discovery will narrow the issues by affording full disclosure of facts and, perhaps, by requiring abandonment of issues which a pleader does not intend in good faith to contest. But there is no indication that discovery was meant to narrow the issues through bringing in by a side door a device which in everything but name so nearly duplicates the rejected New York bill-of-particulars practice.

It is also true that at the pretrial hearing the court is expressly invited to get the parties to consider "the simplification of the issues." It may be urged that this shows the rules were designed to compel detailed statements of claim on the eve of trial, and, that, if such statements are desirable then, the sooner the better; so that the rules should be construed to authorize the compulsion of such statements at an early stage by some appropriate device. To this, two things should be said: (1) The word "simplification" is not apt to describe the process of going into greater detail; indeed it suggests quite the opposite. It is scarcely clear therefore that rule 16 contemplates the compelling of particulars. (2) Even if rule 16 is to be construed as justifying insistence on detailed statements of claim shortly before trial and after full opportunity for the discovery of information, it by no means follows that parties are to be tied down to detail virtually at the pleading stage as bills of particulars would do. Often, perhaps usually in accident litigation, a pleader's claims will concern his adversary's conduct. Especially in such cases there is a substantial difference between compelling particulars before and after an opportunity to probe the adversary's sources of information.

Whether or not the federal rules as they now stand warrant using discovery devices to compel detailed statements of claim, the question remains whether there should be some device for doing this, be it called interrogatory, request for admission, or bill of particulars.

. . . .

The real objection to requiring detailed statements of contentions is that they tie a party down in such a way that he may be deprived of his substantive rights. This is so because even astute counsel are unable always to forecast the vicissitudes of litigation. Time and again some evidence, or some combination of evidence, will emerge for the first time on trial, or will be perceived in its full significance for the first time on trial by the party concerned, or by the tribunal.

True, the discovery devices will and should reduce the possibility of surprise, but they cannot eliminate it. At the trial all the witnesses and evidence are brought together for the first time, and this fact itself may act as a catalyst for eliciting new information and (probably more often) for revealing new insights into the significance and the relationship of things already known. Moreover, at the trial a fresh and most important point of view is brought into play for the first time—that of the tribunal, which is to find and evaluate the facts in terms of the legal theories it finds applicable.

The question, then, is how to resolve the problem of the uncertainty which is inseparable from litigation. Shall its risks be put upon the party who has not had detailed notice of the new possibility, or on the party whose substantive right it unexpectedly supports?

The case for giving judgment according to the substantive law and the facts found to be true by the trier need not be labored. The proponents of detailed particulars would concede it. But they urge that their proposal will narrow the issues and thereby promote administrative efficiency and minimize possible unfairness to the adversary. And they suggest that the danger of substantive injustice can be avoided by amendment. Let us examine these arguments.

Administrative efficiency is of course an important objective of procedure. But it must never be forgotten that the ultimate aim of all procedure should be to secure people their just deserts under the true facts and the appropriate substantive law. The course of law reform is strewn with discarded rules that offered efficiency by narrowing the issues at the cost of justice—witness election of remedies and the common-law rules that demanded production of a single issue on which a case had to stand or fall without opportunity to repair the errors of counsel. Rules which tie a party down to detailed statements of claim would have this vice even if they were efficient; but it is not at all clear that they have the virtue of efficiency.

Administrative efficiency will, to be sure, be promoted by the narrowing of issues, at least if they stay narrow. When discovery devices or a pretrial conference elicit the testimony which will be given at the trial, or an admission that a party intends to abandon contest of an issue made by the pleadings, this purpose will no doubt be served. But experience has shown two reasons why detailed statements of claim fail to promote efficiency to the same extent: (1) The pleader will seek to protect himself by specifying all the details which his imagination suggests as possibilities under the facts which he thinks will or may appear at trial. Thus the detailed statement of contentions may be just as broad as the general pleading, and much more cumbersome. (2) If, however, the pleader has failed to specify some particular contention which would have been within the compass of a generalized pleading and which finds unexpected support or appreciation at trial, then the court is frequently put in a dilemma: It must either refuse to decide the case on the true facts and applicable law, or it must disrupt administrative efficiency to allow a continuance. Either resolution of the dilemma represents an evil. Does fairness to the adversary require this price?

Under the federal rules each party has general notice from the pleadings of the limits of controversy, and full access through discovery devices to all the information and sources of information available to both sides. Each party then knows the framework within which he has to work, and he knows that his adversary may urge his claims and the tribunal may derive its conclusions only from permutations and combinations of facts and legal theories within that framework. A plaintiff, for instance, is entitled to know whether he is charged with contributory negligence and to know the nature of all the sources of information about his conduct and the surrounding circumstances. He is also entitled to have that information. This will narrow the issues a great deal since the nature of the facts themselves will impose severe limits on what may plausibly be claimed.

Further, full discovery of information puts both parties (or their lawyers) in the same position to see what contentions are warranted by the facts. This equalization of the parties enhances the effectiveness of the adversary system to administer justice. In the ordinary case dealing with a single occurrence or transaction like an accident or a breach of contract, where the issues lie within a reasonably narrow compass, it is submitted that fairness to the pleader's adversary requires no more than this.

It may be urged that the adversary should have particulars so as to save him from the unreasonable burden in pretrial preparation of collecting facts upon which no issue will be made. But in many contexts this contention is unrealistic. In accident cases particularly, the adversary's burden will not be alleviated very much by particulars, even when they are not of the shotgun variety. Defendants are nearly always insured or large self-insurers. Those who conduct their defense are familiar with the applicable substantive law and seek to have the accident thoroughly investigated as quickly as possible, well before suit is begun, with a view to careful appraisal of the claim's settlement value as well as to the more remote possibility of litigation. On the other side plaintiffs' attorneys can scarcely afford to neglect a prompt and thorough investigation of their clients' conduct.

The adversary would like, of course, to tie the pleader's contentions down to fine detail. The plaintiff in our illustration, for instance, would like to have the defendant specify the alleged conduct on plaintiff's part which the defendant will contend was negligent. But once the parties have been put on an equal footing, the appeal is less one for fairness than for tactical advantage. The requirement of further particulars of a claim would enable the adversary to prevent the tribunal from giving judgment on the substantive merits whenever the pleader has failed accurately to forecast the course of trial. This carries the implications of the adversary system too far.

---

## SECTION FOUR: THE COURT AS A PHYSICIAN OF ISSUES

In a passage in PHILOSOPHICAL INVESTIGATIONS, Wittgenstein observes that "the philosopher's treatment of a question is like the treatment of an illness." Sec. 225. What he meant was that philosophy's task was not so much to answer certain sorts of questions, but to show why they cannot be answered—to show them as symptoms of an illness in our manner of thinking that had to be treated. Thus, certain questions, like "what is 'length'?" produce in people "a mental cramp", for the form of the question suggests that there must be some substantive—length—which we ought to be able to point to, but, frustratingly, cannot find. By replacing that question with, "how do we measure?", we indicate to the questioner that what he wanted to know about, and what he ought to be investigating is a procedure—how to measure—and not a mysterious thing—length. (See THE BLUE BOOK 1 (1958)). (Consider, in this regard, the analyses of the question "Where is the corporation?" in Chapter 5.)

There is an interesting parallel in Freud. Like Wittgenstein, Freud, albeit for different reasons, is reluctant to suppose that the way the patient portrays the "issues" he faces ought to be accepted at face value and responded to as articulated. Instead, the analyst is to offer a tentative "construction" for the patient to consider as a possible better way to put his "issue" in focus. See Freud, "Construction in Analysis" XXII THE STANDARD EDITION OF THE COMPLETE PSYCHOLOGICAL WORKS OF SIGMUND FREUD 258–259, 260–265 (1964).

From Wittgenstein and Freud to the day-to-day work of the courts may seem a long step. Yet, the function of the courts—as of the analyst—is to resolve conflicts, and often the conflicts that come before them are but symptoms of deeper, unstated conflicts that the society itself may be only dimly aware of. And thus, similarly, some of the most in.portant work of the court system is not to answer, on their face, and in the first instance, questions in the form in which they are put, but to suggest a rephrasing of issues in such manner as to encourage further inquiry into important considerations that will otherwise pass overlooked.

Consider, for example, Terry v. Ohio, 392 U.S. 1 (1969). The case "comes up" framed in terms of whether there had been "probable cause" for a frisking that led to the seizure of evidence and, ultimately, a conviction. But in a footnote to his opinion, Chief Justice Warren brings to the surface a different—and deeper—issue that is involved. "Frisking" he observes

> cannot help but be a severely exacerbating factor in police-community tensions. This is particularly true in situations where the "stop and frisk" of youths or minority group members is "motivated by the officers' perceived need to maintain the power image of the beat officer, an aim sometimes accomplished by humiliating anyone who attempts to undermine police control of the streets.

392 U.S. 1 at 14–15, n. 11, citing to the PRESIDENT'S COMMISSION ON LAW ENFORCEMENT AND ADMINISTRATION OF JUSTICE, TASK FORCE REPORT: THE POLICE (1967). What is the Court *doing* by making this observation? What awarenesses is the Court trying to shift? How is the Court suggesting what Freud might call a "construction" for the sick body politic?

KATZ v. UNITED STATES

389 U.S. 347 (1967)

Mr. Justice STEWART delivered the opinion of the Court.

The petitioner was convicted in the District Court for the Southern District of California under an eight-count indictment charging him with transmitting wagering information by telephone from Los Angeles to Miami and Boston, in violation of a federal statute. At trial the Government was permitted, over the petitioner's objection, to introduce evidence of the petitioner's end of telephone conversations, overheard by FBI agents who had attached an electronic listening and recording device to the outside of the public telephone booth from which he had placed his calls. In affirming his conviction, the Court of Appeals rejected the contention that the recordings had been obtained in violation of the Fourth Amendment, because "[t]here was no physical entrance into the area occupied by [the petitioner]." We granted certiorari in order to consider the constitutional questions thus presented.

The petitioner has phrased those questions as follows:

"A. Whether a public telephone booth is a constitutionally protected area so that evidence obtained by attaching an electronic listening recording device to the top of such a booth is obtained in violation of the right to privacy of the user of the booth.

"B. Whether physical penetration of a constitutionally protected area is necessary before a search and seizure can be said to be violative of the Fourth Amendment to the United States Constitution."

We decline to adopt this formulation of the issues. In the first place, the correct solution of Fourth Amendment problems is not necessarily promoted by incantation of the phrase "constitutionally protected area." Secondly, the Fourth Amendment cannot be translated into a general constitutional "right to privacy." That Amendment protects individual privacy against certain kinds of governmental intrusion, but its protections go further, and often have nothing to do with privacy at all. Other provisions of the Constitution protect personal privacy from other forms of governmental invasion. But the protection of a person's *general* right to privacy—his right to be let alone by other people—is, like the protection of his property and of his very life, left largely to the law of the individual States.

Because of the misleading way the issues have been formulated, the parties have attached great significance to the characterization of the telephone booth from which the petitioner placed his calls. The petitioner has strenuously argued that the booth was a "constitutionally protected area." The Government has maintained with equal vigor that it was not. But this effort to decide whether or not a given "area," viewed in the abstract, is "constitutionally protected" deflects attention from the problem presented by this case. For the Fourth Amendment protects people, not places. What a person knowingly exposes to the public even in his own home or office, is not a subject of Fourth Amendment protection. . . . But what he seeks to preserve as private, even in an area accessible to the public, may be constitutionally protected. . . .

The Government stresses the fact that the telephone booth from which the petitioner made his calls was constructed partly of glass, so that he was as visible after he entered it as he would have been if he had remained outside. But what he sought to exclude when he entered the booth was not the intruding eye—it was the uninvited ear. He did not shed his right to do so simply because he made his calls from a place where he might be seen. No less than an individual in a business office, in a friend's apartment, or in a taxicab, a person in a telephone booth may rely upon the protection of the Fourth Amendment. One who occupies it, shuts the door behind him, and pays the toll that permits him to place a call is surely entitled to assume that the words he utters into the mouthpiece will not be broadcast to the world. To read the Constitution more narrowly is to ignore the vital role that the public telephone has come to play in private communication.

The Government contends, however, that the activities of its agents in this case should not be tested by Fourth Amendment requirements, for the surveillance technique they employed involved no physical penetration of the telephone booth from which the petitioner placed his calls. It is true that the absence of such penetration was at one time thought to foreclose further Fourth Amendment inquiry, Olmstead v. United States, 277 U.S. 438, 457, 464, 466; Goldman v. United States, 316 U.S. 129, 134–136, for that Amendment was thought to limit only searches and seizures of tangible property. But . . . once it is recognized that the Fourth Amendment protects people—and not simply "areas"—against unreasonable searches and seizures, it becomes clear that the reach of that Amendment cannot turn upon the presence or absence of a physical intrusion into any given enclosure. . . . .

. . . The Government's activities in electronically listening to and recording the petitioner's words violated the privacy upon which he justifiably relied while using the telephone booth and thus constituted a "search and seizure" within the meaning of the Fourth Amendment. The fact that the electronic device employed to achieve that end did not happen to penetrate the wall of the booth can have no constitutional significance.

The question remaining for decision, then, is whether the search and seizure conducted in this case complied with constitutional standards. . . .

Accepting [The Government's] account of . . . its actions as accurate, it is clear that this surveillance was so narrowly circumscribed that a duly authorized magistrate, properly notified of the need for such investigation, specifically informed of the basis on which it was to proceed, and clearly apprised of the precise intrusion it would entail, could constitutionally have authorized, with appropriate safeguards, the very limited search and seizure that the Government asserts in fact took place.

. . . .

. . . [T]he judgment must be reversed.

## NOTES AND QUESTIONS

1.   Reformulations of issues by the Supreme Court are by no means rare, and often mark significant shifts in the law.   Justice Brandeis' opening sentence in the landmark decision of Erie Railroad Co. v. Tompkins is "The question for decision is whether the oft-challenged doctrine of Swift v. Tyson shall now be disapproved", 304 U.S. 64, 58 S.Ct. 817, 82 L.Ed. 1188 (1938).   But apparently none of the lawyers had even briefed the question, Brandeis having raised the issue himself in colloquy with counsel.   See WRIGHT, LAW OF FEDERAL COURTS 224 and n. 4 (1970).   In another of the most important cases affecting federal-state relations, Mapp v. Ohio, 367 U.S. 643, 81 S.Ct. 1684, 6 L.Ed.2d 1081 (1961), the Court decided that the issue (or, better, "one way to put the issue") was whether its 1949 opinion in *Wolf v. Colorado*, 338 U.S. 25, should be overruled, so as to impose on the state courts the stricter exclusionary rules that bound federal courts.   Apparently that issue had been raised only by the amicus curiae, and neither by the state of Ohio nor by the appellant.   367 U.S. 646 and n. 3.

2.   Is the judicial "reformulation" of issues peculiar to such Supreme Court landmarks, or is a comparable process, less clearly visible, going on at all levels in all cases?   Even when both sides can agree to a verbalization of "the issue" and the court accepts that verbalization, is it clear that *the meaning* of that verbalization is the same to the court as to the parties; or even that the parties' agreement to the verbalization represents an agreement as to "the issue" in the sense that they wholly agreed to a model for resolution of the differences between them?   Can parties agree to "the issue" and yet disagree as to (a) what rules are applicable, (b) how to interpret the applicable rules; (c) what facts are probative?   If so, what have they agreed to?

Consider any case in which there has been a dissent.   To what extent, in any such case, is the difference that separates the judges one that can be expressed in terms of a different formulation of the issue?

*CHRISTOPHER D. STONE*

## TOWARDS A NEW MODEL OF COURT FUNCTION *

So far I have been addressing myself to the existential humanistic implications of legal instruments and concepts, and to the significance, in those same terms, of a few of the major contemporary developments

---

* From  Existential  Humanism and The Law,  in  Existential  Humanistic  Psy-     chology  152,  169–73.  (Tom  Greening ed. Brooks/Cole 1971).

in law. I would like to close by bringing some of the existential humanist mood to bear on law-making procedures.

To do so, we have to start by reconsidering what the functions of courts are. What first comes to mind is that they serve to resolve disputes between litigants, directing that someone should go to prison, or that a piece of property belongs to Smith rather than to Jones. But courts are importantly involved in a lot more complex processes, though not so evidently. They set an example of how urgently felt needs can be confronted with the claims of principle; they contribute to adjust the social timing that tempers muscular response with reflection; they lead in working out compromises with reality; as important national forums, they stage ceremonies of remembrances—of historical events that hold us together and of crises we managed through; they confirm and question sources of authority; they set a stage on which we can dramatize and act out inner changes that are taking place in senses of morality and mortality; they serve to diffuse hurt and rage, and contribute to a continual redefining of what is to be deemed hurtful in the society.

Part of the function of the courts is thus to shift awareness of what is going on about us and in us, enabling new needs, possibilities and choices to evolve. What this suggests is, that the courts—especially the U. S. Supreme Court, as a paragon—should consciously consider what they could contribute, over and above disposing of the disputes presented to them, by conceiving of themselves as something like a cultural psychotherapist.

This sounds like more radical a reconstrual of Court role than it really is. Actually it is in keeping with much of the tradition of what the Court has, in fact, been doing. By making the effort conscious and systematic, however, the Court may develop its therapeutic potentials a little more fully.

I ought to point out here that the popular conception of how courts operate is far from the mark. The public imagines that the function of courts is simply to issue a series of commands which the litigants and public in turn obey. The image is heavily influenced by—and undoubtedly reinforces—a dominance-submission orientation in the society, giving comfort to forces that need a harsh super-ego for the body politic.

For some time, though, lawyers and court scholars have been pointing out how much of the most important functioning of the court involves avoiding the decision of issues that are tendered to it. The range of such behavior has been well described in BICKEL, THE LEAST DANGEROUS BRANCH (1962), and the rationale for it has been, and can well be, stated in the terms of many models. Of interest to me here is how much of this "non-deciding" behaviour can be described in terms of what a psychotherapist would call non-directive techniques. In the treatment I am referring to, the Supreme Court will not decide cases on the merits, but returns them to the litigants for further consideration—with the Court adding, perhaps, some cues, questions and unobtrusive directions for further explorations. The Court legitimates such unauthoritative behaviour by invoking a series of jurisdictional concepts it has developed, and that number among its most important devices for fulfilling its role. For example, the justices may defer deciding a controversy on the grounds that it is not "ripe" for adjudication (meaning the Court wants to await some further actions that will make the issues clearer); that the party bringing the action has no "standing" to bring it (but some one else might, and perhaps should bring it if the dispute can not be resolved); that the dispute ought first be looked at and considered by some other body—"primary jurisdiction" or "abstention".

The net effect of the Court's invoking these and similar devices is to make itself available in the working out of problems, while yet preserving the autonomy of other decision-making bodies (lower courts, legislatures, commissions, human beings, etc.) which may be able, with further reality-testing, to achieve a better solution on their own.

An obvious example of this is the series of cases involving constitutional attacks on Connecticut's 1879 law prohibiting the use, and counselling as to use, of contraceptives.

The first time controversy over the statute reached the Supreme Court was in 1943. A Connecticut doctor, one Tileston, sought a declaratory judgment to strike down the act on the grounds that if he gave necessary professional advice to three patients whose lives would be endangered by child-rearing, he would be prosecuted. The Court, without dissent, simply dismissed the suit by construing his plea as an attempt to sue upon rights of his patients—not his own—and for the raising of those issues he had no "standing".[2]

Note that the Court did not uphold the statute's constitutionality, and thereby, perhaps, legitimate it in the eyes of the public. It simply listened and refused to direct. But this is not to say that the Court did nothing. Through the suit, many people must have become aware of a statute they had not thought about before, aware that it interfered with the physician's art, and aware that it might result in deaths. Aware, too, of the capacities they had in them, as makers of law, to intrude into the sexual and personal lives of others.

The state of the law being unresolved contributed to further debate in Connecticut, and something of a standoff so far as the statute's effect was concerned: contraceptives were notoriously prescribed and sold, and prosecution was virtually non-existent. But on the other hand, the threat of prosecution still hung over doctors, especially those who might otherwise have set up a clinic.

By 1961 another challenge had worked its way to the Supreme Court. This time, in *Poe v. Ullman*,[3] the plaintiff doctor, Buxton, alleged rights that were clearly his own (to him as a professional, as protected, he claimed, under the Due Process clause of the Fourteenth Amendment). And to be doubly sure of getting an authoritative judgment, his claim was joined (as Tileston's had not been) by his life-endangered patients, who raised their jeopardy in their own right.

2. Tileston v. Ullman, 318 U.S. 44   3. 367 U.S. 497 (1961).
   (1943).

Notwithstanding the carefully mapped out litigation strategy, the Supreme Court still refused to direct a resolution of the problem and resolve the issue. The standing requirement had now been met, allowed Justice Frankfurter for the majority, but since there had been no prosecution,[4] and even the likelihood of prosecution was highly questionable, the case was not ripe; if the Connecticut authorities actually prosecuted and convicted the doctor or his patients, then, and only then, would the Court give further consideration to taking a directive role.

There was now—as there had not been in 1943—a strong division among the Justices. Five were for dismissal on the grounds that no justiciable controversy had yet been presented, but four would have decided the issue on its merits. In all, five separate opinions were written. Each of them, in the course of responding to the jurisdictional questions, served to ventilate the underlying problems— problems not only of the statute, on its merits, but also of the broader institutional framework: where ought responsibility for making a decision to lie—with the people of Connecticut, through their own processes, or with the Supreme Court, imposing its views from above? Justice Douglas, who apparently would have decided the merits (although apparently he had not been prepared to do so at the time of the *Tileston* case), observed:

> The regime of a free society needs room for vast experimentation. Crises, emergencies, experience at the individual and community levels produce new insights; problems emerge in new dimensions; needs, once never imagined, appear. To stop experimentation and the testing of new decrees and controls is to deprive society of a needed versatility. Yet to say that a legislature may do anything not within a specific guarantee of the Constitution may be as crippling to a free society as to allow it to override specific guarantees so long as what it does fails to shock the sensibilities of a majority of the Court.
>
> The present legislation is an excellent example. . . .[5]

The Court, by its disposition of *Poe v. Ullman* had done the following. It had left the State of Connecticut with no choice but to repeal or strongly amend the law; to prosecute someone (if the authorities wanted a final test of constitutionality); or to ignore the unenforcement of a law that everyone in the state was now keenly aware of, at the cost of some loss of respect for—and habit of— obedience to law in general.

The political forces against amendment or repeal were too strong to be overcome, at least with the speed that the statute's opponents demanded. The result was that on November 1, 1961, the opponents very openly set up a clinic in New Haven (the *Poe* opinion having come down June 19) and by the 10th of the same month, they managed

---

4. As in the Tileston case, the doctor and his patients were seeking a declaratory judgment. The aim was to avoid having to wait to be prosecuted and convicted before being able to raise the issue.

5. *Id.* at 518–19.

to get themselves arrested. They were convicted, and by 1965 had gotten their case back up to the Supreme Court, which decided, 85 years after the statute had been enacted, that it was unconstitutional, only two justices dissenting.[6]

Now, from one point of view, the Court's non-directive posture ultimately did not work as well as one might have hoped. The best outcome, in the psychotherapeutic model, would have been for Connecticut itself to have undertaken a genuine and searching analysis of the animus behind the statute, and repealed it without the Court *ordering* it to do so. Viewing this legal sequence in psychotherapeutic terms, we might say that while the Court's action may have gotten rid of the statute (repression), it did not fully facilitate the development of insight—in this instance into the reasons why the statute had found support in Connecticut—as a basis for making visible and getting rid of the underlying needs for it. Still, what the Court did and did not do ought to be viewed from the point of the contributions it made to these processes. It is quite likely that in 1965 the Court was able to do what it could not have done in 1943 or 1879—to resolve the issue effectively—not simply because "times had changed", but because the Court had, by its handling of the prior birth control cases, and similar matters, helped to allow and promote that change. The Court can not, consonant with its more immediate duties, be patient forever, especially while people's lives are endangered. But if the Court consciously thinks of its role as, in part, following the lines of the "psychotherapeutic model", the Court may come to put in a sharper perspective the values that lie on the side of a creative and deferring manner of handling the issues that are tendered to it.

The Court has long been aware of the *realpolitik* values of avoiding rigid rules of decision that may not be carried out (such as when it built into the school integration cases the requirement of "all deliberate speed"). But there are other values as well, values that a fuller development of the psychotherapeutic model would illuminate. These include the Court's refusing to accept more cultural superego functions than is healthy for the balance of the societal decision-making bodies. From this point of view, while Judge Wyzanski's opinion in *United States v. Sisson* [7] was (in these terms) "directive"—laying down, as law, that Sisson could not be drafted—it nonetheless retained large "psychoanalytic" value, for it set up a dialogue as to where decision-making responsibility ought to be allowed to rest at this stage of civilization, and he had the trust to return some of it from the Congress and other remote institutions to the individual human being.

This is how the Court, at best, might aim to conceive its functions: Not as a fount of behavioral edicts, but as partner in a dialogue, as an institution of state systematically engaged in helping the culture to articulate and cope with the tensions that are set up as mankind seeks to work its way to ever-new adjustments in the liberation of its capacities.

---

**6.** Griswold v. Connecticut, 381 U.S. 479 (1965).

**7.** 297 F.Supp. 902 (D.Mass.1969), Chapter 18 *infra*.

## CHAPTER EIGHT

# The Authority of Language

## INTRODUCTORY NOTE

The materials in this chapter respond to a problem which has been raised—both explicitly and implicitly—at a number of earlier points in this book. To what extent, the question might now be framed, is it possible for language to communicate the perceptions, concepts, facts, issues, and prescriptions which people must have in common if human societies—and, specifically, human legal systems— are to function successfully? That most people go about their every-day affairs on the assumption that language can and does work satisfactorily seems to need no argument. But the mere fact of con-sensus would not seem to conclude the matter. In addition, as Cas-sirer's remarks about primitive man suggest, the consensus concerning language has not always been the same. For in other times and other places whole cultures have entertained supernatural ideas about the nature and power of the word which we would consider fantastic. Thus, another way of framing the problem of this chapter is to ask whether current conceptions of language, however modern and civ-ilized they may sound, are not—as were their primitive forerunners— also illusory and mythical.

So far as it has been pursued in the preceding pages, this inquiry has tended to focus on the problem of the interpreter—the person for whom particular linguistic formulations are to provide authoritative direction. The concern has been with whether he can know the law in order that he might follow it. This is, ultimately, the central con-cern of the following pages as well. Before confronting it directly, however, the chapter attempts to expose problems which arise in the initial decision to employ words to control the conduct of others. Here the focus is on the rule-maker and the underlying assumption is that language does work, that it does inform its addressees.

The question posed is not whether, but how and at what cost, language works. Whatever the answer, the inquiry itself should help us to decide when resort to the authority of language is wise. More importantly, knowing these costs helps us to understand and define the role of the interpreter. For if the decision to have a rule is neces-sarily a decision to accept certain costs, it follows that an interpreter who wishes to accept the rule's authority does not have the option— whether it be in the interests of justice, good sense, or whatever—to leave those costs unpaid. An interpreter who refuses to pay them, no matter his protestations to the contrary, is necessarily refusing to follow the rule as well.

Such an analysis—as the remarks of Rawls in Chapter 3 suggest— is by no means novel. It is the theoretical ground on which much criticism of "judicial legislation" is based. It must be remembered, however, that such criticism assumes what this chapter asserts must be proved: that it *is* possible for the good faith interpreter to know what the rules mean. The materials on The Limitations of Rules and of Language make it possible to suggest another way to test the validity of this assumption. For everything can be seen to turn on the nature of the costs which rules entail and whether it is within the power of any interpreter—whatever his intentions—to pay costs of this sort.

One answer to this question may have been offered by Justice Holmes's famous dictum that general propositions do not decide concrete cases. Much of the later material in this chapter can be viewed as an elucidation of the meaning and consequences of Holmes's statement. Section 8(2) (C), for example, seeks to raise questions about the way in which rules operate in human thought, about what it means to *know* a rule, and about the extent to which it is acceptable to say that rules dictate the decision of particular problems and cases. Section 8(3) (A) presents a number of famous justifications for excluding cases from the operation of laws which seem clearly to cover them. One of the questions raised here is whether theories of the sort advanced—and, impliedly, any theory which defends a refusal to follow "the letter of the law"—can be consistent with a commitment to a regime of rules and of authoritative language. Section 8(3) (B), on the other hand, questions whether the alternative to such theories—the strict adherence to "the letter" proposed by men like Kelsen and Augustine—is actually possible given the nature of symbols and their relations to their meanings. Here, among other things, it is asked if there can be a *necessary* connection between a linguistic symbol and any particular object, event or situation.

## SECTION ONE: THE POWER AND MYSTERY OF WORDS

*ERNST CASSIRER*

### LANGUAGE AND MYTH *

The original bond between the linguistic and the mythico-religious consciousness is primarily expressed in the fact that all verbal structures appear as *also* mythical entities, endowed with certain mythical powers, that the Word, in fact, becomes a sort of primary force, in which all being and doing originate. In all mythical cosmogonies, as far back as they can be traced, this supreme position of the Word is found. Among the texts which Preuss has collected among the Uitoto Indians there is one which he has adduced as a direct parallel to the opening passage of St. John, and which, in his translation, certainly seems to fall in with it perfectly: "In the beginning," it says, "the Word gave the Father his origin." . . .

. . . . There must be some particular, essentially unchanging *function* that endows the Word with this extraordinary, religious character, and exalts it *ab initio* to the religious sphere, the sphere of the "holy." In the creation accounts of almost all great

---

* From 44–48, 49, 53–55 (S. Langer transl. Dover ed. 1946). Reprinted       by permission of Yale University Press.

cultural religions, the Word appears in league with the highest Lord of creation; either as the tool which he employs or actually as the primary source from which he, like all other Being and order of Being, is derived.  Thought and its verbal utterance are usually taken directly as one; for the mind that thinks and the tongue that speaks belong essentially together.  Thus, in one of the earliest records of Egyptian theology, this primary force of "the heart and the tongue" is attributed to the creation-god Ptah, whereby he produces and governs all gods and men, all animals, and all that lives.  Whatever is has come into being through the thought of his heart and the command of his tongue; to these two, all physical and spiritual being, the existence of the Ka as well as all properties of things, owe their origin.  Here, as indeed certain scholars have pointed out, thousands of years before the Christian era, God is conceived as a spiritual Being who *thought* the world before he created it, and who used the *Word* as a means of expression and an instrument of creation.  And as all physical and psychical Being rest in him, so do all ethical bonds and the whole moral order.

. . . .

. . . . in India, we find the power of the Spoken Word (Vāc) exalted even above the might of the gods themselves.

"On the Spoken Word all the gods depend, all beasts and men; in the Word live all creatures  . . .  the Word is the Imperishable, the firstborn of the eternal Law, the mother of the Veddas, the navel of the divine world."

As the Word is first in origin, it is also supreme in power.  Often it is the *name* of the deity, rather than the god himself, that seems to be the real source of efficacy.  Knowledge of the name gives him who knows it mastery even over the being and will of the god.

. . . .

. . . .

The essential identity between the word and what it denotes becomes even more patently evident if we look at it not from the objective standpoint, but from a subjective angle.  For even a person's ego, his very self and personality, is indissolubly linked, in mythic thinking, with his name.  Here the name is never a mere symbol, but is part of the personal property of its bearer; property which must be carefully protected, and the use of which is exclusively and jealously reserved to him.

. . .

"The fact that the name functions as proxy for its bearer," says Dieterich in his *Eine Mithrasliturgie*, "and to speak the name may be equal to calling a person into being; that a name is feared because it is a real power; that knowledge of it is sought because being able to speak it bestows control of that power on the knower—all these facts indicate clearly what the early Christians were still feeling and trying to express when they said 'In God's name' instead of 'In God,' or 'In Christ's name' for 'In Christ. . . . The congregation, whose liturgy begins with the words: 'In the name of God,' was thought at the time to be within the bourne of the name's efficacy (no matter how figuratively and formally the phrase is taken). 'Where two or three are gathered together in my name, there am I in the midst of them' (Matthew 18:20) means simply, 'Where they pronounce my name in their assembly, there I am really present.' . . . ."

The "Special god," too, lives and acts only in the particular domain to which his name assigns and holds him. Whoever, therefore, would be assured of his protection and aid must be sure to enter his realm, i. e., to call him by his "right" name. This need explains the phraseology of prayer, and of religious speech in general, both in Greece and in Rome—all the turns of phrase which ring a change on the several names of the god, in order to obviate the danger of missing the proper and essential appellation. . . . for every act of devotion to the god, every appeal directed to him, commands his attention only if he is invoked by his appropriate name . . .

### NOTES AND QUESTIONS

To what extent, if at all, do the ideas about language which Cassirer reports resemble modern civilized conceptions and notions? Do we ever talk as if language were a creative and a coercive force? What is meant, for example, when lawyers speak of rules "dictating" results, "controlling" cases or operating "automatically"? Are these simply metaphors? If they are, is it relatively easy to translate them into literal terms? If so, why do you suppose the literal terms are not used instead of the figurative? If not, how would you account for the difficulty?

Is there any sense in which you would be willing to concede that language has "power"? Consider the pervasive influence of language which we have previously noted in the processes of perception, conception, "fact-finding," and issue formulation. Is there a way of talking about this phenomenon without treating language as a "force"? If so, just what is it that directs us to have certain perceptions—as Henle suggests in Chapter 4—rather than others? Or is this an illegitimate question?

Note the primitive belief that language historically antedates the creation of all material things and, even, in some cultures, the creation of the deity. Is there any parallel to this in the intellectual currency of modern man? Consider Rawls's notion that rules are *logically prior* to cases. Is there a difference between logical priority and historical priority? What is the point Rawls sought to make by establishing the priority of rules to cases? Does his notion that cases somehow fit into "logically" preexisting rules sound plausible to you? If so, is this because that is the way the world is, or because that is the way our culture and our language dispose us to see the world? To what extent does the form of the syllogism reinforce the notion that rules come before cases? Be sure to recur to these questions in the materials on "Rules in Thought and the Logic of Common Law Precedent."

Many thinkers are convinced that magical elements persist in modern man's relationship to his language. The primitive mind's inclination to personify the forces and qualities denoted by names—a phenomenon we have already come across in Chapter 5—is thought to be a continuing feature of modern language. Similarly, the inability to separate names from the particular things they symbolize, as many of the materials in this chapter suggest, apparently continues to characterize instances of legal thinking. The primitive's insistence that everything turns on using the right word is reminiscent, for many, of common law pleading and, if the comments of Stephen in section 2 are still relevant, may continue to have force in the thinking and drafting which lawyers do. Much philosophical, linguistic and semantic thought has been devoted to de-mythologizing language, in order that it might function as a *tool* completely subject to man's pragmatic goals. Other views, however, have apparently resigned themselves to a mythic view of language. Only in these the Word's force is viewed not as divine, but as daemonic. Bacon, for example, admonishes that "words plainly force and overrule the understanding." Philosophy, Wittgenstein asserts, "is a battle against the bewitchment of our intelligence by means of language." A large literature—part of which is represented in the sections which follow—has been produced to expose the ways in which language "overrules" the understanding and the types of mistakes it leads men to make. You should ask yourself when you encounter this material just how devastating is its criticism of language—and just how much authority language can have if these criticisms are valid.

*Bronislaw Malinowski*

## The Language of Magic and Gardening *

. . . . all language in its earliest function within the context of infantile helplessness is proto-magical and pragmatic. It is pragmatic in that it works through the appeal to the child's human surroundings; it is proto-magical in that it contains all the emotional dependence of the child on those to whom it appeals through sound. In the course of long years, during which the pragmatic attitude towards words only gradually develops, the child experiences the power of words and sounds, especially when these are fraught with emotion as well as with the conventional significances of articulation.

. . .

The thesis then which I am putting forward here is that the Trobriand phenomenon of a language of magic, within which we find a masquerading of significant speech under the guise of esoteric and mysterious forms, fits into the theory of language. In Trobriand magic we find hardly a single word, the working of which, that is, the meaning of which, could not be explained on the basis of associations, mythological data or some other aspect of Frazer's principle of sympathy. This, I think, is but part of the universal, essentially human, attitude of all men to all words. From the very use of speech men develop the conviction that the knowledge of a name, the correct

* From 2 Coral Gardens and Their Magic 232–235 (1935). Copyright 1965 by Indiana University Press. Reprinted by permission.

use of a verb, the right application of a particle, have a mystical power which transcends the mere utilitarian convenience of such words in communication from man to man.

The child actually exercises a quasi-magical influence over its surroundings. He utters a word, and what he needs is done for him by his adult entourage. This is a point of view on which I do not need to enlarge. I think that the contributions of such modern child psychologists as Piaget and Buhler, and of older workers such as William Stern, supply us with a rich material for the confirmation of this point of view. . . .

. . . . this early attitude is partly superseded, but to a large extent confirmed, in the further development of the individual. The mastery over reality, both technical and social, grows side by side with the knowledge of how to use words. Whether you watch apprenticeship in some craft within a primitive community or in our own society, you always see that familiarity with the name of a thing is the direct outcome of familiarity with how to use this thing. The right word for an action, for a trick of trade, for an ability, acquires *meaning* in the measure in which the individual becomes capable to carry out this action. The belief that to know the name of a thing is to get a hold on it is thus empirically true. At the same time, it lends itself to obvious distortions in the direction of mysticism. For the genuineness of the process, that is, the genuineness of verbal power over things through manual and intellectual control, is the result of a fine balance. On the one hand we have people who are more effective manually than verbally. This is a handicap. The simple mind, primitive or civilized, identifies difficulty of speech and clumsiness and unreadiness of expression with mental deficiency. In the Trobriands *tonagowa* covers idiocy and defective speech; and among European peasantry the village idiot is very often merely a person who stammers or suffers from inability of clear expression. On the other hand the verbal type and the theoretical type of person surpass in mastery of words while they are backward in manual effectiveness. Even within the most primitive differentiation of activities the man who is better at counsel and advice, at talking and bragging, represents what in more advanced communities will become the schoolman, the talmudist or the baboo. This may be an unhealthy development of learning or of a purely consulting or advisory capacity; but it is rooted in something which functions throughout all human work —I mean the fact that some people must command, advise, plan and coordinate.

So far I have been mainly speaking about arts and crafts. Power through speech in the mastery of social relations, of legal rules and of economic realities, is quite as plain. The child who grows up in a primitive community and becomes instructed gradually in the intricacies of kinship, the taboos, duties and privileges of kindred, of clansmen, of people of higher and lower rank, learns the handling of social relations through the knowledge of sociological terms and phrases. The instruction may take place in the course of initiation ceremonies, a great part of which consists in the sociological apprenticeship of the child, boy or girl, youth or maiden, to tribal citizenship. But obviously there is a long educational process between the small infant, who can name and call for the few people of its immediate surroundings, and the adult tribesman or tribeswoman, who must address a score, a few hundred or even a few thousand people in the proper manner, appeal to them through adequate praise, be able to greet, converse and transact business with them. This process again has two sides: experience in "deportment," manners, practices and abstentions, and the capacity to name, describe and anticipate these things, and also to use the adequate words in these relations. Here also the mastery of social aspect and social terminology runs parallel.

If space allowed, I could enlarge on this side of our subject indefinitely. Take, for instance, the problem of law in its verbal and pragmatic aspects. Here the value of the word, the binding force of a formula, is at the very foundation of order and reliability in human relations. Whether the marriage vows are treated as a sacrament or as a mere legal contract—and in most human societies they have this twofold character—the power of words in establishing a permanent human relation, the sacredness of words and their socially sanctioned inviolability, are absolutely necessary to the existence of social order. If legal phrases, if promises and contracts were not regarded as something more than *flatus vocis*, social order would cease to exist in a complex civilization as well as in a primitive tribe. The average man, whether civilized or primitive, is not a sociologist. He neither needs to, nor can, arrive at the real function of a deep belief in the sanctity of legal and sacral words and their creative power. But he must have this belief; it is drilled into him by the process whereby he becomes part and parcel of the orderly institutions of his community. The stronger this belief, the greater becomes what might be called the elementary honesty and veracity of the citizens. In certain walks of human life speech may develop into the best instrument for the concealment of thought. But there are other aspects—law, contracts, the formulas of sacraments, oaths—in which a complicated apparatus inviolably based on mystical and religious ideas develops in every community as a necessary byproduct of the working of legal and moral institutions and relationships.

This must suffice to establish my proposition that there is a very real basis to human belief in the mystic and binding power of words. We can also see where the truth of this belief really lies. Man rises above his purely animal, anatomical and physiological equipment by building up his culture in cooperation with his fellow beings. He masters his surroundings because he can work with others and through others. Verbal communication from the earliest infantile dependence of the child on his parents to the developed uses of full citizenship, scientific speech and words of command and leadership, is the correlate of this. The knowledge of right words, appropriate phrases and the more highly developed forms of speech, gives man a power over and above his own limited field of personal action. But this power of words, this cooperative use of speech is and must be correlated with the conviction that a spoken word is sacred. The fact also that words add to the power of man over and above their strictly pragmatic effectiveness must be correlated with the belief that words have a mystical influence.

## Notes and Questions

Is it inevitable, according to Malinowski, that men should entertain mythological and magical ideas about language? If the child—even of modern times—develops a magical attitude toward language, will he necessarily retain that attitude throughout his life? Or is the discarding of such attitudes one of the experiences that mark the entrance of the child into adulthood? What is the significance, if true, of Piaget's thesis that in the formation of every mature human mind the organism recapitulates the intellectual development of the species? If this means that each of us is biologically preordained to go through a phase of magical thought, is there reason to believe that such modes of thinking would persist into maturity? Is the answer to this question important?

## Arthur Koestler

## The Ghost in The Machine *

. . . Take a simple example: the farmer's little boy of about three, leaning out of the window, sees the dog snapping at the postman, and the postman retaliating with a vicious kick. All this happens in a flash, so fast that his vocal chords have not even had the time to get innervated; yet he knows quite clearly what happened and feels the urgent need to communicate this as yet unverbalised event, image, idea, thought, or what-have-you, to his mum. So he bursts into the kitchen and shouts breathlessly: 'The postman kicked the dog.' Now the first remarkable fact about this is that he does *not* say, 'The dog kicked the postman,' though he *might* say, 'Doggy *was* kicked *by* the postman'; and again, he will *not* say, 'Was the dog kicked by the postman?', and least of all, 'Dog the by was the kicked postman'.

This was an example of a very simple sentence consisting of four words only ('the' being used twice). Yet a change of the order of two words gave a totally different meaning; a more radical reshuffling, with two new words added, left the meaning unaltered; and most of the ninety-five possible permutations of the original words give no meaning at all. The problem is how a child ever learns the several thousand abstract rules and corollaries necessary to generate and comprehend meaningful sentences—rules which his parents would be unable to name and define; which you and I are equally unable to define; and which nevertheless unfalteringly guide our speech. The few rules of grammar which the child learns at school—long *after* it has learned to speak correctly—and which it promptly for-

* From 28–30 (1968). Copyright 1967 by Arthur Koestler. Reprinted by permission.

gets, are descriptive statements about language, not recipes to generate language. These recipes, or formulae, the child somehow discovers by intuitive processes—probably not unlike the unconscious inferences which go into scientific discovery—by the time it has reached the age of four. By that time 'he will have mastered very nearly the entire complex and abstract structure of the English language. In slightly more than two years, therefore [starting at about the age of two] children acquire full knowledge of the grammatical system of their native tongue. This stunning intellectual achievement is routinely performed by every pre-school child' . . . . another renegade Behaviourist remarked at our Stanford seminar: 'The fact that we can freely produce sentences we had never heard before is amazing. The fact that we can understand them when produced is nothing short of miraculous. . . . A child never has a look at the machinery that produces English sentences. He *could* never have a look at that machinery. Nor is he being told about it since most speakers are completely unaware of it.'

## Note: The Mystery of Language

Perhaps the most outlandish feature of the mythological view of language is its unscientific—its seemingly magical—conception of causation. It is common sense that the world does not rearrange itself at the uttering of a few words or that people cannot be injured simply by calling out their names. Yet, in some way, words and names seem to play a critical role in the modification of nature and the harms that people suffer. Is it clear that we know how or why? Communication, say writers like Noam Chomsky, is a process whose mechanism is largely unknown and there is yet to be developed any system of criteria by which its successes can be "objectively" judged. As Koestler reports, the ability of men to generate and comprehend sentences is considered even by some scientists as "nothing short of miraculous." In the law, some of our linguistic formulations do seem to "work," although we are never quite certain. Others, as we have seen and shall see again, seem to fail us miserably. Are we at all aware of what it is that accounts for these successes and failures? Is it that some times men are clumsy or stupid or careless in the drafting of their regulations, and sometimes they are not? Is it that men are inherently incapable of consistent obedience to rules, however well-made? Can the difficulties be traced to language itself? Does the "tool" by its nature limit the uses to which it can be put? These are some of the questions implicit in all of the materials which follow. As the difficulty of answering them becomes apparent, it may occur to us to wonder whether modern explanations of language and meaning are materially superior to those of primitive mankind.

The Wizard of Id

by Brant parker and Johnny hart

By permission of Johnny Hart and Field Enterprises, Inc.

## Section Two: The Linguistic Urge: Making and Finding Rules

### Introductory Note

Very often rules created with the best of intentions have proved the instruments of injustice, inefficiency and confusion. Even when they seem on the whole to be worthwhile there are inevitably costs which rule-maker and rule-follower must pay. Unfortunately, we are frequently not aware of the costs when the decision to have a rule is initially made. Sometimes, indeed, they remain hidden even as the rule is put into operation. When the consequences are subsequently disappointing it is possible that the policy sought, rather than the method employed to implement it, may unfairly receive the blame.

Rule-making seems so clearly a matter of choice—when we think about it in the abstract—that it might seem superfluous to emphasize the point here. Yet we are constantly making rules without considering that perhaps the best way—or the least bad way—of accomplishing our goals may be to leave their implementation either to our own or somebody else's discretion. Martin v. Herzog, for example, is a case which confronted a judge with the choice of retaining the vague standard of due care or adopting a specific, statutorily decreed rule of conduct. To choose one or the other—or some variant of either—necessarily involved him in a choice between rule and discretion. It is significant that nowhere in his opinion does Cardozo address either his attention or his arguments to that issue. For him it apparently did not exist; it was thus a subject over which he seemed to exercise no conscious choice.

Both the concepts of "rule" and of "discretion"—like all concepts—are by no means simple, straightforward notions and it is possible with minimal analysis to blur the differences between them. Office-holders, for example, are regularly granted discretion by means of a prescriptive phrase, sentence or paragraph. Thus, agencies enjoined to decide cases according to "public convenience and necessity" are ordinarily thought to have much discretion even though their authority derives from a linguistic direction. A law which contained such a standard might technically qualify as a rule. One dictionary, for example, defines "rule" as "a principle or regulation governing conduct." Yet many would argue that a regulation which grants the degree of choice permitted by the above prescription is not sufficiently binding to be a rule. This is apparently the position taken by Rawls in the excerpts which appear in Chapter 3. Rawls distinguishes "summary" from "practice" rules by, *inter alia*, the discretion the former leaves the interpreter to decide each case according to what is "best on the whole." Significantly, it is for "practice" rules that Rawls reserves the description "rules in the strict sense."

The investigation undertaken in this section assumes the validity of distinctions such as the one suggested by Rawls. Rules, therefore, will here be taken to mean those prescriptions which specify definite, isolable conduct and which do not leave the interpreter with freedom to decide for himself whether such conduct is "in the public interest," "best on the whole," or "reasonable." The section assumes—what will ultimately be the question for scrutiny—that linquistic symbols are capable of so defining and describing conduct as to deny "discretion" and to control conduct. The assumption enables one to ask whether, nevertheless, it is always—or, even, often—wise to use language in this way.

In the end, the following materials suggest that this question cannot be profitably studied without taking into account the nature of language and various aspects of its relations to thought. If the purpose of rules is to lay down specific standards of conduct, for example, we need to know just how specific language can get. We need to know if undesired consequences of a law can be precluded by additional words which, because of their specificity, seem to get us closer to the particular problems and situations which called forth the rule in the first place. Similarly, we need to know whether conduct which is ordinarily characterized in vague or ambiguous terms, terms which inevitably invite controversy and uncertainty, can be reduced to unequivocal formulations the meaning of which will be clear to all "reasonable" interpreters. The materials suggest generally that it is necessary to develop some idea of the distinctive features and strengths of language in order to understand why it is possible for it to carry out assignments. It is just as essential to understand the inherent limitations which account for its acknowledged failures. Strangely enough, it frequently seems as if language's strengths are also its major defects. It is apparently a question in any given case, therefore, whether what language is likely to give with one hand will not be retrieved by the other.

For would-be lawyers the problems of rule-making may seem somewhat remote from areas of immediate professional concern. The problems seem to be those of the legislator or of the judge, not of the law student or the soon-to-be practitioner. The latter's problems—at least as the conventional wisdom has it—seem more a matter of rule-finding, rule-studying and rule-following. This, as much of the material in the entire chapter suggests, is misleading in a number of ways. Two of these require notice here. First, lawyers are constantly devising regulations for the conduct of their personal and professional lives as well as for the conduct of their clients. The problem of rule versus discretion, in other words, is pervasive in every phase of everyday living: it arises in the process of deciding what to tell one's son, one's gardener, one's butcher, one's secretary, one's clerk, one's associates. It arises more noticeably in the drafting of contracts, corporate charters, wills, powers of attorney and so forth.

The second way in which the rule-finding conception of the practitioner's function misleads us is that it tends to imply that rule-finding is a qualitatively different process from rule-making. This is seriously challenged by the passages excerpted from Harari. His point is one that can be extended even beyond the particular situation of the doctrine of stare decisis. The lawyer who has found a statute which seems to deal with his problem must still concern himself with the meanings of material words and phrases within it. He must seek a definition which will serve his client's ends. That definition, however, very often will be found in no book. It must be constructed by the attorney himself. Similarly, the reasons advanced for adopting that particular formulation will themselves very likely be new linguistic formulations specially devised for a particular legal occasion. In most instances the form of these constructions will differ in no material way from the form of rules. On the other hand, it is possible that they may and, indeed, that they should. If this is so, then another realm of choice has been exposed to view.

These last observations remind us that rules function not only as directions and guides, but also as vehicles of justification and explanation. We are often expected to justify our conduct, our decisions and our conclusions by reference to some rule to which they conform. We are regularly expected to give reasons and it will often be held against us if we have no reasons to offer. Indeed, it sometimes appears that the very rationality of our thought processes depends upon whether we can point to rules which have been manipulated to reach our intellectual results.

The subject of rule-making, rule-finding, and rule-manipulating thus involves us in the question, what is a "good", an "intelligent", or a "logical" decision? It invites us to ask whether "deciding according to law" is the same as deciding according to rule and, if so, just how one goes about accomplishing the latter task. The degree and nature of the authority which language can have will hopefully be illuminated by the answers to these and similar questions raised in the last part of this section.

## A.  The Decision to Have a Rule

### MARTIN v. HERZOG

228 N.Y. 164 (1920)

CARDOZO, J. The action is one to recover damages for injuries resulting in death.

Plaintiff and her husband, while driving toward Tarrytown in a buggy on the night of August 21, 1915, were struck by the defendant's automobile coming in the opposite direction. They were thrown to the ground, and the man was killed. At the point of the collision the highway makes a curve. The car was rounding the curve when suddenly it came upon the buggy, emerging, the defendant tells us, from the gloom. Negligence is charged against the defendant, the driver of the car, in that he did not keep to the right of the center of the highway (Highway Law, sec. 286, subd. 3; sec. 332; Consol. Laws, ch. 25). Negligence is charged against the plaintiff's intestate, the driver of the wagon, in that he was traveling without lights (Highway Law, sec. 329a, as amended by L.1915, ch. 367). There is no evidence that the defendant was moving at an excessive speed. There is none of any defect in the equipment of his car. The beam of light from his lamps pointed to the right as the wheels of his car turned along the curve toward the left; and looking in the direction of the plaintiff's approach, he was peering into the shadow. The case against him must stand, therefore, if at all, upon the divergence of his course from the center of the highway. The jury found him delinquent and his victim blameless. The Appellate Division reversed, and ordered a new trial.

We agree with the Appellate Division that the charge to the jury was erroneous and misleading. The case was tried on the assumption that the hour had arrived when lights were due. It was argued on the same assumption in this court. In such circumstances, it is not important whether the hour might have been made a question for the jury (Todd v. Nelson, 109 N.Y. 316, 325). A controversy put out of the case by the parties is not to be put into it by us. We say this by way of preface to our review of the contested rulings. In the body of the charge the trial judge said that the jury could consider the absence of light "in determining whether the plaintiff's intestate was guilty of contributory negligence in failing to have a light upon the buggy as provided by law. I do not mean to say that the absence of light necessarily makes him negligent, but it is a fact for your consideration." The defendant requested a ruling that the absence of a light on the plaintiff's vehicle was "*prima facie* evidence of contributory negligence." This request was refused, and the jury were again instructed that they might consider the absence of lights as some evidence of negligence, but that it was not conclusive evidence. The plaintiff then requested a charge that "the fact that the plaintiff's intestate was driving without a light is not negligence in itself," and to this the court acceded. The defendant saved his rights by appropriate exceptions.

We think the the unexcused omission of the statutory signals is more than some evidence of negligence. It *is* negligence in itself. Lights are intended for the guidance and protection of other travelers on the highway. . . . By the very terms of the hypothesis, to omit, willfully or heedlessly, the safeguards prescribed by law for the benefit of another that he may be preserved in life or limb, is to fall short of the standard of diligence to which those who live in organized society are under a duty to conform. That, we think, is now the established rule in this state. . . . Whether the omission of an absolute duty, not willfully or heedlessly, but through unavoidable accident, is also to be characterized as negligence, is a question of nomenclature into which we need not enter, for it does not touch the case before us. There may be times, when if jural niceties are to be preserved, the two wrongs, negligence and breach of statutory duty, must be kept distinct in speech and thought. . . . In the conditions here present they come together and coalesce. A rule less rigid has been applied where the one who complains of the omission is not a member of the class for whose protection the safeguard is designed. . . . Some relaxation there has also been where the safeguard is prescribed by local ordinance, and not by statute. . . . Courts have been reluctant to hold that the police regulations of boards and councils and other subordinate officials create rights of action beyond the specific penalties imposed. This has led them to say that the violation of a statute is negligence, and the violation of a like ordinance is only evidence of negligence. An ordinance, however, like a statute, is a law within its sphere of operation, and so the distinction has not escaped criticism. . . . Whether it has become too deeply rooted to be abandoned, even if it be thought illogical, is a question not now before us. What concerns us at this time is that even in the ordinance cases, the omission of a safeguard prescribed by statute is put upon a different plane, and is held not merely some evidence of negligence, but negligence in itself. . . .

In the case at hand, we have an instance of the admitted violation of a statute intended for the protection of travelers on the highway, of whom the defendant at the time was one. Yet the jurors were instructed in effect that they were at liberty in their discretion to treat the omission of lights either as innocent or as culpable. They were allowed to "consider the default as lightly or gravely" as they would (THOMAS, J., in the court below). They might as well have been told that they could use a like discretion in holding a master at fault for the omission of a safety appliance prescribed by positive law for the protection of a workman. . . . Jurors have no dispensing power by which they may relax the duty that one traveler on the highway owes under the statute to another. It is error to tell them that they have. The omission of these lights was a wrong, and being wholly unexcused was also a negligent wrong. No license should have been conceded to the triers of the facts to find it anything else.

. . . . There may indeed be times when the lights on a highway are so many and so bright that lights on a wagon are superfluous. If that is so, it is for the offender to go forward with the evidence, and prove the illumination as a kind of substituted performance. The plaintiff asserts that she did so here. She says that the scene of the accident was illumined by moonlight, by an electric lamp, and by the lights of the approaching car. Her position is that if the defendant did not see the buggy thus illumined, a jury might reasonably infer that he would not have seen it anyhow. We may doubt whether there is any evidence of illumination sufficient to sustain the jury in drawing such an inference, but the decision of the case does not make it necessary to resolve the doubt, and so we leave it open. It is certain that they were not required to find that lights on the wagon were superfluous. They might reasonably have found the contrary. They ought, therefore, to have been informed what effect they were free to give, in that event, to the violation of the statute. They should have been told not only that the omission of the lights was evidence of negligence, but that it was *"prima facie* evidence of contributory negligence," *i. e.,* that it was sufficient in itself unless its probative force was overcome (THOMAS, J., . . . below) to sustain a verdict that the decedent was at fault (Kelly v. Jackson, 6 Pet. 622, 632). Here, on the undisputed facts, lack of vision, whether excusable or not, was the cause of the disaster. The defendant may have been negligent in swerving from the center of the road, but he did not run into the buggy purposely, nor was he driving while intoxicated, nor was he going at such a reckless speed that warning would of necessity have been futile. Nothing of the kind is shown. The collision was due to his failure to see at a time when sight should have been aroused and guided by the statutory warnings. Some explanation of the effect to be given to the absence of those warnings, if the plaintiff failed to prove that other lights on the car or the highway took their place as equivalents, should have been put before the jury. The explanation was asked for, and refused.

We are persuaded that the tendency of the charge and of all the rulings following it, was to minimize unduly, in the minds of the triers of the facts, the gravity of the decedent's fault. Errors may not be ignored as unsubstantial when they tend to such an outcome. A statute designed for the protection of human life is not to be brushed aside as a form of words, its commands reduced to the level of cautions, and the duty to obey attenuated into an option to conform.

The order of the Appellate Division should be affirmed, and judgment absolute directed on the stipulation in favor of the defendant, with costs in all courts.

## NOTES AND QUESTIONS

1. Does the statute in *Martin* provide that it shall have the effect in negligence cases that Cardozo gives it? Does Cardozo say it so provides? If not, just what is the relevance of the statutory standard in this case? What role does it play in the structure of his argument?

In the law of negligence one of the "elements" of the tort is the failure to exercise "due care" or to act as a "reasonable man" would under the circumstances? Is Cardozo saying that the statutory rule must be taken to set the standard of reasonable conduct in situations to which it applies? Is this what he means in saying that "to omit . . . the safeguards prescribed by law . . . is to fall short of the standard of diligence to which those who live in organized society are under a duty to conform"?

2. How would the standard of conduct required of the plaintiff have been determined had there been no pertinent statute? "[T]he jurors were instructed in effect that they were at liberty in their discretion to treat the omission of lights either as innocent or as culpable." What kind of "discretion" is Cardozo saying the jury was given? Was it a discretion to disregard the omission of lights even if it concluded that the omission amounted to contributory negligence? Is Cardozo saying that the jury was "at liberty" to choose between plaintiff and defendant without regard to law or to general community standards of reasonable conduct? "Jurors have no dispensing power," says Cardozo, "by which they may relax the duty that one traveler on the highway owes under the statute to another. It is error to tell them that they have." Did the lower court judge tell the jury that it could "relax the duty that one traveler . . . owes under the statute to another"? How do you think the lower court judge would describe what he told the jury? Incidentally, did the jury in this case have the *power* to relax "duties" created by the vehicle code, even if it had wanted to?

3.   In connection with the foregoing questions, consider the following remarks of Judge Learned Hand:

> The degree of care demanded of a person by an occasion is the resultant of three factors: the likelihood that his conduct will injure others, taken with the seriousness of the injury if it happens, and balanced against the interest which he must sacrifice to avoid the risk.  All these are practically not susceptible of any quantitative estimate, and the second two are generally not so, even theoretically.  For this reason a solution always involves some preference, or choice between incommensurables, and it is consigned to a jury because their decision is thought most likely to accord with commonly accepted standards, real or fancied.

Conway v. O'Brien, 111 F.2d 611 (2d Cir. 1940).  Is Cardozo saying that the law of negligence, insofar as it leaves the determination of the standard of conduct to a jury, gives it the "liberty" "to treat the omission of lights either as innocent or as culpable"?  Is he saying that the standard of "reasonable" or "ordinary" care is so indeterminate as to permit the jury to act lawlessly?

If the legislature did not decree that the rule it had enacted in its vehicle code should also be the standard of due care in negligence cases, what explanations can be advanced for this?  Having formulated a standard of conduct for traffic code cases, can you think of any reason why it might leave such broad discretion as Hand describes in the jurors?

Why should we ever leave discretion of this breadth in anyone's hands—whether jury, judge, policeman, prosecutor, administrator or, even, legislator?

4.   What are the issues in Martin v. Herzog?  Has Cardozo done them justice?  Has he adequately stated or dealt with them?  How would you describe his view of the issues?  Does he take into account all of the factors and interests at stake?  Which of these do you think he failed to mention?

5.   American courts have devised more than one way of treating statutory violations in negligence cases.  Three alternatives are represented by the opinions in Satterlee v. Orange Glen School District, 29 Cal.2d 581 (1947).  "An act which is performed in violation of an ordinance or statute," the majority held, "is presumptively an act of negligence, but the presumption is not conclusive and may be rebutted by showing that the act was justifiable or excusable under the circumstances."  Justice Traynor, concurring in the decision, argued that "the conduct of the parties must be measured by" the "statutory standard."  He wished to follow the "majority of American courts [which] have adopted the doctrine that the violation of a statute constitutes negligence *per se* . . . . "  Justice Carter dissented contending that "the test should be that of the conduct of a person of ordinary prudence."  He conceded that "the standard provided in the statute . . . is a factor to be considered."  But, he insisted, a "violation of the rule may or may not be negligence *depending upon the circumstances*."  (Italics in original.)

Which of these alternatives would you say Cardozo adopted? Is there language which could support more than one interpretation of his decision? Justice Traynor seemed to think that *Martin* announced a negligence *per se* standard. See his opinion at pp. 594–596. Do you agree? If not, how can you explain Traynor's error?

6. What is the reason that Cardozo gives for holding that plaintiff's omission "*is* negligence in itself"? In what part of the opinion is that reason offered? Can you put the essence of Cardozo's opinion into a syllogism? Would the following be adequate:

*The unexcused violation of a statute is negligence* per se.

*Plaintiff violated a statute and offered no adequate excuse.*

*Plaintiff was guilty of negligence* per se.

Assuming that plaintiff could make out no case for an acceptable "excuse," would such an argument have been satisfactory? If Cardozo had said just that and nothing more, could it be said that he had failed to "explain" his decision? That he had failed to give a "reason" for it? What *is* a reason? Consider the following from Justice Traynor (p. 595):

> Confusion has arisen in the past from a failure to understand why the legislative standard governs civil liability when the statute prescribes criminal sanctions only. The reason is simply that the courts under common law principles make the legislative standard controlling and take the formulation of a standard from the jury . . . .
> [The statutory] standard determines civil liability, not because the Legislature has so provided, but because the courts recognize that, with respect to the conduct in question, the duties of the parties are determined by the statute. . . .

Can you state in your own words the "reason" that Justice Traynor is offering? Is it more or less a "reason" than Cardozo's?

7. Can it be said that Cardozo simply chose the more authoritative expositor of community standards in Martin v. Herzog? Can the decision be read as saying that where the legislature speaks courts and juries must follow? Is this principle really in issue in *Martin*? Does Cardozo write at times as if it is? What major question remains unanswered by an explanation of the sort just advanced for Cardozo's decision? Does Cardozo answer it?

OLIVER WENDELL HOLMES, JR.

THE COMMON LAW *

. . . . any legal standard must, in theory, be one which would apply to all men, not specially excepted, under the same circumstances. It is not intended that the public force should fall upon an individual accidentally, or at the whim of any body of men. The

* From 88–89, 90–91, 96–99, 103 (Harvard ed. 1963). Originally published    in 1881 by Little, Brown and Company.

standard, that is, must be fixed.  In practice, no doubt, one man may have to pay and another may escape, according to the different feelings of different juries.  But this merely shows that the law does not perfectly accomplish its ends.  The theory or intention of the law is not that the feeling of approbation or blame which a particular twelve may entertain should be the criterion.  They are supposed to leave their idiosyncrasies on one side, and to represent the feeling of the community.  The ideal average prudent man, whose equivalent the jury is taken to be in many cases, and whose culpability or innocence is the supposed test, is a constant, and his conduct under given circumstances is theoretically always the same.

Finally, any legal standard must, in theory, be capable of being known.  When a man has to pay damages, he is supposed to have broken the law, and he is further supposed to have known what the law was.

If, now, the ordinary liabilities in tort arise from failure to comply with fixed and uniform standards of external conduct, which every man is presumed and required to know, it is obvious that it ought to be possible, sooner or later, to formulate these standards at least to some extent, and that to do so must at last be the business of the court.  It is equally clear that the featureless generality, that the defendant was bound to use such care as a prudent man would do under the circumstances, ought to be continually giving place to the specific one, that he was bound to use this or that precaution under these or those circumstances.  The standard which the defendant was bound to come up to was a standard of specific acts or omissions, with reference to the specific circumstances in which he found himself. If in the whole department of unintentional wrongs the courts  .  .  . left every case, without rudder or compass, to the jury, they would simply confess their inability to state a very large part of the law which they required the defendant to know, and would assert, by implication, that nothing could be learned by experience.  But neither courts nor legislatures have ever stopped at that point.

From the time of Alfred to the present day, statutes and decisions have busied themselves with defining the precautions to be taken in certain familiar cases;  that is, with substituting for the vague test of the care exercised by a prudent man, a precise one of specific acts or omissions.  .  .  .

The rule of the road and the sailing rules adopted by Congress from England are modern examples of such statutes.  By the former rule, the question has been narrowed from the vague one, Was the party negligent? to the precise one, Was he on the right or left of the road?  To avoid a possible misconception, it may be observed that, of course, this question does not necessarily and under all circumstances decide that of liability; a plaintiff may have been on the wrong side of the road, as he may have been negligent, and yet the conduct of the defendant may have been unjustifiable, and a ground of liability. So, no doubt, a defendant could justify or excuse being on the wrong side, under some circumstances.  .  .  .

The principles of substantive law which have been established by the courts are believed to have been somewhat obscured by having presented themselves oftenest in the form of rulings upon the sufficiency of evidence. When a judge rules that there is no evidence of negligence, he does something more than is embraced in an ordinary ruling that there is no evidence of a fact. He rules that the acts or omissions proved or in question do not constitute a ground of legal liability, and in this way the law is gradually enriching itself from daily life, as it should. Thus, in Crafton v. Metropolitan Railway Co., the plaintiff slipped on the defendant's stairs and was severely hurt. The cause of his slipping was that the brass nosing of the stairs had been worn smooth by travel over it, and a builder testified that in his opinion the staircase was unsafe by reason of this circumstance and the absence of a hand-rail. There was nothing to contradict this except that great numbers of persons had passed over the stairs and that no accident had happened there, and the plaintiff had a verdict. The court set the verdict aside, and ordered a nonsuit. The ruling was in form that there was no evidence of negligence to go to the jury; but this was obviously equivalent to saying and did in fact mean, that the railroad company had done all that it was bound to do in maintaining such a staircase as was proved by the plaintiff. A hundred other equally concrete instances will be found in the text-books.

On the other hand, if the court should rule that certain acts or omissions coupled with damage were conclusive evidence of negligence unless explained, it would, in substance and in truth, rule that such acts or omissions were a ground of liability, or prevented a recovery, as the case might be. Thus it is said to be actionable negligence to let a house for a dwelling knowing it to be so infected with small-pox as to be dangerous to health, and concealing the knowledge. To explain the acts or omissions in such a case would be to prove different conduct from that ruled upon, or to show that they were not, juridically speaking, the cause of the damage complained of. The ruling assumes, for the purposes of the ruling, that the facts in evidence are all the facts.

The cases which have raised difficulties needing explanation are those in which the court has ruled that there was *prima facie* evidence of negligence, or some evidence of negligence to go to the jury.

Many have noticed the confusion of thought implied in speaking of such cases as presenting mixed questions of law and fact. No doubt, as has been said above, the averment that the defendant has been guilty of negligence is a complex one: first, that he has done or omitted certain things; second, that his alleged conduct does not come up to the legal standard. And so long as the controversy is simply on the first half, the whole complex averment is plain matter for the jury without special instructions, just as a question of ownership would be where the only dispute was as to the fact upon which the legal conclusion was founded. But when a controversy arises on the second half, the question whether the court or the jury ought to judge of the defendant's conduct is wholly unaffected by the accident, whether there is or is not also a dispute as to what that conduct was. If there is such a dispute, it is entirely possible to give a series of hypothetical instructions adapted to every state of facts which it is open to the jury to find. If there is no such dispute, the court may still take their opinion as to the standard. The problem is to explain the relative functions of court and jury with regard to the latter.

When a case arises in which the standard of conduct, pure and simple, is submitted to the jury, the explanation is plain. It is that the court, not entertaining any clear views of public policy applicable to the matter, derives the rule to be applied from daily experience, as it has been agreed that the great body of the law of tort has been derived. But the court further feels that it is not itself possessed of sufficient practical experience to lay down the rule intelligently. It conceives that twelve men taken from the practical part of the community can aid its judgment. Therefore it aids its conscience by taking the opinion of the jury.

But supposing a state of facts often repeated in practice, is it to be imagined that the court is to go on leaving the standard to the jury forever? Is it not manifest, on the contrary, that if the jury is, on the whole, as fair a tribunal as it is represented to be, the lesson which can be got from that source will be learned? Either the court will find that the fair teaching of experience is that the conduct complained of usually is or is not blameworthy, and therefore, unless explained, is or is not a ground of liability; or it will find the jury oscillating to and fro, and will see the necessity of making up its mind for itself. There is no reason why any other such question should not be settled, as well as that of liability for stairs with smooth strips of brass upon their edges. The exceptions would mainly be found where the standard was rapidly changing, as, for instance, in some questions of medical treatment.

If this be the proper conclusion in plain cases, further consequences ensue. Facts do not often exactly repeat themselves in practice; but cases with comparatively small variations from each other do. A judge who has long sat at *nisi prius* ought gradually to acquire a fund of experience which enables him to represent the common sense of the community in ordinary instances far better than an average jury. He should be able to lead and to instruct them in detail, even where he thinks it desirable, on the whole, to take their opinion. Furthermore, the sphere in which he is able to rule without taking their opinion at all should be continually growing.

It has often been said, that negligence is pure matter of fact, or that, after the court has declared the evidence to be such that negligence *may* be inferred from it, the jury are always to decide whether the inference shall be drawn. But it is believed that the courts, when they lay down this broad proposition, are thinking of cases where the conduct to be passed upon is not proved directly, and the main or only question is what that conduct was, not what standard shall be applied to it after it is established.

. . . .

The trouble with many cases of negligence is, that they are of a kind not frequently recurring, so as to enable any given judge to profit by long experience with juries to lay down rules, and that the elements are so complex that courts are glad to leave the whole matter in a lump for the jury's determination.

## NOTES AND QUESTIONS

How many separate reasons can you disengage from Holmes's remarks for replacing the broad-based negligence discretion with specific rules and standards? Did Cardozo use any of these reasons to support his decision in Martin v. Herzog? Do you think any of them are responsive to the issue in that case?

Holmes's conception of the jury's role in the determination of the negligence standard of conduct is not the one generally entertained. See, *e. g.*, W. PROSSER, TORTS 191 (1955). The jury's role, however, is confined to "cases where the judgment of reasonable men might differ." Does this suggest another way of reaching the result apparently desired by Cardozo in *Martin*? Was it the omission of lights or the violation of a traffic statute which most irked him? If there had been no statute, do you think he would have permitted the jury to find plaintiff's conduct innocent? If not, and assuming that he had the legal authority to overturn the verdict without committing himself to a doctrinal position on the relation of statutory violations to negligence, why do you think he avoided this route? In what way is the doctrine he announced superior to the case-by-case supervision of jury negligence findings which common law trial judges provide?

Note Holmes's statement that "facts do not often exactly repeat themselves in practice." Do facts *ever* "exactly repeat themselves in practice"? If so, how are you using the word "fact"? Is it easier or harder to believe in the efficacy of specific standards if you believe that at least once in awhile "facts  .  .  .  exactly repeat themselves in practice"?

*JAMES FITZJAMES STEPHEN*

## A HISTORY OF THE CRIMINAL LAW OF ENGLAND *

.  .  .  . The generality of language which is characteristic of the foreign codes would be wholly unsuited to our own country.  .  . There is no doubt something attractive at first sight in broad and apparently plain enactments. Further acquaintance with the matter shows that such enactments are in reality nothing but simple and therefore deceptive descriptions of intricate subjects. If an attempt, for instance, is made to dispose in a few words of such a subject as homicide or madness, the result is, either a vague phrase, such as, "murder is unlawful killing with malice aforethought, which has to be made the subject of all sorts of intricate explanations, and the source of endless technicalities, or else a rule like "l'homicide commis volontairement est qualifie meurtre." This rule has no doubt the merit of being short and, if "volontairement" means "intentionally," clear, but is quite inadequate, and if it is acted upon produces bad results. Homicide, considered as a crime, does not

* From v. III, 355–356 (1883).

admit of a short definition. The subject must be carefully thought out, and all the questions which it raises must be explicitly and carefully dealt with, before the matter can be satisfactorily disposed of. There is, however, abundant proof that when subjects are thus carefully thought out the definitions of crimes may be made quite complete and absolutely perspicuous. To take a single instance, I may refer to the definition of bribery in the Corrupt Practices Act of 1854 (17 & 18 Vic. c. 102, s. 2). It consists of five principal heads,— namely, firstly, paying money for votes; secondly, giving offices for votes; thirdly, doing either of these things with intent to get any person, not to vote for, but to procure the return of, any member to parliament; fourthly, acting upon any such consideration; and lastly, paying money with intent that it shall be employed in any of these ways. Each of these five general heads is carefully elaborated, so that every additional word strikes at some conduct not exactly covered by any other phrase in the whole section, till at last the whole taken collectively, embraces every conceivable case of, what would popularly be described as bribery. After being in force for nearly thirty years, one question only, and that a small one, has arisen as to what acts do or do not fall within the statute. It must, on the other hand, be admitted that such definitions are not pleasant reading, nor can the public at large be expected to follow all their details. As, however, laws are intended mainly for the actual administration of justice, I emphatically prefer our own way of drawing them up.

## Questions

Do Holmes and Stephen have the same reasons for desiring specificity in the law? Can you state clearly what Stephen's reasons are? Are any of these available to Cardozo to support the decision in Martin v. Herzog?

### Jerome Frank

## What Courts Do In Fact *

. . . . There is a delightful intellectual discipline called "formal law" or "law-in-discourse." It is a sort of intellectual game. . .

. . .

It is convenient to express in crude mathematical form the basic thesis of formal law as to how decisions are arrived at. Suppose we call a decision, D; the facts of the case, F; and the so-called rule of law, R. Then

R x F = D (Rules times Facts = Decision).

Thus symbolizing formal law theory, it is revealed that the D will be unknowable in advance in any specific case unless you know both the R and the F. The D is the product of two variables.

. . .

* 26 Ill.L.Rev. 645, 648, 651–656 (1932). Review. Reprinted by permission of Copyright 1932 by the Illinois Law Northwestern University Law School.

.   .   .   .   Formal law explains a jury trial thus: The jury receive their R's from the judge. They arrive at the F by inferences from the evidence. Their general verdict is a product of the Judge's R's times the jury's F.

No description could be more misdescriptive of what really happens. In truth a "contested" jury trial goes thus: The jury is exposed to testimony, to the sight and sound of witnesses, to the dramatic performances of the lawyers; then the judge intones in the jury's presence a treatise on law-in-discourse. This treatise is largely unintelligible to the jury. Most jurymen tell us that the judge's rules are ignored in the jury room. The jury's verdict is often a result of gambling technique—or worse. No attempt is made by juries to separate out the R and the F. They bring in a verdict—their D—finding for Jones in the sum of $15,000. That D becomes the judge's D (through the entry of judgment on the verdict) unless he grants a new trial. If he does so, then a new trial is had before another jury which goes through the same performance. (The judge, that is, either (a) adopts the jury's D or (b) vetoes it and later accepts another jury's D.)

To apply the formal law theory to a jury trial it is therefore necessary to say something like this: Assume (contrary to the obvious truth) that the jury heard and understood the judge's R. Assume (contrary to the obvious truth) that they agreed on an F and then multiplied this F by the judge's R. Making these impossible assumptions, the decision can be explained in terms of R x F = D. But the real truth is that the jury arrives at its D by no such route.

No one knows—and no one is allowed to prove—what was the jury's R or the jury's F. Indeed there is no jury R or jury F—there is only a jury D. Their decision is a composite which formal law later—after the decision—breaks up into an alleged R x F = D.

.   .   .   judges, like juries, usually have composite, undifferentiated reactions to the evidence. The formal law description of the judicial process is false where juries are involved. It is often substantially as false—only less so in degree—with respect to judges.

First note that in most "contested" cases tried before a judge without a jury no opinion is written. So that in most such cases we are never informed by anybody what was the judicial R or F—but only the D.

Sometimes, however, a judge does write a justification, explanation, or apologia for his decision. He phrases it in terms of formal law. He tells us that the "facts" are thus, the "rule" so, and therefore he decided thus and so.

But talks with candid judges have begun to disclose that, whatever is said in opinions, the judge often arrives at his decision before he tries to explain it.   .   .   .   After the judge has so decided, then the judge writes his "opinion." The D has been fixed. The judge's problem is now to find an R and an F that will equal this already-determined D.

The judge's opinion makes it *appear* as if the decision were a result solely of playing the game of law-in-discourse. But this explanation is often truncated, incomplete. Worse, it is frequently unreal, artificial, distorted. It is in large measure an after-thought. It omits all mention of many of the factors which induced the judge to decide the case. Those factors (even to the extent that the judge is aware of them) are excluded from the opinion. So far as opinions are concerned, those factors are tabu, unmentionables.

Opinions, then disclose but little of how judges come to their conclusions. The opinions are often ex post facto; they are *censored expositions*. To study those eviscerated expositions as the principal bases of forecasts of future judicial action is to delude oneself.

How then does a judge arrive at his decision? In terse terms, he does so by a "hunch" as to what is fair and just or wise or expedient. . . . The lawyer's task, then, becomes this: The determination of what produces the judge's hunches. What, then, does produce the judicial hunch? The answer must be vague: The effect of innumerable stimuli on what is loosely termed "the personality of the judge." If you have a liking for mathematical formulas you can let S be the stimuli, P be the judge's personality; D be the decision; you can then say "S x P = D."

. . . . "the personality of the judge" and the "judicial hunch" are not and cannot be described in terms of legal rules and principles. They are therefore not recognized or referred to by formal law—except in jocular asides or allegedly humorous footnotes.

Moreover, to repeat, the judicial hunch does not separate out the F and the R. The hunch is a composite reaction of a multitude of responses to the stimuli set up by witnesses—stimuli which encounter the judge's (or jury's) biases, "stereotypes," preconceptions, and the like. On all this, formal law is silent. This silence makes formal law hopelessly inaccurate and accounts for the smug confidence of its devotees (when they forget that law-in-discourse is a mere game) in the measurable certainty of the judicial process.

## QUESTIONS

Do Frank's comments amount to criticisms of Cardozo or Holmes? At what places in their arguments would Frank's contentions become relevant? Is Frank opposed to rules? Or is he opposed to the way in which rules are employed in the legal system? Or is he simply making a statement about the inefficacy of rules with no necessary implication that they ought to be inefficacious? If so, what is it about rules or about the legal system which makes them inefficacious? Do you think he is right in saying that "the judge intones in the jury's presence a treatise on law-in-discourse" which "is largely unintelligible to the jury"? Do you think that the instructions which the lower court gave in Martin v. Herzog might have been "largely unintelligible to the jury"? Were they more or less so than the instructions Cardozo desired to be given? Try to think of what the trial judge had to tell the jury in *Martin* and imagine how he might do it. Do you think it would be relatively easy to convey a message that was understandable to twelve average members of the community who have no knowledge of the law? If so, why? If not, why not? Is this a factor which judges ought to take into account in deciding whether to proliferate rules and multiply distinctions? What does Stephen think? If Frank is right—and if judges generally know he is right—is the insistence on such instructions a survival of magical attitudes toward language? Is the charge simply a ritualistic incantation?

## B. The Limitations of Rules and of Language

### JOHN DICKINSON

#### ADMINISTRATIVE JUSTICE AND THE SUPREMACY OF LAW *

Where a subject-matter would advantageously admit of reduction to more definite rules and definitions, and is still left open to the unguided operation of a balancing of interests, I do not see how we can escape saying that *pro tanto* we have not a régime of justice according to law. But there is naturally a wide difference in the relative readiness with which different fields of human relations admit of reduction to rules. Commercial transactions and transfers of property lend themselves to it with peculiar facility, for two reasons. They are in the first place artificial in the sense that the attention of the parties is consciously directed toward producing a legal result. Secondly, the need for orderliness in the "game" of business has normally led the participants, of their own accord, to stereotype certain forms of dealing in much the same manner as the law would do. All that remains is for the law to step in and sharpen these distinctions and accentuate the forms already outlined. The test of whether or not a transaction is adapted to the application of a general rule turns on precisely this point of whether or not a limited number of elements naturally stand out in it as marked with dominant significance. If so, the process of generalization and omission can be applied without doing violence to considerations of fairness. On the other hand, in a field where every case involves a multitude of pertinent elements which vary in importance from case to case, it is practically impossible fairly to select any special factor or factors and apply them as criteria over the whole field. This is true of all ordinary matters of conduct not definitely directed, like business transactions, to the production of a legal result. There can be no concrete definition of negligence, because it may occur in every conceivable human situation—crossing a street, handling a barrel, lighting a lamp, riding a bicycle, or hitching a horse. In these cases it is quite possible for the course of time and the run of the cases to carve grooves of classification and issue ultimately, if not in a single definition, at least in particular definitions to fit

* From 145–148 (1927). Copyright 1927 by the President and Fellows of Harvard College, 1955 by John Dickinson.    Reprinted by permission of Harvard University Press.

particular situations. Thus cases of persons injured in crossing railroad tracks are very numerous. The situation is a relatively simple one and the principal ways of exercising due care are within the scope of everyday experience. Some of the cases have accordingly attempted to crystallize a definite rule that a necessary element of due care in such a situation is to stop, look, and listen. So conceivably, the rule might crystallize that it would be negligence to hitch a horse with a rope of less than a certain thickness. Such rules are congenial to the formalistic stage in the early history of jurisprudence. But although it is thus not beyond possibility to develop definite rules in even a field like negligence, there is more than a question as to whether they are desirable. The situation differs in essential respect from that of commercial transactions. Tort cases involve matters of unpremeditated conduct where a legal result is not directly intended by the actors, but is imposed by law. There is a real and practical difference behind the theoretical distinction between a so-called legal transaction and other kinds of juristic acts. In the one case it is not advisable to lay down rules and definitions with the same strictness as in the other, because to do so would be to interfere unwisely with that personal freedom to choose between alternatives of conduct which it is good policy for the law to foster. It is mere formalism to require a man to stop before crossing a railroad track in a case where he could see no more if he stopped than if he did not. Or take the rule suggested as to the thickness of rope. Suppose a new material is discovered for making rope with greater tensile strength than any hitherto used. Shall improvement in manufacture be impeded and industry prevented from reaping its advantage by a legal rule hardened out of circumstances which existed prior to its discovery? Fixed rules cannot profitably govern conduct at points where their effect would be to interfere with the introduction of improved methods of human action.

NOTE: HOLMES, CARDOZO AND THE
"STOP, LOOK AND LISTEN" RULE

In Baltimore & Ohio R. R. v. Goodman, Justice Holmes, speaking for the U. S. Supreme Court, exemplified his disagreement with Dickinson's position as follows:

> When a man goes upon a railroad track he knows that he goes to a place where he will be killed if a train comes upon him before he is clear of the track. He knows he must stop for the train, not the train stop for him. In such circumstances it seems to us that if a driver cannot be sure otherwise whether a train is dangerously near he must stop and get out of his vehicle, although obviously he will not often be required to do more than to stop and look. . . . It is true . . . that the question of due care very generally is left to the jury. But we are dealing with a standard of conduct, and when the standard is clear it should be laid down once for all by the Courts.

275 U.S. 66 (1927). In Pokora v. Wabash Ry., however, where a plaintiff whose vision was obstructed was not required to get out

of his truck, the court, after alluding to consequences of Holmes's rule which might actually add to a driver's danger, held that "to the extent that . . . [*Goodman*] imposes a standard for application by the judge" it was no longer to be followed. 292 U.S. 98 (1934).

The justice who wrote the opinion repudiating Holmes's rule was Cardozo. Do you think he could have written an opinion which was consistent with the decision in Martin v. Herzog? Suppose there had been a statute in *Pokora* which read as follows:

> *Every driver of an automobile, truck or other motor vehicle proceeding to drive through a railroad crossing must before going upon any tracks stop, look and listen for an approaching train. If vision or hearing is obstructed, the driver must leave his vehicle to assure himself that the way is safe.*

Suppose that the only penalty for violation of this statute was a small fine and there was no mention of civil liability. Would Cardozo be required under the reasoning of *Martin* to hold *Pokora* negligent? If *Martin* had involved a statute of the sort hypothesized, rather than the one actually litigated, is it possible that Cardozo would not have announced the Common Law rule he did? If you think so, does this involve you in accepting the position of Frank?

### Note: The Reasons for Codifying Traffic Law

If Dickinson's antipathy to the codification of negligence in specific standards of conduct is justified how does one go about defending codes of traffic law? Isn't this precisely one of those "fields of human relations" which does not "admit of reduction to rules"? Or do the considerations which Dickinson advances to justify "more definite rules and definitions" in commercial and property law apply here as well?

Why do you suppose that legislatures did not leave the enforcement of traffic safety to the Common Law courts under their usual negligence standards? Or, if a statute was desired, why did not legislatures simply enact bills which decreed, *e.g.*, "motorists who engage in conduct which violates community standards of reasonable prudence shall be subject to fine and imprisonment"? Is it because such a standard would be too vague to support the imposition of criminal penalties? Would it be unfair to imprison a person for engaging in "unreasonable" conduct? Suppose that such legislation provided that violations of the traffic safety statute would be punishable only by small fines. Would that eliminate all objections to a traffic statute framed in this way? What other purposes are served by a detailed statement and promulgation of "rules of the road"?

Does negligence law reach all unsafe conduct? Or does it only reach unsafe conduct which eventuates in injuries? Does it even reach all of this conduct? Who has the responsibility under negligence law to see that traffic safety is enforced? Who has this responsibility under a traffic code? Which of the two systems is better adapted to *preventing* accidents? What would be the reaction of many generally law-abiding motorists or pedestrians if told by policemen that they have been stopped, and that they must attend court, because they have engaged in "unreasonable" conduct? Would such a standard be easier or harder to enforce than detailed traffic rules? How efficiently and expeditiously could policemen act under such a standard? Would there be more or fewer traffic cases litigated under a "reasonableness" standard? What would be the economic cost of a system which used it? Assuming that the penalties remained low, could it be argued that the injustice and inexactness of a system of definite, rigid rules was acceptable?

Do any of these reasons also support the use of detailed rules in civil negligence law? Do they engender more or less sympathy for the position that the legislature in its traffic laws has decreed the social standard of safe conduct and this must be used in civil as well as traffic litigation?

## JOSEPH NEEDHAM

### SCIENCE AND CIVILISATION IN CHINA *

The oldest datable codification of Chinese law known to us . . . is that related in the *Tso Chuan* for —535. Here, at the beginning of the story, appears that uncompromising objection to codification which characterised Confucian thought throughout Chinese history. In the text we read:

> In the third month the people of the State of Chêng made (metal cauldrons on which were inscribed the laws relating to) the punishment (of crimes). Shu Hsiang wrote to Tzu-Chhan (i. e. Kungsun Chhiao, prime minister of Chêng), saying:

> 'Formerly, Sir, I took you as my model. Now I can no longer do so. The ancient kings who weighed matters very carefully before establishing ordinances, did not (write down) their system of punishments, fearing to awaken a litigious spirit among the people. But since all crimes cannot be prevented, they set up the barrier of righteousness (*i*), bound the people by administrative ordinances (*chêng*), treated them according to just usage (*li*), guarded them with good faith (*hsin*), and surrounded them with benevolence (*jen*). . . . But when the people know that there are laws regulating punishments, they have no respectful fear of authority. A litigious spirit awakes, invoking the letter of the law, and trusting that evil actions will not fall under its provisions. Government becomes impossible . . . . Sir, I have heard it said that a State has most laws when it is about to perish.'

* From v. 2, 521–522 (1956). Reprinted by permission of the Syndics of Cambridge University Press.

The situation was repeated later in the same century. For the year —512 the *Tso Chuan* says:

> In the winter Ju-Pin was fortified. The inhabitants of the State of Chin were forced to contribute 480 catties of iron to make cauldrons on which the penal laws were inscribed. They were those of Fan Hsüan-Tzu. Confucius said, 'I fear that Chin is going to destruction. If its government would observe the laws which its founder prince received from his brother, it would direct the people rightly . . . Now the people will study the laws on the cauldrons and be content with that; they will have no respect for men of high rank.'

Thus from the beginning the supple and personal relations of *li* were felt to be preferable to the rigidity of *fa*.

## NOTE: CODIFICATION IN THE CRIMINAL LAW

The codification of definite rules in the law of crimes is considered by many in Western democratic societies as a fundamental requirement of liberal democracy.

> They take their stand on the principle that no one shall be punished for anything that is not expressly forbidden by law. *Nullum crimen, nulla poena, sine lege.* They regard that principle as their great charter of liberty.

A. DENNING, FREEDOM UNDER LAW 41 (1949). Common Law crimes, especially those formulated in vague terms, are considered serious threats to liberty. See *id.* at 41–42; H. L. A. HART, LAW, LIBERTY, AND MORALITY 12 (1963): "Perhaps the nearest counterpart to this in modern European jurisprudence is the idea to be found in German statutes of the Nazi period that anything is punishable if it is deserving of punishment according 'to the fundamental conceptions of a penal law and sound popular feeling'." Why is the Nazi rule any more objectionable than the standards of negligence law? Is this what Holmes was getting at? Was this Cardozo's concern as well?

Is the reason that Confucius opposed the codification of criminal law an indifference to "liberty" or "authoritarian repression"? Consider K. MANNHEIM, CRIMINAL JUSTICE AND SOCIAL RECONSTRUCTION 211 (1932):

> As a child of the French Revolution, the principle *nullum crimen sine lege* was mainly designed to favor the *tiers état* as the social class which was the principal usufructuary of Revolution. It has retained this characteristic ever since. As a rule, it is the bourgeois, the business man, the *entrepreneur*, who profits by it, as the member of the community more likely than anybody else to know the law and, with the support of his legal advisers, to find ways and means of getting round it.

Using Dickinson's criteria, is the regulation of crimes one of those "fields of human relations" which does "admit of reduction to rules"? Consider the following:

> Even in something generally supposed to be so much controlled by law as the administration of criminal justice, administrative discretion is far more important than rules. All the rules that call for punishment can be nullified by any one of five sets of discretionary power—the discretion of the police not to arrest, the discretion of the prosecutor not to prosecute or to trade a lesser charge for a plea of guilty, the discretion of the judge in favor of suspended sentence or probation, the discretion of the parole officer to release. . . . Perhaps it is not too much to say that the essence of criminal justice lies in the exercise of discretionary power, despite the continuing importance of the jury trial.

K. Davis, Discretionary Justice 18 (1969). Can you think of additional instances of discretion in the administration of criminal law?

*Joseph Needham*

Science and Civilisation in China *

There is one feature in Legalism which is of particular interest for the historian of science, namely, its tendency towards the quantitative. The word shu, which often appears, means not only number but quantitative degree, and even statistical method. Already in the oldest parts of the *Shang Chün Shu*, says Duyvendak, there is a preference for expressing everything in numerical figures, points, units, degrees of penalties, numbers of granaries, amounts of available fodder, etc. A later part of the same book says:

> Rewards exalt and punishments degrade, but if the superiors have no knowledge of their method, it is as bad as if they had no method at all. But the method for right knowledge is power (*shih*) and quantitative exactness (*shu*). Therefore the early kings did not rely on their strength but their power (*shih*); they did not rely on their beliefs but on their figures (*shu*). Now, for example, a floating seed of the *phêng* plant, meeting a whirlwind, may be carried a thousand li, because it rides on the power of the wind. If, in measuring an abyss, you know that it is a thousand fathoms deep, it is owing to the figures which you have found by dropping a lead line. So by depending on the power of a thing, you will reach your objective, however distant it may be, and by looking at the proper figures, you will find out the depth, however deep it may be. . . .

Again, chapter 14 condemns what it calls 'reliance on private appraisal' and speaks of the folly of trying to weigh things without

* From v. 2, 209–211, 522 (1956). Reprinted by permission of the Syndics of Cambridge University Press.

standard scales, or forming an opinion about lengths in the absence
of accepted units such as feet and inches.  Other schools, such as the
Mohists, had made a good deal of rhetorical play with 'models' and
'measures', but this quantitative element in the Legalists was connected, I would suggest, with the discovery which they made that
positive law, divorced from all ethical considerations enabled them,
and the rulers whom they advised, to achieve enhanced efficiency
by strict regulation of weights, measures and dimensions.  Hu Shih,
indeed, points out that perhaps 'standard' was the oldest meaning of
the word *fa*, since in *Kuan Tzu*, chapter 6, it is defined as including
measures of lengths, weights, volumes of solids and liquids, T-squares
and compasses.  . . .

It is in connection with mathematics, geometry and meteorology
that we come upon the fundamental philosophical flaw in Legalist
thinking.  In their passion for uniformisation, in their reduction of
complex human personal relations to formulae of geometrical simplicity, they made themselves the representatives of mechanistic
materialism, and fatally failed to take account of the levels of organisation in the universe.  . . .  The *Shang Chün Shu* elaborates:

> The former kings hung up balances with standard
> weights and fixed the lengths of the foot and the inch.  Still
> today these are followed as models (*fa*) because the divi-
> sions are clear.  No (practical) merchant would proceed by
> dismissing standard scales and then deciding about the
> weights (of things).  Such (conclusions) would have no
> force (*wei chhi pu pi yeh*).  Turning one's back on models
> and measures (*fa tu*), depending upon private conviction
> (*ssu i*), take away all force and certainty.  Without a model,
> only a Yao could judge knowledge and ability, worth or its
> opposite.  But the world does not consist exclusively of men
> like Yao.  This was why the former kings understood that no
> reliance could be placed on individual opinions or biased ap-
> proval; this is why they set up models and made distinctions
> clear.  Those who fulfilled the standard were rewarded;
> those who harmed the public interest were put to death.

The whole argument, of course, used though it was again and again,
depended on a false analogy, namely, that human conduct and human
emotions could be measured as quantitatively as a picul of salt or
an ell of cloth.  Lian Chhi-Chhao (2), in his discussion of the Legalists, saw this extremely clearly.  The certainty and predictability of
low-level phenomena cannot be found in the realms of 'free-will' at
the higher levels.  And he characterised the Legalist school as mechanistic (*chi hsieh chu-i*), while the Confucians instinctively made allowance for the true organic (*sêng chi thi*) character of man and of
society.

. . .

. . . . .  As one of the inserted chapters of the *Shu Ching*
says, 'Virtue has no invariable rule but fixes on that which is good
as its law.  And goodness itself has no constant resting-place, but
accords only with perfect sincerity.'  Through the centuries there de-
scended the idea enshrined in proverbial wisdom—*Li i fa, sêng i pi*;
'for each new law a new way of circumventing it will arise'.

NOTES AND QUESTIONS

1. In his attack on the "evidence of negligence" rule, Thayer argues that:

> when eminent courts . . . state that the breach of the ordinance is not "negligence per se," but only "evidence of negligence," and leave the question of negligence as a fact to the jury, they are doing nothing less than informing that body that it may properly stamp with approval, as reasonable conduct, the action of one who has assumed to place his own foresight above that of the legislature in respect of the very danger which it was legislating to prevent.

*Public Wrong and Private Action*, 27 Harv.L.Rev. 317, 323 (1914). To what do the words "the very danger" refer? Is it possible that under at least one meaning of these words, the foresight of the ordinance violator was superior to the legislature's? Or is this an inadmissible question because the legislature is our highest law-making body? If the "evidence of negligence" rule is adopted, not only the ordinance violator, but the jury is put in a position of apparent conflict with the legislature. Could it be argued that its conception of "the very danger" is necessarily superior to the legislature's? Or is this question, too, an inadmissible one? What do you think Confucius would say?

2. Is the Confucian attack on codified rules an attack on language generally? Is it an attack on language when used in a particular way, for a particular purpose or in a particular "field"? Or is it an attack on a particular kind of language? Is the Confucian attack more or less sweeping than Dickinson's? Is it based on the same grounds?

*OLIVER WENDELL HOLMES, JR.*

THE COMMON LAW *

The standards of the law are standards of general application. The law takes no account of the infinite varieties of temperament, intellect, and education which make the internal character of a given act so different in different men. It does not attempt to see men as God sees them for more than one sufficient reason. In the first place, the impossibility of nicely measuring a man's powers and limitations is far clearer than that of ascertaining his knowledge of law, which has been thought to account for what is called the presumption that every man knows the law. But a more satisfactory explanation is, that, when men live in society, a certain average of conduct, a sacrifice of individual peculiarities going beyond a certain point, is necessary to the general welfare. If, for instance, a man is born hasty and awkward, is always having accidents and hurting himself or his neighbors, no doubt his congenital defects will be allowed for

* From 86–87 (Harvard ed. 1963).
Originally published in 1881 by Little,
Brown and Company.

in the courts of Heaven, but his slips are no less troublesome to his neighbor than if they sprang from guilty neglect.  His neighbors accordingly require him, at his proper peril, to come up to their standard, and the courts which they establish decline to take his personal equation into account.

The rule that the law does, in general, determine liability by blameworthiness, is subject to the limitation that minute differences of character are not allowed for.  The law considers, in other words, what would be blameworthy in the average man, the man of ordinary intelligence and prudence, and determines liability by that.  If we fall below the level in those gifts, it is our misfortune; so much as that we must have at our peril, for the reasons just given.  But he who is intelligent and prudent does not act at his peril, in theory of law.  On the contrary, it is only when he fails to exercise the foresight of which he is capable, or exercise it with evil intent, that he is answerable for the consequences.

QUESTIONS

When Holmes says "that minute differences of character are not allowed for," what do you think he means by "minute"?  Does he mean "minute" differences, or does he mean *all* differences except the most extreme?  Who is the "average man, the man of ordinary intelligence and prudence"?  Is he "most people"?  Is he "most intelligent and reasonable people"?  Is there any actual, living person who can say, "I am of that class called 'men of ordinary intelligence and prudence'"?  When the law adopts such a standard is it not saying—unless it does take into account those "minute differences"— that it requires of all a type of conduct which would naturally be adopted by no one?

Are the sacrifices which Holmes's conception of law seems to require merely personal sacrifices?  Or is there a way in which they can be viewed as social sacrifices as well?  What response, if any, could Holmes make to the charge that his conception of law and of society is unjust?  That it is inhumane?  Do his remarks bear out the charge—sometimes heard—that Holmes was a "brutalitarian"?  Is it possible to have legal rules which are not to some extent "brutalitarian"?

JAMES FITZJAMES STEPHEN

CODIFICATION IN INDIA AND ENGLAND *

. . . . All language whatever has in it an element of generality, and this circumstance both gives it its chief utility and is the main source of the errors of every kind which arise from its use. Take such a sentence as this, "I saw a man riding down the Strand on a brown horse."  Every one would say, and say truly, that this sentence is perfectly intelligible.  Yet there is not a single word in

* From XVIII The Fortnightly Review
670 (1872).

it which does not leave room for further particulars which in particular cases it might be important to state. "I." Who are you? "Saw." When did you see? How did you see? With your naked eyes, or with spectacles? If with your naked eyes, is your sight long or short? If with spectacles, were they convex or concave? "A man." What sort of man? Can you undertake to say more than that it was a person in man's clothes? "Riding." Was the person you saw riding in the common way, or riding like a carter on the horse's back? "Down." Does this mean going east or west? and so on. So "Thou shalt do no murder" is a very plain proposition, but it has given rise to thousands of questions, not merely in law but in morals. Is suicide murder? Is duelling murder? What sorts of killing in war are murder? and so on. These illustrations, which might be multiplied to any conceivable extent, show that precision in the use of language is a question of degree.

## QUESTIONS

What does Stephen mean by "precision"? Is he saying that "precision" in language "is a question of degree" or is he saying that it is actually impossible? Has Stephen demonstrated in these remarks that "all language whatever has in it an element of generality" or has he simply shown us that two very general statements are indeed very general? What is meant by the word "generality"? What comment might Stephen make on Holmes's statement, "The standards of the law are standards of general application"?

## JAMES FITZJAMES STEPHEN

### A HISTORY OF THE CRIMINAL LAW OF ENGLAND *

The second chapter [of the Indian Penal Code] is entitled not very happily "General Explanations," and consists partly of a series of definitions of the senses in which words are used, and partly of a statement of certain general doctrines of more or less importance. The idea by which the whole Code is pervaded, and which was not unnaturally suggested by parts of the history of the English law, is that every one who has anything to do with the administration of the Code will do his utmost to misunderstand it and evade its provisions; this object the authors of the Code have done their utmost to defeat by anticipating all imaginable excuses for refusing to accept the real meaning of its provisions and providing against them beforehand specifically. The object is in itself undoubtedly a good one, and many of the provisions intended to effect it are valuable as they lay down doctrines which may be needed in order to clear up honest doubts or misunderstandings. For instance, it is perfectly right to say, "a person is said to cause an "effect 'voluntarily' when he causes it by means whereby he intended to cause it," or by means which at the time of "employing those means he knew or had reason to believe to be likely to cause it." It is also quite right to define the expression

* From v. III, 305–306 (1883).

"valuable security," and the word "document," for the extent of these expressions might well be matter of reasonable doubt in good faith.

I think, however, that to go beyond this, and to try to anticipate captious objections, is a mistake. Human language is not so constructed that it is possible to prevent people from misunderstanding it if they are determined to do so, and over-definition for that purpose is like the attempt to rid a house of dust by mere sweeping. You make more dust than you remove. If too fine a point is put upon language you suggest a still greater refinement in quibbling. This I think is a not uncommon fault in Indian legislation, and the Penal Code was the first example of it. For instance it defines "life" as the life of a human being unless the contrary appears from the context. So of death.[1]

## QUESTIONS

Do Stephen's comments here take adequate account of the point he makes in the preceding passage? Is there a better reason, or a better way of stating the reason, for Stephen's criticism of the Indian Penal Code? Incidentally, just what is wrong with the definition of "force" in the Code? Is it simply that it is very laborious reading? Or is there something else?

## JOHN LOCKE

### AN ESSAY CONCERNING HUMAN UNDERSTANDING *

1. All things that exist being particulars, it may perhaps be thought reasonable that words, which ought to be conformed to things, should be so too,—I mean in their signification: but yet we find quite the contrary. The far greatest part of words that make all languages are general terms: which has not been the effect of neglect or chance, but of reason and necessity.

2. First, It is impossible that every particular thing should have a distinct peculiar name. For, the signification and use of words depending on that connexion which the mind makes between its ideas and the sounds it uses as signs of them, it is necessary, in the application of names to things, that the mind should have distinct

---

1. S. 47. The most singular definition in the whole Code is the definition of "force" in § 349. "A person is said to use force to another, if he causes motion, change of motion, or cessation of motion to that other; or if he causes to any substance such motion, or change of motion, or cessation of motion as brings that substance into contact with any part of that other's body, or with any thing which that other is wearing, or carrying, or with any thing so situated that that contact affects that other's sense of feeling, provided that the person causing the motion, or change of motion, or cessation of mo-tion, causes that motion, cessation of motion, or change of motion in one of the three ways hereinafter described first, by his own bodily power; secondly, by disposing any substance in such a manner that the motion, or change or cessation of motion, takes place without any further action on his part, or on the part of any other person; thirdly, by inducing any animal to move, to change its motion, or to cease to move." [Footnote by Stephen.]

* From v. II, 14–16 (A. Fraser ed. Dover ed. 1959).

ideas of the things, and retain also the particular name that belongs to every one, with its peculiar appropriation to that idea. But it is beyond the power of human capacity to frame and retain distinct ideas of all the particular things we meet with: every bird and beast men saw; every tree and plant that affected the senses, could not find a place in the most capacious understanding. If it be looked on as an instance of a prodigious memory, that some generals have been able to call every soldier in their army by his proper name, we may easily find a reason why men have never attempted to give names to each sheep in their flock, or crow that flies over their heads; much less to call every leaf of plants, or grain of sand that came in their way, by a peculiar name.

3. Secondly, If it were possible, it would yet be useless; because it would not serve to the chief end of language. Men would in vain heap up names of particular things, that would not serve them to communicate their thoughts. Men learn names, and use them in talk with others, only that they may be understood: which is then only done when, by use or consent, the sound I make by the organs of speech, excites in another man's mind who hears it, the idea I apply it to in mine, when I speak it. This cannot be done by names applied to particular things; whereof I alone having the ideas in my mind, the names of them could not be significant or intelligible to another, who was not acquainted with all those very particular things which had fallen under my notice.

4. Thirdly, But yet, granting this also feasible, (which I think is not), yet a distinct name for every particular thing would not be of any great use for the improvement of knowledge: which, though founded in particular things, enlarges itself by general views; to which things reduced into sorts, under general names, are properly subservient. These, with the names belonging to them, come within some compass, and do not multiply every movement, beyond what either the mind can contain, or use requires. And therefore, in these, men have for the most part stopped: but yet not so as to hinder themselves from distinguishing particular things by appropriate names, where convenience demands it. And therefore in their own species, which they have most to do with, and wherein they have often occasion to mention particular persons, they make use of proper names; and there distinct individuals have distinct denominations.

5. Besides persons, countries also, cities, rivers, mountains, and other the like distinctions of place have usually found peculiar names, and that for the same reason; they being such as men have often an occasion to mark particularly, and, as it were, set before others in their discourses with them. And I doubt not but, if we had reason to mention particular horses as often as we have to mention particular men, we should have proper names for the one, as familiar as for the other, and Bucephalus would be a word as much in use as Alexander. And therefore we see that, amongst jockeys, horses have their proper names to be known and distinguished by, as commonly as their servants: because, amongst them, there is often occasion to mention this or that particular horse when he is out of sight.

QUESTIONS

Is Locke's position more or less extreme than Stephen's? Does Locke think it is possible to have a particular name for a particular thing, if we really want to? Do you think it is possible? Can one simply designate this particular glass resting on this particular table by the word "glabled" and use that word for nothing else? Does the answer turn on the meaning of such words as "this" and "particular"?

Just why, according to Locke, would many "names of particular things" be "useless" for "the chief end of language"? Why could not people communicate with each other? Is communication with others the only purpose of language? What about communication with oneself? Could "names of particular things" be used for this purpose under Locke's reasoning?

*FRIEDRICH WAISMANN*

LANGUAGE STRATA *

A word may have two altogether different meanings, or better, there may be two words which have the sound in common; thus someone might say, 'How long it is since I have seen the Alps! How I long to see them'. This fact makes possible certain puns—as when a crying child is called 'Prince of Wails'.

QUESTIONS

Is the phenomenon Waismann refers to an instance of the "generality" of language? Or is it something different? Why does Waismann say that it is better to speak of "two words" having a "sound in common"? What is implied about the meaning of the word, "word"?

Why do we permit one sound or group of written marks to have more than one associated "word"? For each distinctive word, why do we not have a distinctive sound or group of marks? Instead of "How I long to see them," why not, "How I desire to see them," or "How intensely I want to see them"? Or, "How deeply and painfully I wish to see them"? If sounds from a given vocabulary will not do, why not invent a new sound? Is this physically possible? Are there enough sounds to go around? Does this raise the same problem to which Locke adverted? Or is this problem more manageable?

NOTE: DRAFTING RULES

Should the features of language to which Stephen, Locke and Waismann call our attention be considered in the drafting of rules? Should they be considered in deciding whether to have a rule in the first place? Can the problems they generate ever be avoided by leaving a field of human conduct to the discretion of some person or body?

* From Logic and Language 227 (A. Flew ed. Anchor ed. 1965). Reprinted by permission of the literary estate of Friedrich Waismann. Originally published by Basil Blackwell.

Suppose that the library has been losing books at a great rate and the librarians wish to impose a strict monitoring system at the exit. Can you draft a rule for the situation? Consider the following:

*No person may leave the library without checking out*
*his books from the monitor at the exit desk.*

Will this rule do? Why? Is it inadequate for more than one reason? Try to frame a better rule. Do you think you could frame one which would be free of all objections to the one proposed above? If so, why? If not, why not? Is the problem only one of knowing more facts? If you could know everything that you wanted about the library, its students and official policy, would it be theoretically possible for you to frame a rule with which you would be completely satisfied? Incidentally, if it is impossible to attain such knowledge are the reasons traceable in any way to the nature of language?

Consider whether the following passages from Bacon have any bearing on the problems of drafting a rule.

*FRANCIS BACON*

Novum Organum *

. . . . it is by discourse that men associate; and words are imposed according to the apprehension of the vulgar. And therefore the ill and unfit choice of words wonderfully obstructs the understanding. Nor do the definitions or explanations wherewith in some things learned men are wont to guard and defend themselves, by any means set the matter right. But words plainly force and overrule the understanding, and throw all into confusion, and lead men away into numberless empty controversies and idle fancies. . . .

. . .

59. . . . For men believe that their reason governs words; but it is also true that words react on the understanding; and this it is that has rendered philosophy and the sciences sophistical and inactive. Now words, being commonly framed and applied according to the capacity of the vulgar, follow those lines of division which are most obvious to the vulgar understanding. And whenever an understanding of greater acuteness or a more diligent observation would alter those lines to suit the true divisions of nature, words stand in the way and resist the change. Whence it comes to pass that the high and formal discussions of learned men end oftentimes in disputes about words and names; with which (according to the use and wisdom of the mathematicians) it would be more prudent to begin, and so by means of definitions reduce them to order. Yet even definitions cannot cure this evil in dealing with natural and material things; since the definitions themselves consist of words, and those words beget others; so that it is necessary to recur to individual instances, and those in due series and order; as I shall say presently when I come to the method and scheme for the formation of notions and axioms.

* From Seventeenth Century Prose and
   Poetry 53–55 (Coffin and Wither-
   spoon eds. 1946).

60.  The Idols imposed by words on the understanding are of two kinds.  They are either names of things which do not exist (for as there are things left unnamed through lack of observation, so likewise are there names which result from fantastic suppositions and to which nothing in reality corresponds), or they are names of things which exist, but yet confused and ill-defined, and hastily and irregularly derived from realities.  Of the former kind are Fortune, the Prime Mover, Planetary Orbits, Element of Fire, and like fictions which owe their origin to false and idle theories.  And this class of idols is more easily expelled, because to get rid of them it is only necessary that all theories should be steadily rejected and dismissed as obsolete.

But the other class, which springs out of a faulty and unskilful abstraction, is intricate and deeply rooted.  Let us take for example such a word as *humid*; and see how far the several things which the word is used to signify agree with each other; and we shall find the word *humid* to be nothing else than a mark loosely and confusedly applied to denote a variety of actions which will not bear to be reduced to any constant meaning.  For it both signifies that which easily spreads itself round any other body; and that which in itself is indeterminate and cannot solidize; and that which readily yields in every direction; and that which easily divides and scatters itself; and that which easily unites and collects itself; and that which readily flows and is put in motion; and that which readily clings to another body and wets it; and that which is easily reduced to a liquid, or being solid easily melts.  Accordingly when you come to apply the word— if you take it in one sense, flame is humid; if in another, air is not humid; if in another, glass is humid.  So that it is easy to see that the notion is taken by abstraction only from water and common and ordinary liquids, without any due verification.

### QUESTIONS

What does Bacon mean that "words are imposed according to the apprehension of the vulgar"?  What is the consequence of his position for a theory that legal rules in a democracy must be intelligible to "the vulgar"?  Is it necessary for legal rules, in order to accomplish their purposes, to go beyond "those lines of division which are most obvious to the vulgar understanding"?

In the passage below is Waismann making the same point as Bacon?

### FRIEDRICH WAISMANN

### HOW I SEE PHILOSOPHY *

.   .   .   .   Existing language, by offering us only certain stereotyped moulds of expression, creates habits of thought which it is almost impossible to break.  Such a mould is, e. g. the actor-action scheme of the Indo-European languages.  How deep their influence

---

* From *Logical Positivism* 362–363 (A.        The Free Press of Glencoe.  Reprint-
Ayer ed. 1959).  Copyright 1959 by        ed by permission.

is can perhaps be surmised from Descartes' conclusion from thinking to the presence of an agent, an ego, different from the thinking, that does the thinking—a conclusion so natural and convincing to us because it is supported by the whole weight of language. Frege's obsession with the question "What is a number?" is another case. As we can speak of "*the* number five," five, Frege argued, must be the proper name of an entity, a sort of Platonic crystal, indicated by means of the definite article. (A Chinese pupil of mine once informed me that Frege's question is unaskable in Chinese, "five" being used there only as a numeral in contexts like "five friends," "five boats," etc.) . . . . A philosopher, instead of preaching the righteousness of ordinary speech, should learn to be on his guard against the pitfalls ever present in its forms. To use a picture: just as a good swimmer must be able to swim up-stream, so the philosopher should master the unspeakably different art of thinking up-speech, against the current of cliches.

Susanne K. Langer

### The Logic of Signs and Symbols *

How are relations expressed in language? For the most part, they are not symbolized by other relations, as in pictures, but are *named*, just like substantives. We name two items, and place the name of a relation between; this means that the relation holds the two items together. "Brutus killed Caesar" indicates that "killing" holds between Brutus and Caesar. Where the relation is not symmetrical, the word-order and the grammatical forms (case, mood, tense, etc.) of the words symbolize its direction. "Brutus killed Caesar" means something different from "Caesar killed Brutus," and "Killed Caesar Brutus" is not a sentence at all. The word-order partly determines the sense of the structure.

The trick of naming relations instead of illustrating them gives language a tremendous scope; one word can thus take care of a situation that would require a whole sheet of drawings to depict it. Consider the sentence, "Your chance of winning is one among a thousand of losing." Imagine a pictorial expression of this comparatively simple proposition! First, a symbol for "you, winning"; another for "you, losing," pictured a thousand times! Of course a thousand anythings would be far beyond clear apprehension on a basis of mere visual *Gestalt*. We can distinguish three, four, five, and perhaps somewhat higher numbers as visible patterns, for instance:

But a thousand becomes merely "a great number." Its exact fixation requires an order of concepts in which it holds a definite place, as

* From *Philosophy in a New Key* 73–75, 76 (3d ed. 1967). Copyright 1942, 1951, 1957 by the President and Fellows of Harvard College. Reprinted by permission of Harvard University Press.

each number concept does in our number system. But to denote such a host of concepts and keep their relations to each other straight, we need a symbolism that can express both terms and relationships more economically than pictures, gestures, or mnesic signs.

It was remarked before that symbol and object, having a common logical form, would be interchangeable save for some psychological factors, namely: that the object is interesting, but hard to fixate, whereas the symbol is easy of apprehension though in itself perhaps quite unimportant. Now the little vocal noises out of which we make our words are extremely easy to produce in all sorts of subtle variations, and easy to perceive and distinguish. As Bertrand Russell has put it, "It is of course largely a matter of convenience that we do not use words of other kinds (than vocal). There is the deaf-and-dumb language; a Frenchman's shrug of the shoulders is a word; in fact, any kind of externally perceptible bodily movement may become a word, if social usage so ordains. But the convention which has given the supremacy to speaking is one which has a good ground, since there is no other way of producing a number of perceptively different bodily movements so quickly or with so little muscular effort. Public speaking would be very tedious if statesmen had to use the deaf-and-dumb language, and very exhausting if all words involved as much muscular effort as a shrug of the shoulders." Not only does speech cost little effort, but above all it requires no instrument save the vocal apparatus and the auditory organs which, normally, we all carry about as part of our very selves; so words are *naturally available* symbols, as well as very economical ones.

. . .

But the greatest virtue of verbal symbols is, probably, their tremendous readiness to enter into *combinations*. There is practically no limit to the selections and arrangements we can make of them. This is largely due to the economy Lord Russell remarked, the speed with which each word is produced and presented and finished, making way for another word. This makes it possible for us to grasp whole groups of meetings at a time, and make a new, total, complex concept out of the separate connotations of rapidly passing words.

NOTE: "EASIER SAID THAN DONE"

To what extent do we tend to think that the world is as manipulable as the symbols we use to describe it? To what extent can this be explained by the fact that words are so manipulable? Some things, we are told, are "easier said than done". Is it also true that other things are "easier done than said"? How could this be so?

## C. Rules in Thought and the Logic Of Common Law Precedent

TEDLA v. ELLMAN

280 N.Y. 124 (1939)

LEHMAN, J. While walking along a highway, Anna Tedla and her brother, John Bachek, were struck by a passing automobile, operated by the defendant Ellman. She was injured and Bachek was killed. Bachek was a deaf-mute. His occupation was collecting and selling junk. His sister, Mrs. Tedla, was engaged in the same occupation. They often picked up junk at the incinerator of the village of Islip. At the time of the accident they were walking along "Sunrise Highway" and wheeling baby carriages containing junk and wood which they had picked up at the incinerator. It was about six o'clock, or a little earlier, on a Sunday evening in December. Darkness had already set in. Bachek was carrying a lighted lantern, or, at least, there is testimony to that effect. The jury found that the accident was due solely to the negligence of the operator of the automobile. The defendants do not, upon this appeal, challenge the finding of negligence on the part of the operator. They maintain, however, that Mrs. Tedla and her brother were guilty of contributory negligence as matter of law.

Sunrise Highway, at the place of the accident, consists of two roadways, separated by a grass plot. There are no footpaths along the highway and the center grass plot was soft. It is not unlawful for a pedestrian, wheeling a baby carriage, to use the roadway under such circumstances, but a pedestrian using the roadway is bound to exercise such care for his safety as a reasonably prudent person would use. The Vehicle and Traffic Law (Cons.Laws, ch. 71) provides that "Pedestrians walking or remaining on the paved portion, or traveled part of a roadway shall be subject to, and comply with, the rules governing vehicles, with respect to meeting and turning out, except that such pedestrians shall keep to the left of the center line thereof, and turn to their left instead of right side thereof, so as to permit all vehicles passing them in either direction to pass on their right. Such pedestrians shall not be subject to the rules governing vehicles as to giving signals." (Section 85, subd. 6.) Mrs. Tedla and her brother did not observe the statutory rule and, at the time of the accident, were proceeding in easterly direction on the eastbound or right-hand roadway. The defendants moved to dismiss the complaint on the ground, among others, that violation of the statutory rule constitutes contributory negligence as matter of law. . . . Upon this appeal, the only question presented is whether, as matter of law, disregard of the statutory rule that pedestrians shall keep to the left of the center line of a highway constitutes contributory negligence which bars any recovery by the plaintiff.

Vehicular traffic can proceed safely and without recurrent traffic tangles only if vehicles observe accepted rules of the road. Such rules, and especially the rule that all vehicles proceeding in one direction must keep to a designated part or side of the road—in this country the right-hand side—have been dictated by necessity and formulated by custom. The general use of automobiles has increased in unprecedented degree the number and speed of vehicles. Control of traffic becomes an increasingly difficult problem. Rules of the road, regulating the rights and duties of those who use highways, have, in consequence, become increasingly important. The Legislature no longer leaves to custom the formulation of such rules. Statutes now codify, define, supplement and, where changing conditions suggest change in rule, even change rules of the road which formerly rested on custom. Custom and common sense have always dictated that vehicles should have the right of way over pedestrians and that pedestrians should walk along the edge of a highway so that they might step aside for passing vehicles with least danger to themselves and least obstruction to vehicular traffic. Otherwise, perhaps, no customary rule of the road was observed by pedestrians with the same uniformity as by vehicles; though, in general, they probably followed, until recently, the same rules as vehicles.

Pedestrians are seldom a source of danger or serious obstruction to vehicles and when horse-drawn vehicles were common they seldom injured pedestrians, using a highway with reasonable care, unless the horse became unmanageable or the driver was grossly negligent or guilty of willful wrong. Swift-moving motor vehicles, it was soon recognized, do endanger the safety of pedestrians crossing highways, and it is imperative that there the relative rights and duties of pedestrians and of vehicles should be understood and observed. The Legislature in the first five subdivisions of section 85 of the Vehicle and Traffic Law has provided regulations to govern the conduct of pedestrians and of drivers of vehicles when a pedestrian is crossing a road. Until, by chapter 114 of the Laws of 1933, it adopted subdivision 6 by section 85, quoted above, there was no special statutory rule for pedestrians walking *along* a highway. Then for the first time it reversed, for pedestrians, the rule established for vehicles by immemorial custom, and provided that pedestrians shall keep to the left of the center line of a highway.

The plaintiffs showed by the testimony of a State policeman that "there were very few cars going east" at the time of the accident, but that going west there was "very heavy Sunday night traffic." Until the recent adoption of the new statutory rule for pedestrians, ordinary prudence would have dictated that pedestrians should not expose themselves to the danger of walking along the roadway upon which the "very heavy Sunday night traffic" was proceeding when they could walk in comparative safety along a roadway used by very few cars. It is said that now, by force of the statutory rule, pedestrians are guilty of contributory negligence as matter of law when they use the safer roadway, unless that roadway is left of the center of the road. Disregard of the statutory rule of the road and observance of a rule based on immemorial custom, it is said, is negligence which as matter of law is a proximate cause of the accident, though observance of the statutory rule might, under the circumstances of the particular case, expose a pedestrian to serious danger from which he would be free if he followed the rule that had been established by custom. If that be true, then the Legislature has decreed that pedestrians must observe the general rule of conduct which it has prescribed for their safety even under circumstances where observance would subject them to unusual risk; that pedestrians are to be charged with negligence as matter of law for acting as prudence dictates. It is unreasonable to ascribe to the Legislature an intention that the statute should have so extraordinary a result, and the courts may not give to a statute an effect not intended by the Legislature.

The Legislature, when it enacted the statute, presumably knew that this court and the courts of other jurisdictions had established the general principle that omission by a plaintiff of a safeguard, prescribed by statute, against a recognized danger, constitutes negligence as matter of law which bars recovery for damages caused by incidence of the danger for which the safeguard was prescribed. The principle has been formulated in the Restatement of the Law of Torts: "A plaintiff who has violated a legislative enactment designed to prevent a certain type of dangerous situation is barred from recovery for a harm caused by a violation of the statute if, but only if, the harm was sustained by reason of a situation of that type." (Section 469.) So where a plaintiff failed to place lights upon a vehicle, as required by statute, this court has said: "we think the unexcused omission of the statutory signals is more than some evidence of negligence. It is negligence in itself. Lights are intended for the guidance and protection of other travelers on the highway. (Highway Law, section 329–a.) By the very terms of the hypothesis, to omit, wilfully or heedlessly, the safeguards prescribed by law for the benefit of another that he may be preserved in life or limb, is to fall short of the standard of diligence to which those who live in organized society are under a duty to conform. That, we think, is now the established rule in this State." (Martin v. Herzog, 228 N.Y. 164, 168, per CARDOZO, J.) The appellants lean heavily upon that and kindred cases and the principle established by them.

The analogy is, however, incomplete. The "established rule" should not be weakened either by subtle distinctions or by extension beyond its letter or spirit into a field where "by the very terms of the hypothesis" it can have no proper application. At times the indefinite and flexible standard of care of the traditional reasonably prudent man may be, in the opinion of the Legislature, an insufficient measure of the care which should be exercised to guard against a recognized danger; at times, the duty, imposed by custom, that no man shall use what is his to the harm of others provides insufficient safeguard for the preservation of the life or limb or property of others. Then the Legislature may by statute prescribe additional safeguards and may define duty and standard of care in rigid terms; and when the Legislature has spoken, the standard of the care required is no longer what the reasonably prudent man would do under the circumstances but what the Legislature has commanded. That is the rule established by the courts and "by the very terms of the hypothesis" the rule applies where the Legislature has prescribed safeguards "for the benefit of another that he may be preserved in life or limb." In that field debate as to whether the safeguards so prescribed are reasonably necessary is ended by the legislative fiat. Obedience to that fiat cannot add to the danger, even assuming that the prescribed safeguards are not reasonably necessary and where the legislative anticipation of dangers is realized and harm results through heedless or willful omission of the prescribed safeguard, injury flows from wrong and the wrongdoer is properly held responsible for the consequent damages.

The statute upon which the defendants rely is of different character. It does not prescribe additional safeguards which pedestrians must provide for the preservation of the life or limb or property of others, or even of themselves, nor does it impose upon pedestrians a higher standard of care. What the statute does provide is rules of the road to be observed by pedestrians and by vehicles, so that all those who use the road may know how they and others should proceed, at least under usual circumstances. A general rule of conduct—and, specifically, a rule of the road—may accomplish its intended purpose under usual conditions, but, when the unusual occurs, strict observance may defeat the purpose of the rule and produce catastrophic results.

Negligence is failure to exercise the care required by law. Where a statute defines the standard of care and the safeguards required to meet a recognized danger, then, as we have said, no other measure may be applied in determining whether a person has carried out the duty of care imposed by law. Failure to observe the standard imposed by statute is negligence, as matter of law. On the other hand, where a statutory general rule of conduct fixes no definite standard of care which would under all circumstances tend to protect life, limb or property but merely codifies or supplements a common-law rule, which has always been subject to limitations and exceptions; or where the statutory rule of conduct regulates conflicting rights and obligations in a manner calculated to promote public convenience and safety, then the statute, in the absence of clear language to the contrary, should not be construed as intended to wipe out the limitations and exceptions which judicial decisions have attached to the common-law duty; nor should it be construed as an inflexible command that the general rule of conduct intended to prevent accidents must be followed even under conditions when observance might cause accidents. We may assume reasonably that the Legislature directed pedestrians to keep to the left of the center of the road because that would cause them to face traffic approaching in that lane and would enable them to care for their own safety better than if the traffic approached them from the rear. We cannot assume reasonably that the Legislature intended that a statute enacted for the preservation of the life and limb of pedestrians must be observed when observance would subject them to more imminent danger.

The distinction in the effect of statutes defining a standard of care or requiring specified safeguards against recognized dangers and the effect of statutes which merely codify, supplement or even change common-law rules or which prescribe a general rule of conduct calculated to prevent accidents, but which under unusual conditions may cause accidents, has been pointed out often. Seldom have the courts held that failure to observe a rule of the road, even though embodied in a statute, constitutes negligence as matter of law where observance would subject a person to danger which might be avoided by disregard of the general rule. "In the United States and in

England certain rules regarding the rights of vehicles and persons meeting or passing in the public highway have been established by long continued custom or usage, or, in many jurisdictions, by statutory regulation. These rules and regulations are usually spoken of as 'the law of the road' or the 'rules of the road.' These rules are, however, not inflexible, and a strict observance should be avoided when there is a plain risk in adhering to them, and one who too rigidly adheres to such rules when the injury might have been averted by variance therefrom, may be charged with fault; . . . the exceptions to the rule of the road depend upon the special circumstances of the case, and in respect to which no general rule can be applied." . . . .

The generally accepted rule and the reasons for it are set forth in the comment to section 286 of the Restatement of the Law of Torts: "Many statutes and ordinances are so worded as apparently to express a universally obligatory rule of conduct. Such enactments, however, may in view of their purpose and spirit be properly construed as intended to apply only to ordinary situations and to be subject to the qualification that the conduct prohibited thereby is not wrongful if, because of an emergency or the like, the circumstances justify an apparent disobedience to the letter of the enactment. . . . The provisions of statutes, intended to codify and supplement the rules of conduct which are established by a course of judicial decision or by custom, are often construed as subject to the same limitations and exceptions as the rules which they supersede. Thus, a statute or ordinance requiring all persons to drive on the right side of the road may be construed as subject to an exception permitting travellers to drive upon the other side, if so doing is likely to prevent rather than cause the accidents which it is the purpose of the statute or ordinance to prevent."

Even under that construction of the statute, a pedestrian is, of course, at fault if he fails without good reason to observe the statutory rule of conduct. The general duty is established by the statute, and deviation from it without good cause is a wrong and the wrongdoer is responsible for the damages resulting from his wrong. . . .

. . .

In each action, the judgment should be affirmed, with costs.

CRANE, Ch. J., HUBBS, LOUGHRAN and RIPPEY, JJ., concur; O'BRIEN and FINCH, JJ., dissent on the authority of Martin v. Herzog (228 N.Y. 164).

Judgments affirmed.

NOTES AND QUESTIONS

1. Consider the method of Judge Lehman's opinion. Does he find it necessary to interpret the decision in Martin v. Herzog? If so, how does the interpretation figure in the structure of his argument? How does it contribute to the justification of his decision? What does Lehman think the rule in *Martin* is? Is his view consistent with the explanation Cardozo himself offers? O'Brien and Finch, JJ., the report tells us, dissented "on the authority of Martin

v. Herzog." How do you think they interpreted Cardozo's opinion? Did they interpret it in the same way as counsel for the defendant? Did they view New York as a "negligence *per se*", a "presumptive negligence," or an "evidence of negligence" state? What language in *Tedla* supports your conclusion? What language in *Martin* supports *their* conclusion?

If Lehman had considered New York a "presumptive negligence" jurisdiction, would it have been easier or harder to have reached the result he apparently desired? What evidence was available to rebut a presumption of negligence on the part of the plaintiffs? Does Lehman himself ultimately use the concept of presumption to help justify his decision? If so, does his conclusion really amount to a "presumptive negligence" rule? Or is there a material difference?

Is Lehman arguing that Cardozo's rule is not applicable? Or is he arguing that the statute is not applicable? Or is he arguing both of these propositions? Is he arguing that the rule in *Martin* is inapplicable because no statute has been violated? Or is he arguing that even though the statute was violated, it is the type of statute whose violation does not amount to negligence? Or is he arguing that although violation of this particular statute can be either negligence in itself or presumptive negligence, this *type* of violation does not have such consequences? Which of these alternatives squares with Lehman's own reading of Cardozo's opinion? Which with the reading of counsel for the defense? Which of the alternatives would be consistent with *your* reading of Martin v. Herzog? Is Lehman saying that the plaintiffs in this case could not have been legally convicted by the traffic court? Is he saying that the plaintiffs are guilty neither of negligence nor of a traffic offense? Or is he only saying that they have not violated the statute for "purposes of negligence law"? Would such reasoning make any sense? How would it square with his interpretation of *Martin*? Does Lehman in a negligence case have authority to say how a traffic case would be decided?

Why, according to Lehman, could not the statute have been intended to cover Mrs. Tedla's case? On what basis does Lehman determine that the conduct directed by the statute would have been unreasonable in Mrs. Tedla's situation? Is his authority for the determination of prudent conduct the same as Cardozo's? If it is not, could it be argued that he is not distinguishing, but overruling the decision in *Martin*? Isn't the point of Cardozo's opinion that the legislative rule *defines* what is reasonable in situations to which it applies? Does Lehman see the legislative rule as playing this role? In some cases, but not in others? Does it play this role for Lehman in *any* of the types of cases which he treats? If it doesn't, what support is left for the reasoning in *Martin*? Would it seem so unreasonable to hold Mrs. Tedla for a violation of the statute if all that was involved was a small traffic fine? Is it the added hardship which negligence law introduces that makes Lehman feel that the legislature could not have intended to reach Mrs. Tedla's case?

2. Is the distinction Lehman draws between different types of statute persuasive to you? Is it clear which of the types that Lehman

describes was involved in Martin v. Herzog? In Tedla v. Ellman? Is it clear that, according to Lehman's catalogue, the same type of statute was *not* involved in each case?

3. Is there only one correct reading of Martin v. Herzog? Is there only one authoritative reading? If your answer is "yes" to either question, how is that reading determined? If your answer is "no" to both, is it possible to view the Common Law as having authority?

4. Was the process by which Lehman ascertained the meaning of Martin v. Herzog—as far as it is reported in his opinion—more like "rule-finding" or "rule-making"? Or was it some combination of both? Was it possible for Lehman to make the process wholly one of "rule-finding"? One in which he was left with no discretion as to what the rule of the Common Law should be?

Could this have been done by confining the inquiry to what Cardozo had said—or thought—the rule was? If so, is this because the ultimate authority in the Common Law is the Common Law judge— just as the ultimate authority in statutory law is the legislature? If not, is this because Cardozo's opinion was too unclear? Too self-contradictory?

*Abraham Harari*

## Negligence in the Law of Torts *

It may be said that in the development of the law of torts . . . a stage has been reached where existing decisions sufficiently cover the field to enable us to decide new cases by merely following the old ones, and that in so far as there is no decision imposing liability there is no liability. This is obviously wrong. New cases coming before the courts are in fact not decided on this basis, and what is more, cannot be decided on this basis, neither today nor at any future time. Logically, legal decisions are

'just particular propositions which only report . . . certain historical events; . . . in order to obtain a general or functional rule or principle we must have a universal proposition.' [2]

No decision can *as such* ever be followed, as no situation, no event, ever completely repeats itself. And since on the view discussed there is no liability where there is no decision imposing liability that can be followed, there never is liability in tort at all. The absurdity of this view is plain: Nor does it become more acceptable if it is slightly varied so that where a case is not 'covered by authori-

---

* From 5–11 (1962). Reprinted by permission of The Law Book Company Limited, Sidney.

2. Stoljar, 'The Logical Status of a Legal Principle', (1953) 20 U.Chi.L. Rev. 181, 188. See also, F. S. Cohen, Ethical Systems and Legal Ideals (1959 reissue), p. 34, n. 47: 'The periodic attempts of students of the common law to put forward logical formulae for discovering "the rule of a case" all betray an elementary ignorance of the logical fact that no particular proposition can imply a general proposition'. [Footnote in original.]

ty', where there is no decision imposing liability which can be followed, the courts are free to impose liability as they think fit. For though on this view the courts would be free to dispense justice of a kind, there would still be no law of torts.

It is important to stress the distinction between a 'judgment' and a 'precedent'. Viewed as a judgment, the decision [3] of a court, when fully stated, will contain many references to factual circumstances which can never be the same in any future case. But the same decision, when viewed as a precedent, will leave out some of these circumstances altogether, and will refer to others only in terms of some wider or narrower class of circumstances to which they belong. It is this transformation of a judgment into a precedent which is now of interest to us. What entitles us to disregard some of the more particular aspects of a case, and what are our criteria for doing this? It is one's notion of the process by which a judgment is transformed into a precedent that determines one's whole conception of the common law; this will become apparent on an examination of the question of how a knowledge of the provisions of the common law is obtained.

To return to our question, 'How do we know the provisions of the law in a system like the common law?', the answer a law student would usually receive would be 'by reading the cases'. But this is of course no answer. Anyone reading the cases on the assumption that all statements made in them regarding the law are correct will soon find himself floundering in a morass of incongruities. For not only will he find contradictory statements of law from one case to another, he will also find decisions in some cases which cannot possibly be reconciled with statements made in others, contradictory statements of law in the same case by judges who agree in the decision, and even in the same opinion statements about the law which it is difficult to square with the decision itself. He will then be told that it is only the *rationes decidendi* which are law, and that is of course when his troubles really start. What are *rationes decidendi*? How does one go about finding them? That all propositions of law which have some relevance to the actual decision are not *rationes decidendi* is pretty obvious, for otherwise we would be back where we started and there would have been no point in confusing our innocent inquirer by the introduction of this notion. On the other hand, if we are to decompose an abstract or generalized proposition of law so as to get rid of all references which were not strictly relevant to the decision, we do not get a rule or a norm, but a history. To take an example from a case often cited in this context, Lord Atkin's proposition of law in Donoghue v. Stevenson,[4] to the effect that one who negligently causes damage to another is liable in torts,[5] very clearly had some relevance to the decision in that case, for by that decision a person

---

3. The word 'decision' is here used in a 'neutral' sense. [Footnote in original.]

4. [1932] A.C. 562. [Footnote in original.]

5. He said: 'You must take reasonable care to avoid acts or omissions which you can reasonably foresee would be likely to injure your neighbour' (at p. 580). [Footnote in original.]

who negligently caused damage to another was held liable. But the proposition equally clearly refers to questions with which the court was not faced, and a pronouncement on which was therefore not relevant to the decision.[6] Let us, therefore, reduce the proposition to what was essential to the decision by restating it in such a way as to exclude all irrelevant references. Starting with the word *damage,* since the damage in question was physical, all reference to non-physical damage must be considered as *obiter,* and excluded; it was not to a chattel or to immovables, but to the body of a person; not external but internal; and so on. Continuing to the end this process of excluding all irrelevant references, the proposition would be converted from a proposition of law to a proposition of fact (a recitation of the facts in the case as found by the court) plus an order directing defendant to pay damages (the decision). It is not even possible to state it in the *form* of a proposition of law. We get a picture of 'what happened' in that case, but we do not get a rule. The *ratio decidendi* therefore has to be something in between a proposition of law which has some relevance to the decision and a mere recitation of 'what happened'.

In this context reference is invariably made to Professor Goodhart's theory, according to which the *ratio decidendi* of a case consists of the *material facts of the case as found by the judge plus the decision thereon.* What this means is that, instead of facing the impossible task of excluding from a proposition of law consciously made by a judge all references which were not necessary for his decision, without thereby reducing a norm to a history, Professor Goodhart would have us perform the same operation on a proposition of law unconsciously or subconsciously made by the judge. For the difference between on the one hand a statement of the facts of a case as found by the judge plus the decision (which as such cannot be converted into a proposition of law), and on the other hand a statement of the *material* facts, etc., plus the decision (which can be converted into a proposition of law), is that in the latter statement generalizations and classifications are made which could just as well have been stated as propositions of law; and if they were stated thus, their reference to questions irrelevant to the decision would be plain. Returning to Donoghue v. Stevenson, if Lord Atkin had said that the defendant had been careless, and that by his carelessness he has caused damage to the plaintiff, and that defendant was therefore liable, what would be the *ratio decidendi*? State the 'material facts plus decision' in whatever way you like, and then convert the whole into a proposition of law, and the irrelevant references will immediately appear. This being so, the modified version of the Goodhart theory, according to which it is for the court on which the precedent is binding to determine what were the material facts, is of no more use than the original version. But if the modified version does not help us to solve our problem any more than the original one, there is at least this to be

6. 'The first key to the discovery of the doctrine of a case is found in the principle that the court making the decision is under a duty to decide the very case presented and has no authority to decide any other'. Wambaugh, The Study of Cases, 2nd ed., p. 8. [Footnote in original.]

said for it, that it does not present the *ratio decidendi*—however determined—as the reason consciously, subconsciously, or unconsciously given by the deciding judge for his decision. In other words, it at least suggests that we are concerned with what the judge did rather than with what he expressly or by implication said that he did, or with his reasons for doing what he did. But even so, it is no advance on what has been called the 'classical theory', that the *ratio decidendi* consists of the principle of law which was necessary for the decision, or which can be abstracted from it. Moreover, it is deceptive, since it correctly describes—as far as it goes—how precedents are in fact manipulated by the courts, and this tends to beguile the inquirer into accepting a superficial or incomplete description where an explanation is required.

'In law as elsewhere, we can know and yet not understand'. We may know what will be regarded as the *ratio decidendi* of one case or another, but unless we understand why it is so regarded, not only are we likely to have insurmountable difficulties in cases where knowledge does not come of itself, but we are also likely to acquire a very distorted view of the law.

The problem then still is to find the basis of this classification (e. g., ginger-beer into 'product') whereby a general rule seems to be obtained from a particular decision. And the answer is of course that this is a spurious problem: by itself a particular decision cannot logically yield a general rule. As there is nothing to determine whether the analogy we are to make is to be wide or narrow, or how far we are to go in either direction, there is no objective basis for such classification or generalization; it must needs be completely arbitrary. The belief that there is some special logical process—even though it cannot be described—whereby particular decisions are made to yield general rules (or what is no less absurd, that the decisions of the courts are in fact arbitrary creations of the judges) can only be ascribed to confused ideas regarding 'concrete' decisions and the 'absence of theory or principles' in the common law.

'Concrete' decisions do not make law. To present a decision in isolation, that is, to hold it forth as a self-contained and self-explanatory unit, is to misrepresent it. Taken out of context and regarded *in vacuo*, it cannot be turned into a precedent as it implies nothing. It can be 'followed' only in the purely chronological sense of the word—in the sense in which night is followed by day.

That this is no gratuitous academic refinement can be demonstrated even to the satisfaction of those who have no patience with 'theories'. 'Everyone knows', they will say, 'that there are facts which are immaterial, and if the academics think otherwise, so much the worse for the academics.' It is surely the merest nonsense to suggest that the decision in Donoghue v. Stevenson might have been different if, for instance, other things being equal, the ginger-beer-cum-snail-drinker had been Mrs. Smith and not Mrs. Donoghue.' Now this may be the merest nonsense, but the question is, why? It is true that the name or identity of the plaintiff in Donoghue v. Stevenson was not a material fact in the sense that the decision might have gone the other way if it had been different. But is this an analytic, or logically necessary, truth? Obviously not. A legal system can easily be imagined in which the identity of the person injured would be very material indeed, in which a name would indicate a status, and in which there would be many and minute differentiations in respect of status. If Mrs. Donoghue had been a slave in ancient Rome she would have been non-suited. As a member of the nobility under King Alfred's laws she would have had a substantially different claim from that of a commoner. If her name had been Cohen in Nazi-Germany he would have been a rash lawyer who would have regarded the name as immaterial. It is then an empirical truth that the identity of the plaintiff in Donoghue v. Stevenson was not a material fact; we know that in the English law of torts of to-day no distinction is made between one individual and another. But what are we affirming here? We are in fact affirming the existence of a number of principles or rules of law, and are regarding the case in the light of those principles.

Logically, this is the only basis on which any factual aspect of a case can be disregarded. In other words, the Goodhartian distinction between 'material' and 'immaterial' facts is not a factual distinction, nor a mixed distinction of facts and law, but a purely legal distinction. To say that the fact that the snail was found in ginger-beer, and not in some other beverage, was immaterial, is as much a proposition of law as to say that the common law of England does not in this context distinguish between one beverage and another.

It is clear that a case cannot serve as a precedent unless at least some of its factual circumstances are disregarded, and it is equally clear that it is only on the basis of a rule or principle of law that any factual circumstance can, logically, be disregarded. To put it differently, it is impossible to speak of the *ratio decidendi* of a case (where *ratio decidendi* means a rule which can be followed) without by implication asserting the existence of certain other rules or principles of law *which are not deducible from this case.*

But since it is one thing to assert the existence of a rule or principle of law, and another to substantiate the assertion, it is clear that one's interpretation of a case, one's view as to its *ratio decidendi,* will depend on one's knowledge of the law. If one has a wrong view of the rules and principles of law established before the decision in the case in question, one's conclusions as to the *ratio decidendi* of the case are very likely to be wrong too. Moreover, they are equally likely to be wrong—as will be shown hereafter—if one has a wrong view of the law established after the decision in the case in question.

We have thus arrived at the seemingly paradoxical position where our student who was told that he would learn the law by reading the cases and finding their *rationes decidendi,* now has to be informed that in order to find the *rationes decidendi* he has to know the law. . . .

QUESTIONS

1. Why do you suppose that the position of the student whom Harari describes is only "seemingly" paradoxical? Can you think of a way of getting out of the paradox?

2. Is Common Law adjudication, in Harari's version, more like rule-making or rule-finding?

Assuming the validity of Harari's analysis, how is it possible to say that the Common Law is knowable? That it can dictate or control the decision of particular cases? Could it be argued that however *prior* Common Law rules may be *historically*, Harari's analysis entails that they are *logically after* the decision of particular cases— that they are in essence, after-, rather than before-, the fact? Can rules of that sort be truly authoritative? Can they be truly "legal"? Would Rawls have to say that they are not "practice" rules?

Does Harari's exposition help us to understand the various movements for codification of the Common Law which have emerged at different times in American history?

3. Can Harari's analysis be taken as a justification of Lehman's treatment of Martin v. Herzog? Does it suggest another way that he might have avoided the authority of that case?

4. Why, according to Harari, are we interested in "what the judge did rather than . . . what he expressly or by implication said that he did"? Is it because of "the principle that the court making the decision is under a duty to decide the very case presented and has no authority to decide any other"? What is the basis of this principle? Is there also a principle that judges must write opinions explaining and justifying their positions? If so, is this principle consistent with the first one? Can an "explanation" or a "justification" decide only "the very case" presented to the court? Does it depend on the meaning of the words, "the very case"? Is it satisfactory to say that "legal decisions" are just "particular propositions" which only report certain historical events? Is there any argument that to state the facts and to announce a decision for the plaintiff actually amounts to a statement of a rule of law? Recall the selections from Stephen and Locke in the foregoing section.

*RUPERT CROSS*

PRECEDENT IN ENGLISH LAW *

. . . . The realists maintain that it is a mistake to pay too great a regard to the vocal as opposed to the non-vocal behaviour of judges. 'Don't worry so much about what the courts say, consider what they do', is one of the chief cries of this school. Its members appear to take seriously a joke made to a Lord Ordinary of Appeal (Lord Asquith) by 'one of our greatest judicial luminaries'. When

* From 45–47 (1961). Reprinted by permission of The Clarendon Press.

asked about the distinction between *ratio decidendi* and *obiter dictum*, he replied:

> The rule is quite simple, if you agree with the other bloke you say it is part of the *ratio*: if you don't you say it is *obiter dictum*, with the implication that he is a congenital idiot.

The same point is made in less vivid terms by the authors of an English textbook on jurisprudence in which some sympathy is expressed with the realist viewpoint. They go so far as to say:

> The division between *ratio* and *dicta* is in fact mainly a device employed by subsequent courts for the adoption or rejection of doctrine expressed in previous cases according to the inclinations of the subsequent courts.

Judges are human, and, as Lord Asquith observed, the joke made to him may well, as a matter of pure psychological fact, have more underlying truth than we know or care to avow'. Moreover, there can be little doubt that conclusions are often reached before the authorities against them are considered. In the words of Lord Wright:

> Sometimes a judge seems to move almost instinctively to the heart of the problem and its solution, though the detailed explanation and justification of what the problem is and how the solution is justified may require some elaborate reasoning and citation of authorities.

Although he was at the time a Lord Ordinary of Appeal, Lord Wright was writing extra-judicially, but the law reports abound in similar observations. When construing the words of a will Sargant J. once said:

> I do not propose to follow the fallacious course, so often deprecated, of looking at the authorities first and then seeing how this will differs from them. I propose to examine the will first, and put my own interpretation on it; and then to see whether there is any principle to be derived from the cases which renders it necessary for me to qualify or alter that interpretation.

When confronted with a case in which the defendants and third party who are respectively the landlord and tenant of a public house were seeking to put the blame for injuries sustained by one Heap on account of a defective cellar flap on to each other, or else to shift it on to a superior landlord who was not a party to the proceedings, McKinnon L.J. said:

> So far as I am concerned I freely avow that, inasmuch as in common sense and decency Heap ought to be able to recover against somebody, and, in the circumstances of this case, and having regard to the correspondence which has taken place, in all common sense and decency he is able to recover against these defendants if the law allows it, my only concern is to see whether, upon the cases, the law does allow him so to recover. I think that it does.

McKinnon L. J. then discussed the cases and showed how they supported the view that Heap was entitled to judgment. Procedure such

**as** this does not warrant the conclusion that, when the authorities do come to be examined, any resort to the distinction between *ratio decidendi* and *obiter dictum* is in the nature of a facade behind which decisions are made on grounds which have little to do with the previous cases. The significance of a piece of reasoning by analogy is not greatly affected by the fact that it succeeds the conclusion which it justifies. From the point of view of the validity of the orthodox theory of the judicial process, the important thing is that a judge should be prepared to alter any provisional decision at which he may have arrived when he considers a case, the *ratio decidendi* of which is binding upon him and which supports a contrary view, and there is no evidence that this is not the current judicial practice in England.

QUESTIONS

Is Cross saying that in any case, there is a presumption in favor of justice and it must be rebutted by a showing that authoritative rules require a different result? If not, what is he saying? If so, how "clear" do you suppose a contrary rule would have to be before the judge declared that it decreed an unjust result? If we consider Harari's remarks on the determination of the *ratio decidendi*, how "important" is it "that a judge should be prepared to alter any provisional decision at which he may have arrived when he considers a . . . *ratio decidendi* . . . . which is binding upon him"? Is Cross sufficiently aware of how one determines what the *ratio decidendi* is?

## 1.   The Authority of Rules in the Process of Decision

JOHN M. ZANE

GERMAN LEGAL PHILOSOPHY *

. . . . The judicial power can only adjudicate. It can render a judgment upon a particular concrete state of facts. Every judicial act resulting in a judgment consists of a pure deduction. The figure of its reasoning is the stating of a rule applicable to certain facts, a finding that the facts of the particular case are those certain facts and the application of the rule is a logical necessity. The old syllogism, "All men are mortal, Socrates is a man, therefore he is mortal", states the exact form of a judicial judgment. The existing rule of law is: Every man who with malice aforethought kills another in the peace of the people is guilty of murder. The defendant with malice aforethought killed A. B. in the peace of the people, therefore the defendant is guilty of murder.

. . . . [I]t must be perfectly apparent to any one who is willing to admit the rules governing rational mental action that unless the rule of the major premise exists as antecedent to the ascertainment of the fact or facts put into the minor premise, there is

* From   16   Mich.L.Rev.   288,   337–8
(1918).   Reprinted by permission of
the Michigan Law Review.

no judicial act in stating the judgment. The man who claims that under our system the courts make law is asserting that the courts habitually act unconstitutionally.

## QUESTIONS

What do you think Zane means by "the rules governing rational mental action"? What does he mean that the "judgment of a court is always this pure deduction"? Does he mean that the opinion must always take the form of a syllogism? Or that the reasoning process must follow the form of a syllogism? Would Zane be satisfied with Cross's defense of rules in the judicial decision-making process?

## JOHN DEWEY

### ART AS EXPERIENCE *

We say of an experience of thinking that we reach or draw a conclusion. Theoretical formulation of the process is often made in such terms as to conceal effectually the similarity of "conclusion" to the consummating phase of every developing integral experience. These formulations apparently take their cue from the separate propositions that are premisses and the proposition that is the conclusion as they appear on the printed page. The impression is derived that there are first two independent and ready-made entities that are then manipulated so as to give rise to a third. In fact, in an experience of thinking, premisses emerge only as a conclusion becomes manifest. The experience, like that of watching a storm reach its height and gradually subside, is one of continuous movement of subject matters. Like the ocean in the storm, there are series of waves; suggestions reaching out and being broken in a clash, or being carried onwards by a cooperative wave. If a conclusion is reached, it is that of a movement of anticipation and cumulation, one that finally comes to completion. A "conclusion" is no separate and independent thing; it is the consummation of a movement.

### NOTE: THE FUNCTION OF ARGUMENT

Consider the following:

.    .    .    So far as proof goes, every argument in and of itself begs the question it is to solve. The classical "proof" that Socrates was mortal exemplifies the point. As its very first step, the conclusion was implicitly assumed for, as soon as we say that all men are mortal, Socrates is implicitly included. This example illustrates the proper function of argument; not to prove the conclusion desired, but to make explicit what is already implicit in one's position on a question.

Oliphant & Hewitt, *Introduction* to J. RUEFF, FROM THE PHYSICAL TO THE SOCIAL SCIENCES (1929). Are the writers saying that the syllogism is an *explanation* rather than a *description* of a decision? Do you agree? What might lead people to think otherwise?

. . .

## GILBERT RYLE

### THE CONCEPT OF MIND *

When we speak of the intellect or, better, of the intellectual powers and performances of persons, we are referring primarily to that special class of operations which constitute theorising. The goal of these operations is the knowledge of true propositions or facts. Mathematics and the established natural sciences are the model accomplishments of human intellects. The early theorists naturally speculated upon what constituted the peculiar excellences of the theoretical sciences and disciplines, the growth of which they had witnessed and assisted. They were predisposed to find that it was in the capacity for rigorous theory that lay the superiority of men over animals, of civilised men over barbarians and even of the divine mind over human minds. They thus bequeathed the idea that the capacity to attain knowledge of truths was the defining property of a mind. Other human powers could be classed as mental only if they could be shown to be somehow piloted by the intellectual grasp of true propositions. To be rational was to be able to recognise truths and the connections between them. To act rationally was, therefore, to have one's non-theoretical propensities controlled by one's apprehension of truths about the conduct of life.

. . .

### (3) *Knowing How and Knowing That.*

When a person is described by one or other of the intelligence-epithets such as 'shrewd' or 'silly', 'prudent' or 'imprudent', the description imputes to him not the knowledge, or ignorance, of this or that truth, but the ability, or inability, to do certain sorts of things. Theorists have been so preoccupied with the task of investigating the nature, the source and the credentials of the theories that we adopt that they have for the most part ignored the question what it is for someone to know how to perform tasks. In ordinary life, on the contrary, as well as in the special business of teaching, we are much more concerned with people's competences than with their cognitive repertoires, with the operations than with the truths that they learn. Indeed even when we are concerned with their intellectual excellences and deficiencies, we are interested less in the stocks of truths that they acquire and retain than in their capacities to find out truths for themselves and their ability to organise and exploit them, when discovered. Often we deplore a person's ignorance of some fact only because we deplore the stupidity of which his ignorance is a consequence.

* From 25–26, 27–31, 32–33, 40–41, 44–45, 48–49 (Barnes & Noble 1949).

There are certain parallelisms between knowing *how* and knowing *that,* as well as certain divergences. We speak of learning how to play an instrument as well as of learning that something is the case; of finding out how to prune trees as well as of finding out that the Romans had a camp in a certain place; of forgetting how to tie a reef-knot as well as of forgetting that the German for 'knife' is *'Messer'.* We can wonder *how* as well as *whether.*

On the other hand, we never speak of a person believing or opining *how,* and though it is proper to ask for the grounds or reasons for someone's acceptance of a proposition, this question cannot be asked of someone's skill at cards or prudence in investments.

What is involved in our descriptions of people as knowing how to make and appreciate jokes, to talk grammatically, to play chess, to fish, or to argue? Part of what is meant is that, when they perform these operations, they tend to perform them well, i. e. correctly or efficiently or successfully. Their performances come up to certain standards, or satisfy certain criteria. But this is not enough. The well-regulated clock keeps good time and the well-drilled circus seal performs its tricks flawlessly, yet we do not call them 'intelligent'. We reserve this title for the persons responsible for their performances. To be intelligent is not merely to satisfy criteria, but to apply them; to regulate one's actions and not merely to be well-regulated. A person's performance is described as careful or skillful, if in his operations he is ready to detect and correct lapses, to repeat and improve upon success, to profit from the examples of others and so forth. He applies criteria in performing critically, that is, in trying to get things right.

This point is commonly expressed in the vernacular by saying that an action exhibits intelligence, if, and only if, the agent is thinking what he is doing while he is doing it, and thinking what he is doing in such a manner that he would not do the action so well if he were not thinking what he is doing. . . . the operation which is characterised as intelligent must be preceded by an intellectual acknowledgment of these rules or criteria; that is, the agent must first go through the internal process of avowing to himself certain propositions about what is to be done ('maxims', 'imperatives' or 'regulative propositions' as they are sometimes called); only then can he execute his performance in accordance with those dictates. He must preach to himself before he can practise. The chef must recite his recipes to himself before he can cook according to them; the hero must lend his inner ear to some appropriate moral imperative before swimming out to save the drowning man; the chess-player must run over in his head all the relevant rules and tactical maxims of the game before he can make correct and skillful moves. To do something thinking what one is doing is, according to this legend, always to do two things; namely, to consider certain appropriate propositions, or prescriptions, and to put into practice what these propositions or prescriptions enjoin. It is to do a bit of theory and then to do a bit of practice.

Certainly we often do not only reflect before we act but reflect in order to act properly. The chess-player may require some time in which to plan his moves before he makes them. Yet the general assertion that all intelligent performance requires to be prefaced by the consideration of appropriate propositions rings unplausibly, even when it is apologetically conceded that the required consideration is often very swift and may go quite unmarked by the agent. . . .

. . .

Efficient practice precedes the theory of it; methodologists presuppose the application of the methods, of the critical investigation of which they are the products. It was because Aristotle found himself and others reasoning now intelligently and now stupidly and it was because Izaak Walton found himself and others angling sometimes effectively and sometimes ineffectively that both were able to give to their pupils the maxims and prescriptions of their arts. It is therefore possible for people intelligently to perform some sorts of operations when they are not yet able to consider any propositions enjoining how they should be performed. Some intelligent performances are not controlled by any anterior acknowledgments of the principles applied in them.

The crucial objection to the intellectualist legend is this. The consideration of propositions is itself an operation the execution of which can be more or less intelligent, less or more stupid. But if, for any operation to be intelligently executed, a prior theoretical operation had first to be performed and performed intelligently, it would be a logical impossibility for anyone ever to break into the circle.

Let us consider some salient points at which this regress would arise. According to the legend, whenever an agent does anything intelligently, his act is preceded and steered by another internal act of considering a regulative proposition appropriate to his practical problem. But what makes him consider the one maxim which is appropriate rather than any of the thousands which are not? Why does the hero not find himself calling to mind a cooking-recipe, or a rule of Formal Logic? Perhaps he does, but then his intellectual process is silly and not sensible. Intelligently reflecting how to act is, among other things, considering what is pertinent and disregarding what is inappropriate. Must we then say that for the hero's reflections how to act to be intelligent he must first reflect how best to reflect how to act? The endlessness of this implied regress shows that the application of the criterion of appropriateness does not entail the occurrence of a process of considering this criterion.

Next, supposing still that to act reasonably I must first perpend the reason for so acting, how am I led to make a suitable application of the reason to the particular situation which my action is to meet? For the reason, or maxim, is inevitably a proposition of some generality. It cannot embody specifications to fit every detail of the particular state of affairs. Clearly, once more, I must be sensible and not stupid, and this good sense cannot itself be a product of the intellectual acknowledgment of any general principle. A soldier does not become a shrewd general merely by endorsing the strategic principles of Clausewitz; he must also be competent to apply them. Knowing how to apply maxims cannot be reduced to, or derived from, the acceptance of those or any other maxims.

To put it quite generally, the absurd assumption made by the intellectualist legend is this, that a performance of any sort inherits all its title to intelligence from some anterior internal operation of planning what to do. Now very often we do go through such a process of planning what to do, and, if we are silly, our planning is silly, if shrewd, our planning is shrewd. It is also notoriously possible for us to plan shrewdly and perform stupidly, i. e. to flout our precepts in our practice. By the original argument, therefore, our intellectual planning process must inherit its title to shrewdness from yet another interior process of planning to plan, and this process could in its turn be silly or shrewd. . . . 'Intelligent' cannot be defined in terms of 'intellectual' or 'knowing *how*' in terms of 'knowing *that*'. . . .

QUESTIONS

1. Would Ryle agree with Zane that there are "rules governing rational mental action"? Would he agree with Zane's conception of what "rational mental action" is?

Consider Zane's assertion that "unless the rule of the major premise exists as antecedent to the ascertainment of the fact or facts put into the minor premise, there is no judicial act in stating the judgment." What comment might Ryle make on this? Is it a statement with which Cross would agree? If not, is it because of the considerations adduced by Ryle? What does Ryle say, if he says anything, as to the *possibility* of deciding Common Law cases other than the way Cross is concerned to defend? What comment might Ryle make on Frank's assertion that judicial opinions—as is the institution of "law-in-discourse"—are rationalizations? Can they, in Ryle's view, be anything else?

2. Can Ryle's arguments be viewed as a justification for the position that in the law of precedent we are interested in "what the judge did rather than . . . what he expressly or by implication said that he did"? Would Ryle's position help justify a bald declaration by Judge Lehman that the case of Martin v. Herzog was to be confined to its facts? Does Ryle give us reason to respect the judge who is often "right, but for the wrong reasons"? What might he say about learned and sophisticated judges who seem often to be "wrong, but for the right reasons"?

3. Recall Koestler's assertion in section 1 that we know how to speak English without knowing the rules for making and understanding English statements. Is it possible to know law in this way as well? Is there, according to Ryle, any other *meaningful* way of knowing something? On the assumption that there is not, and that knowledge of law is something more—or something other—than

knowledge that there are certain legal rules, just how controllable and criticizable does this leave the interpreters of the law?

## NOTE: "I KNOW THE RULES, BUT  . . ."

Every once in a whole some student somewhere will be heard to say, "I know all the rules in the course, but I can't always apply them." Would Ryle have any comment to make on such a statement? What might he say about the notion that the job of law school is to teach students the rules of law? Just what is the difference between "knowing how" and "knowing that"? Does Ryle ever state it in so many words? If he doesn't, what justification could he advance?

### JOHN HOLT

### How CHILDREN FAIL *

Here is Walter  . . .  very eager to do whatever people want him to do, and very good at doing it. (By conventional standards he was a very able pupil, so much so that people called him brilliant, which he most assuredly was not.)

We had the problem, "If you are travelling at 40 miles per hour, how long will it take you to go 10 miles?"

Walter: 4 minutes.

JH (me): How did you get it?

W: Divided the 40 by the 10.

A quick look at my face told him that this would not do. After a while he wrote, "15 minutes." I wanted to check his understanding.

JH: If you were going 50 miles per hour, how far would you go in 24 minutes?

W (quickly): 36 miles.

JH: How did you get that?

W: Subtracted 24 from 60.

He still hadn't gotten it: I tried again.

JH: If you were going 50 miles per hour, how far would you go in 30 minutes?

W: 25 miles. 30 minutes is half an hour, and half of 50 is 25.

It sounded as if he knew what he was doing at last. I thought he would have no trouble with the 24 minutes problem. But it took a long time, with some hinting from me, before he saw that 24 minutes was $\frac{2}{5}$ of an hour, and therefore, that he would go $\frac{2}{5}$ of 50 miles, or 20 miles, in 24 minutes. Would he have discovered it if I had not paved the way with leading questions? Hard to tell.

Most teachers would have assumed, as I would have once, that when he got the 15-minutes problem, he knew what he was doing. Even the skeptical would have been convinced when he gave his ex-

---

* From 18–19, 104, 106–107 (Delta ed. 1964). Copyright 1964 by Pitman Pub-   lishing Corporation. Reprinted by permission.

planation about the 30-minutes problem. Yet in each case he showed that he had not really understood what he was doing, and it is not at all certain that he understands yet.

What was his strategy here? Certainly he was numeral shoving. More than that, he was making up a fairly sensible sounding explanation of how he was doing the problem. And yet, is it not possible, even probable, that in saying that in half an hour you go half of 50 miles, he was merely doing some word shoving to go along with his numeral shoving? The explanation sounded reasonable to me, because, in this case, his way of shoving the numerals happened to be the right way; but he was just as happy with his explanations when he was shoving the numerals the wrong way.

This is a disquieting thought. We say and believe that at this school we teach children to understand the meaning of what they do in math. How? By giving them (and requiring them to give back to us) "explanations" of what they do. But let's take a child's-eye view. Might not a child feel, as Walter obviously did, that in this school you not only have to get the right answer, but you also have to have the right explanation to go with it; the right answer, and the right chatter. Yet we see here that a "successful" student can give the answer and the chatter without understanding at all what he was doing or saying.

.   .   .

There are many   .   .   .   who say that this distinction [between real learning and apparent learning] does not exist. It's their handy way of solving the knotty problem of understanding; just say there is no such thing. Apparently this view is currently in fashion among psychologists. According to many of them, if you can say that 7 x 8=56, you know all there is to know about that particular fact, and you know as much about it as anyone else who can say it. The mathematician, the third grader, and, presumably, a well-trained parrot, would all have an equal and identical understanding of this fact. The only difference between the mathematician and the child is that the mathematician carries around in his head many more such facts. So to make children into mathematicians all we have to do is train them, condition them, until they can say many such facts. Teach them to say everything that Einstein knew, and hey, presto! another Einstein!

It's amazing what nonsense people will believe.

Of course, this notion fits neatly into behaviorism, which is also still very much in fashion, despite all it cannot explain. It is also comforting to teachers, who have felt all along that their job is to drop, or push, one at a time, little bits of information into those largely empty minds that are moving slowly before them down the academic assembly line. And finally, it has set into motion the apparently endless gravy train of programmed instruction and machine teaching, onto which everyone and his brother seem to be happily clambering.

.   .   .

Knowledge, learning, understanding, are not linear. They are not little bits of facts lined up in rows or piled up one on top of another. A field of knowledge, whether it be math, English, history, science, music, or whatever, is a territory, and knowing it is not just a matter of knowing all the items in the territory, but of knowing how they relate to, compare with, and fit in with each other. It is the difference between being able to say that a room in your house has so many tables, so many chairs, so many lamps, and being able to close your eyes and see that this chair goes here and that table there. It is the difference between knowing the names of all the streets in a city and being able to get from any place, by any desired route, to any other place.

Why do we talk and write about the world and our knowledge of it as if they were linear? Because that is the nature of talk. Words come out in a single file, one at a time; there's no other way to talk or write. So, in order to talk about it, we cut the real, undivided world into little pieces, and make these into strings of talk, like beads on a necklace. But we must not be fooled; these strings of talk are not what the world is like. Our learning is not real, not complete, not accurate, above all not useful, unless we take these word strings and somehow convert them in our minds into a likeness of the world, a working mental model of the universe as we know it. Only when we have made such a model, and when there is at least a rough correspondence between that model and reality, can it be said of us that we have learned something.

What happens in school is that children take in these word strings and store them, undigested, in their minds, so that they can spit them back out on demand. But these words do not change anything, fit with anything, relate to anything. They are as empty of meaning as parrot-speech is to a parrot. How can we make school a place where real learning goes on, and not just word swallowing?

## Questions

1. Is it possible to view Walter as the model of a "good judge"? Shouldn't a judge be "very eager to do whatever people want him to do, and very good at doing it"? Isn't this the kind of mentality we need in order to have a rule of law—at least in the sense of a rule of legal rules? Is not the kind of mentality which Holt seems to favor precisely the kind we cannot depend upon to be bound by authoritative directions?

2. Why is it thought to be an advance in education, do you think, to give students the "explanations" of what they are doing? What is the connection between such "explanations" and "the meaning" of "what they do"? Can the Common Law be viewed in the same way as math education at Holt's school—i. e., as a body of reports of what courts have done plus the explanations? If the Common Law, as Holt's and Ryle's remarks seem to imply, cannot be adequately known from the actual decisions with their explanations, could it be adequately known if there were authoritative explanations of the explanations—i. e., authoritative statements of the meaning of each doctrine? Why, according to Ryle, would this be futile?

3. Do you find persuasive Holt's contention that errors about learning and knowledge are attributable to "the nature of talk"? Why should we tend to think that "the world is like" our "strings of talk"? Can you find a parallel between Langer's remarks in the preceding section on the naming of relations and Holt's discussion of language? Does Holt think that knowledge is a thing or a relation— or what? Is he saying that the form of language encourages us to hypostatize the relation that knowledge is?

Can the confusion between the syllogism and the way we think also be attributed to "the nature of talk" or of writing? Why, according to Dewey, do we tend to mistakenly think that the syllogism actually *describes* the process of thought? Is the syllogism and its linguistic expression an hypostatization of the thinking and deciding process?

In Part I it was asked whether the model of the judicial process presented by Zane and others—a model which is probably the authoritative model in American legal thinking—was not based on a disputable assumption about language's communicative efficacy. Do the comments of Langer, Dewey, Ryle and Holt suggest that this model is also in large measure the product of mistaken analogies from the form of language? That the model is an example of what Bacon refers to as words "overruling" the understanding, and what Wittgenstein refers to as "the bewitchment of our intelligence by means of language"?

## 2.　The Force of Logic

*Joseph Heller*

### Catch–22 *

"Men," Colonel Cargill began in Yossarian's squadron, measuring his pauses carefully. "You're American officers. The officers of no other army in the world can make that statement. Think about it."

Sergeant Knight thought about it and then politely informed Colonel Cargill that he was addressing the enlisted men and that the officers were to be found waiting for him on the other side of the squadron.

### Questions

Can the above passages be viewed as a comment about logic? If so, do you see any parallels between that comment and the Logical Positivist position on analytic statements? What, if anything, is funny about Colonel Cargill's words? What, if anything, is funny about his mistake?

JOHN DICKINSON

## ADMINISTRATIVE JUSTICE AND THE SUPREMACY OF LAW *

In the eighteenth century the emphasis shifted, though less in England than elsewhere, from history to reason, from precedent to fundamental justice. That was the golden century of human "reason," when the miraculous was expected of it. In it was found what the Middle Ages had found in religious faith, and what the nineteenth century was to find in science—a key to unlock all doors, a panacea for all the ills of the world, a mechanical toy that kept men agape for what wonders it was going to work next. And for the type of reason, mathematical reason was chosen—a reason working out with inexorable logic the single correct solution for every problem. Such an idea at work in politics produced the Abbé Sieyès, and in law the era of codes. It was believed that the one and only legal rule for every possible situation could be written off in advance by a proper combination of axiomatic first principles with the same accuracy as the answers to all the problems in the Euclidean geometry. Law ceased to be an instrument for working toward certainty—it became certainty itself.

Of course we take no such naive view of law or reason today.[7] We have seen all too clearly how human reason led Germans to one conclusion, and Frenchmen to another, to believe there is aught of the inexorable about it. We have come to realize that logic is but the tool of premises, and that the premises of social intercourse fluctuate with a human equation which contains at least two variables. Logic will not yield us certainties; in fact nothing will.

OLIVER WENDELL HOLMES, JR.

## THE COMMON LAW *

The object of this book is to present a general view of the Common Law. To accomplish the task, other tools are needed besides logic. It is something to show that the consistency of a system requires a particular result, but it is not all. The life of the law has not been logic: it has been experience. The felt necessities of the time,

* From 114–118 (1927). Copyright 1927 by the President and Fellows of Harvard College, 1955 by John Dickinson. Reprinted by permission of Harvard University Press.

7. And still this view has by no means as yet disappeared from legal writers. Compare the following passage from a recent book: "There is not nearly so much doubt about our legal questions as we are prone to believe. In the great majority of cases the solution of them is as certain and exact as an answer to a problem in mathematics, and it brings with it precisely the same intellectual satisfaction," E. V. Abbot, *Justice and the Modern Law*, Boston, (1913), p. 236. This book, throughout, is an excellent example of the mathematical or formally logical view of law. "The judicial process in ascertaining or applying the law is essentially similar to the process by which we acquire our knowledge of geometry," *ibid*, p. 11. [Footnote in Original.]

* From 5 (Harvard ed., 1963). Originally published in 1881 by Little, Brown and Company.

the prevalent moral and political theories, intuitions of public policy, avowed or unconscious, even the prejudices which judges share with their fellowmen, have had a good deal more to do than the syllogism in determining the rules by which men should be governed. The law embodies the story of a nation's development through many centuries, and it cannot be dealt with as if it contained only the axioms and corollaries of a book of mathematics. In order to know what it is, we must know what it has been, and what it tends to become.

### Benjamin N. Cardozo

### The Nature of the Judicial Process *

The directive force of a principle may be exerted along the line of logical progression; this I will call the rule of analogy or the method of philosophy. . . .

I have put first among the principles of selection to guide our choice of paths, the rule of analogy or the method of philosophy. In putting it first, I do not mean to rate it as most important. On the contrary, it is often sacrificed to others. I have put it first because it has, I think, a certain presumption in its favor. Given a mass of particulars, a congeries of judgments on related topics, the principle that unifies and rationalizes them has a tendency, and a legitimate one, to project and extend itself to new cases within the limits of its capacity to unify and rationalize. It has the primacy that comes from natural and orderly and logical succession. Homage is due to it over every competing principle that is unable by appeal to history or tradition or policy or justice to make out a better right. All sorts of deflecting forces may appear to contest its sway and absorb its power. At least, it is the heir presumptive. A pretender to the title will have to fight his way.

. . .

. . . . We must know where logic and philosophy lead even though we may determine to abandon them for other guides. The times will be many when we can do no better than follow where they point.

### Felix S. Cohen

### The Ethical Basis of Legal Criticism *

The ethical responsibilities of the judge have so often been obscured by the supposed duty to be logically consistent in the decision of different cases that it may be pertinent to ask whether any legal decision can ever be logically inconsistent with any other decision. In order to find such an inconsistency we must have two judgments, one for the plaintiff and one for the defendant. But this means that we must have two cases, since a second judgment in the same case would

* From 30, 31–32, 38, 40–43 (1921). Reprinted with permission of Yale University Press.

* From 41 Yale L.J. 201, 215–219 (1931). Reprinted by permission of the Yale Law Journal.

supersede the first judgment. And between the facts of any two cases there must be some difference, so that it will always be logically possible to frame a single legal rule requiring both decisions, given the facts of the two cases. Of course such a rule will seem absurd if the difference between the two cases is unimportant (*e. g.*, in the names or heights of the two defendants). But whether the difference is important or unimportant is a problem not of logic but of ethics, and one to which the opposing counsel in the later case may propose opposite answers without becoming involved in self-contradiction.

The confusion arises when we think of a judicial decision as implying a rule from which, given the facts of the case, the decision may be derived (the logical fallacy of affirming the consequent). That logically startling deduction of the "law of precedents" from judicial precedents, Black's *Handbook of the Law of Judicial Precedents*, thus sums up the matter:

"Even if the opinion of the court should be concerned with unnecessary considerations, or should state the proposition of law imperfectly or incorrectly, yet there is a proposition necessarily involved in the decision and without which the judgment in the case could not have been given; and it is this proposition which is established by the decision (so far as it goes) and for which alone the case may be cited as an authority."

But elementary logic teaches us that every legal decision and every finite set of decisions can be subsumed under an infinite number of different general rules, just as an infinite number of different curves may be traced through any point or finite collection of points. Every decision is a choice between different rules which logically fit all past decisions but logically dictate conflicting results in the instant case. Logic provides the springboard but it does not guarantee the success of any particular dive.

If the doctrine of *stare decisis* means anything, and one can hardly maintain the contrary despite the infelicitous formulations which have been given to the doctrine, the consistency which it demands cannot be a logical consistency. The consistency in question is more akin to that quality of dough which is necessary for the fixing of a durable shape. Decisions are fluid until they are given "morals." It is often important to conserve with new obeisance the morals which lawyers and laymen have read into past decisions and in reliance upon which they have acted. We do not deny that importance when we recognize that with equal logical justification lawyers and laymen might have attached other morals to the old cases had their habits of legal classification or their general social premises been different. But we do shift the focus of our vision from a stage where social and professional prejudices wear the terrible armor of Pure Reason to an arena where human hopes and expectations wrestle naked for supremacy.

No doubt the doctrine of *stare decisis* and the argument for consistency have a significance which is not exhausted by the social usefulness of predictable law. Even in fields where past court decisions play a negligible role in molding expectations, courts may be justified in looking to former rulings for guidance. The time of judges is more limited than the boundaries of injustice. At some risk the results of past deliberation in a case similar to the case at bar must be accepted. But again we invite fatal confusion if we think of this similarity as a logical rather than an ethical relation. To the cold eyes of logic the difference between the names of the parties in the two decisions bulks as large as the difference between care and negligence. The question before the judge is, "Granted that there are differences between the cited precedent and the case at bar, and assuming that the decision in the earlier case was a desirable one, is it desirable to attach legal weight to any of the factual differences between the instant case and the earlier case?" Obviously this is an ethical question. Should a rich woman accused of larceny receive the same treatment as a poor woman? Should a rich man who has accidentally injured another come under the same obligations as a poor man? Should a group of persons, e. g., an unincorporated labor union, be privileged to make all statements that an individual may lawfully make? Neither the ringing hexameters of *Barbara Celarent* nor the logic machine of Jevons nor the true-false patterns of Wittgenstein will produce answers to these questions.

What then shall we think of attempts to frame practical legal issues as conflicts between morality, common sense, history or sociology, and logic (logic playing regularly the Satanic role)? One hesitates to convict the foremost jurists on the American bench of elementary logical error. It is more likely that they have simply used the word "logic" in peculiar ways, as to which they may find many precedents in the current logic textbooks. Bertrand Russell has warned us:

"When it is said, for example, that the French are 'logical', what is meant is that, when they accept a premise, they also accept everything that a person totally devoid of logical subtlety would erroneously suppose to follow from that premise. . . . Logic was, formerly, the art of drawing inferences; it has now become the art of abstaining from inferences, since it has appeared that the inferences we feel naturally inclined to make are hardly ever valid."

If we construe the word "logic" in the light of this warning, we may readily agree with Mr. Justice Holmes when he asserts that "the whole outline of the law is the resultant of a conflict at every point between logic [*viz.* hasty generalization] and good sense", and find some meaning in the statement of Judge Cardozo that "the logic of one principle" prevails over the logic of another [8] or in his pride

---

8. Cardozo, Nature of the Judicial Process, (1921) c. 1 (*Introduction. The Method of Philosophy*) 41. Judge Cardozo illustrates (*op. cit.* 38–39) the method of logic or philosophy, which is distinguished from the methods of history or evolution, of custom or tradition, and of sociology, with the rule that one who contracts to purchase real property must pay for it even though, before the sale is actually completed, the property is substantially destroyed. This, he maintains, is the projection to its logical outcome of the principle that "equity treats that as done which ought to be done," a principle which does not apply to the sale of chattels which did not

that "We in the United States have been readier to subordinate logic to utility."

We may have to interpret the word "logical" as synonymous with "aesthetically satisfying" in order to understand the statement of Mr. Justice Brandeis and Mr. Warren that a distinction between cases where "substantial mental suffering would be the natural and probable result" of an act and cases "where no mental suffering would ordinarily result" is not logical though very practical. Such an identification of the rules of logic with those of intellectual aesthetics seems to be assumed at times by Judge Cardozo as well.

No verbal definition is intrinsically objectionable. But it seems fair to suggest that the use of the word "logic" in the senses exemplified in these typical passages seriously lowers the probability of clear thinking on the relation between law and ethics. Most of us think of logic as the most general and formal of the sciences. Upon that basis we may say, paraphrasing a remark of Mr. Justice Holmes, that conformity with logic is only a necessity and not a duty. The bad judge is no more able to violate the laws of logic than he is to violate the laws of gravitation. He may, of course, ignore both. . . .

QUESTIONS

1. What do you think Black means in saying that "there is a proposition necessarily involved in the decision and without which the judgment in the case could not have been given"? If the "proposition" is not in the opinion, where is it? In the judge's mind? What if the judge never entertained any proposition? Or is this impossible? "Every decision," Cohen says, "is a choice between different rules which logically fit all past decisions . . . ." Does this mean that the judge consciously chooses between rules in making a decision? Even if "every legal decision and every finite set of decisions can be subsumed under an infinite number of different general rules," does this mean that each one of these rules is authoritative? Does Cohen think that each case necessarily involves a conflict between authoritative rules? If so, how does he demonstrate this?

come under the jurisdiction of Chancery. But what sort of principle is this? It is certainly not a logical principle, i.e., a proposition certifiable on logical grounds alone, since it is obviously false. If it were true no plaintiff in equity could ever obtain a judgment since he could never in the face of such a rule show that the defendant had *not* done what he ought to have done. Would it not be quite as logical for a court to say "equity does not treat that as done which has not been done"? If a rule is undesirable we do not make it less undesirable by deducing it from another rule too vague to be liked or disliked and then concentrating our attention on the process of inference rather than the premise. What is in question in the case proposed is not a logical problem or a choice of judicial methods but a conflict of social interests, and there is much that may be said in favor of throwing upon the party who contemplates future enjoyment of a definite piece of real property the risk of its destruction and the necessity of insurance. But what may thus be said bears no peculiar *imprimatur* of logic.

2. What is Cohen saying that Harari did not say earlier? Where do both of these writers leave lower courts which, unlike the highest courts, cannot overturn precedent?

3. What is the meaning that Cohen gives to the word "logic" and precisely how does it differ from that of Holmes and Cardozo in the statements Cohen quotes? How does it differ from the Holmes and Cardozo passages which precede Cohen?

4. Is it possible to argue that what Cardozo and Holmes call the force of logic is really the force of literalism—that it is literal interpretations of controlling rules that give the results supposedly decreed by logic? To what extent does the working of the "apparatus of logic" depend upon the meaning of terms in the major and minor premises? Can a decision be illogical if the major and minor premises use the same terms but their meanings are different? If not, what is meant when the epithet "illogical" is used in such situations?

## Section Three: The Application Of Words And Of Rules

### Note: Tedla v. Ellman on the Classification And Meaning of Statutory Rules

1. *Types of statutes and types of rules.* In *Tedla* we encounter a notion of rules which "apply" in all cases and rules which "apply" only in some cases. Such a distinction should not be unfamiliar to us. Recall Rawls's discussion of practice and summary rules. Is not the distinction between binding and sometimes-binding rules also involved in the debate over the weight of statutory standards in negligence law? Are not courts which consider violation of a statute negligence *per se* saying that the statutory rule must always be used where it is applicable? Are not those who prefer the "presumptive negligence" or "evidence of negligence" approach saying that the rule is a guide which may help, but it is not necessarily binding.

How does Lehman distinguish between those rules which are always to be applied and those which are not? He identifies (1) statutes which fix "no definite standard of care which would under all circumstances tend to protect life, limb or property" and (2) "statutory rule[s] of conduct" which regulate "conflicting rights and obligations in a manner calculated to promote public convenience and safety" as of the type which may be disregarded in some situations. What kind of statutes must be observed in all situations? Can you conceive of any standard "which would under all circumstances tend to protect life, limb or property"? Consider the standard involved in Martin v. Herzog. Would the requirement of lights after dark "tend to protect life, limb or property" no matter what the circumstances? Can you conceive a situation in which it would be safer *not* to have lights after dark? Can you think of any "safeguard" which "under all circumstances" would function *as* a safeguard—*i. e.*, would insure, rather than imperil one's safety? If not, is it still proper to call it a safeguard in those situations where it is not safe? Does it have the name "safeguard" in all situations, even though it is used as one only in some? Or is it a "safeguard" in some situations, but not in others? What answers does usage give us to these questions? Is usage the final authority? Why? Can you think of any characterization which is true of the thing it characterizes in all situations?

Can you think of a statute whose sponsors do not think it regulates "conflicting rights and obligations in a manner calculated to promote public convenience"? Do we arrive at the conclusion that Lehman's exceptions swallow the rule—that in effect all statutes can be disregarded for a "good reason"?

2. *The Meaning of Rules.* What does Lehman think is the "meaning" of the "statutory rule" in Tedla v. Ellman? Does the rule, in his view, "mean" the conduct in which Tedla and Bachek engaged? Or does the rule only *apparently* "mean" that conduct?

Judge Lehman reports that "Mrs. Tedla and her brother did not observe the statutory rule. . . ." He poses the question in *Tedla* as "whether, as matter of law, disregard of the statutory rule . . . constitutes contributory negligence." And he admonishes that "a pedestrian is, of course, at fault if he fails without good reason to observe the statutory rule of conduct." Does all of this mean that Tedla and Bachek violated the statute, but that the court excused them because they had a "good reason"?

Is this interpretation of Lehman's reasoning consistent with his assertion that it "is unreasonable to ascribe to the Legislature an intention that the statute should have so extraordinary a result, and the courts may not give to a statute an effect not intended by the legislature"? Consider also the statement that the court "cannot assume reasonably that the Legislature intended that a statute . . . must be observed when observance would subject them to more imminent danger"? Do these statements indicate that all the court thinks it is doing is interpreting the statute? That rather than permitting the statute to be disregarded, the court is holding that the statute doesn't really say what it seems to say? That, in short, Tedla and Bachek didn't "really" disregard the statutory rule? If so, is it possible to reconcile this reading with the language referred to in the preceding paragraph?

Is Lehman saying, perhaps, that the conduct in which Tedla and Bachek engaged was the *type* the legislature meant to proscribe, but that it did not mean to proscribe their actual conduct? That the legislature prohibited walking on the wrong side of the road but not the specific walking on the road which actually occurred prior to the injuries which Tedla and Bachek suffered? If so, by what kind of evidence or rationale could such a position be justified? Does Lehman present such evidence or offer such a rationale?

Can Lehman's opinion be construed to mean that the statutory rule "covered" the situation in *Tedla*, but that it was not meant to "apply" in that situation? Or that the actions of Tedla and Bachek came within the meaning of the rule's words, but not within the intent of the legislature? Or that the statute "meant" the actions of Tedla and Bachek but did not "apply" to them? Are any of these distinctions logically permissible? Empirically useful?

Is there a distinction between the meaning of a linguistic symbol —be it word or sentence—and the thing, event or situation to which it is actually applied? Is Lehman writing as if he thinks there is such a distinction? If not, can you construct a plausible explanation which accounts for the things he says? If Lehman does seem to be making such a distinction, do you think it has any validity? If so, do Lehman's remarks indicate that he fully understands it? What do you make of the following?

> . . . . in every case involving a statute, the state court must perform . . . two functions essentially different. First the court must construe the statute: that is, determine its meaning and scope. Then it must apply the statute, as so construed, to the facts of the case.[1] [The footnote reads: "The word 'apply' is used in connection with statutes in two senses. When construing a statute, in describing the class of persons, things or functions which are within its scope: as that the statute does not 'apply' to transactions in interstate commerce. When discussing the use made of a statute, in referring to the process by which the statute is made operative; as where the jury is told to 'apply' the statute of limitation if they find that the cause of action arose before a given date. In this opinion it is used in the latter sense."]

Justice Brandeis dissenting in Dahnke-Walker Milling Co. v. Bondurant, 257 U.S. 282, 293 (1921). Do Justice Brandeis's remarks help us better understand Judge Lehman's language in Tedla v. Ellman? How distinct do you think the process of "construing" a statute is from the process of "applying" it? Can you speculate as to why the word "apply" has come to have the meanings which Brandeis distinguishes?

Consider all of these questions again when you reach Langer's discussion of the denotative and connotative meanings of symbols in subsection (b) of this section.

3. *The Legislature's Intention.* How does Lehman reach the conclusion that the legislature could not have intended its rule to apply in Mrs. Tedla's case? From the words of the statute? From the words of other statutes or Common Law rules? Is his authority "common sense"? Is it some generally recognized principle of interpretation?

"The legislature," Lehman says, "presumably knew" of Cardozo's rule. What does it mean for a legislature to know something? Does it mean that each legislator knew it? Or just a majority? Why does Lehman "presume" that the legislature "knew"? Does he offer, even implicitly, some justification for this presumption? Do you think the defendant would be permitted to rebut it?

Is the meaning of a statute, in Learned Hand's words, "exhausted by the specific content of the utterer's mind at the moment"? How does one determine the "specific content" of a legislature's mind at any moment? Is it useful to analyze legal problems in such terms as "legislative knowledge," "legislative intent," or "legislative mind"? Are there any mistakes we are more likely to make because we use such terms? Is there any other way we can arrive at the meaning of a legislature's utterance? Or is a legislature any more capable of "uttering" than it is of "knowing" or "intending"? Are there any other means by which we might express the facts of legislation? Would they make any difference?

## A. The Letter and the Spirit: Traditional Justifications of the Interpreter's Law-Making Functions

### H. L. A. HART

#### THE CONCEPT OF LAW *

In any large group general rules, standards, and principles must be the main instrument of social control, and not particular directions given to each individual separately. If it were not possible to communicate general standards of conduct, which multitudes of individuals could understand, without further direction, as requiring from them certain conduct when occasion arose, nothing that we now recognize as law could exist. Hence the law must predominantly, but by no means exclusively, refer to *classes* of persons, and to *classes* of acts, things, and circumstances; and its successful operation over vast areas of social life depends on a widely diffused capacity to recognize particular acts, things, and circumstances as instances of the general classifications which the law makes.

Two principal devices, at first sight very different from each other, have been used for the communication of such general standards of conduct in advance of the successive occasions on which they are to be applied. One of them makes a maximal and the other a minimal use of general classifying words. The first is typified by what we call legislation and the second by precedent. We can see the distinguishing features of these in the following simple non-legal cases. One father before going to church says to his son, 'Every man and boy must take off his hat on entering a church.' Another baring his head as he enters the church says, 'Look: this is the right way to behave on such occasions.'

The communication or teaching of standards of conduct by example may take different forms, far more sophisticated than our simple case. Our case would more closely resemble the legal use of precedent, if instead of the child being told on the particular occasion

---

* From 121–123 (1961). Reprinted by permission of The Clarendon Press, Oxford.

to regard what his father did on entering the church as an example of the right thing to do, the father assumed that the child would regard him as an authority on proper behaviour, and would watch him in order to learn the way to behave. To approach further the legal use of precedent, we must suppose that the father is conceived by himself and others to subscribe to traditional standards of behaviour and not to be introducing new ones.

Communication by example in all its forms, though accompanied by some general verbal directions such as 'Do as I do', may leave open ranges of possibilities, and hence of doubt, as to what is intended even as to matters which the person seeking to communicate has himself clearly envisaged. How much of the performance must be imitated? Does it matter if the left hand is used, instead of the right, to remove the hat? That it is done slowly or smartly? That the hat is put under the seat? That it is not replaced on the head inside the church? These are all variants of general questions which the child might ask himself: 'In what ways must my conduct resemble his to be right?' 'What precisely is it about his conduct that is to be my guide?' In understanding the example, the child attends to some of its aspects rather than others. In so doing he is guided by common sense and knowledge of the general kind of things and purposes which adults think important, and by his appreciation of the general character of the occasion (going to church) and the kind of behaviour appropriate to it.

In contrast with the indeterminacies of examples, the communication of general standards by explicit general forms of language ('Every man must take off his hat on entering a church') seems clear, dependable, and certain. The features to be taken as general guides to conduct are here identified in words; they are verbally extricated, not left embedded with others in a concrete example. In order to know what to do on other occasions the child has no longer to guess what is intended, or what will be approved; he is not left to speculate as to the way in which his conduct must resemble the example if it is to be right. Instead, he has a verbal description which he can use to pick out what he must do in future and when he must do it. He has only to recognize instances of clear verbal terms, to 'subsume' particular facts under general classificatory heads and draw a simple syllogistic conclusion. He is not faced with the alternative of choosing at his peril or seeking further authoritative guidance. He has a rule which he can apply by himself to himself.

Much of the jurisprudence of this century has consisted of the progressive realization (and sometimes the exaggeration) of the important fact that the distinction between the uncertainties of communication by authoritative example (precedent), and the certainties of communication by authoritative general language (legislation) is far less firm that this naive contrast suggests. Even when verbally formulated general rules are used, uncertainties as to the form of behaviour required by them may break out in particular concrete cases.

NOTE: THE APPLICATION OF STATUTORY RULES

Once an authoritative rule has been enunciated—or, as Hart puts it, "verbally extricated"—what is the judge's duty with respect to it? Must he apply it in every case to which its words are applicable or does he have discretion to disregard it in situations where the costs seem too great? Traditionally, courts in the United States have had the power to modify or even overrule past common law decisions. This is a recognized judicial authority, although there remain controversial questions about the standards and values which should be used in exercising it. It is often said, for example, that the judge is to apply "the community's," rather than his own, conceptions of what is "right," "just," or in "the public interest." In addition, it is frequently contended—Rawls seems to be an example—that a court which disregards a concededly applicable rule must do so for adequately general reasons. If the rule is to be eschewed in one case, it must be eschewed in all—or, at least, in all cases of the same kind.

Whatever the limitations on the common law judge, however, they still seem to leave him a broad discretion to institute or displace legal rules. Many believe that judges ought not to have such power: perhaps Zane is an archetypal representative of this position. Others defend the judicial lawmaking function, pointing to the need for flexible, individualized decisions—a need which we have seen emphasized by writers like Dickinson and Needham. But perhaps the ultimate conventional justification—less orthodox ones may be suggested by the excerpts from Harari and others—is simply that laws which are initially made by judges can be unmade by judges, that there is no compelling reason why the authority of earlier courts should be superior to that of later ones.

However persuasive—or unpersuasive—these justifications may be, they are usually thought to leave unanswered the question of judicial power when the applicable legal rule is statutory rather than decisional. When the law-making authority is not a prior judge, but the legislature, does the court still retain discretion to apply—or not apply—the pertinent law? Traditionally, the short answer is, no. It is a fundamental assumption of Anglo-American law that courts are subordinate to legislatures (save where the constitutionality of legislative enactments is in question). This is supposed to mean that when judge-made law conflicts with statutory law the former must give way. Consequently, it would seem, judges may not disregard legislative rules even when they deplore the consequences of their application.

If courts are forbidden to put aside legislative rules when concededly applicable, the question of their applicability becomes of crucial importance. For the court can only avoid the harsh or unjust result which a statute seems to decree by holding that it does not "really" apply in the particular case. We are by now aware that the meaning of legal rules is not always self-evident. Very often we encounter formulations which seem vague, confused or indefinite. A court which would like to comply meekly with the legislature's authority can be uncertain as to what that authority has decreed. It may have no choice, it would seem, but to choose—among possible alternative meanings. In making that choice, in some cases at least, it may have no criterion available other than its own view of what it or the community thinks is beneficial to the social welfare. Perhaps in these instances, therefore, judges must have the kind of power that comes with their common law jurisdictions.

Yet there is a host of cases in which judges have sought to accomplish the "right" or "just" result but in which the grounds just surveyed seemingly cannot support their exercise of power. In these cases, the statutory words in themselves seem perfectly intelligible, but the consequences of their application in a particular litigation lead judges to revolt. We may then hear judges speak of the statute's "spirit" or the legislature's "intent" or "purpose" in contradistinction to the words used. In Tedla v. Ellman, for example, the court never denies that the plaintiff walked on the side of the road proscribed by the legislature. But it insists that, its words notwithstanding, the legislature could not have intended the statute's application in such a case. Identical arguments are made below in Riggs v. Palmer and Church of the Holy Trinity v. United States. A battery of doctrines, principles, and canons of statutory construction are trotted out to support these decisions, but the underlying theory of justification remains murky. In *Tedla* it is apparently held that some statutes apply only in the "usual" case and are to be disregarded in cases where the results would be undesirable. Statutes of this sort must generally be "observed," but may be ignored for a "good reason." A position of this sort, we are soon to learn, is supported by no lesser authorities than Aristotle, Thomas Aquinas and Learned Hand. Indeed, it is almost as if judicial greatness is partially defined by a propensity to disregard the words of legislative enactments. For along with Judge Hand we find Cardozo and Holmes candidly defending the practice.

It is natural for us to wonder where the courts derive their authority to withhold the application of statutes in cases to which the words concededly apply. Have we been wrong all these years about the supremacy of legislative law to judicial law? Or is there some higher, moral obligation of judges to save the legislature from itself? When we look at the words of Judge Lehman, and, later, Cardozo, it may be difficult to see what other kind of justification can be advanced for their positions. On the other hand, most judicial apologists are not willing to admit that they have measured the law by some "higher" standard and have found it wanting. They contend, instead, that only the letter, not the spirit has been denied. The argument is that they have merely "interpreted" the statute according to the legislature's intention and that the true "meaning" of an enactment can be determined only in this way. For those of a suspicious nature, this may appear to be rank hypocrisy. On the other hand, it is not difficult to imagine cases which seem to fit snugly within a rule's meaning and yet were surely not "intended" to be covered. Perhaps it is asking too much of the interpreter to apply the statute, to ignore as a judge what he knows as a man. Indeed, perhaps, it would be a bad legal system which required him to do so.

In response, it will be said that in most cases the very purpose of embodying policies in legislative rules is to foreclose the possibility of such ad hoc exceptions.  This is what Rawls and Holmes seemed to be telling us in earlier readings.  In a sense, the argument runs, we must sacrifice particular cases for the greater good of certainty and uniformity—and the kind of freedom and fairness which certainty and uniformity secure.  Not always.  There are times, it might be conceded, when the decision is to forego the use of rules or to formulate them in a way which leaves room for discretion.  But when they are enacted in definite, perspicuous terms, the choice thereby expressed should be honored.  Does this argument leave us with the positions of Augustine and of Kelsen?  The former tells us to abide only by the letter, no matter how harsh the result.  The latter claims that there are no "gaps" in the law and thus no room for the play of judicial discretion.  These are severe conclusions and it may only be human to hope that, in some way and somehow, we can have effective rules and still permit enough discretion to avoid particularly distasteful applications.  Whether the famous departures from the letter of the law which appear below adequately tell us how to do this is, perhaps, the major issue of this subsection.

*St. Thomas Aquinas*

Summa Theologica *

.  .  .  .  Hilary says (De Trin. iv.): The meaning of what is said is according to the motive for saying it: because things are not subject to speech, but speech to things.  Therefore we should take account of the motive of the lawgiver, rather than to his very words.

I answer that  .  .  .  every law is directed to the common weal of men, and derives the force and nature of law accordingly. Hence the Jurist says (Pandect.Justin. i.): By no reason of law, or favour of equity, is it allowable for us to interpret harshly, and render burdensome, those useful measures which have been enacted for the welfare of man.  Now it happens often that the observance of some point of law conduces to the common weal in the majority of instances, and yet, in some cases, is very hurtful.  Since then the lawgiver cannot have in view every single case, he shapes the law according to what happens most frequently, by directing his attention to the common good.  Wherefore if a case arise wherein the observance of that law would be hurtful to the general welfare, it should not be observed.  For instance, suppose that in a besieged city it be an established law that the gates of the city are to be kept closed, this is good for public welfare as a general rule: but, if it were to happen that the enemy are in pursuit of certain citizens, who are defenders of the city, it would be a great loss to the city, if the gates were not opened to them; and so in that case the gates ought to be opened, contrary to the letter of the law, in order to maintain

* From pt. II (first part), 74–75 (1915 ed.).

the common weal, which the lawgiver had in view. Nevertheless it must be noted, that if the observance of the law according to the letter does not involve any sudden risk needing instant remedy, it is not competent for everyone to expound what is useful and what is not useful to the state: those alone can do this who are in authority, and who, on account of such like cases, have the power to dispense from the laws. If, however, the peril be so sudden as not to allow of the delay involved by referring the matter to authority, the mere necessity brings with it a dispensation, since necessity knows no law.

## QUESTIONS

Is St. Thomas proposing a method of deriving the meaning of a law or is he describing a situation in which the law may be disregarded? What meaning would you say he is giving to the word "interpret"? Does it mean, in his usage, (a) discovering a law's meaning, or (b) deciding whether to abide by a law whose meaning is conceded? What do you make of such language as "it should not be observed" and "the power to dispense from the laws"?

Is St. Thomas proposing that all laws should be construed so as to promote the general welfare? Does this mean that whenever a judge believes that the general welfare would not be promoted—no matter how clearly the situation may be covered by the statute's words—he may declare the statute inapplicable? Does such a rule of interpretation allow the judge to reopen questions decided by the statute?

St. Thomas was not writing against the background of a strict separation of the judicial and legislative functions. When we consider his statement that everyone "is not competent . . . to expound what is useful . . . to the state," but only those "in authority," what counsel can judges divine from his words? Is it possible that they, too, must refer their questions to authority, except in cases of "necessity"?

## LEARNED HAND

### THE BILL OF RIGHTS *

May I start with some words of my unforgettable master, John Chipman Gray, in his Columbia Lectures on the "Nature and Sources of the Law"? "The difficulties of so-called interpretation arise when the legislature has no meaning at all; when the question which is raised on the statute never occurred to it; when what the judges have to do is, not to determine what the legislature did mean on a point that was not [sic] present to its mind, but to guess what it would have intended on a point not present to its mind, had the point been present." I cannot believe that any of us would say that the "meaning of an utterance is exhausted by the specific content of the utterer's mind at the moment. Do you not all agree with Holmes, J., in

* From 18–25 (1958). Copyright 1958 by the President and Fellows of Harvard College. Reprinted by permission of Harvard University Press.

repudiating that position which he described as follows: "We see what you are driving at, but you have not said it, and therefore we shall go on as before."

. . .

What does a body of men like a legislature "mean" by the words contained in a statute? What "points" are "present" to their minds? Indeed what "points" were common in the minds of a majority of those who voted? These are unanswerable questions. All we know is that a majority has accepted the sequence of words in which the "law" has been couched, and that they expect the judges to decide whether an occasion before them is one of those that the words cover. That is an intricate process made up of many factors; perhaps the single most important one is the general purpose, declared in, or to be imputed to, the command. Gray calls the result a "guess" and indeed it is; but who are we that we should insist upon certainties in a world of no more at best than probabilities? May I break from its setting an epigram of my friend, Bernard Berenson: "In the beginning was the Guess"? Yes, my friends, in the beginning and at the ending let us be content with the "Guess". What we do, and what we must do, when the text baffles us is nowhere better expressed than by Plowden in the much-quoted note to Eyston v. Studd, which I ask your indulgence to repeat in part:

"In order to form a right judgment when the letter of a statute is restrained, and when enlarged by equity, it is a good way, when you peruse a statute, to suppose that the law-maker is present, and that you have passed him the question you want to know touching the equity, then you must give yourself such an answer as you may imagine he would have done, if he had been present. As for example, . . . where the strangers scale the walls, and defend the city, suppose the law-maker to be present with you, and in your mind put this question to him, shall the strangers be put to death? Then give yourself the same answer which you imagine he, being an upright and reasonable man, would have given, and you will find that he would have said "They shall not be put to death" . . . .. And therefore when such cases happen which are within the letter, or out of the letter, of a statute, and yet don't directly fall within the plain and natural purport of the letter, but are in some measure to be conceived in a different idea from that in which the text seems to express, it is a good way to give questions and give answers to yourself thereupon, in the same manner as if you were actually conversing with the maker of such laws, and by this means you will easily find out what is the equity of those cases. And if the law-maker would have followed the equity, notwithstanding the words of the law (as Aristotle says he would, for he says, quod etiam legislator, si adesset, admoneret, etiam si jam legem tulisset) you may safely do the like, for while you do no more than the law-maker would have done, you do not act contrary to the law, but in conformity to it."

As for the passage from Aristotle that he cites it is this:

"All law is universal but about some things it is not possible to make a universal statement which shall be correct. In those cases then in which it is necessary to speak universally but not possible to do so correctly, the law takes the usual case, though it is not ignorant of the possibility of error.  And it is none the less correct; for the error is not in the law nor in the legislator but in the nature of the thing, since the matter of practical affairs is of this kind from the start. When the law speaks universally, then, and a case arises on it which is not covered by the universal statement, then it is right, where the legislator fails us and has erred by oversimplicity, to correct the omission—to say what the legislator himself would have put into his law, if he had known.  Hence the equitable is just, and better than one kind of justice—not better than absolute justice but better than the error that arises from the absoluteness of the statement.  And this is the nature of the equitable, a correction of law where it is defective owing to its universality.  In fact this is the reason why all things are not determined by law, viz, that about some things it is impossible to lay down a law, so that a decree is needed."

And if you are not too averse to more Aristotle, maybe this will also help to pave my way:

"We saw that there are two kinds of right and wrong conduct towards others, one provided by written ordinances, the other by unwritten.  We have now discussed the kind about which the laws have something to say.  The other kind has itself two varieties.  .  .  . The second kind makes up for a community's written code of law.  Its existence partly is, and partly is not, intended by legislators; not intended, where they find themselves unable to define things exactly, and are obliged to legislate as if that held good always which in fact only holds good usually; or where it is not easy to be complete, owing to the endless possible cases presented, such as the kinds and sizes of weapons that may be used to inflict wounds a lifetime would be too short to make out a complete list of these.  If, then, a precise statement is impossible and yet legislation is necessary, the law must be expressed in wide terms; and so, if a man has no more than a finger-ring on his hand when he lifts to strike, or actually strikes, another man, he is guilty of a criminal act according to the written words of the law; but he is innocent really, and it is equity that declares him to be so."

In other words a law couched in general terms *prima facie* includes all occasions that the words cover, and therefore presupposes a choice on each occasion between some value to be attained and some sacrifice to be accepted.  It assumes that its advance appraisal of each value and sacrifice in this equation will not vary too much from the later appraisal.  This assumption is not troublesome, so far as the values and sacrifices do not vary in the different settings in which they appear, but they do vary greatly, so that an occasion may arise that, although it is within the words used, imposes a choice between values and sacrifices altogether different from any that the legislators would have made if they could have foreseen the occasion.

There are two ways of meeting this difficulty.  A statute may rigidly declare those specific occasions to which it will apply, making it plain that it means to cover all occasions within the lexicographic scope of the words and no others. Although that will not indeed avoid all doubts, it will do so in proportion as the language is specific, as for example, when a coined vocabulary is used. It is seldom, however, that the purpose behind a statute is so limited that it is possible in advance to imagine all the occasions which the legislators would wish to include, if they had thought of them.

The other way is to leave the proliferation of the purpose to those who are to be entrusted with effecting it; the "interpreters." This too has its defects, it involves an imaginative projection of the minds of those who uttered the words that in Gray's words can be no better than a "guess," and, as you may recall, he believes that it is usually only a cover for the substitution of the "interpreter's" personal choice, even though it be determined by what he may conceive to be the "principles of morality." (Incidentally, it is not apparent to me why it should be supposed that an "interpreter" if he tries to give the "principles of morality" an objective meaning other than his personal preference, will be more successful than when he tries to imagine how the authors of the statute would have dealt with the occasion.)

However, be the difficulties what they may, there can be no doubt that this second way is that adopted in countless instances in the administration of mature jural systems. Indeed we have carried it so far in the interpretation of statutes that at times in order to effect the obvious design we have actually disregarded words or phrases whose scope admitted of no doubt, and that stood flatly in the path of the reading adopted. A classic paradigm is the supposed acquittal of a surgeon who might bleed a patient contrary to the express prohibition of the statute against drawing blood in the streets of Bologna. Much of the law of torts, including the law of negligence, is based upon just this kind of delegation of an authority, leaving to the "interpreter" the appraisal of the conflicting interests on which the jural choice is to depend.

## QUESTIONS

1. What does Gray mean by "the legislature" having "no meaning at all"? That it had not come to a conclusion on a question put before a court? How does one determine whether a legislature came to such a conclusion? Do the words of the statute have anything to do with it? Do they have everything to do with it? If not, what else is to be considered? What else do Hand and the people he quotes consider?

2. To what is Hand referring in the phrase "when the text baffles us?" In the "classic paradigm" of the surgeon who bled "a patient contrary to the express prohibition of the statute against drawing blood in the streets of Bologna" is it the *text* that "baffles us"? Is the language unclear or confusing? For that matter is the action of the surgeon unclear or confusing? Is there any question that he drew blood in the streets of Bologna? Is it the text which is baffling or is it the dilemma posed by the consequences of applying the statute according to its terms? Is "baffle" the right word to use in this context? Does it misleadingly assimilate the Bolognese statutory prob-

lem to situations in which the exercise of judicial discretion has traditionally been acceptable?

3. How does one recognize "the usual case" when one sees it? Is
it defined any differently from the unusual case, for which the interpreter is to fashion his own solution? If so, what are these defining
differences? Is the "usual" case the one that the legislators specifically had in mind? Is it the case to which the literal terms of the statute apply in "the majority" of instances? What would that mean?

4. Is Hand saying that the judge in interpreting statutes has
the same authority as he or the jury have in negligence cases? What
is the scope of that authority? Does this mean that the "usual" case
is the case in which application of the statute would lead to the right
"appraisal of the conflicting interests"? Which of his words support this interpretation? Which of his words do not?

5. Why does Hand say that the interpreter should imagine what
answer the law-maker would give to his problem? Which law-maker
do you suppose he has in mind? The one who made the law or the
one who is currently making the laws? Should, according to Hand,
the interpreter try to divine the putative desires of the Congress of
1914 in construing the Clayton Act or should it instead attempt to
project the desires of the Congress of 1972? Is Hand saying that the
interpreter must engage in an historical quest? What if the majority
which passed a litigated bill could be mustered for a court appearance?
Would their testimony be admissible? If this is not what Hand means,
why do you think so? And what else could he mean given the language which he adopts?

*BENJAMIN N. CARDOZO*

## THE NATURE OF THE JUDICIAL PROCESS *

If you ask how [the judge] . . . is to know when one interest outweighs another, I can only answer that he must get his
knowledge just as the legislator gets it, from experience and study and
reflection; in brief, from life itself. Here, indeed, is the point of
contact between the legislator's work and his. The choice of methods,
the appraisement of values, must in the end be guided by like considerations for the one as for the other. Each indeed is legislating within the limits of his competence. No doubt the limits for the judge are
narrower. He legislates only between gaps. He fills the open spaces
in the law. How far he may go without traveling beyond the walls
of the interstices cannot be staked out for him upon a chart. He must
learn it for himself as he gains the sense of fitness and proportion
that comes with years of habitude in the practice of an art. Even
within the gaps, restrictions not easy to define, but felt, however im-
palpable they may be, by every judge and lawyer, hedge and circumscribe his action. They are established by the traditions of the centuries, by the example of other judges, his predecessors and his col-

* From 112–115 (1921). Reprinted with
permission of Yale University Press.

leagues, by the collective judgment of the profession, and by the duty of adherence to the pervading spirit of the law. ["He may intervene only to supplement the formal authorities, and even in that field there are limits to his discretion in establishing rules of law. He may neither restrict the scope of the general principles of our juridical organization, explicitly or implicitly sanctioned, nor may he lay down detailed regulations governing the exercise of given rights, by introducing delays, formalities, or rules of publicity."—Charmont, *supra,* transl. in 7 Modern Legal Philosophy Series, p. 120, sec. 91.] None the less, within the confines of these open spaces and those of precedent and tradition, choice moves with a freedom which stamps its action as creative. The law which is the resulting product is not found, but made. The process, being legislative, demands the legislator's wisdom.

## QUESTIONS

1. How does one define or recognize a "gap"? Was there a "gap" in Tedla v. Ellman? Was there a "gap" in the case of the Bolognese surgeon? "Gap" suggests an "open," "uncovered," "empty" space. Do you think Cardozo is talking about that sort of phenomenon? Was there something "empty" or "uncovered" in Tedla v. Ellman? Was it an "area" of conduct which was not "covered" by a law? Was it an "opening" which the legislature had not filled? Didn't the words of the statute "cover" the facts in *Tedla*? Was it the legislature's intention which did not cover the situation? How would a judge know that until after he had made his decision as to the meaning of the statute's words?

2. Note Judge Cardozo says that law is "made" in the "gaps." But it is "found" in all other situations. Is law the kind of thing that can be "found"? Note the very material images expressed by the language of legal interpretation. Statutes "cover" the facts. Rules are "applied" to the facts. Laws "fill" the "gaps." Can this way of describing the process of interpretation lead our thinking astray? Consider the apparent distinction found in the opinions of Lehman and Brandeis between the "meaning" and the "application" of a statute. Consider the distinction between "interpretation" and "application". Is there a distinction between "interpreting" a rule and "following" it? See generally, L. WITTGENSTEIN, PHILOSOPHICAL INVESTIGATIONS secs. 109–115 (1958).

## RIGGS v. PALMER

115 N.Y. 506 (1889)

EARL, J. On the thirteenth day of August, 1880, Francis B. Palmer made his last will and testament, in which he gave small legacies to his two daughters, Mrs. Riggs and Mrs. Preston, the plaintiffs in this action, and the remainder of his estate to his grandson, the defendant Elmer E. Palmer, subject to the support of Susan Palmer, his mother, with a gift over to the two daughters, subject to the support of Mrs. Palmer, in case Elmer should survive him and die under age, unmarried and without any issue. The testator, at the date of his will, owned a farm and considerable personal property. He was a widower, and thereafter, in March, 1882, he was married to Mrs. Bresee, with whom, before his marriage, he entered into an antenuptial contract, in which it was agreed that in lieu of dower and all other claims upon his estate, in case she survived him she should have her support upon his farm during her life, and such support was expressly charged upon the farm. At the date of the will, and subsequently to the death of the testator, Elmer lived with him as a member of his family, and at his death was sixteen years old. He knew of the provisions made in his favor in the will, and that he might prevent his grandfather from revoking such provisions, which he had manifested some intention to do, and to obtain the speedy enjoyment and immediate possession of his property, he willfully murdered him by poisoning him. He now claims the property, and the sole question for our determination is, Can he have it? The defendants say that the testator is dead; that his will was made in due form, and has been admitted to probate, and that, therefore, it must have effect according to the letter of the law.

It is quite true that statutes regulating the making, proof, and effect of wills, and the devolution of property, if literally construed, and if their force and effect can in no way and under no circumstances be controlled or modified, give this property to the murderer.

The purpose of those statutes was to enable testators to dispose of their estates to the objects of their bounty at death, and to carry into effect their final wishes legally expressed; and in considering and giving effect to them, this purpose must be kept in view. It was the intention of the law-makers that the donees in a will should have the property given to them. But it never could have been their intention that a donee who murdered the testator to make the will operative should have any benefit under it. If such a case had been present to their minds, and it had been supposed necessary to make some provision of law to meet it, it cannot be doubted that they would have provided for it. It is a familiar canon of construction that a thing which is within the intention of the makers of a statute is as much within the statute as if it were within the letter; and a thing which is within the letter of the statute is not within the statute, unless it be within the intention of the makers. The writers of laws do not always express their intention perfectly, but either exceed it or fall short of it, so that judges are to collect it from probable or rational conjectures only, and this is called rational interpretation; and Rutherforth, in his Institutes (p. 407), says: "When we make use of rational interpretation, sometimes we restrain the meaning of the writer so as to take in less, and sometimes we extend or enlarge his meaning so as to take in more, than his words express."

Such a construction ought to be put upon a statute as will best answer the intention which the makers had in view; . . . . In Bacon's Abridgment (Statutes, I, 5), Puffendorf (b. 5, c. 12), Rutherforth (pp. 422, 427), and in Smith's Commentaries (814), many cases are mentioned where it was held that matters embraced in the general words of statutes nevertheless were not within the statutes, be-

cause it could not have been the intention of the law-makers that they
should be included.  They were taken out of the statutes by an equitable construction, and it is said in Bacon: "By an equitable construction, a case not within the letter of the statute is sometimes holden to
be within the meaning, because it is within the mischief for which
a remedy is provided.  The reason for such construction is, that the
law-makers could not set down every case in express terms.  In order
to form a right judgment whether a case be within the equity of a
statute, it is a good way to suppose the law-maker present, and that
you have asked him this question, Did you intend to comprehend this
case?  Then you must give yourself such answer as you imagine he,
being an upright and reasonable man, would have given.  If this be
that he did mean to comprehend it, you may safely hold the case to be
within the equity of the statute; for while you do no more than he
would have done, you do not act contrary to the statute, but in conformity thereto."  In some cases the letter of a legislative act is restrained by an equitable construction; in others it is enlarged; in
others the construction is contrary to the letter.  . . .  If the law-
makers could, as to this case, be consulted, would they say that they
intended by their general language that the property of a testator or
of an ancestor should pass to one who had taken his life for the express
purpose of getting his property?  In 1 Blackstone's Commentaries
(91), the learned author, speaking of the construction of statutes,
says: "If there arise out of them any absurd consequences manifestly
contradictory to common reason, they are, with regard to those collateral consequences, void.  . . .  When some collateral matter
arises out of the general words, and happen to be unreasonable, then
the judges are in decency to conclude that the consequence was not
foreseen by the Parliament, and therefore they are at liberty to expound the statute by equity and only *quoad hoc* disregard it"; and he
gives as an illustration, if an act of Parliament gives a man power to
try all causes that arise within his manor of Dale, yet if a cause should
arise in which he himself is party, the act is construed not to extend
to that; because it is unreasonable that any man should determine
his own quarrel.

There was a statute in Bologna that whoever drew blood in the
streets should be severely punished, and yet it was held not to apply to
the case of a barber who opened a vein in the street.  It is commanded
in the Decalogue that no work shall be done upon the sabbath, and
yet, giving the command a rational interpretation founded upon its
design, the infallible judge held that it did not prohibit works of necessity, charity, or benevolence on that day.

What could be more unreasonable than to suppose that it was
the legislative intention in the general laws passed for the orderly,
peaceable, and just devolution of property, that they should have operation in favor of one who murdered his ancestor that he might speedily come into the possession of his estate?  Such an intention is inconceivable.  We need not, therefore, be much troubled by the general
language contained in the laws.

Besides, all laws as well as all contracts may be controlled in
their operation and effect by general, fundamental maxims of the

common law. No one shall be permitted to profit by his own fraud, or to take advantage of his own wrong, or to found any claim upon his own iniquity, or to acquire property by his own crime. These maxims are dictated by public policy, have their foundation in universal law administered in all civilized countries, and have nowhere been superseded by statutes. They were applied in the decision of the case of New York Mutual Life Ins. Co. v. Armstrong, 117 U.S. 591. There it was held that the person who procured a policy upon the life of another, payable at his death, and then murdered the assured to make the policy payable, could not recover thereon. Mr. Justice Field, writing the opinion, said: "Independently of any proof of the motives of Hunter in obtaining the policy, and even assuming that they were just and proper, he forfeited all rights under it when, to secure its immediate payment, he murdered the assured. It would be a reproach to the jurisprudence of the country if one could recover insurance money payable on the death of a party whose life he had feloniously taken. As well might he recover insurance money upon a building that he had willfully fired."

These maxims, without any statute giving them force or operation, frequently control the effect and nullify the language of wills. A will procured by fraud and deception, like any other instrument, may be decreed void and set aside; and so a particular portion of a will may be excluded from probate or held inoperative, if induced by the fraud or undue influence of the person in whose favor it is. . . . So a will may contain provisions which are immoral, irreligious, or against public policy, and they will be held void.

Here there was no certainty that this murderer would survive the testator, or that the testator would not change his will, and there was no certainty that he would get this property if nature was allowed to take its course. He therefore murdered the testator expressly to vest himself with an estate. Under such circumstances, what law, human or divine, will allow him to take the estate, and enjoy the fruits of his crime? The will spoke and became operative at the death of the testator. He caused that death, and thus by his crime made it speak and have operation. Shall it speak and operate in his favor? If he had met the testator, and taken his property by force, he would have had no title to it. Shall he acquire title by murdering him? If he had gone to the testator's house, and by force compelled him, or by fraud or undue influence had induced him, to will him his property, the law would not allow him to hold it. But can he give effect and operation to a will by murder, and yet take the property? To answer these questions in the affirmative, it seems to me would be a reproach to the jurisprudence of our state, and an offense against public policy.

Under the civil law evolved from the general principles of natural law and justice by many generations of jurisconsults, philosophers, and statesmen, one cannot take property by inheritance or will from an ancestor or benefactor whom he has murdered: Domat, pt. 2, b. 1, tit. 1, sec. 3: Code Napoleon, sec. 727; Mackeldy's Roman Law, 530, 550. In the Civil Code of Lower Canada, the provisions on the subject in the Code Napoleon have been substantially copied. But, so far as I can find, in no country where the common law prevails has it been deemed important to enact a law to provide for such a case. Our revisers and law-makers were familiar with the civil law, and they did not deem it important to incorporate into our statutes its provisions upon this subject. This is not a *casus omissus*. It was evidently supposed that the maxims of the common law were sufficient to regulate such a case, and that a specific enactment for that purpose was not needed.

For the same reasons the defendant Palmer cannot take any of this property as heir. Just before the murder he was not an heir, and it was not certain that he ever would be. He might have died before his grandfather, or might have been disinherited by him. He made himself an heir by the murder, and he seeks to take property as the fruit of his crime. What has before been said as to him as legatee applies to him with equal force as an heir. He cannot vest himself with title by crime.

My view of this case does not inflict upon Elmer any greater or other punishment for his crime than the law specifies. It takes from him no property, but simply holds that he shall not acquire property by his crime, and thus be rewarded for its commission.

### NOTES AND QUESTIONS

In Deem v. Millikin, 60 C.C. 357 (Ohio, 1892) the decision in *Riggs* was characterized as one which "judicially added to statutes such conditions or provisions as may be necessary to avert results believed to be inconsistent with the legislative conscience, and, therefore, foreign to the legislative intent." Did the court in *Riggs* think that it had "added" a "condition" or "provision" to the New York statute? On what language will you rely for your answer? The *Millikin* court also said that Bacon's "rule affords no warrant for adding an important exception to a statute which, in clear language, defines a rule of public policy." How did the *Riggs* court interpret the rule from Bacon's Abridgement? How would you interpret it? Did the *Riggs* court think it had power to make exceptions to statutes? If so, how are you using the word "exception"?

"The well-considered cases," says the *Millikin* court, "warrant the pertinent conclusion that when the legislature, not transcending the limits of its power, speaks in clear language upon a question of policy, it becomes the judicial tribunals to remain silent." Does this mean that in cases where such statutes are invoked, courts should say nothing but, "judgment for plaintiff (or defendant)"? If not, what does it mean? Just what should courts remain silent about in such cases? "The decision in Riggs v. Palmer," the Ohio court continues, "is the manifest assertion of a wisdom believed to be superior to that of the legislature upon a question of policy." Is this a fair characterization of the decision in *Riggs*? What arguments did the New York court advance to meet such criticism? What rejoinder would you expect from the *Millikin* court?

## NOTE: THE NATURE AND LEGITIMACY
## OF A LEGISLATOR'S INTENTION

1. *Ascertaining the Legislator's Intention.* As Hand suggests, the problem of ascertaining a legislature's intention is complicated—perhaps, hopelessly—by the fact that legislative bodies are composed of many people who are likely to have different motives for, and understandings of, a given piece of legislation. To speak of *a* legislative intention, then, may be to distort the facts. The importance of the distortion is revealed when the reason for referring to the legislature's "intention" is recalled. Courts engage in this practice, they say, in order to discover what the legislators really thought as opposed to what their legislation apparently said. If the legislature's intention turns out in fact to be a grand fiction, what, then, is left of the court's justification for ignoring a statute's words?

Although it may ultimately be illegitimate to assimilate the phenomenon of group utterances to that of individual utterances, it is instructive to ignore the differences for pedagogical purposes. Let us assume that a statute is the utterance of one person and thus represents only his "intention." Wittgenstein puts the following problem:

> Someone says to me: "Show the children a game."
> I teach them gaming with dice, and the other says, "I didn't mean that sort of game." Must the exclusion of the game with dice have come before his mind when he gave me the order?

*Op. cit. supra,* at 33 ᵉ. Did the utterer "intend" that his addressee not teach "dice" if he did not specifically think of that "exclusion" when the direction was uttered? Hand, you will recall, says that "the 'meaning' of an utterance" is not "exhausted by the specific content of the utterer's mind at the moment." But he puts the word "meaning" in quotation marks. Does he, then, subscribe to Gray's position that when "a point is not present to its mind," "the legislature has no meaning at all"? Does he view the use of the word "meaning" as somewhat illegitimate in his own statement? If so, would he feel the same way about its use in Wittgenstein's example? Does usage brand Wittgenstein's notion illegitimate? If not, what consequences would this have for a theory of interpretation which sought to justify the conduct of Judges Earl and Lehman?

Consider Gray's notion of a "point" being "present" to a "mind." What do you think he means by "point"? Does he mean a particular case which has occurred? Or is likely to occur? Does he mean a particular *question* of interpretation? Are they the same? Does one formulation indicate that we are interested in *that which* the legislator was trying to express? Does the other formulation indicate that we are interested in how the legislator would solve our problem of statutory interpretation—if it were put to him? Are these, in effect, the same questions?

2. *The Nature of Intention.* Consider the "points" which *are* "present" to the legislator's "mind." Or consider "the specific con-

tent of the utterer's mind at the moment." How "specific" is that "content"? Is the "specific content" a particular fact situation or group of fact situations? Will every detail of the fact situation envisaged be present to the legislator's mind? Will there be one case—or group of cases—which will fit exactly his conception, with nothing added or nothing missing? If so, are not all cases which "arise under the statute" likely to be different in some respect from the one he had in mind? In such a case, using Gray's notion of meaning, can it be said that the legislator ever had a meaning? If every case is a new case—in that it is different from all others, containing more or fewer elements than the one envisaged by the legislator—would this mean that every case was also a "gap" case? Judge Hand talks about cases which involve choices which the legislator could not have foreseen. Are there any cases which a legislator could specifically foresee? Will not every such case involve— if we are precise enough—a different choice of values than he could have foreseen? In short, under the tests or concepts proposed by Gray, Cardozo and Hand isn't the judge always justified in legislating?

3. *The Legitimacy of the Search for a Legislator's Intention.* "The purpose of those statutes [regulating the making, proof, and effect of wills]," says the court in *Riggs,* was "to carry into effect their final wishes legally expressed." Suppose that New York's statutes required the signatures of three witnesses to make a will effective. Suppose that only two signed Mr. Smith's will. Suppose, further, that there is overwhelming evidence that Mr. Smith intended the disposition described in his will. Should a court give effect to his intention, even though the formalities have not been satisfied? Do you think the court in *Riggs* would have? What is the significance of the words "legally expressed"? Suppose that in making a disposition to "my cousin Hattie," Mr. Smith really intended to make one to his cousin Mary. Suppose there were statements in his diary and remarks made to intimates which indicated that he had assumed that he had made the disposition to Mary and not Hattie? Do you think the *Riggs* court would have permitted his intention to control? If it adhered to the words and not the intention of the testator, could an argument of any merit be advanced for its position? Could the same argument be advanced for Elmer Palmer's position? Why are not the legislative committee reports and debates which accompany a law considered to be part of that law? Consider again the words "legally expressed"? Is the reason why committee reports which explain a piece of legislation are not part of the law sufficient to preclude using them to overrule the "letter" of the law?

FRIEDRICH WAISMANN

ANALYTIC-SYNTHETIC  V *

. . . . . to talk of *the* ordinary use of language is . . . . unrealistic. Though I would not go so far as Ezra Pound in saying that our whole speech is "churning and chugging" today, the fact remains that language is in a state of flux. But, it will be said, that is the concern of the historian of language, not of the philosopher. All the philosopher needs to know is the *stock* use of a word or phrase, as it is employed at present, in contrast with its nonstock uses. This answer is unsatisfactory. Though it would be silly to pretend that one did not know the stock use of "cat" or "shut the door," there are other cases where one would feel less sure. Is a "taste of onions" the stock use and a "taste for history" derived, secondary, figurative? (But it is not *felt* as a metaphor!) Is only a "brilliant sunshine" standard use and a "brilliant style" nonstandard? Is "day" as opposed to night, or as including night the norm? What about speaking of a "wild laughter," a "brooding silence," or saying that a "recollection of this experience moved in his eyes"? It is easy to see that the "stock use" shifts with the context, and shifts in time. What was stock use may become obsolescent and fall into the limbo of silence, just as new uses may spring up and may, in their turn, become standard language; but where is one to draw the line? It is well to remember that almost all expressions which refer to the mental are derived from others whose primary sense was sensuous and that this is a process which goes on to the present day; just as a good many words, under the influence of science, philosophy, or something still more elusive, have only in fairly recent times undergone a change in meaning—e. g. "organic," "nervous," "unconscious," "original," "creative," "objective," "curiosity," "to entail," etc. There is continuous change and continuous creation in language. Finally, there is such a thing as ambiguity which—except in exceptional cases—mars any attempt to single out one use as the stock one. Exactly how many standard uses has "nature"? What about "in," "on," "about" etc.? "The English prepositions," says Empson, "from being used in so many ways and in combination with so many verbs, have acquired not so much a number of meanings as a body of meaning continuous in several dimensions." If so, or if the uses shade off into one another imperceptibly, how can one peel off and throw away all the nonstock uses and retain the stock ones? Yes, this view *is* unrealistic.

QUESTIONS

Waismann says we know the "stock use" of "cat" and "shut the door," but not of a lot of other words. Does this mean that there are some words which have "stock" uses as well as "non-stock" uses,

* From XIII Analysis 11–12 (1952). Reprinted with permission of Basil Blackwell.

while other words have no "stock" uses at all?  How does one isolate the "stock," from the "non-stock" use of a word?  How does one isolate the words which have stock uses from the ones that don't?

## NOTE: DETERMINING THE "USUAL" CASE

Aristotle speaks of laws which can be applied in the "usual" case, but whose words are to be disregarded when the consequences would be unjust or harsh.  Similarly, Aquinas refers to laws whose consequences are in the public interest in "the majority of cases." Are Aristotle and Aquinas reporting empirical data about the kind of cases which actually arise under statutes?

Are they saying that there are more cases of people maliciously wounding others than there are of surgeons bleeding patients in the streets of Bologna?  Are they saying that there are more cases of people walking along the wrong side of the road for bad reasons than there are of people doing so for good reasons?  Or are they saying something else?

Are they, perhaps, thinking of *the* case that *usually* comes to mind when particular words are uttered?  Assume the Bolognese law read, "No person shall draw blood in the streets of Bologna."  How do we discover the "usual" meaning of these words?  By asking how people usually use them?  *Do* people *usually* use them?  That is, are these words, in this particular order, in general use?  How often have you heard them before?  How often do you think the people of Bologna heard them or used them?  Cf. N. CHOMSKY, LANGUAGE AND MIND 10 (1968): ".  .  .  .  the normal use of language is innovative, in the sense that much of what we say in the course of normal language use is entirely new, not a repetition of anything that we have heard before  .  .  .  ."  Do Judge Hand and Judge Earl in recounting the Bolognese example use precisely the same words in the same order?  Should we look to see how judges have used the law's words?  Would that give us the usual meaning of the words?  What are the difficulties with that approach?  Should we look to the usual meaning of particular words in the statute and then, so to speak, add them up?  What would be the result if we interpreted the word "shall" in its usual sense?  The word "in"? The word "draw"?

Is the "usual" use that of a "reasonable" or "prudent" man? How is that to be determined if not by hypothesizing once again a "usual use" of the word or sentence involved?  Is there a defensible way of distinguishing the "usual" from the "unusual" case?  Just how are we, given the Aristotelian notion of the "unusual" case, to distinguish those situations which are controlled by the "letter" and those which are not?

BENJAMIN N. CARDOZO

THE NATURE OF THE JUDICIAL PROCESS *

. . .

The directive force of logic does not always exert itself . . . along a single and unobstructed path. One principle or precedent, pushed to the limit of its logic, may point to one conclusion; another principle or precedent, followed with like logic, may point with equal certainty to another. In this conflict, we must choose between the two paths, selecting one or the other, or perhaps striking out upon a third, which will be the resultant of the two forces in combination, or will represent the mean between extremes. Let me take as an illustration of such conflict the famous case of Riggs v. Palmer, 115 N.Y. 506. That case decided that a legatee who had murdered his testator would not be permitted by a court of equity to enjoy the benefits of the will. Conflicting principles were there in competition for the mastery. One of them prevailed, and vanquished all the others. There was the principle of the binding force of a will disposing of the estate of a testator in conformity with law. That principle, pushed to the limit of its logic, seemed to uphold the title of the murderer. There was the principle that civil courts may not add to the pains and penalties of crimes. That, pushed to the limit of its logic, seemed again to uphold his title. But over against these was another principle, of greater generality, its roots deeply fastened in universal sentiments of justice, the principle that no man should profit from his own inequity or take advantage of his own wrong. The logic of this principle prevailed over the logic of the others. I say its logic prevailed. The thing which really interests us, however, is why and how the choice was made between one logic and another. In this instance, the reason is not obscure. One path was followed, another closed, because of the conviction in the judicial mind that the one selected led to justice. Analogies and precedents and the principles behind them were brought together as rivals for precedence; in the end, the principle that was thought to be most fundamental, to represent the larger and deeper social interests, put its competitors to flight. I am not greatly concerned about the particular formula through which justice was attained. Consistency was preserved, logic received its tribute, by holding that the legal title passed, but that it was subjected to a constructive trust. A constructive trust is nothing but "the formula through which the conscience of equity finds expression." Property is acquired in such circumstances that the holder of the legal title may not in good conscience retain the beneficial interest. Equity, to express its disapproval of his conduct, converts him into a trustee. Such formulas are merely the remedial devices by which a result conceived of as right and just is made to square with principle and with the symmetry of the legal system. What concerns me now is not the remedial device,

* From 40–43 (1921). Reprinted with
permission of Yale University Press.

but rather the underlying motive, the indwelling, creative energy, which brings such devices into play. The murderer lost the legacy for which the murder was committed because the social interest served by refusing to permit the criminal to profit by his crime is greater than that served by the preservation and enforcement of legal rights of ownership. . . .

### NOTE: CONFLICTING AUTHORITATIVE RULES

1. If two authoritative legal rules conflict, it would seem that the court must have the power to choose between them. As in cases of vague legislative directions, the obedient adjudicator cannot tell what the legislative policy is merely by resort to its words. It becomes important, then, to determine whether there is indeed a conflict and if so whether that conflict is between rules which have the same authoritative status. Suppose two traffic statutes. One reads, "No person shall drive on any road or highway at a speed of more than sixty-five miles an hour." The other reads, "No person shall drive on any road or highway at a speed of more than fifty miles an hour." Do these rules conflict? Can you answer that question without more information? Would it make any difference in what sections of the statute books you found these rules? Let us assume that these rules do conflict. Rarely, if at all, does one find an inconsistency that is so blatant. Consider the more usual situation of two statutes, one prohibiting speeds "in excess of fifty miles an hour" on public highways, the other permitting ambulances to proceed at "speeds necessary to effect their purposes without unreasonably endangering the safety of other drivers." Is there a conflict between these rules? Suppose the ambulance statute read, "at a speed of not more than sixty-five miles an hour"? Would a conflict exist in that case? Suppose this is viewed as a conflict. How should one describe the judge's duty in this case? Is it one of choosing between two rules? Or is it one of determining the meaning of the two rules? Is there an interest in preserving the symmetry of the legal system which requires the judge to say that he is determining the meaning? Should the judges, in Cardozo's words, see that "logic [has] received its tribute"? What would be the point of that strategy?

2. Suppose there were a Common Law rule which permitted suits for "alienating the affections of one to whom a person was betrothed." Suppose, further, that the legislature enacts a statute prohibiting suits "of any kind for the alienation of affections." Is there a conflict between these two rules? If there is, does the judge have discretion to choose between them? Suppose there were a Common Law rule that "no person shall be permitted to profit by his own wrong and actions for recovery of such profit will always be entertained." Would this rule conflict with the legislature's enactment concerning suits for "alienation of affections"? If there is a conflict, would the judge have discretion to choose between these two rules? Suppose the legislature enacted a statute which provided that "no action shall be brought in the courts of this state wherein the amount in controversy is less than $100." Would this conflict

with the Common Law rule which prohibits one from profiting by his own wrong? If so, would judges be free to choose between them?

When Judge Earl says that "all laws . . . may be controlled in their operation and effect by general, fundamental maxims of the common law," is he saying that the Common Law is superior to legislative law—that conflicts between judge-made law and statutory law will be resolved in favor of the former? What does he mean by "may"? That sometimes statutes will be so controlled and sometimes not? If so, does he indicate why this is one of those times? Could Judge Earl mean that in *interpreting* statutes their meaning will be determined so as to consist with "fundamental maxims of the common law"? What would the word "may" mean in that case? That these modes of interpretation are to be used only some times? If so, is there any evidence in the opinion as to when? Should these modes of interpretation be used only when the consequences of applying the statute according to its letter are unjust or harsh, but not otherwise? Or is the determination of injustice or harshness necessarily based on a prior application of the Common Law maxims? Does this mean that the Common Law maxims are always to be used even when the court appears to have before it a "usual" case? How can this result be avoided?

Cardozo says that *Riggs* was a case involving "conflicting principles." Consider two of the principles which conflicted. One, he says, "was the principle of the binding force of a will disposing of the estate of a testator in conformity with law." The opposing principle was "that no man should profit from his own inequity or take advantage of his own wrong." Is this the fairest way to characterize the conflict? Wasn't there involved not only "the binding force of a will," but the "binding force" of a statute? Did the court in *Riggs* have the authority to choose between the principle of enforcing a statute and the principle that no one should profit from his own wrong?

3. If *Riggs* involved a conflict of fundamental principles between which a court must choose, can it be said that *every* case involves a conflict of fundamental principles? Recall the dissenting opinion of Justice Black in Barenblatt v. U. S., *supra*, Chapter 7. Consider the case of a man who kills his wife because "she was always nagging me." Doesn't he have an interest in his mental tranquillity? Doesn't the society have an interest in the mental tranquillity of its members? Is it a fundamental principle that people are allowed to pursue their own happiness without unreasonable interference by others? Can the man who killed his wife claim the protection of this principle? If not, why not? Because there is some higher principle which prevails? Because the principle he invokes does not apply to him? Can you define the ways in which his situation differs from those to whom the principle does apply? Can you think of any situation in which the "violator" of a statute could not invoke some fundamental principle which literally applies to his case? If so, can you see any reason why this should be?

4.  How, according to Cardozo, was the choice between principles accomplished in *Riggs*? Was the choice determined by seeing which principle was "of greater generality"? Does the more specific rule, then, defer to the more general? Could the principle invoked for Elmer's position have been stated more broadly? Could the principle invoked for *Riggs* have been stated more narrowly? Recall the passages from Oliphant *supra*, Chapter 7. Was the choice determined by seeing which principle's "roots [were more] deeply fastened in universal sentiments of justice"? Is it fairly clear which of the principles Cardozo identifies satisfied this standard? Taken in the abstract—out of the context of the *Riggs* case—would you unqualifiedly assent to the proposition that "the social interest served by refusing to permit the criminal to profit by his crime is greater than that served by the preservation and enforcement of legal rights of ownership"? Can you think of a case in which one might wish to choose the latter "social interest" over the former one? If so, what is it that makes one social interest controlling in a given case? Is it some higher rule of selection? Is it intuition? Is it the judge's sense of justice?

5.  How does one go about determining whether the canons which Llewellyn cites below are to be used in a given case? Or are they always in use? How does one choose between them? What, in the end, is their authoritative status?

Karl N. Llewellyn

### Remarks on the Theory of Appellate Decision and the Rules or Canons About How Statutes are to be Construed *

When it comes to presenting a proposed construction in court, there is an accepted conventional vocabulary. As in argument over points of case-law, the accepted convention still, unhappily requires discussion as if only one single correct meaning could exist. Hence there are two opposing canons on almost every point. An arranged selection is appended. Every lawyer must be familiar with them all: they are still needed tools of argument. At least as early as Fortescue the general picture was clear, on this, to any eye which would see.

Plainly, to make any canon take hold in a particular instance, the construction contended for must be sold, essentially, by means other than the use of the canon: The good sense of the situation and a *simple* construction of the available language to achieve that sense, by *tenable means, out of the statutory language.*

* From 3 Vand.L.Rev. 395, 401–406
(1950). Reprinted with permission of
the Vanderbilt Law Review.

## CANONS OF CONSTRUCTION

Statutory interpretation still speaks a diplomatic tongue. Here is some of the technical framework for maneuver.

| THRUST | BUT | PARRY |
|---|---|---|
| 1. A statute cannot go beyond its text.[9] | | 1. To effect its purpose a statute may be implemented beyond its text.[10] |

. . .

| THRUST | BUT | PARRY |
|---|---|---|
| 7. A statute imposing a new penalty or forfeiture, or a new liability or disability, or creating a new right of action will not be construed as having a retroactive effect.[11] | | 7. Remedial statutes are to be liberally construed and if a retroactive interpretation will promote the ends of justice, they should receive such construction.[12] |
| 8. Where design has been distinctly stated no place is left for construction.[13] | | 8. Courts have the power to inquire into real—as distinct from ostensible—purpose.[14] |
| 9. Definitions and rules of construction contained in an interpretation clause are part of the law and binding.[15] | | 9. Definitions and rules of construction in a statute will not be extended beyond their necessary import nor allowed to defeat intention otherwise manifested.[16] |
| 10. A statutory provision requiring liberal construction does not mean disregard of unequivocal requirements of the statute.[17] | | 10. Where a rule of construction is provided within the statute itself the rule should be applied.[18] |

---

9. First National Bank of Webster Springs v. De Berriz, 87 W.Va. 477, 105 S.E. 900 (1921); Sutherland, Statutory Construction § 388 (2d ed. 1904); 59 C.J., Statutes § 575 (1932). [Footnote in original.]

10. Dooley v. Penn. R. R., 250 Fed. 142 (D.Minn.1918); 59 C.J., Statutes § 575 (1932). [Footnote in original.]

11. Keeley v. Great Northern Ry., 139 Wis. 448, 121 N.W. 167 (1909); Black, Construction and Interpretation of Laws § 119 (2d ed. 1911). [Footnote in original.]

12. Falls v. Key, 278 S.W. 893 (Tex. Civ.App.1925); Black, Construction and Interpretation of Laws § 120 (2d ed. 1911). [Footnote in original.]

13. Federoff v. Birks Bros., 75 Cal. App. 345, 242 Pac. 885 (1925); Sutherland, Statutory Construction § 358 (2d ed. 1904); 59 C.J., Statutes § 570 (1932). [Footnote in original.]

14. Coulter v. Pool, 187 Cal. 181, 201 Pac. 120 (1921); 59 C.J., Statutes § 570 (1932). [Footnote in original.]

15. Smith v. State, 28 Ind. 321 (1867); Black, Construction and Interpretation of Laws § 89 (2d ed. 1911); 59 C.J., Statutes § 567 (1932). [Footnote in original.]

16. In re Bissell, 245 App.Div. 395, 282 N.Y.S. 983 (4th Dep't 1935); Black, Construction and Interpretation of Laws § 89 (2d ed. 1911); 59 C.J., Statutes § 566 (1932). [Footnote in original.]

17. Los Angeles County v. Payne, 82 Cal.App. 210, 255 Pac. 281 (1927); Sutherland, Statutory Construction § 360 (2d ed. 1904); 59 C.J., Statutes § 567 (1932). [Footnote in original.]

18. State ex rel. Triay v. Burr, 79 Fla. 290, 84 So. 61 (1920); Sutherland, Statutory Construction § 360 (2d ed. 1904); 59 C.J., Statutes § 567 (1932). [Footnote in original.]

THRUST BUT PARRY

11. Titles do not control meaning; preambles do not expand scope; section headings do not change language.[19]

11. The title may be consulted as a guide when there is doubt or obscurity in the body; preambles may be consulted to determine rationale, and thus the true construction of terms; section headings may be looked upon as part of the statute itself.[20]

12. If language is plain and unambiguous it must be given effect.[21]

. . .

12. Not when literal interpretation would lead to absurd or mischivous consequences or thwart manifest purpose.[22]

. . .

15. Words are to be taken in their ordinary meaning unless they are technical terms or words of art.[23]

15. Popular words may bear a technical meaning and technical words may have a popular signification and they should be so construed as to agree with evident intention or to make the statute operative.[24]

16. Every word and clause must be given effect.[25]

. . .

16. If inadvertently inserted or if repugnant to the rest of the statute, they may be rejected as surplusage.[26]

. . .

19. Westbrook v. McDonald, 184 Ark. 740, 44 S.W.2d 331 (1931); Huntworth v. Tanner, 87 Wash. 670, 152 Pac. 523 (1915); Black, Construction and Interpretation of Laws §§ 83–85 (2d ed. 1911); Sutherland, Statutory Construction §§ 339–42 (2d ed. 1904); 59 C.J., Statutes § 599 (1932); 25 R.C.L. Statutes §§ 266–267 (1919). [Footnote in original.]

20. Brown v. Robinson, 275 Mass. 55, 175 N.E. 269 (1931); Gulley v. Jackson International Co., 165 Miss. 103, 145 So. 905 (1933); Black, Construction and Interpretation of Laws §§ 83–85 (2d ed. 1911); Sutherland, Statutory Construction §§ 339–42 (2d ed. 1904); 59 C.J., Statutes §§ 598–99 (1932); 25 R.C.L. Statutes §§ 266, 267 (1919). [Footnote in original.]

21. Newhall v. Sanger, 92 U.S. 761, 23 L.Ed. 769 (1875); Black, Construction and Interpretation of Laws § 51 (2d ed. 1911); 59 C.J., Statutes § 569 (1932); 25 R.C.L., Statutes §§ 213, 225 (1919).

22. Clark v. Murray, 141 Kan. 533, 41 P.2d 1042 (1935); Sutherland, Statutory Construction § 363 (2d ed. 1904); 59 C.J., Statutes § 573 (1932); 25 R.C.L., Statutes §§ 214, 257 (1919). [Footnote in original.]

23. Hawley Coal Co. v. Bruce, 252 Ky. 455, 67 S.W.2d 703 (1934); Black, Construction and Interpretation of Laws § 63 (2d ed. 1911); Sutherland, Statutory Construction, §§ 390, 393 (2d ed. 1904); 59 C.J., Statutes, §§ 577, 578 (1932). [Footnote in original.]

24. Robinson v. Varnell, 16 Tex. 382 (1856); Black, Construction and Interpretation of Laws § 63 (2d ed. 1911); Sutherland, Statutory Construction § 395 (2d ed. 1904); 59 C.J., Statutes §§ 577, 578 (1932). [Footnote in original.]

25. In re Terry's Estate, 218 N.Y. 218, 112 N.E. 931 (1916); Black, Construction and Interpretation of Laws § 60 (2d ed. 1911); Sutherland, Statutory Construction § 380 (2d ed. 1904). [Footnote in original.]

26. United States v. York, 131 Fed. 323 (C.C.S.D.N.Y. 1904); Black, Construction and Interpretation of Laws § 60 (2d ed. 1911); Sutherland, Stat-

THRUST                    BUT                    PARRY

18. Words are to be interpreted according to the proper grammatical effect of their arrangement within the statute.[27]

18. Rules of grammar will be disregarded where strict adherence would defeat purpose.[28]

19. Exceptions not made cannot be read.[29]

19. The letter is only the "bark." Whatever is within the reason of the law is within the law itself.[30]

20. Expression of one thing excludes another.[31]

20. The language may fairly comprehend many different cases where some only are expressly mentioned by way of example.[32]

. . .

. . .

22. It is a general rule of construction that where general words follow an enumeration they are to be held as applying only to persons and things of the same general kind or class specifically mentioned (*ejusdem generis*).[33]

22. General words must operate on something. Further, *ejusdem generis* is only an aid in getting the meaning and does not warrant confining the operations of a statute within narrower limits than were intended.[34]

---

utory Construction § 384 (2d ed. 1904). [Footnote in original.]

**27.** Harris v. Commonwealth, 142 Va. 620, 128 S.E. 578 (1925); Black, Construction and Interpretation of Laws § 55 (2d ed. 1911); Sutherland, Statutory Construction § 408 (2d ed. 1904). [Footnote in original.]

**28.** Fisher v. Connard, 100 Pa. 63 (1882); Black, Construction and Interpretation of Laws § 55 (2d ed. 1911); Sutherland, Statutory Construction § 409 (2d ed. 1904). [Footnote in original.]

**29.** Lima v. Cemetery Ass'n, 42 Ohio St. 128 (1884); 25 R.C.L., Statutes § 230 (1919). [Footnote in original.]

**30.** Flynn v. Prudential Ins. Co., 207 N.Y. 315, 100 N.E. 794 (1913); 59 C.J., Statutes § 573 (1932). [Footnote in original.]

**31.** Detroit v. Redford Twp., 253 Mich. 453, 235 N.W. 217 (1931); Black, Construction and Interpretation of Laws § 72 (2d ed. 1911); Sutherland, Stat-

utory Construction §§ 491–94 (2d ed. 1904). [Footnote in original.]

**32.** Springer v. Philippine Islands, 277 U.S. 189, 48 S.Ct. 480, 72 L.Ed. 845 (1928); Black, Construction and Interpretation of Laws § 72 (2d ed. 1911); Sutherland, Statutory Construction § 495 (2d ed. 1904). [Footnote in original.]

**33.** Hull Hospital v. Wheeler, 216 Iowa 1394, 250 N.W. 637 (1933); Black, Construction and Interpretation of Laws § 71 (2d ed. 1911); Sutherland, Statutory Construction §§ 422–34 (2d ed. 1904); 59 C.J., Statutes § 581 (1932); 25 R.C.L., Statutes § 240 (1919). [Footnote in original.]

**34.** Texas v. United States, 292 U.S. 522, 54 S.Ct. 819, 78 L.Ed. 1402 (1934); Grosjean v. American Paint Works, 160 So. 449 (La.App.1935); Black, Construction and Interpretation of Laws § 71 (2d ed. 1911); Sutherland, Statutory Construction, §§ 437–41 (2d ed. 1904); 59 C.J., Statutes § 581 (1932); 25 R.C.L., Statutes § 240 (1919). [Footnote in original.]

## CHURCH OF THE HOLY TRINITY v. UNITED STATES

143 U.S. 457 (1896)

Mr. Justice BREWER delivered the opinion of the court.

Plaintiff in error is a corporation, duly organized and incorporated as a religious society under the laws of the State of New York. E. Walpole Warren was, prior to September, 1887, an alien residing in England. In that month the plaintiff in error made a contract with him, by which he was to remove to the city of New York and enter into its service as rector and pastor; and in pursuance of such contract, Warren did so remove and enter upon such service. It is claimed by the United States that this contract on the part of the plaintiff in error was forbidden by the act of February 26, 1885, 23 Stat. 332, c. 164, and an action was commenced to recover the penalty prescribed by that act. The Circuit Court held that the contract was within the prohibition of the statute, and rendered judgment accordingly, (36 Fed.Rep. 303;) and the single question presented for our determination is whether it erred in that conclusion.

The first section describes the act forbidden, and is in these words:

*"Be it enacted by the Senate and House of Representatives of the United States of America in Congress assembled, That from and after the passage of this act it shall be unlawful for any person, company, partnership, or corporation, in any manner whatsoever, to prepay the transportation, or in any way assist or encourage the importation or migration of any alien or aliens, any foreigner or foreigners, into the United States, its Territories, or the District of Columbia, under contract or agreement, parol or special, express or implied, made previous to the importation or migration of such alien or aliens, foreigner or foreigners, to perform labor or service of any kind in the United States, its Territories, or the District of Columbia."*

It must be conceded that the act of the corporation is within the letter of this section, for the relation of rector to his church is one of service, and implies labor on the one side with compensation on the other. Not only are the general words labor and service both used, but also, as it were to guard against any narrow interpretation and emphasize a breadth of meaning, to them is added "of any kind;" and, further, as noticed by the Circuit Judge in his opinion, the fifth section, which makes specific exceptions, among them professional actors, artists, lecturers, singers and domestic servants, strengthens the idea that every other kind of labor and service was intended to be reached by the first section. While there is great force to this reasoning, we cannot think Congress intended to denounce with penalties a transaction like that in the present case. It is a familiar rule, that a thing may be within the letter of the statute and yet not within the statute, because not within its spirit, nor within the intention of its makers. This has been often asserted, and the reports are full of cases illustrating its application. This is not the substitution of the will of the judge for that of the legislator, for frequently words of general meaning are used in a statute, words broad enough to include an act in question, and yet a consideration of the whole legislation, or of the circumstances surrounding its enactment, or of the absurd results which follow from giving such broad meaning to the words, makes it unreasonable to believe that the legislator intended to include the particular act. . . .

In Margate Pier Co. v. Hannam, 3 B. & Ald. 266, 270, Abbott, C. J. quotes from Lord Coke as follows: "Acts of Parliament are to be so construed as no man that is innocent or free from injury or wrong be, by a literal construction, punished or endamaged." . . . In United States v. Kirby, 7 Wall. 482, 486, the defendants were indicted for the violation of an act of Congress, providing "that if any person shall knowingly and wilfully obstruct or retard the passage of the mail, or of any driver or carrier, or of any horse or carriage carrying the same, he shall, upon conviction, for every such offence pay a fine not exceeding one hundred dollars." The specific charge was that the defendants knowingly and wilfully retarded the passage of one Farris, a carrier of the mail, while engaged in the performance of his duty, and also in like manner retarded the steamboat General Buell, at that time engaged in carrying the mail. To this indictment the defendants pleaded specially that Farris had been indicted for murder by a court of competent authority in Kentucky; that a bench warrant had been issued and placed in the hands of the defendant Kirby, the sheriff of the county, commanding him to arrest Farris and bring him before the court to answer to the indictment; and that in obedience to this warrant, he and the other defendants, as his posse, entered upon the steamboat General Buell and arrested Farris, and used only such force as was necessary to accomplish that arrest. The question as to the sufficiency of this plea was certified to this court, and it was held that the arrest of Farris upon the warrant from the state court was not an obstruction of the mail, or the retarding of the passage of a carrier of the mail, within the meaning of the act. In its opinion the court says: "All laws should receive a sensible construction. General terms should be so limited in their application as not to lead to injustice, oppression or an absurd consequence. It will always, therefore, be presumed that the legislature intended exceptions to its language which would avoid results of this character. The reason of the law in such cases should prevail over its letter. The common sense of man . . . . accepts the ruling, cited by Plowden, that the statute of 1st Edward II., which enacts that a prisoner who breaks out when the prison is on fire, 'for he is not to be hanged because he would not stay to be burnt.' And we think that a like common sense will sanction the ruling we make, that the act of Congress which punishes the obstruction or retarding of the passage of the mail, or of its carrier, does not apply to a case of temporary detention of the mail caused by the arrest of the carrier upon an indictment for murder." . . .

Among other things which may be considered in determining the intent of the legislature is the title of the act. We do not mean that it may be used to add to or take from the body of the statute, Hadden v. The Collector, 5 Wall. 107, but it may help to interpret its meaning. In the case of United States v. Fisher, 2 Cranch, 358, 386, Chief Justice Marshall said: "On the influence which the title ought to have in construing the enacting clauses much has been said; and yet it is not easy to discern the point of difference between the opposing counsel in this respect. Neither party contends that the title of an act can control plain words in the body of the statute; and neither denies that, taken with other parts, it may assist in removing ambiguities. Where the intent is plain, nothing is left to construction. Where the mind labors to discover the design of the legislature, it seizes everything from which aid can be derived; and in such case the title claims a degree of notice, and will have its due share of consideration." . . .

. . . . Now, the title of this act is, "An act to prohibit the importation and migration of foreigners and aliens under contract or agreement to perform labor in the United States, its Territories and the District of Columbia." Obviously the thought expressed in this reaches only to the work of the manual laborer, as distinguished from that of the professional man. No one reading such a title would suppose that Congress had in its mind any purpose of staying the coming into this country of ministers of the gospel, or indeed, of any class whose toil is that of the brain. The common understanding of the terms labor and laborers does not include preaching and preachers; and it is to be assumed that words and phrases are used in their ordinary meaning. So whatever of light is thrown upon the statute by the language of the title indicates an exclusion from its penal provisions of all contracts for the employment of ministers, rectors and pastors.

Again, another guide to the meaning of a statute is found in the evil which it is designed to remedy; and for this the court properly looks at contemporaneous events, the situation as it existed, and as it was pressed upon the attention of the legislative body. United States v. Union Pacific Railroad, 91 U.S. 72, 79. The situation which called for this statute was briefly but fully stated by Mr. Justice Brown when, as District Judge, he decided the case of United States v. Craig, 28 Fed.Rep. 795, 798: "The motives and history of the act are matters of common knowledge. It had become the practice for large capitalists in this country to contract with their agents abroad for the shipment of great numbers of an ignorant and servile class of foreign laborers, under contracts, by which the employer agreed, upon the one hand, to prepay their passage, while, upon the other hand, the laborers agreed to work after their arrival for a certain time at a low rate of wages. The effect of this was to break down the labor market, and to reduce other laborers engaged in like occupations to the level of the assisted immigrant. The evil finally became so flagrant that an appeal was made to Congress for relief by the passage of the act in question, the design of which was to raise the standard of foreign immigrants, and to discountenance the migration of those who had not sufficient means in their own hands, or those of their friends, to pay their passage."

It appears, also, from the petitions, and in the testimony presented before the committees of Congress, that it was this cheap unskilled labor which was making the trouble, and the influx of which

Congress sought to prevent.  It was never suggested that we had in this country a surplus of brain toilers, and, least of all, that the market for the services of Christian ministers was depressed by foreign competition.  Those were matters to which the attention of Congress, or of the people, was not directed  So far, then, as the evil which was sought to be remedied interprets the statute, it also guides to an exclusion of this contract from the penalties of the act.

.   .   .

But beyond all these matters no purpose of action against religion can be imputed to any legislation, state or national, because this is a religious people.   .   .   .

.   .   .

If we pass beyond these matters to a view of American life as expressed by its laws, its business, its customs and its society, we find everywhere a clear recognition of the same truth.  Among other matters note the following: The form of oath universally prevailing, concluding with an appeal to the Almighty; the custom of opening sessions of all deliberative bodies and most conventions with prayer; the prefatory words of all wills, "In the name of God, amen;" the laws respecting the observance of the Sabbath, with the general cessation of all secular business, and the closing of courts, legislatures, and other similar public assemblies on that day; the churches and church organizations which abound in every city, town and hamlet; the multitude of charitable organizations existing everywhere under Christian auspices; the gigantic missionary associations, with general support, and aiming to establish Christian missions in every quarter of the globe.  These, and many other matters, which might be noticed, add a volume of unofficial declarations to the mass of organic utterances that this is a Christian nation.  In the face of all these, shall it be believed that a Congress of the United States intended to make it a misdemeanor for a church of this country to contract for the services of a Christian minister residing in another nation?

Suppose in the Congress that passed this act some member had offered a bill which in terms declared that, if any Roman Catholic church in this country should contract with Cardinal Manning to come to this country and enter into its service as pastor and priest; or any Episcopal church should enter into a like contract with Canon Farrar; or any Baptist church should make similar arrangements with Rev. Mr. Spurgeon; or any Jewish synagogue with some eminent Rabbi, such contract should be adjudged unlawful and void, and the church making it be subject to prosecution and punishment, can it be believed that it would have received a minute of approving thought or a single vote?  Yet it is contended that such was in effect the meaning of this statute.  The construction invoked cannot be accepted as correct.  It is a case where there was presented a definite evil, in view of which the legislature used general terms with the purpose of reaching all phases of that evil, and thereafter, unexpectedly, it is developed that the general language thus employed is broad enough to reach cases and acts which the whole history and life of the country affirm could not have been intentionally legislated against.  It is the duty of the courts, under those circumstances, to say that, however broad the language of the statute may be, the act, although within the letter, is not within the intention of the legislature, and therefore cannot be within the statute.

*The judgment will be reversed, and the case remanded for further proceedings in accordance with this opinion.*

## QUESTIONS

As Justice Brewer's opinion reports, Chief Justice Marshall had written that "[w]here the mind labors to discover the design of the legislature, it seizes everything from which aid can be derived." Did the mind labor "to discover the design of the legislature" in the *Holy Trinity Church* case? Should the mind have "labored"? Is it always appropriate, according to Marshall, for the mind to labor in interpreting statutes? Consider his reference to "plain words" and to "ambiguities".

Did the application of the statute to the Church of the Holy Trinity lead to an absurd result? When is a result or consequence absurd? When no good reason can be advanced for it? When it violates fundamental values of the society? Can you advance any rational explanation for including the English minister within the statute's words—in addition to the one that he seems to fall clearly within the statute's words? Was the circuit court's decision against religion? Is the application to a clergyman of a statute prohibiting murder an "action against religion"?

Note the rule of construction cited by Justice Brewer: "Acts of Parliament are to be so construed as no man that is innocent or free from injury or wrong be, by a literal construction, punished or endamaged." How would the judge go about determining whether a man "is innocent or free from injury or wrong"? To what standards or principles would he repair? Do you see any parallels between this rule and the reasoning in Tedla v. Ellman? If this rule of construction were to receive "a literal construction," what would be the consequences?

## HANS KELSEN

## THE PURE THEORY OF LAW *

There is no such thing, of course, as a genuine gap, in the sense that a legal dispute could not be decided according to the valid norms, owing to the omission of a provision directed to the concrete case. Every legal dispute consists in a claim made by one party against another, and the decision confirming or disposing of the claim depends on whether the statute declares it a legal duty or not. As there cannot be a third possibility, a decision is always possible, and on a statutory basis. In the case of a decision disposing of the claim the law is still applied. For in obliging persons to a specific behaviour, the

* From 51 Law Q.Rev. 527, 528 (1935).
Reprinted by permission of Stevens and Sons.

law permits, outside these obligations, freedom.  If one person claims from another a behaviour not laid down in statute, then the latter person has by law a 'right' to forego that behaviour—'right' in the sense of legally permitted freedom.  The law says not only that a person is obliged to a certain behaviour (in so far as the negation of that behaviour is declared to be the condition of the specific penal consequence), but also that a person is free to do or not to do what he is not obliged to.  This negative norm it is which operates in a decision disposing of a claim directed to a behaviour which is not a statutory duty.

When, however, we speak of a 'gap,' what we generally mean is not, as the expression might deceive us into thinking, that a decision is logically impossible for lack of a norm, but only that the logically possible decision, confirming or disposing of the claim, is felt, by the agent competent to decide, that is, to apply the law, to be too inexpedient or too unjust, or so inexpedient or so unjust, as to give rise to the impression that the legislator could never have considered this case, and that, had he considered it, would and could not have decided in this way.  This impression may or may not be true—it is, at any rate, generally problematical: in face of the constitutional obligation to apply the law, however, it is of no importance.  That law also, which the executive agent thinks bad law, is to be applied, which is to say nothing of the fact that what the one thinks bad the other thinks good.  The so-called 'gap' is, therefore, nothing else than the difference between the positive law and some other order considered to be better, truer and juster.  Only by confronting the positive law with some such order, and so revealing its shortcomings, can we speak of any such thing as a 'gap.'  That such a gap cannot be filled by interpretation is obvious as soon as its real nature has been grasped.  The function of interpretation is here not to apply the disputed norm, but on the contrary to sidetrack it and to put in its place a better, truer, juster, in short, that norm which the legal agent desires.

NOTES AND QUESTIONS

Is Kelsen's description of a "gap" supported by the readings and cases preceding it?  What is the criticism that he is making of those who invoke "gaps"?  What do you think he means by "the constitutional obligation to apply the law"?

Is there any room, do you think, in Kelsen's theory for cases in which rules seem to be somewhat vague?  Even if the laws must always be applied, don't there arise cases in which it is not clear whether the law does in fact apply?  In those situations is it possible to distinguish the statement, "the law applies" from the statement, "the law should apply"?  What does Kelsen think?  Consider his references to "interpretation"?

Note that the vague or broad statute has never been a wholly acceptable device in American jurisprudence.  There are Administrative Law cases declaring broad delegations of authority unconstitutional as violations of the separation of powers.  There are cases holding vague statutes invalid precisely because they give an uncontrolled and unguided discretion to some official agency. The "political question" doctrine has been partially explained as a response to situations in which courts did not feel there were any workable standards by which to guide their decisions.

Should the vague statute be prohibited across the board? Could it be? Even if it isn't, does it not remain possible to apply Kelsen's strictures in those situations where the relevant legal rule is not vague?

## ST. THOMAS AQUINAS

### SUMMA THEOLOGICA *

#### Whether He Who Is Under A Law May Act Beside the Letter of the Law?

We proceed thus to the Sixth Article:—

Objection 1. It seems that he who is subject to a law may not act beside the letter of the law. For Augustine says (De Vera Relig. xxxi): Although men judge about temporal laws when they make them, yet when once they are made they must pass judgment not on them, but according to them. But if anyone disregard the letter of the law, saying that he observes the intention of the lawgiver, he seems to pass judgment on the law. Therefore it is not right for one who is under a law to disregard the letter of the law, in order to observe the intention of the lawgiver.

Obj. 2. Further, he alone is competent to interpret the law who can make the law. But those who are subject to the law cannot make the law. Therefore they have no right to interpret the intention of the lawgiver, but should always act according to the letter of the law.

Obj. 3. Further, every wise man knows how to explain his intention by words. But those who framed the laws should be reckoned wise: for Wisdom says (Prov. viii. 15): By Me kings reign, and lawgivers decree just things. Therefore we should not judge of the intention of the lawgiver otherwise than by the words of the law.

#### QUESTIONS

Do we by now see why anyone who disregards "the letter of the law, saying that he observes the intention of the lawgiver . . . seems to pass judgment on the law"? Is it unfair to say that Judges Lehman, Cardozo, Earl and Justice Brewer passed judgment on the laws they were supposed to apply?

What is Augustine's reason for saying, in Aquinas's paraphrase, that "we should not judge of the intention of the lawgiver otherwise than by the words of the law"? Is it a good reason? Can you think of other ones?

* From pt. II (first part), 73 (1915 ed.).

Susanne K. Langer

The Logic of Signs and Symbols *

Another recommendation for words is that they have no value except as symbols (or signs); in themselves they are completely trivial. This is a greater advantage than philosophers of language generally realize. A symbol which interests us *also* as an object is distracting. It does not convey its meaning without obstruction. For instance, if the word "plenty" were replaced by a succulent, ripe, real peach, few people could attend entirely to the mere concept of *quite enough* when confronted with such a symbol. The more barren and indifferent the symbol, the greater is its semantic power. Peaches are too good to act as words; we are too much interested in peaches themselves. But little noises are ideal conveyors of concepts, for they give us nothing but their meaning. That is the source of the "transparency" of language, on which several scholars have remarked. Vocables in themselves are so worthless that we cease to be aware of their physical presence at all, and become conscious only of their connotations, denotations, or other meanings. Our conceptual activity seems to flow *through* them, rather than merely to accompany them, as it accompanies other experiences that we endow with significance. They fail to impress us as "experiences" in their own right, unless we have difficulty in using them as words, as we do with a foreign language or a technical jargon until we have mastered it.

Questions

Can you square Langer's insistence that "words . . . in themselves are completely trivial" with Augustine's insistence that we follow the "letter" of the law? What more precisely is "the letter of the law"? Can one follow it without worrying about such things as "connotations, denotations, or other meanings"?

What does Wittgenstein mean by the following observation?

When one shews someone the king in chess and says: "This is the king," this does not tell him the use of this piece . . . . ."

*op. cit. supra* sec. 31. Or this observation?

. . . . naming and describing do not stand on the same level: naming is a preparation for description . . . . We may say: *nothing* has so far been done, when a thing has been named . . . .

*op. cit. supra* sec. 49.

* From *Philosophy in a New Key* 75–76 (3d ed. 1957). Copyright 1942, 1951, 1957 by the President and Fellows of Harvard College. Reprinted by permission of Harvard University Press.

## B.  Symbol and Meaning

### INTRODUCTORY NOTE

What was it that made the judges in *Tedla, Riggs,* and *Church of the Holy Trinity* so certain that they were not following "the letter of the law"?  Did they have a criterion by which they determined what "the letter" required of them?  Or did they simply inspect the statutory words, inspect the "facts," and "see" if "the latter squared with the former"?  Since they did not tell us, we cannot, of course, know. But if their conception of "following the letter" is anything like Augustine's it would not be surprising to learn that Justice Roberts's method in United States v. Butler, *supra,* Chapter 3, was the one that Judges Lehman and Earl, and Justice Brewer thought that they were using. It is a method which—however unfeasible or inappropriate it may have been in *Butler*—is apparently thought by many to be perfectly proper and useable in most cases involving the application of statutes.  These are cases in which the words of the legislative rule are thought to be "clear" or "plain," or "unambiguous," and the "facts" are thought to fall obviously within them.  The relationship between the words and the things they mean is apparently taken to be simple and straightforward.  The mechanism of decision is thought to be— or to closely resemble—the syllogism.  And the amount of mental energy required to reach a conclusion is thought to be minimal.

Even in the simplest cases of interpretation, is it adequate to describe the process as one of looking at the law and looking at the facts and seeing if one "squares" with the other?  Isn't there more to it than that?  What, for example, does one see when he looks at the terms of a rule?  In what sense does knowing those terms amount to knowing the rule?  "Knowing how to apply maxims," says Gilbert Ryle in a selection presented before, "cannot be reduced to, or derived from, the acceptance of these or any other maxims."  If Ryle is right, would this also be true of the application of legal rules?  Does the acknowledgement that the words of a legal rule are thus and so necessarily imply the ability to apply those words?  Does knowing the words of a rule necessarily involve a knowledge of their meaning?

The Augustinian position seems to say that it is enough to know the words, and it seems to view as illicit any attempt to go further and seek their meaning.  Is it that the meaning is seen as somehow attached to the words, so that any further inquiry would have to be in the service of some spurious, manufactured meaning?  Such a view does seem to account for the phenomenon that we can come across a word or a sentence and, without knowing either the utterer or the circumstances of the utterance, think that it makes some sense to us. On the other hand, does it not sound dangerously like mythological notions of a symbol's meaning?  "You say to me," Wittgenstein hypothesizes, " 'You understand this expression, don't you?  Well then—I am using it in the sense you are familiar with.'—As if the sense were an atmosphere accompanying the word, which it carried with it into every kind of application."  PHILOSOPHICAL INVESTIGATIONS sec. 117 (1958).

Does this conception help us to understand how the application of a statute can be assimilated to the model of a syllogism? We have seen in section 2(C) that the syllogism works so effortlessly because the real energy is expended in ascertaining the major and minor premises. Are there cases of statutory interpretation, for example, where there is no major work involved in determining either the major or minor premise? Are there cases in which both the terms of a statute are "clear" and the facts fall "clearly" within them? Two semantic assumptions seem to be implied when the position is taken that there are such cases. The first is, that no matter what else some words may mean, they always mean at least a certain, definite range of things. That is why when we say one of these words it seems to have some meaning for us right away. The second assumption is that the things we encounter in the external world always have certain fixed names or descriptions no matter how else they may be described in a particular situation. For example, a given material object will in all situations be a man, even though in particular situations it may be described by such varying words as pedestrian, barber, grandfather, testator, batter, thief. It is this phenomenon which, in Professor Hart's words, makes it possible to "recognize instances of clear verbal terms, to 'subsume' particular facts under general classificatory heads and draw a simple syllogistic conclusion." Can you see why the validity of *both* of these assumptions might seem necessary if in any case the application of a statute is to be assimilated to the model of a syllogism?

One object of this subsection is to test the validity of these assumptions, to see what kind of objections are—and can be—made to them, and to see what, if anything, is required to answer the objections. You should ask yourself whether the objections are related, as earlier questions suggested, to the most characteristic features of language. Do the "mobility" and the "generality" of words and sentences, for example, have some necessary connection with the problems of ambiguity, vagueness and open texture? If so, are there any conclusions which follow about the necessity of the relationship which a linguistic symbol has to that which it symbolizes?

SUSANNE K. LANGER

## PHILOSOPHY IN A NEW KEY *

. . . . The analysis of "meaning" has had a peculiarly difficult history; the word is used in many different ways, and a good deal of controversy has been wasted on the subject of *the* correct way, *the* meaning of "meaning." Whenever people find several species of a genus, they look for the prime form, the archetype that is supposed to be differently disguised in each special case; so, for a long time, philosophers hoped to find the true quality of meaning by collecting all its various manifestations and looking for a common ingredient. They talked more and more generally about "symbol-situations," believing

* From Philosophy in a New Key 53–   by the President and Fellows of Har-
54, 55, 56–57, 58–59, 60–62, 63–66 (3d   vard College. Reprinted by permis-
ed. 1957). Copyright 1942, 1951, 1957   sion of Harvard University Press.

that by generalization they might attain to the essential quality which all such situations had in common. But generalizing from vague and muddled special theories can never give us a clear general theory. The sort of generalization that merely substitutes "symbol-situation" for "denotation-or-connotation-or-signification-or-association-etc." is scientifically useless; for the whole purpose of general concepts is to make the distinctions between special classes clear, to relate all subspecies to each other in definite ways; but if such general concepts are simply composite photographs of all known types of meaning, they can only blur, not clarify, the relations that obtain among specialized senses of the word.

Charles Peirce, who was probably the first person to concern himself seriously with semantics, began by making an inventory of all "symbol-situations," in the hope that when all possible meanings of "meaning" were herded together, they would show empirical differentia whereby one could divide the sheep from the goats. But the obstreperous flock, instead of falling neatly into a few classes, each according to its kind, divided and subdivided into the most terrifying order of icons, qualisigns, legisigns, semes, phemes, and delomes, and there is but cold comfort in his assurance that his original 59,049 types can really be boiled down to a mere sixty-six.

    .   .   .

There is in fact no quality of meaning; its essence lies in the realm of logic, where one does not deal with qualities, but only with relations. It is not fair to say: "Meaning is a relation," for that suggests too simple a business. Most people think of a relation as a two-termed affair—"A-in-relation-to-B"; but meaning involves several terms, and different types of meaning consist of different types and degrees of relationship. It is better, perhaps, to say: "Meaning is not a quality, but a *function* of a term." A function is a *pattern* viewed with reference to one special term round which it centers; this pattern emerges when we look at the given term *in its total relation to the other terms about it*.   .   .   .   .

    .   .   .

    .   .   .   . we may view a meaning-pattern from the point of view of any term in it, and our descriptions of the same pattern will differ accordingly. We may say that a certain symbol "means" an object to a person, or that the person "means" the object by the symbol. The first description treats meaning in the logical sense, the second in the psychological sense. The former takes the symbol as the key, and the latter the subject. So, the two most controversial kinds of meaning—the logical and the psychological—are distinguished and at the same time related to each other, by the general principle of viewing meaning *as a function, not a property, of terms*.

In the further analyses that follow, "meaning" will be taken in the objective sense, unless some other is specified; that is to say, I shall speak of terms (such as words) as "meaning" something, not of people as "meaning" this or that. Later we shall have to distinguish various subjective functions; but at present let us consider the *relations of terms to their object*. What *relates* the terms to their objects is, of course, a subject; that is always to be understood.

There are, first of all, two distinct functions of terms, which have both a perfectly good right to the name "meaning": for a significant sound, gesture, thing, event (e. g. a flash, an image), may be either a *sign* or a *symbol.*

A sign indicates the existence—past, present, or future—of a thing, event, or condition. Wet streets are a sign that it has rained. A patter on the roof is a sign that it is raining. A fall of the barometer or a ring round the moon is a sign that it is going to rain. In an unirrigated place, abundant verdure is a sign that it often rains there. A smell of smoke signifies the presence of fire. A scar is a sign of a past accident. Dawn is a herald of sunrise. Sleekness is a sign of frequent and plentiful food.

All the examples here adduced are *natural signs.* A natural sign is a part of a greater event, or of a complex condition, and to an experienced observer it signifies the rest of that situation of which it it a notable feature. It is a *symptom* of a state of affairs.

. . .

Now, just as in nature certain events are correlated, so that the less important may be taken as signs of the more important, so we may also *produce* arbitrary events purposely correlated with important ones that are to be their meanings. A whistle means that the train is about to start. A gunshot means that the sun is just setting. A crêpe on the door means someone has just died. These are artificial signs, for they are not part of a condition of which they naturally signify the remainder or something in the remainder. Their logical relation to their objects, however, is the same as that of natural signs —a one-to-one correspondence of sign and object, by virtue of which the interpretant, who is interested in the latter and perceives the former, may apprehend the existence of the term that interests him.

. . .

A term which is used symbolically and not signally does *not* evoke action appropriate to the presence of its object. If I say: "Napoleon," you do not bow to the conqueror of Europe as though I had introduced him, but merely think of him. If I mention a Mr. Smith of our common acquaintance, you may be led to tell me something about him "behind his back," which is just what you would *not* do in his presence. Thus the symbol for Mr. Smith—his name—may very well initiate an act appropriate peculiarly to his absence. Raised eyebrows and a look at the door, interpreted as a *sign* that he is coming, would stop you in the midst of your narrative; *that* action would be directed toward Mr. Smith in person.

Symbols are not proxy for their objects, but are *vehicles for the conception of objects.* To conceive a thing or a situation is not the same thing as to "react toward it" overtly, or to be aware of its presence. In talking *about* things we have conceptions of them, not the things themselves; *it is the conceptions, not the things, that symbols directly "mean."* Behavior toward conceptions is what words normally evoke; this is the typical process of thinking.

Of course a word may be used as a sign, but that is not its primary role. Its significant character has to be indicated by some special modification—by a tone of voice, a gesture (such as pointing or staring), or the location of a placard bearing the word. In itself it is a symbol, associated with a conception, not directly with a public object or event. The fundamental difference between signs and symbols is this difference of association, and consequently of their *use* by the third party to the meaning function, the subject; signs *announce* their objects to him, whereas symbols *lead him to conceive* their objects. The fact that the same item—say, the little mouthy noise we called a "word"—may serve in either capacity, does not obliterate the cardinal distinction between the two functions it may assume.

The simplest kind of symbolistic meaning is probably that which belongs to proper names. A personal name evokes a conception of something given as a unit in the subject's experience, something concrete and therefore easy to recall in imagination. Because the name belongs to a notion so obviously and unequivocally derived from an individual object, it is often supposed to "mean" that object as a sign would "mean" it. This belief is reinforced by the fact that a name borne by a living person always is at once a symbol by which we think of the person, and a call-name by which we signal him. Through a confusion of these two functions, the proper name is often deemed the bridge from animal semantic, or sign-using, to human language, which is symbol-using. Dogs, we are told, understand names—not only their own, but their masters'. So they do, indeed; but they understand them *only in the capacity of call-names.* If you say "James" to a dog whose master bears that name, the dog will interpret the sound as a sign, and *look for* James. Say it to a person who knows someone called thus, and he will ask: "What about James?" That simple question is forever beyond the dog; signification is the only meaning a name can have for him—a meaning which the master's name shares with the master's smell, with his footfall, and his characteristic ring of the doorbell. In a human being, however, the name evokes the *conception* of a certain man so called, and prepares the mind for further conceptions in which the notion of that man figures; therefore the human being naturally asks: "What about James?"

. . . .

Since a name, the simplest type of symbol, is directly associated with a conception, and is employed by a subject to realize the conception, one is easily led to treat a name as a "conceptual sign," an artificial sign which announces the presence of a certain idea. In a sense this is quite justified; yet it strikes a strained and unnatural note, which is usually a fair warning that the attempted interpretation misses the most important feature in its material. In the present case, it misses *the relation of conceptions to the concrete world*, which is so close and so important that it enters into the very structure of "names." A name, above all, *denotes* something. "James" may represent a conception, but it *names* a certain person. In the case of proper nouns this relation of the symbol to what it denotes is so striking that denotation has been confused with the direct relation of sign and object, signification. As a matter of fact, "James" does not, without further ado, *signify* a person; it *denotes* him—it is associated

with a conception which "fits" the actual person.   The relation between a symbol and an object, usually expressed by "S denotes O," is
not a simple two-termed relation which S has to O; it is a complex
affair: S is coupled, for a certain subject, with a conception that fits
O, i. e. with a notion which O satisfies.

In an ordinary sign-function, there are three essential terms:
subject, sign, and object.  In denotation, which is the commonest kind
of symbol-function, there have to be four: subject, symbol, conception
and object.  The radical difference between sign-meaning and symbol-
meaning can therefore be logically exhibited, for it rests on a difference of pattern, it is strictly a different function.

Denotation is, then, the complex relationship which a name has
to an object which bears it; but what shall the more direct relation
of the name, or symbol, to its associated *concept* be called?  It shall be
called by its traditional name, *connotation*.  The connotation of a word
is the conception it conveys.  Because the connotation remains with
the symbol when the object of its denotation is neither present nor
looked for, we are able to *think about* the object without reacting to
it overtly at all.

Here, then, are the three most familiar meanings of the one word,
"meaning": signification, denotation, and connotation.  All three are
equally and perfectly legitimate, but in no possible way interchangeable.

In every analysis of sign-using or symbol-using, we must be able
to account not only for the genesis of knowledge, but also of that most
human characteristic, error.  How sign-interpretation can miscarry,
has already been shown; but failures of denotation, or confusions of
connotation, are unfortunately just as common, and have a claim to
our attention, too.

There is a psychological act involved in every case of denotation,
which might be called the *application* of a term to an object.  The
word "water," for instance, denotes a certain substance because
people conventionally *apply* it to that substance.  Such application
has fixed its connotation.  We may ask, quite reasonably, whether a
certain colorless liquid is or is not water, but hardly whether water
"really" means that substance which is found in ponds, falls from
the clouds, has the chemical constitution $H_2O$, etc.  The connotation
of the word, though derived from an age-long application, is more
definite now than some cases of the word's applicability.  When we
have *misapplied* a term, i. e. applied it to an object that does not
satisfy its connotation, we do not say that the term "denoted" that
object; one feature in the tetradic meaning-relation is missing, so
there is no real denotation—only a psychological act of application,
and that was a mistake.  The word "water" was never guilty of
*denoting* the drink that undid little Willy, in the pathetic laboratory
rhyme:

> We had a little Willy,
> Now Willy is no more,
> For what he thought was $H_2O$
> Was $H_2SO_4$.

Willy had mistaken one object for another; he *misapplied* a term of which he knew the connotation well enough. But since connotations are normally fixed upon a word, originally, by its application to certain *things*, whose properties are but vaguely known, we may also be mistaken about the connotation, when we use the term as a vehicle of thought. We may know that the symbol "James" applies to our next-door neighbor, and quite mistakenly suppose it connotes a man with all sorts of virtues or frailties. This time we are not mistaking James for someone else, but we are *mistaken about James*.

It is a peculiarity of proper names that they have a *different connotation for every denotation*. Because their connotation is not fixed, they can be arbitrarily applied. In itself, a proper name has no connotation at all; sometimes it acquires a very general sort of conceptual meaning—it connotes a gender, or race, or confession (e. g. "Christian," "Wesley," "Israel")—but there is no actual *mistake* involved in calling a boy "Marion," a girl "Frank," a German "Pierre," or a Jew "Luther." In civilized society the connotation of a proper name is not regarded as a meaning applying to the bearer of the name; when the name is used to denote a certain person it takes on the connotation required by that function. In primitive societies this is less apt to be the case; names are often changed because their accepted connotations do not fit the bearer. The same man may in turn be *named* "Lightfoot," "Hawkeye," "Whizzing Death," etc. In an Indian society, the class of men named "Hawkeye" would very probably be a subclass of the class "sharp-eyed men." But in our own communities ladies named "Blanche" do not have to be albinos or even platinum blondes. A word that functions as a proper noun is excused from the usual rules of application.

## QUESTIONS

If Langer's analysis of meaning is correct, how would it influence your evaluations of the writers on legal interpretation whom you have just read? What is the significance of her emphasis on the "pattern"? Her warning that, even when we are not talking or thinking about him, we must not forget the role of the "subject"? Can you think of instances where writers on meaning have forgotten the role of the subject? What does she mean in saying that meaning is not a "property," but a "function"? Do any of the people you have read seem to view meaning as a property of a term? What is your evidence?

Does Langer's suggestion that "meaning" itself has a number of basic meanings help clear up some of the confusion encountered earlier? Were some of the judges and commentators talking about "connotation" while others were talking about "denotation" or "signification"?

McBoyle v. United States

283 U.S. 25 (1931)

Mr. Justice HOLMES delivered the opinion of the Court.

The petitioner was convicted of transporting from Ottawa, Illinois, to Guymon, Oklahoma an airplane that he knew to have been stolen, and was sentenced to serve three years' imprisonment and to pay a fine of $2,000. The judgment was affirmed by the Circuit Court of Appeals for the Tenth Circuit. 43 F.2d 273. A writ of certiorari was granted by this Court on the question whether the National Motor Vehicle Theft Act applies to aircraft.

. . . . That Act provides: "Sec. 2. That when used in this Act: (a) The term 'motor vehicle' shall include an automobile, automobile truck, automobile wagon, motor cycle, or any other self-propelled vehicle not designed for running on rails; . . . Sec. 3. That whoever shall transport or cause to be transported in interstate or foreign commerce a motor vehicle, knowing the same to have been stolen, shall be punished by a fine of not more than $5,000, or by imprisonment of not more than five years, or both."

Section 2 defines the motor vehicles of which the transportation in interstate commerce is punished in § 3. The question is the meaning of the word 'vehicle' in the phrase "any other self-propelled vehicle not designed for running on rails." No doubt etymologically it is possible to use the word to signify a conveyance working on land, water or air, and sometimes legislation extends the use in that direction, e. g., land and air, water being separately provided for, in the Tariff Act, September 22, 1922, c. 356, § 401(b), 42 Stat. 858, 948. But in every-day speech 'vehicle' calls up the picture of a thing moving on land. Thus in Rev.Stats. § 4, intended, the Government suggests, rather to enlarge than to restrict the definition, vehicle includes every contrivance capable of being used "as a means of transportation on land." And this is repeated, expressly excluding aircraft, in the Tariff Act, June 17, 1930, c. 997, § 401(b); 46 Stat. 590, 708. So here, the phrase under discussion calls up the popular picture. For after including automobile truck, automobile wagon and motor cycle, the words "any other self-propelled vehicle not designed for running on rails" still indicate that a vehicle in the popular sense, that is a vehicle running on land, is the theme. It is a vehicle that runs, not something, not commonly called a vehicle, that flies. Airplanes were well known in 1919, when this statute was passed; but it is admitted that they were not mentioned in the reports or in the debates in Congress. It is impossible to read words that so carefully enumerate the different forms of motor vehicles and have no reference of any kind to aircraft, as including airplanes under a term that usage more and more precisely confines to a different class. . . .

Although it is not likely that a criminal will carefully consider the text of the law before he murders or steals, it is reasonable that a fair warning should be given to the world in language that the common world will understand, of what the law intends to do if a certain line is passed. To make the warning fair, so far as possible the line should be clear. When a rule of conduct is laid down in words that evoke in the common mind only the picture of vehicles moving on land, the statute should not be extended to aircraft, simply because it may seem to us that a similar policy applies, or upon the speculation that, if the legislature had thought of it, very likely broader words would have been used. United States v. Bhagat Singh Thind, 261 U.S. 204, 209.

Judgment reversed.

## Questions

How would you characterize the method of Holmes's argument? Does it remind you of any of the earlier exercises in statutory interpretation that you have encountered? Is Holmes concerned about the legislature's "intention"? Is he concerned about enforcing the "letter" of the law?

Using Langer's terminology, what would be the relationship between the term "motor vehicle" and the object McBoyle transported? What would be the relationship between the term "motor vehicle" and "the picture" which it "calls up"? Who is the "subject" for whom these relationships hold? The legislature? The Supreme Court? Or something else?

What does Justice Holmes mean by "etymologically"? Is he implying that the words "motor vehicle" do not literally mean an airplane? That the extension to them of the object called an airplane would be metaphorical? But, again, what does etymology have to do with it?

Suppose that the airplane was not fit for flight and McBoyle had taxied it across a state line and sold it for junk. Under Holmes's reasoning would the statute then apply to him? If not, why do you think so?

## Terry v. McDaniel

103 Tenn. 415, 53 S.W. 732 (1899)

WILKES, J. This is an action of replevin. It originally involved a barber's chair, a looking-glass, and a map of the world. After the battle of Manila and the close of the Spanish-American War the map of the world was released, presumably because it had become incorrect, obsolete, and valueless. The contest over the chair and the looking-glass, like the war in the Philippines, still continued, however. The contest arose in this manner: Defendant had obtained a judgment against plaintiff for five dollars and some costs. For fear that plaintiff might meet with reverses and become insolvent, she swore out an execution, and put it in the hands of an officer, with instructions to make it. He proceeded to obey instructions, and seized the chair and mirror, when plaintiff replevied them. The officer thereupon stepped out, and left plaintiff and defendant to carry on the fight. Plaintiff says he is married; has a wife and two children;

that he did not own any other looking-glass, and did not have as many chairs as the law allows, counting the barber's chair as one; and he was entitled to hold these necessary articles as exempt to himself, as the head of the family.  He says, also, that he is a barber by occupation, and that he allows his customers to sit in this chair, and look into this glass, while he proceeds to make gentlemen of them; and these, with his razor, are the tools of his trade or occupation, and exempt to him as a mechanic.  The chair is not described fully in the agreed statement of facts, nor is the size and finish of the mirror given, except that it was a large one, and hung on the wall.  The chair is worth $8 and the mirror $11.  It is shown that the plaintiff is a citizen of Roane county, and was engaged in his trade, and had a victim in his chair, when the constable seized it, and he did not have any other barber's chair nor any other mirror of any kind.  The court tried the case without a jury, and thought plaintiff was entitled to the chair and mirror as exempt, and gave judgment for the plaintiff for the costs, inasmuch as the articles had not been taken out of his possession.  Defendant has appealed, and assigned errors.  She says the chair is not a suitable chair for family use, and that, if the plaintiff is as poor as he says he is, the mirror is too large for him, and counsel says that the mirror is larger than his potato patch. Plaintiff demurs to the first proposition, and says the chair is well suited to raise a family in, but candidly admits that he has not a potato patch half as big as the mirror.  Counsel for plaintiff urges upon the court that the statute does not say what sort of a chair a head of a family may have,—whether a split, cane, or wood bottom, straight back or rocker,—nor does it prescribe how large the looking-glass may be, and that he is strictly within the letter of the law in claiming these articles.  The argument is that the law exempts a horse, and under that head it may be a saddle horse, or a harness horse, or a race horse, or even a Spanish horse.  But, if the court should not agree with him on this proposition, still he insists that he is entitled to these articles as a mechanic, and that they are indispensable tools in his trade.  It is argued that no one is a mechanic, except a person who works on wood or metal; but it is replied the barber works upon the head and upon the cheek, so that, while there is a distinction between the two, it seems to be a distinction without any material difference.  Attention is called to the fact, also, that frequently the impression made on the customer's face is similar to that made by a carpenter with his saw.  This appears, however, to be owing more to the razor than the chair or mirror; but (for prudential reasons, no doubt) the constable did not seize the razor.  In Story v. Walker, 11 Lea, 515, it was held that a photographer was not a mechanic, but an artist, and one of such quality that the law required him to pay a privilege tax and take out a license before he could follow the business.  But the legislature has not yet reached the point where they require barbers to pay a privilege tax.  Possibly they may have been overlooked up to this time.  In the case of Waite v. Franciola, 90 Tenn. 191, 16 S.W. 116, it was held that a house and sign painter was both a mechanic and a laborer.  The argument is that if a man who spreads paint on a board, and makes it more attractive, is a mechanic and laboring man, another man, who spreads soap on the face and makes it more presentable, is likewise a mechanic and laboring man. We must confess that we are not able to answer such logic as this. To look at him, the barber appears to be a professional gentleman, and we feel much hesitation in classing him with mechanics, except upon his own request. The decisions of the several states are by no means uniform as to who may be classed as mechanics and what may be treated as mechanics' tools. Thus, in Michigan, a dentist is a mechanic. Maxon v. Perrott, 17 Mich. 332. But in Mississippi he is not. Whitcomb v. Reid, 31 Miss. 567. A pool table in a saloon is held not to be a tool, upon the ground that the saloon could run without a pool table, and a pool table could be run without a saloon, but not very successfully. Goozen v. Phillips, 49 Mich. 7, 12 N.W. 889. In Baker v. Willis, 123 Mass. 194, it was held that a tinner was entitled to a cornet horn, as well as his working tools, and this was on the idea that, while he carried on his trade with his tools occasionally, his chief occupation was blowing the horn. In Illinois it was held that a piano was a tool necessary to a music teacher (Amend v. Murphy, 69 Ill. 337); and in Massachusetts that a fiddle and bow were exempt as tools necessary to a fiddler's occupation (Goddard v. Chaffee, 2 Allen, 395). And so, also, in New Hampshire (Wilkinson v. Alley, 45 N.H. 552); and that a mirror was absolutely necessary to the occupation of a milliner. Now, if a mirror was as necessary to a man as to a woman, this case would be conclusive as to the mirror, but does not touch the question of the chair. In New York a fisherman's boat and net were held to be tools of his trade. Sammis v. Smith, 1 Thomp. & C. 444. So, also, a rope used as a boatman's towline. Fields v. Moul, 15 Abb.Prac. 6. Also a gun in the hands of a hunter. Choate v. Redding, 18 Tex. 581. And in Vermont it is expressly decided that a barber's chair is exempt as a tool (Allen v. Thompson, 45 Vt. 472); and in Texas that a chair, mirror, and table are barber's tools (Fore v. Cooper [Civ.App.] 34 S.W. 341). The cases all hold that the exemption law must be liberally construed to preserve the exemption. Now, there can be no doubt that the law exempts a chair, and there is none that [says] a barber's chair is [not] a chair. There can be no doubt that the law exempts a looking-glass, and a mirror on the wall is a looking-glass, so that defendant comes within the letter of the law. We think, also, that, at his request, he must be classed as a mechanic and laborer, as well as orator and news agent, and is therefore within the spirit of the law, and is entitled to the exemption. We therefore affirm the judgment of the court below, with costs.

## QUESTIONS

Was Terry v. McDaniel an "interpretation" case? Did it involve the ascertainment of the meaning of any word or sentence? Did it involve the interpretation of any legal rule? If it did, can you state the rule? Can you be certain of the word or words that were in issue? Why or why not? If there was a legal rule involved in this case, what kind was it? Why do you suppose the court never states it?

S. *MORRIS ENGEL*

WITTGENSTEIN'S FOUNDATIONS AND ITS RECEPTION *

One of the themes which is almost indispensable for a proper understanding of Wittgenstein's remarks here has to do with his view regarding the way in which our minds are held captive by "pictures." . . . .

. . .

. . . . The fact is that "in an overwhelming number of cases people do have the same sort of images suggested by words. This is a mere matter of fact about what happens in our minds, but a fact of enormous importance." In view of this, it is not difficult to see why and how confusions arise. For all that is really necessary for this to happen is for us to use familiar words in unfamiliar ways. The pictures aroused will be correct enough but, of course, they will be misleading. And it is in such misleading pictures, he concludes here, "that most of the problems of philosophy arise."

In the *Blue Book* he puts this point in this way: "The new expression misleads us," he says, "by calling up pictures and analogies which make it difficult for us to go through with our conventions. And it is extremely difficult to discard these pictures unless we are constantly watchful." We can be so watchful, he goes on to tell us there, by asking ourselves at such times, *"How far does the analogy between these uses go?"* . . . .

We now turn . . . to the *Philosophical Investigations*. Difficulty lies, he explains it there, in our inability "to get away from the idea that using a sentence involves imagining something for every word." We fail to realize that we do all sorts of things with words—turning "them sometimes into one picture, sometimes into another." Unfortunately, such pictures are often "only like an illustration to a story" and from it alone it is mostly impossible "to conclude anything at all"—for only "when one knows the story does one know the significance of the picture." Mainly, however, the trouble with such pictures is that they seem "to fix the sense *unambiguously*" when this is not at all the case. On the contrary, "the actual use, compared with that suggested by the picture" is "muddied."

Now certainly language has this effect on us—"the picture is there"; nor need we necessarily dispute its "validity in any particular case." But we do "want to understand the application of the picture." And not only is this often lacking, but other pernicious effects result as well. Or, as he puts it later: "What this language primarily describes is a picture. What is to be done with the picture, how it is to be used, is still obscure. Quite clearly, however, it must be explored if we want to understand the sense of what we are say-

* From 4 Amer.Phil.Q. 260, 262–263
(1967). Reprinted with permission of
the American Philosophical Quarterly.

ing. But the picture seems to spare us this work: it already points to a particular use. This is how it takes us in."

. . . . These pictures *seem* "to determine what we have to do, what to look for, and how"—but they really do not do so. They *seem* "to make the sense of the expressions unmistakable" but in fact prove to be utterly misleading. For example, "What am I believing in, when I believe that this substance contains two carbon rings? . . . there is a picture in the foreground, but the sense lies far in the background; that is, the application of the picture is not easy to survey." In ordinary circumstances such words and the pictures which they generate "have an application with which we are familiar.—But if we suppose a case in which this application is absent we become as it were conscious for the first time of the nakedness of the words and the picture," of how "idle" such pictures are. In the end we must simply regard them as "illustrated turns of speech" . . . . Philosophy, he concludes, "is a battle against the bewitchment of our intelligence by means of language"; "a simile that has been absorbed into the forms of our language produces a false appearance"; "a picture [holds] us captive."

### NOTE: WORDS AND PICTURES

On the scientific validity of Wittgenstein's position, recall the following quote from Bruner and Goodman, as quoted by Henle, *supra*, Chapter 4:

> . . . . subjects can be conditioned to see and hear things in much the same way as they can be conditioned to perform such overt acts as knee jerking, eye blinking, or salivating. Pair a sound and a faint image frequently enough, fail to present the image, and the subject sees it anyway when the sound is presented. . . . The subject sees what he reports as vividly as he sees the phi-phenomenon.

Do Holmes and Wilkes think that people tend to pair pictures with words? What authority do these pictures have for the respective judges? Is counsel's argument in Terry v. McDaniel explicable in terms of this picture theory? Consider his argument that the barber was a "mechanic." Is counsel, assuming the accuracy of the Court's report, captured by a picture? Or is he afraid that the court might be captured? Besides the word, "mechanic," how many other words can you pick out of the *McDaniel* court's opinion whose interpretation seems to be influenced by a picture? Note the recitation by Wilkes, J. of authorities related to the question in his case. Is the tone of his opinion simply his manner or is he making a comment upon the validity of certain kinds of arguments? What would that comment be? Does the method by which he ultimately resolves the case help you answer the question?

"[I]n every-day speech," Holmes said, " 'vehicle' calls up the picture of a thing moving on land." Do you agree? If someone were to suddenly call out the word "vehicle," are you pretty sure you would envisage "a thing moving on land"? Suppose that an agent says to a producer, "I don't like that vehicle for her". Is the problem with this example that the producer and the agent are not engaging in "every-day speech"? Is it the word "vehicle" or is it the words "motor vehicle" which, in "every-day speech" "calls up the picture of a thing moving on land"? Or is this image called up by the words, "shall include an automobile, automobile truck, automobile wagon, motor cycle, or any other self-propelled vehicle not designed for running on rails"? If so, are these words in "every-day speech"? Can it be argued that Holmes is preferring the "picture" to the literal meaning in interpreting this statute? Once again, what do you think he means by "etymologically"?

## UNITED STATES v. CHURCH OF THE HOLY TRINITY

36 Fed.Rep. 303 (1888)

WALLACE, J. This suit is brought to recover a penalty of $1,000 imposed by the act of congress of February 26, 1885, (23 St. at Large, 332), upon every person or corporation offending against its provisions by knowingly encouraging the migration of any alien into the United States "to perform labor or service of any kind under contract or agreement, express or implied," previously made with such alien. The defendant, a religious corporation, engaged one Warren, an alien residing in England, to come here and take charge of its church as a pastor. The act makes it the duty of the United States district attorney to bring suit to enforce the penalty prescribed. The demurrer interposed to the complaint raises the single question whether such a contract as was made in this case is within the terms of the act. In other words, the question is whether congress intended to prohibit the migration here of an alien who comes pursuant to a contract with a religious society to perform the functions of a minister of the gospel, and to subject to the penalty the religious society making the contract and encouraging the migration of the alien minister. The act is entitled "An act to prohibit the importation and migration of foreigners and aliens under contract or agreement to perform labor in the United States." It was, no doubt, primarily the object of the act to prohibit the introduction of assisted immigrants, brought here under contracts previously made by corporations and capitalists to prepay their passage and obtain their services at low wages for limited periods of time. It was a measure introduced and advocated by the trades union and labor associations, designed to shield the interests represented by such organizations from the effects of the competition in the labor market of foreigners brought here under contracts having a tendency to stimulate immigration and reduce the rates of wages. Except from the language of the statute there is no reason to suppose a contract like the present to be within the evils which the law was designed to suppress; and, indeed, it would not be indulging a violent supposition to assume that no legislative body in this country would have advisedly enacted a law framed so as to cover a case like the present. Nevertheless, where the terms of a statute are plain, unambiguous, and explicit, the courts are not at liberty to go outside of the language to search for a meaning which it does not reasonably bear in the effort to ascertain and give effect to what may be imagined to have been or not to have been the intention of congress. Whenever the will of congress is declared in ample and unequivocal language, that will must be absolutely followed, and it is not admissible to resort to speculations of policy, nor even to the views of members of congress in debate, to find reasons to control or modify the statute. U. S. v. Railroad Co., 91 U.S. 72. If it were permissible to narrow the provisions of the act to correspond with the purport of the title, and restrain its operation to cases in which the alien is assisted to come here under contract "to perform labor," there might be room for interpretation; and the restricted meaning might possibly be given to the word "labor" which signifies the manual work of the laborer, as distinguished from the work of the skilled artisan, or the professional man. But no rule in the construction of statutes is more familiar than the one to the effect that the title cannot be used to extend or restrain positive provisions in the body of the act. In Hadden v. Collector, 5 Wall. 107, it is said: "The title of an act furnishes little aid in the construction of its provisions." The encouragement of migration prohibited by the first section is of aliens under contract or agreement previously made "to perform labor or service of any kind in the United States." The contracts which are declared to be void by the second section are contracts "having reference to the performance of labor or service by any person in the United States" previous to the migration of the alien. The penalty imposed by the third section is imposed on the person or corporation encouraging the migration of the alien under a contract or agreement previously made "to perform labor or service of any kind." No more comprehensive terms could have been employed to include every conceivable kind of labor or avocation, whether of the hand or brain, in the class of prohibited contracts; and, as if to emphasize and make more explicit the intention that the words "labor or service" should not be taken in any restricted sense, they are followed by the words "of any kind." Every kind of industry, and every employment, manual or intellectual, is embraced within the language used. If it were possible to import a narrower meaning than the natural and ordinary one to the language of these sections, the terms of the fifth section would forbid the attempt. That section is a proviso withdrawing from the operation of the act several classes of persons and contracts. Foreigners residing here temporarily, who may engage private secretaries; persons desirous of establishing a new industry not then existing in the United States, who employ skilled workmen therein; domestic servants; and a limited professional class, are thereby exempted from its provisions. The last clause of the proviso is: "Nor shall the provisions of this act apply to professional actors, artists, lecturers, or singers, nor to persons employed strictly as personal or domestic servants." If, without this exemption, the act would apply to this class of persons, because such persons come here under contracts for labor or service, then clearly it must apply to ministers, lawyers, surgeons, architects, and all others who labor in any professional calling. Unless congress supposed the act to apply to the excepted classes, there was no necessity for the proviso.  The office of a proviso is generally to restrain an enacting clause, and to except something which would otherwise have been within it.  Wayman v. Southard, 10 Wheat. 30; Minis v. U. S., 15 Pet. 423.  In the language of the authorities: "A proviso carves special exemptions only out of the enacting clauses." U. S. v. Dickson, 15 Pet. 165; Ryan v. Carter, 93 U.S. 78.  Giving effect to this well-settled rule of statutory interpretation, the proviso is equivalent to a declaration that contracts to perform professional services except those of actors, artists, lecturers, or singers, are within the prohibition of the preceding sections.

The argument based upon the fourth section of the act has not been overlooked.  That section subjects to fine and imprisonment any master of a vessel who knowingly brings within the United States any alien "laborer, mechanic, or artisan," who has previously entered into any contract to perform labor or service in the United States. This section is wholly independent of the others, and the difference in the persons described may reasonably be referred to an intention to mitigate the severity of the act in its application to masters of vessels.  The demurrer is overruled.

## QUESTIONS

What is it that makes "the terms of a statute  .  .  .  plain, unambiguous, and explicit"?  Or that makes the "language" "ample and unequivocal"?  Is it that the language taken in the abstract raises no questions in our minds?  Does this amount to saying that there are some statutes which have no borderline cases whatsoever? So that conduct is either "plainly," "unambiguously," "explicitly," and "unequivocally," within or without the statute?  Does the statute involved in the *Church of the Holy Trinity* case have no borderline cases?  If not, can you construct a statute or rule which has none?

Even if you cannot construct a statute whose meaning would be clear in every case, is it possible to construct one whose meaning would be clear in many cases?  Is the statute in the *Church of the Holy Trinity* case of this sort?  Does the court find it necessary to *demonstrate* that (a) the church was a "person" or "corporation," (b) Warren was an "alien," (c) Warren and the church had made a "contract"?  Why doesn't it view these as issues or questions, do you think?  Is it because the church was "unequivocally" a corporation, Warren was "unambiguously" an alien, and their relationship "plainly" a contract?  Is this because no matter where we find the words "corporation," "alien," and "contract" they will always designate the particular phenomena involved in this case?  If not, how do we know that this is one of those situations in which they do designate those phenomena?

Consider these questions in light of Langer's remarks on the nature of meaning.  Is it clear what her position would be?  What is the significance of the following passages from Beardsley and Bergson?

MONROE BEARDSLEY

## THINKING STRAIGHT *

One of the fundamental facts about words is that the most useful ones in our language have many meanings. That is partly why they are so useful: they work overtime (but, as we shall see, not for nothing). Think of all the various things we mean by the word "foot" on different occasions: one of the lower extremities of the human body, a measure of verse, the ground about a tree, twelve inches, the floor in front of the stairs. The same is true of nearly every common noun or verb. The editors of *The American College Dictionary*, in their preliminary investigation of words most frequently used, found 55 distinct senses of the word "point" in 1,100 occurrences of the word, and they distinguished 109 different senses of the word "run."

### QUESTIONS

Consider the following syllogism:

> Every standard foot has five toes.
>
> The distance between my hands is a foot.
>
> The distance between my hands has five toes.

What has happened in this "syllogism"? Could it also happen in the interpretation of legal rules? How?

HENRI BERGSON

## CREATIVE EVOLUTION **

. . . . In insect societies there is generally polymorphism, the subdivision of labor is natural, and each individual is riveted by its structure to the function it performs. In any case, these societies are based on instinct, and consequently on certain actions or fabrications that are more or less dependent on the form of the organs. So if the ants, for instance, have a language, the signs which compose it must be very limited in number, and each of them, once the species is formed, must remain invariably attached to a certain object or a certain operation: the sign is adherent to the thing signified. In human society, on the contrary, fabrication and action are of variable form, and, moreover, each individual must learn his part, because he is not preordained to it by his structure. So a language is required which makes it possible to be always passing from what is known to what is yet to be known. There must be a language whose signs—which cannot be infinite in number—are extensible to an infinity of things. This tendency of the sign to transfer itself from one object to another is characteristic of human language. It is observable in

---

* From 154 (2d ed. 1956). Copyright 1956 by Prentice-Hall, Inc. Reprinted by permission of Prentice-Hall, Inc., Englewood Cliffs, New Jersey.

** From 157–158 (1911).

the little child as soon as he begins to speak. Immediately and naturally he extends the meaning of the words he learns, availing himself of the most accidental connection or the most distant analogy to detach and transfer elsewhere the sign that had been associated in his hearing with a particular object. "Anything can designate anything;" such is the latent principle of infantile language. This tendency has been wrongly confused with the faculty of generalizing. The animals themselves generalize; and, moreover, a sign—even an instinctive sign—always to some degree represents a genus. But what characterizes the signs of human language is not so much their generality as their mobility. *The instinctive sign is* adherent, *the intelligent sign is* mobile.

## QUESTIONS

Is there any limit to the mobility of words? Can a given word be used for any symbolic function? Can the sound "chair" be used to denote what we usually call "pencil"? Why? Or why not? What do you think Langer's position is on this? Is there evidence going both ways?

Why is the "tendency of the sign to transfer itself from one object to another" sometimes "confused with the faculty of generalizing"? Does generalization also involve transferring a sign "from one object to another"? Recall our earlier readings on the generality of words. Does this characteristic suggest an independent cause of a word's ambiguity? If so, how widespread would the phenomenon of ambiguity be?

## MONROE BEARDSLEY

### THINKING STRAIGHT *

A statement is either true or false; it can't be half-and-half. (A "half-truth" is false.) And an object is either an airplane or it is not; it can't be more or less an airplane. "True" and "airplane" are *either-or* words, but many other words in our language are not either-or words, but *more-or-less* words. . . .

## QUESTIONS

Does Beardsley mean that "an object" is always and in all contexts properly denoted as an airplane? Would this also be true of "chair," "mechanic," "motor vehicle"? Which of these are *"either-or"* words and which are *"more-or-less"* words?

Is an airplane without a propeller an airplane? Or is it a special kind of airplane—*i. e.,* "an airplane without a propeller"? If it cannot fly, why do we still refer to it as an airplane? When we do so refer to it, does the word "airplane" have the same meaning? In the sense of "denotation"? In the sense of "connotation"? Suppose that people were to make a practice of refurbishing old airplanes without pro-

* From 158 (2d ed. 1956). Copyright          by permission of Prentice-Hall, Inc.,
1956 by Prentice-Hall, Inc. Reprinted          Englewood Cliffs, New Jersey.

pellers and using them for warm weather habitations, is it possible that these objects might soon get a new name? Or would people continue to call them "airplanes without propellers"? Or "airplanes without propellers used for warm weather habitations"?

Is a chair that is being used for kindling still a chair? Is a chair that is being used as a weapon? Is a chair whose legs are too rickety to support even a cat's weight still entitled to be called a chair? Does the fact that we give this object the same name mean that we are talking about "the same thing"? Or is the name hiding from us the fact that objects change their nature from context to context, just as words change their meanings? "Of course," says Wittgenstein, "what confuses us is the uniform appearance of words when we hear them spoken or meet them in script and print. For their *application* is not presented to us so clearly." *Op. cit. supra* sec. 11.

## JOHNSON v. UNITED STATES

163 Fed. 30, 31–33 (1908)

HOLMES, Circuit Justice. The plaintiff in error, hereafter called the defendant, was indicted for concealing from the trustee of his estate in bankruptcy property belonging to the estate. He was convicted and sentenced, and the case is here on exceptions to the admission of evidence and to other rulings of the court. . . .

The Government, after putting in the creditors' petition filed against the defendant, the order appointing a receiver, notice to the bankrupt, the adjudication, the appointment of the trustee, the order of reference and the list of debts, offered the schedules of assets and liabilities filed by the bankrupt in the District Court. The defendant objected, the objection was overruled, the schedules were admitted, and the defendant excepted. It is said that the grounds of the objection would have been stated, but we are of opinion that the only possible ground was sufficiently obvious to entitle the defendant in fairness to have it considered by us upon its merits.

The ground, of course, was Rev.St. sec. 860 (U.S.Comp.St.1901, p. 661):

> "No pleading of a party, nor any discovery or evidence obtained from a party or witness by means of a judicial proceeding in this or any foreign country, shall be given in evidence, or in any manner used against him or his property or estate, in any court of the United States, in any criminal proceeding, or for the enforcement of any penalty or forfeiture: Provided, that this section shall not exempt any party or witness from prosecution and punishment for perjury committed in discovering or testifying as aforesaid."

The Government argues that the schedules are not pleadings, discovery or evidence, and that therefore the section does not apply; but we are not satisfied that the fagot can be taken to pieces and broken stick by stick in this manner so easily. We quite agree that vague arguments as to the spirit of a constitution or statute have little worth. We recognize that courts have been disinclined to extend statutes modifying the common law beyond the direct operation of the words used, and that at times this disinclination has been carried very far.  But it seems to us that there may be statutes that need a different treatment.  A statute may indicate or require as its justification a change in the policy of the law, although it expresses that change only in the specific cases most likely to occur to the mind. The Legislature has the power to decide what the policy of the law shall be, and if it has intimated its will, however indirectly, that will should be recognized and obeyed.  The major premise of the conclusion expressed in a statute, the change of policy that induces the enactment, may not be set out in terms, but it is not an adequate discharge of duty for courts to say: We see what you are driving at, but you have not said it, and therefore we shall go on as before.

This section of the Revised Statutes goes beyond and outside of the Fifth Amendment.  It applies, even to a sworn bill or answer in chancery, what is said to be the rule of common law, that pleadings are not evidence against the party concerned.  Langd.Eq.Pl. sec. 33; Boileau v. Rutlin, 2 Exch. 665.  It makes this a general provision, and its object seems to us clear.  We think that object was to prevent the required steps of the written procedure in court preliminary to trial from being used against the party for whom they were filed.  We should be surprised if an allegation in a writ should be held to be outside the protection of the statute, if there should be a case in which that protection was needed.  On the same principle we think that schedules in bankruptcy are protected.  We can see no reason that would apply to an answer in equity that does not apply to them.  They are required by the law.  They are a regular step in the written procedure preliminary to the proof of facts.  If necessary, it might be argued that they are pleadings within the meaning of the act.  Bankruptcy is a proceeding in rem.  The schedules indicate those who are to be made parties to the proceeding, the extent of their supposed claims, and the subject-matter of the distribution.  Bankruptcy Act July 1, 1898, c. 541, sections 7(8), 17(3), 30 Stat. 548, 551 (U.S.Comp. St.1901, pp. 3425, 3428).  They have such characteristics of pleadings as are possible at that stage of a proceeding of this kind against all the world.

It is true that in Tucker v. United States, 151 U.S. 164, 14 S.Ct. 299, 38 L.Ed. 112, the decision takes up the words of the section and discusses them somewhat as the Government has done.  But the affidavit that was admitted in that case fell under the head of evidence, if under any, and therefore by express limitation had to be "obtained from" the prisoner.  As it appeared to have been filed voluntarily it was held to be excluded from the privilege by the very words of the act.  .  .  .

But it is said that filing the schedules was an act.  It was a representation that the property set forth was all the property known to the bankrupt to which the trustee had a right.  If the offense punished by the statute had been an active misrepresentation, there might be force in the argument that there was an implied exception from the statute, even as we read it, analogous to the express exception in the case of perjury.  But the offense is not making a misrepresentation at a given time and place; it is the continuous concealment of the property from the trustee during the whole course of the bankruptcy proceedings or beyond. The omission from the schedule would amount to nothing if the bankrupt had disclosed the property to the trustee. To prove this continued concealment, it is not necessary, of course, to take up each moment of the bankrupt's life while the proceedings lasted, and to prove what he did as a means of proving what he did not. The moment of filing the schedules is no more important than any other moment, and although the fact of a misrepresentation in them would corroborate testimony that certain property was not disclosed, it is like any other corroborative evidence and is not necessary in order to make out the offense. The Government asks what answer it could give to the suggestion that the schedules might disclose the property. The answer is plain. The defendant was free to put them in.

## Notes and Questions

1. Consider Wittgenstein's remarks on a passage from St. Augustine's CONFESSIONS:

> These words, it seems to me, give us a particular picture of the essence of human language. It is this: the individual words in language name objects—sentences are combinations of such names.—In this picture we find the roots of the following idea: Every word has a meaning. This meaning is correlated with the word. It is the object for which the word stands.

*Op. cit. supra* sec. 1. What is Holmes's attitude toward this view of language? Or does he have one?

2. Referring to the interpretation of statutes Holmes has been quoted as saying that he did not "care what their intention was," but only wished "to know what the words mean." See Frankfurter, *Some Reflections on the Reading of Statutes,* 47 Colum.L.Rev. 527, 538–39 (1947). Holmes has also said that "[w]e do not inquire what the legislature meant; we ask only what the statute means." *The Theory of Legal Interpretation,* 12 Harv.L.Rev. 417 (1899). Is his reasoning in the *Johnson* case consistent with these statements?

Can it be said of Holmes that he is adding a term to the Federal statute? "If necessary," he says, "it might be argued that they are pleadings within the meaning of the act." Why doesn't he think it is "necessary"? Holmes says that he "can see no reason that would apply to an answer in equity that does not apply to" schedules in bankruptcy. Even if there are no defensible reasons, what does this have to do with the *meaning* of the statute?

*GILBERT RYLE*

THE THEORY OF MEANING *

. . . . [T]he same argument may be expressed in English or in French or in any other language; and if it is expressed in English, there may still be hosts of different ways of wording it. What the logician is exploring is intended to be indifferent to these differences of wording. He is concerned with what is said by a premiss-sentence or a conclusion-sentence, not with how it is worded.

So, if not in the prosecution of his inquiry, at least in his explanations of what he is doing, he has to declare that his subject matter consists not of the sentences and their ingredient words in which arguments are expressed, but of the propositions or judgments and their constituent terms, ideas, or concepts of which the sentences and words are the vehicles. Sometimes he may say that his subject matter consists of sentence-meanings and their constituent word-meanings or phrase-meanings, though this idiom is interestingly repellent. Why it is repellent we shall, I hope, see later on. So in giving this sort of explanation of his business, he is talking *about* meanings, where in the prosecution of that business he is just operating *upon* them.

For our purposes it is near enough true to say that the first influential discussion of the notion of meaning given by a modern logician was that with which John Stuart Mill opens his *System of Logic* (1843). . . .

. . .

Mill, following Hobbes's lead, starts off his account of the notion of meaning by considering single words. As we have to learn the alphabet before we can begin to spell, so it seemed natural to suppose that the meanings of sentences are compounds of the components, which are the meanings of their ingredient words. Word-meanings are atoms, sentence-meanings are molecules . . . Next Mill, again following Hobbes's lead, takes it for granted that all words, or nearly all words, are names, and this, at first, sounds very tempting. We know what it is for "Fido" to be the name of a particular dog, and for "London" to be the name of a particular town. There, in front of us, is the dog or the town which has the name, so here, one feels, there is no mystery. We have just the familiar relation between a thing and its name. . . .

Mill goes further. Sometimes the grammatical subject of a sentence is not a single word but a many-worded phrase, like "the present Prime Minister" or "the first man to stand on the summit of Mt. Everest." Mill has no qualms in classifying complex expressions like these also as names, what he calls "many-worded names." There do not exist proper names for everything we want to talk about; and sometimes we want to talk about something or somebody whose proper name, though it exists, is unknown to us. So descriptive phrases

* From British Philosophy in the Mid-Century 240–241, 242–247, 248, 249, 254–257 (C. Mace ed. 1957). Reprinted with permission of George Allen and Unwin Ltd.

are coined by us to do duty for proper names. But they are still, according to Mill, names, though the tempting and in fact prevailing interpretation of this assertion differs importantly from what Mill usually wanted to convey. For, when Mill calls a word or phrase a "name," he is using "name" not, or not always, quite in the ordinary way. Sometimes he says that for an expression to be a name it must be able to be used as the subject or the predicate of a subject-predicate sentence—which lets in, e. g., adjectives as names. Sometimes his requirements are more stringent. A name is an expression which can be the subject of a subject-predicate sentence—which leaves only nouns, pronouns and substantival phrases. "Name," for him, does not mean merely "proper name." He often resisted temptations to which he subjected his successors.

    . . . . if every single word were a name, then a sentence composed of five words, say "three is a prime number" would be a list of the five objects named by those five words. But a list, like "Plato, Aristotle, Aquinas, Locke, Berkeley" is not a sentence. It says nothing, true or false. So the words combined into a sentence at least do something jointly which is different from their severally naming the several things that they name if they do name any things. What a sentence means is not decomposable into the set of things which the words in it stand for, if they do stand for things. So the notion of *having meaning* is at least partly different from the notion of *standing for*.

    More than this, I can use the two descriptive phrases "the Morning Star" and "the Evening Star," as different ways of referring to Venus. But it is quite clear that the two phrases are different in meaning. It would be incorrect to translate into French the phrase "the Morning Star" by "l'Etoile du Soir." But if the two phrases have different meanings, then Venus, the planet which we describe by these two different descriptions. cannot be what these descriptive phrases mean. For she, Venus, is one and the same, but what the two phrases signify are different. As we shall see in a moment Mill candidly acknowledges this point and makes an important allowance for it.

    Moreover it is easy to coin descriptive phrases to which nothing at all answers. The phrase "the third man to stand on the top of Mt. Everest" cannot, at present, be used to refer to anybody. There exists as yet no one whom it fits and perhaps there never will. Yet it is certainly a significant phrase, and could be translated into French or German. We know, we have to know, what it means when we say that it fits no living mountaineer. It means *something*, but it does not designate *somebody*. What it means cannot, therefore, be equated with a particular mountaineer. Nor can the meaning conveyed by the phrase "the first person to stand on the top of Mt. Everest" be equated with Hillary, though, we gather, it fits him and does not fit anyone else. We can understand the question, and even entertain Nepalese doubts about the answer to the qustion "Is Hillary the first person to conquer Mt. Everest?" where we could not understand the question "Is Hillary Hillary?"
    . . .

Finally, we should notice that most words are not nouns; they are, e. g. adverbs, or verbs, or adjectives or prepositions or conjunctions or pronouns. But to classify as a name a word which is not even a noun strikes one as intolerable the moment one considers the point. How could "ran" or "often" or "and" or "pretty" be the name of anything? It could not even be the grammatical subject of a sentence. I may ask what a certain economic condition, moral quality or day of the week is called and get the answer "inflation," "punctiliousness" or "Saturday." We do use the word "name" for what something is called, whether it be what a person or river is called, or what a species, a quality, an action or a condition is called. But the answer to the question "What is it called?" must be a noun or have the grammar of a noun. No such question could be answered by giving the tense of a verb, an adverb, a conjunction or an adjective.

Mill himself allowed that some words like "is," "often," "not," "of," and "the" are not names, even in his hospitable use of "name." They cannot by themselves function as the grammatical subjects of sentences. Their function, as he erroneously described it, is to subserve, in one way or another, the construction of many-worded names. They do not name extra things but are ancillaries to the multiverbal naming of things. Yet they certainly have meanings. "And" and "or" have different meanings, and "or" and the Latin "aut" have the same meaning. Mill realized that it is not always the case that for a word to mean something, it must denote somebody or something. But most of his successors did not notice how important this point was.

Even more to Mill's credit was the fact that he noticed and did partial justice to the point, which I made a little while back, that two different descriptive phrases may both fit the same thing or person, so that the thing or person which they both fit or which, in his unhappy parlance, they both name is not to be equated with either (or of course both) of the significations of the two descriptions. . . .

Mill, in effect, met this point with his famous theory of denotation and connotation. Most words and descriptive phrases, according to him, do two things at once. They *denote* the things or persons that they are, as he unhappily puts it, all the names of. But they also *connote* or signify the simple or complex attributes by possessing which the thing or person denoted is fitted by the description.

So to ask for the function of an expression is, on Mill's showing, to ask a double question. It is to ask Which person or persons, thing or things the expression denotes? in one or other of Mill's uses of this verb . . . but it is also to ask What are the properties or characteristics by which the thing or persons is described? . . . As a thing or person can be described in various ways, the various descriptions given will differ in connotation, while still being identical in denotation. They characterize in different ways, even though their denotation is identical. They carry different bits of information or misinformation about the same thing, person or event.

Mill himself virtually says that according to our ordinary natural notion of meaning, it would not be proper to say that, e. g. Sir Winston Churchill is the meaning of a word or phrase. We ordinarily understand by "meaning" not the thing denoted but only what is connoted. That is, Mill virtually reaches the correct conclusions that the meaning of an expression is never the thing or person referred to by means of it; and that descriptive phrases and, with one exception, single words are never names, in the sense of "proper names." The exception is just those relatively few words which really are proper names, i. e. words like "Fido," and "London," the words which do not appear in dictionaries.

.    .    .    .    .    Considering the meaning (or Mill's "connotation") of an expression is considering what can be said with it, i. e. said truly or said falsely, as well as asked, commanded, advised or any other sort of saying. In this, which is the normal sense of "meaning," the meaning of a subexpression like a word or phrase, is a functional factor of a range of possible assertions, questions, commands and the rest.    .    .    .    This precisely inverts the natural assumption with which as I said earlier, Mill and most of us start, the assumption namely that the meanings of words and phrases can be learned, discussed and classified before consideration begins of entire sayings, such as sentences. Word meanings do not stand to sentence meanings as atoms to molecules or as letters of the alphabet to the spellings of words, but more nearly as the tennis racket stands to the strokes which are or may be made with it. This point, which Mill's successors and predecessors half-recognized to hold for such little words as "if," "or," "all," "the" and "note," holds good for all significant words alike. Their significances are their roles inside actual and possible sayings. Mill's two-way doctrine, that nearly all words and phrases both denote, or are names, and connote, i. e. have significance, was therefore, in effect, though unwittingly, a coalition between an atomistic and a functionalist view of words.    .    .    .

.    .    .    .    .    The notion of meaning [was, thanks to Bertrand Russell,]    .    .    .    at long last, partly detached from the notion of naming and re-attached to the notion of saying. It was recognized to belong to, or even to constitute the domain which had always been the province of logic; and as it is at least part of the official business of logic to establish and codify rules, the notion of meaning came now to be seen as somehow compact of rules. To know what an expression means involves knowing what can (logically) be said with it and what cannot (logically) be said with it. It involves knowing a set of bans, fiats and obligations, or, in a word, it is to know the rules of the employment of that expression.

.    .    .    .    When he said "Don't ask for the meaning, ask for the use,"    .    .    .    [Wittgenstein] was imparting a lesson which he had had to teach to himself after he had finished with [his first work] the *Tractatus* [*Logico-Philosophicus*]. The use of an expression, or the concept it expresses, is the role it is employed to perform, not any thing or person or event for which it might be supposed to stand.
.    .    .    Even more instructive is the analogy which Wittgenstein

now came to draw between significant expressions and the pieces with which are played games like chess. The significance of an expression and the powers or functions in chess of a pawn, a knight or the queen have much in common. To know what the knight can and cannot do, one must know the rules of chess, as well as be familiar with various kinds of chess situations which may arise. What the knight may do cannot be read out of the material or shape of the piece of ivory or boxwood or tin of which this knight may be made. Similarly to know what an expression means is to know how it may and may not be employed, and the rules governing its employment can be the same for expressions of very different physical compositions. The word "horse" is not a bit like the word "cheval"; but the way of wielding them is the same. They have the same role, the same sense. Each is a translation of the other. Certainly the rules of the uses of expressions are unlike the rules of games in some important respects. . . . . But still the partial assimilation of the meanings of expressions to the powers or the values of the pieces with which a game is played is enormously revealing. There is no temptation to suppose that a knight is proxy for anything, or that learning what a knight may or may not do is learning that it is a deputy for some ulterior entity. We could not learn to play the knight correctly without having learned to play the other pieces, nor can we learn to play a word by itself, but only in combination with other words and phrases.

## QUESTIONS

Can Holmes use Ryle's arguments to support his method in U. S. v. Johnson? Would it also support him in *McBoyle*? Did Holmes independently interpret the words "motor" and "vehicle" in that case? Does such a method make easier or harder the conclusion reached in *McBoyle*? Do Ryle's arguments help justify Holmes's "adding a term to the law"? Or do they do something else?

Meaning, says Ryle, is not something for which words stand. Is it, in his view, something for which sentences stand? Would it be consistent or inconsistent with his argument to say that legal rules "stand for" the intentions of their makers?

Can Ryle help Holmes justify his concern for the reasons why "an answer in equity" would be included within the Johnson statute while a schedule in bankruptcy would not? Recall Ryle's statement that to "know what an expression means . . . . is to know the rules of the employment of that expression"? Where does one find the content of those rules?

*ARTHUR KOESTLER*

## THE GHOST IN THE MACHINE *

. . . . A sentence taken in isolation conveys no information as to whether it should be interpreted at face value, or meta-

* From 34–35 (1968). Copyright 1967
by Arthur Koestler. Reprinted by
permission.

phorically, or ironically, i. e., meaning the opposite of what it seems to mean; or perhaps containing a veiled message . . . . Such ambiguities of an isolated sentence can once more only be resolved by reference to its context. . . . This is exemplified when we ask at the end of a perfectly intelligible sentence: 'What do you mean by that?' . . .

## NOTES AND QUESTIONS

In *The Theory of Legal Interpretation, supra,* Holmes says, "we ask, not what this man meant, but what those words would mean in the mouth of a normal speaker of English, using them in the circumstances in which they were used . . . . ." This "normal speaker of English," he says, "is merely a special variety, a literary form, so to speak, of our old friend the prudent man." Precisely what question should be put about this "prudent" or "reasonable" man? Should it be asked how he would use particular words? Or a particular sentence? Or should it be asked how he would use an entire paragraph? Or an entire law? How broadly or narrowly could one interpret Holmes's phrase "in the circumstances in which they were used"? Could those circumstances include the entire body of law, written and unwritten? Could it include the customs, manners and mores of the society in general? Could those circumstances include prevailing social institutions and conditions? Are words ever uttered in these kinds of circumstances? How often? If this meaning is given to the word "circumstances," does it become difficult to distinguish the question of what a reasonable man would have *done* in the "circumstances" from what a reasonable man would *mean* by words actually uttered (reasonably or unreasonably) in those circumstances?

## NOTE: WAISMANN ON OPEN TEXTURE

In an article entitled *Verifiability*, Proceedings of the Aristotelian Society, Supp. 123, (1945), Waismann distinguishes "vagueness" from "open texture." "A word which is actually used in a fluctuating way . . . is said to be vague; a term like 'gold', though its actual use may not be vague, is non-exhaustive or of an open texture in that we can never fill up all the possible gaps through which a doubt may seep in." If one attempts to describe one's right hand, he proposes, it will probably be done by stating such things as its size, shape, chemical composition, color, and so forth. No matter how far one goes, however, the description will never be completed. "[L]ogically speaking, it is always possible to extend the description by adding some detail or other." *Id.* at 124.

"A term is defined," Waismann says, "when the sort of situation is described in which it is to be used." But such situations cannot be completely described and thus "we can never be quite sure that we have included in our definition everything that should be included." *Id.* at 125. What is the relationship of "open texture" to the "generality" of language? Is the phenomenon of open texture a consequence of that generality? Is it part of what is meant by "generality"?

When a legal rule states certain conditions, and these conditions are satisfied in the world of human experience, does this necessarily mean that the rule applies? Does it necessarily follow that the rule *means* any piece of experience which satisfies those conditions? Or is it possible that some other condition which is part of the litigated experience will so change its nature as to make it an effectively different thing from what the statute means? Do such experiences usually have conditions or features in addition to those specified by the legal rule? Do such conditions ever make a difference? If they do, how do we know when the unspecified additional conditions are important and when they are immaterial? In other words, when do the differences between cases which fall within the meaning of a rule and those which do not *make* a difference? And who is to decide?

*Felix S. Cohen*

## Field Theory and Judicial Logic *

. . . . dependence of meaning upon a personal frame of reference is something that many of us take for granted when we refuse to argue over affirmations of religious faith. May not the same dependence of meaning and truth upon varying contexts be found in non-religious fields as well, even in the mundane fields which concern lawyers and their clients? May we not say, even, that law as, *par excellence*, the field of controversies, is the field in which the imposition of different meanings upon the same verbal formula is most characteristic and most significant?

. . . . Perhaps, if we look closely enough, a sentence never means exactly the same thing to any two different people. For no two minds bring the same apperceptive mass of understanding and background to bear on the external fact of a sound or a series of marks. Indeed, I doubt whether any sentence means exactly the same thing to me the first time I hear it that it means the tenth time or the hundredth time. Of course, for many practical purposes, we are disposed to overlook such variations of meaning. Each of us is likely to try to fix on a particular segment of our thinking, at a particular time, as "the real meaning" of any sentence. We may then consider all other interpretations as more or less serious aberrations. Perhaps we may be justified in holding that our own specific understanding of the sentence at a particular time is a proposition, and either false or true. But what, then, shall we say of the sentence as a social fact, a source of many interpretations, a matrix of many propositions? Must we not say that the truth of any assertion is a matter of degree, that from certain angles the sentence may give light and that at other angles it may obscure more light than it gives? The angle or perspective and the context are part of the meaning of any proposition, and therefore a part of whatever it is that is true or false.

* From 59 Yale L.J. 238, 240–241 (1950). Reprinted by permission of the Yale Law Journal and Fred B. Rothman & Co., Inc.

The location of words in a context is essential to their meaning and truth. The fallacy of simple location in physical space-time has finally been superseded in physics. We now realize that the Copernican view that the earth moves around the sun and the older Ptolemaic view that the sun moves around the earth can both be true, and that for practical though not aesthetic or religious purposes the Ptolemaic and Copernican astronomics may be used interchangeably. We realize that Euclidean and non-Euclidean geometries can both be true. What is a straight line in one system may be an ellipse in another system, just as a penny may be round in one perspective, oval in a second, and rectangular in a third.

## PART THREE

# SKEPTICISM AND THE NATURE OF KNOWLEDGE

## CHAPTER NINE

## Skepticism and the "Fact-Minded" and Language-Bound Conceptions of Reality

### SECTION ONE: INTRODUCTION: KNOWLEDGE IN ETHICS

#### INTRODUCTORY NOTE

To the extent that the materials in Part II suggest that the influence of individual choice and value is necessarily pervasive in the reaching of decisions, do they also challenge the belief that order is really possible? If the world of things, events, concepts, issues, rules and meanings is, at least in substantial part, determined by the very people—whether officeholders or citizens—who are supposed to be controlled, directed, limited and guided by these "external" authorities, how authoritative, how "controlling" can they really be? In a world so dependent upon the accident of who is doing the deciding and upon the contingency of when and where the decision is to be made, is it meaningful to talk about things that can be known and thoughts that can be communicated? Is it meaningful to talk about officeholders who have acted rightly or wrongly, correctly or incorrectly, legally or illegally?

Are the materials of Part II, in short, to be taken as a denial of the possibility of intersubjective knowledge and meaning? There will no doubt be a segment of opinion which views them in this way. For it is a popular—if not dominant—position that true knowledge and meaning are *defined* by their independence of any given knower or of any particular situation in which they are known. Thus to show that the phases of mental experience discussed in Part II are necessarily "subjective," or "relative," is to deny that they provide us with real knowledge or objective meanings.

It is significant that those who hold this position may well react to Part II in very different ways. Some will be persuaded that there are, "in fact," no facts and no rules which can give us intersubjective meanings. They will conclude that human action and thought are essentially arbitrary and non-justifiable. Judicial decisions, for example, will be characterized as expressions of the judge's "personal preferences," "emotional predispositions," or "gut reactions." Such a position seems to entail—although it is not always carried out to this conclusion—that "law" is no more than the enactment and enforcement of the desires of those who happen to have power. "The

belief in the possibility of a rule of law, of equal justice, of fundamental rights, and a free society," Karl Popper observes,

> can easily survive the recognition that judges are not om-
> niscient and may make mistakes about facts and that, in
> practice, absolute justice is hardly ever realized in any
> particular legal case.  But this belief in the possibility of a
> rule of law, of justice, and of freedom, cannot well survive
> the acceptance of an epistemology which teaches that there
> are no objective facts; not merely in this particular case, but
> in any other case; and that the judge cannot have made a
> factual mistake because he can no more be wrong about the
> facts than he can be right.

## CONJECTURES AND REFUTATIONS 5 (1965).

Others who insist that facts cannot be subjective or relative—
and still be facts—may simply reject the arguments of Part II,
not because they have any specific objections or counterarguments,
but because their own experiences of knowing things and understanding the meaning of things is too real to be denied.  There *must*
be a world of solid fact and a linguistic medium capable of communicating it—and proofs and arguments to the contrary *must* be
sophistries.  Of those who feel this way, there may even be some
who view the kind of criticism presented in Part II as in some way
perverse, subversive, destructive of social and political order—
perhaps because they see it as leading to the "might makes right"
cynicism referred to in the preceding paragraph.  Their response is
therefore likely to be a continued commitment to the authorities
discussed in Part II—with, perhaps, an unarticulated reliance on
"common sense" or "intuition" to correct the relatively few errors
that may be occasioned thereby.

The purpose of this Part is to see what basis there may be for
a position which rejects both the skepticism of the "gut reaction"
theory and the uncritical faith of those who cleave to authority.  Is
there a way to defend the *feeling* that social life is in important
respects orderly and stable, that social and personal relations are
in many ways physically manageable and mentally graspable, and
that language plays an important role in accomplishing this—without accepting the conceptions of perception, concepts, facts, issues
and rules which were criticized in Part II?  Can the materials in
Part II be viewed, in other words, not as an attack on knowledge and
the semantic efficacy of language, but as a critique of a particular
way of conceiving and explaining those experiences of knowing, understanding and communicating which seem to be shared by all of
us and on which everything in our lives seems to depend?

If so, the usefulness of that enterprise will depend upon the
availability of other ways of conceiving and characterizing the nature
of knowledge and the symbolic media by which it is conveyed.  Many
of the readings in this part are included for the purpose of suggesting such alternative epistemological and semantic hypotheses.
They provide conceptions of fact, of symbolism, of the relation be-

tween fact and symbol, and of the nature of thinking which differ
from the ordinary conceptions embedded in the weltanschauung of
the common-sensical lawyer, judge or legislator.  On the other hand,
as later chapters will try to show, they seem to help us account for
and justify much that is thought to be good, or at least standard
operating procedure, in the practice, enforcement, adjudication and
enactment of law.  In addition, insofar as they suggest revisions
of our notions of knowing and communicating, they necessarily give
us some aid in understanding what legal tasks "really" involve and
what must be the nature of legal education, legal knowledge and legal
argument.  In short, they give us some idea of what a "method"
for deciding legal issues would have to look like.

## ROCHIN v. CALIFORNIA

342 U.S. 165 (1952)

Mr. Justice FRANKFURTER delivered the opinion of the Court.

Having "some information that [the petitioner here] was selling
narcotics," three deputy sheriffs of the County of Los Angeles, on
the morning of July 1, 1949, made for the two-story dwelling house
in which Rochin lived with his mother, common-law wife, brothers
and sisters.  Finding the outside door open, they entered and then
forced open the door to Rochin's room on the second floor.  Inside
they found petitioner sitting partly dressed on the side of the bed,
upon which his wife was lying.  On a "night stand" beside the bed
the deputies spied two capsules.  When asked "Whose stuff is this?"
Rochin seized the capsules and put them in his mouth.  A struggle
ensued, in the course of which the three officers "jumped upon him"
and attempted to extract the capsules.  The force they applied proved
unavailing against Rochin's resistance.  He was handcuffed and
taken to a hospital.  At the direction of one of the officers a doctor
forced an emetic solution through a tube into Rochin's stomach against
his will.  This "stomach pumping" produced vomiting.  In the vomit-
ed matter were found two capsules which proved to contain morphine.

Rochin was brought to trial before a California Superior Court,
sitting without a jury, on the charge of possessing "a preparation of
morphine" in violation of the California Health and Safety Code,
1947, section 11,500.  Rochin was convicted and sentenced to sixty
days' imprisonment.  The chief evidence against him was the two
capsules.  They were admitted over petitioner's objection, although
the means of obtaining them was frankly set forth in the testimony
by one of the deputies, substantially as here narrated.

On appeal, the District Court of Appeal affirmed the conviction,
despite the finding that the officers "were guilty of unlawfully breaking into and entering defendant's room and were guilty of unlawfully
assaulting and battering defendant while in the room," and "were
guilty of unlawfully assaulting, battering, torturing and falsely imprisoning the defendant at the alleged hospital."  101 Cal.App.2d
140, 143, 225 P.2d 1, 3.  One of the three judges, while finding that
"the record in this case reveals a shocking series of violations of

constitutional rights," concurred only because he felt bound by decisions of his Supreme Court. These, he asserted, "have been looked upon by law enforcement officers as an encouragement, if not an invitation, to the commission of such lawless acts." *Ibid.* The Supreme Court of California denied without opinion Rochin's petition for a hearing. Two justices dissented from this denial, and in doing so expressed themselves thus: ". . . a conviction which rests upon evidence of incriminating objects obtained from the body of the accused by physical abuse is as invalid as a conviction which rests upon a verbal confession extracted from him by such abuse . . . Had the evidence forced from the defendant's lips consisted of an oral confession that he illegally possessed a drug . . . he would have the protection of the rule of law which excludes coerced confessions from evidence. But because the evidence forced from his lips consisted of real objects the People of this state are permitted to base a conviction upon it. [We] find no valid ground of distinction between a verbal confession extracted by physical abuse and a confession wrested from defendant's body by physical abuse." 101 Cal.App.2d 143, 149–150, 225 P.2d 913, 917–918.

This Court granted certiorari, 341 U.S. 939, because a serious question is raised as to the limitations which the Due Process Clause of the Fourteenth Amendment imposes on the conduct of criminal proceedings by the States.

. . .

. . . . in reviewing a State criminal conviction under a claim of right guaranteed by the Due Process Clause of the Fourteenth Amendment, from which is derived the most far-reaching and most frequent federal basis of challenging State criminal justice, "we must be deeply mindful of the responsibilities of the States for the enforcement of criminal laws, and exercise with due humility our merely negative function in subjecting convictions from state courts to the very narrow scrutiny which the Due Process Clause of the Fourteenth Amendment authorizes." Malinski v. New York, 324 U.S. 401, 412, 418. Due process of law, "itself a historical product," Jackman v. Rosenbaum Co., 260 U.S. 22, 31, is not to be turned into a destructive dogma against the States in the administration of their systems of criminal justice.

However, this Court too has its responsibility. Regard for the requirements of the Due Process Clause "inescapably imposes upon this Court an exercise of judgment upon the whole course of the proceedings [resulting in a conviction] in order to ascertain whether they offend those canons of decency and fairness which express the notions of justice of English-speaking peoples even toward those charged with the most heinous offenses." Malinski v. New York, *supra,* at 416–417. These standards of justice are not authoritatively formulated anywhere as though they were specifics. Due process of law is a summarized constitutional guarantee of respect for those personal immunities which, as Mr. Justice Cardozo twice wrote for the Court, are "so rooted in the traditions and conscience of our people as to be ranked as fundamental," Snyder v. Massachusetts,

291 U.S. 97, 105, or are "implicit in the concept of ordered liberty."
Palko v. Connecticut, 302 U.S. 319, 325.[1]

The Court's function in the observance of this settled conception
of the Due Process Clause does not leave us without adequate guides
in subjecting State criminal procedures to constitutional judgment.
In dealing not with the machinery of government but with human
rights, the absence of formal exactitude, or want of fixity of meaning,
is not an unusual or even regrettable attribute of constitutional provisions. Words being symbols do not speak without a gloss. On the
one hand the gloss may be the deposit of history, whereby a term
gains technical content. Thus the requirements of the Sixth and
Seventh Amendments for trial by jury in the federal courts have a
rigid meaning. No changes or chances can alter the content of the
verbal symbol of "jury"—a body of twelve men who must reach a
unanimous conclusion if the verdict is to go against the defendant.[2]
On the other hand, the gloss of some of the verbal symbols of the
Constitution does not give them a fixed technical content. It exacts
a continuing process of application.

When the gloss has thus not been fixed but is a function of the
process of judgment, the judgment is bound to fall differently at
different times and differently at the same time through different
judges. Even more specific provisions, such as the guaranty of
freedom of speech and the detailed protection against unreasonable
searches and seizures, have inevitably evoked as sharp divisions
in this Court as the least specific and most comprehensive protection
of liberties, the Due Process Clause.

The vague contours of the Due Process Clause do not leave judges
at large.[3] We may not draw on our merely personal and private

1. What is here summarized was
deemed by a majority of the Court,
in Malinski v. New York, 324 U.S.
401, 412, and 438, to be "the controlling principles upon which this
Court reviews on constitutional
grounds a state court conviction for
crime." They have been applied by
this Court many times, long before
and since the *Malinski* case. [Foot-
note by the Court.]

2. This is the federal jury required
constitutionally although England and
at least half of the States have in
some civil cases juries which are composed of less than 12 or whose verdict may be less than unanimous.
See County Courts Act, 1934, 24 &
25 Geo. V, c. 53, section 93; Arizona
State Legislative Bureau, Legislative
Briefs No. 4, Grand and Petit Juries
in the United States, v–vi (Feb. 15,
1940); The Council of State Governments, The Book of the States, 1950–
1951, 515. [Footnote by the Court.]

3. Burke's observations on the method
of ascertaining law by judges are

pertinent: "Your committee do not
find any positive law which binds the
judges of the courts in Westminster-
hall publicly to give a reasoned opinion from the bench, in support of their
judgment upon matters that are stated
before them. But the course hath
prevailed from the oldest times. It
hath been so general and so uniform,
that it must be considered as the
law of the land." Report of the
Committee of Managers on the Causes
of the Duration of Mr. Hastings's
Trial, 4 Speeches of Edmund Burke
(1816) 200–201. And Burke had an
answer for those who argue that the
liberty of the citizen cannot be adequately protected by the flexible conception of due process of law:
". . . the English jurisprudence
has not any other sure foundation,
nor consequently the lives and properties of the subject any sure hold,
but in the maxims, rules, and principles, and juridical traditionary line
of decisions . . ." *Id.*, at 201.
[Footnote by the Court.]

notions and disregard the limits that bind judges in their judicial function. Even though the concept of due process of law is not final and fixed, these limits are derived from considerations that are fused in the whole nature of our judicial process. See Cardozo, The Nature of the Judicial Process; The Growth of the Law; the Paradoxes of Legal Science. These are considerations deeply rooted in reason and in the compelling traditions of the legal profession. The Due Process Clause places upon this Court the duty of exercising a judgment, within the narrow confines of judicial power in reviewing State convictions, upon interests of society pushing in opposite directions.

Due process of law thus conceived is not to be derided as resort to a revival of "natural law." To believe that this judicial exercise of judgment could be avoided by freezing "due process of law" at some fixed stage of time or thought is to suggest that the most important aspect of constitutional adjudication is a function for inanimate machines and not for judges, for whom the independence safeguarded by Article III of the Constitution was designed and who are presumably guided by established standards of judicial behavior. Even cybernetics has not yet made that haughty claim. To practice the requisite detachment and to achieve sufficient objectivity no doubt demands of judges the habit of self-discipline and self-criticism, incertitude that one's own views are incontestable and alert tolerance toward views not shared. But these are precisely the presuppositions of our judicial process. They are precisely the qualities society has a right to expect from those entrusted with ultimate judicial power.

Restraints on our jurisdiction are self-imposed only in the sense that there is from our decisions no immediate appeal short of impeachment or constitutional amendment. But that does not make due process of law a matter of judicial caprice. The faculties of the Due Process Clause may be indefinite and vague, but the mode of their ascertainment is not self-willed. In each case "due process of law" requires an evaluation based on a disinterested inquiry pursued in the spirit of science, on a balanced order of facts exactly and fairly stated, on the detached consideration of conflicting claims, see Hudson County Water Co. v. McCarter, 209 U.S. 349, 355, on a judgment not *ad hoc* and episodic but duly mindful of reconciling the needs both of continuity and of change in a progressive society.

Applying these general considerations to the circumstances of the present case, we are compelled to conclude that the proceedings by which this conviction was obtained do more than offend some fastidious squeamishness or private sentimentalism about combatting crime too energetically. This is conduct that shocks the conscience. Illegally breaking into the privacy of the petitioner, the struggle to open his mouth and remove what was there, the forcible extraction of his stomach's contents—this course of proceeding by agents of government to obtain evidence is bound to offend even hardened sensibilities. They are methods too close to the rack and the screw to permit of constitutional differentiation.

It has long since ceased to be true that due process of law is heedless of the means by which otherwise relevant and credible evidence is obtained. This was not true even before the series of recent cases enforced the constitutional principle that the States may not base convictions upon confessions, however much verified, obtained by coercion. These decisions are not arbitrary exceptions to the comprehensive right of States to fashion their own rules of evidence for criminal trials. They are not sports in our constitutional law but applications of a general principle. They are only instances of the general requirement that States in their prosecution respect certain decencies of civilized conduct. Due process of law, as a historic and generative principle, precludes defining, and thereby confining, these standards of conduct more precisely than to say that convictions cannot be brought about by methods that offend "a sense of justice." See Mr. Chief Justice Hughes, speaking for a unanimous Court in Brown v. Mississippi, 297 U.S. 278, 285–286. It would be a stultification of the responsibility which the course of constitutional history has cast upon this Court to hold that in order to convict a man the police cannot extract by force what is in his mind but can extract what is in his stomach.[4]

To attempt in this case to distinguish what lawyers call "real evidence" from verbal evidence is to ignore the reasons for excluding coerced confessions. Use of involuntary verbal confessions in State criminal trials is constitutionally obnoxious not only because of their unreliability. They are inadmissible under the Due Process Clause even though statements contained in them may be independently established as true. Coerced confessions offend the community's sense of fair play and decency. So here, to sanction the brutal conduct which naturally enough was condemned by the court whose judgment is before us, would be to afford brutality the cloak of law. Nothing would be more calculated to discredit law and thereby to brutalize the temper of a society.

In deciding this case we do not heedlessly bring into question decisions in many States dealing with essentially different, even if related problems. We therefore put to one side cases which have arisen in the State courts through use of modern methods and devices for discovering wrongdoers and bringing them to book. It does not fairly represent these decisions to suggest that they legalize force so brutal and so offensive to human dignity in securing evidence from a suspect as is revealed by this record. Indeed the California Supreme Court has not sanctioned this mode of securing a conviction. It merely exercised its discretion to decline a review of the conviction. All the California judges who have expressed themselves in this case have condemned the conduct in the strongest language.

We are not unmindful that hypothetical situations can be conjured up, shading imperceptibly from the circumstances of this case

---

4. As to the difference between the privilege against self-crimination protected, in federal prosecutions, under the Fifth Amendment, and the limitations which the Due Process Clause of the Fourteenth Amendment imposes upon the States against the use of coerced confessions, see Brown v. Mississippi, *supra*, at 285. [Footnote by the Court.]

and by gradations producing practical differences despite seemingly logical extensions. But the Constitution is "intended to preserve practical and substantial rights, not to maintain theories." Davis v. Mills, 194 U.S. 451, 457.

On the facts of this case the conviction of the petitioner has been obtained by methods that offend the Due Process Clause. The judgment below must be

Reversed.

Mr. Justice MINTON took no part in the consideration or decision of this case.

Mr. Justice BLACK, concurring.

Adamson v. California, 332 U.S. 46, 68–123, sets out reasons for my belief that state as well as federal courts and law enforcement officers must obey the Fifth Amendment's command that "No person . . . shall be compelled in any criminal case to be a witness against himself." I think a person is compelled to be a witness against himself not only when he is compelled to testify, but also when as here, incriminating evidence is forcibly taken from him by a contrivance of modern science. Cf. Boyd v. United States, 116 U.S. 616; Counselman v. Hitchcock, 142 U.S. 547, 562; Bram v. United States, 168 U.S. 532; Chambers v. Florida, 309 U.S. 227. California convicted this petitioner by using against him evidence obtained in this manner, and I agree with Mr. Justice DOUGLAS that the case should be reversed on this ground.

In the view of a majority of the Court, however, the Fifth Amendment imposes no restraint of any kind on the states. They nevertheless hold that California's use of this evidence violated the Due Process Clause of the Fourteenth Amendment. Since they hold as I do in this case, I regret my inability to accept their interpretation without protest. But I believe that faithful adherence to the specific guarantees in the Bill of Rights insures a more permanent protection of individual liberty than that which can be afforded by the nebulous standards stated by the majority.

What the majority hold is that the Due Process Clause empowers this Court to nullify any state law if its application "shocks the conscience," offends "a sense of justice" or runs counter to the "decencies of civilized conduct." The majority emphasize that these statements do not refer to their own consciences or to their senses of justice and decency. For we are told that "we may not draw on our merel personal and private notions"; our judgment must be grounded on "considerations deeply rooted in reason and in the compelling traditions of the legal profession." We are further admonished to measure the validity of state practices, not by our reason, or by the traditions of the legal profession, but by "the community's sense of fair play and decency"; by the "traditions and conscience of our people"; or by "those canons of decency and fairness which express the notions of justice of English-speaking peoples."

If the Due Process Clause does vest this Court with such unlimited power to invalidate laws, I am still in doubt as to why we should consider only the notions of English-speaking peoples to determine what are immutable and fundamental principles of justice. Moreover, one may well ask what avenues of investigation are open to discover "canons" of conduct so universally favored that this Court should write them into the Constitution? All we are told is that the discovery must be made by an "evaluation based on a disinterested inquiry pursued in the spirit of science, on a balanced order of facts."

Some constitutional provisions are stated in absolute and unqualified language such, for illustration, as the First Amendment stating that no law shall be passed prohibiting the free exercise of religion or abridging the freedom of speech or press. Other constitutional provisions do require courts to choose between competing policies, such as the Fourth Amendment which, by its terms, necessitates a judicial decision as to what is an "unreasonable" search or seizure. There is, however, no express constitutional language granting judicial power to invalidate *every* state law of *every* kind deemed "unreasonable" or contrary to the Court's notion of civilized decencies; yet the constitutional philosophy used by the majority has, in the past, been used to deny a state the right to fix the price of gasoline, Williams v. Standard Oil Co., 278 U.S. 235; and even the right to prevent bakers from palming off smaller for larger loaves of bread, Jay Burns Baking Co. v. Bryan, 264 U.S. 504. These cases, and others, show the extent to which the evanescent standards of the majority's philosophy have been used to nullify state legislative programs passed to suppress evil economic practices. What paralyzing role this same philosophy will play in the future economic affairs of this country is impossible to predict. Of even graver concern, however, is the use of the philosophy to nullify the Bill of Rights. I long ago concluded that the accordion-like qualities of this philosophy must inevitably imperil all the individual liberty safeguards specifically enumerated in the Bill of Rights. Reflection and recent decisions of this Court sanctioning abridgment of the freedom of speech and press have strengthened this conclusion.

## NOTES AND QUESTIONS

1. The Due Process Clause of the Fourteenth Amendment provides that "No State shall . . . deprive any person of life, liberty, or property, without due process of law." Are these words adequately accounted for by Justice Black in his critique of Justice Frankfurter's opinion? Do they challenge Black's assertion that, "There is . . . no express constitutional language granting judicial power to invalidate *every* state law of *every* kind deemed 'unreasonable' or contrary to the Court's notion of civilized decencies"? Without further definition of the word, "due," how could one go about ascertaining whether or not the "process of law" accorded someone was "due"— except by asking whether it was "reasonable"?

In Adamson v. California, Justice Black in dissent argued that the Fourteenth Amendment was intended to "incorporate" the Bill of Rights—*i. e.*, that the first eight amendments to the Constitution were to bind the States as well as the Federal government. Even if this interpretation of the Fourteenth Amendment's legislative history is accepted, does it necessarily preclude the use of a general standard of "reasonableness" as well as the more specific standards of the Bill of Rights? Assuming that there is no legislative history which indicates that the Bill of Rights exhausts the "meaning" of the Due Process Clause, is there, nevertheless, some reason of general policy which might call for such an interpretation? Does Justice Black suggest one?

2. Why does Justice Black think that "the Due Process Clause" vests the "Court with such unlimited power to invalidate laws" under Frankfurter's construction of it? Is it because the Clause as so construed provides judges with no information as to what is or is not in violation of it? Is this another way of saying that the clause as so construed has no "meaning"?

3. Can you make an argument that however vague, uninformative, or non-directive a legal injunction may be—as authoritatively formulated—the judges who administer it are under a duty to make it more specific, more informative, more binding? Can you think of social interests that would be served by such a policy? Institutional interests of the judiciary? Of the executive and the police? Of the practicing legal profession? Interests of citizens who wish to know what the law is? Review in this regard the considerations raised in the chapter on The Authority of Language.

Is Justice Frankfurter unwilling to *make* the Due Process Clause more specific? If so, is it because he believes that the framers of the Fourteenth Amendment did not intend for it to be specific? Is it because he thinks there are other reasons, unrelated to the framers' intentions, which would justify a formulation as vague as "due process of law"?

Is it arguable that Justice Frankfurter did wish to reduce "due process of law" to more specific terms? Why, otherwise, did he feel the need to talk about "a sense of justice"? About "conduct which shocks the conscience"? Why did he decide to say anything more than, "on these facts, we find a violation of due process of law"? What did he hope to accomplish, do you think, by saying more?

4. What is "a sense of justice"? Is justice the sort of thing that is "sensed"? Is the ascertainment of justice or injustice a "sensory" exercise? Can one "perceive" injustice? In a way anything like the way one smells or sees or hears?

What is the point of analogizing—if it is only analogizing—the determination of justice to the operation of the senses? Does this help Justice Frankfurter's position vis-à-vis Black's? Does it matter which sense one singles out? Would Frankfurter prefer to analogize the "sense of justice" to the sense of sight? Would Black prefer an analogy to the sense of taste?

5. What, specifically, is shocked when "the conscience" is shocked? Does Justice Frankfurter give any indication? Could you state in your own words what is meant by "shocks the conscience"? Can you frame a statement which would make it easier to determine when conduct shocks the conscience than does Frankfurter's phrase by itself?

6. What, according to Frankfurter, are "the limits that bind judges in their judicial function"? Justice Frankfurter refers to "canons of decency and fairness which express the notions of justice of English-speaking peoples," to "standards of justice," to "considerations . . . fused in the whole nature of our judicial process," to "applications of a general principle," to "certain decencies of civilized conduct," to "these standards of conduct." Does he at any point state what these canons, standards or principles say? If not, does he offer a reason? Is it because he *cannot* state what they say? If so, is it proper to refer to these "things" as canons, standards and principles? Is it implicit in the nature of such phenomena that they are stateable, that they only exist in some definite linguistic form?

If "these standards of justice are not authoritatively formulated anywhere as though they were specifics," how did Justice Frankfurter come to know them? How, according to the justice, would anyone else come to know them?

7. In Griswold v. Connecticut, Justice Black, again dissenting, expanded somewhat on his views in *Rochin*:

> My Brother Goldberg has adopted the recent discovery that the Ninth Amendment as well as the Due Process Clause can be used by this Court as authority to strike down all state legislation which this Court thinks violates "fundamental principles of liberty and justice," or is contrary to the "traditions and [collective] conscience of our people." He also states, without proof satisfactory to me, that in making decisions on this basis judges will not consider "their personal and private notions." One may ask how they can avoid considering them. Our Court certainly has no machinery with which to take a Gallup Poll. And the scientific miracles of this age have not yet produced a gadget which the Court can use to determine what traditions are rooted in the [collective] conscience of our people.

381 U.S. 479, 518–519 (1965). He also cites with approval the following from L. HAND, THE BILL OF RIGHTS 70 (1958):

> Judges are seldom content merely to annul the particular solution before them; they do not, indeed they may not, say that taking all things into consideration, the legislator's solution is too strong for the judicial stomach. On the contrary they wrap up their veto in a protective veil of adjectives such as "arbitrary," "artificial," "normal," "reasonable," "inherent," "fundamental," or "essential," whose office usually, though quite innocently, is to disguise what they are doing and impute to it a derivation far more impressive than their personal preferences, which are all that in fact lie behind the decision.

In light of his opinion in *Rochin*, how would Justice Frankfurter respond to these comments? What is meant, incidentally, by "personal preferences"? Would these "preferences" be "personal" if it could be shown that other people had them, too? Is Justice Frankfurter the only one who has the preferences expressed by his opinion in *Rochin*? Does it matter? What is a "preference"? Can it be expressed in words? If not, is it meaningful to talk about it at all?

8. Would Justice Black agree that "defining" necessarily amounts to "confining" the "standards of conduct" which Frankfurter finds in due process of law? Note his references to "the accordion-like qualities of this philosophy." Compare Frankfurter's declaration that "the Constitution is 'intended to preserve practical and substantial rights, not to maintain theories'" with Professor Wechsler's call for "principled" decisions in Chapter 12 below.

9. Consider Frankfurter's opinion in *Rochin* against the background of two earlier Supreme Court decisions in which he had joined. In Adamson v. California, 332 U.S. 46 (1947), it was held that the Fifth Amendment's self-incrimination privilege was not applicable to the States. The Fourteenth Amendment's Due Process Clause, the majority held, could not be read to "incorporate" any of the specific provisions of the Fifth. Wolf v. Colorado, 338 U.S. 25 (1949), declared that the Fourth Amendment's prohibition of "unreasonable searches and seizures" *was* applicable to the States, but refused to hold that evidence obtained from such acts must be excluded from State criminal trials. The States were free, according to Frankfurter's majority opinion, to use other remedies to enforce the Fourth Amendment right.

Justice Frankfurter's *Rochin* opinion read with his *Wolf* opinion, therefore, seems to say that evidence obtained illegally—*i. e.*, in violation of the Fourteenth and Fourth Amendments—may only be excluded when the method used "shocks the conscience." Does this mean that the intentional violation of Constitutional provisions by governmental officials is not in itself "conduct which shocks the conscience"? Or which violates "a sense of justice"? What, in Frankfurter's own words, could "be more calculated to discredit law and thereby to brutalize the temper of a society"?

In Irvine v. California, 347 U.S. 128 (1954), police repeatedly made illegal entries into the defendant's home and, among other things, installed a microphone into the bedroom with which they were able to overhear conjugal conversations and activities for more than a month. Justice Jackson writing for the Court declared that the conduct of the police "would be almost incredible if it were not admitted." "Few police measures," he said, "have come to our attention that more flagrantly, deliberately, and persistently violated the fundamental principle declared by the Fourth Amendment." Jackson, however, held that the evidence so obtained could not be excluded under *Rochin* because of the absence of physical coercion, violence and brutality. Justice Frankfurter in dissent argued that *Rochin* was controlling.

10. Would Frankfurter be open to the criticisms made by Ayer below? If so, can you frame a critique of his opinion in Ayer's terms? What would you say Justice Black and Professor Ayer have in common? Do they have the same reasons for resisting positions like Frankfurter's? Would Ayer view a finding that Rochin was "compelled in . . . [a] criminal case to be a witness against himself" as factual? As meaningful?

*A. J. AYER*

## ON THE ANALYSIS OF MORAL JUDGMENTS *

"Most of us would agree," said F. P. Ramsey, addressing a society in Cambridge in 1925, "that the objectivity of good was a thing we had settled and dismissed with the existence of God. Theology and Absolute Ethics are two famous subjects which we have realized to have no real objects." There are many, however, who still think that these questions have not been settled; and in the meantime philosophers of Ramsey's persuasion have grown more circumspect. Theological and ethical statements are no longer stigmatized as false or meaningless. They are merely said to be different from scientific statements. They are differently related to their evidence; or, rather, a different meaning is attached to "evidence" in their case. "Every kind of statement," we are told, "has its own kind of logic."

What this comes to, so far as moral philosophy is concerned, is that ethical statements are *sui generis*; and this may very well be true. Certainly, the view, which I still wish to hold, that what are called ethical statements are not really statements at all, that they are not descriptive of anything, that they cannot be either true or false, is in an obvious sense incorrect. For, as the English language is currently used—and what else, it may be asked, is here in question? —it is by no means improper to refer to ethical utterances as statements; when someone characterizes an action by the use of an ethical predicate, it is quite good usage to say that he is thereby describing it; when someone wishes to assent to an ethical verdict, it is perfectly legitimate for him to say that it is true, or that it is a fact, just as, if he wished to dissent from it, it would be perfectly legitimate for him to say that it was false. We should know what he meant and we should not consider that he was using words in an unconventional way. What is unconventional, rather, is the usage of the philosopher who tells us that ethical statements are not really statements at all but something else, ejaculations perhaps or commands, and that they cannot be either true or false.

Now when a philosopher asserts that something "really" is not what it really is, or "really" is what it really is not, that we do not, for example, "really" see chairs and tables, whereas there is a perfectly good and familiar sense in which we really do, or that we cannot "really" step into the same river twice, whereas in fact we really can, it should not always be assumed that he is merely making a mistake. Very often what he is doing, although he may not know it, is to recommend a new way of speaking, not just for amusement, but because he thinks that the old, the socially correct, way of speaking is logically misleading, or that his own proposal brings out certain points more clearly. Thus, in the present instance, it is no doubt correct to say that the moralist does make statements, and, what is more, statements

* From A Modern Introduction to Ethics 537–542, 543, 544, 545, 546 (M. Munitz ed. 1958). Originally published in XX     Horizon No. 117 (1949). Copyright 1949 by A. J. Ayer. Reprinted by permission.

of fact, statements of ethical fact.  It is correct in the sense that if a vote were taken on the point, those who objected to this way of speaking would probably be in the minority.  But when one considers how these ethical statements are actually used, it may be found that they function so very differently from other types of statement that it is advisable to put them into a separate category altogether; either to say that they are not to be counted as statements at all, or, if this proves inconvenient, at least to say that they do not express propositions, and consequently that there are no ethical facts.  This does not mean that all ethical statements are held to be false.  It is merely a matter of laying down a usage of the words "proposition" and "fact," according to which only propositions express facts and ethical statements fall outside the class of propositions.  This may seem to be an arbitrary procedure, but I hope to show that there are good reasons for adopting it.  And once these reasons are admitted the purely verbal point is not of any great importance.  If someone still wishes to say that ethical statements are statements of fact, only it is a queer sort of fact, he is welcome to do so.  So long as he accepts our grounds for saying that they are not statements of fact, it is simply a question of how widely or loosely we want to use the word "fact."  My own view is that it is preferable so to use it as to exclude ethical judgments, but it must not be inferred from this that I am treating them with disrespect.  The only relevant consideration is that of clarity.

The distinctions that I wish to make can best be brought out by an example.  Suppose that someone has committed a murder.  Then part of the story consists of what we may call the police-court details; where and when and how the killing was effected; the identity of the murderer and of his victim; the relationship in which they stood to one another.  Next there are the questions of motive: the murderer may have been suffering from jealousy, or he may have been anxious to obtain money; he may have been avenging a private injury, or pursuing some political end.  These questions of motive are, on one level, a matter of the agent's reflections before the act; and these may very well take the form of moral judgments.  Thus he may tell himself that his victim is a bad man and that the world would be better for his removal, or, in a different case, that it is his duty to rid his country of a tyrant or, like Raskolnikov in *Crime and Punishment*, that he is a superior being who has in these circumstances the right to kill.  A psychoanalyst who examines the case may, however, tell a different story.  He may say that the political assassin is really revenging himself upon his father, or that the man who persuades himself that he is a social benefactor is really exhibiting a lust for power, or, in a case like that of Raskolnikov, that the murderer does not really believe that he has the right to kill.

All these are statements of fact; not indeed that the man has, or has not, the right to kill, but that this is what he tells himself.  They are verified or confuted, as the case may be, by observation.  It is a matter of fact, in my usage of the term, that the victim was killed at such and such a place and at such and such a time and in such and such a manner.  It is also a matter of fact that the murderer had certain conscious motives.  To himself they are known primarily by introspection; to others by various features of his overt behaviour, includng what he says. As regards his unconscious motives the only criterion is his overt behaviour. It can indeed plausibly be argued that to talk about the unconscious is always equivalent to talking about overt behaviour, though often in a very complicated way. Now there seems to me to be a very good sense in which to tell a story of this kind, that this is what the man did and that these were his reasons for doing it, is to give a complete description of the facts. Or rather, since one can never be in a position to say that any such description is complete, what will be missing from it will be further information of the same type; what we obtain when this information is added is a more elaborate account of the circumstances of the action, and of its antecedents and consequences. But now suppose that instead of developing the story in this circumstantial way, one applies an ethical predicate to it. Suppose that instead of asking what it was that really happened, or what the agent's motives really were, we ask whether he was justified in acting as he did. Did he have the right to kill? Is it true that he had the right? Is it a fact that he acted rightly? It does not matter in this connection what answer we give. The question for moral philosophy is not whether a certain action is right or wrong, but what is implied by saying that it is right, or saying that it is wrong. Suppose then that we say that the man acted rightly. The point that I wish to make is that in saying this we are not elaborating or modifying our description of the situation in the way that we should be elaborating if we gave further police-court details, or in the way that we should be modifying it if we showed that the agent's motives were different from what they had been thought to be. To say that his motives were good, or that they were bad, is not to say what they were. To say that the man acted rightly, or that he acted wrongly, is not to say what he did. And when one has said what he did, when one has described the situation in the way that I have outlined, then to add that he was justified, or alternatively that he was not, is not to say any more about what he did; it does not add a further detail to the story. It is for this reason that these ethical predicates are not factual; they do not describe any features of the situation to which they are applied. But they do, someone may object, they describe its ethical features. But what are these ethical features? And how are they related to the other features of the situation, to what we may provisionally call its "natural" features? Let us consider this.

To begin with, it is, or should be, clear that the connection is not logical. Let us assume that two observers agree about all the circumstances of the case, including the agent's motives, but that they disagree in their evaluation of it. Then neither of them is contradicting himself. Otherwise the use of the ethical term would add nothing to the circumstantial description; it would serve merely as a repetition, or partial repetition, of it. But neither, as I hope to show, is the connection factual. There is nothing that counts as observing the *designata* of the ethical predicates, apart from observing the natural features of the situation. But what alternative is left? Certainly it can be said that the ethical features in some way depend upon the natural. We can and do give reasons for our moral judgements, just as we do for our aesthetic judgements, where the same argument applies. We fasten on motives, point to consequences, ask what would happen if everyone were to behave in such a way, and so forth. But the question is: In what way do these reasons support the judgements? Not in a logical sense. Ethical argument is not formal demonstration. And not in a scientific sense either. For then the goodness or badness of the situation, the rightness or wrongness of the action, would have to be something apart from the situation, something independently verifiable, for which the facts adduced as the reasons for the moral judgement were evidence. But in these moral cases the two coincide. There is no procedure of examining the value of the facts, as distinct from examining the facts themselves. We may say that we have evidence for our moral judgements, but we cannot distinguish between pointing to the evidence itself and pointing to that for which it is supposed to be evidence. Which means that in the scientific sense it is not evidence at all.

My own answer to this question is that what are accounted reasons for our moral judgements are reasons only in the sense that they determine attitudes. One attempts to influence another person morally by calling his attention to certain natural features of the situation, which are such as will be likely to evoke from him the desired response. Or again one may give reasons to oneself as a means of settling on an attitude or, more importantly, as a means of coming to some practical decision. . . . [I]n saying that they acted wrongly, I express a resolution not to imitate them, and endeavour also to discourage others. It may be thought that the mere use of the dyslogistic word "wrongly" is not much of a discouragement, although it does have some emotive force. But that is where the reasons come in. I discourage others, or at any rate hope to discourage them, by telling them why I think the action wrong; and here the argument may take various forms. One method is to appeal to some moral principle, as, for example, that human life is sacred, and show that it applies to the given case. It is assumed that the principle is one that already has some influence upon those to whom the argument is addressed. Alternatively, one may try to establish certain facts, as, for example, that the act in question caused, or was such as would be likely to cause, a great deal of unhappiness; and here it is assumed that the consideration of these facts will modify the hearer's attitude. It is assumed that he regards the increase of human misery as something undesirable, something if possible to be avoided. As for the moral judgement itself, it may be regarded as expressing the attitude which the reasons given for it are calculated to evoke. To say, as I once did, that these moral judgements are merely expressive of certain feelings, feelings of approval or disapproval, is an over-simplification. The fact is rather that what may be described as moral attitudes consist in certain patterns of behaviour, and that the expression of a moral judgement is an element in the pattern. The moral judgement expresses the attitude in the sense that it contributes to defining it. Why people respond favourably to certain facts and unfavourably to others is a question for the sociologist, into which I do not here propose to enter.

. . . [M]y concern at present is only to analyse the use of ethical terms, not scientifically to explain it.

At this point it may be objected that I have been excessively dogmatic. What about the people who claim that they do observe ethical properties, non-natural properties, as G. E. Moore once put it, not indeed through their senses, but by means of intellectual intuition? What of those who claim that they have a moral sense, and mean by this not merely that they have feelings of approval and disapproval, or whatever else may go to define a moral attitude, but that they experience such things as goodness or beauty in a way somehow analogous to that in which they experience sounds or colours? What are we to say to them? I may not have any experiences of this sort myself, but that, it may be said, is just my shortcoming. I am surely not entitled to assume that all these honest and intelligent persons do not have the experiences that they say they do. It may be, indeed, that the differences between us lie not so much in the nature of our respective experiences as in our fashion of describing them. I do in fact suspect that the experiences which some philosophers want to describe as intuitions, or as quasi-sensory apprehensions, of good are not significantly different from those that I want to describe as feelings of approval. But whether this be so or not, it does not in any way affect my argument. For let it be granted that someone who contemplates some natural situation detects in it something which he describes as "goodness" or "beauty" or "fittingness" or "worthiness to be approved." How this experience of goodness, or whatever it may be, is supposed to be related to the experiences which reveal the natural features of the situation has not yet been made clear, but I take it that it is not regarded merely as their effect. Rather, the situation is supposed to look good, or fitting, in much the same way as a face may be said to look friendly. But then to say that this experience is an experience of good will be to say no more than that it is this type of experience. The word "good," or whatever other value term may be used, simply comes to be descriptive of experiences of this type, and here it makes no difference whether they are regarded as intuitions or as moral sensations. In neither case does anything whatsoever follow as regards conduct. That a situation has this peculiar property, the property whose presence is established by people's having such experiences, does not entail that it is preferable to other situations, or that it is anyone's duty to bring it into existence. To say that such a situation ought to be created, or that it deserves to exist, will be to say something different from merely saying that it has this property. This point is obscured by the use of an ethical term to describe the property, just because the ethical term is tacitly understood to be normative. It continues to fulfil its function of prescribing the attitude that people are to take. But if the ethical term is understood to be normative, then it does not merely describe the alleged non-natural property, and if it does merely describe this property, then it is not normative and so no longer does the work that ethical terms are supposed to do.

. . . . Those who talk of non-natural qualities, moral intuitions, and all the rest of it, may be giving peculiar descriptions of peculiar experiences; it does not matter which view we take. In either case we are left with the further question whether what is so described is to be valued; and this is not simply equivalent to asking what character it has, whether natural, or non-natural, whatever that may mean. Thus even if an intuitionist does have experiences that others do not have, it makes no difference to the argument. We are still entitled to say that it is misleading for him to use a value-term to designate the content of such experiences; for in this way he contrives to smuggle a normative judgment into what purports to be a statement of fact. A valuation is not a description of something very peculiar; it is not a description at all. . . . [T]alking about values is not a matter of describing what may or may not be there, the problem being whether it really is there. There is no such problem. The moral problem is: What am I to do? What attitude am I to take? And moral judgements are directives in this sense.

We can now see that the whole dispute about the objectivity of values, as it is ordinarily conducted, is pointless and idle. I suppose that what underlies it is the question: Are the things that I value really valuable, and how can I know that they are? Then one party gives the answer: They are really valuable if they reflect, or participate in, or are in some other mysterious way related to an objective world of values; and you can know that they are by inspecting this world. To which their opponents reply that there is no such world, and can therefore be no such inspection. But this sort of argument, setting aside the question whether it is even intelligible, is nothing to the purpose. For suppose that someone did succeed in carrying out such an inspection. Suppose that he had an experience which we allowed him to describe in these terms. He can still raise the questions: Are these values the real ones? Are the objects that I am inspecting themselves really valuable, and how can I know that they are? And how are these questions to be answered? They do not arise, it may be said. These objective values carry the stamp of authenticity upon their faces. You have only to look at them to know that they are genuine. But, in this sense, any natural situation to which we attach value can carry the stamp of authenticity upon its face. That is to say, the value which is attached to it may be something that it does not occur to us to question. But in neither case is it inconceivable that the value should be questioned. Thus, these alleged objective values perform no function. The hypothesis of their existence does no work; or rather, it does no work that is not equally well done without it. Its effect is to answer the question: Are the things that I value really valuable? by Yes, if you have a certain sort of experience in connection with them. Let us assume these experiences can be identified and even that there is some method for deciding between them when they appear to yield contradictory results. Even so, that someone does or does not have them is itself a "natural" fact. Moreover, this answer merely lays down one of many possible standards. It is on a par with saying: "The things that you value are really valuable if they increase human happiness, or they are really valuable if certain persons, your pastors and masters, approve of them." Then either one accepts the standard, or one raises the question again. Why should I value human happiness? Why should I be swayed by my pastors and masters? Why should I attach such great importance just to these experiences? In the end there must come a point where one gets no further answer, but only a repetition of the injunction: Value this because it is valuable.

. . . . What we are given is an injunction not to worry, which may or may not satisfy us. If it does not, perhaps something else will. But in any case there is nothing to be done about it, except look at the facts, look at them harder, look at more of them, and then come to a moral decision. Then, asking whether the attitude that one has adopted is the right attitude comes down to asking whether one is prepared to stand by it. There can be no guarantee of its correctness, because nothing counts as a guarantee. Or rather, something may count for someone as a guarantee, but counting something as a guarantee is itself taking up a moral standpoint.

. . . I hope that I have gone some way towards making clear what the theory which I am advocating is. Let me now say what it is not. In the first place, I am not saying that morals are trivial or unimportant, or that people ought not to bother with them. For this would itself be a judgement of value, which I have not made and do not wish to make. And even if I did wish to make it it would have no logical connection with my theory. For the theory is entirely on the level of analysis; it is an attempt to show what people are doing when they make moral judgments; it is not a set of suggestions as to what moral judgements they are to make.

Again, when I say that moral judgements are emotive rather than descriptive, that they are persuasive expressions of attitudes and not statements of fact, and consequently that they cannot be either true or false, or at least that it would make for clarity if the categories of truth and falsehood were not applied to them, I am not saying that nothing is good or bad, right or wrong, or that it does not matter what we do. For once more such a statement would itself be the expression of a moral attitude. This attitude is not entailed by the theory, nor do I in fact adopt it. It would indeed be a difficult position to maintain. It would exclude even egotism as a policy, for the decision to consult nothing but one's own pleasure is itself a value judgement. . . .

Finally, I am not saying that anything that anybody thinks right is right; that putting people into concentration camps is preferable to allowing them free speech if somebody happens to think so, and that the contrary is also preferable if somebody thinks that it is. If my theory did entail this, it would be contradictory; for two different courses of action cannot each be preferable to the other. But it does not entail anything of the sort. On my analysis, to say that something which somebody thinks right really is right is to range oneself on his side, to adhere to that particular standpoint, and certainly I do not adhere to every standpoint whatsoever. I adhere to some, and not to others, like everybody else who has any moral views at all.
. . . .

But even if there is no logical connection between this meta-ethical theory and any particular type of conduct, may there not be a psychological connection? Does not the promulgation of such a theory encourage moral laxity? Has not its effect been to destroy people's confidence in accepted moral standards? And will not the result of this be that something mischievous will take their place? Such charges have, indeed, been made, but I do not know upon what evidence. The question how people's conduct is actually affected by their accetpance of a meta-ethical theory is one for empirical investigation; and in this case, so far as I know, no serious investigation has yet been carried out. My own observations, for what they are worth, do not suggest that those who accept the "positivist" analysis of moral judgements conduct themselves very differently as a class from those who reject it; and, indeed, I doubt if the study of moral philosophy does, in general, have any very marked effect upon people's conduct. The way to test the point would be to convert a sufficiently large number of people from one meta-ethical view to another and make careful observations of their behaviour before and after their conversions. Assuming that their behaviour changed in some significant way, it would then have to be decided by further experiment whether this was due to the change in their philosophical beliefs or to some other factor. If it could be shown, as I believe it could not, that the general acceptance of the sort of analysis of moral judgements that I have been putting forward would have unhappy social consequences, the conclusion drawn by illiberal persons might be that the doctrine ought to be kept secret. For my part I think that I should dispute this conclusion on moral grounds, but this is a question which I am not now concerned to argue. What I have tried to show is not that the theory I am defending is expedient, but that it is true.

## NOTES AND QUESTIONS

1. Is Ayer's critique of "ethical predicates" applicable to such phrases as "due process of law," "shocks the conscience," and "sense of justice"? How is a determination that one has been denied "due process" related to the "evidence" for such a determination? To the reasons which "support the judgment"? Is it, in Ayer's terms, a "logical" relation? A "factual" relation?

Does Ayer's essay help us understand why legislators should legislate specifically and concretely? Why judges must justify their decisions by reference to definite reasons and rules? Is this the way we can make the application of legal prescriptions capable of being true or false? Is this the way that we can determine whether officeholders are properly carrying out their duties? Or would a program of such specificity in the law ultimately prove futile? Does the answer turn on the relationship between *any* legal determination and the evidence or reasons for it? Are the determinations that X was in possession of Blackacre or Y abandoned his property or that Z was a jaywalker or that A and B have a contract differently related to their evidence and reasons than is the determination that the police in *Rochin* denied "due process of law"?

In what way is any factual determination—*e. g.*, X walked across the street at 3 p. m.; the temperature outside is now 90°—differently related to its evidence and reasons than an ethical determination? A legal determination? What is Ayer's answer to the first question? What answer is suggested by the remarks of Waismann in his piece on *Verifiability*? See Chapter 8(3) (B).

2. Can Ayer's remarks be viewed as a defense of Frankfurter's language and "method" in the *Rochin* case? Would Ayer think that Frankfurter had any choice but to talk and proceed in the way that he did? If so, what difference, if any, is there between the epistemology implicit in Frankfurter's opinion and the explicit statement that Ayer presents?

Can lawyers who try to appeal to a judge's or a jury's emotions, who wax poetic, metaphysical or, even, eschatological, make use of Ayer's analysis to justify their practices? Consider this question again when you read the arguments of Darrow and Crowe in the Leopold and Loeb case. See Part IV, Introduction *infra*.

3. Although he does not specifically invoke the traditional logical positivist vocabulary of "analytic" and "synthetic" statements and of "verifiability," can you see where these conceptions play a role in Ayer's argument? How would you characterize the conception of "fact" which Ayer seems to be using? To which, if any, of the objections earlier considered in Chapter 6 is his conception subject? Can you detect anything in Ayer's argument which would throw light on his notions regarding perception? If so, how do they square with earlier views studied in Chapter 4?

4. Does Ayer adopt a "common sense" view of the "real"? Recall the following:

> . . . . when a philosopher asserts that something "really" is not what it really is . . . that we do not, for example, "really" see chairs and tables, whereas there is a perfectly good and familiar sense in which we really do . . . it should not always be assumed that he is merely making a mistake.

What does the word "really" mean in the usage which Ayer defends? How does one go about determining "reality" of this kind? Is a statement expressing this kind of reality *factual* in Ayer's use of that term? Or is it, instead, "normatively ambiguous"—*i. e.*, does it contain in the form of a descriptive statement a covert prescription?

5. Why, according to Ayer, can one not logically deduce the moral evaluation of a situation from a statement of the details of that situation? Could one deduce a legal evaluation from such a statement? A medical evaluation? What do you think is meant when philosophers, such as Hume, declare that one cannot derive an "ought" from an "is," a prescription from a description? If you agree with the dictum, can you state the grounds which support it? Would it apply to "oughts" other than moral ones?

6. "To say that a man acted rightly or wrongly," says Ayer, "is not to say any more about what he did; it does not add a further de-

tail to the story." Why is it necessary for a moral statement to point to some additional feature of the situation in order for it to be "factual"? Does the requirement turn on the type of "situation" one is considering? Does the statement, "X's act was illegal," add anything to the "factual" story? What kind of a "story" is it that the psychoanalyst tells?

7. Consider the following:

> [The "naturalistic fallacy"] is that if one identifies the meaning of any normative word . . . with any empirical fact whatever, the result is a trivial tautology and this clearly is not what the sentence means.

Northrop, *Law, Language and Morals*, 71 Yale L.J. 1017, 1043 (1962). If, for example, the "good" is defined as what is pleasing, what is perferred, or what is approved, propositions such as "pleasure is good," "my preference is good," or "what I approve is good" could be accurately translated as "pleasure is pleasure," "my preference is my preference," and "what I approve is what I approve." *Id.* at 1023. The notion of "the naturalistic fallacy" was introduced by G. E. Moore. Does Ayer's criticism of "the people who claim that they do observe ethical properties, non-natural properties, as G. E. Moore once put it," amount to the assertion that they have committed "the naturalistic fallacy"? Or is Ayer saying something different from this?

> Essential to Moore's theory [of personal morality] is his distinction between "intrinsically good" and "instrumentally good." A "good" is intrinsic when its goodness depends on nothing other than itself. A "good" is instrumental if its goodness depends on its efficacy in achieving intrinsic goodness. Only intrinsic goodness is non-empirical and not further analyzable.

Northrop at 1024. Does Ayer's criticism of positions such as Moore's take adequate account of this distinction between intrinsic and instrumental goodness? Need it take account of the distinction at all?

8. "Now there seems to be a very good sense," says Ayer, "in which to tell a story of this kind . . . is to give a complete description of the facts." In what sense is he using the word "good" in this sentence? Is the sentence capable of being true or false? How do the reasons which support it function?

9. Ayer's essay responds in one way or another to many of the positions which are presented in the following sections of this chapter. As you come across these positions, repair to Ayer's argument to see just how he takes account of them and assess whether his response is intellectually adequate.

## NOTE: RELATIVISM AND ABSOLUTISM

In assessing the opinion of Justice Frankfurter and the essay of Ayer, consider the following:

> The movement called "relativism" in ethics and aesthetics is still to a large extent negative and destructive in em-

phasis. It is forced to devote the greater part of its energies to combating absolutism, the belief in fixed universal rules and standards of moral and artistic value. Through centuries of philosophical argument, supported by theology and by the natural human tendency to fixed habits and customs, the latter has become so deeply ingrained in theory and practice that it is not to be destroyed in a day. There will long be need of repeated attack upon its speciously impressive arguments, and for protest against its cramping influence in almost every field of thinking and conduct. Under these conditions relativistic theory has wisely emphasized the danger of deciding problems of valuation by appeal to any general standards, and has urged instead that each problem be dealt with afresh, in its own terms, by intelligent analysis of the special conditions involved in it. With regard to aesthetic and moral theory, it has stressed the point that social conditions are too changeable, aims and interests too diverse, every situation too different from any other, to permit of general formulas for valuation.

As usually happens with a moderate view, relativism has been carried to extremes by certain writers. They have construed it as implying a complete anarchy and utter disparity of values, a Sophistic individualism which declares each case to be entirely unique and without precedent in the history of man. No individual's experience is like any other's; no aesthetic moment is comparable to any other; valuation is merely expressing how one feels toward a thing at a particular instant; no general principles can be of the slightest validity from one case to another.

Although it is hard to disprove such views in theory, no one would dream of trying to live up to them in practice, not even their most ardent supporters. Life is too short to analyze and decide every problem from the ground up, and no sane person disregards entirely the testimony of past experience in art or other activities . . . . neither works of art, responses to them, individual tastes, nor problems of appraisal are by any means unique; each is a little different from every other, but common factors recur. Upon this fact rests all continuity of individual action, and all possibility of communicating ideas and preferences. General standards of value are, and always must be, used by every one as a means of bringing to bear the past experience of himself and others.

In so far as relativistic theory seems to ignore their necessity, and to disparage all use of them, it loses touch with facts and urges the impossible. It surrenders the field not only to blind impulse but to absolutism itself. The believers in absolutism have been active in working out principles which, though often excessively restrictive and based on false premises, have had much accumulated wisdom in them, and have performed a useful service in coordinating creative and critical effort. Unless relativism can contribute some positive aid in the use of standards, people will go on employing the old methods *faute de mieux*, and rushing when expedient to the other extreme of admitting no standards at all.

### T. MUNRO, TOWARD SCIENCE IN AESTHETICS 77–79 (1956).*

Is Ayer one of those who has taken the "moderate" doctrine of relativism to an extreme? Is Frankfurter? Or can Munro's remarks be used to defend Frankfurter's opinion in *Rochin*? Consider with respect to this question the excerpts from Munro in section 4 of this chapter.

Is Munro saying that those who reject intersubjective knowledge on the basis of its "subject"-ivity and its relativity, only have the right to reject the *kind* of knowledge "absolutism" seeks? If so, what kind of knowledge *does* "absolutism" seek? What other kind can there be?

## SECTION TWO: STICKING TO THE FACTS

### INTRODUCTORY NOTE

"The legal realist," says Lon L. Fuller, "is emphatically of those called 'tough-minded.' He loves 'things,'—things that are concrete, tangible, *anschaulich*. In Llewellyn's own words, the realists 'want law to deal, they themselves want to deal, with things, with people, with tangibles, with *definite* tangibles, and *observable* relations between definite tangibles—not with words alone; when law deals with words, they want the words to represent tangibles which can be got at beneath the words, and observable relations between those tangibles." *American Legal Realism*, 82 U.Pa.L.Rev. 429, 447 (1934). These observations, we can see, report a tendency of thought of which Ayer and the logical positivists are by no means the sole examples. It is a tendency which expresses itself not only in a demand that the objects of discussion and thought be restricted to the tangible, the concrete, the solid, and the observable. It is a tendency which also exacts requirements of the statements and ideas which report these objects. These must be "clear," "distinct," "definite," "exact," "precise," "specific," "logical." Ayer, you will recall, wishes to limit the notion of "fact" to two kinds of proposition because he "thinks that the old, the socially correct, way of speaking is logically misleading," and "that his own proposal brings out certain points more clearly." And the early Wittgenstein, in perhaps the most thoroughgoing expression of the sentiment, intoned that "Everything that can be thought at all can be thought clearly. Everything that can be put into words can be put clearly." TRACTATUS LOGICO-PHILOSOPHICUS 49–51 (D. Pears & B. McGuinness transl. 1961).

Divorced from the philosophical terms which seek to explain and justify it, it is not too difficult to recognize at least some of the evils to which this "tough-minded" or "fact-minded" tendency may be a response. Consider, for example, the observations of Jacques Barzun:

> . . . . Hokum is the counterfeit of true intellectual currency. It is words without meaning, verbal filler, artificial apples of knowledge. From the necessities of the case, nine tenths of all teaching is done with words, whence the ever-present temptation of hokum.
>
> Words should point to things, seen or unseen. But they can also be used to wrap up emptiness of heart and lack of thought. The student accepts some pompous, false, meaningless formula, and passes it back on demand, to be rewarded with—appropriately enough—a passing grade. All the dull second-rate opinions, all the definitions that don't define, all the moral platitudes that "sound good," all the conventional adjectives ("gentle Shakespeare"), all the pretenses that a teacher makes about the feelings of his students towards him and vice versa, all the intimations that something must be learned because it has somehow got lodged among learnable things (like the Binomial Theorem or the date of Magna Carta)—all this in all its form gives off the atmosphere of hokum, which healthy people everywhere find absolutely unbreathable.
>
> . . .
>
> . . . . I remember once giving a short quiz to a class of young women who had been reading about the Renaissance. I asked for some "identification" of names and put Petrarch in the list. One girl, who had evidently read a textbook, wrote down: "Petrarch—the vanguard of the new emphasis." I spent a good hour trying to explain why this parroting of opinion was not only not "correct" but blind hokum absolute. It was not an easy job because so many teachers and books deal exclusively in that cheap commodity. The child's instinct is first to believe the Word, spoken or printed; then with growing good sense to disbelieve it, but to trust to its hokum value for getting through by "satisfying" the teacher. Great heavens, what satisfactions.

TEACHER IN AMERICA 25–26 (1959)*.

Hokum, or what you will, is surely something to be avoided. But our question is whether the program of "sticking to the facts," especially as it is represented by positivism, is the way to avoid it. We can see, already, why we might want to find another way. For not only do the "fact-minded" shake a skeptical finger at ethics and aesthetics, they also cast an ominous shadow on the language and concepts of law. As Ayer says, however, he is not trying "to show . . . that the theory" he is "defending is expedient, but that it is

---

*Copyright 1944, 1945 by Jacques Barzun.

true." The "truth" of his theory, it would seem, depends to an important degree on the validity of (1) its insistence on the exclusive importance of "fact" and (2) of its conception of the nature of fact. It is to these subjects that this section is devoted. In reading it you should see whether the criticisms made are applicable to the positions adopted by either Ayer or Black's *Rochin* dissent. In what way, if any, do the criticisms support Justice Frankfurter?

### ALFRED NORTH WHITEHEAD

### MODES OF THOUGHT *

The notion of a mere fact is the triumph of the abstractive intellect. It has entered into the explicit thought of no baby and of no animal. Babies and animals are concerned with their wants as projected against the general environment. That is to say, they are immersed in their interest respecting details embedded in externality. There is the merest trace of the abstraction of the detail. A single fact in isolation is the primary myth required for finite thought, that is to say, for thought unable to embrace totality.

This mythological character arises because there is no such fact. Connectedness is of the essence of all things of all types. It is of the essence of types, that they be connected. Abstraction from connectedness involves the omission of an essential factor in the fact considered. No fact is merely itself. The penetration of literature and art at their height arises from our dumb sense that we have passed beyond mythology; namely, beyond the myth of isolation.

. . .

10. Matter-of-fact is an abstraction, arrived at by confining thought to purely formal relations which then masquerade as the final reality. This is why science, in its perfection, relapses into the study of differential equations. The concrete world has slipped through the meshes of the scientific net.

. . .

The concentration of attention upon matter-of-fact is the supremacy of the desert. Any approach to such triumph bestows on learning 'a fugitive, and a cloistered virtue', which shuns emphasis on essential connections such as disclose the universe in its impact upon individual experience.

### QUESTIONS

If Ayer were to accuse Whitehead of uttering meaningless statements, what sort of response do you think the latter might make? Would it hurt Ayer's position if he conceded that the "notion of a mere fact" is "mythological"? Incidentally, how is Whitehead using the word "mythological"? Is he accusing science of being a mythology? If "connectedness is of the essence of all things of all types,"

* From 12–13, 24–26, 27 (Capricorn ed. 1958). Copyright 1938 by The Macmillan Company, renewed 1966 by T. North Whitehead. Reprinted with permission of The Macmillan Company.

what effect will this have on the program to establish clarity, distinctness, definiteness?

*FRIEDRICH WAISMANN*

## How I See Philosophy *

. . . . There is nothing like clear thinking to protect one from making discoveries. It is all very well to talk of clarity, but when it becomes an obsession it is liable to nip the living thought in the bud. This, I am afraid, is one of the deplorable results of Logical Positivism, not foreseen by its founders, but only too striking in some of its followers. Look at these people, gripped by a clarity neurosis, haunted by fear, tongue-tied, asking themselves continually, "Oh dear, now does this make perfectly good sense?" Imagine the pioneers of science, Kepler, Newton, the discoverers of non-Euclidean geometry, of field physics, the unconscious, matter waves or heaven knows what, imagine them asking themselves this question at every step—this would have been the surest means of sapping any creative power. No great discoverer has acted in accordance with the motto, "Everything that can be said can be said clearly." And some of the greatest discoveries have even emerged from a sort of primordial fog. (Something to be said for the fog. For my part, I've always suspected that clarity is the last refuge of those who have nothing to say.)

### Questions

Why is "clarity . . . when it becomes an obsession . . . liable to nip the living thought in the bud"? What is a "living thought," anyhow? Is it a meaningful concept? Can you see why the requirement of "clarity" might discourage creative intuitions? How important are such intuitions? How often do people need to make discoveries?

*D. H. LAWRENCE*

## Studies in Classic American Literature *

. . . . Poe is rather a scientist than an artist. He is reducing his own self as a scientist reduces a salt in a crucible. It is an almost chemical analysis of the soul and consciousness. Whereas in true art there is always the double rhythm of creating and destroying.

. . .

Poe has been so praised for his style. But it seems to me a meretricious affair. "Her marble hand" and "the elasticity of her footfall" seem more like chair-springs and mantel-pieces than a human creature. She never was quite a human creature to him. She was an instrument from which he got his extremes of sensation. His *machine a plaisir*, as somebody says.

All Poe's style, moreover, has this mechanical quality, as his poetry has a mechanical rhythm. He never sees anything in terms of life, almost always in terms of matter, jewels, marble, etc.,—or in terms of force, scientific. And his cadences are all managed mechanically. This is what is called "having a style".

What he wants to do with Ligeia is to analyse her, till he knows all her component parts, till he has got her all in his consciousness. She is some strange chemical salt which he must analyse out in the test-tubes of his brain, and then—when he's finished the analysis— *E finita la commedia!*

But she won't be quite analysed out. There is something, something he can't get. Writing of her eyes, he says: "They were, I must believe, far larger than the ordinary eyes of our own race"—as if anybody would want eyes "far larger" than other folks'. "They were even fuller than the fullest of the gazelle eyes of the tribe of the valley of Nourjahad"—which is blarney. "The hue of the orbs was the most brilliant of black and, far over them, hung jetty lashes of great length"—suggests a whip-lash. "The brows, slightly irregular in outline, had the same tint. The 'strangeness', however, which I found in the eyes, was a nature distinct from the formation, or the colour, or the brilliancy of the features, and must, after all, be referred to the *expression*."—Sounds like an anatomist anatomizing a cat—"Ah, word of no meaning! behind whose vast latitude of mere sound we entrench our ignorance of so much of the spiritual. The expression of the eyes of Ligeia! How for long hours have I pondered upon it! How have I, through the whole of a midsummer night, struggled to fathom it! What was it—that something more profound than the well of Democritus—which lay far within the pupils of my beloved! What *was* it? I was possessed with a passion to discover. . . ."

It is easy to see why each man kills the thing he loves. To *know* a living thing is to kill it. You have to kill a thing to know it satisfactorily. For this reason, the desirous consciousness, the SPIRIT, is a vampire.

One should be sufficiently intelligent and interested to know a good deal about *any* person one comes into close contact with. *About* her. Or *about* him.

But to try to *know* any living being is to try to suck the life out of that being.

Above all things, with the woman one loves. Every sacred instinct teaches one that one must leave her unknown. You know your woman darkly, in the blood. To try to *know* her mentally is to try to kill her. Beware, oh woman, of the man who wants to *find out what you are*. And, oh men, beware a thousand times more of the woman who wants to *know* you, or *get* you, what you are.

It is the temptation of a vampire fiend, is this knowledge.

Man does so horribly want to master the secret of life and of individuality *with his mind*. It is like the analysis of protoplasm. You can only analyse *dead* protoplasm, and know its constituents. It is a death-process.

Keep KNOWLEDGE for the world of matter, force, and function. It has got nothing to do with being.

.  .  .

But poor Ligeia, how could she help it? It was her doom. All the centuries of the SPIRIT, all the years of American rebellion against the Holy Ghost, had done it to her.

## QUESTIONS

Can you derive Lawrence's position from that of Whitehead or of Waismann? What relation, if any, obtains among them? To what extent does the following excerpt from Bergson explain and justify the positions of these three writers? To what extent do the different writers diverge on the *cause* of the evil they attack?

### HENRI BERGSON

### CREATIVE EVOLUTION *

.  .  .  .  the intellect aims, first of all, at constructing. This fabrication is exercised exclusively on inert matter, in this sense, that even if it makes use of organized material, it treats it as inert, without troubling about the life which animated it. And of inert matter itself, fabrication deals only with the solid; the rest escapes by its very fluidity. If, therefore, the tendency of the intellect is to fabricate, we may expect to find that whatever is fluid in the real will escape it in part, and whatever is life in the living will escape it altogether. *Our intelligence, as it leaves the hands of nature, has for its chief object the unorganized solid.*

When we pass in review the intellectual functions, we see that the intellect is never quite at its ease, never entirely at home, except when it is working upon inert matter, more particularly upon solids. What is the most general property of the material world? It is extended: it presents to us objects external to other objects, and, in these objects, parts external to parts. No doubt, it is useful to us, in view of our ulterior manipulation, to regard each object as divisible into parts arbitrarily cut up, each part being again divisible as we like, and so on *ad infinitum*. But it is above all necessary, for our present manipulation, to regard the real object in hand, or the real elements into which we have resolved it, as *provisionally final*, and to treat them as so many *units*. To this possibility of decomposing matter as much as we please, and in any way we please, we allude when we speak of the *continuity* of material extension; but this continuity, as we see it, is nothing else but our ability, an ability that matter allows to us to choose the mode of discontinuity we shall find in it. It is always, in fact, the mode of discontinuity once chosen that ap-

* From 153–155, 161–165 (1911).

pears to us as the actually real one and that which fixes our attention, just because it rules our action. Thus discontinuity is thought for itself; it is thinkable in itself; we form an idea of it by a positive act of our mind; while the intellectual representation of continuity is negative, being, at bottom, only the refusal of our mind, before any actually given system of decomposition, to regard it as the only possible one. *Of the discontinuous alone does the intellect form a clear idea.*

On the other hand, the objects we act on are certainly mobile objects, but the important thing for us to know is *whither* the mobile object is going and *where* it is at any moment of its passage. In other words, our interest is directed, before all, to its actual or future positions, and not to the *progress* by which it passes from one position to another, progress which is the movement itself. In our actions, which are systematized movements, what we fix our mind on is the end or meaning of the movement, its design as a whole—in a word, the immobile plan of its execution. That which really moves in action interests us only so far as the whole can be advanced, retarded, or stopped by any incident that may happen on the way. From mobility itself our intellect turns aside, because it has nothing to gain in dealing with it. If the intellect were meant for pure theorizing, it would take its place within movement, for movement is reality itself, and immobility is always only apparent or relative. But the intellect is meant for something altogether different. Unless it does violence to itself, it takes the opposite course; it always starts from immobility, as if this were the ultimate reality: when it tries to form an idea of movement, it does so by constructing movement out of immobilities put together. This operation, whose illegitimacy and danger in the field of speculation we shall show later on (it leads to dead-locks, and creates artificially insoluble philosophical problems), is easily justified when we refer it to its proper goal. Intelligence, in its natural state, aims at a practically useful end. When it substitutes for movement immobilities put together, it does not pretend to reconstitute the movement such as it actually is; it merely replaces it with a practical equivalent. It is the philosophers who are mistaken when they import into the domain of speculation a method of thinking which is made for action. But of this more anon. Suffice it now to say that to the stable and unchangeable our intellect is attached by virtue of its natural disposition. *Of immobility alone does the intellect form a clear idea.*

. . .

. . . . all the elementary forces of the intellect tend to transform matter into an instrument of action, that is, in the etymological sense of the word, into an *organ*. Life, not content with producing organisms, would fain give them as an appendage inorganic matter itself, converted into an immense organ by the industry of the living being. Such is the initial task it assigns to intelligence. That is why the intellect always behaves as if it were fascinated by the contemplation of inert matter. It is life looking outward, putting itself outside itself, adopting the ways of unorganized nature in principle, in order to direct them in fact. Hence its bewilderment when it turns to the living and is confronted with organization. It does what it can, it resolves the organized into the unorganized, for it cannot, without reversing its natural direction and twisting about on itself, think true continuity, real mobility, reciprocal penetration—in a word, that creative evolution which is life.

Consider continuity. The aspect of life that is accessible to our intellect—as indeed to our senses, of which our intellect is the extension—is that which offers a hold to our action. Now, to modify an object, we have to perceive it as divisible and discontinuous. From the point of view of positive science, an incomparable progress was realized when the organized tissues were resolved into cells. The study of the cell, in its turn, has shown it to be an organism whose complexity seems to grow, the more thoroughly it is examined. The more science advances, the more it sees the number grow of heterogeneous elements which are placed together, outside each other, to make up a living being. Does science thus get any nearer to life? Does it not, on the contrary, find that what is really life in the living seems to recede with every step by which it pushes further the detail of the parts combined? There is indeed already among scientists a tendency to regard the substance of the organism as continuous, and the cell as an artificial entity. But, supposing this view were finally to prevail, it could only lead, on deeper study, to some other mode of analyzing of the living being, and so to a new discontinuity—although less removed, perhaps, from the real continuity of life. The truth is that this continuity cannot be thought by the intellect while it follows its natural movement. It implies at once the multiplicity of elements and the interpenetration of all by all, two conditions that can hardly be reconciled in the field in which our industry, and consequently our intellect, is engaged.

Just as we separate in space, we fix in time. The intellect is not made to think *evolution,* in the proper sense of the word—that is to say, the continuity of a change that is pure mobility. . . . [T]he intellect represents *becoming* as a series of *states,* each of which is homogeneous with itself and consequently does not change. Is our attention called to the internal change of one of these states? At once we decompose it into another series of states which, reunited, will be supposed to make up this internal modification. Each of these new states must be invariable, or else their internal change, if we are forced to notice it, must be resolved again into a fresh series of invariable states, and so on to infinity. Here again, thinking consists in reconstituting, and, naturally, it is with *given* elements, and consequently with *stable* elements, that we reconstitute. So that, though we may do our best to imitate the mobility of becoming by an addition that is ever going on, becoming itself slips through our fingers just when we think we are holding it tight.

Precisely because it is always trying to reconstitute, and to reconstitute with what is given, the intellect lets what is *new* in each moment of a history escape. It does not admit the unforeseeable. It rejects all creation. That definite antecedents bring forth a definite consequent, calculable as a function of them, is what satisfies our intellect. That a definite end calls forth definite means to attain

it, is what we also understand.  In both cases we have to do with
the known which is combined with the known, in short, with the
old which is repeated.  Our intellect is there at its ease; and, whatever be the object, it will abstract, separate, eliminate, so as to substitute for the object itself, if necessary, an approximate equivalent
in which things will happen in this way.  But that each instant is a
fresh endowment, that the new is ever upspringing, that the form
just come into existence (although, *when once produced*, it may be
regarded as an effect determined by its causes) could never have
been foreseen—because the causes here, unique in their kind, are part
of the effect, have come into existence with it, and are determined by
it as much as they determine it—all this we can feel within ourselves and also divine, by sympathy, outside ourselves, but we cannot
think it, in the strict sense of the word, nor express it in terms of pure
understanding.  No wonder at that: we must remember what our
intellect is meant for.  The causality it seeks and finds everywhere
expresses the very mechanism of our industry, in which we go on re-
composing the same whole with the same parts, repeating the same
movements to obtain the same result.  The finality it understands
best is the finality of our industry, in which we work on a model given
in advance, that is to say, old or composed of elements already
known.  As to invention properly so called, which is, however, the
point of departure of industry itself, our intellect does not succeed
in grasping it in its *upspringing*, that is to say, in its indivisibility,
nor in its *fervor*, that is to say, in its creativeness.  Explaining it
always consists in resolving it, it the unforeseeable and new, into
elements old or known, arranged in a different order.  The intellect
can no more admit complete novelty than real becoming; that is to
say, here again it lets an essential aspect of life escape, as if it were
not intended to think such an object.

All our analyses bring us to this conclusion.  But it is hardly
necessary to go into such long details concerning the mechanism of
intellectual working; it is enough to consider the results.  We see
that the intellect, so skilful in dealing with the inert, is awkward the
moment it touches the living.  Whether it wants to treat the life of
the body or the life of the mind, it proceeds with the rigor, the stiffness and the brutality of an instrument not designed for such use.
The history of hygiene or of pedagogy teaches us much in this matter.  When we think of the cardinal, urgent and constant need we
have to preserve our bodies and to raise our souls, of the special facilities given to each of us, in this field, to experiment continually
on ourselves and on others, of the palpable injury by which the
wrongness of a medical or pedagogical practise is both made manifest
and punished at once, we are amazed at the stupidity and especially
at the persistence of errors.  We may easily find their origin in the
natural obstinacy with which we treat the living like the lifeless and
think all reality, however fluid, under the form of the sharply defined
solid.  We are at ease only in the discontinuous, in the immobile, in
the dead.  *The intellect is characterized by a natural inability to comprehend life.*

NOTE

For a critique of the attitudes attacked by Whitehead, Waismann, Lawrence and Bergson which argues that they are irrational, because ultimately self-destructive, attitudes see N. BROWN, LIFE AGAINST DEATH 157, 158, 173–76, 234–39 (1959).

*ERNST CASSIRER*

THE LOGIC OF THE HUMANITIES *

. . . . The world which the self encounters is in the one case a thing-world and in the other a person-world. In the one case, we observe it as a completely spacial object and as the sum total of temporal transformations which complete themselves in this object; whereas, in the other case, we observe it as if it were something "like ourselves." In both cases the otherness persists; but this very fact reveals a characteristic difference. The "it" is an absolute other, an *aliud*; the "you" is an *alter ego*. There can be no mistaking the fact that, always, as we move in the one direction or the other, perception takes on a different significance for us and a distinctive coloring and tone, as it were.

That human beings experience reality in this double mode is unmistakable and indisputable. This is a matter of simple fact which no theory can throw into doubt or annihilate. Why is it so difficult for theory to admit this? Why has theory attempted again and again not only to resort to abstraction from this fact—this is thoroughly justified in point of method—but also to deny and betray it? We discover the basis for this anomaly when we become fully aware of the tendency which all theorizing derives from its origin and which increases in strength as theory advances. This tendency consists, not, to be sure, in completely suppressing, but in limiting one of these factors of perception—forever reclaiming more territory from its opposite. All theoretical explanation finds itself in opposition to another spiritual force—the force of myth. In order to protect themselves against this force, philosophy and science are obliged not only to replace particular mythical explanations but to do battle with the whole mythical interpretation of existence and to reject it *in toto*. It must not only attack the products and configurations of myth but must attack its root.

. . . . Science constructs a world in which expression-qualities—the "characteristics" of the trustworthy, or the fruitful, the friendly or the terrifying—are initially replaced with pure *sense qualities*, with colors, tones, and the like. And even these must be still further reduced. They are only "secondary" properties, based on primary properties, i. e., purely quantitative determinations. These primary properties constitute for cognition all that remains as objective reality. This is the conclusion drawn by physics. And, to

* From 93–94, 95, 101 (C. Howe transl. 1960). Reprinted with permission of Yale University Press.

the extent that philosophy holds to no other testimony than that of physics, it can go no further. . . .

.  .  .  .

It is often held, as an all but self-evident assumption, in need of no further proof, that all entities immediately accessible to knowledge are determinate physical data. In which case, the sensuously given— color, sound, feelings of touch and temperature, smell, and taste—are the only things capable of immediate experience. All else, especially spiritual existence, may indeed be implied by this primary data, but for this very reason it remains uncertain. Yet phenomenological analysis is far from substantiating this assumption. Neither functional nor genetic observation justifies us in giving sense perception primacy over expression-perception. With regard to the purely genetic account, ontogeny as well as phylogeny—the development of consciousness in the individual as well as in the species—shows us that the very data which, above all, were thought to be the starting points of all knowledge of reality, are relatively late products and that a grueling and lengthy process of abstraction is necessary in order to draw them out from the whole of human experience. The perception of "things" and "thing qualities" comes into its own only much later. It is *language*, above all, that first turns the tide. For the capacity for objective representation grows in direct ratio as we [begin to] give linguistic expression to our experience of the world, instead of only experiencing it through passive impressions.

ERNST CASSIRER

AN ESSAY ON MAN *

.  .  .  . we may say that what myth primarily perceives are not objective but *physiognomic* characters. Nature, in its empirical or scientific sense, may be defined as "the existence of things as far as it is determined by general laws." Such a "nature" does not exist for myth. The world of myth is a dramatic world—a world of actions, of forces, of conflicting powers. In every phenomenon of nature it sees the collision of these powers. Mythical perception is always impregnated with these emotional qualities. Whatever is seen or felt is surrounded by a special atmosphere—an atmosphere of joy or grief, of anguish, of excitement, of exultation or depression. Here we cannot speak of "things" as a dead or indifferent stuff. All objects are benignant or malignant, friendly or inimical, familiar or uncanny, alluring and fascinating or repellent and threatening. We can easily reconstruct this elementary form of human experience, for even in the life of the civilized man it has by no means lost its original power. If we are under the strain of a violent emotion we have still this dramatic conception of all things. They no longer wear their usual faces; they abruptly change their physiognomy; they are tinged with the specific color of our passions, of love and hate, of fear or hope.

* From 76–78 (1944). Reprinted with
permission of Yale University Press.

There can scarcely be a greater contrast than between this original direction of our experience and the ideal of truth that is introduced by science. . . . In our scientific concepts we reduce the difference between two colors, let us say red and blue, to a numeric difference. But it is a very inadequate way of speaking if we declare number to be more real than color. What is really meant is that it is more general. The mathematical expression gives us a new and more comprehensive view, a freer and larger horizon of knowledge. But to hypostatize number as did the Pythagoreans, to speak of it as the ultimate reality, the very essence and substance of things, is a metaphysical fallacy. If we argue upon this methodological and epistemological principle even the lowest stratum of our sense experience—the stratum of our "feeling-qualities"—appears in a new light. The world of our sense perceptions, of the so-called "secondary qualities," is in an intermediate position. It has abandoned and overcome the first rudimentary stage of our physiognomic experience, without having reached that form of generalization that is attained in our scientific concepts—our concepts of the physical world. But all these three stages have their definite functional value. None of them is a mere illusion; every one is, in its measure, a step on our way to reality.

The best and clearest statement of this problem has to my mind been given by John Dewey. He was one of the first to recognize and to emphasize the relative right of those feeling-qualities which prove their full power in mythical perception and which are here regarded as the basic elements of reality. It was precisely his conception of the task of a genuine empiricism that led him to this conclusion. "Empirically," says Dewey,

> things are poignant, tragic, beautiful, humorous, settled, disturbed, comfortable, annoying, barren, harsh, consoling, spendid, fearful; are such immediately and in their own right and behalf. . . . These traits stand in themselves on precisely the same level as colors, sounds, qualities of contact, taste and smell. Any criterion that finds the latter to be ultimate and "hard" data will, impartially applied, come to the same conclusion about the former. *Any* quality as such is final; it is at once initial and terminal; just what it is as it exists. It may be referred to other things, it may be treated as an effect or as a sign. But this involves an extraneous extension and use. It takes us beyond quality in its immediate qualitativeness. . . . The surrender of immediate qualities, sensory and significant, as objects of science, and as proper forms of classification and understanding, left in reality these immediate qualities just as they were; since they are *had* there is no need to *know* them. But . . . the traditional view that the object of knowledge is reality *par excellence* led to the conclusion that the object of science was preeminently metaphysically real. Hence, immediate qualities, being extended from the object of science, were left thereby hanging loose from the "real" object. Since their *existence* could not be denied, they were gathered together into a psychic realm of being, set over

against the object of physics. Given this premise, all the problems regarding the relation of mind and matter, the psychic and the bodily, necessarily follow. Change the metaphysical premise; restore, that is to say, immediate qualities to their rightful position as qualities of inclusive situations, and the problems in question cease to be epistemological problems. They become specifiable scientific problems; questions, that is to say, of how such and such an event having such and such qualities actually occurs.

WOLFGANG KOHLER

THE PLACE OF VALUE IN A WORLD OF FACTS *

We should not lose sight of the fact that some philosophers have never been satisfied by theories which localize all value in the self. One reason for it may be that, besides those meanings which I have mentioned, the unfortunate word "objective" has still a third connotation in which it is nearly equivalent to "valid." Convinced that ethics should be a system of strictly *valid* rules these theorists would prefer an objectivistic interpretation of value since "objective" means "outside of us," "independent" and "valid" all at the same time. What is objective phenomenally exhibits, indeed, more steadiness on the average than does the everchanging stream of our subjective life. Besides there seems to be less variability among the objective fields of different people than among their subjective interests and tendencies. I doubt, however, whether this is the only motive of those who insist upon an objectivistic theory of requiredness. . . .

. . . . Charm is a special value-quality; so is loveliness and womanliness. Tell an unsophisticated young man who is very much in love that the object of the case has only neutral properties, and that to speak about her charm is just a synonym for the fact that he is in love. You will hear what he answers. Again, if you make the corresponding observation to a belligerent reactionary who declares that socialism and socialists are bad, he will emphatically refuse to accept the theory that without his hostile interest a socialist is a neutral object. No, he would say, these people themselves are bad. I may go farther and say that we find the same objectivistic conviction everywhere and exemplified in all possible varieties of value. This observation at least raises the question why, if the contrary is true, practically all mankind should not be able to see this simple truth, why they should hold precisely the opposite view, namely that the diverse forms of value are inherent in the objects. It seems to me, by the way, that such apparent objectivity of values is of the very greatest practical importance. It would be ever so much easier to convince somebody that he is on the wrong track, if he could realize that value is equivalent to valuing i. e., only an act of his own. But often he will be much too excited for such a conversion because the bad or the

* From  76,  77–79,  80–82,  83  (1938).    Kohler.  Reprinted with permission of
Copyright renewed 1966 by Wolfgang    Liveright Publishing Company.

great, the mean or the noble, are so clearly before his eyes. And now you, his opponent, pretend that you cannot see what is so obviously there. How blind or stubborn you must be! Is not this our experience almost daily, for instance, in political discussion?

Personally I understand this objectivistic attitude of the layman very well because I find myself exactly in his position. That face looks mean—and I abhor it. Dignity I hear in those words which I have just heard Mr. X. speaking—and I respect him. Her gait is clumsy—and I prefer to look away. Everywhere value-qualities are found residing in such objects as characteristics of them.

If this is true, there are, it seems, three possible interpretations: Just as objects are round or tall, events slow or sudden, so some have charm, some are ugly by themselves, independently. In this case the subjectivistic theory of value would appear to be at least incomplete. Again, if and in so far as interest of any kind is taken in an object, it *acquires* new concrete qualities, viz., value-qualities. This might mean an amplification or completion of the subjectivistic theory. And thirdly: Besides the self and its interests, other factors in a field could perhaps, also by a vectorial influence of some kind, create value-properties in certain objects. In this case, as in the first, the subjectivistic theory of value would be revealed as one-sided.

As to the first possibility I do not see any reason why such "tertiary qualities" should not occur on the objective side of the phenomenal field. Most arguments which have been brought forward against their truly perceptual existence seem to be influenced by the ineradicable tendency which we have to take percepts as pictures of physical realities, if not as somehow identical with them. But no physical sequence of tones has the "minor"-quality. Still, "minor" is an objective property of certain objective auditory events. That the basis of all argument about such questions has been essentially changed by von Ehrenfels and by Gestalt psychology is sufficiently known at present. . . .

. . . . As to the second interpretation it is the path which the subjectivistic theory should follow if, confronted with ample evidence of objective value-attributes, it wishes to preserve its own character. These, the theory would have to say, are products of our acts of interest. And doubtless there are such cases. Even to be a goal in general seems to give a thing a new flavor. Not only is it the end, the terminating part of a circumscribed context, comparable to the edge-quality which a line assumes when a closed figure stands out from the ground. It also begins to dominate in the objective region of the field, to become its center, however unimportant, visually for instance, it would be otherwise. . . .

. . . . After many hours on skis in a sharp frost we come home, and before us there is brown, hot, fat meat just brought in from the kitchen. Can anything look more appetizing than this meat? This is when we are hungry. A short time afterwards—we have eaten too much and too hastily—it may be difficult for us even to stay near by when precisely the same kind of meat is put upon the table for late-comers. It does not look neutral now, it looks decidely repulsive. . . .

So far we are in agreement with Professor Perry. "That feeling," he says, "does somehow color its object is an undeniable fact of experience, and a fact recognized by common speech in so far as all of the familiar feelings assume the form of adjectives." But he is not inclined to accept this objective aspect of interest as genuine: We cannot possibly localize the red of an object in our self; this is therefore a truly objective quality. The "tertiary qualities" on the other hand yield, he believes, to an effort of attention. When we try hard enough we find them separating from the object and tending to unite with the self.

I am afraid that with this argument we approach the procedure of Introspectionism. To the Introspectionist certain phenomena appear as surprising and therefore suspect. In such cases he asks attention to help him find the real sensations. Perhaps attention is successful, in so far as the disturbing fact disappears. Supposing that the change be in the direction of a more customary phenomenon, the Introspectionist will now say that he has found the real fact. More and more psychologists are becoming convinced that they are not entitled to apply this procedure. If, in an analytical attitude, I find an over-tone in a clang which before was phenomenally a completely unitary sound, then my analysis has not corrected an error, an illusion; it has changed one genuine phenomenon into another. Again, if I direct my attention upon some happy feeling in order to find out what it is really like, the chances are that I shall destroy the feeling. All "tertiary qualities," too, may be treated in this way and some of them thus changed or destroyed. But it does not follow that their previous existence was in any sense illusory. That some qualities, e. g., colors, will often show more resistance than many "tertiary qualities" does not decide the point. A bar of steel is not destroyed when we beat it with a hammer, china is. Still china is as real as steel. We might in fact almost deduce from the theory the consequence that such "tertiary qualities" should change or disappear, if we look upon them long enough with the cold scrutiny of scientific analysis. Supposedly they are the objective-looking correlates of definite interest-attitudes. Instead of these we introduce the attitude of sober analysis. From the standpoint of the theory it would be surprising if they should remain unaltered under these circumstances.

But, in this last argument, I may be misrepresenting the theory. "It seems necessary," Professor Perry says, "at some point to admit that the qualities of feeling may be referred where they do not belong." From the point of view of phenomenology I cannot agree. Qualities belong where we find them. And no explanation or theory can convince us that they were not where we found them,—even if it should prove possible to shift them to another place under changed conditions of subjective attitude. The question of their origin is not the question of their present location. The main point, however, is that according to this theory the "tertiary qualities" are said to be misplaced facts of subjective interest. If this were correct, there should be agreement between the "tertiary qualities" and the qualities of those interests which are directed towards the objects in question. That this should be the case in general I find it hard to admit. The charm, womanliness and loveliness which may be found in certain objects are qualitatively altogether different from the present striving of the (male) self, but also from all other interests or conations which he may have at other times. If a face looks brutally stupid, this would be a "tertiary quality" of the negative kind. Certainly the contempt and aversion with which I look upon that face do not show much similarity to this value-quality. Finally may we take a case where the "tertiary quality" is undoubtedly a product of the interest: The goal-character of any object of positive striving is not similar to the striving itself. Therefore it cannot be interpreted as misplaced striving.

. . .

Against the subjectivistic theory the criticism has been raised by Professor Urban that it is circular, as all other forms of relational theory of value are. It describes what happens in value-situations but does not give a definition of value; it actually presupposes the existence of value. It seems to me that the task of a theory of value does not necessarily consist in the reduction of requiredness to something else. In this sense, I think, a definition of value would be impossible. The only thing we can do is to bring into full view the characteristics of a value-situation. When these have been uncovered it becomes possible to see them in their relation to other phenomena, and thus to include the concept of requiredness in a larger theoretical structure. . . .

NOTE: FACT AND AGREEMENT

1. Do you agree that "human beings experience reality" in the "double mode" of which Cassirer speaks? What does he mean that it "is a matter of simple fact which no theory can throw into doubt or annihilate"? Is this an argument or an assertion? If the latter, can its use nevertheless be justified? How do you think Cassirer is using the word "fact"? As a synonym for that which "is unmistakable and indisputable"? For that which "no theory can throw into doubt or annihilate"? Of what other phenomena can these characteristics be predicated? Can they be predicated of material objects, events, colors, sounds? Is Cassirer saying that his "double mode" of observation is as much a fact as the perception of these things? Is he saying that "expression-perception" is as much a fact as "thing-perception"?

Recall Lucas's equation of facts (Chapter 6) with that on which people agree. Are the "expression-perceptions" we experience ever agreed upon? Do we ever agree that a face is ugly, revolting, friendly? Do we ever agree that an action is graceful, sudden, threatening, funny? Is it possible that many would agree with Frankfurter that the actions of the police in *Rochin* were shocking and brutal? Would this agreement be enough to make these "qualities" facts for Ayer? Or are they not facts because they point to no additional "detail" of a "factual" situation? Or because they are not logically necessary? Are they not facts because even if they do point to an additional detail that detail cannot be equated with the "quality"? If, for example, we isolate that portion of a situation which makes it funny, would Ayer argue that the existence of this feature does not establish that one ought to laugh?

Recurring to the more conventional expressions of logical positivism, is a statement about "tertiary" qualities "verifiable" by observation? Even if such a statement is verifiable by observation is it nevertheless too different from statements about "secondary" or "primary" qualities? Is the problem that one cannot state the conditions under which a proposition regarding "tertiary" qualities would be true? Is this a matter of concern to Ayer? To Justice Black? Is it also a requirement of "factuality"—and of cognitivity— that one be able to point to, and engender agreement on, the component conditions which make a statement true? Is this part of the difficulty with Justice Frankfurter's opinion? Is this why it would not be enough—and his unwillingness to invoke a rule indicates *he* thinks it would not be enough—to state that governmental action against individuals violates due process when it shocks the conscience and it shocks the conscience when it is brutal and an affront to human dignity? Are statements regarding "secondary" qualities reducible to statements about component conditions? Is a statement about color? About movement? About smell? What about a statement such as, "I am sitting on a chair"? Is this statement factual because we can reduce it to separate statements about "I", "am", "sitting", "on", "a", "chair"? Can the conditions which establish the truth of "I" (i. e., that it is indeed *me* who is sitting on the chair) be stated? Of "am" or "on" or "a"? What about "chair"? Is it an adequate rejoinder to a statement which presumes to be factual that it cannot be verified by reducing it to its conditions?

If "expression-perception" is a "matter of simple fact which no theory can throw into doubt or annihilate," does this mean that an adequate theory of fact must take it into account? Does Ayer's theory of fact do this? Does Lucas's?

Would a theory which included physical facts and mythic facts also have to include ethical and legal facts? Recall the remarks of Frank, reprinted in Chapter 8, Section 2(a):

> . . . . judges, like juries, usually have composite, undifferentiated reactions to the evidence.

> . . . . whatever is said in opinions, the judge often arrives at his decision before he tries to explain it. . . . After the judge has so decided, then the judge writes his "opinion." The D has been fixed. The judge's problem is now to find an R and an F that will equal this already-determined D.

How is it possible for a judge to decide a case before he determines what the "facts" and the "rules" are? Does he simply perceive the conduct described to him as illegal, as "in violation of the anti-trust laws," as "negligence," etc.? In an unexcerpted part of his article, Frank reports:

> . . . . A member of an upper court once told me that the chief justice said to him after the oral argument of a case, "We'll have to lick that plaintiff somehow and it's up to you to find some theory and authorities that will help us do it."

*What Courts Do In Fact*, 26 Ill.L.Rev. 645, 655 (1932). Assuming that the chief justice had no personal interest in the case, why would he *want* to lick the plaintiff? Because he knew of some *moral* rule that had been violated? Is that the only possible explanation? Consider also the following from Frank:

> . . . . Chancellor Kent . . . explained that in arriving at a judicial decision he first made himself "master of the facts." That done, he wrote, "I saw where justice lay, and the moral sense decided the court half the time."

Why did Kent, do you think, find it necessary to "master . . . the facts"? What does mastering the facts involve? How was it that he "saw" where justice lay? Is this the sort of thing one can "see"? Why, if it isn't, do you think that Kent chose that figure of speech? Why does he speak of "the moral sense"? Is there such a thing? What is Kent *trying* to say? Is he just euphemistically describing a "gut reaction"? Or is there some way of justifying his method of decision?

2. To what extent can it be said that Ayer's theory of knowledge is concerned with the phenomenon of agreement in human life? Could it be said that the logical positivists have staked out for themselves that realm of thought and experience in which agreement is most pronounced and dramatic? Can the issue between Ayer and Lucas be reduced to a difference over the importance of the agreement found in other areas?

KARL R. POPPER

CONJECTURES AND REFUTATIONS *

I approached the problem of induction through Hume. Hume, I felt, was perfectly right in pointing out that induction cannot be logically justified. He held that there can be no valid logical arguments allowing us to establish *'that those instances, of which we have had no experience, resemble those, of which we have had experience'*. Consequently, *'even after the observation of the frequent or constant conjunction of objects, we have no reason to draw any inference concerning any object beyond those of which we have had experience'*. For 'shou'd it be said that we have experience'—experience teaching us that objects constantly conjoined with certain other objects con-

* From 42–47 (Rev. ed. 1965). Copyright © 1963, 1965 by Karl Popper,        Basic Books, Inc. Publishers, New York.

tinue to be so conjoined—then, Hume says, 'I wou'd renew my question, *why from this experience we form any conclusion beyond those past instances, of which we have had experience*'. In other words, an attempt to justify the practice of induction by an appeal to experience must lead to an *infinite regress*. As a result we can say that theories can never be inferred from observation statements, or rationally justified by them.

I found Hume's refutation of inductive inference clear and conclusive. But I felt completely dissatisfied with his psychological explanation of induction in terms of custom or habit.

.   .   .   .

.   .   .   . There are decisive arguments of a *purely logical* nature against his psychological theory.

The central idea of Hume's theory is that of *repetition, based upon similarity* (or 'resemblance'). This idea is used in a very uncritical way. We are led to think of the water-drop that hollows the stone: of sequences of unquestionably like events slowly forcing themselves upon us, as does the tick of the clock. But we ought to realize that in a psychological theory such as Hume's, only repetition-for-us, based upon similarity-for-us, can be allowed to have any effect upon us. We must respond to situations as if they were equivalent; *take* them as similar; *interpret* them as repetitions.   .   .   .

This apparent psychological criticism has a purely logical basis which may be summed up in the following simple argument. (It happens to be the one from which I originally started my criticism.) The kind of repetition envisaged by Hume can never be perfect; the cases he has in mind cannot be cases of perfect sameness; they can only be cases of similarity. Thus *they are repetitions only from a certain point of view*. (What has the effect upon me of a repetition may not have this effect upon a spider.) But this means that, for logical reasons, there must always be a point of view—such as a system of expectations, anticipations, assumptions, or interests—*before* there can be any repetition; which point of view, consequently, cannot be merely the result of repetition. (See now also appendix *x, (1), to my *L.Sc.D.*)

.   .   .   .

To put it more concisely, similarity-for-us is the product of a response involving interpretations (which may be inadequate) and anticipations or expectations (which may never be fulfilled). It is therefore impossible to explain anticipations, or expectations, as resulting from many repetitions, as suggested by Hume. For even the first repetition-for-us must be based upon similarity-for-us, and therefore upon expectations—precisely the kind of thing we wished to explain.

This shows that there is an infinite regress involved in Hume's psychological theory.

.   .   .   .

Thus I was led by purely logical considerations to replace the psychological theory of induction by the following view. Without waiting, passively, for repetitions to impress or impose regularities upon us, we actively try to impose regularities upon the world. We try to discover similarities in it, and to interpret it in terms of laws invented by us. Without waiting for premises we jump to conclusions. These may have to be discarded later, should observation show that they are wrong.

This was a theory of trial and error—of *conjectures and refutations*. It made it possible to understand why our attempts to force interpretations upon the world were logically prior to the observation of similarities. Since there were logical reasons behind this procedure, I thought that it would apply in the field of science also; that scientific theories were not the digest of observations, but that they were inventions—conjectures boldly put forward for trial, to be eliminated if they clash with observations; with observations which were rarely accidental but as a rule undertaken with the definite intention of testing a theory by obtaining, if possible, a decisive refutation.

The belief that science proceeds from observation to theory is still so widely and so firmly held that my denial of it is often met with incredulity. I have even been suspected of being insincere—of denying what nobody in his senses can doubt.

But in fact the belief that we can start with pure observations alone, without anything in the nature of a theory, is absurd; as may be illustrated by the story of the man who dedicated his life to natural science, wrote down everything he could observe, and bequeathed his priceless collection of observations to the Royal Society to be used as inductive evidence. This story should show us that though beetles may profitably be collected, observations may not.

Twenty-five years ago I tried to bring home the same point to a group of physics students in Vienna by beginning a lecture with the following instructions: 'Take pencil and paper; carefully observe, and write down what you have observed!' They asked, of course, *what* I wanted them to observe. Clearly the instruction, 'Observe!' is absurd. (It is not even idiomatic, unless the object of the transitive verb can be taken as understood.) Observation is always selective. It needs a chosen object, a definite task, an interest, a point of view, a problem. And its description presupposes a descriptive language, with property words; it presupposes similarity and classification, which in its turn presupposes interests, points of view, and problems. 'A hungry animal', writes Katz, 'divides the environment into edible and inedible things. An animal in flight sees roads to escape and hiding places. . . . Generally speaking, objects change . . . according to the needs of the animal.' We may add that objects can be classified, and can become similar or dissimilar, *only* in this way— by being related to needs and interests. This rule applies not only to animals but also to scientists. For the animal a point of view is provided by its needs, the task of the moment, and its expectations; for the scientist by his theoretical interests, the special problem under investigation, his conjectures and anticipations, and the theories which he accepts as a kind of background: his frame of reference, his 'horizon of expectations.'

## NOTE: SIMILARITY, FACT, AND VALUE

Is the problem of similarity perhaps even more troublesome than Popper here recognizes? If the way we classify a particular object depends upon a given task, interest, point of view or problem, it remains to be explained how this phenomenon of classification actually occurs. Let us take an apple and a pear. Are they the same or different? The answer, apparently, is that it depends. If some one asks us for an apple, then they are different. If, instead, we are asked for a piece of fruit, they are the same. In the first instance, these two "things" do not come within the same classification. In the second instance they do. But what is it that brings them within the same classification? The usual answer is: these two admittedly different things have certain properties in common. Sometimes these common properties are important for some purpose or from some point of view. When this occurs they are said to be similar. But what are these so-called "common" properties? What is it for a property to be common to more than one object? It would not be argued that the properties of Thing I and of Thing II are identical. But if they are not identical, then apparently they are only similar. And if they are only similar, we have only replaced our initial problem of similarity with a new one.

The point can be made more vividly with another example. What is it that two faces have in common? One might answer, two eyes, a nose, a mouth, a chin, two ears, two cheeks, a forehead, etc. But what does it mean to say that the faces have these features "in common"? They do not *share* the same features. The only thing they share is the *name* of the features. And this can be quite misleading. For when we look, for example, at the two noses, what is it that justifies calling them by the same name? Again, it might be answered, they both have two nostrils, are stationed above the mouth, etc. But this only pushes our regress another step back. For we can now ask, *inter alia*, why these obviously different orifices are called nostrils. The point is, that the closer we look the less sure we are that two objects that are allegedly similar have *anything* in common, no matter what the purpose.

This would seem to leave us with the alternatives of either (1) rejecting the notion of similarity and affirming that everything really is different in every way from everything else (the consequences of which will be left to your imaginations), or (2) rejecting the conventional explanation of the phenomenon of similarity. A way out that has already been seen in this section might be to argue that similarity is itself one of those irreducible facts which cannot be further analyzed. It is a quality which cannot be reduced to its component parts or conditions. Can you see why this might be viewed as a way out? Can you see why it might be viewed as no way at all?

We can see, in any event, that if we wish to adhere to our faith in similarity it has every right to be considered a phenomenon. And

even if it cannot be rigorously explained there are additional remarkable things to be said about it. For example, we may no longer
wish to say that an object is an instance of a class if it satisfies the
conditions which define the class. But this by itself does not preclude
us from viewing the similarity of two objects as dependent upon a
point of view or their utility to achieve a specific task. What are the
consequences of such a view? Is it plausible to say that if they are
similar they are both *good* for the particular job? That one *ought*
to employ them if one wants to get that particular job done? In
other words, to say that an object is a chair—is to say something
about its value. It is, in effect, to evaluate it. In this sense, is not
every statement of fact a "value judgment"? Can you see why?
Or is this whole line of reasoning unacceptable to you? If so, can
you state the reason? If not, what bearing does it have on the validity
of Ayer's thesis? If Ayer were to concede the evaluative character
of factual statements, could he still argue that moral judgments are
not factual? How would such an argument proceed?

*ERNST CASSIRER*

## THE LOGIC OF THE HUMANITIES *

. . . . Strict "physicalism" not only declares all proofs
which have been advanced for the existence of "other selves" to be
unattainable or invalid; it has even denied that it makes any sense
to ask questions concerning a world other than that of the "it"—a
world of the "you." Thus, not only the answer but even the question
is mythical rather than philosophical and must hence be eradicated
without compromise.

. . .

. . . . It is certain that knowledge of physical things
constitutes the foundation and substratum for every other construction of this kind. There is no purely "ideal entity" that can dispense
with this support. The ideal exists only insofar as it presents itself
sensuously and materially in some manner and embodies itself in
this presentation. Religion, language, art—these are never intelligible for us except in the monuments which they themselves have
produced. They are the tokens, memorials, and reminders in which
alone a religious, linguistic, or artistic meaning can be captured. This
very embodiment constitutes the locus in which we come to know
the cultural object.

Like every other object, an object of culture has its place in space
and time. It has its here-and-now. It comes to be and passes away.
Insofar as we describe this here-and-now, this coming-to-be and pass-
ing-away, we have no need to go beyond the sphere of physical determinants. But, on the other hand, in this description even the
physical itself is seen in a new *function*. It not only "is" and "be-

* From 96, 97–100 (C. Howe transl.
1960). Reprinted with permission of
Yale University Press.

comes"; for in this being and becoming something else "emerges." What emerges is a "meaning," which is not absorbed by what is merely physical, but is embodied upon and within it; it is the factor common to all that content which we designate as "culture." To be sure, nothing prevents us from *ignoring* this factor, making us blind to its "symbolic value" through such a leaving-out and overlooking mode of abstraction. We can focus attention upon the composition of the marble of Michelangelo's *David*; we can look upon Raphael's *The School of Athens* as nothing but a canvas covered with flecks of color of determinate quality and spacial arrangement. At such a moment the work has become a thing among things and knowledge of it is subject to the same conditions that hold for any other space-time existent [*Dasein*]. But the moment we become absorbed in the *presentation* and abandon ourselves to it, the difference has emerged once again.

But always we discern in a work of art two fundamental factors, which constitute the whole of the work only by means of their union and interpenetration. The colors in Raphael's painting have a "presentation-function" only insofar as they suggest an object. Here we do not lose ourselves in sheer observation of the colors; we do not see them *as* colors; instead, it is through these colors that we see what is objective—a definite scene, a conversation between two philosophers. But even what is objective in this sense is not the unique, the true subject matter of the painting. The painting is not merely the presentation of an historical scene, a conversation between Plato and Aristotle. For in reality it is not Plato and Aristotle who speak to us here but Raphael himself. These three dimensions—the physical thereness [*Dasein*], the object-presentation, and the evidence of a unique personality—are determining and indispensable in anything that is a genuine "work" ["*Werk*"] and not merely a "result" ["*Wirkung*"] and of all that in this sense belongs not only to "nature" but also to "culture." The exclusion of one of these three dimensions, confinement within a single plane of observation, always yields only a surface image of culture, revealing none of its genuine depth.

Strict positivism is given to denying this depth because it is afraid of losing itself in its obscurity. And it must be admitted that, when one compares expression-perception with thing-perception, an extraordinary difficulty and inconceivability appears to be inherent to expression-perception. But this inconceivability does not exist for the naive world view. Without reserve it entrusts itself to the study of expression and feels completely at home with it. No theoretical argument can shake it in its conviction.

But all this changes as soon as reflection begins to concern itself with the problem. All logical "proofs" for the existence of other selves which have been pursued in the history of philosophy have failed and all psychological explanations that have been given are uncertain and questionable. It is not hard to see through the defect of these proofs and explanations. Skepticism is always able to find the weak point against which to launch its attacks. In the second edition of the *Critique of Pure Reason* Kant added a special refutation

of "psychological idealism."  By means of this refutation he was
determined, as he said, to remove from "philosophy and common
human reason the scandal" of being forced to accept the existence
of external things merely on faith.  This scandal becomes all the more
violent when we turn from the question of external things to that
of other subjects.  Indeed, metaphysical dogmatists—themselves opposed to it, but unable to explain it—have become convinced that at
this point the skeptical arguments are decisive; they have regarded
this doubt as irrefutable, though obviously untenable.  Schopenhauer
says that theoretical egoism which holds all appearances external to
oneself to be mere phantoms can be refuted by countless arguments.

But anyone convinced of this in all seriousness is to be found
only in an insane asylum: in which case, what is needed is not so
much a proof as a cure.  Here, to be sure, solipsism may be viewed as
a small frontier fortress, which may prove increasingly invincible, but
whose garrison is absolutely unable to get out, and which we may
pass and turn our backs on without danger.  But philosophy is surely
in an unsatisfactory state of affairs, if it must appeal here to "healthy
minds" in order to criticize and keep under control what is otherwise
one of its supreme tasks.

It is clear that the process of substantiation cannot go on into
infinity, that at last we must strike on something that is not deductive-
ly demonstrable but which can only be pointed out.  This holds as
well for knowledge of one's own ego as of knowledge of the external
world.  Even the *cogito ergo sum* is, as Descartes emphasized again
and again, no formal argument but a purely intuitive cognition.  In
the area of the really basic problems we cannot leave sole authority
to reflection.  Here we must fall back on sources of knowledge of a
different and more original kind.  What must be demanded is that
the phenomena give rise to no internal contradictions, once we have
moved them into the clear light of reflection, that they harmonize
with each other.  But this requirement is certainly not fulfilled if the
"natural" view of the world irresistibly forces us to the argument
that theory itself must be defined as senseless or as absolutely incapable of being grounded.

## NOTES AND QUESTIONS

1.  In the sense in which Cassirer is using the term, could it be
said that the moral description of Ayer's criminal fact situation is
the "meaning" of that situation?  Or, at least, that it is the *moral*
meaning of the situation?  Would Ayer require us to talk of *The
School of Athens* as "a canvas covered with flecks of color of determinate quality and special arrangement"?  What does it add to the
factual description of this paint-and-canvas phenomenon to say it
is a picture of "a definite scene, a conversation between two philosophers"?

How far can Cassirer's notion of meaning be extended?  Would
it be accurate to view a chair as the meaning of its parts and components?  Or as the meaning of the sense data which contribute to
the effect "chair"?  Does it add anything to the description of these

sense data to call them a "chair"? Does the notion of chair have any independent function or refer to any isolable detail in the phenomenon so described? Consider the following from a later statement by Ayer:

> The assumption behind . . . [the famous slogan that the meaning of a proposition is its method of verification] was that everything that could be said at all could be expressed in terms of elementary statements. All statements of a higher order, including the most abstract scientific hypotheses, were in the end nothing more than shorthand descriptions of observable events. But this assumption was very difficult to sustain. It was particularly vulnerable when the elementary statements were taken to be records of the subject's immediate experiences: for while it has sometimes been maintained that statements about physical objects can be faithfully translated into statements about sense-data, no such translation has ever been achieved: there are, indeed, good reasons for supposing that it is not feasible. Moreover this choice of a basis raised the question of solipsism; the problem of making the transition from the subject's private experiences to the experiences of others and to the public world.

*Editor's Introduction* to LOGICAL POSITIVISM 13 (A. Ayer ed. 1959). Can Ayer consistently hold that "statements about physical objects" cannot be "faithfully translated into statements about sense data," if he also holds that statements about moral fact *can* be translated into statements of physical fact?

2. Can Ayer's position itself overcome the problem of solipsism? Recall his argument that even if ethical descriptions did refer to some independent feature of a situation, one could still ask whether one ought to value that feature? Suppose that the word chair referred to an independent feature of its situation, does Ayer's argument require that we still ask whether that feature ought to be valued for chair purposes? Is there any ultimate justification for saying something is a chair that is different in kind from the ultimate justification for saying something is immoral or ugly? Is Ayer ignoring the "fact" "that the process of substantiation cannot go on into infinity" for any statement? Or is that not a fact?

Ayer concedes (*id.* at 15) that the logical positivist theory of knowledge does not itself satisfy the requirement of verifiability. He admits, therefore, that it is itself a "prescription." The question, says Ayer, "is whether one thinks the difference between metaphysical and common sense or scientific statements to be sufficiently sharp for it to be useful to underline it" in the logical positivist way. *Id.* at 16. Can the question be "whether it is *useful*," for a logical positivist?

## SECTION THREE: THE AUTHORITY
## OF LANGUAGE REVISITED

### INTRODUCTORY NOTE

To what extent can skepticism be answered by revising our conceptions of the role of language in the acquisition, formulation, and communication of knowledge? Is it possible to view the doubts raised by Part II as doubts not about the possibility of knowledge and communication, but about the adequacy of typical conceptions of how language works—of how language functions in the process of thought, and of how it is related to the world of fact? This section raises some traditional objections to language, suggests some possible uncommonplace ways of conceiving of this symbolic medium, and presents arguments for viewing it as only one of many interrelated ways of obtaining access to reality. You should ask yourself as you encounter this material just how it affects the traditional, common-sensical conceptions of the nature of legal decisionmaking and of legal argument? To what extent does it enjoin upon lawyers the need to develop aptitudes, skills, capacities and forms of knowledge which are not usually conceived as part of a lawyer's repertoire? What is the bearing of the materials on the "method" of decision reflected in Justice Frankfurter's *Rochin* opinion? To what extent do these materials suggest that lawyers and judges follow his example?

*SUSANNE K. LANGER*

### DISCURSIVE AND PRESENTATIONAL FORMS *

#### Discursive and Presentational Forms

The logical theory on which this whole study of symbols is based is essentially that which was set forth by Wittgenstein, some twenty years ago, in his *Tractatus Logico-Philosophicus*:

> "One name stands for one thing, and another for another thing, and they are connected together. And so the whole, like a living picture, presents the atomic fact. (4.0311)

> "At the first glance the proposition—say as it stands printed on paper—does not seem to be a picture of the reality of which it treats. But neither does the musical score appear at first sight to be a picture of a musical piece; nor does our phonetic spelling (letters) seem to be a picture of our spoken language. . . . (4.015)

> "In the fact that there is a general rule by which the musician is able to read the symphony out of the score, and that there is a rule by which one could reconstruct the sym-

* From *Philosophy in a New Key* 79–84, 86–88 (3d ed. 1957). Copyright 1942, 1951, 1957 by the President and Fellows of Harvard College. Reprinted by permission of Harvard University Press.

phony from the line on a phonograph record and from this again—by means of the first rule—construct the score, herein lies the internal similarity between the things which at first sight seem to be entirely different. And the rule is the law of projection which projects the symphony into the language of the musical score. It is the rule of translation of this language into the language of the gramophone record." (4.0141)

"Projection" is a good word, albeit a figurative one, for the process by which we draw purely *logical* analogies. Geometric projection is the best instance of a perfectly faithful representation which, without knowledge of some logical rule, appears to be a misrepresentation. A child looking at a map of the world in Mercator projection cannot help believing that Greenland is larger than Australia; he simply *finds* it larger. The projection employed is not the usual principle of copying which we use in all visual comparisons or translations, and his training in the usual rule makes him unable to "see" by the new one. It takes sophistication to "see" the relative sizes of Greenland and Australia on a Mercator map. Yet a mind educated to appreciate the projected image brings the eye's habit with it. After a while, we genuinely "see" the thing as we apprehend it.

Language, our most faithful and indispensable picture of human experience, of the world and its events, of thought and life and all the march of time, contains a law of projection of which philosophers are sometimes unaware, so that their reading of the presented "facts" is obvious and yet wrong, as a child's visual experience is obvious yet deceptive when his judgment is ensnared by the trick of the flattened map. The transformation which facts undergo when they are rendered as propositions is that the relations in them are turned into something like *objects*. Thus, "A killed B" tells of a *way* in which A and B were unfortunately combined; but our only means of expressing this way is to *name* it, and presto!—a new entity, "killing," seems to have added itself to the complex of A and B. The event which is "pictured" in the proposition undoubtedly involved a *succession* of acts by A and B, but not the succession which the proposition seems to exhibit—first A, then "killing," then B. Surely A and B were simultaneous with each other and with the killing. But words have a linear, discrete, successive order; they are strung one after another like beads on a rosary; beyond the very limited meanings of inflections, which can indeed be incorporated in the words themselves, we cannot talk in simultaneous bunches of names. We must name one thing and then another, and symbols that are not names must be stuck between or before or after, by convention. But these symbols, holding proud places in the chain of names, are apt to be mistaken for names, to the detriment of many a metaphysical theory. Lord Russell regrets that we cannot construct a language which would express all relations by analogous relations; then we would not be tempted to misconstrue language, as a person who knows the meaning of the Mercator map, but has not used one freely enough to "see" in its terms, misconstrues the relative sizes of its areas.

. . . . . all language has a form which requires us to string out our ideas even though their objects rest one within the other; as pieces of clothing that are actually worn one over the other have to be strung side by side on the clothesline. This property of verbal symbolism is known as *discursiveness;* by reason of it, only thoughts which can be arranged in this peculiar order can be spoken at all; any idea which does not lend itself to this "projection" is ineffable, incommunicable by means of words. That is why the laws of reasoning, our clearest formulation of exact expression, are sometimes known as the "laws of discursive thought."

Carnap's admirable book, *The Logical Syntax of Language,* carries out the philosophical program suggested by Wittgenstein. . . . . The distinctions between scientific language and everyday speech, which most of us can feel rather than define, are clearly illumined by Carnap's analysis; and it is surprising to find how little of our ordinary communication measures up to the standard of "meaning" which a serious philosophy of language, and hence a logic of discursive thought, set before us.

. . . . The Kantian challenge: "What can I know?" is shown to be dependent on the prior question: "What can I ask?" And the answer, in Professor Carnap's formulation, is clear and direct. I can ask whatever language will express; I can know whatever experiment will answer. A proposition which could not, under any (perhaps ideal, impracticable) conditions, be verified or refuted, is a pseudo-proposition, it has no literal meaning. It does not belong to the framework of knowledge that we call logical conception; it is not true or false, but *unthinkable,* for it falls outside the order of symbolism.

Since an inordinate amount of our talk, and therefore (we hope) of our cerebration too, defies the canons of literal meaning, our philosophers of language—Russell, Wittgenstein, Carnap, and others of similar persuasions—are faced with the new question: What is the true function of those verbal combinations and other pseudo-symbolic structures that have no real significance, but are freely used as though they meant something?

According to our logicians, those structures are to be treated as "expressions" in a different sense, namely, as "expressions" of emotions, feelings, desires. They are not symbols for thought, but symptoms of the inner life, like tears and laughter, crooning, or profanity.

"Many linguistic utterances," says Carnap, "are analogous to laughing in that they have only an expressive function, no representative function. Examples of this are cries like 'Oh, Oh,' or, on a higher level, lyrical verses. The aim of a lyrical poem in which occur the words 'sunshine' and 'clouds,' is not to inform us of certain meteorological facts, but to express certain feelings of the poet and to excite similar feelings in us . . . . . Metaphysical propositions—like lyrical verses—have only an expressive function, but no representative function. Metaphysical propositions are neither true nor false, because they assert nothing . . . . But they are, like laughing, lyrics and music, expressive. They express not so much temporary feelings as permanent emotional and volitional dispositions."

. . .

This is, essentially, the attitude of those logicians who have investigated the limits of language. Nothing that is not "language" in the sense of their technical definition can possess the character of symbolic expressiveness (though it may be "expressive" in the symptomatic way.) Consequently nothing that cannot be "projected" in discursive form is accessible to the human mind at all, and any attempt to understand anything but demonstrable fact is bootless ambition. The knowable is a clearly defined field, governed by the requirement of discursive projectability. Outside this domain is the inexpressible realm of feeling, of formless desires and satisfactions, immediate experience, forever incognito and incommunicado. A philosopher who looks in that direction is, or should be, a mystic; from the ineffable sphere nothing but nonsense can be conveyed, since language, our only possible semantic, will not clothe experiences that elude the discursive form.

But intelligence is a slippery customer; if one door is closed to it, it finds, or even breaks, another entrance to the world. If one symbolism is inadequate, it seizes another; there is no eternal decree over its means and methods. So I will go with the logisticians and linguists as far as they like, but do not promise to go no further. For there is an unexplored possibility of genuine semantic beyond the limits of discursive language.

This logical "beyond," which Wittgenstein calls the "unspeakable," both Russell and Carnap regard as the sphere of subjective experience, emotion, feeling, and wish, from which only *symptoms* come to us in the form of metaphysical and artistic fancies. The study of such products they relegate to psychology, not semantics. And here is the point of my radical divergence from them. Where Carnap speaks of "cries like 'Oh, Oh,' or, on a higher level, lyrical verses", I can see only a complete failure to apprehend a fundamental distinction. Why should we cry our feelings at such high levels that anyone would think we were *talking*? Clearly, poetry means more than a cry; it has reason for being articulate; and metaphysics is more than the croon with which we might cuddle up to the world in a comfortable attitude. We are dealing with symbolisms here, and what they express is often highly intellectual. Only, the form and function of such symbolism are not those investigated by logicians, under the heading of "language." The field of semantics is wider than that of language, as certain philosophers—Schopenhauer, Cassirer, Delacroix, Dewey, Whitehead, and some others—have discovered; but it is blocked for us by the two fundamental tenets of current epistemology, which we have just discussed.

These two basic assumptions go hand in hand: (1) *That language is the only means of articulating thought*, and (2) *That every-*

*thing which is not speakable thought, is feeling.*  They are linked together because all genuine thinking *is* symbolic, and the limits of the expressive medium are, therefore, really the limits of our conceptual powers.  Beyond these we can have only blind feeling, which records nothing and conveys nothing, but has to be discharged in action or self-expression, in deeds or cries or other impulsive demonstrations.

But if we consider how difficult it is to construct a meaningful language that shall meet neo-positivistic standards, it is quite incredible that people should ever *say* anything at all, or understand each other's propositions.  At best, human thought is but a tiny, grammar-bound island, in the midst of a sea of feeling expressed by "oh-oh" and sheer babble.  The island has a periphery, perhaps, of mud—factual and hypothetical concepts broken down by the emotional tides into the "material mode," a mixture of meaning and nonsense.  Most of us live the better part of our lives on this mudflat; but in artistic moods we take to the deep, where we flounder about with symptomatic cries that sound like propositions about life and death, good and evil, substance, beauty, and other non-existent topics.

So long as we regard only scientific and "material" (semi-scientific) thought as really cognitive of the world, this peculiar picture of mental life must stand.  And *so long as we admit only discursive symbolism as a bearer of ideas, thought in this restricted sense must be regarded as our only intellectual activity.*  It begins and ends with language; without the elements, at least, of scientific grammar, conception must be impossible.

## QUESTIONS

1.  Can you think of any ways, other than those described by Langer, by which the form of language might give us a misleading picture of reality?  Does language also have a stability, a repeatability, a logical inevitability, and a distinctness and clarity which we might tend to impose on the "real" world?  Holmes says that "the logical method and form flatter that longing for certainty and for repose which is in every human mind."  Can the same be said for language?

2.  Is it impossible to "know" things that you can't express?  Or is it perhaps a contradiction to speak of knowing something one can't say?  Would this depend on the meaning of the word "know"?  Is there a good reason for excluding from knowledge that which cannot be put into words?  Do we sometimes act as if there were?

3.  Langer has already suggested that if what we know is limited to what we can say, then there is not very much usable knowledge.  In the following readings you should ask yourself just how important language is and what are the consequences of treating it as the only source of knowledge?  How would you use the ideas presented to support a theory of non-linguistic knowledge?  Would such knowledge be subjective or objective, only personal or capable of communication to others?

LUDWIG WITTGENSTEIN

TRACTATUS LOGICO-PHILOSOPHICUS *

6.44    It is not *how* things are in the world that is mystical, but *that* it exists.

6.45    To view the world *subspecie aeterni* is to view it as a whole—a limited whole.

Feeling the world as a limited whole—it is this that is mystical.

6.5    When the answer cannot be put into words, neither can the question be put into words.

*The riddle* does not exist.

If a question can be framed at all, it is also *possible* to answer it.

6.51    Scepticism is *not* irrefutable, but obviously nonsensical, when it tries to raise doubts where no questions can be asked.

For doubt can exist only where a question exists, a question only where an answer exists, and an answer only where something *can be said*.

6.52    We feel that even when *all possible* scientific questions have been answered, the problems of life remain completely untouched. Of course there are then no questions left, and this itself is the answer.

6.521    The solution of the problem of life is seen in the vanishing of the problem.

(Is not this the reason why those who have found after a long period of doubt that the sense of life became clear to them have then been unable to say what constituted that sense?)

6.522    There are, indeed, things that cannot be put into words. They *make themselves manifest*. They are what is mystical.

6.53    The correct method in philosophy would really be the following: to say nothing except what can be said, i. e. propositions of natural science—i. e. something that has nothing to do with philosophy—and then, whenever someone else wanted to say something metaphysical, to demonstrate to him that he had failed to give a meaning to certain signs in his propositions. Although it would not be satisfying to the other person —he would not have the feeling that we were teaching him philosophy—*this* method would be the only strictly correct one.

6.54    My propositions serve as elucidations in the following way: anyone who understands me eventually recognizes them as nonsensical, when he has used them—as steps—to climb

* From 149–151 (D. Pears & B. Mc-Guinness transl. 1961). Reprinted by permission of Humanities Press and Routledge and Kegan Paul Ltd.

up beyond them. (He must, so to speak, throw away the
ladder after he has climbed up it.)

He must transcend these propositions, and then he will
see the world aright.

7       What we cannot speak about we must pass over in silence.

## QUESTIONS

Why do you think that, according to Wittgenstein, "scepticism
is *not* irrefutable, but obviously nonsensical"? Is it that statements
expressing a skeptical position are not capable of being true or false?
How would such an argument run? How would you argue in support of Wittgenstein's assertion that his own "propositions," are "nonsensical"? Are his propositions capable of being verified? Does it
matter if they get you where you want to go? But how can nonsensical propositions take you some place that is worth going and still
be nonsensical? Can they be useful in this way and still be without meaning? What sort of a notion of meaning does Wittgenstein
reveal in these passages? Is it the same one to which Langer refers
in her discussion of the positivist conception of linguistic meaning?

## ALFRED NORTH WHITEHEAD

## MODES OF THOUGHT *

   . . . . The thesis that I am developing conceives 'proof',
in the strict sense of that term, as a feeble second-rate procedure.
When the word 'proof' has been uttered, the next notion to enter
the mind is 'half-heartedness'. Unless proof has produced self-
evidence and thereby rendered itself unnecessary, it has issued in a
second-rate state of mind, producing action devoid of understanding.
Self-evidence is the basic fact on which all greatness supports itself. But 'proof' is one of the routes by which self-evidence is often
obtained.

As an example of this doctrine, in philosophical writings proof
should be at a minimum. The whole effort should be to display the
self-evidence of basic truths, concerning the nature of things and
their connection. It should be noticed that logical proof starts from
premises, and that premises are based upon evidence. Thus evidence
is presupposed by logic; at least, it is presupposed by the assumption
that logic has any importance.

Philosophy is the attempt to make manifest the fundamental evidence as to the nature of things. Upon the presupposition of this
evidence, all understanding rests. A correctly verbalized philosophy
mobilizes this basic experience which all premises presuppose. It
makes the content of the human mind manageable; it adds meaning
to fragmentary details; it discloses disjunctions and conjunctions,

* From 66–67, 68–69 (Capricorn ed.
1958). Copyright 1938 by The Macmillan Company, renewed 1966 by T.
North Whitehead. Reprinted with
permission of The Macmillan Company.

consistencies and inconsistencies. Philosophy is the criticism of abstractions which govern special modes of thought.

It follows that philosophy, in any proper sense of the term, cannot be proved. For proof is based upon abstraction. Philosophy is either self-evident, or it is not philosophy. The attempt of any philosophic discourse should be to produce self-evidence. Of course it is impossible to achieve any such aim. But, none the less, all inference in philosophy is a sign of that imperfection which clings to all human endeavour. The aim of philosophy is sheer disclosure.

.   .   .

Language halts behind intuition. The difficulty of philosophy is the expression of what is self-evident. Our understanding outruns the ordinary usages of words. Philosophy is akin to poetry. Philosophy is the endeavour to find a conventional phraseology for the vivid suggestiveness of the poet. It is the endeavour to reduce Milton's 'Lycidas' to prose; and thereby to produce a verbal symbolism manageable for use in other connections of thought.

This reference to philosophy illustrates the fact that understanding is not primarily based on inference. Understanding is self-evidence. But our clarity of intuition is limited, and it flickers. Thus inference enters as means for the attainment of such understanding as we can achieve. Proofs are the tools for the extension of our imperfect self-evidence. They presuppose some clarity; and they also presuppose that this clarity represents an imperfect penetration into our dim recognition of the world around—the world of fact, the world of possibility, the world as valued, the world as purposed.

## QUESTIONS

Why, in Whitehead's view, is proof inferior to self-evidence? Don't we need proof to justify our feelings of self-evidence? To convince ourselves that a given experience is one of self-evidence? What is the relationship of proof to language? When we ask for a proof are we asking for a linguistic argument and justification? If we are, is this more or less reliable than self-evidence?

*GILBERT RYLE*

## THE CONCEPT OF MIND *

Consider   .   .   .   a boy learning to play chess. Clearly before he has yet heard of the rules of the game he might by accident make a move with his knight which the rules permit. The fact that he makes a permitted move does not entail that he knows the rule which permits it. Nor need the spectator be able to discover in the way the boy makes this move any visible feature which shows whether the move is a random one, or one made in knowledge of the rules. However, the boy now begins to learn the game properly, and this gener-

* From 40–41, 48–49 (Barnes & Noble
ed. 1949). Copyright 1949 by Gilbert
Ryle. Reprinted with permission.

ally involves his receiving explicit instruction in the rules. He probably gets them by heart and is then ready to cite them on demand. During his first few games he probably has to go over the rules aloud or in his head, and to ask now and then how they should be applied to this or that particular situation. But very soon he comes to observe the rules without thinking of them. He makes the permitted moves and avoids the forbidden ones; he notices and protests when his opponent breaks the rules. But he no longer cites to himself or to the room the formulae in which the bans and permissions are declared. It has become second nature to him to do what is allowed and to avoid what is forbidden. At this stage he might even have lost his former ability to cite the rules. If asked to instruct another beginner, he might have forgotten how to state the rules and he would show the beginner how to play only by himself making the correct moves and cancelling the beginner's false moves.

But it would be quite possible for a boy to learn chess without ever hearing or reading the rules at all. By watching the moves made by others and by noticing which of his own moves were conceded and which were rejected, he could pick up the art of playing correctly while still quite unable to propound the regulations in terms of which 'correct' and 'incorrect' are defined. We all learned the rules of hunt-the-thimble and hide-and-seek and the elementary rules of grammar and logic in this way. We learn *how* by practice, schooled indeed by criticism and example, but often quite unaided by any lessons in the theory.

It should be noticed that the boy is not said to know how to play, if all that he can do is to recite the rules accurately. He must be able to make the required moves. But he is said to know how to play if, although he cannot cite the rules, he normally does make the permitted moves, avoid the forbidden moves and protest if his opponent makes forbidden moves. His knowledge *how* is exercised primarily in the moves that he makes, or concedes, and in the moves that he avoids or vetoes. So long as he can observe the rules, we do not care if he cannot also formulate them. It is not what he does in his head or with his tongue, but what he does on the board that shows whether or not he knows the rules in the executive way of being able to apply them. Similarly a foreign scholar might not know how to speak grammatical English as well as an English child, for all that he had mastered the theory of English grammar.

. . .

Underlying all the other features of the operations executed by the intelligent reasoner there is the cardinal feature that he reasons logically, that is, that he avoids fallacies and produces valid proofs and inferences, pertinent to the case he is making. He observes the rules of logic, as well as those of style, forensic strategy, professional etiquette and the rest. But he probably observes the rules of logic without thinking about them. He does not cite Aristotle's formulae to himself or to the court. He applies in his practice what Aristotle abstracted in his theory of such practices. He reasons with a correct method, but without considering the prescriptions of a methodology.  The rules that he observes have become his way of thinking, when he is taking care;  they are not external rubrics with which he has to square his thoughts.  .  .  .

What is true of arguing intelligently is, with appropriate modifications, true of other intelligent operations.  The boxer, the surgeon, the poet and the salesman apply their special criteria in the performance of their special tasks, for they are trying to get things right;  and they are appraised as clever, skillful, inspired or shrewd not for the ways in which they consider, if they consider at all, prescriptions for conducting their special performances, but for the ways in which they conduct those performances themselves.  Whether or not the boxer plans his manoeuvres before executing them, his cleverness at boxing is decided in the light of how he fights.  If he is a Hamlet of the ring, he will be condemned as an inferior fighter, though perhaps a brilliant theorist or critic.  Cleverness at fighting is exhibited in the giving and parrying of blows, not in the acceptance · or rejection of propositions about blows, just as ability at reasoning is exhibited in the construction of valid arguments and the detection of fallacies, not in the avowal of logician's formulae.  Nor does the surgeon's skill function in his tongue uttering medical truths but only in his hands making the correct movements.

A man knowing little or nothing of medical science could not be a good surgeon, but excellence at surgery is not the same thing as knowledge of medical science;  nor is it a simple product of it.  The surgeon must indeed have learned from instruction, or by his own inductions and observations, a great number of truths;  but he must also have learned by practice a great number of aptitudes.  Even where efficient practice is the deliberate application of considered prescriptions, the intelligence involved in putting the prescriptions into practice is not identical with that involved in intellectually grasping the prescriptions.  There is no contradiction, or even paradox, in describing someone as bad at practising what he is good at preaching.  There have been thoughtful and original literary critics who have formulated admirable canons of prose style in execrable prose. There have been others who have employed brilliant English in the expression of the silliest theories of what constitutes good writing.

## QUESTIONS

Is law, which is preeminently a profession of words, an exception to the remarks of Ryle?  Is it meaningful to talk about "knowing the law" or "thinking like a lawyer" if the knower or thinker cannot invoke the applicable rules and linguistic justifications?  Or is knowing the rules only a part of knowing the law and of thinking like a lawyer?  What evidence do we have both from this section and from Chapter 8(2) (C) that knowing the law must involve something— indeed a great deal—more than this?  What could this additional "knowledge" consist of?  Consider this question in light of the readings from Waismann, Langer and Cassirer at the end of this section.

*HENRI BERGSON*

## CREATIVE EVOLUTION *

. . . . In vain, we shall be told, you claim to go beyond intelligence: how can you do that except by intelligence? All that is clear in your consciousness is intelligence. You are inside your own thought; you cannot get out of it. Say, if you like, that the intellect is capable of progress, that it will see more and more clearly into a greater and greater number of things; but do not speak of engendering it, for it is with your intellect itself that you would have to do the work.

The objection presents itself naturally to the mind. But the same reasoning would prove also the impossibility of acquiring any new habit. It is of the essence of reasoning to shut us up in the circle of the given. But action breaks the circle. If we had never seen a man swim, we might say that swimming is an impossible thing, inasmuch as, to learn to swim, we must begin by holding ourselves up in the water and, consequently, already know how to swim. Reasoning, in fact, always nails us down to the solid ground. But if, quite simply, I throw myself into the water without fear, I may keep myself up well enough at first by merely struggling, and gradually adapt myself to the new environment: I shall thus have learnt to swim. So, in theory, there is a kind of absurdity in trying to know otherwise than by intelligence; but if the risk be frankly accepted, action will perhaps cut the knot that reasoning has tied and will not unloose.

Besides, the risk will appear to grow less, the more our point of view is adopted. We have shown that intellect has detached itself from a vastly wider reality, but that there has never been a clean cut between the two; all around conceptual thought there remains an indistinct fringe which recalls its origin. And further we compared the intellect to a solid nucleus formed by means of condensation. This nucleus does not differ radically from the fluid surrounding it. It can only be reabsorbed in it because it is made of the same substance. He who throws himself into the water, having known only the resistance of the solid earth, will immediately be drowned if he does not struggle against the fluidity of the new environment: he must perforce still cling to that solidity, so to speak, which even water presents. Only on this condition can he get used to the fluid's fluidity. So of our thought, when it has decided to make the leap.

But leap it must, that is, leave its own environment. Reason, reasoning on its powers, will never succeed in extending them, though the extension would not appear at all unreasonable once it were accomplished. Thousands and thousands of variations on the theme of walking will never yield a rule for swimming: come, enter the water, and when you know how to swim, you will understand how the mechanism of swimming is connected with that of walking.

* From 192–193 (1911).

Swimming is an extension of walking, but walking would never have pushed you on to swimming. So you may speculate as intelligently as you will on the mechanism of intelligence; you will never, by this method, succeed in going beyond it. You may get something more complex, but not something higher nor even something different. You must take things by storm: you must thrust intelligence outside itself by an act of will.

ARTHUR KOESTLER

THE GHOST IN THE MACHINE *

To unlearn is more difficult than to learn; and it seems that the task of breaking up rigid cognitive structures and reassembling them into a new synthesis cannot, as a rule, be performed in the full daylight of the conscious, rational mind. It can only be done by reverting to those more fluid, less committed and specialised forms of thinking which normally operate in the twilight zones of awareness.

There is a popular superstition, according to which scientists arrive at their discoveries by reasoning in strictly rational, precise, verbal terms. The evidence indicates that they do nothing of the sort. To quote a single example: in 1945, Jacques Hadamard organised a nation-wide inquiry among eminent mathematicians in America to find out their working methods. The result showed that all of them, with only two exceptions, thought neither in verbal terms, nor in algebraic symbols, but relied on visual imagery of a vague, hazy kind. Einstein was among those who answered the questionnaire; he wrote: 'The words of the language as they are written or spoken do not seem to play any role in my mechanism of thought, which relies on more or less clear images of a visual and some of a muscular type. It seems to me that what you call full consciousness is a limit case which can never be fully accomplished because consciousness is a narrow thing.'

Einstein's statement is typical. On the testimony of those original thinkers who have taken the trouble to record their methods of work, *not only verbal thinking but conscious thinking in general plays only a subordinate part in the brief, decisive phase of the creative act itself.* Their virtually unanimous emphasis on spontaneous intuitions and hunches of unconscious origin, which they are at a loss to explain, suggests that the role of strictly rational and verbal processes in scientific discovery has been vastly over-estimated since the age of enlightenment. There are always large chunks of irrationality embedded in the creative process, not only in art (where we are ready to accept it) but in the exact sciences as well.

The scientist who, facing an obstinate problem, regresses from precise verbal thinking to vague visual imagery, seems to follow

* From 179–181 (1968). Copyright 1967 by Arthur Koestler. Reprinted by permission.

Woodworth's advice: 'Often we have to get away from speech in order to think clearly.' Language can become a screen between the thinker and reality; and creativity often starts where language ends, that is, by regressing to pre-verbal levels of mental activity.

Now I do not mean, of course, that there is a little Socratic daemon housed in the scientist's or artist's skull, who does his homework for him; nor should one confuse unconscious mentation with Freud's 'primary process'. The primary process is defined by Freud as devoid of logic, governed by the pleasure-principle, accompanied by massive discharges of affect, and apt to confuse perception and hallucination. It seems that between this very primary process, and the so-called secondary process, governed by the reality-principle, we must interpolate several levels of mental activity which are not just mixtures of 'primary' and 'secondary', but are cognitive systems in their own right, each governed by its own canon of rules. The paranoid delusion, the dream, the daydream, free association, the mentality of children at various ages, and of primates at various stages should not be lumped together, for each has its own logic or rules of the game. But while clearly different in many respects, all these forms of mentation have certain features in common, since they are ontogenetically, and perhaps phylogenetically, older than those of the civilised adult. They are less rigid, more tolerant, ready to combine seemingly incompatible ideas, and to perceive hidden analogies between cabbages and kings. One might call them 'games of the underground', because if not kept under restraint, they would play havoc with the routines of disciplined thinking. But under exceptional conditions, when disciplined thinking is at the end of its tether, a temporary indulgence in these underground games may suddenly produce a solution—some far-fetched, reckless combination of ideas, which would be beyond the reach of, or seem to be unacceptable to, the sober, rational mind. I have proposed the term 'bisociation' for these sudden leaps of creative imagination, to set them apart from the more pedestrian or associative routines. I shall come back to this in a moment; the point to retain is that the creative act in mental evolution again reflects the pattern of *reculer pour mieux sauter*, of a temporary regression, followed by a forward leap. We can carry the analogy further and interpret the Eureka cry as the signal of a happy escape from a blind alley—an act of mental self-repair.

## FRIEDRICH WAISMANN

## LANGUAGE STRATA *

We may set ourselves the task of grouping statements of our language according to the similarity of their usage in distinct domains, in *language-strata* as I shall venture to call them. Thus laws will form one language stratum, material object statements another one,

* From Logic and Language 235–242, 244–247 (A. Flew ed. Anchor ed. 1965). Reprinted by permission of the literary estate of Friedrich Waismann. Originally published by Basil Blackwell.

sense datum statements yet another one, and so on. Now the question which I want to consider is this: Is it possible to develop out of that vague feeling that 'each of them is built in a different logical style' something more precise? Is it possible, say, by characterizing each stratum on the basis of its intrinsic internal fabric or logical texture?

.   .   .

We may first investigate the nature of the concepts which a given stratum contains: whether they are absolutely precise and definable with mathematical rigour, or vague, or of an open texture. We may next consider the statements themselves and ask what sort of logic is valid for them.   .   .   .   Take   .   .   .   the logic of half-faded memory pictures. Here the situation is such that we are often unable to call to mind one or the other point of detail, that is, that we are often unable to decide an alternative. What did that bath-room look like I saw the other day on a visit? Was it ivory, was it cream or pale biscuit or maize? Suppose a pattern-book were shown to me, and I was later asked whether *this* was the colour I had seen, perhaps I would not be able to decide. If I were pressed I might have to say 'I can't remember so distinctly'; if another different shade of yellow were shown to me then I might give the same reply, finally adding, 'all I know is that it was some light yellowish colour'. Notice that, in this case, it is quite natural to use a *vague* term ('light colour') to express the indeterminacy of the impression. If language was such that each and every word was particular and each colour word had a definite, clearly defined meaning, we should find we could not use it. That is, we should come up against alternatives: 'Was it this colour or not?'—which we could not decide. I cannot get back to the impression I had then, it cannot be pinned down and preserved under glass for inspection like a dead beetle. To insist, in these circum-stances, on the law of excluded middle, without any means of deciding the issue, is paying lip service to the laws of logic. There are only two alternatives open to us: We must either be prepared to drop the law of excluded middle when we wish to use a language with precisely defined terms; or we shall have to use a language whose words are in one way or another blurred. But we can't have it both ways. Another way of bringing out this point is to say that, if several colours are shown to me which differ only slightly, they do not necessarily exclude one another. This shows particularly clearly that our attitude towards a half-faded memory image is radically different from that towards a material object. No one would dream of ascribing two different lengths to the table in this room (a *real* table), and saying that both were right. One statement, if it proves true, excludes the other. Whereas it is perfectly correct to say of two slightly different colour statements, when applied to an in-determinate memory picture, that both are compatible; which just shows that the logic of colour words, when applied in this language stratum, is different from their usual logic.

Again, the logic of aphorisms seems to be very peculiar. A man who writes aphorisms may say a thing, and, on another occasion, the very opposite of it without being guilty of a contradiction. For each aphorism, as it stands, is quite complete in itself. Two different aphorisms are not parts of one and the same communication. Suppose you go to a museum where several paintings are hung on the wall. Would you complain that they are not correlated and do not fit into one and the same perspective? Well now, each painting has a pictorial space of its own; what is represented in two paintings, though the paintings may be adjacent, is not in the same pictorial space. It is the first aim of Art, it has been said, to set a frame around Nature. Sometimes the frame is large, sometimes small, but always it is there. An aphorism is Literature and done with ink instead of colours. Of two aphorisms each is in a frame of its own; hence no clash. It would be interesting to penetrate the logic of poems, or of mysticism. Here a contradiction may be a perfectly legitimate means to point to what cannot be said in language. No: seeming contradictions are not always absurd.

To return to our subject: I said that the examples given suggest looking upon a logic as a characteristic which sets its stamp upon a particular language stratum. But there are two further characteristics: truth and verifiability.

### III.   *Systematic Ambiguity of Truth and Verifiability*

Compare a variety of statements such as: a sense-datum statement, a material object statement, a law of nature, description of something half forgotten, a statement of my own motives, a conjecture as to the motives by which someone else was actuated, quotation of the exact words so-and-so was using, brief summary of the tenor of a political speech, characterization of the *Zeitgeist* of a certain historical period, a proverb, a poetic metaphor, a mathematical proposition, and so on. Now what I want to emphasize is that the idea of truth varies with the kind of statement; that it has a systematic ambiguity. Take, for instance, a mathematical proposition, say a theorem of geometry. To say that it is true simply means that it can be deduced from such-and-such axioms. As a consequence of this, it may be true in one system of geometry and false in another. And the axioms themselves? They are no concern of the pure mathematician: all he is concerned with is that *if* these and these axioms apply, *then* the theorems apply too. But whether the axioms actually do apply, is not for him to decide. He leaves that to applied mathematics. Hence Russell's definition of mathematics as 'the subject in which we never know what we are talking about, nor whether what we are saying is true'. Here, then, is a very good case for the 'coherence theory of truth'.

Again, a law of nature is never true in the same sense in which, say, 'There is a fire burning in this room' is, nor in the sense in which 'He is an amusing fellow' may be; and the two latter statements are not true in the same sense in which 'I've got a headache' is. Truth, when applied to a physical law, means roughly speaking that it is well established by experimental evidence or other observation, that it brings widely different things into a close connection and makes us 'understand' what seemed a mystery before; that it simplifies our theoretical system, and further, that it is fruitful in leading us to predictions and new discoveries. (That is, incidentally, why the pragmatist identifies truth with usefulness: he has really got hold of one facet, but of one facet only.) Truth, in this case, it may be said, is not *one* idea but a whole bundle of ideas. Nothing of this applies to truth in the case of a simple observation. Suppose you have to make sure that the light is on in your room. Now when you go and look and say 'All right, it's on', your statement is true, *not* because it brings widely different things into connection, *not* because it simplifies I don't know what, *not* because it is fruitful or suggestive—no, nothing of the sort; it is just true because it says so-and-so is as you say it is.

Again, in what sense is one to say of a proverb that it is true? Have you ever tried to put some rare and subtle experience, or some half-forgotten (but strong) impression into words? If you do, you will find that truth, in this case, is inseparably tied up with the literary quality of your writing: it needs no less than a poet to express fully and faithfully such fragile states of mind. How you say it matters even more than what you say.

Similar remarks apply to verification. A law of nature can be verified by experimental evidence, though not conclusively. Whether a material object statement is capable of conclusive verification is a moot point. Take next a case such as 'I've got a terrible toothache'. Suppose I go to the dentist, he examines my teeth and says, 'All right, there's nothing wrong with them'. Would I then reply, 'Oh, I beg your pardon, I *thought* that I've got a toothache, but now I see that I was mistaken'? My toothache cannot be argued away or refuted by examining my teeth, my nerves, etc. If I were asked how I know that I've got a toothache, I might be tempted to reply, 'Because I *feel* it'. What a queer sort of reply! Is there anything else I can do with a toothache but feel it? What my reply aimed at, however, was something different, namely to *shake off* the whole question as improper, beside the point. How do I know? I've simply got toothache, and that's the end of it. I do not grant that I may have fallen victim to a delusion, I do not recognize a medical examination, an observation of my teeth any psychological tests, a court of experts—no dentist in heaven or earth can refute me. In saying 'I just *feel it*' I am expressing the fact that the toothache is something *given in immediate experience,* not a thing *inferred from something else* on the strength of certain evidences. The first person singular has, amongst other uses, the function to indicate the character of *immediacy* of an experience.

Take the statement, 'There are sea serpents'. How would you verify it? Is it enough that some person has seen them? Perhaps for him; for you the situation is different: you have so far only a man who *says* that he has seen them. So you must check up what he says— you may test his eyesight, go into his past and examine his reliability, and so on. The result of this checking will be a number of statements each of which, in its turn, may again be checked: the expert who examined the man's eyesight may himself be examined, the witnesses who testified may in their turn be scrutinized, etc. In following up the threads of verification we nowhere come to an absolute end, that is we can never say, 'Now it is conclusively proved that the man was right'. What this particular example shows applies in general. At some point we do stop, it is true, for practical reasons, when the evidence seems to be sufficient. But theoretically we may go on checking and re-checking our statements as long as we please. So long as we move amongst statements concerning such evidences as illustrated above, verification has no natural end, but refers continually to ever new statements. In pursuing these fibres, however, we see how secondary lines branch off into other regions: the points where they come to a sudden end represent those immediate experiences which an observer has the moment he experiences them, and which, in this moment, cannot be checked against other evidences. These experiences, expressed in 'I'-sentences, are, so to speak, end points of verification—but of verification in the quite different sense. For if we try to use this verification later, it turns to dust. It lives in the moment, and is gone. Still these experiences are the moments of ultimate fulfilment. It is they from which all light of knowledge flows forth. Or, to change the metaphor, they are the points in which knowledge makes direct contact with reality. Without them all our sentences would float in the air cut off from actual facts. What establishes a connection between sentences and reality are these last points of verification, transitory though they may be. Thus a statement may be verified in two quite different senses: either by checking it against other statements, or by appealing to immediate experience. In the case of material object statement, for instance, some lines refer to other material object statements, i. e. they lead from statement to statement within the same language stratum, the 'I'-statements. Thus verification weaves a complicated net, a ramified pattern of lines.

It is easily seen that the term 'meaningful' displays the same ambiguity: its sense varies with the stratum. For instance, a sentence in a novel is meaningful, if (1) it is correct English, i. e. not a broth of words, and (2) it fits in with the other sentences. This meaningfulness has nothing whatever to do with verifiability. (That, by the way, is why Fiction is not false.) This criterion, however, does not apply to experiential statements where verifiability is of some relevance, although it would not be right to equate meaningfulness with verifiability. Again, in which sense is a rule, a definition, a request, a question meaningful? There may even be a sense in which metaphysical statements have a meaning. The trouble with the Logical Positivists was that they attached too rigid an import to 'meaningfulness' and lost sight of its ambiguity. By virtue of the multiplicity of meaning in this word they lost themselves in a magic cloud out of which they condemned everything that did not conform to their standards. In actual fact they had no machinery, such as they thought they had, by which the senselessness of metaphysics could be *proved*; though it must be admitted that metaphysicians made the greatest efforts to supply them with plausible arguments for such a view. I am afraid what has been said on this subject was of a profound shallowness.

To sum up this point: Statements may be *true* in different senses, *verifiable* in different senses, *meaningful* in different senses. Therefore the attempts at defining 'truth', or at drawing a sharp line between the meaningful and the meaningless, etc., are doomed to fail.

. . .

## V.  A New Picture of Language

We are now in a position to sketch a new picture of language which, though still untried, seems to emerge from all these considerations; a picture of language naturally stratified into layers. This new conception contrasts with such a view as that held by Wittgenstein in his *Tractatus Logico-Philosophicus:* according to that view language consists of statements which can, one and all, be derived from atomic propositions by a uniform process. An atomic proposition is one asserting an atomic fact; an atomic fact is a fact which has no parts that are facts; and the uniform method by which any statement can be constructed is that of building up truth-functions of any selection of atomic propositions. This leads to an amazing simplication of the picture we can make for ourselves of the fabric of language. All statements are, so to speak, on a footing, and all are reducible to the same set of atomic propositions. Or better, the totality of propositions is defined by this method of generation. Too good to be true. Apart from the fact that no one has ever succeeded in producing a single atomic proposition, the whole thing is a myth. Moreover, we know for certain that there are many ways of building up statements which have nothing at all to do with truth-functions; such as unfulfilled conditional statements—'If Hitler had won the war, then . . . .' and many others. No: language does not fit this straitjacket.

There are certain modern trends in Philosophy which seem to have some such background. Phenomenalism, for instance, seems to presuppose that there is one basic language, the sense-datum language, to which any other statement, or at least any material object statement, can be reduced. According to Phenomenalism a material object, say a cat, is a bundle of sense-data tied together and with the edges trimmed off; unless it is a bundle of *sensibilia,* that is the sort of thing which you *would* have seen, if you *had* ever looked, in short, a bundle of highly problematical entities. But no; we have simply to recognize that a statement about a cat is a statement about a cat: and not a truth-function of sense-datum statements, or an infinite class of perspectives, or an infinite group of *sensibilia,* or heaven knows what. A thing is, so to speak, a hard core that resists at any attempt at breaking it up and reducing it to the level of other data, whatever they may be. All this talk about material objects and sense-data is a talk about two language strata, about their relation, about the logic of this relationship. The problem arises along the plane where the two strata make contact, so to speak. The difficulty is to understand in precisely which way a material object statement is related to a sense-datum statement; that is, what sort of relations hold between members of different strata; and that is a problem of logic.

Similarly, Behaviourism is an attempt to reduce psychological statements, e, g., 'What a conceited fellow!' to a very, very long list of statements setting out in which way the person in question would behave under such-and-such circumstances; a very successful way of describing peculiarities of rats which has been transferred to men. The whole thing rests on a *naivete*—that there is one basic language (suitable for describing the behaviour of rats) into which everything else must be translated.  The motto 'Only rats, no men!' overlooks the fact that psychological statements belong to a stratum of their own, with a logic different from that of the language in which you say how a person looks, how he smiles, in short what he has in common with a rat.

We are now in a position to take a further step.  It was hitherto the custom to refer to what I have called 'strata' by indicating their subject-matter, using terms such as: 'material object statements', 'descriptions of vague impressions', 'statements of laws of nature', and the like.  What I now suggest we do—and this is a programme for the future—is to reverse the whole situation by saying: 'The formal motifs which we have been considering all combine to impress a certain stamp on a stratum; they give us the means to characterize each stratum "from within" that is with no reference to the subject'.  If we carefully study the texture of the concepts which occur in a given stratum, the logic of its propositions, the meaning of truth, the web of verification, the senses in which a description may be complete or incomplete—if we consider all that, we may thereby characterize the subject-matter.  We may say, for instance: a material object is something that is describable in a language of such-and-such structure; a sense impression is something which can be described in such-and-such language; a dream is—, a memory picture is—, and so on.  In this way we shall be able to *formalize* these concepts.  The analogy with science is obvious.  The questions, 'What is a point?' 'What is a straight line?' have been debated for more than 2000 years until the solution was found in a reversal of the problem situation. All the time it was thought that we must first define the meaning of the primitive symbols in geometry before we can see that the axioms are 'Self-evident truths' given in intuition.  In modern times the terms 'point', 'straight line', 'plane', 'between', 'congruent', etc., are defined as those things and relations which satisfy the axioms of geometry. That is, the axioms in their totality *determine* (within pure mathematics) the meaning of the primitive symbols.  In like manner we may say that each stratum has a logic of its own and that this logic determines the meaning of certain basic terms.  In some respects this is obvious.  Whether a melody is a sequence of air-vibrations, or a succession of musical notes, or a message of the composer, depends entirely on the way you describe it.  Similarly, you may look at a game of chess, or on the pattern of a carpet from very different aspects and you will then see in them very different things.  Notice how all these words—'melody', 'game of chess', etc.—take on a systematic ambiguity according to the language stratum in which you talk.  The same applies to 'doing a sum', 'writing a letter', or to any action indeed.  An action may be viewed as a series of movements caused by some physiological stimuli in the 'Only rats, no men' sense; or as something that has a purpose or a meaning irrespective of the way its single links are produced.  An action in the first sense is determined by *causes*, an action in the second sense by *motives* or *reasons*.  It is generally believed that an action is determined both by causes and by motives.  But if the causes determine the action, no room is left for motives, and if the motives determine the action, no room is left for causes. Either the system of causes is complete, then it is not possible to squeeze in a motive; or the system of motives is complete, then it is not possible to squeeze in a cause. 'Well, now, do you believe that if you are writing a letter you are engaged in two different activities?' No; I mean that there are two different ways of looking at the thing; just as there are two different ways of looking at a sentence: as a series of noises produced by a human agent; or as a vehicle of thought. For a series of noises there may be causes but no reasons; for a series of words expressing thought there may be reasons but no causes. What we must understand is that the word 'action' has a systematic ambiguity. And yet we are continually invited to regard motives as a special sort of causes; perhaps because we have only the word 'Why?' to ask both for cause and motive. We do not see the ambiguity of the interrogative.

### QUESTIONS

Consider the murder case hypothesized by Ayer. In it he described as facts the "police court" details, the motives of the parties, etc. Are the facts which the lawyer deals with the same as the facts which the psychoanalyst uncovers? Is it possible for the lawyer to describe the "same situation" in terms different from those of the psychoanalyst? Suppose that a chemist were to describe the "facts" in chemical terms. Would his description be more or less factual than the lawyer or the psychoanalyst? Than a doctor? Than a physicist? If all of these people could describe the same situation in different terms, would it be useful to say that they are using different languages? Or language strata? What point—or points—is being made by treating the English language as composed of many sub-languages? How might the man who defends the cognitivity of moral language make use of the point?

*SUSANNE K. LANGER*

### DISCURSIVE AND PRESENTATIONAL FORMS *

. . . . the error which [Logical Positivism] harbors is not in its reasoning. It is in the very premise from which the doctrine proceeds, namely that all articulate symbolism is discursive. . . .

Now, I . . . believe that in this physical, space-time world of our experience there are things which do not fit the grammatical scheme of expression. But they are not necessarily blind, inconceivable, mystical affairs; they are simply matters which require to be conceived through some symbolistic schema other than discursive language. . . .

Our merest sense-experience is a process of *formulation*. The world that actually meets our senses is not a world of "things," about

* From *Philosophy in a New Key* 88–94, 96–101 (3d ed. 1957). Copyright 1942, 1951, 1957 by the President and Fellows of Harvard College. Reprinted by permission of Harvard University Press.

which we are invited to discover facts as soon as we have codified the necessary logical language to do so; the world of pure sensation is so complex, so fluid and full, that sheer sensitivity to stimuli would only encounter what William James has called (in characteristic phrase) "a blooming, buzzing confusion." Out of this bedlam our sense-organs must select certain predominant forms, if they are to make report of *things* and not of mere dissolving sensa. The eye and ear must have their logic—their "categories of understanding," if you like the Kantian idiom, or their "primary imagination," in Coleridge's version of the same concept. An object is not a datum, but a form construed by the sensitive and intelligent organ, a form which is at once an experienced individual thing and a symbol for the concept of it, for *this sort of thing.*

A tendency to organize the sensory field into groups and patterns of sense-data, to perceive forms rather than a flux of light-impressions, seems to be inherent in our receptor apparatus just as much as in the higher nervous centers with which we do arithmetic and logic. But this unconscious appreciation of forms is the primitive root of all abstraction, which in turn is the keynote of rationality; so it appears that the conditions for rationality lie deep in our pure animal experience—in our power of perceiving, in the elementary functions of our eyes and ears and fingers. Mental life begins with our mere physiological constitution. A little reflection shows us that, since no experience occurs more than once, so-called "repeated" experiences are really *analogous* occurrences, all fitting a form that was abstracted on the first occasion. *Familiarity* is nothing but the quality of fitting very neatly into the form of a previous experience. I believe our ingrained habit of hypostatizing impressions, of seeing *things* and not sense-data, rests on the fact that we promptly and unconsciously abstract a form from each sensory experience, and use this form to *conceive* the experience as a whole, as a "thing."

No matter what heights the human mind may attain, it can work only with the organs it has and the functions peculiar to them. Eyes that did not see forms could never furnish it with *images*; ears that did not hear articulated sounds could never open it to *words*. Sense-data, in brief, would be useless to a mind whose activity is "through and through a symbolic process," were they not *par excellence* receptables of meaning. But meaning, as previous considerations have shown, accrues essentially to forms. Unless the *Gestalt*-psychologists are right in their belief that *Gestaltung* is of the very nature of perception, I do not know how the hiatus between perception and conception, sense-organ and mind-organ, chaotic stimulus and logical response, is ever to be closed and welded. A mind that works primarily with meanings must have organs that supply it primarily with forms.

The nervous system is the organ of the mind; its center is the brain, its extremities the sense-organs; and any characteristic function it may possess must govern the work of all its parts. In other words, the activity of our senses is "mental" not only when it reaches the brain, but in its very inception, whenever the alien world outside impinges on the furthest and smallest receptor. All sensitivity bears the stamp of mentality. "Seeing," for instance, is not a passive process, by which meaningless impressions are stored up for the use of an organizing mind, which construes forms out of these amorphous data to suit its own purposes. "Seeing" is itself a process of formulation; our understanding of the visible world begins in the eye.

This psychological insight, which we owe to the school of Wertheimer, Kohler, and Koffka, has far-reaching philosophical consequences, if we take it seriously; for it carries rationality into processes that are usually deemed pre-rational, and points to the existence of forms, i. e., of *possible symbolic material*, at a level where symbolic activity has certainly never been looked for by any epistemologist. The eye and the ear make their own abstractions, and consequently dictate their own peculiar forms of conception. But these forms are derived from exactly the same world that furnished the totally different forms known to physics. There is, in fact, no such thing as *the* form for the "real" world; physics is one pattern which may be found in it, and "appearance," or the pattern of *things* with their qualities and characters, is another. One construction may indeed preclude the other; but to maintain that the consistency and universality of the one brands the other as *false* is a mistake. The fact that physical analysis does not rest in a final establishment of irreducible "qualities" does not refute the belief that there are red, blue, and green things, wet or oily or dry substances, fragrant flowers, and shiny surfaces in the real world. These concepts of the "material mode" are not approximations to "physical" notions at all.  .  .  . The world of physics is essentially the real world construed by mathematical abstractions, and the world of sense is the real world construed by the abstractions which the sense-organs immediately furnish. To suppose that the "material mode" is a primitive and groping attempt at physical conception is a fatal error in epistemology, because it cuts off all interest in the developments of which sensuous conception is capable, and the intellectual uses to which it might be put.

These intellectual uses lie in a field which usually harbors a slough of despond for the philosopher, who ventures into it because he is too honest to ignore it, though really he knows no path around its pitfalls. It is the field of "intuition," "deeper meaning," "artistic truth," "insight" and so forth. A dangerous-looking sector, indeed, for the advance of a rational spirit! To date, I think, every serious epistemology that has regarded mental life as greater than discursive reason, and has made concessions to "insight" or "intuition," has just so far capitulated to *unreason*, to mysticism and irrationalism.  .  .  .

The abstractions made by the ear and the eye—the forms of direct perception—are our most primitive instruments of intelligence. They are genuine symbolic materials, media of understanding, by whose office we apprehend a world of *things*, and of events that are the histories of things. To furnish such conceptions is their prime mission. Our sense-organs make their habitual, unconscious abstractions, in the interest of this *"reifying"* function that underlies ordinary recognition of objects, knowledge of signals, words, tunes, places, and the possibility of classifying such things in the outer world according to their kind. We recognize the elements of this sensuous analysis in all sorts of combination; we can use them imaginatively, to conceive of prospective changes in familiar scenes.

Visual forms—lines, colors, proportions, etc.—are just as capable of articulation, i. e. of complex combination, as words. But the laws that govern this sort of articulation are altogether different from the laws of syntax that govern language. The most radical difference is that visual forms are not discursive. They do not present their constituents successively, but simultaneously, so the relations determining a visual structure are grasped in one act of vision. Their complexity, consequently, is not limited, as the complexity of discourse is limited, by what the mind can retain from the beginning of an apperceptive act to the end of it. Of course such a restriction on discourse sets bounds to the complexity of speakable ideas. An idea that contains too many minute yet closely related parts, too many relations within relations, cannot be "projected" into discursive form; it is too subtle for speech. A language-bound theory of mind, therefore, rules it out of the domain of understanding and the sphere of knowledge.

But the symbolism furnished by our purely sensory appreciation of forms is a *non-discursive symbolism*, peculiarly well suited to the expression of ideas that defy linguistic "projection." Its primary function, that of conceptualizing the flux of sensations, and giving us concrete *things* in place of kaleidoscopic colors or noises, is itself an office that no language-born thought can replace. The understanding of space which we owe to sight and touch could never be developed, in all its detail and definiteness, by a discursive knowledge of geometry. Nature speaks to us, first of all, through our senses; the forms and qualities we distinguish, remember, imagine, or recognize are symbols of entities which exceed and outlive our momentary experience. Moreover, the same symbols—qualities, lines, rhythms—may occur in innumerable presentations; they are abstractable and combinatory. It is quite natural, therefore, that philosophers who have recognized the symbolical character of so-called "sense-data," especially in their highly developed uses, in science and art, often speak of a "language" of the senses, a "language" of musical tones, of colors, and so forth.

Yet this manner of speaking is very deceptive. Language is a special mode of expression, and not every sort of semantic can be brought under this rubric; by generalizing from linguistic symbolism to symbolism as such, we are easily led to misconceive all other types, and overlook their most interesting features. . . .

. . .

. . . . Language in the strict sense is essentially discursive; it has permanent units of meaning which are combinable into larger units; it has fixed equivalences that make definition and translation possible; its connotations are general, so that it requires non-verbal acts, like pointing, looking, or emphatic voice-inflections, to assign specific denotations to its terms. In all these salient characters it differs from wordless symbolism, which is nondiscursive and untranslatable, does not allow of definitions within its own system, and cannot directly convey generalities. The meanings given through language are successively understood, and gathered into a whole by the process called discourse; the meanings of all other symbolic elements that compose a larger, articulate symbol are understood only through the meaning of the whole, through their relations within the total structure. Their very functioning as symbols depends on the fact that they are involved in a simultaneous, integral presentation. This kind of semantic may be called "presentational symbolism," to characterize its essential distinction from discursive symbolism, or "language" proper.

The recognition of presentational symbolism as a normal and prevalent vehicle of meaning widens our conception of rationality far beyond the traditional boundaries, yet never breaks faith with logic in the strictest sense. Wherever a symbol operates, there is a meaning; and conversely, different classes of experience—say, reason, intuition, appreciation—correspond to different types of symbolic mediation. No symbol is exempt from the office of logical formulation, of *conceptualizing* what it conveys; however simple its import, or however great, this import is a *meaning*, and therefore an element for understanding. Such reflection invites one to tackle anew, and with entirely different expectations, the whole problem of the limits of reason, the much-disputed life of feeling and the great controversial topics of fact and truth, knowledge and wisdom, science and art. It brings within the compass of reason much that has been traditionally relegated to "emotion," or to that crepuscular depth of the mind where "intuitions" are supposed to be born, without any midwifery of symbols, without due process of thought, to fill the gaps in the edifice of discursive, or "rational" judgment.

The symbolic materials given to our senses, the *Gestalten* or fundamental perceptual forms which invite us to construe the pandemonium of sheer impression into a world of things and occasions, belong to the "presentational" order. They furnish the elementary abstractions in terms of which ordinary sense-experience is understood. This kind of understanding is directly reflected in the pattern of *physical reaction*, impulse and instinct. May not the order of perceptual forms, then, be a possible principle of symbolization, and hence the conception, expression, and apprehension, of impulsive, instinctive, and sentient life? May not a non-discursive symbolism of light and color, or of tone, be formulative of that life? And is it not possible that the tort of "intuitive" knowledge which Bergson extols above all rational knowledge because it is supposedly not mediated by any formulating (and hence deforming) symbol is itself perfectly rational, but not to be conceived through language—a product of that presentational symbolism which the mind reads in a flash, and preserves in a disposition or an attitude?

This hypothesis, though unfamiliar and therefore somewhat difficult, seems to me well worth exploring. For, quite apart from all questions of the authenticity of intuitive, inherited, or inspired knowledge, about which I do not wish to cavil, the very idea of a *non-rational source* of any knowledge vitiates the concept of mind as an organ of understanding. "The power of reason is simply the power of the whole mind at its fullest stretch and compass," said Professor Creighton, in an essay that sought to stem the great wave of irrationalism and emotionalism following the World War. This assumption appears to me to be a basic one in any study of mentality. Rationality is the essence of mind, and symbolic transformation its elementary process. It is a fundamental error, therefore, to recognize it only in the phenomenon of systematic, explicit reasoning. That is a mature and precarious product.

Rationality, however, is embodied in every mental act, not only when the mind is "at its fullest stretch and compass." It permeates the peripheral activities of the human nervous system, just as truly as the cortical functions.

. . .

The title of Professor Creighton's trenchant little article is "Reason and Feeling." Its central thesis is that if there is something in our mental life besides "reason," by which he means, of course, discursive thinking, then it cannot be an alogical factor, but must be in essence cognitive, too; and since the only alternative to this reason is feeling (the author does not question that axiom of epistemology), feeling itself must somehow participate in knowledge and understanding.

. . .

. . . . *feelings have definite forms*, [says Professor Creighton,] *which become progressively articulated*. Their development is effected through their "interplay with the other aspects of experience"; but the nature of that interplay is not specified. Yet it is here, I think, that cogency for the whole thesis must be sought. *What* character of feeling is "an index of the mind's grasp of its object," and by what tokens is it so? If feeling has articulate forms, what are they like? For what these are *like* determines by what symbolism we might understand them. Everybody knows that language is a very poor medium for expressing our emotional nature. It merely names certain vaguely and crudely conceived states, but fails miserably in any attempt to convey the ever-moving patterns, the ambivalences and intricacies of inner experience, the interplay of feelings with thoughts and impressions, memories and echoes of memories, transient fantasy, or its mere runic traces, all turned into nameless, emotional stuff. If we say that we understand someone else's feeling in a certain matter, we mean that we understand why he should be sad or happy, excited or indifferent, in a general way; that we can see due cause for his attitude. We do not mean that we have insight into the actual flow and balance of his feelings, into that "character" which "may be taken as an index of the mind's grasp of its object." Language is quite inadequate to articulate such a conception. Probably we would not impart our actual, inmost feelings even if they could be spoken. We rarely speak in detail of entirely personal things.

There is, however, a kind of symbolism peculiarly adapted to the explication of "unspeakable" things, though it lacks the cardinal virtue of language, which is denotation. The most highly developed type of such purely connotational semantic is music. We are not talking nonsense when we say that a certain musical progression is significant, or that a given phrase lacks meaning, or a player's rendering fails to convey the import of a passage. Yet such statements make sense only to people with a natural understanding of the medium, whom we describe, therefore, as "musical." Musicality is often regarded as an essentially unintellectual, even a biologically sportive trait. Perhaps that is why musicians, who know that it is the prime source of their mental life and the medium of their clearest insight into humanity, so often feel called upon to despise the more obvious forms of understanding, that claim practical virtues under the names of reason, logic, etc. But in fact, musical understanding is not hampered by the possession of an active intellect, nor even by that love of pure reason which is known as rationalism or intellectualism; and *vice versa*, common-sense and scientific acumen need not defend themselves against any "emotionalism" that is supposed to be inherent in a respect for music. Speech and music have essentially different functions, despite their oft-remarked union in song. . . .

## QUESTIONS

Why is it important for Langer to establish the "mentality" or the "rationality" of nondiscursive symbolisms? Why isn't it enough to demonstrate that these other symbolisms are important and that we cannot very well ignore them? Note that Ayer does not view "morals" or metaphysics as unimportant, nor does he seem to feel that it is useless to argue about them? Indeed, he seems to think that arguing and pointing to facts and general principles may have an effect? If he were to say the same thing about aesthetics, would this satisfy Langer? Or would she want to argue that music and art are as cognitive and rational as physics or common sense experience?

## NOTE

M. McLUHAN, THE GUTENBERG GALAXY (1962) theorizes on the effects on social organization of a general reliance on printed symbols. McLuhan contrasts the written literature tradition with its oral predecessor and sees the alphabet as having "altered the ratio among our senses" in such way as to lead to a split between thought and action. Tribal, non-literate man, McLuhan contends, lives in a "hot hyperesthetic world" whereas the "eye world" is "relatively a cool, neutral world". *Op. cit.* at 28. McLuhan looks to the increasing dominance of electronic media as instituting a new and comparable revolution on social and personal life-styles.

Another view of the broader implications of the reliance on language—written or spoken, presumably—is to be found in Norman O. Brown's LIFE AGAINST DEATH (1959), especially at Chapter 6. Professor Brown presents a psychoanalytic view of language as "a crucial instrument in that general deflection of libido from sexual to social aims which, according to psychoanalytic theory, is sublimation and is culture." *Op. cit.* at 68.

As for the effects of knowing through the senses other than sight or hearing, see H. MARCUSE, EROS AND CIVILIZATION 38–39 (Beacon ed. 1966). Marcuse views the "civilizing" of man as a movement away from, and hence a repression of, the "proximity senses" of touch and smell.

Smell and taste give, as it were, unsublimated pleasure *per se* (and unrepressed disgust). They relate (and separate) individuals immediately, without the generalized and conventionalized forms of consciousness, morality, aesthetics. Such immediacy is incompatible with the effectiveness of organized *domination*, with a society which "tends to isolate people, to put distance between them, and to prevent spontaneous relationships and the 'natural' animal-like expressions of such relations."

*Op. cit.* at 39. What is the relationship between the senses that is presupposed by modern psychotherapy techniques that stress touch and body awareness? Is the assumption that there are non-verbal ways of communicating—with one's self as well as with others—that equally with language lay claim to "meaningfulness" but reach different (perhaps more important) planes of understanding?

## Ernst Cassirer

### Language and Myth *

. . . . What we call myth is, for [Max Muller] . . . something conditioned and negotiated by the agency of language; it is, in fact, the product of a basic shortcoming, an inherent weakness of language. All linguistic denotation is essentially ambiguous—and in this ambiguity, this "paronymia" of words lies the source of all myths. The examples by which Max Muller supports this theory are characteristic of his approach. He cites, as one instance, the legend of Deucalion and Pyrrha, who, after Zeus had rescued them from the great flood which destroyed mankind, became the ancestors of a new race by taking up stones and casting them over their shoulders, whereupon the stones became men. This origin of human beings from stones is simply absurd and seems to defy all interpretation—but is it not immediately clarified as we recall the fact that in Greek men and stones are denoted by identical or at least similar sounding names, that the words . . . are assonant? Or take the myth of Daphne, who is saved from Apollo's embraces by the fact that her mother, the Earth, transforms her into a laurel tree. Again it is only the history of language that can make this myth "comprehensible," and give it any sort of sense. Who was Daphne? In order to answer this question we must resort to etymology, that is to say, we must investigate the history of the word. "Daphne" can be traced back to the Sanskrit Ahana, and Ahana means in Sanskrit the redness of dawn. As soon as we know this, the whole matter becomes clear. The story of Phoebus and Daphne is nothing but a description of what one may observe every day: first, the appearance of the dawnlight in the eastern sky, then the rising of the sun-god who hastens after his bride, then the gradual fading of the red dawn at the touch of the fiery rays, and finally its death or disappearance in the bosom of Mother Earth. So the decisive condition for the development of the myth was not

* From 3–10, 11–14 (S. Langer transl.). Dover ed. 1946). Reprinted by permission of Yale University Press.

the natural phenomenon itself, but rather the circumstance that the Greek word for the laurel and the Sanskrit word for the dawn are related; this entails with a sort of logical necessity the identification of the beings they denote. This, therefore, is his conclusion:

"Mythology is inevitable, it is natural, it is an inherent necessity of language, if we recognize in language the outward form and manifestation of thought; it is in fact the dark shadow which language throws upon thought, and which can never disappear till language becomes entirely commensurate with thought, which it never will. Mythology, no doubt, breaks out more fiercely during the early periods of the history of human thought, but it never disappears altogether. Depend upon it, there is mythology now as there was in the time of Homer, only we do not perceive it, because we ourselves live in the very shadow of it, and because we all shrink from the full meridian light of truth. . . . Mythology, in the highest sense, is the power exercised by language on thought in every possible sphere of mental activity."

It might seem an idle pursuit to hark back to such points of view, which have long been abandoned by the etymology and comparative mythological research of today, were it not for the fact that this standpoint represents a typical attitude which is ever recurrent in all related fields, in mythology as in linguistic studies, in theory of art as well as in theory of knowledge. For Max Muller the mythical world is essentially a world of illusion—but an illusion that finds its explanation whenever the original, necessary self-deception of the mind, from which the error arises, is discovered. This self-deception is rooted in language, which is forever making game of the human mind, ever ensnaring it in that iridescent play of meanings that is its own heritage. And this notion that myth does not rest upon a positive *power* of formulation and creation, but rather upon a mental *defect*—that we find in it a "pathological" influence of speech—this notion has its proponents even in modern ethnological literature.

But when we reduce it to its philosophical lowest terms, this attitude turns out to be simply the logical result of that naive realism which regards the reality of objects as something directly and unequivocally given, literally something tangible. . . . If reality is conceived in this manner, then of course everything which has not this solid sort of reality dissolves into mere fraud and illusion. This illusion may be ever so finely wrought, and flit about us in the gayest and loveliest colors; the fact remains that this image has no independent content, no intrinsic meaning. It does indeed reflect a reality— but a reality to which it can never measure up, and which it can never adequately portray. From this point of view all artistic creation becomes a mere imitation, which must always fall short of the original. Not only simple imitation of a sensibly presented model, but also what is known as idealization, manner, or style, must finally succumb to this verdict; for measured by the naked "truth" of the object to be depicted, idealization itself is nothing but subjective misconception and falsification. And it seems that all other processes of mental gestation involve the same sort of outrageous distortion, the same departure from objective reality and the immediate data of experience. For all mental processes fail to grasp reality itself, and in order to represent it, to hold it at all, they are driven to the use of symbols. But all symbolism harbors the curse of mediacy; it is bound to obscure what it seeks to reveal. Thus the sound of *speech* strives to "express" subjective and objective happening, the "inner" and the "outer" world; but what of this it can retain is not the life and individual fullness of existence, but only a dead abbreviation of it. All that "denotation" to which the spoken word lays claim is really nothing more than mere suggestion; a "suggestion" which, in face of the concrete variegation and totality of actual experience, must always appear a poor and empty shell. That is true of the external as well as the inner world: "When *speaks* the soul, alas, the *soul* no longer speaks!"

From this point it is but a single step to the conclusion which the modern skeptical critics of language have drawn: the complete dissolution of any alleged truth content of language, and the realization that this content is nothing but a sort of phantasmagoria of the spirit. Moreover, from this standpoint, not only myth, art, and language, but even theoretical knowledge itself becomes a phantasmagoria; for even knowledge can never reproduce the true nature of things as they are, but must frame their essence in "concepts." But what are concepts save formulations and creations of thought, which, instead of giving us the true forms of objects, show us rather the forms of thought itself? Consequently all schemata which science evolves in order to classify, organize, and summarize the phenomena of the real world turn out to be nothing but arbitrary schemes—airy fabrics of the mind, which express not the nature of things, but the nature of mind. So knowledge, as well as myth, language, and art, has been reduced to a kind of fiction—to a fiction that recommends itself by its usefulness, but must not be measured by any strict standard of truth, if it is not to melt away into nothingness.

Against this self-dissolution of the spirit there is only one remedy: to accept in all seriousness what Kant calls his "Copernican revolution." Instead of measuring the content, meaning, and truth of intellectual forms by something extraneous which is supposed to be reproduced in them, we must find in these forms themselves the measure and criterion for their truth and intrinsic meaning. Instead of taking them as mere copies of something else, we must see in each of these spiritual forms a spontaneous law of generation; an original way and tendency of expression which is more than a mere record of something initially given in fixed categories of real existence. From this point of view, myth, art, language and science appear as symbols; not in the sense of mere figures which refer to some given reality by means of suggestion and allegorical renderings, but in the sense of forces each of which produces and posits a world of its own. In these realms the spirit exhibits itself in that inwardly determined dialectic by virtue of which alone there is any reality, any organized and definite Being at all. Thus the special symbolic forms are not imitations, but *organs* of reality, since it is solely by their agency that anything real becomes an object for intellectual apprehension, and as such is made visible to us. The question as to what reality is apart from these forms, and what are its independent attributes, becomes irrelevant here. For the mind, only that can be visible which has some definite form; but every form of existence has its source in some peculiar way of seeing, some intellectual formulation and intuition of meaning. Once language, myth, art and science are recognized as such ideational forms, the basic philosophical question is no longer that of their relation to an absolute reality which forms, so to speak, their solid and substantial substratum; the central problem now is that of their mutual limitation and supplementation. Though they all function organically together in the construction of spiritual reality, yet each of these organs has its individual assignment.

From this angle, the relation between language and myth also appears in a new light. It is no longer a matter of simply deriving one of these phenomena from the other, of "explaining" it in terms of the other—for that would be to level them both, to rob them of their characteristic features. If myth be really, as Max Muller's theory has it, nothing but the darkening shadow which language throws upon thought, it is mystifying indeed that this shadow should appear ever as in an aura of its own light, should evolve a positive vitality and activity of its own, which tends to eclipse what we commonly call the immediate reality of *things*, so that even the wealth of empirical, sensuous experience pales before it. As Wilhelm von Humboldt has said in connection with the language problem: "Man lives with his objects chiefly—in fact, since his feeling and acting depends on his perceptions, one may say exclusively—as language presents them to him. By the same process whereby he spins language out of his own being, he ensnares himself in it; and each language draws a magic circle round the people to which it belongs, a circle from which there is no escape save by stepping out of it into another."

This holds, perhaps, even more for the basic mythical conceptions of mankind than for language. Such conceptions are not culled from a ready-made world of Being, they are not mere products of fantasy which vapor off from fixed, empirical, realistic existence, to float above the actual world like a bright mist; to primitive consciousness they present the *totality* of Being. The mythical form of conception is not something superadded to certain definite *elements* of empirical existence; instead, the primary "experience" itself is steeped in the imagery of myth and saturated with its atmosphere. Man lives with these *forms*; he reveals reality to himself, and himself to reality, in that he lets himself and the environment enter into this plastic medium, in which the two do not merely make contact, but fuse with each other.

. . . .

. . . . any symbolic form . . . language, art, or myth . . . is a particular way of seeing, and carries within itself its particular and proper source of light. The function of envisagement, the dawn of a conceptual enlightenment can never be realistically derived from things themselves or understood through the nature of its objective contents. For it is not a question of what we see in a certain perspective, but of the perspective itself. If we conceive the problem in this way, it is certainly clear that a reduction of all myth to one subject matter brings us no nearer to the solution, in fact it removes us further than ever from any hope of a real answer. For now we see in language, art and mythology so many archetypal phenomena of human mentality which can be indicated as such, but are not capable of any further 'explanation' in terms of something else. The realists always assume, as their solid basis for all such explanations, the so-called "given," which is thought to have some definite form, some inherent structure of its own. They accept this reality as an integrated whole of causes and effects, things and attributes, states and processes, of objects at rest and of motions, and the only question for them is which of these elements a particular mental product such as myth, language or art originally embodied. If, for instance, the phenomenon in question is language, their natural line of inquiry must be whether names for things preceded names for conditions or actions, or vice versa—whether, in other words, nouns or verbs were the first "roots" of speech. But this problem itself appears spurious as soon as we realize that the distinctions which here are taken for granted, the analysis of reality in terms of things and processes, permanent and transitory aspects, objects and actions, do not precede language as a substratum of given fact, but that language itself is what initiates such articulations, and develops them in its own sphere. Then it turns out that language could not begin with any phase of "noun concepts" or "verb concepts," but is the very agency that produces the distinction between these forms, that introduces the great spiritual "crisis" in which the permanent is opposed to the transient, and Being is made the contrary of Becoming. So the linguistic fundamental concepts must be realized as something prior to these distinctions, forms which lie between the sphere of noun conception and that of verb conception, between thinghood and eventuality, in a state of indifference, a peculiar balance of feeling.

A similar ambiguity seems to characterize the earliest phases to which we can trace back the development of mythical and religious thought. It seems only natural to us that the world should present itself to our inspection and observation as a pattern of definite forms, each with its own perfectly determinate spatial limits that give it its specific individuality. If we see it as a whole, this whole nevertheless consists of clearly distinguishable units, which do not melt into each other, but preserve their identity that sets them definitely apart from the identity of all the others. But for the mythmaking consciousness these separate elements are not thus separately given, but have to be originally and gradually derived from the whole; the process of culling and sorting out individual forms has yet to be gone through. For this reason the mythic state of mind has been called the "complex" state, to distinguish it from our abstract analytic attitude. Preuss, who coined this expression, points out, for instance, that in the mythology of the Cora Indians, which he has studied exhaustively, the conception of the nocturnal heaven and the diurnal heaven must have preceded that of the sun, the moon, and the separate constellations. The first mythical impulse, he claims, was not toward making a sun-god or a lunar deity, but a community of stars. "The sun-god does indeed hold first rank in the hierarchy of the gods, but . . . the various astral deities can stand proxy for him. They precede him in time, he is created by them, by somebody's jumping into a fire or being thrown into it; his power is influenced by theirs, and he is artificially kept alive by feeding on the hearts of sacrificed victims, i. e., the stars.  The starry night sky is the necessary condition for the existence of the sun; that is the central idea in the whole religious ideation of the Coras and of the ancient Mexicans, and must be regarded as a principal factor in the further development of their religion."

The same function here attributed to the nocturnal heavens seems to be imputed by the Indo-Germanic races to the daylit sky.  Their religions show many traces of the fact that the worship of light as an undifferentiated, total experience preceded that of the individual heavenly bodies, which figure only as its media, its particular manifestations.  In the Avesta, for instance, Mithra is not a sun-god, as he is for later ages; he is the spirit of heavenly light.  He appears on the mountaintops *before* the sun rises, to mount his chariot which, drawn by four white horses, runs the course of heaven during the day; when night comes, he the unsleeping still lights the face of earth with a vague glimmering light.  We are explicitly told that he is neither the sun, nor the moon, nor any or all of the stars, but through them, his thousand ears and ten thousand eyes, he perceives everything and keeps watch over the world.

Here we see in a concrete instance how mythic conception originally grasps only the great, fundamental, qualitative contrast of light and darkness, and how it treats them as *one* essence, one complex whole, out of which definite characters only gradually emerge.  Like the spirit of language, the myth-making genius "has" separate and individualized forms only in so far as it "posits" them, as it carves them out of the undifferentiated whole of its pristine vision.

### Note: Symbolism Versus Reality

In positivism—as in much of everyday thought—the truth or falsity of a statement depends upon the way it measures up to an observable "reality."  Is the difficulty with other symbolisms—such as music, art, poetry, metaphysical and ethical "language"—that there is no way of telling whether they measure up to reality or not?  Is this what is meant when it is said that such symbolisms are nonsensical, have no meaning, do not express facts?  If it is, what is there about language which make *it* capable of being measured against reality?  Does Waismann make an answer to this question in the following passage?

> . . . consider a language in which description does not take the form of sentences.  Examples of such a description would be supplied by a map, a picture language, a film, the musical notation.  A map, for instance, should not be taken as a conjunction of single statements each of which describes a separate fact.  For what, would you say, is the boundary of a fact?  Where does the one end and the other begin?  If we think of such types of description, we are no longer tempted to say that a country, or a story told in a film, or a melody must consist of 'facts'.  Here we begin to see how confusing the idea is according to which the world is a cluster of facts—just as if it were a mosaic made up of little colored stones.  Reality is undivided.  What we may have in mind is perhaps that *language* contains units, viz, *sentences*.

In describing reality, by using sentences, we draw, as it were, lines through it, limit a part and call what corresponds with such a sentence a fact. In other words, language is the knife with which we cut out facts. . . .

*Verifiability* in PROCEEDINGS OF THE ARISTOTELIAN SOCIETY 147–48 (Supp. V. 1945).

Reconsider Cassirer's declaration that "once language, myth, art and science are recognized as such ideational forms, the basic philosophical question is no longer that of their relation to an absolute reality which forms, so to speak, their solid and substantial substratum; the central problem now is that of their mutual limitation and supplementation." Would Waismann agree that the question of meaning is not one of the relation of symbol to external reality? What notion of reality would underlie his position? What is the notion of reality that Cassirer proposes? What does he mean by saying that a symbolic expression must be measured by the standards of the symbolic form of which it is an instance? Would he also think that it is to be judged by its ability to coordinate with the expressions of other symbolic forms? Or would this be the same as measuring the symbol according to its relation to an external reality? Why, exactly, does Cassirer oppose the notion of an external, absolute reality which constitutes a "solid and substantial substratum"? Is it because there is no absolute reality? Or because there is no one presentation of reality which is *a priori* superior to any other?

Let us test the last proposition by recurring to two symbolic expressions of reality which Langer emphasizes—common sense and physics. Is either one of these the criterion for the other? Is the reality of common sense perception and conception always subject to the judgment of physics? Or are the doctrines of physics dependent on common sense? Is Ayer measuring the value of ethical statements against the standards of some other non-ethical symbolism? If so, does he have any alternative? Is there a way for him to follow Cassirer's prescription?

## SECTION FOUR: RATIONALITY IN "COGNITIVE" AND "NON-COGNITIVE" DISCIPLINES

*KARL GEORG WURZEL*

### METHODS OF JURIDICAL THINKING *

. . . . . Pfaff and Hoffmann put at the head of their chapter on interpretation (which is exceedingly thorough and throws much brilliant light on the subject) the proposition (which had been pronounced before upon occasion) that "the interpretation of the Law is an art, not a science; it implies not knowledge but skill; it cannot be learned." As they proceed, practically all rules of interpretation are as a matter of fact abandoned by Pfaff and Hoffmann.

---

* From *Science of Legal Method: Selected Essays by Various Authors* 325–328 (E. Bruncken and L. Register transl. 1921). Reprinted by permission of The Macmillan Company.

Such a proposition, however, means that jurisprudence, the science which above all others deals with phenomena proceeding according to law, is to give up the attempt of understanding the laws to which it itself is subject. Moreover, if this proposition is to be accepted as it stands, it means that jurisprudence must abandon all claims to being a science, a consequence which those who maintain the proposition probably failed to foresee.

Try to realize what is meant by interpretation: the mental reception of the text, the reconstruction of the thought concealed behind the words, briefly the entire mental activity directed upon the words strung together to make the text of a statute, an activity without which the statute would be like a meaningless jumble of words, as a book by Kant would be for a child. This considerable expenditure of mental labor, directed to finding an orderly array of ideas in what otherwise would be a chaos of words without sense, is represented as being subject to no rule or restraint, like the fancy of a poet. (The rules according to which even poetry must proceed were presumably not in the minds of Pfaff and Hoffmann when they formulated their proposition.) This mental activity is represented as purely intuitive, taking shape as it listeth. The lawyer's only guide is tact, as imagination is that of the artist. This tact itself, however, is not susceptible of explanation, its results cannot be controlled by an objective standard. They can be foreseen no more than a future poem about a given subject-matter. If that is to be the meaning of the proposition, what becomes of the claim of jurisprudence to be a method of finding truth, of being a science?

Yet, how could it come about that after all there is such a science as jurisprudence, that this science values the results of its interpretation, its decisions, opinions, and doctrines, according as they appear to be correct, in other words [as they] measure up to the standard of truth; and why is it that notwithstanding numerous differences in detail the practice of the courts and the results of scholarly work do on the whole lead in a single, definite direction? How could it be, moreover, that there is a possibility of legislation?

If as a matter of fact all interpretation were nothing but a sort of artistic function, then nobody could ever foresee how any law would be understood or what effect it would have. Legislation would be a blind rushing to and fro. Regarding particular details, that may really be so, yet the very fact that legislative activity exists and is able to produce effects proves that one can calculate in advance how laws will be understood at least regarding their primary and most general meaning. There can be no doubt about it—a proposition that interpretation is exclusively an art goes far beyond the mark. Such a view is to be explained merely as a reaction against the excess of the rationalistic method formerly in vogue, according to which rules of interpretation were adopted that never went below the surface of legal phenomena.

Interpretation, and juridical thinking in general, are subject, like everything that occurs, to certain laws. They possess their own regularities which at the same time are characteristics. It is immaterial whether these laws are properly considered as jural (which has heretofore been the practice) or natural laws, whether they are merely logical or psychological also; and no more important is the question whether in future jurisprudence itself will consider the exploration of these laws as part of its functions. But the study of these regularities and characteristics must assuredly maintain a place among our scientific interests, if not as a part of legal science, then at all events as part of our knowledge regarding legal science.

## NOTE: THE AUTHORITY OF SCIENCE

Wurzel's unwillingness to let "jurisprudence . . . abandon all claims to being a science" represents one of the characteristic strains in nineteenth and twentieth century thought. The remarkable successes of the natural sciences have spurred thinkers in most disciplines to make their own fields as science-like as possible. For many—and here the logical positivists would seem to be included—an epistemology which identifies knowledge with the scientifically and mathematically knowable seems to follow. The distinction between art and science then comes to include the assumption that the latter is knowable and the former is not. This is an assumption which we seem to find in Wurzel. Yet he does not seem to hold it with complete conviction. He acknowledges that there are "rules according to which even poetry must proceed." The readings in the following section seek to indicate why Wurzel's ambivalence might be justified. They try to show that even the prototypical case of knowledge, scientific knowledge, is not quite as positivism conceives it. To make things more science-like, as positivism would prefer, therefore, would not then lead to the positions which positivism takes and the consequences which positivism envisages.

The attraction of the scientistic model is often explained by the capacity of science to progress. In other areas, such as art and government, it is hard to convince ourselves that we have advanced much beyond the forms that were available to our ancestors. While in science it seems that we are in the process of erecting an edifice of knowledge to which we can continually add, in other areas, we seem incapable of making very much use of conclusions reached in the past. This way of distinguishing science from other fields of thought is explicitly criticized in the pieces by Conant, a Nobel Prize winning chemist, and Kuhn, a noted historian of science. In considering their positions, you might ask yourself just what is the standard of progress which is being invoked by those who emphasize science's progressive nature. Recall Cassirer's dictum that the expressions of any symbolic form must be judged by the standards of that form—and not by those of some other symbolism. How would progress be judged in Cassirer's philosophy? Or is progress an illegitimate concept for him?

Science, finally, is prized for its method. And it sometimes seems that those who criticize a field as being unscientific or unknowable are really making a criticism of the field's methods—or lack of methods. The readings from Munro and Wisdom presented below inquire into the possibility of having a method in fields which are often thought to be method-less. Is there, it is asked, an approach or a procedure which is capable of yielding socially satisfactory results in these fields?

### JAMES B. CONANT

### MODERN SCIENCE AND MODERN MAN *

The fallacy underlying what some might call the eighteenth- and nineteenth-century misconceptions of the nature of scientific investigations seems to lie in a mistaken analogy. Those who said they were investigating the structure of the universe imagined themselves as the equivalent of the early explorers and map makers. The explorers of the fifteenth and sixteenth centuries had opened up new worlds with the aid of imperfect maps; in their accounts of distant lands, there had been some false and many ambiguous statements. But by the time everyone came to believe the world was round, the maps of distant continents were beginning to assume a fairly consistent pattern. By the seventeenth century, methods of measuring space and time had laid the foundations for an accurate geography. The increased success of empirical procedures in improving the work of artisans was already improving men's accuracy of observation. Therefore, by a series of successive approximations, so to speak, maps and descriptions of distant lands were becoming closer and closer to accurate accounts of reality. Why would not the labors of those who worked in laboratories have the same outcome? No one doubted that there were real rivers, mountains, trees, bays with tides, rainfall, snowfall, glaciers; one could doubt any particular map or description, of course, but given time and patience, it was assumed the truth would be ascertained. By the same token there must be a truth about the nature of heat, light, and matter.

To be sure, the map makers had been observing gross objects like rocks and trees, rivers and mountains, while, as science progressed, the force of gravity and atoms and waves in the ether became the preoccupation of the physicist. Still, tentative ideas played a similar part in both enterprises; working hypotheses as to the nature of a river valley, the source of a lake, or the frontier of a mountain range seemed to be the equivalent of the caloric fluid or the early corpuscular theory of light. The early geographers' methods of identification were essentially those of common sense. Any given set of observations might be in error. Yet even erroneous assumptions might serve, at times, a useful purpose. To have assumed the existence of a lake beyond a certain mountain range might prove fortunate; as a "working hypothesis," even if false, it might lead an explorer to important goals.

Of course, the possibility of error exists in all surveys. Indeed, one can image a situation where even in geography no final certainty is possible. Assume an island surrounded by reefs that make direct access out of the question except with special equipment, and assume

* From 92–101 (Anchor ed. 1953). Reprinted with permission of Columbia University Press.

an explorer without such equipment.  He must content himself for the time being with telescopic observations from several angles; he can thus construct a map but with many uncertainties.  For example, are those highly colored areas due to rocks or to vegetation?  On his return with adequate equipment, he can land, go to the colored areas and directly determine their composition.  If before he returns, the island disappears below the surface of the ocean, that makes no difference as to the validity of his methods.  We are all sure that in principle he could have returned and determined the accuracy of his suppositions about the nature of the terrain.

This use of the "in principle" argument, I have already pointeu out, was the basis for the nineteenth-century physicist's confidence in his picture of a gas with its rapidly moving particles.  Those who still hold today with the idea that the universe has a structure which, like the geography of an island, can be discovered by successive approximations, must cling to the "in principle" argument.  Confront them with the phlogiston theory, the caloric fluid, the luminiferous ether— all now obsolete (except for pedagogic purposes)—and they will say, "Yes, the first maps were imperfect, but in principle it is possible to find out what really is the structure of the universe."

On this basic issue there is far from complete agreement among philosophers of science today.  You can, each of you, choose your side and find highly distinguished advocates for the point of view you have selected.  However, in view of the revolution in physics, anyone who now asserts that science is an exploration of the universe must be prepared to shoulder a heavy burden of proof.  To my mind, the analogy between the map maker and the scientist is false.  A scientific theory is not even the first approximation to a map; it is not a creed; it is a policy—an economical and fruitful guide to action by scientific investigators.

But lest my skepticism distort the picture unduly, let me point out how little the new physics has altered some of the older conceptual schemes of physics and chemistry; let me emphasize what an excellent policy the new physics has proved to be in terms of experiments.  What disturbs many people are the difficulties that arise if we accept the map-maker analogy.  That two conceptual schemes should appear so dissimilar as the wave formulation of the laws governing the transmission of light, on the one hand, and the corpuscular theory of light emission, on the other, distresses those who have looked to the physical sciences for an ever increasing degree of explanation as to how matter is "really constructed."  It almost seems as though the modern physicist were like an explorer who, uncertain as to whether the colored areas dimly seen from a distance were rocks or trees, found on landing they were both!  But this is a false parallel; it would be far better to say that the physicist seems now to be in the position of an explorer who can never land on the distant island.  In short, the whole analogy between a map and a scientific theory is without a basis.

One objection to the point of view I am advocating in these lectures may be considered briefly at this point.  It is to the effect that if a scientific theory is not even an approximation to a map of a portion of the universe, the so-called advance of pure science is nothing but a game; from which it would follow, so the objection runs, that the justification of science is to be found only in the application of science to the practical arts. The answer to those who put forward arguments of this type is to remind them of the work of mathematicians, painters, poets, and musical composers. To my mind, the significance of the fabric of scientific theories that have been produced in the last three hundred and fifty years is the same as the significance of the art of the great periods in history, or the significance of the work of the musical composers. For most scientists, I think the justification of their work is to be found in the pure joy of its creativeness; the spirit which moves them is closely akin to the imaginative vision which inspires an artist. To some degree, almost all men today applaud the success of the past in the realm of creative work and do not measure the degree of success by material standards. So too, at some distant time, the advance of science from 1600 to 1950 may be regarded entirely as a triumph of the creative spirit, one manifestation of those vast potentialities of men and women that make us all proud to be members of the human race.

A second objection to the skepticism of those of us who regard all scientific theories as formulations of policy is that our view is only a transitory social phenomenon. One must admit that perhaps the children now in elementary school may in the middle life feel that a picture of the universe that seems no picture is quite a satisfactory model. To be sure, it took generations for people to become accustomed to the concept of a force of gravity acting at a distance without any medium to transmit the force. Certainly by the year 2052, relativity and quantum mechanics will occupy a different position in the total science of that day from that assigned to them at present. When these new ideas have been assimilated into the culture of the times, the idea of science as an inquiry into the structure of the universe may once again become firmly established in people's minds.

My bet as to the future, however, is on the other horse. It seems to me more likely that the average citizen will come to think of science in totally different terms from those employed in explaining science to lay audiences fifty years ago. If I am right, in order to assimilate science into the culture of our twentieth-century highly industrialized society, we must regard scientific theories as guides to human action and thus an extension of common sense. At all events, this is the point of view presented in these lectures.

THOMAS S. KUHN

## THE STRUCTURE OF SCIENTIFIC REVOLUTIONS *

All arguments for a new paradigm [5] discussed so far have been based upon the competitors' comparative ability to solve problems. To

---

* From 154–157 (Phoenix ed. 1964). Copyright 1962 by the University of Chicago Press. Reprinted by permission.

5. At another place, Kuhn describes "paradigms" as "accepted examples of actual scientific practice—examples which include law, theory, application, and instrumentation together—[which] provide models from which spring particular coherent traditions of scientific research." At 10. See also the excerpts reproduced in Chapter 12(1), *infra.*

scientists those arguments are ordinarily the most significant and persuasive. . . . But, for reasons to which we shall shortly revert, they are neither individually nor collectively compelling. Fortunately, there is also another sort of consideration that can lead scientists to reject an old paradigm in favor of a new. These are the arguments, rarely made entirely explicit, that appeal to the individual's sense of the appropriate or the aesthetic—the new theory is said to be "neater," "more suitable," or "simpler" than the old. Probably such arguments are less effective in the sciences than in mathematics. The early versions of most new paradigms are crude. By the time their full aesthetic appeal can be developed, most of the community has been persuaded by other means. Nevertheless, the importance of aesthetic considerations can sometimes be decisive. Though they often attract only a few scientists to a new theory, it is upon those few that its ultimate triumph may depend. If they had not quickly taken it up for highly individual reasons, the new candidate for paradigm might never have been sufficiently developed to attract the allegiance of the scientific community as a whole.

To see the reason for the importance of these more subjective and aesthetic considerations, remember what a paradigm debate is about. When a new candidate for paradigm is first proposed, it has seldom solved more than a few of the problems that confront it, and most of those solutions are still far from perfect. Until Kepler, the Copernican theory scarcely improved upon the predictions of planetary position made by Ptolemy. When Lavoisier saw oxygen as "the air itself entire," his new theory could cope not at all with the problems presented by the proliferation of new gases, a point that Priestley made with great success in his counterattack. . . . Ordinarily, it is only much later, after the new paradigm has been developed, accepted, and exploited that apparently decisive arguments—the Foucault pendulum to demonstrate the rotation of the earth or the Fizeau experiment to show that light moves faster in air than in water—are developed. Producing them is part of normal science, and their role is not in paradigm debate but in postrevolutionary texts.

Before those texts are written, while the debate goes on, the situation is very different. Usually the opponents of a new paradigm can legitimately claim that even in the area of crisis it is little superior to its traditional rival. Of course, it handles some problems better, has disclosed some new regularities. But the older paradigm can presumably be articulated to meet these challenges as it has met others before. Both Tycho Brahe's earth-centered astronomical system and the later versions of the phlogiston theory were responses to challenges posed by a new candidate for paradigm, and both were quite successful. In addition, the defenders of traditional theory and procedure can almost always point to problems that its new rival has not solved but that for their view are no problems at all. Until the discovery of the composition of water, the combustion of hydrogen was a strong argument for the phlogiston theory and against Lavoisier's. And after the oxygen theory had triumphed, it could still not explain the preparation of a combustible gas from carbon, a phenomenon to which the phlogistonists had pointed as strong support for their view. Even in the area of crisis, the balance of argument and counterargument can sometimes be very close indeed. And outside that area the balance will often decisively favor the tradition. Copernicus destroyed a time-honored explanation of terrestrial motion without replacing it; Newton did the same for an older explanation of gravity, Lavoisier for the common properties of metals, and so on. In short, if a new candidate for paradigm had to be judged from the start by hard-headed people who examined only relative problem-solving ability, the sciences would experience very few major revolutions. . . .

But paradigm debates are not really about relative problem-solving ability, though for good reasons they are usually couched in those terms. Instead, the issue is which paradigm should in the future guide research on problems many of which neither competitor can yet claim to resolve completely. A decision between alternate ways of practicing science is called for, and in the circumstances that decision must be based less on past achievement than on future promise. The man who embraces a new paradigm at an early stage must often do so in defiance of the evidence provided by problem-solving. He must, that is, have faith that the new paradigm will succeed with the many large problems that confront it, knowing only that the older paradigm has failed with a few. A decision of that kind can only be made on faith.

That is one of the reasons why prior crisis proves so important. Scientists who have not experienced it will seldom renounce the hard evidence of problem-solving to follow what may easily prove and will be widely regarded as a will-o'-the-wisp. But crisis alone is not enough. There must also be a basis, though it need be neither rational nor ultimately correct, for faith in the particular candidate chosen. Something must make at least a few scientists feel that the new proposal is on the right track, and sometimes it is only personal and inarticulate aesthetic considerations that can do that. Men have been converted by them at times when most of the articulable technical arguments pointed the other way. When first introduced, neither Copernicus' astronomical theory nor De Broglie's theory of matter had many other significant grounds of appeal. Even today Einstein's general theory attracts men principally on aesthetic grounds, an appeal that few people outside of mathematics have been able to feel.

This is not to suggest that new paradigms triumph ultimately through some mystical aesthetic. On the contrary, very few men desert a tradition for these reasons alone. Often those who do turn out to have been misled. But if a paradigm is ever to triumph it must gain some first supporters, men who will develop it to the point where hardheaded arguments can be produced and multiplied. And even those arguments, when they come, are not individually decisive. Because scientists are reasonable men, one or another argument will ultimately persuade many of them. But there is no single argument that can or should persuade them all. Rather than a single group conversion, what occurs is an increasing shift in the distribution of professional allegiances

*HENRY DAVID AIKEN*

### REASON AND CONDUCT *

Another feature of the new approach [in ethics] is its contention that in ethics we are faced with a special sort of reasoning which is different in kind from those employed in formal logic or in empirical science. But here again we do well not to dismiss too soon more traditional views.

Because ethical arguments are, at certain junctures, subject to special "moral" rules of inference, it does not follow that, at other junctures, ordinary deductive and inductive methods do not also apply.

Now one of the reasons why it has been argued that the logic of moral discourse is peculiar is that it has been taken for granted that ordinary deductive and inductive methods are applicable only to statements which are cognitively meaningful. Ethical judgments are, at least in part, noncognitive. Hence, if they are to be regarded as rationally justifiable, there must be special rules of normative inference applicable to them. This conclusion, I am now convinced, is also premature. Philosophers have no very precise notion of what they mean by "cognitive meaning," and hence no clear idea of the range of deductive and inductive procedures, even when it is granted that they are to be restricted to cognitively meaningful statements. But, apart from this, there is no compelling reason to suppose that the application of such procedures to normative statements or to mixed reasonings which are partly cognitive and partly normative is illicit. For example, we all constantly seek to justify particular moral conclusions by subsuming them under general moral principles. Granted that the terms of the conclusion are, as we say, contained in those of the premises, we are all prepared to acknowledge, in certain cases at least, that the conclusion follows logically from the premises. All that is required for deductive methods to apply is that the sentences in question be capable of quantification and of some lawful form of negation or opposition. . . .

. . .

It is possible to reply, however, that such a view is ill advised and question-begging, since it neglects the possibility, brought forcibly to our attention by the emotive theory, that the distinctively non-referential meanings characteristic of ethical terms preclude altogether the application of logical procedures of any sort in the validation of moral conclusions. The logic of the books, whether two-valued or three-valued, applies only to statements which are true, false, or probable. Ethical judgments, however, are or contain recommendations, proposals, prescriptions and incitements to act. These can be neither true nor false nor probable in any intelligible sense. How, then, it may be asked, can one speak of relations of entailment or logical implication holding between them and other expressions? The appeal to general normative principles is not like the appeal to universal premises from

* From 94–97 (1962). Reprinted by permission of Henry David Aiken.

which particular conclusions are inferred. If I accept a universal moral rule, I am bound by no law of logic whatever to accept any particular moral conclusion. It is true that we continually do assert moral principles in support of particular moral conclusions. But here the relation is again purely psychological. When we find ourselves adhering to moral principles which conflict with our particular moral decisions, no question of logical inconsistency is involved. There is merely a material opposition of attitudes which happen to conflict with one another in action.

To this it must be rejoined that, while there can be no logical opposition between individual attitudes, it does not follow from this that there is no logical opposition between sentences which express such attitudes. Again we must focus upon the question whether, as normally used, ethical judgments are related to one another in ways that accord with the syntactical rules of logic. That we do normally so relate them is plain. Nor does formal logic itself preclude the possibility. If all s's are p, and a is an s, then a is a p regardless of whether p is a descriptive predicate such as "yellow" or a normative predicate such as "good." There is no rule that I have been able to discover in the logic books which restricts the values of the variables of any ordinary sentential function to so-called "cognitive" or descriptive terms. There is no formulated condition that they must mean in some particular mode of meaning. If it be replied that there is at any rate a presumption that the sentences derived by substitution from such functions must be either true or false, then it must be rejoined that there is no good reason to deny that ethical judgments are not properly spoken of as true or false. Toulmin tells us that ethical judgments may be valid or invalid but not true or false. But if his appeal is to our ordinary moral practices, as it is, then the reply is clear; it is far more appropriate to say that it is false that I ought to beat my grandmother than to say that is invalid. Toulmin's contention is incompatible with the most obvious facts of ordinary moral discourse. He may then wish to say that, if we so speak, we ought not to do so. But to this the reply must be that in saying this he changes the question and that, when he has given us valid reasons for such a recommendation, we will be delighted to consider them.

For my part, I have discovered no sound reason whatever for denying to our ethical judgments, even if they be admitted not to be factual descriptions or predictions, the right to be regarded as true or false. Notice that no one objects when it is said that a certain statement in formal logic is true or false. Nor does anyone object to the use of the phrase "logical truth." The interesting question is thus not whether moral judgments may be true or false but rather in what sense they are so; nor is the issue whether this sense is identical with that intended when we hold a statement of fact to be true or false but rather whether there is a sufficient analogy to permit the application of logical procedures in both cases. The application of "truth" and "falsity" in either case signifies primarily that the statements in question are validatable or certifiable in accordance with certain governing rules or procedures.

Let me make the point of these remarks more explicit. It is not denied that, in certain respects, the process of justification in morals differs from that involved in formal logic. It is maintained only that there is no sound reason for denying that ordinary deductive methods do apply, not merely to the factual parts of an argument to a moral conclusion, but also to the distinctively normative aspects. Logical subsumption occurs as well in ethics or in the law as in science or pure logic. If this requires us to believe that other than factual statements may have logical implications or relevancies, then we must make the best of it. And if it requires us to adopt the view that words having noncognitive meanings are themselves sometimes subject to proprie- ties, that in the ascription of a noncognitive term we may make significant mistakes, and that we sometimes may be required to with- draw normative judgments on pain of inconsistency and error, then we have our work cut out for us. For my part I welcome the result. What is wanted is a better theory of "noncognitive" terms.

## Notes and Questions

Even if it is assumed that ethical language may properly utilize the syllogism, how far does this go to establish that ethics is a field in which reasoning can take place? Remember that any syllogism is only as good as its premises. For the conclusion of a syllogism to be acceptable, the premises must be acceptable as well. When this point is usually made, emphasis is put on the indeterminacy of the major premise. The minor premise is apparently thought to entail fewer difficulties. We have earlier indicated that this attitude is probably mistaken. For that Socrates is a man for some purposes will be wholly irrelevant if he is not also a man for purposes of the general proposi- tion that "all men are mortal." And whether he is a man for those purposes is dictated by no rule of logic, but only by a judgment of what those purposes are and what they require. It is quite possible, then, to find that both of the premises from which a syllogistic con- clusion follows are unacceptable. Is it possible to "reason" in such a situation? Does reasoning depend to any extent on the likelihood that there will be premises on which people will agree? Can it be said that there is such a likelihood in ethics?

## Thomas Munro

### Toward Science in Aesthetics *

The movement toward a descriptive study of form begins when- ever a critic makes an effort to perceive a work of art clearly and as a whole: to explain his feelings toward it by tracing them to specific observable details in the object.

Such an attitude is intermediate between two extremes. One, that of casual enjoyment or hasty criticism, tends to notice only a few details, or the whole thing in a vague and blurred manner—to sense rather than to perceive it; then to feel an immediate affective response, such as liking or disliking, which may find expression in broad evaluative terms like "beautiful" or "ugly." There the matter

* 18–21, 23–28 (1956). Copyright (c) 1956 by The Liberal Arts Press, Inc. Reprinted by permission of the Lib- eral Arts Press Division of the Bobbs- Merrill Company, Inc.

rests; the judgment expressed is final; attention wanders or remains fragmentary and superficial.

The other extreme is an attempt at a rigorously objective account of the work of art, as a zoologist might describe a butterfly, excluding all affective terms, putting down only what any observer with normal sense organs (and perhaps a microscope) could observe. A critical analysis of a work of art would include, in addition, affective responses and perhaps associated imagery, but with a persistent effort to relate them to perceptible features in the object.

As we have also noted, it is a common human trait to think and speak as if such effects on the beholder were properties inherent in the object which stimulated them. The critic should not be over-anxious to express all his experience in terms of his own responses, in the hope of being more scientific. . . . If the critic were to transfer his attention too much to his own responses, most of them would immediately cease to operate; self-consciousness would stifle them. Another reason is that the structure of the work of art is one of the two main determinants (along with individual personality) of the nature of the response.

It is therefore necessary for aesthetics to observe and describe the various forms of art, not entirely apart from human responses to them, but in their own rights as distinctive stimuli. The experimental way to do this is to take as starting points the affects or "tertiary qualities," roughly distinguished by critical terms; then to work gradually toward a more distinct recognition of those factors in the stimulus which helped to determine them.

In a sense we cannot analyze any aesthetic quality in a work of art, or any other perceptive or affective quality as such. It is present in experience as an irreducible whole, and is different from the sum of any number of psychic elements into which we could try to analyze it. But it does not follow, as some critics have argued, that all analysis of aesthetic form is impossible. In distinguishing the various factors that go to make up a work of art, we are not analyzing the affect itself, but the complex stimulus which produced it. We are thus working toward a partial explanation of it by discovering some of its causal antecedents.

There are two necessary phases in this type of criticism. One is the effort toward clearer perception of form; the other is the effort to express its results in words that will indicate them to others. These phases can proceed hand in hand, each assisting the other.

### 2. *Organic perception of a complex form*

This phase of criticism requires keeping one's attention fixed with some steadiness on a particular work of art, and trying to grasp its chief elements in their interrelations. It is not a passive, dreamy contemplation, or a listing of miscellaneous features, one after the other, but an active, selective scrutiny and co-ordination of details. It involves alternating an analytic with a synthetic attitude: first to dissociate a vaguely sensed complex into its parts, then to reassemble these parts into an organic whole.

The word "form" is often used in one of several narrow senses. In the broad sense intended here, it is any distinctive way of organizing the materials in a work of art. It is not a detachable framework, but (in Pater's words) the distinctive "mode of handling" the subject and materials. In music or poetry, one has not grasped the form in merely identifying a conventional pattern, such as the sonnet or fugue. There is all the difference in the world between sonnets, and to describe the form of one is to recognize and state the distinctive characteristics, of whatever sort, that make it different from all others. If a fugue makes use of peasant folk tunes for its melodies, then to describe it one must recognize not only that fact, but the peculiar mode of handling them, the ways in which they are woven together, varied in rhythm and key, and enriched with harmony. In painting and sculpture, the word "form" is sometimes limited to the linear pattern or to the shapes of masses; but the broader conception would take in also the lines, lights and shadows, colors, spaces, even representative and expressive effects—in so far as they are made to co-operate harmoniously toward producing a single cumulative effect on the beholder.

For the sake of clear perception, however, it is necessary to distinguish to some extent certain main groups of elements in such a total form. These are the sensuous materials (e. g., tones, colors, lines, masses, word sounds, considered as individual units); the same materials as co-operating factors in a design (e. g., a sonnet, facade, or sonata); and the natural objects represented, the ideas or emotions expressed (e. g., trees, houses, and sunlight in a landscape; religious, moral, or dramatic interest, a gay or tragic mood). For a beginner in art appreciation this is especially important, since his usual tendency is to overemphasize representative and expressive effects. At first it is well for him to practice ignoring these effects, and attending only to the others. With a picture, for example, one can stand at a distance, or at an acute angle with the plane of the canvas, or perhaps turn the picture upside down—anything to grasp the effect of the colors, lines, and masses in themselves, without regard to what natural objects they stand for. Afterward, he can return to perceive both elements in their mutual relations. Some critics would have him ignore subject matter forever; but this is an extreme and unnecessary attitude taken by few artists, and destructive of many important values.

. . . .

Perception, like reasoning, can be experimental. Attention can be kept alert but varied in direction; not too rigidly fixed on one aspect or theme, but turned here and there as one would look in a foggy street for outstanding features that may give a clue to the rest. A good order, on the whole, is to experience the object first in a general, unselective way, without looking for anything in particular or trying to recall what anyone has said about it. If it is a picture, stand off at a distance, so that details are merged; if a poem or piece of music, read or hear it first with no definite purpose, merely to let its total effect "sink in" as much as it will in an easy and natural way. Then come back to it later on, to pick out its main constituent parts, its chief themes and distinctive qualities, noticing each of these as a whole without too much attention to subordinate details. Then each of these wholes—say a certain melody composed of several phrases; the complex motives of a single character in a play; the drapery on one painted figure—can be analyzed in turn into its elements. There is a dangerous tendency in perception to let one's attention be caught by some one familiar or conspicuous detail, and thus to miss the larger structure into which it fits. Finally, or at repeated intervals if the task is hard, one should take a general view as at first, but more synthetically, working always towards a more organic perception instead of the first blurred and superficial one.

It is a familiar fact that some objects are more easily perceived as wholes than others. A page containing only a circle, for example, is easier to grasp as a whole than one full of irregular figures; a popular song, than a symphony. Wherever a part is continued or repeated with recognizable similarity, it tends to make the whole form easier to keep track of at once. But it may also tend to become monotonous, like the ticking of a clock; we become anaesthetic toward it, or, if it is forced on our attention, it becomes irritating. In some phases of art, such as architectural ornament, the artist does not care to make us conscious of separate details, and so repeats them with extreme uniformity. In others, he tries to keep our interest stimulated with frequent surprises, and so repeats a theme with minor variations and irregularities. In still others, he wishes to startle and excite us with sudden shocks: a *sforzando* or an unprepared change of key; the extrance of a radically different melody, color, or shape; a quite unexpected turn of events in fiction. In a broad sense, these are examples of disunity; they are breaks in the smooth flow of parts, and in that sense no work of art is a perfect unity. But even these contrasts can be to some extent woven together, reintegrated as parts in a comprehensive scheme. The surprising incident is shown to be one that might logically have happened under the conditions; we hear the first melody again with a sense of familiar recognition, as of coming home after an adventure.

Works of art differ widely as to the extent to which they introduce these sudden breaks, and also as to the extent to which they try to link them up again. The observer should ask himself, then, whether any gaps and shocks that he feels are due to his own failure to perceive the relations which the artist has indicated, whether they are intended by the artist as parts of a total plan, or whether they are unintended faults in the machinery of the work of art itself. Conversely, he should ask if he is noticing all the discontinuities that actually exist in it, and be on the lookout for those of both kinds, the intended and the unintended.

Often after repeated failures, the *raison d'être* of some apparently wrong detail will suddenly flash over one: the distorted tabletop in a Cezanne still life comes into relation with a folded tablecloth in another corner of the picture, as a repetition of line and mass. The larger order into which everything fits has been there all the time, but one has been overlooking some detail that completed the circuit. For this reason it is best not to push perceptive effort to the point of fatigue at any one time, but to come back another day with a fresh viewpoint. Unconsciously, one's nervous mechanism may have kept on organizing the images in the meantime. In the same way a form that seemed solid enough at first glance will disclose weak spots, glaring discrepancies, limping, illogical transitions that were superficially glossed over, as in a thrilling mystery play whose solution one thinks about on the way home.

A form may be made complex, not only by multiplying themes and variations, but by bringing more radically different factors into play. Thus a line drawing may be made more intricate as such, or may be complicated by the addition of light and shade and color. A melody for violin alone may be made into an intricate arabesque, or it may be kept simple and a complex form be built up by adding other voices, each pursuing its own pattern simultaneously. Thus a musical composition may involve co-ordinating melody, harmony, rhythm, counterpoint, and orchestration. In opera, the sense and sound of words, the action, costumes, scenery, and lighting effects are additional factors to be co-ordinated.

The observer's task at any given moment—say the elevation of the Grail in *Parsifal*—is to ask himself what total synthetic effect on the beholder is intended; and how each factor operating at the moment contributes its share—how each previous moment has contributed by leading up to it. He may find that a particular factor is weak: the singing, or the lighting; or that one obtrudes itself on the attention—an overloud orchestra, perhaps; or that the action calls for a mood which the music tends to counteract. In a well-organized work, one is apt to find it harder to think of the factors separately; but comparing the work with others less unified, or imagining how the present one could be changed a little in each factor, will help to reveal the part each is playing in the whole.

3. *Tentative criticism*

One's first experience of a work of art, superficial as it may be, usually includes an immediate feeling over and above mere perception. This may be a positive liking or disliking, an intense emotion, a definite critical judgment, or it may be only mild interest or boredom. To express that feeling in words is not at all a necessary part of aesthetic experience. To persons of a certain temperament, anything more than the proverbial "Hm!" is an annoying distraction. But to others it is a natural and continuous part of appreciation, and it is a necessary phase of both criticism and aesthetics.

. Inadequate as any words are apt to seem, a little effort to find the right ones is often an aid to clear distinction, for oneself as well as for others, of the specific qualities felt. But it is dangerous to try for exact words too quickly; the attempt will distort and stifle other sorts of response. It is best to have the full experience first and then speak or write about it; not a long time afterwards, when it has become a little hazy, but as soon as the response has taken shape, and can lead naturally to expression.

Neither the feeling, nor the finding of words to describe it, is a matter that can be entirely controlled by reason. Both are largely automatic processes of apperception and association, in which the sensory responses start further reverberations through the organism, setting in motion some of the waiting machinery of habit and memory, of innate and acquired predispositions to respond in a certain complex way to a stimulus of that type. The finding of suitable words is a part of this associative process. If in the past certain words have been used or heard in more or less similar situations, they tend now to come to mind as an immediate result of that felt similarity. In proportion as one has become familiar with works of art like the one at hand, forming certain habitual attitudes toward them, and learning to express these attitudes in words, the process will now be quicker and easier, less groping and uncertain.

The chief danger attending it is, as usual, one of habit-fixation. There will be a tendency to pigeonhole the new object at once after glimpsing some few conspicuous features of it; to respond in feelings and words as one usually does to objects having those few features. So standardized, criticism becomes hackneyed and perfunctory. It speaks in cliches, like the term "whimsical" in regard to anything by Barrie. An experimental attitude here would involve a suspension of final judgment, but not necessarily any sense of restraint that would weaken the first spontaneous response. Strong and positive as that response may be, it can be followed up with further investigation.

In exactly the same way, a comment about the present object by some other critic can be followed up as a hypothesis. In going to a play after reading a newspaper criticism of it, this would imply listening for particular lines and incidents in the play which support or contradict that criticism. To work still further toward definite verification would be to read the play later, select these evidential details, and trace their exact bearing on the hypothesis in question. Any general critical or evaluative term suggested will be linked if possible with demonstrable elements; with actual lines or spots of color that one could point to in a painting; to notes that one could point to in a musical score. If the quality alleged is something more pervasive, that cannot be traced to a few definite points, it may at least be possible to find places where it is especially manifest, or bits scattered through the whole which exert a cumulative effect. In a picture there may be a slight but constant tendency to elongate every object; in a piece of music, to reintegrate augmented fourths, briefly and quietly in some inner voice, so that little by little they make themselves felt as a troubled undercurrent.

Still one may have to describe them in emotional terms, such as "troubled." But one is working always toward more distinct recognition of the factors which are contributing most powerfully to that particular emotional effect. Emotions and their causes in the form are recognized and characterized ever more specifically. Things are no longer merely "nice," "unpleasant," or "interesting," as at first. They are "sparkling," "ponderous," "lilting," "harsh," "crisp," "dainty," "melting," "rich," or "barren." More and more of such words come to mind as one contemplates different parts of the object. One has distinguished separate themes and factors and can describe each separately, and the relation of each to others. One melody is wild and tormented; another, grave and sedate, answers and finally dominates it. Bit by bit such comments will grow into a description approximating in organic structure the work of art itself; yet also, in a sense, a narrative or autobiography of one's adventure with it. The account will still be of how one individual sees and feels it, but more and more it will become an account of this particular object as distinct from all others.

In the process, the critic is quite likely to have to alter the snap judgment he began with. What seemed at first confused is now orderly; what seemed ugly and horrible is merely odd, bizarre, and fantastic. He may never come, especially if the work is complex and many-sided, to any way of perceiving or describing it that satisfies him as complete. In each contact with it he will discover new details and relations, and his description of its form will grow with his growing powers of perception. But on some points he will find his first impressions confirmed and traced to definite causes which are there for all the world to see. He will know, now, that his quick feeling of a picture's weakness and confusion was due to the fact that certain objects in it do not take definite positions in space, but appear at the same distance from the eye as other objects which overlap them. He will have traced his feeling of vague disappointment at a story's ending to the realization that a certain conflict was left undecided, or settled in a hasty, arbitrary way.

## QUESTIONS

1. In what sense does Munro bring science into aesthetics? Does a critic who traces his aesthetic feelings "to specific observable details in the object" resemble in any way the scientist who verifies his scientific hunches?

2. To what extent could the method proposed by Munro be used by Frankfurter in *Rochin*? To what extent *was* it used in *Rochin*? Is there a role for Munro's method in establishing the premises of moral and legal argument? If Frankfurter could convince us with it that the actions in *Rochin* were antithetical to our notions of justice and human dignity, would he have discharged his responsibility? Or would it still be necessary for him to state a rule? If so, what additional function is served by rules? How do they add to the authority and legitimacy of a judicial decision?

3. To what extent are Munro's prescriptions applicable to the reading of judicial opinions? Can you translate his remarks into a law student's manual for interpreting and analyzing cases?

JOHN WISDOM

## GODS *

6.5 *In courts of law* it sometimes happens that opposing counsel are agreed as to the facts and are not trying to settle a question

* From XLV Proceedings of the Aristotelian Society (London) 1944/45, 185–206 (193–196). Copyright 1945 by the Aristotelian Society. Reprinted by special permission of the author and the Editor of the Aristotelian Society.

of further fact, are not trying to settle whether the man who admittedly had quarrelled with the deceased did or did not murder him, but are concerned with whether Mr. A who admittedly handed his long-trusted clerk signed blank cheques did or did not exercise reasonable care, whether a ledger is or is not a document, whether a certain body was or was not a public authority.

In such cases we notice that the process of argument is not a *chain* of demonstrative reasoning. It is a presenting and representing of those features of the case which *severally co-operate* in favour of the conclusion, in favour of saying what the reasoner wishes said, in favour of calling the situation by the name by which he wishes to call it. The reasons are like the legs of a chair, not the links of a chain. Consequently although the discussion is *a priori* and the steps are not a matter of experience, the procedure resembles scientific argument in that the reasoning is not *vertically* extensive but *horizontally* extensive—it is a matter of the cumulative effect of several independent premises, not of the repeated transformation of one or two. And because the premises are severally inconclusive the process of deciding the issue becomes a matter of weighing the cumulative effect of one group of severally inconclusive items against the cumulative effect of another group of severally inconclusive items, and thus lends itself to description in terms of conflicting 'probabilities'. This encourages the feeling that the issue is one of fact—that it is a matter of guessing from the premises at a further fact, at what is to come. But this is a muddle. *The dispute does not cease to be* a priori *because it is a matter of the cumulative effect of severally inconclusive premises.* The logic of the dispute is not that of a chain of deductive reasoning as in a mathematic calculation. But nor is it a matter of collecting from several inconclusive items of information an expectation as to something further, as when a doctor from a patient's symptoms guesses at what is wrong, or a detective from many clues guesses the criminal. It has its own sort of logic and its own sort of end—the solution of the question at issue is a decision, a ruling by the judge. But it is not an arbitrary decision though the rational connections are neither quite like those in vertical deductions nor like those in inductions in which from many signs we guess at what is to come; and though the decision manifests itself in the application of a name it is no more merely the application of a name than is the pinning on of a medal merely the pinning on of a bit of metal. Whether a lion with stripes is a tiger or a lion is, if you like, merely a matter of the application of a name. Whether Mr. So-and-So of whose conduct we have so complete a record did or did not exercise reasonable care is not merely a matter of the application of a name or, if we choose to say it is, then we must remember that with this name a game is lost and won and a game with very heavy stakes. With the judges' choice of a name for the facts goes an attitude, and the declaration, the ruling, is an exclamation evincing that attitude. But *it is an exclamation which not only has a purpose but also has a logic,* a logic surprisingly like that of 'futile', 'deplorable', 'graceful', 'grand', 'divine'.

6.6 *Suppose two people are looking at a picture or natural scene.* One says 'Excellent' or 'Beautiful' or 'Divine'; the other says 'I don't see it'. He means he doesn't see the beauty. And this reminds us of how we felt the theist accuse the atheist of blindness and the atheist accuse the theist of seeing what isn't there. And yet surely each sees what the other sees. It isn't that one can see part of the picture which the other can't see. So the difference is in a sense not one as to the facts. And so it cannot be removed by the one disputant discovering to the other what so far he hasn't seen. It isn't that the one sees the picture in a different light and so, as we might say, sees a different picture. Consequently the difference between them cannot be resolved by putting the picture in a different light. And yet surely this is just what can be done in such a case—not by moving the picture but by talk perhaps. To settle a dispute as to whether a piece of music is good or better than another we listen again, with a picture we look again. Someone perhaps points to emphasize certain features and we see it in a different light. Shall we call this 'field work' and 'the last of observation' or shall we call it 'reviewing the premises' and 'the beginning of deduction (horizontal)'?

If in spite of all this we choose to say that a difference as to whether a thing is beautiful is not a factual difference we must be careful to remember that there is a procedure for settling these differences and that this consists not only in reasoning and redescription as in the legal case, but also in a more literal re-setting-before with re-looking or re-listening.

6.7 *And if we say as we did at the beginning that when a difference as to the existence of a God is not one as to future happenings, it is not experimental and therefore not as to the facts, we must not forthwith assume that there is no right and wrong about it,* no rationality or irrationality, no appropriateness or inappropriateness, no procedure which tends to settle it, *nor even that this procedure is in no sense a discovery of new facts.* . . .

The difference as to whether a God exists involves our feelings more than scientific disputes and in this respect is more like a difference as to whether there is beauty in a thing.

NOTE: THE MEANING OF A PAINTING

1. Compare the difficulties of communication by means of language with the difficulties of communication by means of a painting, such as Tooker's "The Subway" (Figure 1.). Is the understanding of a work of art any less subjective an enterprise than the understanding of a linguistic direction or description? Yet, is it unreasonable to say that, in an important sense, Tooker is *telling us something*? And is it impossible to know, within some significant range, what that something is? Does each person looking at the painting simply see "what he wants to see," uninfluenced by Tooker's prior decisions? Would Tooker have evoked the same responses had he simply thrown ink on canvas, attaining an effect something like that of a Rorschach test?

2.  Describe the painting.  Is it possible to talk at least generally about its "subject matter"?  Is it unreasonable to say that it conveys ideas about fear, isolation (virginity), the barriers between strangers, the concrete sterility of modern life?  How much of what the woman sees is "really" outside her mind and how much of what she "sees" reflects the inside to which she has withdrawn? (Does Tooker's selection of the subway subtly turn our minds towards contemplation of the role of the subconscious—the buried underground?)  How much of what you see in the painting is influenced by what is in your mind and how much by what is in Tooker's?  Did Tooker just see a scene and paint it, leaving it to the viewer to decide what it meant, or does the painting reflect and convey *Tooker's* thoughts about life?  If the latter, how does the painting "reflect and convey" the artist's thoughts?  If such thoughts can be conveyed by a picture—notwithstanding the range for "subjectivity"—how impossible is it for, say, a legislature to "reflect and convey" its ideas, by printed symbols, to judges and administrators?

3.  How do you come to know what Tooker meant to state, so far as you feel that you can know it?  Does your understanding improve upon *reflection*?  If so, what does reflection involve?  Try to describe the process of your understanding.  Does your understanding "grow" by looking serially at one segment of the painting after the other, *e.g.*, one face after the other?  Or is there constant feedback between parts and whole?  Does the title of the painting add to your understanding (what other titles might the painting have, and how would each influence your estimate of what the author meant)?  How *do* titles come to have such an effect on the work "itself"?  Is part of the process of understanding the painting a putting ourselves in the place of the artist?  How do we put ourselves "in the place of" someone we have never met?  What is involved?  Is the attempt meaningful even though we can never *know* we were right?  What influence does the effort have on our thoughts?

4.  Would your understanding of the painting be different depending upon your previous study of the art?  How?

5.  Compare now the process of interpreting a legal rule with the process of interpreting a painting.  How are the processes of reflection by which one seeks to understand a work of art like the processes by which one seeks to understand legislative intent?  What corresponds, in statutory interpretation, to the process of going from the whole to its parts and back again?  For further discussion of these questions, see Chapter 15, especially section 1(b).

FIGURE I.

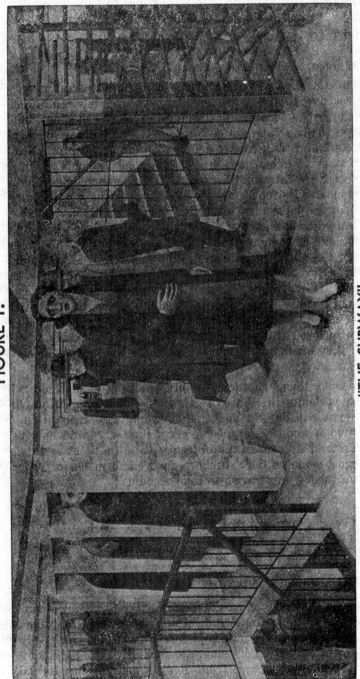

"THE SUBWAY"
George Tooker *

• Egg tempera on composition board. 18⅛ x 36⅛. (1950). Julian Force Purchase. Collection Whitney Museum of Modern Art, New York. Photo: Geoff Clements. With the kind permission and co-operation of the Whitney Museum.

## CHAPTER TEN

# The Facts of Life

## NOTE: FREEDOM AND ORDER

When it is argued that knowledge—and therefore any given decision—is relative to the individual knower and the conditions in which his knowledge occurs, a spectre of disorder, even chaos, is likely to appear. This relativism seems to leave individuals unchecked and undirected, and thus free to act as their immediate impulses declare. For many thinkers, it is precisely this consequence which provides the decisive refutation of a relativistic epistemology. No matter how persuasive its tenets, they will argue, it cannot overcome the simple fact of common experience that the alternatives available to men are limited and that there are paths which they must follow. To this, of course, some relativists will respond that this "simple fact" is no fact at all: it is only an illusion fostered by a false philosophy and devised to soothe egos which cannot bear to face the "true" facts of life. Other relativists will argue, however, that it is the absolutist or literalist position which leads to chaos, to a skepticism which calls into question the theoretical possibility of personal and social organization. Thus, their position is that if there is any order at all—and they emphatically insist that there is—it *must* be a relativistic one.

Most people, then, whether absolutist or relativist, would reject a theory which denies the sense of givenness and organization which seems to pervade life. No doubt, they would also insist that any theory of human knowledge must express this sense and help us to better understand its causes and objects. It is the point of this section to suggest some of the "stubborn facts" and modes of order of which such a theory might wish to take account.

## SECTION ONE: STUBBORN FACTS

*ALEXANDER BICKEL*

### THE LEAST DANGEROUS BRANCH *

In the vast majority of cases—barring those that are dismissed outright as not suitable for adjudication—the normal and expected judgment of the Court is a crisp and specific writing which tells one of the parties exactly what he must do, such as pay a judgment, deliver certain real estate, cease from doing something, or, indeed, go to jail. The equivalent in  . . .  [the Segregation cases] would have been a decree ordering the named children, and perhaps, since these were class actions, all children in the five school districts affected who were similarly situated, to be admitted forthwith to the white schools of their choice.  The question is, why should the Court not have issued such a decree?  Indeed, one might have asked whether the Court could do other than issue such a decree?

If the Court, at the other extreme from merely composing for the anthologies, sat merely to render *ad hoc* judgments applicable solely to the precise circumstances of a controversy immediately before it, then also it would not be the powerful institution it is, and its function would need no elaborate justification.  The matrix paradox of all paradoxes concerning the Court is, as I have noted, that the Court may only decide concrete cases and may not pronounce general principles at large; but it may decide a constitutional issue only on the basis of general principle.  In the performance of this function—to use a fittingly lofty phrase of Chief Justice Hughes—the Court's "mental vision embraces distant scenes."  Hence, while the cases immediately before the Court exemplified and concretized the issue of principle, they could not be treated as if they involved only the admission of three or four dozen children to a dozen schools.  Rather, these five cases did necessarily bring into view the total situation in all the states having school districts which are organized on a segregated basis.

The admission of a few dozen children to a few dozen schools would have presented no very grave difficulties calling for a study of means of gradual adjustment.  Seen in its totality, however, as involving some 5,000 school districts, nearly nine million white children and nearly three million colored, the situation exhibited great variety and complexity.  To begin with, a vast number of statutes and regulations, incorporating centrally or marginally the rule of segregation, would require change in order to conform to the new principle.  In most places, pupils are assigned to schools in accordance with the location of their homes.  Where there were two schools, one white and one Negro, residential lines would now have to be drawn purely on a geographical basis, rather than, as previously, in accordance with both geography and race.  But the two schools may not have been of equal size or otherwise of equal character.  Thus elimination of the racial criterion may create a new and expensive problem before solving the old one.  In general, running two segregated school systems is more expensive than running a single integrated one.  But that is not to say that the process of integration might not require some immediate additional expenditures.  And the cost of money is either money or time.  Further complications: New assignments and other administrative arrangements for teachers, including Negro teachers, would have to be made.  School transportation would have to be rearranged.  No doubt, since Negro schools had seldom been fully equal to white ones, and since many Negro pupils come from economically and culturally depressed families, differences in educational background and aptitudes would be found between Negro and white pupils, and allowance might have to be made for these in the process of integration.

These and yet additional problems varied greatly from place to place, from cities to rural districts, and in relation, among other things, to the ratio of Negro to white pupils in a given district.  No solution could be fabricated and made effective overnight, no matter what anyone might wish. Moreover, the Court itself bore some responsibility for the situation it now faced. The practice of segregation was no invention of the Court, to be sure. But segregation had prospered and come to full flower at least partly in reliance upon the Court's decision, in 1896, that it conformed to constitutional principle. No one hearing the late John W. Davis, who argued to the Court in behalf of South Carolina, emphasize how pervasive and how solidly founded the present order was could fail to be sensible of the difficulties to be encountered in uprooting it. "Sometime to every principle," Mr. Davis remarked, "comes a moment of repose when it has been so often announced, so confidently relied upon, so long continued, that it passes the limits of judicial discretion and disturbance." Mr. Davis was intimating that the existing order was no longer subject to judicial change, that no principle of its alteration could now be announced. This was to deny the essence of the Court's function, and on the basis of no more than an inadmissibly static view of society. But the suggestion that judicial alteration of so deep-rooted an order of things raises special problems to which the Court must have due regard—that could not be ignored.

It is unusual but not unheard of for the Court—for all courts, in the general run of business, constitutional and otherwise—to be faced with practical factors that make it impossible to achieve immediately a result called for by the Court's decision. Thus in applying the antitrust laws the Court may find—has in fact found—that a large corporation, the American Tobacco Company, for example, was a near-monopoly and violated the antitrust laws, and that it should be dissolved and split into its component parts. Or the Court may find, as it recently did, that ownership by the DuPont Corporation of a potentially controlling block of shares in the General Motors Corporation violates the antitrust laws, and that the relationship should be severed. But such things cannot be made to happen in a day. Here is the elemental demonstration of the truth that very often society can only strive to attain the rule of principle through a tangle of perverse and intractable existing facts, which are themselves man-made but which are not any the less real for that. Pupil-assignment rules were willfully scrambled by men pursuing racist ends rather than ordained of god; but that does not render them any easier to unscramble overnight, once the racist principle has been extracted. There is embedded in Anglo-American law, quite aside from the peculiar function of constitutional adjudication, the recognition that, on occasion, the law proposes but, for a time at least, the facts of life dispose. The mainstream of Anglo-American legal development has been the common law, administered by judges who evolved and reasoned from principle. But there soon flowed alongside the common law another stream, the equity jurisdiction, whose headwaters were in the discretionary royal prerogative. Equity was a more flexible process, more unprincipled, initially quite *ad hoc*. It often worked the accommodation that made the rigorous principles of the common law fit to live with. Our courts in general now combine both functions—common law and equity—and so does the process of judicial review.

. . .

It was argued to the Court by the National Association for the Advancement of Colored People, which represented the Negro children, that the task of making the Court's principle accepted and effective would be facilitated by a sort of shock treatment, an order of immediate and sudden execution, rather than by allowing time for accommodation. The argument was that "gradualism, far from facilitating the process, may actually make it more difficult; that, in fact, the problems of transition will be a good deal less complicated than might be forecast. . . . Our submission is that this, like many wrongs, can be easiest and best undone, not by 'tapering off' but by forthright action." Conceivably this might have been so, but certainly it was not a broadly shared view. What the Court was more widely urged to do, especially by the Solicitor General, and what it did was in effect to require the local school boards to submit to the lower federal courts plans providing for a start toward integration— that is, to begin with, the admission of a few children here and there on some staged scheme. Any such plan would have to contain also the promise of eventual full compliance, meaning an eventually unified school system in which children would be assigned to schools without distinction of race, although other criteria, including residential ones, might still be effective. The Court set no deadlines. None was seriously urged, it being realized as the Solicitor General pointed out, that conditions vary and "that maximum periods tend to become minimum periods." The test for each plan would be whether it was moving in good faith toward integration "with all deliberate speed."

QUESTIONS

1. Why didn't the Court order immediate desegregation of Southern schools? How could it answer the argument that Black children were entitled to "justice now" or "freedom now"? Did the Court choose order over justice and freedom? If so, how are you using the words "justice" and "freedom"? Could it be argued that it would be unjust and a denial of freedom to immediately desegregate? How would such an argument run?

2. How could the Court reconcile its remedial order with its substantive declaration that state-enforced segregation was a violation of the Equal Protection Clause? Did not its decree permit Southern school districts to continue breaking the law? Does the Court have the power to permit someone to break the law? Is the Court's only answer that it is best on the whole in this case to permit lawbreaking? Or is there a way in which it could be argued that the decree did not permit law-breaking?

Could it be argued that if the decree is right, the substantive declaration is wrong? That if the remedial decision takes into account the "stubborn facts" of life, the substantive rule should as well?

ALFRED NORTH WHITEHEAD

## SYMBOLISM: ITS MEANING AND EFFECT *

Time is known to us as the succession of our acts of experience, and thence derivatively as the succession of events objectively perceived in those acts. But this succession is not pure succession: it is the derivation of state from state, with the later state exhibiting conformity to the antecedent. Time in the concrete is the conformation of state to state, the later to the earlier; and the pure succession is an abstraction from the irreversible relationship of settled past to derivative present. The notion of pure succession is analogous to the notion of colour. There is no mere colour, but always some particular colour such as red or blue: analogously there is no pure succession, but always some particular relational ground in respect to which the terms succeed each other. The integers succeed each other in one way, and events succeed each other in another way; and, when we abstract from these ways of succession, we find that pure succession is an abstraction of the second order, a generic abstraction omitting the temporal character of time and the numerical relation of integers. The past consists of the community of settled acts which, through their objectifications in the present act, establish the conditions to which that act must conform.

. . . . the immediate present has to conform to what the past is for it, and the mere lapse of time is an abstraction from the more concrete relatedness of 'conformation.' The 'substantial' character of actual things is not primarily concerned with the predication of qualities. It expresses the stubborn fact that whatever is settled and actual must in due measure be conformed to by the self-creative activity. The phrase 'stubborn fact' exactly expresses the popular apprehension of this characteristic. Its primary phase, from which each actual thing arises, is the stubborn fact which underlies its existence. According to Hume there are no stubborn facts. Hume's doctrine may be good philosophy, but it is certainly not common sense. In other words, it fails before the final test of obvious verification.

### 2. Kant and Causal Efficacy.

The school of transcendental idealists, derived from Kant, admit that causal efficacy is a factor in the phenomenal world; but hold that it does not belong to the sheer data presupposed in perception. It belongs to our ways of thought about the data. Our consciousness of the perceived world yields us an objective system, which is a fusion of mere data and modes of thought about those data.

The general Kantian reason for this position is that direct perception acquaints us with particular fact. Now particular fact is what simply occurs as particular datum. But we believe universal principles about all particular facts. Such universal knowledge cannot be

* From 35–44, 45–46 (Capricorn ed. 1959). Copyright 1927 by The Macmillan Company; copyright renewed 1955 by Evelyn Whitehead. Reprinted with permission.

derived from any selection of particular facts, each of which has just simply occurred. Thus our ineradicable belief is only explicable by reason of the doctrine that particular facts, as consciously apprehended, are the fusion of mere particular data with thought functioning according to categories which import their own universality in the modified data. Thus the phenomenal world, as in consciousness, is a complex of coherent judgments, framed according to fixed categories of thought, and with a content constituted by given data organized according to fixed forms of intuition.

This Kantian doctrine accepts Hume's naive presupposition of 'simple occurrence' for the mere data. I have elsewhere called it the assumption of 'simple location,' by way of applying it to space as well as to time.

I directly deny this doctrine of 'simple occurrence.' There is nothing which 'simply happens.' Such a belief is the baseless doctrine of time as 'pure succession.' The alternative doctrine, that the pure succession of time is merely an abstract from the fundamental relationship of conformation, sweeps away the whole basis for the intervention of constitutive thought, or constitutive intuition, in the formation of the directly apprehended world. Universality of truth arises from the universality of relativity, whereby every particular actual thing lays upon the universe the obligation of conforming to it. Thus in the analysis of particular fact universal truths are discoverable, those truths expressing this obligation. The given-ness of experience —that is to say, all its data alike, whether general truths or particular sensa or presupposed forms of synthesis—expresses the specific character of the temporal relation of that act of experience to the settled actuality of the universe which is the source of all conditions. The fallacy of 'misplaced concreteness' abstracts from time this specific character, and leaves time with the mere generic character of pure succession.

3. *Direct Perception of Causal Efficacy.*

The followers of Hume and the followers of Kant have thus their diverse, but allied, objections to the notion of any direct perception of causal efficacy, in the sense in which direct perception is antecedent to thought about it. Both schools find 'causal efficacy' to be the importation, into the data, of a way of thinking or judging about those data. One school calls it a habit of thought; the other school calls it a category of thought. Also for them the mere data are the pure sense-data.

If either Hume or Kant gives a proper account of the status of causal efficacy, we should find that our conscious apprehension of causal efficacy should depend to some extent on the vividness of the thought or of the pure intuitive discrimination of sense-data at the moment in question. For an apprehension which is the product of thought should sink in importance when thought is in the background. Also, according to this Humian-Kantian account, the thought in question is thought about the immediate sense-data. Accordingly a certain vividness of sense-data in immediate presentation should be favourable to apprehension of causal efficacy. For according to these accounts, causal efficacy is nothing else than a way of thinking about sense-data, given in presentational immediacy. Thus the inhibition of thought and the vagueness of sense-data should be extremely unfavourable to the prominence of causal efficacy as an element in experience.

The logical difficulties attending the direct perception of causal efficacy have been shown to depend on the sheer assumption that time is merely the generic notion of pure succession. This is an instance of the fallacy of 'misplaced concreteness.' Thus the way is now open to enquire empirically whether in fact our apprehension of causal efficacy does depend either on the vividness of sense-data or on the activity of thought.

According to both schools, the importance of causal efficacy, and of action exemplifying its presupposition, should be mainly characteristic of high-grade organisms in their best moments. Now if we confine attention to long-range identification of cause and effect, depending on complex reasoning, undoubtedly such high-grade mentality and such precise determination of sense-data are required. But each step in such reasoning depends on the primary presupposition of the immediate present moment conforming itself to the settled environment of the immediate past. We must not direct attention to the inferences from yesterday to today, or even from five minutes ago to the immediate present. We must consider the immediate present in its relationship to the immediate past. The overwhelming conformation of fact, in present action, to antecedent settled fact is to be found here.

My point is that this conformation of present fact to immediate past is more prominent both in apparent behaviour and in consciousness, when the organism is low grade. A flower turns to the light with much greater certainty than does a human being, and a stone conforms to the conditions set by its external environment with much greater certainty than does a flower. A dog anticipates the conformation of the immediate future to his present activity with the same certainty as a human being. When it comes to calculations and remote inferences, the dog fails. But the dog never acts as though the immediate future were irrelevant to the present. Irresolution in action arises from consciousness of a somewhat distant relevant future, combined with inability to evaluate its precise type. If we were not conscious of relevance, why is there irresolution in a sudden crisis?

Again a vivid enjoyment of immediate sense-data notoriously inhibits apprehension of the relevance of the future. The present moment is then all in all. In our consciousness it approximates to 'simple occurrence.'

Certain emotions, such as anger and terror, are apt to inhibit the apprehension of sense-data; but they wholly depend upon a vivid apprehension of the relevance of immediate past to the present, and of the present to the future. Again an inhibition of familiar sense-data provokes the terrifying sense of vague presences, effective for good or evil over our fate. Most living creatures, of daytime habits, are more nervous in the dark, in the absence of the familiar visual sense-data.

But according to Hume, it is the very familiarity of the sense-data which is required for causal inference. Thus the sense of unseen effective presences in the dark is the opposite of what should happen.

### 4. *Primitiveness of Causal Efficacy.*

The perception of conformation to realities in the environment is the primitive element in our external experience. We conform to our bodily organs and to the vague world which lies beyond them. Our primitive perception is that of 'conformation' vaguely, and of the yet vaguer relata 'oneself' and 'another' in the undiscriminated background. Of course if relationships are unperceivable, such a doctrine must be ruled out on theoretic grounds. But if we admit such perception, then the perception of conformation has every mark of a primitive element. One part of our experience is handy, and definite in our consciousness; also it is easy to reproduce at will. The other type of experience, however insistent, is vague, haunting, unmanageable. The former type, for all its decorative sense-experience, is barren. It displays a world concealed under an adventitious show, a show of our own bodily production. The latter type is heavy with the contact of the things gone by, which lay their grip on our immediate selves. This latter type, the mode of causal efficacy, is the experience dominating the primitive living organisms, which have a sense for the fate from which they have emerged, and for the fate towards which they go—the organisms which advance and retreat but hardly differentiate any immediate display. It is a heavy, primitive experience. The former type, the presentational immediacy, is the superficial product of complexity, of subtlety; it halts at the present, and indulges in a manageable self-enjoyment derived from the immediacy of the show of things. . . .

Anger, hatred, fear, terror, attraction, love, hunger, eagerness, massive enjoyment, are feelings and emotions closely entwined with the primitive functioning of 'retreat from' and of 'expansion towards.'

. . .

These primitive emotions are accompanied by the clearest recognition of other actual things reacting upon ourselves. The vulgar obviousness of such recognition is equal to the vulgar obviousness produced by the functioning of any one of our five senses. When we hate, it is a man that we hate and not a collection of sense-data—a causal, efficacious man. This primitive obviousness of the perception of 'conformation' is illustrated by the emphasis on the pragmatic aspect of occurrences, which is so prominent in modern philosophical thought. There can be no useful aspect of anything unless we admit the principle of conformation, whereby what is already made becomes a determinant of what is in the making. The obviousness of the pragmatic aspect is simply the obviousness of the perception of the fact of conformation.

In practice we never doubt the fact of the conformation of the present to the immediate past. It belongs to the ultimate texture of experience, with the same evidence as does presentational immediacy. The present fact is luminously the outcome from its predecessors, one quarter of a second ago. Unsuspected factors may have intervened;

dynamite may have exploded. But, however that may be, the present event issues subject to the limitations laid upon it by the actual nature of the immediate past. If dynamite explodes, then present fact is that issue from the past which is consistent with dynamite exploding. Further, we unhesitatingly argue backwards to the inference, that the complete analysis of the past must disclose in it those factors which provide the conditions for the present. If dynamite be now exploding, then in the immediate past there was a charge of dynamite unexploded.

### NOTES AND QUESTIONS

1. Hume, as Whitehead here—and Popper earlier—reports, held that there could be no *necessary* connection between one event in time and any subsequent event, even if by *habit* we view the former as cause and the latter as effect. If A punches B in the nose and B's nose begins to bleed there is no way of demonstrating that the relations between these two phenomena are anything but coincidental. If you do not have Hume's reason for this clearly in mind, review it now. Kant would find a necessary connection between A's act and B's injury, but, as Whitehead reports, it is a necessity which is decreed by the nature of the mind. The structure of the mind, says Kant, requires us to see a causal connection between two events, to impose it upon the data of experience. What is Whitehead's rejoinder to this position? To what extent does the validity of his rejoinder depend on the position we have earlier seen him take in MODES OF THOUGHT— namely, that the notion of a "mere fact" is mythological? Be sure to review precisely what Whitehead means by the term. To what extent does the Humian and Kantian position on causality reflect a belief in mere fact? To which of the three philosophers—Hume, Kant or Whitehead—is Popper closest? What do you think his position is on "mere fact"?

If we "consider the immediate present in its relationship to the immediate past," is it easier to understand Whitehead's point? Consider the moment at which you are now reading these words and the moment one-tenth of a second prior to that. Are these two distinct states of affairs, two isolable facts? Do you *perceive* them as separate? Would you refer to them as separate? Or would you treat them as the *same* fact? What is it that would make you right or wrong?

2. Why is it important for Whitehead that low-grade organisms experience "conformation of present fact to immediate past . . . both in apparent behavior and in consciousness"? Is it because the Humian and Kantian notion of causality emphasizes elements which are peculiarly human? Are Hume's "habit" and Kant's "categories" to be found in low-grade organisms? And if they are, are they to be found at the same stage of development?

3. Can you make an argument to support Whitehead's contention that relationships are perceivable? What is the significance of this point? Could Hume and Kant concede that relationships are "directly" perceptible? What do you think Whitehead means by "direct perception"?

JOHN DEWEY

## ART AS EXPERIENCE *

There are two sorts of possible worlds in which esthetic experience would not occur. In a world of mere flux, change would not be cumulative; it would not move toward a close. Stability and rest would have no being. Equally is it true, however, that a world that is finished, ended, would have no traits of suspense and crisis, and would offer no opportunity for resolution. Where everything is already complete, there is no fulfillment. We envisage with pleasure Nirvana and a uniform heavenly bliss only because they are projected upon the background of our present world of stress and conflict. Because the actual world, that in which we live, is a combination of movement and culmination, of breaks and re-unions, the experience of a living creature is capable of esthetic quality. The live being recurrently loses and reestablishes equilibrium with his surroundings. The moment of passage from disturbance into harmony is that of intensest life. In a finished world, sleep and waking could not be distinguished. In one wholly perturbed, conditions could not even be struggled with. In a world made after the pattern of ours, moments of fulfillment punctuate experience with rhythmically enjoyed intervals.

. . .

An environment that was always and everywhere congenial to the straightaway execution of our impulsions would set a term to growth as surely as one always hostile would irritate and destroy. Impulsion forever boosted on its forward way would run its course thoughtless, and dead to emotion. For it would not have to give an account of itself in terms of the things it encounters, and hence they would not become significant objects. The only way it can become aware of its nature and its goal is by obstacles surmounted and means employed; means which are only means from the very beginning are too much one with an impulsion, on a way smoothed and oiled in advance, to permit of consciousness of them. Nor without resistance from surroundings would the self become aware of itself; it would have neither feeling nor interest, neither fear nor hope, neither disappointment nor elation. Mere opposition that completely thwarts, creates irritation and rage. But resistance that calls out thought generates curiosity and solicitous care, and, when it is overcome and utilized, eventuates in elation.

That which merely discourages a child and one who lacks a matured background of relevant experiences is an incitement to intelligence to plan and convert emotion into interest, on the part of those who have previously had experiences of situations sufficiently akin to be drawn upon. Impulsion from need starts an experience that does not know where it is going; resistance and check bring about the conversion of direct forward action into re-flection; what is turned back upon is the relation of hindering conditions to what the self possesses

* From 16–17, 59–62 (Capricorn ed. 1958). Copyright 1934 by John Dewey; copyright renewed 1961 by Roberta L. Dewey. Reprinted by permission of the estate of Roberta L. Dewey.

as working capital in virtue of prior experiences. As the energies thus involved reenforce the original impulsion, this operates more circumspectly with insight into end and method. Such is the outline of every experience that is clothed with meaning.

That tension calls out energy and that total lack of opposition does not favor normal development are familiar facts. In a general way, we all recognize that a balance between furthering and retarding conditions is the desirable state of affairs—provided that the adverse conditions bear intrinsic relation to what they obstruct instead of being arbitrary and extraneous. Yet what is evoked is not just quantitative, or just more energy, but is qualitative, a transformation of energy into thoughtful action, through assimilation of meanings from the background of past experiences. The junction of the new and old is not a mere composition of forces, but is a re-creation in which the present impulsion gets form and solidity while the old, the "stored," material is literally revived, given new life and soul through having to meet a new situation.

It is this double change which converts an activity into an act of expression. Things in the environment that would otherwise be mere smooth channels or else blind obstructions become means, media. At the same time, things retained from past experience that would grow stale from routine or inert from lack of use, become coefficients in new adventures and put on a raiment of fresh meaning. Here are all the elements needed to define expression. The definition will gain force if the traits mentioned are made explicit by contrast with alternative situations. Not all outgoing activity is of the nature of expression. At one extreme, there are storms of passion that break through barriers and that sweep away whatever intervenes between a person and something he would destroy. There is activity, but not, from the standpoint of the one acting, expression. An onlooker may say "What a magnificent expression of rage!" But the enraged being is only raging, quite a different matter from *expressing* rage. Or, again, some spectator may say "How that man is expressing his own dominant character in what he is doing or saying." But the last thing the man in question is thinking of is to express his character; he is only giving way to a fit of passion. Again the cry or smile of an infant may be expressive to mother or nurse and yet not be an act of expression of the baby. To the onlooker it is an expression because it tells something about the state of the child. But the child is only engaged in doing something directly, no more expressive from his standpoint than is breathing or sneezing—activities that are also expressive to the observer of the infant's condition.

Generalization of such instances will protect us from the error—which has unfortunately invaded esthetic theory—of supposing that the mere giving way to an impulsion, native or habitual, constitutes expression. Such an act is expressive not in itself but only in reflective interpretation on the part of some observer—as the nurse may interpret a sneeze as the sign of an impending cold. As far as the act itself is concerned, it is, if purely impulsive, just a boiling over. While there is no expression, unless there is urge from within outwards, the welling up must be clarified and ordered by taking into itself the values of prior experiences before it can be an act of expression. And these values are not called into play save through objects of the environment that offer resistance to the direct discharge of emotion and impulse. Emotional discharge is a necessary but not a sufficient condition of expression.

There is no expression without excitement, without turmoil. Yet an inner agitation that is discharged at once in a laugh or cry, passes away with its utterance. To discharge is to get rid of, to dismiss; to express is to stay by, to carry forward in development, to work out to completion. A gush of tears may bring relief, a spasm of destruction may give outlet to inward rage. But where there is no administration of objective conditions, no shaping of materials in the interest of embodying the excitement, there is no expression. What is sometimes called an act of self-expression might better be termed one of self-exposure; it discloses character—or lack of character—to others. In itself, it is only a spewing forth.

The transition from an act that is expressive from the standpoint of an outside observer to one intrinsically expressive is readily illustrated by a simple case. At first a baby weeps, just as it turns its head to follow light; there is an inner urge but nothing to express. As the infant matures, he learns that particular acts effect different consequences, that, for example, he gets attention if he cries, and that smiling induces another definite response from those about him. He thus begins to be aware of the *meaning* of what he does. As he grasps the meaning of an act at first performed from sheer internal pressure, he becomes capable of acts of true expression. The transformation of sounds, babblings, lalling, and so forth, into language is a perfect illustration of the way in which acts of expression are brought into existence and also of the difference between them and mere acts of discharge.

## QUESTIONS

If the Supreme Court had ordered the immediate desegregation —say, the next day—of Southern schools, how might Dewey characterize this action? Would he view it as an "act of expression" or as a "mere giving way to an impulsion"? Or does it matter so long as justice is done?

## SECTION TWO: THE GIVEN ORDER

### NOTE

Are there forms of order and ways of seeing which are given and which insure that people will be able to achieve certain minimal degrees of community and cooperation? Is there any other way one can account for the phenomena of persistent human life and of continuing human societies? If not, do these forms and ways also give us some reason to believe that individual decision-makers will not be totally at large when they are called upon to affect our lives? And is it possible that in these modes of organization we can find at least some of the ultimate points of orientation by which to guide human and social conduct? These are questions which are raised in the following materials. In them you will also find some of the possible answers. The ordering factors treated here, however, although perhaps the most important, are probably the most overlooked. Indeed, we are usually so unaware of them that philosophical theories by which they are mooted often gain acceptance without any indication that they threaten something worthy of defense. You should ask yourself whether any of the epistemological positions so far advanced fall within this class.

## IVES v. SOUTH BUFFALO RAILWAY

201 N.Y. 271 (1911)

This is an action brought by an employee against his employer to recover compensation under article 14–a of the Labor Law, being Chapter 674 of the Laws of 1910, entitled "An act to amend the labor law, in relation to workmen's compensation in certain dangerous employments."

The complaint alleges, in substance, that on the second day of September, 1910, while the plaintiff was engaged in his work as a switchman on defendant's steam railroad, he was injured solely by reason of a necessary risk or danger of his employment; that at the time of the commencement of the action he had been totally incapacitated for labor for a period of three weeks, and that such incapacity would continue for four weeks longer, and demands judgment for compensation in accordance with the provisions of said act for a period of five weeks. The answer, after admitting all the allegations of the complaint, pleads as a defense the unconstitutionality of article 14–a of the Labor Law, upon the ground that it contravenes certain provisions of the Federal and State Constitutions. . . .

. . .

WERNER, J. . . .

The statute, judged by our common-law standards, is plainly revolutionary. Its central and controlling feature is that every employer who is engaged in any of the classified industries shall be liable for any injury to a workman arising out of and in the course of the employment by "a necessary risk or danger of the employment or one inherent in the nature thereof; * * * provided that the employer shall not be liable in respect of any injury to the workman which is caused in whole or in part by the serious and willful misconduct of the workman." This rule of liability, stated in another form, is that the employer is responsible to the employee for every accident in the course of the employment, whether the employer is at fault, or not, and whether the employee is at fault or not, except when the fault of the employee is so grave as to constitute serious and willful misconduct on his part. The radical character of this legislation is at once revealed by contrasting it with the rule of the common law, under which the employer is liable for injuries to his employee only when the employer is guilty of some acts or acts of negligence which caused the occurrence out of which the injuries arise, and then only when the employee is shown to be free from any negligence which contributes to the occurrence. . . .

. . .

. . . . When our Constitutions were adopted it was the law of the land that no man who was without fault or negligence could be held liable in damages for injuries sustained by another. That is still the law, except as to the employers enumerated in the new statute, and as to them it provides that they shall be liable to their employees for personal injury by accident to any workman arising out of and in the course of the employment which is caused in whole or in part, or is contributed to, by a necessary risk or danger of the employment or one inherent in the nature thereof, except that there shall be no liability in any case where the injury is caused in whole or in part by the serious and willful misconduct of the injured workman. It is conceded that this is a liability unknown to the common law and we think it plainly constitutes a deprivation of liberty and property under the Federal and State Constitutions. . . . In arriving at this conclusion we do not overlook the cogent economic and sociological arguments which are urged in support of the statute. There can be no doubt as to the theory of this law. It is based upon the proposition that the inherent risks of an employment should in justice be placed upon the shoulders of the employer, who can protect himself against loss by insurance and by such an addition to the price of his wares as to cast the burden ultimately upon the consumer; that indemnity to an injured employee should be as much a charge upon the business as the cost of replacing or repairing disabled or defective machinery, appliances or tools; that, under our present system, the loss falls immediately upon the employee who is almost invariably unable to bear it, and ultimately upon the community which is taxed for the support of the indigent; and that our present system is uncertain, unscientific and wasteful, and fosters a spirit of antagonism between employer and employee which it is to the interests of the state to remove. We have already admitted the strength of this appeal to a recognized and widely prevalent sentiment, but we think it is an appeal which must be made to the people and not to the courts. The right of property rests not upon philosophical or scientific speculations nor upon the commendable impulses of benevolence or charity, nor yet upon the dictates of natural justice. The right has its foundation in the fundamental law. That can be changed by the people, but not by legislatures. In a government like ours theories of public good or necessity are often so plausible or sound as to command popular approval, but courts are not permitted to forget that the law is the only chart by which the ship of state is to be guided. Law as used in this sense means the basic law and not the very act of legislation which deprives the citizen of his rights, privileges or property. Any other view would lead to the absurdity that the Constitutions protect only those rights which the legislatures do not take away. If such economic and sociologic arguments as are here advanced in support of this statute can be allowed to subvert the fundamental idea of property, then there is no private right entirely safe, because there is no limitation upon the absolute discretion of legislatures, and the guarantees of the Constitution are a mere waste of words. . . . If the argument in support of this statute is sound we do not see why it cannot logically be carried much further. Poverty and misfortune from every cause are detrimental to the state. It would probably conduce to the welfare of all concerned if there could be a more equal distribution of wealth. Many persons have much more property than they can use to advantage and many more find it impossible to get the means for a comfortable existence. If the legislature can say to an employer, "you must compensate your employee for an injury not caused by you or by your fault," why can it not go further and say to the man of wealth, "you have more property than you need and your neighbor is so poor that he can barely subsist; in the interest of natural justice you must divide with your neighbor so that he and his dependents shall not become a charge upon the State?" The argument that the risk to an employee should be borne by the employer because it is inherent in the employment, may be economically sound, but it is at war with the legal principle that no employer can be compelled to assume a risk which is inseparable from the work of the employee, and which may exist in spite of a degree of care by the employer far greater than may be exacted by the most drastic law. If it is competent to impose upon an employer, who has omitted no legal duty and has committed no wrong, a liability based solely upon a legislative fiat that his business is inherently dangerous, it is equally competent to visit upon him a special tax for the support of hospitals and other charitable institutions, upon the theory that they are devoted largely to the alleviation of ills primarily due to his business. In its final and simple analysis that is taking the property of A and giving it to B, and that cannot be done under our Constitutions. Practical and simple illustrations of the extent to which this theory of liability might be carried could be multiplied *ad infinitum*, and many will readily occur to the thoughtful reader. There is, of course, in this country no direct legal authority upon the subject of the liability sought to be imposed by this statute, for the theory is not merely new in our system of jurisprudence, but plainly antagonistic to its basic idea. . . .

SUSANNE K. LANGER

## PHILOSOPHY IN A NEW KEY *

Every age in the history of philosophy has its own preoccupation. Its problems are peculiar to it, not for obvious practical reasons—political or social—but for deeper reasons of intellectual growth. If we look back on the slow formation and accumulation of doctrines which mark that history, we may see certain *groupings* of ideas within it, not by subject-matter, but by a subtler common factor which may be called their "technique." It is the mode of handling problems, rather than what they are about, that assigns them to an age. Their subject-matter may be fortuituous, and depend on con-

* From 4–8 (3d ed. 1957). Copyright 1942, 1951, 1957 by the President and Fellows of Harvard College. Reprint- ed by permission of Harvard University Press.

quests, discoveries, plagues, or governments; their treatment derives from a steadier source.

The "technique," or treatment, of a problem begins with its first expression as a question. The way a question is asked limits and disposes the ways in which any answer to it—right or wrong—may be given. If we are asked: "Who made the world?" we may answer: "God made it," "Chance made it," "Love and hate made it," or what you will. We may be right or we may be wrong. But if we reply: "Nobody made it," we will be accused of trying to be cryptic, smart, or "unsympathetic." For in this last instance, we have only seemingly given an answer; in reality we have *rejected the question*. The questioner feels called upon to repeat his problem. "Then how did the world become as it is? If now we answer: "It has not 'become' at all," he will be really disturbed. This "answer" clearly repudiates the very framework of his thinking, the orientation of his mind, the basic assumptions he has always entertained as common-sense notions about things in general. Everything has become what it is; everything has a cause; every change must be to some end; the world is a thing, and must have been made by some agency, out of some original stuff, for some reason. These are natural ways of thinking. Such implicit "ways" are not avowed by the average man, but simply followed. He is not conscious of assuming any basic principles. They are what a German would call his "Weltanschauung," his attitude of mind rather than specific articles of faith. They constitute his outlook; they are deeper than facts he may note or propositions he may moot.

But, though they are not stated, they find expression in the *forms of his questions*. A question is really an ambiguous proposition; the answer is its determination. There can be only a certain number of alternatives that will complete its sense. In this way the intellectual treatment of any datum, any experience, any subject, is determined by the nature of our questions, and only carried out in the answers.

In philosophy this disposition of problems is the most important thing that a school, a movement, or an age contributes. This is the "genius" of a great philosophy; in its light, systems arise and rule and die. Therefore a philosophy is characterized more by the *formulation* of its problems than by its solution of them. Its answers establish an edifice of facts; but its questions make the frame in which its picture of facts is plotted. They make more than the frame; they give the angle of perspective, the palette, the style in which the picture is drawn—everything except the subject. In our questions lie our *principles of analysis*, and our answers may express whatever those principles are able to yield.

There is a passage in Whitehead's *Science and the Modern World*, setting forth this predetermination of thought, which is at once its scaffolding and its limit. "When you are criticizing the philosophy of an epoch," Professor Whitehead says, "do not chiefly direct your attention to those intellectual positions which its exponents feel it necessary explicitly to defend. There will be some fundamental assumptions which adherents of all the variant systems within the epoch unconsciously presuppose. Such assumptions appear so obvious that people do not know what they are assuming because no other way of putting things has ever occurred to them. With these assumptions a certain limited number of types of philosophic systems are possible, and this group of systems constitutes the philosophy of the epoch."

Some years ago, Professor C. D. Burns published an excellent little article called "The Sense of the Horizon," in which he made a somewhat wider application of the same principle; for here he pointed out that every civilization has its limits of knowledge—of perceptions, reactions, feelings, and ideas. To quote his own words, "The experience of any moment has its horizon. Today's experience, which is not tomorrow's, has in it some hints and implications which are tomorrow on the horizon of today. Each man's experience may be added to by the experience of other men, who are living in his day or have lived before; and so a common world of experience, larger than that of his own observation, can be lived in by each man. But however wide it may be, that common world also has its horizon; and on that horizon new experience is always appearing . . . . ."

"Philosophers in every age have attempted to give an account of as much experience as they could. Some have indeed pretended that what they could not explain did not exist; but all the great philosophers have allowed for more than they could explain, and have, therefore, signed beforehand, if not dated, the death-warrant of their philosophies."

". . . The history of Western philosophy begins in a period in which the sense of the horizon lifts men's eyes from the myths and rituals, the current beliefs and customs of the Greek tradition in Asia Minor . . . . In a settled civilization, the *regularity* of natural phenomena and their connection over large areas of experience became significant. The myths were too disconnected; but behind them lay the conception of Fate. This perhaps provided Thales and the other early philosophers with the first hint of the new formulation, which was an attempt to allow for a larger scale of certainty in the current attitude toward the world. From this point of view the early philosophers are conceived to have been not so much disturbed by the contradictions in the tradition as attracted by certain factors on the horizon of experience, of which their tradition gave no adequate account. They began the new formulation in order to include the new factors, and they boldly said that 'all' was water or 'all' was in flux."

The formulation of experience which is contained within the intellectual horizon of an age and a society is determined, I believe, not so much by events and desires, as by the *basic concepts* at people's disposal for analyzing and describing their adventures to their own understanding. Of course, such concepts arise as they are needed, to deal with political or domestic experience; but the same experiences could be seen in many different lights, so the light in which they do appear depends on the genius of a people as well as on the demands of the external occasion.  Different minds will take the same events in very different ways.  A tribe of Congo Negroes will react quite differently to (say) its first introduction to the story of Christ's passion, than did the equally untutored descendants of Norsemen, or the American Indians.  Every society meets a new idea with its own concepts, its own tacit, fundamental way of seeing things;  that is to say, *with its own questions*, its peculiar curiosity.

The horizon to which Professor Burns makes reference is the limit of clear and sensible questions that we can ask.  When the Ionian philosophers, whom he cites as the innovators of Greek thought, asked what "all" was made of, or how "all" matter behaved, they were assuming a general notion, namely that of a parent substance, a final, universal *matter* to which all sorts of accidents could happen.  This notion dictated the terms of their inquiries:  what things were, and how they changed.  Problems of right and wrong, of wealth and poverty, slavery and freedom, were beyond their scientific horizon.  On these matters they undoubtedly adopted the wordless, unconscious attitudes dictated by social usage.  The concepts that preoccupied them had no application in those realms, and therefore did not give rise to new, interesting, leading questions about social or moral affairs.

(Professor Burns regards all Greek thought as one vast formulation of experience.  "In spite of continual struggles with violent reversals in conventional habits and in the use of words," he says, "work upon the formulation of Greek experience culminated in the magnificent doctrines of Plato and Aristotle.  Both had their source in Socrates.  He had turned from the mere assertions of the earlier philosophers to the question of the validity of any assertion at all. Not what the world was but how one could know what it was, and therefore what one could know about one's self seemed to him to be the fundamental question  .  .  .  .   The formulation begun by Thales was completed by Aristotle."

I think the historical continuity and compactness of Hellenic civilization influences this judgment.  Certainly between Thales and the Academy there is at least one further shift of the horizon, namely with the advent of the Sophists.  The questions Socrates asked were as new to Greek thought in his day as those of Thales and Anaximenes had been to their earlier age.)  .  .  .  Socrates did not continue and complete Ionian thought;  he cared very little about the speculative physics that was the very breath of life to the nature-philosophers, and his lifework did not further that ancient enterprise by even a step.  He had not new answers, but new questions, and therewith he brought a new conceptual framework, an entirely different perspective, into Greek philosophy.  His problems had arisen in the law-courts and the Sophists' courses of oratory;  they were, in the main, and in their significant features, irrelevant to the academic tradition.  The validity of knowledge was only one of his new puzzles;  the *value* of knowing, the *purpose* of science, of political life, practical arts, and finally of the course of nature, all became problematical to him.  For he was operating with a new idea.  Not prime matter and its disguises, its virtual products, its laws of change and its ultimate identity, constituted the terms of his discourse, but the notion of *value*. That everything had a value was too obvious to require statement. It was so obvious that the Ionians had not even given it one thought, and Socrates did not bother to state it; but his questions centered on what values things had—whether they were good or evil, in themselves or in their relations to other things, for all men or for few, or for the gods alone. In the light of that newly-enlisted old concept, *value*, a whole world of new questions opened up. The philosophical horizon widened in all directions at once, as horizons do with every upward step.

The limits of thought are not so much set from outside, by the fullness or poverty of experiences that meet the mind, as from within, by the power of conception, the wealth of formulative notions with which the mind meets experiences. Most new discoveries are suddenly-seen things that were always there. A new idea is a light that illuminates presences which simply had no form for us before the light fell on them. We turn the light here, there, and everywhere, and the limits of thought recede before it. A new science, a new art, or a young and vigorous system of philosophy, is generated by such a basic innovation. Such ideas as identity of matter and change of form, or as value, validity, virtue, or as outer world and inner consciousness, are not theories; they are the terms in which theories are conceived; they give rise to specific questions, and are articulated only in the form of these questions. Therefore one may call them *generative ideas* in the history of thought.

## QUESTIONS

Are the ideas of "fault" and of "property" which Werner uses in *Ives* v. *South Buffalo Railway* "generative" ideas, in Langer's use of the word? How would you characterize or describe Werner's notion of the "basic idea" of "our system of jurisprudence"? Is this idea considered basic by anyone other than Werner? By any large number of people other than Werner? Is the idea one that has any remaining force in 1972? To the extent that it does not, are there other ideas which now are used for the ranges of experience formerly left to Werner's "basic idea"?

## ERNST CASSIRER

### AN ESSAY ON MAN *

We can still when learning a foreign language subject ourselves to an experience similar to that of the child. Here it is not sufficient to acquire a new vocabulary or to acquaint ourselves with a system of abstract grammatical rules. All this is necessary but it is only the first and less important step. If we do not learn to think in the new language all our efforts remain fruitless. In most cases we find it extremely difficult to fulfil this requirement. Linguists and psy-

* From 133–135 (1944). Reprinted with permission of Yale University Press.

chologists have often raised the question as to how it is possible for a child by his own efforts to accomplish a task that no adult can ever perform in the same way or as well. . . In a later and more advanced state of our conscious life we can never repeat the process which led to our first entrance into the world of human speech. In the freshness, in the agility and elasticity of early childhood this process had a quite different meaning. Paradoxically enough the real difficulty consists much less in the learning of the new language than in the forgetting of a former one. We are no longer in the mental condition of the child who for the first time approaches a conception of the objective world. To the adult the objective world already has a definite shape as a result of speech activity, which has in a sense molded all our other activities. Our perceptions, intuitions, and concepts have coalesced with the terms and speech forms of our mother tongue. Great efforts are required to release the bond between words and things. And yet, when we set about to learn a new language, we have to make such efforts and to separate the two elements. Overcoming this difficulty always marks a new important step in the learning of a language. When penetrating into the "spirit" of a foreign tongue we invariably have the impression of approaching a new world, a world which has an intellectual structure of its own. It is like a voyage of discovery in an alien land, and the greatest gain from such a voyage lies in our having learned to look upon our mother tongue in a new light. . . . So long as we know no foreign languages we are in a sense ignorant of our own, for we fail to see its specific structure and its distinctive features. A comparison of different languages shows us that there are no exact synonyms. Corresponding terms from two languages seldom refer to the same objects or actions. They cover different fields which interpenetrate and give us many-colored views and varied perspectives of our experience.

### CHARLES S. PEIRCE

### ESSAYS IN THE PHILOSOPHY OF SCIENCE *

. . . . The first stating of a hypothesis and the entertaining of it, whether as a simple interrogation or with any degree of confidence, is an inferential step which I propose to call *abduction*. This will include a preference for any one hypothesis over others which would equally explain the facts, so long as this preference is not based upon any previous knowledge bearing upon the truth of the hypotheses, nor on any testing of any of the hypotheses, after having admitted them on probation. I call all such inference by the peculiar name, *abduction*, because its legitimacy depends upon altogether different principles from those of other kinds of inference.

* From 236–238, 239, 244, 245–46 (V. Tomas ed. 1957).

## II  [ON SELECTING HYPOTHESES]

If we are to give the names of Deduction, Induction, and Abduction to the three grand classes of inference, then Deduction must include every attempt at mathematical demonstration, whether it relate to single occurrences or to "probabilities," that is, to statistical ratios; Induction must mean the operation that induces an assent, with or without quantitative modification, to a proposition already put forward, this assent or modified assent being regarded as the provisional result of a method that must ultimately bring the truth to light; while Abduction must cover all the operations by which theories and conceptions are engendered.

How is it that man ever came by any correct theories about nature? We know by Induction that man has correct theories; for they produce predictions that are fulfilled. But by what process of thought were they ever brought to his mind? A chemist notices a surprising phenomenon. Now if he has a high admiration of Mill's *Logic*, as many chemists have, he will remember that Mill tells him that he must work on the principle that, under precisely the same circumstances, like phenomena are produced. Why does he then not note that this phenomenon was produced on such a day of the week, the planets presenting a certain configuration, his daughter having on a blue dress, he having dreamed of a white horse the night before, the milkman having been late that morning, and so on? The answer will be that in early days chemists did use to attend to some such circumstances, but that they have learned better. How have they learned this? By an induction. Very well, that induction must have been based upon a theory which the induction verified. How was it that man was ever led to entertain that true theory? You cannot say that it happened by chance, because the possible theories, if not strictly innumerable, at any rate exceed a trillion—or the third power of a million; and therefore the chances are too overwhelmingly against the single true theory in the twenty or thirty thousand years during which man has been a thinking animal, ever having come into any man's head. Besides, you cannot seriously think that every little chicken that is hatched, has to rummage through all possible theories until it lights upon the good idea of picking up something and eating it. On the contrary, you think the chicken has an innate idea of doing this; that is to say, that it can think of this, but has no faculty of thinking anything else. The chicken you say pecks by instinct. But if you are going to think every poor chicken endowed with an innate tendency toward a positive truth, why should you think that to man alone this gift is denied? If you carefully consider with an unbiased mind all the circumstances of the early history of science, and all the other facts bearing on the question, which are far too various to be specifically alluded to in this lecture, I am quite sure that you must be brought to acknowledge that man's mind has a natural adaptation to imagining correct theories of some kinds, and in particular to correct theories about forces, without some glimmer of which he could not form social ties and consequently could not reproduce his kind. In short, the instincts conducive to assimilation of food, and the instincts conducive to reproduction, must have involved from the beginning certain tendencies to think truly about physics, on the one hand, and about psychics, on the other. It is somehow more than a mere figure of speech to say that nature fecundates the mind of man with ideas which, when those ideas grow up, will resemble their father, Nature.

.    .    .    .

The question is what theories and conceptions we *ought* to entertain. Now the word "ought" has no meaning except relatively to an *end*. That ought to be done which is conducive to a certain end. The inquiry therefore should begin with searching for the *end* of thinking. What do we think *for*? What is the physiological function of thought? If we say it is action, we must mean the government of action to some end. To what end? It must be something, good or admirable, regardless of any ulterior reason. This can only be the esthetically good. But what is esthetically good? Perhaps we may say the full expression of an idea? Thought, however, is in itself essentially of the nature of a sign. But a sign is not a sign unless it translates itself into another sign in which it is more fully developed. Thought requires achievement for its own development, and without this development it is nothing. Thought must live and grow in incessant new and higher translations, or it proves itself not to be genuine thought.

.    .    .

.    .    .    . If man had not had the gift, which every other animal has, of a mind adapted to his requirements, he not only could not have acquired any knowledge, but he could not have maintained his existence for a single generation. But he is provided with certain instincts, that is, with certain natural beliefs that are true. They relate in part to forces, in part to the action of minds. The manner in which he comes to have this knowledge seems to me tolerably clear. Certain uniformities, that is to say certain general ideas of action, prevail throughout the universe, and the reasoning mind is [it]self a product of this universe. These same laws are thus, by logical necessity, incorporated in his own being. . . .

In this way, general considerations concerning the universe, strictly philosophical considerations, all but demonstrate that if the universe conforms, with any approach to accuracy, to certain highly pervasive laws, and if man's mind has been developed under the influence of those laws, it is to be expected that he should have a *natural light*, or *light of nature*, or *instinctive insight*, or genius, tending to make him guess those laws aright, or nearly aright. This conclusion is confirmed when we find that every species of animal is endowed with a similar genius. For they not only one and all have some correct notions of force, that is to say, some correct notions, though excessively narrow, of phenomena of force, and some similarly correct notions about the minds of their own kind and of other kinds, which are the two sufficient cotyledons of all our science, but they all have, furthermore, wonderful endowments of genius in other directions. Look at the little birds, of which all species are so nearly identical in their physique, and yet what various forms of genius do they not display in modelling their nests? This would be impossible unless the ideas that are naturally predominant in their minds were true.  It would be too contrary to analogy to suppose that similar gifts were wanting to man.  Nor does the proof stop here.  The history of science, especially the early history of modern science, on which I had the honor of giving some lectures in this hall some years ago, completes the proof by showing how few were the guesses that men of surpassing genius had to make before they rightly guessed the laws of nature.  . . .

NOAM CHOMSKY

## LANGUAGE AND MIND *

.    .    .    .    it seems that knowledge of a language—a grammar—can be acquired only by an organism that is "preset" with a severe restriction on the form of grammar.  This innate restriction is a precondition, in the Kantian sense, for linguistic experience, and it appears to be the critical factor in determining the course and result of language learning.  The child cannot know at birth which language he is to learn, but he must know that its grammar must be of a predetermined form that excludes many imaginable languages.  Having selected a permissible hypothesis, he can use inductive evidence for corrective action, confirming or disconfirming his choice.  Once the hypothesis is sufficiently well confirmed, the child knows the language defined by this hypothesis; consequently, his knowledge extends enormously beyond his experience and, in fact, leads him to characterize much of the data of experience as defective and deviant.

### NOTE: THE POSSIBILITY OF COMMUNICATION

The dilemma of intersubjective communication might be framed in the following way.  People seem to be able to communicate with each other and yet since each person is different from every other and each situation is a new one, how is it possible to explain their apparent agreement on the meanings of common symbols?  Do Peirce and Chomsky help to answer this question?  Could we postulate an innate mechanism whereby people are predestined to see basically the same things when they are pointed out?  Would this help resolve the dilemma?

CLAUDE LEVI-STRAUSS

## The Savage Mind *

A . . . recent observer seems . . . to believe that the native gives names and forms to concepts solely in accordance with his needs:

I well remember the hilarity of Marquesan friends. . . . over the (to them) fatuous interest of the botanist of our expedition in 1921, who was collecting nameless ('useless') 'weeds' and asking their names (Handy and Pukui, Part VI, p. 127n).

However, Handy compares this indifference to that which specialists in our civilization show towards phenomena which have no immediate bearing on their field. When his native collaborator stressed the fact that in Hawaii 'every botanical, zoological or inorganic form that is known to have been named (and personalized), was *some thing* . . . used', she is careful to add 'in some way'. She goes on to say that the reason why 'there was an infinite variety of living things in forest and sea, of meteorological or marine phenomena, which were unnamed' was that they were regarded as being of no 'use or interest' —terms which are not equivalent, as 'use' concerns practical, and 'interest' theoretical, matters. What follows confirms this by concentrating on the latter aspect at the expense of the former: 'Living was experience fraught with exact and definite significance' (id., p. 126–7).

. . .

The proliferation of concepts, as in the case of technical languages, goes with more constant attention to properties of the world, with an interest that is more alert to possible distinctions which can be introduced between them. This thirst for objective knowledge is one of the most neglected aspects of the thought of people we call 'primitive'. Even if it is rarely directed towards facts of the same level as those with which modern science is concerned, it implies comparable intellectual application and methods of observation. In both cases the universe is an object of thought at least as much as it is a means of satisfying needs.

. . .

. . . . E. Smith Bowen scarcely exaggerates in the amusing description she gives of her confusion when, on her arrival in an African tribe, she wanted to begin by learning the language. Her informants found it quite natural, at an elementary stage of their instruction, to collect a large number of botanical specimens, the names of which they told her as they showed them to her. She was unable to identify them not because of their exotic nature but because she had never taken an interest in the riches and diversities of the plant world. The natives on the other hand took such an interest for granted.

* From 1–3, 6–10 (University of Chicago Press 1966). Copyright 1962 by Librairie Plon, 8, rue Garanciere, Paris-6 e. English transl. copyright 1966 by George Weidenfeld and Nicolson Ltd. Reprinted by permission.

> These people are farmers: to them plants are as impor-
> tant and familiar as people. I'd never been on a farm and
> am not even sure which are begonias, dahlias, or petunias.
> Plants, like algebra, have a habit of looking alike and being
> different, or looking different and being alike; consequently
> mathematics and botany confuse me. For the first time in
> my life I found myself in a community where ten-year-old
> children weren't my mathematical superiors. I also found
> myself in a place where every plant, wild or cultivated, had a
> name and use, and where every man, woman and child knew
> literally hundreds of plants  . . .  (my instructor) sim-
> ply could not realize that it was not the words but the plants
> which baffled me (Smith Bowen, p. 19).

The reaction of a specialist is quite different. In a monograph in
which he describes nearly three hundred species or varieties of medicinal or toxic plants used by certain peoples of Northern Rhodesia, Gilges
writes:

> It has always been a surprise to me to find with what
> eagerness the people in and around Balovale were ready and
> willing to talk about their medicines. Was it that they found
> my interest in their methods pleasing? Was it an exchange
> of information amongst colleagues? Or was it to show off
> their knowledge? Whatever the reason, information was
> readily forthcoming. I remember a wicked old Luchozi who
> brought bundles of dried leaves, roots and stems and told me
> about their uses. How far he was a herbalist and how far a
> witch-doctor I could never fathom, but I regret that I shall
> never possess his knowledge of African psychology and his
> art in the treatment of his fellow men, that, coupled with my
> scientific medical knowledge, might have made a most useful
> combination (Gilges, p. 20).

Conklin quotes the following extract from his field notes to illustrate
the intimate contact between man and his environment which the native is constantly imposing on the ethnologist:

> At 0600 and in a light rain, Langba and I left Parina for
> Binli  . . .  At Aresaas, Langba told me to cut off sev-
> eral 10 x 50 cm. strips of bark from an *anapla kilala* tree
> (*Albizzia procera* (Roxb.) Benth.) for protection against
> the leeches. By periodically rubbing the cambium side of the
> strips of saponaceous (and poisonous: Quisumbling, 1947,
> 148) bark over our ankles and legs—already wet from the
> rain-soaked vegetation—we produced a most effective leech-
> repellent lather of pink suds. At one spot along the trail
> near Aypud, Langba stopped suddenly, jabbed his walking
> stick sharply into the side of the trail and pulled up a small
> weed, *tawag kugum buladlad* (*Buchnera urticifolia* R. Br.)
> which he told me he will use as a lure  . . .  for a spring-
> spear boar trap. A few minutes later, and we were going at
> a good pace, he stopped in a similar manner to dig up a small
> terrestrial orchid (hardly noticeable beneath the other fo-

liage) known as *liyamliyam* (*Epipogum roseum* (D. Don.)
Lindl.) This herb is useful in the magical control of insect pests which destroy cultivated plants. At Binli, Langba
was careful not to damage those herbs when searching
through the contents of his palm leaf shoulder basket for
*apug* 'slaked lime' and *tabaku* (*Nicotiana tabacum* L.) to
offer in exchange for other betel ingredients with the Binli
folk. After an evaluative discussion about the local forms
of betel pepper (*Piper betle* L.) Langba got permission to cut
sweet potato (*Ipomoea batatas* (L.) Poir.) vines of two vege-
tatively distinguishable types, *kamuti inaswang* and *knauti
lupaw* . . . In the camote patch, we cut twenty-five
vine-tip sections (about 75 cm. long) of each variety, and
carefully wrapped them in the broad fresh leaves of the cultivated *saging saba* (*Musa sapientum compressa*) (Blco. Teo-
foro) so that they would remain moist until we reached Langba's place. Along the way we munched on a few stems of
*tubu minuma*, a type of sugar cane (*Saccharum officinarum*
L.), stopped once to gather fallen bunga area nuts (*Areca
catechu* L.), and another time to pick and eat the wild cherry-
like fruits from some *bugnay* shrubs (*Antidesma brunius*
(L.) Spreng). We arrived at the Mararim by mid-after-
noon having spent much of our time on the trail discussing
changes in the surrounding vegetation in the last few decades! (Conklin I, pp. 15–17) . . .

. . . .

Knowledge as systematically developed as this clearly cannot relate just to practical purposes. The ethnologist who has made the best
study of the Indians of the north-eastern United States and Canada
(the Montagnais, Naskapi, Micmac, Malecite, Penobscot) emphasizes
the wealth and accuracy of their zoological and botanical knowledge
and then continues:

> Such knowledge, of course, is to be expected with respect
> to the habits of the larger animals which furnish food and
> the materials of industry to primitive man. We expect, for
> instance, that the Penobscot hunter of Maine will have a
> somewhat more practical knowledge of the habits and char-
> acter of the moose than even the expert zoologist. But when
> we realize how the Indians have taken pains to observe and
> systematize facts of science in the realm of lower animal life,
> we may perhaps be pardoned a little surprise.
>
> The whole class of reptiles . . . affords no eco-
> nomic benefit to these Indians; they do not eat the flesh of
> any snakes or batrachians, nor do they make use of other
> parts except in a very few cases where they serve in the prep-
> aration of charms against sickness or sorcery (Speck I, p.
> 273).

And nevertheless, as Speck has shown, the northeastern Indians have
developed a positive herpetology, with distinct terms for each genus
of reptile and other terms applying to particular species and varieties.

. . .

.   .   .   .   Classifying, as opposed to not classifying, has a value of its own, whatever form the classification may take.  As a recent theorist of taxonomy writes:

> Scientists do tolerate uncertainty and frustration, because they must.  The one thing that they do not and must not tolerate is disorder.  The whole aim of theoretical science is to carry to the highest possible and conscious degree the perceptual reduction of chaos that began in so lowly and (in all probability) unconscious a way with the origin of life.  In specific instances it can well be questioned whether the order so achieved is an objective characteristic of the phenomena or is an artifact constructed by the scientist.  That question comes up time after time in animal taxonomy   .   .   .   Nevertheless, the most basic postulate of science is that nature itself is orderly   .   .   .   .   All theoretical science is ordering and if, systematics is equated with ordering, then systematics is synonymous with theoretical science (Simpson, p. 5).

The thought we call primitive is founded on this demand for order. This is equally true of all thought but it is through the properties common to all thought that we can most easily begin to understand forms of thought which seem very strange to us.

A native thinker makes the penetrating comment that 'All sacred things must have their place' (Fletcher 2, p. 34).  It could even be said that being in their place is what makes them sacred for if they were taken out of their place, even in thought, the entire order of the universe would be destroyed.  Sacred objects therefore contribute to the maintenance of order in the universe by occupying the places allocated to them.  Examined superficially and from the outside, the refinements of ritual can appear pointless.  They are explicable by a concern for what one might call 'microadjustment'—the concern to assign every single creature, object or feature to a place within a class.  The ceremony of the Hako among the Pawnee is particularly illuminating in this respect, although only because it has been so well analysed.  The invocation which accompanies the crossing of a stream of water is divided into several parts, which correspond, respectively to the moment when the travellers put their feet in water, the moment when they move them and the moment when the water completely covers their feet.  The invocation to the wind separates the moment when only the wet parts of the body feel cool: 'Now, we are ready to move forward in safety' (id., pp. 77–8). As the informant explains: 'We must address with song every object we meet, because Tira'wa (the supreme spirit) is in all things, everything we come to as we travel can give us help   .   .   .' (id., pp. 73, 81).

*John Holt*

## How Children Fail *

My seventeen-month-old niece . . . is a kind of scientist. She is always observing and experimenting. She is hardly ever idle. Most of her waking time she is intensely and purposefully active, soaking up experience and trying to make sense out of it, trying to find how things around her behave, and trying to make them behave as she wants them to.

In the face of what looks like unbroken failure, she is so persistent. Most of her experiments, her efforts to predict and control her environment, don't work. But she goes right on, not the least daunted. Perhaps this is because there are no penalties attached to failure, except nature's—usually, if you try to step on a ball, you fall down. A baby does not react to failure as an adult does, or even a five-year-old, because she has not yet been made to feel that failure is shame, disgrace, a crime. Unlike her elders, she is not concerned with protecting herself against everything that is not easy and familiar; she reaches out to experience, she embraces life.

Watching this baby, it is hard to credit the popular notion that without outside rewards and penalties children will not learn. There are some rewards and penalties in her life; the adults approve of some things she does, and disapprove of others. But most of the time she lives beyond praise or blame, if only because most of her learning experiments are unobserved. After all, who thinks about the meaning of what a baby is doing, so long as she is quiet and contented? But watch a while and think about it, and you see that she has a strong desire to make sense of the world around her. Her learning gives her great satisfaction, whether anyone else notices it or not.

### Notes and Questions

In PHILOSOPHY IN A NEW KEY, Susanne Langer argues that men have a need to symbolize that is as real as their more generally recognized requirements—such as eating, sleeping, procreating, etc. See *id.* at 40–41. People do not symbolize only to satisfy these other needs, she contends. Indeed, these other activities are often vehicles for satisfying the need to symbolize. Compare also LON L. FULLER, THE MORALITY OF LAW:

> Communication is something more than a means of staying alive. It is a way of being alive. . . .

> If I were asked . . . to discern one central indisputable principle of what may be called substantive natural law . . . I would find it in the injunction:

---

> Open up, maintain, and preserve the integrity of the chan-
> nels of communication  .   .   .   .

*Id.* at 186 (1964).  Do these positions answer in any way the view
that it is futile to attempt to solve the problems of human and social
existence through the use of mind?  That progress in moral and
social life is not possible?

## PART FOUR

# THE RECONSTRUCTION OF LEGAL METHOD

### INTRODUCTORY NOTE

As we have seen, to equate the *difficulty* of finding limits on authority with the *impossibility* of doing so is to fall, from a philosophical perspective, into a sort of solipsism, and, from a "political" perspective, into a cynicism about the wielding of power,—"might makes right". Is there any intermediate ground between the unrealizable simplicity of a decision maker "squaring" the Constitution with a statute, and the cynicism of supposing he must adopt the other extreme—deciding "what he wants to decide"? How, and to what extent, can people reach agreement and make decisions subject to the considerations that ought to limit them? What limits, realistically, can we hope for?

Let us take, for example, a decision that appears as "unbounded" as any in the law: the decision of a trial judge as to sentence. Here, the range of discretion afforded by "the law" is not even covert. In *State v. Leopold and Loeb*, described more fully below, two young men had pleaded guilty to murder in the first degree. The state requested the death penalty. The defense pleaded for life imprisonment. Under the law, the judge could give either.

Ought Leopold and Loeb to be hanged? How does a judge go about deciding such a question? How do lawyers go about arguing to him? Are those who say that the judge will ultimately "decide what he wants to decide" saying that there is no possibility of *method* in the decision?—that the arguments are a waste of time, or "meaningless". How and to what extent, is it possible for the judge to be constrained by those considerations that we want peculiarly to constrain *him*? If some such constraints are possible, what are the dynamics of the processes that are involved?

CHAPTER ELEVEN

# The Art of Legal Method: Closing Arguments in State v. Leopold and Loeb

*CLARENCE S. DARROW*

**CLOSING ARGUMENT FOR THE DEFENSE IN THE LEOPOLD-LOEB MURDER TRIAL \***

## BIOGRAPHICAL NOTES

Clarence S. Darrow was born in Kinsman, Ohio, on April 18, 1857. Admitted to the Ohio bar in 1875, he was for many years attorney for the Northwestern Railroad. In 1902, he was a member of the Illinois Legislature. He was counsel for the anthracite miners in the coal strike arbitration at Scranton and Philadelphia; for the McNamara brothers in the Los Angeles Times dynamite case; and for the defendants in the Moyer, Haywood and Pettibone trial for the murder of ex-governor Steunenberg of Idaho.

## STATEMENT OF FACTS

On May 21, 1924, in Chicago, Nathan F. Leopold, nineteen years old, son of a wealthy box manufacturer, and Richard A. Loeb, eighteen years old, son of the vice-president of Sears, Roebuck and Company, murdered Robert Franks, fourteen years old, son of a manufacturer of watches. Leopold was a graduate of the University of Chicago, and Loeb of the University of Michigan.

Within less than ten days, the murderers were arrested. On Sunday, June 1st, while they were still under the control of the State's Attorney, they as well as many of their acquaintances were examined by three physicians, Drs. Patrick, Church and Krohn, employed by the Prosecutor. Subsequently they were examined and observed over a period of nineteen days by two physicians employed by the defense, Drs. Hulbert and Bowman. These physicians prepared a written report, called the Hulbert-Bowman report, from which Mr. Crowe quoted extensively in his closing argument.

The defendants were indicted for murder in the first degree and for kidnapping.

The trial began about the middle of July before Judge John R. Caverly in the Criminal Court of Cook County. The case for the People was conducted by Robert E. Crowe, State's Attorney, and the following Assistant State's Attorneys: Joseph P. Savage, Milton D. Smith, John Sbarbaro, Robert E. McMillan, Bert Cronson and Thomas Marshall. The defense was represented by Clarence S. Darrow, defender in 104 murder cases, and Walter and Benjamin Bachrach.

\* From *Famous American Jury Speeches* 992–1004, 1007–1009, 1013–16, 1020–23, 1027, 1028–33, 1037, 1044–45, 1048–49, 1053–54, 1057–58, 1060–61, 1075– 77, 1082, 1084. (C. E. Hicks ed. West Publishing Co. 1925). With permission of West Publishing Company.

The defendants plead guilty and chose to submit their case to Judge Caverly without a jury. Under the Illinois statute, the court could have sentenced them to be hanged, or to be imprisoned for any period from fourteen years to life imprisonment. 110 witnesses for the state were examined to show the aggravated character of the crime, the motive, and that the murderers were mentally responsible. The defense, arguing in mitigation of sentence, plead for life imprisonment instead of death by hanging. They relied on the youth of the criminals, upon evidence to show lack of motive, and upon expert testimony that they were mentally abnormal. No plea of insanity was however made. Eight medical experts were employed by the defense including Dr. White of Washington, D. C., Dr. Healy of Boston, and Dr. Glueck, of New York, referred to in Mr. Crowe's argument as "the three wise men from the East."

## MR. DARROW'S CLOSING ARGUMENT

Your Honor, it has been almost three months since the great responsibility of this case was assumed by my associates and myself. I am willing to confess that it has been three months of great anxiety. A burden which I gladly would have been spared excepting for my feelings of affection toward some of the members of one of these unfortunate families. This responsibility is almost too great for any one to assume; but we lawyers can no more choose than the court can choose.

Our anxiety over this case has not been due to the facts that are connected with this most unfortunate affair, but to the almost unheard of publicity it has received; to the fact that newspapers all over this country have been giving it space such as they have almost never before given to any case. The fact is that day after day the people of Chicago have been regaled with stories of all sorts about it, until almost every person has formed an opinion.

And when the public is interested and demands a punishment, no matter what the offense, great or small, it thinks of only one punishment, and that is death.

It may not be a question that involves the taking of human life; it may be a question of pure prejudice alone; but when the public speaks as one man it thinks only of killing.

We have been in this stress and strain for three months. We did what we could and all we could to gain the confidence of the public, who in the end really control, whether wisely or unwisely.

It was announced that there were millions of dollars to be spent on this case. Wild and extravagant stories were freely published as though they were facts. Here was to be an effort to save the lives of two boys by the use of money in fabulous amounts, amounts such as these families never even had.

We announced to the public that no excessive use of money would be made in this case, neither for lawyers nor for psychiatrists, or in any other way. We have faithfully kept that promise.

The psychiatrists, as has been shown by the evidence in this case, are receiving a per diem, and only a per diem, which is the same as is paid by the State.

The attorneys, at their own request, have agreed to take such amount as the officers of the Chicago Bar Association may think is proper in this case.

If we fail in this defense it will not be for lack of money. It will be on account of money. Money has been the most serious handicap that we have met. There are times when poverty is fortunate.

I insist, your Honor, that had this been the case of two boys of these defendants' age, unconnected with families supposed to have great wealth, there is not a State's Attorney in Illinois who would not have consented at once to a plea of guilty and a punishment in the penitentiary for life. Not one.

No lawyer could have justified any other attitude. No prosecution could have justified it.

We could have come into this court without evidence, without argument, and this court would have given to us what every judge in the City of Chicago has given to every boy in the City of Chicago since the first capital case was tried. We would have had no contest.

We are here with the lives of two boys imperiled, with the public aroused. For what?

Because, unfortunately, the parents have money. Nothing else.

I told your Honor in the beginning that never had there been a case in Chicago, where on a plea of guilty a boy under twenty-one had been sentenced to death. I will raise that age and say, never has there been a case where a human being under the age of twenty-three has been sentenced to death. And, I think I am safe in saying, although I have not examined all the records and could not—but I think I am safe in saying—that never has there been such a case in the State of Illinois.

And yet this court is urged, aye, threatened, that he must hang two boys contrary to precedents, contrary to the acts of every judge who ever held court in this state.

Why?

Tell me what public necessity there is for this.

Why need the State's Attorney ask for something that never before has been demanded?

Why need a judge be urged by every argument, moderate and immoderate, to hang two boys in the face of every precedent in Illinois, and in the face of the progress of the last fifty years?

Lawyers stand here by the day and read cases from the Dark Ages, where Judges have said that if a man had a grain of sense left and a child if he was barely out of his cradle, could be hanged because he knew the difference between right and wrong. Death sentences for eighteen, seventeen, sixteen and fourteen years have been cited.

Brother Marshall has not half done his job.  He should read his beloved Blackstone again.

I have heard in the last six weeks nothing but the cry for blood. I have heard from the office of the State's Attorney only ugly hate.

I have heard precedents quoted which would be a disgrace to a savage race.

I have seen a court urged almost to the point of threats to hang two boys, in the face of science, in the face of philosophy, in the face of humanity, in the face of experience, in the face of all the better and more humane thought of the age.

Why did not my friend, Mr. Marshall, who dug up from the relics of the buried past these precedents that would bring a blush of shame to the face of a savage, read this from Blackstone:

"Under fourteen, though an infant shall be judged to be incapable of guile prima facie, yet if it appeared to the court and the jury that he was capable of guile, and could discern between good and evil, he may be convicted and suffer death."

Thus a girl thirteen has been burned for killing her mistress.

How this case would delight Dr. Krohn!

He would lick his chops over that more gleefully than over his dastardly homicidal attempt to kill these boys.

One boy of ten, and another of nine years of age, who had killed his companion were sentenced to death; and he of ten actually hanged.

Why?

He knew the difference between right and wrong.  He had learned that in Sunday School.

Age does not count.

Why, Mr. Savage says age makes no difference, and that if this court should do what every other court in Illinois had done since its foundation, and refuse to sentence these boys to death, no one else would ever be hanged in Illinois.

Well, I can imagine some results worse than that.  So long as this terrible tool is to be used for a plaything, without thought or consideration, we ought to get rid of it for the protection of human life.

My friend Marshall has read Blackstone by the page, as if it had something to do with a fairly enlightened age, as if it had something to do with the year 1924, as if it had something to do with Chicago, with its boys' courts and its fairly tender protection of the young.

Now, your Honor, I shall discuss that more in detail a little later, and I only say it now because my friend Mr. Savage—did you pick him for his name or his ability or his learning?—because my friend Mr. Savage, in as cruel a speech as he knew how to make, said to this court that we plead guilty because we were afraid to do anything else.

Your Honor, that is true.

It was not correct that we would have defended these boys in this court; we believe we have been fair to the public. Anyhow, we have tried, and we have tried under terribly hard conditions.

We have said to the public and to this court that neither the parents, nor the friends, nor the attorneys would want these boys released. That they are as they are. Unfortunate though it be, it is true, and those the closest to them know perfectly well that they should not be released, and that they should be permanently isolated from society. We have said that; and we mean it. We are asking this court to save their lives, which is the least and the most that a judge can do.

We did plead guilty before your Honor because we were afraid to submit our cause to a jury. I would not for a moment deny to this court or to this community a realization of the serious danger we were in and how perplexed we were before we took this most unusual step.

I can tell your Honor why.

I have found that years and experience with life tempers one's emotions and makes him more understanding of his fellow man.

When my friend Savage is my age, or even yours, he will read his address to this court with horror.

I am aware that as one grows older he is less critical. He is not so sure. He is inclined to make some allowance for his fellow man. I am aware that a court has more experience, more judgment and more kindliness than a jury.

Your Honor, it may be hardly fair to the court, I am aware that I have helped to place a serious burden upon your shoulders. And at that, I have always meant to be your friend. But this was not an act of friendship.

I know perfectly well that where responsibility is divided by twelve, it is easy to say:

"Away with him."

But, your Honor, if these boys hang, you must do it. There can be no division of responsibility here. You can never explain that the rest overpowered you. It must be by your deliberate, cool, premeditated act, without a chance to shift responsibility.

It was not a kindness to you. We placed this responsibility on your shoulders because we were mindful of the rights of our clients, and we were mindful of the unhappy families who have done no wrong.

Now, let us see, your Honor, what we had to sustain us. Of course, I have known your Honor for a good many years. Not intimately. I could not say that I could even guess from my experience what your Honor might do, but I did know something. I knew, your Honor, that ninety unfortunate human beings had been hanged by the neck until dead in the city of Chicago in our history. We would not have civilization except for those ninety that were hanged, and if we can not make it ninety-two shall we have to shut up shop? Some ninety human beings have been hanged in the history of Chicago, and of those only four have been hanged on the plea of guilty—one out of twenty-two.

I know that in the last ten years four hundred and fifty people have been indicted for murder in the city of Chicago and have plead guilty. Four hundred and fifty have pleaded guilty in the city of Chicago, and only one has been hanged!—And my friend who is prosecuting this case deserves the honor of that hanging while he was on the bench. But his victim was forty years old.

Your Honor will never thank me for unloading this responsibility upon you, but you know that I would have been untrue to my clients if I had not concluded to take this chance before a court, instead of submitting it to a poisoned jury in the city of Chicago. I did it knowing that it would be an unheard of thing for any court, no matter who, to sentence these boys to death.

And, so far as that goes, Mr. Savage is right. I hope, your Honor, that I have made no mistake.

I could have wished that the State's Attorney's office had met this case with the same fairness that we have met it.

It has seemed to me as I have listened to this case five or six times repeating the story of this tragedy, spending days to urge your Honor that a condition of mind could not mitigate, or that tender years could not mitigate, it has seemed to me that it ought to be beneath the representative of a proud state like this to invoke the dark and cruel and bloody past to affect this court and compass these boys' death.

Your Honor I must for a moment criticize the arguments that have preceded me. I can read to you in a minute my friend Marshall's argument, barring Blackstone. But the rest of his arguments and the rest of Brother Savage's argument, I can sum up in a minute: *Cruel; dastardly; premeditated; fiendish; abandoned and malignant heart;*—sounds like a cancer—*cowardly,*—cold-blooded!

Now that is what I have listened to for three days against two minors, two children, who have no right to sign a note or make a deed.

Cowardly?

Well, I don't know. Let me tell you something that I think is cowardly, whether their acts were or not. Here is Dickie Loeb, and Nathan Leopold, and the State objects to anybody calling one "Dickie" and the other "Babe" although everybody does, but they think they can hang them easier if their names are Richard and Nathan, so, we will call them Richard and Nathan.

Eighteen and nineteen years old at the time of the homicide.

Here are three officers watching them. They are led out and in this jail and across the bridge waiting to be hanged. Not a chance to get away. Handcuffed when they get out of this room. Not a chance. Penned like rats in a trap; and for a lawyer with physiological eloquence to wave his fist in front of their faces and shout "Cowardly!" does not appeal to me as a brave act. It does not commend itself to me as a proper thing for a State's Attorney or his assistant; for even defendants not yet hanged have some rights with an official.

Coldblooded? and arranged, and fixed? But I don't know, your Honor. I will discuss that a little later,—whether it was cold-blooded or not.

Cold-blooded? Why? Because they planned, and schemed.

Yes. But here are the officers of justice, so-called, with all the power of the State, with all the influence of the press, to fan this community into a frenzy of hate; with all of that, who for months have been planning and scheming, and contriving, and working to take these two boys' lives.

You may stand them up on a trap-door of the scaffold, and choke them to death, but that act will be infinitely more cold-blooded whether justified or not, than any act that these boys have committed or can commit.

Cold-blooded!

Let the State, who is so anxious to take these boys' lives, set an example in consideration, kindheartedness and tenderness before they call my clients cold-blooded.

I have heard this crime described; this most distressing and unfortunate homicide, as I would call it;—this cold-blooded murder, as the State would call it.

I call it a homicide particularly distressing because I am defending.

They call it a cold-blooded murder because they want to take human lives.

Call it what you will.

I have heard this case talked of, and I have heard these lawyers say that this is the coldest-blooded murder that the civilized world ever has known. I don't know what they include in the civilized world. I suppose Illinois. Although they talk as if they did not. But we will assume Illinois. This is the most cold-blooded murder, says the State, that ever occurred.

Now, your Honor, I have been practicing law a good deal longer than I should have, anyhow, for forty-five or forty-six years, and during a part of that time I have tried a good many criminal cases, always defending. It does not mean that I am better. It probably means that I am more squeamish than the other fellows. It means neither that I am better nor worse. It means the way I am made. I can not help it.

I have never yet tried a case where the state's attorney did not say that it was the most cold-blooded, inexcusable, premeditated case that ever occurred. If it was murder, there never was such a murder. If it was robbery, there never was such a robbery. If it was conspiracy, it was the most terrible conspiracy that ever happened since the Star-Chamber passed into oblivion. If it was larceny, there never was such a larceny.

Now, I am speaking moderately. All of them are the worse. Why? Well, it adds to the credit of the State's Attorney to be connected with a big case. That is one thing. They can say,—

"Well, I tried the most cold-blooded murder case that ever was tried, and I convicted them, and they are dead."

"I tried the worst forgery case that ever was tried, and I won that. I never did anything that was not big."

Lawyers are apt to say that.

And then there is another thing, your Honor: Of course, I generally try cases to juries, and these adjectives always go well with juries; bloody, cold-blooded, despicable, cowardly, dastardly, cruel, heartless,—the whole litany of the State's Attorney's office generally goes well with a jury. The twelve jurors, being good themselves, think it is a tribute to their virtue if they follow the litany of the State's Attorney.

I suppose it may have some effect with the court; I do not know. Anyway, those are the chances we take when we do our best to save life and reputation.

"Here, your clients have pleaded guilty to the most cold-blooded murder that ever took place in the history of the world. And how does a judge dare to refuse to hang by the neck until dead two cowardly ruffians who committed the coldest-blooded murder in the history of the world?"

That is a good talking point.

I want to give some attention to this cold-blooded murder, your Honor.

Was it a cold-blooded murder?

Was it the most terrible murder that ever happened in the State of Illinois?

Was it the most dastardly act in the annals of crime?

No.

I insist, your Honor, that under all fair rules and measurements, this was one of the least dastardly and cruel of any that I have known anything about.

Now, let us see how we should measure it.

They say that this was a cruel murder, the worst that ever happened. I say that very few murders ever occurred that were as free from cruelty as this.

There ought to be some rule to determine whether a murder is exceedingly cruel or not.

Of course, your Honor, I admit that I hate killing, and I hate it no matter how it is done,—whether you shoot a man through the heart, or cut his head off with an axe, or kill him with a chisel or tie a rope around his neck, I hate it. I always did. I always shall.

But there are degrees, and if I might be permitted to make my own rules I would say that if I were estimating what was the most cruel murder, I might first consider the sufferings of the victim.

Now, probably the State would not take that rule. They would say the one that had the most attention in the newspapers. In that way they have got me beaten at the start.

But I would say the first thing to consider is the degree of pain to the victim.

Poor little Bobby Franks suffered very little. There is no excuse for his killing. If to hang these two boys would bring him back to life, I would say let them go, and I believe their parents would say so, too. But:

The moving finger writes, and having writ,
Moves on; nor all your piety nor wit
Shall lure it back to cancel half a line,
Nor all your tears wash out a word of it.

Robert Franks is dead, and we cannot call him back to life. It was all over in fifteen minutes after he got into the car, and he probably never knew it or thought of it. That does not justify it. It is the last thing I would do. I am sorry for the poor boy. I am sorry for his parents. But, it is done.

Of course I cannot say with the certainty of Mr. Savage that he would have been a great man if he had grown up. At fourteen years of age I don't know whether he would or not. Savage, I suppose, is a mind reader, and he says that he would. He has a phantasy, which is hanging. So far as the cruelty to the victim is concerned, you can scarce imagine one less cruel.

Now, what else would stamp a murder as being a most atrocious crime?

First, I put the victim, who ought not to suffer; and next, I would put the attitude of those who kill.

What was the attitude of these two boys?

It may be that the State's Attorney would think that it was particularly cruel to the victim because he was a boy.

Well, my clients are boys, too, and if it would make more serious the offense to kill a boy, it should make less serious the offense of the boys who did the killing.

What was there in the conduct of these two boys which showed a wicked, malignant, and abandoned heart beyond that of anybody else, who ever lived? Your Honor, it is simply foolish.

Everybody who thinks knows the purpose of this. Counsel know that under all the rules of the courts they have not the slightest right to ask this court to take life. Yet they urge it upon this court by falsely characterizing this as being the cruelest act that every occurred. What about these two boys,—the second thing that would settle whether it was cruel or not?

Mr. Marshall read case after case of murders and he said: "Why, those cases don't compare with yours. Yours is worse." Worse, why? What were those cases? Most of his cases were robbery cases,—where a man went out with a gun to take a person's money and shot him down. Some of them were cases where a man killed from spite and hatred and malice. Some of them were cases of special atrocities, mostly connected with money. A man kills someone to get money, he kills someone through hatred. What is this case?

This is a senseless, useless, purposeless, motiveless act of two boys. Now, let me see if I can prove it. There was not a particle of hate, there was not a grain of malice, there was no opportunity to be cruel except as death is cruel,—and death *is* cruel.

There was absolutely no purpose in it all, no reason in it at all, and no motive for it all.

Now, let me see whether I am right or not.

I mean to argue this thoroughly, and it seems to me that there is no chance for a court to hesitate upon the facts in this case.

I want to try to do it honestly and plainly, and without any attempt at frills or oratory; to state the facts of this case just as the facts exist, and nothing else.

What does the State say about it?

In order to make this the most cruel thing that ever happened, of course they must have a motive. And what, do they say, was the motive?

Your Honor, if there was ever anything so foolish, so utterly futile as the motive claimed in this case, then I have never listened to it.

What did Tom Marshall say?

What did Joe Savage say?

"The motive was to get ten thousand dollars," say they.

These two boys, neither one of whom needed a cent, scions of wealthy people, killed this little inoffensive boy to get ten thousand dollars?

. . . .

Your Honor, jurors sometimes make mistakes, and courts do, too. If on this evidence the court is to construe a motive out of this case then I insist that human liberty is not safe and human life is not safe. A motive could be construed out of any set of circumstances and facts that might be imagined.

In addition to that, these boys' families were extremely wealthy. The boys had been reared in luxury, they had never been denied anything; no want or desire left unsatisfied; no debts; no need of money; nothing.

And yet they murdered a little boy, against whom they had nothing in the world, without malice, without reason, to get five thousand dollars each. All right. All right, your Honor, if the court believes it, if anyone believes it, I can't help it.

That is what this case rests on. It could not stand up a minute without motive. Without it, it was the senseless act of immature and diseased children, as it was; a senseless act of children, wandering around in the dark and moved by some emotion, that we still perhaps have not the knowledge or the insight into life to throughly understand.

Now, let me go on with it. What else do they claim?

I want to say to your Honor that you may cut out every expert in this case, you may cut out every lay witness in this case, you may decide this case upon the facts as they appear here alone; and there is no sort of question but what these boys were mentally diseased.

I do not believe that there is any man who knows this case, who does not know that it can be accounted for only on the theory of the mental disease of these two lads.

First, I want to refer to something else. Mr. Marshall argues to this court that you can do no such thing as to grant us the almost divine favor of saving the lives of two boys, that it is against the law, that the penalty for murder is death; and this court, who, in the fiction of the lawyers and the judges, forgets that he is a human being and becomes a court, pulseless, emotionless, devoid of those common feelings which alone make men; that this court as a human machine must hang them because they killed.

Now, let us see. I do not need to ask mercy from this court for these clients, nor for anybody else, nor for myself; though I have never yet found a person who did not need it.

But I do not ask mercy for these boys. You Honor may be as strict in the enforcement of the law as you please and you cannot hang these boys. You can only hang them because back of the law and back of justice and back of the common instincts of man, and back of the human feeling for the young, is the hoarse voice of the mob which says, "Kill." I need ask nothing. What is the law of Illinois?

If one is found guilty of murder in the first degree by a jury, or if he pleads guilty before a court, the court or jury may do one of three things: He may hang; he may imprison for life; or, he may imprison for a term of not less than fourteen years. Now, why is that the law?

Does it follow from the statute that a court is bound to ascertain the impossible, and must necessarily measure the degrees of guilt? Not at all. He may not be able to do it. A court may act from any reason or from no reason. A jury may fix any one of these penalties as they separate. Why was this law passed? Undoubtedly in recognition of the growing feeling in all the forward-thinking people of the United States against capital punishment. Undoubtedly, through the deep reluctance of courts and juries to take human life.

Without any reason whatever, without any facts whatever, your Honor must make the choice, and you have the same right to make one choice as another, no matter what Mr. Justice Blackstone says. It is your Honor's province; you may do it, and I need ask nothing in order to have you do it. There is the statute. But there is more than that in this case.

We have sought to tell this court why he should not hang these boys. We have sought to tell this court, and to make this court believe, that they were diseased of mind, and that they were of tender age. However, before I discuss that, I ought to say another word in reference to the question of motive in this case. If there was no motive, except the senseless act of immature boys, then of course there is taken from this case all of the feeling of deep guilt upon the part of these defendants.

. . . .

Why did they kill little Bobby Franks?

Not for money, not for spite; not for hate. They killed him as they might kill a spider or a fly, for the experience. They killed him because they were made that way. Because somewhere in the infinite processes that go to the making up of the boy or the man something slipped, and those unfortunate lads sit here hated, despised, outcasts, with the community shouting for their blood.

Are they to blame for it? There is no man on earth who can mention any purpose for it all or any reason for it all. It is one of those things that happened; that happened, and it calls not for hate but for kindness, for charity, for consideration.

I heard the State's Attorney talk of mothers.

Mr. Savage is talking for the mothers, and Mr. Crowe is thinking of the mothers, and I am thinking of the mothers. Mr. Savage, with the immaturity of youth and inexperience, says that if we hang them there will be no more killing. This world has been one long slaughter house from the beginning until today, and killing goes on and on and on, and will forever. Why not read something, why not study something, why not think instead of blindly shouting for death?

Kill them. Will that prevent other senseless boys or other vicious men or vicious women from killing? No!

It will simply call upon every weak minded person to do as they have done. I know how easy it is to talk about mothers when you want to do something cruel. But I am thinking of the mothers, too. I know that any mother might be the mother of a little Bobby Franks, who left his home and went to his school, and who never came back. I know that any mother might be the mother of Richard Loeb and Nathan Leopold, just the same. The trouble is this, that if she is the mother of a Nathan Leopold or of a Richard Loeb, she has to ask herself the question,

"How came my children to be what they are? From what ancestry did they get this strain? How far removed was the poison that destroyed their lives? Was I the bearer of the seed that brings them to death?"

Any mother might be the mother of any of them. But these two are the victims. I remember a little poem that gives the soliloquy of a boy about to be hanged, a soliloquy such as these boys might make:

> "The night my father got me
> His mind was not on me;
> He did not plague his fancy
> To muse if I should be
> The son you see.

The day my mother bore me
She was a fool and glad,
For all the pain I cost her,
That she had borne the lad
That borne she had.

My father and my mother
Out of the light they lie;
The warrant would not find them,
And here, 'tis only I
Shall hang so high.

O let not man remember
The soul that God forgot,
But fetch the county sheriff
And noose me in a knot,
And I will rot.

And so the game is ended,
That should not have begun.
My father and my mother
They had a likely son,
And I have none."

No one knows what will be the fate of the child he gets or the child she bears; the fate of the child is the last thing they consider. This weary old world goes on, begetting, with birth and with living and with death; and all of it is blind from the beginning to the end. I do not know what it was that made these boys do this mad act, but I do know there is a reason for it. I know they did not beget themselves. I know that any one of an infinite number of causes reaching back to the beginning might be working out in these boys' minds, whom you are asked to hang in malice and in hatred and injustice, because someone in the past has sinned against them.

I am sorry for the fathers as well as the mothers, for the fathers who give their strength and their lives for educating and protecting and creating a fortune for the boys that they love; for the mothers who go down into the shadow of death for their children, who nourish them and care for them, and risk their lives, that they may live, who watch them with tenderness and fondness and longing, and who go down into dishonor and disgrace for the children that they love.

All of these are helpless. We are all helpless. But when you are pitying the father and the mother of poor Bobby Franks, what about the fathers and mothers of these two unfortunate boys, and what about the unfortunate boys themselves, and what about all the fathers and all the mothers and all the boys and all the girls who tread a dangerous maze in darkness from birth to death?

Do you think you can cure it by hanging these two? Do you think you can cure the hatreds and the mal-adjustments of the world by hanging them? You simply show your ignorance and your hate when you say it. You may here and there cure hatred with love and understanding, but you can only add fuel to the flames by cruelty and hate.

What is my friend's idea of justice? He says to this court, whom he says he respects—and I believe he does—your Honor, who sits here patiently, holding the lives of these two boys in your hands:

"Give them the same mercy that they gave to Bobby Franks."

Is that the law? Is that justice? Is this what a court should do? Is this what a State's Attorney should do? If the state in which I live is not kinder, more human, more considerate more intelligent than the mad act of these two boys, I am sorry that I have lived so long.

.   .   .   .

And still, your Honor, on account of its weirdness and its strangeness, and its advertising, we are forced to fight. For what? Forced to plead to this court that two boys, one eighteen and the other nineteen, may be permitted to live in silence and solitude and disgrace and spend all their days in the penitentiary. Asking this court and the State's Attorney to be merciful enough to let these two boys be locked up in a prison until they die.

I sometimes wonder if I am dreaming—if in the first quarter of the twentieth century there has come back into the hearts of men, the hate and feeling and the lust for blood which possesses the primitive savage of barbarous lands.

What do they want? Tell me, is a life time for the young boys spent behind prison bars,—is that not enough for this mad act? And is there any reason why this great public should be regaled by a hanging?

I cannot understand it, your Honor. It would be past belief, excepting that to the four corners of the earth the news of this weird act has been carried and men have been stirred, and the primitive has come back, and the intellect has been stifled, and men have been controlled by feelings and passions and hatred which should have died centuries ago.

My friend Savage pictured to you the putting of this dead boy in this culvert. Well, no one can minutely describe any killing and not make it shocking. It is shocking. It is shocking because we love life and because we instinctively draw back from death. It is shocking wherever it is and however it is, and perhaps all death is almost equally shocking.

But here is the picture of a dead boy, past pain, when no harm can come to him, put in a culvert, after taking off his clothes, so that the evidence would be destroyed; and that is pictured to this court as a reason for hanging. Well, your Honor, that does not appeal to me as strongly as the hitting over the head of little Robert Franks with a chisel. The boy was dead.

I could say something about the death penalty that, for some mysterious reason, the state wants in this case. Why do they want it? To vindicate the law? Oh, no. The law can be vindicated without killing anyone else. It might shock the fine sensibilities of the

State's counsel that this boy was put into a culvert and left after he was dead, but, your Honor, I can think of a scene that makes this pale into insignificance. I can think, and only *think*, your Honor, of taking two boys, one eighteen and the other nineteen, irresponsible, weak, diseased, penning them in a cell, checking off the days and the hours and the minutes, until they will be taken out and hanged. Wouldn't it be a glorious day for Chicago? Wouldn't it be a glorious triumph for the State's Attorney? Wouldn't it be a glorious triumph for justice in this land? Wouldn't it be a glorious illustration of Christianity and kindness and charity? I can picture them, wakened in the gray light of morning, furnished a suit of clothes by the state, led to the scaffold, their feet tied, black caps drawn over their heads, stood on a trap door, the hangman pressing a spring, so that it gives way under them; I can see them fall through space—and—stopped by the rope around their necks.

This would surely expiate placing Bobbie Franks in the culvert after he was dead. This would doubtless bring immense satisfaction to some people. It would bring a greater satisfaction because it would be done in the name of justice. I am always suspicious of righteous indignation. Nothing is more cruel than righteous indignation. To hear young men talk glibly of justice. Well, it would make me smile if it did not make me sad. Who knows what it is? Does Mr. Savage know? Does Mr. Crowe know? Do I know? Does your Honor know? Is there any human machinery for finding it out? Is there any man can weigh me and say what I deserve? Can your Honor? Let us be honest. Can your Honor appraise yourself, and say what you deserve? Can your Honor appraise these two young men and say what they deserve? Justice must take account of infinite circumstances which a human being cannot understand.

If there is such a thing as justice it could only be administered by one who knew the inmost thoughts of the man to whom they were meting it out. Aye, who knew the father and mother and the grandparents and the infinite number of people back of him. Who knew the origin of every cell that went into the body, who could understand the structure, and how it acted. Who could tell how the emotions that sway the human being affected that particular frail piece of clay. It means more than that. It means that you must appraise every influence that moves them, the civilization where they live, and all society which enters into the making of the child or the man! If your Honor can do it—if you can do it you are wise, and with wisdom goes mercy.

No one with wisdom and with understanding, no one who is honest with himself and with his own life whoever he may be, no one who has seen himself the prey and the sport and the plaything of the infinite forces that move man, no one who has tried and who has failed,—and we have all tried and we have all failed,—no one can tell what justice is for someone else or for himself—and the more he tries and the more responsibility he takes the more he clings to mercy as being the one thing which he is sure should control his judgment of men.

It is not so much mercy either, your Honor. I can hardly understand myself pleading to a court to visit mercy on two boys by shutting them into a prison for life.

For life! Where is the human heart that would not be satisfied with that?

Where is the man or woman who understands his own life and who has a particle of feeling that could ask for more. Any cry for more roots back to the hyena; it roots back to the hissing serpent; it roots back to the beast and the jungle. It is not a part of man. It is not a part of that feeling which, let us hope, is growing, though scenes like this sometimes make me doubt that it is growing; it is not a part of that feeling of mercy and pity and understanding of each other which we believe has been slowly raising man from his low estate. It is not a part of the finer instincts which are slow to develop; of the wider knowledge which is slow to come, and slow to move us when it comes. It is not a part of all that makes the best there is in man. It is not a part of all that promises any hope for the future and any justice for the present. And must I ask that these boys get mercy by spending the rest of their lives in prison, year following year, month following month, and day following day, with nothing to look forward to but hostile guards and stone walls? It ought not to be hard to get that much mercy in any court in the year 1924 . . . .

. . . . .

Can you administer law without consideration? Can you administer what approaches justice without it? Can this court or any court administer justice by consciously turning his heart to stone and being deaf to all the finer instincts which move men? Without those instincts I wonder what would happen to the human race?

If a man could judge a fellow in coldness without taking account of his own life, without taking account of what he knows of human life, without some understanding,—how long would we be a race of real human beings? It has taken the world a long time for man to get even where he is today. If the law was administered without any feeling of sympathy or humanity or kindliness, we would begin our long, slow journey back to the jungle that was formerly our home.

. . . . .

We are satisfied with justice, if the court knows what justice is, or if any human being can tell what justice is. If anybody can look into the minds and hearts and the lives and the origin of these two youths and tell what justice is, we would be content. But nobody can do it without imagination, without sympathy, without kindliness, without understanding, and I have faith that this court will take this case, with his conscience, and his judgment and his courage and save these boys' lives.

Now, your Honor, let me go a little further with this. I have gone over some of the high spots in this tragedy. This tragedy has not claimed all the attention it has had on account of its atrocity. There is nothing to that. Why is it? There are two reasons, and only two that I can see. First is the reputed extreme wealth of these families; not only the Loeb and Leopold families, but the Franks family, and of course it is unusual. And next is the fact that it is weird and uncanny and motiveless. That is what attracted the attention of the world. Many may say now that they want to hang these boys; but I know that giving the people blood is something like giving them their dinner. When they get it they go to sleep. They may for the time being have an emotion, but they will bitterly regret it. And I undertake to say that if these two boys are sentenced to death, and are hanged, on that day there will be a pall settle over the people of this land that will be dark and deep, and at least cover every humane and intelligent person with its gloom. I wonder if it will do good. I wonder if it will help the children—and there is an infinite number like these. I marveled when I heard Mr. Savage talk. I do not criticize him. He is young and enthusiastic. But has he ever read anything? Has he ever thought? Was there ever any man who had studied science, who has read anything of criminology or philosophy,—was there ever any man who knew himself who could speak with the assurance with which he speaks?

What about this matter of crime and punishment, anyhow?· I may know less than the rest, but I have at least tried to find out, and I am fairly familiar with the best literature that has been written on that subject in the last hundred years. The more men study, the more they doubt the effect of severe punishment on crime. And yet Mr. Savage tells this court that if these boys are hanged, there will be no more murder.

Mr. Savage is an optimist. He says that if the defendants are hanged there will be no more boys like these.

I could give him a sketch of punishment, punishment beginning with the brute which killed something because something hurt it; the punishment of the savage; if a person is injured in the tribe, they must injure somebody in the other tribe; it makes no difference who it is, but somebody. If one is killed, his friends or family must kill in return.

You can trace it all down through the history of man. You can trace the burnings, the boilings, the drawings and quarterings, the hanging of people in England at the crossroads, carving them up and hanging them as examples for all to see.

We can come down to the last century when nearly two hundred crimes were punishable by death, and by death in every form; not only hanging—that was too humane—but burning, boiling, cutting into pieces, torturing in all conceivable forms.

You can read the stories of the hangings on a high hill, and the populace for miles around coming out to the scene, that everybody might be awed into goodness. Hanging for picking pockets—and more pockets were picked in the crowd that went to the hanging than had been known before. Hangings for murder—and men were murdered on the way there and on the way home. Hangings for poaching, hangings for everything and hangings in public, not shut up cruelly and brutally in a jail, out of the light of day, wakened in the night time and led forth and killed, but taken to the shire town on a high hill, in the presence of a multitude, so that all might see that the wages of sin were death.

What happened? I have read the life of Lord Shaftesbury, a great nobleman of England, who gave his life and his labors toward modifying the penal code. I have read of the slow, painful efforts through all the ages for more humanity of man to his fellowman. I know what history says, I know what it means, and I know what flows from it, so far as we can tell, which is not with certainty.

I know that every step in the progress of humanity has been met and opposed by prosecutors, and many times by courts. I know that when poaching and petty larceny was punishable by death in England, juries refused to convict. They were too humane to obey the law; and judges refused to sentence. I know that when the delusion of witchcraft was spreading over Europe, claiming its victims by the millions, many a judge so shaped his cases that no crime of witchcraft could be punished in his court. I know that these trials were stopped in America because juries would no longer convict. I know that every step in the progress of the world in reference to crime has come from the humane feelings of man. It has come from that deep well of sympathy, that in spite of all our training and all our conventions and all our teaching, still lives in the human breast. Without it there could be no human life on this weary old world.

Gradually the laws have been changed and modified, and men look back with horror at the hangings and the killings of the past. What did they find in England? That as they got rid of these barbarous statutes crimes decreased instead of increased; as the criminal law was modified and humanized, there was less crime instead of more. I will undertake to say, your Honor, that you can scarcely find a single book written by a student—and I will include all the works on criminology of the past—that has not made the statement over and over again that as the penal code was made less terrible, crimes grew less frequent.

Now let us see a little about the psychology of man. It is easy, your Honor. Anybody can understand it if he just looks into himself. This weird tragedy occurred on the 21st of May. It has been heralded broadcast through the world. How many attempted kidnappings have come since then? How many threatening letters have been sent out by weak-minded boys and weak-minded men since then? How many times have they sought to repeat again and again this same crime because of the effect of publicity upon the mind? I can point to examples of killing and hanging in the city of Chicago which have been repeated in detail over and over again, simply from the publicity of the newspapers and the public generally.

Let us take this case. Let's see whether we can guess about it. Still it is not a guess.

If these two boys die on the scaffold, which I can never bring myself to imagine,—if they do die on the scaffold, the details of this will be spread over the world. Every newspaper in the United States will carry a full account. Every newspaper of Chicago will be filled with the gruesome details. It will enter every home and every family.

Will it make men better or make men worse? I would like to put that to the intelligence of man, at least such intelligence as they have. I would like to appeal to the feelings of human beings so far as they have feelings,—would it make the human heart softer or would it make hearts harder? How many men would be colder and crueler for it? How many men would enjoy the details, and you cannot enjoy human suffering without being affected for better or for worse; those who enjoyed it would be affected for the worse.

What influence would it have upon the millions of men who will read it? What influence would it have upon the millions of women who will read it, more sensitive, more impressionable, more imaginative than men? Would it help them if your Honor should do what the State begs you to do? What influence would it have upon the infinite number of children who will devour its details as Dicky Loeb has enjoyed reading detective stories? Would it make them better or would it make them worse? The question needs no answer. You can answer it from the human heart. What influence, let me ask you, will it have for the unborn babes still sleeping in their mother's womb? And what influence will it have on the psychology of the fathers and mothers yet to come? Do I need to argue to your Honor that cruelty only breeds cruelty?—that hatred only causes hatred; that if there is any way to soften this human heart which is hard enough at its best, if there is any way to kill evil and hatred and all that goes with it, it is not through evil and hatred and cruelty; it is through charity, and love and understanding.

How often do people need to be told this? Look back at the world. There is not a man who is pointed to as an example to the world who has not taught it. There is not a philosopher, there is not a religious leader, there is not a creed that has not taught it. This is a Christian community, so-called, at least it boasts of it, and yet they would hang these boys in a Christian community. Let me ask this court, is there any doubt about whether these boys would be safe in the hands of the founder of the Christian religion? It would be blasphemy to say they would not. Nobody could imagine, nobody could even think of it. And yet there are men who want to hang them for a childish, purposeless act, conceived without the slightest malice in the world.

Your Honor, I feel like apologizing for urging it so long. It is not because I doubt this court. It is not because I do not know something of the human emotions and the human heart. It is not that I do not know that every result of logic, every page of history, every line of philosophy and religion, every precedent in this court, urges this court to save life. It is not that. I have become obsessed with this deep feeling of hate and anger that has swept across this city and this land. I have been fighting it, battling with it, until it has fairly driven me mad, until I sometimes wonder whether every righteous human emotion has not gone down in the raging storm.

I am not pleading so much for these boys as I am for the infinite number of others to follow, those who perhaps cannot be as well defended as these have been, those who may go down in the storm, and the tempest, without aid. It is of them I am thinking, and for them I am begging of this court not to turn backward toward the barbarous and cruel past.

Now, your Honor, who are these two boys?

Leopold, with a wonderfully brilliant mind; Loeb, with an unusual intelligence;—both from their very youth, crowded like hothouse plants, to learn more and more and more. Dr. Krohn says that they are intelligent. In spite of that, it is true:—they are unusually intelligent. But it takes something besides brains to make a human being who can adjust himself to life.

.  .  .  .

There can be no question on the evidence in this case. Dr. Church and Dr. Patrick both testified that these boys have no emotional reactions in reference to this crime. Every one of the alienists on both sides has told this court, what no doubt this court already knew, that the emotions furnish the urge and the drive to life. A man can get along without his intellect, and most people do, but he cannot get along without his emotions. When they did make a brain for man, they did not make it good enough to hurt, because emotions can still hold sway. He eats and he drinks, he works and plays and sleeps, in obedience to his emotional system. The intellectual part of man acts only as a judge over his emotions, and then he generally gets it wrong, and has to rely on his instincts to save him.

These boys—I do not care what their mentality—that simply makes it worse—are emotionally defective.

.  .  .  .

They wanted to commit a perfect crime. There had been growing in this brain, dwarfed and twisted—as every act in this case shows it to have been dwarfed and twisted—there had been growing this scheme, not due to any wickedness of Dickie Loeb, for he is a child. It grew as he grew; it grew from those around him; it grew from the lack of the proper training until it possessed him. He believed he could beat the police. He believed he could plan the perfect crime. He had thought of it and talked of it for years. Had talked of it as a child; had worked at it as a child, and this sorry act of his, utterly irrational and motiveless, a plan to commit a perfect crime which must contain kidnapping, and there must be ransom, or else it could not be perfect, and they must get the money.

The state itself in opening this case said that it was largely for experience and for a thrill, which it was. In the end the state switched it on to the foolish reason of getting cash.

Every fact in this case shows that cash had almost nothing to do with it, except as a factor in the perfect crime; and to commit the perfect crime there must be a kidnapping, and a kidnapping where they could get money, and that was all there was of it. .  .  .  .

.  .  .  .

But, your Honor, that is not all there is to boyhood. Nature is strong and she is pitiless. She works in her own mysterious way, and we are her victims. We have not much to do with it ourselves. Nature takes this job in hand, and we play our parts. In the words of old Omar Khayyam, we are only

> "Impotent pieces in the game He plays
> Upon this checkerboard of nights and days,
> Hither and thither moves, and checks, and slays,
> And one by one back in the closet lays."

. . . .

There was a time in England, running down as late as the beginning of the last century, when judges used to convene court and call juries to try a horse, a dog, a pig, for crime. I have in my library a story of a judge and jury and lawyers trying and convicting an old sow for lying down on her ten pigs and killing them.

What does it mean? Animals were tried. Do you mean to tell me that Dickie Loeb had any more to do with his making than any other product of heredity that is born upon the earth?

. . . .

For God's sake, are we crazy? In the face of history, of every line of philosophy, against the teaching of every religionist and seer and prophet the world has ever given us, we are still doing what our barbaric ancestors did when they came out of the caves and the woods.

From the age of fifteen to the age of twenty or twenty-one, the child has the burden of adolescence, of puberty and sex thrust upon him. Girls are kept at home and carefully watched. Boys without instruction are left to work the period out for themselves. It may lead to excess. It may lead to disgrace. It may lead to perversion. Who is to blame? Who did it? Did Dickie Loeb do it?

. . . .

Babe took to philosophy. I call him Babe, not because I want it to affect your Honor, but because everybody else does. He is the youngest of the family and I suppose that is why he got his nickname. We will call him a man. Mr. Crowe thinks it is easier to hang a man than a boy, and so I will call him a man if I can think of it.

He grew up in this way. He became enamoured of the philosophy of Nietzsche.

. . . Nietzsche believed that some time the superman would be born, that evolution was working toward the superman.

He wrote one book, "Beyond Good and Evil," which was a criticism of all moral codes as the world understands them; a treatise holding that the intelligent man is beyond good and evil; that the laws for good and the laws for evil do not apply to those who approach the superman. He wrote on the will to power. He wrote some ten or fifteen volumes on his various philosophical ideas. Nathan Leopold is not the only boy who has read Nietzsche. He may be the only one who was influenced in the way that he was influenced.

. . . .

Now, I have said that, as to Loeb, if there is anybody to blame it is back of him. Your Honor, lots of things happen in this world that nobody is to blame for. In fact, I am not very much for settling blame myself. If I could settle the blame on somebody else for this special act, I would wonder why that somebody else did it, and I know if I could find that out, I would move it back still another peg.

I know, your Honor, that every atom of life in all this universe is bound up together. I know that a pebble cannot be thrown into the ocean without disturbing every drop of water in the sea. I know that every life is inextricably mixed and woven with every other life. I know that every influence, conscious and unconscious, acts and re-acts on every living organism, and that no one can fix the blame. I know that all life is a series of infinite chances, which sometimes result one way and sometimes another. I have not the infinite wisdom that can fathom it, neither has any other human brain. But I do know that if back of it is a power that made it, that power alone can tell, and if there is no power, then it is an infinite chance, which man can-not solve.

Why should this boy's life be bound up with Frederick Nietzsche, who died thirty years ago, insane, in Germany? I don't know.

I only know it is. I know that no man who ever wrote a line that I read failed to influence me to some extent. I know that every life I ever touched influenced me, and I influenced it; and that it is not given to me to unravel the infinite causes and say, "this is I, and this is you." I am responsible for so much; and you are responsible for so much. I know—I know that in the infinite universe everything has its place and that the smallest particle is a part of all. Tell me that you can visit the wrath of fate and chance and life and eternity upon a nineteen-year-old boy! If you could, justice would be a travesty and mercy a fraud.

* · ·. · ·

There is something else in this case, your Honor, that is stronger still. There is a large element of chance in life. I know I will die. I don't know when; I don't know how; I don't know where; and I don't want to know. I know it will come. I know that it depends on in-finite chances. Do I live to myself? Did I make myself? And con-trol my fate? Can I fix my death unless I suicide—and I cannot do that because the will to live is too strong; I know it depends on in-finite chances.

Take the rabbit running through the woods; a fox meets him at a certain fence. If the rabbit had not started when it did, it would not have met the fox and would have lived longer. If the fox had started later or earlier it would not have met the rabbit and its fate would have been different.

My death will depend upon chances. It may be by the taking in of a germ; it may be a pistol; it may be the decaying of my facul-ties, and all that makes life; it may be a cancer; it may be any one of an indefinite number of things, and where I am at a certain time, and whether I take in that germ, and the condition of my system when

I breathe is an accident which is sealed up in the book of fate and which no human being can open.

These boys, neither one of them, could possibly have committed this act excepting by coming together. It was not the act for one; it was the act of two. It was the act of their planning, their conniving, their believing in each other; their thinking themselves supermen. Without it they could not have done it. It would not have happened. Their parents happened to meet, these boys happened to meet; some sort of chemical alchemy operated so that they cared for each other, and poor Bobby Franks' dead body was found in the culvert as a result. Neither of them could have done it alone.

. . . .

I have a list of executions in Cook County beginning in 1840, which I presume covers the first one, because I asked to have it go to the beginning. Ninety poor unfortunate men have given up their lives to stop murder in Chicago. Ninety men have been hanged by the neck until dead, because of the ancient superstition that in some way hanging one man keeps another from committing a crime. The ancient superstition, I say, because I defy the State to point to a criminologist, a scientist, a student, who has ever said it. Still we go on, as if human conduct was not influenced and controlled by natural laws the same as all the rest of the Universe is the subject of law. We treat crime as if it had no cause. We go on saying, "Hang the unfortunates, and it will end." Was there ever a crime without a cause? And yet all punishment proceeds upon the theory that there is no cause; and the only way to treat crime is to intimidate every one into goodness and obedience to law. We lawyers are a long way behind.

Crime has its cause. Perhaps all crimes do not have the same cause, but they all have some cause. And people today are seeking to find out the cause. We lawyers never try to find out. Scientists are studying it; criminologists are investigating it; but we lawyers go on and on and on, punishing and hanging and thinking that by general terror we can stamp out crime.

It never occurs to the lawyer that crime has a cause as certainly as disease, and that the way to rationally treat any abnormal condition is to remove the cause.

. . . .

As a rule, lawyers are not scientists. They have learned the doctrine of hate and fear, and they think that there is only one way to make men good, and that is to put them in such terror that they do not dare to be bad. They act unmindful of history, and science, and all the experience of the past.

Still, we are making some progress. Courts give attention to some things that they did not give attention to before.

Once in England they hanged children seven years of age; not necessarily hanged them, because hanging was never meant for punishment; it was meant for exhibition. If somebody committed crime, he would be hanged by the head or the heels, it didn't matter much which, at the four cross roads, so that everybody could look at him until his bones were bare, and so that people would be good because they had seen the gruesome result of crime and hate.

. . . .

We have raised the age of hanging. We have raised it by the humanity of courts, by the understanding of courts, by the progress in science which at last is reaching the law; and in ninety men hanged in Illinois from its beginning, not one single person under twenty-three was ever hanged upon a plea of guilty—not one. If your Honor should do this, you would violate every precedent that has been set in Illinois for almost a century. There can be no excuse for it, and no justification for it, because this is the policy of the law which is rooted in the feelings of humanity, which are deep in every human being that thinks and feels. There have been two or three cases where juries have convicted boys younger than this, and where courts on convictions have refused to set aside the sentence because a jury had found it.

. . . .

Your Honor, if in this court a boy of eighteen and a boy of nineteen should be hanged on a plea of guilty, in violation of every precedent of the past, in violation of the policy of the law to take care of the young, in violation of all the progress that has been made and of the humanity that has been shown in the care of the young; in violation of the law that places boys in reformatories instead of prisons,—if your Honor in violation of all that and in the face of all the past should stand here in Chicago alone to hang a boy on a plea of guilty, then we are turning our faces backward toward the barbarism which once possessed the world. If your Honor can hang a boy eighteen, some other judge can hang him at seventeen, or sixteen, or fourteen. Some day, if there is any such thing as progress in the world, if there is any spirit of humanity that is working in the hearts of men, some day men would look back upon this as a barbarous age which deliberately set itself in the way of progress, humanity and sympathy, and committed an unforgiveable act.

. . . .

Now, your Honor, I have spoken about the war. I believed in it. I don't know whether I was crazy or not. Sometimes I think perhaps I was. I approved of it; I joined in the general cry of madness and despair. I urged men to fight. I was safe because I was too old to go. I was like the rest. What did they do? Right or wrong, justifiable or unjustifiable—which I need not discuss to-day—it changed the world. For four long years the civilized world was engaged in killing men. Christian against Christian, barbarians uniting with Christians to kill Christians; anything to kill. It was taught in every school, aye in the Sunday schools. The little children played at war. The toddling children on the street. Do you suppose this world has ever been the same since then? How long, your Honor, will it take for the world to get back the humane emotions that were daily growing before the war? How long will it take the calloused hearts of men before the scars of hatred and cruelty shall be removed?

We read of killing one hundred thousand men in a day. We read about it and we rejoiced in it—if it was the other fellows who were killed. We were fed on flesh and drank blood. Even down to the prattling babe. I need not tell your Honor this, because you know; I need not tell you how many upright, honorable young boys have come into this court charged with murder, some saved and some sent to their death, boys who fought in this war and learned to place a cheap value on human life. You know it and I know it. These boys were brought up on it. The tales of death were in their homes, their playgrounds, their schools; they were in the newspapers that they read; it was a part of the common frenzy—what was a life? It was nothing. It was the least sacred thing in existence and these boys were trained to this cruelty.

It will take fifty years to wipe it out of the human heart, if ever. I know this, that after the Civil War in 1865, crimes of this sort increased, marvelously. . . .

Your Honor knows that in this very court crimes of violence have increased growing out of the war. Not necessarily by those who fought but by those that learned that blood was cheap, and human life was cheap, and if the State could take it lightly why not the boy? There are causes for this terrible crime. There are causes, as I have said, for everything that happens in the world. War is a part of it; education is a part of it; birth is a part of it; money is a part of it,—all these conspired to compass the destruction of these two poor boys.

Has the court any right to consider anything but these two boys? The State says that your Honor has a right to consider the welfare of the community, as you have. If the welfare of the community would be benefited by taking these lives, well and good. I think it would work evil that no one could measure. Has your Honor a right to consider the families of these two defendants? I have been sorry, and I am sorry for the bereavement of Mr. and Mrs. Franks, for those broken ties that cannot be healed. All I can hope and wish is that some good may come from it all. But as compared with the families of Leopold and Loeb, the Franks are to be envied,—and everyone knows it.

I do not know how much salvage there is in these two boys. I hate to say it in their presence, but what is there to look forward to? I do not know but what your Honor would be merciful if you tied a rope around their necks and let them die; merciful to them, but not merciful to civilization, and not merciful to those who would be left behind. To spend the balance of their days in prison is mighty little to look forward to, if anything. Is it anything? They may have the hope that as the years roll around they might be released. I do not know. I do not know. I will be honest with this court as I have tried to be from the beginning. I know that these boys are not fit to be at large. I believe they will not be until they pass through the next stage of life, at forty-five or fifty. Whether they will be then, I cannot tell. I am sure of this; that I will not be here to help them. So far as I am concerned, it is over.

. . . .

I care not, your Honor, whether the march begins at the gallows or when the gates of Joliet close upon them, there is nothing but the night, and that is little for any human being to expect.

But there are others to be considered. Here are these two families, who have led honest lives, who will bear the name that they bear, and future generations must carry it on.

Here is Leopold's father—and this boy was the pride of his life. He watched him, he cared for him, he worked for him; the boy was brilliant and accomplished, he educated him, and he thought that fame and position awaited him, as it should have awaited. It is a hard thing for a father to see his life's hopes crumble into dust.

Should he be considered? Should his brothers be considered? Will it do society any good or make your life safer, or any human being's life safer, if it should be handed down from generation to generation, that this boy, their kin, died upon the scaffold?

And Loeb's the same. Here is the faithful uncle and brother, who have watched here day by day, while Dickie's father and his mother are too ill to stand this terrific strain, and shall be waiting for a message which means more to them than it can mean to you or me. Shall these be taken into account in this general bereavement?

Have they any rights? Is there any reason, your Honor, why their proud names and all the future generations that bear them shall have this bar sinister written across them? How many boys and girls, how many unborn children will feel it? It is bad enough as it is, God knows. It is bad enough, however it is. But it's not yet death on the scaffold. It's not that. And I ask your Honor, in addition to all that I have said, to save two honorable families from a disgrace that never ends, and which could be of no avail to help any human being that lives.

Now, I must say a word more and then I will leave this with you where I should have left it long ago. None of us are unmindful of the public; courts are not, and juries are not. We placed our fate in the hands of a trained court, thinking that he would be more mindful and considerate than a jury. I cannot say how people feel. I have stood here for three months as one might stand at the ocean trying to sweep back the tide. I hope the seas are subsiding and the wind is falling, and I believe they are, but I wish to make no false pretense to this court. The easy thing and the popular thing to do is to hang my clients. I know it. Men and women who do not think will applaud. The cruel and the thoughtless will approve. It will be easy today; but in Chicago, and reaching out over the length and breadth of the land, more and more fathers and mothers, the humane, the kind and the hopeful, who are gaining and understanding and asking questions not only about these poor boys, but about their own,—these will join in no acclaim at the death of my clients. These would ask that the shedding of blood be stopped, and that the normal feelings of man resume their sway. And as the days and the months and the years go on, they will ask it more and more. But, your Honor, what they shall ask may not count. I know the easy way. I know your Honor stands between the future and the past.

I know the future is with me, and what I stand for here; not merely for the lives of these two unfortunate lads, but for all boys and all girls; for all of the young, and as far as possible, for all of the old. I am pleading for life, understanding, charity, kindness, and the infinite mercy that considers all. I am pleading that we overcome cruelty with kindness and hatred with love. I know the future is on my side. Your Honor stands between the past and the future. You may hang these boys; you may hang them by the neck until they are dead. But in doing it you will turn your face toward the past. In doing it you are making it harder for every other boy who in ignorance and darkness must grope his way through the mazes which only childhood knows. In doing it you will make it harder for unborn children. You may save them and make it easier for every child that some time may stand where these boys stand. You will make it easier for every human being with an aspiration and a vision and a hope and a fate. I am pleading for the future; I am pleading for a time when hatred and cruelty will not control the hearts of men. When we can learn by reason and judgment and understanding and faith that all life is worth saving, and that mercy is the highest attribute of man.

I feel that I should apologize for the length of time I have taken. This case may not be as important as I think it is, and I am sure I do not need to tell this court, or to tell my friends that I would fight just as hard for the poor as for the rich. If I should succeed in saving these boys' lives and do nothing for the progress of the law, I should feel sad, indeed. If I can succeed, my greatest reward and my greatest hope will be that I have done something for the tens of thousands of other boys, for the countless unfortunates who must tread the same road in blind childhood that these poor boys have trod, —that I have done something to help human understanding, to temper justice with mercy, to overcome hate with love.

I was reading last night of the aspiration of the old Persian poet, Omar Khayyam. It appealed to me as the highest that I can vision. I wish it was in my heart, and I wish it was in the hearts of all.

> "So I be written in the Book of Love,
> I do not care about that Book above,
> Erase my name or write it as you will,
> So I be written in the Book of Love."

### ROBERT E. CROWE

### CLOSING ARGUMENT FOR THE PROSECUTION IN THE LEOPOLD-LOEB MURDER TRIAL *

### BIOGRAPHICAL NOTES

Robert Emmett Crowe was born in Peoria, Illinois, on January 22, 1879. He was graduated from the Yale Law School in 1901, and

---

\* From *Famous American Jury Speeches* 1090–1102, 1105–06, 1110, 1115, 1127–29, 1131–32, 1134–35, 1149–50, 1157–63, 1164. (C. E. Hicks ed. West Publishing Co. 1925). With permission of West Publishing Company.

began the practice of law in Chicago. From 1908 to 1912, he was Assistant State's Attorney; in 1915, he became Assistant Corporation Counsel; and from 1916 to 1921, he was Judge of the Circuit Court of Cook County. He [became] State's Attorney of Cook County [in] 1921.

## MR. CROWE'S CLOSING ARGUMENT

Before entering into a discussion of the case at bar, I desire to express to your Honor our appreciation for the uniform courtesy and patience with which you have treated me and the representatives of my office.

Before going into a discussion of the merits of the case, there is a matter that I would like to refer to. The distinguished gentleman whose profession it is to protect murder in Cook County, and concerning whose health thieves inquire before they go out to commit crime, has seen fit to abuse the State Attorney's office, and particularly my assistants, Mr. Marshall and Mr. Savage, for their conduct in this case. He has even objected to the State's Attorney referring to two self-confessed murderers, who have pleaded guilty to two capital offenses, as criminals. And he says that Marshall has no heart or, if he has, that it must be a heart of stone. He says that Savage was probably selected on account of his name and not on account of his attainments; that they have dared to tell your Honor that this is a cold-blooded murder; have violated all the finer sensibility of this distinguished attorney whose profession it is to protect murder in this community, by representing this crime as a dastardly, cruel, premeditated crime.

That is their business, if they refer to this case at all. Bachrach, however, in his closing argument said that I haven't any right after a plea of guilty has been entered and the evidence presented, to talk to your Honor; that this case should be taken under advisement by you. With merely the plea of the defense the State's Attorney ought to go back to his office. He has no business to argue on behalf of the People of the State of Illinois at all. Their arguments must go uncontradicted and without a reply.

We ought not to refer to these two young men, the poor sons of multimillionaires, with any coarse language. Savage and Marshall should have come up here and tried them with kindness and with consideration.

I can imagine, your Honor, when this case was called for trial and your Honor began to warn these two defendants of the consequences of their plea, and when you said we may impose the death penalty, Savage and Marshall both rushing up and saying:

"Now, Judge! now Judge! not so fast! We don't intend to be cruel in this case. We don't intend to be harsh. We want to try these boys, these kiddies, with kindness and consideration. Your Honor ought not to shock their ears by such a cruel reference to the laws of this State, to the penalty of death. Why, don't you know that one of them has to shave every day of the week, and that is a bad sign? The other one has to shave twice a week only and that is a bad sign. One is short and one is tall, and it is equally a bad sign in both of them. When they were children they played with 'Teddy bears.' One of them has three moles on his back. One is over developed sexually and the other not quite so good."

My God, if one of them had a hare lip I suppose Darrow would want me to apologize for having had them indicted.

Can you imagine Savage and Marshall making a plea of that sort to your Honor, and saying: "Instead of sending these two mad boys, who are wandering around in the dark, to prison for life, parole them to us. Marshall will take 'Dickie' and Savage will take 'Babe.' And we will try to get them out of this 'fantasy life.' We will try to wake them up, out of their dreams."

I know what your Honor would have said if they had pursued that line of conduct. You would have said:

"Mr. Sheriff, search these men, find out how much money they have in their pockets."

And if they had not any money in their pockets, your Honor would tell the sheriff to take them to the psychopathic hospital and you would send for me and say:

"Crowe, send up somebody who has got some brains to prosecute a murder case in my court room."

If we are cold-blooded, we have, according to Mr. Darrow, planned for three months, and conspired to take the lives of two little boys who are wandering around in dreamland. We have been held up to the world as men who desire blood, who have no kindly instincts within our hearts at all.

I do not believe that is fair to Tom Marshall. Tom Marshall has lived in this community for years. He is a kindly man in private life; he is a man of family; he enjoys the respect and confidence of every person who has been fortunate enough to know him.

Joe Savage is a decent man, a clean living man, a man of kindly instincts. He is a man of family also, and he enjoys the confidence and respect of everybody in this community.

I do not believe that even Mr. Darrow, who has known me for years, or any other person who knows me, would tell you that Bob Crowe is a cruel, vicious, heartless monster. I am a man of family; I love my children, four of them, and I love my wife, and I believe they love me. I have never been cruel or vicious to any living person in my life. I have never prosecuted any person for any wrong that he did me personally, and I have been grievously wronged in the past. I have never sued any person for any debt he owed me, although I have many debts now owing me.

I believe in God,—and that is a fault in this case—a fault not only of the two murderers, but a fault of the master pleader whose profession it is to protect murder in this country. I believe in the laws of this state. There is nothing personal in this prosecution with me. If I were not a State's attorney or if I were not on the bench, I would have absolutely no feeling in my heart against these two as individuals. When they were in my care and custody, where it was a matter of man to man, I treated them with kindness and consideration. That is the sworn testimony in this case, that while they were in my custody they were treated with kindness and consideration.

When I first got Leopold's name as a possible owner of these glasses, when I got the name of a lady of this community of respectability and refinement, when I got the name of a prominent lawyer, who might have been the owner of these glasses, I treated all three of them with kindness and consideration. I did not bring them into the State's Attorney's office so that their names would be headlined across the newspapers, as connected with this terrible crime, and where they would have their pictures taken by every newspaper in the country. I brought them over to the La Salle Hotel, so that, if none of them had any connection with this case, no disgrace or notoriety would have attached to any one of them. I think the State's Attorney of this county is just as kindly a man as the paid humanitarian, the man who believes in doing his fellow citizens good,—after he has done them good and plenty.

But, when I had fastened this crime upon these defendants, then I had a duty to perform, a sworn duty to perform the same as your Honor has.

I have a right to forgive those who trespass against me, as I do, in the hopes that I in the hereafter will be forgiven my trespasses. As a private citizen I have that right, and as a private citizen I live that religion. But, as a public official, elected by the people, charged with the duty of enforcing the laws of my country, I have no right to forgive those who violate their country's laws. It is my duty to prosecute them.

Your Honor has no right to forgive those who trespass against the State of Illinois. You have a right to, and I know you do, forgive those who trespass against John R. Caverly. But sitting here as the Chief Justice of this great court, you have no right to forgive anybody who violates the law. You have got to deal with him as the law prescribes.

And I want to say to you, your Honor, in this case, with the mass of evidence presented by the State, if a jury were sitting in that box and they returned a verdict and did not fix the punishment at death, every person in this community, including your Honor and myself, would feel that that verdict was founded in corruption.

And I will tell you why. I have taken quite a trip during the last four or five weeks.

I thought I was going to be kept in Chicago all summer trying this case, and that most of my time would be spent in the Criminal Court Building.

And I find I have been mistaken. I did come up to your Honor's court room five weeks ago, and after I was there a little while old Doc Yak—is that his name?—the man from Washington—oh, Dr. White—took me by the hand and led me into the nursery of two poor, rich young boys, and he introduced me to a Teddy bear. Then he told me some bedtime stories, and after I got through listening to them, he took me into the kindergarten and he presented to me little "Dickie" and "Babe," and he wanted to know if I had any objection to calling them that, and I said no, if he had no purpose.

And after he had wandered between the nursery and the kindergarten for quite a while, I was taken in hand by the Bachrach brothers and taken to a psychopathic laboratory, and there I received quite a liberal education in mental diseases, and particularly what certain doctors did not know about them.

The three wise men from the East, who came on to tell your Honor about these little babes,—being three wise men brought on from the East, they want to make the picture a little more perfect. One of them was sacrilegious enough to say this pervert, this murderer, this kidnapper thought that he was the Christ child and his mother the Madonna, and that—without a syllable of evidence any place to support the blasphemous and sacrilegious statement.

Who said that this young pervert ever thought he was the Christ child? He has proclaimed since he was eleven years of age that there is no God. "The fool in his heart hath said there is no God." I wonder now, Nathan, whether you think there is a God or not. I wonder whether you think it is pure accident that this discipline of Nietzschian philosophy dropped his glasses or whether it was an act of Divine Providence to visit upon your miserable carcasses the wrath of God in the enforcement of the laws of the State of Illinois.

After the Bachrachs had completed my education in the psychopathic laboratories, then my good friend Clarence Darrow took me on a Chautauqua trip, visiting various towns, we would go to social settlements, such as the Hull House, and Clarence would expound his peculiar philosophy of life; and we would meet with communists and anarchists, and Clarence would regale them with his philosophy of the law, which means there ought not to be any law and there ought not to be any enforcement of the law.

And he even took me to Springfield, where he argued before the legislature that you ought to abolish capital punishment in the State of Illinois.

I don't know whether the fact that he had a couple of rich clients who were dangerously close to the gallows prompted that trip or not. I know when he was a member of the legislature he did not abolish capital punishment or introduce a bill for that purpose.

Yes, and on this tour he criticized the State's Attorney of this county severely because he, in a humane way, wanted to correct the law so that men of this sort could be dealt with before somebody lay cold in death, and that the children of this community might be protected.

When I occupied the position that your Honor now graces, I had an unfortunate man come before me. He was a man of my own race, of my own faith. I don't know whether his pineal gland was calcified or ossified. I don't know whether he had club feet or not, and I did not inspect his back to find out whether he had a couple of moles. I don't know whether he developed sexually at 14 or 16. I knew under the law he had committed a dastardly crime. He had taken a little six-year-old girl, a daughter of the poor, and he was a poor man, and he outraged her and he took her into the basement and he covered her over with coal. He did not even have the decency or the heart to put a handkerchief over that little dead face as he heaped the coal on it.

The law says in extreme cases death shall be the penalty. If I were in the legislature I might vote against such a law. I don't know. But as a judge, I have no right to set aside that law. I have no right to defeat the will of the people, as expressed by the legislature of Illinois. I have no right to be a judicial anarchist, even if Clarence Darrow is an anarchistic advocate. He says that hanging does not stop murder. I think he is mistaken.

From the time Thomas Fitzgerald expiated his crime upon the gallows, I have not heard of any little tot in Chicago who met a like fate to that which Janet Wilkinson met. He says hanging does not stop murder.

I will direct your Honor's attention to the year 1920, when Judge Kavanagh, Judge Brentano, Judge Barrett and Judge Scanlan came over here at my request and from the 5th day of May until the first day of July tried nothing but murder cases.

In addition to the many men that they sent to the penitentiary for manslaughter or a term of years for murder, in that brief period of less than sixty days, fifteen men were sentenced to death in the Criminal Court of Cook County. The records of the Police Department, the records of the Chicago Crime Commission, show that as a result of that, murder fell 51 per cent in Cook County during the year 1920.

We had a time here when every night in every newspaper there was a column devoted to the number of automobiles stolen. We established an automobile court, and I presided in it, and after we had sent several hundred to penal institutions for stealing automobiles, the Rolls Royce became just as safe as the flivver on the streets of Chicago.

We had a reign of terror inaugurated here for years by criminals who dominated labor unions. They were above and beyond the law. They laughed at it, and spat in its face, just as do these two poor young sons of multimillionaires. Forty-nine of them were convicted in the courts of Cook County. The building industry, that had been strangled for years, began to revive and take on life, and we have not heard anything more of the Maders, or the Murphys, or the Walshes since. Punishment in jail does not deter crime? Why are there so few violations of the laws of the United States? When a man files his income schedule, why does he hire an auditor to see that he makes no mistake? And yet he goes before the Board of Assessors and Board of Review on his personal property and conceals millions. Why? Because when you get into the United States court, your Honor, for having violated the laws of the United States, if you are guilty, no plea of mercy, however eloquent or by whomsoever delivered, will cheat the law there.

You have heard a lot about England. Well, I was never very enthusiastic about England myself. That is due to heredity in me. I never had any liking or respect for her laws as they applied to my ancestors and people in an adjoining isle; but I have learned to have a wholesome respect for the manner in which they enforce the laws of England in England.

There murder is murder; it is not a fantasy. There, justice is handed out swiftly and surely, and as a result there are less murders in the entire Kingdom of Great Britain yearly than there are in the City of Chicago.

The police of England do not carry weapons. What would happen to the Chicago police if, after giving notice, they all went out one night without a weapon?

. . . .

Treat them with kindness and consideration? Call them babes? Call them children? Why, from the evidence in this case, if your Honor please, they are as much entitled to the sympathy and the mercy of this court as a couple of rattlesnakes flushed with venom, coiled, read to strike. They are entitled to as much mercy at the hands of your Honor as two mad dogs are entitled to.

They are no good to themselves. The only purpose for which they are of any use is to debase themselves. They are a disgrace to their honored families, and they are a menace to this community. The only useful thing that remains for them now in life is to go out of this life and to go out of it as quickly as possible, under the law.

. . . .

Bobby Franks kidnapped! When we had not the slightest information who was guilty of the dastardly crime, the papers were full of it. It was the only topic of conversation. It remained the only topic of conversation for a week before the State's Attorney of this county called in Nathan Leopold, Jr.

Their wealth, in my judgment, has nothing to do with this. It permits a defense here seldom given to men in the Criminal Court. Take away the millions of the Loebs and Leopolds, and Clarence Darrow's tongue is as still as the tongue of Julius Caesar. Take away their millions, and the wise men from the East would not be here to tell you about fantasies, Teddy bears and about bold boys who had their pictures taken in cowboy uniform. Take away their money, and what happens? The same as has happened to all other men who have been tried in this building that had no money:

A plea of guilty; a police officer sworn; a Coroner's physician sworn; the parents of the murdered boy sworn; a sentence.

I used to wonder what the poet Gray meant when he talked about the short and simple annals of the poor. Clarence Darrow once said that the poor man on trial was usually disposed of in fifteen minutes. But if he was rich and committed some crime, and he got a good lawyer, his trial would last twenty-one days. Well, they have three good lawyers, and it has lasted just a little bit longer; and in addition they had three wise men from the East.

Are we trying here, if your Honor please, a murder case? And what is the evidence presented by the State upon which they ask the extreme penalty? A murder. The result of a drunken brawl, a murder committed in hot blood, that there would have been some injury, either real or fanciful, a man shooting down another because he debauched his wife and destroyed his home? A murder the result of impulse or passion?

No; one of the most carefully planned murder cases that your Honor or I, from all our long experience, have ever heard about. A murder committed by some young gamin of the streets, whose father was a drunkard and his mother loose, who was denied every opportunity and brought up in the slums, never had a decent example set before him? No; but a murder committed by two superintellects, coming from the members of the most respected families in Chicago; every advantage that love, money and wealth and position could give them was theirs.

A man's conduct, I believe, your Honor, depends upon his philosophy of life. Those who want to grow up to be respected citizens in the community, to be useful citizens, have a correct philosophy of life. Those who want to excel in crime, those who want to tear down instead of build up, select the wrong philosophy of life. That is all there is to this. They had the power of choice, and they deliberately chose to adopt the wrong philosophy and to make their conduct correspond with it.

Away last November, after these two defendants had had a quarrel and made it up—but I will not go into the nature of that quarrel as I have before—there has been a lot of evidence in this case that has not come out, and I do not intend to repeat it to shock any person who may be listening. These two defendants were perverts, Loeb the victim and Leopold the aggressor, and they quarreled. Then they entered into a "childish compact." "A childish compact," Dr. Healy says, a compact between these two, so that these unnatural crimes might continue. Dr. Healy says that this is a childish compact; and I say if Dr. Healy is not ashamed of himself, he ought to be. My God! I was a grown man before I knew of such depravity.

They talk about what lawyers will do for money, but my God! I am glad I don't know of any lawyer who would sit on the witness stand and under oath characterize an unnatural agreement between these two perverts as a childish compact. Mr. Bachrach says that is an evidence of insanity. The statute of Illinois says that crimes against nature are crimes punishable by imprisonment in the penitentiary. It is not a defense to a murder charge.

Mitigation. Mitigation. I have heard so many big words, and foreign words in this case that I sometimes thought that probably we are letting error creep into the record. So many strange, foreign words have been used here; and the Constitution provides that the trial must be conducted in the English language. I don't know; maybe I have got aggravation and mitigation mixed up.

It is a mitigating circumstance, if your Honor pleases, that when they were outlining the plan of this conspiracy and murder, they wanted to take a little girl, the daughter of the rich, and first rape her and then murder her, and then collect the ransom. If that evidence had been put in by the State, I would have thought it was an aggravation.

These three wise men, with their distorted theories, hired by the defense, put that evidence in. Clarence Darrow calls it a mitigating circumstance. Why, when they murder a boy, they ought to be treated with kindness and consideration. If they had taken a little tot, a little girl, debauched her and raped her, I suppose we ought to give them each a medal and tell them to go on their ways. . . .

.  .  .  .  .  .

Mr. Darrow says that there is no motive, that this is a senseless crime; the $10,000 has absolutely nothing to do with it. I will undertake to prove,—not by argument, but by sworn testimony,—that the $10,000 had everything to do with it. I will show that this was not the crime of diseased emotion, but this was a crime planned in all its minuteness by more than ordinary intellect.

.  .  .  .  .  .

.  .  . Mr. Darrow .  .  . guessed that maybe after I knew they had no defense on the fact, and I knew how much money they had, that I might think that they were going to put in some kind of a fancy insanity defense. And that is the reason I sent for the four best alienists in the City of Chicago, while I still had these young, egotistical, smart alecs—that is all they are, they are not supermen, they are not men of superintelligence, they are just a couple of spoiled smart alecs, spoiled by the twaddling and petting of their folks and by the people who fawn upon them on account of their wealth. They repeat, parrot like, things that they have remembered and assume the solemn expression of an owl and talk about supermen.

In one breath one of these wise men from the East will tell you that the two defendants still believe in Santa Claus, and then in the next breath Mr. Darrow will tell you that they do not believe even in God.

.  .  .  .  .  .

The only explanation I can give of the testimony of Dr. White is that he is in his second childhood. I would hate to think a man of his attainments would prostitute his profession and prostitute his learning to tell the story that he told to your Honor.

One of the very significant and distinguishing things the eminent doctor says was the fact that little Dick had his picture taken in a cowboy's uniform when he was four years of age; and that is a distinguishing thing and stamped him as a man of diseased mind, with homicidal tendencies; and I saw a shudder go through every woman in the court room that has a "kid" four or five years of age, and I began to think of my four "kids."

I suppose Marshall Field's sale of cowboy suits must have fallen off at least one hundred thousand since that doctor testified.

When the other doctors saw how ridiculous and silly it all was, they said they paid no attention to it; and one by one, all, each doctor discharged this silly bosh that the preceding doctor had testified to, as distinguishing matter; and finally the Grand Old Man of defense, Clarence Darrow, seeing how absolutely absurd it was, discarded all of their testimony and substituted as a defense in this case his peculiar philosophy of life, of which we will talk later on.

. . . .

In all probability the present mental disease of these two defendants would disappear very rapidly if the causes for its existence were removed. If the glasses had never been found, if the State's Attorney had not fastened the crime upon these two defendants, Nathan Leopold would be over in Paris or some other of the gay capitals of Europe, indulging his unnatural lust with the $5,000 he had wrung from Jacob Franks.

If they were to be discharged today, through some technicality in the law, this present disturbance would all disappear very rapidly, if the causes for its existence were removed. I used to wonder why they got Doc White—and this explains it.

. . . .

A crime by mad boys without a purpose, without any thought of revenge, without any thought of money? Let's see. The first boy they contemplated killing was a boy he did not like. Hatred, revenge, was the motive in his mind at that time, but a desire for money overcame that.

"The patient did not like this boy or his family." The details of which were not brought out. Why not? Because the details might show that the hate and the anger were strong enough to compel him to kill him, but he does not tell you that the first boy was one he did not like and he did not like his family.

"He was the patient's own age, rather large for his age. The patient's idea was to get hold of this boy when he was coming back from a party and lure him into an automobile. He could not figure any safe way of getting the money and because he could not figure of any safe way of getting the money he brushed aside his hate and his desire upon his enemy."

Money is the motive in this case, and I will prove it repeatedly by their own evidence. He could not figure any safe way of getting the money. "The patient and his companion discussed this idea quite frequently. Neither of them, however, could think of any simple and certain method of securing the money." All through this case it is money, money, money—blood.

"Neither of them, however, could think of any simple, certain way of securing the money. They continued to discuss the matter, weighing the pros and cons, suggesting methods only to pick flaws in them. In March, 1924, the patient conceived the idea of securing"—What? Thrill? The excitement? No. "Conceived the idea of securing the money by having it thrown off a moving train."

This idea was discussed in great detail and gradually developed into a carefully systematized plan. But Mr. Darrow disagrees with the doctor. This was not carefully discussed and gone into in great detail and gradually developed into a carefully systematized plan. This was just a mad act of mad boys, wandering around in the dark, looking for a Teddy bear.

"It was figured out first that the money should be thrown off of a moving train when it was dark somewhere in the country. He and his companion spent many uncomfortable afternoons—" (I really sympathize with you dear little boys for all the discomfort you have suffered on those afternoons. It is too bad that in this weird, uncanny scheme of yours of murder, you had to spend many uncomfortable afternoons)—"going over the Illinois Central tracks looking for suitable location. Finally his companion—" that is Leopold, your Honor) —"suggested the idea of studying upon a certain brick factory on the left side of the tracks as a landmark. There was considerable discussion as to what car to use, but the patient and his companion felt that it was not safe to use either of their own cars."

Mad boys in the dark and dreamland, doing a mad act without any thought of the consequences of it, and least of all not considering their personal safety at all? Too crazy to know that it was wrong and too crazy to care whether they were caught.

"They both felt that it was not safe to use either of their own cars. The patient developed an intense interest in the plan and found also that it gave him a very pleasant topic of consideration [sic] when he and his companion were together drinking or driving about."

When he and his companion were drinking they would gloat over the perfection of their plan to murder and murder for money.

I used to think that the most impelling motive in life was passion, but in this case passion and a desire for revenge is swept aside for money. Money is the controlling motive in this case. If they merely wanted to kill for a thrill, if they merely wanted to kill to satisfy anger, and hate for this companion if he had been the victim,—but they could not figure out how they could safely get the money.

. . . .

Doctors Hulbert and Bowman were told by these defendants, as I told your Honor, that the killing had no significance here, except to prevent their being apprehended and convicted if the victim escaped.

That is the motive for the murder: self-preservation; the same as a thief at night in your house, when suddenly surprised, shoots to kill. Why? He did not go into your house to kill; he went in to rob. The killing had no significance, except he did not want to be apprehended. The desire, the urge of self-preservation. And that is the only significance that the murder in this case has. Not the thrill, as we have been told, but a desire for excitement; but they killed for exactly the same reason that the burglar caught at night kills; exactly the same reason that Krauser killed when he was robbing the Atlantic & Pacific Tea Store. He did not go into the A. & P. store with murder in his heart; he went in with greed, just as they went into this kidnapping.

He killed because he did not want to be apprehended.

See whether they took the delight and pleasure in this killing for the mere wantonness of killing; see whether the mere wantonness of killing gave them the thrill that they tried to make you believe. They anticipated a few unpleasant minutes, not pleasant minutes, not the thrill and the delight and the fast-beating heart that they tell you that Dickie Loeb has—if he has got a heart at all—"They anticipated a few unpleasant minutes in strangling him."

And I might tell you at this point, Your Honor, and will develop later that the original plan of Loeb was not to kill him with a chisel, but they were to strangle him to death with the ropes that they procured. He was to pull one end and Leopold the other; and the reason he wanted that done was, as I will demonstrate as we go on, Leopold had something on him. Leopold knew about the crimes A, B, C, and D, and in this murder he was going to make Leopold pull the rope, so he would have something equal on Leopold.

"They anticipated a few unpleasant minutes in strangling him." And then the doctor says, in parentheses, "The patient's face registered the expression of disgust."

No emotions; no, his emotions were split from his intellect. And again the doctor says he showed emotion, showed disgust at the plot to strangle that boy.

"And they planned for each of them, namely, the patient and his associate, to have hold of one end of the strangling rope, and they would pull at the same time, so that both would be equally guilty of murder. They did not seem to think that this would give them a closer tie in their friendship.

. . . .

. . . Well, let's see what Dickie says about it:

"I had quite a time quieting down my associate (after the murder). I cooled him down in five minutes, after we got him (Bobby Franks) into the back seat thinking he was alive. I got calmer while quieting my associate. Franks was hit on the head several times. My associate said, 'This is terrible, this is terrible.' "

Emotion, or totally devoid of emotion? When he saw Loeb knocking out the life of this boy, it took Loeb five minutes to quiet him down.

He said, "This is terrible, this is terrible."

I will tell your Honor, if you don't think they have emotions, of another instance. Some of us didn't think that Harvey Church had. He told his story with the air of braggadocio, and he gloated, apparently, while he was telling the authorities how tough a fellow he was. But when he was told to begin his march to the gallows, they carried him there in a stupor.

And if it is the fate of these two perverts that they must pay the penalty of this crime upon the gallows, when they realize it, you will find that they have emotions, and you will find they have fear, and you will find these cowardly perverts will have to be carried to the gallows.

To calm him? No. "I told him it was all right and joked and laughed, and possibly to calm myself, too."

Cold blooded? How did they put this poor little Franks boy into the culvert?

"Unfortunately, the body was not kicked far enough into this hole."

There is that little dead body, naked, and after they shoved it in they kicked it in. And the unfortunate part of it was, according to Loeb, "Unfortunately the body was not kicked far enough into this hole, because a foot remained protruding, visible to a passerby."

That was the only unfortunate thing about this, that a foot stuck out. The body was found the next day; and they are sitting before Your Honor on a plea of guilty to this murder.

He did not have any emotions. He first told the doctor, in accordance with his own ideas or his training, that he got a kick out of the whole thing; and then he began to get a little more truthful to the doctor.

On page 110: "He first stated that he got more of a kick out of discussing it with his own family; but later changed his statement, and said that he felt he got a little less kick, because he had some slight remorse. His mother said that whoever did it should be tarred and feathered."

What does that mean? A mob ought to take him? We have heard Mr. Darrow talk repeatedly of the hoarse cry of the angry mob.

There is no danger or fear about hearing the hoarse cry of the angry mob, if the extreme penalty is visited here. I am not so sure, otherwise.

.   .   .   .

The same argument was made by Mr. Darrow with reference to Leopold as was made about Loeb. First he began to blame the old German philosopher Nietzsche, although every student in every university for the last 25 years has read his philosophy. And then I guess he thought that would not do because if reading this philosophy would be an excuse for this crime, how about the countless thousands who have gone before and who are still reading this philosophy who lead decent, honorable lives?

He did not have a poor old nurse in this case to blame, and he was not quite satisfied in blaming some remote ancestor, so he blames their parents, respectable, decent law-abiding citizens.

The only unfortunate think that ever came into their lives was to have a snake like Leopold in that decent family. Casting blame where blame was not due, but where sympathy should go out as it does go from the heart of every person in this community, to the respected families of these men.

But Darrow says, "No. Save your sympathy for the boys. Do not place the blame on the boys. Place it on their families. This is the result of heredity."

.   .   .   .

Mr. Darrow relies upon the facts, first he says there was no motive, second upon the youth of the defendants, and third upon their mental condition.

I strongly suspect that the real defense in this case is not any of those at all.

The real defense in this case is Clarence Darrow and his peculiar philosophy of life. I quite agree with the senior Bachrach when he was closing that they brought in a man who was an expert on punishment to instruct Your Honor just what punishment you should mete out in this case. In other words, the real defense in this case is Clarence Darrow, and those things which he has urged upon Your Honor as a defense I would like to take up in detail.

. . . .

Mr. Darrow criticised Mr. Marshall for his quotations from Blackstone, and seemed to be under the impression that we were trying to try this case under the ancient British law.

We are trying this case, if Your Honor please, under the statutes of the State of Illinois in the year 1924.

They say that a boy between 10 and 14 may have sufficient capacity to commit a crime and be answerable for it, but it is the duty of the State to prove beyond a reasonable doubt that he has sufficient capacity.

The Statute that Your Honor is bound to enforce in this case, and the statute under which we are trying these defendants further provides that from 14 years of age up the law presumes that he has the capacity to commit a crime and is entirely and thoroughly responsible for it.

Let us see at what age some of these men have been hanged.

Buff Higgins was hanged at the age of 23.

Butch Lyons was 25.

Henry Foster, 24.

Albert C. Fields, 24.

Windreth, 29.

Mannow, 27.

Dan McCarty, 27.

William T. Powers, 23.

Chris Murray, 28.

John Drugan, 22.

Robert Howard, 30.

Louis Pesant, sentenced on a plea of guilty April 15, 1904, by Judge Kernsten, was 23.

Peter Neidermeyer, 23 and hanged.

Gustave Marks, 21.

Harvey Van Dine, 21.

These were not the poor sons of multimillionaires; these were the sons of poor men, who had no advantages in life, men who had no education, men who had been brought up in the gutter and the slums, and men who did not develop intellectually at the early age that these men have developed at.

Richard Ivens, 24.

Andrew Williams, 22.

Thomas Jennings, 28.

Thomas Schultz, 19.

Frank Shiblewski, 22, and his brother hanged the same day.

Ewald, 23.

Smith, 27.

Lundgren, 25.

Dennis Anderson, 21.

Lloyd Bopp, 23.

Albert Johnson, 25.

Earl Dear, 26.

Jack O'Brien, 22.

Mills, 21.

Champion, 22.

Zander, 22.

Haensel, a man who fought for his country, who was syphilitic, who was hit in the service of his country in the head by a chain weighing a thousand pounds, and who was discharged from further service physically unfit, was hanged in Cook County at the age of 27.

The little songbird from Italy, Viani, 17.

Brislane, 27.

Sam Ferrari, 26.

Oscar McDavit, a colored man who thought that the Lord had appointed him to lead his race back to Africa, 23.

George Brown, 29.

Antonio Lopez, 26.

Harry Ward, 25.

Carl Wanderer, 25.

Ligregni, 27.

Harvey Church, 23.

Pastoni, 26.

Dalton, sentenced by Your Honor, a colored boy, without any of the advantages that these men had, whose ancestors were slaves, only two or three generations removed from savagery in Africa, and yet he paid the penalty for the violation of the laws.

Walter Krauser, marking off the days between now and the day he hangs, 21.

Bernard Grant, sitting in the County Jail, waiting for October 17, when he will pay the penalty upon the gallows.

Oh, but Mr. Darrow says there are only six men who have been hanged on pleas in Cook County.

Now, Your Honor and I are familiar enough with the practice over here not to be fooled by that.

What happens when a man gets a guilty client and there is no defense?

He generally goes to the State's Attorney, and he says, "If you will waive the death penalty I will plead guilty." If there is in the nature of the case any mitigating circumstance the State's Attorney says:

"Yes, we will waive the death penalty. Let's go upstairs and plead him guilty, and I will recommend life."

But if the case is of such a nature that the State's Attorney cannot in conscience and in law waive the extreme penalty, he says:

"No, that man has got to go to a jury."

And then sometimes they do as Walter Stanton did this summer.

We went before the State's Attorney and asked him, would he waive the death penalty?

The State's Attorney said:

"No, this is a hanging case."

Walter Stanton then went in and stated the facts to Judge Steffen, and Judge Steffen said:

"If you plead him guilty I am going to hang him."

Walter Stanton then went before another judge, and there apparently was some misunderstanding, because he pleaded the man guilty, and when he got through the judge indicated he was going to sentence him to hang, and then Walter Stanton nearly collapsed and begged the Court for God's sake to let him go to a jury.

The reason that courts do not hang any oftener than they do is because hanging cases always go to juries. Where the attorney cannot make an agreement in advance, he says:

"Well, then, I am going to take a chance with 12 men. They can't do any worse than the court can do on a plea, and I am going to give my client a run for his money."

Now, Your Honor and I know that that is the case, and Mr. Darrow knows it is the case, and everybody who is familiar with procedure in the Criminal Court knows it is the case.

It is not because there is one law for the judge and another law for the jury. It is not because juries must execute the law to the uppermost, and the Court has a right to sit as a friendly father.

It is a matter of fact, known to everybody, that when they cannot make an agreement with either the Court or the State's Attorney, they go to juries. That is why we have only six hanged on pleas, and so many hanged on verdicts.

. . . .

The law, if Your Honor please, is made to protect the innocent, and it is made to protect the innocent by punishing the guilty and in no other way can we protect the innocent or protect society.

I think, if Your Honor please, I have now covered the three defenses set forth by Mr. Darrow, their age, lack of motive and physical and mental condition.

When we get all through, Mr. Darrow says that Your Honor ought to be merciful and finally, and that is his concluding defense, he appeals to your heart and your sympathy and not to your mind or your conscience.

When I was listening to Mr. Darrow plead for sympathy for these two men who showed no sympathy, it reminded me of the story of Abraham Lincoln, about a young boy about their age whose parents were wealthy and he murdered both of them. He was an only child and he did it so that he might inherit their money.

His crime was discovered the same as this crime has been discovered, and the court asked him for any reason he might have why sentence of death should not be passed upon him and he promptly replied, he hoped the court would be lenient to a poor orphan.

Robert Franks had a right to live. He had a right to the society of the family and his friends and they had a right to his society.

These two young law students of superior intelligence, with more intelligence than they have heart, decided that he must die.

He was only 14.

These two law students knew under the law if you had a right to take a life you had a right to take it at 14 and they thought that they had a right to take his life, and they proceeded to take it.

Mr. Darrow quoted considerable poetry to you, and I would like again to be indulged while I read a little bit of prose:

"Crime and Criminals. If I looked at jails and crime and prisoners in the way the ordinary person does, I should not speak on this subject to you." (This was an address delivered to the prisoners in the County Jail, if Your Honor please.)

"The reason I talk to you on the question of crime, its cause and cure, is because I really do not believe in the least in crime.

"There is no such thing as a crime, as the word is generally understood. I do not believe that there is any sort of distinction between the real moral condition in and out of jail. One is just as good as the other.

"The people here can no more help being here than the people outside can avoid being outside. I do not believe that people are in jail because they deserve to be. They are in jail simply because they cannot avoid it, on account of circumstances which are entirely beyond their control, and for which they are in no way responsible.

.   .   .   .   .

"When I ride on the street cars, I am held up; I pay five cents a ride for what is worth two and a half cents, simply because a body of men have bribed the City Council and the Legislature so that all the rest of us have to pay tribute to them. If I don't want to fall into the clutches of the gas trust, and choose to burn oil instead of gas, then good Mr. Rockefeller holds me up.

"Let me see whether there is any connection between the crime of the respectable classes and your presence in the jail. Many of you I believe are in jail because you have really committed burglary; many of you because you have stolen something within the meaning of the law, you have taken some other person's property. Some of you may have entered a store and carried off a pair of shoes because you did not have the price. Possibly some of you have committed murder. I cannot tell what all of you did. There are a great many people here who have done some of these things, who really don't know themselves why they did them.

"I think I know why you did them, every one of you. You did these things because you were bound to do them.   .   .   .

"I think all this has nothing whatever to do with right conduct. Some so-called criminals—and I will use that word, because it is handy, it means nothing to me; I speak of the criminal who gets caught as distinguished from the criminal who catches them,—some of these so-called criminals are in jail for the first offense; but nine-tenths of you are in jail because you did not have a good lawyer; and of course you did not have a good lawyer because you did not have enough money to pay a good lawyer. There is no very great danger of a rich man going to jail.

"There is a bill before the Legislature of this State, to punish the kidnapping of children with death. We have wise members of the Legislature. They know the gas trust when they see it—and they always see it. They can furnish light enough to be seen. And this Legislature thinks it is going to stop kidnapping of children, by making a law punishing kidnappers of children with death.

"I believe that progress is purely a question of the pleasurable units that we get out of life. The pleasure-and-paid theory is the only correct theory of morality, and the only way of judging life."

That is the doctrine of Leopold. That is the doctrine expounded last Sunday in the press of Chicago by Clarence Darrow.

I want to tell you the real defense in this case, Your Honor; it is Clarence Darrow's dangerous philosophy of life. He said to Your Honor that he was not pleading alone for these two young men. He said he was looking to the future; that he was thinking of the ten thousand young boys who in the future would fill the chairs his clients filled, and he wants to soften the law. He wants them treated, not with the severity that the law of his State prescribes, but he wants them treated with kindness and consideration.

I want to tell Your Honor that it would be much better if God had not caused this crime to be disclosed; it would be much better if it had gone unsolved, and these men went unwhipped of justice; it would not have done near the harm to this community that will be done if Your Honor, as Chief Justice of this great Court, puts your official seal of approval upon the doctrines of anarchy preached by Clarence Darrow as a defense in this case.

Society can endure, the law can endure, if criminals escape; but if a court such as this court should say that he believes in the doctrines of Darrow, that you ought not to hang when the law says you should, a greater blow has been struck to our institutions than by a hundred, aye, a thousand murders.

Mr. Darrow has preached in this case that one of the handicaps the defendants are under is that they are rich, the sons of multi-millionaires. I have already stated to Your Honor that if it was not for their wealth, Darrow would not be here and the Bachrachs would not be here. If it was not for their wealth we would not have been regaled by all this tommy-rot by the three wise men from the East. I don't want to refer to this, anymore than Mr. Darrow did; but he referred to it, and it is in evidence, and he tried to make your Honor believe that somebody lied, that Gortland lied, when he talked about a friendly judge.

On June 10, 1924, in the Chicago-Herald and Examiner—that was before this case had been assigned to anybody, that was when Darrow was announcing, and he did announce in this, same article, that they were going to plead not guilty,—there was an article written by Mr. Slattery, sitting back there, on June 10th.

"The friendly-judge resort suggested for the defense will be of no avail.

"It was mentioned as a possibility that a plea of guilty might be entered, on the understanding it would result in life sentences. If this becomes an absolute probability, Crowe announced that he will nolle prosse the case and re-indict the slayers."

Did Gortland lie? He gave the name of witness after witness that he told the story to, as he told it to Slattery, before the case was even assigned. He says that was told to him by Leopold. I don't know whether Your Honor believes that officer or not; but I want to tell you if you have observed these two defendants during the trial, if you have observed the conduct of their attorneys and their families,—with one honorable exception, and that is the old man who sits in sackcloth and ashes, and who is entitled to the sympathy of everybody, old Mr. Leopold,—with that one honorable exception, everybody connected with the case has laughed and sneered and jeered; and if the defendant Leopold did not say that he would plead guilty before a friendly judge, his actions demonstrate that he thinks he has got one.

You have listened with a great deal of patience and kindness and consideration to the State and the defense. I am not going to trespass unduly upon Your Honor's time, and I am going to close for the State.

I believe that the facts and circumstances proved in this case demonstrate that a crime has been committed by these two defendants, and that no other punishment except the extreme penalty of the law will fit it; and I leave the case with you on behalf of the State of Illinois, and I ask Your Honor in the language of Holy Writ to "Execute justice and righteousness in the land."

## QUESTIONS

1. What is the question for the court to decide in the sentencing of Leopold and Loeb? How many ways are there—in Fisher's terms (Chapter 7, *supra*)—to "fractionate the issue"? What alternative statements of the issue do counsel offer, *e. g.*, "the state vs. two mad dogs," "Progress vs. Barbarism," "ought killing be discouraged," "ought God or Darrow's 'philosophy of life' to prevail"? What other

statements of the issue run through the arguments? Does this array of possibilities mean that the judge is at large to pick whatever issue he wants?

2.  What are the fears that people are expressing when they object that a judge should not "decide what he wants to decide"? What are the restraints on Judge Caverly? How far do they go towards keeping his thinking out of the objectionable area?

3.  To what extent *is* Judge Caverly the one who is deciding? In what way is the decision more *his* than that of the lawyers? of society at large? of the press? of past judges? of the language, basic concepts, and other trappings of the culture?

4.  In regard to the relationship between the personality of the judge and the decision, does the judge *have* a static personality? What supposition do the lawyers seem to be making? How meaningful is it to speak of who Judge Caverly *is* independent of what the decision in this case will *make him*?

5.  Even though no remark of Judge Caverly is reported, can you nevertheless get some sense of him as a person—of what his aspirations may be—at least in the estimates of the lawyers? What do the lawyers assume about him? To what extent are the arguments of the lawyers a *telling* to Judge Caverly of who he is, a *defining* for him of his self? What image of Judge Caverly does Darrow offer him? What image does Crowe offer him? How do the lawyers' respective presentations of Caverly's image cohere with the balance of their presentations?

6.  Is the judge "unbound" in his decision because the lawyers' appeal is "emotional"? Consider, in this regard, the poems Darrow reads and the picture he verbally paints of what the hanging scene will look like. Are these emotional appeals wrong because a judge should decide according to reason, and when he leaves reason for emotion he is "at large"? *Can* "reason" be separated out from "emotion"? What are we asking someone to do when we say, "don't be emotional"? What are we saying different from "don't invoke *those* emotions" ("repress *these* emotions in favor of *these*")? Is there no "logic" to an appeal to "emotions"? Is there no systematic method for the development of new responses? What would a composer, painter or author say—or literary critic?

7.  To what extent is Judge Caverly unconstrained by any "facts"? Are there no happenings, or descriptions of happenings, that are uncontroverted? Even where there is controversy—that is, even where, on the surface, the lawyers are taking issue with one another— can you find a deeper level on which they are agreeing? For example, Darrow and Crowe disagree on what the motive was, but are they not therefore implicitly agreeing that a reconstruction of the motive is important to the decision? Is not each disagreement in life testimony to—on a deeper level—an agreement? Consider, in this regard, the lawyers' respective appeals to progress; to kindness; to utilitarianism; to freedom and determinism. Can you find, here, *agreement* even in the midst of disagreement?

Consider the lawyers' arguments in light of the questions they *do not* raise, *i. e.*, does anyone ask whether a killing like that of Bobby Franks might not be just? What other major unasked questions can you think of? What is the cause of these unasked questions? What effect do they have on the arguments and on the decision?

To what extent can you identify in the lawyers' arguments a sort of structure of agreements that would enable a future historian to piece together the world-view of America in the 1920s? What is the significance of your answer?

How does this underlying structure of agreement give structure to the lawyers' method? Compare how, in the sciences, a structure of agreement as to, *e. g.*, how light "travels" (in "waves" or "particles" or "wavicles") gives structure to the further method of scientists.

8. Consider the selection from John Wisdom, *Gods, supra* at p. 635.

> If . . . we choose to say that a difference as to whether a thing is beautiful is not a factual difference we must be careful to remember that there is a procedure for settling these differences [i. e., as to "beauty"—Ed.] and this consists not only in reasoning and a redescription as in the legal case but also in a more literal re-setting-before with re-looking or re-listening.

In what ways does the procedure for judging whether a work of art is "beautiful" depend upon a "re-setting"—a "re-looking" at the painting from one angle and then from another? What effect does this procedure have on the judges of the art? How different is the "art" case from the "legal" case of *State v. Leopold and Loeb*? Can you find in the lawyers' arguments "redescriptions" that practically amount to a "re-setting" of the picture before Judge Caverly?

Consider, for example, the way in which the opposing lawyers set and reset before the judge the picture of Bobby Franks in the culvert: how do they point up differences in what are (at least in one sense) the same "facts"? How do they "make" these "differences"? How is their procedure like the procedure of art critics? Is the procedure one of making random "pot-shots" from their own point of view, or is their method intellectual, organized and part of a larger coherent presentation?

From this point of view, go back over the arguments and note how the opposing lawyers present, describe, redescribe and "re-set" before the judge the crime; the defendants; the judge as a person; the judge's role; themselves (as people and lawyers); the punishment. What other areas of the total picture do the lawyers describe and redescribe, set, and re-set? What determines the manner of their presentations?

9. Why did Darrow not submit his clients to a jury? Why does he tell this to Judge Caverly? What is the function of his underscoring the point by the remark, "it was not a kindness to you"? What does Darrow hope to achieve? What are the dynamics of "responsibility", *i. e.*, how does *feeling responsible* translate itself into a different intellectual management of a problem?

Is Darrow consistent in placing the burden on Judge Caverly? Consider his repeated references to precedent. Is not an appeal to precedent a dividing of responsibility through time? Is Darrow being "illogical"?

10. What is the function of Crowe's telling Judge Caverly:

You have a right to, and I know you do, forgive those who trespass against John R. Caverly. But sitting here as the Chief Justice of this great court, you have no right to forgive anybody who violates the law.

Does Crowe figure that this reminder of the judge's role will be translated into a different intellectual management of the problem the judge faces? In what respects? Will the judge repress certain emotions and bring others to the fore? Does Crowe conceive that the judge has, in Quine's terminology (Chapter 6) a different "force-field" *qua* judge than *qua* ordinary human?

11. Why are the counsel concerned with defendants' motive (or lack of motive)? What is it that one is looking for when one looks for "motive"—a picture that the defendants had in their mind? Or something more complex? What sorts of considerations does a search for motive force the judge to take into account in his judgment? How does this process keep the judge in touch with the considerations that the society wants a judge to consult?

12. To what extent are the lawyers' arguments an invitation to the judge to identify with them? Consider, for example, Darrow's references to one of the prosecutors being named "Savage," and Crowe's response to this. Is every decision a man makes an identifying, on some level, with other men and with mankind? If so, how does this tendency exercise a "binding" effect on the judge's deliberations?

13. What determines when someone faced with a decision will stop taking evidence and suspend deliberations and *decide*? How must his considerations fit together before he can say, "hang" or "life imprisonment"? What is it that must "fit together"—facts about the crime with facts about the punishment?—facts about the punishment with facts about one's self? What is the relationship between emotional attitudes and beliefs which allows one to feel satisfied with a tentative conclusion and adopt it as one's own? (It may be useful, in this regard, to refer back to the materials on the coherence theory of truth in Chapter 6).

---

## DECISION OF JUDGE CAVERLY ON SENTENCING *

In view of the profound and unusual interest that this case has aroused not only in this community but in the entire country and even beyond its boundaries, the court feels it his duty to state the reasons which have led him to the determination he has reached.

* Reprinted in M. McKernan, The Amazing Crime and Trial of Leopold and      Loeb (The New American Library 1957).

It is not an uncommon thing that pleas of guilty are entered in criminal cases, but almost without exception in the past such pleas have been the result of a virtual agreement between the defendants and the State's Attorney whereby in consideration of the plea the State's Attorney consents to recommend to the court a sentence deemed appropriate by him, and, in the absence of special reasons to the contrary, it is the practice of the court to follow such recommendations.

In the present case the situation is a different one. A plea of guilty has been entered by the defense without a previous understanding with the prosecution and without any knowledge whatever on its part. Moreover, the plea of guilty did not in this particular case, as it usually does, render the task of the prosecution easier by substituting the admission of guilt for a possibly difficult and uncertain chain of proof. Here the State was in possession not only of the essential substantiating facts but also of voluntary confessions on the part of the defendants. The plea of guilty, therefore, does not make a special case in favor of the defendant.

Since both the cases—that, namely, of murder and that of kidnapping for ransom—were of a character which invested the court with discretion as to the extent of the punishment, it became his duty under the statute to examine witnesses as to the aggravation and mitigation of the defense. This duty has been fully met. By consent of counsel for the State and for the defendants, the testimony in the murder case has been accepted as equally applicable to the case of kidnapping for ransom. In addition, a prima facie case was made out for the kidnapping case as well.

The testimony introduced, both by the prosecution and the defense, has been as detailed and elaborate as though the case had been tried before a jury. It has been given the widest publicity and the public is so fully familiar with all its phases that it would serve no useful purpose to restate or analyze the evidence.

By pleading guilty, the defendants have admitted legal responsibility for their acts; the testimony has satisfied the court that the case is not one in which it would have been possible to set up successfully the defense of insanity as insanity is defined and understood by the established law of this state for the purpose of the administration of criminal justice.

The court, however, feels impelled to dwell briefly on the mass of data produced as to the physical, mental and moral condition of the two defendants. They have been shown in essential respects to be abnormal; had they been normal they would not have committed the crime. It is beyond the province of this court, as it is beyond the capacity of humankind in its present state of development, to predicate ultimate responsibility for human acts.

At the same time, the court is willing to recognize that the careful analysis made of the life history of the defendants and of their present mental, emotional and ethical condition has been of extreme interest and is a valuable contribution to criminology. And yet the court feels strongly that similar analyses made of other persons accused of crime will probably reveal similar or different abnormalities. The value of such tests seems to lie in their applicability to crime and criminals in general.

Since they concern the broad question of human responsibility and legal punishment and are in no wise peculiar to the individual defendants, they may be deserving of legislative but not judicial consideration. For this reason the court is satisfied that his judgment in the present case cannot be affected thereby.

The testimony in this case reveals a crime of singular atrocity. It is, in a sense, inexplicable, but is not thereby rendered less inhuman or repulsive. It was deliberately planned and prepared for during a considerable period of time. It was executed with every feature of callousness and cruelty. And here the court will say, not for the purpose of extenuating guilt but merely with the object of dispelling a misapprehension that appears to have found lodgment in the public mind, that he is convinced by conclusive evidence that there was no abuse offered to the body of the victim.

But it did not need that element to make the crime abhorrent to every instinct of humanity, and the court is satisfied that neither in the act itself, nor in its motives or lack of motives, or in the antecedents of the offenders, can he find any mitigating circumstances.

For the crime of murder and of kidnapping for ransom the law prescribes different punishments in the alternatives.

For the crime of murder the statute declares: "Whoever is guilty of murder shall suffer the punishment of death or imprisonment in the penitentiary for his natural life or for a term not less than fourteen years. If the accused is found guilty by a jury they shall fix the punishment by their verdict; upon a plea of guilty, the punishment shall be fixed by the court."

For the crime of kidnapping for ransom the statute reads: "Whoever is guilty of kidnapping for ransom shall suffer death or be punished by imprisonment in the penitentiary for life, or for any term not less than five years."

Under the pleas of guilty, the duty of determining the punishment devolves upon the court, and the law indicates no rule or policy for the guidance of his discretion. In reaching his decision the court would have welcomed the counsel and support of others. In some states the legislature, in its wisdom, has provided for a bench of three judges to determine the penalty in cases such as this. Nevertheless, the court is willing to meet his responsibilities. It would have been the task of least resistance to impose the extreme penalty of the law. In choosing imprisonment instead of death, the court is moved chiefly by the consideration of the age of the defendants, boys of eighteen and nineteen years.

It is not for the court to say that he will not, in any case, enforce capital punishment as an alternative, but the court believes it is within his province to decline to impose the sentence of death on persons who are not of full age.

This determination appears to be in accordance with the progress of criminal law all over the world and with the dictates of enlightened humanity. More than that, it seems to be in accordance with the precedents hitherto observed in this State. The records of Illinois show only two cases of minors who were put to death by legal process . . . to which number the court does not feel inclined to make an addition.

Life imprisonment, at the moment, strikes the public imagination as forcibly as would death by hanging, but to the offenders, particularly of the type they are, the prolonged suffering of years of confinement may well be the severest form of retribution and expiation.

The court feels it proper to add a final word concerning the effect of the parole law upon the punishment of these defendants. In the case of such atrocious crimes it is entirely within the discretion of the department of public welfare, never to admit these defendants to parole.

To such a policy the court urges them strictly to adhere. If this course is persevered in in the punishment of these defendants, it will both satisfy the ends of justice and safeguard the interests of society.

In No. 33,623, indictment for murder, the sentence of the court is that you, Nathan F. Leopold, Jr., be confined in the penitentiary at Joliet for the term of your natural life. The court finds that your age is 19.

In No. 33,623, indictment for murder, the sentence of the court is that you, Richard Loeb, be confined in the penitentiary at Joliet for the term of your natural life. The court finds that your age is 18.

In 33,624, kidnapping for ransom, it is the sentence of the court that you, Nathan F. Leopold, Jr., be confined in the penitentiary at Joliet for the term of 99 years. The court finds your age at 19.

In 33,624, kidnapping for ransom, the sentence of the court is that you, Richard Loeb, be confined in the penitentiary at Joliet for the term of 99 years.

## CHAPTER TWELVE

# The Role of Rule

## INTRODUCTORY NOTE

"Frequently," wrote Roscoe Pound in *The Theory of Judicial Decision*, "application of the legal precept, as found and interpreted, is intuitive." And, he continued,

However repugnant to our nineteenth century notions it may be to think of anything anywhere in the judicial administration of justice as proceeding otherwise than on rule and logic, we cannot conceal from ourselves that in at least three respects the trained intuition of the judge does play an important role in the judicial process. One is in the selection of grounds of decision—in finding the legal materials that may be made both to furnish a legal ground of decision and to achieve justice in the concrete case. . . . Another place where the judge's intuition comes into play is in development of the grounds of decision, or interpretation. This is especially marked when it becomes necessary to apply the criterion of the intrinsic merit of the possible [alternative] interpretations. A third [place where the judge's intuition comes into play] is in the application of the developed grounds of decision to the facts.

36 Harv.L.Rev. 940, 951 (1923). Pound's recognition of the importance and pervasiveness of intuition at each stage of the adjudicative process would, according to many of the readings in Parts II and III, require only the qualification that it is not "frequently," but *always* and *inevitably* that "application of the legal precept, as found and interpreted, is intuitive." Those readings would require us to reject an earlier statement by Pound that there are cases in which "[a]pplication of the abstract grounds of decision to the facts of the particular case may be purely mechanical" (*id.* at 950). For however much we may think that a particular problem can be resolved solely by resort to "rule and logic," the very nature of language and thought precludes such a view. "General propositions do not"—and, it might be added, cannot—"decide concrete cases."

If this is so, however, just what effect or importance can linguistic formulations—which are necessarily general—have? If it is acknowledged that intuition—and/or some non-linguistic image, idea or symbolism—is involved in the decision of any problem or case, does this mean that rules, theories, principles, statements of fact, etc., are simply forms of "window dressing"? That they "really" have no part in the decisions and the processes by which they are reached? Or is it possible to argue that however essential the non-linguistic or non-articulated element may be in any decision, there is also in innumerable cases a useful and often critical role to be played by language? Is it possible to argue, in other words, that "general propositions" *contribute* to—though they do not "decide"—

"concrete cases"?  Such a position no doubt invites resistance because of its vagueness.  People want to be told *precisely* how a
linguistic formulation "contributes to" or "plays a role in" the
resolution of problems and cases.  They want to be told *exactly* how
intuition interacts with rules and statements of fact to yield a decision.  This, however, may be the sort of information that is just
not available.  If that is the case, would it establish that talk of
language's "contribution" or "role" is simply "a lot of words"?
Or would it leave room for other hypotheses—for example, that we
are still at an early stage in the investigation and study of language?
Or that the relationship of language to thought is the type of phenomenon that can, at best, be described only in vague and metaphorical terms?

One of those who insists on the usefulness of discursive language
—despite its dangers—is Wittgenstein in his PHILOSOPHICAL IN-
VESTIGATIONS.  "If I tell someone 'Stand roughly here,'" he says,
"may not this explanation work perfectly?  And cannot every other
one fail too?"  Even if such an explanation is considered "inexact,"
Wittgenstein suggests, that does not mean it is "unusable".  At 41e
(1958 ed.).  Perhaps if we try to conceive Wittgenstein's hypothetical
situation—whatever its details may be—with and without the verbal
direction, "Stand roughly here," it may help us to find some things
to say about language's function in the making of decisions.  If we
"subtract" the statement from the situation, will it make any difference?  Will something be lost that language is supposed to provide?  Consider Wittgenstein's observation that "A rule stands there
like a sign-post."  *Id.* at 39e.  What function can a rule have, if, as
Wittgenstein implies, like a sign-post it leaves a "doubt open about
the way I have to go" and fails to "shew which direction I am to take
when I have passed it; whether along the road or the footpath or
cross-country"?  *Id.* at 39e.  Consider a sign post with the words
"Los Angeles" written on it.  Consider one to which "25 miles" is
added.  Do these words *make a difference*?  Would the "situation"
be the same "in reality" with or without these additional markings?
If there is a difference, what is it?  Can it be stated in exact, precise
or specific terms?  Or is it necessary to resort to vagaries and
metaphors?  If there is a difference, is it possible to express it in
words that will themselves *make* a difference?

These last questions, in a sense, pose the problems of this chapter: What difference does the symbolic mode called language—especially when it takes the form of rules—make?  What is gained by
using it?  What can be meaningfully *said* about the manner and
occasions of its use?

*John Dickinson*

## Legal Rules: Their Function
## In the Process of Decision *

.  .  .  . [It is said that] in fact the judge reaches his decisions on the basis of his personal reaction towards a case as a whole in its individual uniqueness, and then simply casts about and finds one or another of the forms of words called legal rules which he can attach to his conclusion for the purpose of rationalizing it.  This argument against the effectiveness of legal rules is much in the mouth of law-school teachers.  The reason why it appeals to them is not far to seek.  It is approximately true when applied to decisions of appellate courts which establish creative precedents, and these are precisely the decisions which find their way into "case-books".  Here a court in deciding a new case to which one or more rules seem applicable with equal plausibility purports to bring the case under one rule rather than another, and it is quite true in such instances that it is not a rule of law but some non-legal consideration which ultimately accounts for the decision.  This type of case, however, by no means exhausts or even fairly represents the operation of legal rules, and even in cases of this type the influence of rules has often a somewhat larger part than at first sight appears.

There is, however, a large and important class of cases in which it is not too much to say that the outcome is in fact directly dictated by a legal rule without the intervention of judicial discretion in the smallest degree.  Suppose for example that a purported will is offered for probate which bears the signature of but one witness in a jurisdiction where two are required by the statute.  The rule of law which requires that the witnesses shall be two operates with the deadly inevitability of a guillotine to decide the question of probate.  Similarly where land is claimed under a deed from a married woman not signed by her husband, in a jurisdiction where the law requires the husband to join in the deed.  The automatic operation of direct specific rules of law of this character is seldom sufficiently brought home to professional teachers of law and students in law-schools.  It does not always appear from a study of litigation, because cases where the rule thus leaves absolutely no doubt are seldom litigated.  But this does not mean that the automatic operation of legal rules in situations of this kind is not of the utmost importance from the standpoint of the value of law as an agency of social order.  It is one of the great preventives of litigation.  It enables counsel to advise their clients with an assurance which does not need to be tested by resort to the courts in every instance.  It operates with equal value in another way.  Clean-cut and specific rules make it possible for men to accomplish in their business dealings the legal results they intend without the necessity of constant recourse to the courts to resolve doubts.  Thus it is well established that a deed expressed

* From  79  U.Pa.L.Rev.  833, 846–848      the University of Pennsylvania Law
  (1931).  Reprinted with permission of      Review.

in certain words and executed, acknowledged and recorded in a certain way will have the legal effect of transferring land from one person to another without having to be adjudicated. Similarly a check will serve to transfer a right to money in such a way that no doubt will arise about the validity of the transfer. These results are made possible by the practically automatic operation of legal rules which are so simple and specific that legal scholars do not ordinarily find them interesting.

Where the bar is reasonably well educated, cases which reach the stage of litigation are all cases presenting a substantial element of doubt. This doubt is not necessarily, however, as to the legal rule or rules applicable; often the rule is clear, but doubt exists as to the facts of the situation to which it is sought to be applied. This is true of perhaps the largest number of controversies litigated in *nisi prius* courts which are not carried forward into courts of appeal. Thus the rule is clear that if an individual requests another to supply him with specific goods at a certain price and the other agrees to do so, and in accordance with the agreement does supply the goods, the former is legally bound to pay the agreed price. There may, however, be doubt as to the facts of a given case,—doubt, that is, whether the defendant did actually request the plaintiff to supply the goods, or whether the plaintiff did actually supply them. The decision of the case will turn on the conclusion reached as to what happened between the parties. The case is accordingly one which may well be taken into court, but it comes there not because of any uncertainty in the applicable rule, but solely because of uncertainty about the facts. Such a case will almost never get beyond a lower court except on a point of evidence or procedure; and therefore the vast mass of litigation of this character is seldom impressed on the attention of teachers who teach from case-books. The conditions of their work invite them, unless consciously vigilant, to overlook the obvious.

## Note: Rules in "Clear" Cases and in "Hard" Cases

Are rules capable of "dictating" anything? Can they operate "with the deadly inevitability of a guillotine"? Can it ever be accurate to speak of the "automatic operation of direct specific rules of law"? In a very important sense, as indicated by the materials in Chapter 8, the answers to all these questions seem to be, "no." People, not rules, decide "outcomes" and neither operate "automatically" or "with the deadly inevitability of a guillotine." No rule *necessarily* applies to any given situation, precisely because of the very nature of language— namely, its characteristics of generality and mobility. To review earlier ground, suppose a statute which provides that "no will shall be valid unless it bears the signatures of two witnesses." Suppose further that a will is offered for probate which bears the signatures of *three* witnesses. Literally, the will fails to satisfy the statute's requirements. For the statute did not say "at least" two witnesses. It simply said, "two witnesses." Does the statute operate automatically or inevitably in such a case? Does it *dictate* the outcome? Or consider the case which Dickinson puts? Does the statutory rule tell us how to apply the words "one witness" to any actual, particular factual situation? Does it tell us whether "one witness" for purposes of everyday, non-legal usage is the same as "one witness" for purposes of a technical legal rule?

Yet the results of cases like these do sometimes seem "inevitable" or certain. Is this an illusion? Or is it one of those "simple facts" which, Cassirer tells us, no theory can refute? Our assumption is that the phenomenon of the clear or certain case *is* one of the facts of life. Our critique is aimed only at language which makes it appear that rules *by themselves* can account for such a phenomenon. The nature of language precludes that explanation. But it does not prevent rules from playing a major *part*. It does not deny the datum of experience that the introduction of rules makes it possible to decide a host of cases almost without thinking. And the importance of this, as you should readily see, is inestimable. It might be fair to say, in fact, that the help rules—legal or otherwise—give us in making most of our everyday decisions without much, if any, conscious deliberation, constitute their primary function. It is a function on which much of our intellectual and social cohesion necessarily depends and thus one which must be emphasized. For this reason there are materials in this chapter and in Chapter 15 which try to cast some light on the conditions under which rules are able to carry it out. But the major concern here are those cases in which outcomes are *not* certain, deliberation *is* necessary, and, naturally, the presence of choice is obvious. Here, some have thought, rule really can have no role. Analysis would probably show, however, that such a view is founded on the assumption that rules are only effective *qua* rules (as opposed to rationalizations, devices of deception, etc.) when they "dictate" outcomes. If the fact is that rules never dictate outcomes, yet often play crucial roles in the ordering of human life, this view loses its main support. And once rejected, the value of rules in situations where the decision-maker seems to have discretion should be easier to perceive.

For this purpose the analogies of science and of "the scientific method" may offer worthwhile instruction. In science, as in law, there are rules, laws, theories, hypotheses, explanations, justifications, reasons. To be sure, scientific rules and scientific laws, as Dickinson declares below, seem to be radically different from legal rules and legal laws. In essence, the former are simply types of theory or hypothesis. They are so to speak after-, and subject-to-, the-fact. Their viability depends upon their capacity to explain and to conform to the facts. Legal rules, on the other hand, seem to be before-the-fact. It is fact which must conform to them. All of this, however, stems directly from those uncritical linguistic conceptions which we have come to suspect. For legal rules, as much of the material in Chapter 8 indicated, can be disturbingly after-the-fact. And, as will be suggested in this chapter, there are grounds for believing that scientific rules are very often before-the-fact. Science and law have in common, therefore, a very complex problem of the relation of rules to the individual instances of their application. In a sense, it could be said that this is the paradigmatic problem of this chapter. For to solve it is to tell what rules do and how they do it. It is to suggest criteria for the initial decision to have a rule and for the selection of a particular rule from among competing candidates.  It is to tell us when a rule should be applied and if a rule ought to be repudiated.  The solution of the problem—if ever it were to be found—would, in short, tell us what the role of rule is.

## Section One: Principles and Principled Decisions

*Herbert Wechsler*

### Toward Neutral Principles of Constitutional Law *

If courts cannot escape the duty of deciding whether actions of the other branches of the government are consistent with the Constitution, when a case is properly before them in the sense I have attempted to describe, you will not doubt the relevancy and importance of demanding what, if any, are the standards to be followed in interpretation.  Are there, indeed, any criteria that both the Supreme Court and those who undertake to praise or to condemn its judgments are morally and intellectually obligated to support?

Whatever you may think to be the answer, surely you agree with me that I am right to state the question as the same one for the Court and for its critics.  An attack upon a judgment involves an assertion that a court should have decided otherwise than as it did.  Is it not clear that the validity of an assertion of this kind depends upon assigning reasons that should have prevailed with the tribunal; and that any other reasons are irrelevant?  That is, of course, not only true of a critique of a decision of the courts; it applies whenever a determination is in question, a determination that it is essential to make either way.  Is it the irritation of advancing years that leads me to lament that our culture is not rich with critics who respect these limitations of the enterprise in which they are engaged?

.   .   .   .   the problem of criteria   .   .   .   arises for both courts and critics—   .   .   .   criteria that can be framed and tested as an exercise of reason and not merely as an act of willfulness or will.  Even to put the problem is, of course, to raise an issue no less old than our culture.  Those who perceive in law only the element of fiat, in whose conception of the legal cosmos reason has no meaning or no place, will not join gladly in the search for standards of the kind I have in mind.   .   .   .   So too must I anticipate dissent from those more numerous among us who, vouching no philosophy to warranty, frankly or covertly make the test of virtue in interpretation whether its result in the immediate decision seems to hinder or advance the interests or the values they support.

I shall not try to overcome the philosophic doubt that I have mentioned, although to use a phrase that Holmes so often used—"it hits me where I live."  That battle must be fought on wider fronts than that

* From  Principles, Politics and Fundamental Law 15–36 (1961).  Copyright 1961 by the President and Fellows of Harvard College.  Reprinted by permission of Harvard University Press.

of constitutional interpretation; and I do not delude myself that I can qualify for a command, great as is my wish to render service. The man who simply lets his judgment turn on the immediate result may not, however, realize that his position implies that the courts are free to function as a naked power organ, that it is an empty affirmation to regard them, as ambivalently he so often does, as courts of law. If he may know he disapproves of a decision when all he knows is that it has sustained a claim put forward by a labor union or a taxpayer, a Negro or a segregationist, a corporation or a Communist—he acquiesces in the proposition that a man of different sympathy but equal information may no less properly conclude that he approves.

You will not charge me with exaggeration if I say that this type of *ad hoc* evaluation is, as it has always been, the deepest problem of our constitutionalism, not only with respect to judgments of the courts but also in the wider realm in which conflicting constitutional positions have played a part in our politics.

Did not New England challenge the embargo that the South supported on the very ground on which the South was to resist New England's demand for a protective tariff? Was not Jefferson in the Louisiana Purchase forced to rest on an expansive reading of the clauses granting national authority of the very kind that he had steadfastly opposed in his attacks upon the Bank? Can you square his disappointment about Burr's acquittal on the treason charge and his subsequent request for legislation with the attitude towards freedom and repression most enduringly associated with his name? Were the abolitionists who rescued fugitives and were acquitted in defiance of the evidence able to distinguish their view of the compulsion of a law of the United States from that advanced by South Carolina in the ordinance that they despised?

. . .

I have cited these examples from the early years of our history since time has bred aloofness that may give them added force. What a wealth of illustration is at hand today! How many of the constitutional attacks upon congressional investigations of suspected Communists have their authors felt obliged to launch against the inquiries respecting the activities of Goldfine or of Hoffa or of others I might name? How often have those who think the Smith Act, as construed, inconsistent with the first amendment made clear that they also stand for constitutional immunity for racial agitators fanning flames of prejudice and discontent? Turning the case around, are those who in relation to the Smith Act see no virtue in distinguishing between advocacy of merely abstract doctrine and advocacy which is planned to instigate unlawful action, equally unable to see virtue in the same distinction in relation, let us say, to advocacy of resistance to the judgments of the courts, especially perhaps to judgments vindicating claims that equal protection of the laws has been denied? I may live a uniquely sheltered life but am I wrong in thinking I discerned in some extremely warm enthusiasts for jury trial a certain diminution of enthusiasm as the issue was presented in the course of the debate in 1957 on the bill to extend federal protection of our civil rights?

All I have said, you may reply, is something no one will deny, that principles are largely instrumental as they are employed in politics, instrumental in relation to results that a controlling sentiment demands at any given time. Politicians recognize this fact of life and are obliged to trim and shape their speech and votes accordingly, unless perchance they are prepared to step aside; and the example that John Quincy Adams set somehow is rarely followed.

That is, indeed, all I have said but I now add that whether you are tolerant, perhaps more tolerant than I, of the *ad hoc* in politics, with principle reduced to a manipulative tool, are you not also ready to agree that something else is called for from the courts? I put it to you that the main constituent of the judicial process is precisely that it must be genuinely principled, resting with respect to every step that is involved in reaching judgment on analysis and reasons quite transcending the immediate result that is achieved. To be sure, the courts decide, or should decide, only the case they have before them. But must they not decide on grounds of adequate neutrality and generality, tested not only by the instant application but by others that the principles imply? Is it not the very essence of judicial method to insist upon attending to such other cases, preferably those involving an opposing interest, in evaluating any principle avowed?

Here too I do not think that I am stating any novel or momentous insight. But now, as Holmes said long ago in speaking of "the unrest which seems to wonder vaguely whether law and order pay," we "need education in the obvious." We need it more particularly now respecting constitutional interpretation, since it has become a commonplace to grant what many for so long denied: that courts in constitutional determinations face issues that are inescapably "political"—political in the third sense that I have used that word—in that they involve a choice among competing values or desires, a choice reflected in the legislative or executive action in question, which the court must either condemn or condone.

I should be the last to argue otherwise or to protest the emphasis upon the point  .  .  .  But what is crucial, I submit, is not the nature of the question but the nature of the answer that may validly be given by the courts. No legislature or executive is obligated by the nature of its function to support its choice of values by the type of reasoned explanation that I have suggested is intrinsic to judicial action—however much we may admire such a reasoned exposition when we find it in those other realms.

Does not the special duty of the courts to judge by neutral principles addressed to all the issues make it inapposite to contend, as Judge Hand does, that no court can review the legislative choice—by any standard other than a fixed "historical meaning" of constitutional provisions—without becoming "a third legislative chamber"? Is there not, in short, a vital difference between legislative freedom to appraise the gains and losses in projected measures and the kind of principled appraisal, in respect of values that can reasonably be asserted to have constitutional dimension, that alone is in the province of the courts? Does not the difference yield a middle ground between a judicial House of Lords and the abandonment of any limitation on the other branches —a middle ground consisting of judicial action that embodies what are surely the main qualities of law, its generality and its neutrality? This must, it seems to me, have been in Mr. Justice Jackson's mind when in his chapter on the Supreme Court "as a political institution" he wrote in words that I find stirring, "Liberty is not the mere absence of restraint, it is not a spontaneous product of majority rule, it is not achieved merely by lifting underprivileged classes to power, nor is it the inevitable by-product of technological expansion. It is achieved only by a rule of law." Is it not also what Mr. Justice Frankfurter must mean in calling upon judges for "allegiance to nothing except the effort, amid tangled words and limited insights, to find the path through precedent, through policy, through history, to the best judgment that fallible creatures can reach in that most difficult of all tasks: the achievement of justice between man and man, between man and state, through reason called law"?

You will not understand my emphasis upon the role of reason and of principle in the judicial, as distinguished from the legislative or executive, appraisal of conflicting values to imply that I depreciate the duty of fidelity to the text of the Constitution, when its words may be decisive—though I would certainly remind you of the caution stated by Chief Justice Hughes: "Behind the words of the constitutional provisions are postulates which limit and control." Nor will you take me to deny that history has weight in the elucidation of the text, though it is surely subtle business to appraise it as a guide. Nor will you even think that I deem precedent without importance, for we surely must agree with Holmes that "imitation of the past, until we have a clear reason for change, no more needs justification than appetite." But after all, it was Chief Justice Taney who declared his willingness "that it be regarded hereafter as the law of this court, that its opinion upon the construction of the Constitution is always open to discussion when it is supposed to have been founded in error, and that its judicial authority should hereafter depend altogether on the force of the reasoning by which it is supported." Would any of us have it otherwise, given the nature of the problems that confront the courts?

At all events, is not the relative compulsion of the language of the Constitution, of history and precedent—where they do not combine to make an answer clear—itself a matter to be judged, so far as possible, by neutral principles—by standards that transcend the case at hand? I know, of course, that it is common to distinguish, as Judge Hand did, clauses like "due process," cast "in such sweeping terms that their history does not elucidate their contents," from other provisions of the Bill of Rights addressed to more specific problems. But the contrast, as it seems to me, often implies an overstatement of the specificity or the immutability these other clauses really have—at least when problems under them arise.

No one would argue, for example, that there need not be indictment and a jury trial in prosecutions for a felony in district courts. What made a question of some difficulty was the issue whether service wives charged with the murders of their husbands overseas could be tried there before a military court. Does the language of the double-jeopardy clause or its preconstitutional history actually help to decide whether a defendant tried for murder in the first degree and convicted of murder in the second, who wins a reversal of the judgment on appeal, may be tried again for murder in the first or only murder in the second?  Is there significance in the fact that it is "jeopardy of life or limb" that is forbidden, now that no one is in jeopardy of limb but only of imprisonment or fine?  The right to "have the assistance of counsel" was considered, I am sure, when the sixth amendment was proposed, a right to defend by counsel if you have one, contrary to what was then the English law.  That does not seem to me sufficient to avert extension of its meaning to imply a right to court-appointed counsel when the defendant is too poor to find such aid—though I admit that I once urged the point sincerely as a lawyer for the Government.  It is difficult for me to think the fourth amendment freezes for all time the common law of search and of arrest as it prevailed when the amendment was adopted, whatever the exigencies of police problems may now be or may become.  Nor should we, in my view, lament the fact that "the" freedom of speech or press that Congress is forbidden by the first amendment to impair is not determined only by the scope such freedom had in the late eighteenth century, though the word "the" might have been taken to impose a limitation to the concept of that time—a time when, President Wright has recently reminded us, there was remarkable consensus about matters of this kind.

Even "due process," on the other hand, might have been confined, as Mr. Justice Brandeis urged originally, to a guarantee of fair procedure, coupled perhaps with prohibition of executive displacement of established law—the analogue for us of what the barons meant in Magna Carta.  Equal protection could be taken as no more than an assurance that no one may be placed beyond the safeguards of the law, outlawing, as it were, the possibility of outlawry, but nothing else.  Here too I cannot find it in my heart to regret that interpretation did not ground itself in ancient history but rather has perceived in these provisions a compendious affirmation of the basic values of a free society, values that must be given weight in legislation and administration at the risk of courting trouble in the courts.

So far as possible, to finish with my point, I argue that we should prefer to see the other clauses of the Bill of Rights read as an affirmation of the special values they embody rather than as statements of a finite rule of law, its limits fixed by the consensus of a century long past, with problems very different from our own.  To read them in the former way is to leave room for adaptation and adjustment if and when competing values, also having constitutional dimension, enter on the scene.

Let me repeat what I have thus far tried to say.  The courts have both the title and the duty when a case is properly before them to review the actions of the other branches in the light of constitutional provisions, even though the action involves value choices, as invariably action does.  In doing so, however, they are bound to function otherwise than as a naked power organ; they participate as courts of law. This calls for facing how determinations of this kind can be asserted to have any legal quality. The answer, I suggest, inheres primarily in that they are—or are obliged to be—entirely principled. A principled decision, in the sense I have in mind, is one that rests on reasons with respect to all the issues in the case, reasons that in their generality and their neutrality transcend any immediate result that is involved. When no sufficient reasons of this kind can be assigned for overturning value choices of the other branches of the Government or of a state, those choices must, of course, survive. Otherwise, as Holmes said in his first opinion for the Court, "a constitution, instead of embodying only relatively fundamental rules of right, as generally understood by all English-speaking communities, would become the partisan of a particular set of ethical or economical opinions . . . ."

The virtue or demerit of a judgment turns, therefore, entirely on the reasons that support it and their adequacy to maintain any choice of values it decrees, or, it is vital that we add, to maintain the rejection of a claim that any given choice should be decreed. . . .

## NOTES AND QUESTIONS

1. How, if at all, do the phenomena which Wechsler calls "neutral principles" differ from rules? From reasons or justifications? From theories or explanations? What, if anything, do all of these have in common?

What are the reasons that Wechsler favors "principled" decisions? Are they the same reasons Holmes advances in favor of codifying the Common Law? As the reasons Stephen advances? See Chapter 8(2) (A) above. Does Wechsler emphasize the necessity of "principle" in order to insure that people will know what the law is or that like cases will be treated alike? Or are his reasons different from these?

2. What is it that makes the judicial process "principled"? Can a *process* be principled? Was the "judicial process" of Justice Frankfurter in *Rochin* unprincipled? Note that both Wechsler and Frankfurter seem to insist on a close interrelationship between law and reason. Indeed, Wechsler quotes Frankfurter's reference to "reason called law." Is *Rochin* an example of Frankfurter's abandonment of reason? Recall his assertion there that "the Constitution is 'intended to preserve practical and substantial rights, not to maintain theories'." Is there any way that such a statement can be reconciled with Wechsler's position? Again, is this consistent with a call for reason in law? Does the answer depend on whether reason is equivalent to principle?

3. If neutral and general principles are required for a lawful judicial decision, does this mean that any poorly reasoned decision is not law? What would be the consequences of such a position? Is there a neutral and general principle by which Wechsler can avoid adopting it? "When no sufficient reasons can be assigned," says Wechsler, the "value choices of the other branches . . . must, of course, survive." Does this mean that the judges must be able to assign such reasons when their decision comes down? Or is it enough that someone else, perhaps a later commentator, could assign such

reasons? Must a judge uphold, because he can find no principle, an act he feels certain is unconstitutional?

4. How can Wechsler "argue that we should prefer to see the other clauses of the Bill of Rights read as an affirmation of the special values they embody rather than as statements of a finite rule of law"? Doesn't this conception of constitutional interpretation lead to inconsistent constitutional principles over time? Would Wechsler defend the proposition that the Court must keep the Constitution in tune with the times? Could he do so consistently with his general position?

## SHELTON v. TUCKER

### 364 U.S. 479 (1960)

Mr. Justice STEWART delivered the opinion of the Court.

An Arkansas statute compels every teacher, as a condition of employment in the state-supported school or college, to file annually an affidavit listing without limitation every organization to which he has belonged or regularly contributed within the preceding five years. At issue in these two cases is the validity of that statute under the Fourteenth Amendment to the Constitution. . . .

The statute in question is Act 10 of the Second Extra-ordinary Session of the Arkansas General Assembly of 1958. The provisions of the Act are summarized in the opinion of the District Court as follows (174 F.Supp. 353):

"Act 10 provides in substance that no person shall be employed or elected to employment as a superintendent, principal or teacher in any public school in Arkansas, or as an instructor, professor or teacher in any public institution of higher learning in that State until such person shall have submitted to the appropriate hiring authority an affidavit listing all organizations to which he at the time belongs and to which he has belonged during the past five years, and also listing all organizations to which he is at the time paying regular dues or is making regular contributions, or to which within the past five years he has paid such dues or made such contributions. * * * The filing of a false affidavit is denounced as perjury, punishable by a fine of not less than five hundred nor more than one thousand dollars, and, in addition, the person filing the false affidavit is to lose his teaching license."

These provisions must be considered against the existing system of teacher employment required by Arkansas law. Teachers there are hired on a year-to-year basis. They are not covered by a civil service system, and they have no job security beyond the end of each school year. . . .

. . .

## I.

It is urged here, as it was unsuccessfully urged throughout the proceedings in both the federal and state courts, that Act 10 deprives teachers in Arkansas of their rights to personal, associational, and academic liberty, protected by the Due Process Clause of the Fourteenth Amendment from invasion by state action.  In considering this contention, we deal with two basic postulates.

*First.*  There can be no doubt of the right of a State to investigate the competence and fitness of those whom it hires to teach in its schools, as this Court before now has had occasion to recognize.  "A teacher works in a sensitive area in a schoolroom.  There he shapes the attitude of young minds towards the society in which they live.  In this, the state has a vital concern."  Adler v. Board of Education.
. . .

This controversy is thus not of a pattern with such cases as N. A. A. C. P. v. Alabama, 357 U.S. 449, 78 S.Ct. 1163, 2 L.Ed.2d 1488, and Bates v. Little Rock, 361 U.S. 516, 80 S.Ct. 412, 4 L.Ed.2d 480.  In those cases the Court held that there was no substantially relevant correlation between the governmental interest asserted and the State's effort to compel disclosure of the membership lists involved.  Here, by contrast, there can be no question of the relevance of a State's inquiry into the fitness and competence of its teachers.

*Second.*  It is not disputed that to compel a teacher to disclose his every associational tie is to impair that teacher's right of free association, a right closely allied to freedom of speech and a right which, like free speech, lies at the foundation of a free society.  De Jonge v. Oregon; Bates v. Little Rock, supra.  Such interference with personal freedom is conspicuously accented when the teacher serves at the absolute will of those to whom the disclosure must be made— those who any year can terminate the teacher's employment without bringing charges, without notice, without a hearing, without affording an opportunity to explain.

The statute does not provide that the information it requires be kept confidential.  Each school board is left free to deal with the information as it wishes.  The record contains evidence to indicate that fear of public disclosure is neither theoretical nor groundless.  Even if there were no disclosure to the general public, the pressure upon a teacher to avoid any ties which might displease those who control his professional destiny would be constant and heavy.  Public exposure, bringing with it the possibility of public pressures upon school boards to discharge teachers who belong to unpopular or minority organizations, would simply operate to widen and aggravate the impairment of constitutional liberty.

The vigilant protection of constitutional freedoms is nowhere more vital than in the community of American schools. . . .

## II.

The question to be decided here is not whether the State of Arkansas can ask certain of its teachers about all their organizational relationships.  It is not whether the State can ask all of its teachers about certain of their associational ties.  It is not whether teachers can be asked how many organizations they belong to, or how much time they spend in organizational activity.  The question is whether the State can ask every one of its teachers to disclose every single organization with which he has been associated over a five-year period. The scope of the inquiry required by Act 10 is completely unlimited. The statute requires a teacher to reveal the church to which he belongs, or to which he has given financial support. It requires him to disclose his political party, and every political organization to which he may have contributed over a five-year period. It requires him to list, without number, every conceivable kind of associational tie—social, professional, political, avocational, or religious. Many such relationships could have no possible bearing upon the teacher's occupational competence or fitness.

In a series of decisions this Court has held that, even though the governmental purpose be legitimate and substantial, that purpose cannot be pursued by means that broadly stifle fundamental personal liberties when the end can be more narrowly achieved. The breadth of legislative abridgment must be viewed in the light of less drastic means for achieving the same basic purpose.

.   .   .

As recently as last Term we held invalid an ordinance prohibiting the distribution of handbills because the breadth of its application went far beyond what was necessary to achieve a legitimate governmental purpose. Talley v. California.

.   .   .

The unlimited and indiscriminate sweep of the statute now before us brings it within the ban of our prior cases. The statute's comprehensive interference with associational freedom goes far beyond what might be justified in the exercise of the State's legitimate inquiry into the fitness and competency of its teachers. The judgments in both cases must be reversed.

It is so ordered.

Judgments reversed.

Mr. Justice FRANKFURTER, dissenting.

.   .   .

In the present case the Court strikes down an Arkansas statute requiring that teachers disclose to school officials all of their organizational relationships, on the ground that "Many such relationships could have no possible bearing upon the teacher's occupational competence or fitness." Granted that a given teacher's membership in the First Street Congregation is, standing alone, of little relevance to what may rightly be expected of a teacher, is that membership equally irrelevant when it is discovered that the teacher is in fact a member of the First Street Congregation *and* the Second Street Congregation *and* the Third Street Congregation *and* the 4–H Club *and* the 3–H Club *and* half a dozen other groups? Presumably, a teacher may have so many divers associations, so many divers commitments, that they consume his time and energy and interest at the expense of his work or even of his professional dedication. Unlike wholly individual interests, organizational connections—because they involve obligations undertaken with relation to other persons—may become inescapably demanding and distracting. Surely, a school board is entitled to inquire whether any of its teachers has placed himself, or is placing himself, in a condition where his work may suffer. Of course, the State might ask: "To how many organizations do you belong?" or "How much time do you expend at organizational activity?" But the answer to such questions could reasonably be regarded by a state legislature as insufficient, both because the veracity of the answer is more difficult to test, in cases where doubts as to veracity may arise, than in the case of the answers required by the Arkansas statute, and because an estimate of time presently spent in organizational activity reveals nothing as to the quality and nature of that activity, upon the basis of which, necessarily, judgment or prophesy of the extent of future involvement must be based. A teacher's answers to the questions which Arkansas asks, moreover, may serve the purpose of making known to school authorities persons who come into contact with the teacher in all of the phases of his activity in the community, and who can be questioned, if need be, concerning the teacher's conduct in matters which this Court can certainly not now say are lacking in any pertinence to professional fitness. It is difficult to understand how these particular ends could be achieved by asking "certain of [the State's] teachers about all their organizational relationships," or "all of its teachers about certain of their associational ties," or all of its teachers how many associations currently involve them, or during how many hours; and difficult, therefore, to appreciate why the Court deems unreasonable and forbids what Arkansas does ask.

If I dissent from the Court's disposition in these cases, it is not that I put a low value on academic freedom. . . . It is because that very freedom in its most creative reaches, is dependent in no small part upon the careful and discriminating selection of teachers. This process of selection is an intricate affair, a matter of fine judgment, and if it is to be informed, it must be based upon a comprehensive range of information. I am unable to say, on the face of this statute, that Arkansas could not reasonably find that the information which the statute requires—and which may not be otherwise acquired than by asking the question which it asks—is germane to that selection. Nor, on this record, can I attribute to the State a purpose to employ the enactment as a device for the accomplishment of what is constitutionally forbidden. Of course, if the information gathered by the required affidavits is used to further a scheme of terminating the employment of teachers solely because of their membership in unpopular organizations, that use will run afoul of the Fourteenth Amendment. It will be time enough, if such use is made, to hold the application of the statute unconstitutional. . . .

I am authorized to say that Mr. Justice CLARK, Mr. Justice HARLAN and Mr. Justice WHITTAKER agree with this opinion.

*Alexander Bickel*

## The Least Dangerous Branch *

. . . . [Professor Wechsler's rule of neutral principles] is an indispensable elaboration of any general justification of judicial review as a process for the injection into representative government of a system of enduring basic values.  One recent case in which the rule of the neutral principles failed of vindication may serve to illustrate its continued utility and importance.  [This was] Shelton v. Tucker . . . .

It was clear, the Court said, that a state should have power "to investigate the competence and fitness of those whom it hires to teach in its schools," and in general . . . there was sufficient rational connection between that permissible purpose and an inquiry into a teacher's out-of-school associations.  On the other hand, it was clear also that the duty to disclose such associations would have a tendency to impair the average teacher's indulgence of the spontaneous urge to join, especially where employment was renewable at such short periods as in Arkansas and where there was no guarantee that the information obtained by the state would be kept confidential.  Public exposure, of course, would work a further inhibition upon the freedom to join unpopular groups.  Moreover, these inhibitions are particularly harmful in the case of teachers, in whose freedom of intellectual inquiry society has a great stake.  Yet the Court did not hold that the state should be forbidden to make its inquiries into associations under these conditions or that it should be fore-closed from inquiring into particularly unpopular associations or into certain classes of them, such as religious or political.  Rather, the Court implicitly rested on the premise of previous decisions that the state's interest in the fitness of its employees generally outweighs the desirability of sustaining an atmosphere of freedom of private association.

On what ground, then, did the Court strike down the statute?  It said that the question was not whether Arkansas could ask certain of its teachers about all their organizational associations; nor whether the state could ask all of its teachers about certain associations; nor whether teachers could be asked how many associations they had or how much time they spent on them.  The decisive point was the broad scope of the disclosures Arkansas required of all teachers.  Many of the associations of which disclosure was required "could have no possible bearing upon the teacher's occupational competence or fitness."  But we were not told which.  If this were so, then it was not true, as the Court had just said, that Arkansas could "ask certain of its teachers about all their organizational relationships."  Moreover, it could scarcely be that Arkansas had a permissible interest in finding out how much time they spent in organizational activity but might not verify that information by inquiring into the names of the organizations that a teacher had joined.

The Court, however, reasoned by analogy to certain earlier cases in which it had struck down ordinances prohibiting the distribution of literature in public places without a license. These ordinances had fallen because the state's interest in good order and in the prevention of fraud, littering of the streets, and like inconveniences was held not to justify the broad restrictions on freedom of speech that were actually imposed. In other words, in those cases, the Court had weighed the rather limited purpose the state was allowed to pursue against the total effect of the action taken and had found that the ordinances were broader than their purpose immediately required and that, since in their breadth they affected other important values, they should be struck down, leaving to the state the alternative of enacting a narrower measure to achieve its allowable end. The analogy to present case would have been apt had the Court been able to hold that Arkansas had only a limited interest in informing itself of the extracurricular activities of its teachers and that the broad statute in question went beyond that limited interest. But the Court did not so hold. It affirmed as permissible on principle the state's interest in investigating the full range of its teachers' outside activities. Then it superimposed the holding that the inquiry made by the present statute was nevertheless too broad. The Court did not say in what respect, and it did not take back one whit of its previous concessions as to the range of the permissible state interest. Such a decision lacks neutral principle because it lacks intellectual coherence.

The decisive factor in the Court's judgment may have been the more-than-tenable surmise that Arkansas would dismiss teachers whom it had found to be members of the NAACP, and that dismissals would actually rest on such membership even though other, spurious grounds would be formally assigned. Despite the Court's assumption that the state may inquire into a teacher's commitments and use of his free time and may require him to disclose the totality of his affiliations, including one with the NAACP, a dismissal for NAACP membership would lack rationality, at least in the absence of a showing of some particular interference with the teacher's professional effectiveness. For in light of the "conventional wisdom" of the day —which must qualify as rational, although experience may have disproved it two decades hence—inferences as to loyalty and even as to an individual's intellectual integrity and freedom may be drawn, say, from Communist Party membership. But little beyond a peaceable dedication to the ideal of equality of the races can be inferred from adherence to the NAACP, and such an inference without more is not relevant to any purpose the state is permitted to pursue. This problem, however, was not present in the case and might never arise. The plaintiff here had failed to file his affidavit and had been dismissed for that reason. Hence there was no call as yet to decide questions of dismissal for NAACP membership, or dismissal at will, without any procedural safeguards, and the Court in fact did not deal with such questions.

"Of course," as Justice Harlan said in dissent, "this decision has a natural tendency to enlist support, involving as it does an un-

usual statute that touches constitutional rights whose protection in
the context of the racial situation in various parts of the country demands the unremitting vigilance of the courts." But it is evident
on the face of the opinion that the Court was unable to evolve a principle on which to dispose of this case.

To tell the legislature of Arkansas that it must act rationally;
to have told it, if such a principle were tenable, that it must employ
as teachers all comers; to have told it that it may not permit the
public disclosure of the private associations of its employees, although
it may find out about them for itself; to have told it that certain associations (as, for example, family or religious ones) are so private
that they may under no circumstances be inquired into; or to have
made any or all of these injunctions applicable to teachers but not
the generality of public employees—a decision based on any of these,
and perhaps other, principles, although some are less and some more
tenable, might have been within the proper function of a Court empowered to enunciate and apply fundamental values. But to tell the
legislature of Arkansas only that for inscrutable reasons a teacher
named Shelton may not be fired, or that inquiries into membership
in the NAACP, but not necessarily in any other organization, are not
permitted—that is to revise, even if out of the most laudable of motives, a mere judgment of expediency; it is merely to disagree with
the legislature on the thoroughness with which the fitness of Mr.
Shelton should be inquired into, or on whether the NAACP is a worthi-
er organization than the Elks or the Masons or the John Birch Society
and should therefore be protected by special legislative exemptions.

There are other such examples, although, of course, not one or
a dozen of them can be taken to characterize the present Court's discharge of its office. They do, however, demonstrate the utility of
the principle of the neutral principles, the rule, in Justice Frankfurter's words, that the Court must not "sit like a kadi under a tree
dispensing justice according to considerations of individual expediency." The rule is a timely reminder that the inviting garden of what
Cardozo, following Geny, called "judicial impressionism" is forbidden
territory. The Justices must not benevolently constitute themselves
"*les bons juges*" and do in each case what seems just for it alone.
Rather, as Cardozo enjoined them to do, they must hold "fast to
Kant's categorical imperative, 'Act on a maxim which thou canst
will to be law universal.' " They must refuse "to sacrifice the larger
and more universal good to the narrower and smaller . . . .
We look beyond the particular to the universal, and shape our judgment in obedience to the fundamental interest of society. . . ."

QUESTIONS

1. Is Bickel saying that the Court decided this case in Shelton's
favor for no reason more general than that it wanted him to win?
Or that it wanted the NAACP to win? If not, what might lead one
to think that this is what he is saying?

2. What would be wrong with a principle that all cases in which
Negroes are parties shall be decided in favor of the Black litigant?

Would this be a general principle? Would this be a neutral principle? If not, why not? Can one state a principle that does not aid some interest or other? If so, how useful a principle would it be? If not, what bearing would this have on the requirement that principles be "neutral"?

Is the principle which decrees that Negroes shall win all cases in which they participate a bad one because it will often lead to bad results? Is that a final test of the validity of a rule or principle? Are there any rules or principles which do not lead to bad results in some cases? Note the remark of Bickel in the excerpt below that "a neutral principle is a rule of action that will be authoritatively enforced without adjustment or concession and without let-up. If it sometimes hurts, nothing is better proof of its validity."

3.   Why, according to Bickel, was it not enough for the Court to label the statutory inquiry too broad? Suppose that the Federal government wished to place television cameras in every citizen's home in order to prevent espionage. Would the government's obvious and paramount interest in internal security justify this kind of action? Couldn't arguments of the sort used by Justice Frankfurter be adduced to support such legislation? Would the Court be justified in declaring such legislation unconstitutional on the grounds that it required an overly broad surveillance? Even though it was conceded that this was the most effective way of accomplishing the governmental purpose? Or would the Court have to explain why it was overly broad as well?

What reasons might the Court have for requiring the legislature to accomplish its purpose through more specific regulations, assuming that it really was the breadth of these to which it objected? What does a Court learn from more specific legislation?

## BROWN v. BOARD OF EDUCATION

347 U.S. 483 (1954)

Mr. Chief Justice WARREN delivered the opinion of the Court.

These cases come to us from the States of Kansas, South Carolina, Virginia, and Delaware. They are premised on different facts and different local conditions, but a common legal question justifies their consideration together in this consolidated opinion.

In each of the cases, minors of the Negro race, through their legal representatives, seek the aid of the courts in obtaining admission to the public schools of their community on a nonsegregated basis. In each instance, they have been denied admission to schools attended by white children under laws requiring or permitting segregation according to race. This segregation was alleged to deprive the plaintiffs of the equal protection of the laws under the Fourteenth Amendment. In each of the cases other than the Delaware case, a three-judge federal district court denied relief to the plaintiffs on the so-called "separate but equal" doctrine announced by this Court in Plessy v. Ferguson, 163 U.S. 537. Under that doctrine, equality of treatment is accorded when the races are provided substantially equal facilities, even though these facilities be separate. In the Delaware case, the Supreme Court of Delaware adhered to that doctrine, but ordered that the plaintiffs be admitted to the white schools because of their superiority to the Negro schools.

The plaintiffs contend that segregated public schools are not "equal" and cannot be made "equal," and that hence they are deprived of the equal protection of the laws. Because of the obvious importance of the question presented, the Court took jurisdiction. Argument was heard in the 1952 Term, and reargument was heard this Term on certain questions propounded by the Court.

Reargument was largely devoted to the circumstances surrounding the adoption of the Fourteenth Amendment in 1868. It covered exhaustively consideration of the Amendment in Congress, ratification by the states, then existing practices in racial segregation, and the views of proponents and opponents of the Amendment. This discussion and our own investigation convince us that, although these sources cast some light, it is not enough to resolve the problem with which we are faced. At best, they are inconclusive. The most avid proponents of the post-War Amendments undoubtedly intended them to remove all legal distinctions among "all persons born or naturalized in the United States." Their opponents, just as certainly, were antagonistic to both the letter and the spirit of the Amendments and wished them to have the most limited effect. What others in Congress and the state legislatures had in mind cannot be determined with any degree of certainty.

An additional reason for the inconclusive nature of the Amendment's history, with respect to segregated schools, is the status of public education at that time. In the South, the movement toward free common schools, supported by general taxation, had not yet taken hold. Education of white children was largely in the hands of private groups. Education of Negroes was almost nonexistent, and practically all of the race were illiterate. In fact, any education of Negroes was forbidden by law in some states. Today, in contrast, many Negroes have achieved outstanding success in the arts and sciences as well as in the business and professional world. It is true that public school education at the time of the Amendment had advanced further in the North, but the effect of the Amendment on Northern States was generally ignored in the congressional debates. Even in the North, the conditions of public education did not approximate those existing today. The curriculum was usually rudimentary; ungraded schools were common in rural areas; the school term was but three months a year in many states; and compulsory school attendance was virtually unknown. As a consequence, it is not surprising that there should be so little in the history of the Fourteenth Amendment relating to its intended effect on public education.

In the first cases in this Court construing the Fourteenth Amendment, decided shortly after its adoption, the Court interpreted it as proscribing all state-imposed discriminations against the Negro race. The doctrine of "separate but equal" did not make its appearance in this Court until 1896 in the case of Plessy v. Ferguson, supra, involving not education but transportation. American courts have since labored with the doctrine for over half a century. In this Court, there have been six cases involving the "separate but equal" doctrine in the field of public education. In Cumming v. Board of Education of Richmond County, 175 U.S. 528, and Gong Lum v. Rice, 275 U.S. 78, the validity of the doctrine itself was not challenged. In more recent cases, all on the graduate school level, inequality was found in that specific benefits enjoyed by white students were denied to Negro students of the same educational qualifications. State of Missouri ex rel. Gaines v. Canada, 305 U.S. 337; Sipuel v. Board of Regents of University of Oklahoma, 332 U.S. 631; Sweatt v. Painter, 339 U. S. 629; McLaurin v. Oklahoma State Regents, 339 U.S. 637. In none of these cases was it necessary to re-examine the doctrine to grant relief to the Negro plaintiff. And in Sweatt v. Painter, supra, the Court expressly reserved decision on the question whether Plessy v. Ferguson should be held inapplicable to public education.

In the instant cases, that question is directly presented. Here, unlike Sweatt v. Painter, there are findings below that the Negro and white schools involved have been equalized, or are being equalized, with respect to buildings, curricula, qualifications and salaries of teachers, and other "tangible" factors. Our decision, therefore, cannot turn on merely a comparison of these tangible factors in the Negro and white schools involved in each of the cases. We must look instead to the effect of segregation itself on public education.

In approaching this problem, we cannot turn the clock back to 1868 when the Amendment was adopted, or even to 1896 when Plessy v. Ferguson was written. We must consider public education in the light of its full development and its present place in American life throughout the Nation. Only in this way can it be determined if segregation in public schools deprives these plaintiffs of the equal protection of the laws.

Today, education is perhaps the most important function of state and local governments. Compulsory school attendance laws and the great expenditures for education both demonstrate our recognition of the importance of education to our democratic society. It is required in the performance of our most basic public responsibilities, even service in the armed forces. It is the very foundation of good citizenship. Today it is a principal instrument in awakening the child to cultural values, in preparing him for later professional training, and in helping him to adjust normally to his environment. In these days, it is doubtful that any child may reasonably be expected to succeed in life if he is denied the opportunity of an education. Such an opportunity, where the state has undertaken to provide it, is a right which must be made available to all on equal terms.

We come then to the question presented: Does segregation of children in public schools solely on the basis of race, even though the physical facilities and other "tangible" factors may be equal, deprive the children of the minority group of equal educational opportunities? We believe that it does.

In Sweatt v. Painter, supra, in finding that a segregated law school for Negroes could not provide them equal educational opportunities, this Court relied in large part on "those qualities which are incapable of objective measurement but which make for greatness in a law school." In McLaurin v. Oklahoma State Regents, supra, the Court, in requiring that a Negro admitted to a white graduate school be treated like all other students, again resorted to intangible consideration: ". . . his ability to study, to engage in discussions and exchange views with other students, and, in general, to learn his profession." Such considerations apply with added force to children in grade and high schools. To separate them from others of similar age and qualifications solely because of their race generates a feeling of inferiority as to their status in the community that may affect their hearts and minds in a way unlikely ever to be undone. The effect of this separation on their educational opportunities was well stated by a finding in the Kansas case by a court which nevertheless felt compelled to rule against the Negro plaintiffs:

"Segregation of white and colored children in public schools has a detrimental effect upon the colored children. The impact is greater when it has the sanction of the law; for the policy of separating the races is usually interpreted as denoting the inferiority of the negro group. A sense of inferiority affects the motivation of a child to learn. Segregation with the sanction of law, therefore, has a tendency to [retard] the educational and mental development of negro children and to deprive them of some of the benefits they would receive in a racial[ly] integrated school system." Whatever may have been the extent of psychological knowledge at the time of Plessy v. Ferguson, this finding is amply supported by modern authority.[1] Any language in Plessy v. Ferguson contrary to this finding is rejected.

We conclude that in the field of public education the doctrine of "separate but equal" has no place. Separate educational facilities are inherently unequal. Therefore, we hold that the plaintiffs and others similarly situated for whom the actions have been brought are, by reason of the segregation complained of, deprived of the equal protection of the laws guaranteed by the Fourteenth Amendment. . . .

1.  K. B. Clark, Effect of Prejudice and Discrimination on Personality Development (Midcentury White House Conference on Children and Youth, 1950); Witmer and Kotinsky, Personality in the Making (1952), c. VI; Deutcher and Chein, The Psychological Effects of Enforced Segregation: A Survey of Social Science Opinion, 26 J. Psychol. 259 (1948); Chein, What are the Psychological Effects of Segregation Under Conditions of Equal Facilities?, 3 Int.J.Opinion and Attitude Res. 229 (1949); Brameld, Educational Costs, in Discrimination and National Welfare (MacIver, ed., 1949), 44–48; Frazier, The Negro in the United States (1949), 674–681. And see generally Myrdal, An American Dilemma (1944). [This is the much-discussed Footnote 11 in the original opinion.]

HERBERT WECHSLER

TOWARD NEUTRAL PRINCIPLES OF CONSTITUTIONAL LAW *

. . . . I come to the school decision, which for one of my persuasion stirs the deepest conflict I experience in testing the thesis I propose. . . .

. . .

The problem [there] inheres strictly in the reasoning of the opinion, an opinion which is often read with less fidelity by those who praise it than by those by whom it is condemned. The Court did not declare, as many wish it had, that the fourteenth amendment forbids all racial lines in legislation, though subsequent per curiam decisions may . . . now go that far. Rather . . . the separate-but-equal formula was not overruled "in form" but was held to have "no place" in public education on the ground that segregated schools are "inherently unequal," with deleterious effects upon the colored children in implying their inferiority, effects which retard their educational and mental development. So, indeed, the district court had found as a fact in the Kansas case, a finding which the Supreme Court embraced, citing some further "modern authority" in its support.

Does the validity of the decision turn then on the sufficiency of evidence or of judicial notice to sustain a finding that the separation harms the Negro children who may be involved? There were, indeed, some witnesses who expressed that opinion in the Kansas case, as there were also witnesses in the companion Virginia case, including Professor Garrett of Columbia, whose view was to the contrary. Much depended on the question that the witness had in mind, which rarely was explicit. Was he comparing the position of the Negro child in a segregated school with his position in an integrated school where he was happily accepted and regarded by the whites; or was he comparing his position under separation with that under integration where the whites were hostile to his presence and found ways to make their feelings known? And if the harm that segregation worked was relevant, what of the benefits that it entailed: sense of security, the absence of hostility? Were they irrelevant? Moreover, was the finding in Topeka applicable without more to Clarendon County, South Carolina, with 2,799 colored students and only 295 whites? Suppose that more Negroes in a community preferred separation than opposed it? Would that be relevant to whether they were hurt or aided by segregation as opposed to integration? Their fates would be governed by the change of system quite as fully as those of the students who complained.

I find it hard to think the judgment really turned upon the facts. Rather, it seems to me, it must have rested on the view that racial segregation is, in principle, a denial of equality to the minority

* From Principles, Politics and Fundamental Law 43–47 (1961). Copyright 1961 by the President and Fellows of     Harvard College. Reprinted by permission of Harvard University Press.

against whom it is directed; that is, the group that is not dominant politically and, therefore, does not make the choice involved. For many who support the Court's decision this assuredly is the decisive ground. But this position also presents problems. Does it not involve an inquiry into the motive of the legislature, which is generally foreclosed to the courts? Is it alternatively defensible to make the measure of validity of legislation the way it is interpreted by those who are affected by it? In the context of a charge that segregation *with equal facilities* is a denial of equality, is there not a point in *Plessy* in the statement that if "enforced separation stamps the colored race with a badge of inferiority" it is solely because its members choose "to put that construction upon it"? Does enforced separation of the sexes discriminate against females merely because it may be the females who resent it and it is imposed by judgments predominantly male? Is a prohibition of miscegenation a discrimination against the colored member of the couple who would like to marry?

For me, assuming equal facilities, the question posed by state-enforced segregation is not one of discrimination at all. Its human and its constitutional dimensions lie entirely elsewhere, in the denial by the state of freedom to associate, a denial that impinges in the same way on any groups or races that may be involved. I think, and I hope not without foundation, that the Southern white also pays heavily for segregation, not only in the sense of guilt that he must carry but also in the benefits he is denied. In the days when I was joined with Charles H. Houston in a litigation in the Supreme Court, before the present building was constructed, he did not suffer more than I in knowing that we had to go to Union Station to lunch together during the recess. Does not the problem of miscegenation show most clearly that it is the freedom of association that at bottom is involved, the only case, I may add, where it is implicit in the situation that association is desired by the only individuals involved?
. . . .

But if the freedom of association is denied by segregation, integration forces an association upon those for whom it is unpleasant or repugnant. Is this not the heart of the issue involved, a conflict in human claims of high dimension, not unlike many others that involve the highest freedoms. . . . Given a situation where the state must practically choose between denying the association to those individuals who wish it or imposing it on those who would avoid it, is there a basis in neutral principles for holding that the Constitution demands that the claims for association should prevail? I should like to think there is, but I confess that I have not yet written the opinion. To write it is for me the challenge of the school-segregation cases.

## NOTES AND QUESTIONS

1. The Fourteenth Amendment reads in part as follows: "nor shall any State deprive any person of life, liberty or property, without due process of law; nor deny to any person within its jurisdic-

tion the equal protection of the laws." In the first Wechsler excerpt, you will recall, he suggests that "Equal protection" might have been "taken as no more than an assurance that no one may be placed beyond the safeguards of the law, outlawing, as it were, the possibility of outlawry, but nothing else." What does this mean? Examine the phrase "the equal protection of the laws"? What idea would it convey to you if you had no previous knowledge of the term's legal applications? Why have judges found it necessary to say that "equal protection of the laws" also includes "the protection of equal laws"? Is this a gloss which the Court in *Brown* would have to accept?

If "equal protection of the laws" means that the laws themselves must be "equal", just what does that mean? What is it for a law or a rule to be equal? Suppose that a state statute requires lawyers to pay an annual license fee, but makes no such requirement of doctors. Would the laws of that state be unequal? Consider typical voting legislation which denies the franchise to persons under age 18. Is a 17 year old thereby denied the protection of equal laws? Consider children in the fifth grade of an elementary school who are divided into classes on the basis of performance on mathematical and reading aptitude tests. Are the children in the class for lower aptitude students denied any benefits thereby? If so, would this fact in itself establish that they are being denied the protection of equal laws? The *Brown* Court says that separate schools are inherently unequal? Can such a proposition be established simply by pointing out that separation involves a harm to the Negro children that is not suffered by the white children? Or must the equal protection clause require something more? Do these questions help you to see how Wechsler's remarks about the actual harm suffered by Negro children under segregation bear on the question of whether the Fourteenth Amendment was violated?

2. Can any act of the State be declared invalid simply because it harms someone? Are there any laws which don't harm some interest or person in some way? Does the answer depend on the meaning of the word "harm"? Can the word "cost" be substituted for "harm" in some of the latter's uses? Or is "harm" always something different from "cost"? Consider the sentence, "His actions cost him something, but he was certainly not harmed." Or the sentence, "The harm I suffered was outweighed by the benefits." Is the word "harm" being used in the same way in these sentences?

Can a rule or principle exist, or have any use, if it exacts no costs? Can a rule or reason adequately justify a decision if it refers only to the costs involved in a challenged action? Is it enough to say that segregation hurts the Blacks without also dealing with the ways in which it might help them? Alternatively, is it enough to say that "on the whole" segregation harms the Blacks without also dealing with the assertion that integration harms the Whites? Do these questions tell us anything about the conditions necessary for an adequate rule?

3. If two boys are constantly fighting and school officials decree that they shall be put in separate classes and kept from mingling

during school hours, does this amount to a denial of equal protection? Would it matter if one boy was Black and the principal was white—assuming that each boy had equal facilities available to him?

4. Can you state more elaborately Wechsler's objections to "the view that racial segregation is, in principle, a denial of equality to the minority against whom it is directed"? Why does this view "involve an inquiry into the motive of the legislature"? Is it because the practice on its face and in its effects does not treat one group differently from the other? What, incidentally, is wrong with looking at the legislature's "motive"? Why would it not be "defensible to make the measure of validity of legislation the way it is interpreted by those who are affected by it"? Would that be a bad "maxim" to "will as law universal"?

Why do you suppose, incidentally, that this minority tends to view "enforced separation" as stamping "the colored race with a badge of inferiority"? Is it "solely because its members choose to put that construction upon it"? Are we dealing, then, with a group of paranoids? Or is this an irrelevant question?

5. Why are discriminations against people solely because of race and color violations of the "equal protection" clause? If all legislation involves discriminations, what is it that makes these invalid? Is it that the standard employed is wholly unacceptable, unreasonable, arbitrary, etc.? Is that true? In all cases?

6. What interests do you think the "equal protection" clause should be construed to protect? Would it be fair to say that the clause insures that people's rights are determined according to rule? That their problems are resolved by rules? Is this the same thing as saying that the "equal protection" clause is meant to insure that "like" cases are treated alike?

Should there be a Constitutional principle that "like cases must be treated alike" or that "all cases must be disposed of according to rule"? Since all cases are different, wouldn't it be juster to treat them differently—i. e., individually and on their own merits? Is it possible to implement such a policy? Does the Fourteenth Amendment require its implementation? What is the effect of the Segregation decisions? Is it to make all Blacks be treated like all Whites? Is it to make all Blacks be treated alike? Is it arguable that the effect of those decisions is to enable Blacks to be treated differently —i. e., individually and on their own merits? If so, is there any necessary, though paradoxical, relation between equality and individualization? Between rules and individualization? Between language and individualization? Consider these questions again in studying the materials in the next two sections. Do they provide any support for the proposition that language and rules help make it possible to conceive and to deal with cases in their individuality? See, especially, the selection from Church in the following section.

ALEXANDER BICKEL

## THE LEAST DANGEROUS BRANCH *

As Mr. Wechsler concedes, the *School Segregation Cases*, read in conjunction with certain brief orders that followed after them, have made clear that the principle in question is that racial segregation constitutes, *per se,* a denial of equality to the minority group against whom it is directed. . . . Mr. Wechsler sees segregation statutes as regulations of the freedom to associate. . . . [And he asks if there is] "a basis in neutral principles for holding that the Constitution demands that the claims for association should prevail?"

The reply question is this: What, on the score of generality and neutrality, is wrong with the principle that a legislative choice in favor of a freedom not to associate is forbidden, when the consequence of such a choice is to place one of the groups of which our society is constituted in a position of permanent, humiliating inferiority; when the consequence beyond that is to foster in the whites, by authority of the state, self-damaging and potentially violent feelings of racial superiority—feelings, that as Lincoln knew, find easy transference from Negroes to other groups as their particular objects? It may be that this principle is wrong or is on other grounds ill suited for pronouncement and application by the Court. But wherein is it lacking on the score of neutrality, . . .?

The point that the Court must necessarily rely on an estimate of legislative motive or of the subjective feelings of Negroes affected by segregation fails, in my judgment, entirely. Granted that it would be relatively novel, and in that degree *ad hoc,* as well as extremely difficult for the Court so to rely. But it is unnecessary. To determine that segregation establishes a relationship of the inferior to the superior race is to take objective notice of a fact of our national life and of experience elsewhere in the world, now and in other times, quite without reference to legislative motives and without reliance on subjective and perhaps idiosyncratic feelings. It is no different from a similarly experiential judgment that official inquiries into private associations inhibit the freedom to join, or that hearsay evidence, reported at second or third hand, has a tendency to become distorted. And so one is led to the surmise that if the judgment embodied in the *Segregation Cases* lacks neutrality for Mr. Wechsler, it must be because he understands the concept in some additional sense, beyond [the generality and coherence we have so far discussed]. . . .

More recently, Mr. Wechsler has shed further light on his position. If the Fourteenth Amendment is read to outlaw race or color as allowable legislative grounds of classification, the principle must be tested, he has said, not only by its effect on straight-out segregation, "but also by its impact upon measures that take race into account to equalize job opportunity or to reduce *de facto* segregation, as in New York City's schools." By its effect also, one might add, on such proposals as the benevolent quota in housing. Mr. Wechsler carries this suggestion no further, but it is pregnant with an elaboration of the idea of neutrality which is of the very first importance.

Our point of departure, like Mr. Wechsler's, has been that judicial review is the principled process of enunciating and applying certain enduring values of our society. These values must, of course, have general significance and even-handed application. When values conflict—as they often will—the Court must proclaim one as overriding, or find an accommodation among them. The result is a principle, or a new value, if you will, or an amalgam of values, or a compromise of values; it must in any event also have general significance and even-handed application. For, again, the root idea is that the process is justified only if it injects into representative government something that is not already there; and that is principle, standards of action that derive their worth from a long view of society's spiritual as well as material needs and that command adherence whether or not the immediate outcome is expedient or agreeable. It follows, and I take it Mr. Wechsler suggests, that once the Court has arrived at a principle, it must apply that principle without compromise. Therefore, the Court should not rest judgment on a "principle" which may be incapable of uniform application. If, in order to be workable in our society as it actually exists, a rule of action must be modulated by pragmatic compromises, then that rule is not a principle; it is no more than a device of expediency. And it is for legislatures, not courts, to impose what are merely solutions of expediency. Courts must act on true principles, capable of unremitting application. When they cannot find such a principle, they are bound to declare the legislative choice valid. No other course is open to them.

This is an idea exquisitely poised on the brink of logomachy, but I think that it has substance and that it is crucial. A true principle may carry within itself its own flexibility, but—and this is the important thing—flexibility on its own terms. For example, one may lay it down that in all criminal proceedings the accused must have the assistance of counsel in order to ensure the protection of his rights. Or one may say, as the Court has in fact said, that the assistance of counsel is constitutionally required in all cases, except in relatively simple ones in the state courts, where the accused seems to have been able to cope for himself, so that his rights were in fact adequately protected. This is not a mere device of expediency; it is a principle with flexibility built in, within its own terms. But a "principle" that speech is not a fit subject for legislative regulation because it is a sacred and untrammeled right of Everyman, except that sometimes some laws may be allowed to restrict it—that would be no more than an invitation to judgments of expediency. So also must one view as a device of expediency a "principle" that race is a proscribed ground of legislative classification, except that it may be used sometimes.

Earlier we saw the rule of the neutral principles as foreclosing *ad hoc* constitutional judgments which express merely the judge's transient feeling of what is fair, convenient, or congenial in the particular circumstances of a litigation. The *Shelton* case was an apt illustration, because it was decided without reference to any standard that could be stated in terms one whit more general than its own result. A neutral principle, by contrast, is an intellectually coherent statement of the reason for a result which in like cases will produce a like result, whether or not it is immediately agreeable or expedient. Now the demand for neutral principles is carried further. It is that the Court rest judgment only on principles that will be capable of application across the board and without compromise, in all relevant cases in the foreseeable future: absolute application of absolute—even if sometimes flexible—principles. The flexibility, if any, must be built into the principle itself, in equally principled fashion. Thus a neutral principle is a rule of action that will be authoritatively enforced without adjustment or concession and without let-up. If it sometimes hurts, nothing is better proof of its validity. If it must sometimes fail of application, it won't do. Given the nature of a free society and the ultimate consensual basis of all its effective law, there can be but very few such principles.

But it may be argued that the exceptions to the principle of the *Segregation Cases* which Mr. Wechsler foresees are themselves principled ones, quite like the exception to the right-to-counsel rule mentioned above. Benevolent quotas, for example, differ from segregation. They do not completely deny the Negro's freedom of association, with the inevitable consequence of keeping him in a situation of permanent inferiority. Rather, they take account of an ineluctable fact in his present situation—that whites will move out of a neighborhood in which the Negro population has risen above a certain percentage point—to the end that some integration may be obtainable now, and that in time, perhaps, the prejudices that result in segregation in any degree may be eradicated altogether. Aware of these facts, the state decrees, let us say, that 33.3% of units in a public housing project must be allocated to Negro tenants and the rest to whites. In other words, the present situation is that it is not within the power of the state to enforce genuine integration unless it is prepared to dictate where people must live and work. This might well be thought unwise, counter-productive, perhaps unenforceable, and wrong on yet additional grounds. Therefore, if it wishes to go beyond the ineffectual removal of legal bars to integration, the state or the federal government may have to legislate some degree of controlled segregation.

. . . . The questions concerning benevolent quotas . . . must be whether their effect can be squared with the principle of the *Segregation Cases,* and, if not, whether a purpose conforming to some other, not inconsistent principle can be attributed to them. It is clear that the principle of the *Segregation Cases* cannot be made to fit. The benevolent quota, like segregation, is a classification by race. Is a principled modification of the principle possible?

That there should be no distinctions of race ordained by the state —that is a principle. That there should be no distinctions of race ordained by the state except when their consequence may be that the racial prejudices of the people are mitigated in the long run—that comes in the end only to this: that the state should try, in the ways best suited to prevailing conditions, to draw the races into a closer relationship. And this, in turn, is not a principled rule of behavior; it is the statement of a goal whose attainment will call for a great many prudential judgments, aimed at the goal, to be sure, but not proceeding immediately from principle. The question of which arrangement, based on the invidious criterion of race, is consistent with ultimate attainment of the goal will most often be answerable only by a doubtful and variable judgment of expediency. Not always; perhaps not at the extremes, and perhaps absolute segregation is such an extreme. But most often.

Tested against the great judicial event of the century, the general justification of judicial review which was outlined in the previous chapter, and which is also Mr. Wechsler's point of departure, may thus appear to fail. If judicial review is to remain a process of principled decision, it would seem that it must here either impose upon the country a rigidly doctrinaire rule of behavior which will appear almost ludicrous to anyone who has any sense of the actualities of the situation and of its different aspects in different states; or it must uphold the segregation of the races by law. Otherwise it meddles with insoluble questions, either of motive or of mere expediency.

I believe that Mr. Wechsler suggests something like such a conclusion, and the fact that he does so gives one much pause. If Mr. Wechsler is right, then the decision in the *Segregation Cases* leads straight to disaster, for the Court or for the country. The Court—if Mr. Wechsler is right—either has set out to be a third legislative chamber or is imposing on the country an absolute rule of absolute principle. Thus it is either totally at war with the theory and practice of democracy or, far from being a stabilizing influence, it is leading the country to ruin by intractable, doctrinaire stages of irrepressible conflict. Or both, for the absolute rule of principle is also at war with a democratic system. But Mr. Wechsler, I believe, is not right.

No society, certainly not a large and heterogeneous one, can fail in time to explode if it is deprived of the arts of compromise, if it knows no ways of muddling through. No good society can be unprincipled; and no viable society can be principle-ridden. But it is not true in our society that we are generally governed wholly by principle in some matters and indulge a rule of expediency exclusively in others. There is no such neat dividing line. . . . Most often . . . and as often as not in matters of the widest and deepest concern, such as the racial problem, both requirements exist most imperatively side by side; guiding principle and expedient compromise. The role of principle, when it cannot be the immutable governing rule, is to affect the tendency of policies of expediency. And it is a potent role.

Is it not clear our nation would be severely damaged—inwardly, not merely in its external relations—if in the second half of the twentieth century it believed that segregation of the races was neither right nor wrong; if it were committed to no principle in the matter, one way or the other? But is it not equally clear—as the example of the benevolent quota may show—that the problem of the association of the black and white races will not always yield to principled resolution, that it must proceed through phases of compromise and expedient muddling-through, or else fail of an effective and peaceable outcome?

NOTES AND QUESTIONS

1. Would Wechsler agree that the consequence of segregation *with equal facilities* "is to place one of the groups of which our society is constituted in a position of permanent, humiliating inferiority"? Would he agree that the determination of this consequence simply depends on taking "objective notice of a fact of our national life and of experience elsewhere . . . ."? Do segregated schools necessarily and inevitably place the minority group in the position Bickel reports? What if the minority schools were given additional and better facilities—the better to bring minority pupils up to the level of the white pupils intellectually? Is separation *inherently* unequal?

2. Is Bickel defining "principle" as "standards of action that derive their worth from a long view of society's spiritual as well as material needs and that command adherence whether or not the immediate outcome is expedient or agreeable"? Is this a definition of "principle" or only of "good principle"? Or is it a constituent element of a principle that it take "a long view"? Or that it take account of "society's spiritual as well as material needs"? Can you suggest any reasons why such criteria might have something to do with whether something was or was not a principle? Or at least was a social, political or legal principle? What do you think Bickel means by the "long view"? By "spiritual needs"? Is there a relationship between these two concepts other than the one Bickel specifically states?

In order for something to be a principle does it have to "command adherence whether or not the immediate outcome is expedient or agreeable"? Can't something still be a principle even if it does not command adherence of this sort?

3. When Bickel envisages that adherence to a principle may lead to an "immediate outcome" which is neither "expedient or agreeable", what is his criterion for determining expediency or agreeableness? When he says that there is no better proof of a principle's validity than that "it sometimes hurts," what is his standard for determining hurt? From the point of view expressed in the principle can *any* of its applications be inexpedient, disagreeable, injurious or painful? If one agrees to the principle, hasn't one also agreed to its applications? If one thinks the principle is good, are not its applications good as well?

4. What does Bickel mean by a "compromise"? By an "exception"? How does one distinguish a "principled exception" from a "compromise"?

5. What is the difference between "a principle with flexibility built in, within its own terms" and the "principle" that speech cannot be regulated, "except that sometimes some laws may be allowed to restrict it"? What is it that makes the latter "no more than an invitation to judgments of expediency"? Does your answer tell you anything about the requirements for a proposition to qualify as a rule or a principle?

6. Do you agree that benevolent quotas are inconsistent with the *Segregation Cases?* "The benevolent quota, like segregation," says Bickel, "is a classification by race." Is Bickel telling us that the principle of the *Segregation Cases* is that there shall be no classifications by race? Is that equivalent to his earlier statement that "the principle in question is that racial segregation constitutes, *per se*, a denial of equality to the minority group against whom it is directed"? Is there any way you can distinguish those two principles?

In an omitted portion of his book, Professor Bickel elaborates on the Constitutional deficiencies of the benevolent quota:

> Yet it cannot be denied that in its objective operation, a benevolent quota is as invidious as straight-out segregation. The difference in immediate effect is that some Negroes will not be denied their freedom to associate. But most Negroes will be, and the others will be allowed to associate only on the basis of special arrangements that proclaim their apartness and hence inferiority. What may be hoped for from the benevolent quota is that association of the races —limited to begin with—will allay the fears and other irrationalities on which white prejudice is nurtured. Especially in the young. But only experience will show whether this hope can be sustained. And meanwhile, limited segregation may provide as much nourishment for prejudice as a complete prohibition against association of the races. . . .

THE LEAST DANGEROUS BRANCH 61 (1962). Does the benevolent quota fall within the principle that Bickel earlier stated, namely that practices which "place one of the groups of which our society is constituted in a position of permanent, humiliating inferiority" are forbidden? Is the benevolent quota such a practice? Mr. Bickel apparently thinks that it may not be, for the thrust of his argument is that even though it raises serious Constitutional questions it ought to be given a chance—in the hope that it will help in achieving a truly integrated society. Does all of this involve him in a contradiction?

7. Why, according to Bickel, can there be but few "neutral principles"? Is he arguing for more principles, even though they may not be neutral?

*"The role of principle, when it cannot be the immutable governing rule, is to affect the tendency of policies of expediency. And it is a potent role."* Consider this proposition as you read the remain-

ing materials in this chapter. Ask yourself how it is possible for a rule which does not govern "to affect the tendency of policies of expediency." How does one go about determining when the rule should govern and when a compromise is in order? How does one determine the terms of the compromise? How does one avoid the fear that Bickel's critique of neutral principles is an invitation to cynical implementation of the desires of personal and vested interests?

THOMAS S. KUHN

THE STRUCTURE OF SCIENTIFIC REVOLUTIONS *

In this essay, 'normal science' means research firmly based upon one or more past scientific achievements, achievements that some particular scientific community acknowledges for a time as supplying the foundation for its further practice. Today such achievements are recounted, though seldom in their original form, by science textbooks, elementary and advanced. These textbooks expound the body of accepted theory, illustrate many or all of its successful applications, and compare these applications with exemplary observations and experiments. Before such books became popular early in the nineteenth century (and until even more recently in the newly matured sciences), many of the famous classics of science fulfilled a similar function. Aristotle's *Physica,* Ptolemy's *Almagest,* Newton's *Principia* and *Opticks,* Franklin's *Electricity,* Lavoisier's *Chemistry,* and Lyell's *Geology*—these and many other works served for a time implicitly to define the legitimate problems and methods of a research field for succeeding generations of practitioners. They were able to do so because they shared two essential characteristics. Their achievement was sufficiently unprecedented to attract an enduring group of adherents away from competing modes of scientific activity. Simultaneously, it was sufficiently open-ended to leave all sorts of problems for the redefined group of practitioners to resolve.

Achievements that share these two characteristics I shall henceforth refer to as 'paradigms,' a term that relates closely to 'normal science.' By choosing it, I mean to suggest that some accepted examples of actual scientific practice—examples which include law, theory, application, and instrumentation together—provide models from which spring particular coherent traditions of scientific research. These are the traditions which the historian describes under such rubrics as 'Ptolemaic astronomy' (or 'Copernican'), 'Aristotelian dynamics' (or 'Newtonian'), 'corpuscular optics' (or 'wave optics'), and so on. The study of paradigms, including many that are far more specialized than those named illustratively above, is what mainly prepares the student for membership in the particular scientific community with which he will later practice. Because he there joins men who learned the bases of their field from the same concrete models, his subsequent practice will seldom evoke overt disagreement

* From 10–13, 15, 23–25, 42, 43–44, 46–47 (Phoenix ed. 1964). Copyright 1962    by the University of Chicago Press. Reprinted by permission.

Bishin & Stone, Law, Language & Ethics UCB—48

over fundamentals. Men whose research is based on shared paradigms are committed to the same rules and standards for scientific practice. That commitment and the apparent consensus it produces are prerequisites for normal science, i. e., for the genesis and continuation of a particular research tradition.

Because in this essay the concept of a paradigm will often substitute for a variety of familiar notions, more will need to be said about the reasons for its introduction. Why is the concrete scientific achievement, as a locus of professional commitment, prior to the various concepts, laws, theories, and points of view that may be abstracted from it? In what sense is the shared paradigm a fundamental unit for the student of scientific development, a unit that cannot be fully reduced to logically atomic components which might function in its stead? . . . .

If the historian traces the scientific knowledge of any selected group of related phenomena backward in time, he is likely to encounter some minor variant of a pattern here illustrated from the history of physical optics. Today's physics textbooks tell the student that light is photons, i. e., quantum-mechanical entities that exhibit some characteristics of waves and some of particles. Research proceeds accordingly, or rather according to the more elaborate and mathematical characterization from which this usual verbalization is derived. That characterization of light is, however, scarcely half a century old. Before it was developed by Planck, Einstein, and others early in this century, physics texts taught that light was transverse wave motion, a conception rooted in a paradigm that derived ultimately from the optical writings of Young and Fresnel in the early nineteenth century. Nor was the wave theory the first to be embraced by almost all practitioners of optical science. During the eighteenth century the paradigm for this field was provided by Newton's *Opticks*, which taught that light was material corpuscles. At that time physicists sought evidence, as the early wave theorists had not, of the pressure exerted by light particles impinging on solid bodies.

These transformations of the paradigms of physical optics are scientific revolutions, and the successive transition from one paradigm to another via revolution is the usual developmental pattern of mature science. It is not, however, the pattern characteristic of the period before Newton's work, and that is the contrast that concerns us here. No period between remote antiquity and the end of the seventeenth century exhibited a single generally accepted view about the nature of light. Instead there were a number of competing schools and subschools, most of them espousing one variant or another of Epicurean, Aristotelian, or Platonic theory. One group took light to be particles emanating from material bodies; for another it was a modification of the medium that intervened between the body and the eye; still another explained light in terms of an interaction of the medium with an emanation from the eye; and there were other combinations and modifications besides. Each of the corresponding schools derived strength from its relation to some particular metaphysic, and each emphasized, as paradigmatic observations, the particular cluster of optical phenomena that its own theory could do most to explain. Other observations were dealt with by *ad hoc* elaborations, or they remained as outstanding problems for further research.

At various times all these schools made significant contributions to the body of concepts, phenomena, and techniques from which Newton drew the first nearly uniformly accepted paradigm for physical optics. Any definition of the scientist that excludes at least the more creative members of these various schools will exclude their modern successors as well. Those men were scientists. Yet anyone examining a survey of physical optics before Newton may well conclude that, though the field's practitioners were scientists, the net result of their activity was something less than science. Being able to take no common body of belief for granted, each writer on physical optics felt forced to build his field anew from its foundations. In doing so, his choice of supporting observation and experiment was relatively free, for there was no standard set of methods or of phenomena that every optical writer felt forced to employ and explain. Under these circumstances, the dialogue of the resulting books was often directed as much to the members of other schools as it was to nature. That pattern is not unfamiliar in a number of creative fields today, nor is it incompatible with significant discovery and invention . . . .

. . .

. . . . History suggests that the road to a firm research consensus is extraordinarily arduous.

History also suggests, however, some reasons for the difficulties encountered on that road. In the absence of a paradigm or some candidate for paradigm, all of the facts that could possibly pertain to the development of a given science are likely to seem equally relevant. As a result, early fact-gathering is a far more nearly random activity than the one that subsequent scientific development makes familiar. Furthermore, in the absence of a reason for seeking some particular form of more recondite information, early fact-gathering is usually restricted to the wealth of data that lie ready to hand. The resulting pool of facts contains those accessible to casual observation and experiment together with some of the more esoteric data retrievable from established crafts like medicine, calendar making, and metallurgy. . . .

. . .

. . . . Paradigms gain their status because they are more successful than their competitors in solving a few problems that the group of practitioners has come to recognize as acute. To be more successful is not, however, to be either completely successful with a single problem or notably successful with any large number. The success of a paradigm—whether Aristotle's analysis of motion, Ptolemy's computations of planetary position, Lavoisier's application of the balance, or Maxwell's mathematization of the electromagnetic field—is at the start largely a promise of success discoverable in selected and still incomplete examples. Normal science consists in the actualization of that promise, an actualization achieved by extending the knowledge of those facts that the paradigm displays as particularly revealing, by increasing the extent of the match between those facts and the paradigm's predictions, and by further articulation of the paradigm itself.

Few people who are not actually practitioners of a mature science realize how much mop-up work of this sort a paradigm leaves to be done or quite how fascinating such work can prove in the execution. And these points need to be understood. Mopping-up operations are what engage most scientists throughout their careers. They constitute what I am here calling normal science. Closely examined, whether historically or in the contemporary laboratory, that enterprise seems an attempt to force nature into the preformed and relatively inflexible box that the paradigm supplies. No part of the aim of normal science is to call forth new sorts of phenomena; indeed those that will not fit the box are often not seen at all. Nor do scientists normally aim to invent new theories, and they are often intolerant of those invented by others. Instead, normal-scientific research is directed to the articulation of those phenomena and theories that the paradigm already supplies.

Perhaps these are defects. The areas investigated by normal science are, of course, minuscule; the enterprise now under discussion has drastically restricted vision. But those restrictions, born from confidence in a paradigm, turn out to be essential to the development of science. By focusing attention upon a small range of relatively esoteric problems, the paradigm forces scientists to investigate some part of nature in a detail and depth that would otherwise be unimaginable. And normal science possesses a built-in mechanism that ensures the relaxation of the restrictions that bound research whenever the paradigm from which they derive ceases to function effectively. At that point scientists begin to behave differently, and the nature of their research problems changes. In the interim, however, during the period when the paradigm is successful, the profession will have solved problems that its members could scarcely have imagined and would never have undertaken without commitment to the paradigm. And at least part of that achievement always proves to be permanent.

. . .

. . . . Though there obviously are rules to which all the practitioners of a scientific specialty adhere at a given time, those rules may not by themselves specify all that the practice of those specialists has in common. Normal science is a highly determined activity, but it need not be entirely determined by rules. That is why, at the start of this essay, I introduced shared paradigms rather than shared rules, assumptions, and points of view as the source of coherence for normal research traditions. Rules, I suggest, derive from paradigms, but paradigms can guide research even in the absence of rules.

. . .

The determination of shared paradigms is not . . . the determination of shared rules. That demands a second step and one of a somewhat different kind.  When undertaking it, the historian must compare the community's paradigms with each other and with its current research reports.  In doing so, his object is to discover what isolable elements, explicit or implicit, the members of that community may have *abstracted* from their more global paradigms and deployed as rules in their research.  Anyone who has attempted to describe or analyze the evolution of a particular scientific tradition will necessarily have sought accepted principles and rules of this sort.  Almost certainly, as the preceding section indicates, he will have met with at least partial success.  But, if his experience has been at all like my own, he will have found the search for rules both more difficult and less satisfying than the search for paradigms.  Some of the generalizations he employs to describe the community's shared beliefs will present no problems.  Others, however, including some of those used as illustrations above, will seem a shade too strong.  Phrased in just that way, or in any other way he can imagine, they would almost certainly have been rejected by some members of the group he studies.  Nevertheless, if the coherence of the research tradition is to be understood in terms of rules, some specification of common ground in the corresponding area is needed.  As a result, the search for a body of rules competent to constitute a given normal research tradition becomes a source of continual and deep frustration.

Recognizing that frustration, however, makes it possible to diagnose its source.  Scientists can agree that a Newton, Lavoisier, Maxwell, or Einstein has produced an apparently permanent solution to a group of outstanding problems and still disagree, sometimes without being aware of it, about the particular abstract characteristics that make those solutions permanent.  They can, that is, agree in their *identification* of a paradigm without agreeing on, or even attempting to produce, a full *interpretation* or *rationalization* of it.  Lack of a standard interpretation or of an agreed reduction to rules will not prevent a paradigm from guiding research.  Normal science can be determined in part by the direct inspection of paradigms, a process that is often aided by but does not depend upon the formulation of rules and assumptions.  Indeed, the existence of a paradigm need not even imply that any full set of rules exists.

. . .

. . . . Scientists, it should already be clear, never learn concepts, laws, and theories in the abstract and by themselves.  Instead, these intellectual tools are from the start encountered in a historically and pedagogically prior unit that displays them with and through their applications.  A new theory is always announced together with applications to some concrete range of natural phenomena; without them it would not be even a candidate for acceptance.  After it has been accepted, those same applications or others accompany the theory into the textbooks from which the future practitioner will learn his trade.  They are not there merely as embroidery or even as documentation.  On the contrary, the process of learning a theory depends upon the study of applications, including practice problem-solving both with a pencil and paper and with instruments in the laboratory.  If, for example, the student of Newtonian dynamics ever discovers the meaning of terms like 'force,' 'mass,' 'space,' and 'time,' he does so less from the incomplete though sometimes helpful definitions of his text than by observing and participating in the application of these concepts to problem-solution.

That process of learning by finger exercise or by doing continues throughout the process of professional initiation. As the student proceeds from his freshman course to and through his doctoral dissertation, the problems assigned to him become more complex and less completely precedented. But they continue to be closely modeled on previous achievements as are the problems that normally occupy him during his subsequent independent scientific career. One is at liberty to suppose that somewhere along the way the scientist has intuitively abstracted rules of the game for himself, but there is little reason to believe it. Though many scientists talk easily and well about the particular individual hypotheses that underlie a concrete piece of current research, they are little better than laymen at characterizing the established bases of their field, its legitimate problems and methods. If they have learned such abstractions at all, they show it mainly through their ability to do successful research. That ability can, however, be understood without recourse to hypothetical rules of the game.

### Note: Scientific and Legal Thought

Can you discern any similarities between "normal science" and the day-to-day administration of the law? Consider the way in which students of science come to know their field. Are there any resemblances between the learning of science and the learning of law? Is there anything in law which might correspond to the phenomenon of "paradigms" in scientific research? To what extent do law students learn their rules together with their applications?

Roscoe Pound has observed:

> . . . It is an everyday experience of those who study judicial decisions that the results are usually sound, whether the reasoning from which the results purport to flow is sound or not. The trained intuition of the judge continually leads him to right results for which he is puzzled to give unimpeachable legal reasons.

*The Theory of Judicial Decision,* 36 Harv.L.Rev. 940, 951 (1923). If the phenomena which Pound reports actually do occur, what explanations would you advance to account for it? Would Kuhn's observations be of any help in framing such an explanation? It is an everyday occurrence in the decision of cases that judges will agree not only on the result, but also on the doctrinal authority which decrees that result—with the area of disagreement confined solely to the reasons *why* the conceded authority requires the conceded result? Thus, judges may dispute vehemently over the meaning of the First Amendment while impliedly agreeing that (a) it is the authoritative rule for the case in hand, and (b) it "requires" a particular decision in that case. Is *Rochin* an example of this phenomenon? Note that Frankfurter, Black and Douglas not only agree that (1) the evidence must be excluded, and (2) that the police conduct was unconstitutional, but also (3) that it was the 14th Amendment which had been violated, and, more particularly, (4) the "due process" clause. Is there a point in trying to account for all of this agreement? Or should it be viewed as a coincidence given the disagreement over the reasons why the "due process" clause applied? Is there any reason to believe that the existence of a "due process" clause made any difference in the process by which all nine justices came to the same ultimate conclusion? How, if at all, do Kuhn's observations bear on this question?

Somewhat later you will encounter Dickinson's attempt to distinguish legal from scientific rules and you should ask yourself then whether his conception of science accords with the one Kuhn expresses. First, however, a problem will be posed which in one sense is logically prior to that raised by articulated rules and theories—although it necessarily involves many of the same considerations. If it is not possible, the question might be framed, to justify a judicial—or any other legal—decision by reference to a rule, is there a point in saying anything at all? Apparently Justice Frankfurter thought there was something to be accomplished in *Rochin* by describing the facts and values which determined his decision, even though he explicitly refused to state a rule. Note that Kuhn may offer some support for Frankfurter in this. Normal science, he says, can progress by mere inspection of a paradigm. Rules are not required. Yet how does one "inspect" such a paradigm? How is it made accessible to cognition? Paradigms, you will recall, are scientific achievements. How are these achievements made known to other scientists? One important symbolism for accomplishing this is language, even though it may not take the form of exhaustive definitions which account for the paradigm's nature and function. If this is true in science, it may also be true in law—if we are willing to concede that something akin to paradigms can be found there, too. Can Justice Frankfurter's opinion be viewed as an attempt to describe or invoke a "legal paradigm"? What arguments can you marshall for such a proposition?

## Section Two: The Social and Intellectual Function of the Opinion

*Herbert Wechsler*

### Toward Neutral Principles of Constitutional Law *

.  .  .  .  [There are] two important fields of present interest in which the Court has been decreeing value choices in a way that makes it quite impossible to speak of principled determinations or the statement and evaluation of judicial reasons, since the Court has not disclosed the grounds on which its judgments rest.

* From Principles, Politics and Fundamental Law (1961). Copyright 1961 by the President and Fellows of Harvard College. Reprinted by permission of Harvard University Press.

The first of these involves the sequel to the *Burstyn* case, in which, as you recall, the Court decided that the motion picture is a medium of expression included in the "speech" and "press" to which the safeguards of the first amendment, made applicable to the states by the fourteenth, apply. But *Burstyn* left open, as it was of course obliged to do, the extent of the protection that the movies are accorded, and even the question whether any censorship is valid, involving as it does prior restraint. The judgment rested, and quite properly, upon the vice inherent in suppression based upon a finding that the film involved was "sacrilegious"—with the breadth and vagueness that that term had been accorded in New York. "[W]hether a state may censor motion pictures under a clearly drawn statute designed and applied to prevent the showing of obscene films" was said to be "a very different question" not decided by the Court. In five succeeding cases, decisions sustaining censorship of different films under standards variously framed have been reversed, but only by per curiam decisions. In one of these, in which I should avow I was of counsel, the standard was undoubtedly too vague for any argument upon the merits. I find it hard to think that this was clearly so in all the others. Given the subtlety and difficulty of the problem, the need and opportunity for clarifying explanation, are such unexplained decisions in a new domain of constitutional interpretation consonant with standards of judicial action that the Court or we can possibly defend? I realize that nine men often find it easier to reach agreement on result than upon reasons and that such a difficulty may be posed within this field. Is it not preferable, however, indeed essential, that if this is so the variations of position be disclosed?

The second group of cases to which I shall call attention involves what may be called the progeny of the school-segregation ruling of 1954. Here again the Court has written on the merits of the constitutional issue posed by state segregation only once; its subsequent opinions on the form of the decree and the defiance in Arkansas deal, of course, with other matters. The original opinion, you recall, was firmly focused on state segregation in the public schools, its reasoning accorded import to the nature of the educational process, and its conclusion was that separate educational facilities are "inherently unequal."

What shall we think then of the Court's extension of the ruling to other public facilities, such as public transportation, parks, golf courses, bath houses, and beaches, which no one is obliged to use— by per curiam decisions? That these situations present a weaker case against state segregation is not, of course, what I am saying. I am saying that the question whether it is stronger, weaker, or of equal weight appears to me to call for principled decision. I do not know, and I submit you cannot know, whether the per curiam affirmance in the *Dawson* case, involving public bath houses and beaches, embraced the broad opinion of the circuit court that all state-enforced racial segregation is invalid or approved only its immediate result and, if the latter, on what ground. Is this "process of law," to borrow the words Professor Brown has used so pointedly in writing of such unexplained decisions upon matters far more technical—the process that alone affords the Court its title and its duty to adjudicate a claim that state action is repugnant to the Constitution?

NOTES AND QUESTIONS

1. Is the fact that unexplained decisions occur "in a new domain of constitutional interpretation" a mitigation or an aggravation of the vice inherent in deciding cases without opinions? Could it be argued that it is in the "new domain" that judges are least likely to be articulate and certain of the grounds of decision? How would such an argument run? On what view of language and thought would it be based? If a judge is certain of his result, but not of his reason, should he abandon his result because he cannot state that reason? Cassirer says that all "thought must prove itself in language". Does this support Wechsler's position? Consider the following from Koestler:

> . . . . it is . . . . true that ideas are often airy nothings until they crystallize into verbal concepts and acquire tangible shape. . . . [B]ut that does not justify the fallacy of identifying language with thought and of denying the importance of non-verbal images and symbols, particularly in the creative thinking of artists and scientists.
> . . . Often some promising intuition is nipped in the bud by prematurely exposing it to the acid bath of verbal definitions; others may never develop without such verbal exposure.

THE GHOST IN THE MACHINE 39–40 (1968). Is a "new domain" of constitutional law one in which lawyers and judges, like artists and scientists, must engage in "creative thinking"? If so, ought the courts to stay out of such domains precisely because Wechsler's requirements cannot be fulfilled? If this presents a dilemma does Frankfurter's approach help resolve it?

2. The view that written opinions are simply rationalizations of decisions reached on other, non-legal, grounds tends naturally to deemphasize the importance of an articulated judicial justification. The following excerpts seek to show that the tradition of the judicial opinion may be explicable in terms of elemental social, intellectual and legal functions—even though one can never depend on such a writing to unequivocally tell us what the law *is*. These functions, it is suggested, are precisely the functions that language generally serves and thus the inability to perceive their importance or character stems ultimately from a mistaken view of the nature of language and its relation to both social and intellectual organization.

As you read the material in this section try to enumerate the legitimate fears which might be occasioned by the absence of a written or verbal justification for particular action? See if the readings help to explain why language is in an importance sense the dominant or primary symbolism of the law. Do they help you see if there is any necessary connection between what Wechsler calls "process of law" and linguistic symbolization? Consider what is special about the symbolism of language that might make it particularly useful in the organization of people.  In this regard, recall some of the materials in Chapter 8(2)(B).

## JOHN LOCKE

### AN ESSAY CONCERNING HUMAN UNDERSTANDING *

1.   Man though he have great variety of thoughts, and such from which others as well as himself might receive profit and delight; yet they are all within his own breast, invisible and hidden from others, nor can of themselves be made to appear.  The comfort and advantage of society not being to be had without communication of thoughts, it was necessary that man should find out some external sensible signs, whereof those invisible ideas, which his thoughts are made up of, might be made known to others.  For this purpose nothing was so fit, either for plenty or quickness, as those articulate sounds, which with so much ease and variety he found himself able to make.  Thus we may conceive how *words*, which were by nature so well adapted to that purpose, came to be made use of by men as the signs of their ideas; not by any natural connexion that there is between particular articulate sounds and certain ideas, for then there would be but one language amongst all men; but by a voluntary imposition, whereby such a word is made arbitrarily the mark of such an idea.  The use, then, of words, is to be sensible marks of ideas; and the ideas they stand for are their proper and immediate signification.

2.   The use men have of these marks being either to record their own thoughts, for the assistance of their own memory; or, as it were, to bring out their ideas, and lay them before the view of others: words, in their primary or immediate signification, stand for nothing but *the ideas in the mind of him that uses them*, how imperfectly soever or carelessly those ideas are collected from the things which they are supposed to represent.  When a man speaks to another, it is that he may be understood: and the end of speech is, that those sounds, as marks, may make known his ideas to the hearer.  .  .  .

### NOTES AND QUESTIONS

1.   In Locke's observations we find one of the clearer statements of a conception which seems to recur constantly in everyday thought, although it is a conception to which everyday thought is not always loyal.  The conception is that thought is something different from language and that language serves simply as a sign or symbol of this other phenomenon.  What are the theoretical consequences of such a conception?  To what extent do the following readings moot it?  Is there any way of avoiding the Lockeian position without adopting the Wittgensteinian position of the TRACTATUS LOGICO-PHILOSOPHICUS?

2.   GENESIS reports that after God had finished his labors on the sixth day he looked upon his work and "saw that it was good."  Why was it necessary for God to implement his intention before he

* From v. II, 8–9 (A. Fraser ed. Dover ed. 1959).

knew that it was satisfactory? Is this consistent with the implications of Locke's position? Recall the quotation from Koestler above.

3. What is the bearing of the following remarks on Locke's position:

> [The] trick of talking to oneself in silence is acquired neither quickly nor without effort; and it is a necessary condition of our acquiring it that we should have previously learned to talk intelligently aloud and have heard and understood other people doing so. Keeping our thoughts to ourselves is a sophisticated accomplishment. It was not until the Middle Ages that people learned to read without reading aloud. Similarly a boy has to learn to read aloud before he learns to read under his breath, and to prattle aloud before he prattles to himself. Yet many theorists have supposed that the silence in which most of us have learned to think is a defining property of thought. Plato said that in thinking the soul is talking to itself. But silence, though often convenient, is inessential, as is the restriction of the audience to one recipient.

G. RYLE, THE CONCEPT OF MIND 27 (1949).

*SAMUEL BUTLER*

## THOUGHT AND LANGUAGE *

As regards our being able to think and reason without words, the Duke of Argyll has put the matter as soundly as I have yet seen it stated. "It seems to me," he wrote, "quite certain that we can and do constantly think of things without thinking of any sound or word as designating them. Language seems to me to be necessary for the progress of thought, but not at all for the mere act of thinking. It is a product of thought, an expression of it, a vehicle for the communication of it, and an embodiment which is essential to its growth and continuity; but it seems to me altogether erroneous to regard it as an inseparable part of cogitation."

The following passages, again, are quoted from Sir William Hamilton in Professor Max Muller's own book, with so much approval as to lead one to suppose that the differences between himself and his opponents are in reality less than he believes them to be.

"Language," says Sir W. Hamilton, "is the attribution of signs to our cognitions of things. But as a cognition must have already been there before it could receive a sign, consequently that knowledge which is denoted by the formation and application of a word must have preceded the symbol that denotes it. A sign, however, is necessary to give stability to our intellectual progress—to establish each step in our advance as a new starting-point for our advance to another

---

\* From The Importance of Language 34–
35 (M. Black ed. Cornell Paperback
ed. 1969).

beyond. A country may be overrun by an armed host, but it is only conquered by the establishment of fortresses. Words are the fortnesses of thought. They enable us to realize our dominion over what we have already overrun in thought; to make every intellectual conquest the base of operations for others still beyond."

"This," says Professor Max Muller, "is a most happy illustration," and he proceeds to quote the following, also from Sir William Hamilton, which he declares to be even happier still.

"You have all heard," says Sir William Hamilton, "of the process of tunnelling through a sandbank. In this operation it is impossible to succeed unless every foot, nay, almost every inch of our progress be secured by an arch of masonry before we attempted the excavation of another. Now language is to the mind precisely what the arch is to the tunnel. The power of thinking and the power of excavation are not dependent on the words in the one case or on the mason-work in the other; but without these subsidiaries neither could be carried on beyond its rudimentary commencement. Though, therefore, we allow that every movement forward in language must be determined by an antecedent movement forward in thought, still, unless thought be accompanied at each point of its evolutions by a corresponding evolution of language, its further development is arrested."

## QUESTIONS

Can you make an argument based on the very material quoted by Butler that thought is dependent on language? Or that the process of thought necessarily involves the use of language?

*ERNST CASSIRER*

## AN ESSAY ON MAN *

. . . . In what . . . consists that fundamental difference between the mental attitude which we may ascribe to a speechless creature—a human being before the acquisition of speech or an animal—and that other frame of mind which characterizes an adult who has fully mastered his mother tongue?

Curiously enough it is easier to answer this question on the basis of abnormal instances of speech development. Our consideration of the cases of Helen Keller and Laura Bridgman illustrated the fact that with the first understanding of the symbolism of speech a real revolution takes place in the life of the child. From this point on his whole personal and intellectual life assumes an entirely new shape. Roughly speaking, this change may be described by saying that the child passes from a more subjective state to an objective state, from a merely emotional attitude to a theoretical attitude. The same change may be noted in the life of every normal child, though in a much less spectacular way. The child himself has a clear sense of the significance of the new instrument for his mental development. He is not

* From 131–133 (1944). Reprinted with
permission of Yale University Press.

satisfied with being taught in a purely receptive manner but takes an active share in the process of speech which is at the same time a process of progressive objectification. The teachers of Helen Keller and Laura Bridgman have told us with what eagerness and impatience both children, once they had understood the use of names, continued to ask for the particular names of all the objects in their environment. This, too, is a general feature in the normal development of speech. "By the beginning of the twenty-third month," says D. R. Major, "the child had developed a mania for going about naming things, as if to tell others their names, or to call our attention to the things he was examining. He would look at, point toward, or put his hand on an article, speak its name, then look at his companions." Such an attitude would not be understandable were it not for the fact that the name, in the mental growth of the child, has a function of the first importance to perform. If a child when learning to talk had simply to learn a certain vocabulary, if he only had to impress on his mind and memory a great mass of artificial and arbitrary sounds, this would be a purely mechanical process. It would be very laborious and tiresome, and would require too great conscious effort for the child to make without a certain reluctance since what he is expected to do would be entirely disconnected from actual biological needs. The "hunger for names" which at a certain age appears in every normal child and which has been described by all students of child psychology proves the contrary. It reminds us that we are here confronted with a quite different problem. By learning to name things a child does not simply add a list of artificial signs to his previous knowledge of ready-made empirical objects. He learns rather to form the concepts of those objects, to come to terms with the objective world. Henceforth the child stands on firmer ground. His vague, uncertain, fluctuating perceptions and his dim feelings begin to assume a new shape. They may be said to crystallize around the name as a fixed center, a focus of thought. Without the help of the name every new advance made in the process of objectification would always run the risk of being lost again in the next moment. The first names of which a child makes conscious use may be compared to a stick by the aid of which a blind man gropes his way. And language, taken as a whole, becomes the gateway to a new world. All progress here opens a new perspective and widens and enriches our concrete experience. Eagerness and enthusiasm to talk do not originate in a mere desire for learning or using names; they mark the desire for the detection and conquest of an objective world.

## Note

In addition to Cassirer, consider the following:

Watch a young child that is just learning to speak play with a toy; he says the name of the object, e. g.: "Horsey! horsey! horsey!" over and over again, looks at the object, moves it, always saying the name to himself or to the world at large. It is quite a time before he talks to anyone in particular; he talks first of all to himself. This is his way of forming and fixing the *conception* of the object in his mind, and around this conception all his knowledge of it grows. *Names* are the essence of language; for the name is what abstracts the conception of the horse from the horse itself, and lets the mere idea recur at the speaking of the name. This permits the conception gathered from one horse experience to be exemplified again by another instance of a horse, so that the notion embodied in the name is a general notion.

Langer, *The Lord of Creation*, 29 Fortune, No. 1, pp. 143–144 (1944).*

*ALDOUS HUXLEY*

## WORDS AND THEIR MEANINGS **

Human behavior as we know it became possible only with the establishment of relatively stable systems of relationships between things and events on the one hand and words on the other. In societies where no such relationship has been established, that is to say, where there is no language, behavior is nonhuman. Necessarily so; for language makes it possible for men to build up the social heritage of accumulated skill, knowledge and wisdom, thanks to which it is possible for us to profit by the experiences of past generations, as though they were our own. There may be geniuses among the gorillas; but since gorillas have no conceptual language, the thoughts and achievements of these geniuses cannot be recorded and so are lost to simian posterity. In those limited fields of activity where some form of progress is possible, words permit of progress being made.

Nor is this all. The existence of language permits human beings to behave with a degree of purposefulness, perseverance and consistency unknown among the other mammals and comparable only to the purposefulness, perseverance and consistency of insects acting under the compulsive force of instinct. Every instant in the life, say, of a cat or a monkey tends to be irrelevant to every other instant. Such creatures are the victims of their moods. Each impulse as it makes itself felt carries the animal away completely. Thus, the urge to fight will suddenly be interrupted by the urge to eat; the all-absorbing passion of love will be displaced in the twinkling of an eye by a no less absorbing passion to search for fleas. The consistency of human behavior, such as it is, is due entirely to the fact that men have formulated their desires, and subsequently rationalized them, in terms of words. The verbal formulation of a desire will cause a man to go on pressing towards his goal, even when the desire itself lies dormant. Similarly, the rationalization of his desire in terms of some theological or philosophical system will convince him that he does well to persevere in this way  .   .    .    .

---

* Reprinted by permission.                ** From 13–16 (1940). Reprinted with
permission of Laura Archera Huxley.

JOSEPH CHURCH

## LANGUAGE AND THE DISCOVERY OF REALITY *

. . . . . In our society, the children of symbol-minded parents quickly pick up styles of analytical, logical, playful, critical language and begin the slow and painful but rewarding venture of working and reworking their experience symbolically until they have achieved rational thought. In so doing, the individual carries a step further the evolutionary internalization of the environment: he internalizes it symbolically and can carry his experience around with him, since every act of thematization increases his ability to recreate, by his own action, any part of his known reality.

Still, we must understand how thematization transforms the appearance of reality. The very act of naming designates an object or an attribute or a relationship as a restricted region of space. But it is in the explication of experience—in saying something about it— that it becomes a part of the schematic framework in which we live. In verbalizing reality, we make explicit the properties of and the connections between things, properties and connections which previously were only dynamistically implicit or wholly hidden. Once language has called our attention—has mobilized us—to previously latent features of the landscape, they remain permanently accessible to us. Needless to say, the child does not do all his own thematizing. Adults tell him about things and explain things to him. In addition, they impart typical verbal operations which he takes over and uses for himself: making comparisons, passing judgment, pretending the contrary of what is so, narration, generalizing, exaggeration, wishing, classification, hypothesizing, and so forth.

Thematic learning leads us, of course, not only to facts but to general principles and perspectives. The child is unimpressed by monetary worth, by antiquity, by esthetic values, by high estate, and so forth. The adult may be excessively impressed by all of these. In any event, our way of looking at things shifts, sometimes abruptly and sometimes cumulatively, and the appearance of things shifts accordingly. To the child, the department-store Santa Claus seems a majestic figure compounded of jollity, abundant generosity, stern justice, omniscience and omnipotence, and so on. To the adult, the same Santa Claus looks seedy, meretricious, pathetic, and altogether implausible. Similarly, when the adult pays a sentimental visit, after a long absence, to the scenes of his childhood, he finds that memory and present perception are oddly out of joint. Our present perceptual experience is subordinated to a whole conception of reality, a conception built up out of countless concrete events, verbalizations, and verbalizations about verbalizations, whereby successive environments are woven into a world.

* From 107–107 (Vintage ed. 1961). Reprinted with permission of Joseph Church.

The way that perception changes with knowledge can be illustrated by what happens when we solve a problem. Figure 2 shows a square moat, the same width on all four sides. For purposes of the problem, the moat is infinitely deep. The task is to make a usable bridge across the moat. The *only* materials are two boards, each just shorter than the width of the moat. Once this problem has been solved, the moat will never look the same again.

What we are saying is that full consciousness of reality is possible only to the extent that it has been verbalized. We must remember that realistic-phenomenalistic-dynamistic experience is without depth, without wonder, and without subtlety, and that the world becomes marvelous only as we grasp its complexities.

### ALFRED NORTH WHITEHEAD

## MODES OF THOUGHT *

Language has two functions. It is converse with another, and it is converse with oneself. The latter function is too often overlooked, so we will consider it first. Language is expression from one's past into one's present. It is the reproduction in the present of sensa which have intimate association with the realities of the past. Thus the experience of the past is rendered distinct in the present, with a distinctness borrowed from the well-defined sensa. In this way, an articulated memory is the gift of language, considered as an expression from oneself in the past to oneself in the present.

Again by the aid of a common language, the fragmentary past experiences of the auditor, as enshrined in words, can be recombined into a novel imaginative experience by the reception of the coherent sentences of the speaker. Thus in both functions of language the immediate imaginative experience is enormously increased, and is stamped with a sense of realization, or of possible realization.

. . .

The essense of language is that it utilizes those elements in experience most easily abstracted for conscious entertainment, and most easily reproduced in experience. By the long usage of humanity, these elements are associated with their meanings which embrace a large variety of human experiences. Each language embalms an historic tradition. Each language is the civilization of expression in the social systems which use it. Language is the systematization of expression.

Of all the ways of expressing thought, beyond question language is the most important. . . .

. . . . Apart from language, the retention of thought, the easy recall of thought, the interweaving of thought into higher complexity, the communication of thought, are all gravely limited. Human civilization is an outgrowth of language, and language is the

* From 46, 48, 49, 57 (Capricorn ed. 1958). Copyright 1938 by The Macmillan Company, renewed 1966 by T. North Whitehead. Reprinted by permission of The Macmillan Company.

product of advancing civilization.  Freedom of thought is made possible by language: we are thereby released from complete bondage to the immediacies of mood and circumstance.  It is no accident that the Athenians from whom we derive our Western notions of freedom enjoyed the use of a language supreme for its delicate variety.

.  .  .

.  .  .  .  the mentality of mankind and the language of mankind created each other.  If we like to assume the rise of language as a given fact, then it is not going too far to say that the souls of men are the gift from language to mankind.

The account of the sixth day should be written, He gave them speech, and they became souls.

## C. WRIGHT MILLS

### LANGUAGE, LOGIC AND CULTURE *

The function of words is the mediation of social behavior, and their meanings are dependent upon this social and behavioral function. Semantical changes are surrogates and foci of cultural conflicts and group behavior.  Because language functions in the organization and control of behavior patterns, these patterns are determinants of the meanings in a language.  Words carry meanings by virtue of dominant interpretations placed upon them by social behavior.  Interpretations or meanings spring from the habitual modes of behavior which pivot upon symbols.  Such social patterns of behavior constitute the meanings of the symbols.  Nonlinguistic behaviors are guided or manipulated by linguistic materials, and language is the ubiquitous string in the web of patterned human behavior.

We can view language functionally as a system of social control.  A symbol, a recurrent language form, gains its status as a symbol, an event with meaning, because it produces a similar response from both the utterer and the hearer.  Communication must set up common modes of response in order to be communication; the meaning of language is the common social behavior evoked by it.  Symbols are the "directing pivots" of social behaviors.  They are also the indispensable condition of human mentality.  The meanings of words are formed and sustained by the interactions of human collectivities, and thought is the manipulation of such meanings.  Mind is the interplay of the organism with social situations mediated by symbols. The patterns of social behavior with their "cultural drifts," values, and political orientations extend a control over thought by means of language.  It is only by utilizing the symbols common to his group that a thinker can think and communicate.  Language, socially built and maintained, embodies implicit exhortations and social evaluations.  By acquiring the categories of a language, we acquire the structured

* From Power, Politics and People 432–433, 434–435 (I. Horowitz ed. Ballantine ed. 1963).  Originally published in IV Amer. Soc. Rev. No. 5 (Oct. 1939).  Reprinted by permission of The American Sociological Association.

"ways" of a group, and along with the language, the value-implicates of those "ways." Our behavior and perception, our logic and thought, come within the control of a system of language. Along with language, we acquire a set of social norms and values. A vocabulary is not merely a string of words; immanent within it are societal textures— institutional and political coordinates. Back of a vocabulary lie sets of collective action.

.  .  .

We must recognize the priority of a system of meanings to a thinker. Thinking influences language very little, but thought, as Malinowski has indicated, "having to borrow from (social) action its tool, is largely influenced thereby." No thinker can assign arbitrary meanings to his terms and be understood. Meaning is antecedently *given;* it is a collective "creation." In manipulating a set of socially given symbols, thought is itself manipulated. Symbols are impersonal and imperative determinants of thought because they manifest collective purposes and evaluations. New nuances of meaning which a thinker may give to words are, of course, socially significant in themselves; but such "new" meanings must in their definition draw upon the meanings and organization of collectively established words in order that they may be understood, and they are conditioned thereby; and so is the acceptance and/or rejection of them by others.

Here, again, the thinker is "circumscribed" by his audience because, in order to communicate, to be understood, he must "give" symbols such meanings that they call out the same responses in his audience as they do in himself. The process of "externalizing" his thought in language is thus, by virtue of the commonness essential to meaning, under the control of the audience. Socialization is accompanied by revision of meaning. Seldom do identical interpretations obtain. Writings get reinterpreted as they are diffused across audiences with different nuances of meanings. We call the tendency to telescope (by variations of interpretation) the meaning of concepts into a given set of social habits, ethnocentricism of meaning. Functionally, *i. e.*, as far as communication obtains, the reader is a factor determining what the thinker writes.

*EDWARD STEVENS ROBINSON*

LAW AND THE LAWYERS *

.  .  .  .  "thought is reorganized and mind is reconstituted through the instrumentality of linguistic process into human reason and logical structure." The fact that the mental attitudes of Abraham Lincoln toward the Civil War had not previously been stated just as he stated them in the Gettysburg Address by no means indicates that he was representing facts that were ineffective elements in his

* From 173–174, 175–178 (1935). Reprinted with permission of the estate of Edward Stevens Robinson.

conduct. A man has come to a general decision with nothing but fleeting ideas and attitudes present in the immediate deliberative consciousness. For the purposes of communication, or perhaps for his personal satisfaction, he feels the need of exploring his own mind in respect to that decision. And so he talks or writes about the subject and in this talking and writing he discovers why he came to think as he did. There is no absolute guarantee that this verbal exploration will reveal the whole truth or that it will avoid the fabrication of satisfying fictions. On the other hand, there is every reason to believe that it will clarify factors that were only implicitly present in the original process of inarticulate deliberation. Whether, in his explicit statement of his reasons for concluding thus and so, a man gives a largely accurate or a largely fictitious account of himself is another one of those matters of fact. They are not always easy to settle, but certainly they can never be settled by the loose, lazy, and frequently cynical use of such terms as *unconscious complexes* and *rationalization*.

The possibility of a man discovering ideas and motives simply because he is impelled to talk about them has excellent illustration in many of those psychogenic disorders known as the psychoneuroses.

. . . .

. . . .

The situation is similar in respect to those conclusions ordinarily called intellectual. We present an economist with the question as to whether the business cycle has turned. He concludes after a merely momentary hesitation that it has. Of course he may be relying upon a conclusion that has already been thoroughly thought out, but suppose that we are the first to force him to make up his mind upon this question, and suppose that after he has given us his verdict we ask him why he thinks so. He will immediately begin an exploration of his own information and conceptions which may explain his intellectual result. In that process he may think of a wide variety of *reasons* backing his conclusion, many of which were functionally present in his mental attitude toward this problem even if they did not rise to conscious thought prior to the articulation of his judgment. Or turn back to that earlier and simpler example whether dogs fly. At once he answers, "No" without being aware of any of the considerations entering into the determination of that answer. Yet such considerations may be found after the fact and they are not all post-rationalizations.

In earlier pages we examined the prevalent theory that formal discourse is never more than a disguise for deep-seated impulses. If this were true, judicial opinions would hold no direct evidence of the psychological make-up of the judge. But psychologists are becoming increasingly suspicious of the instincts and urges which are supposed to be the underlying reality of overt behavior. Such instincts and urges remind us too much of the natural man of earlier political theory. There are also grounds for suspecting the reality of class prejudice and many other goblins that are assumed to be the moving spirits back of judicial discourse. We would not take such discourse at its face value, but it is at all times necessary to realize that the mere establishment of logical congruence between a judicial argument and some large division of public interest does not justify the conclusion that the utterance is a merely superficial symptom of the more general underlying trend.

We should also recall in this connection, that though the utterance of an argument in favor of a certain course of thought or action may at first be an ineffective element in the total dynamic pattern of a deliberation, such arguments soon become deepset habits. The idea that is at first added to an argument simply as a kind of pious gesture frequently becomes a powerful motive in the mind of him who has employed it. What the judge himself recognizes as mere dicta may, by virtue of the fact that they are expressed, gradually increase in apparent relevance until they become real determinants of a later decision.

. . .

While the expressed opinion of a judge may add arguments that were not present in that private deliberation by means of which he first came to his conclusion, these new ideas frequently perform a direct psychological function. When one threads one's way through a host of facts and principles to a final decision one seeks not only to arrive at a decision, but also to attain conviction both for oneself and for all others who may be concerned. The concept of rationalization ordinarily implies that the actual, motivating influences of thought are being distorted into acceptable form, but these new arguments brought forward in the search for personal and social conviction may not distort anything. In the struggle for convicting expression the judge may discover notions which, though they did not influence him in his preliminary thinking, actually do so now. The jurist finds himself mentally hemmed in by formal doctrines that seem to force him to an inhumane decision. In such a case he sees clearly what his decision should be but he feels that he must find a way to believe in that decision.

In many instances a happy word or phrase may be achieved which is more than mere rhetoric; it may actually constitute a discovery of fact. "The last clear chance," "the imminent danger," "the attractive nuisance" are more than metaphors. When first employed they probably came out of the struggle for conviction rather than out of the primary struggle for decision, but they nevertheless raised into prominence obviously relevant facts. . . . "Metaphors in law are to be narrowly watched, for starting as devices to liberate thought, they end often by enslaving it." But the criticism cannot be justified on the general grounds that the phrase is old. Ancient, half-forgotten words may bring to view facts crucial to a modern problem.

. . .

## QUESTIONS

To what extent does Robinson retain the conception of the relation between thought and language expressed by Locke? To what extent does he abandon that conception? See if you can support your answers by references to his specific observations?

## Section Three:  Rules, Paradigms
## And Working Hypotheses

*Karl N. Llewellyn*

### The Common Law Tradition *

. . . .  The wise place to search thoroughly for what is a right and fair solution is the *recurrent problem-situation* of which the instant case is *typical*.  For in the first place this presses, this drives, toward formulating a solving and *guiding rule*; and to address oneself to the rule side of the puzzle is of necessity both to look back upon the heritage of doctrine and also to look forward into prospective consequences and prospective further problems—and to account to each.  In that work, the tang of the case at bar gives feel and flavor, and stimulates the imagination; but the immediate equities fall into a wider, paler frame which renders it much easier both to feel and to see how much and what parts of them are typical and so are proper shapers of policy, how much and what part on the other hand is too individual for legal cognizance or appeals rather to sentimentality than to the sensitivity and sense proper to a legal-governmental scheme.  It is not to appellate courts that our polity commits the pardoning power, nor yet the dispensing power, to be exercised along any lines which cannot be put into a form significantly general.

It seems to me obvious at sight that this order of approach to the problem of deciding an appellate case *must* materially raise the level of reckonability, make results more even, make the operating factors easier to foresee and forefeel, make the ways of handling prior doctrine stand forth, make the new formulations so reached increase in adequacy both of content and of phrasing.  It seems to me no less obvious at sight that this same order of approach *must* at the same time raise the level of wisdom of result.  . . .

### Questions

Would an analogy be proper between Llewellyn's "recurrent problem-situation" and Kuhn's "paradigms"?  Do these notions have anything in common?  Would the notion of a "recurrent problem-situation" have a place in cases involving the interpretation of a statute?

---

\* From 43–44 (1960).  Reprinted with permission of the estate of Karl N. Llewellyn.

JOHN DICKINSON

## LEGAL RULES: THEIR FUNCTION IN THE PROCESS OF DECISION *

The reason why the sceptical school so strongly object to the fact that courts in reaching their decisions employ rules which are stamped as authoritative appears to be primarily because this method is not followed by modern thought in other fields than the adjudication of legal controversies, and particularly because it is not followed in scientific thinking. The modern scientist when called upon to solve a problem does not feel obliged to reason from any particular propositions because they bear the *imprimatur* of authority. Time was, in the history of science, when the contrary was true; when the scientist felt bound to reach conclusions, irrespective of what the facts might show, which were in accordance with settled and authoritative propositions [2] in the same way that a judge feels bound to reach his decision of a case in accordance with settled legal rules. It is clear that in the case of science the abandonment of this procedure was essential to progress, and that so long as it persisted it made any real science impossible. Under the influence of analogy progressive jurists assume that what has been good for science must be good also for law, and that the abandonment of reasoning from legal rules will make possible a corresponding advance in the administration of justice. This conclusion involves failure to note the difference between the objectives of scientific thinking and the nature of the problems to which it addresses itself, as contrasted with the judicial thinking which is directed toward deciding litigated controversies in accordance with law. The distinction is fundamental. It needs to be elaborated in view of the fact that most of the attention which has recently been given to questions connected with human thought-processes has been in relation to scientific thinking, and that conclusions reached in connection with scientific thinking have been unreflectingly transferred and applied to judicial thinking.

Some of the confusion between scientific thinking and the judicial thinking which is directed towards deciding controversies has no doubt been promoted by the insistence of Dewey and his followers that the objective of scientific thought is action,—is to inform human beings what to do. Clearly the objective of judicial thinking is also action, in the sense that it aims to inform the judge how to act with reference to the case before him. From this point of view the objectives of the two types of thought seem superficially the same. But on analysis there becomes apparent an essential difference which was

---

* From 79 U.Pa.L.Rev. 833, 858–862 (1931). Reprinted with permission of the University of Pennsylvania Law Review.

2. An interesting illustration of this attitude is the story recounted by Myerson (L'Explication Dans Les Sciences, V. I, 119) of Father Scheiner who reported his discovery of sun-spots to the provincial of his order and was told by the latter that such a thing could not be. "I have read," said the latter, "my entire Aristotle several times and I can assure you that I never found there anything of the sort. Go, my Son, calm yourself and be sure that it is defects in your lenses or in your eyes which you take for spots in the sun." [Footnote in original.]

set in clearer relief by the older conception of scientific thinking. According to the older form of statement, the object of scientific thinking is not to inform an actor how to act, but rather to describe what will happen if a given situation is left undisturbed, or is disturbed in a particular way. Dewey's conception does not affect the validity of this conception,—it merely adds to it by emphasizing why men may wish to know what will happen. Since it is true that men are dominantly interested in what will happen because they may wish to adapt their conduct to the future situation, it is to this extent true that men's ultimate interest in action stimulates and to a certain exent may be said to account for scientific thought. It remains true, however, that scientific thought itself is not directly concerned, and indeed, so far as it is scientific, is not concerned at all, with how men may choose to act in view of the situation disclosed by science; it stops with disclosing the situation.

The aim of science may therefore still be accurately described as discovery. The scientific procedure of discovery rests on the assumption that, given identical conditions, what has happened once will happen invariably. Scientific thought, therefore, concerns itself with analyzing and classifying the elements of given fact-situations and determining their relations to one another for the purpose of acquiring ability to predict the relations between these elements if recurring in a future situation. This procedure involves the same basic thought-processes which are also involved in the procedure of judicial thinking,—the isolation of identities, their formulation in general propositions, and the application of these propositions to specific situations. Here, however, the resemblance ends.[3] The aim of science being discovery, its concern with its general formulations is primarily to test them for their conformity to future situations. The interest of the scientist in a scientific "law" is to determine the degree of accuracy with which it turns out to describe a future case, and if possible to supersede it with a new generalization which will make possible a description having a higher degree of accuracy. In a sense therefore the generalization is created with the idea of being

---

**3.** Of course, in cases when there is doubt as to what the rule of law *is*, then under a system of law which adopts the doctrine of precedent it is necessary to "discover" the rule from past adjudications. The method of doing this seemed to Hammond and Bishop, and apparently still seems to Llewellyn and Cook, the same method as that whereby scientific laws are discovered. Legal rules seem to Llewellyn discoveries of what "is". Thus he writes: "Real rules . . . are descriptive, not prescriptive, except insofar as there may be occasionally implied that the courts ought to continue in their practices. Real rules, if I had my way with words, would by legal scientists be called the practices of the courts, and not rules at all. . . . Factual terms. No more. . . . They are on the level of *isness* and not of *oughtness*. . . . Their intent and effort is to describe." . . . Llewellyn, *op. cit. supra* note 6, at 448. It is important to note, however, that a legal rule, even though derived by generalization from what has been done, is not a rule of "isness" because it either may or may not be applied in the next case, *i. e.*, the case for which the rule is sought, depending on the volition of the judge. There is thus no possibility as in the case of a scientific rule of testing the "correctness" of the rule by seeing whether the instant case conforms to it. In other words the uniformity between cases is an imitated, not a scientific or physically necessitated, uniformity.

overthrown; it is created with specific understanding that its application to future cases shall be for the purpose of testing its validity. Each specific case thus controls the generalization; each future happening supplies a standard to which a scientific proposition must conform at the risk of being rejected for some other proposition which will state the observed facts more closely.

This whole procedure is radically different in intent and method from the kind of reasoning which is directed toward deciding controversies by the application of law. Once more the distinction can best be explained by recourse to older conceptions, in this instance the long-established distinction between scientific and so-called "normative" thinking. The decision of controversies by recourse to authoritative rules is an instance of normative thinking. The goal of normative thinking is not discovery; the judge who is called on to decide whether or not to award damages to a plaintiff is not, like the scientist, engaged in the discovery of new truth, or in adding to the sum total of human knowledge. The judge does not employ the case before him as a means of testing the validity of the rules which he employs in reasoning towards his decision. The whole theory of decision according to law is that the rules are to govern the case, and not, like scientific laws, to be governed by it. Normative thinking rests on the assumption that it is socially beneficial that action shall be taken which is in accordance with a rule primarily because it is in conformity to observed fact, and the reason for applying the rule raises a different issue which is not for the moment in question.

In the case of a scientific rule, the problem of applying the rule and the problem of testing its "correctness" are substantially one and the same problem, since "correctness" means only conformity to observed fact and the reason for applying the rule in scientific experiment is primarily to determine its conformity to fact. In the case of a normative rule, on the other hand, the problems are distinct. The reason for applying the rule is not directly or immediately concerned with determining its "correctness". This is not the task of ordinary judicial thinking, which is concerned with deciding in accordance with rules because they happen to be the established rules, but is the task of what, for the purpose of emphasizing the distinction, may be called "constructive juristic thought," which is concerned with the criticism and formulation of rules. This constructive thought must at one time or another be performed by practically all judges in dealing with difficult or unprovided cases,—*i. e.*, cases not falling clearly under an existing rule; but it does not form the principal function of *nisi prius* judges, or even of appellate courts except in connection with new and difficult cases. It is, however, an essential factor in the judicial process, and as such can only be understood in connection and contrast with the more usual type of normative thinking which is concerned with the application of rules.

The term "correctness" has a different meaning when applied to a scientific and to a normative rule. Normative rules, which are statements that in certain kinds of fact-situations certain action is to be taken, are not statements that any fact-situations will occur, and therefore cannot be tested by conformity between actual and predicted occurrence. What we mean by saying that they are correct is that the action which they prescribe will produce a result which for one reason or another we regard as the result that ought to be produced in contrast with other results which are physically capable of being produced. To determine the correctness of a rule in this sense, a double process is necessary. There must first be determined the fact-consequences which the application of the rule can be expected to produce; secondly there must be determined whether this result should be regarded as desirable.

### NOTES AND QUESTIONS

1.   Would Kuhn agree that the scientist no longer feels "bound to reach conclusions, irrespective of what the facts might show, which" are "in accordance with settled and authoritative propositions"? Would Kuhn agree that "the abandonment of this procedure was essential to progress, and so long as it persisted it made any real science impossible"?

2.   Is it satisfactory to say that all science is interested in is "disclosing the situation" or seeing what will happen? Is Dickinson taking adequate account of the scientist's wish to know in order to determine the course of his own, scientific action? Does his account recognize the scientist's desire to reconcile his conclusions with the structure of his science and the body of currently established propositions? Or are these wishes and desires non-existent or simply irrelevant? Would they tend to make science look more or less like law?

3.   Dickinson says that scientists do not have to decide "litigated cases in accordance with law." Is there at least a figurative sense in which he is wrong? Consider Kuhn's discussion of "normal science."

4.   Legal rules, says Dickinson, are not rules of "isness," because the judge always has the "volition" to choose to ignore the generalizations derived from past cases. Is this true of lower court judges who must apply the law laid down by their highest courts? Incidentally, can an analogy be drawn between normal science and lower court adjudication of the law? Or is it inaccurate to limit such an analogy to lower court practice?

5.   Is there no sense in which "the [legal] generalization is created with the idea of being overthrown"? Recall Wechsler's quotation of Taney in Section 1. Is it possible to argue that at least Common Law rules will be tested against the facts of social and economic life and if found wanting will be rejected? Is this at all a legitimate metaphor? How could courts go about testing their rules against the facts? Where are their laboratories? Is it the absence in courts of the power to reject statutory and Constitutional rules that makes the "working hypothesis" metaphor inappropriate in these areas of the law? Or is there a way of expressing the statutory and Constitutional jurisdictions which would justify the use of such a conception?

6.  Consider Dickinson's assertion that the judge "is not, like the scientist, engaged in the discovery of new truth, or in adding to the sum total of human knowledge"?  Is there nothing in law which corresponds to "truth"?  What theory of truth do you think Dickinson holds?  Are there theories which would support the notion that there is a "legal" truth?  Recall the materials in Chapter 6.

BIRD v. JONES

7 Q.B. 742 (1845)

COLERIDGE, J. . . .

This point is, whether certain facts, which may be taken as clear upon the evidence, amount to an imprisonment.  These facts, stated shortly, and as I understand them, are in effect as follows.

A part of a public highway was inclosed, and appropriated for spectators of a boat race, paying a price for their seats.  The plaintiff was desirous of entering this part, and was opposed by the defendant: but, after a struggle, during which no momentary detention of his person took place, he succeeded in climbing over the inclosure.  Two policemen were then stationed by the defendant to prevent, and they did prevent, him from passing onwards in the direction in which he declared his wish to go: but he was allowed to remain unmolested where he was, and was at liberty to go, and was told that he was so, in the only other direction by which he could pass.  This he refused for some time, and, during that time, remained where he had thus placed himself.

These are the facts: and, setting aside those which do not properly bear on the question now at issue, there will remain these: that the plaintiff, being in a public highway and desirous of passing along it, in a particular direction, is prevented from doing so by the orders of the defendant, and that the defendant's agents for the purpose are policemen, from whom, indeed, no unnecessary violence was to be anticipated, or such as they believed unlawful, yet who might be expected to execute such commands as they deemed lawful with all necessary force, however, resisted.  But, although thus obstructed, the plaintiff was at liberty to move his person and go in any other direction, at his free will and pleasure: and no actual force or restraint on his person was used, unless the obstruction before mentioned amounts to so much.

. . . . I lay out of consideration the question of right or wrong between these parties.  The acts will amount to imprisonment neither more nor less from their being wrongful or capable of justification.

And I am of opinion that there was no imprisonment.  To call it so appears to me to confound partial obstruction and disturbance with total obstruction and detention.  A prison may have its boundary large or narrow, visible and tangible, or, though real, still in the conception only; it may itself be moveable or fixed: but a boundary it must have; and that boundary the party imprisoned must be prevented from passing; he must be prevented from leaving that place, within the ambit of which the party imprisoning would confine him, except by prison-breach. Some confusion seems to me to arise from confounding imprisonment of the body with mere loss of freedom: it is one part of the definition of freedom to be able to go whithersoever one pleases; but imprisonment is something more than the mere loss of this power; it includes the notion of restraint within some limits defined by a will or power exterior to our own.

In Com. Dig. Imprisonment (G), it is said: "Every restraint of the liberty of a free man will be an imprisonment." For this the authorities cited are 2 Inst. 482, Cro. Car. 210(*a*). But, when these are referred to, it will be seen that nothing was intended at all inconsistent with what I have ventured to lay down above. In both books, the object was to point out that a prison was not necessarily what is commonly so called, a place locally defined and appointed for the reception of prisoners. Lord Coke is commenting on the Statute of Westminster 2d "in persona," and says, "Every restraint of the liberty of a freeman is an imprisonment, although he be not within the walls of any common prison." The passage in Cro. Car. (*b*), is from a curious case of an information against Sir Miles Hobart and Mr. Stroud for escaping out of the Gate House prison, to which they had been committed by the King. The question was, whether, under the circumstances, they had ever been there imprisoned. Owing to the sickness in London, and through the favour of the keeper, these gentlemen had not, except on one occasion, ever been within the walls of the Gate House: the occasion is somewhat singularly expressed in the decision of the Court, which was "that their voluntary retirement to the close stool" in the Gate House "made them to be prisoners." The resolution, however, in question is this: "That the prison of the King's Bench is not any local prison confined only to one place, and that every place where any person is restrained of his liberty is a prison; as if one take sanctuary and depart thence, he shall be said to break prison."

On a case of this sort, which, if there be difficulty in it, is at least purely elementary, it is not easy nor necessary to enlarge: and I am unwilling to put any extreme case hypothetically: but I wish to meet one suggestion, which has been put as avoiding one of the difficulties which cases of this sort might seem to suggest. If it be said that to hold the present case to amount to an imprisonment would turn every obstruction of the exercise of a right of way into an imprisonment, the answer is, that there must be something like personal menace or force accompanying the act of obstruction, and that, with this, it will amount to imprisonment. I apprehend that is not so. If, in the course of a night, both ends of a street were walled up, and there was no egress from the house but into the street, I should have no difficulty in saying that the inhabitants were thereby imprisoned; but, if only one end were walled up, and an armed force stationed outside to prevent any scaling of the wall or passage that way, I should feel equally clear that there was no imprisonment. If there were, the street would obviously be the prison; and yet, as obviously, none would be confined to it.

. . . .

WILLIAMS, J. . . . .

A part of Hammersmith Bridge, which is generally used as a public footway, was appropriated for seats to view a regatta on the river, and separated for that purpose from the carriage way by a temporary fence. The plaintiff insisted upon passing along the part so appropriated, and attempted to climb over the fence. The defendant (clerk of the Bridge Company) pulled him back; but the plaintiff succeeded in climbing over the fence. The defendant then stationed two policemen to prevent, and they did prevent, the plaintiff from proceeding forwards along the footway in the direction he wished to go. The plaintiff, however, was at the same time told that he might go back into the carriage way and proceed to the other side of the bridge, if he pleased. The plaintiff refused to do so, and remained where he was so obstructed, about half an hour.

And, if a partial restraint of the will be sufficient to constitute an imprisonment, such undoubtedly took place. He wished to go in a particular direction, and was prevented; but, at the same time, another course was open to him. About the meaning of the word imprisonment, and the definitions of it usually given, there is so little doubt that any difference of opinion is scarcely possible. Certainly, so far as I am aware, none such exists upon the present occasion. The difficulty, whatever it may be, arises when the general rule is applied to the facts of a particular case.

"Every confinement of the person" (according to Blackstone (3Bl. C. 127), "is an imprisonment, whether it be in a common prison, or in a private house, or in the stocks, or even by forcibly detaining one in the public street," which, perhaps, may seem to imply the application of force more than is really necessary to make an imprisonment. Lord Coke, in his Second Institute (2 Inst. 589), speaks of "a prison in law" and "a prison in deed:" so that there may be a constructive, as well as an actual, imprisonment: and, therefore, it may be admitted that personal violence need not be used in order to amount to it. "If the bailiff" (as the case is put in Bull.N.P. 62) "who has a process against one, says to him," " 'You are my prisoner, I have a writ against you,' upon which he submits, turns back or goes with him, though the bailiff never touched him, yet it is an arrest, because he submitted to the process." So, if a person should direct a constable to take another in custody, and that person should be told by the constable to go with him, and the orders are obeyed, and they walk together in the direction pointed out by the constable, that is, constructively, an imprisonment, though no actual violence be used. In such cases, however, though little may be said, much is meant and perfectly understood. The party addressed in the manner above supposed feels that he has no option, nor more power of going in any but the one direction prescribed to him than if the constable or bailiff had actually hold of him: no return or deviation from the course prescribed is open to him. And it is that entire restraint upon the will which, I apprehend, constitutes the imprisonment. In the passage cited from Buller's Nisi Prius it is remarked that, if the party addressed by the bailiff, instead of complying, had run away, it could be no arrest, unless the bailiff actually laid hold of him, and for obvious reasons. Suppose (and the supposition is perhaps objectionable, as only putting the case before us over again) any person to erect an obstruction across a public passage in a town, and another, who had a right of passage, to be refused permission by the party obstructing, and, after some delay, to be compelled to return and take another and circuitous route to his place of destination: I do not think that, during such detention, such person was under imprisonment, or could maintain an action for false imprisonment, whatever other remedy might be open to him.

I am desirous only to illustrate my meaning and explain the reason why I consider the imprisonment in this case not to be complete. The reason shortly is, that I am aware of no case, nor of any definition, which warrants the supposition of a man being imprisoned during the time that an escape is open to him if he chooses to avail himself of it.

PATTESON, J. . . . .

.    .    .    . A part of Hammersmith Bridge which is ordinarily used as a public footway was appropriated for seats to view a regatta on the river, and separated for that purpose from the carriage way by a temporary fence. The plaintiff insisted on passing along the part so appropriated, and attempted to climb over the fence. The defendant, being clerk of the Bridge Company, seized his coat, and tried to pull him back: the plaintiff, however, succeeded in climbing over the fence. The defendant then stationed two policemen to prevent and, they did prevent, the plaintiff from proceeding forwards along the footway; but he was told that he might go back into the carriage way, and proceed to the other side of the bridge, if he pleased. The plaintiff would not do so, but remained where he was above half an hour: and then, on the defendant still refusing to suffer him to go forwards along the footway, he endeavoured to force his way, and, in so doing, assaulted the defendant: whereupon he was taken into custody.

.    .    .

I have no doubt that, in general, if one man compels another to stay in any given place against his will, he imprisons that other just as much as if he locked him up in a room: and I agree that it is not necessary, in order to constitute an imprisonment, that a man's person should be touched. I agree, also that the compelling a man to go in a given direction against his will may amount to imprisonment. But I cannot bring my mind to the conclusion that, if one man merely obstructs the passage of another in a particular direction, whether by threat of personal violence or otherwise, leaving him at liberty to stay where he is or to go in any other direction if he pleases, he can be said thereby to imprison him. He does him wrong, undoubtedly, if there was a right to pass in that direction, and would be liable to an action on the case for obstructing the passage, or of assault, if, on the party persisting in going in that direction, he touched his person, or so threatened him as to amount to an assault. But imprisonment is, as I apprehend, a total restraint of the liberty of the person, for however short a time, and not a partial obstruction of his will, whatever inconvenience it may bring on him. The quality of the act cannot, however, depend on the right of the opposite party. If it be an imprisonment to prevent a man passing along the public highway, it must be equally so to prevent him passing further along a field into which he has broken by a clear act of trespass.

A case was said to have been tried before Lord Chief Justice Tindal involving this question: but it appears that the plaintiff in that case was compelled to stay and hear a letter read to him against his will, which was doubtless a total restraint of his liberty whilst the letter was read.

I agree to the definition in Selwyn's Nisi Prius, title Imprisonment (vol. ii. p. 915, 11th ed.): "False imprisonment is a restraint on the liberty of the person without lawful cause; either by confinement in prison, stocks, house, &c., or even by forcibly detaining the party in the streets, against his will." He cites 22 Ass. fol. 104, B, pl. 85, per Thorpe, C. J. The word there used is "arrest," which appears to me to include a "detaining," as Mr. Selwyn expresses it, and not to mean merely the preventing a person from passing.

Upon the whole, I am of opinion that the only imprisonment proved in this case was that which occurred when the plaintiff was taken into custody after he had assaulted the defendant. . . .

Lord Denman, C. J. I have not drawn up a formal judgment in this case, because I hoped to the last that the arguments which my learned brothers would produce in support of their opinion might alter mine. We have freely discussed the matter both orally and in written communications; but, after hearing what they have advanced, I am compelled to say that my first impression remains. If, as I must believe, it is a wrong one, it may be in some measure accounted for by the circumstances attending the case. A company unlawfully obstructed a public way for their own profit, extorting money from passengers, and hiring policemen to effect this purpose. The plaintiff, wishing to exercise his right of way, is stopped by force, and ordered to move in a direction which he wished not to take. He is told at the same time that a force is at hand ready to compel his submission. That proceeding appears to me equivalent to being pulled by the collar out of the one line and into the other.

There is some difficulty perhaps in defining imprisonment in the abstract without reference to its illegality; nor is it necessary for me to do so, because I consider these acts as amounting to imprisonment. That word I understand to mean any restraint of the person by force. In Buller's Nisi Prius (p. 22) it is said: "Every restraint of a man's liberty under the custody of another, either in a gaol house, stocks or in the street, is in law an imprisonment; and whenever it is done without a proper authority, is false imprisonment, for which the law gives an action; and this is commonly joined to assault and battery; for every imprisonment includes a battery, and every battery an assault." It appears, therefore, that the technical language has received a very large construction, and that there need not be any touching of the person: a locking up would constitute an imprisonment, without touching. From the language of Thorpe, C. J., which Mr. Selwyn (vol. ii. p. 915, 11th ed., tit. Imprisonment), cites from the Book of Assizes (22 Ass. fol. 104, B, pl. 85), it appears that, even in very early times, restraint of liberty by force was understood to be the reasonable definition of imprisonment.

I had no idea that any person in these times supposed any particular boundary to be necessary to constitute imprisonment, or that the restraint of a man's person from doing what he desires ceases to be an imprisonment because he may find some means of escape.

It is said that the party here was at liberty to go in another direction. I am not sure that in fact he was, because the same unlawful power which prevented him from taking one course might, in case of acquiescence, have refused him any other. But this liberty to do something else does not appear to me to affect the question of imprisonment. As long as I am prevented from doing what I have a right to do, of what importance is it that I am permitted to do something else? How does the imposition of an unlawful condition show that I am not restrained? If I am locked in a room, am I not imprisoned because I might effect my escape through a window, or because I might find an exit dangerous or inconvenient to myself, as by wading through water or by taking a route so circuitous that my necessary affairs would suffer by delay?

It appears to me that this is a total deprivation of liberty with reference to the purpose for which he lawfully wished to employ his liberty: and, being effected by force, it is not the mere obstruction of a way, but a restraint of the person. The case cited as occurring before Lord Chief Justice Tindal, as I understand it, is much in point. He held it an imprisonment where the defendant stopped the plaintiff on his road till he had read a libel to him. Yet he did not prevent his escaping in another direction.

### NOTES AND QUESTIONS

1. Examine the reasons given by the three judges for holding that the plaintiff was not falsely imprisoned. Do they amount to or express an adequate legal theory? Note Williams's declaration that "there is so little doubt" about "the meaning of the word imprisonment" that "any difference of opinion is scarcely possible." Do the opinions in *Bird* bear him out? Does Williams himself tell us what that meaning is on which there is so little doubt?

2.   The RESTATEMENT OF TORTS, 2d provides:

To make the actor liable for false imprisonment, the other's confinement within the boundaries fixed by the actor must be complete.

Section 36 (1965).   Does it help us in trying to understand the nature of a confinement for purposes of false imprisonment to be told that it must be "complete"?   Would an "incomplete" confinement *be* a confinement?   Consider the requirement that there be an "entire restraint upon the will."   How useful a rule or reason is this?   Is a man confined to a maximum security penitentiary imprisoned under this definition?   Is a person in such circumstances entirely restrained?   Is he deprived of all choice?   Or are there avenues of liberty open to him even in this most typical of prisons?   Does "entire restraint" refer to a restraint of any and every liberty or of a particular liberty?   If the latter, wouldn't the plaintiff's case fall within the majority's conception of false imprisonment?

3.   Does a prison lose its character as a prison if there is a means of escape?   Are the only prisons those which are wholly and completely escape-proof?   How many prisons of this sort are there?   Do the opinions of the majority indicate that they view "imprisonment" in this way?   Is such a view consistent with the cases they cite?   Would it be possible to frame the issue in this case as involving the question of what is an "escape" for false imprisonment purposes?   If so, how would such a formulation help us to resolve the case?

4.   Compare the statements of the facts provided by Coleridge, Williams, Denman.   How do they differ?   How might you account for the differences?   Do the differences tell us anything about the theories of false imprisonment each judge is using?   Consider, for example, Williams's reference to the carriageway.   Can you think of any reason why he might mention this?   And why Coleridge did not?   That is, can you think of any reason why the existence of the carriageway might matter?

5.   If the majority judges do not have an adequate theory of false imprisonment, can their agreement be accounted for by a common "picture" of what an imprisonment essentially is?   Is this a picture derived from everyday usage or from legal usage?   Or both?   Why doesn't Denman share the same image, do you think?

6.   Assume that the area appropriated by the Bridge Company was enclosed on every side.   Could Plaintiff not argue that the walls of this enclosure imprisoned him in the rest-of-the-world?   That his complaint was not his inability to get into the enclosure, but his inability to get out of the rest-of-the-world?   Would not this argument satisfy the criteria laid down by the majority judges?

7.   Can the problem of what is an imprisonment in the law of torts be viewed as a parable of the problem of what is an adequate rule?   Consider Wittgenstein's remarks:

.  .  .  .   An indefinite sense—that would really not be a sense *at all*.—This is like: An indefinite boundary is not really a boundary at all.

PHILOSOPHICAL INVESTIGATIONS 45ᵉ (1958 ed.)   One who holds this
view, says Wittgenstein, would think that locking up a person in
a room is a "sham" if after locking everything else the door was
left open.   "One would be inclined to say here: 'You haven't done
anything at all'.   An enclosure with a hole in it is as good as *none.*—
But is that true?" *Ibid.*

## A.   *The Choice of Rule*

ALFRED NORTH WHITEHEAD

### MODES OF THOUGHT *

.   .   .   .   in every consideration of a single fact there is the
suppressed presupposition of the environmental coordination requisite
for its existence.   This environment, thus coordinated, is the whole
universe in its perspective to the fact.   .   .   .

In this way the finite intellect deals with the myth of finite facts.
There can be no objection to this procedure, provided that we remember what we are doing.   We are presupposing an environment
which, in its totality, we are unable to define.   For example, science
is always wrong, so far as it neglects this limitation.   The conjunction of premises, from which logic proceeds, presupposes that no difficulty will arise from the conjunction of the various unexpressed presuppositions involved in these premises.   Both in science and in logic
you have only to develop your argument sufficiently, and sooner or
later you are bound to arrive at a contradiction, either internally
within the argument, or externally in its reference to fact.

Judging from the history of European science, about three or four
thousand years of continuous thought by a sufficient number of able
people suffice to uncover some contradiction latent in any logical
train of thought.   As to physical science, the unguarded Newtonian
doctrines survived for three hundred years.   The span of life for
modern scientific schemes is about thirty years.   The father of European philosophy, in one of his many moods of thought, laid down the
axiom that the deeper truths must be adumbrated by myths.   Surely,
the subsequent history of Western thought has amply justified his
fleeting intuition.

It is to be noticed that none of these logical or scientific myths
is wrong, in an unqualified sense of that term.   It is unguarded.   Its
truth is limited by unexpressed presuppositions; and as time goes
on we discover some of these limitations.   The simple-minded use of
the notions 'right or wrong' is one of the chief obstacles to the progress of understanding.

ALFRED NORTH WHITEHEAD

ADVENTURES OF IDEAS *

. . . . every method is a happy simplification. But only truths of a congenial type can be investigated by any one method, or stated in the terms dictated by the method. For every simplification is an over-simplification. Thus the criticism of a theory does not start from the question, True or false? It consists in noting its scope of useful application and its failure beyond that scope. It is an unguarded statement of a partial truth. Some of its terms embody a general notion with a mistaken specialization, and others of its terms are too general and require discrimination of their possibilities of specialization.

. . .

. . . . Speculative Philosophy can be defined as the endeavour to frame a coherent, logical, necessary system of general ideas in terms of which every element of our experience can be interpreted. Here 'interpretation' means that each element shall have the character of a particular instance of the general scheme.

Thus speculative philosophy embodies the method of the 'working hypothesis'. The purpose of this working hypothesis for philosophy is to coordinate the current expressions of human experience, in common speech, in social institutions, in actions, in the principles of the various special sciences, elucidating harmony and exposing discrepancies. No systematic thought has made progress apart from some adequately general working hypothesis, adapted to its special topic. Such an hypothesis directs observation, and decides upon the mutual relevance of various types of evidence. In short, it prescribes method. To venture upon productive thought without such an explicit theory is to abandon oneself to the doctrines derived from one's grandfather.

In the preliminary stages of knowledge a haphazard criterion is all that is possible. Progress is then very slow, and most of the effort is wasted. Even an inadequate working hypothesis with some conformation to fact is better than nothing. It coordinates procedure.

The advance of any reasonably developed science is twofold. There is the advance of detailed knowledge within the method prescribed by the reigning working hypothesis; and there is the rectification of the working hypothesis dictated by the inadequacies of the current orthodoxy.

Sometimes it is necessary for a science to entertain concurrently two—or more—working hypotheses, each with its own success and its own failure. Such hypotheses are contradictory as stated: and science awaits their conciliation by the production of a working hypothesis with a wider sweep. When a new working hypothesis is proposed, it must be criticized from its own point of view. For example, it is futile to object to the Newtonian dynamics that, on the Aristotelian system, the loose things on the earth's surface must be left behind by the earth's motion.

Philosophy has been afflicted by the dogmatic fallacy, which is the belief that the principles of its working hypotheses are clear, obvious, and irreformable. Then, as a reaction from this fallacy, it has swayed to the other extreme which is the fallacy of discarding method. Philosophers boast that they uphold no system. They are then a prey to the delusive clarities of detached expressions which it is the very purpose of their science to surmount. Another type of reaction is to assume, often tacitly, that if there can be any intellectual analysis it must proceed according to some one discarded dogmatic method, and thence to deduce that intellect is intrinsically tied to erroneous fictions. This type is illustrated by the anti-intellectualism of Nietzsche and Bergson, and tinges American Pragmatism.

## QUESTIONS

1. Is Whitehead saying that scientific laws are myths? If so, what is the conception of myth that Whitehead is using?

2. Does Whitehead accept the conventional criteria by which the adequacy of theories and rules is judged? If not, in what ways does he depart from these criteria? What criteria does he use himself? How do his remarks bear on the positions taken by Wechsler and Bickel regarding "neutral principles"?

3. To what extent is it necessary for a theory to be an oversimplification? Or a partial truth? How useful would a theory be which adequately accounted for everything? What form would it take? What degree of generality would its terms have? Consider these questions in relation to the materials which follow in this section.

4. Why does the absence of "an explicit theory" require one "to abandon oneself to the doctrines derived from one's grandfather"? Recall the material above concerning thought and language.

5. To what extent do Whitehead's remarks about theories resemble Kuhn's about paradigms? To what extent can legal rules be viewed and judged in the same way? Consider these questions as you study the remaining material in this chapter.

## JAMES B. CONANT

### MODERN SCIENCE AND MODERN MAN *

Let me ask you to consider  .  .  . heat, and to recall that somewhat more than a hundred years ago popular lecturers on science fascinated their audiences by demonstrating that heat was a "mode of motion." The notion of a subtle caloric fluid that flowed from hot bodies to cooler ones could be shown to be totally unnecessary; in-

---

* From 67–71, 91–92 (Anchor ed. 1953).
Reprinted with permission of Columbia University Press.

deed, not only unnecessary but also quite incapable of accounting for a number of experimental results, such as the generation of heat by friction. Therefore, the caloric theory of heat which had been useful in its day was disproved and in its place was firmly established the concept that heat was associated with the motion of particles. Nevertheless, the caloric theory of heat has remained a useful pedagogic device. We still talk of the flow of heat and even set up mathematical expressions to formulate this flow as though there were a caloric fluid. Within a limited range of experimental facts in physics and chemistry, the caloric theory of heat is still the most convenient way of ordering these facts. Note that I said "limited range of facts," for it was the introduction of other experimental situations that destroyed the overall usefulness of the notion of a caloric fluid. To retain this theory and yet account for all these new facts, one would have had to add arbitrary assumption to assumption. On the other hand, when the theory was discarded and heat formulated in terms of the motions of particles, a vast new set of possibilities opened up. In short, experiments settled conclusively, so we say, which one of two theories of heat was "true."

At the end of the last century the nature of light seemed to be as definitely settled as did the nature of heat. Light was an electromagnetic disturbance in all-pervading ether; it was a wave phenomenon. The older idea that light was corpuscular—a stream of bullets—had been destroyed, so it was said, by a certain set of famous experiments that proved that light was in fact undulatory. Then along came certain new experimental phenomena which were as difficult to fit into a wave theory of light as had been the older set to fit into the framework of the corpuscular theory. About 1910 a highly unsatisfactory situation had developed which could be summarized by saying that light is emitted and received as though it consisted of a stream of particles and it is transmitted as though it were a set of waves. To the scientists of forty years ago this was the equivalent of saying a box was both full and empty; it was impossible, so they maintained, for light to be both undulatory and corpuscular. The fact that this appeared to be the case could only be a temporary situation. It would surely be only a matter of time before a set of experiments would be devised that would resolve the difficulty, for such a sequence of events had occurred throughout the history of science.

One is tempted to say that what has happened in the last forty years is that physicists have learned to love a situation they once thought to be intolerable. It is as though their predecessors had been forced to retain the caloric fluid not only as a matter of convenience in formulating certain experiments, but also as a matter of necessity, and yet the evidence against the theory remained unshaken. Furthermore, it is as though their predecessors had decided that the very nature of energy and matter was such that it was impossible to decide for or against the two ideas of heat: the caloric theory or heat as a mode of motion. But such a decision on the part of early-nineteenth-century scientists would have been a negation of science itself—at least, so people would have declared until very recent years. The progress of science consisted in testing the deductions from various hypotheses and discarding the hypothesis the deductions from which were contradicted by experiment. The idea that there could be two diametrically opposed theories as to the nature of heat, or of light, or of matter, and that both could be rejected and confirmed as a consequence of experiments would have been considered nonsense to almost all sane people fifty years ago. In regard to heat we can still agree that the caloric fluid is obsolete, make no mistake about that; in regard to light, however, we can hardly do better than say that light is in a sense both undulatory and corpuscular. . . . .

If I tried to sum up in a sentence what seems to me the philosophic implications of the new physics I should be inclined to paraphrase Sir J. J. Thomson. A mass of experimental evidence in the twentieth century has provided powerful ammunition to those who look upon a scientific theory as a policy and has made untenable at least one theory [which would regard it] as a creed. A policy suggests always a guide to action, and of the various interpretations of science that are current today, those seem to me to be the most useful that emphasize the dynamic nature of science. There are philosophers, I realize, who draw a sharp line between knowing and doing and look askance at all philosophizing that seems to tie the search for truth in any way to practical undertakings. But for me, at least, any analysis of the process of testing a statement made in a scientific context leads at once to a series of actions. Therefore, I venture to define science as a series of interconnected concepts and conceptual schemes arising from experiment and observation and fruitful of further experiments and observations. The test of a scientific theory is, I suggest, its fruitfulness—in the words of Sir J. J. Thomson, its ability "to suggest, stimulate, and direct experiment."

## Notes and Questions

Compare Conant's conception of scientific rules with Dickinson's.

What is it precisely that makes it possible for two inconsistent theories to exist together? Why does not such a situation lead to intolerable confusion? Recall the materials in Chapter 8 on conflicting authoritative rules and canons of statutory construction. What bearing might Conant's remarks have on the problems raised therein?

## Note: The Value of Political Theory

In *The Language of Political Theory,** Margaret MacDonald suggests that the important differences between competing theories of political organization and obligation may lie not in their relative abilities to be confirmed by fact, but rather in their practical and psychological effects. In one sense, for example, the theory which views government as based on an original compact between the governed and the governors, and the theory which views the state as an organic, higher entity of which the individual is only a part are both incapable of empirical verification. In another sense, there is prob-

---

* Logic and Language 174–194 (A. Flew ed. Anchor ed. 1965).

ably no "fact" of political and social life—e. g., the "fact" that people feel obligated to obey legal rules or the "fact" that people expect
their governments to be responsive to their needs—for which account
cannot be taken by either theory.  Thus, says MacDonald, such
theories cannot be differentiated from each other either by "their
truth or falsity" nor, even, by their comprehensiveness.  "Yet the
'contractual' and the 'organic' views of political relations," she notes,
"would never be ordinarily said to mean the same and they have had
very different effects."  These differences she attributes to their
"picturing political relationships with the help of two very different
images."  One theory invokes the image of equal contracting parties
agreeing to the terms of their polity; the other projects a mystical,
higher entity from whom all is derived and to whom all is owed.

People who "picture the relation between themselves, the State
and the Government" as one of contract "will probably tend to stress
the fact of or the need for the *consent* of the governed to its governors."  They will consider the governors *responsible* to the governed
and "their attitude to rulers will be critical rather than reverential."
Further, the "contract" image "encourages the view that social arrangements of all kinds are made by men for their own ends and can
be altered and even ended at their will and pleasure."  This does not
mean, says MacDonald, that the contract theory is inconsistent with
great respect for existing institutions of government or "for the customs and traditions of the past and the welfare of the future."  In any
political or social decision which is to be made these elements may
have great, even decisive weight.  The contract view says "only that
if, in spite of all this," proposed changes "are *consented* to by a majority of the present members of a society, no higher authority can be
found with a *right* to prevent them."  Thus, concludes MacDonald,
"the 'contract' view can take account of every fact stressed by other
views, but its own difference of emphasis alters their point or effects."

The "organic" image has a very different character.  The relation of a part to an entire organism is not viewed as one of free choice.
In Burke's words,

> The State ought not to be considered as nothing better than
> a partnership agreement in a trade of pepper and coffee,
> calico or tobacco, or some other such low concern, to be taken
> up for a little temporary interest, and to be dissolved by the
> fancy of the parties.  It is to be looked on with other rev-
> erence.  .  .  .  It is a partnership in all science, a partner-
> ship in all art, a partnership not only between those who are
> living, but between those who are living, those who are dead,
> and those who are to be born  .  .  .  linking the lower
> with the higher natures, connecting the visible and invisible
> world, according to a fixed compact sanctioned by the inviola-
> ble oath which holds all physical and all moral natures each
> in their appointed place.

Such an image subordinates the individual and tends toward an
attitude of submission to and reverence for Authority.  Yet, according to MacDonald, the "organic" theory does not have to deny any of

the elements which form such an important part of the "contract" image. There is still room for "consent, freedom, criticism," although they may be minimized or reinterpreted. When the word "liberty" is used, for example, it will often be accompanied by the word "order."

The practical and psychological effects which these theories have, MacDonald proposes, may encourage people to "go on using them, although they learn nothing much [thereby] . . . about political affairs." For many people the role of a small part in a very large whole satisfies and reassures them. They do not like to view themselves as constantly making decisions, holding representatives to account, taking responsibility for the general direction of their lives. Other people would be wholly unable to accept such a role. They must feel, apparently, that they have some effective control of their destiny. MacDonald notes that considerations of this sort may account even for the choice of a particular scientific theory. Ptolemaic astronomy, for example, could if properly complicated describe the motions of planets just as well as the Copernican system. Yet this by itself could not explain the enormous resistance which the latter encountered. Such resistance indicates that people could not accept the image of man in relation to the universe which Copernicus's conception suggested.

MacDonald takes issue with the notion that political theories "explain certain puzzles about social life." One of these puzzles, she reports, arises from the fact that the many so easily allow themselves to be governed by the few. Philosophers want to know why they do this and if they should. They are thus led to ask very general questions about the nature of man, of the State, of political obligation. Some of the answers at which they have arrived have already been mentioned. The many obey the few because they have so contracted— and they will continue to do so as long as the contract's terms are observed by the other side. Or, the organic view might hold, the many obey the few because the latter represent that higher entity which possesses a greater wisdom and value than any or all of its particular members. These answers, says MacDonald, are really quite unsatisfactory. There is no historical evidence of an original contract and even if there were the question of its obligatory force centuries later would remain unanswered. That there is a State which in some sense is above the individual, on the other hand, may be conceded. Yet this does not establish that what the State does is right or ought to be obeyed. Both theories, thus, seem hopelessly inadequate to provide us with a general account of political obligation. For they rely either on entities of which there is no empirical evidence or on assertions which beg the question.

Even more modern, less mythical-sounding, theories, MacDonald insists, will not adequately explain the "social puzzles" to which they are addressed. Utilitarianism views the State as an institution for promoting the interests of its members. One gets the impression, therefore, that it can be judged like any other association—by whether and how it carries out its purposes. The difficulty is that the ordinary association has very definite, specifiable aims. The State does not. What are the "interests of its members" and how do we know when they are being satisfied? Once again, political theory speaks as if it rested on some accessible, definable datum, but analysis shows that it does not.

The fundamental error that political theorists make, says Mac-Donald, is their assumption that it "is either possible or necessary" to provide a general criterion of political obligation. There is no more reason to suppose this than to suppose that a general proof of the existence of material objects or of the rightness of human actions is possible. Yet the political theorists insist on "an answer which is always and infallibly right." They wish "to reduce all political obligation to the application of an almost magical formula." They seem to believe "that we can know once and for all almost by learning a single sentence" when we ought and ought not to accede to governmental authority. And the result of their attempts is that language is stretched "beyond the bounds of significance." In short, the theories they devise are literally meaningless.

Such theories, however, do have value. They "call attention in a very vivid way to facts and experiences of whose existence we all know but which, for some reason, it seems important to emphasize." They stress at a critical historical moment a criterion of legitimacy "which is tending to be overlooked or denied." For consent, tradition, authority, satisfaction of needs are all proper desiderata of political obligation. Even though no one of them is always the final arbiter of legitimacy, any one of them may be decisive in a large number of cases. The value of a political theory depends on its ability to remind us of this when the reminder is needed.

If the value of political theories rests on their ability to stress certain facts and criteria, why don't those theories simply state these, establish their importance, and avoid the invocation of myths and fictions? Why is it necessary to talk of social contracts when one can talk of consent, freedom, etc.? In some sense, it would seem, such notions as contract and organism *justify* the emphasis which they place on certain aspects of experience—or at least the theorists seem to think so. But, as MacDonald implies, such justifications do not seem to hold up by the ordinary tests of theoretical adequacy. Is there nevertheless a use of the notion of "justification" which might support the political theorist's practice? Can you find anything in the excerpts from Whitehead which might support them?

Compare MacDonald's position to the following:

> . . . . . we are not justified in regarding one view of the judicial role as more valuable than another simply be-cause it, more frequently than the other, produces substantive results with which we agree. We might well prefer such a theory, but we could regard it as demonstrably better than other views only on the basis of the criterion by which all theories are judged: the ability satisfactorily to account for a range of phenomena. Thus, when we say that the value of a theory concerning the Court rests on its application to particular decisions, what we mean is that successful theories

satisfactorily account for results that alternative hypotheses fail to explicate.

Deutsch, *Neutrality, Legitimacy, and the Supreme Court*, 20 Stan.L. Rev. 169, 171 (1968). What qualifications might MacDonald make to this? Would Whitehead and Kuhn agree with Deutsch's test for the adequacy of theories? What about Wechsler and Bickel?

## B. The Value of Error

### NOAM CHOMSKY

### SYNTACTIC STRUCTURES *

. . . . The search for rigorous formulation in linguistics has a much more serious motivation than mere concern for logical niceties or the desire to purify well-established methods of linguistic analysis. Precisely constructed models for linguistic structure can play an important role, both negative and positive, in the process of discovery itself. By pushing a precise but inadequate formulation to an unacceptable conclusion, we can often expose the exact source of this inadequacy and, consequently, gain a deeper understanding of the linguistic data. More positively, a formalized theory may autocatically provide solutions for many problems other than those for which it was explicitly designed. Obscure and intuition-bound notions can neither lead to absurd conclusions nor provide new and correct ones, and hence they fail to be useful in two important respects. I think that some of those linguists who have questioned the value of precise and technical development of linguistic theory may have failed to recognize the productive potential in the method of rigorously stating a proposed theory and applying it strictly to linguistic material with no attempt to avoid unacceptable conclusions by *ad hoc* adjustments or loose formulation.

### THOMAS S. KUHN

### THE STRUCTURE OF SCIENTIFIC REVOLUTIONS **

. . . . No natural history can be interpreted in the absence of at least some implicit body of intertwined theoretical and methodological belief that permits selection, evaluation, and criticism. If that body of belief is not already implicit in the collection of facts—in which case more than "mere facts" are at hand—it must be externally supplied, perhaps by a current metaphysic, by another science, or by personal and historical accident. No wonder, then, that in the early stages of the development of any science different men confronting the same range of phenomena, but not usually all the same particular phenomena, describe and interpret them in different ways. What is surprising, and perhaps also unique in its degree to the fields we call science, is that such initial divergences should ever largely disappear.

For they do disappear to a very considerable extent and then apparently once and for all. Furthermore, their disappearance is usually caused by the triumph of one of the pre-paradigm schools, which, because of its own characteristic beliefs and preconceptions, emphasized only some special part of the too sizable and inchoate pool of information. Those electricians who thought electricity a fluid and therefore gave particular emphasis to conduction provide an excellent case in point. Led by this belief, which could scarcely cope with the known multiplicity of attractive and repulsive effects, several of them conceived the idea of bottling the electrical fluid. The immediate fruit of their efforts was the Leyden jar, a device which might never have been discovered by a man exploring nature casually or at random, but which was in fact independently developed by at least two investigators in the early 1740's. Almost from the start of his electrical researches, Franklin was particularly concerned to explain that strange and, in the event, particularly revealing piece of special apparatus. His success in doing so provided the most effective of the arguments that made his theory a paradigm, though one that was still unable to account for quite all the known cases of electrical repulsion. To be accepted as a paradigm, a theory must seem better than its competitors, but it need not, and in fact never does, explain all the facts with which it can be confronted.

What the fluid theory of electricity did for the subgroup that held it, the Franklinian paradigm later did for the entire group of electricians. It suggested which experiments would be worth performing and which, because directed to secondary or to overly complex manifestations of electricity, would not. Only the paradigm did the job far more effectively, partly because the end of interschool debate ended the constant reiteration of fundamentals and partly because the confidence that they were on the right track encouraged scientists to undertake more precise, esoteric, and consuming sorts of work. Freed from the concern with any and all electrical phenomena, the united group of electricians could pursue selected phenomena in far more detail, designing much special equipment for the task and employing it more stubbornly and systematically than electricians had ever done before. Both fact collection and theory articulation became highly directed activities. The effectiveness and efficiency of electrical research increased accordingly, providing evidence for a societal version of Francis Bacon's acute methodological dictim: "Truth emerges more readily from error than from confusion."

NOTE: THE "PANIC OF ERROR"

His pupils, says John Holt, persist in thinking that a "*yes* answer" is the only good answer to a question. This is because they have been miseducated, because they have been taught that "right answers" "are the only ones that pay off." They are completely unaware that one can learn from mistakes. Remarkably, his pupils will groan at a "no" answer which gives them just as much information as a "yes" answer. "The more anxious ones will, over and over again, ask questions that have already been answered, just for the satisfaction of hearing a *yes.*" See How Children Fail 34 (1964).

## C. Rules, Method and Issues

ALFRED NORTH WHITEHEAD

### ADVENTURES OF IDEAS *

. . . . theory dictates method, and . . . any particular method is only applicable to theories of one correlate species. An analogous conclusion holds for the technical terms. This close relation of theory to method partly arises from the fact that the relevance of evidence depends on the theory which is dominating the discussion. This fact is the reason why dominant theories are also termed 'working hypotheses'.

. . . . A great deal of confused philosophical thought has its origin in obliviousness to the fact that the relevance of evidence is dictated by theory. For you cannot prove a theory by evidence which that theory dismisses as irrelevant. This is also the reason that in any science which has failed to produce any theory with a sufficient scope of application, progress is necessarily very slow. It is impossible to know what to look for, and how to connect the sporadic observations. Philosophical discussion in the absence of a theory has no criterion of the validity of evidence. . . .

### QUESTIONS

To what extent are Whitehead's statements applicable to law as well as philosophy. Recall again the differing statements of fact in Bird v. Jones. Can they be accounted for by different theories? Can they, in some degree, be accounted for by the absence of any coherent theory?

JOHN DICKINSON

### LEGAL RULES: THEIR FUNCTION IN THE PROCESS OF DECISION †

. . . . legal rules, even if of a highly specific character, operate on the decision mainly by determining whether or not any issues, and if so which ones remain to be decided in order to reach an ultimate decision of the case,—operate, that is by guiding the attention of the adjudicating official to certain particular issues rather than others, and by making his ultimate decision of the case as a whole meet the test of consistency with the decisions which are de-

* From 221, 222 (Mentor ed. 1955). Copyright 1933 by The Macmillan Company, renewed 1961 by Evelyn Whitehead. Reprinted by permission of The Macmillan Company.

† From 79 U.Pa.L.Rev. 833, 849 (1931). Reprinted with permission of the University of Pennsylvania Law Review.

termined or influenced by the pertinent rules as to these particular issues. In the absence of rules, the attention of the official would be free to wander at large over the manifold elements of the case so that the ultimate decision might be reached on the basis of any factor or factors which for the time being loomed largest to the judge's mind. The operation of rules is to make certain factors the primary elements before the judge's attention, and to push other considerations into the background until he has reached conclusions on those which the rules single out as primary. It thus helps him to decide without making the ultimate decision for him; it supplies a structure for his thought to follow, it draws a sketch map for him of the way into and through a case.

*John Dewey*

## Moral Commands, Rules and Systems *

A rule does not tell what to do or what to leave undone. The Golden Rule, for example, does not tell me how to act in any specific case. *A rule is a tool of analysis.* The moral situation, or capacity in its relation to environment, is often an extremely complicated affair. How shall the individual resolve it? How shall he pick it to pieces, so as to see its real nature and the act demanded by it? It is evident that the analysis will be the more truly and speedily performed if the agent has a method by which to attack it, certain principles in the light of which he may view it, instruments for cross-questioning it and making it render up its meaning. Moral rules perform this service. While the Golden Rule does not of itself give one jot of information as to what I should do in a given case, it does, if accepted, immensely simplify the situation. Without it I should perhaps have to act blindly; with it the question comes to this: What should I, under the given circumstances, like to have done to me? This settled, the whole question of what should be done is settled.

It is obvious, then, that the value of a moral rule depends upon its potency in revealing the inner spirit and reality of individual deeds. Rules in the negative form, rules whose application is limited in scope because of an attempt to be specific, are midway between commands proper and rules. The Golden Rule, on the other hand, is positive, and not attempting to define any specific act, covers in its range all relations of man to man. It is indeed only a concrete and forcible statement of the ethical principle itself, the idea of a common good, or of a community of persons. This is also a convenient place for considering the practical value of ethical systems. We have already seen that no system can attempt to tell what in particular should be done. The principle of a system, however, may be of some aid in analyzing a specific case. In this way, a system may be regarded as a highly generalized rule. It attempts to state some fundamental principle which lies at the basis of moral conduct. So far as it suc-

* From Outlines of a Critical Theory of
Ethics in 3 The Early Works of John
Dewey 1882–1898, at 366–368 (1969).

ceeds in doing this, there is the possibility of its practical application in particular cases, although, of course, the mediate rules must continue to be the working tools of mankind—on account of their decided concrete character, and because they have themselves taken shape under the pressure of practice rather than of more theoretical needs.

## D. Rules, Change and Recalcitrant Facts

ALFRED NORTH WHITEHEAD

### THE FUNCTION OF REASON *

. . . . The trained body of physiologists under the influence of the ideas germane to their successful methodology entirely ignore the whole mass of adverse evidence. We have here a colossal example of anti-empirical dogmatism arising from a successful methodology. Evidence which lies outside the method simply does not count.

. . . . The dawn of brilliant epochs is shadowed by the massive obscurantism of human nature. Obscurantism is the inertial resistance of the practical Reason, with its millions of years behind it, to the interference with its fixed methods arising from recent habits of speculation. This obscurantism is rooted in human nature more deeply than any particular subject of interest. It is just as strong among the men of science as among the clergy, and among professional men and business men as among the other classes. Obscurantism is the refusal to speculate freely on the limitations of traditional methods. It is more than that: it is the negation of the importance of such speculation, the insistence on incidental dangers. A few generations ago the clergy, or to speak more accurately, large sections of the clergy were the standing examples of obscurantism. Today their place has been taken by scientists—

*By merit raised to that bad eminence.* The obscurantists of any generation are in the main constituted by the greater part of the practitioners of the dominant methodology. Today scientific methods are dominant, and scientists are the obscurantists.

. . .

The antagonism between science and metaphysics has, like all family quarrels, been disastrous. It was provoked by the obscurantism of the metaphysicians in the later Middle Ages. Of course, there were many exceptions. For example, the famous Cardinal, Nicholas of Cusa, illustrated the fact that quite a different turn might have been given the history of European thought. But the understanding of the proper functions of speculative thought was hampered by the fallacy of dogmatism. It was conceived that metaphysical thought started from principles which were individually clear, distinct, and certain. The result was that the tentative methods of science seemed quite at variance with dogmatic habits of metaphysicians. Also science itself was not quite so certain of its tentative procedure. The

* From 11, 34–35, 39–41 (1957). Copyright 1929 (c) 1957 by Princeton University Press. Reprinted by permission of Princeton University Press.

triumph of the Newtonian physics settled science upon a dogmatic foundation of materialistic ideas which lasted for two centuries. Unfortunately this approach to the metaphysical dogmatism did not produce a sense of fellowship even in evil habits. For if scientific materialism be the last word, metaphysics must be useless for physical science. The ultimate truths about nature are then not capable of any explanatory interpretation. On this theory, all that there is to be known is that inexplicable bits of matter are hurrying about with their motions correlated by inexplicable laws expressible in terms of their spatial relations to each other. If this be the final dogmatic truth, philosophy can have nothing to say to natural science.

In addition to the natural human tendency to turn a successful methodology into a dogmatic creed, the two sciences of mathematics and theology must bear the blame of fostering the dogmatic habit in European thought. The premises of mathematics seem clear, distinct, and certain. Arithmetic and geometry, as it seemed, could not be otherwise and they applied throughout the realm of nature. Also theology, by reason of its formulation of questions concerning our most intimate, sensitive interests, has always shrunk from facing the moments of bewilderment inherent in any tentative approach to the formulation of ideas.

The separation of philosophy and natural science, due to the dominance of Newtonian materialism, is indicated by the division of science into "moral science" and "natural science." For example, the University of Cambridge has inherited the term "moral science" for its department of philosophic studies. The notion is that philosophy is concerned with topics of the mind, and that natural science takes care of topics concerning matter. The whole conception of philosophy as concerned with the discipline of the speculative Reason, to which nothing is alien, has vanished. Newton himself was one of the early scientists who most emphatically repudiated the intrusion of metaphysics into science. There is plenty of evidence that, like many another man of genius, his nerves were delicately balanced. For such men the intrusion of alien considerations into the narrow way of a secure technology produces mere bewildered irritation, by reason of its disturbance of the sense of supreme mastery within the methods of their technique. Of course it would be foolish to believe that any man should dissipate his energies by straying beyond his own best lines of activity. But the pursuit of knowledge is a co-operative enterprise, and the repudiation of the relevance of diverse modes of approach to the same topic requires more justification than appeal to the limitations of individual activities.

## NOTE: KEEPING OUR RULES UP-TO-DATE

In Griswold v. Connecticut, Justice Black, dissenting, commented:

I realize that many good and able men have eloquently spoken and written, sometimes in rhapsodical strains, about the duty of this Court to keep the Constitution in tune with the times. The idea is that the Constitution must be changed from time to time and that this Court is charged with a

duty to make those changes. For myself, I must with all
deference reject that philosophy. The Constitution makers
knew the need for change and provided for it. Amendments
suggested by the people's elected representatives can be submitted to the people or their selected agents for ratification.
That method of change was good for our Fathers, and being
somewhat old-fashioned I must add that it is good enough
for me. . . .

381 U.S. 479, 522 (1965). Can an argument be made that Justice
Black is guilty of obscurantism? Does the answer depend on the
conception of legal rules that one adopts? Note that as times change
the conduct to which authoritative rules apply can change radically
in character. Can you think of examples? If so, what is the significance of a radical change in the facts presupposed by an unre-
pealed authoritative rule? Does it have any effect on the meaning
of such a rule? What might lead one to think so?

Constitutional rules are the only kind which judges ultimately
cannot abandon. Yet they do have the power to modify and reconstruct the theories of meaning by which those rules are interpreted.
This is a device which is not restricted to Constitutional adjudication,
however. Rather than abandon a statutory rule by invoking the
Constitution or a Common Law rule the courts often reinterpret the
rule to make it serviceable for the circumstances in which they find
themselves. Is this in principle a legitimate device, or is it a dishonest
trick? Is it as Justice Black seems to think a mode of camouflaging
a lawless grab for legislative power? The following readings from
Fuller, Waismann, and Barfield should help you to answer this question.


*Lon L. Fuller*

## Legal Fictions *

. . . . the fiction represents the pathology of the law. When
all goes well and established legal rules encompass neatly the social
life they are intended to regulate, there is little occasion for fictions.
There is also little occasion for philosophizing, for the law then proceeds with a transparent simplicity suggesting no need for reflective
scrutiny. Only in illness, we are told, does the body reveal its complexity. Only when legal reasoning falters and reaches out clumsily
for help do we realize what a complex undertaking the law is.

Changing the figure, we may liken the fiction to an awkward
patch applied to a rent in the law's fabric of theory. Lifting the patch
we may trace out the patterns of tension that tore the fabric and
at the same time discern elements in the fabric itself that were previously obscured from view. In all this we may gain a new insight
into the problems involved in subjecting the recalcitrant realities

* From viii–xi (1967). Reprinted with
permission of Professor Fuller.

of human life to the constraints of a legal order striving toward unity and systematic structure.

In a talk given before the American Philosophical Association in 1912, Morris Cohen urged his professional colleagues to give more attention to the philosophy of law. In discussing the relevance of jurisprudence for epistemology and metaphysics he said:

> Consider how much would our controversy over the nature of truth have been enriched if, instead of our easy dichotomous division of propositions into the true and false, we had taken notice of what lawyers call legal fictions. Such propositions occur, for instance, when we say that the constitution is the will of the people, or that the judges simply declare and never make the law, or when we say that the innocent purchaser of a chattel subject to mortgage has had notice of this fact if only the mortgage is duly recorded. These propositions, like the statement of the actor, "I am thy father's spirit," are not adequately characterized when we say merely that they are true or that they are false.

The fiction, in other words, forces upon our attention the relation between theory and fact, between concept and reality, and reminds us of the complexity of that relation. Curiously enough, the fiction finds its most pervasive application in two subjects that seem in other respects at opposite poles from one another: physics and jurisprudence. To be sure, fictions are to be found in other subjects, such as political science and economics, where we encounter the fictions of the social compact and the economic man. But these may be called Big Fictions. They furnish a kind of general starting point, an original impetus, to thought; they are not like the numerous little fictions of law and physics, which proliferate into the interstices of their subject and enter intimately into its everyday concerns. Thus the physicist may say, "For this purpose we regard light as corpuscular; for this other purpose we must regard it as wavelike." The judge, in turn, may find himself forced to declare, "For purpose $x$ we must deem the marriage between A and B to be valid; for purpose $y$ it is to be deemed null and void." There is nothing like this—certainly not in the same measure—in chemistry, botany, sociology, political science, or economics.

What is the reason for this difference? What characteristic sets law and physics apart from other branches of human study? I suggest it is their commitment to *comprehensive system*. When in actual life men are observed behaving in ways that seem to contradict the motives of the economic man, economists can say, "This simply illustrates the limitations of our science. We do not assert that men are motivated exclusively by the desire for economic advantage; we simply say that economics is concerned with their actions only insofar as they are so motivated." No such easy way out is available to law and physics. The physicist cannot—at least openly and comfortably—say, "Of course this newly observed phenomenon does not fit our theories, but this simply means that it falls outside the area of our concern." The judge cannot say, "For the litigation now before me there happen to be no clearly formulated legal rules, so I shall simply leave it undecided."

To be sure, the physicist can, as it were, put the observed irregularity on the shelf and reserve it for later treatment. The judge can say, "The facts of the case before me fall outside the constraints of established law; I shall therefore decide for the defendant and dismiss the plaintiff's complaint." But at best these easy dispositions can only be temporary. In physics new discoveries are likely to break down any neat division between established theory and the inconvenient facts of nature; sooner or later, the scientist knows, he will have to face a reexamination of his whole body of theory. In law the pressure of new cases, presenting varied situations of fact, will in time compel the judge either to clarify rules previously obscure or to draw with some precision the line at which the constraints of law leave off. Neither task is easy.

*FRIEDRICH WAISMANN*

## ANALYTIC-SYNTHETIC V *

Nothing is so opposed as day and night; yet there is a sense, as when we speak of a "three days' journey," in which "day" includes night. "Man" is used in contrast to woman, but occasionally as a term including woman; and a similar shift of sense is perceptible in "he" and "she"—as an arguer, also woman is "he." We say of a child that he is two years "old," not two years "young," just as we inquire "How *long* (not how *short*) will you stay?" or "How *far* (not how *near*) is it from here to the station?" The word "quality," while for the most part used indifferently, is sometimes uttered in a peculiar tone—as when we say "He has quality." White and black are commonly contrasted with colors in the strict and proper sense ("illustrations in color" *versus* "illustrations in black and white"), yet in certain contexts we are inclined to reckon them amongst the colors; as when we say "Look round you—everything you see has some color or other," thinking, perhaps, that even air and vapor, or glass and water are possessed by some very pale, some very pearly tone. Thus "color" tends to absorb into its meaning all shades, even black and white, the otherwise "colorless" hues. But these are instances betraying a deeper drift. In the ordinary sense, motion is opposed to rest, speed to slowness, size to littleness, numerous to a few, depth to shallowness, strength to weakness, value to worthlessness, just as far is opposed to near, hot to cold, dry to wet, dark to bright, heavy to light, and true to false. And this was, roughly, the way in which Greek philosophers regarded such contrasts. "Up" for them was simply "not-down," "soft" "not-hard," "dry" "not wet," and so on. The fact that two polar terms were in use may have played a role in underpinning the belief that things which are hot and cold, or hard and soft, etc., are different, not in degree, but in kind—a fateful belief,

* From XIII Analysis 3–5 (1952). Reprinted with permission of Basil Blackwell.

for on it hinged their understanding—no, their lack of understanding of change. They signally failed to penetrate it. The Greeks never mastered the problem of motion—which is but the simplest case—they never evolved a science of dynamics, which is surprising enough in view of their genius for mathematics. They give the impression that they somehow got started on the wrong track—for them heavenly and terrestrial motion were entirely different, the one governed by law, eternal and unchanging, the other lawless, corrupt, confused; if faced with a change, such as a thing getting heated, they thought that one quality must be destroyed to let the opposite quality take its place. Thus they were, perhaps as a consequence of their quaint ideas, mightily impeded in coming to grips with the problem of change.

In science a language has come into use in which those contrasted terms are looked upon as degrees of one and the same quality—darkness as light intensity of illumination, slowness as the lower range of speed, rest as the limiting case of motion; there is a scale only of hardness, not of softness, only a physical theory of heat, not a theory of coldness; what we measure is the strength of a rope, a current, etc., not its weakness, what we count is number, not fewness; the air has a degree of moisture, not of dryness; and everything has weight and mass, even an electron. Again, we speak of health irrespective of whether it is good or bad health, and of the value of things which are of no value. Under the influence of such examples, it would seem, a term like "truth-value" has been coined to cover both truth and falsity of a statement, just as "verification" is, prevalently, used to include falsification. "Distance," "width," "wealth," "intelligence" are further nouns which had the same career; though the same is not so true of the adjectives—"distant," "wealthy," "intelligent" are not yet relativized, any more than "hard," "hot," "speedy," "weighty" are, or "healthy," "valuable" and "worthy"; on the contrary, they retain the original sense. Adjectives, it would appear, have a much tougher life than nouns, and not only in English. But that only in passing.

Here we see a whole array of terms shifting in a parallel way, and in a way which is of farreaching consequence: for the construction of modern science is bound up with it and would not have been possible without it. The changeover from the static view—where the adjective is seen as the expression of a permanent quality—to a dynamic which apprehends quality as a variable degree within a certain scale made possible "functional thinking" (I use the word as mathematicians do), the kind of thinking that can cope with change and the conceptual difficulties it presents. What happened was obviously this: one term of a pair of contraries had a tendency to swallow up the other and stand for the whole range of variation. Whether this tendency can be traced to the rationalizing influence of science, or whether it is prior to science and has itself given an impetus to that revolution of thought is a question still undecided.

Owen Barfield

## Poetic Diction and Legal Fiction *

. . . . if we proceed to study language with a more definitely historical bias, and look into the etymologies and derivations of words, then the vast majority even of those meanings which we normally regard as "literal" are seen to have originated either in metaphors or in something like them. Such words as *spirit, sad, humor, perceive, attend, express, understand,* and so on immediately spring to mind as examples. Indeed the difficulty here would rather be to find words that are *not* examples. There is no doubt that they were once metaphorical. The question which a good many people have asked themselves, a little uneasily, is Are they *still* metaphors? And, if not, when—and still more *how*—precisely, did they cease to be so?

What is essential to the nature and growth of language is clearly essential to the nature and growth of our thought, or rather of our consciousness as a whole. In what way then is metaphor or tarning [4] essential to that nature and that growth? Here we begin to tread on metaphysical ground and here I think the analogy of legal fictions can really help us by placing our feet on one or two firmer tufts in the quaking bog. It can help us to realize in firmer outlines certain concepts which, like all those relating to the nature of thought itself, are tenuous, elusive, and difficult of expression.

Students of history will have observed that rebellions and agitations arising out of dissatisfaction with the law tend, at any rate in the earlier stages of society, to demand, not so much a reform of the law as its *publication*. People complain that they do not know what the law is. They want to know what it is, because otherwise they cannot be sure that it will be the same tomorrow as it is today. In fact it is the very essence of a law that it should apply to every case. It follows that the forms of action must be limited in number, and they must not change from day to day. If there is a different law for every case that arises, then what is being administered is simply not law at all but the arbitrary (though not necessarily unjust) decisions of those who govern us. But that is exactly what the word law *means* —something which is *not* such a series of arbitrary decisions or events, something which will be *the same* for the next case as it was for the last. This is where the difficulty arises; for it is the nature of life itself (certainly of human life) never to repeat itself exactly. Phenomena exactly repeated are not life, they are mechanism. Life varies, law is of its nature unvarying. Yet at the same time it is the function of law to serve, to express, and indeed partly to *make* the social life of the community. That is the paradox, the diurnal solution of which constitutes the process called society. One solution is legislation, the other is fiction. Legislation is drastic, *a priori*, and necessary. Fiction is flexible, empirical, and also necessary. Without the Fiction

* From *Essays Presented to Charles Williams* 121–125 (1947). Published by Oxford University Press and reprinted with its permission.

4. The writer's neologism for "saying one thing and meaning another."

of Adoption," says Maine in his *Ancient Law*, "it is difficult to understand how Society would ever have escaped from its swaddling-clothes."

In the paradoxical relation of law to social life I think we have a useful picture of the paradoxical relation of language to consciousness. Formal logic is not much studied nowadays, but that does not alter the fact that logic is essential to the very existence of language and the forms of proposition and syllogism underlie all expression. Now logic presupposes first and foremost that the same word means the same thing in one sentence as it does in another. Humpty Dumpty may speak of making his words "mean" what he chooses, and if somebody made a noise never heard before or since he might possibly manage to convey some sort of vague sympathetic impression of the state of his feelings. Yet repetition is inherent in the very meaning of the word "meaning." To say a word "means" something implies that it means that same something more than once.

Here then is the paradox again. The logical use of language presupposes the meanings of the words it employs and presupposes them constant. I think it will be found to be a corollary of this, that the logical use of language can never add any meaning to it. The conclusion of a syllogism is implict already in the premises, that is, in the *meanings* of the *words* employed; and all the syllogism can do is to make that meaning clearer to us and remove any misconception or confusion. But life is not constant. Every man, certainly every original man, has something new to say, something new to mean. Yet if he wants to express that meaning (and it may be that it is only when he tries to express it, that he knows what he means) he must use language—a vehicle which presupposes that he must either mean what was meant before or talk nonsense!

If therefore he would say anything really new, if that which was hitherto unconscious is to become conscious, he must resort to tarning. He must talk what is nonsense on the face of it, but in such a way that the recipient may have the new meaning suggested to him. This is the true importance of metaphor. I imagine this is why Aristotle, in calling metaphor "the most important," gives as a reason that "it alone does not mean borrowing from someone else." In terms of mixed law and logic we might perhaps say that the metaphorical proposition contains a judgment, but a judgment pronounced with a wink at the Court. Bacon put it more clearly in the *Advancement of Learning* when he said:

> Those whose conceits are seated in popular opinions need only but to prove or dispute; but those whose conceits are beyond popular opinions have a double labour; the one *to make themselves conceived*, and the other to prove and demonstrate. So that it is of necessity with them to have recourse to similitudes and translations to express themselves.

If we consider Bacon's position in the history of thought, it will not surprise us that the problem should have presented itself to him so clearly. Himself a lawyer, was he not attempting to do for science the very thing which Maitland tells us those old legal fictions were contrived for, that is, "to get modern results out of medieval premisses"?

At all events there is a sentence in the *Novum Organum* which provides one of the most striking illustrations of tarning that it would be possible to imagine. It is a double illustration: first, there was an attempt at deliberate and fully conscious meaning-making, which failed: Bacon tried to inject new meaning into a word by *saying* precisely what he wanted it to mean. But we have seen that what is said precisely cannot convey new meaning. But, since his meaning *was* really new, there had at some point in the process to be a piece of actual tarning. There was—and it succeeded. He did in fact inject new meaning into another word—not by saying, but by just meaning it!

> [Although it is true that in nature nothing exists beyond
> separate bodies producing separate motions according to law;
> still for the *study* of nature that very law and its investiga-
> tion, discovery and exposition are the essential thing, for
> the purpose both of science and of practice. Now it is that
> law and its clauses which we understand by the term
> "forms"—principally because this word is a familiar one
> and has become generally accepted. *Novum Organum, ii. 2.*]

The "forms" of which Bacon here speaks were none other than the Platonic ideas, in which Bacon, of course, did not believe. What he did believe in was that system of abstract causes or uniformity which we have long since been accustomed to express by the phrase "the laws of nature," but for which there was then no name, because the meaning was a new one. He therefore tried deliberately by way of a *simile* to put this new meaning into the old word *"forma"*; but he failed, inasmuch as the new meaning never came into general use. Yet at the same time, more unconsciously, and by way of *metaphor*, he was putting the new meaning into the word *"lex"* itself—that curious meaning which it now bears in the expression "the laws of nature." This is one of those pregnant metaphors which pass into the language, so that much of our subsequent thinking is based on them.

## CHAPTER THIRTEEN

# The Rule of Role

## INTRODUCTORY NOTE

In his *Rochin* opinion Justice Frankfurter insisted that it was possible for judges to "practice the requisite detachment and to achieve sufficient objectivity" even when their decisions could not be shown to derive from, or be justified by, a specific legal rule. Among other factors which make such judicial action responsible, objective, and externally controllable, he said, are widely-held cultural presuppositions and attitudes, the limited nature of judicial jurisdiction, and the habits of mind and methods of work which characterize the judicial office. These are factors, however, whose force and importance are often questioned. Many people simply do not believe that they materially limit the conduct of judges or, for that matter, any other power-wielders. You should ask yourself whether, and to what extent, your own views coincide with this position. Consider also the evidence on which the position rests and what it is—if it is something other than wishful thinking—which has led many to adopt Justice Frankfurter's view.

The forces and conditions which Justice Frankfurter invokes, however, do not have to be dismissed out of hand in order to reject the method of his *Rochin* opinion. Social customs, institutions, taboos, etc. must play a crucial role in judicial decisions, it might be argued—but only as expressed in an authoritative, official statement: *i. e.*, a legal rule. The reason for this critical reservation is that social and institutional forces are multifarious, complex, contradictory, and often very difficult to discern. To let a judge determine *de novo* what they require, therefore, is to leave him without adequate guidance and direction. The result will necessarily be an essentially personal, emotionally derived decision. The last chapter's attempts to suggest the critical social importance of language and of rules should not obscure the difficulties presented by such reasoning. For if rules are the sole means by which to achieve objectivity and public control in the formulation and execution of social policies then the prospects for such objectivity and control must be dim, indeed. Situations are constantly arising for which no preexisting rules can be found. And of these situations, furthermore, there are many for which acceptable rules cannot be *devised*. In addition, there are areas where it is difficult to determine which of a number of apparently applicable rules should in fact be applied—and there is usually no metarule with which the choice can be made. Finally, what is ultimately most disturbing on reflection, even when there is general agreement as to which rule is the applicable one, there may still be substantial doubts. For the question of the rule's meaning can always arise and there can be no ultimate rule which decisively answers it. When all of this is remembered—and taken into account—it would seem that a position which denies objectivity to decisions in which rules do not play the decisive role must treat much of the law as arbitrary and idiosyncratic.

If we are unwilling to accept such a conclusion, other sources of objectivity are obviously necessary. We have already seen in Chapter 10 that certain elementary modes of intellectual organization—biologically and culturally given—may account to some extent for the degree of community which human beings have in fact achieved. Such factors support the dictum that men necessarily are social animals and that none of their decisions can be wholly personal. Yet, for purposes of law certainly, the limits and channels which such modes of intellectual organization provide are not likely to be enough. The range of decisions they leave open remains uncomfortably wide. Other, more specific expressions of social need and interest are probably required. In the search for these, it is hard to ignore the considerations on which Justice Frankfurter so heavily relied. Traditional social attitudes, customary ways of implementing social and personal purposes, institutions devised to deal with recurring problems—all of these embody to some extent important, public, socially-shared decisions. They are not necessarily decisions consciously made at a definite time—the process by which they develop may more nearly resemble a gradual and subliminal dialectic. Yet just as one constructs a useable, socially responsive theory of "the law" from the heterogeneous opinions which make up the body of common law precedent, one might also formulate helpful propositions expressing a society's social values from its time-tested responses to the needs of people living together. At any rate, this is an hypothesis to be examined in this chapter. The specific focus will be the phenomenon of role, a subject of special importance to lawyers, who frequently must ask themselves what the obligations of their various legal roles—judge, legislator, practitioner, trustee, corporate counsel—entail. The extent to which such questions further the social interest in intelligent, responsible and reckonable decisionmaking may be viewed as one of the central concerns of the chapter.

Roles, unlike rules, cannot be seen and are by no means as easy to grasp or manipulate intellectually. This may be one reason why their importance—even their existence—is often discounted. But after encountering, among other things, corporations and paradigms, the invisibility and elusiveness of a phenomenon should not alone keep us from appreciating it. Actually, it is possible to discern important parallels between roles and rules. A role can be viewed as a master rule which reconciles and directs the actions of those who take it. It is a rule, however, only in the sense that it seems to exhibit a logic, a consistency, and a structure which enable us to conceive it as a unit or entity. It is likely that any specific, articulate linguistic formulation would strike us as a fatally inadequate expression of its character and scope. On the other hand, a typical role very often consists of many specific rules which the role-player will have to follow. It can be said, therefore, that a major function of roles is to help us decide, when in doubt, just what rules are applicable to situations with which we must deal.

There is more, however, to role than these rules. With them, it has been argued, come attitudes, prejudices, points of view, goals, policies, motives, fears, wishes, concerns, pleasures, etiquettes which distinguish the different forms of role-conduct from each other. A system of stereotyped emotions and value preferences, of course, is likely to offend those who demand that people's actions be authentic and genuine. Decisions based on generalized feelings may be excoriated as inhuman and insincere just as rule-guided decisions are condemned as unjust because they ignore the individuality of particular cases. The objections to this position, it should be clear, will be very much like those traditionally advanced in defense of rules. The maintenance of personal and social organization requires that feelings take a definite, manageable, reckonable form. We must be able to recognize them when we have them and we must be able to have them when we need them. The incidence of feelings must be generally consistent. Although, as with rules, there may be room for interpretation and for change, one must usually have the same feelings when confronted with essentially the same situation. To test these remarks consider physical pain. How important is it that this feeling take a definite, recognizable form? Consider affection or disgust. How important is the reckonability of their appearances?

Roles, their defenders will contend, make it possible to formulate, organize and select appropriate emotions. They help the role-player decide what he should and should not get excited about—what facts he should view as settled, what assumptions he should challenge, what issues he should raise. They invite study as one of the devices which purport to make it possible for men to resolve *some* problems without having to resolve *all possible* problems.

## SECTION ONE: ROLE AND SOCIALIZED COGNITION

### EDWARD G. BUDD MFG. v. N.L.R.B.

138 F.2d 86 (3d Cir. 1943)

BRIGGS, Circuit Judge.

On charges filed by International Union, United Automobile, Aircraft and Agricultural Workers of America, an affiliate of the Congress of Industrial Organizations, with the National Labor Relations Board, a complaint issued dated November 26, 1941, alleging that the petitioner was engaging in unfair labor practices within the meaning of Section 8(1), (2) (3) of the National Labor Relations Act, 49 Stat. 449, 29 U.S.C.A. section 158(1), (2), (3). The complaint, as subsequently amended, alleges that the petitioner, in September, 1933, created and foisted a labor organization, known as the Budd Employee Representation Association, upon its employees and thereafter contributed financial support to the Association and dominated its activities. The amended complaint also alleges that in July, 1941, the petitioner discharged an employee, Walter Weigand, because of his activities on behalf of the union, and in October of that year refused to reinstate another employee, Milton Davis, for similar reasons. The petitioner denies these charges as does the Association which was permitted to intervene. After extensive hearings before a trial examiner the Board on June 10, 1942 issued its decision and order, requiring the disestablishment of the Association and the reinstatement of Weigand and Davis.

. . .

Another indication of the dependent nature of the Association should be referred to. We think it is symptomatic. The petitioner treated the employee representatives with extraordinary leniency. The testimony shows to what very great lengths the employer went in its parental treatment of the Association and its officers. The petitioner permitted the employee representatives to conduct themselves about as they wished. They left the plant at will whether on personal business or on the business of the Association. Some of them did very little or no work but they received full pay. It is clear that some of them, Walter Weigand for example, were not disciplined because they were representatives. We can scarcely believe that the petitioner would have displayed such an attitude toward officers of an undominated "adversary" labor organization.

In our opinion the decision of the Board to the effect that the Association was and is subject to the petitioner's domination and control is amply supported by the evidence.

. . .

The case of Walter Weigand is extraordinary. If ever a workman deserved summary discharge it was he. He was under the influence of liquor while on duty. He came to work when he chose and he left the plant and his shift as he pleased. In fact, a foreman on one occasion was agreeably surprised to find Weigand at work and commented upon it. Weigand amiably stated that he was enjoying it.[1] He brought a woman (apparently generally known as the "Duchess") to the rear of the plant yard and introduced some of the employees to her. He took another employee to visit her and when this man got too drunk to be able to go home, punched his time-card for him and put him on the table in the representatives' meeting room in the plant in order to sleep off his intoxication. Weigand's immediate superiors demanded again and again that he be discharged, but each time higher officials intervened on Weigand's behalf because as was naively stated he was "a representative." In return for not working at the job for which he was hired, the petitioner gave him full pay and on five separate occasions raised his wages. One of these raises was general; that is to say, Weigand profited by a general wage increase throughout the plant, but the other four raises were given Weigand at times when other employees in the plant did not receive wage increases.

The petitioner contends that Weigand was discharged because of cumulative grievances against him. But about the time of the discharge it was suspected by some of the representatives that

---

1. Weigand stated that he was carried on the payroll as a "rigger". He was asked what was a rigger. He replied: "I don't know; I am not a rigger." [Footnote in Court's opinion.]

Weigand had joined the complaining CIO union. One of the representatives taxed him with this fact and Weigand offered to bet a hundred dollars that it could not be proved. On July 22, 1941 Weigand did disclose his union membership to the vice-chairman (Rattigan) of the Association and to another representative (Mullen) and apparently tried to persuade them to support the union. Weigand asserts that the next day he with Rattigan and Mullen, were seen talking to CIO organizer Reichwein on a street corner. The following day, according to Weigand's testimony, Mullen came to Weigand at the plant and stated that Weigand, Rattigan and himself had been seen talking to Reichwein and that he, Mullen, had just had an interview with Personnel Director McIlvain and Plant Manager Mahan. According to Weigand, Mullen said to him, "Maybe you didn't get me in a jam." And, "We were seen down there." The following day Weigand was discharged.

As this court stated in National Labor Relations Board v. Condenser Corp., supra, 3 Cir., 128 F.2d at page 75, an employer may discharge an employee for a good reason, a poor reason or no reason at all so long as the provisions of the National Labor Relations Act are not violated. It is, of course, a violation to discharge an employee because he has engaged in activities on behalf of a union. Conversely an employer may retain an employee for a good reason, a bad reason or no reason at all and the reason is not a concern of the Board. But it is certainly too great a strain in our credulity to assert, as does the petitioner, that Weigand was discharged for an accumulation of offenses. We think that he was discharged because his work on behalf of the CIO had become known to the plant manager. That ended his sinecure at the Budd plant. The Board found that he was discharged because of his activities on behalf of the union. The record shows that the Board's finding was based on sufficient evidence.

### NOTES AND QUESTIONS

1. Although the National Labor Relations Act [2] protects the organizational rights [3] of "employees," not all those employed by a business fall within this category. See, e. g., Section 2(2). Roughly speaking, the Act is usually thought to protect "labor" employees, but not "management" employees—of whom obvious examples are executives, less obvious examples are plant foremen.

What kind of "employee" was Weigand? Is the answer clear? Does the fact that he was listed as a rigger or that he sometimes

2. 29 U.S.C.A. § 141 (1964).

3. See, e.g., sections 8(a)(1) and 8(a)(3):

. . . It shall be an unfair labor practice—

(1) to interfere with, restrain, or coerce employees in the exercise of the rights guaranteed in section 7 [including "the right to self-organization, to form, join, or assist labor organizations"];

. . .

(3) by discrimination in regard to hire or tenure of employment . . . to encourage or discourage membership in any labor organization. . . .

29 U.S.C.A. §§ 158(a)(1), 158(a)(2) (1964).

worked in the plant conclude the matter? Could it be argued that his plant job was not his "real" job? How would one go about arguing such a proposition? To what does one look in order to determine what one's job is? Is the evidence always spelled out in definite rules and directions?

2.    Could it be argued that although Weigand was fired for his C.I.O. activity this was because such activity directly interfered, indeed, made impossible the performance of his job? Thus, he was fired not because of union membership *per se*, but for failure to do his job? What conception of Weigand's job would be necessary to make such an argument tenable? What kind of job would be inconsistent with union activity and membership?

3.    Why do you suppose "Weigand's immediate superiors demanded again and again that he be discharged"? Did they understand the nature of his job? Why, after being rebuffed repeatedly, should they have persisted in their demands? What difference did it make to them what Weigand did if "higher officials" were aware of it and were willing to permit it?

4.    Can you offer some speculations as to why Weigand joined the C.I.O. given the sinecure he had at the Budd plant? What pressures, if any, might have been on him to "go straight"? Would these pressures have been external? Internal? Both?

GARDNER MURPHY

## PERSONALITY *

A factor often neglected in the study of perception and thought has been motivation. As blurred percepts give way to differentiated ones, and these in turn give way to integrated ones, the underlying principle is that of *need*, or *drive*, or *tension*. The latent aspects in a percept—as yet unresolved and lacking recognizable individuality—which have a stable relation to tension reduction, to satisfaction of a craving, tend more and more to stand out as figure against the background of other attributes; with each successive tension resolution and each change in the qualities of the total, perceptual sharpening is accelerated. If the blurred total is related, as it often is, to two or more needs, and if on some occasions certain parts of it are relevant to one need, other parts relevant to another, it is only by focusing the sensory and cortical apparatus at the time that the immediate need is cared for; only through neglecting some parts and emphasizing others is adaptive behavior possible.

The principle of controlling the perceptual processes through tension or needs is evident in the earliest childhood problem of differentiating between friendly and hostile voices  . . .

* From 345–353, 365–366, 379–380, 559–560, 770, 903–904 (1947). Copyright (c) 1947 by Harper & Bros. Reprinted with permission of Gardner Murphy.

## ANCHORAGE

As soon as differentiation has occurred, *anchorage* appears; this is the tendency of percepts to take on a form which gives one feature of the situation special prominence. This one feature, the "figure," stands out against the "ground," and it is upon the figure that the percept is said to be "anchored." Subjectively this is a phenomenon of attention; objectively it is the law of dominance. The response that is dominant is the one that represents the prevailing anchorage.

To discover the dominance relations of drives is to discover the anchorage of ambiguous figures. Anchorage is also illustrated by the Skinner tautophone which Shakow and Rosenzweig used to bring out, in each individual subject, the tendency to anchor upon that aspect of a blurred stimulus which is most directly relevant to his personality. A phonograph record containing only vowel sounds is played over at such a distance or under such conditions that it is impossible to hear the record distinctly: the subject hears in the fluid sound pattern what his own needs and interests predispose him to hear.

Anchorage is not an ideal term for this process. Whereas a physical anchor leaves the structure of the anchored ship unaffected, psychological anchorage depends upon the entire structure of the perceptual situation; each aspect is part of the context of every other aspect, and helps to "anchor" the rest. The context of which we are dimly aware may help to determine the meaning of a sound which thereafter appears as figure; nevertheless the meaning, when once clearly perceived, serves as the anchor for interpreting other parts of the stimulus field.

The nature of the *context* or *ground* in giving a specific meaning to the *figure* is well illustrated in the "autokinetic effect." When a single star breaks through the mist on a dark night and is closely watched for a moment, it appears to move. The star may be brought into the laboratory in the form of a tiny point of light shining from a black box; the night, in the form of a darkroom. The light wavers or swings. At first, the movements seem chaotic. But they are remarkably responsive to the experimenter's suggestions; his instructions may cause the light to move rapidly to the right, slowly upward, etc. The movements are, moreover, very responsive to autogenous direction; the light moves as one expects it to move. This "autokinetic" effect, long explored by astronomers as well as experimental psychologists, has been used by Sherif to demonstrate that perceptual fields may be structured by social forces in a manner whose lawfulness and quantitative relations can be explored. The fact that *external* structure is wanting allows maximum play for *inner* structure-giving factors and for all those which arise in the subject from the verbal and other suggestions of those present. The phenomenon obeys all the laws of prestige suggestion and negativism. A mature and experienced subject, instructed to distribute his judgments around his own predetermined mean, influenced a young and naive subject to bring her range of judgments nearer his own and to raise the mean. At times a subject, setting himself against the effect, saw no motion. . . . We conclude, then, that motives in the broad sense control perceptual responses exactly as they control motor responses. . . .

The little child learns to see ambiguous situations much as Sherif's subjects learned to see the moving light. The greater the ambiguity, the more coercive the parental influence; and when others disagree, the child is *impelled* by opposing buffets to occupy a middle region, the safe region of the mores, that is as far as possible from the deviants, the "lunatic fringe." For in this and all other cases of anchoring, the figure-ground relations depend on the tension system; hence specific needs play a huge role in determining these relations, as we shall try to show in detail. . . .

The *internal* anchors must not be forgotten. Unstable though it may be, the inner organization has regions of relative fixity; one moves forward to the tune given by the organic condition, while moving also in response to the changing accompaniment provided by the stimulus field. The need to keep in intimate contact with the environment is thus the need to discover relevant anchors in the outer world—anchors that move to reduce tension. What is called the *psychology of attention* and is often treated without much reference to inner needs often proves to be the psychology of this quest for anchorage. Just as the structured world is the end result of the evolution of practical necessity, the selective awareness of the individual child or adult is less a matter of sense organs and permanent brain dispositions than of needs for peace, stability, satisfaction.

Thus in contrast to the common assertion that the Gestalt principle of organization has been over-emphasized, we are inclined to say that it has not been emphasized enough. One of the attributes of outer stimulus fields which makes them capable of the organization described by Gestaltists is their dependence upon the character of inner fields. The principle of isomorphism which the Gestaltists have emphasized (the correspondence in *formal organization* between outer stimulus pattern and inner bodily response) is not merely an isomorphism of psychological and physiological structure. It is true that the same organizing principles are discovered with the tools of the physiologist as with those of the psychologist; but there is a still deeper unity of perceptual and motivational structure. This lies in the fact that the structure of motive patterns tends to become the structure of cognitive patterns; the perceived world pattern mirrors to a considerable degree the organized need pattern within. The more tightly organized, the better structured the world pattern, the less it can be controlled by the inner pattern; the more lowly organized, the more lowly structured, the more the inner pattern controls it.

This is not to say that a momentary need must take precedence over others which have functioned before. Personality patterns involve habituation, and cognitive patterns need much reworking in order to be stable, dependable satisfiers of enduring needs. Percepts solidify and resist change; new evidence, new phenomena are frequently unassimilable. Here is embodied what we might call the

fallacy of expert opinion, or what Stefansson has called the "standardization of error." New ways of perceiving in science, as in other fields, must often be valiantly sought by the novice or the crackpot individualist among the scientists. Unless a new movement in psychology, for example, carries with it the immense prestige of the better-established aspects of the physical sciences, it is unassimilable.
. . .

We have been working our way slowly toward a definition of perception in bipolar terms, as an organized process which is both outer and inner, which is organized in terms of saliences both of the world without and of the world within. Organization is not molded exclusively by the need pattern or by the stimulus pattern. This definition, stemming chiefly from Koffka and Sherif, makes perception an *individual process*. The outer world can never be so completely unstructured as to make perception depend solely upon the perceiver; but it can never be so sharply and clearly organized as to obliterate individual differences among perceivers. Experimental techniques can therefore be formulated which cover the entire continuum from extreme fluidity, as in the autokinetic effect used by Sherif, to a definite structure, like an illuminated page of print, in which deviations of individual percepts from the "standard" are slight and can be explored only with patient analysis.

The cultural molding of perception must be viewed in these terms. It is true that group pressure can profoundly modify the individual's habits of perceiving or recalling or reasoning; but it must be emphasized that almost everything depends upon the clarity and tightness of the structure involved, and that there are huge individual differences in the clarity of the inner structure that is brought to bear on the outer pattern. Thus Lewis and Asch have shown that the effects of suggestion, marked though they may be in subjects who have only an extremely fluid inner social attitude, are negligible in subjects with clear-cut convictions. The latter respond in two contrasting ways: either by redefining the suggestion stimulus, giving it a meaning which makes sense in terms of their own inner structure and thus enables them to make sense out of it (instead of being bowled over by it), or by elaborating a fresh context to surround the suggestion stimulus and interpreting it as a natural mistake or a deliberate frame-up. . . .

The molding of perception or thought or memory in the drive-satisfying direction follows directly from the satisfying or frustrating quality of past perception; one learns to perceive, think, or remember in this way or that because such a habit is satisfying, just as one learns to *behave* this way or that because such behavior is satisfying. All cognitive processes are apparently continually shaped in greater or lesser degree by the pressure of wants.

This movement of the cognitive processes in the direction of need satisfaction is called autism. The term comes from Bleuler, who was especially concerned with autism in adult phychotics, yet saw clearly the almost universal role of the process in human life. Although the individual drive patterns vary, and the learning history of each individual is unique, a cardinal problem in personality study is the acquisition of individual autisms.

## THE BEGINNINGS OF AUTISTIC RESPONSE

At the first stage of perception, as we have already seen, drive satisfaction or drive frustration yields affects that are fused or blurred with cognitive dispositions in the physiognomic process, the whole being a global reaction. . . .

At the second stage, the cognitive structure begins to move into the foreground, and objects are recognized but are *acceptable* or *unacceptable* (or good at one time and bad at another, depending not upon the cognitive structure but upon dynamic contexts, i. e., varying needs). Here, again, there is no occasion for referring to autism, since the cognitive elements are relatively independent of the affective.

At the third stage, *affective elements are wrought into the total picture in which cognitive integration has been or is being achieved.* In the bipolar organization of perception there is a constant shift between emphasis on outer factors and emphasis on inner factors, so that there is constant variation in the degree to which drive-satisfying qualities act to influence the organization of the cognitive ingredients. It is precisely when the affective ingredients markedly distort the cognitive picture of reality, so that the observer is markedly mislead by the distortion, that true autism appears. Typical autism is thus not merely an expression of the third level of perceptual development; it is an expression of those phases of third-level perception in which the interaction of affective and cognitive elements goes on without the observer's being sharply aware of what is happening. As the blood stream, for example, bathes the brain with varying endocrine products, one sees (or remembers, or imagines) in accordance with the changing thresholds.

. . .

## SOCIALLY SHARED AUTISMS

So far as individuals share the factors that make for uniformity of outlook, they share their autisms. And not only do they tend to anchor perception in the same way and to derive the same satisfactions for their way of seeing the world; their community status depends in large degree upon their being able to see as sound, sensible people see. It should be easy, if this is so, to define and measure experimentally the autism of a socially defined group. Such an attempt has been made in a study by Proshansky, which aimed to evaluate the end result of the three types of autism which we should expect to discover, namely, autism of perception, of memory, and of thought. College students whose social attitudes had been measured were briefly shown pictures of social situations which they then had to describe in five-minute essays. Autistic factors were evidently present all the way through from the first appearance of the picture on the screen to the last word of the written report. Thus, commenting on a picture of "poor people," one subject says: "They seem to be messy, sloppy people, who seem to enjoy dwelling in their own trash."

As we turn to the way in which individuals come to share the same autistic outlook, we find abundant evidence in observations of children, which show that if an adult calls a child's attention to a feature of a complex situation to which the child already has a strongly positive or negative response, through anchorage the whole perceived situation becomes good or bad. But even if the child has no predisposition in the matter, an adult can supply it by strongly indicating his own attitude; the child by identification with the adult both anchors when he does and assigns a disvalue when the adult assigns it. If we are interested in observing quantitatively the way in which an adult comes to share the outlook of other adults, data from Sherif's original experiment answer precisely this question. It will be recalled that when three experimental subjects were jointly tested in the darkroom, giving their judgments orally, each tended quickly to assimilate his judgments somewhat to those of the others, the one giving the largest estimates and the one giving the smallest both moving toward agreement with the subject in the middle position. This "funnel-shaped relationship" seems to be characteristic of most group conduct, for the individual's approximation to group standards must occur gradually. Such data suggest indeed that security, the need to be safe in the midst of the group rather than be a lone dissenter, is the central motivating factor, and that socially shared autisms in general, as brought out in the studies of Horowitz mentioned below, derive basically from the need to be accepted by others.

From this point of view we can hardly be surprised that the individual who has built up his autistic perceptions in the group retains them, at least for a considerable period, when tested in isolation. Socially shared autisms express chiefly the needs that relate to commonly accepted standards of social adjustment. . . .

We are reminded of Ralph Linton's clear demonstration that it is not to the culture as a whole, but to specific roles that the cultural phase of personality owes its origin. Roles in terms of age, sex, occupation, etc., are assigned to the child, and through such serially enacted roles, as through a tube, he makes his way to old age. Personality is in considerable degree a matter of role behavior; even more, however, it is a matter of role perception and of self-perception in the light of the role. Bateson's contribution enables us to see more clearly the complexity of roles to be enacted by one person within a given period of his life, and also the dependence of each person's roles upon those enacted by others, the interdependence of complex role patterns by virtue of which the individual's self-portrait varies both with tasks and with the fulfillment of tasks by others.

. . .

The study of roles is a very literal application of Gestalt psychology. Roles make up a social configuration, and each person who enacts them must make adjustments between his various roles, integrate them in terms of a figure-ground pattern with a high degree of organization. One task stands out for him as figure, and every other task seems subsidiary.

.  .  .

Reviewing and condensing much that has been said heretofore, we find four ways in which personality is molded by social pressures.

(1) The signals used by society to call forth any given response can be almost indefinitely varied. Signals can secure results in terms of behavior by virtue of a limitless number of words, gestures, flags, pictures; new symbols appear from day to day. Tabus and restrictions depend similarly on an infinite variety of symbols; one society shows disapproval by signals made in one's face, whereas another uses words that threaten corporal punishment. The individual is very effectively molded by being sensitized to a particular system of signals, so much so that he is frequently unaware of these signals, these fleeting and truncated gestures and inflections of approval and disapproval.

(2) The value system of the individual begins in large part with canalizations that are referable to the current modes of satisfaction which society provides for each need. If the child responds positively to the music he hears, society has ways of repeating that experience day in and day out. In the course of time, structured music, with its diatonic or pentatonic scale, its characteristic melodic sequences, its simple or complex harmony, becomes the accepted music and all other music becomes queer. This is accomplished not by arousing in the individual any completely new wants, but by reinforcing and deepening the satisfactions first given to the primitive childhood needs. Every developed art form is the elaboration of responses to socially patterned tone, form, color, rhythm, etc. The curiosity satisfactions, as in scientific thought, can also be traced from child to adult in these terms; society acts not by adding something but by molding something that is already there, giving it characteristic direction.

(3) Somewhat more surprisingly, there is the fact that the impulsive life of the individual can be qualitatively changed to some extent. By emphasizing the legitimacy of one type of satisfaction and the illegitimacy of another within the realm of the accepted drives, society can fuse and pattern the needs and can consequently change their quality. For example, the way in which food is prepared and served involves more than the molding of food preferences by society; it changes the nature of hunger, e. g., emphasis passes from olfactory and gustatory to tactual qualities of food. Food tastes become "coarse," "refined," etc.

(4) Because of this third process, the ethos, the predominant feeling tone, depends upon the cultural process through which the individual goes. Not only are the impulses molded, but the inner core and the flow of feeling into the cognitive outlook are likewise shaped.

## NOTES AND QUESTIONS

1. Consider Murphy's remarks in relation to Justice Frankfurter's argument in *Rochin*. How many of the separate points

which Murphy makes could Frankfurter use to support his position? Which, if any, of Murphy's statements might account for the force of the specifically *legal* traditions, institutions, and roles on which much of Frankfurter's argument depends?

Is it possible to explain judicial action in terms of autisms? What would such an explanation look like? Consider that the relative independence of the judiciary leaves judges freer than other men of traditional motivations—such as the desire for economic security and prestige. Does this suggest that the judiciary is therefore freer to implement its personal preferences? What, incidentally, would Murphy think of the notion of a "purely personal preference"?

2. Would Murphy argue that one's role could affect one's perception of reality? If so, how would such an argument run? Would there be a place in such an argument for the notion of autism? If not, why? If so, just what would that part be? Are there any specifically *role-defined* motives? If so, can you think of any connected with judicial office? If not, does this mean that judicial cognition is not autistic?

Would Murphy contend that people *share* ways of seeing things? If so, how would he account for such a phenomenon? Would Murphy entertain the notion that judges—or, for that matter, members of any professional group—share modes of perception that other people do not? What makes you think so?

3. Consider the notion of anchorage. Is it applicable to anything other than perception? Would it be useful to speak of the interpretation of rules in terms of figure, ground and anchorage? Just how would those terms apply? What would be figure, what ground? What would be anchored on the figure? Consider these questions later in relation to the materials on The Language of Meaning, Chapter 15.

"One task," says Murphy, "stands out . . . as figure, and every other task seems subsidiary." If this means that a role can be figure, what would be the ground? Just what would be anchored on the figure?

### Note: The Social Function of Motives

In CHARACTER AND SOCIAL STRUCTURE,* Hans Gerth and C. Wright Mills suggest that it is possible to view motives not as "subjective 'springs' of action lying in the psychic structure or organism of the individual," but "as the terms which persons typically use in their interpersonal relations." A motive, they continue, "is a term in a vocabulary which appears to the actor himself and/or to the observer to be an adequate reason for his conduct."

As human beings grow, according to Gerth and Mills, motives are imputed to them by others. This occurs before individuals are themselves aware of having motives. Parents, for example, offer their children their first interpretations of inter-personal experience,

---

* (Harbinger ed. 1964). See, especially, *id.* at 114–123.

interpretations which are stereotyped, socially derived, and limited in number. These apparently provide the growing person with mental sets which organize his inter-personal world in an intrinsically social way. Furthermore, as the child learns new modes of conduct appropriate for various occasions, he is also taught the motives which will be viewed as acceptable justifications of such conduct. All of this, no doubt, makes it possible for individuals to rationalize their conduct and to devise modes of deception. But it also limits and directs human conduct, because the number of available motives is restricted by the relevant "vocabulary of motives acceptable for given situations by given social circles." In any given situation, for example, there may be only a few motives which would be credible and of these only one or two might be socially acceptable.

Acceptable motives, say Gerth and Mills, vary with the role an individual is playing. The differences are obvious when the more intimate roles are contrasted with the more public ones, but, these writers suggest, the differences between any two public roles or any two intimate roles may also be very wide. "Different motives may be employed for roles involving one's wife and for those involving one's acquaintance on the commuter train."

All of this means that an individual will have to internalize different, and very often conflicting, "vocabularies of motive." He must be careful to restrict the use of some motives to special situations or subject himself to a variety of social penalties. Some motives, for example, may appear "beautiful" to some in certain situations and "silly" to others. In addition, these varying vocabularies may make it difficult for the individual to decide himself on an adequate explanation of his drives and conduct. He may actually find himself unable to determine whether "he does this or that for love or for duty, for 'selfish' economic gain or for civic betterment."

Consider the position of Gerth and Mills in light of the passages from Murphy. Is Murphy one of those who views motives as "subjective 'springs' of action lying in the psychic structure or organism of the individual"? On what evidence is your answer based? In what ways do Gerth and Mills modify or elaborate the general position which Murphy wishes to take? Do they help or hinder the progress of Frankfurter's argument in *Rochin*? Do they strengthen or weaken the proposition that human cognition is socially determined? More or less so than Murphy?

## C. WRIGHT MILLS

### LANGUAGE, LOGIC AND CULTURE *

Problems of a sociology of knowledge arise when certain conceptions and findings of the cultural sciences are confronted by theories of knowing and methodology. Awareness of the social and economic

* From Power, Politics and People 423, 426–430 (I. Horowitz ed. Ballantine ed. 1963). Originally published in IV Amer. Soc. Rev. No. 5 (Oct. 1939). Reprinted by permission of The American Sociological Association.

factors operative in the reflective process has arisen within American sociology as peripheral notations on specific researches and as implicit in psychology when sociologically approached. However, the relevant sociological materials, particularly as they bear on the nature of mind and language, are as yet unexploited by those interested in sociological theories of knowledge and in the cultural careers of ideas.

.  .  .

Even if we grant that "thought" in some manner involves social processes, the thought is, nevertheless, a lingual performance of an individual thinker. We cannot "functionalize" reflection in social terms by postulating a "collective subject;" nor can we avoid the fact that there is no "group mind" by conveniently using implicit conceptions of "collective subjects." We can socially functionalize a given thinker's production only when we have made explicit, and systematically applied, a sound hypothesis of the specific socio-psychic mechanisms by which cultural determinants are operative. Without a thorough-going social theory of mind, there is real danger that research in the sociology of knowledge may become a set of mere historical enumerations and a calling of names. Only with such construction can we gain a clear and dynamic conception of the relations imputed between a thinker and his social context. Until we build a set of theoretically substantial hypotheses of socio-psychological nature, our research is likely to remain frustrated and our larger theoretical claims feeble. I wish to advance two such hypotheses.

The first is derived from the social statement of mind presented by G. H. Mead. It is his concept of the "generalized other" which, with certain modification and extension, we may employ to show how societal processes enter as determinants into reflection. The generalized other is the internalized audience with which the thinker converses: a focalized and abstracted organization of attitudes of those implicated in the social field of behavior and experience. The structure and contents of selected and subsequently selective social experiences imported into mind constitute the generalized other with which the thinker converses and which is socially limited and limiting.

Thinking follows the pattern of conversation. It is a give and take. It is an interplay of meanings. The audience conditions the talker; the other conditions the thinker and the outcome of their interaction is a function of both interactants. From the standpoint of the thinker, the socialization of his thought is coincidental with its revision. The social and intellectual habits and character of the audience, as elements in this interaction, condition the statement of the thinker and the fixation of beliefs evolving from that interplay. Thought is not an interaction as between two impenetrable atoms; it is conversational and dynamic; *i. e.*, the elements involved interpenetrate and modify the existence and status of one another. Imported into mind, this symbolic interplay constitutes the structure of mentality.

It is conversing with this internalized organization of collective attitudes that ideas are logically, *i. e.*, implicitly, "tested." Here they meet recalcitrance and rejection, reformulation and acceptance. Reasoning, as C. S. Peirce has indicated, involves deliberate approval of one's reasoning. One operates logically (applies standardized critiques) upon propositions and arguments (his own included) from the standpoint of a generalized other. It is from this socially constituted viewpoint that one approves or disapproves of given arguments as logical or illogical, valid or invalid.

No individual can be logical unless there be agreement among the members of his universe of discourse as to the validity of some general conception of good reasoning. Deliberate logical approval is based upon comparison of the argument approved with some common idea of how good argument should appear. The "laws of logic" impose a restriction upon assertion and argument. They are the rules we must follow if we would socialize our thought. They are not arrived at intuitively, nor are they *given*, "innate within the mind." They are not to be "taken as formulating generic characters of existences outside of inquiry or the traits of all possible being." Rather, the principles of logic are "the rules by means of which the meanings of our terms are explicated  .  .  .  the principles of logic are  .  .  . conventional without being arbitrary ,  .  .  .  they are shaped and selected by the instrumental character of discourse, by the goals of inquiry and discourse."

There is evidence that the so-called laws of proof may be merely the conventional abstract rules governing what are accepted as valid conversational extensions. What we call illogicality is similar to immorality in that both are deviations from norms. We know that such thought-ways change. Arguments which in the discourse of one group or epoch are accepted as valid, in other times and conversations are not so received. That which was long meditated upon is now brushed aside as illogical. Problems set by one logic are, with a change in interests, outgrown, not solved. The rules of the game change with a shift in interests, and we must accept the dominant rules if we would make an impress upon the profile of thought. Our logical apparatus is formulated by the rebuffs and approvals received from the audiences of our thought. When we converse with ourselves in thought, a generalized other as the carrier of a socially derived logical apparatus restricts and governs the directions of that thought. Although not always the ultimate critique, logical rules serve as an ultimatum for most ideas. Often on this basis are selected out those ideas which will not be spoken, but forgotten; those that will not be experimentally applied, but discarded as incipient hypotheses. In general, conformity to current principles of logic is a necessary condition for the acceptance and diffusion of ideas. This is true because principles of logic are the abstracted statements of social rules derived from the dominant diffusion patterns of ideas. In attempting to implement the socialization of our interests and thought, we acquire and utilize a socially derived logical apparatus. Within the inner forum of reflection, the generalized other functions as a socially derived mechanism through which logical evaluation operates.

Social habits are not only overt and social actions which recur,—they leave residues, "apperceptive masses," which conform to dominant and recurring activities and are built by them. In human communities, such dominant fields of behavior have implications in terms of systems of value. The interest-evaluative implication of a social structure has been termed its ethos. Dominant activities (*e. g.*, occupations) determine and sustain modes of satisfaction, mark definitions of value preference; embodied in language, they make perception discriminatory. The stuff of ideas is not merely sensory experiences, but meanings which have back of them collective habits.

## Questions

Is the "generalized other" at all a plausible concept for you? Does it correspond to anything in your own experience? What facts of human personal and interpersonal life does it try to account for?

Do Mills's remarks in this passage add anything to the discussion presented by Murphy? Does he tell us anything about motives that is not told to us by Murphy? Does he tell us anything about the operation of roles that we have not yet encountered? Does he provide any further grist for Justice Frankfurter's mill?

Does the concept of "the generalized other" help us to understand the function of a written judicial opinion? Is "the generalized other" of the judge different from that of the lawyer? Of the plumber? Try to defend your answer.

## Note: The Cultural Apparatus

To understand the human condition, says C. Wright Mills in *The Cultural Apparatus*,* we must recognize "that men live in second-hand worlds." What they "know" is much more than they have personally experienced and their personal "experience is always indirect." The meanings which shape and color their lives come from without. These "meanings and designs and communications" stand between men's consciousness and their existence. They "decisively influence such consciousness as men have of their existence." "Every man, to be sure, *observes* nature, social events, and his own self: but he does not, he has never, observed most of what he takes to be fact, about nature, society, or self." And the very terms by which each man interprets his observations are not his own: "he has not personally formulated or even tested them." These standard facts and stereotyped meanings, says Mills, are increasingly monopolized "by means of what I am going to call the cultural apparatus."

The cultural apparatus produces our science, our art, our learning, our entertainment, our news, our hokum. It devises the modes of their distribution and consumption. It is composed of the institutions —schools, theatres, newspapers, census bureaus, laboratories, museums, etc.—which do this producing and this distributing and which determine the modes of consumption. "Inside this apparatus, standing between men and events, the images, meanings, slogans that define the worlds in which men live are organized and compared, maintained and revised, lost and cherished, hidden debunked, celebrated. Taken

---

* In Power, Politics and People 405–422
(I. Horowitz ed. Ballantine ed. 1963).

as a whole, the cultural apparatus is the lens of mankind through which men see; the medium by which they interpret and report what they see. It is the semiorganized source of their very identities and of their aspirations. It is the source of The Human Variety—of styles of living and of ways to die." The cultural apparatus tells us what reason, sensibility, technique, beauty, and goodness are and when they are properly to be invoked. And it is so dominant in the formulation of men's personal experience that they will often hold in doubt what they have seen with their own eyes until it has been confirmed or denied by some accredited interpreter of social events. "With such means, each nation tends to offer a selected, closed-up and official version of world reality."

Do you agree that men live in second-hand worlds? How much of your own thinking is unmediated by the cultural apparatus? To what extent would it be possible to obtain a greater degree of direct, immediate personal experience? Is it possible? Desirable?

Note the legal rule which prohibits the introduction of hearsay testimony into evidence. If we live in second-hand worlds what is the point of such a rule? The traditional justification is that hearsay evidence deprives the opposing party of his right to cross-examine the witness whose observations are being reported. What makes the right to cross-examine so important?

*Edward Stevens Robinson*

## Law and the Lawyers *

The deliberative processes that will constitute essential psychological subject matter for a naturalistic jurisprudence are of many varieties. The most familiar and accessible is the deliberative process of the appellate court. This is the type of deliberation which conventional legal science has seen most fit to record. It has been, as we have noted, the principal subject matter of conventional legal study. Actually the picture of appellate deliberation furnished by legal scholarship has been over-simplified. The process has been discussed mostly as though it were a ratiocination of an individual mind whereas it has more often been a process of social dispute. There needs to be added to the play of ideas the play of personality upon personality, of judge upon judge. The psychological principles of leadership, of jeolousy, of positive and negative suggestibility must ultimately be taken into account if we are to gain an adequate understanding of the judicial process.

.   .   .

In our efforts to understand the process of deliberation **as it** occurs in the judicial mind we cannot set aside as mere argumentative devices all those elements of expression that imply an audience. The contents of the self are largely social. A man's most intimate thoughts deal with what he thinks others think about him. Whenever a man

* From    170–174,    175–178,    179–180        the estate of Edward Stevens Robin-
  (1935).  Reprinted with permission of      son.

feels that his conduct is important he looks upon it as though through the eyes of another person; he stands, a spectator, upon the curb and watches himself march by. Whenever a man accepts or rejects an opinion he feels his act of judgment being judged by others. These critics who permeate a man's thinking, may be hypothetical; their evaluations may not correspond with those that actual persons would make; but they are in a very real sense social influences. In overt controversy one may distinguish between one's own opinions and those of other persons, but the segregation of self is never more than partial. One who is content with opinions that are approved by none of his fellow men assumes the grave psychic risks of paranoia.

And so the judge in his expressed opinion orders his thoughts and puts them in becoming dress not simply with the design of reducing an argumentative adversary nor yet with that of disguising his own real meaning. The atmosphere of sobriety, of modesty, of conscientious effort that he seeks to cast about his written words are frequently no more than is required for the maintenance of his own essentially social nature. Those words, if they are properly to represent himself, must also represent his colleagues, whether or not they have participated in the case, and also a larger world of men in which the court is an instrument of the good and decent life.

NOTES AND QUESTIONS

1. Do you agree that "one who is content with opinions that are approved by none of his fellow men assumes the grave psychic risks of paranoia"? Is such a view consistent with notions of individual integrity? Why do we make our judges so independent of external coercion if they are still bound to worry over and be controlled by "what other people think"? Insofar as the written opinion requires the judge to expose himself to the critical scrutiny of other people does it defeat the goal of making judges independent?

2. In connection with the passages from Robinson consider also the following:

> The deciding is, in the main, done under felt pressure or even compulsion to follow up with a published "opinion" which tells any interested person what the cause is and why the decision—under the authorities—is right, and perhaps why it is wise.

> This opinion is addressed also to the losing party and counsel in an effort to make them feel at least that they have had a fair break—a matter of importance to the polity and the law, and often enough (as is suggested by long Per Curiams in some touchy cases) of political importance also re a judge's re-election. The "single *right* answer" idea still has some tendency to dominate the form of the opinion, and the need for an opinion, often enough the opinion itself, often casts its shadow before, into the process of the actual deciding.

> In our law the opinion has in addition a central forward-looking function which reaches far beyond the cause in hand: the opinion has as one if not its major office to show

how like cases are properly to be decided in the future. **This**
also frequently casts its shadow before, and affects the deciding of the cause in hand. (If I cannot give a reason I
should be willing to stand to, I must shrink from the very
result which otherwise seems good.) Thus the opinion serves
as a steadying factor which aids reckonability. Its preparation affords not only back-check and cross-check on any contemplated decision by way of continuity with the law to date
but provides also a due measure of caution by way of contemplation of effects ahead.

More: the effort is to make this opinion an opinion of
the court, a group expression, at the worst one which will
command adherence of the group. This, like the process of
consultation and vote, goes some distance to smooth the unevenness of individual temper and training into a moving
average more predictable than the decisions of diverse single
judges.

In another fashion the dissent and its possibility press
toward reckonability of result. . . . In real measure . . . the dissent, by forcing or suggesting full
publicity, rides herd on the majority, and helps to keep constant the due observance of [traditional limitations]. . . .

## K. LLEWELLYN, THE COMMON LAW TRADITION 26 (1960) *

Note the references to the *form* of the judicial opinion in both Robinson and Llewellyn. The former speaks of the "atmosphere of sobriety, of modesty, of conscientious effort that" the judge "seeks to
cast about his written words." The latter adverts to opinions which
proceed as if there were a "single right answer" to the problem confronting the court. How can you account for such phenomena? Do
they help or hinder the courts in reaching socially satisfactory legal
solutions? Is the "'single right answer' idea" a good idea? How
does it comport with the material concerning the nature of rules which
you recently encountered?

## KARL N. LLEWELLYN

### THE COMMON LAW TRADITION †

The men who do the deciding hold office; they hold judicial office as full-time professionals. This is not a simple matter to be just
glanced at or indeed assumed without a glance. Neither is it to be
casually dismissed as a mere illustration, say, of role theory, or with
such a vague concept and label as "impartiality." . . .

In our tradition *judicial* office is with peculiar intensity *office*,
and is perhaps unmatched in the doggedness with which it presses
upon the officeholder a demand to be selfless. Time, place, archi-

---

* Reprinted with permission of the es-    † From 46–50 (1960). Reprinted with
  tate of Karl N. Llewellyn.            permission of the estate of Karl N.
                                        Llewellyn.

tecture and interior arrangement, supporting officials, garb, ritual combine to drive these matters home. The pressures are unremitting, time gives them further power; I hold this shaping force to be as important as the skill-values of bench-experience in making the case against unnecessary replacement of appellate personnel.

Various aspects of the role have indeed rooted deep in the folkways and moral judgments even of childhood: an umpire is *not* to "take sides"; "wait a minute, we gotta see what *he* has to say." And a deep and rich as-of-course grasp of the idea and ideal of this office is revealed when our language to describe it has no need to strike close to the mark.   .   .   .

.   .   .

.   .   .   . The intermediate court of appeal is subject to the pat or slap of affirmance or reversal. And on any appellate court there sit beside a man, as already mentioned, his breathren of the particular bench, with their example, their warmth or aloofness, their praise or even remonstrance. Also to be felt are the bar and the vocal portion of the public; one recalls the impact of recorded vote and signed opinion. These days, the law reviews, too, manage to smooth or ruffle pride—or vanity. Even those judges who make and file notes and write letters for posterity with the care and hope which Pliny lavished on his "letters"—even they are steadied into greater predictability by their conscious need to seem to themselves consistent, and duly noble.

In the net, our appellate bench has been strikingly self-corrective in morale as well as manner. Despite all mistakes and despite all passions of the day, they have either maintained or speedily regained a standing with the lay public hardly rivaled by any scattered, unorganized aggregation of equivalent size in all recorded history. I think of only one period when the supreme courts at large (in contrast to the Supreme Court of the United States) have come under general and continuous attack—the period which culminated in Theodore Roosevelt's onslaught on "government by injunction" and in that movement for recall of judges which captured seven States before it ebbed. But we have with us today two legal generations for whom that story no longer has a meaning, while despite ups and downs of particular persons and particular benches, honesty, reasonable effort, and reasonable dignity remain, along with position, prestige-attributes of the appellate bench. Odd, individual delinquencies fade out like the ripples from a flung stone: for instance, even the continued self-will and corruption and final public disgrace of a Manton left the Second Circuit still for decades with the most distinguished and admired bench in these United States. All of which means that the *office* waits and then moves with majestic power to shape the man. An image so poignantly perceived, so imperiously held up for imitation, is not to be escaped. It sorts and lifts out of a man the best he has to offer, with a degree of consistency foreign to the past of all but a few; it builds that initial best up to levels which were not in him when he first became a judge; with every robing he renews a silent covenant with self and office. This is not merely a matter of squeezing or cutting away the idiosyncratic and so shaping the man more nearly to an average; it is a matter, no less, of so dealing with idiosyncratic might or vision that, without loss of character, it is yet channeled into service of the whole, no longer of the part, and channeled into teamwork; channeled therefore into a new reckonability. There is in this last phenomenon at once a mystic and no mystic quality. You can "explain" it, if you will, in relative comfort by a dozen or so of such things as I have been discussing, and come close to understanding the result. But for myself, I feel more to be there than the sum of such factors, taken even in dynamic interaction, will explain. I think of how a second injection of judicial office and responsibility transformed the rhinoceros-hided and-tempered McReynolds, so resistant to the normal shaping forces that his mannerlessness in the robing or consulting room and on the bench had become a by-word; so "judicial" that he would stalk out of court when a lawyer rose at the bar who was a Jew or was a Negro or was a woman. Yet when the chief was sick and McReynolds came to preside, he was decorous to a woman advocate and even gave her extra time, and we have it from Stone that there had not in his time been fairer or more courteous conduct of the consultation.

(b) It is true—to put a semi-contra, and as the stage itself reminds us—that neither role, costume, setting, nor training means uniformity, nor do the four together. Add ritual, add ingrained felt tradition and ideal and what have you more, still men will differ in temper, background, eyes to see, wit to judge, tongue to say, persuasiveness with their brethren. As a matter of horse sense it is thus clear that the factor of person is still important, even when we limit observation to that overwhelming bulk of the appellate judges to whom improper conduct in office would be unthinkable: Else how could you by their work tell a Brandeis from a Butler, a Hough or Hand or Swan from a Rogers, a Mansfield from an Ellenborough, a Coke from a Jeffreys, a Cardozo or Cuthbert Pound from an O'Brien or McLaughlin? How, indeed, could you justify allowing an appeal from any honest and diligent trial judge to any appellate court; or, especially, from any immediate appellate bench to any other court; or permit dissent save at penalty of impeachment? So that any conception of appellate deciding done "by *laws and not* by men" is patent error.

But this does not mean lack of effect in those factors which work like a flywheel for stability. I am minded of Kinsey-Pomeroy-Martin on "un"-chastity among American husbands: for at least half of those husbands, during the lifetime, at least one extramarital orgasm! K–P–M were here wringing their evidence dry; but has anyone ever offered more powerful testimony on the degree to which men—many or most of this 50 per cent and all of the other half—*can* be shaped in conduct by the channeling pressures of a culture? We must expect with the appellate judges a materially greater effect from the molding factors because in the main those influences are accepted by them, not resisted, are welcome, are to only a slight degree a source of trouble or conflict with individual or even queerish aspects of the person, call for no release of resistance-tensions—as sex-control does in so many persons and cultures—by way of breakover or carnival or convention

or binge.  Let me say this again: over the vast bulk of persons and
of occasions for each person, appellate judges labor to be judicial, appellate judges learn to be judicial, appellate judges like to be judicial.
It seems to me obvious that this is much more nearly universal among
them than among the judges who sit at trial or as magistrates; certainly the working team, the bench of which each appellate judge is
but one working part, goes far to elicit these attitudes and to restrain
or root out any contrary tendency.  Where, as occasionally, this fails
to work out, the matter is largely one of individual insensitivity: an
anteater-hide stuffed with either egotism or naive bigotry or both.

### NOTES AND QUESTIONS

1.  Consider also the following:

> Few judges "make" the American appellate bench
> without twenty and more years of active work in some as-
> pect of the law, in addition to their schooling.  The judges
> are therefore not mere Americans.  They have been law-
> conditioned.  They *see* things, they see *significances*, through
> law-spectacles, in terms of torts and trusts and corporations
> and due process and motions to dismiss; and this is the way
> they sort and size up any welter of facts.  Moreover, they
> *think* like lawyers, not like laymen; and more particularly
> like *American* lawyers, not like German lawyers or Brazilian
> lawyers. . . .
>
> . . .
>
> The Court before which the cause is to come has issued
> opinions which do more than lay down "law" on particular
> points; they also and especially cumulate to show ways of
> looking at things, ways of sizing things up, ways of handling
> authorities, attitudes in one area of life-conflict and another.
> Over a five-year, indeed over a one-year, stretch these facets
> of the opinions furnish a revealing and appealing study which
> no appellate lawyer can afford to do without.  For one must
> not forget that a particular bench tends strongly to develop
> a characteristic going tradition not only of ways of work
> but of outlook, and of working attitudes of one judge toward
> another.  New judges get broken in to all of this; each nor-
> mally adjusts largely to the harness which the going tradi-
> tion seeks to fit upon him.  Of course the tradition changes.
> Occasionally, it can change with relative speed.  Thus a Car-
> dozo joining the New York Court of Appeals, a Schaefer join-
> ing the Illinois Supreme Court, can be felt within a year or
> two, and though with strong men beside them can within a
> few years have strong impact upon the tradition; but even
> this is a process which leaves its marks upon the published
> record, so that the going tradition of the moment, though in
> transition, can be somewhat known and to a greater degree
> felt.
>
> . . .
>
> . . . . the men of our appellate bench are human
> beings.  I have never understood why the cynics talk and

think as if this were not so.  For it is so.  And one of the more obvious and obstinate facts about human beings is that they operate in and respond to traditions, and especially to such traditions as are offered to them by the crafts they follow.  Tradition grips them, shapes them, limits them, guides them; not for nothing do we speak of *ingrained* ways of work or thought, of men *experienced* or case-hardened, of *habits* of mind.  Tradition, moreover, wreaks these things upon human beings notwithstanding that in a real degree men also make use of the tradition, reshape it in the very use, sometimes manipulate it to the point of artifice or actual evasion if need, duty, or both, seem so to require.

LLEWELLYN, THE COMMON LAW TRADITION 19–20, 34–35, 53 (1960).*

2.  Llewellyn's major emphasis is on the "reckonability" of judicial decisions.  In spite of the inadequacies of language and the divergencies of personality, he contends, there are forces and forms which make the law a field in which intelligence can be profitably used.  It is meaningful, in other words, to talk about what the law is, even though no linguistic proposition can be treated as its final and absolute expression.  Do his arguments seem plausible to you?  Do you concede the force of the social factors, conditions and structures which he invokes?  If so, why?  If not, why not?

Is the importance of role, according to Llewellyn, confined only to the problem of predictability in law?  Do the roles people take sacrifice justice, freedom, happiness, etc., for order?  What do you think Llewellyn would say?

## SECTION TWO: THE DEFINITION OF THE JOB

### *LEARNED HAND*

### THE CONTRIBUTION OF AN INDEPENDENT JUDICIARY TO CIVILIZATION †

In considering the contributions of an independent judiciary to our kind of civilization, I should like to distinguish between its customary law and constitution on the one hand and what I shall call its "enacted law" on the other.  By "enacted law" I mean any authoritative command of an organ of government purposely made responsive to the pressure of interests affected.  I shall assume that before "enacted law" is passed these interests have opportunity in the press, in public meeting, by appearance before committees or the like and in any other lawful way, to exert their influence.  "Enacted law" in that sense is ordinarily a compromise of conflicts and its success depends upon how far mutual concessions result in an adjust-

* Reprinted with permission of the estate of Karl N. Llewellyn.

† From Massachusetts Bar Association, The Supreme Judicial Court of Massachusetts 1692–1942, at 59–67 (1942). Reprinted with permission of the Massachusetts Bar Association.

ment which brings in its train the most satisfaction and leaves the least acrimony. I am not sure that an independent judiciary would be desirable in a society where law was enacted by a different process. For example, Gallup polls may in the end become so accurate that, if we should wish a government by referendum, we could accept them as reliable and speedy equivalents. It might be best not to make independent a judiciary called upon to interpret the answers so obtained. Nobody can capture the implications of his purposes, or really know what he wants till they have been tried out in experience; but, although political controversy is poor makeshift, it is the best we can get in advance, and law must speak in futuro. Those vague stirrings of mass feeling which many who pride themselves upon their democracy mistake for the popular will must always be made concrete before they can become law in any practical sense, and the process of definition is as important as the dumb energy which provokes it, perhaps more so. In a society governed by Gallup polls it might be well to submit the judiciary to a Gallup poll, too; the definition of the popular command would be too much like the command itself.

But an independent judiciary is an inescapable corollary of "enacted law" in the sense I am using it. Such laws do not indeed represent permanent principles of jurisprudence—assuming that there are any such—but they can be relatively stable; and, provided that the opportunity always exists to supplant them when there is a new shift in political power, it is of critical consequence that they should be loyally enforced until they are amended by the same process which made them. That is the presupposition upon which the compromises were originally accepted; to disturb them by surreptitious, irresponsible and anonymous intervention imperils the possibility of any future settlements and pro tanto upsets the whole system. Such laws need but one canon of interpretation, to understand what the real accord was. The duty of ascertaining its meaning is difficult enough at best, and one certain way of missing it is by reading it literally, for words are such temperamental beings that the surest way to lose their essence is to take them at their face. Courts must reconstruct the past solution imaginatively in its setting and project the purposes which inspired it upon the concrete occasions which arise for their decision. To interject into the process the fear of displeasure or the hope of favor of those who can make their will felt, is inevitably to corrupt the event, and could never be proposed by anyone who really comprehended the issue. This was long held a truism, but it must be owned that the edge of our displeasure at its denial has of late been somewhat turned. In the name of a more loyal fealty to the popular will, we are asked to defeat the only means by which that will can become articulate and be made effective. To this, the first aspect of our question, I submit that there is but one answer: an unflinching resistance.

The respect all men feel in some measure for customary law lies deep in their nature; we accept the verdict of the past until the need for change cries out loudly enough to force upon us a choice between the comforts of further inertia and the irksomeness of action.

Through the openings given by that disposition, the common law has been fabricated bit by bit without express assent and under the ministrations of those who have always protested that, like the Bourbons, they learn nothing and forget nothing. Logically, the irresponsibility of an independent judiciary is here an anomaly, like the common law itself; in a pitilessly consistent democracy judges would not be making law at all. Why then do we not resent it? In earlier times when the parturition of statutes was slow and painful, judicial license was tolerated partly for that reason and partly because judges fairly represented the governing classes. While the king was supreme, or nearly so, he could remove them at pleasure, and even when after the fall of the Stuarts, they began to hold upon good behavior, they were still for long in harmony with those who had succeeded to the reins. Occasionally—Lord Mansfield is the classic example—they could without offence make radical changes in the customary law. That is no longer true; both the need and the unison have gone; legislation has become easy, judges no longer speak for the ruling classes. The price of their continued power must therefore be a self-denying ordinance which forbids change in what has not already become unacceptable. To compose inconsistencies, to unravel confusions, to announce unrecognized implications, to make, in Holmes' now hackneyed phrase, "interstitial" advances; these are the measure of what they may properly do, and there is not indeed much danger of their exceeding this limit; rather the contrary, for they are curiously timid about innovations. A judge who will hector the bar and browbeat the witnesses and who can find a warrant in the Fourteenth Amendment for stifling a patently reasonable legislative experiment, will tremble at the thought of introducing a new exception into the hearsay rule. And so, although precisionists and purists might repine, in the end things work out very well as they are, for the advantages of leaving step by step amendments of the customary law in the hands of those trained in it, outweigh the dangers.

You may well think that I have so far been merely skirmishing in a rather obvious effort to avoid the main engagement. For, unless I am deceived, those who proposed the subject of the evening were really thinking about judges and constitutions, perhaps more especially the United States Constitution; and unless I am a skulker, I must now advance to the attack. Nevertheless, I shall first attempt one more diversion. A constitution is primarily an instrument to distribute political power; and so far as it is, it is hard to escape the necessity of some tribunal with authority to declare when the prescribed distribution has been disturbed. Otherwise those who hold the purse will be likely in the end to dominate and absorb everything else, except as astute executives may from time to time check them by capturing and holding popular favor. Obviously the independence of such a tribunal must be secure; and there seems to be nothing to add to what I have been saying about "enacted law." I do not mean that courts should approach such constitutional questions as they approach statutes, and they have never done so when they knew their business; constitutions can only map out the terrain roughly, inevitably leaving much to be filled in. The scope of the interstate commerce power of Congress is an ever present instance. It is impossible to avoid all such occasions, but it was a daring expedient to meet them with judges, deliberately put beyond the reach of popular pressure. And yet, granted the necessity of some such authority, probably independent judges were the most likely to do the job well. Besides, the strains that decisions on these questions set up are not ordinarily dangerous to the social structure. For the most part the interests involved are only the sensibilities of the officials whose provinces they mark out, and usually their resentments have no grave seismic consequences.

But American constitutions always go further. Not only do they distribute the powers of government, but they assume to lay down general principles to insure the just exercise of those powers. This is the contribution to political science of which we are proud, and especially of a judiciary of Vestal unapproachability which shall always tend the Sacred Flame of Justice. Yet here we are on less firm ground. It is true that the logic which has treated these like other provisions of a constitution seems on its face unanswerable. Are they not parts in the same document? Did they not originally have a meaning? Why should not that meaning be found in the same way as that of the rest of the instrument? Nevertheless there are vital differences. Here history is only a feeble light, for these rubrics were meant to answer future problems unimagined and unimaginable. Nothing which by the utmost liberality can be called interpretation describes the process by which they must be applied. Indeed if law be a command for specific conduct, they are not law at all; they are cautionary warnings against the intemperance of faction and the first approaches of despotism. The answers to the questions which they raise demand the appraisal and balancing of human values which there are no scales to weigh. Who can say whether the contributions of one group may not justify allowing it a preference? How far should the capable, the shrewd or the strong be allowed to exploit their powers? When does utterance go beyond persuasion and become only incitement? How far are children wards of the state so as to justify its intervention in their nurture? What limits should be imposed upon the right to inherit? Where does religious freedom end and moral obliguity begin? As to such questions one can sometimes say what effect a proposal will have in fact, just as one can foretell how much money a tax will raise and who will pay it. But when that is done, one has come only to the kernel of the matter, which is the choice between what will be gained and what will be lost. The difficulty here does not come from ignorance, but from the absence of any standard, for values are incommensurable. It is true that theoretically, and sometimes practically, cases can arise where courts might properly intervene, not indeed because the legislature has appraised the values wrongly, for it is hard to see how that can be if it has honestly tried to appraise them at all; but because that is exactly what it has failed to do, because its action has been nothing but the patent exploitation of one group whose interests it has altogether disregarded. But the dangers are always very great. What seems to the losers mere spoliation usually appears to the gainers less than a reasonable relief from manifest injustice.  Moreover, even were there a hedonistic rod by which to measure loss or gain, how could we know that the judges had it; or—what is more important—would enough people think they had, to be satisfied that they should use it?  So long as law remains a profession (and certainly there is no indication that its complexities are decreasing) judges must be drawn from a professional class with the special interests and the special hierarchy of values which that implies.  And even if they were as detached as Rhadamanthus himself, it would not serve unless people believed that they were.  But to believe that another is truly a Daniel come to judgment demands almost the detachment of a Daniel; and whatever may be properly said for the judges, among whom there are indeed those as detached as it is given men to be, nobody will assert that detachment is a disposition widespread in any society.

It is not true, as you may be disposed at first blush to reply, that all this can be said with equal force of any other decision of a court.  Constitutions are deliberately made difficult of amendment; mistaken readings of them cannot be readily corrected.  Moreover, if they could be, constitutions must not degenerate into vade mecums or codes; when they begin to do so, it is a sign of a community unsure of itself and seeking protection against its own misgivings.  And that is especially true of such parts of a constitution as I am talking about; these particularly must be left imprecise.  If a court be really candid, it can only say: "We find that this measure will have this result; it will injure this group in such and such ways, and benefit that group in these other ways.  We declare it invalid, because after every conceivable allowance for differences of outlook, we cannot see how a fair person can honestly believe that the benefits balance the losses."  Practically, it is very seldom possible to be sure of such a conclusion; practically, it is very seldom possible to say that a legislature has abdicated by surrendering to one faction; the relevant factors are too many and too incomparable.

Nor need it surprise us that these stately admonitions refuse to subject themselves to analysis.  They are the precipitates of "old, unhappy, far-off things, and battles long ago," originally cast as universals to enlarge the scope of the victory, to give it authority, to reassure the very victors themselves that they have been champions in something more momentous than a passing struggle.  Thrown large upon the screen of the future as eternal verities, they are emptied of the vital occasions which give them birth, and become moral adjurations, the more imperious because inscrutable, but with only that content which each generation must pour into them anew in the light of its own experience.  If an independent judiciary seeks to fill them from its own bosom, in the end it will cease to be independent.  And its independence will be well lost, for that bosom is not ample enough for the hopes and fears of all sorts and conditions of men, nor will its answers be theirs; it must be content to stand aside from these fateful battles.  There are two ways in which the judges may forfeit their independence, if they do not abstain.  If they are intransigent but honest, they will be curbed; but a worse fate will befall them if they learn to trim their sails to the prevailing winds. A society whose judges have taught it to expect complaisance will exact complaisance; and complaisance under the pretense of interpretation is rottenness. If judges are to kill this thing they love, let them do it, not like cowards with a kiss, but like brave men with a sword.

And so, to sum up, I believe that for by far the greater part of their work it is a condition upon the success of our system that the judges should be independent; and I do not believe that their independence should be impaired because of their constitutional function. But the price of this immunity, I insist, is that they should not have the last word in those basic conflicts of "right and wrong—between whose endless jar justice resides." You may ask what then will become of the fundamental principles of equity and fair play which our constitutions enshrine; and whether I seriously believe that unsupported they will serve merely as counsels of moderation. I do not think that anyone can say what will be left of those principles; I do not know whether they will serve only as counsels; but this much I think I do know—that a society so riven that the spirit of moderation is gone, no court can save; that a society where that spirit flourishes, no court need save; that in a society which evades its responsibility by thrusting upon the courts the nurture of that spirit, that spirit in the end will perish. What is the spirit of moderation? It is the temper which does not press a partisan advantage to its bitter end, which can understand and will respect the other side, which feels a unity between all citizens—real and not the factitious product of propaganda—which recognizes their common fate and their common aspirations—in a word, which has faith in the sacredness of the individual. If you ask me how such a temper and such a faith are bred and fostered, I cannot answer. They are the last flowers of civilization, delicate and easily overrun by the weeds of our sinful human nature; we may even now be witnessing their uprooting and disappearance until in the progress of the ages their seeds can once more find some friendly soil. But I am satisfied that they must have the vigor within themselves to withstand the winds and weather of an indifferent and ruthless world; and that it is idle to seek shelter for them in a courtroom. Men must take that temper and that faith with them into the field, into the marketplace, into the factory, into the council-room, into their homes; they cannot be imposed; they must be lived. Words will not express them; arguments will not clarify them; decisions will not maintain them. They are the fruit of the wisdom that comes of trial and a pure heart; no one can possess them who has not stood in awe before the spectacle of this mysterious Universe; no one can possess them whom that spectacle has not purged through pity and through fear—pity for the pride and folly which inexorably enmesh men in toils of their own contriving, fear, because that same pride and that same folly lie deep in the recesses of his own soul.

## NOTES AND QUESTIONS

1. As Hand notes, "the logic which has treated" the Bill of Rights "like other provisions of a constitution seems on its face un-

answerable." On what basis, according to Hand, can a judge decide to enforce one part of an authoritative document, but refuse to enforce another? Could it be argued that a judge who does this is abdicating the responsibilities which attach to his office—in short, that he is not doing his job? Is Hand aware of such an argument? Does anything he says serve to meet it?

Can it be argued that Hand is putting the interests of the judiciary over those of the society in general? Is he proposing a constitutional theory which insures the continuance of independent courts while sacrificing the more fundamental interests of freedom and justice? Or has Hand simply decided that what is good for the judiciary is good for the country—just as a former president of the United States asserted that what's good for business is good for the country? Is this the kind of attitude toward one's role or job that we should wish to foster?

2. When a judge refuses to notice the unconstitutionality of legislation which is involved in a case before him, does he not become responsible for the illegal action which the legislation decrees? Does a judge who allows an executive officer to suppress an individual's freedom of speech make himself a party to that suppression? Is such judicial action moral? Is it legal? Consider the following:

> The courts refuse to convict an entrapped defendant, not because his conduct falls outside the proscription of the statute, but because, even if his guilt be admitted, the methods employed on behalf of the Government to bring about conviction cannot be countenanced. As Mr. Justice Holmes said in Olmstead v. United States, 277 U.S. 438, 470 (dissenting), in another connection, "It is desirable that criminals should be detected, and to that end that all available evidence should be used. It is also desirable that the Government should not itself foster and pay for other crimes, when they are the means by which the evidence is to be obtained. . . . [F]or my part I think it a less evil that some criminals should escape than that the Government should play an ignoble part." Insofar as they are used as instrumentalities in the administration of criminal justice, the federal courts have an obligation to set their face against enforcement of the law by lawless means or means that violate rationally vindicated standards of justice, and to refuse to sustain such methods by effectuating them. They do this in the exercise of a recognized jurisdiction to formulate and apply "proper standards for the enforcement of the federal criminal law in the federal courts," McNabb v. United States, 318 U.S. 332, 342, an obligation that goes beyond the conviction of the particular defendant before the court. Public confidence in the fair and honorable administration of justice, upon which ultimately depends the rule of law, is the transcending value at stake.

Sherman v. United States, 356 U.S. 369 (Concurring opinion). What response do you think Judge Hand might make to this? Would he be willing to sacrifice the "rule of law" in order to preserve the independence of the judiciary?

3. What, according to Judge Hand, is the courts' job? To find the "real accord" embodied in "enacted law" and then to faithfully enforce it? Does this mean that—except in those rare cases of one branch usurping the powers of another—the courts are to view themselves as instruments of the legislature? If so, how would one justify such a conception of the judicial role? By reference to history— *i. e.*, how the role has been carried out in the past? By reference to prevailing notions of judicial jurisdiction—*i. e.*, what people generally think the court does and should do? By reference to the Constitution, which, as Hand notes, allocates power between the branches? Does Hand use any of these sources of justification to support his position? If so, which ones? If not, what, if anything, does he use?

Note, again, that for Hand there is one area in which courts *can* check the legislative and executive branches. "A constitution," says Hand, "is primarily an instrument to distribute political power; and so far as it is, it is hard to escape the necessity of some tribunal with authority to declare when the prescribed distribution has been disturbed." If the necessity of some tribunal to adjudicate interdepartmental disputes justifies the placement of such power in the judiciary, could it be argued as well that the necessity of protecting the individual—whose "sacredness" Hand ultimately proclaims—also justifies a judicial checking power? Is, in other words, Hand being unduly discriminatory in his argument from necessity? Or would he say, do you think, that there is no such necessity, because legislators and executives can be trusted with the rights of individuals?

4. Does Hand have a right to expect that "the spirit of moderation" will survive if the responsibility for its survival is left to no particular agency of government or institution of society? Is a society which thrusts "upon the courts the nurture of that spirit" *necessarily* evading its responsibility and insuring that "that spirit in the end will perish"? Or is there an argument that by such delegation and concentration of authority the society is effectively discharging its responsibility? Is a society which thrusts upon the police the job of preventing and detecting crime, evading its responsibility for law and order and insuring the ultimate demise of an organized community? Does Hand's argument lead him to deny the efficacy of such social devices as the division of labor and the delegation of governmental powers? Or is there something special about "the spirit of moderation" such that it is not capable of being fostered in the same way as "the spirit of law and order"? Is there something about the "freedom of speech," for example, such that its protection cannot be given to a particular office as a special job of that office? What is ordinarily achieved by making some task the specific job of a particular agency or office? What is likely to be lost?

5. "The discussion of problems and the declaration of broad principles by the courts," says Dean Rostow, "is a vital element in the community experience through which American policy is made. The Supreme Court is, among other things, an educational body, and

the Justices are inevitably teachers in a vital national seminar."
*The Democratic Character of Judicial Review,* 66 Harv.L.Rev. 193,
208 (1952). What is it that makes this—as it was meant to be—a response to Judge Hand? With what particular assumption or position is Rostow taking issue?

Compare A. BICKEL, THE LEAST DANGEROUS BRANCH 24–27
(1962)*:

> .  .  .  .  many actions of government have two as-
> pects: their immediate, necessarily intended, practical ef-
> fects, and their perhaps unintended or unappreciated bear-
> ing on values we hold to have more general and permanent
> interest. It is a premise we deduce not merely from the
> fact of a written constitution but from the history of the
> race, and ultimately as a moral judgment of the good society,
> that government should serve not only what we conceive
> from time to time to be our immediate material needs but
> also certain enduring values. This in part is what is meant
> by government under law. But such values do not present
> themselves ready-made. They have a past always, to be sure,
> but they must be continually derived, enunciated, and seen
> in relevant application. And it remains to ask which insti-
> tution of our government—if any single one in particular—
> should be the pronouncer and guardian of such values.
>
> Men in all walks of public life are able occasionally to
> perceive this second aspect of public questions. Sometimes
> they are also able to base their decision on it; that is one
> of the things we like to call acting on principle. Often they
> do not do so, however, particularly when they sit in legisla-
> tive assemblies. There, when the pressure for immediate re-
> sults is strong enough and emotions ride high enough, men
> will ordinarily prefer to act on expediency rather than take
> the long view. Possibly legislators—everything else being
> equal—are as capable as other men of following the path of
> principle, where the path is clear or at any rate discerni-
> ble. Our system, however, like all secular systems, calls for
> the evolution of principle in novel circumstances, rather than
> only for its mechanical application. Not merely respect for
> the rule of established principles but the creative establish-
> ment and renewal of a coherent body of principled rules—
> that is what our legislatures have proven themselves ill
> equipped to give us.
>
> Initially, great reliance for principled decision was plac-
> ed in the Senators and the President, who have more extend-
> ed terms of office and were meant to be elected only indi-
> rectly. Yet the Senate and the President were conceived of
> as less closely tied to, not as divorced from, electoral re-
> sponsibility and the political marketplace. And so even then

the need might have been felt for an institution which stands altogether aside from the current clash of interests, and which, insofar as is humanly possible, is concerned only with principle. . . . [I]t is arguable also that the partial separation of the legislative and judicial functions—and it is not meant to be absolute—is beneficial in any event, because it makes it possible for the desires of various groups and interests concerning immediate results to be heard clearly and unrestrainedly in one place. It may be thought fitting that somewhere in government, at some stage in the process of law-making, such felt needs should find unambiguous expression. Moreover, and more importantly, courts have certain capacities for dealing with matters of principle that legislatures and executives do not possess. Judges have, or should have, the leisure, the training and the insulation to follow the ways of the scholar in pursuing the ends of government. This is crucial in sorting out the enduring values of a society, and it is not something that institutions can do well occasionally, while operating for the most part with a different set of gears. It calls for a habit of mind, and for undeviating institutional customs. Another advantage that courts have is that questions of principle never carry the same aspect for them as they did for the legislature or the executive. Statutes, after all, deal typically with abstract or dimly foreseen problems. The courts are concerned with the flesh and blood of an actual case. This tends to modify, perhaps to lengthen, everyone's view. It also provides an extremely salutary proving ground for all abstractions; it is conducive, in a phrase of Holmes, to thinking things, not words, and thus to the evolution of principle by a process that tests as it creates.

Their insulation and the marvelous mystery of time give courts the capacity to appeal to men's better natures, to call forth their aspirations, which may have been forgotten in the moment's hue and cry. This is what Justice Stone called the opportunity for "the sober second thought." Hence it is that the courts, although they may somewhat dampen the people's and the legislatures' efforts to educate themselves, are also a great and highly effective educational institution. Judge Gibson, . . . took account of this. "In the business of government," he wrote, "a recurrence to first principles answers the end of an observation at sea with a view to correct the dead reckoning; and, for this purpose, a written constitution is an instrument of inestimable value. It is of inestimable value also, in rendering its principles familiar to the mass of the people. . . ." The educational institution that both takes the observation to correct the dead reckoning and makes it known is the voice of the Constitution: the Supreme Court exercising judicial review. The Justices, in Dean Rostow's phrase, "are inevitably teachers in a vital national seminar." No other branch of the American government is nearly so well equipped to conduct one. And such a seminar can do a great deal to keep our society from becoming so riven that no court will be able to save it. Of course, we have never quite been that society in which the spirit of moderation is so richly in flower that no court need save it.

Thus, as Professor Henry M. Hart, Jr., has written, and as surely most of the profession and of informed laity believe; for if not this, what and why?—thus the Court appears "predestined in the long run, not only by the thrilling tradition of Anglo-American law but also by the hard facts of its position in the structure of American institutions, to be a voice of reason, charged with the creative function of discerning afresh and of articulating and developing impersonal and durable principles. . . ."

To what extent does Bickel's argument respond to the objections raised by Hand to the Bill of Rights jurisdiction of the courts? Elsewhere Hand says that the exercise of such a jurisdiction makes courts a third legislative chamber—for such exercise inevitably involves the same legislative value selection as one finds in the other chambers. Is Bickel responding to this argument?

6. Compare the methods by which Bickel and Hand seek to establish the nature of a court's role? Do these methods have anything in common? What is the nature of the supporting premises which they attempt to establish? Do they resemble each other at all? Are arguments about role wholly at large or is there anything in the positions of Bickel and Hand which suggests that there are boundaries which limit the scope and nature of such disputes. If there are such limits does this mean that the notion of role may serve a useful intellectual function—that it may help to focus and limit discussion and controversy? Is anything gained, for example, by asking, "What is my role?" "What has been my role?" "What can be my role?" "What should be my role?" "What is his role?" "What is the relation of his role to my role?"

7. Assuming that Gallup polls could be made satisfactorily accurate, would Hand prefer to see governmental decisions determined by them? What does he mean in saying that "Those vague stirrings of mass feeling which many who pride themselves upon their democracy mistake for the popular will must always be made concrete before they can become law in any practical sense, and the process of definition is as important as the dumb energy which provokes it, perhaps more so"? Suppose that a Gallup poll showed that a majority of the people did not want a particular law to be enforced. Would Hand, assuming his confidence in the poll's accuracy, ignore the law and implement the popular will? Consider: "In the name of a more loyal fealty to the popular will, we are asked to defeat the only means by which that will can become articulate and be made effective. To this . . . I submit that there is but one answer: an unflinching resistance."

What reasons does Hand give for this resistance to the popular will? How are they related to the needs of his role? Is he, again, confusing the interests of his office with the interests of society—which (by definition?) always amount to what the majority wills? What is his answer and how does he defend it? Does it have anything to do with maintaining a rule of law?

Is Hand consistent? Why is he willing to defer to the popular will in Bill of Rights litigation but not in the kind of situation suggested above? What is the distinction he draws? Can you state the fundamental social interest which Hand believes is served by his conception of the judiciary's function? How is this related to his interest in an independent judiciary?

8. To what extent does Hand's notion of judicial role rest on a particular epistemological position? Does his emphasis on the importance of "enacted law" reveal a particular philosophical theory of society and government?

Note Hand's reference to "human values which there are no scales to weigh." Note his reference to the temper of good faith open-mindedness, human feeling and the faith in the sacredness of the individual—of which he says: "Words will not express them; arguments will not clarify them; decisions will not maintain them." If words cannot express these values, does this mean that they cannot be taught? Does it mean that society has no way of propagating them? Does it mean that they are essentially innate? Or that they are the accidental creation of particular individuals confronting peculiar and unusual circumstances? Do Hand's remarks adequately account for *his* own words? Is he, according to his own terms, talking nonsense? Do his remarks account for the numbers of people who would accept his values as the right ones?

Compare Hand's remarks to Frankfurter's argument in *Rochin*. Does Frankfurter have the same conception of the judicial office? What are the differences? Compare Hand's epistemological position to Wechsler's or to Bickel's as represented by the readings in Chapter 12. Do these writers believe that the Bill of Rights is law? What kind of law? Is their conception of the judge's intellectual task the same as Hand's?

9. Hand's position is elaborated in THE BILL OF RIGHTS (1958), from which excerpts are reproduced in Chapter 15, *infra*. This book is viewed as one of the most extreme statements of "judicial self-restraint" recently presented. One writer has wondered whether Hand's point of view was not influenced by the fact that throughout his entire career he was a lower court judge. What is this supposed to explain? Is there likely to be a difference in viewpoint, in attitude, in motives, in values emphasized between a trial judge or an intermediate appellate judge and a United States Supreme Court justice? What is the difference in the nature of the work—in non-Constitutional as well as Constitutional cases?

*Arthur Koestler*

## The Ghost in the Machine *

Let me start with a parable. I owe it to Professor H. A. Simon, designer of logic computers and chess-playing machines, but I have taken the liberty of elaborating on it.

There were once two Swiss watchmakers named Bios and Mekhos, who made very fine and expensive watches. . . . Although their watches were in equal demand, Bios prospered, while Mekhos just struggled along; in the end he had to close his shop and take a job as a mechanic with Bios. . . .

The watches they made consisted of about one thousand parts each, but the two rivals had used different methods to put them together. Mekhos had assembled his watches bit by bit—rather like making a mosaic floor out of small coloured stones. Thus each time when he was disturbed in his work and had to put down a partly assembled watch, it fell to pieces and he had to start again from scratch.

Bios, on the other hand, had designed a method of making watches by constructing, for a start, sub-assemblies of about ten components, each of which held together as an independent unit. Ten of these sub-assemblies could then be fitted together into a sub-system of a higher order; and ten of these sub-systems constituted the whole watch. This method proved to have two immense advantages.

In the first place, each time there was an interruption or a disturbance, and Bios had to put down, or even drop, the watch he was working on, it did not decompose into its elementary bits; instead of starting all over again, he merely had to reassemble that particular sub-assembly on which he was working at the time; so that at worst (if the disturbance came when he had nearly finished the sub-assembly in hand) he had to repeat nine assembling operations, and at best none at all. Now it is easy to show mathematically that if a watch consists of a thousand bits, and if some disturbance occurs at an average of once in every hundred assembling operations—then Mekhos will take four thousand times longer to assemble a watch than Bios. Instead of a single day, it will take him eleven years. And if for mechanical bits, we substitute amino acids, protein molecules, organelles, and so on, the ratio between the time-scales becomes astronomical; some calculations indicate that the whole lifetime of the earth would be insufficient for producing even an amoeba—unless he becomes converted to Bios' method and proceeds hierarchically, from simple sub-assemblies to more complex ones. Simon concludes: 'Complex systems will evolve from simple systems much more rapidly if there are stable intermediate forms than if there are not. The resulting complex forms in the former case will be hierarchic. We have only to turn the argument around to explain the observed predominance of hierarchies among the complex systems Nature presents to us.  Among possible complex forms, hierarchies are the ones that have the time to evolve.'

A second advantage of Bios' method is of course that the finished product will be incomparably more resistant to damage, and much easier to maintain, regulate and repair, than Mekhos' unstable mosaic of atomic bits.  We do not know what forms of life have evolved on other planets in the universe, but we can safely assume that *where-ever there is life, it must be hierarchically organised.*

## Enter Janus

If we look at any form of social organisation with some degree of coherence and stability, from insect state to Pentagon, we shall find that it is hierarchically ordered.  The same is true of the structure of living organisms and their ways of functioning—from instinctive behaviour to the sophisticated skills of piano-playing and talking.  And it is equally true of the processes of becoming—phylogeny, ontogeny, the acquisition of knowledge. . . .

The first universal characteristic of hierarchies is the relativity, and indeed ambiguity, of the terms 'part' and 'whole' when applied to any of the sub-assemblies.  Again it is the very obviousness of this feature which makes us overlook its implications.  A 'part', as we generally use the word, means something fragmentary and incomplete, which by itself would have no legitimate existence.  On the other hand, a 'whole' is considered as something complete in itself which needs no further explanation.  But *'wholes' and 'parts in this absolute sense just do not exist anywhere,* either in the domain of living organisms or of social organisations.  What we find are intermediary structures on a series of levels in an ascending order of complexity:  sub-wholes which display, according to the way you look at them, some of the characteristics commonly attributed to wholes and some of the characteristics commonly attributed to parts.  We have seen the impossibility of the task of chopping up speech into elementary atoms or units, either on the phonetic or on the syntactic level.  Phonemes, words, phrases, are wholes in their own right, but parts of a larger unit; so are cells, tissues, organs; families, clans, tribes.  The members of a hierarchy, like the Roman god Janus, all have two faces looking in opposite directions:  the face turned towards the subordinate levels is that of a self-contained whole; the face turned upward towards the apex, that of a dependent part.  One is the face of the master, the other the face of the servant.  This *'Janus effect'* is a fundamental characteristic of sub-wholes in all types of hierarchies.

But there is no satisfactory word in our vocabulary to refer to these Janus-faced entities:  to talk of sub-wholes (or sub-assemblies, sub-structures, sub-skills, sub-systems) is awkward and tedious.  It seems preferable to coin a new term to designate these nodes on the hierarchic tree which behave partly as wholes or wholly as parts, according to the way you look at them.  The term I would propose is 'holon', from the Greek *holos* = whole, with the suffix *on* which, as in pro*ton* or neu*tron*, suggests a particle or part.

. . . .

The individual, *qua* biological organism, constitutes a nicely integrated hierarchy of molecules, cells, organs, and organ systems. Looking inward into the space enclosed by the boundaries of his skin, he can rightly assert that he is something complete and unique, a whole. But facing outward, he is constantly—sometimes pleasantly, sometimes painfully—reminded that he is a part, an elementary unit in one or several social hierarchies.

.  .  .

A society without hierarchic structurings would be as chaotic as the random motions of gas molecules flying, colliding, and rebounding in all directions. But the structuring is obscured by the fact that no advanced human society—not even the totalitarian state—is a monolithic structure, patterned into one single hierarchy. This may be the case in some very 'unspoilt' tribal societies, where the exigencies of the family-kinship-clan-tribe hierarchy completely control the individual's existence. The medieval church and modern totalitarian nations have tried to establish equally effective monolithic hierarchies, with only limited success. Complex societies are structured by several types of interlocking hierarchies, and control of higher authority is only one among them. I shall call these authority-yielding hierarchies 'control hierarchies'. Obvious examples are government administrations, military, ecclesiastic, academic, professional and business hierarchies.  .  .  .

Entwined with these control hierarchies are others, based on social cohesion, geographical distribution, etc. There are the family—clan—sub-caste—caste hierarchies, and their modern versions. Interlocking with them are the hierarchies based on geographical neighbourhood. Old towns like Paris, Vienna or London have their *quartiers,* each of them relatively self-sufficient, with its local shops, familiar cafes, pubs, milkmen and sweeps. Each is a kind of local village, a social holon, which again is part of a larger division—Left Bank and Right Bank, City and West End, amusement centre and civic centre, parks, suburbs. Old towns, notwithstanding their architectural diversity, seem to have grown like organisms, and to have an individual life of their own. Towns which have mushroomed up too fast have a depressing amorphousness because they lack the hierarchic structure of organic development. They seem to have been built not by Bios but by Mekhos.

.  .  .  .  We must distinguish  .  .  .  between the rules which govern individual behavior and those which guide the activities of the group as a whole. The individual may even be unaware of the fact that his behaviour is rule-governed, and no more able to name the rules which guide his conduct than he is able to name those which guide his speech. The activities of the social holon, on the other hand, depend not only on the complex interactions between its parts, but also on its interaction as a whole with other holons on its own, higher level of the hierarchy; and these cannot be inferred from the lower level any more than the function of the nervous system can be inferred from the level of individual nerve cells, or the rules of syntax can be inferred from the rules of phonology. We can 'dissect' a complex whole into its composite holons of the second and third order, and so on, but we cannot 'reduce' it to a sum of its parts, nor predict its properties from those of its parts. The hierarchy concept of 'levels of organisation' in itself implies a rejection of the reductionist view that all phenomena of life (consciousness included) can be reduced to and explained by physico-chemical laws.

Thus a stable social holon has an individuality or 'profile'— whether it is a Papuan tribe or a Treasury department. Every closely knit social body sharing a common territory and/or a code of explicit and implicit laws, customs and beliefs tends to preserve and assert its pattern—or else it could not qualify as a stable holon. In a primitive society the tribe might be the highest unit of the shallow hierarchy, a more or less self-contained whole. But in a complex society, with its many-levelled hierarchies, it is equally essential that each holon—whether an administrative department, a local government or the fire brigade—should operate as an autonomous, self-contained unit; without division of labour and delegation of powers, according to the hierarchic schema, no society can function effectively.

. . . . In order to operate as a self-reliant unit, the department must be equipped with a set of instructions and regulations enabling it to take routine contingencies in its stride, without having to consult higher authority in each particular case. In other words, what enables the department to function in this efficient way, as an autonomous holon, is . . . a set of fixed rules, its *canon*. But . . . there will be cases where the rules can be interpreted in this way or that, and so leave room for more than one decision. Whatever the nature of a hierarchic organisation, its constituent holons are defined by *fixed rules* and *flexible strategies*.

. . . . it is essential for the stability and efficient functioning of the body social that each of its sub-divisions should operate as an autonomous, self-reliant unit which, though subject to control from above, must have a degree of independence and take routine contingencies in its stride, without asking higher authority for instructions. Otherwise the communication channels would become overloaded, the whole system clogged up, the higher echelons would be kept occupied with petty detail and unable to concentrate on more important factors.

However, the rules, or codes, which govern a social holon act not merely as negative *constraints* imposed on its actions, but also as positive *precepts*, maxims of conduct or moral imperatives. As a consequence, every holon will tend to persist in and assert its particular pattern of activity. This *self-assertive tendency* is a fundamental and universal characteristic of holons, which manifests itself on every level of the social hierarchy (and, as we shall see, in every other type of hierarchy).

On the level of the individual, a certain amount of self-assertiveness—ambition, initiative, competition—is indispensable in a dynamic society. At the same time, of course, he is dependent on, and must be integrated into, his tribe or social group. If he is a well-adjusted person, the self-assertive tendency and its opposite, the *integrative tendency*, are more or less equally balanced; he lives, so long as things are normal, in a kind of dynamic equilibrium with his social environment. Under conditions of stress, however, the equilibrium is upset, leading to emotionally disorderd behaviour.

No man is an island—he is a holon. A Janus-faced entity who, looking inward, sees himself as a self-contained unique whole, looking outward as a dependent part. His *self-assertive tendency* is the dynamic manifestation of his unique *wholeness*, his autonomy and independence as a holon. Its equally universal antagonist, the *integrative tendency*, expresses his dependence on the larger whole to which he belongs: his '*part-ness*'.

NOTES AND QUESTIONS

1. Would a court be viewed as a social holon by Koestler? If so, what would be the consequences? In what respects is it a part? In what respects a whole?

2. Note Koestler's insistence that all holons need independence and autonomy? Do they need it, would you say, for the same reasons Hand says that courts need it? How serious would it be if a holon lost its independence? Would it nevertheless be able to serve *some* function? Would it still be a holon—*i. e.*, are independence and autonomy constituent elements of the concept of holon? Is it possible to conceive of an entity which has *no* independence or autonomy? Could it satisfy the requirements even of a *part* of something else if it had no independence or autonomy? Or would it simply be *no*-thing?

3. Consider the characteristic of self-assertiveness. Would a court that followed Hand's recommendations be self-assertive or would it instead be, to coin a phrase, "self-integrative"? Put another way, is "judicial self-restraint" an assertive or an integrative position? What would be the value of a holon which never tended "to persist in and assert its particular pattern of activity"? Is this another way of inquiring into the validity of the notion that what's good for a particular holon is good for the country? What do you think Bios's position would be on this issue? Mekhos's position?

4. Is it possible to have a holon which is neutral or impartial—in the sense that it is unbiased or unprejudiced? What implications does your answer have for the problem of a neutral or impartial judiciary? What implications for the notion that bias and prejudice are necessarily bad things?

5. To what extent does consistent loyalty to a role make possible better ways of carrying out the role's characteristic tasks? Recall Kuhn's discussion of paradigms and his conclusion that adherence to them makes possible a depth and detail of knowledge which would otherwise be unimaginable. Also, recall Whitehead's dictum that even a bad theory is better than none because it coordinates procedures. See Chapter 12. Can anything of the same sort be said of roles? What does Koestler's holon theory suggest?

Will the answer to these questions help us decide whether it might be wise for a society to give one institution the special job of protecting principle? Or civil liberties? Or the "spirit of moderation"? Or the rule of law?

6. It is sometimes said that the Supreme Court is "equal" to the other branches of the Federal government. What could this possibly mean? Does Koestler suggest an answer? What is the hierarchical relationship, would you say, between courts and legislatures? What does Hand think it is? Could it be argued that his notion does not recognize the equality of the courts?

7. To what extent do Koestler's remarks help us to understand and describe the problems raised by the Correspondence of the Justices and Muskrat v. United States?

## THE CORRESPONDENCE OF THE JUSTICES (1793) *

Letter from Thomas Jefferson, Secretary of State, to Chief Justice Jay and Associate Justices:

Philadelphia, July 18, 1793.

Gentlemen:

The war which has taken place among the powers of Europe produces frequent transactions within our ports and limits, on which questions arise of considerable difficulty, and of greater importance to the peace of the United States. These questions depend for their solution on the construction of our treaties, on the laws of nature and nations, and on the laws of the land, and are often presented under circumstances *which do not give a cognizance of them to the tribunals of the country*. Yet, their decision is so little analogous to the ordinary functions of the executive, as to occasion much embarrassment and difficulty to them. The President therefore would be much relieved if he found himself free to refer questions of this description to the opinions of the judges of the Supreme Court of the United States, whose knowledge of the subject would secure us against errors dangerous to the peace of the United States, and their authority insure the respect of all parties. He has therefore asked the attendance of such of the judges as could be collected in time for the occasion, to know, in the first place, their opinion, whether the public may, with propriety, be availed of their *advice on these questions*? And if they may, to present, for their advice, the abstract questions which have already occurred, or may soon occur, from which they will themselves strike out such as any circumstances might, in their opinion, forbid them to pronounce on. I have the honour to be with sentiments of the most perfect respect, gentlemen,

Your most obedient and humble servant,

Thos. Jefferson

The following are some of the questions submitted by the President to the Justices:

1. Do the treaties between the United States and France give to France or her citizens a *right*, when at war with a power with whom the United States are at peace, to fit out originally in and from the

* From H. Hart & H. Wechsler, The Federal Courts and the Federal System 75–77 (1953). Reprinted with permission of the Foundation Press.

ports of the United States vessels armed for war, with or without commission?

2. If they give such a *right*, does it extend to all manner of armed vessels, or to particular kinds only? If the latter, to what kinds does it extend?

3. Do they give to France or her citizens, in the case supposed, a right to refit or arm anew vessels, which, before their coming within any port of the United States, were armed for war, with or without commission?

4. If they give such a right, does it extend to all manner of armed vessels, or to particular kinds only? If the latter, to what kinds does it extend? Does it include an *augmentation* of force, or does it only extend to replacing the vessel *in statu quo?*

17. Do the laws of neutrality, considered as aforesaid, authorize the United States to permit France, her subjects, or citizens, the sale within their ports of prizes made of the subjects or property of a power at war with France, before they have been carried into some port of France and there condemned, refusing the like privilege to her enemy?

18. Do those laws authorize the United States to permit to France the erection of courts within their territory and jurisdiction for the trial and condemnation of prizes, refusing that privilege to a power at war with France?

19. If any armed vessel of a foreign power at war with another, with whom the United States are at peace, shall make prize of the subject or property of its enemy within the territory or jurisdiction of the United States, have not the United States a right to cause restitution of such prizes? Are they bound, or not, by the principles of neutrality to do so, if such prize shall be within their power?

20. To what distance, by the laws and usages of nations, may the United States exercise the right of prohibiting the hostilities of foreign powers at war with each other within rivers, bays, and arms of the sea, and upon the sea along the coasts of the United States?

21. Have vessels, armed for war under commission from a foreign power, a right, without the consent of the United States, to engage within their jurisdiction seamen or soldiers for the service of such vessels, being citizens of that power, or of another foreign power, or citizens of the United States?

22. What are the articles, by name, to be prohibited to both or either party?

25. May we, within our own ports, sell ships to both parties, prepared merely for merchandise? May they be pierced for guns?

26. May we carry either or both kinds to the ports of the belligerent powers for sale?

27. Is the principle, that free bottoms make free goods, and enemy bottoms make enemy goods, to be considered as now an established part of the law of nations?

28. If it is not, are nations with whom we have no treaties, authorized by the law of nations to take out of our vessels enemy passengers, not being soldiers, and their baggage?

29.  May an armed vessel belonging to any of the belligerent powers follow *immediately* merchant vessels, enemies, departing from our ports, for the purpose of making prizes of them? If not, how long ought the former to remain, after the latter have sailed? And what shall be considered as the place of departure, from which the time is to be counted? And how are the facts to be ascertained?

On July 20, 1793, Chief Justice Jay and the Associate Justices wrote to President Washington expressing their wish to postpone the answer to Jefferson's letter until the sitting of the Court. On August 8, 1793, they wrote to the President as follows:

Sir:

We have considered the previous questions stated in a letter written by your direction to us by the Secretary of State on the 18th of last month, [regarding] the lines of separation drawn by the Constitution between the three departments of the government. These being in certain respects checks upon each other, and our being judges of a court in the last resort, are considerations which afford strong arguments against the propriety of our extra-judicially deciding the questions alluded to, especially as the power given by the Constitution to the President, of calling on the heads of departments for opinions, seems to have been *purposely* as well as expressly united to the *executive* departments.

We exceedingly regret every event that may cause embarrassment to your administration, but we derive consolation from the reflection that your judgment will discern what is right, and that your usual prudence, decision, and firmness will surmount every obstacle to the preservation of the rights, peace, and dignity of the United States.

NOTES AND QUESTIONS

1.  Article III of the United States Constitution provides in relevant part as follows:

Section. 1.  The judicial Power of the United States, shall be vested in one supreme Court, and in such inferior Courts as the Congress may from time to time ordain and establish. The Judges, both of the supreme and inferior Courts, shall hold their Offices during good Behavior, and shall, at stated Times, receive for their Services, a Compensation, which shall not be diminished during their Continuance in Office.

Section 2.  The judicial Power shall extend to all Cases, in Law and Equity, arising under this Constitution, the Laws of the United States, and Treaties made, or which shall be made, under their Authority;—to all Cases affecting Ambassadors, other public Ministers and Consuls;—to all Cases of admiralty and maritime Jurisdiction;—to Controversies to which the United States shall be a Party;—to Controversies between two or more States;—between a State and Citizens of another State;—between Citizens of different States;—between Citizens of the same State claiming Lands under Grants of different States, and between a State, or the Citizens thereof, and foreign States, Citizens or Subjects.

In all Cases affecting Ambassadors, other public Ministers and Consuls, and those in which a State shall be Party, the supreme Court shall have original Jurisdiction. In all the other Cases before mentioned, the supreme Court shall have appellate Jurisdiction, both as to Law and Fact, with such Exceptions, and under such Regulations as the Congress shall make.

Is there anything in Article III which prohibits the Justices of the Supreme Court from giving the type of advice which Washington and Jefferson sought? Does the response of the Justices say there is? Is it clear whether the "strong arguments against the propriety of our extra-judicially deciding the questions alluded to" are legal or Constitutional arguments?

Is it arguable that Jefferson did not present the Justices with a "case" or "controversy" and for this reason they could not satisfy his request? Is there no conceivable usage of the word "case" that would include Jefferson's questions? Could it not be said that Jefferson was putting a number of hypothetical cases to the Justices? Does Article III say that cases must be "actual" or "ripe" for decision before the Court can decide them? Could not Article III be construed simply as a statement of the kinds of legal *questions* or *issues* which Federal courts have the power to act upon? How should one go about determining whether this or any other construction is the right one? Note that it was not unknown for English courts in the eighteenth century to give advisory opinions or to offer *obiter dicta*? Does such historical information have a bearing on the question of what a case or controversy is? Note, further, that some State judiciaries have given advisory opinions. Does this evidence of the practices of other American courts bear on the question of case or controversy? Note incidentally that the Massachusetts Constitution of 1780, Art. 2, Ch. 3, gave "each branch of the legislature as well as the governor and council" the "authority to require the opinions of the justices of the supreme judicial court upon important questions of law" fully seven years before the Constitution was framed. In view of the Justices' reliance on the separation of powers in its response to Jefferson and Washington, it should be noted that Massachusetts has—and had—a Constitutional provision which is far more explicit and emphatic:

In the government of this Commonwealth, the legislative department shall never exercise the executive and judicial powers or either of them; The executive shall never exercise the legislative and judicial powers, or either of them; The judicial shall never exercise the legislative and executive, or either of them; to the end it may be a government of laws and not of men.

Article XXX, Constitution of Commonwealth of Massachusetts (1780).

Assuming that Jefferson did not present the Justices with a "case" or "controversy" would this necessarily mean that they were prohibited by Article III from answering his questions? Could it be argued that in answering they would not be exercising "judicial power" precisely because the questions did not arise in an actual case between litigants? That judicial power is the power to *decide* concrete disputes between contesting parties and since the justices were not *deciding* anything the limitations of Federal judicial power would say nothing about the Justices' power to give advisory opinions?

2. Assuming that the Justices' rejection of Jefferson's request was neither compelled by Constitutional language nor by judicial practice, how does one explain their apparent selfishness with their office? The questions put to them were legal questions and Jefferson made it clear that they would be rendering the executive branch and the country a great service by answering them. What justifications could they give for their refusal? Could any of them rise to the level of importance of the reasons advanced by Jefferson?

3. Consider the foregoing question in terms of the specifically institutional interests of the Supreme Court. Would the Court lose power by giving advisory opinions? Would the sources of its authority be undermined? Could it gain power by carefully delineating the boundaries of its jurisdiction and holding itself strictly within them? Consider the Court's position in the structure of the Federal government. In how many different ways could the legislature, for example, coerce the Court if it wished? Note the power of appropriation, the power over the appellate jurisdiction, the power to confirm Justices and to determine how many there shall be? Just what power does the Court have?

4. What institutional considerations are revealed by the following:

> Would it be sound to conclude that the judicial function is essentially the function (in such cases as may be presented for decision) of authoritative application to particular situations of general propositions drawn from preexisting sources—including as a necessary incident the function of determining the facts of the particular situation and of resolving uncertainties about the content of the applicable general propositions? Would it be sound to conclude, in addition, that this function is an inescapable one in any regime of law?

> If so, in what respects, if any, would the Court have performed a significantly different function had it undertaken to reply to the questions of the President?

> In considering this question, take into account:

> (a) The sheer multiplication of matters to which attention must be directed, and the resulting dispersion of thought, when a legal proposition is being formulated in the abstract;

> (b) The special disadvantages of dispersion of thought when a legal proposition is being formulated in the abstract;

(c) The importance, in the judicial development of law, of a concrete set of facts as an aid to the accurate formulation of the legal issue to be decided—the weight, in other words, which should be given to the maxim, *ex facto ius oritur*;

(d) The importance of an adversary presentation of evidence as an aid to the accurate determination of the facts out of which the legal issue arises;

(e) The importance of an adversary presentation of argument in the formulation and decision of the legal issue;

(f) The importance of a concrete set of facts in limiting the scope of the legal determination and as an aid to its accurate interpretation;

(g) The diminished scope for the play of personal convictions or preferences with respect to public policy when decision is focussed upon a definite legal issue derived from a concrete set of facts;

(h) The value of having courts function as organs of the sober second thought of the community appraising action already taken, rather than as advisers at the front line of governmental action at the stage of initial decision;

(i) The importance of all the factors enumerated in maximizing the acceptability of decisions, and the importance of acceptable decisions.

H. Hart & H. Wechsler, The Federal Courts and the Federal System 78–79 (1953).*

5. To what extent can the action of the Justices be defended in the terms employed by Koestler?

## United States ex rel. Klonis v. Davis

13 F.2d 630 (2d Cir. 1926)

HAND, J. . . . .

The [alien] was born in Poland, and at an age variously fixed at six or seven months and ten years was brought here by his parents. He has lived here continuously since his original immigration, can read English, and professes to be a carpenter. He has been twice convicted of burglary, and has served two terms in prison of more than one year each. The last conviction was in August, 1923, and the last sentence for two years and six months. A warrant of arrest for deportation was issued by the Secretary of Labor on July 13, 1924, while the [alien] was in prison, on the ground that, having been twice convicted of a crime involving moral turpitude, and having been sentenced each time to more than one year's imprisonment, he was deportable under section 19 of the act of 1917 . . . .

* Reprinted with permission of the
Foundation Press.

Learning of this proceeding, the [alien's] attorneys applied to the judge who imposed the last sentence [for burglary], and on January 16, 1925, procured an order, entered "nunc pro tunc," amending the sentence by recommending that the [alien] be not deported. . . .

The language of the section avoids deportation if the alien "has been pardoned," or "if the court, or judge thereof, sentencing such alien, . . . shall, at the time of imposing . . . sentence or within thirty days thereafter" make a recommendation to that effect. We do not see how we can interpolate as a condition that the recommendation may be made within 30 days after the effect of the sentence is realized [the alien having made application to the judge to amend his sentence by the appropriate recommendation within thirty days of the time the alien realized the effect of his having failed to do so]. Apparently during its course through the House an amendment was offered and rejected which extended the judge's power indefinitely. . . . Even without that, we should have felt bound to read the words as they are written. Possibly it was thought that those who for any reason failed to get a timely recommendation would be protected by a pardon, but at any rate the power of the court was exactly circumscribed, and we may not enlarge it. Fortunately it may still be possible to secure a pardon here, the sentence having been served. We cannot suppose that opportunity will not be given for an application.

At any rate we think it not improper to say that deportation under the circumstances would be deplorable. Whether the [alien] came here in arms or at the age of ten, he is as much our product as though his mother had borne him on American soil. He knows no other language, no other people, no other habits, than ours; he will be as much a stranger in Poland as any one born of ancestors who immigrated in the seventeenth century. However heinous his crimes, deportation is to him exile, a dreadful punishment, abandoned by the common consent of all civilized peoples. Such, indeed, it would be to any one, but to one already proved to be incapable of honest living, a helpless waif in a strange land, it will be utter destruction. That our reasonable efforts to rid ourselves of unassimilable immigrants should in execution be attended by such a cruel and barbarous result would be a national reproach.

Order affirmed.

## NOTES AND QUESTIONS

1. Might anyone think it "improper" for Hand "to say that deportation under the circumstances would be deplorable"? Could it be argued that this was an opinion he should have kept to himself? That it was none of his business? Has Hand in the last paragraph confused his role as judge with his role as concerned citizen? Can he offer a justification for including this last paragraph which reconciles it with his judicial office? Would such a justification be consistent with his analysis of "the contribution of an independent judiciary to civilization"?

2. What forms of social harm can be caused by actions such as Hand's? Can you think of ways in which the organizing and stabilizing function of role—whether judicial or other—could be damaged by such actions?

3. To whom is Hand's last paragraph addressed? To the people generally? If so, what would be the purpose? Would it be a legitimate purpose for a judge acting as judge?

Is the last paragraph directed to the legislature? If not, what might lead one to think so? If so, what would the purpose be? To criticize it for bad lawmaking? To urge a revision? Are these proper purposes? How does one go about deciding?

Is the last paragraph directed to the executive branch? If not, what might make one think so? If so, what would be the purpose? Would it be a legitimate one?

4. Could it be argued that Hand was giving an advisory opinion? How, if at all, would it differ from the advice sought in the Correspondence of the Justices?

## MUSKRAT v. UNITED STATES

219 U.S. 346 (1911)

Mr. Justice DAY delivered the opinion of the court.

These cases arise under an act of Congress undertaking to confer jurisdiction upon the Court of Claims, and upon this court on appeal, to determine the validity of certain acts of Congress hereinafter referred to.

Case No. 330 was brought by David Muskrat and J. Henry Dick in their own behalf and in behalf of others in a like situation to determine the constitutional validity of the act of Congress of April 26, 1906, c. 1876, 34 Stat. 137, as amended by the act of June 21, 1906, c. 3504, 34 Stat. 325 *et seq.*, and to have the same declared invalid in so far as the same undertook to increase the number of persons entitled to share in the final distribution of lands and funds of the Cherokees beyond those enrolled on September 1, 1902, in accordance with the act of Congress passed July 1, 1902, c. 1375, 32 Stat. 716–720, 721. The acts subsequent to that of July 1, 1902, have the effect to increase the number of persons entitled to participate in the division of the Cherokee lands and funds, by permitting the enrollment of children who were minors living on March 4, 1906, whose parents had theretofore been enrolled as members of the Cherokee tribe or had applications pending for that purpose.

Case No. 331 was brought by Brown and Gritts on their own behalf and on behalf of other Cherokee citizens having a like interest in the property allotted under the act of July 1, 1902, c. 1368, 32 Stat. 710. Under this act, Brown and Gritts received allotments. The subsequent act of March 11, 1904, c. 505, 33 Stat. 65, empowered the Secretary of the Interior to grant rights of way for pipe lines over lands allotted to Indians under certain regulations. Another act, that of April 26, 1906, c. 1876, 34 Stat. 137, purported to extend to a period of twenty-five years the time within which full-blooded Indians of the Cherokee, Choctaw, Chickasaw, Creek and Seminole tribes were forbidden to alienate, sell, dispose of or encumber certain of their lands.

The object of the petition of Brown and Gritts was to have the subsequent legislation of 1904 and 1906 declared to be unconstitutional and void, and to have the lands allotted to them under the original act of July 1, 1902, adjudged to be theirs free from restraints upon the rights to sell and convey the same. From this statement it is apparent that the purpose of the proceedings instituted in the Court of Claims and now appealed to this court is to restrain the enforcement of such legislation subsequent to the act of July 1, 1902, upon the ground that the same is unconstitutional and void. The Court of Claims sustained the validity of the acts and dismissed the petitions. 44 C. Cls. 137, 283.

These proceedings were begun under the supposed authority of an act of Congress passed March 1, 1907 (a part of the Indian appropriation bill), c. 2285, 34 Stat. 1015, 1028. As that legislation is important in this connection so much of the act as authorized the beginning of these suits is here inserted in full.

"That William Brown and Levi B. Gritts, on their own behalf and on behalf of all other Cherokee citizens, having like interests in the property allotted under the act of July first, nineteen hundred and two, entitled 'An act to provide for the allotment of lands of the Cherokee Nation, for the disposition of townsites therein, and for other purposes,' and David Muskrat and J. Henry Dick, on their own behalf, and on behalf of all Cherokee citizens enrolled as such for allotment as of September first, nineteen hundred and two, be, and they are hereby, authorized and empowered to institute their suits in the Court of Claims to determine the validity of any acts of Congress passed since the said act of July first, nineteen hundred and two, in so far as said acts, or any of them, attempt to increase or extend the restrictions upon alienation, encumbrance, or the right to lease the allotments of lands of Cherokee citizens, or to increase the number of persons entitled to share in the final distribution of lands and funds of the Cherokees beyond those enrolled for allotment as of September first, nineteen hundred and two, and provided for in the said act of July first, nineteen hundred and two.

"And jurisdiction is hereby conferred upon the Court of Claims, with the right of appeal, by either party, to the Supreme Court of the United States, to hear, determine, and adjudicate each of said suits.

"The suits brought hereunder shall be brought on or before September first, nineteen hundred and seven, against the United States as a party defendant, and, for the speedy disposition of the questions involved, preference shall be given to the same by said courts, and by the Attorney General, who is hereby charged with the defense of said suits.

"Upon the rendition of final judgment of the Court of Claims or the Supreme Court of the United States denying the validity of any portion of the said acts authorized to be brought into question.

in either or both of said cases, the Court of Claims shall determine the amount to be paid the attorneys employed by the above-named parties in the prosecution thereof for services and expenses, and shall render judgment therefor, which shall be paid out of the funds in the United States Treasury belonging to the beneficiaries under the said act of July first, nineteen hundred and two."

This act is the authority for the maintenance of these two suits.

The first question in these cases, as in others, involves the jurisdiction of this court to entertain the proceeding, and that depends upon whether the jurisdiction conferred is within the power of Congress, having in view the limitations of the judicial power as established by the Constitution of the United States.

Section 1 of Article III of the Constitution provides:

"The judicial power of the United States shall be vested in one Supreme Court and in such inferior courts as the Congress may from time to time ordain and establish."

Section 2 of the same Article provides:

"The judicial power shall extend to all cases, in law and equity, arising under this Constitution, the laws of the United States, and treaties made, or which shall be made, under their authority;—to all cases affecting ambassadors, other public ministers, and consuls;—to all cases of admiralty and maritime jurisdiction;—to controversies to which the United States shall be a party;—to controversies between two or more States;—between a State and citizens of another State;—between citizens of different States;—between citizens of the same State claiming lands under grants of different States and between a State, or the citizens thereof, and foreign states, citizens or subjects."

It will serve to elucidate the nature and extent of the judicial power thus conferred by the Constitution to note certain instances in which this court has had occasion to examine and define the same. As early as 1792, an act of Congress, March 23, 1792, c. 11, 1 Stat. 243, was brought to the attention of this court, which undertook to provide for the settlement of claims of widows and orphans barred by the limitations theretofore established regulating claims to invalid pensions. The act was not construed by this court, but came under consideration before the then Chief Justice and another Justice of this court and the District Judge, and their conclusions are given in the margin of the report of Hayburn's Case, 2 Dall. 409. The act undertook to devolve upon the Circuit Court of the United States the duty of examining proofs, of determining what amount of the monthly pay would be equivalent to the disability ascertained, and to certify the same to the Secretary of War, who was to place the names of the applicants on the pension list of the United States in conformity thereto, unless he had cause to suspect imposition or mistake, in which event he might withhold the name of the applicant and report the same to Congress.

In the note to the report of the case in 2 Dall. it appeared that Chief Justice Jay, Mr. Justice Cushing and District Judge Duane unanimously agreed:

"That by the Constitution of the United States, the government thereof is divided into three distinct and independent branches, and that it is the duty of each to abstain from, and to oppose, encroachments on either.

"That neither the legislative nor the executive branches can constitutionally assign to the judicial any duties but such as are properly judicial, and to be performed in a judicial manner.

"The duties assigned to the Circuit Courts, by this act, are not of that description, and that the act itself does not appear to contemplate them as such; inasmuch as it subjects the decisions of these courts, made pursuant to those duties, first to the consideration and suspension of the Secretary of War, and then to the revision of the legislature; whereas by the Constitution, neither the Secretary of War, nor any other executive officer, nor even the legislature, are authorized to sit as a court of errors on the judicial acts or opinions of this court."

A further history of the case—and of another brought under the same act but unreported—will be found in United States v. Ferreira, 13 How. 40, in which the opinion of the court was by the Chief Justice, and the note by him on page 52 was inserted by order of the court. Concluding that note it was said:

"In the early days of the Government, the right of Congress to give original jurisdiction to the Supreme Court, in cases not enumerated in the Constitution, was maintained by many jurists, and seems to have been entertained by the learned judges who decided Todd's case. But discussion and more mature examination has settled the question otherwise; and it has long been the established doctrine, and we believe now assented to by all who have examined the subject, that the original jurisdiction of this court is confined to the cases specified in the Constitution, and that Congress cannot enlarge it. In all other cases its power must be appellate."

In the *Ferreira case* this court determined the effect of proceedings under an act of Congress, authorizing the District Judge of the United States for the Northern District of Florida to receive and adjudicate claims for losses for which this Government was responsible under the treaty of 1819 between the United States and Spain; decisions in favor of claimants, together with evidence given in connection therewith, to be reported to the Secretary of the Treasury, who, being satisfied that the same were just and equitable and within the treaty, was to pay the amount thereof. It was held that an award of the District Judge under that act was not the judgment of a court and did not afford a basis of appeal to this court.

In 1793, by direction of the President, Secretary of State Jefferson addressed to the Justices of the Supreme Court a communication soliciting their views upon the question whether their advice to the executive would be available in the solution of important questions of the construction of treaties, laws of nations and laws of the land, which the Secretary said were often presented under circumstances which *"do not give a cognizance of them to the tribunals of the country."* The answer to the question was postponed until the subsequent sitting of the Supreme Court, when Chief Justice Jay and his associates answered to President Washington that in consideration of the lines of separation drawn by the Constitution between the three departments of government, and being judges of a court of last resort, afforded strong arguments against the propriety of extrajudicially deciding the questions alluded to, and expressing the view that the power given by the Constitution to the President of calling on heads of departments for opinions "seems to have been purposely, as well as expressly, united to the executive departments." Correspondence & Public Papers of John Jay, vol. 3, p. 486.

The subject underwent a complete examination in the case of Gordon v. United States, reported in an appendix to 117 U.S. 697, in which the opinion of Mr. Chief Justice Taney, prepared by him and placed in the hands of the clerk, is published in full. It is said to have been his last judicial utterance, and the whole subject of the nature and extent of the judicial power conferred by the Constitution is treated with great learning and fullness. In that case an act of Congress was held invalid which undertook to confer jurisdiction upon the Court of Claims and thence by appeal to this court, the judgment, however, not to be paid until an appropriation had been estimated therefor by the Secretary of the Treasury; and, as was said by the Chief Justice, the result was that neither court could enforce its judgment by any process, and whether it was to be paid or not depended on the future action of the Secretary of the Treasury and of Congress. "The Supreme Court," says the Chief Justice, "does not owe its existence or its powers to the legislative department of the government. It is created by the Constitution, and represents one of the three great divisions of power in the Government of the United States, to each of which the Constitution has assigned its appropriate duties and powers, and made each independent of the other in performing its appropriate functions. The power conferred on this court is exclusively judicial, and it cannot be required or authorized to exercise any other."

Concluding his discussion of the subject, the Chief Justice said, after treating of the powers of the different branches of the Government, and laying emphasis upon the independence of the judicial power as established under our Constitution, p. 706: "These cardinal principles of free government had not only been long established in England, but also in the United States from the time of their earliest colonization, and guided the American people in framing and adopting the present Constitution. And it is the duty of this court to maintain it unimpaired as far as it may have the power. And while it executes firmly all the judicial powers entrusted to it, the court will carefully abstain from exercising any power that is not strictly judicial in its character, and which is not clearly confided to it by the Constitution."

At the last term of the court, in the case of Baltimore & Ohio R. R. Co. v. Interstate Commerce Commission, 215 U.S. 216, this court declined to take jurisdiction of a case which undertook to extend its appellate power to the consideration of a case in which there was no judgment in the court below. In that case former cases were reviewed by Mr. Chief Justice Fuller, who spoke for the court, and the requirement that this court adhere strictly to the jurisdiction, original and appellate, conferred upon it by the Constitution, was emphasized and enforced. It is therefore apparent that from its earliest history this court has consistently declined to exercise any powers other than those which are strictly judicial in their nature.

It therefore becomes necessary to inquire what is meant by the judicial power thus conferred by the Constitution upon this court, and with the aid of appropriate legislation upon the inferior courts of the United States. "Judicial power," says Mr. Justice Miller in his work on the Constitution, "is the power of a court to decide and pronounce a judgment and carry it into effect between persons and parties who bring a case before it for decision." Miller on the Constitution, 314.

As we have already seen by the express terms of the Constitution, the exercise of the judicial power is limited to "cases" and "controversies." Beyond this it does not extend, and unless it is asserted in a case or controversy within the meaning of the Constitution, the power to exercise it is nowhere conferred.

What, then, does the Constitution mean in conferring this judicial power with the right to determine "cases" and "controversies"? A "case" was defined by Mr. Chief Justice Marshall as early as the leading case of Marbury v. Madison, 1 Cranch, 137, to be a suit instituted according to the regular course of judicial procedure. And what more, if anything, is meant in the use of the term "controversy"? That question was dealt with by Mr. Justice Field, at the circuit, in the case of In re Pacific Railway Commission, 32 Fed.Rep. 241, 255. Of these terms that learned Justice said:

"The judicial article of the Constitution mentions cases and controversies. The term 'controversies,' if distinguishable at all from 'cases,' is so in that it is less comprehensive than the latter, and includes only suits of a civil nature. Chisholm v. Georgia, 2 Dall. 431, 432; 1 Tuck.Bl.Comm.App. 420, 421. By cases and controversies are intended the claims of litigants brought before the courts for determination by such regular proceedings as are established by law or custom for the protection or enforcement of rights, or the prevention, redress, or punishment of wrongs. Whenever the claim of a party under the Constitution, laws, or treaties of the United States takes such a form that the judicial power is capable of acting upon it, then it has become a case. The term implies the existence of present or possible adverse parties whose contentions are submitted to the court for adjudication."

The power being thus limited to require an application of the judicial power to cases and controversies, is the act which undertook to authorize the present suits to determine the constitutional validity of certain legislation within the constitutional authority of the court? This inquiry in the case before us includes the broader question, When may this court, in the exercise of the judicial power, pass upon the constitutional validity of an act of Congress? That question has been settled from the early history of the court, the leading case on the subject being Marbury v. Madison, *supra*.

In that case Chief Justice Marshall, who spoke for the court, was careful to point out that the right to declare an act of Congress unconstitutional could only be exercised when a proper case between opposing parties was submitted for judicial determination; that there was no general veto power in the court upon the legislation of Congress; and that the authority to declare an act unconstitutional sprung from the requirement that the court, in administering the law and pronouncing judgment between the parties to a case, and choosing between the requirements of the fundamental law established by the people and embodied in the Constitution and an act of the agents of the people, acting under authority of the Constitution, should enforce the Constitution as the supreme law of the land. The Chief Justice demonstrated, in a manner which has been regarded as settling the question, that with the choice thus given between a constitutional requirement and a conflicting statutory enactment, the plain duty of the court was to follow and enforce the Constitution as the supreme law established by the people. And the court recognized, in Marbury v. Madison and subsequent cases, that the exercise of this great power could only be invoked in cases which came regularly before the courts for determination, for, said the Chief Justice, in Osborn v. Bank of United States, 9 Wheat. 819, speaking of the third Article of the Constitution conferring judicial power:

"This clause enables the judicial department to receive jurisdiction to the full extent of the Constitution, laws, and treaties of the United States, when any question respecting them shall assume such a form that the judicial power is capable of acting on it. That power is capable of acting only when the subject is submitted to it by a party who asserts his rights in the form prescribed by law. It then becomes a case, and the Constitution declares that the judicial power shall extend to all cases arising under the Constitution, laws, and treaties of the United States."

Again, in the case of Cohens v. Virginia, 6 Wheat. 264, Chief Justice Marshall, amplifying and reasserting the doctrine of Marbury v. Madison, recognized the limitations upon the right of this court to declare an act of Congress unconstitutional, and granting that there might be instances of its violation which could not be brought within the jurisdiction of the courts, and referring to a grant by a State of a patent of nobility as a case of that class, and conceding that the court would have no power to annul such a grant, said, p. 405:

"This may be very true; but by no means justifies the inference drawn from it. The article does not extend the judicial power to every violation of the Constitution which may possibly take place, but to 'a case in law or equity' in which a right under such law is asserted in a court of justice. If the question cannot be brought into a court, then there is no case in law or equity, and no jurisdiction is given by the words of the article. But if, in any controversy pending in a court, the cause should depend on the validity of such a law, that would be a case arising under the Constitution, to which the judicial power of the United States could extend. The same observation applies to the other instances with which the counsel who opened the cause has illustrated this argument. Although they show that there may be violations of the Constitution of which the courts can take no cognizance, they do not show that an interpretation more restrictive than the words themselves import ought to be given to this article. They do not show that there can be 'a *case* in law or equity' arising under the Constitution, to which the judicial power does not extend."

See also in this connection Chicago & Grand Trunk Railway Company v. Wellman, 143 U.S. 339. On page 345 of the opinion in that case the result of the previous decisions of this court was summarized in these apposite words by Mr. Justice Brewer, who spoke for the court:

"Whenever, in pursuance of an honest and actual antagonistic assertion of rights by one individual against another, there is presented a question involving the validity of any act of any legislature, State or Federal, and the decision necessarily rests on the competency of the legislature to so enact, the court must, in the exercise of its solemn duties, determine whether the act be constitutional or not; but such an exercise of power is the ultimate and supreme function of courts. It is legitimate only in the last resort, and as a necessity in the determination of real, earnest and vital controversy between individuals. It never was the thought that, by means of a friendly suit, a party beaten in the legislature could transfer to the courts an inquiry as to the constitutionality of the legislative act."

Applying the principles thus long settled by the decisions of this court to the act of Congress undertaking to confer jurisdiction in this case, we find that William Brown and Levi B. Gritts, on their own behalf and on behalf of all other Cherokee citizens having like interest in the property allotted under the act of July 1, 1902, and David Muskrat and J. Henry Dick, for themselves and representatives of all Cherokee citizens enrolled as such for allotment as of September 1, 1902, are authorized and empowered to institute suits in the Court of Claims to determine the validity of acts of Congress passed since the act of July 1, 1902, in so far as the same attempt to increase or extend the restrictions upon alienation, encumbrance, or the right to lease the allotments of lands of Cherokee citizens, or to increase the number of persons entitled to share in the final distribution of lands and funds of the Cherokees beyond those enrolled for allotments as of September 1, 1902, and provided for in the said act of July 1, 1902.

The jurisdiction was given for that purpose first to the Court of Claims and then upon appeal to this court. That is, the object and purpose of the suit is wholly comprised in the determination of the constitutional validity of certain acts of Congress; and furthermore, in the last paragraph of the section, should a judgment be rendered in the Court of Claims or this court, denying the constitutional validity of such acts, then the amount of compensation to be paid to attorneys employed for the purpose of testing the constitutionality of the law is to be paid out of funds in the Treasury of the United States belonging to the beneficiaries, the act having previously provided that the United States should be made a party and the Attorney General be charged with the defense of the suits.

It is therefore evident that there is neither more nor less in this procedure than an attempt to provide for a judicial determination, final in this court, of the constitutional validity of an act of Congress. Is such a determination within the judicial power conferred by the Constitution, as the same has been interpreted and defined in the authoritative decisions to which we have referred? We think it is not. That judicial power, as we have seen, is the right to determine actual controversies arising between adverse litigants, duly instituted in courts of proper jurisdiction. The right to declare a law unconstitutional arises because an act of Congress relied upon by one or the other of such parties in determining their rights is in conflict with the fundamental law. The exercise of this, the most important and delicate duty of this court, is not given to it as a body with revisory power over the action of Congress, but because the rights of the litigants in justiciable controversies require the court to choose between the fundamental law and a law purporting to be enacted within constitutional authority, but in fact beyond the power delegated to the legislative branch of the Government. This attempt to obtain a judicial declaration of the validity of the act of Congress is not presented in a "case" or "controversy," to which, under the Constitution of the United States, the judicial power alone extends. It is true the United States is made a defendant to this action, but it has no interest adverse to the claimants. The object is not to assert a property right as against the Government, or to demand compensation for alleged wrongs because of action upon its part. The whole purpose of the law is to determine the constitutional validity of this class of legislation, in a suit not arising between parties concerning a property right necessarily involved in the decision in question, but in a proceeding against the Government in its sovereign capacity, and concerning which the only judgment required is to settle the doubtful character of the legislation in question. Such judgment will not conclude private parties, when actual litigation brings to the court the question of the constitutionality of such legislation. In a legal sense the judgment could not be executed, and amounts in fact to no more than an expression of opinion upon the validity of the acts in question. Confining the jurisdiction of this court within the limitations conferred by the Constitution, which the court has hitherto been careful to observe, and whose boundaries it has refused to transcend, we think the Congress, in the act of March 1, 1907, exceeded the limitations of legislative authority, so far as it required of this court action not judicial in its nature within the meaning of the Constitution.

Nor can it make any difference that the petitioners had brought suits in the Supreme Court of the District of Columbia to enjoin the Secretary of the Interior from carrying into effect the legislation subsequent to the act of July 1, 1902, which suits were pending when the jurisdictional act here involved was passed. The latter act must depend upon its own terms and be judged by the authority which it undertakes to confer. If such actions as are here attempted, to determine the validity of legislation, are sustained, the result will be that this court, instead of keeping within the limits of judicial power and deciding cases or controversies arising between opposing parties, as the Constitution intended it should, will be required to give opinions in the nature of advice concerning legislative action, a function never conferred upon it by the Constitution, and against the exercise of which this court has steadily set its face from the beginning.

The questions involved in this proceeding as to the validity of the legislation may arise in suits between individuals, and when they do and are properly brought before this court for consideration they, of course, must be determined in the exercise of its judicial functions. For the reasons we have stated, we are constrained to hold that these actions present no justiciable controversy within the authority of the court, acting within the limitations of the Constitution under which it was created. As Congress, in passing this act as a part of the plan involved, evidently intended to provide a review of the judgment of the Court of Claims in this court, as the constitutionality of important legislation is concerned, we think the act cannot be held to intend to confer jurisdiction on that court separately considered.

NOTES AND QUESTIONS

1.   In what respects is the "case" which came before the Supreme Court in *Muskrat* different from the one presented by Jefferson to Chief Justice Jay and his Associate Justices? Are the differences significant?

Are you sure of the reason the Court found no "case" or "controversy" in *Muskrat*? Are the definitions of "case" which the court advances decisive of the issue in the case? Or could an argument be made that under all of them *Muskrat* would be a proper case for judicial jurisdiction?

Why wasn't *Muskrat* one of those "actual controversies arising between adverse litigants, duly instituted in courts of proper jurisdiction"? Wasn't the controversy between Muskrat and the United States an "actual" one? Was it in any sense specious, feigned or trivial? Did Muskrat have anything important at stake? Did the United States? Did the Attorney General's interest in protecting the validity of a duly enacted Federal law really not amount to an interest "adverse" to Muskrat's? Is it true that Muskrat is not asserting a "property right" against the United States government? Is it far-fetched to say that Congress had deprived Muskrat of property?

What do you think is meant by saying that "the judgment could not be executed"? That it would not be binding on the United States in any future litigation? Is that so? Does the Court say it is so? How does the judgment differ from the judgment one receives in a declaratory judgment action?

2.   When *Muskrat* came down there was no Federal Declaratory Judgment Act and the institution of declaratory judgments had not yet developed in the States. To what extent can the Supreme Court's decision be explained, do you think, by the novelty of the remedy of declaratory judgments? Does *Muskrat* represent a kind of mindless conversatism and/or does it represent a protection of important institutional interests? Consider Justice Stone's defense of a state de-

claratory judgment act twenty-two years later in Nashville, C. & St. L. Ry. v. Wallace:

> While the ordinary course of judicial procedure results in a judgment requiring an award of process or execution to carry it into effect, such relief is not an indispensable adjunct to the exercise of the judicial function. . . . This Court has often exerted its judicial power to adjudicate boundaries between states, although it gave no injunction or other relief beyond the determination of the legal rights which were the subject of controversy between the parties, Louisiana v. Mississippi, 202 U.S. 1 . . . ., and to review judgments of the Court of Claims, although no process issues against the Government. United States v. Jones, 119 U.S. 477. . . . As we said in Fidelity National Bank & Trust Co. v. Swope, supra, "Naturalization proceedings, Tutun v. United States, 270 U.S. 568; suits to determine a matrimonial or other status; suits for instructions to a trustee or for the construction of a will, Traphagen v. Levy, 45 N.J. Eq. 448, 18 A. 222; bills of interpleader so far as the stakeholder is concerned, Wakeman v. Kingsland, 46 N.J.Eq. 113, 18 A. 680; bills to quiet title where the plaintiff rests his claim on adverse possession, Sharon v. Tucker, 144 U.S. 533; are familiar examples of judicial proceedings which result in an adjudication of the rights of litigants, although execution is not necessary to carry the judgment into effect, in the sense that damages are required to be paid or acts to be performed by the parties." . . .

> The issues raised here are the same as those which under old forms of procedure could be raised only in a suit for an injunction or one to recover the tax after its payment. But the Constitution does not require that the case or controversy should be presented by traditional forms of procedure, invoking only traditional remedies. The judiciary clause of the Constitution defined and limited judicial power, not the particular method by which that power might be invoked. It did not crystallize into changeless form the procedure of 1789 as the only possible means for presenting a case or controversy otherwise cognizable by the federal courts. Whenever the judicial power is invoked to review a judgment of a state court, the ultimate constitutional purpose is the protection, by the exercise of the judicial function, of rights arising under the Constitution and laws of the United States. The states are left free to regulate their own judicial procedure. Hence, changes merely in the form or method of procedure by which federal rights are brought to final adjudication in the state courts are not enough to preclude review of the adjudication by this Court, so long as the case retains the essentials of an adversary proceeding, involving a real, not a hypothetical, controversy, which is finally determined by the judgment below. . . . .

288 U.S. 249 (1933). What kind of a judgment, incidentally, does a defendant get in a civil or criminal case? Can it be compared to a declaratory judgment?

In Aetna Life Insurance Co. v. Haworth, 300 U.S. 227 (1937), the Supreme Court upheld the Federal Declaratory Judgment Act. Consider the following passages from Chief Justice Hughes's opinion with regard to the action brought in *Muskrat*.

> . . . . The Declaratory Judgment Act of 1934, in its limitation to "cases of actual controversy," manifestly has regard to the constitutional provision and is operative only in respect to controversies which are such in the constitutional sense. The word "actual" is one of emphasis rather than of definition. Thus the operation of the Declaratory Judgment Act is procedural only. In providing remedies and defining procedure in relation to case and controversies in the constitutional sense the Congress is acting within its delegated power over the jurisdiction of the federal courts which the Congress is authorized to establish. . . . Exercising this control of practice and procedure the Congress is not confined to traditional forms or traditional remedies. . . . In dealing with methods within its sphere of remedial action the Congress may create and improve as well as abolish or restrict. The Declaratory Judgment Act must be deemed to fall within this ambit of congressional power, so far as it authorizes relief which is consonant with the exercise of the judicial function in the determination of controversies to which under the Constitution the judicial power extends.
>
> A "controversy" in this sense must be one that is appropriate for judicial determination. . . . A justiciable controversy is thus distinguished from a difference or dispute of a hypothetical or abstract character; from one that is academic or moot. . . . The controversy must be definite and concrete, touching the legal relations of parties having adverse legal interests. . . . It must be a real and substantial controversy admitting of specific relief through a decree of a conclusive character, as distinguished from an opinion advising what the law would be upon a hypothetical state of facts. . . . Where there is such a concrete case admitting of an immediate and definite determination of the legal rights of the parties in an adversary proceeding upon the facts alleged, the judicial function may be appropriately exercised although the adjudication of the rights of the litigants may not require the award of process or the payment of damages.

Can you use this language to support the constitutionality of the legislation in *Muskrat*?

4. Try to list the ways in which *Muskrat* differed from "typical" legal cases. What are the attributes which might make it appear suspect or queer to the Justices? To what extent do we want judges—

or, for that matter, any office-holder or role-player—to resist new and strange-sounding forms of procedure? New and strange-sounding tasks? Is there really any choice as to whether such resistance will occur?

### NOTE: THE SATISFACTIONS OF THE ROLE EXPERIENCE

It is easy to view a job or a role simply as a means to an end—the particular rational-utilitarian task with which the role may be associated. As we have seen, this can be a dangerous oversimplification, for jobs and roles will not meet the demands we make upon them unless to a large extent—perhaps in *most* instances—the role-player is permitted to treat the role itself as the end, as the final statement of relevant values. Or, for those who prefer a different terminology, one might say that roles cannot work unless they are ordinarily treated as the *authoritative* expressions of the higher or more abstract purposes which they serve.

Whichever way one may choose to talk, it is important to note that either formulation continues to assume that the role is simply a means. Although it is treated *as if* it were the end in most instances, it is only treated as such in order to serve some higher end. Its value as a means, that is, depends on its *use* as an end. This may be a perfectly proper way of viewing the matter, but it tends to make us forget that for the role-player the maintenance of the role and its peculiar structure may well be the primary value. For it is *his* role and the degree of personal satisfaction he will experience in his life will largely depend upon the type of experience that role permits him to have. The roles he chooses are likely to be ones that meet his needs; the modifications in their structure and the idiosyncrasies of performing them which he adopts will similarly serve some personal interest.

It can, of course, be said that when roles function in this way they are still means to a higher end—although this time the end is not a definite, overt, social one, but a highly personal,—one might even say non-rational—one. These are not the ends, however, with which we ordinarily associate our roles, and so in a certain sense they are not what is meant by "ends" in that context. Again, however one chooses to speak, in any examination of the nature, function and performance of roles one cannot have fully understood his subject matter, unless he has investigated the degree to which role decisions are a function of the type and quality of role experience which is being sought. To what extent, for example, are the rules, techniques, prejudices, and values which make roles socially useful—*e. g.*, as ways of organizing cognitive and social life—"needed" by the role-player, so that in fulfilling personal goals he is led to satisfy social ones as well? The following readings from Llewellyn, Shklar, Huizinga, and Kuhn are meant to pose and to pursue questions of this type?

*KARL N. LLEWELLYN*

## THE COMMON LAW TRADITION *

.  .  .  [T]he bar is bothered about our appellate courts—not the much discussed Supreme Court alone, but our appellate courts in general.  The bar is so much bothered about these courts that we face a crisis in confidence which packs danger.  Of course, ever since lawyers began to lawyer, there have been losing counsel aplenty who have so believed in their causes that they have bitterly blamed the court.  And, of course, ever since issues in court have had political flavor, i. e., roughly since before Genesis, each new crucial decision has been, for some vocal citizens, the brink of perdition.  And of course ever since men began to generalize, the particular decisions of the day or week have been enough to make many see the whole system as in decay.  And of course and as usual, "never in history" has there been a crisis to match today's crisis.  Despite all this, the bar *is* bothered these days with a bother which has a new corrosiveness.  For all the old worries centered on things which at least left to a man his pride in himself and his craftsmanship, and his skill to fight and fight back with, though he might be overpowered.  The evil used to lie in results basically political: the ravening demagogues were taking over, or the vested exploiters were too deeply entrenched; or else the ring or the syndicate or the racketeers had spread their tentacles; or, perhaps, some particular court (contrary to the manner of our courts at large) was corrupt.  And a man equipped with the skills of craftsmanship and a high heart may suffer, and may have to suffer it out, but he can fight; and a healthy body will in time cast out corruption; and in this country political monsters, however gruesome, seem to have a limited span of life.

But today the worry has a novel corrosiveness.  In most it no longer inspires healthy fighting reaction to effect its cure; for most it has come to lay a pall and palsy on heart and hand because it goes to whether there is any reckonability in the work of our appellate courts, any real stability of footing for the lawyer, be it in appellate litigation or in counseling, whether therefore there is any effective craftsmanship for him to bring to bear to serve his client and to justify his being.  A right man cannot be a man and feel himself a trickster or a charlatan.  It is the appellate court, it is particularly the highest court in any given hierarchy, which is the organ and even more importantly the symbol of reckonable recognition and reward for decent careful craftsmanship in law.  It is that court—those courts— in whom as persons, but also and no less importantly in whose ways of work, and finally further and again no less vitally, in whose general run of results, the man at the bar must have *confidence* on pain of feeling his own sustaining faith in his craft, in his craftsmanship, in his very office and utility as a lawyer, to ooze and seep away from him until he stands naked and hollow, helpless and worthless, a nothing, or a medicine man who has discovered his medicine to be a cheat.

* From 3–4 (1960).  Reprinted with permission of the estate of Karl N. Llewellyn.

QUESTIONS

What does Llewellyn mean by "reckonability in the work of our appellate courts"? Is he referring to knowledge of the exact outcome of particular cases? Is the absence of this the cause of the lawyer's crisis of confidence? If not, what is it that the lawyer wants to know? What is it that will enable the lawyer to sustain his "faith in his craft, in his craftsmanship, in his very office and utility as a lawyer"?

Should courts worry about the effect of their decisions on lawyers? Or should they simply do justice and protect freedom? What difference does it make if a lawyer feels "himself a trickster or a charlatan"? Recall Weigand in the *Budd* case.

THOMAS S. KUHN

THE STRUCTURE OF SCIENTIFIC REVOLUTIONS *

Perhaps the most striking feature of the normal research problems we have . . . encountered is how little they aim to produce major novelties, conceptual or phenomenal. Sometimes, as in a wave-length measurement, everything but the most esoteric detail of the result is known in advance, and the typical latitude of expectation is only somewhat wider. . . .

. . . . Even the project whose goal is paradigm articulation does not aim at the *unexpected* novelty.

But if the aim of normal science is not major substantive novelties—if failure to come near the anticipated result is usually failure as a scientist—then why are these problems undertaken at all? Part of the answer has already been developed. To scientists, at least, the results gained in normal research are significant because they add to the scope and precision with which the paradigm can be applied. That answer, however, cannot account for the enthusiasm and devotion that scientists display for the problems of normal research. No one devotes years to, say, the development of a better spectrometer or the production of an improved solution to the problem of vibrating strings simply because of the importance of the information that will be obtained. The data to be gained by computing ephemerides or by further measurements with an existing instrument are often just as significant, but those activities are regularly spurned by scientists because they are so largely repetitions of procedures that have been carried through before. That rejection provides a clue to the fascination of the normal research problem. Though its outcome can be anticipated, often in detail so great that what remains to be known is itself uninteresting, the way to achieve that outcome remains very much in doubt. Bringing a normal research problem to a conclusion is achieving the anticipated in a new way, and it requires the solution of all sorts of complex instrumental, conceptual, and mathematical puzzles.

The man who succeeds proves himself an expert puzzle-solver, and the challenge of the puzzle is an important part of what usually drives him on.

The terms 'puzzle' and 'puzzle-solver' highlight several of the themes that have become increasingly prominent in the preceding pages. Puzzles are, in the entirely standard meaning here employed, that special category of problems that can serve to test ingenuity or skill in solution. Dictionary illustrations are 'jigsaw puzzle' and 'crossword puzzle,' and it is the characteristics that these share with the problems of normal science that we now need to isolate. One of them has just been mentioned. It is no criterion of goodness in a puzzle that its outcome be intrinsically interesting or important. On the contrary, the really pressing problems, e. g., a cure for cancer or the design of a lasting peace, are often not puzzles at all, largely because they may not have any solution. Consider the jigsaw puzzle whose pieces are selected at random from each of two different puzzle boxes. Since that problem is likely to defy (though it might not) even the most ingenious of men, it cannot serve as a test of skill in solution. In any usual sense it is not a puzzle at all. Though intrinsic value is no criterion for a puzzle, the assured existence of a solution is.

We have already seen, however, that one of the things a scientific community acquires with a paradigm is a criterion for choosing problems that, while the paradigm is taken for granted, can be assumed to have solutions. To a great extent these are the only problems that the community will admit as scientific or encourage its members to undertake. Other problems, including many that had previously been standard, are rejected as metaphysical, as the concern of another discipline, or sometimes as just too problematic to be worth the time. A paradigm can, for that matter, even insulate the community from those socially important problems that are not reducible to the puzzle form, because they cannot be stated in terms of the conceptual and instrumental tools the paradigm supplies. Such problems can be a distraction, a lesson brilliantly illustrated by several facets of seventeenth-century Baconianism and by some of the contemporary social sciences. One of the reasons why normal science seems to progress so rapidly is that its practitioners concentrate on problems that only their own lack of ingenuity should keep them from solving.

If, however, the problems of normal science are puzzles in this sense, we need no longer ask why scientists attack them with such passion and devotion. A man may be attracted to science for all sorts of reasons. Among them are the desire to be useful, the excitement of exploring new territory, the hope of finding order, and the drive to test established knowledge. These motives and others besides also help to determine the particular problems that will later engage him. Furthermore, though the result is occasional frustration, there is good reason why motives like these should first attract him and then lead him on. The scientific enterprise as a whole does from time to time prove useful, open up new territory, display order, and test long-accepted belief. Nevertheless, *the individual* engaged on a normal research problem *is almost never doing any one of these things.* Once engaged, his motivation is of a rather different sort.  What then challenges him is the conviction that, if only he is skillful enough, he will succeed in solving a puzzle that no one before has solved or solved so well.  Many of the greatest scientific minds have devoted all of their professional attention to demanding puzzles of this sort.  On most occasions any particular field of specialization offers nothing else to do, a fact that makes it no less fascinating to the proper sort of addict.

Turn now to another, more difficult, and more revealing aspect of the parallelism between puzzles and the problems of normal science. If it is to classify as a puzzle, a problem must be characterized by more than an assured solution.  There must also be rules that limit both the nature of acceptable solutions and the steps by which they are to be obtained.  To solve a jigsaw puzzle is not, for example, merely "to make a picture."  Either a child or a contemporary artist could do that by scattering selected pieces, as abstract shapes, upon some neutral ground.  The picture thus produced might be far better, and would certainly be more original, than the one from which the puzzle had been made.  Nevertheless, such a picture would not be a solution.  To achieve that all the pieces must be used, their plain sides must be turned down, and they must be interlocked without forcing until no holes remain.  Those are among the rules that govern jigsaw-puzzle solutions.  Similar restrictions upon the admissible solutions of crossword puzzles, riddles, chess problems, and so on, are readily discovered.

## QUESTIONS

To what extent do lawyers and judges with their rules of procedure, their rules of jurisdiction, their rules of evidence, their rules of rule selection and rule interpretation attempt to create a field in which the puzzle-solver's appetite may be satiated?

*JOHAN HUIZINGA*

## HOMO LUDENS *

The great archetypal activities of human society are all permeated with play from the start.  Take language, for instance—that first and supreme instrument which man shapes in order to communicate, to teach, to command.  Language allows him to distinguish, to establish, to state things; in short, to name them and by naming them to raise them into the domain of the spirit.  In the making of speech and language the spirit is continually "sparking" between matter and mind, as it were, playing with this wondrous nominative faculty.  Behind every abstract expression there lie the boldest of metaphors, and every metaphor is a play upon words.  Thus in giving expression to life man creates a second, poetic world alongside the world of nature.

* From 4–6, 9–13, 18, 19–20, 76–79, 206–208 (Beacon ed. 1955).  Reprinted with permission of Beacon Press, Publishers, Boston.

Or take myth. This, too, is a transformation or an "imagination" of the outer world, only here the process is more elaborate and ornate than is the case with individual words. In myth, primitive man seeks to account for the world of phenomena by grounding it in the Divine. In all the wild imaginings of mythology a fanciful spirit is playing on the border-line between jest and earnest. Or finally, let us take ritual. Primitive society performs its sacred rites, its sacrifices, consecrations and mysteries, all of which serve to guarantee the well-being of the world, in a spirit of pure play truly understood.

Now in myth and ritual the great instinctive forces of civilized life have their origin: law and order, commerce and profit, craft and art, poetry, wisdom and science. All are rooted in the primaeval soil of play.

The object of the present essay is to demonstrate that it is more than a rhetorical comparison to view culture *sub specie ludi*. The thought is not at all new. There was a time when it was generally accepted, though in a limited sense quite different from the one intended here: in the 17th century, the age of world theatre. Drama, in a glittering succession of figures ranging from Shakespeare and Calderon to Racine, then dominated the literature of the West. It was the fashion to liken the world to a stage on which every man plays his part. Does this mean that the play-element in civilization was openly acknowledged? Not at all. On closer examination this fashionable comparison of life to a stage proves to be little more than an echo of the Neo-platonism that was then in vogue, with a markedly moralistic accent. It was a variation on the ancient theme of the vanity of all things. The fact that play and culture are actually interwoven with one another was neither observed nor expressed, whereas for us the whole point is to show that genuine, pure play is one of the main bases of civilisation.

To our way of thinking, play is the direct opposite of seriousness. At first sight this opposition seems as irreducible to other categories as the play-concept itself. Examined more closely, however, the contrast between play and seriousness proves to be neither conclusive nor fixed. We can say: play is non-seriousness. But apart from the fact that this proposition tells us nothing about the positive qualities of play, it is extraordinarily easy to refute. As soon as we proceed from "play is non-seriousness" to "play is not serious", the contrast leaves us in the lurch—for some play can be very serious indeed. Moreover we can immediately name several other fundamental categories that likewise come under the heading "non-seriousness" yet have no correspondence whatever with "play". Laughter, for instance, is in a sense the opposite of seriousness without being absolutely bound up with play. Children's games, football, and chess are played in profound seriousness; the players have not the slightest inclination to laugh. It is worth noting that the purely physiological act of laughing is exclusive to man, whilst the significant function of play is common to both men and animals. The Aristotelian *animal ridens* characterizes man as distinct from the animal almost more absolutely than *homo sapiens.*

.   .   .

Play is distinct from "ordinary" life both as to locality and duration.  This is the third main characteristic of play:  its secludedness, its limitedness.  It is "played out" within certain limits of time and place.  It contains its own course and meaning.

Play begins, and then at a certain moment it is "over".  It plays itself to an end.  While it is in progress all is movement, change, alternation, succession, association, separation.  But immediately connected with its limitation as to time there is a further curious feature of play:  it at once assumes fixed form as a cultural phenomenon.  Once played, it endures as a new-found creation of the mind, a treasure to be retained by the memory.  It is transmitted, it becomes tradition.  It can be repeated at any time, whether it be "child's play" or a game of chess, or at fixed intervals like a mystery.  In this faculty of repetition lies one of the most essential qualities of play.  It holds good not only of play as a whole but also of its inner structure.  In nearly all the higher forms of play the elements of repetition and alternation (as in the *refrain*), are like the warp and woof of a fabric.

More striking even than the limitation as to time is the limitation as to space.  All play moves and has its being within a playground marked off beforehand either materially or ideally, deliberately or as a matter of course.  Just as there is no formal difference between play and ritual, so the "consecrated spot" cannot be formally distinguished from the play-ground.  The arena, the card-table, the magic circle, the temple, the stage, the screen, the tennis court, the court of justice, etc., are all in form and function play-grounds, i. e. forbidden spots, isolated, hedged round, hallowed, within which special rules obtain.  All are temporary worlds within the ordinary world, dedicated to the performance of an act apart.

Inside the play-ground an absolute and peculiar order reigns.  Here we come across another, very positive feature of play:  it creates order, *is* order.  Into an imperfect world and into the confusion of life it brings a temporary, a limited perfection.  Play demands order absolute and supreme.  The least deviation from it "spoils the game", robs it of its character and makes it worthless.  The profound affinity between play and order is perhaps the reason why play, as we noted in passing, seems to lie to such a large extent in the field of aesthetics.  Play has a tendency to be beautiful.  It may be that this aesthetic factor is identical with the impulse to create orderly form, which animates play in all its aspects.  The words we use to denote the elements of play belong for the most part to aesthetics, terms with which we try to describe the effects of beauty:  tension, poise, balance, contrast, variation, solution, resolution, etc.  Play casts a spell over us; it is "enchanting", "captivating".  It is invested with the noblest qualities we are capable of perceiving in things:  rhythm and harmony.

The element of tension in play to which we have just referred plays a particularly important part. Tension means uncertainty, chanciness; a striving to decide the issue and so end it. The player wants something to "go", to "come off"; he wants to "succeed" by his own exertions. Baby reaching for a toy, pussy patting a bobbin, a little girl playing ball—all want to achieve something difficult, to succeed, to end a tension. Play is "tense", as we say. It is this element of tension and solution that governs all solitary games of skill and application such as puzzles, jig-saws, mosaic-making, patience, target-shooting, and the more play bears the character of competition the more fervent it will be. In gambling and athletics it is at its height. Though play as such is outside the range of good and bad, the element of tension imparts to it a certain ethical value in so far as it means a testing of the player's prowess: his courage, tenacity, resources and, last but not least, his spiritual powers—his "fairness"; because, despite his ardent desire to win, he must still stick to the rules of the game.

These rules in their turn are a very important factor in the play-concept. All play has its rules. They determine what "holds" in the temporary world circumscribed by play. The rules of a game are absolutely binding and allow no doubt. Paul Valery once in passing gave expression to a very cogent thought when he said: "No scepticism is possible where the rules of a game are concerned, for the principle underlying them is an unshakable truth. . . . ." Indeed, as soon as the rules are transgressed the whole play-world collapses. The game is over. The umpire's whistle breaks the spell and sets "real" life going again.

The player who trespasses against the rules or ignores them is a "spoil-sport". The spoil-sport is not the same as the false player, the cheat; for the latter pretends to be playing the game and, on the face of it, still acknowledges the magic circle. It is curious to note how much more lenient society is to the cheat than to the spoil-sport. This is because the spoil-sport shatters the play-world itself. By withdrawing from the game he reveals the relativity and fragility of the play-world in which he had temporarily shut himself with others. He robs play of its *illusion*—a pregnant word which means literally "in-play" (from *inlusio, illudere* or *inludere*). Therefore he must be cast out, for he threatens the existence of the play-community. The figure of the spoil-sport is most apparent in boys' games. The little community does not inquire whether the spoil-sport is guilty of defection because he dares not enter into the game or because he is not allowed to. Rather, it does not recognize "not being allowed" and calls it "not daring". For it, the problem of obedience and conscience is no more than fear of punishment. The spoil-sport breaks the magic world, therefore he is a coward and must be ejected. In the world of high seriousness, too, the cheat and the hypocrite have always had an easier time of it than the spoil-sports, here called apostates, heretics, innovators, prophets, conscientious objectors, etc. It sometimes happens, however, that the spoil-sports in their turn make a new community with rules of its own. The outlaw, the revolutionary, the cabbalist or member of a secret society, indeed heretics of all kinds are of a highly associative if not sociable disposition, and a certain element of play is prominent in all their doings.

. . .

The exceptional and special position of play is most tellingly illustrated by the fact that it loves to surround itself with an air of secrecy. Even in early childhood the charm of play is enhanced by making a "secret" out of it. This is for *us*, not for the "others". What the "others" do "outside" is no concern of ours at the moment. Inside the circle of the game the laws and customs of ordinary life no longer count. We are different and do things differently. This temporary abolition of the ordinary world is fully acknowleged in child-life, but it is no less evident in the great ceremonial games of savage societies. During the great feast of initiation when the youths are accepted into the male community, it is not the neophytes only that are exempt from the ordinary laws and regulations: there is a truce to all fueds in the tribe. All retaliatory acts and vendettas are suspended. This temporary suspension of normal social life on account of the sacred play-season has numerous traces in the more advanced civilizations as well. Everything that pertains to saturnalia and carnival customs belongs to it. Even with us a bygone age of robuster private habits than ours, more marked class-privileges and a more complaisant police recognized the orgies of young men of rank under the name of a "rag". The saturnalian licence of young men still survives, in fact, in the ragging at English universities, which the *Oxford English Dictionary* defines as "an extensive display of noisy and disorderly conduct carried out in defiance of authority and discipline".

The "differentness" and secrecy of play are most vividly expressed in "dressing up". Here the "extra-ordinary" nature of play reaches perfection. The disguised or masked individual "plays" another part, another being. He *is* another being. The terrors of childhood, open-hearted gaiety, mystic fantasy and sacred awe are all inextricably entangled in this strange business of masks and disguises.

. . .

. . . . Ritual is seriousness at its highest and holiest. Can it nevertheless be play? We began by saying that all play, both of children and of grown-ups, can be performed in the most perfect seriousness. Does this go so far as to imply that play is still bound up with the sacred emotion of the sacramental act? Our conclusions are to some extent impeded by the rigidity of our accepted ideas. We are accustomed to think of play and seriousness as an absolute antithesis. It would seem, however, that this does not go to the heart of the matter.

Let us consider for a moment the following argument. The child plays in complete—we can well say, in sacred—earnest. But it plays and knows that it plays. The sportsman, too, plays with all the fervour of a man enraptured, but he still knows that he is playing. The actor on the stage is wholly absorbed in his playing, but is all the time conscious of "the play". The same holds good of the violinist, though he may soar to realms beyond this world.  The play-character, therefore, may attach to the sublimest forms of action.  . . .

. . .

We found that one of the most important characteristics of play was its spatial separation from ordinary life.  A closed space is marked out for it, either materially or ideally, hedged off from the everyday surroundings.  Inside this space the play proceeds, inside it the rules obtain.  Now, the marking out of some sacred spot is also the primary characteristic of every sacred act.  This requirement of isolation for ritual, including magic and law, is much more than merely spatial and temporal.  Nearly all rites of consecration and initiation entail a certain artificial seclusion for the performers and those to be initiated.  Whenever it is a question of taking a vow or being received into an Order or confraternity, or of oaths and secret societies, in one way or another there is always such a delimitation of room for play.  The magician, the augur, the sacrificer begins his work by circumscribing his sacred space.  Sacrament and mystery presuppose a hallowed spot.

Formally speaking, there is no distinction whatever between marking out a space for a sacred purpose and marking it out for purposes of sheer play.  The turf, the tennis-court, the chess-board and pavement-hopscotch cannot formally be distinguished from the temple or the magic circle.  The striking similarity between sacrificial rites all over the earth shows that such customs must be rooted in a very fundamental, an aboriginal layer of the human mind.  As a rule people reduce this over-all congruity of cultural forms to some "reasonable", "logical" cause by explaining the need for isolation and seclusion as an anxiety to protect the consecrated individual from noxious influences—because, in his consecrated state, he is particularly exposed to the malign workings of ghosts, besides being himself a danger to his surroundings.  Such an explanation puts intellection and utilitarian purpose at the beginning of the cultural process: the very thing Frobenius warned against.  Even if we do not fall back here on the antiquated notion of a priestcraft inventing religion, we are still introducing a rationalistic element better avoided.  If, on the other hand, we accept the essential and original identity of play and ritual we simply recognize the hallowed spot as a playground, and the misleading question of the "why and the wherefore" does not arise at all.

. . .

At first sight few things would seem to be further apart than the domain of law, justice and jurisprudence, and play.  High seriousness, deadly earnest and the vital interests of the individual and society reign supreme in everything that pertains to the law.  The etymological foundation of most of the words which express the ideas of law and justice lies in the sphere of setting, fixing, establishing, stating, appointing, holding, ordering, choosing, dividing, binding, etc.  All these ideas would seem to have little or no connection with, indeed to be opposed to, the semantic sphere which gives rise to the words for play.  However, as we have observed all along, the sacredness and seriousness of an action by no means preclude its play-quality.

That an affinity may exist between law and play becomes obvious to us as soon as we realize how much the actual practice of the law, in other words a lawsuit, properly resembles a contest whatever the ideal foundations of the law may be. . . .

. . . . The pronouncement of justice takes place in a "court", for a start. This court is still, in the full sense of the word . . . the sacred circle within which the judges are shown sitting, in the shield of Achilles. Every place from which justice is pronounced is a veritable *temenos*, a sacred spot cut off and hedged in from the "ordinary" world. The old Flemish and Dutch word for it is *vierschaar*, literally a space divided off by four ropes or, according to another view, by four benches. But whether square or round it is still a magic circle, a play-ground where the customary differences of rank are temporarily abolished. . . .

Judges about to administer justice step outside "ordinary" life as soon as they don wig and gown. I do not know whether the costume of the English judge and barrister has been the subject of ethnological investigation. It seems to me that it has little to do with the vogue for wigs in the 17th and 18th centuries. The judge's wig is rather a survival of the mediaeval head-dress worn by lawyers in England, called the coif, which was originally a close-fitting white cap. A vestige of this is still present in the little white edging at the rim of the wig. The judge's wig, however, is more than a mere relic of antiquated professional dress. Functionally it has close connections with the dancing masks of savages. It transforms the wearer into another "being". And it is by no means the only very ancient feature which the strong sense of tradition so peculiar to the British has preserved in law. The sporting element and the humour so much in evidence in British legal practice is one of the basic features of law in archaic society. Of course this element is not wholly lacking in the popular tradition of other countries as well. Even law proceedings on the Continent, though much more persistently serious than in England, bear traces of it. The style and language in which the juristic wranglings of a modern lawsuit are couched often betray a sportsmanlike passion for indulging in argument and counter-argument, some of them highly sophistical, which has reminded a legal friend of mine, a judge, of the Javanese *adat*. Here, he says, the spokesmen poke little sticks into the ground at each well-aimed argument, so that he who has accumulated most sticks carries the day victoriously. . . .

. . . . The judicial contest is always subject to a system of restrictive rules which, quite apart from the limitations of time and place, set the lawsuit firmly and squarely in the domain of orderly, antithetical play. The active association of law and play, particularly in archaic culture, can be seen from three points of view. The lawsuit can be regarded as a game of chance, a contest, or a verbal battle.

We moderns cannot conceive justice apart from abstract righteousness, however feeble our conception of it may be. For us, the lawsuit is primarily a dispute about right and wrong; winning and losing take only a second place. Now it is precisely this preoccupation with ethical values that we must abandon if we are to understand archaic justice. Turning our eyes from the administration of justice in highly developed civilizations to that which obtains in less advanced phases of culture, we see that the idea of right and wrong, the ethical-juridical conception, comes to be over-shadowed by the idea of winning and losing, that is, the purely agonistic conception. It is not so much the abstract question of right and wrong that occupies the archaic mind as the very concrete question of winning or losing. Once given this feeble ethical standard the agonistic factor will gain enormously in legal practice the further back we go; and as the agonistic element increases so does the element of chance, with the result that we soon find ourselves in the play-sphere. We are confronted by a mental world in which the notion of decision by oracles, by the judgment of God, by ordeal, by sortilege—i. e., by *play*—and the notion of decision by judicial sentence, fuse in a single complex of thought. Justice is made subservient—and quite sincerely—to the rules of the game. We still acknowledge the incontrovertibility of such decisions when, failing to make up our minds, we resort to drawing lots or "tossing up".

. . .

More and more the sad conclusion forces itself upon us that the play-element in culture has been on the wane ever since the 18th century, when it was in full flower. Civilization to-day is no longer played, and even where it still seems to play it is false play—I had almost said, it plays false, so that it becomes increasingly difficult to tell where play ends and non-play begins. This is particularly true of politics. Not very long ago political life in parliamentary democratic form was full of unmistakable play-features. One of my pupils has recently worked up my observations on this subject into a thesis on parliamentary eloquence in France and England, showing how, ever since the end of the 18th century, debates in the House of Commons have been conducted very largely according to the rules of a game and in the true play-spirit. Personal rivalries are always at work, keeping up a continual match between the players whose object is to checkmate one another, but without prejudice to the interests of the country which they serve with all seriousness. The mood and manners of parliamentary democracy were, until recently, those of fair play both in England and in the countries that had adopted the English model with some felicity. The spirit of fellowship would allow the bitterest opponents a friendly chat even after the most virulent debate. It was in this style that the "Gentleman's Agreement" arose. Unhappily certain parties to it were not always aware of the duties implicit in the word gentleman. There can be no doubt that it is just this play-element that keeps parliamentary life healthy, at least in Great Britain, despite the abuse that has lately been heaped upon it. The elasticity of human relations underlying the political machinery permits it to "play", thus easing tensions which would otherwise be unendurable or dangerous—for it is the decay of humour that kills. We need hardly add that this play-factor is present in the whole apparatus of elections.

In American politics it is even more evident. Long before the two-party system had reduced itself to two gigantic teams whose political differences were hardly discernible to an outsider, electioneering in America had developed into a kind of national sport. The presidential election of 1840 set the pace for all subsequent elections. The party then calling itself Whig had an excellent candidate, General Harrison of 1812 fame, but no platform. Fortune gave them something infinitely better, a symbol on which they rode to triumph: the log cabin which was the old warrior's modest abode during his retirement. Nomination by majority vote, i. e. by the loudest clamour, was inaugurated in the election of 1860 which brought Lincoln to power. The emotionality of American politics lies deep in the origins of the American nation itself: Americans have ever remained true to the rough and tumble of pioneer life. There is a great deal that is endearing in American politics, something naive and spontaneous for which we look in vain in the dragoonings and drillings, or worse, of the contemporary European scene.

## Judith N. Shklar

### Legalism *

What is legalism? It is the ethical attitude that holds moral conduct to be a matter of rule following, and moral relationships to consist of duties and rights determined by rules. Like all moral attitudes that are both strongly felt and widely shared it expresses itself not only in personal behaviour but also in philosophical thought, in political ideologies, and in social institutions. . . . Legalism, so understood, is thus often an inarticulate, but nonetheless consistently followed, individual code of conduct. It is also a very common social ethos, though by no means the only one, in Western countries. To a great extent it has provided the standards of organization and the operative ideals for a vast number of social groups, from governmental institutions to private clubs. Its most nearly complete expression is in the great legal systems of the European world. Lastly, it has also served as the political ideology of those who cherish these systems of law, and, above all, those who are directly involved in their maintenance—the legal profession, both bench and bar. The court of law and the trial according to law are the social paradigms, the perfection, the very epitome, of legalistic morality. They are, however, far from being its only expressions. Indeed, they are inconceivable without the convictions, mores, and ideologies that must permeate any society which wishes to maintain them. . . .

Legalism is the operative outlook of the legal profession, both bench and bar. Moreover, most legal theory, whether it be analytical

* From 1–2, 8–10, 12, 14–15, 16–18 (1964). Copyright 1964 by the President and Fellows of Harvard College.     Reprinted by permission of Harvard University Press.

positivism or natural law thinking, depends on categories of thought derived from this shared professional outlook. The tendency to think of law as "there", as a discrete entity, discernibly different from morals and politics, has its deepest roots in the legal profession's views of its own functions, and forms the very basis of most of our judicial institutions and procedures. That lawyers have particularly pronounced intellectual habits peculiar to them has often been noticed, especially by historians and other students of society whose views differ sharply from those of the legal profession. As one English lawyer has put it, "A lawyer is *bound* by certain habits of belief . . . by which lawyers, however dissimilar otherwise, are more closely linked than they are separated. . . . A man who has had legal training is never quite the same again . . . is never able to look at institutions or administrative practices or even social or political policies, free from his legal habits or beliefs. It is not easy for a lawyer to become a political scientist. It is very difficult for him to become a sociologist or a historian. . . . He is interested in relationships, in rights in something and against somebody, in relation to others. . . . This is what is meant by the legalistic approach. . . . [A lawyer] will fight to the death to defend legal rights against persuasive arguments based on expediency or the public interest or the social good. . . . He distrusts them. . . . He believes, as part of his mental habits, that they are dangerous and too easily used as cloaks for arbitrary action."

. . .

The dislike of vague generalities, the preference for case-by-case treatment of all social issues, the structuring of all claims under established rules, and the belief that the rules are "there"—these combine to make up legalism as a social outlook. When it becomes self-conscious, when it challenges other views, it is a full-blown ideology. Since lawyers are engaged in their daily lives with political or social conflicts of some kind, they are bound to run up against perspectives radically different from their own. As law serves ideally to promote the security of established expectations, so legalism with its concentration on specific cases and rules is, essentially, conservative. It is not, however, a matter of "masking" a specific class and economic interest. Not only do lawyerly interests often differ from those of other conservative social groups, businessmen's, for example, but legalism is no mask for anything. It is an openly, instrinsically, and quite specifically conservative view, because law is itself a conservatizing ideal and institution. . . .

. . .

Both natural law theories and analytical positivism allow judges to believe that there always is a rule somewhere for them to follow. The consensus of society or of its wise men, a statute (however broadly interpreted), a precedent (however twisted in meaning), all are somehow present to serve as rationalizations to which a judge must resort if his decisions are to meet the demands that a legalistic conscience and his office make upon him. . . .

To seek rules, or at least a public consensus that can serve in place of a rule, must be the judge's constant preoccupation, and it affects his choices in ways that are unknown to less constrained political agents. To avoid the appearance of arbitrariness is a deep inner necessity for him. . . .

An A.B.A.-sponsored survey of the American legal profession concluded that when it came to reforming procedure, for instance, lawyers were unreasonably obstinate. Observers of the English bar have reached the same conclusion. The English barrister tends to regard the common law as an inheritance to be preserved and technically perfected without being in any way altered. The changes that the bar wants, if any, are not those that the public is interested in. It is, moreover, doubtful that change of any kind is to its liking. "The lawyers could no doubt reform their education and training, reform the practice and processes of the law, even reform the law itself, if they felt like it. But probably they will not feel like it." On the contrary, the more the bar concentrates on formal perfection of established rules and procedures, the more removed it may become from the social ends that law serves. . . .

Antiquity of legalism as an ideology is, in fact, one of the wonders of history. It is itself the expression of the continuity of the legal profession and its basic tasks. Whereas science has rendered the practice of modern medicine quite unlike the pre-nineteenth-century profession of the same name, the heirs of Coke resemble him closely in vocabulary, outlook, and concerns. De Tocqueville's description of the legalistic ethos is as accurate today as it was when it was written. Order and formality being the marks of the legal mind, he wrote, it is natural for lawyers to support the established social order. As long as they are not deprived of the authority which they regard as their due they will rally to the regime in power. The radical village lawyer of the French Revolution was an aberration that the aristocracy foolishly brought upon itself. In the normal course of events conservatism is inseparable from legalism. "If they prize freedom much, they generally value legality still more: they are less afraid of tyranny, than of arbitrary power." One might add that, if they fear tyranny, it is because it tends to be arbitrary, not because it is repressive. The fear of the arbitrary, however, is what gives legalism its political use. That is why it is not a conservatism without content. To the extent that change means uncertainty, the hatred of the arbitrary is inevitably conservative, but it is a conservatism that has a specific direction which distinguishes it from other conservatisms, especially on those occasions when the independence and professional standing of the bench and bar are directly involved; for they, and they alone, stand to protect "justice" against the arbitrariness and "expedience" of politics.

Almost a hundred years after de Tocqueville wrote, Max Weber could still present a picture of the ideology of the legal profession that was virtually unaltered. Lawyers remained as wedded to formal justice as ever and so to all the interests that relied on permanence and predictability in social procedures. . . . A legal caste, once it had established the "rule of law" securely against threats from absolutist arbitrariness, was bound to prefer order to liberty. What de Tocqueville called aristocratic habits of thought, Weber believed (rightly) to be more a matter of "internal professional ideology." The importance of the inner dynamic of legal reasoning and the professional preferences of lawyers tend to separate them from other social groups. Capitalist entrepreneurs have their own interest in stability and calculability, but the excessive formalities of lawyers' law are uncongenial to them. The conflict between jurists and pyschiatrists is another example of tension engendered by incompatible professional views. As Weber was quick to note, these are not class struggles but acute differences between groups which belong to the same economic stratum in society. Looking at German lawyerdom mainly, he thought that its self-absorption, the extreme formalism of the legalistic spirit, would make it inevitably hostile not only to all radical social reform but to democracy in general. Since democracy was a radical ideal in Imperial Germany, he was quite right. However, as de Tocqueville noted, democracy is not necessarily incompatible with legalism. Law in America, then as now, is a profession open to talent, the poor boy's classifical road to middle-class eminence. One might add that political democracy in America has been so conservative, in general, as to give the legalistic consciousness relatively little cause for complaint. Only occasionally, in the fear of radical state legislation and the Progressive movement for popular recall of the judiciary in the decades before the First World War, have legalism and democratic ideology clashed directly. Nevertheless, the main thrust of legalistic ideology is toward orderliness, and formalism can readily reinforce an inherent preference for authority. The ease with which German lawyers accepted "Adolf Légalité's" pretensions to legitimacy, the support they gave Nazism until its radical anti-legalistic tendencies revealed themselves (and even after), more than justify de Tocqueville's and Weber's suspicions. It cannot be repeated often enough that procedurally "correct" repression is perfectly compatible with legalism. That is the cost of conservative adaptability.

If traditionalism tends to favor liberal constitutionalism in America and England, as it did not in Germany, other aspects of legalism transcend the historic differences which Weber stressed so much and which certainly are very important. The differences in the respective attitudes of American lawyers, psychiatrists, and businessmen are still much as he described them. If the American corporation lawyer, the "house lawyer," comes to identify himself completely with the "organization" for which he works, there are lawyers who are wary of the informality of businessmen. There are, moreover, plenty of businessmen who find "lawyer's law," and expenses, unwelcome and not only crude robber barons like Ryan and Whitney at that. The resort to arbitration under chamber of commerce auspices, from which lawyers were at first explicitly excluded, represented a significant preference for direct negotiations over formalism and, worse, litigation. On another level, businessmen do not want regulatory governmental agencies to become too courtlike, but prefer to maintain direct access to them in order to bargain with officials. The official program of the A.B.A., on the other hand, calls for judicialization. In this the lawyers, true to their ideology and habits, express their traditional distaste for the politics of negotiation, expediency, and arbitrariness.

It is the popular acceptance of this legalism in America that surely contributes its share to the general cynicism toward politics as inevitably "dirty". The belief that negotiations aiming at peaceful settlements represent defeats for justice, for the politics of legalism, has led the official American bar to take at least one stand that separates it noticeably from most other conservative groups. From the first it has lent its support to international law, and especially to the International Court of Justice, on the ground that adjudication alone can prevent war and establish the reign of justice. Here, as in domestic politics, disputes between states are treated in isolation, apart from world politics in general. Here, too, the adjudicative process is held up as the model for government, the substitute for politics. So devoted a business lawyer as Joseph Choate headed the American delegation to the Second Hague Conference, and the "World Peace Through World Law" movement has today the ardent support of the A.B.A. This in itself would suffice to demonstrate the existence of a professional ideology among lawyers.

## QUESTIONS

Does Shklar offer a reason different from Llewellyn's for the bar's failure of confidence in the appellate courts? Is the basis of complaint the loss of structure necessary to practice a craft—or to perform coherently a role—or is the complaint directed at the *kind* of craft which today's judges would have lawyer's ply? Is the lawyer's craft likely to have the same character in an era of relatively static law as it has in an era of rapid change and of wholesale repudiation of precedent? Is it possible to have a craft at all under the latter conditions?

Does Shklar help us understand such cases as Muskrat v. United States? If so, what explanation for the result in that case might she offer?

Is there anything good to be said about "legalism"? Does it serve any important social purposes? Is it, at the least, an exaggeration or perversion of tendencies which have some social value?

To what extent are the things Shklar is talking about explicable in the terms used by Llewellyn, Kuhn, and Huizinga? That is, do these writers help us better understand the phenomenon of legalism?

SECTION THREE: DISPASSIONATENESS, RESPONSIBILITY, AND THE ETHIC OF ROLE PERFORMANCE

### PUBLIC UTILITIES COMMISSION V. POLLAK

343 U.S. 451, 466 (1952)

A street railway company in the District of Columbia, whose service and equipment are subject to regulation by the Public Utilities Commission of the District of Columbia, receives and amplifies radio programs through loudspeakers in its streetcars and busses. The programs consist generally of 90% music, 5% announcements, and 5% commercial advertising. The Commission, after an investigation and public hearings disclosing substantial grounds for doing so, concluded that the radio service is not inconsistent with public convenience, comfort and safety; and permitted it to continue despite protests of some passengers that their constitutional rights are thereby violated. *Held:* Neither the operation of the radio service nor the action of the Commission permitting its operation is precluded by the Federal Constitution.

. . .

Mr. Justice FRANKFURTER, for reasons stated by him took no part in the consideration or decision of this case.

. . .

Mr. Justice FRANKFURTER.

The judicial process demands that a judge move within the framework of relevant legal rules and the covenanted modes of thought for ascertaining them. He must think dispassionately and submerge private feeling on every aspect of a case. There is a good deal of shallow talk that the judicial robe does not change the man within it. It does. The fact is that on the whole judges do lay aside private views in discharging their judicial functions. This is achieved through training, professional habits, self-discipline and that fortunate alchemy by which men are loyal to the obligation with which they are entrusted. But it is also true that reason cannot control the subconscious influence of feelings of which it is unaware. When there is ground for believing that such unconscious feelings may operate in the ultimate judgment, or may not unfairly lead others to believe they are operating, judges recuse themselves. They do not sit in judgment. They do this for a variety of reasons. The guiding consideration is that the administration of justice should reasonably appear to be disinterested as well as be so in fact.

This case for me presents such a situation. My feelings are so strongly engaged as a victim of the practice in controversy that I had better not participate in judicial judgment upon it. I am explicit as to the reason for my non-participation in this case because I have for some time been of the view that it is desirable to state why one takes himself out of a case.

## QUESTIONS

1. Why did Justice Frankfurter find it necessary to disqualify himself? Do the reasons he gives adequately account for his action? Conceding "that reason cannot control the subconscious influence of feelings of which it is unaware," was Justice Frankfurter unaware of the influences which caused him to recuse himself? If Justice Frankfurter knew that he didn't like the transit company's practice, what was there about this particular disaffection which made him unable to "lay aside private views in discharging" his judicial function?

2. Is Justice Frankfurter saying that there are some emotions which even the "judicial robe" cannot eliminate? Or is he saying that there are emotions which cannot be transformed or controlled

by a change of role or office? Are these formulations the same? If not, what is the difference? Does it have anything to do with the function of roles in the organization of human experience? Do the different formulations indicate a difference in the way the mechanism of role is conceived?

3. To what, do you suppose, Frankfurter is contrasting "private views"? "Public views"? What is the difference?

4. Suppose, as may very well have been the case, every Justice was "a victim of the practice in controversy." Should each of them, therefore, have disqualified himself? Or should only those Justices whose feelings were "so strongly engaged" as Justice Frankfurter's? Would those Justices whose feelings were not "so strongly engaged" be more impartial, more detached, more judicial in the adjudication of this case? If so, would this be because they have *no* emotions concerning the transit company's practice? Or because they have different emotions? If the latter, what would be the difference?

5. Is Justice Frankfurter saying that his "feelings are so strongly engaged" that he cannot follow the rules of his role? Or that he cannot adopt the emotions which his role requires of its performers? If this is the case, does this raise doubts about Justice Frankfurter's suitability for the judiciary? Consider this question in connection with the remarks from Hand below.

6. Is Frankfurter saying that he ought not to participate in the *Pollak* case because people will think he was biased? Why would people think that? Because of earlier, unofficial positions he might have taken on the issue? If so, should judges always recuse themselves when an issue arises on which they have earlier expressed an opinion? Would that be a practicable general rule?

KARL GEORG WURZEL

## METHODS OF JURIDICAL THINKING *

**Dispassionateness of the Judge.** Every emotion, whether of the kind psychologists call sthenic, or of the asthenic sort, implies a narrowing of the field of conscious action. It favors unreasoned, associative (i. e., determined by external factors), or impulsive mental activity over a form of thinking proceeding with due consideration according to the categories of logic, especially the principle of causality (apperceptive thinking, to use the terminology of Wundt). Briefly, every emotion lessens the capacity of the intellect to see the truth, it makes partially blind. Passionless absence of emotion is a prerequisite of all scientific thinking, that is, thinking directed to the recognition of external truths.

The reason why this requirement was insisted on by lawyers at so early a period must be sought in the circumstance that the judge is exposed more than any other thinker to emotional influences. He

* From Science of Legal Method: Select Essays by Various Authors 298–300 (E. Bruncken and L. Register transl. 1921). Reprinted by permission of The Macmillan Company.

must come to his conclusion among the struggles of contending parties.   While in the case of other sciences conflicts of wills mean annoying interference, they are the natural environment for jurisprudence, in which it carries on its life functions.   Moreover, the results of juridical thinking at once become matters of practical importance and touch the very nerve of life.   Errors produced by emotion are felt most often and easiest in the field of legal thinking, and it is for this reason that lawyers were the first and the most emphatic in insisting on the absence of emotional bias.

The general public, with its deficient understanding of psychology, includes in this requirement merely the absence of individual emotions in the widest sense, "prejudice and bias for or against either party."   That amounts, generally speaking, to the reasons which make a judge or juror incapable of acting according to most codes of procedure, such as personal interest, kinship, and the like.   Modern social science, however, has shown that there exist, in addition to the influence of such individual emotions, a multitude of social feelings which exercise a determining influence on the way we think of and judge other persons.   Such social feelings may be of a national or political, professional, religious character, may be produced by class, occupation, or other circumstances that produce a feeling of solidarity;   or they may be based on ethical tendencies, historical traditions, inherited value judgments, and so forth.   The more general and constant nature of such feelings is the reason why they do not usually take the form of an acute emotion and do not, generally speaking, enter into individual consciousness at all but remain below its threshold.   Just the same, or perhaps for that very reason, they are apt to obscure the logical quality of thought and judgment in a manner quite obvious to a really unbiased observer.   Anyone who desires a large number of examples showing how it is by no means enough, in order to be unbiased in regard to social currents by which one is himself carried along, if one has the intention of being unbiased, cannot do better than to turn to Spencer's "the Study of Sociology." [4] There he will learn how our attitude towards the world, our whole way of thinking, is covered by a network of tendencies and cross-tendencies, how under their influence the same phenomenon may meet with the most various judgments although the critics are all imbued with the most upright desire for the truth.   Modern logic (see the writings of Wundt, Erdmann, Sigwart, etc.) which has generally come close to psychology, explains these unconscious disturbances of correct thinking very well indeed.

In this connection a question arises which cannot be answered until we have progressed farther with our inquiry.   Does the requirement of lack of bias mean that the judge must also disengage his rea-

---

**4.** I cannot resist the temptation to recall an excellent observation of Nietzsche to the effect that we are by no means indifferent to our own concepts and mental images, but are fond of some and constantly recall them, while we have a dislike for others and try to exclude them as much as possible.  We may mention such ideas as death and illness.  In the face of every mathematical calculation the chances of winning always look greater than they are to the gambler, because he is constantly calling them up in his mind.  This is the reason why lotteries, raffles, and the like are so immensely profitable.

soning from the influence of all these social feelings? Must we take the saying "pereat mundus, fiat justitia," not ironically but pathetically? Should the judge actually comply with the demand of Spinoza and never blame or praise anything human but only understand it? Must he purify his thought of everything but logical reasoning and get rid of all feeling, whether individual or social, that may disturb his logic? Is such purification possible to all? Does it ever exist?

## QUESTIONS

1. Where, if at all, does the "feeling" which incapacitates Justice Frankfurter receive consideration by Wurzel?

2. What do you think Wurzel means by "a really unbiased observer"? Can there be such a person? Is there anything in Wurzel himself which suggests a negative answer? If one could find a "really" unbiased observer, what could he do that others could not? Is there anything he could not do which others could?

3. Are there any roles or jobs other than the judge's which require dispassionateness? Are there some which clearly do not? Consider the advocate. The husband. The father. The businessman. The politician.

4. Is the best thinking carried on without emotion? Is this what Wurzel is saying?

*LEARNED HAND*

## MR. JUSTICE CARDOZO *

. . . . the wise man is the detached man. By that I mean more than detached from his grosser interests—his advancement and his gain. Many of us can be that—I dare to believe that most judges can be, and are. I am thinking of something far more subtly interfused. Our convictions, our outlook, the whole make-up of our thinking, which we cannot help bringing to the decision of every question, is the creature of our past; and into our past have been woven all sorts of frustrated ambitions with their envies, and of hopes of preferment with their corruptions, which, long since forgotten, still determine our conclusions. A wise man is one exempt from the handicap of such a past; he is a runner stripped for the race; he can weigh the conflicting factors of his problem without always finding himself in one scale or the other. Cardozo was such a man; his gentle nature had in it no acquisitiveness; he did not use himself as a measure of value; the secret of his humor—a precious gift that he did not wear upon his sleeve—lay in his ability to get outside of himself, and look back. Yet from this self-effacement came a power greater than the power of him who ruleth a city. He was wise because his spirit was uncontaminated, because he knew no violence, or

* From The Spirit of Liberty (Dilliard ed. Vintage ed. 1959). Reprinted by permission of the Harvard and Columbia Law Reviews and the Yale Law Journal. Originally published in 52 Harv.L.Rev. 361 (1939); 39 Colum. L.Rev. 9 (1939); 48 Yale L.J. 379 (1939).

hatred, or envy, or jealousy, or ill-will.  I believe that it was this purity that chiefly made him the judge we so much revere; more than his
learning, his acuteness, and his fabulous industry.  In this America
of ours where the passion for publicity is a disease, and where swarms
of foolish, tawdry moths dash with rapture into its consuming fire,
it was a rare good fortune that brought to such eminence a man so
reserved, so unassuming, so retiring, so gracious to high and low, and
so serene.

## QUESTIONS

1.  Can you distinguish the influences which Hand adduces from
those Wurzel mentions?  Or are they talking about precisely the same
thing?

2.  Does wisdom involve an emotion?  Or is it an absence of
emotion?  Does detachment connote an absence of emotion?  Of commitment?  Of conviction?  Do commitment and conviction involve
emotions?  If so, in what way?  Is a wise man one who has no
commitments?  Who has no convictions?

3.  Is wisdom one of the attributes we demand of judges?  Of
all judges?  Are there any other jobs or roles which require it as
well?  Are there any roles for which wisdom would be inappropriate?

4.  Consider some dictionary definitions of wisdom: "knowledge
of what is true or right coupled with just judgment as to action";
"sagacity, discernment, or insight".  Can you square these with
Hand's conception of wisdom?  What does "detachment" or "impartiality" have to do with such mental qualities as are usually connoted
by the notion of wisdom?

5.  Is a wise man simply one who is "stripped for the race"?
Or is this too negative a notion of wisdom?  Is there nothing that the
wise man gains from his past, from "the frustrated ambitions with
their envies" and "hopes of preferment with their corruptions"?

*BENEDICT DE SPINOZA*

## ETHICS *

PROP. II.  If we remove disturbance of the mind or emotion
from the thought of an external cause and unite it to other thoughts,
then love or hatred towards the external cause, as well as waverings
of the mind which arise from these emotions, are destroyed.

Proof.—Now that which constitutes the form of love or hatred is
pleasure or pain accompanied by the idea of an external cause.  .   .
When this then is removed, the form of love or hatred is also removed: and therefore these emotions and those which arise from
them are destroyed.  Q. e. d.

PROP. III.  An emotion which is a passion ceases to be a
passion as soon as we form a clear and distinct idea of it.

* New York, E. P. Dutton, from 202–
205, 210 (Boyle transl. 1910).

Proof.—An emotion which is a passion is a confused idea.  .  .
If, therefore, we form a clear and distinct idea of this emotion, this
idea will be distinguished from the emotion in so far as it has reference to the mind alone by reason alone   .   .  .:   and therefore
.  .  .   the emotion will cease to be a passion.  Q. e. d.

Corollary.—Therefore, the more an emotion becomes known to
us, the more it is within our power and the less the mind is passive
to it.

PROP. IV.   There is no modification of the body of which we
cannot form some clear and distinct conception.

.  .  .

Note.—Since there is nothing from which some effect does not
follow   .   .  .,   and whatever follows from an idea which is adequate in us we understand clearly and distinctly   .  .  .,   it follows
that every one has power of understanding himself and his emotions,
if not absolutely at least in part clearly and distinctly, and consequently of bringing it about that he is less passive to them.  For this
purpose care must be taken especially that we understand clearly
and distinctly each emotion and to what extent it may grow, so that
the mind may be determined by the emotion to think those things
which it clearly and distinctly perceives and in which it acquiesces
entirely: and thus the emotion is separated from the thought of an
external cause and united to true thoughts.  From which would happen not only that love, hatred, etc., would be destroyed  .  .  .,  but
also that appetites and desires which are wont to arise from such
emotion could have no excess.  .  .  .   For it must be noted above
all that it is one and the same appetite through which a man is said to
be active and passive.  E. G., we have shown that human nature is so
disposed that each one desires that others should live according to his
idea of life   .   .  .  .:  and this desire in a man who is not guided by
reason is a passion which is called ambition, and which differs very
little from pride; and, on the contrary, in a man who is guided by
reason it is an action or virtue which is called piety.  .  .  .   And
in this manner all appetites or desires are only passions in so far as
they arise from inadequate ideas, and they are accredited to virtue
when they are excited or generated by adequate ideas.  .  .  .   And
this remedy for emotions (to return from my digression), and which
consists in a true knowledge of them, is excelled by nothing in our
power we can think of, since no other power of the mind is granted
than that of thinking and forming adequate ideas, as we showed
above.  .  .  .

.  .  .

PROP. VI.   In so far as the mind understands all things as necessary it has more power over the emotions or is less passive to them.

Proof.—The mind understands all things as necessary   .   .  .,
and to be determined for existing and acting by the infinite connection of causes   .   .  .:  and therefore  .  .  .  it brings it about
that it is less passive to the emotions which arise from them and
.  .  .   it will be affected less towards them.  Q. e. d.

Note.—The more this knowledge, namely that things are necessary, is applied to individual things which we imagine more distinctly and vividly, the greater is this power of the mind over the emotions, which is borne witness to by experience. For we see the pain caused by the loss of some good to be lessened or mitigated as soon as he who lost it considers that it could have been preserved in no manner. Thus also we see that no one pities an infant for that it cannot talk, walk, reason, or lastly, that it lives so many years almost unconscious of self. But if most were born full grown and only one now and then an infant, then we should pity each infant: for then we should regard infancy not as a thing natural and necessary, but as a flaw or mishap in nature. And to this we may refer many other things.

.   .   .

PROP. XVII.   God is free from passions, nor is he affected with any emotion of pleasure or pain.

Proof.—All ideas, in so far as they have reference to God, are true   .   .   ., that is   .   .   ., they are adequate: and therefore (Gen.Def.Emo.) God is without passions.   .   .   .

QUESTIONS

1.   Does Spinoza help us to understand the connection between wisdom and detachment which Hand postulates?

2.   Does Spinoza seek the elimination of emotions from human thought? What is the connection he sees between emotions and ideas? When the mind has achieved complete mastery over the emotions, according to Spinoza, will there be any emotions left?

3.   Consider Frankfurter's opinion in *Pollak* in light of Spinoza. Was his problem that he did not "form a clear idea" of his emotion? Is that what judges are supposed to do with their emotions?

KARL N. LLEWELLYN

THE COMMON LAW TRADITION *

.   .   .   .   The typical word, used as a sufficient word, is "impartial," which describes a condition: "not on either side, and without personal interest or desire re the outcome" is about as far as that word really takes you, though the dictionaries tend to add "just." But we mean when we use the word about a man in judicial *office* a great deal more. We mean, and definitely in addition, "upright." We also mean—and if we stop to think we know that we mean—not a passive but a positive and active attitude: the judge must be *seeking*, as best he can, to see the matter fairly, and with an eye not to the litigants merely but to All-of-Us as well. We mean further, and importantly, still another attitude: "Open, truly open, to listen, to get informed, to be persuaded, to respond to good reason." Nay, more; we gather into

* From 47 (1960). Reprinted with permission of the estate of Karl N. Llewellyn.

this one weak, bleak word "impartial" a drive: an idea of effort, of self-denying labor, toward patience, toward understanding sympathy, toward quest for wisdom in the result.

It is very queer that our fraternity of appellate judges whose professional skill is centered on sharp verbal definition of the duty and breach of duty of any other citizen, should remain more inadequate than the man in the street when it comes to fixing in words the limits of permissible judicial behavior. The man in the street cuts straight to the heart on this one: "Hell, is that any way for a *judge* to act?!" But the judges themselves have not progressed even to adapting from the military such a phrase as "conduct materially unbecoming a judge and a gentleman," or from the bar such a phrase as "flagrantly unjudicial." Thus Thacher, ex-name-partner in a major Wall Street firm, ex-solicitor-general, ex-district-judge, ex-president of the Association of the Bar, when chosen to frame charges against Capshaw, a judge whose conduct in office skunk-stank, came up with—as a crux —"*He has decided cases on considerations outside the record*"—a procedure which, used rightly and wisely, had made the glory of a Mansfield, a Marshall, a Cardozo. . . .

## QUESTIONS

1. Why does Llewellyn insist that the judge's attitude must be "not a passive but a positive and active attitude"? What consequences does he think will ensue if the attitude is not viewed as "positive and active"? How does this notion square with the views expressed by Frankfurter, Wurzel, Hand?

2. Would Llewellyn concede that the judicial attitude should be devoid of emotion?

3. Does it matter that judges do not have an articulated conception of "the limits of permissible judicial behavior"?

4. To what extent can it be said that impartiality is a problem of "considerations outside the record"? To what extent can it be argued that one's role defines, among other things, what should and should not be considered in the solution of a role problem? Consider this question in light of Justice Frankfurter's opinion in Dennis v. United States.

## DENNIS v. UNITED STATES

341 U.S. 494, 517 (1951)

Mr. Justice FRANKFURTER, concurring in affirmance of the judgment.

The defendants were convicted under section 3 of the Smith Act for conspiring to violate section 2 of that Act, which makes it unlawful "to organize or help to organize any society, group, or assembly of persons who teach, advocate, or encourage the overthrow or destruction of any government in the United States by force or violence." Act of June 28, 1940, section 2(a) (3), 54 Stat. 670, 671, 18 U.S.C. section 10, now 18 U.S.C. section 2385. The substance of the indictment is that the defendants between April 1, 1945, and July 20, 1948, agreed to bring about the dissolution of a body known as the Communist Political Association and to organize in its place the Communist Party of the United States; that the aim of the new party was "the overthrow and destruction of the Government of the United States by force and violence"; that the defendants were to assume leadership of the Party and to recruit members for it and that the Party was to publish books and conduct classes, teaching the duty and the necessity of forceful overthrow. . . .

. . . . In enacting a statute which makes it a crime for the defendants to conspire to do what they have been found to have conspired to do, did Congress exceed its constitutional power?

Few questions of comparable import have come before this Court in recent years. The appellants maintain that they have a right to advocate a political theory, so long, at least, as their advocacy does not create an immediate danger of obvious magnitude to the very existence of our present scheme of society. On the other hand, the Government asserts the right to safeguard the security of the Nation by such a measure as the Smith Act. Our judgment is thus solicited on a conflict of interests of the utmost concern to the well-being of the country. This conflict of interests cannot be resolved by a dogmatic preference for one or the other, nor by a sonorous formula which is in fact only a euphemistic disguise for an unresolved conflict. If adjudication is to be a rational process, we cannot escape a candid examination of the conflicting claims with full recognition that both are supported by weighty title-deeds.

. . .

The language of the First Amendment is to be read not as barren words found in a dictionary but as symbols of historic experience illumined by the presuppositions of those who employed them. Not what words did Madison and Hamilton use, but what was it in their minds which they conveyed? Free speech is subject to prohibition of those abuses of expression which a civilized society may forbid. As in the case of every other provision of the Constitution that is not crystallized by the nature of its technical concepts, the fact that the First Amendment is not self-defining and self-enforcing neither impairs its usefulness nor compels its paralysis as a living instrument.

"The law is perfectly well settled," this Court said over fifty years ago, "that the first ten amendments to the Constitution, commonly known as the Bill of Rights, were not intended to lay down any novel principles of government, but simply to embody certain guaranties and immunities which we had inherited from our English ancestors, and which had from time immemorial been subject to certain well-recognized exceptions arising from the necessities of the case. In incorporating these principles into the fundamental law there was no intention of disregarding the exceptions, which continued to be recognized as if they had been formally expressed." Robertson v. Baldwin, 165 U.S. 275, 281. That this represents the authentic view of the Bill of Rights and the spirit in which it must be construed has been recognized again and again in cases that have come here within the last fifty years. Absolute rules would inevitably lead to absolute exceptions, and such exceptions would eventually corrode the rules. The demands of free speech in a democratic society as well as the interest in national security are better served by candid and informed weighing of the competing interests, within the confines of the judicial process, than by announcing dogmas too inflexible for the non-Euclidian problems to be solved.

But how are competing interests to be assessed? Since they are not subject to quantitative ascertainment, the issue necessarily resolves itself into asking, who is to make the adjustment?—who is to balance the relevant factors and ascertain which interest is in the circumstances to prevail? Full responsibility for the choice cannot be given to the courts. Courts are not representative bodies. They are not designed to be a good reflex of a democratic society. Their judgment is best informed, and therefore most dependable, within narrow limits. Their essential quality is detachment, founded on independence. History teaches that the independence of the judiciary is jeopardized when courts become embroiled in the passions of the day and assume primary responsibility in choosing between competing political, economic and social pressures.

Primary responsibility for adjusting the interests which compete in the situation before us of necessity belongs to the Congress. The nature of the power to be exercised by this Court has been delineated in decisions not charged with the emotional appeal of situations such as that now before us. We are to set aside the judgment of those whose duty it is to legislate only if there is no reasonable basis for it. We are to determine whether a statute is sufficiently definite to meet the constitutional requirements of due process, and whether it respects the safeguards against undue concentration of authority secured by separation of power. We must assure fairness of procedure, allowing full scope to governmental discretion but mindful of its impact on individuals in the context of the problem involved. And, of course, the proceedings in a particular case before us must have the warrant of substantial proof. Beyond these powers we must not go; we must scrupulously observe the narrow limits of judicial authority even though self-restraint is alone set over us. Above all we must remember that this Court's power of judicial review is not "an exercise of the powers of a super-legislature" Mr. Justice Brandeis and Mr. Justice Holmes, dissenting in Burns Baking Co. v. Bryan, 264 U.S. 504, 534.

A generation ago this distribution of responsibility would not have been questioned. But in recent decisions we have made explicit what has long been implicitly recognized. In reviewing statutes which restrict freedoms protected by the First Amendment, we have emphasized the close relation which those freedoms bear to maintenance of a free society. Some members of the Court—and at times a majority—have done more. They have suggested that our function in reviewing statutes restricting freedom of expression differs sharply from our normal duty in sitting in judgment on legislation. It has been said that such statutes "must be justified by clear public interest, threatened not doubtfully or remotely, but by clear and present danger. The rational connection between the remedy provided and the evil to be curbed, which in other contexts might support legislation against attack on due process grounds, will not suffice." Thomas v. Collins, 323 U.S. 516, 530. It has been suggested, with the casualness of a footnote, that such legislation is not presumptively valid, see United States v. Carolene Products Co., 304 U.S. 144, 152, n. 4, and it has been weightily reiterated that freedom of speech has a "preferred position" among constitutional safeguards. Kovacs v. Cooper, 336 U.S. 77, 88.

The precise meaning intended to be conveyed by these phrases need not now be pursued. It is enough to note that they have recurred in the Court's opinions, and their cumulative force has, not without justification, engendered belief that there is a constitutional principle, expressed by those attractive but imprecise words, prohibiting restriction upon utterance unless it creates a situation of "imminent" peril against which legislation may guard. It is on this body of the Court's pronouncements that the defendants' argument here is based.

In all fairness, the argument cannot be met by reinterpreting the Court's frequent use of "clear" and "present" to mean an entertainable "probability." In giving this meaning to the phrase "clear and present danger," the Court of Appeals was fastidiously confining the rhetoric of opinions to the exact scope of what was decided by them. We have greater responsibility for having given constitutional support, over repeated protests, to uncritical libertarian generalities.

Nor is the argument of the defendants adequately met by citing isolated cases. Adjustment of clash of interests which are at once subtle and fundamental is not likely to reveal entire consistency in a series of instances presenting the clash. It is not too difficult to find what one seeks in the language of decisions reporting the effort to reconcile free speech with the interests with which it conflicts. The case for the defendants requires that their conviction be tested against the entire body of our relevant decisions. Since the significance of every expression of thought derives from the circumstances evoking it, results reached rather than language employed give the vital meaning. See Cohens v. Virginia, 6 Wheat. 264, 442; Wambaugh, The Study of Cases, 10.

There is an added reason why we must turn to the decisions. "Great cases," it is appropriate to remember, "like hard cases make bad law. For great cases are called great, not by reason of their real importance in shaping the law of the future, but because of some accident of immediate overwhelming interest which appeals to the feelings and distorts the judgment. These immediate interests exercise a kind of hydraulic pressure which makes what previously was clear seem doubtful, and before which even well settled principles of law will bend." Mr. Justice Holmes, dissenting in Northern Securities Co. v. United States, 193 U.S. 197, 400–401.

This is such a case. Unless we are to compromise judicial impartiality and subject these defendants to the risk of an *ad hoc* judgment influenced by the impregnating atmosphere of the times, the constitutionality of their conviction must be determined by principles established in cases decided in more tranquil periods.  If those decisions are to be used as a guide and not as an argument, it is important to view them as a whole and to distrust the easy generalizations to which some of them lend themselves.

.  .  .

On the one hand is the interest in security.  The Communist Party was not designed by these defendants as an ordinary political party.  For the circumstances of its organization, its aims and methods, and the relation of the defendants to its organization and aims we are concluded by the jury's verdict.  The jury found that the Party rejects the basic premise of our political system—that change is to be brought about by nonviolent constitutional process.  The jury found that the Party advocates the theory that there is a duty and necessity to overthrow the Government by force and violence.  It found that the Party entertains and promotes this view, not as a prophetic insight or as a bit of unworldly speculation, but as a program for winning adherents and as a policy to be translated into action.

In finding that the defendants violated the statute, we may not treat as established fact that the Communist Party in this country is of significant size, well-organized, well-disciplined, conditioned to embark on unlawful activity when given the command.  But in determining whether application of the statute to the defendants is within the constitutional powers of Congress, we are not limited to the facts found by the jury.  We must view such a question in the light of whatever is relevant to a legislative judgment.  We may take judicial notice that the Communist doctrines which these defendants have conspired to advocate are in the ascendency in powerful nations who cannot be acquitted of unfriendliness to the institutions of this country.  We may take account of evidence brought forward at this trial and elsewhere, much of which has long been common knowledge.  In sum, it would amply justify a legislature in concluding that recruitment of additional members for the Party would create a substantial danger to national security.

In 1947, it has been reliably reported, at least 60,000 members were enrolled in the Party.  Evidence was introduced in this case that the membership was organized in small units, linked by an intricate chain of command, and protected by elaborate precautions designed to prevent disclosure of individual identity.  There are no reliable data tracing acts of sabotage or espionage directly to these defendants.  But a Canadian Royal Commission appointed in 1946 to investigate espionage reported that it was "overwhelmingly established" that "the Communist movement was the principal base within which the espionage network was recruited."  The most notorious spy in recent history was led into the service of the Soviet Union through Communist indoctrination.  Evidence supports the conclusion that members of the Party seek and occupy positions of importance in political and labor organizations.  Congress was not barred by the Constitution from believing that indifference to such experience would be an exercise not of freedom but of irresponsibility.

On the other hand is the interest in free speech. The right to exert all governmental powers in aid of maintaining our institutions and resisting their physical overthrow does not include intolerance of opinions and speech that cannot do harm although opposed and perhaps alien to dominant, traditional opinion. The treatment of its minorities, especially their legal position, is among the most searching tests of the level of civilization attained by a society. It is better for those who have almost unlimited power of government in their hands to err on the side of freedom. We have enjoyed so much freedom for so long that we are perhaps in danger of forgetting how much blood it cost to establish the Bill of Rights.

Of course no government can recognize a "right" of revolution, or a "right" to incite revolution if the incitement has no other purpose or effect. But speech is seldom restricted to a single purpose, and its effects may be manifold. A public interest is not wanting in granting freedom to speak their minds even to those who advocate the overthrow of the Government by force. For, as the evidence in this case abundantly illustrates, coupled with such advocacy is criticism of defects in our society. Criticism is the spur to reform; and Burke's admonition that a healthy society must reform in order to conserve has not lost its force. Astute observers have remarked that one of the characteristics of the American Republic is indifference to fundamental criticism. Bryce, The American Commonwealth, c. 84. It is a commonplace that there may be a grain of truth in the most uncouth doctrine, however false and repellent the balance may be. Suppressing advocates of overthrow inevitably will also silence critics who do not advocate overthrow but fear that their criticism may be so construed. No matter how clear we may be that the defendants now before us are preparing to overthrow our Government at the propitious moment, it is self-delusion to think that we can punish them for their advocacy without adding to the risks run by loyal citizens who honestly believe in some of the reforms these defendants advance. It is a sobering fact that in sustaining the convictions before us we can hardly escape restriction on the interchange of ideas.

We must not overlook the value of that interchange. Freedom of expression is the well-spring of our civilization—the civilization we seek to maintain and further by recognizing the right of Congress to put some limitation upon expression. Such are the paradoxes of life. For social development of trial and error, the fullest possible opportunity for the free play of the human mind is an indispensable prerequisite. The history of civilization is in considerable measure the displacement of error which once held sway as official truth by beliefs which in turn have yielded to other truths. Therefore the liberty of man to search for truth ought not to be fettered, no matter what orthodoxies he may challenge. Liberty of thought soon shrivels without freedom of expression. Nor can truth be pursued in an atmosphere hostile to the endeavor or under dangers which are hazarded only by heroes.

"The interest, which [the First Amendment] guards, and which gives it its importance, presupposes that there are no orthodoxies—

religious, political, economic, or scientific—which are immune from debate and dispute.  Back of that is the assumption—itself an orthodoxy, and the one permissible exception—that truth will be most likely to emerge, if no limitations are imposed upon utterances that can with any plausibility be regarded as efforts to present grounds for accepting or rejecting propositions whose truth the utterer asserts, or denies."  International Brotherhood of Electrical Workers v. Labor Board, 181 F.2d 34, 40.  In the last analysis it is on the validity of this faith that our national security is staked.

It is not for us to decide how we would adjust the clash of interests which this case presents were the primary responsibility for reconciling it ours.  Congress has determined that the danger created by advocacy of overthrow justifies the ensuing restriction on freedom of speech.  The determination was made after due deliberation, and the seriousness of the congressional purpose is attested by the volume of legislation passed to effectuate the same ends.

Can we then say that the judgment Congress exercised was denied it by the Constitution?  Can we establish a constitutional doctrine which forbids the elected representatives of the people to make this choice?  Can we hold that the First Amendment deprives Congress of what it deemed necessary for the Government's protection?

To make validity of legislation depend on judicial reading of events still in the womb of time—a forecast, that is, of the outcome of forces at best appreciated only with knowledge of the topmost secrets of nations—is to charge the judiciary with duties beyond its equipment.  We do not expect courts to pronounce historic verdicts on bygone events.  Even historians have conflicting views to this day on the origins and conduct of the French Revolution, or, for that matter, varying interpretations of "the glorious Revolution" of 1688.  It is as absurd to be confident that we can measure the present clash of forces and their outcome as to ask us to read history still enveloped in clouds of controversy.

In the light of their experience, the Framers of the Constitution chose to keep the judiciary dissociated from direct participation in the legislative process.  In asserting the power to pass on the constitutionality of legislation, Marshall and his Court expressed the purposes of the Founders.  See Charles A. Beard, The Supreme Court and the Constitution.  But the extent to which the exercise of this power would interpenetrate matters of policy could hardly have been foreseen by the most prescient.  The distinction which the Founders drew between the Court's duty to pass on the power of Congress and its complementary duty not to enter directly the domain of policy is fundamental.  But in its actual operation it is rather subtle, certainly to the common understanding.  Our duty to abstain from confounding policy with constitutionality demands perceptive humility as well as self-restraint in not declaring unconstitutional what in a judge's private judgment is deemed unwise and even dangerous.

Even when moving strictly within the limits of constitutional adjudication, judges are concerned with issues that may be said to involve vital finalities.  The too easy transition from disapproval of what is undesirable to condemnation as unconstitutional, has led some of the wisest judges to question the wisdom of our scheme in lodging such authority in courts.  But it is relevant to remind that in sustaining the power of Congress in a case like this nothing irrevocable is done.  The democratic process at all events is not impaired or restricted.  Power and responsibility remain with the people and immediately with their representatives.  All the Court says is that Congress was not forbidden by the Constitution to pass this enactment and that a prosecution under it may be brought against a conspiracy such as the one before us.

### IV.

The wisdom of the assumptions underlying the legislation and prosecution is another matter.  In finding that Congress has acted within its power, a judge does not remotely imply that he favors the implications that lie beneath the legal issues.  Considerations there enter which go beyond the criteria that are binding upon judges within the narrow confines of their legitimate authority.  The legislation we are here considering is but a truncated aspect of a deeper issue.  For me it has been most illuminatingly expressed by one in whom responsibility and experience have fructified native insight, the Director-General of the British Broadcasting Corporation:

"We have to face up to the fact that there are powerful forces in the world today misusing the privileges of liberty in order to destroy her.  The question must be asked, however, whether suppression of information or opinion is the true defense.  We may have come a long way from Mill's famous dictum that:

" 'If all mankind minus one were of one opinion, and only one person were of the contrary opinion, mankind would be no more justified in silencing that one person, than he, if he had the power, would be justified in silencing mankind,'

but Mill's reminders from history as to what has happened when suppression was most virulently exercised ought to warn us that no debate is ever permanently won by shutting one's ears or by even the most Draconian policy of silencing opponents.  The *debate* must be won. And it must be won with full information.  Where there are lies, they must be shown for what they are.  Where there are errors, they must be refuted.  It would be a major defeat if the enemies of democracy forced us to abandon our faith in the power of informed discussion and so brought us down to their own level.  Mankind is so constituted, moreover, that if, where expression and discussion are concerned, the enemies of liberty are met with a denial of liberty, many men of goodwill will come to suspect there is something in the proscribed doctrine after all.  Erroneous doctrines thrive on being expunged.  They die if exposed."  Sir William Haley, What Standards for Broadcasting?  Measure, Vol. I, No. 3, Summer 1950, pp. 211–212.

In the context of this deeper struggle, another voice has indicated the limitations of what we decide today. No one is better equipped than George F. Kennan to speak on the meaning of the menace of Communism and the spirit in which we should meet it.

"If our handling of the problem of Communist influence in our midst is not carefully moderated—if we permit it, that is, to become an emotional preoccupation and to blind us to the more important positive tasks before us—we can do a damage to our national purpose beyond comparison greater than anything that threatens us today from the Communist side. The American Communist party is today, by and large, an external danger. It represents a tiny minority in our country; it has no real contact with the feelings of the mass of our people; and its position as the agency of a hostile foreign power is clearly recognized by the overwhelming mass of our citizens.

"But the subjective emotional stresses and temptations to which we are exposed in our attempt to deal with this domestic problem are not an external danger: they represent a danger within ourselves—a danger that something may occur in our own minds and souls which will make us no longer like the persons by whose efforts this republic was founded and held together, but rather like the representatives of that very power we are trying to combat: intolerant, secretive, suspicious, cruel, and terrified of internal dissension because we have lost our own belief in ourselves and in the power of our ideals. The worst thing that our Communists could do to us, and the thing we have most to fear from their activities, is that we should become like them.

"That our country is beset with external dangers I readily concede. But these dangers, at their worst, are ones of physical destruction, of the disruption of our world security, of expense and inconvenience and sacrifice. These are serious, and sometimes terrible things, but they are all things that we can take and still remain Americans.

"The internal danger is of a different order. America is not just territory and people. There is lots of territory elsewhere, and there are lots of people; but it does not add up to America. America is something in our minds and our habits of outlook which causes us to believe in certain things and to behave in certain ways, and by which, in its totality, we hold ourselves distinguished from others. If that once goes there will be no America to defend. And that can go too easily if we yield to the primitive human instinct to escape from our frustrations into the realms of mass emotion and hatred and to find scapegoats for our difficulties in individual fellow-citizens who are, or have at one time been, disoriented or confused." George F. Kennan, Where Do You Stand on Communism? New York Times Magazine, May 27 1951, pp. 7, 53, 55.

Civil liberties draw at best only limited strength from legal guaranties. Preoccupation by our people with the constitutionality, instead of with the wisdom, of legislation or of executive action is preoccupation with a false value. Even those who would most freely use the judicial brake on the democratic process by invalidating legislation that goes deeply against their grain, acknowledge, at least by paying lip service, that constitutionality does not exact a sense of proportion or the sanity of humor or an absence of fear. Focusing attention on constitutionality tends to make constitutionality synonymous with wisdom. When legislation touches freedom of thought and freedom of speech, such a tendency is a formidable enemy of the free spirit. Much that should be rejected as illiberal, because repressive and envenoming, may well be not unconstitutional. The ultimate reliance for the deepest needs of civilization must be found outside their vindication in courts of law; apart from all else, judges, howsoever they may conscientiously seek to discipline themselves against it, unconsciously are too apt to be moved by the deep undercurrents of public feeling. A persistent, positive translation of the liberating faith into the feelings and thoughts and actions of men and women is the real protection against attempts to strait-jacket the human mind. Such temptations will have their way, if fear and hatred are not exorcised. The mark of a truly civilized man is confidence in the strength and security derived from the inquiring mind. We may be grateful for such honest comforts as it supports, but we must be unafraid of its incertitudes. Without open minds there can be no open society. And if society be not open the spirit of man is mutilated and becomes enslaved.

## NOTES AND QUESTIONS

1. If Judges are supposed to be wise doesn't this give them some special expertise on the wisdom of legislation? Is this an argument for permitting them a broader area of review than Frankfurter would accept?

Considering the earlier excerpts from Wechsler, Bickel, and Frankfurter in *Rochin*, could you make an argument that the determination of an official act's constitutionality is necessarily and precisely a determination of its wisdom?

2. To what extent does one's job tell one what biases to have? Is this something that the judicial job tells judges? Note that both the presumption of constitutionality, which Frankfurter upholds, and the "clear and present danger test" which Frankfurter derogates, enact a bias—a bias which is justified by reference to a particular conception of the judge's role. Can you see how?

3. What considerations or consequences, do you think, is a judge precluded from entertaining in deciding a Constitutional Law case? Any other case? What questions can he legitimately ask himself? What questions can he not ask himself? Consider the following. "Will this law help me?" "Will it help a friend?" "Will society hold together if I enforce this law in this case?" "Does this law really ac-

complish its purpose?" "Does the evil which this law presupposes actually exist?" "Does this law reflect the majority's will?"

4. What was the Supreme Court's role in the *Dennis* case? Did Frankfurter adequately understand it? Was Frankfurter's decision a responsible decision? Or was it an irresponsible decision? Did he decide according to the dictates of his role? Or was his invocation of the terminology of role merely a way of escaping the duty which his role actually imposed?

Given the encomiums which Frankfurter heaps on freedom of speech, thought and inquiry, how could he feel that he had adequately discharged his duty to society by the decision which he reached? Can you construct a justification for Frankfurther which is consistent with his emphasis on the unwisdom of restricting speech as the Smith Act had done? Given Frankfurter's personal commitment to the values which he was unwilling to uphold in *Dennis,* could it be said that the justice was not "true to himself"? That he had violated his own personal integrity?

When the role-player finds it difficult to determine what his role requires solely by consulting the traditions and values which the role emphasizes where else can he look? Must he consult—or construct—some broader generalization about society and humanity? Must he consult—or construct—some broader generalization about the duties he owes to himself? What other alternatives are open to him?

## CHAPTER FOURTEEN

# Self-Knowledge and Self-Deception

## INTRODUCTORY NOTE

In the interpretation of language, James Fitzjames Stephen once remarked, "something must always be left to the good faith and good sense of the persons addressed, and this is one of the reasons why judges and courts of justice are necessary." Since the various elements which limit and define judicial—as well as other legal—authority cannot be so marshalled as to *prove* in any given case that a particular result is required, officials often, if not always, can devise a plausible justification for any of a number of opposing decisions. What makes a decision compelling, socially "right" or fitting apparently cannot be isolated effectively by means of words, so that it is extraordinarily difficult, if not impossible, to judge the "good faith," let alone the correctness, of a decision. To an important degree, therefore, the lawfulness of an official decision will depend on the *willingness* of the deciding officer to seek the "right" decision. In a sense, that is, no matter the wording of rules, the tradition and structure of his role, the general cultural institutions, ideas, and symbolisms which he shares with other members of the community, it may not be possible to wholly prevent any decisionmaker from deciding "what he wants to decide." And so the decision will not be completely understandable if it is not viewed to some extent as an expression of the individual needs, interests, and values of the decider.

For many—perhaps for all of us to some degree—such a conclusion presents an ominous spectre. Insofar as official decisions contain an element of "personal preference," it is often assumed, they are to that extent capricious, arbitrary, productive of disorder, antisocial, lawless. Even among those who believe that cultural conditions, social rules and roles, and other social phenomena do effectively channel and organize individual conduct, such cultural forces are viewed as effective only insofar as they are able to *overcome* personal desires, needs, and predispositions. The conception is one of a disruptive, recalcitrant element which is imprisoned, hedged-in, channeled by external forces and conditions.

When the forms and modes of social order are viewed, *inter alia*, as ways of preventing individuals—whether officials or laymen—from "doing what they want" or "deciding what they want to decide," at least two critical assumptions often seem to be present. One is that what people want will have no necessary relation to what the society has decided it wants and that there will inevitably be an unacceptable divergence between the policy of the individual and the policy of the society or culture. The second assumption is that what people want is always changing—from mood to mood, from circumstance to circumstance—and nothing stable can be built upon it. If the importance and inevitability of "the individual element" in formulating, interpreting and implementing the various modes of social order are conceded, these assumptions present us with a critical philosophical dilemma which we have faced before.  For, if accepted, they require us to dismiss as illusions the phenomenological experiences of social organization and stability that we all seem to share.  In addition, these assumptions about individual wants do not seem to account for the subliminal effect of cultural forces—including rules and roles —in the individual's perception of and thought about his social environment.  To the extent that what he sees, feels and thinks is culturally conditioned, as many of the materials throughout this book suggest, it is hard to escape the conclusion that there *is* a necessary relationship between personal preferences and social needs.

The materials in this chapter inquire into the relation of the individual—or, to speak more technically and perhaps more obscurely, of the relation of "self"—to social organization.  Not only do they provide reasons for reconsidering the conception of the individual as a force in conflict with the social interest in security, they present and investigate the hypothesis that the "self" is itself a form or agency of social order.  Thus, instead of regarding it as necessarily antithetical to such socializing devices as rules and roles, the materials inquire into the paradoxical possibility that it is an essential part of the process by which these devices become effective.  "To thine ownself be true," Shakespeare's Polonius told his son, "and it must follow as the night the day, Thou canst not then be false to any man." The relationship that holds between being "true" to oneself and being "true" to the rest of mankind may be a particularly illuminating alternative way of describing the subject matter of this chapter's inquiry.  For when looked at in this way, it makes it easier to see that the Delphic injunction, "Know thyself" may be as important an educational imperative for lawyers, judges and other officials as the more traditional professional admonitions to know one's rules and one's role.

## Section One: The Concept of Self: Is it a Meaningful Posit?

*Michel de Montaigne*

### Of the Inconsistency of Our Actions *

Those who make a practice of comparing human actions are never so much at a loss as to put them together and in the same light; for they commonly contradict each other so strangely that it seems impossible that they have come from the same shop.  One moment Marius the Younger is a son of Mars, another moment a son of Venus.  Pope Boniface the Eighth, they say, entered office like a fox, behaved in it like a lion, and died like a dog.  And who would believe that it was Nero, that living image of cruelty, who said, when they brought him in customary fashion the sentence of a condemned criminal to sign: "Would to God I had never learned to write!"  So much his heart was wrong at condemning a man to death!

* From  Selected  Essays  117–118,  119–
   120, 121–124, 126 (D. Frame ed. and        transl. 1943).  Reprinted with permis-
                                              sion of Walter J. Black, Inc.

All the world is so full of such examples, each man, in fact, can supply himself with so many, that sometimes I find it strange to see intelligent men going to great pains to match these pieces; seeing that irresolution seems to me the most common and apparent defect of our nature, as witness that famous line of Publius, the farce writer:

>*Bad is the plan that never can be changed.*
>[Publius Syrus]

There is some justification for basing a judgment of a man on the most ordinary acts of his life; but in view of the natural instability of our conduct and opinions, it has often seemed to me that even good authors are wrong to insist on weaving a consistent and solid fabric out of us.  They choose one general characteristic, and go and arrange and interpret all a man's actions to fit their picture; and if they cannot twist them enough, they go and set them down to dissimulation.  Augustus has escaped them; for there is in this man throughout the course of his life such an obvious, abrupt, and continual variety of actions, that even the boldest judges have had to let him go, untouched and unsolved.  It is harder for me to believe in men's consistency than in anything, and easier to believe in their inconsistency.  He who would judge them in detail and distinctly, bit by bit, would more often hit upon the truth.

.  .  .

Our ordinary practice is to follow the inclinations of our appetite, to the right, to the left, up hill and down, as the wind of chance carries us.  We think of what we want only at the moment we want it, and we change like that animal which takes the color of the place you set it on.  What we have just now planned, we presently change, and presently again we retrace our steps: nothing but oscillation and inconstancy:

>*Like puppets we are moved by outside strings.*
>[Horace]

We do not go; we are carried away, like floating objects, now gently, now violently, according as the water is angry or calm:

>*Do we not see all humans unaware*
>*Of what they want, and always searching everywhere,*
>*And changing place, as if to drop the load they bear?*
>
>[Lucretius]

Every day a new fancy, and our humors shift with the shifts in the weather:

>*Such are the minds of men, as is the fertile light*
>*That Father Jove himself sends down to make earth bright.*
>
>[Homer]

We float between different minds; we wish nothing freely, nothing absolutely, nothing constantly.  If any man had prescribed and established definite laws and a definite regime in his head, we

should see shining throughout his life an evenness of habits, an order and infallible relation between his principles and his practice.
.    .    .
.    .    .

This man would be easy to understand, as is the younger Cato: he who has touched one chord of him has touched all; he is a harmony of perfectly concordant sounds, which cannot conflict. With us, on the contrary, for so many actions, we need so many individual judgments. The surest thing, in my opinion, would be to trace them to the neighboring circumstances, without getting into any further research and without drawing from them any other conclusions.
.    .    .

Antigonus, having taken a liking to one of his soldiers for his virtue and valor, ordered his physicians to treat him for a persistent internal malady that had long tormented him; and perceiving after his cure that he was going to work much more coldly, asked him what had changed him and made him such a coward. "You yourself, Sire," he answered him, "by delivering me from the ills because of which I took no account of my life." A soldier of Lucullus, having been robbed of everything by the enemy, made a bold attack on them for revenge. When he had retrieved his loss, Lucullus, having formed a good opinion of him, urged him to some dangerous exploit with all the fine expostulations he could think of,

*With words that might have stirred a coward's heart.*

[Horace]

"Urge some poor soldier who has been robbed to do it," he replied;

> *Though but a rustic lout,*
> "He'll  go  where'er  you  wish  who's  lost  his  money," he called out;

[Horace]

and resolutely refused to go.

When we read that Mohammed having outrageously berated Chasan, leader of his Janissaries, because he saw his troops driven back by the Hungarians and himself behaving like a coward in the fight, Chasan's only reply was to go and hurl himself madly, alone, just as he was, arms in hand, into the first body of enemies that he met, by whom he was promptly swallowed up; this was perhaps not so much self-justification as a change of mood, nor so much his natural prowess as fresh spite.

That man whom you saw so adventurous yesterday, do not think it strange to find him such a coward the day after: either anger, or necessity, or company, or wine, or the sound of a trumpet, had put his heart in his belly. This was not a courage shaped by reason; these circumstances have made it firm; it is no wonder if he has now been made different by other, contrary circumstances.

These supple variations and contradictions that are seen in us have made some imagine that we have two souls, and others, two powers which accompany us and drive us, each one in its own way, one toward good, the other toward evil; for such sudden diversity cannot well be reconciled with one simple subject.

Not only does the wind of accident move me at will, but, besides, I move and disturb myself by the instability of my position; and anyone who observes carefully can hardly find himself twice in the same state. I give my soul now one face, now another, according to the direction in which I turn it. If I speak of myself in different ways, that is because I look at myself in different ways. All contradictions may be found in me by some twist and in some fashion. Bashful, insolent; chaste, lascivious; talkative, taciturn; tough, delicate; clever, stupid; surly, affable; lying, truthful; learned, ignorant; and liberal and miserly and prodigal: all this I see in myself to some extent according to how I turn; and whoever studies himself really attentively finds in himself, yes, even in his judgment, this gyration and discord. I have nothing to say about myself absolutely, simply, and solidly, without confusion and without mixture, or in one word. *Distinguo* is the most universal member of my logic.

. . .

Therefore one courageous deed must not be taken to prove a man valiant; a man who was really valiant would be so always and on all occasions. If it were a habit of virtue, and not a sally, it would make a man equally resolute in any accident, the same alone as in company, the same in single combat as in battle; for, whatever they say, there is not one valor for the pavement and another for the camp. As bravely would he bear an illness in his bed as a wound in camp, nor would he fear death more in his home than in an assault. We would not see the man charging into the breach with brave assurance, and later tormenting himself, like a woman, over the loss of a lawsuit or a son. When, though a coward against infamy, he is brave against poverty; when, though weak against the surgeons' knives, he is steadfast against the enemy's swords, the action is praiseworthy, not the man.

Many Greeks, says Cicero, cannot look at the enemy, and are brave in sickness; the Cimbrians and Celtiberians, just the opposite: *for nothing can be uniform that does not spring from a firm principle.* [Cicero]

There is no more extreme valor of its kind than Alexander's; but it is only of one kind, and not complete and universal enough. Incomparable though it is, it still has its blemishes; which is why we see him worry so frantically when he conceives the slightest suspicion that his men are plotting against his life, and behaves in these investigations with such violent and indiscriminate injustice and a fear that upsets his natural judgment. Also superstition, with which he was so badly tainted, bears some stamp of pusillanimity. And the excessiveness of the penance he did for the murder of Clytus is also evidence of the unevenness of his temper.

Our actions are nothing but a patchwork—*they despise pleasure, but are too cowardly in pain; they are indifferent to glory, but infamy breaks their spirit*—and we want to gain honor under false colors. Virtue will not be followed except for her own sake; and

if we sometimes borrow her mask for some other purpose, she promptly snatches it from our face.  It is a strong and vivid dye, once the
soul is steeped in it, and will not go without taking the flesh with it.
That is why, to judge a man, we must follow his traces long and carefully.  If he does not maintain consistency for her own sake, *whose
way of life has been well considered and preconcerted* [Cicero];  if
changing circumstances make him change his pace (I should say his
path, for his pace may be hastened or slowed), let him go:  that man
goes before the wind, as the motto of our Talbot says.

. . .

.  .  .  .  .   it is not a matter for a calm mind to judge us simply
by our outward actions;  we must sound the inside and see what
springs set us in motion.  But since this is a high and hazardous
undertaking, I wish fewer people would meddle with it.

## Notes and Questions

1.  Compare Montaigne's remarks to the Humian and the
Buddhist position concerning the concept of "self" which you encountered in Chapter 5.  Is Montaigne saying anything about the
concept of self?  If so, what leads you to think so?  If not, is there
anything that might lead one to think so?

2.  Why do you think Montaigne cares about "the inconsistency
of our actions"?  Is it important that human actions be consistent?
What is gained by such consistency?

How would one determine whether two human actions were inconsistent?  Is my cowardliness inconsistent with your bravery?
If so, what is the explanation?  If not, what criterion of inconsistency
has not been satisfied?  Conversely, what is required for two actions
to be regarded as consistent?  Could it be argued that Hume and the
Buddhists hold consistency in human conduct to be an impossibility?
If not, what would lead one to think so?  If so, is this a logical or an
empirical impossibility?  Would one who believed in the possibility of
consistent human conduct adopt a position different from the Humian
or Buddhist one on the "reality" of "self"?  What position does Montaigne adopt on this question?

3.  Is it foolish, according to Montaigne, to make judgments of
personal character?  If it is, what are the consequences?  Where
and when do we ordinarily make such judgments?  Could we carry on
our affairs without making them?  Consider especially the sentencing phase of criminal trials, decisions on child custody, recruitment
of business personnel.  Could the decisions required by such activities be made by referring *solely* to specific acts and the circumstances
in which they occurred?  Is it possible to "judge them in detail and
distinctly, bit by bit"?  Is it possible for "the action" to be "praiseworthy not the man"?  How is Montaigne using the word "action"?

4.  Why does Montaigne refer to Lucretius's assertion that "all
humans [are] unaware of what they want"?  Does Montaigne think
that humans are unaware of what they want or that what they want
is always changing?  Could it be argued that these amount to the same
thing?  Is there a relationship between "knowing who one is" and

"knowing what one wants"?  Is there a relationship between knowledge of self and the consistency of human action?

Consider the statement, "He doesn't know *what* he wants."  Is this a useful or meaningful statement?  Is it more or less meaningful than, "He doesn't know who he is," or "He doesn't know himself," or "He doesn't know his self"?

5.  What is "a courage shaped by reason"?  What does "reason" have to do with "courage"?  Is there a relationship between actions which "spring from a firm principle" and courage?

Is bravery in the face of a lost son or a lost lawsuit the same kind of thing as bravery in the thick of battle?  If so, how would you state the principle under which they fall?  If not, is there any basis for Montaigne's metaphor?  What do people mean by "moral" courage or cowardice?  "Intellectual" courage or cowardice?  Do they have anything in common with battlefield courage and cowardice? What, if any, kinds of bravery or cowardice are lawyers and judges called upon to have?

6.  Is the inconsistency which Montaigne remarks as pervasive as he suggests?  Is it possible that, for example, the bashfulness and insolence which alternately characterize him have in common that they are *his* bashfulness and *his* insolence?  If Montaigne has "nothing to say about myself absolutely, simply, and solidly, without confusion and without mixture, or in one word" does this conclude the question of whether he *has* a self?  Or could it be argued that it only tells us something about the kind of selves which are possible?


*Gordon Allport*

### Becoming *

Since the time of Wundt, the central objection of psychology to *self*, and also to *soul*, has been that the concept seems question-begging.  It is temptingly easy to assign functions that are not fully understood to a mysterious central agency, and then to declare that "it" performs in such a way as to unify the personality and maintain its integrity.  Wundt, aware of this peril, declared boldly for "a psychology without a soul."  It was not that he necessarily denied philosophical or theological postulates, but that he felt psychology as science would be handicapped by the *petitio principii* implied in the concept.   For half a century few psychologists other than Thomists have resisted Wundt's reasoning or his example.  Indeed we may say that for two generations psychologists have tried every conceivable way of accounting for the integration, organization, and striving of the human person without having recourse to the postulate of a self.

---

* From   36–37  (Paperbd.  ed.  1960).    Press and reprinted with its permission.
Copyright (c) 1955 by Yale University

Questions

1.   Is Allport in accord with Montaigne?  If not, how would you express the disagreement?  Does Montaigne think it necessary to account "for the integration, organization, and striving of the human person"?  Just how, incidentally, *does* "the postulate of a self" account for such phenomena?

2.   Why was the concept of self thought to beg the question? What was the question which was begged?  Is Allport still begging it?  Does Allport answer the objections of such as Hume?

Herbert Fingarette

The Self in Transformation *

.  .  .

What is the chief, the defining function of that which we call ego? The ego is ordinarily spoken of as the mental system which perceives, judges, synthesizes, and executes.  It is, especially as used in the context of this discussion, the set of highest order psychic organizing functions of the human being, Waelder's "human ego."  The ego by definition is the set of powers which organizes the discharge of innergenerated drive in such a way as to take account of "external reality" and in such a style as tends to maintain reasonable long-term integrity of the person as autonomous agent.

To postulate the existence of ego is to postulate that these powers do exist in the normal human being, that they do *function*.  Where, as in the case of neonates, there is energy but little or no use of it in a psychically organized way, there is no ego and no experience.  Ego is the name of these integrating functions, not a mysterious entity which "performs" them.

Questions

1.   Is Fingarette begging the question to which Allport adverted?  Is his notion of ego the same as Allport's notion of self?

2.   When Fingarette refers to "the set of highest order psychic organizing functions of the human being," what does he mean by "highest order"?  Can you think of any *lower* order psychic organizing functions?  What is the difference between the higher and lower orders—*i. e.*, what is it that makes one order higher than another?

* From 76 (Torchbook ed. 1965).  Originally published by Basic Books, Inc., and reprinted with its permission.

GORDON ALLPORT

## BECOMING *

The prevailing psychological theory of conscience treats it chiefly as a phenomenon of opportunistic learning. It tells us that we learn conscience as we learn any cultural practice, though in the case of conscience it is punishment rather than reward that seems to be the decisive agent. The argument is simple and, up to a point, convincing. The young child receives punishment when he violates a parental taboo. Commands, admonitions, scoldings accompany the infraction and the punishment. After sufficient repetition of this sequence, the child hears the voice of authority whenever he is tempted, and suffers a modified pain when he transgresses.

.   .   .

While applicable to the early stages of the growth of conscience, this theory is not convincing for later stages. For one thing, it is not often the violation of tribal taboos or of parental prohibitions that makes us as adults feel most guilty. We now have our private codes of virtue and sin; and what we feel guilty about may have little relation to the habits of obedience we once learned. If conscience were merely a matter of self-punishment for breaking an established habit taught with authority, then we could not account for the fact that we do often discard codes imposed by parents and by culture, and devise codes of our own.

.   .   .   .   conscience somehow shifts its center from ad hoc habits of obedience to the proprium—that is to say, from opportunistic becoming to oriented becoming. In the course of this shift there occurs an important phenomenological change. The "feel" of conscience in adulthood is seldom tied to the fear of punishment, whether external or self-administered. It is rather an experience of value-related obligation. According to most current psychological theories the essence of conscience is a "must"—a dread of punishment if one commits or omits an action. As we have seen, the early conscience of the child *is* undoubtedly of this order. But when conflicts and impulses come to be referred to the self-image and to propriate striving we find that the sense of obligation is no longer the same as a sense of compulsion; ought is not the same as must. I *must* be careful with matches; I *must* obey traffic regulations; I *ought* to pick up the picnic litter; I *ought* to pursue the good as I conceive it. Whenever I make a self-referred value judgment—as if to say, "This is in keeping with my self-image, that is not"—then I feel a sense of obligation that has no trace of fear in it. To argue that I fear future pangs of conscience is to confuse a possible negative outcome with the wholly positive and immediate sense of obligation, of self-consistency, that is clearly primary.

.   .   .   .   To say that a person performs certain acts and abstains from others because he fears God's punishment would be to

* From 69, 71–73, 78–79 (Paperbd. ed. 1960). Copyright (c) 1955 by Yale    University Press and reprinted with its permission.

travesty the experience of most religious people, whose consciences have more to do with love than with fear.  An inclusive path of life is adopted that requires discipline, charity, reverence, all experienced as lively obligations by a religious person.  If we encounter in a personality fear of divine punishment as the sole sanction for right doing, we can be sure we are dealing with a childish conscience, with a case of arrested development.

Conscience in personality is by no means always religiously toned.  High moral character is found among the nonreligious.  Conscience presupposes only a reflective ability to refer conflicts to the matrix of values that are felt to be one's own.  I experience "ought" whenever I pause to relate a choice that lies before me to my ideal self-image.  Normally when inappropriate decisions are made, I feel guilt.  Guilt is a poignant suffering, seldom reducible in an adult to a fear of, or experience of, punishment.  It is rather a sense of violated value, a disgust at falling short of the ideal self-image.

. . .

The juvenile conscience is fragmentary, consisting of a series of musts as unrelated as brushing one's teeth, avoiding the jam pot, and saying one's prayers—all arbitrary and meaningless precriptions imposed by the inscrutable will of the parent or other dominant authority.  Early conscience is  . . .  an opportunistic conscience.  Our later generic conscience, on the other hand, reflects the growing conviction that a state of wholeness is possible even though we continually fight the battle between our impulsive nature and our ideals.

## QUESTIONS

Does Allport's distinction between childish and adult conscience correspond to phenomena you have actually experienced?  Do you accept the legitimacy of such notions as "a childish decision," "a mature decision," "acting like a child," "acting like an adult," "acting like a boy," "acting like a man"?  What distinctions, if any, are embodied in these terms?  Are they the same distinctions that Allport adduces?  To what extent, if any, does the postulate of self help us to talk about the distinction between childish and adult human action, mature and immature human beings?

## NOTE: TWO CONCEPTS OF SELF

"The experience of 'conscience'," says Hans Gerth and C. Wright Mills, "is not the experience of a self-image; it is the experience of the appraisals of others who are not immediately present, but who, nevertheless, restrain or facilitate our own appraisals and images of our self."  CHARACTER AND SOCIAL STRUCTURE 95 (1953).  How, if at all, does this terminology differ from Allport's?  Does Allport maintain a sharp distinction between conscience and self-image?  For the child?  For the adult?  Do children have self-images or, at the least, selves?  If Allport conceded that they do, would this require him to concede that he is using the term "self" in two different ways—that he is talking about two different concepts?

In everyday speech the word "self" may be used in apparently paradoxical ways.  Consider, for example, expressions such as, "I was not myself" and "He is not acting like himself." How, it might be asked, can one help but act like himself? Would the paradox disappear if we were willing to entertain the possibility that there is more than one common notion of self? Sometimes, it can be argued, self refers to all the tendencies, traits, actions which could be included in a person's biography. For example, "I know myself: my weaknesses, prejudices, fears, inconsistencies, ambivalences, etc." Other times, as in the examples above, self seems to function as a standard by which are criticized those biographical tendencies, traits, and actions. Sometimes, in other words, self is all that a man is. Other times, it is only a selected part.

Consider these two conceptions of self. Is it arguable that they are meaningless? That the expressions in which they occur are simply nonsense? Which of the two concepts is easier to reduce to its constituent elements? Can either of them be so reduced without any loss? Try to imagine some common situations in which the word "self" is used. Can the situations be stated in more specific terms, which do not require the use of the term—or any similar one, e. g., "ego," "personality," "character," "conscience"?

## SECTION TWO: THE NEED TO KNOW ONE'S SELF

*JEROME N. FRANK*

### LAW AND THE MODERN MIND *

To many persons, like Salmond, it is unthinkable that not the rules but the personalities of the judges are of transcendent importance in the working of the judicial process. They suggest that the judge's peculiar biases must and can be obliterated by having the judge "follow the law" or consider himself "bound by the law." Often such writers ascribe the intrusion of the judge's personality to what is called an unwarrantable exercise of "discretion." If, they argue, the bench is deprived of the power to exercise discretion, then the personal equation can be eliminated and the law will be uniform, definite and certain. "The discretion of a judge," said Lord Camden, "is the law of tyrants; it is always unknown; it is different in different men; it is casual, and depends on constitution, temper and passion. At best it is often caprice. In the worst it is every vice, folly and passion to which human nature can be liable."

In an amusing opinion Judge Peters of Alabama quotes Lord Camden's language with approval:

"It may be extreme," he says, "but every practitioner of experience knows that it is not without much truth. The writer of this opinion has known a popular judicial officer grow quite angry with a suitor in his court, and threaten him with imprisonment, for no sensible reason save the fact that he wore an overcoat made of wolf skins. Moreover, *it cannot*

* From 136–139, 141–143 (1930). Copyright 1930 by Brentano's, Inc.

*safely be denied that mere judicial discretion is sometimes very much interfered with by prejudice, which may be swayed and controlled by the merest trifles such as the tooth-ache, the rheumatism, the gout, or a fit of indigestion, or even through the very means by which indigestion is frequently sought to be avoided."* And the opinion then goes on to decry "the uncertain security of a power so uncontrollable and liable to error as mere judicial discretion—a power that may possibly be misdirected by a fit of temporary sickness, a mint julep, or the smell or look of a peculiar overcoat, or things more trivial than those."

Now, Judge Peters was close to the truth. He set forth with what many lawyers would think unbecoming candor, some of the un-named and ofter undiscerned springs of judicial conduct. But, al-though he was unconventional in his manner of describing them, he represented the typical point of view in assuming that they were to be done away with by destroying discretionary judicial powers and requiring the judges to apply undeviating rules. He is at one with Salmond, who, we have seen, is apprehensive that, if a judge were al-lowed to take account of the merits of a particular case, he would be exposed "to all the perverting impulses of his emotional nature, to all his prejudices, and to the unconscious bias of his mental constitution and  .  .  .  would be led astray by the temptation which beset the 'arbitrium judicis.' "

Surely here again we are confronting mythical thinking. All judges exercise discretion, individualize abstract rules, make law. Shall the process be concealed or disclosed? The fact is, and every lawyer knows it, that *those judges who are most lawless, or most swayed by the "perverting influences of their emotional natures," or most dishonest, are often the very judges who use most meticulously the language of compelling mechanical logic, who elaborately wrap about themselves the pretense of merely discovering and carrying out existing rules, who sedulously avoid any indications that they indi-vidualize cases.* If every judicial opinion contained a clear exposi-tion of all the actual grounds of the decision, the tyrants, the bigots and the dishonest men on the bench would lose their disguises and become known for what they are.

It is time that we gave up the notion that indirection and evasion are necessary to legal technique and that in law we shall better achieve our ends if lawyers and judges remain half-ignorant, not only of these ends, but of the means of achieving them.

No, the pretense that judges are without the power to exercise an immense amount of discretion and to individualize controversies, does not relieve us of those evils which result from the abuse of that judicial power. On the contrary, it increases the evils. The honest, well-trained judge with the completest possible knowledge of the char-acter of his powers and of his own prejudices and weaknesses is the best guaranty of justice. Efforts to eliminate the personality of the judge are doomed to failure. The correct course is to recognize the necessary existence of this personal element and to act accordingly.

Indeed, as Ehrlich puts it, this personal element "should not be tolerated as something unavoidable but should be gladly welcomed. For the one important desideratum is that his (the judge's) personality must be great enough to be properly intrusted with such functions." The central problem of adequate administration of justice is "how to organize the judiciary so as to give plenty of scope to strong personalities."

The attempt to cut down the discretion of the judge, if it were successful, would remove the very creativeness which is the life of the law. For try as men will to avoid it, judging involves discretion and individualization. The judge, in determining what is the law of the case, must choose and select, and it is virtually impossible to delimit the range of his choice and selection. But many have feared that discretionary element in justice, and even when they come to see that it is unavoidable, treat it as something to be deplored and not altogether *comme il faut.*

   .   .   . when, more or less detachedly, one observes what goes on in court one is led rather to say that, if there must be a better or a worse, a more or less important aspect of legal processes, then what Pound calls the non-legal is the dominant, the more important, the more truly legal, for it is found at the very core of the whole business; as against Aristotle and Pound it would be wiser to go to the other extreme and to say that the law is at its best when the judges are wisely and consciously exercising their discretion, their power to individualize cases.

Let us take stock at this point. The childish desire to rediscover an all-knowing, strict father-judge in the law leads to a demand for impossible legal inflexibility and infallibility. Thence follow assiduous efforts to make law static and therefore to reduce the power of the judge, to deny to him creativeness. These efforts are unavailing—fortunately so, since justice depends on a creative judiciary. But the compulsion to make the appearances deny the fact of judicial innovation and individualization means that the most important task of the judge must be done in a sneaking, hole-in-corner manner. The judicial genius must do his work on the sly: a Mansfield modernizes and vastly improves English commercial law, but, while doing so, feels obliged to reiterate that the certainty of the law is of much more importance than its reasonableness.

The methods of the lawyers depart markedly in this respect from those of the natural scientists. Among scientists there is a determination to eliminate the personal equation not by concealing it but, on the contrary, by the most persistent efforts to drag it into the light, carefully note its effects and thereby to reduce its consequences. If this is the practice in astronomy where the personal equation is relatively slight, does it not seem clear that it should be the method in the law, where the personal equation inevitably looms large? The unavoidable intrusion of the judge's personality has its evil aspects. But the evils are not to be abated by the method of covering up the fact of this intrusion but by going in precisely the opposite direction—by bringing into the sunlight of free and unembarrassed discussion the truth that the obscure personal traits of our judges are of vast significance in shaping our law.

Not, of course, that it will ever be possible for judges to become completely emotionless. The nature of the subject-matter with which the judge deals makes the elimination of the personal equation peculiarly difficult. There are few tangled emotions involved in determining the parallax of a distant star. Passion and prejudice may play some part in deciding whether one will adhere to or break away from a particular theory about electrons or light waves, but the emotions involved are less numerous and far more simple than those of the judge deciding a complicated dispute about the conduct of the officers of a corporation, the rate of fare to be charged by a street-railway company, the constitutionality of a statute affecting labor, the meaning of a tax law. The judge is trying to decide what is just; his judgment is a "value judgment" and most value judgments rest upon obscure antecedents. We cannot, if we would, get rid of emotions in the field of justice. The best we can hope for is that the emotions of the judge will become more sensitive, more nicely balanced, more subject to his own scrutiny, more capable of detailed articulation.

## QUESTIONS

1. How might Frank defend the proposition that there is a "need" to know one's self? What does one know, would he say, when one knows one's self? Which of the concepts of self mentioned in the preceding Note is Frank discussing?

2. What do you think Frank means by a "strong" personality? What is it, if anything, that makes a strong personality more likely to be creative? Why does he want judges to have strong personalities? What would be the social and legal consequences of judging by "weak" personalities? Is there a connection, incidentally, between strength of personality and knowledge of self? Is there any reason why a weak personality would not know as much about his self as a strong personality?

3. Why is it, according to Frank, that "justice depends on a creative judiciary"? If Frank does not agree "that the certainty of the law is of much more importance than its reasonableness," does this explain his preference for strong judicial personalities? Are strong personalities more likely to be reasonable? Does this depend on one's use of the word "strong"? Are strong personalities less likely to respect the interest of certainty?

*KARL N. LLEWELLYN*

## THE COMMON LAW TRADITION *

.   .   .   [T]he inarticulateness of the vast body of appellate judges about how they do their work and why—their inarticulateness

* From 43–44 (1960). Reprinted with permission of the estate of Karl N. Llewellyn.

even to themselves—leaves them man by man somewhat soul-troubled, albeit their consciences are clear. This tells against reckonability of result; case by case, a troubled man is less certain in his action than a man who, like James Stephen's salmon, "is all one piece from his head to his tail." There obviously results some waste of effort, some waste of energy in internal friction, and especially an unevenness in operation which lessens predictability for the most skilled observer, whether at the bar or outside.

But the biggest single effect of the inarticulateness is that it tends to focus the court's known duty to justice—to what is right and fair—on the particular case and on the particular parties who happen to be in hand. This is a better way of going at decision than to discard the earthy concreteness of the case and to ignore the starry-eyed or knave-fool equities; but it is for all that a half-baked technique and one which strains toward both discontinuity and unwisdom.

. . .

## Questions

1. To what extent do Llewellyn and Frank agree? Is Llewellyn one who recognizes a need to know one's self? Or is he simply concerned with knowledge of role? Does one's mode of carrying out one's role necessarily raise problems of self? In other words, is there reason for judges to be left "man by man somewhat soul-troubled, albeit their consciences are clear"? Why, incidentally, should one be "soul-troubled" if he is not conscience-troubled? On this question see the next section.

2. Is Llewellyn willing—as is Frank—to sacrifice certainty for justice? Can you elucidate the connection between soul-trouble and "reckonability of result"? Just what does one have to do with the other?

3. For the technique of deciding cases that Llewellyn recommends, see Chapter 12, section 3.

*Thomas Munro*

## Toward Science in Aesthetics *

Any but the most naive of critics will realize that his feelings and criticism depend in part on his own personality. Any but the most dogmatic will desire in certain important cases to be especially fair and impartial; to guard against possible prejudice and other factors that might distort his judgment. If he is not interested in explicit judgments, he may at least be curious to understand more clearly the whole relationship between himself and the object: just how it affects him, and why in that particular way. "This Wagner opera," he may say, "is boresome and heavy to me, but some people enthuse over it. I am not going to be awed by authority and try

* From 70–73 (1956). Copyright (c) 1956 by The Liberal Arts Press, Inc. Reprinted by permission of the Liberal    Arts Press Division of the Bobbs-Merrill Company, Inc.

to convince myself that I like it; but I would like to know what it is in myself, and what in the opera, that don't get along together."

Such a desire to understand a relationship would not be gratified by an intensive analysis of the form alone, or of one's own nature apart from the form. Attention might divide itself about evenly between self and object. It is unlikely that in practice one would wish to carry either line of analysis into the amount of detail that we have considered in the last two chapters. There the interest was a scientific one, in working toward generalizations. Here we are considering a difficulty that is purely practical and local: a desire for light on the components of a particularly puzzling situation.

Any consequent reflection will be likely to go a little way toward form-analysis, and a little way toward self-analysis, without much, if any, attempt to distinguish between the two lines of inquiry. Is it the orchestra, the singing, or the acting that bothers me most? The number of things to keep track of at once? The long drawn-out monologues? Am I perhaps listening in the wrong way, straining too hard to recognize each *leit-motiv*, or to understand every German word? Have I become so used to Italian opera that I listen for obvious tunes, and am disappointed not to hear them? Such questioning can go on until one strikes a reason or combination of reasons that seems adequate, or until one loses interest in the problem. If the importance of the case seemed to warrant it, one could go indefinitely far along both lines of analysis.

By far the greater part of our mental workings cannot possibly be brought to consciousness by our own unaided efforts, as psychoanalysis has abundantly demonstrated. Fundamentally, one's response to a work of art as to anything else is determined by the long history of habit formation stretching back into infancy, whose cumulative steps cannot be consciously remembered. One's most intense fascinations and repulsions may be caused by some long-forgotten shock, or the habitual repression of a strong tendency. Many of the customary standards of one's social group, moreover, are so much taken for granted as to be unconscious and not recognizable as distinct factors in motivation. But to some extent it is possible for anyone to bring into consciousness motives which are near its threshold, especially by reading about or observing such motives in others, or noticing marked differences between their preferences and his.

It is usually not difficult to recognize major peculiarities in one's physical condition which may affect aesthetic responses. These may be basic, like color-blindness or tone-deafness; or transitory, like a headache or the fatigue and satiety caused by overstimulation of one set of nerves. A person who has heard a brass band practicing in the next room all day would do well to take the fact into account if he has to hear and criticize a band concert that evening.

Granted a genuine desire for intellectual honesty, it is sometimes possible to make oneself admit that one's valuation of a work of art has been influenced by extraneous associations. The artist, or someone who has praised or attacked his work, may be a friend or relative, or an enemy. Some pleasant or unpleasant experience may have happened to one in connection with the present object, with a similar one, or even with something suggesting a detail in this one. Oftentimes a vague but strong emotion toward an object is due to such a memory, halfway or altogether buried: a dance tune, a perfume, a pictured garment will convey some poignant but unidentifiable association. A strong dislike for a color or pattern may be due to the fact that it was in the wallpaper of a sickroom during an illness long ago. Sometimes these associations can be recaptured by effort, and sometimes not; but they can at least be recognized as factors in one's own personality, and not in the work of art one is criticizing.

By frank self-analysis one can also, at times, come face to face with some other unrealized cause of an aesthetic judgment. Perhaps it is due to a desire to win approval through showing one's up-to-date tastes; through appearing erudite, radical, or conservative. Perhaps it is due to an excessive respect for some authority on the subject, whose positive attitude is making one repress a feeling inconsistent with it. Perhaps one has publicly expressed a strong opinion about an artist, in a way identifying oneself with that attitude, and hesitates to admit a change of mind. One's judgment has perhaps been a perfunctory deduction from some supposed law or standard of good art rather than an expression of one's actual feelings. Some associated belief or bit of knowledge is perhaps being confused with the direct appeal of the object as it stands—that the work is by a famous artist; has had a romantic history; was a great step in advance for its time; was much influenced by some other work; is said to have been retouched or copied. All these points may be relevant to a comprehensive account or valuation of the object; but it is confusion of thinking to mistake them for directly perceivable qualities of form. A good way to clarify a situation of this sort is to ask oneself whether one's feeling and judgment would be affected by incontrovertible proof that the object is of a much later (or earlier) date than it is supposed to be. As a general practice, one can guard against the confusion by criticizing works of art without knowing the name or date of the artist; by listening to music before consulting the program; by judging pictures before looking at the labels underneath.

Still another variety of confusion in direct criticism arises from introducing speculations in regard to the object's future and indirect effects. What effect would it have on a person to keep on exposing himself to this sort of art? Would it improve his morals or his general culture? Is this a rather trivial, ephemeral piece of work (such as a popular tune, an amusing short story, or a bit of journalistic cleverness) of which one would grow tired if forced to hear or read it many times? Once more, these are important questions in themselves. But clarity of thinking would consist in considering them as fairly distinct from an estimate of the object's present direct appeal; confusion would consist in mistaking answers to them for the direct response and criticism.

These suggestions for self-examination are not given with the implication that all art criticism should be so careful and analytic. Quick snap judgments on scanty evidence, with no consciousness of self, are the life of practical enterprise in art criticism as elsewhere. It is not implied, furthermore, that if one discovers a certain peculiar motivation or dubious inference behind a judgment, that judgment should forthwith be altered. Certain peculiar preferences, certain habits, faiths, and assumptions, strong emotional associations, one may accept as integral parts of one's character. Their dictates in aesthetic judgment will then be upheld even when consciously recognized. Everyone has such peculiarities; there is no such thing as a completely objective valuation of a work of art.

But from a practical standpoint, a desire for greater care in appraising immediate values may be achieved through a combination of form-analysis and self-analysis. The former can help the individual to be more confident that he is judging the work of art itself as a whole, and not some fragment of it, or some associated fancy. The latter can help him to be more confident that his response represents the more basic and permanent elements in his character, and not merely a transitory mood or caprice, or a single mistaken reference. By comparing his judgment with those of others, he can further discover the extent to which it is in accord with the consensus of social experience. If he then still reaffirms his first judgment, it will be a more conscious and tested one, and less a product of blind impulse.

## Questions

1.  What are the situations in which, as Munro says, one might "at least be curious to understand more clearly the whole relationship between himself and the object: just how it affects him, and why in that particular way"? If one ought not to like a Wagner opera because "some people enthuse over it," is there nevertheless some obligation in the face of such authority to justify one's own reaction? A social obligation? A personal obligation? Recall Robinson's assertion in Chapter 12 that "the contents of the self are largely social." Does this statement imply any particular answer to these questions? "By comparing his judgment with those of others," says Munro, one "can further discover the extent to which it is in accord with the consensus of social experience. If he then still reaffirms his first judgment, it will be a more conscious and tested one, and less a product of blind impulse." Could it also be said that the judgment, though still contrary to the consensus, has become a more social one?

2.  Why, if at all, is it important for one "to be more confident that his response represents the more basic and permanent elements in his character"? Is there a necessary relationship between "self-analysis" and "the more basic and permanent elements" in one's character?

JOSEPH CHURCH

## LANGUAGE AND THE DISCOVERY OF REALITY *

. . . . each individual, on the basis of firsthand experience and of original and secondhand thematizations, builds up schematic principles according to which reality is organized and defined. The individual's total schematic orientation to reality is, in effect, a concrete theory from which he draws inferences and makes predictions, and in terms of which he values or disvalues, believes or disbelieves, attends or ignores, is amused or irritated or untouched by the things he encounters or hears about. Now we can try stating the converse proposition, that what we think of as theories are in fact personal orientations to all or part of reality. No matter how impersonally phrased, a theory has its origins in an individual faced with an array of phenomena. It is only this that permits a difference of opinion about theories along with full accord on the facts. In this view, logical implication is not a property of propositions but of a relationship between proposition and person. A theory is always an ordering of facts into figure and ground, important and unimportant, and such an ordering may follow from personal predilections and emotional investments as well as from the dictates of reality. Thus, it is probably inaccurate to say that a scientist derives logical hypotheses from his theory; rather, he has intuitions which can then be phrased as hypotheses—complete, if need be, with ex post facto justifications. It seems likely, too, that adherence to and defense of theories long since and repeatedly shown to be inadequate can best be explained by the personal nature of theories. For to question a theory is to question the theorist's grip on reality— as we have said, in the final analysis all our arguments are *ad hominem*.

## QUESTIONS

1. What arguments might Church adduce, if he would adduce any, for the proposition that there is a need to know one's self? What, according to him, does one know when one know's one's self?

2. Does Church offer an explanation for the phenomena which Koestler discusses below? Can you make an argument that the agony of Kepler or Bruner's experimental subjects is an indispensable element of human life? Is there anything that Church says which might help you?

* From 211 (Vintage ed. 1961). Reprinted with permission of Joseph Church.

ARTHUR KOESTLER

## THE GHOST IN THE MACHINE *

. . . . to undo a mental habit sanctified by dogma or tradition one has to overcome immensely powerful intellectual and emo-

tional obstacles. I mean not only the inertial forces of society; the primary locus of resistance against heretical novelty is inside the skull of the individual who conceives of it. It reverberates in Kepler's agonised cry when he discovered that the planets move not in circular but in elliptical pathways: 'Who am I, Johannes Kepler, to destroy the divine symmetry of the circular orbits!' On a more down-to-earth level the same agony is reflected in Jerome Bruner's experimental subjects who, when shown for a split second a playing card with a *black* queen of hearts, saw it as red, as it should be; and when the card was shown again, reacted with nausea at such a perversion of the laws of Nature.

GORDON ALLPORT

## BECOMING †

. . . . No theory of motivation explains why we learn at all; at best it accounts for the urge but not for the modifiability of conduct. Nor does any so-called "learning theory" tell why we learn, but only how we learn. Everyone knows *that* we learn, but few psychologists, least of all the Lockeans, seem to wonder about the nature of the underlying disposition to adapt and to modify behavior. Now whatever else learning may be it is clearly *a disposition to form structures*. Such structures include simple habits and sequences of habits; but they also include more complex and less rigid structures such as moral conscience, one's conception of oneself, pre-emptive traits and interests, schemata of meaning, and even one's embracing philosophy of life. Up to now few concepts pertaining to learning give proper recognition to its structural nature. . . .

Learning, as it operates on instinct and inheritance, thus leads to the formation of more or less stable structures, among which we have listed the moral conscience, a self-concept, and a hierarchical organization of personality. But it would not do so unless these stadia too were carried in our natures as inherent possibilities. They likewise comprise a type of "given" in human nature, much neglected in personality theory today.

We maintain therefore that personality is governed not only by the impact of stimuli upon a slender endowment of drives common to the species. Its process of becoming is governed, as well, by a disposition to realize its possibilities, i. e., to become characteristically

* From 179 (1968). Copyright 1967 by Arthur Koestler. Reprinted by permission.

† From 26–28 (Paperbd. ed. 1960). Copyright (c) 1955 by Yale University Press and reprinted with its permission.

human at all stages of development. And one of the capacities most urgent is individuation, the formation of an individual style of life that is self-aware, self-critical, and self-enhancing.

HERBERT FINGARETTE

## THE SELF IN TRANSFORMATION *

. . . . meaning-structure is constitutive in experience. It is also assumed that the disposition to increase the meaningfulness of life is fundamental to the human being. Where this fails, the distinctively human is gone. Freud spoke of it as "the irresistible advance toward a unification of mental life." This specific drive toward meaning may be viewed in relation to the total biologic drive, the drive from organismic stress toward organismic homeostasis: a variant on the theme "where id was, there shall ego be." However, we must not lose sight of the distinctively human aspect of this process —the symbol structure, the aspect of "meaning"—which is the proper focus of insight therapy. On this symbol level the drive toward integration is a drive toward that state where, according to Freud, "all the enigmatic products of life (have been) elucidated." It is, that is to say, a drive toward meaning.

QUESTIONS

1. Compare the remarks of Allport and Fingarette to those excerpted from Levi-Strauss's THE SAVAGE MIND in Chapter 10, section 3.

2. Is there a relationship between the need to know one's self and the particular needs and dispositions which Allport and Fingarette discuss? How might an argument run that there needs all amount to the same thing? Would such an argument have to view what Munro calls "self-analysis" as involving some kind of "self-synthesis"?

## SECTION THREE: CONSCIENCE: THE DISCOVERY OF SELF IN A SOCIETY OF ROLE

A. *Role For and Against Self*

DAVID SHAW

## "THE SHOWOFF JUDGE"—COURT REFORMS GET MIXED REVIEWS †

He was 23, accused of raping a 15-year-old girl at knife-point.

"Do you know what rape is?" the judge asked him.

"Yes, I think so."

* From 26 (Torchbook ed. 1965). Originally published by Basic Books, Inc., and reprinted with its permission.

† From L. A. Times, Feb. 18, 1971, Pt. 1, at 1, col. 1. Reprinted with permission of The Los Angeles Times.

The judge looked away, and when he spoke again, a mischievous gleam lit his eye.

"Do you know the difference between rape and rapture?"

The defendant shook his head.

"Salesmanship," the judge cracked.

Spectators in the courtroom snickered and bailiffs and clerks grinned and nudged each other.

It was a typical performance for 57-year-old Harry Shafer.

Earlier in the day, he had warned a youth cited for driving without a license to "get one, so you can buy your own car and drive it legally. How you gonna make time with your girl if you don't have a car?"

Later, after fining a drunk $35, Shafer quipped, "Will you drink to that?"

And he asked another defendant that same day if he wanted him to act as his lawyer.

"I guess so."

"Good," Shafer said. "Case dismissed. Now see what a good lawyer you got?"

In the five years since former Gov. Edmund G. Brown appointed him to the Municipal Court bench, Shafer has sparked considerable controversy with his blustery courtroom behavior. His liberal reforms and lenient sentences have even further aroused the antagonism of many in law enforcement.

"Shafer's a buffoon, a disgrace to the bench," says one police official. "He's a wheeling and dealing politician who disparages the police, coddles criminals and runs a circus instead of a courtroom."

Shafer, who drives a $10,000 Rolls Royce he bought from Red Skelton, admits, even boasts, that he's "a big showoff" and "the softest judge in the county."

But he insists his methods give defendants—"and, in the long run, society, too"—more justice than many conventional judges render.

"Everyone gets a fair shake from me and they know it, even if we do have a little fun in the process," he says. "That's particularly important here, where people are so suspicious of law enforcement and the Establishment."

"Here" is Compton, Shafer's court—lower-middle class and 60% black—and many of the men who defend Shafer's antics and rulings do so primarily because he is in Compton.

John Gottes, a South Gate attorney, calls him "a great humanitarian, someone who understands human problems and the causes of crime—just what an area like Compton needs."

Toward that end, Shafer has instituted a number of courtroom programs. Among them:

—He often uses high school students as mock juries in traffic cases.

("They hear the evidence and get 15 minutes to reach a verdict," he says. "My decision is binding, of course, but this gives the young people some understanding of the legal system and a sense of participation in it.")

—Last month, he began allowing third-year UCLA law students to advise indigent defendants of their constitutional rights and, perhaps, to represent them.

("What better way to get a feel for the law, and maybe even learn what you'd like to specialize in—and help other people while you're at it?")

—He releases most defendants without bail or on very low bail.

("It's ridiculous to make some guy without money sit in jail for 30 days, waiting for trial, when the worst sentence he could possibly get if he's guilty is five days. I know police say they don't come back if you let them go without bail. Well, I checked on the first 320 guys I let go. Only five didn't come back. Pretty damn good record, I'd say.")

—He has one court official and one poverty project worker in court to help explain defendants' rights to them and even make telephone calls for them, at county expense, to raise bail, contact relatives or witnesses and find an attorney.

("A lot of these poor guys just don't know what's going on in court. All they want is to get out of here—fast. They'll even plead guilty to something they didn't do if it'll speed things up. I want them to know what's happening. If they're innocent, we stand a better chance of finding out that way. If they're guilty, maybe they'll learn enough not to do it again.")

In addition to these changes, already in effect, Shafer is seeking:

—Selection of juries from telephone directory lists instead of voter registration roles.

("A lot of poor people don't register, so we always get a defendant from Watts being tried by a jury from Palos Verdes. That's not a jury of his peers.")

—Permission to require defendants with some money, but not enough to hire a private attorney, to pay whatever they can afford to have a public defender represent them.

("I'm politically liberal but financially very conservative. If a guy can afford to pay a little, I don't want the county to carry him for free. Besides, he'll have more respect for his attorney if he's paying him than if he gets him for nothing.")

The holder and promulgator of these often heretical views is a short, squat, graying man who wears an $1,800 watch and $160 alligator shoes and speaks in a voice that is, alternately, a growl of gruff self-confidence and a shrill appeal for attention and acceptance.

He is the son of a Russian immigrant who sold dry goods from a pushcart to put his eight children through school successfully enough for young Harry to spend his undergraduate days at Yale and get his law degree at Columbia.

After practicing law briefly in his native New Haven, Conn., Shafer spent three years in the Army during World War II—and came to California when he was discharged in 1946.

While waiting for the results of his California Bar exam, Shafer sold linen and women's apparel door to door in San Pedro, but once back in law practice, his shrewd, aggressive tactics and long hours quickly built his reputation—and his bank account.

He became Compton's city prosecutor, then—as an active financial backer of key Democratic politicians—a natural court selection for Gov. Brown.

"I was making $70,000 a year in private practice," Shafer says. "[A] judge was paid $23,000. Now it's $30,000. But money isn't everything. I didn't want to be doing the same kind of work all my life, and I thought I'd be able to help people . . . as a judge.

"Besides," he says, smiling broadly, "I've still got about $30,000, maybe $35,000 a year in outside income. I'm not hurting."

One of the first problems Shafer encountered as a judge was his affiliation with liberal socio-political groups.

He was—and is—a life member of the NAACP. He is also a sustaining member of the American Civil Liberties Union (ACLU). And he is active in the Welfare Planning Council, and heads two chapters of Neighborhood Legal Services, a group formed to provide legal aid to the poor.

Some critics say Shafer should withdraw from those organizations to avoid the appearance of judicial bias. The ACLU itself has made such a suggestion.

"If I can't be impartial, I don't belong on the bench," says Shafer. "Taking my name off a membership list isn't going to change how I feel anyway."

As an attorney, Shafer handled more than 4,000 divorce cases, and one of the most noticeable carryovers from those days now that he's a judge is his firm, almost fanatic belief in the sanctity of the family.

He thinks the breakdown of the family unit, particularly among blacks, is a major contributor to the spiraling crime rate, and he's determined to preserve the family wherever possible.

When one woman came before him recently, her face bruised and her left eye blackened from a beating by her husband, Shafer tried desperately to encourage a reconciliation, despite the woman's angry insistence that her husband be "put in jail or in a hospital."

"How long you two been married?" Shafer asked at her husband's arraignment.

"Twenty-five years," she replied.

"One beating in 25 years? That's not so bad," Shafer said.

The woman told him they had never gotten along together.

"Never? How many kids you got?"

"Six."

"Six? You must've gotten along at least six times."

Almost invariably, Shafer asks defendants who come before him, regardless of their age, if they have a friend or relative in court.

If someone is there, he invites him to come forward to "the high-priced seats," and says, "You don't have to be a lawyer to speak in my court, you know." And he is often even more lenient than usual if the defendant has a supporter present.

"I figure the guy has a better chance of making it if he knows someone cares enough to show up when he's in trouble," Shafer says. "I also figure he won't want to let that person down. It gives him extra incentive not to screw up again."

Occasionally, Shafer will try an alternative to this ploy.

"The bail is $60," he told one indigent defendant recently. "We'll get on the phone with you, and see if we can find a friend or someone who'll put up $20 today. Then I'll give you six weeks to bring in the other $40.

"I don't know you and I'm willing to trust you for $40. You ought to be able to get someone who knows you to trust you for $20."

When not setting bail, Shafer tells defendants they're being released on their "own honor," instead of the customary legal term "own recognizance."

"Who the hell knows what 'recognizance' means?" he asks. " 'Honor' is something everyone understands. It puts a moral burden on them to come back in."

But it isn't all generosity—or even social philosophy.

"It costs the county $10 a day to keep a guy in jail," Shafer says. "Why waste the taxpayers' money like that when the guy, if he's guilty, probably won't be fined that much?"

"He might lose his job while he's in jail. He'd have to go on welfare or unemployment when he gets out. More tax money wasted. I'd rather have the guy out right away, if he's not dangerous.

"He can keep his job, try to find an attorney and line up witnesses. The county saves money and he gets a better trial."

Shafer is convinced there's "more to crime than just greed or meanness," and he says he tries to understand and act on the "underlying factors—poverty and family break-ups and racial discrimination and other social pressures.

"That's why my sentences are so light," he says. "I want to rehabilitate the guy, help him, not just punish him and wind up having him do the same thing—or worse—next time."

Some defendants try to take advantage of Shafer's compassion. That's a mistake. A Mexican-American defendant, for example, may shrug his shoulders at Shafer's questions as if he doesn't understand English.

If Shafer's suspicious, he'll say, "Dismissed."

Often, the defendant will smile, and start to walk away.

"Oh, so you speak English after all," a smirking Shafer will say —and start the case over.

.   .   .

More often than not in Shafer's court, someone with a good record who is accused of drunk driving will be invited to plead guilty to the lesser charge of reckless driving. ("My New Year's special," he called it last month.)

Come back a second time though, and—like the defendant who tries to con him or violates the terms of a light sentence—you're not likely to meet with mercy again.

"You got a lawyer?" he snapped at a two-time drunk-driver.

"Yes."

"Good.  His name better be Houdini, buddy.  You're in real trouble this time."

When the befuddled defendant asked Shafer if he could give him Houdini's telephone number, Shafer muttered, "My mother told me there'd be days like this," then glared at the defendant and said:

"He's in Forest Lawn.  He hasn't answered his phone in 40 years. And you might not either."

Like many of Shafer's barbs, this one left the defendant confused and unhappy—almost, it seems, with a feeling that he was extraneous to the proceedings, there only as a straight man for Shafer rather than as the defendant in a criminal lawsuit.

Once, not too long ago, in fact, Shafer interrupted a defendant to tell a joke, and when the defendant tried to resume his narrative before Shafer was through, Shafer actually told him to "wait a minute;  don't kill the joke."

"Shafer," says one critic, "carries his informality so far that he ends up ridiculing the defendant."

Shafer is well aware of the discomfort his irrepressible and often sarcastic humor inflicts on defendants, and he is equally aware of the criticism.

"I gotta be myself," he says.  "I don't know why I show off; I just do.  But I think the relaxed, easy-going atmosphere we have in my court is better than the cold, impersonal courts you usually see."

Though his critics in law enforcement say his banter undercuts their efforts ("How do you make a guy realize he's done something wrong if you joke with him about it?" one asks), Shafer insists he's "a friend" of the police and prosecutors.

"We just have different jobs to do, so we look at our roles and the results differently," he says.

To aid his understanding of police problems, Shafer rides with them on patrol every few months.  And he makes it a point to speak favorably of them in court, especially when a defendant criticizes them.

In confiscating a gun from one defendant, for example, he said, "I think guns belong in the hands of police, not private citizens. The police do a good job."

For all his abrasive self-indulgence, Shafer is generally well thought of by other judges and by many, if not most, in the profession.

He is chairman of a 10-court Judges Study Group in Orange and southeast Los Angeles counties. He lectures at a Long Beach school for alcoholics. He teaches at a law school in Orange County that he and two others bought, then donated to conservative, fundamentalist Pepperdine College.

Moreover, when he ran for Superior Court in the elections last year, he finished second in a field of eight before losing the runoff.

The loss didn't bother him, he says—a little too often and too loudly to be convincing, perhaps—and he insists he doesn't know if he'll run again.

But six of his seven foes attended a big "Losers, No Weepers" party Jan. 31, at which he provided food and drink for almost 300 people, with part of his campaign surplus (the balance went to charity).

It was clear, at the party, that Shafer was in his element—the laughing, shouting, joking, cigar-smoking, back-slapping center of attention.

"Harry," says one friend, "is a good man, but he'll always sound like he just stepped out from behind a New York delicatessen counter."


*Jean-Paul Sartre*

## Being and Nothingness *

Let us consider this waiter in the cafe. His movement is quick and forward, a little too precise, a little too rapid. He comes toward the patrons with a step a little too quick. He bends forward a little too eagerly; his voice, his eyes express an interest a little too solicitous for the order of the customer. Finally there he returns, trying to imitate in his walk the inflexible stiffness of some kind of automaton while carrying his tray with the recklessness of a tight-rope-walker by putting it in a perpetually unstable, perpetually broken equilibrium which he perpetually reestablishes by a light movement of the arm and hand. All his behaviour seems to us a game. He applies himself to chaining his movements as if they were mechanisms, the one regulating the other, his gestures and even his voice seem to be mechanisms, he gives himself the quickness and pitiless rapidity of things. He is playing, he is amusing himself. But what is he playing? We need not watch long before we can explain it: he is playing *at being* a waiter in a cafe. There is nothing there to surprise us. The game

* From 59 (H. Barnes transl. 1956). Copyright 1956 by Philosophical Library, Inc., New York and reprinted with its permission.

is a kind of marking out and investigation.  The child plays with his body in order to explore it, to take inventory of it; the waiter in the cafe plays with his condition in order to *realize* it.  This obligation is not different from that which is imposed on all tradesmen.  Their condition is wholly one of ceremony.  The public demands of them that they realize it as a ceremony: there is a dance of the grocer, of the tailor, of the auctioneer, by which they endeavour to persuade their clientele that they are nothing but a grocer, an auctioneer, a tail- or.  A grocer who dreams is offensive to the buyer, because such a grocer is not wholly a grocer.  Society demands that he limit himself to his function as a grocer, just as the soldier at attention makes himself into a soldier-thing with a direct regard which does not see at all, which is no longer meant to see, since it is the rule and not the in- terest of the moment which determines the point he must fix his eyes on (the sight "fixed at ten paces").  There are indeed many precau- tions to imprison a man in what he is, as if we lived in perpetual fear that he might escape from it, that he might break away and suddenly elude his condition.

GORDON ALLPORT

## BECOMING *

While the child needs and wants love and security, he does not want them to interfere with his impulses, his freedom, or his preferred ways of acting.  From the very start of his life he is resistant to the smothering effects of his social environment.  Affiliation alone would make for slavish obedience to family or tribal living which provide the child with his early standards of conduct and with his definitions of the world around him.  If these influences were the only ones acting upon him they would lead to conduct always conventional and stereo- typed.  It is a limitation of current theories of socialization that they do in fact deal only with the mirror-like character of the so-called superego, that they tend to define socialization exclusively in terms of conformity, and not also in terms of creative becoming.

The truth of the matter, however, is that the moral sense and life-styles of most people reach far beyond the confines of domestic and community mores in which they were first fashioned.  If we look into ourselves we observe that our tribal morality seems to us some- how peripheral to our personal integrity.  True, we obey conventions of modesty, decorum, and self-control, and have many habits that fashion us in part as mirror-images of our home, class, and cultural ways of living.  But we know that we have selected, reshaped, and transcended these ways to a marked degree.

Thus there seem to be two contrary forces at work.  The one makes for a closed tribal being.  It takes its start in the dependence of the child upon those who care for him.  His gratifications and his security come from the outside; so too do all the first lessons he

* From 34–35 (Paperbd. ed. 1960). Copy- right (c) 1955 by Yale University      Press and reprinted with its permis- sion.

learns: the times of day when he may have meals, the activities for which he is punished and those that bring reward. He is coerced and cajoled into conformity but not, we note, with complete success. He shows a capacity even from birth to resist the impact of material and tribal demands. While to a certain degree his group shapes his course, at the same time it seems to antagonize him, as if he realized its threat to his integrity.

If the demand for autonomy were not a major force we could not explain the prominence of negativistic behavior in childhood. The crying, rejecting, and anger of a young infant as well as the negativistic behavior of the two-year-old are primitive indications of a being bent on asserting itself. All his life long this being will be attempting to reconcile these two modes of becoming, the tribal and the personal: the one that makes him into a mirror, the other that lights the lamp of individuality within.

PAUL N. SAVOY

## TOWARD A NEW POLITICS OF LEGAL EDUCATION *

When I first came to teaching two years ago, I had it in mind to emulate the style of some of my own teachers whose verbal art had made them so deadly, so omnipotent in the classroom. But, I find that pedagogical *mimesis*—teaching as an imitation of teaching—does not work very well for me. The only time that anything really happens in my classes is when I start being the person I really am—with feelings, doubts, expectations, fears—and not the incarnation of some professional or academic role. Lawyers and law students, though, are especially resistant to efforts to get them in touch with their feelings. Of all the admonitions of the Greek philosopher, the one which we self-styled Socratics most persistently and flagrantly ignore is: Know thyself. Between law teacher and law student there is a silent conspiracy to preserve what Alan Watts calls "the taboo against knowing who you are."

Teachers and students must meet face to face, but that will never happen until we remove our academic masks and put an end to those degradation ceremonies we politely call the "Socratic method."

* From 79 Yale L.J. 444, 456–457 (1970). Reprinted with permission of the Yale Law Journal and Fred B. Rothman, Inc.

*F. H. Bradley*

## My Station and Its Duties *

.    .    .    .    we have found ourselves, when we have found our station and its duties, our function as an organ in the social organism.

.    .    .

.    .    .    To know what a man is  .  .  .    you must not take him in isolation.   He is one of a people, he was born in a family, he lives in a certain society, in a certain state.   What he has to do depends on what his place is, what his function is, and that all comes from his station in the organism.   Are there then such organisms in which he lives, and if so, what is their nature?   Here we come to questions which must be answered in full by any complete system of Ethics, but which we can not enter on.   We must content ourselves by pointing out that there are such facts as the family, then in a middle position a man's own profession and society, and, over all, the larger community of the state.   Leaving out of sight the question of a society wider than the state, we must say that a man's life with its moral duties is in the main filled up by his station in that system of wholes which the state is, and that this, partly by its laws and institutions, and still more by its spirit, gives him the life which he does live and ought to live.   That objective institutions exist is of course an obvious fact; and it is a fact which every day is becoming plainer that these institutions are organic, and further, that they are moral. The assertion that communities have been manufactured  by the addition of exclusive units is, as we have seen, a mere fable; and if, within the state, we take that which seems wholly to depend on individual caprice, e. g., marriage, yet even here we find that a man does give up his self so far as it excludes others; he does bring himself under an unity which is superior to the particular person and the impulses that belong to his single existence, and which makes him fully as much as he makes it.   In short, man is a social being; he is real only because he is social, and can realize himself only because it is as social that he realizes himself.   The mere individual is a delusion of theory; and the attempt to realize it in practice is the starvation and mutilation of human nature, with total sterility or the production of monstrosities.

.    .    .

.    .    .    [A]lthough within certain limits I may choose my station according to my own liking, yet I and every one else must have some station with duties pertaining to it, and those duties do not depend on our opinion or liking.   Certain circumstances, a certain position, call for a certain course.   How I in particular know what my right course is, is a question we shall recur to hereafter—but at present we may take it as an obvious fact that in my station my particular duties are prescribed to me, and I have them whether I wish to or not. And secondly, it is concrete.   The universal to be realized is no abstraction, but an organic whole; a system where many spheres are

---

* From  163,  173–174,  176–177  (2d ed. 1927).

subordinated to one sphere, and particular actions to spheres. This system is real in the detail of its functions, not out of them, and lives in its vital processes, not away from them. The organs are always at work for the whole, the whole is at work in the organs. And I am one of the organs. The universal then which I am to realize is the system which penetrates and subordinates to itself the particulars of all lives, and here and now in my life has this and that function in this and that case, in exercising which through my will it realizes itself as a whole, and me in it.

NOTE: ROLE FOR AND AGAINST SELF

One theme that has recurred throughout this book is that of the conflict between duty to self and duty to role. More than once situations have been presented in which some particular role-obligation seems to contradict a deeper feeling of rightness or justice. Reasons for acceding to role demands are readily forthcoming—as portions of Part I and Chapter 13 should indicate—but it should also be clear after reading the foregoing sections of this Chapter that loyalty to self may be of equal or greater importance. It is easy to overlook this as long as we frame the problem in the discredited, but not discarded, terms of an opposition between the interests of the individual and the society. For in the end, the interests of the greater whole are likely to seem compelling. But if we are willing to entertain the proposition that social order and development depend on the vitality of individual personal organization, that there can be no order at higher social levels if there is none at the individual's level, the importance of loyalty to self should disclose itself dramatically.

Ordinarily, conflicts between self and role are viewed as inevitable products of any civilizing process. The individual is viewed as one who must make some sacrifice of self in order to insure the community's greater good. In some sense of the notion of self—perhaps that inclusive one mentioned, *supra*, in the Note: Two Concepts of Self—this may be a useful mode of expression. But if self is viewed as the peculiar form of organization of an individual life, then it seems possible to argue that a sacrifice of self necessarily must be a social loss not a gain. In a sense, one who chooses role over self in fact chooses against role as well.

From another standpoint, it could be argued that one cannot choose self over role without losing both. Even if one is unwilling to go as far as Bradley, his remarks may help us understand the reason. A self, it could be argued, expresses itself primarily through the forms of role. A man without roles, therefore, if conceivable at all, must be a man without a self of any substance. This is a position, you should be able to see, which should not sit well with Sartre or Savoy. Can you suggest an argument in their defense?

All of this, it is hoped, may provoke you into a deeper and more complicated consideration of the problems raised by a conflict between self and role. You may even wish to reconsider the phenomenon's characterization as (1) a conflict and (2) between self and role. Perhaps this way of viewing the phenomenon is itself the cause of the intellectual and moral paradoxes which seem to accompany it. To make your musings more concrete, consider the conduct of Judge Shafer who insists on being a judge as well as being himself. Try to hypothesize the criticisms and defenses which his conduct would likely engender. Can you construct arguments which do not beg the question? What, incidentally, is the question?

## B.  Judicial Self-Restraint:  A Problem In the Meaning of Responsibility

### Note: Judicial Self-Restraint or Judicial Abdication?

Learned Hand and Felix Frankfurter were perhaps the two most famous and thorough-going American counselors of judicial abnegation. For characteristic statements of their views see Hand's *The Contribution of an Independent Judiciary to Civilization* and Frankfurter's concurring opinion in Dennis v. U. S., reprinted in the preceding chapter. Their positions were particularly impressive because both had in their times been eloquent defenders of the civil liberties they refused to protect in their courts. See, *e. g.*, Hand, *A Plea for the Open Mind and Free Discussion* in The Spirit of Liberty (I. Dilliard ed. 1959). It is easy to suspect the sincerity of people who insist that they are duty-bound to do what they would rather not. Often enough such people personally prefer to do what they choose to do. Hand and Frankfurter, however, possessed libertarian credentials which lend their protestations credibility. Nevertheless, their positions have been attacked as apologies for judicial abdication of responsibility. As you consider the following excerpts you should ask yourself how much the justifications which Hand and Frankfurter use resemble the characteristics attributed to those who are and those who are not "responsible." Who—the defenders or the critics of judicial self-restraint—do you think would find these pieces most congenial?

*Walter Kaufmann*

### From Shakespeare to Existentialism *

> They that have power to hurt and will do none,
> That do not do the thing they most do show,
> Who, moving others, are themselves as stone,
> Unmoved, cold, and to temptation slow:
> They rightly do inherit heaven's graces
> And husband nature's riches from expense,
> They are the lords and owners of their faces,
> Others, but stewards of their excellence.
> The summer's flower is to the summer sweet,
> Though to itself it only live and die,

---

\* From 5–8, 9–11 (Anchor ed. 1960). Reprinted with permission of Walter Kaufmann.

But if that flower with base infection meet,
The basest weed outbraves his dignity:
For sweetest things turn sourest by their deeds;
Lilies that fester smell far worse than weeds.

This sonnet, XCIV, celebrates Shakespeare's un-Christian ideal, which was also the ideal of Nietzsche, who expressed it, not quite three centuries later, in the chapter "On Those Who Are Sublime" in *Zarathustra*. Those who find Shakespeare's first two lines puzzling will find an excellent commentary in Nietzsche:

> One who was sublime I saw today, one who was solemn, an ascetic of the spirit; oh, how my soul laughed at his ugliness! . . . As yet he has not overcome his deed. . . . As yet his torrential passion has not become still in beauty. Verily, it is not in satiety that his desire shall grow silent and be submerged, but in beauty. Gracefulness is part of the graciousness of the great-souled. . . . There is nobody from whom I want beauty as much as from you who are powerful: let your kindness be your final self-conquest. Of all evil I deem you capable: therefore I want the good from you. Verily, I have often laughed at the weaklings who thought themselves good because they had no claws.

In a note published posthumously in *The Will to Power* (1893), Nietzsche compressed this vision into half a dozen words: "the Roman Caesar with Christ's soul." Shakespeare, too, celebrates the man who has claws but does not use them. Or, as he put it in *Measure for Measure* (II, ii):

                                    O, it is excellent
To have a giant's strength; but it is tyrannous
To use it like a giant.

In a good book on *The Sense of Shakespeare's Sonnets*, Edward Hubler tells us that "On first reading the [ninety-fourth] sonnet, we shall, of course, notice the irony of the first eight lines. . . . It is preposterous on the face of things to proclaim as the inheritors of heaven's graces those who are 'as stone.' It can be other than ironical only to the cynic. . . ."

What seems "preposterous" to a Christian reader need not have struck a Roman or a Spartan as unseemly. We need only to recall some of the heroes of republican Rome—the first Brutus or Scaevola. Caesar, too, was one of those "who, moving others, are themselves as stone." Notice the difference between his affair with Cleopatra and poor Antony's. Shaw underlined this point: his Caesar knows he has forgotten something as he is about to leave Egypt, but cannot remember what it is. And then he realizes that he almost left without saying goodbye to Cleopatra. The historical Caesar literally moved Cleopatra to Rome, without letting her interfere with his work.

Caesar, to cite Nietzsche's great tribute to Goethe from his *Twilight of the Idols*, "might dare to afford the whole range and wealth of being natural, being strong enough for such freedom."

And not only Caesar and Goethe but Shakespeare himself might well be characterized in Nietzsche's words as "the man of tolerance, not from weakness but from strength, because he knows how to use to his advantage even that of which the average nature would perish."

Poetic liberties that would have ruined a lesser poet are used to advantage by Shakespeare, whose moral tolerance does more to educate the heart than a whole library of sermons. And Shakespeare, no less than Caesar, was one of those "that have power to hurt and will do none" and "who, moving others, are themselves as stone." Cassius was irritated by Caesar's excessive power to hurt without appreciating that Caesar had no mind to use his power like a giant. And how much hurt could Shakespeare have inflicted with his rarely equalled power to express himself! Those romantic souls who would rather not believe that Shakespeare, the poet, moving others, was himself as stone, might well recall that Shakespeare was an actor, too.

The interpretation that insists that the first eight lines must be ironical depends on the strange assertion that "The first line is tauntingly obscure, and an understanding of the poem cannot proceed without an interpretation of it." The second half of that sentence is true enough, but the first line is not at all obscure. As Edward Dowden understands it rightly in his standard edition of the sonnets, it refers to those "who can hold their passions in check, who can refuse to wrath its outbreak" or, to approximate the wording of the line, to those who have power to hurt but refrain from using it to hurt. There is no irony at all in praising men like that. As Dowden says, "True, these self-contained persons may seem to lack generosity; but then, without making voluntary gifts, they give inevitably, even as the summer's flower is sweet to the summer, though it live and die only to itself."

Such self-sufficiency is not a part of popular morality. "Physician, help yourself: thus you help your patient, too. Let this be his best help that he may behold with his eyes the man who heals himself," says Nietzsche's Zarathustra in his discourse "On the Gift-giving Virtue"; and the chapter "On The Friend" is a fine commentary on Shakespeare's sonnets, too.

It is only in a world view that does not seek a meaning for this life and this world beyond, after death, that experience becomes an end in itself, especially the experience of those who embody mature perfection, "though to itself it only live and die."

The apprehension may remain that such perfection and such power are profoundly dangerous. Cassius considered Caesar dangerous, and Coriolanus, Macbeth, and Othello met "with base infection." But that is part of the point of this sonnet and of Shakespeare's tragic view: "Lilies that fester smell far worse than weeds."

.   .   .

.   .   .   .   A simple reading of a couple of pages from Aristotle's *Nicomachean Ethics* is sufficient to give anyone a new perspective on Shakespeare's ninety-fourth sonnet, his *Coriolanus*, and his other tragedies, and on Goethe and Nietzsche, too.

> The good man ought to be a lover of self, since he will then act nobly, and so benefit himself and aid his fellows; but the bad man ought not to be a lover of self, since he will follow his base passions, and so injure both himself and his neighbors.  (IX, 8)

> A person is thought to be great-souled if he claims much and deserves much. . . . He that claims less than he deserves is small-souled. . . . Greatness of soul seems . . . a crowning ornament of all the virtues. . . . Great honours accorded by persons of worth will afford [the great-souled man] pleasure in a moderate degree: he will feel he is receiving only what belongs to him, or even less, for no honour can be adequate to the merits of perfect virtue, yet all the same he will deign to accept their honours, because they have no greater tribute to offer him.  Honour rendered by common people and on trivial grounds he will utterly despise. . . . He . . . will be indifferent to other things as well.  Hence great-souled men are thought to be haughty. . . . The great-souled man is justified in despising other people—his estimates are correct; but most proud men have no good ground for their pride. . . He is fond of conferring benefits, but ashamed to receive them. . . . He returns a service done to him with interest, since this will put the original benefactor into his debt in turn. . . . The great-souled are said to have a good memory for any benefit they have conferred, but a bad memory for those which they have received. . . . It is also characteristic of the great-souled men never to ask help from others, or only with reluctance, but to render aid willingly; and to be haughty towards men of position and fortune, but courteous towards those of moderate station . . . and to adopt a high manner with the former is not ill-bred, but it is vulgar to lord it over humble people. . . He must . . . care more for the truth than for what people will think; . . . he is outspoken and frank, except when speaking with ironical self-depreciation, as he does to common people. . . . He does not bear a grudge. . . . He is . . . not given to speaking evil himself, even of his enemies, except when he deliberately intends to give offence.  (IV, 3)

Most modern admirers of Aristotle pass over such passages in embarrassment though they offer nothing less than Aristotle's notion of ideal manhood—and then Shakespeare's ninety-fourth sonnet seems "preposterous" to them.  For it does not celebrate the Christian saint but Aristotle's great-souled man.

QUESTIONS

1. Would Aristotle's great-souled man be sympathetic to judicial self-restraint? Or can you not answer the question? If so, why? What more would you want to know? About Aristotle? About judicial self-restraint?

2. Recall Frank's desire for judges with strong personalities. Does Kaufmann cast any doubt on the proposition that a necessary and sufficient condition of the kind of judging Frank wants is a strong personality?

*PAUL TILLICH*

THE COURAGE TO BE *

. . . The anxiety of becoming guilty, the horror of feeling condemned, are so strong that they make responsible decisions and any kind of moral action almost impossible. But since decisions and actions cannot be avoided they are reduced to a minimum which, however, is considered absolutely perfect; and the sphere where they take place is defended against any provocation to transcend it. Here also the separation from reality has the consequence that the consciousness of guilt is misplaced. The moralistic self-defense of the neurotic makes him see guilt where there is no guilt or where one is guilty only in a very indirect way. Yet the awareness of real guilt and the self-condemnation which is identical with man's existential self-estrangement are repressed, because the courage which could take them into itself is lacking.

*HERBERT FINGARETTE*

THE SELF IN TRANSFORMATION †

. . . . Responsibility is the readiness to face the absence of meaning, the nonbeing of self. It requires that a self *be* formed, a meaning be instated, a policy adopted. The crisis exists precisely because there is no a priori decisive resolution of the situation.

Responsibility is the willingness to "leap into nothingness." But it is more than this: it is the willingness to accept—and accept in a very special sense—the consequences of one's act. Responsibility is, in its primary sense, commitment, not obligation. Indeed, genuine obligations arise out of such commitments. Hence it is in a derivative sense that we say: "He is responsible about carrying out his obligations." . . .

We flinch from this leap, this commitment without decisive justification. We would prefer to *know*. We prefer security. And the heart of responsibility is revealed when we see that, faced with anxiety and the need for choice, precisely what we wish to know

* From 75–76 (1952). Reprinted with
    permission of Yale University Press.

† From 101 (Torchbook ed. 1965). Originally published by Basic Books, Inc., and reprinted with its permission.

is what we *cannot* know. We establish meaning and regulative principle by our act—if we have the courage to accept and identify ourselves with the act and its import.

QUESTIONS

1.   Is there any evidence that either Hand or Frankfurter "flinch from this leap, this commitment without decisive justification"? That not only would they "prefer to *know*," but that they refuse to act in the absence of such knowledge? Or can they refuse to act? Is that a choice open to them?

2.   If responsibility "requires that a self *be* formed, a meaning be instated, a policy adopted," does this mean that responsibility is ultimately reducible to the requirement that one know one's self? Reconsider the excerpts from Allport and Fingarette in the preceding section.


PAUL TILLICH

THE COURAGE TO BE *

.   .   .   .   *Neurosis is the way of avoiding nonbeing.*  In the neurotic state self-affirmation is not lacking; it can indeed be very strong and emphasized. But the self which is affirmed is a reduced one. Some or many of its potentialities are not admitted to actualization, because actualization of being implies the acceptance of nonbeing and its anxiety. He who is not capable of a powerful self-affirmation in spite of the anxiety of nonbeing is forced into a weak, reduced self-affirmation. He affirms something which is less than his essential or potential being. He surrenders a part of his potentialities in order to save what is left  .   .   .   .

NOTES AND QUESTIONS

1.   When judicial self-restraint is viewed not only as a check on the power to overturn legislation, but also as a restrictive jurisdictional policy, recall *Muskrat,* does it bear any resemblance to the anxiety symptoms Tillich describes? Does it reduce "decisions and actions  .   .   .   to a minimum which, however, is considered absolutely perfect"? Is "the sphere where they take place  .   .   . defended against any provocation to transcend it"? Review Hand's *Contribution of an Independent Judiciary to Civilization* and Frankfurter's concurrence in Dennis v. United States.

2.   What would an argument look like—what evidence would it adduce—which proposed that advocates and practitioners of judicial self-restraint "see guilt where there is no guilt"?

3.   With Tillich's description of the neurotic compare John Holt's description of his pupils. HOW CHILDREN FAIL 41 (1964). Holt at one time was puzzled that students who did the worst work were often

* From 66, 75 (1952). Reprinted with
permission of Yale University Press.

the first ones to turn in their papers—in spite of his admonitions that those who finish early should use their time to verify their conclusions and redo some of the problems. Holt finally concluded that this was like asking them "to flap their wings and fly." The children were turning in their papers early in order to relieve the tension. Although they wished to do well and worried about failure it was a worry which did not have the same sting, "it didn't contain the agonizing element of choice." "Worrying about whether you did the right thing, while painful enough, is less painful than worrying about the right thing to do." *Ibid.*

   4.   Consider the following:

   Thus conscience does make cowards of us all;
   And thus the native hue of resolution
   Is sicklied o'er with the pale cast of thought;
   And enterprises of great pith and moment,
   With this regard, their current turn awry,
   And lose the name of action.

W. SHAKESPEARE, HAMLET, PRINCE OF DENMARK, Act III, Scene I.


*PAUL TILLICH*

THE COURAGE TO BE *

      .   .   .   .   "If there is," says Seneca, "no other attribute which belongs to man as man except reason, then reason will be his one good, worth all the rest put together." This means that reason is man's true or essential nature, in comparison with which everything else is accidental. The courage to be is the courage to affirm one's own reasonable nature over against what is accidental in us. It is obvious that reason in this sense points to the person in his center and includes all mental functions. Reasoning as a limited cognitive function, detached from the personal center, never could create courage. One cannot remove anxiety by arguing it away. This is not a recent psychoanalytical discovery; the Stoics, when glorifying reason, knew it as well. They knew that anxiety can be overcome only through the power of universal reason which prevails in the wise man over desires and fears. Stoic courage presupposes the surrender of the personal center to the Logos of being; it is participation in the divine power of reason, transcending the realm of passions and anxieties. The courage to be is the courage to affirm our own rational nature, in spite of everything in us that conflicts with its union with the rational nature of being-itself.

      .   .   .

      .   .   .   .   Although the Stoics emphasized that all human beings are equal in that they participate in the universal Logos, they could not deny the fact that wisdom is the possession of only an infinitely small elite. The masses of people, they acknowledged, are "fools," in the

* From 12–13, 16 (1952). Reprinted with permission of Yale University Press.

bondage of desires and fears. While participating in the divine Logos with their essential or rational nature, most human beings are in a state of actual conflict with their own rationality and therefore unable to affirm their essential being courageously.

## NOTES AND QUESTIONS

1. To what extent do the Stoics offer a solution to problems raised by the conflicts of role against role and of role against self? Do they tell us which roles and which conceptions of self we ought to choose? Does the choice of role or self involve a choice between "the bondage of desires and fears" and the affirmation of "our own rational nature"? Can it be argued that certain interpretations (or constructions) of role or self express that bondage? That others express that affirmation?

2. What is the conception of wisdom which, according to Tillich, the Stoics entertained? How does it resemble or differ from the conception of wisdom which Frankfurter's *Dennis* opinion implies? Compare the Stoic position on wisdom to the conception of the judicial function which Bickel describes in Chapter 12.

3. Can you conceptualize what Tillich means by Reason? Does it help to consider the conception of mind which Langer defends in Chapter 9, section 3? Does it have anything to do with the conception of mind implied by Cassirer's piece in the same section?

## NOTE: THE RECOGNITION OF RESPONSIBILITY

The problem of responsibility, as we saw even in the opening pages of this book, arises not only in the obvious situations where judges refuse to exercise the power to declare statutes unconstitutional, but also in the most pedestrian exercises of rule interpretation. Since many of the materials you have encountered may be taken as pleas for responsible conduct, it may be worthwhile to pause for a moment and question the purposes of the pleaders. Just why do they wish to make people recognize their responsibility? What changes in attitude or method do they expect to achieve by convincing decision-makers that they are responsible for the consequences of their decisions? In what way do they hope to make such decisions better? What standard of goodness do they assume?

Be sure to consider the readings in this section as you try to work out answers to these questions. Insofar as they help us to define the concept of responsibility, do they also help us understand the motives of those who urge us to responsible action? Consider also the existentialist position that man is responsible for every choice he makes. What notion of responsibility does such a statement imply? What alteration of human conduct is it trying to accomplish? What would be the consequences if everyone *felt* responsible for every decision he had to make? Does the answer depend on the meaning of the word "decision" or of the word "make"? How many decisions do men make each day?

SECTION FOUR: THE COURAGE TO BE: RESISTING
THE TABOO AGAINST KNOWING WHO YOU ARE

PAINTER V. BANNISTER

258 Iowa 1390 (1966)

STUART, J.—We are here setting the course for Mark Wendell
Painter's future.  Our decision on the custody of this seven-year-old
boy will have a marked influence on his whole life.  The fact that we
are called upon many times a year to determine custody matters does
not make the exercising of this awesome responsibility any less difficult.  Legal training and experience are of little practical help in
solving the complex problems of human relations.  However, these
problems do arise and under our system of government the burden of
rendering a final decision rests upon us.  It is frustrating to know
we can only resolve, not solve, these unfortunate situations.

The custody dispute before us in this habeas corpus action is between the father, Harold Painter, and the maternal grandparents,
Dwight and Margaret Bannister.  Mark's mother and younger sister
were killed in an automobile accident on December 6, 1962, near Pullman, Washington.  The father, after other arrangements for Mark's
care had proved unsatisfactory, asked the Bannisters to take care of
Mark.  They went to California and brought Mark to their farm home
near Ames in July 1963.  Mr. Painter remarried in November 1964
and about that time indicated he wanted to take Mark back.  The
Bannisters refused to let him leave and this action was filed in June
1965.  Since July 1965 he has continued to remain in the Bannister
home under an order of this court staying execution of the judgment
of the trial court awarding custody to the father until the matter
could be determined on appeal.  For reasons hereinafter stated, we
conclude Mark's better interests will be served if he remains with the
Bannisters.

Mark's parents came from highly contrasting backgrounds.  His
mother was born, reared and educated in rural Iowa.  Her parents are
college graduates.  Her father is agricultural information editor for
the Iowa State University Extension Service.  The Bannister home is
in the Gilbert community and is well kept, roomy and comfortable.
The Bannisters are highly respected members of the community.  Mr.
Bannister has served on the school board and regularly teaches a Sunday school class at the Gilbert Congregational Church.  Mark's mother
graduated from Grinnell College.  She then went to work for a newspaper in Anchorage, Alaska, where she met Harold Painter.

Mark's father was born in California.  When he was two and
one-half years old, his parents were divorced and he was placed in a
foster home.  Although he has kept in contact with his natural parents, he considers his foster parents, the McNellys, as his family.  He
flunked out of a high school and a trade school because of a lack of
interest in academic subjects, rather than any lack of ability.  He
joined the navy at 17.  He did not like it.  After receiving an honorable discharge, he took examinations and obtained his high school

diploma. He lived with the McNellys and went to college for two and one-half years under the G. I. bill. He quit college to take a job on a small newspaper in Ephrata, Washington, in November 1955. In May 1956 he went to work for the newspaper in Anchorage which employed Jeanne Bannister.

Harold and Jeanne were married in April 1957. Although there is a conflict in the evidence on the point, we are convinced the marriage, overall, was a happy one, with many ups and downs as could be expected in the uniting of two such opposites.

We are not confronted with a situation where one of the contesting parties is not a fit or proper person. There is no criticism of either the Bannisters or their home. There is no suggestion in the record that Mr. Painter is morally unfit. It is obvious the Bannisters did not approve of their daughter's marriage to Harold Painter and do not want their grandchild reared under his guidance. The philosophies of life are entirely different. As stated by the psychiatrist who examined Mr. Painter at the request of Bannisters' attorneys: "It is evident that there exists a large difference in ways of life and value systems between the Bannisters and Mr. Painter, but in this case there is no evidence that psychiatric instability is involved. Rather, these divergent life patterns seem to represent alternative normal adaptations."

It is not our prerogative to determine custody upon our choice of one of two ways of life within normal and proper limits and we will not do so. However, the philosophies are important as they relate to Mark and his particular needs.

The Bannister home provides Mark with a stable, dependable, conventional, middle-class, middlewestern background and an opportunity for a college education and profession, if he desires it. It provides a solid foundation and secure atmosphere. In the Painter home Mark would have more freedom of conduct and thought with an opportunity to develop his individual talents. It would be more exciting and challenging in many respects, but romantic, impractical and unstable.

Little additional recitation of evidence is necessary to support our evaluation of the Bannister home. It might be pointed out, however, that Jeanne's three sisters also received college educations and seem to be happily married to college graduates.

Our conclusion as to the type of home Mr. Painter would offer is based upon his Bohemian approach to finances and life in general. We feel there is much evidence which supports this conclusion. His main ambition is to be a free-lance writer and photographer. He has had some articles and picture stories published, but the income from these efforts has been negligible. At the time of the accident, Jeanne was willingly working to support the family so Harold could devote more time to his writing and photography. In the ten years since he left college he has changed jobs seven times. He was asked to leave two of them; two he quit because he did not like the work; two because he wanted to devote more time to writing and the rest for better pay. He was contemplating a move to Berkeley at the time of trial.

His attitude toward his career is typified by his own comments concerning a job offer:

"About the Portland news job, I hope you understand when I say it took guts not to take it; I had to get behind myself and push. It was very, very tempting to accept a good salary and settle down to a steady, easy routine. As I approached Portland, with the intention of taking the job, I began to ask what, in the long run, would be the good of the job: 1, it was not *really* what I wanted; 2, Portland is just another big farm town, with none of the stimulation it takes to get my mind sparking. Anyway, I decided Mark and myself would be better off if I went ahead with what I've started and the hell with the rest, sink, swim or starve."

There is general agreement that Mr. Painter needs help with his finances. Both Jeanne and Marilyn, his present wife, handled most of them. Purchases and sales of books, boats, photographic equipment and houses indicate poor financial judgment and an easy come easy go attitude. He dissipated his wife's estate of about $4300, most of which was a gift from her parents and which she had hoped would be used for the children's education.

The psychiatrist classifies him as "a romantic and somewhat of a dreamer". An apt example is the plan he related for himself and Mark in February 1963: "My thought now is to settle Mark and myself in Sausilito, near San Francisco; this is a retreat for wealthy artists, writers, and such aspiring artists and writers as can fork up the rent money. My plan is to do expensive portraits ($150 and up), sell prints ($15 and up) to the tourists who flock in from all over the world * * *."

The house in which Mr. Painter and his present wife live, compared with the well kept Bannister home, exemplifies the contrasting ways of life. In his words "it is a very old and beat-up and lovely home * * *". They live in the rear part. The interior is inexpensively but tastefully decorated. The large yard on a hill in the business district of Walnut Creek, California, is of uncut weeds and wild oats. The house "is not painted on the outside because I do not want it painted. I am very fond of the wood on the outside of the house."

The present Mrs. Painter has her master's degree in cinema design and apparently likes and has had considerable contact with children. She is anxious to have Mark in her home. Everything indicates she would provide a leveling influence on Mr. Painter and could ably care for Mark.

Mr. Painter is either an agnostic or atheist and has no concern for formal religious training. He has read a lot of Zen Buddhism and "has been very much influenced by it". Mrs. Painter is Roman Catholic. They plan to send Mark to a Congregational Church near the Catholic Church, on an irregular schedule.

He is a political liberal and got into difficulty in a job at the University of Washington for his support of the activities of the American Civil Liberties Union in the university news bulletin.

There were "two funerals" for his wife. One in the basement of his home in which he alone was present. He conducted the service and wrote her a long letter. The second at a church in Pullman was for the gratification of her friends. He attended in a sport shirt and sweater.

These matters are not related as a criticism of Mr. Painter's conduct, way of life or sense of values. An individual is free to choose his own values, within bounds, which are not exceeded here. They do serve however to support our conclusions as to the kind of life Mark would be exposed to in the Painter household. We believe it would be unstable, unconventional, arty, Bohemian and probably intellectually stimulating.

Were the question simply which household would be the most suitable in which to rear a child, we would have unhesitatingly chosen the Bannister home. We believe security and stability in the home are more important than intellectual stimulation in the proper development of a child. There are, however, several factors which have made us pause.

First, there is the presumption of parental preference, which, though weakened in the past several years, exists by statute. Code of Iowa, section 668.1, Code, 1962; Finken v. Porter, 246 Iowa 1345, 72 N.W.2d 445; Kouris v. Lunn, 257 Iowa 1267, 136 N.W.2d 502; Vanden Heuvel v. Vanden Heuvel, 254 Iowa 1391, 1399, 121 N.W.2d 216. We have a great deal of sympathy for a father who, in the difficult period of adjustment following his wife's death, turns to the maternal grandparents for their help and then finds them unwilling to return the child. There is no merit in the Bannister claim that Mr. Painter permanently relinquished custody. It was intended to be a temporary arrangement. A father should be encouraged to look for help with the children from those who love them without the risk of thereby losing the custody of the children permanently. This fact must receive consideration in cases of this kind. However, as always, the primary consideration is the best interest of the child and if the return of custody to the father is likely to have a seriously disrupting and disturbing effect upon the child's development, this fact must prevail. Vanden Heuvel v. Vanden Heuval, supra; In re Gaurdianship of Plucar, 247 Iowa 394, 403, 72 N.W.2d 455; Carrere v. Prunty, 257 Iowa 525, 531, 133 N.W.2d 692, 696; Finken v. Porter and Kouris v. Lunn, both supra; rule 344(f) 15, Rules of Civil Procedure.

Second, Jeanne's will named her husband guardian of her children and, if he failed to qualify or ceased to act, named her mother. The parent's wishes are entitled to consideration. Finken v. Porter, supra.

Third, the Bannisters are 60 years old. By the time Mark graduates from high school they will be over 70 years old. Care of young children is a strain on grandparents and Mrs. Bannister's letters indicate as much.

We have considered all of these factors and have concluded that Mark's best interest demands that his custody remain with the Bannisters. Mark was five when he came to their home. The evidence clearly shows he was not well adjusted at that time. He did not distinguish fact from fiction and was inclined to tell "tall tales" emphasizing the big "I". He was very aggressive toward smaller children, cruel to animals, not liked by his classmates and did not seem to know what was acceptable conduct. As stated by one witness: "Mark knew where his freedom was and he didn't know where his boundaries were." In two years he made a great deal of improvement. He now appears to be well disciplined, happy, relatively secure and popular with his classmates, although still subject to more than normal anxiety.

We place a great deal of reliance on the testimony of Dr. Glenn R. Hawks, a child psychologist. The trial court, in effect, disregarded Doctor Hawks' opinions, stating: "The court has given full consideration to the good doctor's testimony, but cannot accept it at full face value because of exaggerated statements and the witness' attitude on the stand." We, of course, do not have the advantage of viewing the witness' conduct on the stand, but we have carefully reviewed his testimony and find nothing in the written record to justify such a summary dismissal of the opinions of this eminent child psychologist.

Doctor Hawks is head of the Department of Child Development at Iowa State University. However, there is nothing in the record which suggests that his relationship with the Bannisters is such that his professional opinion would be influenced thereby. Child development is his specialty and he has written many articles and a textbook on the subject. He is recognized nationally, having served on the staff of the 1960 White House Conference on Children and Youth and as consultant on a Ford Foundation program concerning youth in India. He is now educational consultant on the project "Head Start". He has taught and lectured at many universities and belongs to many professional associations. He works with the Iowa Children's Home Society in placement problems. Further detailing of his qualifications is unnecessary.

Between June 15 and the time of trial he spent approximately 25 hours acquiring information about Mark and the Bannisters, including appropriate testing of and "depth interviews" with Mark. Doctor Hawks' testimony covers 70 pages of the record and it is difficult to pinpoint any bit of testimony which precisely summarizes his opinion. He places great emphasis on the "father figure" and discounts the importance of the "biological father". "The father figure is a figure that the child sees as an authority figure, as a helper, he is a nutrient figure, and one who typifies maleness and stands as maleness as far as the child is concerned."

His investigation revealed: " * * * the strength of the father figure before Mark came to the Bannisters is very unclear. Mark is confused about the father figure prior to his contact with Mr. Bannister." Now, "Mark used Mr. Bannister as his father figure. This is very evident. It shows up in the depth interview, and it shows up in the description of Mark's life given by Mark. He has a very warm feeling for Mr. Bannister."

Doctor Hawks concluded that it was not for Mark's best interest to be removed from the Bannister home. He is criticized for reaching this conclusion without investigating the Painter home or finding out more about Mr. Painter's character  He answered:

"I was most concerned about the welfare of the child, not the welfare of Mr. Painter, not about the welfare of the Bannisters. Inasmuch as Mark has already made an adjustment and sees the Bannisters as his parental figures in his psychological makeup, to me this is the most critical factor. Disruption at this point, I think, would be detrimental to the child even though Mr. Painter might well be a paragon of virtue. I think this would be a kind of thing which would not be in the best interest of the child. I think knowing something about where the child is at the present time is vital. I think something about where he might go, in my way of thinking, is essentially untenable to me, and relatively unimportant. It isn't even helpful. The thing I was most concerned about was Mark's view of his own reality in which he presently lives. If this is destroyed I think it will have rather bad effects on Mark. I think then if one were to make a determination whether it would be to the parents' household, or the McNelly household, or X-household, then I think further study would be appropriate.

Doctor Hawks stated: "I am appalled at the tremendous task Mr. Painter would have if Mark were returned to him because he has got to build the relationship from scratch. There is essentially nothing on which to build at the present time. Mark is aware Mr. Painter is his father, but he is not very clear about what this means. In his own mind the father figure is Mr. Bannister. I think it would take a very strong person with everything in his favor in order to build a relationship as Mr. Painter would have to build at this point with Mark."

It was Doctor Hawks' opinion "the chances are very high [Mark] will go wrong if he is returned to his father." This is based on adoption studies which "establish that the majority of adoptions in children who are changed, from ages six to eight, will go bad, if they have had a prior history of instability, some history of prior movement. When I refer to instability I am referring to where there has been no attempt to establish a strong relationship." Although this is not an adoption, the analogy seems appropriate, for Mark who had a history of instability would be removed from the only home in which he has a clearly established "father figure" and placed with his natural father about whom his feelings are unclear.

We know more of Mr. Painter's way of life than Doctor Hawks. We have concluded that it does not offer as great a stability or security as the Bannister home. Throughout his testimony he emphasized Mark's need at this critical time is stability. He has it in the Bannister home.

Other items of Doctor Hawks' testimony which have a bearing on our decision follow. He did not consider the Bannisters' age anyway disqualifying. He was of the opinion that Mark could adjust to a change more easily later on, if one became necessary, when he would have better control over his environment.

He believes the presence of other children in the home would have a detrimental effect upon Mark's adjustment whether this occurred in the Bannister home or the Painter home.

The trial court does not say which of Doctor Hawks' statements he felt were exaggerated. We were most surprised at the inconsequential position to which he relegated the "biological father". He concedes "child psychologists are less concerned about natural parents than probably other professional groups are." We are not inclined to so lightly value the role of the natural father, but find much reason for his evaluation of this particular case.

Mark has established a father-son relationship with Mr. Bannister, which he apparently had never had with his natural father. He is happy, well adjusted and progressing nicely in his development. We do not believe it is for Mark's best interest to take him out of this stable atmosphere in the face of warnings of dire consequences from an eminent child psychologist and send him to an uncertain future in the father's home. Regardless of our appreciation of the father's love for his child and his desire to have him with him, we do not believe we have the moral right to gamble with this child's future. He should be encouraged in every way possible to know his father. We are sure there are many ways in which Mr. Painter can enrich Mark's life.

For the reasons stated, we reverse the trial court and remand the case for judgment in accordance herewith.—Reversed and remanded.

All JUSTICES concur except THORNTON, J., who concurs in result.

## NOTES AND QUESTIONS

1. Can you state concisely the reason given by the court for granting custody of Mark Painter to the Bannisters? Is there anything in the opinion which would lend credence to the charge that Harold Painter lost his son because he was a "political liberal"? Because he was a Bohemian? Because the Bannisters were Iowans? What would one look for in order to investigate the validity of such a charge? Can an argument be made that, despite the court's disclaimer, the custody decision was based on the Iowa judges' "choice of one of two ways of life"?

2. What is the relevance to the custody decision of Harold Painter's politics? His religion? The religion of his wife? The religious education planned for Mark? What is the relevance of the kind of house the Painter family would live in—so long as the "interior is inexpensively but tastefully decorated" and no question was raised as to its suitability as a shelter? What is the relevance of the "uncut weeds and wild oats," of Painter's desire to keep the outside of the house unpainted? What do the two funerals tell us about Harold Painter that we should want to know in making a custody decision?

Is, perhaps, all of this relevant because everything is relevant to determining the kind of person Harold is? If so, did the court consider "everything" in its decision?

Do all of these considerations establish that Mark would not have "security and stability" in his father's home? That his life there would be *insecure* and *unstable*? What are the conceptions of security and stability which the court entertains? Are they the only conceptions you can think of? Is there anything that Painter could say which would establish that despite his politics, his "Bohemianism," his job record, his religion, he still could offer his son stability and security? What conception of these notions might he offer?

Is there any relation, incidentally, between the Bannisters' age and their ability to provide Mark with "security and stability"? Note Dr. Hawks's statement that Mark "has a very warm feeling for Mr. Bannister." Is that the strongest kind of emotion one can feel for his "father figure"? Does the emotional relationship between a child and his "father figure" have anything to do with the child's "security and stability"?

3. If the Bannisters had been wholly unrelated to Mark—if for example he had been left with them by a kidnapper—would the court's analysis have been the same? Even though the Bannisters' had all of the material advantages and modes of living which the court held to be in Mark's "best interests"? Is it adequate to view the court's responsibility solely as one of determining the best interests of the child? Or are there other important interests involved?

What are the arguments which the court uses to rebut the statutorily prescribed "presumption of parental preference"? What are the kind of arguments which you would expect to qualify as adequate rebuttal? How would you go about determining whether a particular factor was given a presumption at all? How would you defend the proposition that the court in this case gave "parental preference" a presumption?

4. What evidence is adduced by the court to support the conclusion that "the return of custody to the father is likely to have a seriously disrupting and disturbing effect upon the child's development"? Is this conclusion based primarily on psychological studies? On the testimony of the child psychologist? Is there anything to indicate that these were *not* the bases of the court's decision?

5. Should the court have placed "a great deal of reliance on the testimony of Dr. Glenn R. Hawks, a child psychologist," given the trial court's assessment of his evidence? In Iowa child custody cases may be reviewed *de novo*—is this sufficient reason to disregard the findings on credibility below?

Was there "nothing in the written record to justify" the lower court's "summary dismissal of the opinions of this eminent child psychologist"? "Nothing" at all? Did the court itself accept all of the testimony of Dr. Hawks? What criterion did it use to choose between the testimony it accepted and the testimony it rejected? Why is that criterion important to an adequate understanding of the court's decision in this case?

Is it sufficient that "there is nothing in the record which suggests that" Dr. Hawks's "relationship with the Bannisters is such that his professional opinion would be influenced thereby"? How difficult is it for a party to come up with a favorable expert witness even when he is *not* a personal acquaintance?

Consider Dr. Hawks's statement that he was not interested in "where he [Mark] might go," that "it isn't even helpful"? Does that statement give cause to question the psychologist's authority? Did the court actually accept it? Would you think that Harold Painter's personality and home would be relevant to the conclusion which Dr. Hawks ultimately reached, namely that "the chances are very high [Mark] will go wrong if he is returned to his father"?

How would the court know whether the analogy to adoptions "seems appropriate"? Is this a matter for common sense? Can you think of any differences between Mark's case and the adoption cases on which the court relies?

Consider Dr. Hawks's position that he did not think "the Bannisters' age anyway disqualifying"? Is this a conclusion with which you are comfortable? Is there no way in which the Bannisters' age would constitute some kind of drawback?

Consider Dr. Hawks's conclusion that the "presence of other children in the home would have a detrimental effect upon Mark's adjustment." Do you think this is a debatable point? Or is it settled by Dr. Hawks's authority?

Is child psychology the kind of field in which one is likely to find overwhelming uniformity of opinion? Is it a field whose practitioners are entitled to declaim with certainty their conclusions? Did the court in fact treat it as such a field?

What remaining evidence did the court have to support its decision to take a child from a concededly normal, morally fit parent and give him to his grandparents? Was it strong enough to support the conclusions the court reaches? In light of a presumption in favor of the parent?

6.  Note that the court begins its opinion with a fairly elaborate statement of its responsibility in this case? Does the opinion support the notion discussed in the last section that recognition of responsibility will lead to better judicial method and better judicial decisions?

Could it be argued that the court acted responsibly precisely because it imposed its own values on Harold and Mark Painter— values which it thought were important to society? Consider this question in light of the materials which follow in this chapter.

NOTE: PSYCHOANALYTIC AND SPIRITUAL CATEGORIES

In the following sections you will encounter a number of psychoanalytic, psychological, and spiritual statements about the human condition. They are meant to provide a basis for criticism and fuller understanding of such phenomena as Painter v. Bannister. You should ask yourself whether they open up avenues of inquiry that did not occur to you as you read the *Painter* case. On the answer to this, it may be, will hinge your personal decision as to the usefulness of the kind of statements psychoanalytic, existentialist and other thinkers make. To what extent do the phenomena which are described by Frenkel-Brunswik and Sartre correspond to portions of your own experience? To what extent do they help you to understand inarticulate judgments and predispositions which you have noted in yourself? To what extent do they help you to make actual decisions?

To what extent were the concepts and experiences which these writings present available to the persons involved in *Painter*? To Harold Painter? To his lawyer? To the Bannisters? To the child psychologist? To the court? What avenues of inquiry might you have expected to see in the court's opinion if the court had recently read these writers? What unsaid would have been said? What said unsaid?

## A.  Self-Obliviousness

JOSEPH CHURCH

### LANGUAGE AND THE DISCOVERY OF REALITY *

While the adolescent's self-esteem continues to be dependent on public opinion, he is beginning, too, to define more abstract, ideal standards to which he compares himself. The adolescent's self-judgments include some which are factually quite accurate, some which are much too harsh, and some which give him rather more credit than he deserves.

Like the adult, the adolescent seeks self-understanding only up to a point. There are some things he would rather not know about, because they conflict with either the standards of the group or his own professed ideals. In addition, to acknowledge some impulses is tantamount to approving them, and approving them to acting on them. In short, a portion of the adolescent's (and adult's) self-knowledge is cast in the form of the "defense mechanisms" mentioned earlier —denial, reaction formation, rationalization, projection, displacement, and so forth. The defense mechanisms work in either of two ways. One can refuse to give a name to a wish, impulse, attitude, or idea, thus denying its existence; or else one can give it a verbal formulation which masks its true nature and so neutralize it. We can see an early defense mechanism in the legalistic quibble of the school-age child: "You said not to hit him. I only gave him a little shove."

### QUESTIONS

Is the court's assertion in Bannister that it is not choosing between alternative ways of life, but only seeking security and stability in the best interests of Mark, simply a "defense mechanism"? Is the position that Harold Painter's life is normal, but unstable a mode of expression by which the court seeks to deceive itself? What evidence is there to support such a thesis? What motive would the court be trying to avoid acknowledging? What is wrong with such a motive?

* From 105 (Vintage ed. 1961). Reprinted with permission of Joseph Church.

*Else Frenkel-Brunswik*

## Sex, People and Self as Seen Through the Interviews *

### 2. Moralistic Condemnation vs. Permissiveness

High-scoring individuals were found to tend toward a *moralistic condemnation* of other people while *permissiveness towards individuals* is more common in our low scorers. . . .

It is easy to understand why condemnation of people, based on an external and conventional set of values, should be closely connected with prejudice; in fact, such an attitude seems close to being the very essence of prejudice.

The records, quoted below, of subjects scoring high on overt ethnocentrism illustrate a readiness to condemn others on such external bases as absence of good manners, uncleanliness, "twitching the shoulders," saying "inappropriate" things (inappropriate, as will be seen, on a superficial level only), and so forth.

The statements show a great deal of indulgence in what is seen as "righteous indignation" about people considered as inferior. This indignation seems to serve the double purpose of externalizing what is unacceptable in oneself, and of displacing one's hostility which otherwise might turn against powerful groups," e. g., the parents.

Furthermore, the subsequent records presented . . . contain statements referring to a positive ideal of how one should behave, the essence of which is expressed by one of the subjects in this group who demands that everybody should have a "set of rules"; these rules turn out to be determined either by convention or by a shallow interpretation of church dogma. The emphasis on conventional values is found in the respectable as well as in the delinquent high scorer. . . .

### 3. Extrapunitiveness

Another attitude, quite directly akin to prejudice, is that of extrapunitiveness, to use Rosenzweig's term, i. e., a tendency to blame other people rather than oneself. As has been repeatedly pointed out in this volume, lack of insight into one's own shortcomings and the projection of one's own weaknesses and faults onto others is often found in high-scoring subjects. It probably represents the essential aspect of the mechanism of scapegoating.

An opposite variant to extrapunitiveness is *impunitiveness*, i. e., the tendency to refrain from blaming altogether, be it others or oneself. . . .

. . .

### 4. Conventionalism and Moralism

Likewise in line with some of the findings reported earlier is the tendency of high-scoring men and women to think of themselves as basically highly moral and controlled and to consider any conduct which contradicts this norm as a "break-through" of tendencies which cannot be explained or influenced. The above quotations illustrate the tendency these individuals have to describe themselves as honest and as possessing high ideals and self-control in the sense of a *conventional moralism*. Low-scoring subjects, on the other hand, more readily admit *fallibility of self-control* without trying to explain it away as a break-through of something foreign to their basic nature.

. . .

. . .

### 5. *Conformity of Self and Ideal*

Lack of insight and of self-criticism on the part of the typical high scores is revealed in their tendency to mention as the type of person they would wish to be, as their *self-ideal, the same set of traits which they actually ascribe to themselves.* There is hardly any discrepancy between their image of what they ought to be and their conception of what they really are.

Thus, high-scoring men tend to mention as their ego-ideal the combination of traits characterized above as "pseudo-masculine" (determination, energy, industry, independence, decisiveness, will power, no passivity) as well as the syndrome of "moralistic conventionalism," likewise mentioned above.

An example of a more worrisome adoption of this type of ego-ideal in a high-scoring man is the following:

M52: (Worries?) "Well, I had worries, I remember that. I think my greatest desire was to be somebody in life. I did a lot of reading as a kid . . . . I was sort of a hero worshipper—nobody particularly—I wanted to be a success in business. I used to plan, and sometimes worried about whether I would."

The following quotations illustrate the admiration high-scoring men have for men of action and success, such as MacArthur and Andrew Carnegie who "amounted to so much":

M47: "And then another one I like real well . . . this Patton. I like him for the same reason I like MacArthur. He went right up to the front. . . . He wouldn't send his men anywhere he wouldn't go himself."

M51: "Andrew Carnegie, I guess, I got from some of my relatives. . . . His coming over here with so little and amounting to so much. . . ."

High-scoring women likewise tend to list as the ideal the same traits which they mentioned in their self-description and which were summarized under the heading "pseudo-femininity" and "conventional moralism."

Low-scoring subjects, on the other hand, tend to mention, as their ideal, traits which are different from, or at least differently conceived from those which they ascribe to themselves. Being basically more secure, it seems, they can more easily afford to see a discrepancy between ego-ideal and actual reality. Seeing this discrepancy enables them to strive toward a better fulfillment of the ego-ideal. A study dealing with mechanisms of self-deception seems to indicate that the more aware subjects are of falling short of their ideals, the nearer they actually are to the realization of these ideals.  (See 33)

. . .

Regardless of whether the specific topic was that of ambivalence, or aggression, or passivity, or some other related feature of personality dynamics, the outstanding finding was that the extremely unprejudiced individual tends to manifest a greater readiness to become aware of unacceptable tendencies and impulses in himself.  The prejudiced individual tends to manifest a greater readiness to become aware of unacceptable tendencies and impulses in himself.  The prejudiced individual, on the other hand, is more apt not to face these tendencies openly and thus to fail in integrating them satisfactorily with the conscious image he has of himself.  The resultant break between the conscious and the unconscious layers in the personality of the high scorers, as compared with the greater fluidity of transition and of intercommunication between the different personality strata in the low scorers, appears to have the greatest implications for their respective personality patterns.

### 3.  Externalization vs. Internalization

Among the tendencies which the typical high scorer attempts to keep in a repressed state (but which nonetheless find indirect expression in the interview) are mainly fear, weakness, passivity, sex impulses, and aggressive feeling against authoritative figures, especially the parents.  Among the rigid defenses against these tendencies there is, above all, the mechanism of projection, by which much of what cannot be accepted as part of one's own ego is externalized.  Thus it is not oneself but others that are seen as hostile and threatening.  Or else one's own weakness leads to an exaggerated condemnation of everything that is weak; one's own weakness is thus fought outside instead of inside.  At the same time there is a compensatory —and therefore often compulsive—drive for power, strength, success, and self-determination.

Repression and externalization of the instinctual tendencies mentioned reduces their manageability and the possibility of their control by the individual, since it is now the external world to which the feared qualities of the unconscious are ascribed.  As long as social conditions are conducive to and furnish acceptable outlets for compensatory tendencies, a relative mental balance within the individual may well be achieved in this manner.

Another aspect of externalization may be found in a tendency toward avoidance of introspection and of insight in general, thus rendering the content of consciousness relatively narrow.  Since the energy of the person is in this case largely devoted either to keeping instinctual tendencies out of consciousness or to striving for external success and status, there appears to be relatively little left for genuine libidinization of one's interpersonal relationships, or of one's work, as ends in themselves.  The comparatively impoverished potentialities for interpersonal relationships may exhibit themselves either in a relatively restricted, conventional, but dependable approach to people, as found primarily in the more conservative subgroup of the high scorers, or in a ruthless, manipulative approach, as found in the more delinquent subgroup.

There also seems to be relatively little enjoyment of sensuality or of passive pleasure such as affection, companionship, or art and music on the part of the typical high scorer. Instead of these internalized pleasures, there is an inclination toward mobility and activity, and a striving for material benefits.

The composite picture of the low scorer, on the other hand, not only reveals greater readiness to accept and to face one's impulses and weaknesses, but also to ruminate about them. While for the high scorer possible loss of energy is connected with his tendency toward rigid repressions, the low scorer is apt to waste energies by indulging in often unfruitful introspection and by placing the blame for mishaps too much upon himself. In contrast to the high scorer's tendency toward externalization, the typical low scorer is prone to internalize in an excessive manner, and this is turn may lead to open anxiety, feelings of guilt, and other neurotic features.

The positive aspects of this latter kind of orientation are a more closely knit integration within the individual and a more internalized and more intensive, though not conflict-free, relation to others. The low scorer also tends to be oriented, more than is the high scorer, toward real achievement, toward intellectual or aesthetic goals, and toward the realization of socially productive values. His great capacity for intensive interpersonal relationships goes hand in hand with greater self-sufficiency. He struggles for the establishment of inner harmony and self-actualization whereas the high scorer is concentrated on an effort to adjust to the outside world and to gain power and success within it.

One of the results of greater internalization is the generally more creative and imaginative approach of the low scorer both in the cognitive and in the emotional sphere, as compared with a more constricted, conventional and stereotypical approach in the high scorer.

*4. Conventionalism vs. Genuineness*

. . .

Conformity to externalized values in the extremely prejudiced can be observed in a variety of spheres of life. One of the earliest expressions of this conventionality is to be found, probably, in the high scorer's attitude toward his parents. It is one of stereo-typical admiration, with little ability to express criticism or resentment. There are many indications that there actually is often considerable underlying hostility toward the parents which—though not always expressed—prevents the development of a truly affectionate relationship.

The greater genuineness of the low scorer is evident in his attitude toward the parents. His is an equalitarian conception of the parent-child relationship. This makes it possible for him to express criticism and resentment openly, and at the same time to have a more positive and affectionate relation with the parents. The descriptions of the parents given by the low scorers have an aspect of spontaneity: they depict real people with all their inherent assets and shortcomings.

## QUESTIONS

Does Frenkel-Brunswik describe symptoms which could be attributed to the persons involved in Painter v. Bannister? To Harold Painter? To the Bannisters? To the child psychologist? To the court? To what extent ought we to be concerned with the neurotic tendencies which Frenkel-Brunswik describes? Should they have any bearing on the decision in Painter? On our judgment of the court's performance? Of the court's criteria of decision?

*MAX LERNER*

### THE UNSOLD CONSTITUENCY *

For anyone who believes that even senators are not simpletons it has been heartening to watch the response of the Senate to the Carswell nomination.

After the Haynsworth fiasco the Nixon-Mitchell-Thurmond axis was certain it had found in Judge Carswell the sure thing: A young Florida judge, a strict constructionist, with none of the financial shenanigans in his record that had plagued the Haynsworth nomination. For a time it looked as if he had renounced his early vow, as a fledgling politician, that he would never desert the cause of white supremacy.

But then came the erosion. . . .

There is a motion to recommit—to bury the nomination decently and permanently in the Judiciary Committee. It would be the kindest thing, both to Carswell and to Nixon. . . .

How did it happen? The obvious answer is Carswell's attitude toward the blacks, and there is little question that his hapless early speech and his role as an incorporator of a lily-white club counted against him, along with his civil rights rulings.

Important as this was . . ., I doubt whether the civil rights issue was in itself decisive. In the defeat of Judge Haynsworth there had to be another issue, the financial one. In Carswell's case it is the dismal mediocrity of his legal mind and judicial record and—beyond that—the slipperiness he showed in rebutting and minimizing the charges against him.

Any one of these—the race issue, the mediocrity, the lack of candor—might have been shrugged off. The three together cannot be.

One cross that poor Carswell had to bear was the intellectual quality of his managers. The argument of his chief defender, Sen. Roman L. Hruska, is likely to go down as a historic gem: "Even if he

* From L. A. Times, March 30, 1970, Part II, at 9. Copyright, Los Angeles Times. Reprinted by permission.

were mediocre, there are a lot of mediocre judges and people and lawyers, and they are entitled to a little representation, aren't they? We can't have all Brandeises, Frankfurters and Cardozos." Carswell can survive his opponents, but can he survive his defenders?

*Jean-Paul Sartre*

## Reflections on the Jewish Question *

The antisemite willingly admits that the Jew is intelligent and hard-working. He will even admit that he is inferior to him in this respect. This concession costs him little. He has put these qualities, as it were, in parentheses. Or rather, they draw their merit from the man who possesses them: the more virtues a Jew has, the more dangerous he is. He considers himself an average man, modestly average, and in the last analysis a mediocre person. There is no example of an antisemite claiming individual superiority over the Jews. But do not believe for a second that this mediocrity is a cause for shame. On the contrary, he is well satisfied with it, I might even say he has chosen it. This man is afraid of any kind of solitude, that of the genius as well as that of the murderer: he is the man of the mob: no matter how short he is, he still takes the precaution of stooping for fear of standing out from the herd and of finding himself face to face with himself. If he has become an antisemite, it is because one cannot be antisemitic alone. This sentence: "I hate the Jews," is a sentence which is said in chorus; by saying it one connects oneself with a tradition and a community: that of the mediocre man. It is also well to recall that by consenting to mediocrity one is not necessarily humble, nor even modest. It is just the opposite: there is a passionate pride in being mediocre and antisemitism is an attempt to make mediocrity as such a virtue, to create an elite of the mediocre. For the antisemite, intelligence is Jewish, he can therefore disdain it in all tranquility, like all other Jewish virtues: these are all ersatz qualities which the Jews use to replace the well-balanced mediocrity which they will always lack. The true Frenchman, rooted in his province, in his country, carried along by a tradition of twenty centuries, having the advantage of ancestral wisdom, guided by proved customs, *does not need* intelligence. The basis of his virtue is the assimilation of the qualities which the work of a hundred generations has lent to objects which surround him, i. e., property. But it goes without saying that this refers to hereditary property and not to that which one buys for oneself. The antisemite misunderstands the principle of the diverse forms of modern property: money, stocks, etc. These are abstractions, things of reason which ally themselves to the abstract intelligence of the Jew. A stock belongs to no one since it can belong to everyone and then it is a sign of wealth, not a concrete piece of property. The antisemite can conceive of but one type of primitive and landowning appropriation based on a veritable magical connection with possession, in which the object possessed and its pos-

* From Existentialism from Dostoevsky to Sartre 276–277, 286–287 (W. Kaufmann ed. 1956). Reprinted by permission of Schocken Books, Inc.

sessor are linked by a mystical participation; he is the poet of land-holding.  It transfigures the owner, endowing him with a particular and concrete sensitivity.  Of course, this sensitivity is not addressed to the eternal verities, to universal values: the universal is Jewish since it has to do with the intelligence.  What this subtle sense will seize upon is just what the intelligence cannot discern.  In other words, the principle of antisemitism is that concrete possession of a particular object magically conveys its meaning.

.  .  .  .  He is a man who is afraid.  Not of the Jews, of course, but of himself, of his conscience, his freedom, of his instincts, of his responsibilities, of solitude, of change, of society and the world; of everything except the Jews.  He is a coward who does not want to admit his cowardice to himself; a murderer who represses and censures his penchant for murder without being able to restrain it and who nevertheless does not dare to kill except in effigy or in the anonymity of a mob; a malcontent who dares not revolt for fear of the consequences of his rebellion.  By adhering to antisemitism, he is not only adopting an opinion, he is choosing himself as a person.  He is choosing the permanence and the impenetrability of rock, the total irresponsibility of the warrior who obeys his leaders—and he has no leader.  He chooses to acquire nothing, to deserve nothing but that everything be given him as his birthright—and he is not noble.  He chooses finally, that good be readymade, not in question, out of reach; he dare not look at it for fear of being forced to contest it and seek another form of it.  The Jew is only a pretext: elsewhere it will be the Negro, the yellow race; the Jew's existence simply allows the antisemite to nip his anxieties in the bud by persuading himself that his place has always been cut out in the world, that it was waiting for him and that by virtue of tradition he has the right to occupy it.  Antisemitism, in a word, is fear of man's fate.  The antisemite is the man who wants to be pitiless stone, furious torrent, devestating lightning: in short, everything but a man.

## Notes and Questions

1.  Do you accept the connection between ethnic prejudice and mediocrity which Sartre proposes?  Try to spell out the intermediate propositions which support such a connection?  What kind of mediocrity is Sartre treating?  An emotional mediocrity?  A moral mediocrity?  A spiritual mediocrity?  Or would he draw a distinction between these?  What about intellectual mediocrity?  Is this also his subject?

2.  According to the writers in this section, is the neurotic or mediocrity more or less well-suited to deal with the problems of living?  Is he more or less able to achieve a life of "security and stability"?  How would they defend their answers?  What requirement of success-ful living would they focus on?

3.  Is the appointment of mediocre judges the beginning of the end of an independent judiciary?  How would you argue that it was?  What institutional need is denied by choosing mediocre judges?  Con-sider Hand's warnings and Frank's recommendation for strong

judicial personalities.  Does such strength ultimately lead to a demand by the public for weak judges?  If so, is this because the judges are irresponsible or the people are neurotic?  Is there any relationship between weakness and mediocrity?  Review Sartre's remarks above.

4.  What intellectual mistake does the neurotic's rule of action resemble.  Recall Whitehead's remarks on obscurantism in Chapter 12.  Consider this question in conjunction with the discussion of the plain meaning rule in Chapter 15.

## B.  Self-Consciousness

ELSE FRENKEL-BRUNSWIK

### SEX, PEOPLE AND SELF AS SEEN THROUGH THE INTERVIEWS *

The record of another low scorer gives evidence, over and above the absence of conventional morals, and a stressing of intrinsic values, of a tendency not to think very highly of oneself:

> M3: (Ideal wife?)  "Attractive, at least average.  I can't ask for too much there, with my looks.  At least as much intelligence as I have.  Fairly intelligent, in other words.  I don't care about religion and morals, as long as they are not too bad.  Her own damn business whether she is a virgin or not  .   .   .   .   Essential that she be a good companion, keep me well amused; companionship includes everything from conversation to sex, with emphasis on congeniality."

Some of the low scorers come close to a tendency toward obsessional rumination about their faults and the mistakes they have made.  The exaggerated feelings of guilt and self-deprecation constitute some of the major neurotic features common in low scorers.  They are frequently accompanied by depressions.  Instead of aggressive self-assertion, there is often an unhealthy trend toward withdrawal in the face of difficulties.

JEAN-PAUL SARTRE

### BEING AND NOTHINGNESS †

.   .   .   .   A homosexual frequently has an intolerable feeling of guilt and his whole existence is determined in relation to this feeling.  One will readily foresee that he is in self-deception.  In fact it frequently happens that this man, while recognizing his homosexual inclination, while avowing each and every particular misdeed which he has committed, refuses with all his strength to consider himself "a pederast."  His case is always "different," peculiar; there enters into it something of a game, of chance, of bad luck; the mistakes are

---

* From T. Adorno et al., The Authoritarian Personality 412 (Norton Lib. ed. 1969).  Copyright 1950 by The American Jewish Committee.  Reprinted by permission of Harper & Row, Publishers, Inc.

† From 63–65 (H. Barnes transl. 1956).  Copyright 1956 by Philosophical Library, Inc., New York and reprinted with its permission.

all in the past; they are not explained by a certain conception of the beautiful which women can not satisfy; we should see in them the results of a restless search, rather than the manifestations of a deeply rooted tendency, *etc., etc.* Here is assuredly a man in self-deception who borders on the comic since, acknowledging all the facts which are imputed to him, he refuses to draw from them the conclusion which they impose. His friend who is his most severe critic, becomes irritated with this duplicity. The critic asks only one thing—and perhaps then he will show himself indulgent: that the guilty one recognize himself as guilty, that the homosexual declare frankly—whether humbly or boastfully matters little—*"I am a pederast."* We ask here: Who is in self-deception? The homosexual or the champion of sincerity?

The homosexual recognizes his faults, but he struggles with all his strength against the crushing view that his mistakes constitute for him *a destiny.* He does not wish to let himself be considered as a thing. He has an obscure but strong feeling that an homosexual is not an homosexual as this table is a table or as this red-haired man is red-haired. It seems to him that he has escaped from each mistake as soon as he has posited it and recognized it; he even feels that the psychic duration by itself cleanses him from each misdeed, constitutes for him an undetermined future, causes him to be born anew. Is he wrong? Does he not recognize in himself the peculiar, irreducible character of human reality? His attitude includes then an undeniable comprehension of truth. But at the same time he needs this perpetual rebirth, this constant evasion in order to live; he must constantly put himself beyond reach in order to avoid the terrible judgement of collectivity. Thus he plays on the word *being.* He would be right actually if he understood the phrase, "I am not a pederast" in the sense of "I am not what I am." That is, if he declared to himself, "To the extent that a pattern of conduct is defined as the conduct of a pederast and to the extent that I have taken on this conduct, I am a pederast. But to the extent that human reality can not be finally defined by patterns of conduct, I am not one." But instead he slides surreptitiously towards a different connotation of the word "being." He understands "not being" in the sense of "not being in itself." He lays claim to "not being a pederast" in the sense in which this table *is not* an inkwell. He is in self-deception.

But the champion of sincerity is not ignorant of the transcendence of human reality and he knows how at need to appeal to it for his own advantage. He makes use of it even and brings it up in the present argument. Does he not wish, first in the name of sincerity, then of freedom, that the homosexual reflect on himself and acknowledge himself as an homosexual? Does he not let the other understand that such a confession will win indulgence for him? What does this mean if not that the man who will acknowledge himself as an homosexual will no longer be *the same* as the homosexual whom he acknowledges being, and that he will escape into the region of freedom and of good will. The critic asks the man then to be what he is in order no longer to be what he is. It is the profound meaning of the saying, "A sin confessed is half pardoned." He demands of the guilty one that he constitute himself as a thing, precisely in order no longer to treat him as a thing.  And this contradiction is constitutive of the demand of sincerity.  Who can not see how offensive to the other and how reassuring for me is a statement such as, "He's just a pederast," which removes a disturbing freedom from a trait and which aims at henceforth constituting all the acts of the other as consequences following strictly from his essence.  That is actually what the critic is demanding of his victim—that he constitute himself as a thing, that he should entrust his freedom to his friend as a fief, in order that the friend should return it to him subsequently—like a suzerain to his vassal.

.   .   .   .

The man who confesses that he is evil has exchanged his disturbing "freedom-for-evil" for an inanimate character of evil; he *is* evil, he clings to himself, he is what he is.  But by the same stroke, he escapes from that *thing*, since it is he who contemplates it, since it depends on him to maintain it under his glance or to let it collapse in an infinity of particular acts.  He derives a *merit* from his sincerity, and the deserving man is not the evil man as he is evil but as he is beyond his evilness.  At the same time the evil is disarmed since it is nothing, save on the plane of determinism, and since in confessing it, I posit my freedom in respect to it; my future is virgin; everything is allowed to me.

Thus the essential structure of sincerity does not differ from that of self-deception since the sincere man constitutes himself as what he is *in order not to be it.*  This explains the truth recognized by all, that one can fall into self-deception through being sincere.   .   .   . Total, constant sincerity as a constant effort to adhere to oneself is by nature a constant effort to dissociate oneself from oneself.  A person frees himself from himself by the very act by which he makes himself an object for himself.  To draw up a perpetual inventory of what one is means constantly to redeny oneself and to take refuge in a sphere where one is no longer anything put a pure, free regard.  The goal of self-deception, as we said, is to put oneself out of reach, it is an escape.  Now we see that we must use the same terms to define sincerity.

## C.   *Social and Personal Determinants of Self-Deception*

ERICH FROMM

### ESCAPE FROM FREEDOM *

It is important to consider how our culture fosters this tendency to conform, even though there is space for only a few outstanding examples.  The suppression of spontaneous feelings, and thereby of the development of genuine individuality, starts very early, as a matter of fact with the earliest training of a child.  This is not to say that training must inevitably lead to suppression of spontaneity if the real aim of education is to further the inner independence and individuality of the child, its growth and integrity. The restrictions which such a kind of education may have to impose upon the growing child are only transitory measures that really support the process of growth and expansion. In our culture, however, education too often results in the elimination of spontaneity and in the substitution of original psychic acts by superimposed feelings, thoughts, and wishes. (By original I do not mean, let me repeat, that an idea has not been thought before by someone else, but that it originates in the individual, that it is the result of his own activity and in this sense is *his* thought.) To choose one illustration somewhat arbitrarily, one of the earliest suppressions of *feelings* concerns hostility and dislike. To start with, most children have a certain measure of hostility and rebelliousness as a result of their conflicts with a surrounding world which tends to block their expansiveness and to which, as the weaker opponent, they usually have to yield. It is one of the essential aims of the educational process to eliminate this antagonistic reaction. The methods are different; they vary from threats and punishments, which frighten the child, to the subtler methods of bribery or "explanations," which confuse the child and make him give up his hostility. The child starts with giving up the expression of his feeling and eventually gives up the very feeling itself. Together with that, he is taught to suppress the awareness of hostility and insincerity in others; sometimes this is not entirely easy, since children have a capacity for noticing such negative qualities in others without being so easily deceived by words as adults usually are. They still dislike somebody "for no good reason" —except the very good one that they feel the hostility, or insincerity, radiating from that person. This reaction is soon discouraged; it does not take long for the child to reach the "maturity" of the average adult and to lose the sense of discrimination between a decent person and a scoundrel, as long as the latter has not committed some flagrant act.

On the other hand, early in his education, the child is taught to have feelings that are not at all "his"; particularly is he taught to like people, to be uncritically friendly to them, and to smile. What education may not have accomplished is usually done by social pressure in later life. If you do not smile you are judged lacking in a "pleasing personality"—and you need to have a pleasing personality if you want to sell your services, whether as a waitress, a salesman, or a physician. Only those at the bottom of the social pyramid, who sell nothing but their physical labor, and those at the very top do not need to be particularly "pleasant." Friendliness, cheerfulness, and everything that a smile is supposed to express, become automatic responses which one turns on and off like an electric switch.

To be sure, in many instances the person is aware of merely making a gesture; in most cases, however, he loses that awareness and thereby the ability to discriminate between the pseudo feeling and spontaneous friendliness.

It is not only hostility that is directly suppressed and friendliness that is killed by superimposing its counterfeit. A wide range of spontaneous emotions are suppressed and replaced by pseudo feelings.

Freud has taken one such suppression of sex. Although I believe that the discouragement of sexual joy is not the only important suppression of spontaneous reactions but one of many, certainly its importance is not to be underrated. Its results are obvious in cases of sexual inhibitions and also in those where sex assumes a compulsive quality and is consumed like liquor or a drug, which has no particular taste but makes you forget yourself. Regardless of the one or the other effect, their suppression, because of the intensity of sexual desires, not only affects the sexual sphere but also weakens the person's courage for spontaneous expression in all other spheres.

In our society emotions in general are discouraged. While there can be no doubt that any creative thinking—as well as any other creative activity—is inseparably linked with emotion, it has become an ideal to think and to live without emotions. To be "emotional" has become synonymous with being unsound or unbalanced. By the acceptance of this standard the individual has become greatly weakened; his thinking is impoverished and flattened. On the other hand, since emotions cannot be completely killed, they must have their existence totally apart from the intellectual side of the personality; the result is the cheap and insincere sentimentality with which movies and popular songs feed millions of emotion-starved customers.

There is one tabooed emotion that I want to mention in particular, because its suppression touches deeply on the roots of personality: the sense of tragedy. As we saw in an earlier chapter, the awareness of death and of the tragic aspect of life, whether dim or clear, is one of the basic characteristics of man. Each culture has its own way of coping with the problem of death. For those societies in which the process of individuation has progressed but little, the end of individual existence is less of a problem since the experience of individual existence itself is less developed. Death is not yet conceived as being basically different from life. Cultures in which we find a higher development of individuation have treated death according to their social and psychological structure. The Greeks put all emphasis on life and pictured death as nothing but a shadowy and dreary continuation of life. The Egyptians based their hopes on a belief in the indestructibility of the human body, at least of those whose power during life was indestructible. The Jews admitted the fact of death realistically and were able to reconcile themselves with the idea of the destruction of individual life by the vision of a state of happiness and justice ultimately to be reached by mankind in this world. Christianity has made death unreal and tried to comfort the unhappy individual by promises of a life after death. Our own era simply denies death and with it one fundamental aspect of life. Instead of allowing the awareness of death and suffering to become one of the strongest incentives for life, the basis for human solidarity, and an experience without which joy and enthusiasm lack intensity and depth, the individual is forced to repress it. But, as is always the case with repression, by being removed from sight the repressed elements do not cease to exist. Thus the fear of death lives an illegitimate existence among us. It remains alive in spite of the attempt to deny it, but being repressed it remains sterile.  It is one source of the flatness of other experiences, of the restlessness pervading life, and it explains, I would venture to say, the exorbitant amount of money this nation pays for its funerals.

In the process of tabooing emotions modern psychiatry plays an ambiguous role.  On the one hand its greatest representative, Freud, has broken through the fiction of the rational, purposeful character of the human mind and opened a path which allows a view into the abyss of human passions.  On the other hand psychiatry, enriched by these very achievements of Freud, has made itself an instrument of the general trends in the manipulation of personality.  Many psychiatrists, including psychoanalysts, have painted the picture of a "normal" personality which is never too sad, too angry, or too excited.  They use words like "infantile" or "neurotic" to denounce traits or types of personalities that do not conform with the conventional pattern of a "normal" individual.  This kind of influence is in a way more dangerous than the older and franker forms of name-calling.  Then the individual knew at least that there was some person or some doctrine which criticized him and he could fight back.  But who can fight back at "science"?

The same distortion happens to original *thinking* as happens to feelings and emotions.  From the very start of education original thinking is discouraged and ready-made thoughts are put into people's heads.  .   .   .

*DAVID RIESMAN WITH NATHAN GLAZER AND REUEL DENNEY*

## THE LONELY CROWD *

.   .   .

This is a book about social character and about the differences in social character between men of different regions, eras, and groups.  It considers the ways in which different social character types, once they are formed at the knee of society, are then deployed in the work, play, politics, and child-rearing activities of society.  More particularly, it is about the way in which one kind of social character, which dominated America in the nineteenth century, is gradually being replaced by a social character of quite a different sort.  Why this happened; how it happened; what are its consequences in some major areas of life: this is the subject of this book.

.   .   .

.   .   .

### 1.  *Character and Society*

What is the relation between social character and society?  How is it that every society seems to get, more or less, the social character it "needs"?  Erik H. Erikson writes, in a study of the social character of the Yurok Indians, that ".   .   .   systems of child

* From 3, 5-7, 8-9, 11-12, 13-25 (1964).    Yale University Press and reprinted
  Copyright (c) 1950, 1953, 1961 by    with its permission.
  Bishin & Stone Law, Language & Ethics UCB—61

training  .  .  .  represent unconscious attempts at creating out of human raw material that configuration of attitudes which is (or once was) the optimum under the tribe's particular natural conditions and economic-historic necessities."

From "economic-historic necessities" to "systems of child training" is a long jump. Much of the work of students of social character has been devoted to closing the gap and showing how the satisfaction of the largest "needs" of society is prepared, in some half-mysterious way, by its most intimate practices. Erich Fromm succinctly suggests the line along which this connection between society and character training may be sought: "In order that any society may function well, its members must acquire the kind of character which makes them *want* to act in the way they *have* to act as members of the society or of a special class within it. They have to *desire* what objectively is necessary for them to do. *Outer force* is replaced by *inner compulsion,* and by the particular kind of human energy which is channeled into character traits."

Thus, the link between character and society—certainly not the only one, but one of the most significant, and the one I choose to emphasize in this discussion—is to be found in the way in which society ensures some degree of conformity from the individuals who make it up. In each society, such a mode of ensuring conformity is built into the child, and then either encouraged or frustrated in later adult experience. (No society, it would appear, is quite prescient enough to ensure that the mode of conformity it has inculcated will satisfy those subject to it in every stage of life.) I shall use the term "mode of conformity" interchangeably with the term "social character"—though certainly conformity is not all of social character: "mode of creativity" is as much a part of it. However, while societies and individuals may live well enough—if rather boringly—without creativity, it is not likely that they can live without some mode of conformity—even be it one of rebellion.

My concern in this book is with two revolutions and their relation to the "mode of conformity" or "social character" of Western man since the Middle Ages. The first of these revolutions has in the last four hundred years cut us off pretty decisively from the family- and the clan-oriented traditional ways of life in which mankind has existed throughout most of history; this revolution includes the Renaissance, the Reformation, the Counter-Reformation, the Industrial Revolution, and the political revolutions of the seventeenth, eighteenth, and nineteenth centuries. This revolution is, of course, still in process, but in the most advanced countries of the world, and particularly in America, it is giving way to another sort of revolution—a whole range of social developments associated with a shift from an age of production to an age of consumption.

The first revolution we understand moderately well; it is, under various labels, in our texts and our terminology; this book has nothing new to contribute to its description, but perhaps does contribute something to its evaluation. The second revolution, which is just beginning, has interested many contemporary observers, including social scientists, philosophers, and journalists.  Both description and evaluation are still highly controversial; indeed, many are still preoccupied with the first set of revolutions and have not invented the categories for discussing the second set.  In this book I try to sharpen the contrast between, on the one hand, conditions and character in those social strata that are today most seriously affected by the second revolution, and, on the other hand, conditions and character in analogous strata during the earlier revolution; in this perspective, what is briefly said about the traditional and feudal societies which were overturned by the first revolution is in the nature of backdrop for these later shifts.

One of the categories I make use of is taken from demography, the science that deals with birth rates and death rates, with the absolute and relative numbers of people in a society, and their distribution by age, sex, and other variables, for I tentatively seek to link certain social and charaterological developments, as cause and effect, with certain population shifts in Western society since the Middle Ages.

. . .

The society of high growth potential develops in its typical members a social character whose conformity is insured by their tendency to follow tradition: these I shall term *tradition-directed* people and the society in which they live *a society dependent on tradition-direction*.

The society of transitional population growth develops in its typical members a social character whose conformity is insured by their tendency to acquire early in life an internalized set of goals. These I shall term *inner-directed* people and the society in which they live *a society dependent on inner-direction*.

Finally, the society of incipient population decline develops in its typical members a social character whose conformity is insured by their tendency to be sensitized to the expectations and preferences of others.  These I shall term *other-directed* people and the society in which they live one *dependent on other-direction*.

Let me point out, however, before embarking on a description of these three "ideal types" of character and society, that I am not concerned here with making the detailed analysis that would be necessary before one could prove that a link exists between population phase and character type.  Rather, the theory of the curve of population provides me with a kind of shorthand for referring to the myriad institutional elements that are also—though usually more heatedly—symbolized by such words as "industrialism," "folk society," "monopoly capitalism," "urbanization," "rationalization," and so on.  Hence when I speak here of traditional growth or incipient decline of population in conjunction with shifts in character and conformity, these phrases should not be taken as magical and comprehensive explanations.

. . .

*A definition of tradition-direction.*  Since the type of social order we have been discussing is relatively unchanging, the conformity of the individual tends to reflect his membership in a particular age-grade, clan, or caste; he learns to understand and appreciate patterns which have endured for centuries, and are modified but slightly as the generations succeed each other.   The important relationships of life may be controlled by careful and rigid etiquette, learned by the young during the years of intensive socialization that end with initiation into full adult membership.   Moreover, the culture, in addition to its economic tasks, or as part of them, provides ritual, routine, and religion to occupy and to orient everyone.   Little energy is directed toward finding new solutions of the age-old problems, let us say, of agricultural technique or medicine, the problems to which people are acculturated.

It is not to be thought, however, that in these societies, where the activity of the individual member is determined by characterologically grounded obedience to traditions, the individual may not be highly prized and, in many instances, encouraged to develop his capabilities, his initiative, and even, within very narrow time limits, his aspirations.   Indeed, the individual in some primitive societies is far more appreciated and respected than in some sectors of modern society.   For the individual in a society dependent on tradition-direction has a well-defined functional relationship to other members of the group.   If he is not killed off, he "belongs"—he is not "surplus," as the modern unemployed are surplus, nor is he expendable as the unskilled are expendable in modern society.   But by very virtue of his "belonging," life goals that are *his* in terms of conscious choice appear to shape his destiny only to a very limited extent, just as only to a limited extent is there any concept of progress for the group.

In societies in which tradition-direction is the dominant mode of insuring conformity, relative stability is preserved in part by the infrequent but highly important process of fitting into institutionalized roles such deviants as there are.   In such societies a person who might have become at a later historical stage an innovator or rebel, whose belonging, as such, is marginal and problematic, is drawn instead into roles like those of the shaman or sorcerer.   That is, he is drawn into roles that make a socially acceptable contribution, while at the same time they provide the individual with a more or less approved niche.   The medieval monastic orders may have served in a similar way to absorb many characterological "mutations."

In some of these societies certain individuals are encouraged toward a degree of individuality from childhood, especially if they belong to families of high status.   But, since the range of choice, even for high-status people, is minimal, the apparent social need for an individuated type of character is also minimal.   It is probably accurate to say that character structure in these societies is very largely "adjusted," in the sense that for most people it appears to be in tune with social institutions.   Even the few misfits "fit" to a degree; and only very rarely is one driven out of his social world.

This does not mean, of course, that the people are happy; the society to whose traditions they are adjusted may be a miserable one, ridden with anxiety, sadism, and disease. The point is rather that change, while never completely absent in human affairs, is slowed down as the movement of molecules is slowed down at low temperature; and the social character comes as close as it ever does to looking like the matrix of the social forms themselves.

. . .

## TRANSITIONAL GROWTH: INNER-DIRECTED TYPES

Except for the West, we know very little about the cumulation of small changes that can eventuate in a breakup of the tradition-directed type of society, leading it to realize its potential for high population growth. As for the West, however, much has been learned about the slow decay of feudalism and the subsequent rise of a type of society in which inner-direction is the dominant mode of insuring conformity.

Critical historians, pushing the Renaissance ever back into the Middle Ages, seem sometimes to deny that any decisive change occurred at all. On the whole, however, it seems that the greatest social and characterological shift of recent centuries did indeed come when men were driven out of the primary ties that bound them to the western medieval version of tradition-directed society. All later shifts, including the shift from inner-direction to other-direction, seem unimportant by comparison, although of course this latter shift is still under way and we cannot tell what it will look like when—if ever—it is complete.

A change in the relatively stable ratio of births to deaths which characterizes the period of high growth potentials, is both the cause and consequence of other profound social changes. In most of the cases known to us a decline takes place in mortality prior to a decline in fertility; hence there is some period in which the population expands rapidly. The drop in death rate occurs as the result of many interacting factors, among them sanitation, improved communications (which permit government to operate over a wider area and also permit easier transport of food to areas of shortage from areas of surplus), the decline, forced or otherwise, of infanticide, cannibalism, and other inbred kinds of violence. Because of improved methods of agriculture the land is able to support more people, and these in turn produce still more people.

Notestein's phrase, "transitional growth," is a mild way of putting it. The "transition" is likely to be violent, disrupting the stablized paths of existence in societies in which tradition-direction has been the principal mode of insuring conformity. The imbalance of births and death puts pressure on the society's customary ways. A new slate of character structures is called for or finds its opportunity in coping with the rapid changes—and the need for still more changes—in the social organization.

*A definition of inner-direction.* In western history the society that emerged with the Renaissance and Reformation and that is only now vanishing serves to illustrate the type of society in which inner-direction is the principal mode of securing conformity. Such a society is characterized by increased personal mobility, by a rapid accumulation of capital (teamed with devastating technological shifts), and by an almost constant *expansion:* intensive expansion in the production of goods and people, and extensive expansion in exploration, colonization, and imperialism. The greater choices this society gives—and the greater initiatives it demands in order to cope with its novel problems—are handled by character types who can manage to live socially without strict and self-evident tradition-direction. These are the inner-directed types.

The concept of inner-direction is intended to cover a very wide range of types. Thus, while it is essential for the study of certain problems to differentiate between Protestant and Catholic countries and their character types between the effects of the Reformation and the effects of the Renaissance, between the puritan ethic of the European north and west and the somewhat more hedonistic ethic of the European east and south, while all these are valid and, for certain purposes, important distinctions, the concentration of this study on the development of modes of conformity permits their neglect. It allows the grouping together of these otherwise distinct developments because they have one thing in common: *the source of direction for the individual is "inner" in the sense that it is implanted early in life by the elders and directed toward generalized but nonetheless inescapably destined goals.*

We can see what this means when we realize that, in societies in which tradition-direction is the dominant mode of insuring conformity, attention is focused on securing strict conformity in generally observable words and actions, that is to say, behavior. While behavior is minutely prescribed, individuality of character need not be highly developed to meet prescriptions that are objectified in ritual and etiquette—though to be sure, a social character *capable* of such behavioral attention and obedience is requisite. By contrast, societies in which inner-direction becomes important, though they also are concerned with behavioral conformity, cannot be satisfied with behavioral conformity alone. To many novel situations are presented, situations which a code cannot encompass in advance. Consequently the problem of personal choice, solved in the earlier period of high growth potential by channeling choice through rigid social organization, in the period of transitional growth is solved by channeling choice through a rigid though highly individualized character.

This rigidity is a complex matter. While any society dependent on inner-direction seems to present people with a wide choice of aims—such as money, possessions, power, knowledge, fame, goodness—these aims are ideologically interrelated, and the selection made by any one individual remains relatively unalterable throughout his life. Moreover, the means to those ends, though not fitted into as tight a frame of social reference as in the society dependent on tradition-direction, are nevertheless limited by the new voluntary associations—for instance, the Quakers, the Masons, the Mechanics' Associations—to which people tie themselves. Indeed, the term "tradition-direction" could be misleading if the reader were to conclude that the force of tradition has no weight for the inner-directed character. On the contrary, he is very considerably bound by traditions: they limit his ends and inhibit his choice of means. The point is rather that a splintering of tradition takes place, connected in part with the increasing division of labor and stratification of society. Even if the individual's choice of tradition is largely determined for him by his family, as it is in most cases, he cannot help becoming aware of the existence of competing traditions—hence of tradition as such. As a result he possesses a somewhat greater degree of flexibility in adapting himself to ever changing requirements and in return requires more from his environment.

As the control of the primary group is loosened—the group that both socializes the young and controls the adult in the earlier era— a new psychological mechanism appropriate to the more open society is "invented": it is what I like to describe as a psychological gyroscope. This instrument, once it is set by the parents and other authorities, keeps the inner-directed person, as we shall see, "on course" even when tradition, as responded to by his character, no longer dictates his moves. The inner-directed person becomes capable of maintaining a delicate balance between the demands upon him of his life goal and the buffeting of his external environment.

This metaphor of the gyroscope, like any other, must not be taken literally. It would be a mistake to see the inner-directed man as incapable of learning from experience or as insensitive to public opinion in matters of external conformity. He can receive and utilize certain signals from outside, provided that they can be reconciled with the limited maneuverability that his gyroscope permits him. His pilot is not quite automatic.

Huizinga's *The Waning of the Middle Ages* gives a picture of the anguish and turmoil, the conflict of values, out of which the new forms slowly emerged. Already by the late Middle Ages people were forced to live under new conditions of awareness. As their self-consciousness and their individuality developed, they had to make themselves at home in the world in novel ways. They still have to.

## INCIPIENT DECLINE OF POPULATION: OTHER-DIRECTED TYPES

The problem facing the societies in the stage of transitional growth is that of reaching a point at which resources become plentiful enough or are utilized effectively enough to permit a rapid accumulation has to be achieved even while the social product is being drawn on at an accelerated rate to maintain the rising population and satisfy the consumer demands that go with the way of life that has already been adopted. For most countries, unless capital and techniques can be imported from other countries in still later phases of the population curve, every effort to increase national resources at a rapid rate must actually be at the expense of current standards of living. We have seen this occur in the U.S.S.R., now in the stage of transitional growth.

For western Europe this transition was long-drawn-out and painful. For America, Canada, and Australia—at once beneficiaries of European techniques and native resources—the transition was rapid and relatively easy.

The tradition-directed person, as has been said, hardly thinks of himself as an individual. Still less does it occur to him that he might shape his own destiny in terms of personal, lifelong goals or that the destiny of his children might be separate from that of the family group. He is not sufficiently separated psychologically from himself (or, therefore, sufficiently close to himself), his family, or group to think in these terms. In the phase of transitional growth, however, people of inner-directed character do gain a feeling of control over their own lives and see their children also as individuals with careers to make. At the same time, with the shift out of agriculture and, later, with the end of child labor, children no longer become an unequivocal economic asset. And with the growth of habits of scientific thoughts, religious and magical views of human fertility—views that in an earlier phase of the population curve made sense for the culture if it was to reproduce itself—give way to "rational," individualistic attitudes. Indeed, just as the rapid accumulation of productive capital requires that people be imbued with the "Protestant ethic" (as Max Weber characterized one manifestation of what is here termed inner-direction), so also the decreased number of progeny requires a profound change in values—a change so deep that, in all probability, it has to be rooted in character structure.

As the birth rate begins to follow the death rate downward, societies move toward the epoch of incipient decline of population. Fewer and fewer people work on the land or in the extractive industries or even in manufacturing. Hours are short. People may have material abundance and leisure besides. They pay for these changes however—here, as always, the solution of old problems gives rise to new ones—by finding themselves in a centralized and bureaucratized society and a world shrunken and agitated by the contacted—accelerated by industrialization—of races, nations, and cultures.

The hard enduringness and enterprise of the inner-directed types are somewhat less necessary under these conditions. Increasingly, *other people* are the problem, not the material environment. And as people mix more widely and become more sensitive to each other, the surviving traditions from the stage of high growth potential—much disrupted, in any case, during the violent spurt of industrialization—become still further attenuated. Gyroscopic control is no longer sufficiently flexible, and a new psychological mechanism is called for.

Furthermore, the "scarcity psychology" of many inner-directed people, which was socially adaptive during the period of heavy capital accumulation that accompanied transitional growth of population, needs to give way to an "abundance psychology" capable of "wasteful" luxury consumption of leisure and of the surplus product. Unless people want to destroy the surplus product in war, which still does require heavy capital equipment, they must learn to enjoy and engage in those services that are expensive in terms of man power but not of capital—poetry and philosophy, for instance. Indeed, in the period of incipient decline, non-productive consumers, both the increasing number of old people and the diminishing number of as yet untrained young, form a high proportion of the population, and these need both the economic opportunity to be prodigal and the character structure that allows it.

Has this need for still another slate of character types actually been acknowledged to any degree? My observations lead me to believe that in America it has.

*A definition of other-direction.* The type of character I shall describe as other-directed seems to be emerging in very recent years in the upper middle class of our larger cities; more prominently in New York than in Boston, in Los Angeles than in Spokane, in Cincinnati than in Chillicothe. Yet in some respects this type is strikingly similar to the American, whom Tocqueville and other curious and astonished visitors from Europe, even before the Revolution, thought to be a new kind of man. Indeed, travelers' reports on America impress us with their unanimity. The American is said to be shallower, freer with his money, friendlier, more uncertain of himself and his values, more demanding of approval than the European. It all adds up to a pattern which, without stretching matters too far, resembles the kind of character that a number of social scientists have seen as developing in contemporary, highly industrialized, and bureaucratic America: Fromm's "marketer," Mill's "fixer," Arnold Green's "middle class male child."

It is my impression that the middle-class American of today is decisively different from those Americans of Tocqueville's writings who nevertheless strike us as so contemporary, and much of this book will be devoted to discussing these differences. It is also my impression that the conditions I believe to be responsible for other-direction are affecting increasing numbers of people in the metropolitan centers of the advanced industrial countries. My analysis of the other-directed character is thus at once an analysis of the American and of contemporary man. Much of the time I find it hard or impossible to say where one ends and the other begins. Tentatively, I am inclined to think that the other-directed type does find itself most at home in America, due to certain unique elements in American society, such as its recruitment from Europe and its lack of any feudal past. As against this, I am also inclined to put more weight on capitalism, industrialism, and urbanization—these being international tendencies —than on any character-forming peculiarities of the American scene.

Bearing these qualifications in mind, it seems appropriate to treat contemporary metropolitan America as our illustration of a society—so far, perhaps, the only illustration—in which other-direction is the dominant mode of insuring conformity. It would be premature, however, to say that it is already the dominant mode in America as a whole. But since the other-directed types are to be found among the young, in the larger cities, and among the upper income groups, we may assume that, unless present trends are reversed, the hegemony of other-direction lies not far off.

If we wanted to cast our social character types into social class molds, we could say that inner-direction is the typical character of the "old" middle class—the banker, the tradesman, the small entrepreneur, the technically oriented engineer, etc.—while other-direction is becoming the typical character of the "new" middle class—the bureaucrat, the salaried employee in business, etc. Many of the economic factors associated with the recent growth of the "new" middle class are well known. They have been discussed by James Burnham, Colin Clark, Peter Drucker, and others. There is a decline in the numbers and in the proportion of the working population engaged in production and extraction—agriculture, heavy industry, heavy transport—and an increase in the numbers and the proportion engaged in white-collar work and the service trades. People who are literate, educated, and provided with the necessities of life by an ever more efficient machine industry and agriculture, turn increasingly to the "tertiary" economic realm. The service industries prosper among the people as a whole and no longer only in court circles.

Education, leisure, services, these go together with an increased consumption of words and images from the new mass media of communications. While societies in the phase of transitional growth step up the process of distributing words from urban centers, the flow becomes a torrent in the societies of incipient population decline. This process, while modulated by profound national and class differences, connected with differences in literacy and loquacity, takes place everywhere in the industrialized lands. Increasingly, relations with the outer world and with oneself are mediated by the flow of mass communication. For the other-directed types political events are likewise experienced through a screen of words by which the events are habitually atomized and personalized—or pseudo-personalized. For the inner-directed person who remains still extent in this period the tendency is rather to systematize and moralize this flow of words.

These developments lead, for large numbers of people, to changes in paths to success and to the requirement of more "socialized" behavior both for success and for marital and personal adaptation. Connected with such changes are changes in the family and in child-rearing practices. In the smaller families of urban life, and with the spread of "permissive" child care to ever wider strata of the population, there is a relaxation of older patterns of discipline. Under these newer patterns the peer-group (the group of one's associates of the same age and class) becomes much more important to the child, while the parents make him feel guilty not so much about violation of inner standards as about failure to be popular or otherwise to manage his relations with these other children. Moreover, the pressures of the school and the peer-group are reinforced and continued—in a manner whose inner paradoxes I shall discuss later—by the mass medias movies, radio, comics, and popular culture media generally. Under these conditions types of character emerge that we shall here term other-directed. To them much of the discussion in the ensuing chapters is devoted. *What is common to all the other-directed people is that their contemporaries are the source of direction for the individual —either those known to him or those with whom he is indirectly ac-*

quainted, through friends and through the mass media.  This source is of course "internalized" in the sense that dependence on it for guidance in life is implanted early.  The goals toward which the other-directed person strives shift with that guidance; it is only the process of striving itself and the process of paying close attention to the signals from others that remain unaltered throughout life.  This mode of keeping in touch with others permits a close behavioral conformity, not through drill in behavior itself, as in the tradition-directed character, but rather through an exceptional sensitivity to the actions and wishes of others.

Of course, it matters very much who those "others" are: whether they are the individual's immediate circle or a "higher" circle or the anonymous voices of the mass media; whether the individual fears the hostility of chance acquaintances or only of those who "count." But his need for approval and direction from others—and contemporary others rather than ancestors—goes beyond the reasons that lead most people in any era to care very much what others think of them. While all people want and need to be liked by some of the people some of the time, it is only the modern other-directed types who make this their chief source of direction and chief area of sensitivity.

It is perhaps the insatiable force of this psychological need for approval that differentiates people of the metropolitan, American upper middle class, whom we regard as other-directed, from very similar types that have appeared in capital cities and among other classes in previous historical periods, whether in Imperial Canton, in eighteenth and nineteenth–century Europe, or in ancient Athens, Alexandria, or Rome.  In all these groups fashion not only ruled as a substitute for morals and customs, but it was a rapidly changing fashion that held sway.  It could do so because, although the mass media were in their infancy, the group corresponding to the American upper middle class was comparably small and the elite structure was extremely reverberant.  It can be argued, for example, that a copy of *The Spectator* covered its potential readership more thoroughly in the late eighteenth century than *The New Yorker* covers its readership today.  In eighteenth- and nineteenth-century English, French, and Russian novels, we find portraits of the sort of people who operated in the upper reaches of bureaucracy and had to be prepared for rapid changes of signals.  Stepan Arkadyevitch Oblonsky in *Anna Karenina* is one of the more likable and less opportunistic examples, especially striking because of the way Tolstoy contrasts him with Levin, a moralizing, inner-directed person.  At any dinner party Stepan manifests exceptional social skills; his political skills as described in the following quotation are also highly social:

> Stepan Arkadyevitch took in and read a liberal news-paper, not an extreme one, but one advocating the views held by the majority.  And in spite of the fact that science, art, and politics had no special interest for him, he firmly held those views on all subjects which were held by the majority and by his paper, and he only changed them when the majority changed them—or, more strictly speaking, he did not

*change them, but they imperceptively changed of themselves within him.*

*Stepan Arkadyevitch had not chosen his political opinions or his views; these political opinions and views had come to him of themselves, just as he did not choose the shapes his hats or coats, but simply took those that were being worn. And for him, living in a certain society—owing to the need, ordinarily developed at years of discretion, for some degree of mental activity—to have views was just as indispensable as to have a hat. If there was a reason for his preferring liberal to conservative views, which were held also by many of his circle, it arose not from his considering liberalism more rational, but from its being in closer accord with his manner of life . . . And so liberalism had become a habit of Stepan Arkadyevitch's, and he liked his newspaper, as he did his cigar after dinner, for the slight fog it diffused in his brain.*

Stepan, while his good-natured gregariousness makes him seem like a modern middle-class American, is not fully other-directed. This gregariousness alone, without a certain sensitivity to others as individuals and as a source of direction, is not the identifying trait. Just so, we must differentiate the nineteenth-century American—gregarious and subservient to public opinion though he was found to be by Tocqueville, Bryce, and others—from the other-directed American as he emerges today, an American who in his character is more capable of and more interested in maintaining responsive contact with others both at work and at play. This point needs to be emphasized, since the distinction is easily misunderstood. The inner-directed person, though he often sought and sometimes achieved a relative independence of public opinion and of what the neighbors thought of him, was in most cases very much concerned with his good repute and, at least in America, with "keeping up with the Joneses." These conformities, however, were primarily external, typified in such details as clothes, curtains, and bank credit. For, indeed, the conformities were to a standard, evidence of which was provided by the "best people" in one's milieu. In contrast with this pattern, the other-directed person, though he has his eye very much on the Joneses, aims to keep up with them not so much in external details as in the quality of his inner experience. That is, his great sensitivity keeps him in touch with others on many levels than the externals of appearance and propriety. Nor does any ideal of independence or of reliance on God alone modify his desire to look to the others—and the "good guys" as well as the best people—for guidance in what experiences to seek and in how to interpret them.

*The three types compared.* One way to see the structural differences that mark the three types is to see the differences in the emotional sanction or control in each type.

The tradition-directed person feels the impact of his culture as a unit, but it is nevertheless mediated through the specific, small number of individuals with whom he is in daily contact. These expect of him not so much that he be a certain type of person but that he behave in the approved way.   Consequently, the sanction for behavior tends to be the fear of being *shamed.*

The inner-directed person has early incorporated a psychic gyroscope which is set going by his parents and can receive signals later on from other authorities who resemble his parents.  He goes through life less independent than he seems, obeying this internal piloting. Getting off course, whether in response to inner impulses or to the fluctuating voices of contemporaries, may lead to the feeling of *guilt.*

Since the direction to be taken in life has been learned in the privacy of the home from a small number of guides and since principles, rather than details of behavior, are internalized, the inner-directed person is capable of great stability.  Especially so when it turns out that his fellows have gyroscopes too, spinning at the same speed and set in the same direction.  But many inner-directed individuals can remain stable even when the reinforcement of special approval is not available—as in the upright life of the stock Englishman isolated in the tropics.

Contrasted with such a type as this, the other-directed person learns to respond to signals from a far wider circle than is constituted by his parents.  The family is no longer a closely knit unit to which he belongs but merely part of a wider social environment to which he early becomes attentive.  In these respects the other-directed person resembles the tradition-directed person: both live in a group milieu and lack the inner-directed person's capacity to go it alone.  The nature of this group milieu, however, differs radically in the two cases. The other-directed person is cosmopolitan.  For him the border between the familiar and the strange—a border clearly marked in the societies depending on tradition-direction—has broken down.  As the family continuously absorbs the strange and reshapes itself, so the strange becomes familiar.  While the inner-directed person could be "at home abroad" by virtue of his relative insensitivity to others, the other-directed person is, in a sense, at home everywhere and nowhere, capable of a rapid if sometimes superficial intimacy with and response to everyone.

The tradition-directed person takes his signals from others, but they come in a cultural monotone; he needs no complex receiving equipment to pick them up.  The other-directed person must be able to receive signals from far and near; the sources are many, the changes rapid.  What can be internalized, then, is not a code of behavior but the elaborate equipment needed to attend to such messages and occasionally to participate in their circulation.  As against guilt-and-shame controls, though of course these survive, one prime psychological lever of the other-directed person is a diffuse *anxiety.*  This control equipment, instead of being like a gyroscope, is like a radar.

### QUESTIONS

Suppose it were conceded that the court in Painter v. Bannister chose the Bannisters over Harold Painter because it preferred the kind of people and the way of life which the former represented.

Does Riesman provide any justification for such a course of judicial conduct? Ought the courts to help their society (or sub-society) "get . . . the social character it 'needs'"? Do the courts have any choice about participating in the formation of "social character"? Could they choose not to participate in it? Could they choose not to involve themselves in its very statement and definition? If so, ought they to so choose? If not, how should they go about defining and stating the nature of a given social character? Ought it to be a conscious or an unconscious process? A relatively passive expression of social forces and predispositions or an active, constructive formulation of social needs, interests, relationships, and goals?

NORMAN O. BROWN

LIFE AGAINST DEATH *

There is one word which, if we only understand it, is the key to Freud's thought. That word is "repression." The whole edifice of psychoanalysis, Freud said, is based upon the theory of repression. Freud's entire life was devoted to the study of the phenomenon he called repression. The Freudian revolution is that radical revision of traditional theories of human nature and human society which becomes necessary if repression is recognized as a fact. In the new Freudian perspective, the essence of society is repression of the individual, and the essence of the individual is repression of himself.

The best way to explore the notion of repression is to review the path which led Freud to his hypothesis. Freud's breakthrough was the discovery of meaningfulness in a set of phenomena theretofore regarded, at least in scientific circles, as meaningless: first, the "mad" symptoms of the mentally deranged; second, dreams; and third, the various phenomena gathered together under the title of the psychopathology of everyday life, including slips of the tongue, errors, and random thoughts.

Now in what sense does Freud find meaningfulness in neurotic symptoms, dreams, and errors? He means, of course, that these phenomena are determined and can be given a causal explanation. He is rigorously insisting on unequivocal allegiance to the principle of psychic determinism; but he means much more than that. For if it were possible to explain these phenomena on behavioristic principles, as the result of superficial associations of ideas, then they would have a cause but no meaning. Meaningfulness means expression of a purpose or an intention. The crux of Freud's discovery is that neurotic symptoms, as well as the dreams and errors of everyday life, do have meaning, and that the meaning of "meaning" has to be radically revised because they have meaning. Since the purport of these purposive expressions is generally unknown to the person whose purpose they express, Freud is driven to embrace the paradox they express, Freud is driven to embrace the paradox that there are

* From 1–10, 55, 56, 57–62, 63–67 (Vintage ed. 1959). Copyright 1959 by Wesleyan University and reprint-ed by permission of Wesleyan University Press.

in a human being purposes of which he knows nothing, involuntary purposes, or, in more technical Freudian language, "unconscious ideas." From this point of view a new world of psychic reality is opened up, of whose inner nature we are every bit as ignorant as we are of the reality of the external world, and of which our ordinary conscious observation tells us no more than our sense organs are able to report to us of the external world. Freud can thus define psycho-analysis as "nothing more than the discovery of the unconscious in mental life."

But the Freudian revolution is not limited to the hypothesis of an unconscious psychic life in the human being in addition to his conscious life. The other crucial hypothesis is that some unconscious ideas in a human being are incapable of becoming conscious to him in the ordinary way, because they are strenuously disowned and re-sisted by the conscious self. From this point of view Freud can say that "the whole of psychoanalytic theory is in fact built up on the perception of the resistance exerted by the patient when we try to make him conscious of his unconscious." The dynamic relation be-tween the unconscious and the conscious life is one of conflict, and psychoanalysis is from top to bottom a science of mental conflict.

The realm of the unconscious is established in the individual when he refuses to admit into his conscious life a purpose or desire which he has, and in doing so establishes in himself a psychic force opposed to his own idea. This rejection by the individual of a purpose or idea, which nevertheless remains his, is repression. "The essence of repression lies simply in the function of rejecting or keeping some-thing out of consciousness." Stated in more general terms, the es-sence of repression lies in the refusal of the human being to recognize the realities of his human nature. The fact that the repressed pur-poses nevertheless remain his is shown by dreams and neurotic symp-toms, which represent an irruption of the unconscious into conscious-ness, producing not indeed a pure image of the unconscious, but a compromise between the two conflicting systems, and thus exhibiting the reality of the conflict.

Thus the notion of the unconscious remains an enigma without the theory of repression; or, as Freud says, "We obtain our theory of the unconscious from the theory of repression." To put it another way, the unconscious *is* "the dynamically unconscious repressed." Repression is the key word in the whole system; the word is chosen to indicate a structure dynamically based on psychic conflict. Freud illustrates the nature of psychic repression by a series of metaphors and analogies drawn from the social phenomena of war, civil war, and police action.

From neurotic symptoms, dreams, and errors to a general theory of human nature may seem like a long step. Granting that it is a long step, Freud could argue that he is entitled to explore the widest possible application of a hypothesis derived from a narrow field. He could take the offensive and claim that traditional theories of human nature must be regarded as unsatisfactory because they have nothing to say about these peripheral phenomena. What theory of human nature, except Freud's, does have anything significant to say about dreams or insanity? And are dreams and insanity really negligible factors on the periphery of human life?

But the truth of the matter is that Freud maintains that to go from neurotic symptoms, dreams, and errors, to a new theory of human nature in general involves no further step at all. For the evidence on which the hypothesis of the repressed unconscious is based entails the conclusion that it is a phenomenon present in all human beings. The psychopathological phenomena of everyday life, although trivial from a practical point of view, are theoretically important because they show the intrusion of unconscious intentions into our everyday and supposedly normal behavior.

Even more theoretically important are dreams. For dreams, also "normal" phenomena, exhibit in detail not only the existence of the unconscious but also the dynamics of its repression (the dream-censorship). But since the same dynamics of repression explained neurotic symptoms, and since the dreams of neurotics, which are a clue to the meaning of their symptoms, differ neither in structure nor in content from the dreams of normal people, the conclusion is that a dream is itself a neurotic symptom. We are all therefore neurotic. At least dreams show that the difference between neurosis and health prevails only by day; and since the psychopathology of everyday life exhibits the same dynamics, even the waking life of the "healthy" man is pervaded by innumerable symptom-formations. Between "normality" and "abnormality" there is no qualitative but only a quantitative difference, based largely on the practical question of whether our neurosis is serious enough to incapacitate us for work.

Or perhaps we are closer to the Freudian point of view if we give a more paradoxical formulation; the difference between "neurotic" and "healthy" is only that the "healthy" have a socially usual form of neurosis. At any rate, to quote a more technical and cautious formulation of the same theorem, Freud says that from the study of dreams we learn that the neuroses make use of a mechanism already in existence as a normal part of our psychic structure, not of one that is newly created by some morbid disturbance or other.

Thus Freud's first paradox, the existence of a repressed unconscious, necessarily implies the second and even more significant paradox, the universal neurosis of mankind. Here is the *pons asinorum* of psychoanalysis. Neurosis is not an occasional aberration; it is not just in other people; it is in us, and in us all the time. It is in the psychoanalyst: Freud discovered the Oedipus complex, which he regarded as the root of all neurosis, by self-analysis. *The Interpretation of Dreams* is one of the great applications and extensions of the Socratic maxim, "Know thyself." Or, to put it another way, the doctrine of the universal neurosis of mankind is the psychoanalytical analogue of the theological doctrine of original sin.

The crucial point in Freud's basic hypothesis is the existence of psychic conflict; the hypothesis cannot be meaningfully formulated without some further specification of the nature of the conflict and the conflicting forces. Now Freud made repeated analyses of the fundamental psychic conflict, at several different levels and from several points of view. Let us at this point try to abstract the common core from these various accounts.

In our first description of Freud's theory of repression we used the word "purpose" to designate that which is repressed into the unconscious. This excessively vague word conceals a fundamental Freudian axiom. The psychic conflict which produces dreams and neuroses is not generated by intellectual problems but by purposes, wishes, desires. Freud's frequent use of the term "unconscious idea" can be misleading here. But as Freud says, "We remain on the surface so long as we treat only of memories and ideas. The only valuable things in psychic life are, rather, the emotions. All psychic forces are significant only through their aptitude to arouse emotions. Ideas are repressed only because they are bound up with releases of emotions, which are not to come about; it would be more correct to say that repression deals with the emotions, but these are comprehensible to us only in their tie-up with ideas." Freud is never tired of insisting that dreams are in essence wish-fulfillments, expressions of repressed unconscious wishes, and neurotic symptoms likewise.

Now if we take "desire" as the most suitably abstract of this series of terms, it is a Freudian axiom that the essence of man consists, not, as Descartes maintained, in thinking, but in desiring. Plato (and, *mutatis mutandis*, Aristotle) identified the *summum bonum* for man with contemplation; since the *telos* or end is the basic element in definition, this amounts to saying that the essence of man is contemplation. But ambiguously juxtaposed with this doctrine of man as contemplator is the platonic doctrine of Eros, which, as elaborated by Plato in the *Symposium* and the *Phaedrus*, suggests that the fundamental quest of man is to find a satisfactory object for his love. A similar ambiguity between man as contemplator and man as lover is to be found in Spinoza and Hegel. The turning point in the Western tradition comes in the reaction to Hegel. Feuerbach, followed by Marx, calls for the abandonment of the contemplative tradition in favor of what he calls "practical-sensuous activity"; the meaning of this concept, and its relation to Freud, would take us far afield. But Schopenhauer, in his notion of the primacy of will—however much he may undo his own notion by his search for an escape from the primacy of the will—is a landmark, seceding from the great, and really rather insane, Western tradition that the goal of mankind is to become as contemplative as possible. Freudian psychology eliminates the category of pure contemplation as nonexistent. Only a wish, says Freud, can possibly set our psychic apparatus in motion.

With this notion of desire as the essence of man is joined a definition of desire an energy directed toward the procurement of pleasure and avoidance of pain. Hence Freud can say, "Our entire psychical activity is bent upon procuring pleasure and avoiding pain, is automatically regulated by the pleasure-principle." Or, "It is simply the pleasure-principle which draws up the programme of life's purpose." At this level of analysis, the pleasure-principle implies no complicated hedonistic theory nor any particular theory as to the sources of pleasure. It is an assumption taken from common sense, and means much the same as Aristotle's dictum that all men seek happiness: Freud says that the goal of the pleasure-principle is happiness.

But man's desire for happiness is in conflict with the whole world. Reality imposes on human beings the necessity of renunciation of pleasures; reality frustrates desire. The pleasure-principle is in conflict with the reality-principle, and this conflict is the cause of repression. Under the conditions of repression the essence of our being lies in the unconscious, and only in the unconscious does the pleasure-principle reign supreme. Dreams and neurotic symptoms show that the frustrations of reality cannot destroy the desires which are the essence of our being: the unconscious is the unsubdued and indestructible element in the human soul. The whole world may be against it, but still man holds fast to the deep-rooted, passionate striving for a positive fulfillment of happiness.

The conscious self, on the other hand, which by refusing to admit a desire into consciousness institutes the process of repression, is, so to speak, the surface of ourselves mediating between our inner real being and external reality. The nucleus of the conscious self is that part of the mind or system in the mind which receives perceptions from the external world. This nucleus acquires a new dimension through the power of speech, which makes it accessible to the process of education and acculturation. The conscious self is the organ of adaptation to the environment and to the culture. The conscious self, therefore, is governed not by the pleasure-principle but by the principle of adjustment to reality, the reality-principle.

From this point of view dreams and neurotic symptoms, which we previously analyzed as produced by the conflict between the conscious and unconscious systems, can also be analyzed as produced by the conflict between the pleasure-principle and the reality-principle. On the one hand, dreams, neurotic symptoms, and all other manifestations of the unconscious, such as fantasy, represent in some degree or other a flight or alienation from a reality which is found unbearable. On the other hand, they represent a return to the pleasure-principle; they are substitutes for pleasures denied by reality. In this compromise between the two conflicting systems, the pleasure desired is reduced or distorted or even transformed to pain. Under the conditions of repression, under the domination of the reality-principle, the pursuit of pleasure is degraded to the status of a symptom.

But to say that reality or the reality-principle causes repression defines the problem rather than solves it. Freud sometimes identifies the reality-principle with the "struggle for existence," as if repression could be ultimately explained by some objective economic necessity to work. But man makes his own reality and various kinds of reality (and various compulsions to work) through the medium of culture or society. It is therefore more adequate to say that society imposes repression, though even this formula in Freud's early writings is connected with the inadequate idea that society, in imposing repression, is simply legislating the demands of objective economic necessity. This naive and rationalistic sociology stands, or rather falls, with Freud's earlier version of psychoanalysis.  The later Freud, as we shall see, in his doctrine of anxiety is moving toward the position that man is the animal which represses himself and which creates culture or society in order to repress himself. Even the formula that society imposes repression poses a problem rather than solves it; but the problem it poses is large.  For if society imposes repression, and repression causes the universal neurosis of mankind, it follows that there is an intrinsic connection between social organization and neurosis.  Man the social animal is by the same token the neurotic animal.  Or, as Freud puts it, man's superiority over the other animals is his capacity for neurosis, and his capacity for neurosis is merely the obverse of his capacity for cultural development.

Freud therefore arrives at the same conclusion as Nietzsche ("the disease called man"), but by a scientific route, by a study of the neuroses.  Neurosis is an essential consequence of civilization or culture.  Here again is a harsh lesson in humility, which tender-minded critics and apostles of Freud evade or suppress.  We must be prepared to analyze clinically as a neurosis not only the foreign culture we dislike, but also our own.

. . .

Psychoanalysis has not developed an adequate theory of art.  That psychoanalysis has made fundamental contributions to the study of art is a proposition denied only by the willfully ignorant.  Psychoanalysis has introduced revolutionary new ideas as to the nature of the thematic content of art.  The thematic content of art is always in some sense man; the psychoanalytical contribution to the content-analysis of art is no more than, and no less than, its contribution to the understanding of human nature.  Psychoanalysis has introduced equally important, though less generally recognized, ideas as to the technique of art.  The technique of art, so radically different from the technique of science and rational discourse, is rooted in what Freud called the primary process—the procedures of the unconscious which, Freud insists, are radically different from the logical procedures of the conscious system, and which, though in this sense illogical, are nevertheless in their own way meaningful and purposive. Trilling is justified in saying, "Freud discovered in the very organization of the mind those mechanisms by which art makes its effects, such devices as the condensations of meanings and the displacement of accent."

. . .

Psychoanalysis will continue to be no more than a tantalizing or disturbing possibility on the fringes of artistic criticism as long as it has no adequate general theory of art and of the place of art in life.  Freud's own statements on this subject are unsatisfactory. Not without justification does Trilling conclude that Freud's general statements bespeak a contempt for art; not without justification does he maintain that Freud's notion of art as a "substitute-gratification" and as an "illusion in contrast to reality" suggests that art is essentially an opiate of the people, an escape into an unreal world of fantasy indistinguishable from a full-blown neurosis, both art and neurosis having the basic dynamic of a flight from reality.

Now neither the doctrine that art provides pleasures which compensate for the harshness of life, nor the doctrine that art has affinity with madness, can be ruled out as false or insignificant. But anyone who has had experience of art knows that this is not the whole story. It is clear that Freud himself knows that this is not the whole story: hence the vacillations in his statements about art. . . .

    . . . . Freud's vacillations must be understood as the reflection of a deeper ambiguity at the heart of psychoanalytical theory —the question whether man's ultimate allegiance is to the reality-principle or to the pleasure-principle. The issue here is not a technical or factual question as to the relative weight of these two principles in the dynamics of the human psyche. It is rather a practical one of individual or social therapy; or, to use another terminology, the issue is eschatological. The question is: What shall man do to be saved?

Freud's writings, taken as a whole, vacillate between two opposite answers to this perpetual question of unhappy humanity. Sometimes the council is instinctual renunciation: Grow up and give up your infantile dreams of pleasure, recognize reality for what it is. And sometimes the counsel is instinctual liberation: Change this harsh reality so that you may recover lost sources of pleasure. . . .

The basic dialectic in Freud is the tension between his deep humanitarian desire to help mankind and his intellectual realism, which refused to accept a cheap and easy solution. His realism and his humanitarianism could come together only on the platform of instinctual liberation. All Freud's work demonstrates that the allegiance of the human psyche to the pleasure-principle is indestructible and that the path of instinctual renunciation is the path of sickness and self-destruction. When, therefore, in his later writings he counsels instinctual renunciation, it is a counsel of despair; and a careful reading of his later writings shows Freud still trying to find a way out of the prison.

But art is inseparably wedded to the pleasure-principle, and is in fact the most powerful evidence in support of Freud's doctrine of man's indestructible allegiance to the pleasure-principle:

A thing of beauty is a joy for ever:
Its loveliness increases, it will never
Pass into nothingness; but still will keep
A bower quiet for us, and a sleep
Full of sweet dreams, and health, and quiet breathing.
Therefore, on every morrow, are we wreathing
A flowery band to bind us to the earth,
Spite of despondence, of the inhuman dearth,
Of noble natures, of the gloomy days,
Of all the unhealthy and o'er-darkened ways
Made for our searching: yes, in spite of all,
Some shape of beauty moves away the pall
From our dark spirits.

This is the truth contained in Freud's formula of art as substitute-gratification. Compare Nietzsche's doctrine of the necessary connection between suffering and art: "What must this people have suffered, that they might become thus beautiful."

If man's salvation lies in instinctual renunciation laid at the feet of the reality-principle, then Freud is being characteristically consistent and courageous when he offends Trilling and betrays contempt for art, which he loved. Judged at the bar of the reality-principle, the consolations of art are childish, and they reinforce mankind's willful refusal to put away childish things. But if man's destiny is to change reality until it conforms to the pleasure-principle, and if man's fate is to fight for instinctual liberation, then art appears, in the words of Rilke, as the *Weltanschauung* of the last goal. Its contradiction of the reality-principle is its social function, as a constant reinforcement of the struggle for instinctual liberation; its childishness is to the professional critic a stumbling block, but to the artist its glory.

Freud's evaluation of art shifts with his shifting mood as to the possibility of making room for the pleasure-principle in the real world. At the outset of his career, when he was still under the spell of Charcot's famous diagnosis ("*C'est toujours la chose gènitale, toujours—toujours—toujours*"), he tended to identify instinctual liberation and a recovery of sanity with a relaxation of Victorian sexual morality, with sexual liberation in the ordinary sense of the term—a point of view which can be best studied in Wilhelm Reich, who essentially remained with it and who broke with Freud in order to remain with it. This oversimplified view of the problem naturally engendered an oversimplified optimism with regard to its solution. At this stage, Freud's realism and his humanitarianism could come together on a program of oversimplified sexual liberation.

With this tentative theoretical synthesis—perhaps also influenced by the political upheavals of 1903–1905–Freud wrote his most socially critical, even rebellious, book, *Wit and the Unconscious*. But *Wit and the Unconscious* is also his most significant contribution to the theory of art, although it has not been exploited as such. It is true that Freud disclaims any intention of offering a general theory of art, limits himself strictly to the problem of wit, and even denies that humor and comedy in general involve that contribution from the sphere of the unconscious which he claims to be essential in wit. But like all of Freud, this is a pioneer work which invites, even requires, extension and modification. It is also Freud's earliest work in applied psychoanalysis, and it is written with a cautiousness which the later Freud would not have felt necessary. It is doubtful if the later Freud would have maintained that humor and comedy involve no contribution from the unconscious; a quite different analysis of the psychogenesis of humor is offered in an essay written in 1928. If we take courage and explore *Wit and the Unconscious* for suggestions as to the general nature of art, we get a quite different picture from that which emerges from those later passages, written by a more pessimistic Freud, in which art seems to be regarded as childishness and as a narcotic.

In *Wit and the Unconscious* Freud affirms the connection between art and the pleasure-principle, but the pursuit, through art, of pleasure incompatible with the reality-principle is not despised but glorified. When the psychic apparatus is not used to satisfy one of our indispensable instinctual gratifications, he says, we let it work for pleasure; we even try to derive pleasure from its very activity. Herein, he suspects, is the true basis of all aesthetic thinking.

Freud also affirms the connection between art and childishness; however childishness is not a reproach, but the ideal kingdom of pleasure which art knows how to recover. What we are striving to obtain, he says, is a sort of euphoria—a return to the bygone state in which we were accustomed to satisfy our psychic needs with scant effort. This was the state of childhood, when we needed neither wit nor humor to make us happy, and indeed we knew nothing about them. The function of art—Freud says "wit"—is to help us find our way back to sources of pleasure that have been rendered inaccessible by the capitulation to the reality-principle which we call education or maturity—in other words, to regain the lost laughter of infancy.

This notion of art as driving at a recovery of childhood needs philosophical elaboration. It opens the way for a psychoanalytical reformulation of the truth contained in the Platonic doctrine of *anamnesis*. Plato in the *Phaedrus*—one of the greatest explorations of the psychology of beauty—not only gives full recognition to the affinity between love of beauty and madness, but also sees in the fevered pursuit of beauty a struggle to recover a lost vision of perfection. Those who do not join in the conclusion that

.. . . trailing clouds of glory do we come
From God, who is our home

have been haunted by the force of the Platonic notion of *anamnesis*, and at a loss how to explain it. Hence the persuasiveness of mystical formulations ultimately rooted in Platonism, such as the following from Poe: "Inspired by an ecstatic prescience of the glories beyond the grave, we struggle, by multiform combinations among the things and thoughts of Time, to attain a portion of that Loveliness whose very elements, perhaps, appertain to eternity alone." The Freudian doctrine of the archetypal status of childhood can put the Platonic doctrine of *anamnesis* on a naturalistic basis. Max Scheler has noted that the Freudian emphasis on childhood opened up a way to resolve the old philosophic controversy between empiricism and the doctrine of innate ideas.

In *Wit and the Unconscious* Freud also suggests that art, both as a return to the pleasure-principle and as a return to childhood, must be essentially a play activity. He uses the category of play to establish a connection between the techniques of art and the techniques of the primary process, the infantile and the unconscious. Play on words—the technique of wit—is recovered when thought is allowed to sink into the unconscious. In returning to the unconscious in the quest for the materials of wit, our thoughts are only revisiting the old home where in infancy word play reigned. It takes only the reflection that metaphor, which is the building block of all poetry, is nothing but a playing with words, to see how readily Freud's analysis of wit invites extension to the whole domain of art.

Freud does not merely connect art with the unconscious and the infantile; he also distinguishes it from other manifestations of the unconscious and the infantile, such as dreams and neurosis. He distinguishes art from dreams by insisting that art has a social reference and an element of conscious control:

> The dream is a completely asocial psychical product . . . it remains unintelligible to the person himself and therefore completely without interest to anyone else. . . . Wit, on the other hand, is the most social of all pleasure-seeking psychic functions. . . . It must therefore bind itself to the condition of intelligibility; it may utilize the distortion that is possible in the unconscious by means of condensation and displacement, but not to the point that the intelligence of the third person cannot still detect the meaning.

Thus Freud here takes the same position as Charles Lamb, quoted by Trilling as a contradiction of Freud: "The poet dreams being awake. He is not possessed by his subject but he has dominion over it." With the reference to the indispensable third person (an audience), Freud relates the demand for intelligibility to the demand for communication. The implication is that art has the function of making public the contents of the unconscious. In another passage Freud says that the indispensable third person must be suffering from the same repressions which the creative artist has overcome by finding a way of expressing the repressed unconscious. And in his essay on Jensen's novella, also written in the same early phase of his thought, Freud says that the author "directs his attention to the unconscious in his own psyche, is alive to its possibilities of development and grants them artistic expression." Thus art, like psychoanalysis itself, appears to be a way of making the unconscious conscious. Freud many times quotes the artists in support of his psychoanalytical discoveries. At his seventieth birthday celebration he disclaimed the title of "discoverer of the unconscious," saying that "the poets and philosophers before me discovered the unconscious; what I discovered was the scientific method by which the unconscious can be studied." But while psychoanalysis tries to reach the unconscious by extending the conscious, art represents an irruption from the unconscious into the conscious. Art has to assert itself against the hostility of the reality-principle and of reason, which is enslaved to the reality-principle. Hence its aim, in Freud's words, is the veiled presentation of deeper truth; hence it wears a mask, a disguise which confuses and fascinates our reason. The mask which seduces us is derived from the play of the primary process.

. . . . .

Art differs from dreaming not only because it makes the unconscious conscious—a purely cognitive relation—but also because it liberates repressed instincts—a libidinal relation. Because of the repression that arises from civilized life, we have lost many of the primary pleasures of which censorship disapproves. But we find renunciation regressive and thus to regain what we have lost. Its object from the beginning is the same: to rid us of our inhibitions, and thereby to make those sources of pleasure that have long been blocked once more accessible for our gratification. As such, art struggles against repressive reason and the reality-principle in an effort to regain lost liberties. A special pleasure in wit is derived from an *"economy in the expenditure of inhibitions or suppressions."* Our normal orderly responsible selves, dominated by the reality-principle, are sustained by a constant expenditure in psychic energy devoted to the maintenance of the repression of our fundamental desires. Art, by overcoming the inhibition and by activating the playful primary process, which is intrinsically easier and more enjoyable than the procedures of normal responsible thought, on both counts effects a saving in psychic expenditure and provides relief from the pressures of reason.

Art, if its object is to undo repressions, and if civilization is essentially repressive, is in this sense subversive of civilization. Some of Freud's formulations on the role of the indispensable third person suggest that the function of art is to form a subversive group, the opposite of that authoritarian group the structure of which Freud analyzed in *Group Psychology and the Analysis of the Ego.* The indispensable third person must be suffering from the same repressions as the creative artist. The relation between the artist and the third person is one of identification, and identification is the relation which, according to *Group Psychology,* binds together the members of an authoritarian group. In contrast with the repressive structure of the authoritarian group, the aim of the partnership between the artist and the audience is instinctual liberation.

Freud works out the relation between the element of pure play and the element of instinctual liberation in wit by means of the analogy of the distinction between fore-pleasure and end-pleasure in sexual intercourse. In sexual intercourse the fore-pleasure is in the preliminary play with all parts of the body, and it represents a perpetuation of the pure polymorphous perverse play of infantile sexuality; the end-pleasure in the orgasm is purely genital and post-pubertal. Freud says that the element of pure play in wit serves as an "alluring premium" which makes possible the much greater pleasure of liberating repressed desires. It seems to me that the word "art" can be substituted for the word "wit" in the following passage, allowing for a few minor changes:

> It begins as play, in order to derive pleasure from the free use of words and ideas. As soon as the strengthening reason forbids this play with words as senseless and with ideas as foolish, it turns to the joke in order to retain these sources of pleasure and to be able to gain new pleasure from the liberation of the nonsensical. As real but nontendentious wit it assists ideas and strengthens them against the assault of the critical judgment, utilizing in this process the principle of interchange of pleasure-sources; and finally it joins with the major tendencies struggling against repression, in order

to remove inner inhibitions according to the principle of fore-pleasure.

Art seduces us into the struggle against repression.

This notion of art as a mode of instinctual liberation suggests a further distinction between art on the one hand and dreams and neurosis on the other. Dreams and neurosis give expression to the repressed unconscious, but they do not liberate it. The distinction between giving expression to the unconscious and liberating the unconscious is difficult. Perhaps we should say that neurosis and dreams are the determinate outcome of the unconscious, while art is its conscious articulation. For the liberation in art is connected with the element of consciousness in it. Freud compares humor to psychoneurotic defense mechanisms inaugurated, like humor, to protect from pain; but at the same time he distinguishes humor from the neurotic defense mechanism. Indeed he calls it the highest of all defense functions; quite unlike repression, humor openly confronts ideas that are in themselves painful or are connected with painful images, and thus it is instrumental in overcoming the automatic machinery of defense.

The neurotic mechanism involves repression and a shutting of the eye of consciousness, and a resultant psychic automatism. Art does not withdraw the eye of consciousness, does not repress, and attains some freedom. And by liberating the instincts, art attains a positive pleasure denied to dreams and neurosis. Dreams are wish-fulfillment fantasies; neurotic symptoms are substitutes for forbidden pleasures, but as compromises they never satisfy. Art, on the other hand, not being a compromise with the unconscious either in the cognitive or in the libidinal sense, affords positive satisfaction, and cannot be simply classed, as in Freud's later formulations, with dreams and neurosis as a "substitute-gratification." This I take to the meaning of the contrast between dream and wit stated in *Wit and the Unconscious*: that the one primarily guards against pain, while the other seeks pleasure. This formulation must be understood in the light of the distinction which Freud drew between avoidance of pain and positive happiness, the distinction which made him say love is not "content to strive for avoidance of pain—that goal of weary resignation; rather it passes that by heedlessly and holds fast to the deep-rooted passionate striving for a positive fulfillment of happiness." Art gives us this positive pleasure in so far as it attains that goal which must always remain the goal of humanity—conscious play. Freud has seen that the category of conscious play gives the final distinction between dreams and neurosis and art; the dream is always a wish, but wit is actualized play.

The conception of art derived from what Freud says about wit is substantial enough to constitute at least the outline of a psychoanalytical theory of art. Art as pleasure, art as play, art as the recovery of childhood, art as making conscious the unconscious, art as a mode of instinctual liberation, art as the fellowship of men struggling for instinctual liberation—these ideas plainly fit into the system of psychoanalysis. . . .

. . . .

Thus the dialectic between art and society derives from the artist's contact with the ultimate essence of humanity, which is also humanity's ultimate goal: "History is the index of men born too soon." And as for the artist, "Again and again someone in the crowd wakes up, he has no ground in the crowd, and he emerges according to much broader laws. He carries strange customs with him and demands room for bold gestures. The future speaks ruthlessly through him." But as spokesmen for the essence and for the future, artists are the spokesmen for what is repressed in the present: "Their winged heart everywhere beats against the walls of their time; their work was that which was not resolved in the lives they lived."

The artist is compared by Rilke to "a dancer whose movements are broken by the constraint of his cell. That which finds no expression in his steps and the limited swing of his arms, comes in exhaustion from his lips, or else he has to scratch the unlived lines of his body into the walls with his wounded fingers." Art is a way of life faithful to the natural instincts, and therefore faithful to childhood: "Not any self-control or self-limitation for the sake of specific ends, but rather a carefree letting go of oneself: not caution, but rather a wise blindness; not working to acquire silent, slowly increasing possessions, but rather a continuous squandering of all perishable values. This way of being has something naive and instinctive [*Unwillkurliches*] about it, and resembles that period of the unconscious [*des Unbewussten*] best characterized by a joyous confidence, namely the period of childhood." The child "has no anxiety about losing things." Everything the child has sensed passes through his love, and is illuminated by it: "And whatever has once been lit up in love remains as an image, never more to be lost, and the image is possession; that is why children are so rich." (Rilke's thought is complemented by Freud's remark on happiness: "Happiness is the deferred fulfillment of a prehistoric wish. That is why wealth brings so little happiness; money is not an infantile wish.") The artist is the man who refuses initiation through education into the existing order, remains faithful to his own childhood being, and thus becomes "a human being in the spirit of all times, an artist." Hence the artist tree is distinguished by profounder roots in the dark unconscious: "Artists extend much farther down into the warmth of all Becoming; in them other juices rise into fruit."

Perhaps Rilke needs to be supplemented by psychoanalysis. It is certain, on the other hand, that psychoanalytical formulations seem like a scrannel pipe of wretched straw when set beside Rilke. Psychoanalysts should, like Freud, envy the capacity of poets, "with hardly an effort to salve from the whirlpool of their own emotions the deepest truths, to which we others have to force our way, ceaselessly groping amid torturing uncertainties."

QUESTION

Does Brown help us understand why a court might consider the life and character of an artist—or one of artistic motives and inclinations—suspect of "instability"?

## CHAPTER FIFTEEN

# The Language of Meaning

## INTRODUCTORY NOTE

Intellectual posits such as rules, roles and selves function, we have seen, in two distinguishable, if critically-related, ways. On the one hand, they are modes of symbolizing and explaining—of making accessible to the conscious intelligence—the exemplifications of intellectual and social organization which we phenomenologically experience. A rule, a role, or a self is an intellectual way of expressing the often taken-for-granted phenomena of similarity, regularity, functional interdependence, personal achievement, and interpersonal agreement. And insofar as we insist that the value of such constructs is compelling and indisputable we affirm that order and organization are possible and that analytic critiques of knowledge and meaning which lead to a different conclusion are necessarily wrong.

In one sense, then, rules, roles and selves are devices for reporting certain crucial facts of life. In another sense—the one with which the preceding chapters were most concerned—these constructs are devices of personal and social orientation. They are structure-giving and method-giving posits which help make problems manageable indeed, comprehendable. They provide anchors and frames of reference in a world of otherwise incomprehensible flux and heterogeneity.

To say that rules, roles and selves are useful in this way is to say that they help solve particular, concrete dilemmas. The problem of deciding how and when they are relevant to such dilemmas and what they tell us to do about them is the problem of interpretation or of meaning. And it would seem elementary that the means by which interpretation is carried on must be one that does not defeat the stabilizing and organizing functions which rules, roles, selves—and, for that matter, any other posits—have. The problem of interpretation has, therefore, often been posed as one of finding a way to preserve the defining functions of such constructs, while at the same time meeting certain other standards. Among these, some of the most familiar are: the standard that a construct should be construed so as to carry out the policy or achieve the goals which account for its formulation; the standard that a construct should be construed so as to take account of the circumstances in which it was formulated; the standard that a construct should be construed so as to avoid absurd or unjust applications. On the other hand, this way of framing the central dilemma of interpretation is rejected either explicitly or, more often, implicitly by many critics and performers of the interpretive function. For a few, apparently, the function of the interpretive process is to reach the right, good or just result whatever may be the direction and structure provided by a concededly authoritative construct. For a much larger number, the function of the interpretive process is to seek the construct's meaning and this assumes that there is no necessary connection between that entity and such notions as purpose, intention, circumstances, good sense, justice or public policy. Indeed, it is usually assumed by those who hold rigorously to the latter position that these notions are merely smokescreens by which to obscure official disregard of a relevant construct and to thereby defeat its stabilizing and organizing function.

Both of these semantic positions, it should by now be clear, are extreme ones. But it is not always easy to pinpoint what it is that makes them extreme and why it is a mistake to defend either of them unconditionally and without reservation. Part of the purpose of this chapter is to investigate these questions: to see and test the assumptions which support the two positions. More importantly, however, the concern is with those elements in the two positions which account for the continuing allegiance which so many have to them. Is there something in both of the positions for which any adequate theory of meaning and of interpretive method must account? To what extent do the theories of meaning which are presented below attempt such an account? To what extent do they do so adequately?

In pursuing these inquiries the initial focus is on the interpretation of legal words and rules. But this, as the sections on "The Language of Meaning" and on "Reality, Mind and Common Sense" suggest, does not mean that the chapter focuses solely, or even primarily, on the meaning of authoritative legal language. It is concerned as much with the general problem of interpreting things and facts—conditions, acts, events, as well as linguistic and other conventional symbols—and with the question of whether there is an interpretive method, an interpretive attitude, and a set of interpretive skills which is appropriate to any situation in which meaning is sought. The chapter is concerned with the extent to which the problems of interpretation isolated by lawyers, judges and legal commentators can be viewed as instances of generic semantic problems. Is there, it asks, a general approach to meaning from which legal interpretation can profit and by which legal interpreters can be judged?

## Section One: The Hart-Fuller Debate

*H. L. A. Hart*

### Positivism and the Separation of Law and Morals *

I now turn to a distinctively American criticism of the separation of the law that is from the law that ought to be. It emerged from the critical study of the judicial process with which American jurisprudence has been on the whole so beneficially occupied. The most skeptical of these critics— the loosely named "Realists" of the 1930's— perhaps too naively accepted the conceptual framework of the natural sciences as adequate for the characterization of law and for the analysis of rule-guided action of which a living system of law at least partly consists. But they opened men's eyes to what actually goes on

* From 71 Harv.L.Rev. 593, 606–615 (1958). Copyright 1958 by The Harvard Law Review Association. Reprinted by permission.

when courts decide cases, and the contrast they drew between the actual facts of judicial decision and the traditional terminology for describing it as if it were a wholly logical operation was usually illuminating; for in spite of some exaggeration the "Realists" made us acutely conscious of one cardinal feature of human language and human thought, emphasis on which is vital not only for the understanding of law but in areas of philosophy far beyond the confines of jurisprudence. The insight of this school may be presented in the following example. A legal rule forbids you to take a vehicle into the public park. Plainly this forbids an automobile, but what about bicycles, roller skates, toy automobiles? What about airplanes? Are these, as we say, to be called "vehicles" for the purpose of the rule or not? If we are to communicate with each other at all, and if, as in the most elementary form of law, we are to express our intentions that a certain type of behavior be regulated by rules, then the general words we use—like "vehicle" in the case I consider—must have some standard instance in which no doubts are felt about its application. There must be a core of settled meaning, but there will be, as well a penumbra of debatable cases in which words are neither obviously applicable nor obviously ruled out. These cases will each have some features in common with the standard case; they will lack others or be accompanied by features not present in the standard case. Human invention and natural processes continually throw up such variants on the familiar, and if we are to say that these ranges of facts do or do not fall under existing rules, then the classifier must make a decision which is not dictated to him, for the facts and phenomena to which we fit our words and apply our rules are as it were *dumb*. The toy automobile cannot speak up and say, "I am a vehicle for the purpose of this legal rule," nor can the roller skates chorus, "We are not a vehicle." Fact situations do not await us neatly labeled, creased, and folded, nor is their legal classification written on them to be simply read off by the judge. Instead, in applying legal rules, someone must take the responsibility of deciding that words do or do not cover some case in hand with all the practical consequences involved in this decision.

We may call the problems which arise outside the hard core of standard instances or settled meaning "problems of the penumbra"; they are always with us whether in relation to such trivial things as the regulation of the use of the public park or in relation to the multidimensional generalities of a constitution. If a penumbra of uncertainty must surround all legal rules, then their application to specific cases in the penumbral area cannot be a matter of logical deduction, and so deductive reasoning, which for generations has been cherished as the very perfection of human reasoning, cannot serve as a model for what judges, or indeed anyone, should do in bringing particular cases under general rules. In this area men cannot live by deduction alone. And it follows that if legal arguments and legal decisions of penumbral questions are to be rational, their rationality must lie in something other than a logical relation to premises. So if it is rational or "sound" to argue and to decide that for the purposes of this rule an airplane is not a vehicle, this argument must be sound or rational without being logically conclusive. What is it then that makes such decisions correct or at least better than alternative decisions? Again, it seems true to say that the criterion which makes a decision sound in such cases is some concept of what the law ought to be; it is easy to slide from that into saying that it must be a moral judgment about what law ought to be. So here we touch upon a point of necessary "intersection between law and morals" which demonstrates the falsity or, at any rate, the misleading character of the Utilitarians' emphatic insistence on the separation of law as it is and ought to be. Surely, Bentham and Austin could only have written as they did because they misunderstood or neglected this aspect of the judicial process, because they ignored the problems of the penumbra.

The misconception of the judicial process which ignores the problems of the penumbra and which views the process as consisting pre-eminently in deductive reasoning is often stigmatized as the error of "formalism" or "literalism." My question now is, how and to what extent does the demonstration of this error show the utilitarian distinction to be wrong or misleading? Here there are many issues which have been confused, but I can only disentangle some. The charge of formalism has been leveled both at the "positivist" legal theorist and at the courts, but of course it must be a very different charge in each case. Leveled at the legal theorist, the charge means that he has made a theoretical mistake about the character of legal decision; he has thought of the reasoning involved as consisting in deduction from premises in which the judges' practical choices or decisions play no part. It would be easy to show that Austin was guiltless of this error; only an entire misconception of what analytical jurisprudence is and why he thought it important has led to the view that he, or any other analyst, believed that the law was a closed logical system in which judges deduced their decisions from premises. On the contrary, he was very much alive to the character of language, to its vagueness or open character; he thought that in the penumbral situation judges must necessarily legislate, and, in accents that sometimes recall those of the late Judge Jerome Frank, he berated the common-law judges for legislating feebly and timidly and for blindly relying on real or fancied analogies with past cases instead of adapting their decisions to the growing needs of society as revealed by the moral standard of utility. The villians of this piece, responsible for the conception of the judges as an automaton, are not the Utilitarian thinkers. The responsibility, if it is to be laid at the door of any theorist, is with thinkers like Blackstone and, at an earlier stage, Montesquieu. The root of this evil is preoccupation with the separation of powers and Blackstone's "childish fiction" (as Austin termed it) that judges only "find," never "make," law.

But we are concerned with "formalism" as a vice not of jurists but of judges. What precisely is it for a judge to commit this error, to be a "formalist," automatic," a "slot machine"? Curiously enough the literature which is full of denunciation of these vices never makes this clear in concrete terms; instead we have only descriptions which cannot mean what they appear to say: it is said that in the formalist error courts make an excessive use of logic, take a thing to "a dryly logical extreme," or make an excessive use of analytical methods. But just how in being a formalist does a judge make an excessive use of logic? It is clear that the essence of his error is to give some general term an interpretation which is blind to social values and consequences (or which is in some other way stupid or perhaps merely disliked by critics). But logic does not prescribe interpretation of terms; it dictates neither the stupid nor intelligent interpretation of any expression. Logic only tells you hypothetically that *if* you give a certain term a certain interpretation then a certain conclusion follows. Logic is silent on how to classify particulars—and this is the heart of a judicial decision. So this reference to logic and to logical extremes is a misnomer for something else, which must be this. A judge has to apply a rule to a concrete case—perhaps the rule that one may not take a stolen "vehicle" across state lines, and in this case an airplane has been taken. He either does not see or pretends not to see that the general terms of this rule are susceptible of different interpretations and that he has a choice left open uncontrolled by linguistic conventions. He ignores, or is blind to, the fact that he is in the area of the penumbra and is not dealing with a standard case. Instead of choosing in the light of social aims, the judge fixes the meaning in a different way. He either takes the meaning that the word most obviously suggests in its ordinary nonlegal context to ordinary men, or one which the word has been given in some other legal context, or, still worse, he thinks of a standard case and then arbitrarily identifies certain features in it—for example, in the case of a vehicle, (1) normally used on land, (2) capable of carrying a human person, (3) capable of being self-propelled—and treats these three as always necessary and always sufficient conditions for the use in all contexts of the word "vehicle," irrespective of the social consequences of giving it this interpretation. This choice, not "logic," would force the judge to include a toy motor car (if electrically propelled) and to exclude bicycles and the airplane. In all this there is possibly great stupidity but no more "logic," and no less, than in cases in which the interpretation given to a general term and the consequent application of some general rule to a particular case is consciously controlled by some identified social aim.

Decisions made in a fashion as blind as this would scarcely deserve the name of decisions; we might as well toss a penny in applying a rule of law. But it is at least doubtful whether any judicial decisions (even in England) have been quite as automatic as this. Rather, either the interpretations stigmatized as automatic have resulted from the conviction that it is fairer in a criminal statute to take a meaning which would jump to the mind of the ordinary man at the cost even of defeating other values, and this itself is a social policy (though possibly a bad one); or much more frequently, what is stigmatized as "mechanical" and "automatic" is a determined choice made indeed in the light of a social aim but of a conservative social aim. Certainly many of the Supreme Court decisions at the turn of the century which have been so stigmatized represent clear choices in the penumbral area to give effect to a policy of a conservative type. This is peculiarly true of Mr. Justice Peckham's opinions defining the spheres of police power and due process.

But how does the wrongness of deciding cases in an automatic and mechanical way and the rightness of deciding cases by reference to social purposes show that the utilitarian insistence on the distinction between what the law is and what it ought to be is wrong? I take it that no one who wished to use these vices of formalism as proof that the distinction between what is and what ought to be is mistaken would deny that the decisions stigmatized as automatic are law; nor would he deny that the system in which such automatic decisions are made is a legal system. Surely he would say that they are law, but they are bad law, they ought not to be law. But this would be to use the distinction, not to refute it; and of course both Bentham and Austin used it to attack judges for failing to decide penumbral cases in accordance with the growing needs of society.

Clearly, if the demonstration of the errors of formalism is to show the utilitarian distinction to be wrong, the point must be drastically restated. The point must be not merely that a judicial decision to be rational must be made in the light of some conception of what ought to be, but that the aims, the social policies and purposes to which judges should appeal if their decisions are to be rational, are themselves to be considered as part of the law in some suitably wide sense of "law" which is held to be more illuminating than that used by the Utilitarians. This restatement of the point would have the following consequence: instead of saying that the recurrence of penumbral questions shows us that legal rules are essentially incomplete, and that, when they fail to determine decisions, judges must legislate and so exercise a creative choice between alternatives, we shall say that the social policies which guide the judges' choice are in a sense there for them to discover; the judges are only "drawing out" of the rule what, if it is properly understood, is "latent" within it. To call this judicial legislation is to obscure some essential continuity between the clear cases of the rule's application and the penumbral decisions. I shall question later whether this way of talking is salutary, but I wish at this time to point out something obvious, but likely, if not stated, to tangle the issues. It does not follow that, because the opposite of a decision reached blindly in the formalist or literalist manner is a decision intelligently reached by reference to some conception of what ought to be, we have a junction of law and morals. We must, I think, beware of thinking in a too simple-minded fashion about the word "ought." This is not because there is no distinction to be made between law as it is and ought to be. Far from it. It is because the distinction should be between what is and what from many different points of view ought to be. The word "ought" merely reflects the presence of some standard of criticism; one of these standards is a moral standard but not all standards are moral. We say to our neighbour, "You ought not to lie," and that may certainly be a moral judgment, but we should remember that the baffled poisoner may say, "I ought to have given her a second dose." The point here is that intelligent decisions which we oppose to mechanical or formal decisions are not necessarily identical with decisions defensible on moral grounds. We may say of many a decision: "Yes, that is right; that is as it ought to be," and we may mean only that some accepted purpose or policy has been thereby advanced; we may not mean to endorse the moral propriety of the policy or the decision. So the contrast between the mechanical decision and the intelligent one can be reproduced inside a system dedicated to the pursuit of the most evil aims. It does not exist as a contrast to be found only in legal systems which, like our own, widely recognize principles of justice and moral claims of individuals.

An example may make this point plainer. With us the task of sentencing in criminal cases is the one that seems most obviously to demand from the judge the exercise of moral judgment. Here the factors to be weighed seem clearly to be moral factors: society must not be exposed to wanton attack; too much misery must not be inflicted on either the victim or his dependents; efforts must be made to enable him to lead a better life and regain a position in the society whose laws he has violated. To a judge striking the balance among these claims, with all the discretion and perplexities involved, his task seems as plain an example of the exercise of moral judgment as could be; and it seems to be the polar opposite of some mechanical application of a tariff of penalties fixing a sentence careless of the moral claims which in our system have to be weighed. So here intelligent and rational decision is guided however uncertainly by moral aims. But we have only to vary the example to see that this need not necessarily be so and surely, if it need not necessarily be so, the Utilitarian point remains unshaken. Under the Nazi regime men were sentenced by courts for criticism of the regime. Here the choice of sentence might be guided exclusively by consideration of what was needed to maintain the state's tyranny effectively. What sentence would both terrorize the public at large and keep the friends and family of the prisoner in suspense so that both hope and fear would cooperate as factors making for subservience? The prisoner of such a system would be regarded simply as an object to be used in pursuit of these aims. Yet, in contrast with a mechanical decision, decision on these grounds would be intelligent and purposive, and from one point of view the decision would be as it ought to be. Of course, I am not unaware that a whole philosophical tradition has sought to demonstrate the fact that we cannot correctly call decisions or behavior truly rational unless they are in conformity with moral aims and principles. But the example I have used seems to me to serve at least as a warning that we cannot use the errors of formalism as something which per se demonstrates the falsity of the utilitarian insistence on the distinction between law as it is and law as *morally* it ought to be.

We can now return to the main point. If it is true that the intelligent decision of penumbral questions is one made not mechanically but in the light of aims, purposes, and policies, though not necessarily in the light of anything we would call moral principles, is it wise to express this important fact by saying that the firm utilitarian distinction between what the law is and what it ought to be should be dropped? Perhaps the claim that it is wise cannot be theoretically refuted for it is, in effect, an *invitation* to revise our conception of what a legal rule is. We are invited to include in the "rule" the various aims and policies in the light of which its penumbral cases are decided on the ground that these aims have, because of their importance, as much right to be called law as the core of legal rules whose meaning is settled. But though an invitation cannot be refuted, it may be refused and I would proffer two reasons for refusing this invitation. First, everything we have learned about the judicial process can be expressed in other less mysterious ways. We can say laws are incurably incomplete and we must decide the penumbral cases rationally by reference to social aims. I think Holmes, who had such a vivid appreciation of the fact that "general propositions do not decide concrete cases," would have put it that way. Second, to insist on the utilitarian distinction is to emphasize that the hard core of of settled meaning is law in some centrally important sense and that even if there are borderlines, there must first be lines. If this were not so the notion of rules controlling courts' decisions would be senseless as some of the "Realists"—in their most extreme moods, and, I think, on bad grounds—claimed.

By contrast, to soften the distinction, to assert mysteriously that there is some fused identity between law as it is and as it ought to be, is to suggest that all legal questions are fundamentally like those of the penumbra. It is to assert that there is no central element of actual law to be seen in the core of central meaning which rules have, that there is nothing in the nature of a legal rule inconsistent with *all* questions being open to reconsideration in the light of social policy. Of course, it is good to be occupied with the penumbra. Its problems are rightly the daily diet of the law schools. But to be occupied with the penumbra is one thing, to be preoccupied with it another. And preoccupation with the penumbra is, if I may say so, as rich a source of confusion in the American legal tradition as formalism in the English. Of course we might abandon the notion that rules have authority; we might cease to attach force or even meaning to an argument that a case falls clearly within a rule and the scope of a precedent. We might call all such reasoning "automatic" or "mechanical," which is already the routine invective of the courts. But until we decide that this *is* what we want, we should not encourage it by obliterating the Utilitarian distinction.

### Questions

Consider Professor Hart's remarks in the light of earlier excerpts from Felix Cohen's *The Ethical Basis of Legal Criticism* and *Field Theory and Judicial Logic*. See Chapters 1 and 8, *infra*. Is Hart taking issue with Cohen? If so, in what way? If not, what might lead one to think he is?

Lon L. Fuller

## Positivism and Fidelity to Law—A Reply to Professor Hart *

### VII.  The Problem of Interpretation: The Core and the Penumbra

It is essential that we be just as clear as we can be about the meaning of Professor Hart's doctrine of "the core and the penumbra," because I believe the casual reader is likely to misinterpret what he has to say.  Such a reader is apt to suppose that Professor Hart is merely describing something that is a matter of everyday experience for the lawyer, namely, that in the interpretation of legal rules it is typically the case (though not universally so) that there are some situations which will seem to fall rather clearly within the rule, while others will be more doubtful.  Professor Hart's thesis takes no such jejune form.  His extended discussion of the core and the penumbra is not just a complicated way of recognizing that some cases are hard, while others are easy.  Instead, on the basis of a theory about language meaning generally, he is proposing a theory of judicial interpretation which is, I believe, wholly novel.  Certainly it has never been put forward in so uncompromising a form before.

As I understand Professor Hart's thesis (if we add some tacit assumptions implied by it, as well as some qualifications he would no doubt wish his readers to supply) a full statement would run something as follows: The task of interpretation is commonly that of determining the meaning of the individual words of a legal rule, like "vehicle" in a rule excluding vehicles from a park.  More particularly, the task of interpretation is to determine the range of reference of such a word, or the aggregate of things to which it points.  Communication is possible only because words have a "standard instance," or a "core of meaning" that remains relatively constant, whatever the context in which the word may appear.  Except in unusual circumstances, it will always be proper to regard a word like "vehicle" as embracing its "standard instance," that is, that aggregate of things it would include in all ordinary contexts, within or without the law.  This meaning the word will have in any legal rule, whatever its purpose.  In applying the word to its "standard instance," no creative role is assumed by the judge.  He is simply applying the law "as it is."

In addition to a constant core, however, words also have a penumbra of meaning which, unlike the core, will vary from context to context.  When the object in question (say, a tricycle) falls within this penumbral area, the judge is forced to assume a more creative role.  He must now undertake, for the first time, an interpretation of the rule in the light of its purpose or aim.  Having in mind what was sought by the regulation concerning parks, ought it to be considered as barring tricycles?  When questions of this sort are decided there is at least an "intersection" of "is" and "ought," since the judge, in de-

* From 71 Harv.L.Rev. 630, 661–669 (1958).  Coyright 1958 by The Har-    vard Law Review Association.  Reprinted by permission.

ciding what the rule "is," does so in the light of his notions of what "it ought to be" in order to carry out its purpose.

If I have properly interpreted Professor Hart's theory as it affects the "hard core," then I think it is quite untenable. The most obvious defect of this theory lies in its assumption that problems of interpretation typically turn on the meaning of individual words. Surely no judge applying a rule of the common law ever followed any such procedure as that described (and, I take it, prescribed) by Professor Hart; indeed, we do not normally even think of his problem as being one of "interpretation." Even in the case of statutes, we commonly have to assign meaning, not to a single word, but to a sentence, a paragraph, or a whole page or more of text. Surely a paragraph does not have a "standard instance" that remains constant whatever the context in which it appears. If a statute seems to have a kind of "core meaning" that we can apply without a too precise inquiry into its exact purpose, this is because we can see that, however one might formulate the precise objective of the statute, *this* case would still come within it.

Even in situations where our interpretive difficulties seem to head up in a single word, Professor Hart's analysis seems to me to give no real account of what does or should happen. In his illustration of the "vehicle," although he tells us this word has a core of meaning that in all contexts defines unequivocally a range of objects embraced by it, he never tells us what these objects might be. If the rule excluding vehicles from parks seems easy to apply in some cases. I submit this is because we can see clearly enough what the rule "is aiming at in general" so that we know there is no need to worry about the difference between Fords and Cadillacs. If in some cases we seem to be able to apply the rule without asking what its purpose is, this is not because we can treat a directive arrangement as if it had no purpose. It is rather because, for example, whether the rule be intended to preserve quiet in the park, or to save carefree strollers from injury, we know, "without thinking," that a noisy automobile must be excluded.

What would Professor Hart say if some local patriots wanted to mount on a pedestal in the park a truck used in World War II, while other citizens, regarding the proposed memorial as an eyesore, support their stand by the "no vehicle" rule? Does this truck, in perfect working order, fall within the core or the penumbra?

Professor Hart seems to assert that unless words have "standard instances" that remain constant regardless of context, effective communication would break down and it would become impossible to construct a system of "rules which have authority." If in every context words took on a unique meaning, peculiar to that context, the whole process of interpretation would become so uncertain and subjective that the ideal of a rule of law would lose its meaning. In other words, Professor Hart seems to be saying that unless we are prepared to accept his analysis of interpretation, we must surrender all hope of giving an effective meaning to the ideal of fidelity to law. This presents a very dark prospect indeed, if one believes, as I do, that we cannot accept his theory of interpretation. I do not take so gloomy a view of the future of the ideal of fidelity to law.

An illustration will help to test, not only Professor Hart's theory of the core and the penumbra, but its relevance to the ideal of fidelity to law as well. Let us suppose that in leafing through the statutes, we come upon the following enactment: "It shall be a misdemeanor, punishable by a fine of five dollars, to sleep in any railway stations." We have no trouble in perceiving the general nature of the target toward which this statute is aimed. Indeed, we are likely at once to call to mind the picture of a disheveled tramp, spread out in an ungainly fashion on one of the benches of the station, keeping weary passengers on their feet and filling their ears with raucous and alcoholic snores. This vision may fairly be said to represent the "obvious instance" contemplated by the statute, though certainly it is far from being the "standard instance" of the physiological state called "sleep."

Now let us see how this example bears on the ideal of fidelity to law. Suppose I am a judge, and that two men are brought before me for violating this statute. The first is a passenger who was waiting at 3 A. M. for a delayed train. When he was arrested he was sitting upright in an orderly fashion, but was heard by the arresting officer to be gently snoring. The second is a man who had brought a blanket and pillow to the station and had obviously settled himself down for the night. He was arrested, however, before he had a chance to go to sleep. Which of these cases presents the "standard instance" of the word "sleep"? If I disregard that question, and decide to fine the second man and set free the first, have I violated a duty of fidelity to law? Have I violated that duty if I interpret the word "sleep" as used in this statute to mean something like "to spread oneself out on a bench or floor to spend the night, or as if to spend the night"?

Testing another aspect of Professor Hart's theory, is it really ever possible to interpret a word in a statute without knowing the aim of the statute? Suppose we encounter the following incomplete sentence: "All improvements must be promptly reported to. . . . ." Professor Hart's theory seems to assert that even if we have only this fragment before us we can safely construe the word "improvement" to apply to its "standard instance," though we would have to know the rest of the sentence before we could deal intelligently with "problems of the penumbra." Yet surely in the truncated sentence I have quoted, the word "improvement" is almost as devoid of meaning as the symbol "X."

The word "improvement" will immediately take on meaning if we fill out the sentence with the words, "the head nurse," or, "the Town Planning Authority," though the two meanings that come to mind are radically dissimilar. It can hardly be said that these two meanings represent some kind of penumbral accretion to the word's "standard instance." And one wonders, parenthetically, how helpful the theory of the core and the penumbra would be in deciding whether, when the report is to be made to the planning authorities, the word "improvement" includes an unmortgageable monstrosity of a house that lowers the market value of the land on which it is built.

It will be instructive, I think, to consider the effect of other ways of filling out the sentence. Suppose we add to, "All improvements must be promptly reported to . . ." the words, "the Dean of the Graduate Division." Here we no longer seem, as we once did, to be groping in the dark; rather, we seem now to be reaching into an empty box. We achieve a little better orientation if the final clause reads, "to the Principal of the School," and we feel completely at ease if it becomes, "to the Chairman of the Committee on Relations with the Parents of Children in the Primary Division."

It should be noted that in deciding what the word "improvement" means in all these cases, we do not proceed simply by placing the word in some general context, such as hospital practice, town planning, or education. If this were so, the "improvement" in the last instance might just as well be that of the teacher as that of the pupil. Rather, we ask ourselves, What can this rule be for? What evil does it seek to avert? What good is it intended to promote? When it is "the head nurse" who receives the report, we are apt to find ourselves asking, "Is there, perhaps, a shortage of hospital space, so that patients who improve sufficiently are sent home or are assigned to a ward where they will receive less attention?" If "Principal" offers more orientation than "Dean of the Graduate Division," this must be because we know something about the differences between primary education and education on the postgraduate university level. We must have some minimum acquaintance with the ways in which these two educational enterprises are conducted, and with the problems encountered in both of them, before any distinction between "Principal" and "Dean of the Graduate Division" would affect our interpretation of "improvement." We must, in other words, be sufficiently capable of putting ourselves in the position of those who drafted the rule to know what they thought "ought to be." It is in the light of this "ought" that we must decide what the rule is."

Turning now to the phenomenon Professor Hart calls "preoccupation with the penumbra," we have to ask ourselves what is actually contributed to the process of interpretation by the common practice of supposing various "borderline" situations. Professor Hart seems to say, "Why, nothing at all, unless we are working with problems of the penumbra." If this is what he means, I find his view a puzzling one, for it still leaves unexplained why, under his theory, if one is dealing with a penumbral problem, it could be useful to think about other penumbral problems.

Throughout his whole discussion of interpretation, Professor Hart seems to assume that it is a kind of cataloguing procedure. A judge faced with a novel situation is like a library clerk who has to decide where to shelve a new book. There are easy cases: the *Bible* belongs under Religion, *The Wealth of Nations* under Economics, etc. Then there are hard cases, when the librarian has to exercise a kind of creative choice, as in deciding whether *Das Kapital* belongs under Politics or Economics, *Gulliver's Travels* under Fantasy or Philosophy. But whether the decision where to shelve is easy or hard, once it is made all the librarian has to do is to put the book away. And so it is with judges, Professor Hart seems to say, in all essential particulars.

Surely the judicial process is something more than a cataloguing procedure. The judge does not discharge his responsibility when he pins an apt diagnostic label on the case. He has to do something about it, to treat it, if you will. It is this larger responsibility which explains why interpretative problems almost never turn on a single word, and also why lawyers for generations have found the putting of imaginary borderline cases useful, not only "on the penumbra," but in order to know where the penumbra begins.

These points can be made clear, I believe, by drawing again on our example of the statutory fragment which reads, "All improvements must be promptly reported to. . . . " Whatever the concluding phrase may be, the judge has not solved his problems simply by deciding what kind of improvement is meant. Almost all of the words in the sentence may require interpretation, but most obviously this is so of "promptly" and "reported." What kind of "report" is contemplated: a written note, a call at the office, entry in a hospital record? How specific must it be? Will it be enough to say "a lot better," or "a big house with a bay window"?

Now it should be apparent to any lawyer that in interpreting words like "improvement," "prompt," and "report," no real help is obtained by asking how some extralegal "standard instance" would define these words. But, much more important, when these words are all parts of a single structure of thought, they are in interaction with one another during the process of interpretation. "What is an 'improvement'? Well, it must be something that can be made the subject of a report. So, for purposes of this statute 'improvement' really means 'reportable improvement.' What kind of 'report' must be made? Well, that depends upon the sort of 'improvement' about which information is desired and the reasons for desiring the information."

When we look beyond individual words to the statute as a whole, it becomes apparent how the putting of hypothetical cases assists the interpretative process generally. By pulling our minds first in one direction, then in another, these cases help us to understand the fabric of thought before us. This fabric is something we seek to discern, so that we may know truly what it is, but it is also something that we inevitably help create as we strive (in accordance with our obligation of fidelity to law) to make the statute a coherent, workable whole.

I should have considered all these remarks much too trite to put down here if they did not seem to be demanded in an answer to the theory of interpretation proposed by Professor Hart, a theory by which he puts such store that he implies we cannot have fidelity to law in any meaningful sense unless we are prepared to accept it. Can it be possible that the positivistic philosophy demands that we abandon a view of interpretation which sees as its central concern, not words, but purpose and structure? If so, then the stakes in this battle of schools are indeed high.

I am puzzled by the novelty Professor Hart attributes to the lessons I once tried to draw from Wittgenstein's example about teaching a game to children. I was simply trying to show the role reflection plays in deciding what ought to be done. I was trying to make such simple points as that decisions about what ought to be done are improved by reflection, by an exchange of views with others sharing the same problems, and by imagining various situations that might be presented. I was assuming that all of these innocent and familiar measures might serve to sharpen our perception of what we were trying to do, and that the product of the whole process might be, not merely a more apt choice of means for the end sought, but a clarification of the end itself. I had thought that a famous judge of the English bench had something like this in mind when he spoke of the common law as working "itself pure." If this view of the judicial process is no longer entertained in the country of its origin, I can only say that, whatever the vicissitudes of Lord Mansfield's British reputation may be, he always remain for us in this country a heroic figure of jurisprudence.

I have stressed here the deficiencies of Professor Hart's theory as that theory affects judicial interpretation. I believe, however, that its defects go deeper and result ultimately from a mistaken theory about the meaning of language generally. Professor Hart seems to subscribe to what may be called "the pointer theory of meaning." [1] a theory which ignores or minimizes the effect on the meaning of words of the speaker's purpose and the structure of language. Characteristically, this school of thought embraces the notion of "common usage." The reason is, of course, that it is only with the aid of this notion that it can seem to attain the inert datum of meaning it seeks, a meaning isolated from the effects of purpose and structure.

It would not do to attempt here an extended excursus into linguistic theory. I shall have to content myself with remarking that the theory of meaning implied in Professor Hart's essay seems to me to have been rejected by three men who stand at the very head of modern developments in logical analysis: Wittgenstein, Russell, and Whitehead. Wittgenstein's posthumous *Philosophical Investigations* constitutes a sort of running commentary on the way words shift and transform their meanings as they move from context to context. Russell repudiates the cult of "common usage," and asks what "in-

1. I am speaking of the linguistic theory that seems to be implied in the essay under discussion here. In Professor Hart's brilliant inaugural address, *Definition and Theory in Jurisprudence*, 70 L.Q.Rev. (1954), the most important point made is that terms like "rule," "right," and "legal person" cannot be defined by pointing to corresponding things or actions in the external world, but can only be understood in terms of the function performed by them in the larger system, just as one cannot understand the umpire's ruling, "Y're out!" without having at baseball. Even in the analysis presented in the inaugural address, however, Professor Hart seems to think that the dependence of meaning on function and context is a peculiarity of formal and explicit systems, like those of a game or a legal system. He seems not to recognize that what he has to say about explicit systems is also true of the countless informal and overlapping systems that run through language as a whole. These implicit systematic or structural elements in language often enable us to understand at once the meaning of a word used in a wholly novel sense, as in the statement, "Experts regard the English Channel as the most difficult swim in the world." In the essay now being discussed, Professor Hart seems nowhere to recognize that a rule or statute has a structural or systematic quality that reflects itself in some measure into the meaning of every principal term in it.

stance" of the word "word" itself can be given that does not imply some specific intention in the use of it. Whitehead explains the appeal that "the deceptive identity of the repeated word" has for modern philosophers; only by assuming some linguistic constant (such as the "core of meaning") can validity be claimed for procedures of logic which of necessity move the word from one context to another.

## NOTES AND QUESTIONS

1. Do you agree with Professor Fuller's criticisms of Professor Hart? Do you think that Hart views himself as "proposing a theory of judicial interpretation"? Does Hart say that the "task of interpretation is commonly that of determining the meaning of the individual words of a legal rule"? Does Hart hold that the "core of meaning" "remains relatively constant, whatever the context in which the word may appear" or that this "meaning the word will have in any legal rule, whatever its purpose"? If Hart does not say this—or any rough equivalent—how do you account for Fuller's criticisms? Could Fuller argue that no matter what Hart explicitly says, his position as a whole amounts to the thesis which Fuller is attributing to him? Is there any evidence to support such a contention?

Consider the following from a later work of Professor Hart:

> . . . . There will indeed be plain cases constantly recurring in similar contexts to which general expressions are clearly applicable ('If anything is a vehicle a motor-car is one') . . . . The plain case, where the general terms seem to need no interpretation and where the recognition of instances seems unproblematic or 'automatic,' are only the familiar ones, constantly recurring in similar contexts, where there is general agreement in judgments as to the applicability of the classifying terms.

> General terms would be useless to us as a medium of communication unless there were such familiar, generally unchallenged cases. . . .

THE CONCEPT OF LAW 123 (1961). Do these remarks show that Professor Fuller was wrong about Professor Hart's "thesis"? Or do they show that Professor Hart has *changed* his thesis? Just what are the differences between the statement just quoted and its counterpart in the essay Fuller criticizes? Does Hart still believe that if "we are to communicate with each other at all, . . . then the general words we use . . . must have some standard instance in which no doubts are felt about its [sic] application"? What is the function of the phrase, "constantly recurring in similar contexts"? How often is it used? Is there anything like it in the earlier piece?

2. What is it that makes a case "plain," "clear," or "easy" for Hart? Does he explain how it is that some cases are "clear"? Or does he simply report that there are such cases? How does Fuller account for easy cases? Why does he feel it is necessary to do so?

3. What does Hart tell us about the characteristics of a core, as opposed to a penumbral, meaning case? In describing the penumbral

case is he contrasting it with core cases? If so, which—if any—of the following things is he saying about core cases? (1) Core cases possess no features in addition to those possessed by the "standard instance," nor do they lack features which the standard instance possesses. (2) In core cases the interpreter "must make a decision which" *is* "dictated to him." (3) In core cases "the facts and phenomena to which we fit our words and apply our rules are [not] . . . dumb." Automobiles *can* "speak up and say, 'I am a vehicle for the purpose of this legal rule.'" (4) In core cases "fact situations" do "await us neatly labeled, creased, and folded." (5) In core cases the interpreter does not have to "take the responsibility of deciding that words do or do not cover some case in hand." (6) The realm of core meaning is one in which men *can* "live by deduction alone." (7) Core cases are those which *are* controlled "by linguistic conventions." They are the cases in which rules "determine" or control "courts' decisions." Are these positions which can fairly be attributed to Professor Hart? If not, why not? And what might lead one to consider such an attribution? At one point in THE CONCEPT OF LAW, Professor Hart suggests that it is possible to "freeze the meaning of the rule so that its general terms must have the same meaning in every case where its application is in question." To do this, he says, one can fasten "on certain features present in the plain case and insist that these are both necessary and sufficient to bring anything which has them within the scope of the rule . . . ." *Id.* at 126. Does this observation tell us anything about Hart's conception of meaning?

4. Consider the following cases in light of the theories of meaning advanced by Hart and Fuller. Do these cases in any way illustrate the positions taken by the two professors? Do they suggest objections to, or justifications for, those positions?

### PEOPLE v. HALL

4 Cal.Rep. 399 (1854)

Mr. Ch. J. MURRAY delivered the opinion of the Court, Mr. J. HEYDENFELDT concurred.

The appellant, a free white citizen of this State, was convicted of murder upon the testimony of Chinese witnesses.

The point involved in this case, is the admissibility of such evidence.

The 394th section of the Act Concerning Civil Cases, provides that no Indian or Negro shall be allowed to testify as a witness in any action or proceeding in which a White person is a party.

The 14th section of the Act of April 16th, 1850, regulating Criminal Proceedings, provides that "No Black, or Mulatto person, or Indian, shall be allowed to give evidence in favor of, or against a white man."

The true point at which we are anxious to arrive, is the legal signification of the words, "Black, Mulatto, Indian and White person," and whether the Legislature adopted them as generic terms, or intended to limit their application to specific types of the human species.

Before considering this question, it is proper to remark the difference between the two sections of our Statute, already quoted, the latter being more broad and comprehensive in its exclusion, by use of the word "Black," instead of Negro.

Conceding, however, for the present, that the word "Black," as used in the 14th section, and "Negro," in 394th, are convertible terms, and that the former was intended to include the latter, let us proceed to inquire who are excluded from testifying as witnesses under the term "Indian."

When Columbus first landed upon the shores of this continent, in his attempt to discover a western passage to the Indies, he imagined that he had accomplished the object of his expedition, and that the Island of San Salvador was one of those Islands of the Chinese sea, lying near the extremity of India, which had been described by navigators.

Acting upon the hypothesis, and also perhaps from the similarity of features and physical conformation, he gave to the Islanders the name of Indians, which appellation was universally adopted, and extended to the aboriginals of the New World, as well as of Asia.

From that time, down to a very recent period, the American Indians and the Mongolian, or Asiatic, were regarded as the same type of the human species.

In order to arrive at a correct understanding of the intention of our Legislature, it will be necessary to go back to the early history of legislation on this subject, our Statute being only a transcript of those of older States.

At the period from which this legislation dates, those portions of Asia which include India proper, the Eastern Archipelago, and the countries washed by the Chinese waters, as far as then known, were denominated the Indies, from which the inhabitants had derived the generic name of Indians.

Ethnology, at that time, was unknown as a distinct science, or if known, had not reached that high point of perfection which it has since attained by the scientific inquiries and discoveries of the master minds of the last half century. Few speculations had been made with regard to the moral or physical differences between the different races of mankind. These were general in their character, and limited to those visible and palpable variations which could not escape the attention of the most common observer.

The general, or perhaps universal opinion of that day was, that there were but three distinct types of the human species, which, in their turn, were subdivided into varieties or tribes. This opinion is still held by many scientific writers, and is supported by Cuvier, one of the most eminent naturalists of modern times.

Many ingenious speculations have been resorted to for the purpose of sustaining this opinion. It has been supposed, and not without plausibility, that this continent was first peopled by Asiatics, who crossed Behring's Straits, and from thence found their way down to the more fruitful climates of Mexico and South America. Almost every tribe has some tradition of coming from the North, and many of them, that their ancestors came from some remote country beyond the ocean.

From the eastern portions of Kamchatka, the Aleutian Islands form a long and continuous group, extending eastward to that portion of the North American Continent inhabited by the Esquimaux. They appear to be a continuation of the lofty volcanic ranges which traverse the two continents, and are inhabited by a race who resemble, in a remarkable degree, in language and appearance, both the inhabitants of Kamtschatka (who are admitted to be the Mongolian type,) and the Esquimaux, who again, in turn, resemble other tribes of American Indians. The similarity of the skulls and pelvis, and the general configuration of the two races; the remarkable resemblance in eyes, beard, hair, and other peculiarities, together with the contiguity of the two Continents, might well have led to the belief that this country was first peopled by the Asiatics, and that the difference between the different tribes and the parent stock was such as would necessarily arise from the circumstances of climate, pursuits, and other physical causes, and was no greater than that existing between the Arab and the European, both of whom were supposed to belong to the Caucasian race.

Although the discoveries of eminent Archeologists, and the researches of modern Geologists, have given to this Continent an antiquity of thousands of years anterior to the evidence of man's existence, and the light of modern science may have shown conclusively that it was not peopled by the inhabitants of Asia, but that the Aborigines are a distinct type, and as such claim a distinct origin, still, this would not, in any degree, alter the meaning of the term, and render that specific which was before generic.

We have adverted to these speculations for the purpose of showing that the name of Indian, from the time of Columbus to the present day, has been used to designate, not alone the North American Indian, but the whole of the Mongolian race, and that the name, though first applied probably through mistake, was afterwards continued as appropriate on account of the supposed common origin.

That this was the common opinion in the early history of American legislation, cannot be disputed, and therefore, all legislation upon the subject must have borne relation to that opinion.

Can, then, the use of the word "Indian," because at the present day it may be sometimes regarded as a specific, and not as a generic term, alter this conclusion? We think not; because at the origin of the legislation we are considering, it was used and admitted in its common and ordinary acceptation, as a generic term, distinguishing the great Mongolian race, and as such, its meaning then became fixed by law, and in construing Statutes the legal meaning of words must be preserved.

Again: the words of the Act must be construed in *pari materia*. It will not be disputed that "White" and "Negro," are generic terms, and refer to two of the great types of mankind. If these, as well as the word "Indian," are not to be regarded as generic terms, including the two great races which they were intended to designate, but only specific, and applying to those Whites and Negroes who were inhabitants of this Continent at the time of the passage of the Act, the most anomalous consequences would ensue. The European white man who comes here would not be shielded from the testimony of the degraded and demoralized caste, while the Negro, fresh from the coast of Africa, or the Indian of Patagonia, the Kanaka, South Sea Islander, or New Hollander, would be admitted, upon their arrival, to testify against white citizens in our courts of law.

To argue such a proposition would be an insult to the good sense of the Legislature.

The evident intention of the Act was to throw around the citizen a protection for life and property, which could only be secured by removing him above the corrupting influences of degraded castes.

It can hardly be supposed that any Legislature would attempt this by excluding domestic Negroes and Indians, who not unfrequently have correct notions of their obligations to society; and turning loose upon the community the more degraded tribes of the same species, who have nothing in common with us, in language, country or laws.

We have, thus far, considered this subject on the hypothesis that the 14th section of the Act Regulating Criminal Proceedings, and the 394th section of the Practice Act, were the same.

As before remarked, there is a wide difference between the two. The word "Black" may include all Negroes, but the term "Negro" does not include all Black persons.

By the use of this term in this connection, we understand it to mean the opposite of "White," and that it should be taken as contradistinguished from all White persons.

In using the words, "No Black, or Mulatto person, or Indian shall be allowed to give evidence for or against a White person," the Legislature, if any intention can be ascribed to it, adopted the most comprehensive terms to embrace every known class of shade or color, as the apparent design was to protect the White person from the influence of all testimony other than that of persons of the same caste. The use of these terms must, by every sound rule of construction, exclude every one who is not of white blood.

The Act of Congress in defining what description of aliens may become naturalized citizens, provides that every "free white citizen," &c. In speaking of this subject, Chancellor Kent says, that "the Act confines the description to "white" citizens, and that it is a matter of doubt, whether, under this provision, any of the tawny races of Asia can be admitted to the privileges of citizenship." 2 Kent's Com. 72.

We are not disposed to leave this question in any doubt. The word "White" has a distinct signification, which *ex vi termini*, excludes black, yellow, and all other colors. It will be observed, by reference to the first section of the second article of the Constitution of this State, that none but white males can become electors, except in the case of Indians, who may be admitted by special Act of the Legislature. On examination of the constitutional debates, it will be found that not a little difficulty existed in selecting these precise words, which were finally agreed upon as the most comprehensive that could be suggested to exclude all inferior races.

If the term "White," as used in the Constitution, was not understood in its generic sense as including the Caucasian race, and necessarily excluding all others, where was the necessity of providing for the admission of Indians to the privilege of voting, by special legislation?

We are of the opinion that the words "White," "Negro," "Mulatto," "Indian," and "Black person," wherever they occur in our Constitution and laws, must be taken in their generic sense, and that, even admitting the Indian of this Continent is not of the Mongolian type, that the words "Black person," in the 14th section must be taken as contradistinguished from White, and necessarily excludes all races other than the Caucasian.

We have carefully considered all the consequences resulting from a different rule of construction, and are satisfied that even in a doubtful case we would be impelled to this decision on grounds of public policy.

The same rule which would admit them to testify, would admit them to all the equal rights of citizenship, and we might soon see them at the polls, in the jury box, upon the bench, and in our legislative halls.

This is not a speculation which exists in the excited and overheated imagination of the patriot and statesman, but it is an actual and present danger.

The anomalous spectacle of a distinct people, living in our community, recognizing no laws of this State except through necessity, bringing with them their prejudices and national feuds, in which they indulge in open violation of law; whose mendacity is proverbial; a race of people whom nature has marked as inferior, and who are incapable of progress or intellectual development beyond a certain point, as their history has shown; differing in language, opinions, color, and physical conformation; between whom and ourselves nature has placed an impassable difference, is now presented, and for them is claimed, not only the right to swear away the life of a citizen, but the further privilege of participating with us in administering the affairs of our Government.

These facts were before the Legislature that framed this Act, and have been known as matters of public history to every subsequent Legislature.

There can be no doubt as to the intention of the Legislature, and that if it had ever been anticipated that this class of people were not embraced in the prohibition, then such specific words would have been employed as would have put the matter beyond any possible controversy.

For these reasons, we are of opinion that the testimony was inadmissible.

The judgment is reversed and the cause remanded.

INTERPRETATION OF THE 1919 CONVENTION CONCERNING EMPLOYMENT OF WOMEN DURING THE NIGHT

Perm. Ct. Intl. Just., 1932, 3 Hudson, World Court Reports 99 (1938)

[Difficulties having arisen regarding the proper interpretation of the 1919 Convention Concerning Employment of Women at Night (1 Hudson, Internation Legislation 412 (1931)) and a proposed revision to clarify the point having failed of adoption at the Fifteenth International Labor Conference in 1931, the International Labor Office asked the Council of the League of Nations to obtain an advisory opinion on the question:

"Does the Convention concerning employment of women during the night, adopted in 1919 by the International Labour Conference, apply, in the industrial undertakings covered by the said Convention, to women who hold positions of supervision or management and are not ordinarily engaged in manual work?"]

Pursuant to Article 424 of the Treaty of Versailles, the first meeting of the "International Labour Conference," the creation of which was provided for in Part XIII of the Treaty, was to take place in October 1919; according to an annex to Article 426, the Conference was to meet at Washington and its agenda was to include the following points: "(3) Women's employment: . . . (b) during the night; . . . (5) Extension and application of the international conventions adopted at Berne in 1906 on the prohibition of night work for women employed in industry. . . ."

Although the Treaty of Versailles had not yet come into force, the Conference was held as provided in Article 424 of the Treaty. On November 28th, 1919, it adopted, in accordance with the procedure laid down in Part XIII of the Treaty of Versailles, a draft convention concerning employment of women during the night; in accordance with Article II, this Convention came into force, so far as concerned the first Members of the International Labour Organization which had registered their ratifications with the Secretariat of the League of Nations, on June 13th, 1921. It contains, inter alia, the following clause:

"Article 3. Women without distinction of age shall not be employed during the night in any public or private industrial undertaking, or in any branch thereof, other than an undertaking in which only members of the same family are employed."

According to the written Statement submitted to the Court on behalf of the International Labour Organization, as the result of the foregoing, "one thing alone remained clear; and that was that the terms of the Convention were interpreted in two very different ways. Some governments read into Article 3 a prohibition against night work for all women. Others thought they were entitled to exempt certain categories of working women from the application of the Convention."

The wording of Article 3, considered by itself, gives rise to no difficulty; it is general in its terms and free from ambiguity or obscurity. It prohibits the employment during the night in industrial establishments of women without distinction of age. Taken by itself, it necessarily applies to the categories of women contemplated by the question submitted to the Court. If, therefore, Article 3 of the Washington Convention is to be interpreted in such a way as not to apply to women holding posts of supervision and management and not ordinarily engaged in manual work, it is necessary to find some valid ground for interpreting the provision otherwise than in accordance with the natural sense of the words.

The terms of Article 3 of the Washington Convention, which are in themselves clear and free from ambiguity, are in no respect inconsistent either with the title, or with the Preamble, or with any other provisions of the Convention. The title refers to "employment of women during the night." The Preamble speaks of "women's employment during the night." . . . Article 2 states what is meant by the term "night." These provisions, therefore, do not affect the scope of Article 3, which provides that "women shall not be employed during the night either in any public or private industrial undertaking, or in any branch thereof."

The question which the Court is now called upon to answer amounts therefore to deciding whether there exist, in respect of this Convention concerning the employment of women during the night, good grounds for restricting the operation of Article 3 to women engaged in manual work.

The first ground which the Court has considered is whether any such restriction results from the fact that the Convention is a Labour convention, i. e., one prepared within the framework of Part XIII of the Treaty of Versailles of 1919, and in accordance with the procedure provided for therein, and whether in consequence a clause, such as Article 3, which is couched in general terms, must be interpreted as intended to apply only to manual workers, upon the ground that it was the improvement of the lot of the manual worker which was the principal object of Part XII. . . .

But the Court has considered whether it could be maintained that, in view of the fact that the improvement of the lot of the manual worker was the aim of Part XIII, a provision in a Labour convention couched in general terms must be assumed to be intended to apply only to manual workers unless the opposite intention is made manifest by the terms of the Convention. This would be tantamount to saying that, as no such contrary intention is shown to exist in the case of this Convention, Article 3 must be regarded as applying only to manual workers.

The Court holds that it would not be sound to argue thus.

It is certainly true that the amelioration of the lot of the manual worker was the main preoccupation of the authors of Part XIII of the Treaty of Versailles of 1919; but the Court is not disposed to regard the sphere of activity of the International Labour Organization as circumscribed so closely, in respect of the persons with which it was to concern itself, as to raise any presumption that a Labour convention must be interpreted as being restricted in its operation to manual workers, unless a contrary intention appears.  .  .  .

To justify the adoption of a rule for the interpretation of Labour conventions to the effect that words describing general categories of human beings such as "persons" or "women" must prima facie be regarded as referring only to manual workers, it would be necessary to show that it was only with manual workers that the Labour Organization was intended to concern itself  .  .  .

The words used in the Preamble and in the operative articles of Part XIII—both in the French and English texts—to describe the individuals who are the subjects of the International Labour Organization's activities are not words which are confined to manual workers.  The words are *"travailleurs,"* "workers," "work-people," *"travailleurs salaries,"* "wage-earners," words which do not exclude employed persons doing non-manual work, as perhaps might have been held to be the case if the words used had been *"ouvrier"* or "labourer." In this connection, the wording of Article 393—providing for the election of Members of the Governing Body of the International Labour Office—is noteworthy.  In paragraph 5 of that article, the word "workers" in the English text is represented by *"employés et ouvriers"* in the French text.

The text, therefore, of Part XIII does not support the view that it is workers doing manual work—to the exclusion of other categories of workers—with whom the International Labour Organization was to concern itself.  This being so, the fact that the Washington Convention is a Labour convention does not provide sufficient reason for interpreting "women" in Article 3 of that Convention as confined to women doing manual work.

It has further been maintained that the circumstances in which the Convention was adopted at Washington afford sufficient reason for confining the operation of Article 3 to female workers doing manual work.  The argument is as follows:

The business before the Washington Conference in 1919 was (as regards this subject of the employment of women at night) that of the extension and application of the Berne Convention of 1906 on the prohibition of night work for women employed in industry.  As the Berne Convention covered only women engaged in manual work, Article 3 of the Washington Convention, however general in its terms, must be interpreted in the light of the corresponding provision in the Berne Convention, and must be restricted to female workers.  The limitation in the meaning of Article 3 results, according to this view, from the work in which the Washington Conference was engaged. The Convention should be read in the light of the agenda of the Conference as fixed by Part XIII of the Treaty of Versailles. This argument is not based on the "preparatory work" or *travaux préparatoires* of the Convention, but on the fact that the programme of the Conference was fixed and on the contents of that programme.

The weakness of this line of argument is that the agenda of the Washington Conference as laid down in Part XIII contained two items, each of which would cover the Convention concerning employment of women during the night. Item 3 was: "Women's employment . . . (b) during the night." Item 5 was: "Extension and application of the international conventions adopted at Berne in 1906 on the prohibition of night work for women employed in industry. . . . " The text of the Convention as adopted made no reference to the Berne Convention. The third paragraph of the Preamble of the Washington Convention connects this Convention with the third item in the agenda and not with the fifth; this paragraph runs as follows: "Having decided upon the adoption of certain proposals with regard to 'women's employment during the night,' which is part of the third item in the agenda for the Washington meeting of the Conference. . . . "

The Washington Convention cannot therefore be said, by reason of the work on which the 1919 Conference was engaged, to be so intimately linked with the Berne Convention as to require that the terms of the Washington Convention should bear the same meaning as the terms of the Berne Convention. . . .

It has been stated that in 1919, when the Convention was adopted at Washington, very few women actually held positions of supervision or management in industrial undertakings, and that the application of the Convention to women holding such posts was never considered. Even if this were so, however, it does not by itself afford sufficient reason for ignoring the terms of the Convention. The mere fact that, at the time when the Convention on Night Work of Women was concluded, certain facts or situations, which the terms of the Convention in their ordinary meaning are wide enough to cover, were not thought of, does not justify interpreting those of its provisions which are general in scope otherwise than in accordance with their terms.

The grounds considered above upon which it has been suggested that the natural meaning of the text of the Convention can be displaced, do not appear to the Court to be well founded.

The Court has been so struck with the confident opinions expressed by several delegates with expert knowledge of the subject at Geneva during the discussions in 1930 and 1931 on the proposal to revise the Washington Convention on Night Work of Women to the effect that the Convention applied only to working women—ouvrieres—that the Court has been led to examine the preparatory work of the Convention in order to see whether or not it confirmed the opinions expressed at Geneva.

In doing, so, the Court does not intend to derogate in any way from the rule which it has laid down on previous occasions that there is no occasion to have regard to preparatory work if the text of a convention is sufficiently clear in itself.

The history of this Convention as shown by the preparatory work is as follows:

The task of organizing the First Labour Conference was entrusted to an international Committee, the membership of which, like the agenda of the Conference, was fixed by Part XIII of the Treaty of Versailles. The recommendation of this Organizing Committee was that the Conference should urge all States, Members of the League of Nations, to accede to the Convention of Berne.

A Committee was appointed by the Conference to deal with the subject of the employment of women. As regards the employment of women by night, this Committee went beyond the proposals of the Organizing Committee and recommended a new convention which was to supersede that of Berne, but was to follow it in outline, while effecting a series of changes which are indicated in the Committee's report. Whether it was the intention of the members of the Committee that the new convention which they recommended for adoption should follow so closely the Convention it was to supersede as to carry into the new convention any agreed interpretation of phrases and words in the old Convention, is a matter which the Committee's report is insufficient to determine. As many phrases can be found which tell one way as the other. On the other hand, the wording of the report does not seem sufficient to show in the French text only, six times words are used which are consistent with the view that *"femmes"* means *"femmes"* and not *"ouvrieres,"* and once only the word used in *"ouvrieres,"* and that only in the general statement at the end of the report that an effective prohibition of night work for women will constitute a marked progress in the *"protection de la sante des ouvrieres."* As to this last sentence, it is well to note that the French and English texts do not correspond, that the English word is the phrase "women workers," and that Miss Smith, who submitted the report, was English and used her own language.

The report of the Committee was adopted unanimously and was referred to the Drafting Committee of the Conference with instructions to prepare a new convention on the lines of the Convention of Berne, embodying the amendments adopted, and to add new formal paragraphs.

. . .

The preparatory work thus confirms the conclusion reached on a study of the text of the Convention that there is no good reason for interpreting Article 3 otherwise than in accordance with the natural meaning of the words . . . .

The similarity both in structure and in expression between the various draft Conventions adopted by the Labour Conference at Washington in 1919 leads the Court to attach some importance to the presence in one of the other Conventions of a specific exception that the provisions of that Convention should not apply to persons holding positions of supervision or management, nor to persons employed in a confidential capacity.

The Convention in question is that limiting the hours of work in industrial undertakings to eight in the day, usually known as the Eight Hour Day Convention  . . . .

If in the Eight Hour Day Convention, after a prohibition applicable to "persons," it was necessary to make an exception in respect of persons holding positions of supervision or management, it was equally necessary to make a corresponding exception in respect of women in the Convention on Night Work of Women, if it was intended that women holding positions of supervision or management should be excluded from the operation of the Convention.

*For these reasons, the Court,* by six votes to five, is of opinion that the Convention concerning employment of women during the night, adopted in 1919 by the International Labour Conference, applies in the industrial undertakings covered by the said Convention, to women who hold positions of supervision or management and are not ordinarily engaged in manual work.  . . .

Baron Rolin-Jacquemyns, Count Rostworowski, MM. Fromageot and Schucking, Judges, declare that, in their opinion, the agenda, documents and minutes of the Washington Conference which refer to the Berne Convention of 1906 on the prohibition of night work for women employed in industry, do not permit them to subscribe to the grounds and conclusions of the present opinion.

### Note: The Subject of the Hart-Fuller Debate

As Professor Hart indicates, his treatment of the "core" and the "penumbra" is part of a larger discussion of "the separation of the law that is from the law that ought to be."  That there is such a separation is asserted in the following remarks by John Austin:

> The existence of law is one thing; its merit or demerit is another. Whether it be or be not is one inquiry; whether it be or be not conformable to an assumed standard, is a different inquiry. A law, which actually exists, is a law though we happen to dislike it  . . . .

The Province of Jurisprudence Determined 184–185 (Hart ed. 1954). Confusion between "the law that is" and "the law that ought to be," according to Hart, may lead to either or both of the following attitudes toward law. (1) An undue reverence toward existing law, because the very fact of its existence signifies that it *ought to be.* (2) An undue irreverence toward the rules laid down by the accepted authorities, because only those rules which conform to morality are law. The first attitude leads to a conservative "quietism" which impedes reform. The second leads to a rebelliousness which threatens order. Can you see why reformers such as Austin—and his mentor, Jeremy Bentham—would be concerned to dissipate both of these attitudes? The distinction between what the law is and what it ought to be, says Austin, is a "truth  . . .  so simple and glaring that it seems idle to insist upon." Yet, he continues, "the enumeration of the instances in which it has been forgotton would fill a volume." Why is it, do you think, that "so simple and glaring" a "truth" should be "forgotten" so often? How can Professor Fuller and others take the position that it is not a truth at all?

Note Professor Hart's contention that those who wish to drop the distinction between what the law is and what it ought to be are inviting us "to revise our conception of what a legal rule is." How does Hart support this contention? Could it also be argued that those who would abandon the "is-ought" distinction are inviting us to revise our conception of how a legal rule means? Is there some necessary connection between the problem of the separation of the is and the ought and the problem of the nature of meaning? Is it true that, in Fuller's words, Hart "implies we cannot have fidelity to law in any meaningful sense unless we are prepared to accept" his "theory of interpretation"? Is this another way of saying that if Hart's theory is false there can be no such thing as law "in any meaningful sense"? That there can be no such thing as communication? Is Hart's theory of interpretation a necessary corrollary of the position that the "is" and the "ought" are distinguishable? If so, does this mean that communication would not be possible if there were no distinction between "is" and "ought"?

Note the distinctions Hart draws between "stupid," "mechanical," or "blind" interpretive decisions and "intelligent" interpretive decisions. Is he saying that "formalism" or "literalism" is a "stupid" mode of interpretation? If so, what is it that makes it stupid? What error or errors do formalists characteristically make? Can you see any relationship in Hart's exposition between "intelligent" interpretation and "contextual" interpretation? Between "intelligent" interpretation and "purposive" interpretation? What is the relationship for Hart between "intelligence" and "morality"? Are they as separable as law and morality? If they were not, what effect would it have on Hart's general position? Consider the following from Professor Fuller:

> . . . . Professor Hart seems to assume that evil aims may have as much coherence and inner logic as good ones. I, for one, refuse to accept that assumption. I realize that I am here raising, or perhaps dodging, questions that lead into the most difficult problems of the epistemology of ethics. Even if I were competent to undertake an excursus in that direction, this is not the place for it. I shall have to rest on the assertion of a belief that may seem naive, namely, that coherence and goodness have more affinity than coherence and evil.

*Positivism and Fidelity to Law,* 71 Harv.L.Rev. 630, 636 (1958). Recall, also, the following from Hart:

> Of course, I am not unaware that a whole philosophical tradition has sought to demonstrate the fact that we cannot correctly call decisions or behavior truly rational unless they are in conformity with moral aims and principles.

What is the relevance of this "philosophical tradition" to Hart's argument? Does he have any intellectual obligation to discuss it? Or could he justifiably argue that "this is not the place" for "an excursus in that direction"? If so, what would be the place for such an excursus?

The subject of the Hart-Fuller debate was advertised as the distinction between "law and morals" or the "is" and the "ought." Which of the following might also be considered "the subject" of that debate: (1) the nature of law; (2) the nature of morality; (3) the nature of language, meaning, and communication; (4) the nature of intelligence? How would you defend your answer? Are there any other subjects which might plausibly be viewed as involved in the Hart-Fuller debate? If so, what obligations were the disputants under to discuss them? What factors might justify their refusal to do so?

## SECTION TWO: THE MEANING OF LANGUAGE

### STATE V. DANIEL

136 No.Car. 415 (1904)

Edgar Alston, a witness for the State, testified: "I went to my hog-pen one Sunday at Littleton, about two months ago, taking them slops. Just below the hog-pen, when I got there, was the defendant and his brother-in-law, Mr. Burton. After I fed the hogs and started towards the house the defendant called me to come to him. I told him I was in a hurry to get back home to dress and go to preaching. He called me again, and said 'You come here.' I replied, 'Yes, boss man, of course if you order me to come I'll come.' I pulled off my hat and went on to him, and he cursed me and said 'Why can't you come to me when I call you?' I told him I did. I always obey a white man when he calls me, and I knew he meant for me to come. Just about that time he snatched a knife out of his right hand coat pocket that was open and put the blade right up against my throat and told me if I moved my hands he would cut my damned throat, and then he tapped me on the head with the handle of it. I stood there with my hands right down by my sides until he told me to put my hat on and go to the house. Mr. Burton was standing near there, (572) but did not try to stop him. I think the defendant was kind of intoxicated. I do not think if he had been sober he would have done so." On cross-examination the witness stated: "It was between eleven and twelve o'clock. I pulled my hat off as I started to him, and just as I got up to him I put my hat on, and he asked me why I did not come up to him when he called, and told me to take off my hat like a damn negro ought when he came up to talk to him, and then drew his knife and pulled off my hat."

The defendant, in his testimony, denied that he had used a knife, but admitted that he cursed the prosecutor, and stated that he had merely asked him to bring him a match and when he came told him he was too damned slow.

J. H. Burton, a witness for the defendant, testified that he is a brother-in-law of the defendant, and that the latter merely asked the prosecutor to bring him a match, and as the prosecutor started back to get it the defendant cursed him several times. The witness was with Daniel at the time, but saw no knife, though he may have had one without the witness seeing it. The prosecutor took off his hat after he came up to the defendant. The witness admitted that he did not say anything about a match at the trial before the magistrate.

There was evidence tending to show that the defendant was under the influence of liquor at the time of the alleged assault, and also at the trial before the magistrate, when he drew a stick back at his own father.

The prosecutor was recalled and testified that the defendant did not ask him for a match and did not state at the magistrate's trial that he had done so. The defendant was convicted of a simple assault, and appealed from the judgment rendered upon the verdict.

. . .

Walker, J. . . . .

The first instruction was that if the defendant cursed the prosecutor, Alston, and ordered him to come to him, and Alston obeyed through fear, the defendant was guilty of an assault. Before the prosecutor reached the place near the hog pen where the defendant was standing, the latter had made no threat nor had he offered or attempted any violence to the person of the prosecutor, nor was there any display or exhibition of force of any kind, so far as the evidence here shows. In this state of the case we are unable to sustain this instruction as a correct statement of the law of assault. It would seem, says READE, J., that there ought to be no difficulty in determining whether any given state of facts amounts to an assault, but the behavior of men towards each other varies by such mere shades that it is sometimes very difficult to characterize properly their acts and words. S. v. Hampton, 63 N.C., 14. While the law relating to this crime would seem to be simple and of easy application, we are often perplexed in our attempt to discriminate between what is and what is not an assault. But in (574) this case we have no such difficulty, as the law applicable to the facts has been clearly stated and well settled by the decisions of this Court.

An assault is an intentional offer or attempt by violence to do any injury to the person of another. There must be an offer or attempt. Mere words, however insulting or abusive, will not constitute an assault, nor will a mere threat or violence menaced, as distinguished from violence begun to be executed. Where an unequivocal purpose of violence is accompanied by any act which, if not stopped or diverted, will be followed by personal injury, the execution of the purpose is then begun and there has been a sufficient offer or attempt. S. v. Davis, 23 N.C., 125, 35 Am.Dec., 735; S. v. Reavis, 113 N.C., 677. This principle, as stated by Judge GASTON in the first case cited, has been adopted as a correct exposition of the law of assault, not only in subsequent decisions of this Court, but in numerous cases decided in the courts of the other States. There must, therefore, be not only threatening words or violence menaced, but the defendant must have committed some act in execution of his purpose. It is not necessary at all that his words should be accompanied or followed by an actual battery, for a mere assault excludes the idea of a battery, but he must either offer to do violence, as by drawing back his fist or raising a stick, or attempt to do it, as by aiming a blow at another which does not take effect because it is warded off by a third person, or by shooting at another and missing the mark —all of which is clearly and fully explained by PEARSON, C. J., in S. v. Myerfield, 61 N.C., 108. It is not necessary, in view of the facts of this case, that we should stop here to state how these acts can be qualified by words or otherwise, and with what restrictions or exceptions, so as to relieve the accused of any guilt. The law in this respect is also discussed in Myerfield's case, *supra*.

The principle is well established that not only is a person who offers or attempts by violence to injure the person of another guilty of an assault, but no one by the show of violence has the right to put another in fear and thereby force him to leave a place where he has the right to be. . . . . It is not always necessary to constitute an assault that the person whose conduct is in question should have the present capacity to inflict injury, for if by threats or a menace of violence which he attempts to execute, or by threats and a display of force, he causes another to reasonably apprehend imminent danger and thereby forces him to do otherwise than he would have done, or to abandon any lawful purpose or pursuit, he commits an assault. It is the apparently imminent danger that is threatened rather than the present ability to inflict injury which distinguishes violence menaced from an assault. S. v. Jeffries and S. v. Martin, *supra*. It is sufficient if the aggressor, by his conduct, lead another to suppose that he will do that which he apparently attempts to do. 1 Archb.Cr. Pr., Pl. & Ev. (8 Ed. by Pomeroy), 907, 908.

If, therefore, the defendant had threatened the prosecutor with violence and the threat had been accompanied by any show of force, such as drawing a sword or knife, or if he had advanced towards the prosecutor in a menacing attitude, even without any weapon, and had been stopped before he delivered a blow, and the prosecutor had been put in fear and compelled to leave the place where he had the lawful right to be, the assault would have been complete, although he was not at the time in striking distance. But in this case, so far as the facts recited in the first instruction should be considered, (576) there was not even violence menaced, but, at most, only offensive and profane words. There must be an overt act or an attempt, or the unequivocal appearance of an attempt, with force and violence, to do a corporal injury—such an act as will convey to the mind of the other person a well grounded apprehension of personal injury. Bare words will never do, for, however violent they may be, they can not take the place of that force which is necessary to complete the offense. They are often the exhibition of harmless passion and do not by themselves constitute a breach of the peace, as the law supposes that against mere rudeness of language ordinary firmness will be a sufficient protection. . . .

It may be, as suggested, that the positions of the two parties were relatively unequal, as the defendant belonged to a strong and dominant and the prosecutor to a weak and servile race, and it may further be that the words of the prosecutor as he approached the defendant were the cringing utterances of servility and showed great humility and submissiveness because of the lowliness of his station in life as compared with that of the defendant, and therefore he abjectly obeyed the latter's command to come to him.  All this may be true;  and while it reflects little credit upon the defendant, whose conduct as it now appears to us can not be too severely condemned, it can not have the effect of reversing a long established principle of the law to which we must adhere, it being founded upon reason and justice and treated by the courts and the text writers as one of universal application.  S. v. Milsaps, 82 N.C., 549, illustrates the extent to which the principle has been carried.  In that case it appeared that the defendant addressed grossly insulting language to the prosecutor and then picked up a stone about twelve feet from the prosecutor, but did not offer to throw it, and the Court held that it was not an assault, but only violence menaced, and it was therefore error for the lower Court to charge the jury that if the acts and (577) words of the defendant were such as to put a man of ordinary firmness in fear of immediate danger, and the defendant had the ability at the time to inflict an injury, he would be guilty.  Substantially to the same effect is S. v. Mooney, 61 N.C., 434.  See also, Johnson v. State, 43 Texas, 576.  In neither of those cases, though, was the prosecutor deterred from doing what he had a right to do, or in any respect unlawfully restrained in his action or conduct or constrained to act contrary to his wishes.

NOTES AND QUESTIONS

1.  Although State v. Daniel is a criminal assault case, in some jurisdictions the injunction against "bare words" is applied to the law of tortious assaults as well.  Suppose that the prosecutor in *Daniel* had sued in tort, do you think that the court's reasoning would have been the same?  Is there any reason why it should not be?

Prosser describes a tortious assault as follows:

The defendant is liable for the apprehension of immediate harmful or offensive contact with the plaintiff's person, caused by acts intended to result in such contacts, or the apprehension of them, directed at the plaintiff or a third person.

HANDBOOK OF THE LAW OF TORTS 34 (1955).  Is a court which intones that "bare words will never do" saying that words cannot be "acts intended to result in  .  .  .  the apprehension" of "immediate harmful or offensive contact with the plaintiff's person"?  Is this because words are not used in that way?  Is it because words cannot be used in that way?  Is it because words are not acts?  Is there implicit in Walker's opinion the assumption that speech is different from conduct—and that the difference is material?  Walker speaks of "an act as will convey to the mind of the other person a well grounded apprehension of personal injury." Could he be arguing that utterances are not acts of the sort which convey "well grounded" apprehensions? Is he saying that *actions speak louder than words?* With regard to what do actions speak louder than words? How is the word "louder" being used? How is the word "speak" being used? In what way do actions "speak"?

2. Consider the applicability of Professor Fuller's emphasis on purpose. Should Walker's method of decision have included an examination of the "purpose" of the law of assault? Did it include such an examination? What would you say is the purpose of the law of assault? "The interest in freedom from apprehension of a harmful or offensive contact with the person," says Prosser, "as distinguished from the contact itself, is protected by an action for the tort known as assault." Is this "interest" also the "purpose" of the law of assault, in Fuller's use of the term? If it is, should it matter what means are used to create the "apprehension," so long as (a) it was intended to occur, (b) it was reasonably likely to occur, and (c) it in fact did occur? If it doesn't matter, is there nevertheless something erroneous in the trial court's charge to the jury? Suppose that the trial court had given the following instruction:

> If the defendant intended by his words to make the prosecutor apprehend imminent danger to his person and the defendant did in fact suffer such an apprehension, the defendant is guilty of an assault.

Is there any reason that Walker advances why the law of assault could not be stated in this way? Is it accurate to say that this is what the law of assault "means" or "provides," given the statement of its purpose hypothesized earlier? What would Fuller say? Is the meaning of the word "purpose" the same in the phrase "purpose of the statute" as it is in "purpose of the law of assault"? Can a body of law have a purpose in the same way as a specific legal rule? What might make us think so? What might make us think not?

3. Consider the statements "mere words, however insulting or abusive, will not constitute an assault" and "bare words will never do" in light of the excerpts from Whitehead and Allport which follow.

*Alfred North Whitehead*

## An Enquiry Concerning the Principles Of Natural Knowledge *

'Significance' is the relatedness of things. To say that significance is experience, is to affirm that perceptual knowledge is nothing else than an apprehension of the relatedness of things, namely of things in their relations and as related. Certainly if we commence

* From 12–13 (1919). Reprinted with permission of Cambridge University Press.

with a knowledge of things, and then look around for their relations we shall not find them. 'Causal connection' is merely one typical instance of the universal ruin of relatedness. But then we are quite mistaken in thinking that there is a possible knowledge of things as unrelated. It is thus out of the question to start with a knowledge of things antecedent to a knowledge of their relations. The so-called properties of things can always be expressed as their relatedness to other things unspecified, and natural knowledge is exclusively concerned with relatedness.

3.6  The relatedness which is the subject of natural knowledge cannot be understood without reference to the general characteristics of perception. Our perception of natural events and natural objects is a perception from within nature, and is not an awareness contemplating all nature impartially from without. When Dr. Johnson 'surveyed mankind from China to Peru,' he did it from Pump Court in London at a certain date. Even Pump Court was too wide for his peculiar *locus standi*; he was really merely conscious of the relations of his bodily events to the simultaneous events throughout the rest of the universe. Thus perception involves a percipient object, a percipient event, the complete event which is all nature simultaneous with the percipient event, and the particular events which are perceived as parts of the complete event. . . . The point here to be emphasised is that natural knowledge is a knowledge 'from within nature,' and is an awareness of the natural relations of one element in nature (namely, the percipient event) to the rest of nature. Also what is known is not barely the things but the relations of things, and not the relations in the abstract but specifically those things as related.

QUESTIONS

1.  Is Whitehead saying that "significance" and "perceptual knowledge" are the same thing? Or is he saying that "perceptual knowledge" is "an apprehension" of "significance"? What is the point of specifying that "the relatedness of things" means "things in their relations and as related"? Is there a difference between "things in their relations" and "things . . . as related"? What does Whitehead mean by a "knowledge of things as unrelated"? Do you agree that it is impossible to have such knowledge? Even if Whitehead is right, why does he find it necessary to say so? What attitudes or positions assume that it is possible to know things "as unrelated"?

Is it true that the "properties of things can always be expressed as their relatedness to other things unspecified"? Can the color of a wall "be expressed" as the "relatedness" of the wall "to other things unspecified"? Is the wall's color the "significance" of the wall in its relations "to other things"? Can this way of talking be defended?

What is the connection between the error "that there is a possible knowledge of things as unrelated" and the error that "perception of natural events and natural objects" is "an awareness contemplating all nature impartially from without"? If Whitehead is right, what turns on the fact that all "perception . . . is a perception from within nature"?

2. What would Whitehead say, do you think, about the notions of "mere words" or "bare words"? Could something be a word if it was bare? Can anything be known at all, according to Whitehead, if it is "bare"? Can you reformulate Walker's statement in *Daniel* so that it would not be open to Whitehead's criticism?

FLOYD H. ALLPORT

THEORIES OF PERCEPTION AND THE CONCEPT OF STRUCTURE *

A perception, said Tichener, consists, in its earlier stage, of the three following items: (1) a number of sensations consolidated and incorporated into a group under the laws of attention and the special principles of sensory connection; (2) images from past experience that supplement the sensations; and (3) meaning. The sensations are integrated and fused with the images so that the two are often indistinguishable. What then is meaning? Meaning is something that the sensations or images provide for one another. That is to say, meaning is *context*. One group of sensations is usually focal— this is spoken of as the "core." Other sensations or images that accompany the focal group provide, as its context, the *logical meaning* of the focal group. In the case of new perceptions it thus takes at least two sensations to make a meaning. One mental process is the meaning of another if it is that other's context. As to the question of what provides these contextual processes that accompany the focal experiences, the answer is that they are aroused through the total situation in which the organism finds itself and to which it reacts.

Examples of meaning through context can be readily given. The significance of a gesture or facial expression is often conveyed by accompanying aspects of the situation. The experience of auditory rhythm comes from kinaesthetic sensations resulting from movements of stress upon the accentuated beat, such muscularly aroused sensations providing a context for the focal auditory group. In learning to read a foreign language we are often painfully aware of contextual clues that we are summoning in order to find the meaning of a particular word. Word-imagery of equivalents in our mother-tongue are also present as context in these early stages.

Titchener used the notion of context to explain individual differences in perceiving. The sensory core would be the same for different individuals, but the imagery supplied as context (and hence the meaning) would be different for different persons according to their past experience. Boring (op. cit.) treated the context more broadly as something that modifies or corrects the data of the core as the perception is being formed. For example, the size of the retinal image of an object decreases with the distance of the object, a

* From 77–79 (1955). Reprinted with permission of John Wiley & Sons.

fact which would produce a false shrinkage in the object's perceived size if we had to depend on the size of the retinal image alone. The data from this image, however, becomes altered by other visual clues (context) that are associated with apparent distance, with the result that the object appears approximately in its actual (physical) size. It will thus be seen that the core-context theory can be applied to the perceptual constancies.

In Titchener's view there is one special type of sensation that is paramount as a contextual, meaning-providing process, namely, kinaesthesis. As the organism faces the situation it adopts an attitude toward it, and the kinaesthetic sensations resulting from this attitude (assuming it to be a muscular tension or reaction) give the context and meaning of the object to which the organism is reacting. Here we have the beginnings of a motor theory of perception. Kinaesthetic images may come to replace these bodily sensations in later perceptions of the object, so that the meaning may depend upon a context purely of imagery. Word responses are also important as providers of meaningful contexts. The process of recognition, in its earlier but not its later stages, is likely to be one in which the *name* of an object or a person is associated with the core of visual experience.

## QUESTIONS

1.  What is the relationship between what Allport calls "meaning" and Whitehead calls "significance"? Would Whitehead agree that "meaning is context"? If so, what language supports your answer? If not, is he at all interested in what Allport calls "context"?

2.  Is Allport's theory of the "core" akin to Hart's? Would Fuller be more sympathetic to Titchener's treatment of context or to Boring's? Can you argue that Hart would be sympathetic to neither?

3.  What do you think Allport's position toward "mere" or "bare" words would be?

## A.   *Certainty, Clarity and Extrinsic Context*

### LIPPMAN v. SEARS ROEBUCK

271 P.2d 891 (1954).

MOSK, Justice pro tem.

This is an appeal from a judgment in favor of the plaintiff landlord against the defendant tenant for rental due pursuant to a lease.

The lease in question was executed by Lazard Lippman as lessor and Sears, Roebuck & Co., a New York corporation, as lessee, on December 13, 1940, to run from January 1, 1941 to December 31, 1950. It provided for a monthly rental in the sum of $285 plus 2½ per cent of the appellant company's annual sales of the first $163,200 in excess of $136,800, and 2 per cent of the remainder.

The lease further provided that the premises were "to be occupied for the sale and storage of general merchandise and for servicing automobiles, automobile tires, batteries and accessories." In the event the tenant assigned the lease or sublet all of the premises the monthly rent was to be equal to the average monthly rent paid during the preceding twelve months. In the event of abandonment of the premises the tenant was to pay the difference between the rent collected by the landlord upon reletting and the rent reserved.

The complaint alleged that the appellant ceased doing business on the premises on January 1, 1950, that the average rental for the preceding twelve months was $20,424.82, that only $3,400.08 was paid, leaving a balance due of $17,024.74.

The trial court found that the appellant ceased to occupy the premises for sales on November 1, 1949, that the sum of $3,420 was paid, leaving a balance due the respondent of $17,004.82.

It is significant that the respondent sued entirely in reliance upon the provisions of the lease. Neither reformation of the lease nor other equitable relief was sought.

Over objection of appellant, testimony was permitted regarding negotiations between the parties leading up to execution of the lease. Despite our ultimate conclusion that this evidence was inadmissible, we shall review it briefly.

In 1940 the appellant corporation (hereinafter sometimes referred to as Sears) was operating a store in a building owned by a Mrs. Russell in the city of San Fernando. The lease between appellant and Mrs. Russell called for a flat rental of $285 per month and in 1940 the lease had eight more years to run.

During that year the building was substantially destroyed by fire and since Mrs. Russell was not insured, she was either unable or unwilling to rebuild the structure. Shortly thereafter Samuel Edward Jones, for many years in charge of Sears' property department for the Pacific Coast, called respondent to his office and suggested that it might be profitable for him to purchase this property, construct a building and lease it to Sears. At this time respondent was leasing a building to Sears in El Centro and apparently their relationship was mutually satisfactory.

Pursuant to that suggestion respondent conducted negotiations with Mrs. Russell and ascertained costs for reconstructing the store. He testified he subsequently indicated to Jones that to undertake the proposition he would need a rental of $800 a month. There were further conversations relative to the amount of the rental, during which Jones stated the company would not pay that amount but would agree to a minimum guarantee of $285 against a percentage of sales. Mail order sales were to be excluded from the computation.

Thereafter plans and specifications for the building were prepared in Chicago by the construction department of Sears. The building was completed November 1, 1940, and Sears immediately occupied the premises with a retail store. The parties did not enter into the written lease until December 13, 1940; it was to become effective January 1, 1941, and to run until the end of 1950.

Respondent testified he paid $38,000 for the land and the building in its damaged condition, that it cost $8,000 to tear down and remove the structure and debris, that his cost of rebuilding, not including any sum for his own services as a contractor, was $29,255.82. Thus, excluding any consideration of respondent's time, overhead, interest and taxes during construction, he expended $75,255.82.

In 1945, Russell A. Veach, Jones' successor at Sears, requested the use of four lots which respondent had acquired near the San Fernando store. He declined to pay any rent therefor, maintaining that the use of the lots for parking facilities would increase the sales in the store and consequently the percentage return to respondent. The latter acquiesced.

During January of each year respondent received a statement showing the prior year's net sales made on the premises. For the calendar year preceding the one involved herein, Sears, under the terms of the lease, paid to respondent the minimum rental payment of $3,420 and additional rent in the sum of $17,424.82, upon net sales of $981.440.92.

On November 1, 1949, Sears ceased to transact sales on the leased premises and began business operations a block away from the premises involved herein. During the remaining fourteen months of the term Sears used the premises for the storage of general merchandise and during that period paid rent at the rate of $285 a month.

Upon expiration of the lease on December 31, 1950, Sears continued to occupy and use the premises for the storage of merchandise pursuant to a later agreement. During this period the agreed rental was $300 per month.

After discussions for the subsequent occupancy had been concluded, Veach requested of his staff preparation of a letter memorandum for respondent's signature. When prepared, this document contained language which could be construed to be a release by respondent of all claims he might have under the lease of December 13, 1940. Upon assurance of Veach that this letter, dated January 2, 1951, did not refer to rental claims under the prior lease but merely to eliminating the possibility of a percentage claim during the holdover period, the respondent signed the instrument.

Apparently this letter of January 2, 1951, was not produced at the trial for the purpose of urging seriously a waiver of any rights by respondent, but merely to indicate conduct of the parties.

The trial court found that the minimum monthly rental of $285 "was intended to be and was, in fact, a nominal rental and was not a substantial or adequate minimum rental." The court further found that the lease provided "In the event the defendant did not occupy said premises for the sale of general merchandise but used said premises for the storage of merchandise, it was to pay plaintiff a monthly rental equal to the average monthly rental it had paid for the twelve months immediately preceding the month in which it ceased to use said premises for the sale of merchandise."

The court further found that the letter of January 2, 1951, was not a complete satisfaction of the existing controversies between the parties.

The appellant has assigned as error each of the foregoing findings on the ground that they are not supported by the evidence and are contrary to law.

The trial court, over objection of appellant, permitted parol evidence to disclose negotiations precedent to the execution of the written lease. In this it fell into unfortunate error. For in the construction of an instrument, the office of the judge is simply to ascertain and declare what is in terms or in substance contained therein, not to insert what has been omitted, or to omit what has been inserted. Code Civ.Proc. section 1858.

Morgan v. Green, 86 Cal.App. 216, at page 222, 260 P. 596, at page 598, succinctly relates the principle: "The rule is found in section 1856, Code of Civil Procedure, which declares that when the terms of an agreement have been reduced to writing it is presumed to embrace all the terms agreed upon. The decisions are all in harmony with the section of the Code running from Harrison v. McCormick, 89 Cal. 327, 330, 26 P. 830, 23 Am.St.Rep. 469, to Thoroman v. David, 199 Cal. 386, 390, 249 P. 513. We cannot improve upon the language of Thompson v. Libbey, 34 Minn. [374,] 377, 26 N.W. 1, quoted in the Harrison Case and approved in the later decisions:

" 'If it imports on its face to be a complete expression of the whole agreement—that is, contains such language as imports a complete legal obligation—it is to be presumed that the parties have introduced into it every material item and term; and parol evidence cannot be admitted to add another term to the agreement, although the writing contains nothing on the particular one to which the parol evidence is directed.'

"Upon the theory first advanced by respondents that the evidence was inadmissible because the writing did not include all the terms agreed upon—the rule is uniform that evidence of such collateral agreements is admissible only when the circumstances attending the execution of the writing show that the parties did not intend it to be a complete and final statement of the whole transaction. 10 Cal.Juris. p. 927. The lease here does not come within this exception. It appears upon the face to be a complete statement of the undertakings of the respective legal obligations within the rule of Harrison v. McCormick, supra. Gardiner v. McDonogh, 147 Cal. 313, 319, 81 P. 964, and Germain Fruit Co. v. [j. K.] Armsby Co., 153 Cal. 585, 595, 96 P. 319."

Of course, no rule is inviolately exempt from exception, and in this the parol evidence rule is itself no exception. Where the instrument on its face bears an ambiguity or uncertainty, then testimony may be permitted to relate the circumstances under which the document was executed. The purpose is to enable the trier of fact to fathom the intent of the parties, not at the present time, but at the moment of the meeting of minds.

.   .   .

A few jurisdictions permit parol evidence to indicate the intended use of premises when the lease is silent on the subject.   .    .    .

But the vast majority hold that where the lease does not restrict the use of the premises, it may not be shown that there was an oral understanding of restriction.   .    .    .

On this appeal we are not prevented from inquiring into the propriety of the admission of parol.  For it is well settled in construing a contract, the question as to whether an uncertainty or ambiguity exists is one of law, and the lower court's finding on this issue is not binding on appeal.  Brant v. California Dairies, Inc., 4 Cal.2d 128, 133, 48 P.2d 13.

The admission of parol is not discretionary with the trial court. For the parol evidence rule is in no sense a rule of evidence; it does not concern a probative mental process, but declares that certain kinds of fact are legally ineffective in the substantive law.  Wigmore on Evidence, 3d. Ed. section 2400.

In the instant case, respondent has called to our attention no ambiguous or uncertain language in the lease, and we have found none. What he has proposed is to provide omitted terms relating to the use and occupancy required of appellant, and rental to be exacted from it in the event of a breach.

Hoffman v. Seidman, 101 N.J.L. 106, 127 A. 199, at page 200, presents a markedly analogous situation, revealed in the following quotation: "the written lease was complete on its face, and oral testimony, either to contradict it or to supply terms with respect to which the writing was silent (as the testimony offered would have done), will not be permitted, in the absence of fraud or illegality.  (Cases cited).

"But the defendant argues that the phrase, 'nor use or permit any part thereof to be used for any other purpose than a dwelling and a hardware and paint store,' is ambiguous.  We think it is not.  We think it perfectly clear that the whole purpose of that clause was to exclude any other use, but to permit the uses mentioned, not necessarily conjunctively, but either of them or both, and at such times as the tenant sees fit to so use them, and that he was under no obligation to use the premises at all, or at any time to reside there, or at any time to keep a store there.  The language used is restrictive, not mandatory.  *  *  *  Of course, it does not follow, because the parties used the conjunctive instead of the disjunctive, that they thereby rendered their lease ambiguous, and opened the door to oral testimony.  When, as here, the meaning of the language of the lease is plain and unambiguous when read in connection with the context, parol evidence as to its meaning is not admissible."

The words of caution expressed in Payne v. Commercial Nat. Bank, 177 Cal. 68, 72, 169 P. 1007, 1008, L.R.A.1918C, 328, must be heeded: "no authority sustains the proposition that under the guise of construction or explanation a meaning can be given to the instrument which is not to be found in the instrument itself, but is based entirely upon direct evidence of intention independent of the instrument. It has been well said that in the admission of extrinsic evidence the line which separates evidence which aids the interpretation of what is in the instrument from direct evidence of intention independent of the instrument must be kept steadily in view, the duty of the court being to declare the meaning of what is written in the instrument, and not what was intended to be written."

An implication cannot rest solely upon an inference to be drawn from the facts surrounding the execution of the lease. It must have a basis in the lease itself. Stockton Dry Goods Co. v. Girsh, 36 Cal.2d 677, 680, 227 P.2d 1, 22 A.L.R.2d 1460.

When a person takes part in a bilateral act, a transaction in which other persons share, he must accept a common standard. He cannot claim to enforce his individual standard of meaning. Wigmore on Evidence, 3d Ed., section 2466. That common standard is the language employed in the instrument reduced to writing. The parties, having dealt on a basis of equality in its negotiation, are bound by its terms.

## QUESTIONS

1. Consider the statement from Payne v. Commercial Nat. Bank that no "meaning can be given to the instrument which is not to be found in the instrument itself . . . ." What do you suppose would be the reaction of Whitehead or Allport to the notion of a meaning to be found "in" the instrument? Are the meanings of things inside or outside of the things themselves? In connection with these questions, reconsider the materials in Chapter 8, Section 3.

2. "An implication cannot rest solely upon an inference to be drawn from the facts surrounding the execution of the lease," says Mosk, J., but "must have a basis in the lease itself." Was there no basis at all "in the lease itself" for plaintiff's contention? Mosk reports that "the vast majority [of jurisdictions] hold that where the lease does not restrict the use of the premises, it may not be shown that there was an oral understanding of restriction." Does the lease in *Lippman* restrict the uses of the premises? Are the stipulations regarding subletting, assigning and abandoning "restrictions"? If not, can one say that plaintiff is contending for an unstated "restriction"? Suppose that a lease provides that rent shall be based solely on a percentage of sales and makes no provision regarding uses other than the sale of goods. If the lessee then uses the premises only for storage, is he, under the reasoning in *Lippman*, free of any claims for damages? Does he have no claim with a "basis in the lease itself"?

"In the construction of an instrument," says the court in *Lippman*, "the office of the judge is simply to ascertain and declare what is in terms or in substance contained therein, not to insert what has been omitted, or to omit what has been inserted." Was Lippman attempting to insert a new provision or to omit an old one? Can you state the provision? Do you think there was a provision in the contract reading substantially as follows:

> In the event that lessee uses the premises for storage only, his rent payments will be $285 per month.

If not, could the court's decision be construed as the insertion of such a provision? If so, does the court have any more right to insert provisions on behalf of the lessee than on behalf of the lessor? Is there anything in the opinion which indicates that the court might think it has such a right?

In order to "fathom the intent of the parties . . . at the moment of the meeting of minds," says Justice Mosk, testimony of "the circumstances under which the document was executed" will be permitted if "the instrument on its face bears an ambiguity or uncertainty." Does this mean that the court is not concerned with "the intent of the parties" when the instrument "on its face" bears *no* ambiguity or uncertainty? If not, why not? Would it be fair to characterize plaintiff's claim as an attempt "to enforce his individual standard of meaning"? Is that the only possible explanation for the effort to introduce extrinsic evidence?

Is it useful to distinguish different kinds of extrinsic evidence? Is parol evidence of "negotiations precedent to the execution of the written lease" the same as parol evidence of "the circumstances under which the document was executed"? If there is a difference, should it matter for purposes of the parol evidence rule?

LAURENCE P. SIMPSON

## HANDBOOK OF THE LAW OF CONTRACTS *

When a contract is expressed in a writing which is intended to be the complete and final expression of the rights and duties of the parties, parol evidence, of prior oral or written negotiations or agreements of the parties or of their contemporaneous oral agreements, which varies or contradicts the written contract, is not admissible. But the parol evidence rule does not relate to and does not prevent proof of oral contracts entered into subsequent to the formal written contract, varying it or discharging it, even though the written contract expressly provides that it can only be changed or discharged by a subsequent agreement in writing. In a few states, however, this is made effective by statute. The purpose of the parol evidence rule is to carry out the presumed intention of the parties, who have put their contract in written form, thus to achieve certainty and finality as to their rights and duties and to exclude fraudulent and perjured claims.

### QUESTIONS

Under the parol evidence rule as Simpson states it, could Lippman have introduced evidence of the cost of land and construction? Does his version of the parol evidence rule include, if only by implication, the doctrine of interpretation enunciated by Mosk? Is that doctrine a necessary part of the rule or is it a separate, independent

---

\* From § 63 (1964). Reprinted with
permission of West Publishing Company.

rule in its own right? How do you suppose Professor Fuller would go about answering this question?

If it is conceded that the "purpose of the parol evidence rule is to carry out the presumed intention of the parties," what would you want to know in order to decide whether the rule had the *effect* of carrying out the parties' intention? Or does use of the word "presumed" indicate that such intentions are only a fictitious concern of the parol evidence rule? If so, what purpose would you say does explain the rule's existence?

Why is the parol evidence rule needed "to achieve certainty and finality" and "to exclude fraudulent and perjured claims"? Why would the introduction of evidence which the rule prohibits lead to uncertainty? Are the checks in the Anglo-American system of civil trials inadequate "to exclude fraudulent and perjured claims"? What are the objections to giving judge and jury all the evidence "relevant" to a comprehensive understanding of the litigated transaction—and then let them decide the parties' intentions therefrom?

JOHN HENRY WIGMORE

A TREATISE ON EVIDENCE *

. . . . *the* [parol evidence] *rule is in no sense a rule of Evidence,* but a rule of Substantive Law. It does not exclude certain data because they are for one or another reason untrustworthy or undesirable means of evidencing some fact to be proved. It does not concern a probative mental process,—the process of believing one fact on the faith of another. What the rule does is to declare that certain kinds of fact are legally ineffective in the substantive law; and this of course (like any other ruling of substantive law) results in forbidding the fact to be proved at all (*ante,* 2). But this prohibition of proving it is merely the dramatic aspect of the process of applying the rule of substantive law. When a thing is not to be proved at all, the rule of prohibition does not become a rule of Evidence merely because it comes into play when the counsel offers to "prove" it or "give evidence" of it; otherwise, any rule of law whatever might be reduced to a rule of Evidence; a ruling (for example) that on a plea of self-defence, in an action of battery, no evidence of the plaintiff's insulting words is to be received, would become the legitimate progeny of the law of Evidence. This employment of terms of evidence for rulings of substantive law, by reason of the constant dramatic presentation of the latter in the course of a trial, is an old and natural failing of the profession. . . .

NOTES AND QUESTIONS

1. Can you state Wigmore's distinction between "a rule of evidence" and "a rule of substantive law"? What is it, according to

---

* From 3–4 (3d ed. 1940). Reprinted
with permission of the estate of John
Henry Wigmore.

Wigmore, that the parol evidence rule has in common with the rule "that on a plea of self-defense, in an action of battery, no evidence of the plaintiff's insulting words is to be received"?

Why do you suppose that Wigmore deems it important to emphasize (note his italics) that the parol evidence rule "is in no sense" a rule of evidence? Is he making the point for the same reason that the court in *Lippman* quotes him? Is there anything in Mosk's opinion which would support the assertion that the parol evidence rule *does* "concern a probative mental process,—the process of believing one fact on the faith of another"? Is there anything in Simpson's statement that would support such an assertion? Note his remark on the need to "exclude fraudulent and perjured claims."

2.   What does it mean for "certain kinds of fact" to be "legally ineffective in the substantive law"? Which "kinds of fact" are made "legally ineffective" by the parol evidence rule?

If the parol evidence rule is not itself a "rule of evidence" mustn't the exclusion of such evidence at trial necessarily involve *some* rule as to the admissibility of evidence? Consider the following from Thayer:

> .   .   .   . There is a principle—not so much a rule of evidence as a presupposition involved in the very conception of a rational system of evidence  .   .   . which forbids receiving anything irrelevant, not logically probative.  .   .   .
>
> There is another precept which should be laid down as preliminary, in stating the law of evidence; namely, that unless excluded by some rule or principle of law, all that is logically probative is admissible. This general admissibility, however, of what is logically probative is not, like the former principle, a necessary presupposition in a rational system of evidence; there are many exceptions to it.  .   .   .
>
> .   .   .   . we must not fall into the error of supposing that relevancy, logical connection, real or supposed, is the only test of admissibility; for so we should drop out of sight the chief part of the law of evidence.  .   .   . Some things are rejected as being of too slight a significance, or as having too conjectural and remote a connection; others, as being dangerous, in their effect on the jury, and likely to be misused or overestimated by that body; others, as being impolitic, or unsafe on public grounds  .   .   . . It is this sort of thing  .   .   .—the rejection on one or another practical ground, of what is really probative,—which is the characteristic thing in the law of evidence; stamping it as the child of the jury system.

PRELIMINARY TREATISE ON EVIDENCE 264–266 (1898). Is parol evidence excluded, according to Wigmore, for any of the reasons suggested by Thayer? Is he arguing that it is irrelevant? Consider James: "evidence may be excluded as 'irrelevant' for either of  .   .   . two .   .   . reasons: because it is not probative of the proposition at which it is directed, or because that proposition is not provable in the case." *Relevancy, Probability and the Law*, 29 Calif.L.Rev. 689, 691 (1941). Is it possible to formulate a rationale of the parol evidence rule which would involve "stamping it as" a "child of the jury system"? What about the rule of assault law that "bare words will never do"?

ARTHUR LINTON CORBIN

## A Comprehensive Treatise on The Rules of Contract Law *

No parol evidence that is offered can be said to vary or contradict a writing until by process of interpretation it is determined what the writing means. The "parol evidence rule" is not, and does not purport to be, a rule of interpretation or a rule as to the admission of evidence for the purpose of interpretation. Even if a written document has been assented to as the complete and accurate integration of the terms of the contract, it must still be interpreted; and all those factors that are of assistance in this process may be proved by oral testimony.

It is true that the language of some agreements has been believed to be so plain and clear that the court needs no assistance in interpeting. Even in these cases, however, it will be found that the court has had the aid of parol evidence of the surrounding circumstances. The meaning to be discovered and applied is that which each party had reason to know would be given to the words by the other party. Antecedent and surrounding factors that throw light upon this question may be proved by any kind of relevant evidence.

. . . . As long as the court is aware that there may be doubt and ambiguity and uncertainty in the meaning and application of agreed language, it will welcome testimony as to antecedent agreements, communications, and other factors that may help to decide the issue. Such testimony does not vary or contradict the written words; it determines that which cannot be varied or contradicted. Nor is it made inadmissible by the fact that it has the effect of filling out the terms of a promise and of determining the character and extent of the performance promised.

## Notes and Questions

1. Is Corbin accurately reporting the law? Can it be said that the court in *Lippman* "had the aid of parol evidence of the surrounding circumstances"? Did Mosk think that "the meaning to be discovered and applied is that which each party had reason to know would be given to the words by the other party"? Or does Mosk think that "each party to a contract has notice that the other will understand his words according to the usage of the normal speaker of English under the circumstances, and therefore cannot complain if his words are taken in that sense"? Holmes, *The Theory of Legal Interpretation*, 12 Harv.L.Rev. 417, 419 (1899). Could it be argued

* From v. 3, § 579 (1960). Reprinted with permission of West Publishing Company and Yale University Press.

that Holmes and Corbin are in agreement?  Consider Holmes, J. in Goode v. Riley, 153 Mass. 585 (1891):

> .  .  .  .  You cannot prove a mere private convention between the two parties to give language a different meaning from its common one.  .  .  .  An artificial construction cannot be given to plain words by express agreement.  .  .  .

2.  Can it be said that Corbin has confused "what the law is" with "what the law ought to be"?  If so, can a defense for Corbin be found in the following remarks written fourteen years after those reprinted above?

> .  .  .  .  It is still being said  .  .  .  that extrinsic evidence is not admissible to aid the court in the interpretation of a written contract (an integration) if the written words are themselves plain and clear and unambiguous. This is said even by a court that declares the rule to be a rule of substantive law and not a rule of evidence.
>
> Is not this continuous repetition in itself sufficient to make the statement a well settled rule of substantive law [?]
> .  .  .  .  Is not an author  .  .  .  guilty of the utmost temerity (and even of folly) to deny the accuracy, the justice, and the necessity of the repeated rule?
>
> There are times when an author is incompetent, and even intellectually and morally dishonest, if he fails to attack an often repeated statement of law.  This is such a case .  .  .  .  There are many court decisions, made by highly respected courts, that are inconsistent with the repeated rule.  .  .  .  There are many cases, practically never subjected to criticism, in which the court has considered extrinsic evidence as a basis for finding that the written words are ambiguous;  instead of ambiguity admitting the evidence, the evidence establishes the ambiguity.  .  .  .
>
> There are general rules that are universally accepted that are inconsistent with the stated rule here criticized. The cardinal rule with which all interpretation begins is that its purpose is to ascertain the intention of the parties.  The criticized rule, if actually applied, excludes proof of their actual intention.  It is universally agreed that it is the first duty of the court to put itself in the position of the parties at the time the contract was made; it is wholly impossible to do this without being informed by extrinsic evidence of the circumstances surrounding the making of the contract. .  .  .

*The Interpretation of Words and the Parol Evidence Rule*, 50 Corn. L.Q. 161–162 (1965).*  Why would Corbin be "incompetent, and even intellectually and morally dishonest" if he failed to attack the "often repeated statement of law"?  What does competence have to do with it? Or intellectual or moral honesty? Is he saying that he would be incompetent for failing to report how the law "ought to be"? Is that a matter of competence? Or honesty? If not, what would be?

3. Does Mosk think that the parol evidence rule "is not, and does not purport to be, a rule of interpretation or a rule as to the admission of evidence for the purpose of interpretation"? Does Corbin suggest a rule of interpretation? Is Corbin suggesting that when the contract is interpreted we must recur to general principles of construction? Is Mosk saying that a special rule of interpretation necessarily accompanies the parol evidence rule? Or is he invoking a general rule of construction? If so, does it have a name?

JOHN HENRY WIGMORE

A TREATISE ON EVIDENCE *

The real strength of the argument [for the plain meaning rule] is . . . found in the practical statement of Mr. Justice Holmes that "it would open too great risks [*i. e.* of false pretenses] if evidence were admissible to show that when they said 'five hundred feet' they agreed that it should mean one hundred inches, or that 'Bunker Hill Monument' should signify the Old South Church." Now the interesting feature of this illustration is that in important instances the very opposite fact is daily and hourly illustrated,—in the private cipher-codes of commercial houses. By these agreements words *are* employed in a sense totally alien, and sometimes exactly opposite, to the ordinary meaning. In one of the printed cable codes now in use, for example, "Innovate" is made to mean "We all unite in sending you our heartiest congratulations"! No doubt, too, some brokers who are particularly apprehensive of the interception of their messages are accustomed to agree that "buy" shall mean "do *not* buy." There are, then, abundant instances in which not only is there no "great risk," but there is an absolute necessity, of accepting proof of these private conventions; and these instances shatter the whole argument for the rule as a rule. The fallacy of the person who declared that "He was open to conviction, but he would like to meet the person who could convince him," is here reversed; for the judicial attitude thus illustrated is that "We are not open to conviction, because we are afraid that somebody will sometimes convince us."

The truth is that whatever virtue and strength lies in the argument for the antique rule leads not to a fixed rule of law, but only to a general maxim of prudent discretion. In the felicitous alliteration of that great judge, Lord Justice Bowen, it is "not so much a canon of construction as a counsel of caution." The distinguished Master of the Rolls, Sir George Jessel, once wittily declared to coun-

* From 193–194 (3d ed. 1940). Reprinted with permission of the estate of John Henry Wigmore.

sel that "nobody could convince *him* that black [selvedge] was white!"; and yet the Court of Appeals reversed his judgment because they were after all convinced of that precise proposition. To say that it would be difficult to convince him, and upon the evidence to fail to be convinced, would have been a rational attitude. But that is very different from an arbitrary rule declaring 'a priori' that the judicial mind is legally not open to conviction.

## QUESTIONS

Why do the instances adduced by Wigmore "shatter the whole argument for the [plain meaning] rule as a rule"? Reconsider the earlier materials in this book on the "role of rule." What is the distinction Wigmore is drawing between "a fixed rule of law" and "a general maxim of prudent discretion"? Why is such a maxim necessary at all?

## NOTE: PLAIN MEANINGS AND CORE MEANINGS

Compare the persistent invocation of a plain meaning rule in parol evidence cases with Professor Hart's contention that "to communicate with each other at all  .  .  .  the general words we use .  .  .  must have some standard instance in which no doubts are felt about its application." Would Hart's reasoning permit him to introduce extrinsic evidence in cases which fall within the "core of settled meaning"? Is Corbin one of those who assumes "that all legal questions are fundamentally like those of the penumbra"? Or, at least, that all problems of contractual interpretation are?

If, as Simpson says, the parol evidence rule is meant to achieve certainty and finality, does Corbin's method of interpretation effectively vitiate this aim? If parol evidence can always be introduced to support a particular party's peculiar theory of meaning, what is left of the parol evidence rule? Is there any function which it can then perform?

Suppose a person with whom you were conversing should turn from the conversation and, pointing to a man who had just come over the horizon, say: "I'm going to kill that man." He then picks up a rifle, fires and kills him. Is there any question that he has committed murder? Is this one of those cases where the meaning of a person's actions is "plain" or "perfectly clear"? Would any of the following facts if added to the account cast doubt? (1) He was joking and had reason to believe the gun was a toy, or was unloaded. (2) The victim was an outlaw, wanted dead or alive. (3) The killer meant only to frighten the man and to fool you, but never intended to hit him. (4) The killer had reason to believe that the victim was returning from an assignation with his wife. (5) The killer was mentally deranged. If the killer were tried for murder, should he be permitted to vary or contradict the actions he took by introducing extrinsic evidence of this sort? Should he be permitted to complicate his case in this way and thereby imperil the certainty of the criminal law? If cases become clear by restricting the facts we take into account is there a constant danger of distorted meaning and consequently, of injustice? Is it fair to say that Corbin wishes to sacrifice order and stability in order to achieve justice? Would Corbin agree with this description?


MONROE BEARDSLEY

THINKING STRAIGHT *

Considering the number of ways of taking a particular word, the task of speaking clearly and being understood would seem pretty hopeless if it were not for another very important fact about language. Though a word may have many senses, these senses can be controlled, up to a point, by the *context* in which the word is used. When we find the word in a particular verbal setting—that is, take it with the words that come before and after it in a discourse—we can usually decide quite definitely which of the many senses of the word is relevant. If a poet says his verse has three feet, it doesn't occur to you that he could mean it's a yard long or is three-legged (unless perhaps you are a critic planning to puncture the poet with a pun about his "limping verse"). The context rules out these maverick senses quite decisively.

We might be puzzled if we read in a newspaper that "in the suicide's pocket the police found a large envelope full of bills." In this sentence, as it stands, the word "bills" can easily be taken in two very different senses. But if the context were expanded so as to read, "The police were surprised to find in the suicide's pocket a large envelope full of bills of various denominations," we should understand that "bills" meant *paper money*, and we might wonder whether it was indeed suicide or accident. Or if the context were expanded differently, so as to read, "The police were surprised to find in the suicide's pocket a large envelope full of unpaid bills," we should understand that "bills meant *requests for payment of a debt*, and we might wonder whether that explains the suicide.

This is a rather simple illustration of the way in which the context of a word helps to pick out one of its senses and fix that sense. But of course "context" is used broadly here: it may be the rest of a sentence (the *immediate* context), a page, a whole book, or a newspaper file. A "shady street" is one thing; a "shady neighborhood" is something else. The word "strike" means one action on the front page of a paper and another action on the sports page; the words "liberal" and "patriotic" mean certain attitudes in *The New York Times* and mostly different ones in *The Chicago Tribune*. When some time ago a British physicist announced with pleasure that the hydrogen bomb is "safe," his statement caused gasps of surprise; in the technical talk of atomic scientists, "safe" apparently means that it couldn't set off a chain reaction that might destroy the earth itself. This is not the way the man in the street uses the word.

Many common words like "line," "pipe," "stock," and "head," have acquired many serviceable meanings in different occupational contexts—say, in the shoptalk of plumbers, pitchers, or plastic engineers. Think of what the word "wing" means to a birdwatcher, an airman, a stagehand, a general, or an architect. But just because these meanings are so completely distinct—no one can confuse the wing of an airplane with the wing of a house—it is easy to control them by very light contextual pressure. A word or two makes it clear that it is the airman's wing rather than the architect's that is referred to. But when the differences between the senses of a word are slighter and subtler (they may be even more important, however), the most careful management of the context may be required to get and keep one sense in focus. The exact meaning of a word like "middle class" or "evolution" or "justice" may depend upon the whole book in which it appears.

That is why it is often easy to misrepresent what someone has said by quoting some of his remarks out of their context. The words may not, strictly speaking, be *mis*quoted, but their meaning has been changed. The political candidate's promise to obtain peace or balance the budget is echoed and attacked by his opponent—who is careful to leave out the conditions and qualifications that originally surrounded it. Even if a writer is scrupulous enough to put in dots to indicate that something has been left out, he may not be *quite* scrupulous enough to stick to the original meaning. You have seen advertisements of a new play, with a few words from a review. The phrase " . . . emotional subtlety . . . (Bridgeport *Post*)" may be from a sentence that goes: "It has all the emotional subtlety of a barroom brawl." The phrase " . . . great drama . . . (New Haven *Register*)" may be from a sentence that goes: "No doubt it was considered a great drama when it first appeared in 1927, but . . . " And this is nothing to what a professional wiretapper can do if he records a telephone conversation and picks out words to re-record on a new tape.

Representative Wayne L. Hays, a member of the Special House Committee set up by the 83rd Congress to investigate tax-exempt foundations, frequently argued during the committee's hearings that the "research directors" of the committee were willing to make judgments on passages torn out of contexts that might change their meaning considerably. He finally made a dramatic demonstration of this by producing three paragraphs which the associate research director testified were "closely comparable" with, and parallel to, Communist literature that he had read. They were excerpts from two papal encyclicals.

## NOTES AND QUESTIONS

In Beardsley's view, does the addition of context make the meaning of a word more or less certain? Do plain meaning judges wish to exclude this kind of context? Or does "extrinsic evidence" refer not to the words which surround the terms to be interpreted but only the circumstances in which the terms were uttered or written? Is this a defensible distinction?

Consider the following:

> Imagine a picture representing a boxer in a particular stance. Now, this picture can be used to tell someone how he should stand, should hold himself; or how he should not hold himself; or how a particular man did stand in such-and-such a place; and so on. . . .

L. WITTGENSTEIN, PHILOSOPHICAL INVESTIGATIONS 11ᵉ (1953). How many other ways could this picture be used? If you had time, could you list them all? How do you know in any instance the particular use of such a picture? Would it help to know who used it and when and where?

## NOTE: THE NATURE OF A CLEAR CASE

If it is conceded that "communication" depends on there being clear cases to which words or rules apply, is it important to know why the words or rules are clearly applicable to such cases? That is, must one who proposes a theory of interpretation account for the phenomenon of the clear or easy case in his theory? Or is it enough for him to merely report it? Professor Fuller offers some observations about clear cases. Was it necessary for him to do so? Is it a requisite of any adequate theory of interpretation that it be consistent with the "fact" of "clear" or "easy" cases? Is Fuller's theory consistent with that "fact"? Does Hart think it is? What language are you relying on for your answer?

How does the account of clear cases differ in the theories of Hart and Fuller? Do they both agree that a clear case is one that can be decided "without thinking"—or without much thinking? What is the relationship of the context of a word to its "easiness" or "difficulty"? Does the following excerpt from Allport shed any light on the nature of a "clear" case?

*FLOYD H. ALLPORT*

## THEORIES OF PERCEPTION AND THE CONCEPT OF STRUCTURE *

Thus far we have spoken mainly of "new" perceptions, perceptual activities in the earlier stages of their formation. With repeated perceptions of the same object or situation there is a decay of the imagery. The context of sensations or images supplementing the core becomes less and less necessary. Images may reduce to some common denominator or a symbolic kind of shorthand. Thus when we greet a familiar acquaintance we no longer need to recall his name or other context in order to have a meaningful experience of his identity. The trained musician is not aware in sensory or imaginal terms of the key-signature of the piece of music he is reading. One glance at the signature at the beginning was enough to render the key-meaning automatic and to guide his fingers accordingly. Words of our mother-tongue do not require supporting context; we perceive

---

* From 79 (1955). Reprinted with permission of John Wiley & Sons.

their meaning immediately. The fact that context has thus faded out does not, of course, indicate that meaning has ceased to exist. It is now carried, said Titchener, in purely physiological terms. It lies in the physiological organization of the brain processes and can be immediately recalled in the form of context if required. The musician can always tell, if asked, the key in which he is playing. We can paraphrase, if asked to do so, the meaning of what we have just read. One might add here that if the stimulus situation had contained other contextual material not compatible with the meaning that was afoot, it would at once have been noted. An incongruous word in the text stands out like a sore thumb. These cases clearly signalize that meaning is present, that it represents an ongoing process in the nervous system even though it be totally outside of consciousness.

### Questions

If meaning is context, as Allport said in an earlier excerpt, how can he say that when the "context has  .  .  .  faded out" this "does not, of course, indicate that meaning has ceased to exist"? Can context be carried "in purely physiological terms"?

## B.  *Authoritative Parts and Authoritative Wholes*

### Griswold v. Connecticut

381 U.S. 479 (1965)

Mr. Justice DOUGLAS delivered the opinion of the Court.

Appellant Griswold is Executive Director of the Planned Parenthood League of Connecticut. Appellant Buxton is a licensed physician and a professor at the Yale Medical School who served as Medical Director for the League at its Center in New Haven—a center open and operating from November 1 to November 10, 1961, when appellants were arrested.

They gave information, instruction, and medical advice to *married persons* as to the means of preventing conception. They examined the wife and prescribed the best contraceptive device or material for her use. Fees were usually charged, although some couples were serviced free.

The statutes whose constitutionality is involved in this appeal are 53–32 and 54–196 of the General Statutes of Connecticut (1958 rev.). The former provides:

"Any person who uses any drug, medicinal article or instrument for the purpose of preventing conception shall be fined not less than fifty dollars or imprisoned not less than sixty days nor more than one year or be both fined and imprisoned."

Section 54–196 provides:

"Any person who assists, abets, counsels, causes, hires or commands another to commit any offense may be prosecuted and punished as if he were the principal offender."

The appellants were found guilty as accessories and fined $100 each, against the claim that the accessory statute as so applied violated the Fourteenth Amendment. . . .

. . .

. . . . we are met with a wide range of questions that implicate the Due Process Clause of the Fourteenth Amendment. Overtones of some arguments suggest that Lochner v. New York, 198 U.S. 45, should be our guide. But we decline that invitation . . . . We do not sit as a super-legislature to determine the wisdom, need, and propriety of laws that touch economic problems, business affairs, or social conditions. This law, however, operates directly on an intimate relation of husband and wife and their physician's role in one aspect of that relation.

The association of people is not mentioned in the Constitution nor in the Bill of Rights. The right to educate a child in a school of the parent's choice—whether public or private or parochial—is also not mentioned. Nor is the right to study any particular subject or any foreign language. Yet the First Amendment has been construed to include certain of those rights.

By Pierce v. Society of Sisters, *supra*, the right to educate one's children as one chooses is made applicable to the States by the force of the First and Fourteenth Amendments. By Meyer v. Nebraska, *supra*, the same dignity is given the right to study the German language in a private school. In other words, the State may not, consistently with the spirit of the First Amendment, contract the spectrum of available knowledge. The right of freedom of speech and press includes not only the right to utter or to print, but the right to distribute, the right to receive, the right to read . . . and freedom of inquiry, freedom of thought, and freedom to teach . . . indeed the freedom of the entire university community. . . Without those peripheral rights the specific rights would be less secure. And so we reaffirm the principle of the *Pierce* and the *Meyer* cases.

In NAACP v. Alabama, 357 U.S. 449, 462, we protected the "freedom to associate and privacy in one's associations," noting that freedom of association was a peripheral First Amendment right. Disclosure of membership lists of a constitutionally valid association, we held, was invalid "as entailing the likelihood of a substantial restraint upon the exercise by petitioner's members of their right to freedom of association." . . In other words, the First Amendment has a penumbra where privacy is protected from governmental intrusion. In like context, we have protected forms of "association" that are not political in the customary sense but pertain to the social, legal, and economic benefit of the members. NAACP v. Button, 371 U.S. 415, 430–431. In Schware v. Board of Bar Examiners, 353 U.S. 232, we held it not permissible to bar a lawyer from practice, because he had once been a member of the Communist Party. The man's "association with that Party" was not shown to be "anything more than a political faith in a political party" (*id.*, at 244) and was not action of a kind proving bad moral character. . .

Those cases involved more than the "right of assembly"—a right that extends to all irrespective of their race or ideology. DeJonge

v. Oregon, 299 U.S. 353. The right of "association," like the right of belief (Board of Education v. Barnette, 319 U.S. 624), is more than the right to attend a meeting; it includes the right to express one's attitudes or philosophies by membership in a group or by affiliation with it or by other lawful means. Association in that context is a form of expression of opinion; and while it is not expressly included in the First Amendment its existence is necessary in making the express guarantees fully meaningful.

The foregoing cases suggest that specific guarantees in the Bill of Rights have penumbras, formed by emanations from those guarantees that help give them life and substance. . . Various guarantees create zones of privacy. The right of association contained in the penumbra of the First Amendment is one, as we have seen. The Third Amendment in its prohibition against the quartering of soldiers "in any house" in time of peace without the consent of the owner is another facet of that privacy. The Fourth Amendment explicitly affirms the "right of the people to be secure in their persons, houses, papers, and effects, against unreasonable searches and seizures." The Fifth Amendment in its Self-Incrimination Clause enables the citizen to create a zone of privacy which government may not force him to surrender to his detriment. The Ninth Amendment provides: "The enumeration in the Constitution, of certain rights, shall not be construed to deny or disparage others retained by the people."

The Fourth and Fifth Amendments were described in Boyd v. United States, . . . as protection against all governmental invasions "of the sanctity of a man's home and the privacies of life." [2] We recently referred in Mapp v. Ohio, . . . to the Fourth Amendment as creating a "right to privacy, no less important than any other right carefully and particularly reserved to the people." See Beaney, The Constitutional Right to Privacy, 1962 Sup.Ct.Rev. 212; Griswold, The Right to be Let Alone, 55 Nw.U.L.Rev. 216 (1960).

We have had many controversies over these penumbral rights of "privacy and repose." See, e. g., Breard v. Alexandria, 341 U.S. 622, 626, 644; Public Utilities Comm'n v. Pollak, 343 U.S. 451; Monroe v. Pape, 365 U.S. 167; Lanza v. New York, 370 U.S. 139; Frank v.

---

**2.** The Court said in full about this right of privacy:

"The principles laid down in this opinion [by Lord Camden in Entick v. Carrington, 19 How.St.Tr. 1029] affect the very essence of constitutional liberty and security. They reach farther than the concrete form of the case then before the court, with its adventitious circumstances; they apply to all invasions on the part of the government and its employes of the sanctity of a man's home and the privacies of life. It is not the breaking of his doors, and the rummaging of his drawers, that constitutes the essence of the offence; but it is the invasion of his indefeasible right of personal security, personal liberty and private property, where that right has never been forfeited by his conviction of some public offence,—it is the invasion of this sacred right which underlies and constitutes the essence of Lord Camden's judgment. Breaking into a house and opening boxes and drawers are circumstances of aggravation; but any forcible and compulsory extortion of a man's own testimony or of his private papers to be used as evidence to convict him of crime or to forfeit his goods, is within the condemnation of that judgment. In this regard the Fourth and Fifth Amendments run almost into each other." 116 U.S., at 630. [Footnote in Court's opinion.]

Maryland, 359 U.S. 360; Skinner v. Oklahoma, 316 U.S. 535, 541. These cases bear witness that the right of privacy which presses for recognition here is a legitimate one.

The present case, then, concerns a relationship lying within the zone of privacy created by several fundamental constitutional guarantees. And it concerns a law which, in forbidding the *use* of contraceptives rather than regulating their manufacture or sale, seeks to achieve its goals by means having a maximum destructive impact upon that relationship. Such a law cannot stand in light of the familiar principle, so often applied by this Court, that a "governmental purpose to control or prevent activities constitutionally subject to state regulation may not be achieved by means which sweep unnecessarily broadly and thereby invade the area of protected freedoms." NAACP v. Alabama, 377 U.S. 288, 307. Would we allow the police to search the sacred precincts of marital bedrooms for telltale signs of the use of contraceptives? The very idea is repulsive to the notions of privacy surrounding the marriage relationship.

We deal with a right of privacy older than the Bill of Rights— older than our political parties, older than our school system. Marriage is a coming together for better or for worse, hopefully enduring, and intimate to the degree of being sacred. It is an association that promotes a way of life, not causes; a harmony in living, not political faiths; a bilateral loyalty, not commercial or social projects. Yet it is an association for as noble a purpose as any involved in our prior decisions.

Reversed.

Mr. Justice GOLDBERG, concurring.

. . . . In reaching the conclusion that the right of marital privacy is protected as being within the protected penumbra of specific guarantees of the Bill of Rights, the Court refers to the Ninth Amendment, *ante*, at 484. I add these words to emphasize the relevance of that Amendment to the Court's holding.

. . . . The language and history of the Ninth Amendment reveal that the Framers of the Constitution believed that there are additional fundamental rights, protected from governmental infringement, which exist alongside those fundamental rights specifically mentioned in the first eight constitutional amendments.

The Ninth Amendment reads, "The enumeration in the Constitution, of certain rights, shall not be construed to deny or disparage others retained by the people." The Amendment is almost entirely the work of James Madison. It was introduced in Congress by him and passed the House and Senate with little or no debate and virtually no change in language. It was proffered to quiet expressed fears that a bill of specifically enumerated rights could not be sufficiently broad to cover all essential rights and that the specific mention of certain rights would be interpreted as a denial that others were protected.

In presenting the proposed Amendment, Madison said:

"It has been objected also against a bill of rights, that, by enumerating particular exceptions to the grant of power, it would disparage those rights which were not placed in that enumeration; and it might follow by implication, that those rights which were not singled out, were intended to be assigned into the hands of the General Government, and were consequently insecure. This is one of the most plausible arguments I have ever heard urged against the admission of a bill of rights into this system; but, I conceive, that it may be guarded against. I have attempted it, as gentlemen may see by turning to the last clause of the fourth resolution [the Ninth Amendment]." I Annals of Congress 439 (Gales and Seaton ed. 1834).

Mr. Justice Story wrote of this argument against a bill of rights and the meaning of the Ninth Amendment:

. . .

"This clause was manifestly introduced to prevent any perverse or ingenious misapplication of the well-known maxim, that an affirmation in particular cases implies a negation in all others; and *e converso*, that a negation in particular cases implies an affirmation in all others." *Id.*, at 651.

. . .

While this Court has had little occasion to interpret the Ninth Amendment, "[i]t cannot be presumed that any clause in the constitution is intended to be without effect." Marbury v. Madison, 1 Cranch 137, 174. In interpreting the Constitution, "real effect should be given to all the words it uses." Myers v. United States, 272 U.S. 52, 151. The Ninth Amendment to the Constitution may be regarded by some as a recent discovery and may be forgotten by others, but since 1791 it has been a basic part of the Constitution which we are sworn to uphold. To hold that a right so basic and fundamental and so deep-rooted in our society as the right of privacy in marriage may be infringed because that right is not guaranteed in so many words by the first eight amendments to the Constitution is to ignore the Ninth Amendment and to give it no effect whatsoever. Moreover, a judicial construction that this fundamental right is not protected by the Constitution because it is not mentioned in explicit terms by one of the first eight amendments or elsewhere in the Constitution would violate the Ninth Amendment, which specifically states that "[t]he enumeration in the Constitution, of certain rights, shall not be *construed* to deny or disparage others retained by the people." (Emphasis added.)

. . .

I agree fully with the Court that, applying these tests, the right of privacy is a fundamental personal right, emanating "from the totality of the constitutional scheme under which we live." . . . Mr. Justice Brandeis, dissenting in Olmstead v. United States, 277 U.S. 438, 478, comprehensively summarized the principles underlying the Constitution's guarantees of privacy:

"The protection guaranteed by the [Fourth and Fifth] Amendments is much broader in scope. The makers of our

Constitution undertook to secure conditions favorable to the pursuit of happiness. They recognized the significance of man's spiritual nature, of his feelings and of his intellect. They knew that only a part of the pain, pleasure and satisfactions of life are to be found in material things. They sought to protect Americans in their beliefs, their thoughts, their emotions and their sensations. They conferred, as against the Government, the right to be let alone—the most comprehensive of rights and the right most valued by civilized men."

The Connecticut statutes here involved deal with a particularly important and sensitive area of privacy—that of the marital relation and the marital home. This Court recognized in Meyer v. Nebraska, *supra*, that the right "to marry, establish a home and bring up children" was an essential part of the liberty guaranteed by the Fourteenth Amendment. 262 U.S., at 399. In Pierce v. Society of Sisters, 268 U.S. 510, the Court held unconstitutional an Oregon Act which forbade parents from sending their children to private schools because such an act "unreasonably interferes with the liberty of parents and guardians to direct the upbringing and education of children under their control." 268 U.S., at 534–535. As this Court said in Prince v. Massachusetts, 321 U.S. 158, at 166, the *Meyer* and *Pierce* decisions "have respected the private realm of family life which the state cannot enter."

I agree with Mr. Justice HARLAN's statement in his dissenting opinion in Poe v. Ullman, 367 U.S. 497, 551–552: "Certainly the safeguarding of the home does not follow merely from the sanctity of property rights. The home derives its pre-eminence as the seat of family life. And the integrity of that life is something so fundamental that it has been found to draw to its protection the principles of more than one explicitly granted Constitutional right . . . . Of this whole 'private realm of family life' it is difficult to imagine what is more private or more intimate than a husband and wife's marital relations."

The entire fabric of the Constitution and the purposes that clearly underlie its specific guarantees demonstrate that the rights to marital privacy and to marry and raise a family are of similar order and magnitude as the fundamental rights specifically protected.

Although the Constitution does not speak in so many words of the right of privacy in marriage, I cannot believe that it offers these fundamental rights no protection. The fact that no particular provision of the Constitution explicitly forbids the State from disrupting the traditional relation of the family—a relation as old and as fundamental as our entire civilization—surely does not show that the Government was meant to have the power to do so. Rather, as the Ninth Amendment expressly recognizes, there are fundamental personal rights such as this one, which are protected from abridgment by the Government though not specifically mentioned in the Constitution.

. . . .

Mr. Justice BLACK, with whom Mr. Justice STEWART joins, dissenting.

.   .   .   .   There is no single one of the graphic and eloquent strictures and criticisms fired at the policy of this Connecticut law either by the Court's opinion or by those of my concurring Brethren to which I cannot subscribe—except their conclusion that the evil qualities they see in the law make it unconstitutional.

.   .   .

The Court talks about a constitutional "right of privacy" as though there is some constitutional provision or provisions forbidding any law ever to be passed which might abridge the "privacy" of individuals. But there is not. There are, of course, guarantees in certain specific constitutional provisions which are designed in part to protect privacy at certain times and places with respect to certain activities. Such, for example, is the Fourth Amendment's guarantee against "unreasonable searches and seizures."   .   .   .

One of the most effective ways of diluting or expanding a constitutionally guaranteed right is to substitute for the crucial word or words of a constitutional guarantee another word or words, more or less flexible and more or less restricted in meaning. This fact is well illustrated by the use of the term "right of privacy" as a comprehensive substitute for the Fourth Amendment's guarantee against "unreasonable searches and seizures." "Privacy" is a broad, abstract and ambiguous concept which can easily be shrunken in meaning but which can also, on the other hand, easily be interpreted as a constitutional ban against many things other than searches and seizures. I have expressed the view many times that First Amendment freedoms, for example, have suffered from a failure of the courts to stick to the simple language of the First Amendment in construing it, instead of invoking multitudes of words substituted for those the Framers used.   .   .   .   For these reasons I get nowhere in this case by talk about a constitutional "right of privacy" as an emanation from one or more constitutional provisions. I like my privacy as well as the next one, but I am nevertheless compelled to admit that government has a right to invade it unless prohibited by some specific constitutional provision.   .   .   .

### Questions

1. Is Douglas saying that although the Supreme Court does "not sit as a super-legislature to determine the wisdom, need and propriety of laws that touch economic problems, business affairs, or social conditions," it does sit as a "super-legislature" regarding laws which operate "directly on an intimate relation of husband and wife"? What is the evidence that this is what he is saying? What is the evidence that it is not? Does Douglas think he is using the Due Process Clause in the same way that Frankfurter used it in Rochin v. California? Does he think he is using the Clause in the way required by Black's dissent in *Rochin*?

How does Douglas justify the existence of the unstated, but nevertheless protected, "peripheral" or "penumbral" rights which "emanate" from explicit Constitutional provisions? From which explicit Constitutional provision or provisions, according to Douglas, does the "right of marital privacy" emanate? Does he say that this "right" is such an emanation for the same reason that, for example, "freedom to distribute" or "freedom to associate" are emanations of the First Amendment? Would such an argument hold up?

2.  Note the characterizations of "peripheral" or "penumbral" rights that Douglas advances.

   a.  Those rights without which "the specific rights would be less secure."

   b.  Those rights whose "existence is necessary in making the express guarantees fully meaningful."

   c.  Those "guarantees that help give" specific guarantees "life and substance"?

Do these characterizations amount to the same thing or do they differ materially? What is the relationship between making "secure," making "meaningful," and giving "life"? To which provisions of the Bill of Rights does the right of marital privacy give greater security, meaningfulness, and life? Does Douglas tell us how the right does this?

3.  Can it be argued that both Douglas and Goldberg concede that the "right of marital privacy" is not provided for by the Constitution? Can you cite language from their opinions which seems to say this? If this is their position, is there any way to avoid Black's charge that they are resting their conclusions on a higher, natural law?

4.  Are you sympathetic to Justice Black's complaint that "constitutionally guaranteed" rights have been expanded or diluted by substituting "for the crucial word or words of a constitutional guarantee another word or words, more or less flexible and more or less restricted in meaning"? How easy is it "to stick to the simple language of the First Amendment in construing it, instead of invoking multitudes of words substituted for those the Framers used"? What theory of meaning is disclosed by such a conception of interpretation or construction?

## Note: Authoritative Parts of Authoritative Wholes

Legal issues are usually framed as questions about the "meaning" of some particular, isolable linguistic entity. Fuller attacked Hart's "assumption that problems of interpretation typically turn on the meaning of individual words." "Even in the case of statutes," he said, "we commonly have to assign meaning, not to a single word, but to a sentence, a paragraph, or a whole page or more of text." Yet sentences, paragraphs, and "whole pages or more of text" are themselves, despite varying degrees of length and complexity, conceptually distinct entities. And it is possible to argue—perhaps by following Fuller's own line of reasoning—that even these are illegitimate subjects of interpretive attention. Determining the legal acceptability of a labor union's actions, for example, does not simply involve the applicability of a particular rule of labor law. It necessarily implicates an interpretation of the statute of which the provision is a part. But why stop with the statute? If the statute, why not the whole body of labor legislation? If all labor legislation, why not the entire body of enacted law? And if all enacted law, why not the entire social system of which that law is only a part?

Can the decision in *Griswold* be defended by such reasoning? Could it be argued that the Court's refusal to view its problem as one of the meaning of a specific rule or provision actually represents semantic sophistication rather than—as Justice Black thought—judicial lawlessness? At points—especially in the opinion of Justice Goldberg—the Court appears to invalidate Connecticut's law because of its inconsistency with "the totality of the constitutional scheme under which we live." Elsewhere it seems that the Bill of Rights *as a whole* somehow proscribes anti-contraception statutes. If the Court had made either of these grounds the explicit justification of its action, would Justice Black have been appeased? Suppose that Justice Douglas had begun his opinion in the case with the words, "The issue in this case is whether Connecticut's ban on contraceptive devices is consistent with the structure of American society." Do you think that would have been an acceptable statement of the issue to most lawyers? If not, consider whether you can propose an explanation for their disapproval? Are there any situations in which the explanation would not be applicable? Consider Goldberg's discussion of the Ninth Amendment. Is he saying that it creates a right of marital privacy? Or is he saying that it prescribes a canon of linguistic interpretation? Could it be argued that this Amendment is an authoritative declaration that the Constitution is something more—or something other—than the sum of its parts?

Whether the method of Griswold v. Connecticut—if method it be—is ultimately justifiable, it must be emphasized again that it is not the approach ordinarily used by those who deal with legal problems. Decisionmakers are constantly isolating words, rules, contracts, cases and asking what they mean. In so doing, they raise questions about the legal context—*e. g.*, the surrounding legal words, rules, enactments, etc.—from which these particular focal terms are isolated. Unlike the extrinsic matter with which the plain meaning rule is concerned this context is as authoritative as the particular entity which has been chosen for interpretation. It is not so easy, therefore, to shunt it aside and proceed with the task of construction. On the other hand, for many jurists it seems equally difficult to decide what should be done with it. Fuller's discussion of the relationship of words to the sentences in which they are found dramatizes the most obvious example of the dependency of an authoritative part on its authoritative whole. But it is the less obvious examples that perhaps cause the most difficulties for interpreters of legal language. As you read the Electrical Workers case, therefore, ask yourself whether the court recognizes and treats these difficulties or simply sweeps them under the rug.

INTERNATIONAL BROTHERHOOD OF ELECTRICAL WORKERS
ET AL. V. NATIONAL LABOR RELATIONS BOARD

341 U.S. 694 (1951)

Mr. Justice BURTON delivered the opinion of the Court.

The principal question here is whether a labor organization and its agent committed an unfair labor practice, within the meaning of section 8(b)(4)(A) of the National Labor Relations Act, 49 Stat. 449, 29 U.S.C. section 151, as amended by the Labor Management Relations Act, 1947,[3] when, by peaceful picketing, the agent induced employees of a subcontractor on a construction project to engage in a strike in the course of their employment, where an object of such inducement was to force the general contractor to terminate its contract with another subcontractor. For the reasons hereafter stated, we hold that an unfair labor practice was committed.

In December, 1947, the Giorgi Construction Company, a partnership (here called Giorgi), having its principal place of business at Port Chester, New York, contracted to build a private dwelling in Greenwich, Connecticut. The contract price was $15,200. Giorgi did part of the work with its own employees but subcontracted the electrical work to Samuel Langer and the carpentry work to Nicholas Deltorto, the principal place of business of each of whom was also at Port Chester, Langer's subcontract was for $325.

Langer in the past had employed union men but, prior to this project, had become involved in a dispute with petitioner, International Brotherhood of Eectrical Workers, Local 501, A. F. of L., here called the Electricians Union, because of his employment of nonunion men. By the middle of April, 1948, Langer's two electricians, neither of whom was a member of the Electricians Union, had completed the roughing in of the electrical work which was necessary before the walls of the house could be completed. At that point, on two days when no employees of Langer were present on the project, but before the completion of Langer's subcontract, William Patterson, the other petitioner herein, visited the project in his capacity of agent and business representative of the Electricians Union. The only workmen then present were Deltorto and his two carpenters, each of whom was a member of Local 543, United Brotherhood of Carpenters & Joiners of America, A. F. of L., here called the Carpenters

---

3. 61 Stat. 140–141, 29 U.S.C. (Supp. III) section 158(b) (4) (A). "Sec. 8

. . . .

"(b) It shall be an unfair labor practice for a labor organization or its agents—

. . . .

"(4) to engage in, or to induce or encourage the employees of any employer to engage in, a strike or a concerted refusal in the course of their employment to use, manufacture, process, transport, or otherwise handle or work on any goods, articles, materials, or commodities or to perform any services, where an object thereof is: (A) forcing or requiring any employer or self-employed person to join any labor or employer organization or any employer or other person to cease using, selling, handling, transporting, or otherwise dealing in the products of any other producer, processor, or manufacturer, or to cease doing business with any other person; . . . ." 61 Stat. 140–141, 29 U.S.C. (Supp. III) section 158(b) (4) (A). [Footnote in Court's opinion.]

Union.  Patterson informed Deltorto and one or both of his workmen that the electrical work on the job was being done by nonunion men. Deltorto and his men expressed ignorance of that fact, but Patterson, on the second day of his visits, repeated the statement and proceeded to picket the premises himself, carrying a placard which read "This job is unfair to organized labor: I.B.E.W. 501 A. F. L." Deltorto and his men thereupon stopped work and left the project. Deltorto promptly telephoned Giorgi, the general contractor, that his carpenters had walked off the job because the electrical delegate had picketed it.  Patterson also telephoned Giorgi saying that Langer was "unfair" and that Giorgi would have to replace Langer with a union contractor in order to complete the job.  He added that if Giorgi did not replace Langer, he would not receive any skilled trades to finish the rest of the work.

No communication was had with Langer by either of petitioners.  The next day, Giorgi recited these circumstances to Langer and the latter released Giorgi from the electrical subcontract, saying that he would step aside so that a union subcontractor could take over.  He did no further work on the project.  Giorgi informed Deltorto that the trouble had been straightened out, and the latter's carpenters returned to the project.

On a charge filed by Langer, based upon these events, the Regional Director of the National Labor Relations Board issued a complaint against the Electricians Union and Patterson.  It alleged that they had induced and encouraged the employees of Deltorto to engage in a strike or a concerted refusal in the course of their employment to perform services for him, an object thereof being to force or require Giorgi to cease doing business with Langer in violation of section 8(b)(4)(A).

With the consent of the present petitioners, a restraining order was issued against them by the United States District Court for the Southern District of New York, pursuant to section 10(1).  The . . . trial examiner . . . . recommended dismissal of the complaint on the ground that petitioners' action here was permissible under section 8(c), despite the provisions of section 8(b) (4) (A). . . . The majority of the Board . . . then affirmed the rulings which the examiner had made during the hearings, adopted certain of his findings, conclusions and recommendations, attached his intermediate report to its decision, but declined to follow his recommendation to dismiss the complaint.  The Board expressly held that section 8(c) did not immunize petitioners' conduct from the proscriptions of section 8(b) (4) (A).  82 N.L.R.B. 1028.  It ordered petitioners to—

> "Cease and desist from inducing or encouraging the employees of Nicholas Deltorto or any employer, by picketing or related conduct, to egage in a strike or a concerted refusal in the course of their employment to perform any services, where an object thereof is to force or require Giorgi Construction Co. or any other employer or person to cease doing business with Samuel Langer."  *Id.*, at 1030.

Petitioners asked the United States Court of Appeals, under section 10(f), to review and set aside that order. The Board answered and asked enforcement of it. With one judge dissenting, the court below ordered enforcement. 181 F.2d 34. We granted certiorari.

. . .

. . . . In the instant case, a labor dispute had been pending for some time between Langer and the Electricians Union, but no demands were made upon him directly by either of petitioners in connection with this project. There are no findings that the picketing was aimed at Langer to force him to employ union workmen on this job. On the contrary, the findings demonstrate that the picketing was directed at Deltorto's employees to induce them to strike and thus force Deltorto, the carpentry subcontractor, to force Giorgi, the general contractor, to terminate Langer's electrical subcontract.

. . .

4. The principal feature of the instant case . . . is that there is no finding here that the picketing and other activities of petitioners were mere signals in starting and stopping a strike in accordance with by-laws or other controlling practices of the Electricians and Carpenters Unions. The complaint here is not that petitioners . . . themselves *engaged in* or called a strike of Deltorto's carpenters in order to force the general contractor to cease doing business with the electrical subcontractor. Here the complaint is that petitioners, by peaceful picketing, rather than by prearranged signal, induced or encouraged the employees of Deltorto to strike (or to engage in a concerted refusal to perform any services for Deltorto) in the course of their employment to force Giorgi, the contractor, to cease doing business with Langer, the electrical subcontractor.

While in the *Denver* case we have held that section 8(c)[4] had no application to a strike signal, there are other considerations that enter into the decision here. The question here is what effect, if any, shall be given to section 8(c) in its application to peaceful picketing conducted by a labor organization or its agents merely as an inducement or encouragement of employees to engage in a secondary boycott. Petitioners contend that section 8(c) immunizes peaceful picketing, even though the picketing induces a secondary boycott made unlawful by section 8(b) (4). The Board reached the opposite conclusion and the court below approved the Board's order as applied to the facts of this case which it recognized as amounting to "bare instigation" of the secondary boycott. We agree with the Board.

a. To exempt peaceful picketing from the condemnation of section 8(b) (4) (A) as a means of bringing about a secondary boycott is contrary to the language and purpose of that section. The words "induce or encourage" are broad enough to include in them every

4. "The expressing of any views, argument, or opinion, or the dissemination thereof, whether in written, printed, graphic, or visual form, shall not constitute or be evidence of an unfair labor practice under any of the provisions of this Act, if such expression contains no threat of reprisal or force or promise of benefit." 61 Stat. 142, 29 U.S.C.A. (Supp. III) section 158(c). [Footnote in Court's opinion.]

form of influence and persuasion.[5] There is no legislative history to justify an interpretation that Congress by those terms has limited its proscription of secondary boycotting to cases where the means of inducement or encouragement amount to a "threat of reprisal or force or promise of benefit." Such an interpretation would give more significance to the means used than to the end sought. If such were the case there would have been little need for section 8(b) (4) defining the proscribed objectives, because the use of "restraint and coercion" for any purpose was prohibited in this whole field by section 8(b) (1) (A).

"Induce or encourage" appear in like context in section 303. The action proscribed by the terms of section 8(b) (4) is made in section 303 the basis for the recovery of damages in a civil action. Because section 8(c) is in terms limited to unfair labor practice proceedings and section 303 refers only to civil actions for damages,[6] it seems clear that section 8(c) does not apply to an action under section 303. That section does not mention unfair labor practices through which alone the provisions of section 8(c) become applicable. If section 8(c) were given the effect which petitioners urge, it would limit section 8(b) (4) (A) so as to give the words "induce or encourage" a meaning in that section different than they have in section 303. We think that the words are entitled to the same meaning in sections 8(b) (4) and 303.

b. The intended breadth of the words "induce or encourage" in section 8(b) (4) (A) is emphasized by their contrast with the restricted phrases used in other parts of section 8(b). For example, the unfair labor practice described in section 8(b) (1) is one "to restrain or coerce" employees; in section 8(b) (2) it is to "cause or attempt to cause an employer"; in section 8(b) (5) it is to "require of em-

---

5. Induce: "1. To lead on; to influence; to prevail on; to move by persuasion or influence. Encourage: "1. To give courage to; to inspire with courage, spirit, or hope; to raise the confidence of; to animate; hearten; . . . .
"2. To embolden, incite, or induce as by inspiration, recommendation, etc.; hence, to advise; . . . .
"3. To give help or patronage to, as an industry; to foster; . . . ."
Webster's New Int'l Dict., Unabridged (2d ed. 1945). [Footnote in Court's opinion.]

6. Sec. 303. (a) It shall be unlawful, for the purposes of this section only, in an industry or activity affecting commerce, for any labor organization to engage in, or to induce or encourage the employees of any employer to engage in, a strike or a concerted refusal in the course of their employment to use, manufacture, process, transport, or otherwise handle or work on any goods, articles, materials, or commodities or to perform any services, where an object thereof is—
"(1) forcing or requiring any employer or self-employed person to join any labor or employer organization or any employer or other person to cease using, selling, handling, transporting, or otherwise dealing in the products of any other producer, processor, or manufacturer, or to cease doing business with any other person:

·    ·    ·    ·    ·

(b) Whoever shall be injured in his business or property by reason of any violation of subsection (a) may sue therefor in any district court of the United States subject to the limitations and provisions of section 301 hereof without respect to the amount in controversy, or in any other court having jurisdiction of the parties, and shall recover the damages by him sustained and the cost of the suit." 61 Stat. 158–159, 29 U.S.C.A. (Supp. III) section 187. [Footnote in Court's opinion.]

ployees"; and in section 8(b) (6) it is to "cause or attempt to cause an employer." The scope of "induce" and especially of "encourage" goes beyond each of them.

c. To exempt peaceful picketing from the reach of section 8(b) (4) would be to open the door to the customary means of enlisting the support of employees to bring economic pressure to bear on their employer. The Board quickly recognized that to do so would be destructive of the purpose of section 8(b) (4) (A). It said "To find that peaceful picketing was not thereby proscribed would be to impute to Congress an incongruous intent to permit, through indirection, the accomplishment of an objective which it forbade to be accomplished directly." United Brotherhood of Carpenters, 81 N.L.R.B. 802, 811. Also—

> It was the *objective* of the unions' secondary activities.
> . . . and not the *quality of the means* employed to accomplish that objective, which was the dominant factor motivating Congress in enacting that provision . . . . In these circumstances, to construe Section 8(b) (4) (A) as qualified by Section 8(c) would practically vitiate its underlying purpose and amount to imputing to Congress an unrealistic approach to the problem." (Emphasis in original.) *Id.*, at 812.

The legislative history does not sustain a congressional purpose to outlaw secondary boycotts under section 8(b) (4) and yet in effect to sanction them under section 8(c).

d. We find no indication that Congress thought that the kind of picketing and related conduct which was used in this case to induce or encourage a strike for an unlawful object was any less objectionable than engaging directly in that strike. The court below, after finding that there was "bare instigation" here rather than an appeal to reason by "the expressing of any views, argument, or opinion," traced the development of the doctrine that he who provokes or instigates a wrong makes himself a party to it. That court then reached the conclusion that it is "highly unlikely that by section 8(c) Congress meant to abolish a doctrine, so deeply embedded in our civil and criminal law." 181 F.2d at 39.

e. The remedial function of section 8(c) is to protect noncoercive speech by employer and labor organization alike in furtherance of a lawful object. It serves that purpose adequately without extending its protection to speech or picketing in furtherance of unfair labor practices such as are defined in section 8(b) (4). The general terms of section 8(c) appropriately give way to the specific provisions of section 8(b) (4).

. . .

The judgment of the Court of Appeals accordingly is

Affirmed.

Mr. Justice REED, Mr. Justice DOUGLAS and Mr. Justice JACKSON would reverse the judgment of the Court of Appeals.

## QUESTIONS

1.   Is Burton right in saying that the "principal question
.   .   .   is whether" defendant "committed an unfair labor practice, within the meaning of section 8(b)(4)(A)"?   Or is the principal question whether defendant's conduct was protected by section
8(c)?   Or does it make any difference?

2.   What is the significance for Burton of the fact that the words
"induce or encourage" are "broad enough" to cover "every form of
influence and persuasion"?   Just what has been decided when it is
determined that words are "broad enough" to include some phenomenon?

3.   What role does the dictionary play in Burton's opinion?   Is
it treated as an authority?   What do dictionaries tell us about the
meanings of words?   Can they ever give us the answer to a problem
of legal interpretation?   Which of the two, Hart or Fuller would be
more sympathetic to the use of dictionaries in the solution of legal
problems?   Why?

4.   Does Burton offer a reason for thinking "that the words are
entitled to the same meaning in sections 8(b)(4) and 303"?   Can you
offer a reason why they are not "entitled" to the same meaning?   Even
if they should have the same meaning, does it necessarily follow that
the sections should have the meaning which Burton gives to them?

5.   What is the purpose which the Court attributes to Congress?
Is it the purpose of 8(b)(4)(A) or of 8(c) or of something else which
the Court invokes?   Does it offer any justification for this attribution of purpose?   What sorts of justifications would be acceptable?
Should 8(c) have a role in the determination of Congress's purpose?

6.   Why do the "general terms of section 8(c) appropriately give
way to the specific provisions of section 8(b)(4)"?   Is it a canon of
statutory interpretation that general terms defer to more specific
ones?   If so, is it a defensible canon?   What does it mean, do you think,
for one term to be more specific than another one?   Is it clear that
8(b)(4) is the more specific of the two sections discussed by Justice
Burton?

7.   Are the Electrical Workers arguing that Congress's "purpose
was to outlaw secondary boycotts under section 8(b)(4) and yet in
effect to immunize them under section 8(c)"?   Does it make sense to
speak of one section of a statute contradicting another?

*ABRAHAM HARARI*

## NEGLIGENCE IN THE LAW OF TORTS *

It has been shown that 'concrete' decisions are not law, that the
propositions of law found in the opinions of judges cannot, as such, be
considered authoritative, that no case when viewed in isolation will

---

* From 11–18 (1962).   Reprinted by permission of The Law Book Company
Limited, Sidney.

yield a *ratio decidendi*, that one's conception of the *ratio decidendi* of any case is determined by one's knowledge of the law.[7] Yet it is clear that it is only from the cases that the law can be learned, and it is equally clear that a not inconsiderable number of people do in fact succeed in learning it.

Let us therefore pass from a consideration of the method by which our student was advised that he would learn the law, to a consideration of the method by which he does in fact learn it. He reads both textbooks and cases. In both he finds propositions in the form of rules and principles of law. He knows that neither the propositions found in textbooks nor those found in cases are authoritative. But he accepts them tentatively as correct statements of the law. In the course of his reading he may find that a rule as formulated in the textbook, or in the opinion of a judge, cannot be squared with a decision or a number of decisions. He then checks the 'authorities'—that is, the cases—on the basis of which the rule was formulated. He may find that they did not necessitate the formulation in question, that is to say, that they could be explained on the basis of a wider or narrower rule. He will then reformulate the rule so as to make it consistent with those other decisions, and he will henceforth regard that modified or reformulated rule as correctly stating the law. If he finds that the rule as formulated in the textbook is fully supported by the authorities cited for it, he may conclude either that those 'authorities' have in the meantime been 'deprived of authority' to some extent. That is, if the conflicting decisions were the later decisions, he will conclude that the law has changed; or, if the conflicting decisions were the earlier ones, that the authorities cited have in effect deprived the conflicting decision of authority. If neither of these views is tenable he will conclude that the law is not yet settled, and that the rule as formulated in the textbook cannot therefore be accepted as correctly stating the law. In other words, the propositions of law found in textbooks and cases—in fact, all propositions regarding the provisions of the common law—are generalizations based on existing decisions, hypotheses as to what existing decisions imply or express *when they are co-ordinated*.

An analogy which throws some light on the process of finding the law is that between the law and the character of a person. If we liken the common law to the character of a person we get a fairly clear idea of its logical structure, of the way in which we arrive at propositions regarding its provisions, and of the logical status of these propositions.

What do we mean by 'character of a person', and how do we determine or discover it? Taking a multitude of 'particular facts' about a man we construct out of them what appears to be a consistent whole, a pattern, which in turn colours the 'facts' by which it was suggested and explains them. The basic assumption is that of consistency; all the actions of the man under consideration are interrelated, and the true significance of any of them is found only when all of them have been 'pieced together', when we have found the pattern. His character

---

7. For Harari's preceding discussion, see Chapter 8(2) (C), *infra.*

is the pattern which shows the consistency of his behaviour. If there is no way of fitting a given action into a suggested pattern, if the pattern does not explain the action, then the pattern is bad. In other words, our hypothesis regarding the man's character was wrong; it has either to be modified or to be replaced.

The same basic assumption—or, in this context, principle—is at the root of our idea of the common law: every decision of a court whose decisions are binding as precedents, which has not been reversed by a superior court, is in accordance with our pre-existing notions of the provisions of the law . . . . what we mean by 'the law' are all these decisions pieced together.

The decisions can of course be read in a way which will make them appear mutually inconsistent and contradictory, but if our purpose is to find the law such a reading would obviously be self-frustrating. For even if we invoke the time factor and regard the later decisions as overruling the earlier ones, we do not arrive at the kind of law we are after; rather we enter the cul-de-sac of 'realism' at its worst. By breaking all continuity we would have to regard as law the latest pronouncement from the bench . . . . 'The law' would literally be 'what the judge says', and there would be no point in reading what he says, for we would only be finding what the law *was* and not what it *is*. It is true that facts have to be faced whether they are palatable or not, but the question is 'What are the facts?' One fact which would probably not be disputed by anyone is that we are in the great majority of cases (taking into account cases which do not reach the courts) able to predict accurately what the courts' decisions will or would be, without studying the mental or psychic history or make-up of the particular judges, and without any knowledge about the state of their digestion. The obvious conclusion to which this points is that there is such a thing as 'law' in the old-fashioned sense of the word. It is our task to find it and to state it.

The logical relation between any single decision and 'the law' is exactly the same as that between any single act of a man and 'his character'. Just as 'his character' merely means a notional pattern which shows the consistency of his behaviour, so 'the law' merely means a notional pattern which shows the consistency of the decisions. And just as our view of the significance of any single act is determined by our view of his character, so our view of the significance of any given decision is determined by our view of the law.

The process of discovering a man's character, the technique employed, is similar to that by which we arrive at our notion of the law. We make generalizations suggested by the premises, that is by descriptions of any of the actions of the man, and we 'test' them by their consistency with his other actions. Let us say we have observed a man and made notes of all his actions over a period of time, and that one of our items reads: 'lovingly stroked a cat'. With no additional information available concerning his relations with our dumb friends, we may, on starting to make a character-sketch, write down: 'loves cats/animals?' This is a generalization suggested by the description of a single act. It is like reading Donoghue v. Stevenson [8] and making a marginal note such as 'negligently causing gastro-enteritis/damage? to another is a tort'. If we obtain additional information about our man, say that he is afraid of dogs, cannot stand the smell of horses, and enjoys shooting at birds, we may strike out 'animals'. On further being told that he allows no cats into his house and continually complains about his neighbours' cats, we will probably also change our view as to his regard for cats, and may even write down: 'dislikes animals'. By then moreover we will have realized that there is something wrong with our initial 'fact', that we must, to use a homely phrase, 'have got the wrong impression' when we note that he 'lovingly stroked a cat'. Reconstructing the scene, we may recall that we observed him stroking the cat while he was sitting in the drawing-room of his aunt, an elderly spinster of not inconsiderable means, who was at the time holding forth on the sensitivity and intelligence of cats in general, and of the said pet in particular, as against the coarseness and stupidity of the greater part of humanity. Obviously he stroked the cat out of consideration for the old lady, and it was she, and not the cat, who inspired the love and devotion which so clearly animated his face. We have to modify our initial view of the 'facts': he did not 'lovingly stroke a cat', he only went through the motions of doing so.

Legal decisions are dealt with in the same way. Having read Donoghue v. Stevenson, let us say that we now read Cattle v. Stockton Waterworks and Candler v. Crane, Christmas and Co. We might make the following marginal notes:

> CATTLE: 'Negligently making the performance of a contract more onerous for a contractor, or negligently depriving a person of the profits of his contract, is no tort'.

> CANDLER: 'Negligently causing pecuniary damage to another is no tort'.

It should be noted that with regard to *Cattle's* case the generalization 'negligently causing damage to another is no tort' does not suggest itself, because we already have before us Donoghue v. Stevenson, which negatives so wide a proposition. The same applies to *Candler's* case, but with this difference, that having now an additional case before us, and one in which there was no liability for negligence (namely, *Cattle's* case), we should be looking for a more inclusive proposition, one that would account for both these cases in which there was no liability; hence we are not likely to read *Candler's* case as merely establishing that 'negligently causing damage to another by inducing him to invest his money in worthless shares is no tort'.

The point of all this, however, is not so much how we read our third case in the light of the two cases which we read earlier, but that we would now go back to our first case and correct our marginal note: the proposition 'negligently causing damage to another is a tort' is now

8. See Harari's earlier discussion of
this case in Chapter 8(2) (c), *infra*.

ruled out. In other words, taking the individual decisions as the data from which we construct the law, our conception of the data themselves is subject to continual change and adjustment in the process of co-ordination.

This brings us to the concept of 'the *ratio decidendi* of a case'. It has been seen that the process of finding the law, like the process of discovering the character of a person, consists of collecting data and correlating them. In the case of the law the data are the decisions; in the case of a person's character the data are his actions, his behaviour. It has also been seen that what we regard as our data are in both cases, not unimpeachable or incontrovertible facts, but rather hybrids of observations and interpretations, mere working hypotheses constantly subject to qualification and modification. In much the same way as the significance of the observed behaviour—e. g., the stroking of the cat—emerges only when it is seen both in the special context of the man's behaviour generally, the significance of any given decision emerges only when it is seen both in the special context of the case in which it was given and in the wider context of all other relevant decisions.

The 'significance' of an action in this context is its significance with regard to the man's character: what it tells us about his character, what light it throws on his other known actions, and what we can learn from it with a view to predicting his future conduct. In the same way, the significance of a decision in this context is its significance for the law, what it tells us about the law, what light it throws on other decisions, and what we can learn from it with a view to predicting future decisions.

It was said that the significance of the observed behaviour only emerges when this behaviour is seen both in the special context in which it occurred and in the wider context of the man's behaviour generally. It may therefore be assumed that there is a certain point in time at which the data crystallize, as it were, at which we can make a proposition about the significance of a given act in the sure knowledge that we will not have to qualify or modify it subsequently. This is not so. Firstly, 'the man's behaviour generally' of course includes his future behaviour, so while he is still alive it is logically impossible to make such a proposition—if it is borne in mind that by 'his character' we mean a pattern which shows the consistency of *all* his actions, and by the significance of an act we mean what the act stands for within this pattern. As long as we cannot take account of all the man's actions every pattern which we construct must necessarily be a provisional one, subject to modification as additional data become available. It follows that any placing of a given act within such pattern must also be provisional. Secondly, even if the difficulty presented by future behaviour is removed (as by removing the man from this world), the profusion and complexity of the data to be processed, quite apart from the question of their availability, is such that it is practically impossible to attain certainty. We always remain in the sphere of hypotheses.

The same applies to the data from which we construct the law, except that here there are no practical means of removing the difficulty presented by future decisions. In other words, just as there is no way of determining once and for all the significance of a decision, that is, what it tells us about the law, how it affects our view of other decisions, and what conclusions we can draw from it with regard to future decisions; in short, its *ratio decidendi*.

The *ratio decidendi* of a case is the proposition of law the case supports when it is co-ordinated with all other cases. Once it is conceded that the law is not static, but develops and changes, it must also be conceded that the *rationes decidendi* of the cases change. If this is not generally recognized it is only because the notion of a changing law is still a relatively new one.

The concept *ratio decidendi* emerged at a time when it was seriously thought that the judges merely 'discover' the law, when there seemed to be a valid distinction between 'the law as such' and 'our conception of the law'. With *ratio decidendi* as a vague concept meaning 'the principle of law applied by the decision', and with a refusal to recognize that the judges were constantly making law, a distinction between 'the *ratio decidendi* of the case' and our conception of its *ratio decidendi* was inevitable. A case would be regarded as establishing a certain rule of law, which would be modified when additional cases further 'clarified' the law: the *ratio decidendi* of the old case obviously was not what it appeared to be—that has been conclusively shown by the new decisions. Since the judges were not regarded as making or changing law it was quite logical to regard as the true *ratio decidendi* of the old case the rule of law which the new case seemed to imply.

Today, when we no longer believe in 'the law as such' and when it is recognized that the law is not static, there is no room for the old concept of *ratio decidendi*. When looking for the *ratio decidendi* of a case we are not trying to discover the pre-existing rule of law which was applied in the case. What we are trying to determine is the *rule of law the decision will support when all other existing lawmaking decisions have been taken into account*. As new law-making decisions are given and taken into account, a given decision may no longer support a given rule. For example, since Lloyd v. Grace Smith and Co., Barwick v. English Joint Stock Bank can only be regarded as an authority for the proposition that a master is liable for a wrong committed by a servant in the course of the service; whereas before that decision *Barwick's* case would have been—and in fact was—regarded as an authority for a much narrower rule. It is therefore correct to say that until the decision in *Lloyd's* case the *ratio decidendi* of *Barwick's* case was X, and since *Lloyd's* case it is Y. To say, as Goodhart does, that the *ratio decidendi* of *Barwick's* case was misunderstood until the decision in *Lloyd's* case, is to use *ratio decidendi* in the old sense as 'the rule of law applied by the decision', implying the fiction of a pre-existing law which only has to be discovered and applied.[9]  The static *ratio decidendi* or 'principle of a case' seen by Goodhart is no less a mirage than the static law seen by him

## NOTE: THE SUSCEPTIBILITY OF *"All* QUESTIONS . . . TO RECONSIDERATION IN THE LIGHT OF SOCIAL POLICY"

To view "all legal questions" as "fundamentally like those of the penumbra," said Hart, amounts to the position "that there is no central element of actual law to be seen in the core of central meaning which rules have, that there is nothing in the nature of a legal rule inconsistent with *all* questions being open to reconsideration in the light of social policy."  If the meanings of words and cases are always open to question, would this mean, as Hart seems to imply, that communication would be impossible?  If we never know the meaning of a word until we have studied its context, and its context includes words whose meanings are similarly dependent on their contexts, how is it possible to ever reach a conclusion?  Do the readings from Lucas, Quine and Blanshard, reprinted in Chapter 6, Section 3, suggest a solution to this dilemma?

## SECTION THREE:  THE LANGUAGE OF MEANING

### GARRATT v. DAILEY

46 Wash.2d 197 (1955)

HILL, J.—The liability of an infant for an alleged battery is presented to this court for the first time.  Brian Dailey (age five years, nine months) was visiting with Naomi Garratt, an adult and a sister of the plaintiff, Ruth Garratt, likewise an adult, in the backyard of the plaintiff's home, on July 16, 1951.  It is plaintiff's contention that she came out into the backyard to talk with Naomi and that, as she started to sit down in a wood and canvas lawn chair, Brian deliberately pulled it out from under her.  The only one of the three persons present so testifying was Naomi Garratt.  (Ruth Garratt, the plaintiff, did not testify as to how or why she fell.)  The trial court, unwilling to accept this testimony, adopted instead Brian Dailey's version of what happened, and made the following findings:

"III.  .  .  .  that while Naomi Garratt and Brian Dailey were in the back yard the plaintiff, Ruth Garratt, came out of her house into the back yard.  Some time subsequent thereto defendant, Brian Dailey, picked up a lightly built wood and canvas lawn chair which was then and there located in the back yard of the above described premises, moved it sideways a few feet and seated himself therein, at which time he discovered the plaintiff, Ruth Garratt, about to sit down at the place where the lawn chair had formerly been, at which time he hurriedly got up from the chair and attempted to move it

---

**9.**  See *Essays*, p. 129: 'It will be necessary to quote at some length from the opinions of the judges in this case, so as to determine as *definitely* as possible the exact *ratio decidendi* of each decision.'  (Italics mine).  [Footnote in original.]

toward Ruth Garratt to aid her in sitting down in the chair; that due to the defendant's small size and lack of dexterity he was unable to get the lawn chair under the plaintiff in time to prevent her from falling to the ground. That plaintiff fell to the ground and sustained a fracture of her hip, and other injuries and damages as hereinafter set forth.

"IV. That the preponderance of the evidence in this case establishes that when the defendant, Brian Dailey, moved the chair in question *he did not have any wilful or unlawful purpose in doing so*; that *he did not have any intent to injure the plaintiff, or any intent to bring about any unauthorized or offensive contact with her person* or any objects appurtenant thereto; that the circumstances which immediately preceded the fall of the plaintiff established that the defendant, *Brian Dailey, did not have purpose, intent or design to perform a prank or to effect an assault and battery upon the person of the plaintiff.*" (Italics ours, for a purpose hereinafter indicated.)

It is conceded that Ruth Garratt's fall resulted in a fractured hip and other painful and serious injuries. To obviate the necessity of a retrial in the event this court determines that she was entitled to a judgment against Brian Dailey, the amount of her damage was found to be eleven thousand dollars. Plaintiff appeals from a judgment dismissing the action and asks for the entry of a judgment in that amount or a new trial.

The authorities generally, but with certain notable exceptions (see Bohlen, "Liability in Tort of Infants and Insane Persons," 23 Mich.L.Rev. 9), state that, when a minor has committed a tort with force, he is liable to be proceeded against as any other person would be. . . . .

In our analysis of the applicable law, we start with the basic premise that Brian, whether five or fifty-five, must have committed some wrongful act before he could be liable for appellant's injuries.

. . .

It is urged that Brian's action in moving the chair constituted a battery. A definition (not all-inclusive but sufficient for our purpose) of a battery is the intentional infliction of a harmful bodily contact upon another. The rule that determines liability for battery is given in 1 Restatement, Torts, 29, sec. 13, as:

"An act which, directly or indirectly, is the legal cause of a harmful contact with another's person makes the actor liable to the other, if

"(a) the act is done with the intention of bringing about a harmful or offensive contact or an apprehension thereof to the other or a third person, and

"(b) the contact is not consented to by the other or the other's consent thereto is procured by fraud or duress, and

"(c) the contact is not otherwise privileged."

We have in this case no question of consent or privilege. We therefore proceed to an immediate consideration of intent and its place in the law of battery.  In the comment on clause (a), the Restatement says:

"*Character of actor's intention.*  In order that an act may be done with the intention of bringing about a harmful or offensive contact or an apprehension thereof to a particular person, either the other or a third person, the act must be done for the purpose of causing the contact or apprehension or with knowledge on the part of the actor that such contact or apprehension is substantially certain to be produced."

See, also, Prosser on Torts 41, sec. 8.

We have here the conceded volitional act of Brian, *i. e.*, the moving of a chair.  Had the plaintiff proved to the satisfaction of the trial court that Brian moved the chair while she was in the act of sitting down, Brian's action would patently have been for the purpose or with the intent of causing the plaintiff's bodily contact with the ground, and she would be entitled to a judgment against him for the resulting damages.  .  .  .

The plaintiff based her case on that theory, and the trial court held that she failed in her proof and accepted Brian's version of the facts rather than that given by the eyewitness who testified for the plaintiff.  After the trial court determined that the plaintiff had not established her theory of a battery (*i. e.*, that Brian had pulled the chair out from under the plaintiff while she was in the act of sitting down), it then became concerned with whether a battery was established under the facts as it found them to be.

In this connection, we quote another portion of the comment on the "Character of actor's intention," relating to clause (a) of the rule from the Restatement heretofore set forth:

"It is not enough that the act itself is intentionally done and this, even though the actor realizes or should realize that it contains a very grave risk of bringing about the contact or apprehension.  Such realization may make the actor's conduct negligent or even reckless but unless he realizes that to a substantial certainty, the contact or apprehension will result, the actor has not that intention which is necessary to make him liable under the rule stated in this Section."

A battery would be established if, in addition to plaintiff's fall, it was proved that, when Brian moved the chair, he knew with substantial certainty that the plaintiff would attempt to sit down where the chair had been.  If Brian had any of the intents which the trial court found, in the italicized portions of the findings of fact quoted above, that he did not have, he would of course have had the knowledge to which we have referred.  The mere absence of any intent to injure the plaintiff or to play a prank on her or to embarrass her, or to commit an assault and battery on her would not absolve him from liability if in fact he had such knowledge.  .  .  Without such knowledge, there would be nothing wrongful about Brian's act in moving the chair, and, there being no wrongful act, there would be no liability.

While a finding that Brian had no such knowledge can be inferred from the findings made, we believe that before the plaintiff's action in such a case should be dismissed there should be no question but that the trial court had passed upon that issue; hence, the case should be remanded for clarification of the findings to specifically cover the question of Brian's knowledge, because intent could be inferred therefrom. If the court finds that he had such knowledge, the necessary intent will be established and the plaintiff will be entitled to recover, even though there was no purpose to injure or embarrass the plaintiff. . . . If Brian did not have such knowledge, there was no wrongful act by him, and the basic premise of liability on the theory of a battery was not established.

It will be noted that the law of battery as we have discussed it is the law applicable to adults, and no significance has been attached to the fact that Brian was a child less than six years of age when the alleged battery occurred. The only circumstance where Brian's age is of any consequence is in determining what he knew, and there his experience, capacity, and understanding are of course material.

From what has been said, it is clear that we find no merit in plaintiff's contention that we can direct the entry of a judgment for eleven thousand dollars in her favor on the record now before us.

Nor do we find any error in the record that warrants a new trial.

What we have said concerning intent in relation to batteries caused by the physical contact of a plaintiff with the ground or floor as the result of the removal of a chair by a defendant, furnishes the basis for the answer to the contention of the plaintiff that the trial court changed its theory of the applicable law after the trial, and that she was prejudiced thereby.

It is clear to us that there was no change in theory so far as the plaintiff's case was concerned. The trial court consistently from beginning to end recognized that, if the plaintiff proved what she alleged and her eyewitness testified, namely, that Brian pulled the chair out from under the plaintiff while she was in the act of sitting down and she fell to the ground in consequence thereof, a battery was established. Had she proved that state of facts, then the trial court's comments about inability to find any intent (from the connotation of motivation) to injure or embarrass the plaintiff, and the italicized portions of his findings as above set forth, could have indicated a change of theory. But what must be recognized is that the trial court was trying in those comments and in the italicized findings to express the law applicable, not to the facts as the plaintiff contended they were, but to the facts as the trial court found them to be. The remand for clarification gives the plaintiff an opportunity to secure a judgment even though the trial court did not accept her version of the facts, if from all the evidence the trial court can find that Brian knew with substantial certainty that the plaintiff intended to sit down where the chair had been before he moved it, and still without reference to motivation.

The plaintiff-appellant urges as another ground for a new trial that she was refused the right to cross-examine Brian. Some twenty pages of cross-examination indicate that there was no refusal of the right of cross-examination. The only occasion that impressed us as being a restriction on the right of cross-examination occurred when plaintiff was attempting to develop the fact that Brian had had chairs pulled out from under him at kindergarten and had complained about it. Plaintiff's counsel sought to do this by asking questions concerning statements made at Brian's home and in a court reporter's office. When objections were sustained, counsel for plaintiff stated that he was asking about the conversations to refresh the recollection of the child, and made an offer of proof. The fact that plaintiff was seeking to develop came into the record by the very simple method of asking Brian what had happened at kindergarten. Consequently, what plaintiff offered to prove by the cross-examination is in the record, and the restriction imposed by the trial court was not prejudicial.

.   .   .

The plaintiff complains, and with some justice, that she was not permitted to take a pretrial deposition of the defendant, Brian Dailey. While Rule of Pleading, Practice, and Procedure 30(b), 34A Wn. (2nd) 91, gives the trial court the right "for good cause shown" to prevent the taking of a deposition, it seems to us that though it might well have been taken under the supervision of the court to protect the child from leading, misleading, and confusing questions, the deposition should have been allowed, if the child was to be permitted to testify at the trial. If, however, the refusal to allow the taking of the deposition was an abuse of discretion, and that we are not prepared to hold, it has not been established that the refusal constituted prejudicial error.   .   .   .

The cause is remanded for clarification, with instructions to make definite findings on the issue of whether Brian Dailey knew with substantial certainty that the plaintiff would attempt to sit down where the chair which he moved had been, and to change the judgment if the findings warrant it.

Costs on this appeal will abide the ultimate decision of the superior court. If a judgment is entered for the plaintiff, Ruth Garratt, appellant here, she shall be entitled to her costs on this appeal. If, however, the judgment of dismissal remains unchanged, the respondent will be entitled to recover his costs on this appeal.

Remanded for clarification.

## Questions

1. Why did the appellate court remand "for clarification"? What precisely had to be clarified? Did the appellate court conclude that the trial judge had erroneously found the facts? Or that it had misapplied the law? Or was it that the lower tribunal's decision was too confusing to be understood? Is there anything in Hill's opinion which would justify such a characterization?

2. On what portion of the record does Hill base the assertion that "the trial court determined that the plaintiff had not established her theory of a battery (*i. e.*, that Brian had pulled the chair out from

under the plaintiff while she was in the act of sitting down)"? Is there any way of interpreting finding "III" which would permit the inference that Brian *did* pull "the chair out from under the plaintiff while she was in the act of sitting down"?

Why would "Brian's action . . . patently have been for the purpose or with the intent of causing the plaintiff's bodily contact with the ground" if he had moved the chair while Ruth Garratt was in the act of sitting down? Would the fact that Ruth was in the act of seating herself when Brian moved the chair necessarily establish that he *knew* she was engaged in that process? Or is knowledge of the consequences of one's act not always necessary to establish "purpose" or "intent" under the law of battery? Is there anything in Hill's opinion which would support such an hypothesis? Or in the passages from the Restatement of Torts which Hill quotes? Even if Brian moved the chair knowing that Ruth was seating herself is that enough to warrant a finding of battery? Recall the Restatement definition referred to by Hill:

> . . . . the act [must be] . . . done with the intention of bringing about a harmful or offensive contact
> . . . .

Would Brian's action necessarily have been "with the intention of bringing about a . . . contact"? A contact that was "harmful or offensive"?

"A battery would be established," Justice Hill says, "if, in addition to plaintiff's fall, it was proved that, when Brian moved the chair, he knew with substantial certainty that the plaintiff would attempt to sit down where the chair had been." If this were proved would it mean necessarily that Brian knew Ruth would fall? That she would make contact with the ground? That any contact would be harmful or offensive? Would it mean necessarily that Brian "intended" Ruth to fall? Or to make contact with the ground? Or to make contact in a way which would be harmful or offensive? Is it important that these questions be answered? Given the Restatement's discussion of intention, would it be possible to reach a correct result without answering these questions?

3. Is there anything in the lower court's decision which supports Hill's declaration that "a finding that Brian had no . . . knowledge [that the plaintiff would attempt to sit down where the chair had been] can be inferred from the findings made"? If there is language which supports such an inference, what is the language which puts it in doubt, which justifies the remand "for clarification"? What specifically does Hill want the trial judge to *say* in order to convince him that "the trial court had passed upon that issue"? What characteristic of this new statement would make it superior to the old one? Can you make an argument that a more specific statement would be less satisfactory than the one under examination?

4. Do the words "intention" and "purpose" have the same or different meanings in the usage of the trial court? Of the appellate court? Of the Restatement of Torts? Note that the Restatement would find the requisite "intention" if the act were done (1) "for the

purpose of causing the contact . . . *or"* (emphasis added) (2) "with knowledge on the part of the actor that such contact . . . is substantially certain to be produced." Does this mean that "purpose" is a type of "intention"? That "intention" is the broader category? Does it mean that one can have "the purpose of causing the contact," even though one does not have "knowledge . . . that such contact . . . is substantially certain to be produced"? If so, how does one go about determining whether one has the purpose of causing a harmful or offensive contact? According to Hill, Naomi testified that Brian "deliberately pulled . . . out [the chair] from under" Ruth. How could Naomi have reached such a conclusion? Is the process different from the one used by Brian to reach the opposite conclusion? Is it different from the one used by the trial judge in deciding that Brian was not liable?

Suppose that Brian moved the chair, because he was tired and wanted to sit down. Suppose further that he knew Ruth would attempt to sit down and thereby injure herself. Would ordinary usage support his assertion that he did not "intend" to injure her? Would ordinary usage support Ruth's intention that he did so intend? What functions would such words as "purpose" and "motive" have in a description of Brian's "state of mind"? Suppose that Brian declared that he did not "desire" or "want" Ruth to be hurt; he only wished to have the chair for his own use. Would ordinary usage justify the meanings which Brian gave to these words?

GILBERT RYLE

## THE CONCEPT OF MIND *

. . . . when we describe people as exercising qualities of mind, we are not referring to occult episodes of which their overt acts and utterances are effects; we are referring to those overt acts and utterances themselves. There are, of course, differences, crucial for our inquiry, between describing an action as performed absent-mindedly and describing a physiologically similar action as done on purpose, with care or with cunning. But such differences of description do not consist in the absence or presence of an implicit reference to some shadow-action covertly prefacing the overt action. They consist, on the contrary, in the absence or presence of certain sorts of testable explanatory-cum-predictive assertions.

. . .

It is, of course, perfectly true that when we characterize as witty or tactful some piece of overt behaviour, we are not considering only the muscular movements which we witness. A parrot might have made the same remark in the same situation without our crediting it with a sense of humour, or a lout might have done precisely what the tactful man did, without our thinking him tactful. But if one and the same vocal utterance is a stroke of humour from the humorist, but a mere noise-response, when issuing from the parrot, it is tempting to say that we are ascribing wit not to something that we hear but to something else that we do not hear. We are accordingly tempted to say that what makes one audible or visible action witty, while another audibly or visibly similar action was not, is that the former was attended by another inaudible and invisible action which was the real exercise of wit. But to admit, as we must, that there may be no visible or audible difference between a tactful or witty act and a tactless or humourless one is not to admit that the difference is constituted by the performance or non-performance of some extra secret acts.

The cleverness of the clown may be exhibited in his tripping and tumbling. He trips and tumbles just as clumsy people do, except that he trips and tumbles on purpose and after much rehearsal and at the golden moment and where the children can see him and so as not to hurt himself. The spectators applaud his skill at seeming clumsy, but what they applaud is not some extra hidden performance executed 'in his head'. It is his visible performance that they admire, but they admire it not for being an effect of any hidden internal causes but for being an exercise of a skill. Now a skill is not an act. It is therefore neither a witnessable nor an unwitnessable act. To recognise that a performance is an exercise of a skill is indeed to appreciate it in the light of a factor which could not be separately recorded by a camera. But the reason why the skill exercised in a performance cannot be separately recorded by a camera is not that it is an occult or ghostly happening, but that it is not a happening at all. It is a disposition, or complex of dispositions, and a disposition is a factor of the wrong logical type to be seen or unseen, recorded or unrecorded. Just as the habit of talking loudly is not itself loud or quiet, since it is not the sort of term of which 'loud' and 'quiet' can be predicated, or just as a susceptibility to headaches is for the same reason not itself unendurable or endurable, so the skills, tastes and bents which are exercised in overt or internal operations are not themselves overt or internal, witnessable or unwitnessable. . . .

.   .   .

Epistemologists, among others, often  .   .   .   .  postulate that, for example, a man who believes that the earth is round must from time to time be going through some unique proceeding of cognising, 'judging', or internally re-asserting, with a feeling of confidence, 'The earth is round'. In fact, of course, people do not harp on statements in this way, and even if they did so and even if we knew that they did, we still should not be satisfied that they believed that the earth was round, unless we also found them inferring, imagining, saying and doing a great number of other things as well. If we found them inferring, imagining, saying and doing these other things, we should be satisfied that they believed the earth to be round, even if we had the best reasons for thinking that they never internally harped on the original statement at all. However often and stoutly a skater avers to us or to himself, that the ice will bear, he shows that he has his qualms, if he keeps to the edge of the pond, calls his children away from the middle, keeps his eye on the life-belts or continually speculates what would happen, if the ice broke.

. . . . [Thus,] when we speak of a person's mind, we are not speaking of a second theatre of special-status incidents, but of certain ways in which some of the incidents of his one life are ordered. His life is not a double series of events taking place in two different kinds of stuff; it is one concatenation of events, the differences between some and other classes of which largely consist in the applicability or inapplicability to them of logically different types of law-propositions and law-like propositions. Assertions about a person's mind are therefore assertions of special sorts about that person. So questions about the relations between a person and his mind, like those about the relations between a person's body and his mind are improper questions. They are improper in much the same way as is the question, 'What transactions go on between the House of Commons and the British Constitution?'

It follows that it is a logical solecism to speak, as theorists often do, of someone's mind knowing this, or choosing that. The person himself knows this and chooses that, though the fact that he does so can, if desired, be classified as a mental fact about that person. In partly the same way it is improper to speak of my eyes seeing this, or my nose smelling that; we should say, rather, that I see this, or I smell that, and that these assertions carry with them certain facts about my eyes and nose. But the analogy is not exact, for while my eyes and nose are organs of sense, 'my mind' does not stand for another organ. It signifies by ability and proneness to do certain sorts of things and not some piece of personal apparatus without which I could or would not do them. Similarly the British Constitution is not another British political institution functioning alongside of the Civil Service, the Judiciary, the Established Church, the Houses of Parliament and the Royal Family. Nor is it the sum of these institutions, or a liaison-staff between them. We can say that Great Britain has gone to the polls; but we cannot say that the British Constitution has gone to the polls, though the fact that Great Britain has gone to the polls might be described as a constitutional fact about Great Britain.

. . .

The questions 'What knowledge can a person get of the workings of his own mind?' and 'How does he get it?' by their very wording suggest absurd answers. They suggest that, for a person to know that he is lazy, or has done a sum carefully, he must have taken a peep into a windowless chamber, illuminated by a very peculiar sort of light, and one to which only he has access. And when the question is construed in this sort of way, the parallel questions, 'What knowledge can one person get of the workings of another mind?' and 'How does he get it?' by their very wording seem to preclude any answer at all; for they suggest that one person could only know that another person was lazy, or had done a sum carefully, by peering into another secret chamber to which, *ex hypothesi*, he has no access.

In fact the problem is not one of this sort. It is simply the methodological question, how we establish, and how we apply, certain sorts of lawlike propositions about the overt and the silent behaviour of persons. I come to appreciate the skill and tactics of a chess-player by watching him and others playing chess, and I learn that a certain pupil of mine is lazy, ambitious and witty by following his work, noticing his excuses, listening to his conversation and comparing his performances with those of others. Nor does it make any important difference if I happen myself to be that pupil. I can indeed then listen to more of his conversations, as I am the addressee of his un-spoken soliloquies; I notice more of his excuses, as I am never absent, when they are made. On the other hand, my comparison of his per-formances with those of others is more difficult, since the examiner is himself taking the examination, which makes neutrality hard to preserve and precludes the demeanour of the candidate, when under interrogation, from being in good view.

.   .   .   .   after listening to an argument, you aver that you understand it perfectly; but you may be deceiving yourself, or trying to deceive me. If we then part for a day or two, I am no longer in a position to test whether or not you did understand it perfectly. But still I know what tests would have settled the point. If you had put the argument into your own words, or translated it into French; if you had invented appropriate concrete illustrations of the generalisa-tions and abstractions in the argument; if you had stood up to cross-questioning;   .   .   .   then I should have required no further evidence that you understood it perfectly. And exactly the same sorts of tests would satisfy me that I had understood it perfectly; the sole differ-ences would be that I should probably not have voiced aloud the ex-pressions of my deductions, illustrations, etc., but told them to myself more perfunctorily in silent sililoquy; and I should probably have been more easily satisfied of the completeness of my understanding than I was of yours.

In short it is part of the *meaning* of 'you understood it' that you could have done so and so and would have done it, if such and such, and the *test* of whether you understood it is a range of performances satisfying the apodoses of these general hypothetical statements. It should be noticed, on the one hand, that there is no single nuclear performance, overt or in your head, which would determine that you had understood the argument. Even if you claimed that you had experienced a flash or click of comprehension and had actually done so, you would still withdraw your other claim to have understood the argument, if you found that you could not paraphrase it, illustrate, expand or recast it; and you would allow someone else to have under-stood it who could meet all examination-questions about it, but re-ported no click of comprehension.   .   .   .

I discover my or your motives in much, though not quite the same way as I discover my or your abilities. The big practical difference is that I cannot put the subject through his paces in my inquiries into his inclinations as I can in my inquiries into his competences. To discover how conceited or patriotic you are, I must still observe your conduct, remarks, demeanour and tones of voice, but I cannot subject you to examination-tests or experiments which you recognise as such. You would have a special motive for responding to such experiments in a particular way. From mere conceit, perhaps, you would try to behave self-effacingly, or from mere modesty you might try to behave con-ceitedly. None the less, ordinary day to day observation normally serves swiftly to settle such questions.  To be conceited is to tend to boast of one's own excellences, to pity or ridicule the deficiencies of others, to day-dream about imaginary triumphs, to reminisce about actual triumphs, to weary quickly of conversations which reflect unfavourably upon oneself, to lavish one's society upon distinguished persons and to economise in association with the undistinguished. The tests of whether a person is conceited are the actions he takes and the reactions he manifests in such circumstances.  Not many anecdotes, sneers or sycophancies are required from the subject for the ordinary observer to make up his mind, unless the candidate and the examiner happen to be identical.

## QUESTIONS

1.  In light of what Ryle says thereafter is it correct to say that "when we describe people as exercising qualities of mind, we are not referring to occult episodes of which their overt acts and utterances are effects; we are referring to those overt acts and utterances themselves"?  Are "we referring" solely "to those overt acts and utterances" or are we also referring to "certain sorts of testable explanatory-cum-predictive assertions"?  What is the relationship, according to Ryle, between the "overt acts and utterances" and these "assertions"?

Compare Ryle's "qualities of mind" with Whitehead's "properties of things."  Do you think Whitehead would view the qualities of a mind as specific properties of a specific thing?  Is intelligence a property of the mind?  Is knowledge?  Is intention?  If not, why not?  Could the intelligence of an action "be expressed as  .  .  . [its] relatedness to other things unspecified"?  Would Ryle concur in this form of expression?  If so, which term in his vocabulary corresponds to Whitehead's "relatedness"?

2.  Is there anything in *Garratt* which indicates that the law— or at least some lawyers—view the problem of determining intention as one of "peep[ing] into a windowless chamber," rather than (a) establishing and (b) applying "certain sorts of law-like propositions about the overt and the silent behaviour of persons"?  Would the judges and authorities in *Garratt* agree "that there is no single nuclear performance, overt or in your head, which would determine that you had understood" something?  Would they think that "intention" or "purpose" was determined by whether the subject "had experienced a flash or click" of determination?

## NOTE: HOW TO READ AN OPINION

On the remand of Garratt v. Dailey, the trial judge decided that "it was necessary for him to consider carefully the time sequence, as he had not done before; and this resulted in his finding that the arthritic woman had begun the slow process of being seated when the defendant quickly removed the chair and seated himself upon it, and that he knew, with substantial certainty, at that time that she would attempt to sit in the place where the chair had been."  The plaintiff obtained a judgment which was affirmed by the Supreme Court of Washington, 49 Wash.2d 499 (1956).

Was this finding a reversal of an earlier finding? Or was it simply an additional finding? Did the trial court judge do what the appellate court had directed? Or did it do something else? Did the appellate court ask the trial court to "consider carefully the time sequence"? If not, why was it *"necessary"* (emphasis added) to consider it on remand? Do you have any comment on the admission that "he had not done [so] before"?

By now you have probably realized that Garratt v. Dailey raises questions about "intention" that go beyond the law of battery. It may be instructive for you to compare the concept of intention which obtains in Torts with the concepts of intention found in, for example, the law of contracts and of statutory interpretation? Can you see how Ryle's remarks dissolve some of the distinguishing features which are usually thought to separate these forms of intention? More immediately, however, *Garratt* raises questions about the intentions of the trial court judge and the appellate tribunal which reviewed him. Is there anything unusual about the way the Supreme Court of Washington interpreted the lower court's decision? Is there anything strange about the lower court's construction of the appellate opinion? Consider the following passages from Robinson and Schroeder. Do they explain or justify in any way the actions of the judges in Garratt v. Dailey?

EDWARD STEVENS ROBINSON

LAW AND THE LAWYERS *

.   .   .   .   only a judge can secure a direct, introspective approach to the judicial consciousness. The judicial opinions, it is widely recognized, depart far from the original deliberative processes. The author of an appellate opinion sets forth a train of thought which seems to him a sound defense of the court's conclusion; he makes no direct effort to describe the actual deliberative processes either of his own mind or those in the minds of his colleagues.

The situation is probably not quite so hopeless as it first appears. Freud was early confronted with the objection that, during the psychoanalysis, his patients might tell him of dreams and fantasies which actually they never had. But what of it? A lie about a dream is actually as significant as a dream that one actually has had, providing only that the lie is properly interpreted. Indeed one could even press the point and say that dreams and fantasies are always lies anyway and that that is why they are so important. In other words Freud always assumes a latent meaning or implication under every act or thought or feeling that is worthy of psychoanalytic notice. Thus one is forced to get behind the obvious contents of a patient's report whether or not it is upon its surface obviously false. Similarly the private, inarticulate deliberations of the judge can hardly be taken

* From 171–173 (1935). Reprinted with
permission of the estate of Edward
Stevens Robinson.

more literally than can their public expression. In either case there is a task of psychological interpretation.

And, after all, whatever discrepancies may exist between judicial thoughts and judicial words, it is through words alone that the lawyer can make any practical impression upon the judicial mind. Professor Gray put the matter clearly: "The student of jurisprudence is at times troubled by the thought that he is dealing not with things, but with words, that he is busy with the shape and size of counters in a game of logomachy, but when he fully realizes how these words have been passed and are still being passed as money not only by fools and on fools, but by and on some of the acutest minds, he feels that there is work worthy of being done, if only it can be done worthily."

There is, as a matter of fact, some ground for questioning the assumption that the articulate cogitations of the court, that is to say, the expressed opinions, are in any sense secondary. Descartes, in the days of an immature but vigorous physical science, saw no place within the system of physical nature for such intangibles as the ideas and passions. He therefore relegated them to a spiritual level of reality. While subsequent modern thought has not retained all of Descartes' theological tenets regarding the status of psychological facts, it has held fairly slavishly to the belief that, for the psychologist, the more subtle facts like toothaches and daydreams must have a primacy which objective behavior can never have. The story of the behavioristic movement in this country has had as its central theme the contradiction of this attitude and the counterclaim that overt speech and bodily movements are not psychologically insignificant simply because they are as susceptible to direct examination as are the facts of the nonpsychological sciences. The assumption, therefore, that the written judicial opinions cannot be important data for psychology is hardly in line with the present attitude of psychologists toward other similar problems. The present tendency in psychology is to begin an inquiry by examining the plainest and most accessible facts. The written discourse of the courts would thus seem to be a proper rather than a makeshift starting point for an empirical investigation of judicial deliberation.

It was in many ways a great achievement when scholars came to recognize that a man's talk is not a mirror-image of his motivation. But like most other essentially negative scientific conclusions, this one has tended to divert interest from the more constructive question as to what his talk does reflect. There has been a tendency to use too glibly such terms as *rationalization* without pushing forward to inquire what rationalization does besides affording an immediate relief to psychological tensions.

Consider first the certain fact that the expressed reasons for coming to a decision are to a degree at least indicative of the impulses that actually did play a part in reaching that decision. In many instances these reasons are more reliable symptoms of previous thinking. They may give a psychological analysis of that thinking which could not have been found in the thinking itself. Much of what goes on in private deliberation is not only dim and fragmentary to the thinker himself; much of it must be interpreted before it can be intelligibly described. . . .

*THEODORE SCHROEDER*

## THE PSYCHOLOGIC STUDY OF JUDICIAL OPINIONS *

. . . . Analytic psychology can uncover . . . potent yet submerged early impulses governing our acts as adults. It is my purpose to expound and to illustrate this psycho-analytic method as a means of studying judicial opinions.

. . . . this new theory can be applied to reshaping our understanding of juridical action. By the deductive application of the general psycho-analytic principles we come to the conclusion that every judicial opinion necessarily is the justification of the personal impulses of the judge, in relation to the situation before him, and that the character of these impulses is determined by the judge's life-long series of previous experiences, with their resultant integration in emotional tones.

. . . . every choice of conclusion, argument, precedent, phrase or word, is expressive of a dominant personal motive and is symptomatic of the evolutionary status of the judge's mentality. His choices must be studied in the light of their alternatives, and we expect to find that from the standpoint of motive these choices possess some elements of unification. . . . [E]very opinion is unavoidably a fragment of autobiography for those who know how to read the impulses and experiences behind the words, unconsciously expressed in their choice, by methods that are not at the command of the ordinary reader. Every opinion thus amounts to a confession. . . . In the interplay of human motives, the choices, even unconsciously expressed in the rulings of the court, necessarily reveal as much of the character of the judge, as of the prisoner at the bar.

. . . . From this viewpoint we treat the judicial opinion as a mere intellectualization or justification of the judge's desires, which we can rate according to an evolutionary classification. These desires are only the surface manifestations of a life-long chain of influences. . . .

From this standpoint the written opinion is little more than a special plea made in defense of impulses which are largely unconscious, at least, so far as concerns their origin or the immediate power of the past experiences. . . . These unconscious confessions never lie, though inefficient observers may be oblivious of their true meaning. In the light of genetic psychology the judicial intellect is to be studied, not according to the results of decisions, but according to the conscious and unconscious motivation which predetermined the result, and the relative degree of the consciousness of those im-

* From 6 Calif.L.Rev. 89, 93–98 (1918).    Review, Inc.    Reprinted by permission
  Copyright (c) 1918, California Law    sion and Fred B. Rothman Co., Inc.

pulses, that is, according to the relative maturity of the mental process involved in the justification or checking of the desires.

.   .   .   .   [W]e must forget our own emotional or other sanction of "justice," or expediency, and fix our attention wholly upon the discovery and understanding of the character-impulses which the opinion always defends. Only thus can we discover what the decision means as a revelation of the emotions, the phantasies, the desires, the persistent past life and the present intellectual status of the judge.

.   .   .

Every judicial opinion necessarily reveals a variety of choice. There is a choice of materials from that offered in evidence, as well as among possible precedents and arguments. A choice is made in that which is approved, as well as that which is ignored, or expressly disapproved. There is a choice of material brought in by the judge and not a matter of record. There is choice in all that is emphasized, slighted or distorted. A choice is evinced in the very words by which these other choices are expressed. Every such choice is a fragment of autobiography because it reveals not only the present conscious motive, but also the still potent, past and immature experiential causes, which determined the unconscious impulses submerged in, but controlling the avowed motive. To the extent to which we have become familiar with psychic evolution, and with mental mechanism in general, we can efficiently and genetically analyze the manifest desires expressed in the final opinion.

By such methods the psycho-analyst comes to see that which is concealed from the ordinary observer and which if often operating from the subconscious, though determining the immediate conscious action. In other words this is only applying a scientific efficiency toward the genetic understanding of human nature as developed and revealed in the judge. If the judge is momentarily unconscious of these past experiences and of their present influences, probably this is so because he had some unhappy conflict about them at the time, which conflict made it pleasant for him to exclude these experiences from consciousness and from memory. That is to say, he is happier in forgetting the painful aspects of those experiences and perhaps the experiences themselves. Therefore, they are quite permanently excluded from consciousness, are forgotten.

The tendency of these internal conflicts is to create two or more inconsistent, inharmonious, distinctly separate aspects to our character; that is we tend measureably toward a condition which in the extreme is known as dual or multiple personality. One of these aspects of our character remains as a submerged personality, operating subconsciously and is dissociated from that conventional part which is the more pleasing. Because of this we are impelled to thrust it unduly upon the public notice, unconsciously hoping thereby to divert the attention away from the suppressed and painful personality. Just to the extent of such a division in his personality, the judge is relatively incapable of adequately and consciously co-ordinating all the factors of a problem, or to give to each part such influence as is due to it from the relatively impersonal or objective viewpoint. This is one way in which he reveals himself to us, because his conflicts make him feel so intensely about some factor of each present problem as to distort his sense of proportion. This intensity of feeling originates in an anxiety concerning that part of his life which he is least anxious to reveal, most anxious to keep submerged even below the apex of his own consciousness. That in the presence of the public he can not bear to think about it is only another way to saying that he is unwilling, emotionally unable, to allow the public to look this other personality square in the face, or to face himself for what he really is.

Even when such a person is perfectly conscious of the desire to conceal his past the accompanying anxiety will always betray him. So long as it exists, this emotional fear will show itself by compelling an over-emphasis in the relatively unimportant matter behind which he seeks to screen himself. Because of the intensity of the anxiety which exists as suppressed energy, he is unable to treat all the persons, the evidence or the argument, with equal candor, equal calm, or equal fulness and fairness, according to objective standards. When we see what is avoided, slighted, or emphasized we already see the submerged personality unconsciously revealing itself.

LEARNED HAND

## THE BILL OF RIGHTS *

When the Constitution emerged from the Convention in September, 1787, the structure of the proposed government, if one looked to the text, gave no ground for inferring that the decisions of the Supreme Court, and *a fortiori* of the lower courts, were to be authoritative upon the Executive and the Legislature. Each of the three "Departments" was an agency of a sovereign, the "People of the United States." Each was responsible to that sovereign, but not to one another; indeed, their "Separation" was still regarded as a conditon of free government, whatever we may think of that notion now. Moreover, it is impossible to have any assurance how the Convention would have voted at the time, had the question been put to it whether the Supreme Court should have a conclusive authority to construe the Constitution. Although this was the opinion of a number of the most influential members, the issue was highly controversial, and there can be no certainty what would have been the outcome of a vote. True, under the "Supremacy Clause" state courts would at times have to decide whether state laws and constitutions, or even a federal statute, were in conflict with the federal constitution; but the fact that this jurisdiction was confined to such occasions, and that it was thought necessary specifically to provide such a limited jurisdiction, looks rather against than in favor of a general jurisdiction. The arguments deducing the court's authority from the structure of the new government, or from the implications of any government, were not valid, in spite of the deservedly revered names of their authors.

.  .  .

It is significant that when Hamilton, who, as I have said, and as was in any event to be expected, had apparently been among those who supported the power, came to defend it as he did in the well-known 78th number of the Federalist, he did not suggest that the conclusion followed from anything in the text; but rather from the ordinary function of courts to construe statutes.  .  .  .

.  .  .

It is interesting to observe how closely Marshall's reasoning in Marbury v. Madison followed Hamilton's.

"It is, emphatically, the province and duty of the judicial department, to say what the law is. Those who apply the rule to particular cases, must of necessity expound and interpret that rule. If two laws conflict with each other, the courts must decide on the operation of each. So, if a law be in opposition to the constitution; if both the law and the constitution apply to a particular case, so that the court must either decide that case, conformable to the law, disregarding the constitution; or conformable to the constitution, disregarding the law; the court must determine which of these conflicting rules governs the case; this is of the very essence of judicial duty. If then, the courts are to regard the constitution, and the constitution is superior to any ordinary act of the legislature, the constitution, and not such ordinary act, must govern the case to which they both apply."

.  .  .

It is of course true that, when a court decides whether a constitution authorizes a statute, it must first decide what each means, and that, so far, is the kind of duty that courts often exercise, just as they decide conflicts between earlier and later precedents. But if a court, having concluded that a constitution did not authorize the statute, goes on to annul it, its power to do so depends upon an authority that is not involved when only statutes or precedents are involved. For a later statute will prevail over an earlier, if they conflict, because a legislature confessedly has authority to change the law as it exists. So too when a court finds two precedents in conflict, it must follow the later one, if that be a decision of a higher court, and it is free to do so if it be one of its own, because, again, confessedly it has authority to change its mind. But when a court declares that a constitution does not authorize a statute, it reviews and reverses an earlier decision of the legislature; and, however well based its authority to do so may be, it does not follow from what it does in the other instances in which the same question does not arise.

.  .  .

There was nothing in the United States Constitution that gave courts any authority to review the decisions of Congress; and it was a plausible—indeed to my mind an unanswerable—argument that it invaded that "Separation of Powers" which, as so many then believed, was the condition of all free government. That there were other reasons, not only proper but essential, for inferring such a power in the Constitution seems to me certain; but for the moment I am only concerned to show that the reasoning put forward to support the inference will not bear scrutiny.

As an approach, let us try to imagine what would have been the result if the power did not exist. There were two alternatives, each prohibitive, I submit. One was that the decision of the first "Department" before which an issue arose should be conclusive whenever it arose later. That doctrine, coupled with its conceded power over the purse, would have made Congress substantially omnipotent, for by far the greater number of issues that could arise would depend upon its prior action.

Hamilton in the 71st number of the Federalist forecast what would probably have been the result. He was speaking of what he called the "tendency of legislative authority to absorb every other." "In governments purely republican, this tendency is almost irresistible. The representatives of the people in a popular assembly seem sometimes to fancy that they are the people themselves, and betray strong symptoms of impatience and disgust at the least sign of opposition from any other quarter; as if the exercise of its rights by either the executive or the judiciary were a breach of their privilege and an outrage on their dignity. They often appear disposed to exert an imperious control over the other departments; and, as they commonly have the people on their side, they always act with such momentum as to make it very difficult for the other members of the government to maintain the balance of the Constitution."

It was unfair to ascribe to a mere lust for power this disposition of legislators to expand their powers. As Hamilton intimated, every legislator is under constant pressure from groups of constituents whom it does not satisfy to say, "Although I think what you want is right and that you ought to have it, I cannot bring myself to believe that it is within my constitutional powers." Such scruples are not convincing to those whose interests are at stake; and the voters at large will not usually care enough about preserving "the balance of the Constitution" to offset the votes of those whose interests will be disappointed.

The issues that arise are often extremely baffling, and the answers are not obvious. They demand, not only a detached approach, but a training in verbal analysis by no means general among legislators, even though they are usually lawyers. The uncertainties that so often arise are shown by the differences in the answers of the judges themselves.

.   .   .

What I have called the first alternative would have meant that the interpretation of the Constitution on a given occasion would be left to that "Department" before which the question happened first to come; and such a system would have been so capricious in operation, and so different from that designed, that it could not have endured. Moreover, the second alternative would have been even worse, for under it each "Department" would have been free to decide constitutional issues as it thought right, regardless of any earlier decision of the others.   Thus it would have been the President's privilege, and indeed his duty, to execute only those statutes that seemed to him to be constitutional, regardless even of a decision of the Supreme Court.   The courts would have entered such judgments as seemed to them consonant with the Constitution; but neither the President, nor Congress, would have been bound to enforce them if he or it disagreed, and without their help the judgments would have been waste paper.

For centuries it has been an accepted canon in interpretation of documents to interpolate into the text such provisions, though not expressed, as are essential to prevent the defeat of the venture at hand;   and this applies with especial force to the interpretation of constitutions, which, since they are designed to cover a great multitude of necessarily unforeseen occasions, must be cast in general languages, unless they are constantly amended.   If so, it was altogether in keeping with established practice for the Supreme Court to assume an authority to keep the states, Congress, and the President within their prescribed powers.   Otherwise the government could not proceed as planned;   and indeed would almost certainly have foundered, as in fact it almost did over that very issue.

However, since this power is not a logical deduction from the structure of the Constitution but only a practical condition upon its successful operation, it need not be exercised whenever a court sees, or thinks that it sees, an invasion of the Constitution.   It is always a preliminary question how importunately the occasion demands an answer.   It may be better to leave the issue to be worked out without authoritative solution;   or perhaps the only solution available is one that the court has no adequate means to enforce.

QUESTIONS

1.   Can you reconcile Hand's statement that "the structure of the  . . . .  government [proposed by the Constitution], if one looked to the text, gave no ground for inferring that the decisions of the Supreme Court   . . .   were to be authoritative upon the Executive and the Legislature," with the statement that "the government could not proceed as planned;   and indeed would almost certainly have foundered, as in fact it almost did . . . ." if "the Supreme Court [had not seen fit] to assume an authority to keep the states, Congress, and President within their prescribed powers"?   Or is there any need to reconcile the statements?

2.   When Hand says that the power of judicial review "is not a logical deduction from the structure of the Constitution but only a practical condition upon its successful operation" what does this amount to?   (a) That the power is not "in" the Constitution but one must act as if it were?   (b) That the Constitution does not "mean" judicial review, but through a fiction courts must act as if it does? Consider the following passages from Allport and Waismann in an-

swering these questions. Does Allport have the same standard for determining whether something is a part of something else? Does Waismann describe a theory of meaning which is consistent with Hand's language?

Suppose that judicial review was "a logical deduction from the structure of the Constitution," but would nevertheless have had bad consequences. Would Hand feel free to reverse his canon of interpretation so as to disregard the Constitution's "actual" meaning? Who would find it easier to do this, Professor Hart or Professor Fuller? Whose side do you think Hand would take?

## FLOYD H. ALLPORT

### THEORIES OF PERCEPTION AND THE CONCEPT OF STRUCTURE *

The writer has found that an excellent test of whether some item belongs in an aggregate is to omit that item and then see whether the aggregate will be essentially the same and will "operate," dynamically speaking, without it. We might call this method the "negative-causation test" of the aggregate. If a part is taken away, or if conditions are established under which it cannot operate, and if the whole aggregate then breaks down, would we not have to assume that that part is an essential item of the aggregate and that under normal conditions it is actually present and operating? This would certainly be a logical supposition in physiology; and it would be no less true if the part concerned were not clearly recognized in consciousness or were subordinated to the experience of the whole. Now if we were to apply this test, for example, in the perception of a brick house, and were thinking of the perceptual meaning of the house, we would set ourselves to suppose an instance of perception in which the elements representing "bricks," "roof," "window frames," and the like were either in part or totally taken away from the percept's physiological basis and thus from the percept, or else were so modified that they no longer had a representative relation to bricks, roof, or windows. Would we then have a perceptual meaning of "house"? It seems highly doubtful.

## FRIEDRICH WAISMANN

### LANGUAGE STRATA †

Then there is such a thing as *systematic ambiguity*. This expression was first coined by Bertrand Russell in connection with his Theory of Types. Without entering into it here we can say that his idea, roughly speaking, is that we must distinguish between different *logical types of symbols*. Beginning with names which stand for 'individuals', we come next to predicates which possibly apply to those names, and then to second-order predicates which possibly apply to the

* From 76–77 (1955). Reprinted with permission of John Wiley & Sons.

† From Logic and Language 232–234 (A. Flew ed. Anchor ed. 1965). Reprinted by permission of the literary estate of Friedrich Waismann. Originally published by Basil Blackwell.

first-order predicates, and so on. We are thus led to consider a hierarchy of symbols which, theoretically, goes on without end. This hierarchy corresponds to a similar hierarchy of *statements*. And statements are divided into different types according to whether they are statements about an individual, or statements about a class of individuals, or statements about a class of classes of individuals, and so on. A statement such as 'Socrates is mortal' is true when there is a corresponding fact, and false when there is no corresponding fact. But take now such a statement as 'All men are mortal'. The truth of it can no longer consist in its correspondence to a single fact, for there are indefinitely many facts such as 'Socrates is mortal', 'Plato is mortal', etc. Now Russell's point is that the meaning of 'truth' which is applicable to the latter sort of proposition is *not the same* as the meaning of 'truth' which is applicable to the proposition 'All men are mortal'; i. e. each type of statement has its own sort of truth.

The main ground for accepting that distinction is that it offers an escape from the paradoxes or antinomies which were a threat to logic.

> The imaginary sceptic, who asserts that he knows nothing, and is refuted by being asked if he knows that he knows nothing, has asserted nonsense, and has been fallaciously refuted by an argument which involves a vicious-circle fallacy. In order that the sceptic's assertion may become significant, it is necessary to place some limitation upon the things of which he is asserting his ignorance, because the things of which it is possible to be ignorant form an illegitimate totality. *Principia Mathematica* (Vol. I, Introduction).

Take the case of the Liar, that is of a man who says 'I am lying'; if he is lying he is speaking the truth, and if he is speaking the truth he is lying. We may interpret his statement as saying, 'All propositions which I assert are false'. Is this proposition itself true or false? To clear up the paradox we must distinguish between elementary propositions which do not refer to a totality of propositions, first-order propositions which do refer to a totality of elementary propositions, second-order propositions which do refer to a totality of first-order propositions, and so on. Now if the liar asserts that all propositions which he asserts are false he is making a first-order statement which does not fall within its own scope, and therefore no contradiction emerges. The decisive point to realize is that the phrase 'all propositions' is an illegitimate totality. As soon as a suitable limitation has been put upon the collection of propositions we are considering, as soon as they are broken up into different orders, the contradiction disappears. We may put it like this: if somebody were to tell us that he is a liar, we could ask him, 'Well, a liar of what order?' If he says he is a liar of the first order he is making a statement of the second order, and this statement may be perfectly true. When he says 'I am a liar of the second order' (including the totality of first-order statements) this would be a statement of the third order; and so on. However far he may extend the scope of propositions to which he is referring, his statement about their falsehood will represent a proposition of higher order.  Once we reach this stage, there is no contradiction.

Russell's solution is thus based on the ground that 'true' and 'false' are ambiguous, and that, in order to make them unambiguous, we must specify the order of truth or falsehood which we ascribe to a proposition.  Similar considerations apply to negation and disjunction, and indeed to any logical particle.  It might seem that they were symbols which had throughout the same meaning.  But this is due to a systematic ambiguity in the meanings of 'not', 'or', etc., by which they adjust themselves to propositions of any order.

## QUESTIONS

Would it be fair to say that Russell, like Hand, has invoked a fictive mode of interpretation in order to get out of a logical dilemma?  Or does his method of determining meaning have more legitimate credentials?  Compare it to the methods invoked by Collingwood and Fingarette below.

## R. G. COLLINGWOOD

### THE IDEA OF HISTORY *

.   .   .   .   Like every science, history is autonomous.  The historian has the right, and is under an obligation, to make up his own mind by the methods proper to his own science as to the correct solution of every problem that arises for him in the pursuit of that science.  He can never be under any obligation, or have any right, to let someone else make up his mind for him.  If anyone else, no matter who, even a very learned historian, or an eyewitness, or a person in the confidence of the man who did the thing he is inquiring into, or even the man who did it himself, hands him on a plate a ready-made answer to his question, all he can do is to reject it:  not because he thinks his informant is trying to deceive him, or is himself deceived, but because if he accepts it he is giving up his autonomy as an historian and allowing someone else to do for him what, if he is a scientific thinker, he can only do for himself.   .   .   .

When the historian accepts a ready-made answer to some question he has asked, given him by another person, this other person is called his 'authority,' and the statement made by such an authority and accepted by the historian is called 'testimony.'  In so far as an historian accepts the testimony of an authority and treats it as historical truth, he obviously forfeits the name of historian;  but we have no other name by which to call him.

Now, I am not for a moment suggesting that testimony ought never to be accepted.  In the practical life of every day, we constantly and rightly accept the information that other people offer us, believing them to be both well informed and truthful, and having, sometimes, grounds for this belief.  I do not even deny, though I do not assert it,

* From  256–259, 260, 263–265, 266–268,    1956).  Reprinted  by  permission  of
269–273, 274–276, 280–282 (Galaxy ed.    the Clarendon Press, Oxford.

that there may be cases in which, as perhaps in some cases of memory, our acceptance of such testimony may go beyond mere belief and deserve the name of knowledge. What I assert is that it can never be historical knowledge, because it can never be scientific knowledge. It is not scientific knowledge because it cannot be vindicated by appeal to the grounds on which it is based. . . .

(iv) *Scissors and paste*

There is a kind of history which depends altogether upon the testimony of authorities. As I have already said, it is not really history at all, but we have no other name for it. The method by which it proceeds is first to decide what we want to know about, and then to go in search of statements about it, oral or written, purporting to be made by actors in the events concerned, or by eyewitnesses of them, or by persons repeating what actors or eyewitnesses have told them, or have told their informants, or those who informed their informants, and so on. Having found in such a statement something relevant to his purpose, the historian excerpts it and incorporates it, translated if necessary and recast into what he considers a suitable style, in his own history. As a rule, where he has many statements to draw upon, he will find that one of them tells him what another does not; so both or all of them will be incorporated. Sometimes he will find that one of them contradicts another; then, unless he can find a way of reconciling them, he must decide to leave one out; and this, if he is conscientious, will involve him in a critical consideration of the contradictory authorities' relative degree of truthworthiness. And sometimes one of them, or possibly even all of them, will tell him a story which he simply cannot believe, a story characteristic, perhaps, of the superstitions or prejudices of the author's time or the circle in which he lived, but not credible to a more enlightened age, and therefore to be omitted.

History constructed by excerpting and combining the testimonies of different authorities I call scissors-and-paste history. I repeat that it is not really history at all, because it does not satisfy the necessary conditions of science; but until lately it was the only kind of history in existence, and a great deal of the history people are still reading to-day, and even a good deal of what people are still writing, belongs to this type. Consequently people who know little about history (some of whom, in spite of my recent farewell, may still be reading these pages) will say with some impatience: 'Why, this thing that you say is not history, is just history itself; scissors and paste, that is what history is; and that is why history is not a science, which is a fact that everybody knows, in spite of groundless claims by professional historians magnifying their office'. I shall therefore say a little more about the vicissitudes of scissors-and-paste history.

Scissors and paste was the only historical method known to the later Greco-Roman world or the Middle Ages. It existed in its simplest form. An historian collected testimony, spoken or written, using his own judgment as to its truthworthiness, and put it together for publication: the work which he did on it being partly literary—the presentation of his material as a connected, homogeneous, and convincing narrative—and partly rhetorical, if I may use that word to indicate the fact that most ancient and medieval historians aimed at proving a thesis, in particular some philosophical or political or theological thesis.

It was only in the seventeenth century, when the post-medieval reform of natural science had attained completion, that historians began to think their house also needed to be set in order. Two new movements in historical method now began. One was a systematic examination of authorities, in order to determine their relative credibility, and in particular to establish principles according to which this determination should be carried out. The other was a movement to broaden the basis of history by making use of non-literary sources, such as coins and inscriptions and such like relics of antiquity which hitherto had been of interest not to historians but only to collectors of curiosities.

The first of these movements did not overstep the limits of scissors-and-paste history, but it permanently altered its character. As soon as it became understood that a given statement, made by a given author, must never be accepted for historical truth until the credibility of the author in general and of this statement in particular had been systematically inquired into, the word 'authority' disappeared from the vocabulary of historical method, except as an archaistic survival; for the man who makes the statement came henceforth to be regarded not as someone whose word must be taken for the truth of what he says, which is what was meant by calling him an authority, but as someone who has voluntarily placed himself in the witnessbox for cross-examination. The document hitherto called an authority now acquired a new status, properly described by calling it a 'source', a word indicating simply that it contains the statement, without any implications as to its value. That is *sub judice*; and it is the historian who judges.

This is 'critical history', as it was worked out from the seventeenth century onwards, and officially acclaimed in the nineteenth as the apotheosis of the historical consciousness. There are two things to observe about it: that it was still only a form of scissors and paste; and that it had already, in principle, been superseded by something very different.

(1) The problem of which historical criticism offers a solution is a problem interesting to nobody but the practitioner of scissors-and-paste history. The presupposition of the problem is that in certain source we have found a certain statement which bears on our subject. The problem is: Shall we incorporate this statement in our own narrative or not? The methods of historical criticism are intended to solve this problem in one or other of two ways: affirmatively or negatively. In the first case, the excerpt is passed as fit for the scrapbook; in the second, it is consigned to the waste-paper basket.

(2) But many historians in the nineteenth century, and even in the eighteenth, were aware that this dilemma was fallacious. It was by now a commonplace that if in some source you found a statement which for some reason could not be accepted as literally true, you must

not on that account reject it as worthless. It might be a way, perhaps a well-established way according to the custom of the time when it was written, of saying something which you, through ignorance of that custom, did not recognize as its meaning.

The first person to make this point was Vico, at the beginning of the eighteenth century.  .  .  .  anyone who had read Vico, or even a second-hand version of some of his ideas, must have known that the important question about any statement contained in a source is not whether it is true or false, but what it means. And to ask what it means is to step right outside the world of scissors-and-paste history into a world where history is not written by copying out the testimony of the best sources, but by coming to your own conclusions.

.  .  .

### (vi) *Pigeon-holing*

Scissors-and-paste historians who have become disgusted with the work of copying out other people's statements, and, conscious of having brains, feel a laudable desire to use them, are often found satisfying this desire by inventing a system of pigeon-holes in which to arrange their learning. This is the origin of all those schemes and patterns into which history has again and again, with surprising docility, allowed itself to be forced by such men as Vico, with his pattern of historical cycles based on Greco-Roman speculations; Kant, with his proposal for a 'universal history from a cosmopolitan point of view'; Hegel, who followed Kant in conceiving universal history as the progressive realization of human freedom; Comte and Marx, two very great men who followed Hegel's lead each in his own way; and so on down to Flinders Petrie, Oswald Spengler, and Arnold Toynbee in our own time, whose affinities are less with Hegel than with Vico.

Although we find it as late as the twentieth century and as early as the eighteenth, not to mention isolated occurrences even earlier, this impulse towards arranging the whole of history in a single scheme (not a chronological scheme merely, but a qualitative scheme, in which 'periods' each with its own pervasive character follow one another in time, according to a pattern which may be necessary *a priori* on logical grounds, or may be forced upon our minds by the fact of its frequent repetition, or may be a bit of both) is in the main a nineteenth-century phenomenon. It belongs to the period when scissors-and-paste history was on its last legs; when people were becoming dissatisfied with it but had not yet broken away from it. This is why the people who have indulged it have been, in general, men with a high degree of intelligence and a real talent for history, but a talent which has been to some extent thwarted and baffled by the limitations of scissors and paste.

It is typical of this condition that some of them described their pigeon-holing enterprise as 'raising history to the rank of a science'. History as they found it meant scissors-and-paste history; that, obviously, was no science, because there was nothing autonomous, nothing creative, about it; it was merely the transshipment of ready-made information from one mind into another. They were conscious that history might be something more than this. It might have, and it ought to have, the characteristics of a science. But how was this to be brought about? At this point the analogy of the natural sciences came, they thought, to their aid. It had been a commonplace ever since Bacon that a natural science began by collecting facts, and then went on to construct theories, that is, to extrapolate the patterns discernible in the facts already collected. Very well: let us put together all the facts that are known to historians, look for patterns in them, and then extrapolate these patterns into a theory of universal history.

It proved to be not at all a difficult task for anybody with an active mind and a taste for hard work. For there was no need to collect all the facts known to historians. Any large collection of facts, it was found, revealed patterns in plenty; and extrapolating such patterns into the remote past, about which there was very little information, and into the future, about which there was none, gave the 'scientific' historian just that sense of power which scissors-and-paste history denied him. After being taught to believe that he, as an historian, could never know anything except what his authorities told him, he found himself discovering, as he fancied, that this lesson had been a fraud; that by converting history into a science he could ascertain, entirely for himself, things that his authorities had concealed from him or did not know.

This was a delusion. The value of each and all of these pigeon-holing schemes, if that means their value as means for discovering historical truths not ascertainable by the interpretation of evidence, was exactly nil. And in fact none of them ever had any scientific value at all: for it is not enough that science should be autonomous or creative, it must also be cogent or objective: it must impress itself as inevitable on anyone who is able and willing to consider the grounds upon which it is based, and to think for himself what the conclusions are to which they point. That is what none of these schemes can do. They are the offspring of caprice. If any of them has ever been accepted by any considerable body of persons beside the one who invented it, that is not because it has struck them as scientifically cogent, but because it has become the orthodoxy of what is in fact, though not necessarily in name, a religious community. . . .

(vii) *Who killed John Doe?*

When John Doe was found, early one Sunday morning, lying across his desk with a dagger through his back, no one expected that the question who did it would be settled by means of testimony. It was not likely that anyone saw the murder being done. It was even less likely that someone in the murderer's confidence would give him away. It was least likely of all that the murderer would walk into the village police-station and denounce himself. In spite of this, the public demanded that he should be brought to justice, and the police had hopes of doing it; though the only clue was a little fresh green paint on the handle of the dagger, like the fresh green paint on the iron gate between John Doe's garden and the rector's.

This was not because they hoped that, in time, testimony would be forthcoming. On the contrary, when it did come, in the shape of a visit from an elderly neighbouring spinster asserting that she killed John Doe with her own hand because he had made a dastardly attempt upon her virtue, even the village constable (not an exceptionally bright lad, but kindly) advised her to go home and have some aspirin.  Later in the day the village poacher came along and said that he had seen the squire's gamekeeper climbing in at John Doe's study window; testimony which was treated with even less deference.  Finally the rector's daughter, in a state of great agitation, rushed in and said she had done it herself; the only effect of which was to make the village constable ring up the local Inspector and remind him that the girl's young man, Richard Roe, was a medical student, and presumably knew where to find a man's heart; and that he had spent Saturday night at the rectory, within a stone's throw of the dead man's house.

There had been a thunderstorm that night, with heavy rain, between twelve and one; and the Inspector, when he questioned the rectory parlour-maid (for the living was a good one), was told that Mr. Roe's shoes had been very wet in the morning.  Questioned, Richard admitted having gone out in the middle of the night, but refused to say where or why.

John Doe was a blackmailer.  For years he had been blackmailing the rector, threatening to publish the facts about a certain youthful escapade of his dead wife.  Of this escapade the rector's supposed daughter, born six months after marriage, was the fruit; and John Doe had letters in his possession that proved it.  By now he had absorbed the whole of the rector's private fortune, and on the morning of the fatal Saturday he demanded an installment of his wife's which she had left to him in trust for her child.  The rector made up his mind to end it.  He knew that John Doe sat at his desk late into the night; he knew that behind him as he sat, there was a french window on the left and a trophy of Eastern weapons on the right; and that on hot nights the window was left open until he went to bed.  At midnight, wearing gloves, he slipped out, but Richard, who had noticed his state of mind and was troubled about it, happened to be leaning out of his window and saw the rector cross the garden.  He hurried into his clothes and followed; but by the time he reached the garden the rector was gone.  At this moment the thunderstorm broke.  Meanwhile the rector's plan had succeeded perfectly.  John Doe was asleep, his head fallen forward on a pile of old letters.  Only after the dagger had reached his heart did the rector look at them, and see his wife's handwriting.  The envelopes were addressed 'John Doe, Esq.'  Until that moment, he had never known who his wife's seducer had been.

It was Detective-Inspector Jenkins of Scotland Yard, called in by the Chief Constable at the entreaty of his old friend's little girl, who found in the rectory dustbin a lot of ashes, mostly from writing paper, but including some from leather, probably a pair of gloves.  The wet paint on John Doe's garden gate—he had painted it himself that day, after tea—explained why the gloves might have been destroyed; and among the ashes were metal buttons bearing the name of a famous glove-maker in Oxford Street whom the rector always patronized.  More of John Doe's paint was found on the right cuff of a jacket, ruined as to shape by a recent wetting, which on Monday the rector bestowed on a deserving parishioner.  The Detective-Inspector was

severely blamed, later on, for allowing the rector to see in what direction his inquiries were tending, and thus giving him an opportunity to take cyanide and cheat the hangman.

.    .    .    .

### (viii) *The question*

Francis Bacon, lawyer and philosopher, laid it down in one of his
memorable phrases that the natural scientist must 'put Nature to the
question'. What he was denying, when he wrote this, was that the
scientist's attitude towards nature should be one of respectful attentiveness, waiting upon her utterances and building his theories on the
basis of what she chose to vouchsafe him. What he was asserting was
two things at once: first, that the scientist must take the initiative,
deciding for himself what he wants to know and formulating this in
his own mind in the shape of a question; and secondly, that he must
find means of compelling nature to answer, devising tortures under
which she can no longer hold her tongue. Here, in a single brief epigram, Bacon laid down once for all the true theory of experimental
science.

It is also, though Bacon did not know this, the true theory of historical method. In scissors-and-paste history the historian takes up a
pre-Baconian position. His attitude towards his authorities, as the
very word shows, is one of respectful attentiveness. He waits to hear
what they choose to tell him, and lets them tell it in their own way and
at their own time. . . . The scientific historian no doubt spends
a great deal of time reading the same books that the scissors-and-
paste historian used to read—Herodotus, Thucydides, Livy, Tacitus,
and so forth—but he reads them in an entirely different spirit; in
fact, a Baconian spirit. The scissors-and-paste historian reads them
in a simply receptive spirit, to find out what they said. The scientific
historian reads them with a question in his mind, having taken the
initiative by deciding for himself what he wants to find out from them.
Further, the scissors-and-paste historian reads them on the understanding that what they did not tell him in so many words he would
never find out from them at all; the scientific historian puts them to
the torture, twisting a passage ostensibly about something quite different into an answer to the question he has decided to ask. Where
the scissors-and-paste historian said quite confidently 'There is nothing in such-and-such an author about such-and-such a subject', the
scientific or Baconian historian will reply 'Oh, isn't there? Do you
not see that in this passage about a totally different matter it is implied that the author took such-and-such a view of the subject about
which you say this text contains nothing?'

To illustrate from my fable. The village constable does not arrest the rector's daughter and beat her periodically with a rubber
truncheon until she tells him that she thinks Richard did the murder.
What he tortures is not her body, but her statement that she killed
John Doe. He begins by using the methods of critical history. He says
to himself: 'The murder was done by somebody with a good deal of
strength and some knowledge of anatomy. This girl certainly hasn't
the first, and probably hasn't the second; at any rate, I know she has

never attended ambulance classes. Further, if she had done it she wouldn't be in such a hurry to accuse herself. The story is a lie.'

At this point the critical historian would lose interest in the story and throw it in the waste-paper basket: the scientific historian begins to be interested in it, and tests it for chemical reactions. This he is able to do because, being a scientific thinker, he knows what questions to ask. 'Why is she telling a lie? Because she is shielding someone. Whom is she shielding? Either her father or her young man. Is it her father? No; fancy the rector! Therefore it is her young man. Are her suspicions of him well founded? They might be; he was here at the time; he is strong enough; and he knows enough anatomy.' The reader will recollect that in criminal detection probability is required, of a degree sufficient for the conduct of daily life, whereas in history we demand certainty. Apart from that, the parallel is complete. The village constable (not a clever lad, as I explained; but a scientific thinker does not have to be clever, he has to know his job, that is, know what questions to ask) has been trained in the elements of police work, and this training enables him to know what questions to ask and thus to interpret the untrue statement that she did it herself into evidence for the true conclusion that she suspects Richard Roe.

The constable's only mistake was that in the excitement of answering the question 'Whom does this girl suspect?' he lost sight of the question 'Who killed John Doe?' This is where Inspector Jenkins, not so much because he was a cleverer man as because he had learned the job more thoroughly, had the advantage of him. The way I see the Inspector going to work is like this.

'Why does the rector's daughter suspect Richard Roe? Probably because she knows that he was involved in something queer which happened at the rectory that night. We know that one queer thing happened at the rectory: Richard was out in the storm, and that was quite enough to make the girl suspicious. But what we want to know is, did he kill John Doe? If he did, when did he do it? After the thunderstorm broke, or before? Not before, because here are his tracks going both ways in the mud of the rectory garden path: You see them beginning a few yards from the garden door, going away from the house; so that is where he was, and that is the direction he was going in, when the downpour began. Well, did he carry mud into John Doe's study? No: none there. Did he take off his shoes before going in? Think a moment. What position was John Doe in when he was stabbed? Was he leaning back or sitting upright in his chair? No; because the chair would have protected his back. He must have been leaning right forward. Possibly, indeed probably, asleep in the position in which he still lies. How exactly did the murder proceed? If Doe was asleep, nothing easier: step quietly inside, take the dagger and in it goes. If Doe was awake and merely leaning forward, the same might be done, but not so easily. Now, did the murderer pause outside to take off his shoes? Impossible. In either case, speed was the first thing necessary: the job had to be done before he leaned back, or woke up. So the absence of mud in the study lets Richard out.

'Then, once more, why did he go into the garden? For a walk? Not with that thunderstorm growling about. For a smoke? They smoke all over the house. To meet the girl? No signs that she was in the garden; and why should he? They had had the drawingroom to themselves ever since dinner, and the rector isn't one to shoo young people off to bed. Broadminded sort of chap. Had trouble, I shouldn't wonder. Now, why did young Richard go into that garden? Something must have been going on there. Something queer. A second queer thing that night at the rectory, one we don't know about.

'What could it have been? If the murderer had come from the rectory, which that paint suggests he did, and if Richard saw him from his window, it might have been that; because the murderer got to Doe's house before the rain began, and Richard was caught in it ten yards from the garden door. Just time. Let's see what would follow, if the murderer did come from the rectory. Probably he went back there afterwards. No tracks in the mud; why? Because he knew the garden well enough to keep on the grass all the way, even in that pitch darkness. If so, he knew the rectory very well and also spent the night there. Was it the rector himself?

'Now why does Richard refuse to say what made him go into the garden? It must be to keep somebody out of trouble; almost certainly, trouble about the murder. Not himself, because I've told him we know he didn't do it. Somebody else. Who? Might be the rector. Can't think of anybody else it might be. Suppose it was the rector; how would he have worked it? Very easy. Go out about midnight, in tennis shoes and gloves. Quite silent on the rectory paths—no gravel on them. Reach that little iron gate into John Doe's garden. Does he know it's wet paint? Probably not; it was only painted after tea. So he grabs it. Paint on glove. Probably paint on jacket too. Walk on the grass to Doe's study window. Doe is leaning forward in his chair, or likelier asleep. Now for a bit of quick work, easy for a good tennis-player. Left foot inside, right foot to the right, grab that dagger thing, left foot forward, in it goes.

'But what had John Doe been doing at that desk? Nothing on it, you know. Queer. Does a man spend the evening sitting at an empty desk? There must have been something there. What do we know about the chap at the Yard? Blackmailer, that's it. Had he been blackmailing the rector? and gloating over the letters, or what not, all evening? And did the rector, if it was the rector, find him asleep on top of them? Well, that's not our business. We'll pass it on to the defence for what it's worth. I'd rather not use a motive like that in prosecution.

'Now then, Jonathan, don't go ahead too fast. You've got him in there, you've got to get him out again. What exactly does he do? About now it begins to rain cats and dogs. Back he goes through it. More paint at the gate. Walk on grass, no mud brought in. Back in the house. All soaked: gloves covered with paint, too. Wipe paint off door-knob. Lock up. Put letters (if it was letters), and anyhow gloves, in the hot-water furnace—the ashes may be in the dustbin now. Put all clothes in the bathroom cupboard; they will be dry by morning.

And so they are; but the jacket will be hopelessly out of shape. Now what did he do with that jacket? First, he'd look for paint on it. If he found paint, he'd have to destroy the thing; and I pity the man who tries to destroy a jacket in a house overrun with women. If he didn't find any, he would certainly give it away on the quiet to a poor man.

'Well, well: there's a pretty story for you; but how can we tell whether it's true or not? There are two questions we've got to ask. First: can we find the ashes of those gloves? And the metal buttons, if they are like most of his gloves? If we can, the story is true. And if we can find a lot of writing-paper ash as well, the blackmail bit is true, too. Second: where is that jacket? Because if we can find the tiniest speck of John Doe's paint on it, there's our case.'

.   .   .

(1) Every step in the argument depends on asking a question. The question is the charge of gas, exploded in the cylinder-head, which is the motive force of every piston-stroke. But the metaphor is not adequate, because each new piston-stroke is produced not by exploding another charge of the same old mixture but by exploding a charge of a new kind. No one with any grasp of method will go on asking the same question all the time, 'Who killed John Doe?' He asks a new question every time. And it is not enough to cover the ground by having a catalogue of all the questions that have to be asked, and asking every one of them sooner or later: they must be asked in the right order.   .   .   .

(2) These questions are not put by one man to another man, in the hope that the second man will enlighten the first man's ignorance by answering them. They are put, like all scientific questions, to the scientist by himself. This is the Socratic idea which Plato was to express by defining thought as 'the dialogue of the soul with itself', where Plato's own literary practice makes it clear that by dialogue he meant a process of question and answer. When Socrates taught his young pupils by asking them questions, he was teaching them how to ask questions of themselves, and showing them by examples how amazingly the obscurest subjects can be illuminated by asking oneself intelligent questions about them instead of simply gaping at them, according to the prescription of our modern anti-scientific epistemologists, in the hope that when we have made our minds a perfect blank we shall 'apprehend the facts'.

### (ix) *Statement and evidence*

It is characteristic of scissors-and-paste history, from its least critical to its most critical form, that it has to do with readymade statements, and that the historian's problem about any one of these statements is whether he shall accept it or not: where accepting it means reasserting it as a part of his own historical knowledge. Essentially, history for the scissors-and-paste historian means repeating statements that other people have made before him. Hence he can get to work only when he is supplied with ready-made statements on the subjects about which he wants to think, write, and so forth. It is the fact that these statements have to be found by him readymade in his sources that makes it impossible for the scissors-and-paste historian to claim the title of a scientific thinker, for this fact makes it impossible to attribute to him that autonomy which is everywhere essential to scientific thought; where by autonomy I mean the condition of being one's own authority, making statements or taking action on one's own initiative and not because those statements or actions are authorized or prescribed by anyone else.

It follows that scientific history contains no ready-made statements at all. The act of incorporating a ready-made statement into the body of his own historical knowledge is an act which, for a scientific historian, is impossible. Confronted with a ready-made statement about the subject he is studying, the scientific historian never asks himself: 'Is this statement true or false?', in other words 'Shall I incorporate it in my history of that subject or not?' The question he asks himself is: 'What does this statement mean?' And this is not equivalent to the question 'What did the person who made it mean by it?', although that is doubtless a question that the historian must ask, and must be able to answer. It is equivalent, rather, to the question 'What light is thrown on the subject in which I am interested by the fact that this person made this statement, meaning by it what he did mean?' This might be expressed by saying that the scientific historian does not treat statements as statements but as evidence: not as true or false accounts of the facts of which they profess to be accounts, but as other facts which, if he knows the right questions to ask about them, may throw light on those facts. Thus in my fable the rector's daughter tells the constable that she killed John Doe. As a scientific historian, he begins attending seriously to this statement at the point where he stops treating it as a statement, that is, as a true or false account of her having done the murder, and begins treating the fact that she makes it as a fact which may be of service to him. It is of service to him because he knows what questions to ask about it, beginning with the question: 'Now why does she tell this story?' The scissors-and-paste historian is interested in the 'content', as it is called, of statements: he is interested in what they state. The scientific historian is interested in the fact that they are made.

A statement to which an historian listens, or one which he reads, is to him a ready-made statement. But the statement that such a statement is being made is not a ready-made statement. If he says to himself 'I am now reading or hearing a statement to such and such effect', he is himself making a statement; but it is not a second-hand statement, it is autonomous. He makes it on his own authority. And it is this autonomous statement that is the scientific historian's starting-point. The evidence from which the constable infers that the rector's daughter suspects Richard Roe is not her statement 'I killed John Doe', but his own statement 'the rector's daughter tells me that she killed John Doe'.

If the scientific historian gets his conclusions not from the statement that he finds ready-made, but from his own autonomous statement of the fact that such statements are made, he can get conclusions even when no statements are made to him. The premisses of his argument are his own autonomous statements: there is no need for these autonomous statements to be themselves statements about other statements. To illustrate once more from the story of John Doe. The premisses from which the Detective-Inspector argued to the innocence of Richard Roe were all premisses of the Detective-Inspector's own stating, autonomous statements resting on no authority but his own: and not one of them was a statement about statements made by anybody else. The essential points were that Richard Roe had got his shoes muddy while going away from the rectory, that no mud was to be seen in John Doe's study, and that the circumstances of the murder had been such that he would not have stopped to clean or remove his shoes. Each of these three points, in its turn, was the conclusion of an inference, and the statements upon which they severally rested were no more statements about other people's statements than were these three points themselves. Again: the ultimate case against the rector did not logically depend upon any statements made by the Detective-Inspector about statements made by other persons. It depended upon the presence of certain objects in a certain dustbin, and of certain paint-smears on the cuff of a jacket made in the conventional clerical style and shrunk by wetting; and these facts were vouched for by his own observation. I do not mean that the scientific historian can work better when no statements are made to him about the subjects on which he is working; it would be a pedantical way of avoiding scissors-and-paste history, to avoid occasions of this type which might be a trap for the weaker brethren; what I mean is that he is not dependent on such statements being made.

.   .   .

## (x)  *Question and Evidence*

.   .   .

In my fable there is only one obvious characteristic common to all the pieces of evidence used by the Detective-Inspector in his argument: they are all things observed by himself. If we ask what kind of things, it is not easy to give an answer. They include such things as the existence of certain footprints in certain mud, their number, position, and direction, their resemblance to any others; the absence of mud on the floor of a certain room; the position of a dead body, the position of a dagger in its back, and the shape of the chair in which it is sitting; and so on, a most variegated collection. This, I think, we can safely say about it: that no one could possibly know what could or could not find a place in it until he had got all his questions not only formulated but answered. In scientific history anything is evidence which is used as evidence, and no one can know what is going to be useful as evidence until he has had occasion to use it.

Let us put this by saying that in scissors-and-paste history, if we allow ourselves to describe testimony—loosely, I admit—by the name of evidence, there is potential evidence and there is actual evidence. The potential evidence about a subject is all the extant statements about it. The actual evidence is that part of these statements which we decide to accept. But in scientific history the idea of potential evidence disappears; or, if we like to put the same fact in these other words, everything in the world is potential evidence for any subject whatever. This will be a distressing idea to anyone whose notions of historical method are fixed in a scissors-and-paste mould; for how, he will ask, are we to discover what facts are actually of service to us, unless we can first of all round up the facts that might be of service to us? To a person who understands the nature of scientific thinking, whether historical or any other, it will present no difficulty. He will realize that, every time the historian asks a question, he asks it because he thinks he can answer it: that is to say, he has already in his mind a preliminary and tentative idea of the evidence he will be able to use. Not a definite idea about potential evidence, but an indefinite idea about actual evidence. To ask questions which you see no prospect of answering is the fundamental sin in science, like giving orders which you do not think will be obeyed in politics, or praying for what you do not think God will give you in religion. Question and evidence, in history, are correlative. Anything is evidence which enables you to answer your question—the question you are asking now. A sensible question (the only kind of question that a scientifically competent man will ask) is a question which you think you have or are going to have evidence for answering. If you think you have it here and now, the question is an actual question, like the question 'What position was John Doe in when he was stabbed?' If you think you are going to have it the question is a deferred question, like the question 'Who killed John Doe?'

It was a correct understanding of this truth that underlay Lord Acton's great precept, 'Study problems, not periods'. Scissors-and-paste historians study periods; they collect all the extant testimony about a certain limited group of events, and hope in vain that something will come of it. Scientific historians study problems: they ask questions, and if they are good historians they ask questions which they see their way to answering. It was a correct understanding of the same truth that led Monsieur Hercule Poirot to pour scorn on the 'human bloodhound' who crawls about the floor trying to collect everything, no matter what, which might conceivably turn out to be a clue; and to insist that the secret of detection was to use what, with possibly wearisome iteration, he called 'the little grey cells'. You can't collect your evidence before you begin thinking, he meant: because thinking means asking questions (logicians, please note), and nothing is evidence except in relation to some definite question. The difference between Poirot and Holmes in this respect is deeply significant of the change that has taken place in the understanding of historical method in the last forty years. Lord Acton was preaching his doctrine in the hey day of Sherlock Holmes, in his inaugural lecture at Cambridge in 1895; but it was caviare to the general. In Monsieur Poirot's time, to judge by his sales, the general cannot have too much of it. The revolution which dethroned the principles of scissors-and-paste history, and replaced them by those of scientific history, had become common property.

NOTES AND QUESTIONS

1.   Recall the following words of Professor Hart:

the facts and phenomena to which we fit our words and apply
our rules are as it were *dumb*.  The toy automobile cannot
speak up and say, "I am a vehicle for the purpose of this legal
rule," nor can the roller skates chorus, "We are not a vehicle."
Fact situations do not await us neatly labeled, creased and
folded, nor is their legal classification written on them to
be simply read off by the judge.  .  .  .

Suppose that the toy automobile could speak up and tell us what
it is.  What would Collingwood's reaction be?

2.   How would Collingwood go about determining the intention
of Brian in Garratt v. Dailey?  The intention of the trial judge?  Of
the appellate judge?  Would he do it in the same way as Ryle?  On
what points generally do you think Ryle and Collingwood would agree?
On what points would they disagree?  To what extent would Collingwood be sympathetic to the positions taken by Robinson and Schroeder?
Which of the three presents the more general—*i. e.*, more widely applicable—approach?  Would they all agree with Collingwood's conception of scientific method?

3.   In the readings on "The Meaning of Language," three different methods of interpretation were exposed: the literalist, the
plain meaning, and the contextualist.  In the passages from Collingwood three different methods of the historian were described: scissors-
and-paste, critical, and scientific.  Can you see any parallels between
these two triads?  Does the fact that Collingwood views the problems
of history as problems of meaning suggest that there ought to be
parallels?

4.   What is involved, according to Collingwood, in using "the
little grey cells"?  If this is what he is advocating, how does it square
with the declaration that "a scientific thinker does not have to be
clever, he has to know his job, that is, know what questions to ask"?
Is knowing what questions to ask a matter of memorization?  If not,
can it be distinguished from cleverness?  Or from intelligence?  Can
you see any similarities between Hart's conception of intelligence and
Collingwood's?

5.   How is Collingwood using the word "meaning"?  Is it the
same usage as Fingarette's below?  Try to trace the differences and
similarities between the methods of Fingarette and of Collingwood?
Which is the more general of the two and why?


*HERBERT FINGARETTE*

THE SELF IN TRANSFORMATION *

Let us think  .  .  .  of a crude analogy to an insightful interpretation, an analogy already suggested in the previous discussion.

* From 20–23, 25, 28, 29, 38 (Torchbook         Basic Books, Inc., and reprinted with
  ed. 1965).  Originally published by           its permission.

A person sees a rabbit in a cloud. But it is not a very good "fit." Some of the visible shapes don't "belong." A friend remarks: "Why, it's really a ship!" *This* way of looking at it does fit; there are no significant shapes unaccounted for.

Let us move, without comment, to a more complex analogy. A man reads a poem. He reads the poem through, every word of it, and memorizes it. Although the words and phrases are familiar to him and understood in ordinary contexts, he feels his "understanding" of the poem, as a poem, is inadequate; his enjoyment of it is meager. He fails in his attempts at a conception of the poem which will "work" by tying together all the elements. Now a friend, a trained and sensitive critic of poetry, suggests to him an over-all organization or unifying meaning-scheme which had not occurred to him. Suddenly, it "clicks."

We can illustrate this familiar experience and also add one complication. I once had the kind of experience just mentioned, and in this case the poet himself gave me the key meaning-scheme after I had failed to find it. Then, everything fit; I was impressed and delighted. The scheme was based on the very rational philosophic speculations of the great philosopher Berkeley. Some time later I suddenly saw the poem in the light of a meaning-scheme quite alien to that which the poet mentioned, in fact a mystical meaning. The poem "clicked" again—and the impact and delight were much more than were provided by what the poet himself had consciously had in mind.

The words, without some unifying scheme of meanings, are not a poem. A poem is an experience which is generated only as there is also brought to bear some unifying scheme by the one who interprets.

Now I propose that the patient in insight therapy plays a role analogous to that of the reader of the poem: what the patient "reads" are the bits and pieces of his life. He brings these fragments of his life to the therapist who then suggests a meaning-scheme in terms of which to reorganize and unify the patient's experience. The poet had merely to mention the name Berkeley to me as a cue to the whole very familiar pattern of meanings, the philosophy of Berkeley. So the therapist has merely to make a brief comment, offer a key phrase, in order to suggest to the patient a familiar but, in this context, a hitherto unused pattern of meanings in terms of which to view the situation.

Such meaning-schemes have conceptual, conative, and affective aspects, although it is the conceptual aspect which is distinctive. They are woven into the fabric of human response—indeed they are the constitutive structure of that response insofar as it is typically human and not merely animal. This is to re-enunciate the familiar principle that man is the animal whose responses are characteristically mediated by signs, symbols, and concepts. It is true that we often think of concepts being used to reflect or to report about our experience; and for many purposes this way of speaking is just right. But concepts do not only "reflect" and report our experience; as meanings, not merely as verbalistic structures, they are *constitutive* of experience. Human experience is further distinguished from all other biological behavior in that meaning-structure is not only constitutive of the experience-content, it is efficacious with regard to the course of that content's transformations. "Meaning-scheme," as this phrase is used here, points to patterns for behavior and experience, never just patterns of words, although words and concepts are the distinctive marks and peculiarly essential elements of meaning-schemes.

It will help to turn to the analogy between the meaning-systems which give structure to experience and the rules, strategies, and piece-names in a game. When we shift from poker to bridge, we do not say we are playing the same game with different rules, principles, and piece-names. They are different games. They are different games because *the rules, principles, and piece-names establish the game.* Analogously, human experience is brought into being by language and its syntax. As Kant said in introducing his "transcendental logic," "Percepts without concepts are blind." We might add that if no concepts make us blind, an inadequate meaning-scheme makes us shortsighted. Inadequate meaning-schemes institute fragmented, erratic experience. We are faced with patches of the meaningless. From this standpoint, it is easy to see that the therapist's effective introduction of a different meaning-scheme from that formerly used by the patient is a way of *directly* acting upon, a way of reorganizing the current experience rather than a way of revealing the truth about a hidden past. Let us at once balance things by paraphrasing the rest of Kant's famous dictum. Meaning-schemes divorced from the experience in which they function are psychotherapeutically empty, are merely verbal schemes; they are, in Wittgenstein's happy image, like an engine idling. In psychoanalytic informal jargon, they are merely "intellectual" insights.

In psychotherapy, we must assume the patient's former meaning-scheme did not work; it did not tie together enough of experience. The therapist's interventions aim at suggesting schemes which do work; everything "fits" and takes on a new value when cast into this mold . . .

A therapeutic interpretation given to the patient is, as has been said, a suggestion that a new conception of one's life may be worth trying, a new "game" played. But it is more than a suggestion about a "conception": it is the dynamic (existential) offering of the conception at the appropriate moment of dramatic involvement. It is more than the suggestion of a new way of talking about one's life descriptively; it is the proposal to *experience* genuinely and *see* one's life in terms of the meaning-scheme suggested by the words. It involves the hint that the structure of experience will be more unified, i. e., that there will be fewer meaningless gaps if this new scheme can become the very frame of one's being.

During the course of therapy, a woman patient comes to the therapeutic session suffering from a headache. The headache had developed after the patient had been offered an extra week's vacation by her employer. After some preliminary discussion, the therapist suggests that she feels that the gratitude due her boss puts her in his debt. He suggests that she resents this. It threatens her typical and intense efforts to maintain her independence. This view of the matter is accepted by her.  After some further discussion, the therapist proposes that her desire to be independent is in turn really a way of overreacting to a severe temptation, the temptation to give in to strong but unacceptable (unconscious) dependency needs.  At this point the headache has begun to disappear.

.   .   .

The therapist, in catalyzing psychoanalytic insight, is helping to generate a kind of imaginative reliving of the situation.  In this relived situation, the former key, organizing meaning-scheme is *now* replaced with another.  Originally, the patient had seen the offer of a vacation, the past event, as an act falling within the more comprehensive web of meanings centering around the concepts of generosity and friendliness.  Feelings of discomfort and headaches make no sense in that context.  Such responses are not a part of the "game" of being befriended.  Hence they are symptoms.  Now, in therapy, it is suggested that she experience the event in terms of a new meaning-scheme, one having such key organizing concepts as "frustration," "dependency," "temptation," and "fear."  Both schemes, the "generosity" meaning-scheme and the "temptation" meaning-scheme, though complex, are, in general, quite familiar to her.  But the "temptation" scheme never before presented itself as a "live" option in terms of which to construe the events.

We need here note only one result: since frustration, fearful temptation, and resentment are meaning-structures in experience which "imply" or meaningfully lead to the possibility of unpleasant affect, the formerly incomprehensible headache begins to loom over the horizon of the meaningful.  Thus a meaning-pattern hitherto not entertained by the patient turns out to be more comprehensive and consistent in relation to the stuff of experience than her former interpretative schemes  .   .   .

.   .   .

Insight therapy may now be viewed as the attempt to provide integrating meanings where before we had the "disconnected and unintelligible."  It is the attempt to reweave instead of putting what Freud called a "patch on the spot where there was a rent."  Insight therapy is the attempt to elucidate "all the enigmatic products of life." The therapist and patient seek schemes which not only make sense of the symptom-behavior but also tie it into the main, integrated body of meanings constituting the ego.  There is achieved thus the first of the two chief justifications for speaking of the unconscious: "a gain in meaning."  As a result, energy discharges which were isolated are integrated within the core of the psychic system.  This means that we achieve the other chief ground for speaking of the unconscious: it "enables us to construct a successful procedure by which we can exert an effective influence upon the course of conscious processes."

WILLIAM JAMES

REFLEX ACTION AND THEISM *

.   .   .   .   In a general way, all educated people know what reflex action means.

It means that the acts we perform are always the result of outward discharges from the nervous centres, and that these outward discharges are themselves the result of impressions from the external world, carried in along one or another of our sensory nerves. Applied at first to only a portion of our acts, this conception has ended by being generalized more and more, so that now most physiologists tell us that every action whatever, even the most deliberately weighed and calculated, does, so far as its organic conditions go, follow the reflex type. There is not one which cannot be remotely, if not immediately, traced to an origin in some incoming impression of sense. There is no impression of sense which, unless inhibited by some other stronger one, does not immediately or remotely express itself in action of some kind. There is no one of those complicated performances in the convolutions of the brain to which our trains of thought correspond, which is not a mere middle term interposed between an incoming sensation that arouses it and an outgoing discharge of some sort, inhibitory if not exciting, to which itself gives rise. The structural unit of the nervous system is in fact a triad, neither of whose elements has any independent existence. The sensory impression exists only for the sake of awaking the central process of reflection, and the central process of reflection exists only for the sake of calling forth the final act. All action is thus *re*-action upon the outer world; and the middle stage of consideration or contemplation or thinking is only a place of transit, the bottom of a loop, both whose ends have their point of application in the outer world. If it should ever have no roots in the outer world, if it should ever happen that it led to no active measures, it would fail of its essential function, and would have to be considered either pathological or abortive. The current of life which runs in at our eyes or ears is meant to run out at our hands, feet, or lips. The only use of the thoughts it occasions while inside is to determine its direction to whichever of these organs shall, on the whole, under the circumstances actually present, act in the way most propitious to our welfare.

The willing department of our nature, in short, dominates both the conceiving department and the feeling department; or, in plainer English, perception and thinking are only there for behavior's sake.

.   .   .

.   .   .   .   let me ask you to linger a moment longer over .   .   .   the reflex theory of mind, so as to be sure that we understand it absolutely before going on to consider those of its conse-

---

* From The Will to Believe and Other
Essays 113–114, 117–120 (Dover ed.
1956).

quences of which I am more particularly to speak. I am not quite sure that its full scope is grasped even by those who have most zealously promulgated it. I am not sure, for example, that all physiologists see that it commits them to regarding the mind as an essentially teleological mechanism. I mean by this that the conceiving or theorizing faculty—the mind's middle department—functions *exclusively for the sake of ends* that do not exist at all in the world in impressions we receive by way of our senses, but are set by our emotional and practical subjectivity altogether. It is a transformer of the world of our impressions into a totally different world,—the world of our conception; and the transformation is effected in the interests of our volitional nature, and for no other purpose whatsoever. Destroy the volitional nature, the definite subjective purposes, preferences, fondnesses for certain effects, forms, orders, and not the slightest motive would remain for the brute order of our experience to be remodelled at all. But, as we have the elaborate volitional constitution we do have, the remodelling must be effected; there is no escape.

. . . . The real world as it is given objectively at this moment is the sum total of all its beings and events now. But can we think of such a sum? Can we realize for an instant what a cross-section of all existence at a definite point of time would be? While I talk and the flies buzz, a sea-gull catches a fish at the mouth of the Amazon, a tree falls in the Adirondack wilderness, a man sneezes in Germany, a horse dies in Tartary, and twins are born in France. What does that mean? Does the contemporaneity of these events with one another and with a million others as disjointed, form a rational bond between them, and unite them into anything that means for us a world? Yet just such a collateral contemporaneity, and nothing else, is the real order of the world. It is an order with which we have nothing to do but to get away from it as fast as possible. As I said, we break it: we break it into histories, and we break it into arts, and we break it into sciences; and then we begin to feel at home. We make ten thousand separate serial orders of it, and on any one of these we react as though the others did not exist. We discover among its various parts relations that were never given to sense at all (mathematical relations, tangents, squares, and roots and logarithmic functions), and out of an infinite number of these we call certain ones essential and lawgiving, and ignore the rest. Essential these relations are, but only *for our purpose*, the other relations being just as real and present as they; and our purpose is to *conceive simply* and to *foresee*. Are not simple conception and prevision subjective ends pure and simple? They are the ends of what we call science; and the miracle of miracles, a miracle not yet exhaustively cleared up by any philosophy, is that the given order lends itself to the remodelling. It shows itself plastic to many of our scientific, to many of our aesthetic, to many of our practical purposes and ends.

When the man of affairs, the artist, or the man of science fails, he is not rebutted, He tries again. He says the impressions of sense *must* give way, *must* be reduced to the desiderated form.[10]  They all postulate in the interests of their volitional nature a harmony between the latter and the nature of things.  The theologian does no more.  And the reflex doctrine of the mind's structure, though all theology should as yet have failed of its endeavor, could but confess that the endeavor itself at least obeyed in form the mind's most necessary law.

## Questions

With whom do you think James would side, Professor Hart or Professor Fuller?  Would he think that purposes are only to be considered in penumbral cases?

## John Dewey

### Art as Experience *

Why is the attempt to connect the higher and ideal things of experience with basic vital roots so often regarded as betrayal of their nature and denial of their value?  Why is there repulsion when the high achivements of fine art are brought into connection with common life, the life that we share with all living creatures?  Why is life thought of as an affair of low appetite, or at its best a thing of gross sensation, and ready to sink from its best to the level of lust and harsh cruelty?  A complete answer to the question would involve the writing of a history of morals that would set forth the conditions that have brought about contempt for the body, fear of the senses, and the opposition of flesh to spirit.

One aspect of this history is so relevant to our problem that it must receive at least passing notice.  The institutional life of mankind is marked by disorganization.  This disorder is often disguised by the fact that it takes the form of static division into classes, and this static separation is accepted as the very essence of order as long as it is so fixed and so accepted as not to generate open conflict.  Life is compartmentalized and the institutionalized compartments are classified as high and as low; their values as profane and spiritual, as material and ideal.  Interests are related to one another externally and mechanically, through a system of checks and balances.  Since

---

10.  "No amount of failure in the attempt to subject the world of sensible experience to a thorough-going system of conceptions, and to bring all happenings back to cases of immutably valid law, is able to shake our faith in the rightness of our principles.  We hold fast to our demand that even the greatest apparent confusion must sooner or later solve itself in transparent formulas.  We begin the work ever afresh; and, refusing to believe that nature will permanently withhold the reward of our exertions, think rather that we have hitherto only failed to push them in the right direction.  And all this pertinacity flows from a conviction that we *have no right* to renounce the fulfilment of our task.  What, in short sustains the courage of investigators is the force of obligation of an ethical idea."  Sigwart: Logik, bd. ii., p. 23)

religion, morals, politics, business has each its own compartment, within which it is fitting each should remain, art, too, must have its peculiar and private realm.  Compartmentalization of occupations and interests brings about separation of that mode of activity commonly called "practice" from insight, of imagination from executive doing, of significant purpose from work, of emotion from thought and doing.  Each of these has, too, its own place in which it must abide.  Those who write the anatomy of experience then suppose that these divisions inhere in the very constitution of human nature.

Of much of our experience as it is actually lived under present economic and legal institutional conditions, it is only too true that these separations hold.  Only occasionally in the lives of many are the senses fraught with the sentiment that comes from deep realization of intrinsic meanings.  We undergo sensations as mechanical stimuli or as irritated stimulations, without having a sense of the reality that is in them and behind them: in much of our experience our different senses do not unite to tell a common and enlarged story.  We see without feeling; we hear, but only a second-hand report, second hand because not reenforced by vision.  We touch, but the contact remains tangential because it does not fuse with qualities of senses that go below the surface.  We use the senses to arouse passion but not to fulfill the interest of insight, not because that interest is not potentially present in the exercise of sense but because we yield to conditions of living that force sense to remain an excitation on the surface.  Prestige goes to those who use their minds without participation of the body and who act vicariously through control of the bodies and labor of others.

Under such conditions, sense and flesh get a bad name.  The moralist, however, has a truer sense of the intimate connections of sense with the rest of our being than has the professional psychologist and philosopher, although his sense of these connections takes a direction that reverses the potential facts of our living in relation to the environment.  Psychologist and philosopher have in recent times been so obsessed with the problem of knowledge that they have treated "sensations" as mere elements of knowledge.  The moralist knows that sense is allied with emotion, impulse and appetition.  So he denounces the lust of the eye as part of the surrender of spirit to flesh.  He identifies the sensuous with the sensual and the sensual with the lewd.  His moral theory is askew, but at least he is aware that the eye is not an imperfect telescope designed for intellectual reception of material to bring about knowledge of distant objects.

### QUESTIONS

1.  Are James and Dewey in agreement about the nature of "order" or "organization"?  Can you reconcile James's statement that we must "break" the "collateral contemporaneity . . . of the world" into histories, arts, and sciences with Dewey's attack on compartmentalization?  Is James one of those who accepts the "static division into classes . . . as the very essence of order"?  Why is such "static separation," according to Dewey, really a disguise for "disorder"?

2.   Is there any connection between the "separation of  .  .  . 'practice' from insight, of imagination from executive doing, of significant purpose from work, of emotion from thought and doing" and the "separation of the law as it is from the law as it ought to be"?   Does Hart's position necessarily involve him in making the separations which Dewey criticizes?   If not, what would lead one to think so?   Does Hart think that the differentiation of "is" from "ought" leads to more or less order?   Is Fuller's insistence on the importance of purpose derived from a concern, at least partially, with order?   Or is it based on a judgment that in the end order must defer to other values, such as justice?   Recall Fuller's "assertion .  .  .   that coherence and goodness have more affinity than coherence and evil."

Do you think that James believes "that we *have no right* to renounce" "the attempt to subject the world of sensible experience to a thoroughgoing system of conceptions"?   What kind of an ethical theory would justify such a statement?   Does Dewey see a connection between order and morality?   What is the distinction between "moralism" and "morals" that Dewey assumes?   Would Hart's position be weaker or stronger if his attack were leveled at the confusion of "law and moralism" rather than that of "law and morals"?   What, incidentally, is the relation, if any, between positions which are "moralistic" and positions which are "legalistic"?   Do moralistic positions differ from moral positions in the same way that legalistic positions differ from legal positions?

3.   What is the relation between meaning and reality which Dewey's remarks imply?   The relation between meaning and order?   Reality and order?   What, in Dewey's view, does the fact that "in much of our experience our different senses do not unite to tell a common and enlarged story" have to do with the meaningfulness, the orderliness, or the reality of such a "story"?

Do James and Dewey have the same view of what is "real"?   Consider James's contention that "such a collateral contemporaneity is the real order of the world."   Consider James's reference to "other relations  .  .  .   just as real and present" as the "certain ones [we call] essential and lawgiving."   Would Dewey agree that the relations which are *essential* "for our purpose" are no more real than the ones which are not essential?

## SECTION FOUR:  REALITY, MIND AND COMMON SENSE

### NOTE: MYSTERY, MEANING AND REALITY

Professor Hart suggests, you will recall, that those who would abandon the "distinction between what the law is and what it ought to be" are inviting us "to revise our conception of what a legal rule is."   "We are invited," he says, "to include in the 'rule' the various aims and policies in the light of which its penumbral cases are decided on the ground that these aims have, because of their import-ance, as much right to be called law as the core of legal rules whose meaning is settled." One reason that Hart rejects the invitation is that "everything we have learned about the judicial process can be expressed in other less mysterious ways. We can say laws are incurably incomplete and we must decide the penumbral cases rationally by reference to social aims." A little later Hart criticizes the American tradition's "preoccupation with the penumbra" as a rich "source of confusion." Penumbral cases, apparently, are the unusual, non-routine, non-familiar cases. Is Professor Hart suggesting that the American emphasis on the unusual cases leads to a strange or "mysterious" conception of legal rules?

It will perhaps be instructive to wonder how one determines whether a particular mode of expression qualifies as "mysterious." Is the criterion involved that of the ordinary man using words in ordinary situations? Or of the average lawyer in ordinary legal circumstances? If either of these is the proper criterion, what is to be said of Hart's notion of the "core" and the "penumbra" or of laws which "are incurably incomplete"? Are these conceptions of legal rules and of legal meanings the ordinary or average ones? Consider again the notion of a law which is "incurably incomplete"? Would it be unfair to call this a "mysterious" mode of expression? Professor Hart apparently feels that an explanation's strangeness is a mark against it. Is he unusual in this regard? Or is there a general tendency to prefer explanations which sound like things we have heard before? Are we inclined to believe that the real world is something with which we are comfortable and at home so that descriptions which make it appear alien and strange are rejected as unreal? Lionel Trilling speaks of "the chronic American belief that there exists an opposition between reality and mind and that one must enlist oneself in the party of reality." If he is right, is this because "mind" is constantly making reality seem new and surprising? Consider the intellectual approaches recommended by the writers in the last subsection. Are the results which they are designed to achieve likely to be familiar? What will their relation be to the common sense view of things? Consider the following from Pepper:

> There appear to be two broad types of evidence: uncriticized, and criticized or refined evidence. Socially and individually, knowledge begins with the former. . . .
>
> We often call this sort of evidence common sense. Plato called it "opinion." It has been called "preanalytical data," and "middle-sized fact." . . . .
>
> Uncriticized, common-sense facts are the sort of things we think of when we ordinarily read the daily papers or novels depicting the ordinary life of men or the sort of things we see and hear and smell and feel as we walk along the street or in the country. . . .
>
> . . .
>
> If we examine material of this sort, we note certain traits. First, it is not definitely cognizable. Any attempt to exhibit, or describe, or specify any of this material definitely in

detail generally carries us out of the material.  What was uncriticized fact immediately turns into criticized fact, and generally a transformation of the material takes place as a result of the attempt.  .  .  .

.  .  .  .  There is no implication in this assertion, of course, that whatever is the fact or the truth in a common-sense matter is not what it is.  We simply cannot have any assurance that we know what it is without criticism.  But then the matter ceases to be uncriticized and generally considerably changes in appearance.

WORLD HYPOTHESES * 39–40 (1966 ed.)  Does this explain why even Hart's theory of meaning, try as it might to be common sensical, is bound to be "mysterious"?

It is arguable that the strongest resistance to positions such as Collingwood's or Fingarette's stems from a feeling that they are too "intellectual," too removed from immediate experience, and, therefore, too distortive of reality.  Systematic theory is necessarily abstract and so, perhaps by definition, it takes us away from the brute, concrete data of existence.  Furthermore, the ultimate value of particular theories seems usually to be determined by some final resort to a portion of our unrefined experience.  In the end, somehow, the best theories must be practical which probably means that they must comport with at least a part of our common sense.  Yet as Trilling has indicated, and the following excerpts reiterate, systematic theory seems to be at war with common sense.  You should ask yourself whether such an opposition is necessary and, if so, whether it implies an opposition between systematic theory and reality.

*LEO STEINBERG*

### THE EYE IS A PART OF THE MIND †

.  .  .  .  Representational art for [Malraux] is weighted with extraneous content and transcribed appeal, with reference to things and situations that exist outside the picture frame in general experience.  Manet pries art loose from the world.  "Modern art," says Malraux, "has liberated painting which is now triumphantly a law unto itself."  No longer must a painting borrow its validity from natural analogues.  Its meaning—if self-significance can be called meaning—lies wholly within itself.  Wherever art is seen with modern eyes—seen, that is to say, as "a certain compelling balance in colors and lines"—there, says Malraux, "a magic casement opens on another world  .  .  .  a world incompatible with the world of reality."  .  .  .

.  .  .

. . . . This is the [view] . . . of such continental crit- ics as Ortega y Gasset and Malraux, who endorse the meaning ele- ments in the historic styles, yet claim for modern art exemption from associated values. It is also (aesthetics makes strange bedfellows!) the view of the bourgeois who repudiates all modern art as an un- funny and too long protracted hoax.

. . .

. . . . about half the great art generated by mankind is dedicated to the accurate transcription of the sensible world. This is as true of the best paleolithic art as of Egyptian at its finest mo- ments. It applies to the entire Hellenic effort down to third-century Rome. It applies equally to the great Western wave that lies be- tween Giotto and the Post-Impressionists. Nor is it any the less true of Chinese painting—so self-conscious that it operated for a thou- sand years within six explicit canons; of which the third called for "conformity with nature," or "the drawing of forms which answer to natural forms." All of these schools—and there are as many more— strove for the mastery of nature by convincing imitation.

Perhaps it will be said that artists closer to us in time would not have subscribed to this errant quest. Here is a sampling of their depositions: Manet declared (Malraux notwithstanding) that he painted what he saw. Van Gogh's avowed aim was to be "simply honest before nature." Cezanne exclaims: "Look at that cloud! I would like to be able to paint that!" And he says: "We must give the picture of what we see, forgetting everything that has appeared in the past." Even for Matisse "the problem is to maintain the in- tensity of the canvas whilst getting near to verisimilitude."

. . .

Yet artists and critics, for half a century and more, have been denouncing the representation of nature as a fatal side-stepping of artistic purpose. . . . The picturing of overt nature is written off as mere factual reportage, worthy only of the amateur photogra- pher, a mechanical skill, patently uncreative and therefore alien to the essence of art.

The objection to this view is not far to seek. To begin with, "technical capacity in imitation" implies what no one seriously be- lieves: that nature confronts man with a fixed, invariant look. For what else does it mean to speak of "mere skill in copying the model" (the words a re Malraux's), but that the model's appearance is an ob- jective fact susceptible of mechanical reproduction? We know better than that. Appearances reach us through the eye, and the eye— whether we speak with the psychologist or the embryologist—is part of the brain and therefore hopelessly involved in mysterious cerebral operations. Thus nature presents every generation (and every person who will use his eyes for more than nodding recognitions) with a unique and unrepeated facet of appearance. And the Ineluctible Modality of the Visible—young Dedalus' hypnotic phrase—is a myth that evaporates between any two works of representation. The en- croaching archaism of old photographs is only the latest instance of an endless succession in which every new mode of nature-representation eventually resigns its claim to co-identity with natural appear-ance. And if appearances are thus unstable in the human eye, their representation in art is not a matter of mechanical reproduction but of progressive revelation.

We can therefore assert with confidence that "technical capacity in the imitation of nature" simply does not exist. What does exist is the skill of reproducing handy graphic symbols for natural ap-pearances, of rendering familiar facts by set professional conventions. We have cited a canon from the beginning phase of Chinese painting; here is another from nearer its dead end:

There are ten ways, say the Chinese academicians, of depicting a mountain: by drawing wrinkles like the slashes of a large axe, or wrinkles like the hair on a cow's hide; by brushstrokes wrinkled like a heap of firewood, or like the veins of lotus leaves. The rest are to be wrinkled like the folds of a belt, or the twists of a rope; or like raindrops, or like convoluted clouds, etc.

With rigorous training the Ming painters could, and did, ac-quire a dazzling proficiency in drawing the right wrinkles and so suggesting the available, respectable, familiar facts about natural panoramas. They had mastered the skill of applying certain academic tricks for the drawing of mountains—but this is most emphatically not the same as skill in drawing actual mountains. The mechanical, the uncreative element lies not therefore in imitating nature, but in academicism, which is the passionless employment of performed devices. Representation in art is the fashioning of graphic symbols to act as analogues for certain areas of visual experience. There is a mightly difference between this fashioning of symbols, this trans-mutation and reduction of experience to symbolic pattern, and the use of symbols readymade. In words that seem to duplicate a visible aspect of nature we must therefore distinguish between the recitation of a known fact and the discovery thereof, between the dexterous use of tools and their invention.

This distinction must be upheld for all representational art. Seen in this light it becomes quite absurd to charge Victorian academicians with too fastidious an eye for natural forms. Their fault was not, as Roger Fry maintained, "the fervid pursuit of naturalistic appear-ances," but that they continued to see and represent the facts of na-ture in terms of a spent convention. The so-called naturalism of the nineteenth-century academicians was worthless because it was im-pelled by precept and by meritorious example, instead of by pure visual apprehension. These men never imitated nature; they copied earlier imitations and applied those formal principles which, they believed, had made their models so effective. That they sometimes painted from life is, of course, beside the point; for they still saw life in the aspect which their vision was conditioned to expect. Thus the malady of Victorian art (and of some lingering official art to-day, notably in Soviet Russia) is not naturalism, nor literal repre-sentation, but the presumption to create living art out of impulses long dead and mummified; which ailment is not confined to realistic art. For academicism will blight non-objective figurations and abstract designs as readily as illustrative, anecdotal pictures. One has only to walk into an up-to-date New York art school to see how academic are those repetitious canvases that imitate Braque and Picasso down to the planimetric mandolin.

This is not to say that a convention invariably chokes artistic creativity. It does so only when too fully conned and understood, when the uphill drive of aspiration is relaxed and the professors of the brush can settle down to mass production. An artist searches for true vision, but having found it, leaves in his successors' hands the blueprint of a new academy. Almost anyone with a modicum of talent and sufficient application can possess himself of another man's mode of representation. (Were this not so, the forger's craft would not exist.) But he cannot discover it. He can learn after one lesson in perspective how to give an illusion of depth to a design (an illusion, by the way, based largely on our habit of routine consent). But this lesson shall not arm him with the passion of an early Florentine who first ventures through the picture plane and, like daydreaming Alice, finds a wonderland beyond. The same rules of perspective mean one thing at the Beaux Arts; in Mantegna's studio, in Uccello's workshop, they meant quite another. Space, that had congealed into a solid crust during the Middle Ages, was here dented, pierced and vaporized. Bodies were inserted and, against resisting pressure, as on reluctant hinges, pivoted into depth. There is in Uccello's work a tensity which springs directly from his craving to know how bodies will behave in the *terra incognita* known as the third dimension. And the reports of his discoveries, such as the bold foreshortenings in "The Battle of San Romano," are proclaimed in tense and urgent gestures. And what is true of perspective applies equally to anatomy. The gulf that separates a Pollaiuolo nude from one by Bouguereau is not all a matter of significant design. The one was born of nature's union with an avid sensibility; the other makes a parade of a habitual skill. One says, pointing to the array of anatomic facts—"Here lies the mystery"; the other says—"Here lies no mystery, I know it all."

The modern critic who belittles all representational concerns, because he sees them only as solved problems, underrates their power to inflame the artist's mind and to intensify his vision and his touch. He will fail of appreciation if he cannot appropriate the artist's will to state his concept of reality. Nor need he know how much of anatomic ignorance prevailed in Pollaiuolo's time to judge the measure of the artist's revelation. For Pollaiuolo's effort to articulate each muscular inflection is permanently sealed in the form. Like all works connected with discoveries of representation, his pictures lack the sweet ease of accomplishment. His images are ever aborning, swelling into space and taking life, like frozen fingers tingling as they warm. It is not facts they purvey; it is the thrill and wonder of cognition.

.    .    .

In realistic art,  .    .    .    it is the ever-novel influx of visual experience which incites the artist's synthesizing will, summons his energies and so contributes to the generation of aesthetic form. And this perhaps explains why periods of expanding iconography, of deepening observation and growing imitative skill so often coincide with supreme aesthetic achievement. When the limits of the depictable in nature suddenly recede before the searching gaze, when earlier works come to seem inadequately representative of truth, then the artist's power multiplies. Hence the beauty of those Fifth Dynasty reliefs in Egypt, when, almost suddenly, all life comes to be taken for the artist's province; or the unsurpassed grandeur of the Middle Kingdom heads, when the uniqueness of the human face is first perceived. Hence the upsurge of aesthetic force in Sixth and Fifth Century Greece, when new insights into human nature call for embodiment; or in Quattrocento art when the untamed reality of space has to be disciplined and reduced to the coordinate system of the plane canvas or wall.

.  .  .

.  .  .  .  Nowadays every schoolboy knows that Cezanne was interested in picture construction. We incline to forget that he was just as concerned with the construction of Mont Sainte-Victoire and the vibration of sunlight; that he studied the subterranean geologic energies which had rolled up the landscape of Provence, and pondered those pervasive unities of nature in which forms are compacted despite their apparent edges. Today's fashionable cant represses Cezanne's deep obsession with reality, "the spectacle that the Pater Omnipotens spreads before our eyes." When he warns his friend Emile Bernard, to "beware of the literary spirit which so often causes painting to deviate from its true path—the concrete study of nature—to lose itself all too long in intangible speculations," he seems to be speaking not so much of the critics he knew, as of those more recent who profess to know him. The truth is that Cezanne's work embodies profound insights into nature. And the inner logic of his form is unthinkable without his ardent apprehension of natural fact.

.  .  .

.  .  .  .  the arts discussed in the foregoing section  .  .  .  . endorsed Constable's plea for the pure apprehension of natural fact.

But natural fact can be purely apprehended only where the human mind has first endowed it with the status of reality. Only then is the act of seeing backed by a passion, being focused on ultimate truth. From Masaccio to Cezanne men prized overt nature as the locus of reality, and to it they directed their capacities of apprehension. But if we invoke a civilization for whom nature was a pale and immaterial reflection of ideal types, we shall expect to find it careless of the outer shapes of things. Its art will strive to incarnate those forms which are the permanent exemplars behind the drift of sensuous appearances. This indeed is the course taken by Christian art after the fall of pagen Rome.

We can now modify Constable's dictum and propose that art seeks the pure apprehension of natural fact wherever natural fact, as registered by the senses, is regarded as meaningful reality. Where it it not so interpreted we shall find some form of anti-humanist distortion, of hieratic stylization or abstraction. But—and this is crucial—such abstraction will continue to apprehend and to express reality. Though it rejects the intimations of mere sense perception, it does not thereby cease to be representational. Only the matter that now calls for representation is drawn from a new order of reality.

Let us list briefly some of the formal features governing Early Christian and Byzantine art. Comparing it to the preceding style. of disenchanted Hellenism, we are struck by a rigid frontality in the disposition of figures, by a minimum of variation in gesture, and the replacement of individual likeness by canonic type. We note that movement is arrested, that the natural bulk of things is flattened and all forms are gathered in a single plane; distance is eliminated in favor of ideal space, purple or gold; color becomes pure, unmodulated, and the shadow—that negating spirit who haunts only the art of the West—vanishes in the diffusion of an unremitting light.

These devices sound, as indeed they look, other-worldly. Yet we can say without paradox that their employment proves how deeply involved was the art of Byzantium, and of the Western Dark and Middle Ages, in the effort at truthful representation. This is readily verified by reference to Neo-Platonist aesthetics.

The most valuable source here is Plotinus, whose thought, by way of Dionysius and Augustine, shaped the spirituality of the first Christian millennium. What, asks Plotinus, speaking of the plastic arts, are true distance and true size? And his answer is a philosophic premonition of the Byzantine manner. If we see two men, the one close by, the other far away, the latter will appear ridiculously dwarfted, and the interval between the two will seem absurdly shrunken. A given distance, therefore, is so many measures of falsification. Since deep space is the occasion of delusion, true distance can exist only within the nearest facing plane; true size is the dimension of each form within that plane.

The argument may be extended to true color. If the red of a red object fades in distance, this effaced, degraded color is not "true." The truth must be an even red in the proximate plane. Furthermore, shadows are to be shunned for doing violence to truthful color, for there can be neither truth nor reality where there is not illumination. Thus to Plotinus the proper rendering of a red sphere would be a disk of pure, ungraduated hue. It is the chiaroscurist—a pander to the sense of sight—who mistakes the nature of reality and therefore sins against the light. "We dare not keep ourselves set toward the images of sense," Plotinus says.

Do Byzantine images seem incorporeal? How else should they represent the truly real? "The body is brute," says Plotinus; "the true man is the other, going pure of body." And he proceeds to reprove them who on the evidence of thrust and resistance identify body with real being.

Do Early Christian figures seem monotonously like, immobile and unchanging? We are forewarned by Plotinus that "bodies live in the species, and the individual in the whole class; from them they derive their life and maintenance, for life here is a thing of change, but in that prior realm it is unmoving."

Finally, do the eyes in medieval faces seem excessively prominent? The eye sees the sun, says Plotinus, because it is itself sun-like. Window of the soul, it bespeaks the presence in the body of that radiant emanation which sustains matter in being. Should not the artist therefore state the eye's true nature rather than comparative size? Values having more reality than facts, it is they that determine the ethos and technique of medieval art.

Clearly, then, the formal conventions of this Christian art came into being in the interest of representational truth; not, to be sure, of direct visual facts, since such facts were metaphysically discredited, but of an ideal, extra-sensory reality.

Obedient to its mystic vision, Christian art proceeded to erect a system of representation by abstraction. Here a certain limited affinity to our own contemporary art suggests itself. There is indeed striking resemblance between the repudiation of naturalism in our time and Plotinus' day. The latter had written that "the arts give no bare reproduction of the thing seen but go back to the ideas from which nature herself derives." Compare this with Paul Klee's: "The modern artist places more value on the powers that do the forming, than on the final forms (of nature) themselves." And even Roger Fry, who had no stomach for mystical speculation, says of Cezanne— who was all modern art to him—that he rendered "not appearances, but the causes of appearance in structure."

As the greatest apostle of the modern aesthetic faith, the case of Roger Fry is a rewarding study. And it is noteworthy that he was unaware of his own implications. He fervently believed that the prime business of art, in fact its sole legitimate concern, was "abstract unity of design." "Painting," he exclaimed, "has thrown representation to the winds; literature should do the same and follow suit!" Yet, gazing at an academic portrait, he passed this elegant quip (quoted in Virginia Woolf's biography): "I cannot," he said, "see the man for the likeness."

This went far deeper than Fry would have granted. He had meant to say that he could not see the essential man beneath the clutter of external traits. But he unwittingly confessed that he did want to see this inner man. While affirming that the valuable image did not manifest itself in mere visibility, he also admitted that the truth which lay concealed behind the model's mask, could and should be represented by some graphic symbol. It will be seen at once that Fry was speaking from a philosophic premise for which his formalistic theorizing left no room. He mistook for an aesthetic doctrine what was actually a shift in philosophic orientation. And he was not calling for the end of representation in art, but for the representation of a different content, to be tapped from a new order of reality.

Fry's sensitive recoil from Victorian academicism—or naturalism, to give it his preferred misnomer—was therefore based on two objections, neither of which he acknowledged. First, that it substituted standard commonplaces for pure vision, and second, that it continued to portray an aspect of nature which in the philosophic conscience of his age had lost reality and meaning. For the inversions of modern psychology and the iconoclasm of contemporary physics have once again, as in the Middle Ages, subverted our faith in the reality of palpable appearances. And it is right and proper for the modern artist who is worthy of his time that he should turn his back on the apparent, since he holds with Plotinus that "all perceptible things are but signs and symbols of the imperceptible." Thus the revelance of naturalistic representation to art depends on no aesthetic doctrines, but on prior metaphysical commitments. And the argument for and against representation, which has agitated critics for so long, has rarely been fought at its proper level.

## IV

Has modern art, then, like Byzantium, broken with the sensible world? Is it true that art, having paid its debt to nature, is now finally at liberty? Let us consider first those modern works which still maintain natural forms at some degree of recognizability. To the formalist their distortions seem sufficiently justified as serving the higher needs of design. Yet in these works the illustrative element is there, and—no matter how abstracted—takes its point from its residual resemblance to familiar sights. "The deformation of natural forms" of which Klee speaks in his journals presupposes in us a conception of natural forms undeformed. Meyer Schapiro, speaking of Picasso's "Girl before a Mirror," points out that "Picasso and other moderns have discovered for art the internality of the body," that is, the inner image of the body as conjured up by fear and desire, pleasure and pain. But this inner image is communicable only as related contrast to the outer. Everyone knows how clumsy the human foot feels when pursuing a bird. The mammoth foot in Miro's "Man Throwing a Stone at a Bird" is thus an eloquent hyperbole, a piece of graphic gigantism. It makes its point not as largeness—a pure, abstract value—but as enlargement which implies an external referent. The distance which the form has traveled in the way of distortion is apprehended by the beholder and becomes a vital element of the narrative structure. Familiar nature is not, after all, ignored. It survives as the distanced, but implicit, norm.

This principle of representation by distortion and exaggeration for expressive ends is found, of course, throughout the history of art. It is the common device of all caricatures. No matter how remotely they have ventured into fantasy, it is the stretch and span between norm and distortion that constitutes their wit. The same is true of expressionism and of much so-called abstract art. A term of reference still lies outside the picture frame in human recollection and experience, as it does for the most clinically realistic pictures.

To an eye still immersed in the visual habits of the nineteenth century, the abstract way often seems willful and offensive. To a mind indoctrinated with modern aesthetic theory, it often looks like— "simply painting," the projection of inbred phantasmagoria. Both judgments, we believe, are failures of appreciation, since abstraction *from* nature is still a telling mode of representation, whose hyphen with common reality is stretched but never snapped, except in the most thinly decorative works.

There is another feature in contemporary abstract art which ties it to the world of sense and separates it from all anti-naturalistic styles of the past—its boundless freedom of selection from natural sights. The conceptualism of ancient Egypt or Byzantium had constrained itself to show every form from a preferred angle, convinced that one aspect alone could reveal its essential nature. Thus the Egyptian foot appears persistently in profile, as though the human foot in essence were a profile form, all other postures being accidentals. Domiciled in eternity, the Egyptian or Byzantine foot is not susceptible of change.

Modern abstraction brooks no such restraints. Six centuries of arduous research into the changing nature of appearance are not so easily dismissed. Accordingly, in modern abstract art, a difficult, foreshortened front view of a foot is met head-on, and finds its abstract formulation as readily as the diagrammatic profile. The modern painter, if caught in the orbit of Picasso or Paul Klee, discovers a formative principle not in the foot as such, but in the foot in every possible predicament. He sees not one transcendent, universal formula for man, but a distinct abbreviation for man in every pose, mood, situation. Klee himself finds a symbolic cipher not for Woman, the Eternal Feminine, but for a certain middle-aged lady coming home loaded with packages.

It is quite true that Klee seeks ever the form-giving principle behind the thing, and strips it, like the mystic, of its superfluity; his representations rest upon his vision of a world whose surface forms conceal an occulted reality. In his own words, he seeks "a distant point at the source of creation, a kind of formula for man, earth, fire, water, air, and all the circling forces." Klee here seems to repeat a commonplace of mysticism. And yet his work, one of the most potent influences behind modern abstraction, is of devastating originality, utterly destructive of the mystic premise that there is one immutable reality available to detached contemplation. For Klee finds his occult reality incarnate in each fleeting, perjured gesture of this world. In his intuition the nature of man is not to be found in any timeless essence, soaring like Egyptian or Byzantine man above vicissitudes. Man, to Paul Klee, is what he does and where he is. Man is a "Juggler in April," an "Old Man Figuring," a "Mocker Mocked," an "Omphalocentric Lecturer." Vainly you scan these works for any single pictographic type; in every sketch the symbol is freshly apprehended and fashioned anew. If this is mysticism it is certainly not of the medieval, contemplative kind. It is a restless, existential mysticism, peculiarly our own.

Or watch Picasso's "Three Musicians" in the Philadelphia version. Despite an apparently remote cubistic formalism we can say with confidence that the three men in the picture are furnished with six hands. But saying this we have already said too much. Having availed ourselves of the non-visual concept of *the human hand*, we have implied that Picasso here deals with a six-fold repetition of a single item. But he does nothing of the kind. He knows, or knew in 1921, that a man's hand may manifest itself as rake, pestle, mallet, cup, cantilever, pincer, vise or broom; as waving banner or as decorative fringe; that it is a nubile and unstable element, contracting easy marriages with other forms to build up into compound entities. In actual vision the hand is an infinity of variegated forms. Its common factor is not any ontological handshape, but a protean energy with only a positional and functional relation to the arm, and to the object handled. Thus, in the "Three Musicians," a fist hugging a fiddle's neck is one sort of efficient force expressed by one decorative shape; four digits flat upon a keyboard are of another sort entirely. Picasso here banishes the *a priori* vision which must ever find conceptual permanence despite visible change. His manual formulae stand not for Being, but for function, operation. Adaptability and change are the sole measure of reality. And it is on behalf of such reality, as well as of design, that his sleights of hand are wrought. To describe the "Three Musicians" as a finely patterned abstraction of invented anatomies is an injustice to the matter of Picasso's revelation.

It follows that the modern abstractionist does not necessarily write off the "accidents" of visual appearance. He welcomes their occurrence, but pictures them as the negotiable shapes assumed by transient energy. And in this adaptability to every optic impulse modern art is more closely linked to its naturalistic ancestry than to the unworldly stylizations of the past. Its affinity with medieval art remains, after all, purely negative. Modern and medieval art agree that reality is not so much revealed as masked by surfaces. But, as at a carnival, the choice of a mask may betray the reveler's characteristic nature, so surfaces bespeak something as to the truth below. And the truths inferred by modern and by medieval artists lie at opposite poles of interpretation.

## V

It remains to speak of so-called non-objective art. Here surely all connection with the outer world is cut. The forms that here emerge mean nothing, we are told, but private states of feeling; and, for the rest, they are pure form, a music for the optic nerve. The following passage from Ortega y Gasset ("On Point of View in the Arts," *Partisan Review*, August 1949) may serve as an example of the common view: "Painting," Ortega writes, "completely reversed its function and, instead of putting us within what is outside, endeavored to pour out upon the canvas what is within: ideal invented objects . . . . The [artist's] eyes, instead of absorbing things, are converted into projectors of private flora and fauna. Before, the real world drained off into them; now they are reservoirs of irreality."

This seems to us an open question still. For we are forced to ask: by what faculty of mind or eye does the artist discover and distill the forms of his private irreality? Whence come the plastic symbols of his unconditioned subjectivity? Surely no amount of introspection will yield shapes to put on canvas. And if this is so, from what external quarter proceed those visual stimuli which the artist can identify as apt and corresponding to his inner state?

Obviously, any attempt to answer such a question will be so highly speculative as almost to vindicate in advance the voices of dissent.

Yet it seems worth considering the testimony of those artists and critics who have pointed to the impact of science on contemporary art.

The impact operates on several levels and takes various forms. There is, first, a constant stream of suggestion issuing from the laboratories. Wittingly, or through unconscious exposure, the nonobjective artist draws much of his iconography from the visual data of the scientist—from magnifications of minute natural textures, from telescopic vistas, submarine scenery and X-ray photographs. Not that he undertakes to render a particular bacterial culture or pattern of refracted light. The shapes of his choice are recruited in good faith for their suggestiveness as shapes, and for their obscure correspondence to his inner state. But it is significant how often the morphology he finds analogous to his own sentient being is such as has revealed itself to human vision scientifically multiplied. It is apparently in these gestating images, shapes antecedent to the visible, that many abstract painters recognize an intenser mode of natural truth. On these uncharted realms of form they must impose aesthetic unity; from them they wrest new decorative principles—such as the "biomorphic" motif in modern ornament and applied design. Nature they imitate no less than did Masaccio. But where the Renaissance haᴅ turned to nature's display windows, and to the finished forms of man and beast, the men of our time descend into nature's laboratories.

But the affinity with science probably goes further still. It has been suggested that the very conceptions of twentieth-century science are finding expression in modern abstract art. The scientist's sense of pervasive physical activity in space, his intuition of immaterial functions, his awareness of the constant mutability of forms, of their indefinable location, their mutual interpenetration, their renewal and decay—all these have found a visual echo in contemporary art; Not because painters illustrate scientific concepts, but because an awareness of nature in its latest undisguise seems to be held in common by science and art.

The question is, of course, whether nature as the modern scientist conceives it can be represented at all, except in spectral mathematical equations. Philosophers of science concur in saying it cannot. Even such divergent thinkers as A. N. Whitehead and Bertrand Russell join hands when they declare that the abstractions of contemporary science have irrevocably passed beyond man's visual imagination. "Our understanding of nature has now reached a stage," says J. W. N. Sullivan, "when we cannot picture what we are talking about."

But this utterance of the philosophers contains an unwarranted assumption, to wit, that whereas man's capacity for intellectual abstraction is ever widening, his visual imagination is fixed and circumscribed. Here the philosophers are reckoning without the host, since our visualizing powers are determined for us not by them but by the men who paint. And this our visual imagination, thanks to those in whom it is creative, is also in perpetual growth, moving *pari passu* with the extension of thought.

Thus the art of the last half-century may well be schooling our eyes to live at ease with the new concepts forced upon our credulity by scientific reasoning. What we may be witnessing is the gradual condensation of abstract ideas into images that fall within the range of our sensory imagination. Modern painting inures us to the aspect of a world housing not discrete forms but trajectories and vectors, lines of tension and strain. Form in the sense of solid substance melts away and resolves itself into dynamic process. Instead of bodies powered by muscle, or by gravity, we get energy propagating itself in the void. If, to the scientist, solidity and simple location are illusions born of the grossness of our senses, they are so also to the modern painter. His canvases are fields of force; his shapes the transient aggregates of energies that seem impatient to be on their way. In the imagery of modern art waves of matter have usurped the place of tangible, visible things. And the perpetual form, whether in motion or at rest, is dispossessed by forms of transition.

The representation of the trajectory in art has its own history, like the representation of the visage of Christ. Emerging in certain Rembrandt drawings as a scribbled flourish in the wake of a volatile angel, it comes in the late work of Turner to invade painting itself. And in Brancusi's "Bird in Space" the path of motion at last claims the full sculptured dignity of mass. It is senseless to call such a work non-representational, for there is no ignoring here of nature. The trail of a projectile is, after all, as real as the object flung. And though it wants tangibility, it is as surely part of the natural world.

    .   .   .

It takes some effort to concede the heroic creativity of such envisionings. Granted that they do not depict what we normally see. But to call them "simply painting," as though they had no referent outside themselves, is to miss both their meaning and their continuity with the art of the past. If our suggestion is valid, then even non-objective art continues to pursue art's social role in fixating thought in aesthetic form, pinning down the most ethereal conceptions of the age in vitalized designs, and rendering them accessible to the apparatus of sense.

QUESTIONS

How does the conception of reality used by Steinberg differ from or resemble the one with which you are generally familiar?

Trilling speaks of those who conceive themselves "to be opposed to the genteel and the academic and in alliance with the vigorous and the actual." THE LIBERAL IMAGINATION 1 (1953). Is Steinberg one of these? Does it depend on the meaning which you give to the word "academic"? Consider to what extent the following excerpts from Bradley and Trilling exemplify and emphasize points made by Steinberg. Can you find points which are effectively new?

## A. C. BRADLEY

### SHAKESPEAREAN TRAGEDY *

.    .    .    . It is sometimes said that Hamlet's character is not only intricate but unintelligible. Now this statement might mean something quite unobjectionable and even perhaps true and important. It might mean that the character cannot be *wholly* understood. As we saw, there may be questions which we cannot answer with certainty now, because we have nothing but the text to guide us, but which never arose for the spectators who saw *Hamlet* acted in Shakespeare's day; and we shall have to refer to such questions in these lectures. Again, it may be held without any improbability that, from carelessness or because he was engaged on this play for several years, Shakespeare left inconsistencies in his exhibition of the character which must prevent us from being certain of his ultimate meaning. Or, possibly, we may be baffled because he has illustrated in it certain strange facts of human nature, which he had noticed but of which we are ignorant. But then all this would apply in some measure to other characters in Shakespeare, and it is not this that is meant by the statement that Hamlet is unintelligible. What is meant is that Shakespeare *intended* him to be so, because he himself was feeling strongly, and wished his audience to feel strongly, what a mystery life is, and how impossible it is for us to understand it. Now here, surely we have mere confusion of mind. The mysteriousness of life is one thing, the psychological unintelligibility of a dramatic character is quite another; and the second does not show the first, it shows only the incapacity or folly of the dramatist. If it did show the first, it would be very easy to surpass Shakespeare in producing a sense of mystery: We should simply have to portray an absolutely nonsensical character. Of course *Hamlet* appeals powerfully to our sense of the mystery of life, but so does *every* good tragedy; and it does so not because the hero is an enigma to us, but because, having a fair understanding of him, we feel how strange it is that strength and weakness should be so mingled in one soul, and that this soul should be doomed to such misery and apparent failure.

### QUESTIONS

What, according to Bradley, must an artist *not* do in order to make the state of confusion or chaos intelligible to us? What kind of a theory of reality must those people have who argue for the "psychological unintelligibility" of Hamlet's character? Can you speculate on how they might come up with such a theory?

* From 81–82 (Meridian ed. 1957).

LIONEL TRILLING

## A GATHERING OF FUGITIVES *

. . . . I had been, as people used to say, brought up on Dickens, or at least I had been brought up on the myth of being brought up on Dickens, and there seemed to me no possibility that so familial a figure could have any true virtue for an intelligent and advanced person . . . .

But the literary sophistication of one day is the literary obscurantism of the next. We have come to accept, and even to demand, degrees of intensity and distortion which, to refined minds, once seemed inadmissible. Our own advanced tastes have taught us how to read the work of Dickens that was naturally and easily accessible to the simplest reader of a hundred years ago. What Dostoievski learned from Dickens has revealed to us what Dickens had to teach. The young Henry James denounced *Our Mutual Friend* for Mrs. Wilfer's gloves and the psychological impossibilities of the story—it was necessary for him to reject what he thought to be Dickens's extravagances in order to make room for his own; but James's extravagances have in turn helped us in our acceptance of Dickens's. Indeed, there is scarcely a cherished modern text that does not instruct us in this way—we cannot read Kafka or Lawrence or Faulkner without learning a little better how to read Dickens.

. . . . our contemporary literature has had the effect of bringing to light, of developing as on a photographic film, our sense of the importance and profundity and accuracy of Dickens. In that last difficult matter of accuracy, events have played their part in settling the question in Dickens's favor. We who have seen Hitler, Goering, and Goebbels put on the stage of history, and Pecksniffery institutionalized in the Kremlin, are in no position to suppose that Dickens ever exaggerated in the least the extravagance of madness, absurdity, and malevolence in the world—or, conversely, when we consider the resistance to these qualities, the amount of goodness. "When people say Dickens exaggerates, it seems to me that they can have no eyes and ears. They probably have only *notions* of what things and people are"—thus, in justified irritation, Santayana: and who now, with the smallest experience of life, would fail to agree with him?

*LIONEL TRILLING*

## THE LIBERAL IMAGINATION *

Like any great artist of story, like Shakespeare or Balzac or Dickens or Dostoevski, James crowds probability rather closer than we nowadays like. It is not that he gives us unlikely events but that he sometimes thickens the number of interesting events beyond our ordinary expectation. If this, in James or in any storyteller, leads to a straining of our sense of verisimilitude, there is always the defense to be made that the special job of literature is, as Marianne Moore puts it, the creation of "imaginary gardens with real toads in them." The reader who detects that the garden is imaginary should not be led by his discovery to a wrong view of the reality of the toads. In settling questions of reality and truth in fiction, it must be remembered that, although the novel in certain of its forms resembles the accumulative and classificatory sciences, which are the sciences most people are most at home with, in certain other of its forms the novel approximates the sciences of experiment. And an experiment is very like an imaginary garden which is laid out for the express purpose of supporting a real toad of fact. The apparatus of the researcher's bench is not nature itself but an artificial and extravagant contrivance, much like a novelist's plot, which is devised to force or foster a fact into being. This seems to have been James's own view of the part that is played in his novels by what he calls "romance." He seems to have had an analogy with experiment very clearly in mind when he tells us that romance is "experience liberated, so to speak; experience disengaged, disembroiled, disencumbered, exempt from the conditions that usually attach to it." Again and again he speaks of the contrivance of a novel in ways which will make it seem like illegitimate flummery to the reader who is committed only to the premises of the naturalistic novel, but which the intelligent scientist will understand perfectly.

Certainly *The Princess Casamassima* would seem to need some such defense as this, for it takes us, we are likely to feel, very far along the road to romance, some will think to the very point of impossibility. It asks us to accept a poor young man whose birth is darkly secret, his father being a dissipated but authentic English lord, his mother a French courtesan-seamstress who murders the father; a beautiful American-Italian princess who descends in the social scale to help "the people"; a general mingling of the very poor with persons of exalted birth; and then a dim mysterious leader of revolution, never seen by the reader, the machinations of an underground group of conspirators, an oath taken to carry out an assassination at some unspecified future day, the day arriving, the hour of the killing set, the instructions and the pistol given.

---

* From 61–64 (Anchor ed. 1953). Originally published by The Macmillan Company in H. James, The Princess Casamassima xiii–xvii (1948). Copyright 1948 by The Macmillan Company and reprinted with its permission.

Confronted by paraphernalia like this, even those who admire the book are likely to agree with Rebecca West when, in her exuberant little study of James she tells us that it is "able" and "meticulous" but at the same time "distraught" and "wild," that the "loveliness" in it comes from a transmutation of its "perversities"; she speaks of it as a "mad dream" and teases its vast unlikelihood, finding it one of the big jokes in literature that it was James, who so prided himself on his lack of naivete, who should have brought back to fiction the high implausibility of the old novels which relied for their effects on dark and stormy nights, Hindu servants, mysterious strangers, and bloody swords wiped on richly embroidered handkerchiefs.

Miss West was writing in 1916, when the English naturalistic novel, with its low view of possibility, was in full pride. Our notion of political possibility was still to be changed by a small group of quarrelsome conspiratorial intellectuals taking over the control of Russia. Even a loyal Fabian at that time could consider it one of the perversities of *The Princess Casamassima* that two of its lower-class characters should say of a third that he had the potentiality of becoming Prime Minister of England; today Paul Muniment sits in the Cabinet and is on the way to Downing Street. In the thirties the book was much admired by those who read it in the light of knowledge of our own radical movements; it then used to be said that although James had dreamed up an impossible revolutionary group he had nonetheless managed to derive from it some notable insights into the temper of radicalism; these admirers grasped the toad of fact and felt that it was all the more remarkably there because the garden is so patently imaginary.

Yet an understanding of James's use of "romance"—and there is "romance" in Hyacinth's story—must not preclude our understanding of the striking literal accuracy of *The Princess Casamassima*. James himself helped to throw us off the scent when in his preface to the novel he told us that he made no research into Hyacinth's subterranean politics. He justified this by saying that "the value I wished most to render and the effect I wished most to produce were precisely those of our not knowing, of society's not knowing, but only guessing and suspecting and trying to ignore, what 'goes on' irreconcilably, subversively, beneath the vast smug surface." And he concludes the preface with the most beautifully arrogant and truest thing a novelist ever said about his craft: "What it all came back to was, no doubt, something like *this* wisdom—that if you haven't, for fiction, the root of the matter in you, haven't the sense of life and the penetrating imagination, you are a fool in the very presence of the revealed and assured; but that if you *are* so armed, you are not really helpless, not without your resource, even before mysteries abysmal." If, to learn about the radical movement of his time, James really did no more than consult his penetrating imagination—which no doubt was nourished like any other on conversation and the daily newspaper—then we must say that in no other novelist did the root of the matter go so deep and so wide. For the truth is that there is not a political event of *The Princess Casamassima,* not a detail of oath or mystery or danger, which is not confirmed by multitudinous records.

NOTES AND QUESTIONS

Noam Chomsky reports that "Viktor Shklovskij in the early 1920's developed the idea that the function of poetic art is that of 'making strange' the object depicted." The most familiar forms of experience, according to Shklovskij, tend to fall below the limen of notice; to bring them to our attention they must be deprived of their quality of familiarity. LANGUAGE AND MIND 21 (1968). Can you relate this point to that of the "imaginary gardens with real toads in them"? Does one make an object more or less "real" by making it strange? What is the meaning of "real" that you are using to answer the question? In what sense could it be said that we understand best those things which are most familiar to us? In what sense could it be said that we understand these things less than others?

*CHARLES DICKENS*

HARD TIMES *

"Now, what I want is, Facts. Teach these boys and girls nothing but Facts. Facts alone are wanted in life. Plant nothing else, and root out everything else. You can only form the minds of reasoning animals upon Facts: nothing else will ever be of any service to them. This is the principle on which I bring up my own children, and this is the principle on which I bring up these children. Stick to Facts, Sir!"

The scene was a plain, bare, monotonous vault of a schoolroom, and the speaker's square forefinger emphasized his observations by underscoring every sentence with a line on the schoolmaster's sleeve. The emphasis was helped by the speaker's square wall of a forehead, which had his eyebrows for its base, while his eyes found commodious cellarage in two dark caves, overshadowed by the wall. The emphasis was helped by the speaker's mouth, which was wide, thin, and hard set. The emphasis was helped by the speaker's voice, which was inflexible, dry, and dictatorial. The emphasis was helped by the speaker's hair, which bristled on the skirts of his bald head, a plantation of firs to keep the wind from its shining surface, all covered with knobs, like the crust of a plum pie, as if the head had scarcely warehouse-room for the hard facts stored inside. The speaker's obstinate carriage, square coat, square legs, square shoulders,—nay, his very neckcloth, trained to take him by the throat with an unaccommodating grasp, like a stubborn fact, as is was,—all helped the emphasis.

"In this life, we want nothing but Facts, Sir; nothing but Facts!"

The speaker, and the schoolmaster, and the third grown person present, all backed a little, and swept with their eyes the inclined plane of little vessels then and there arranged in order, ready to have

---

* From 3–10 (1965 ed).

imperial gallons of facts poured into them until they were full to the brim.

. . .

Thomas Gradgrind, Sir. A man of realities. A man of facts and calculations. A man who proceeds upon the principle that two and two are four, and nothing over, and who is not to be talked into allowing for anything over. Thomas Gradgrind, Sir—peremptorily Thomas —Thomas Gradgrind. With a rule and a pair of scales, and the multiplication table always in his pocket, Sir, ready to tell you exactly what it comes to. It is a mere question of figures, a case of simple arithmetic. You might hope to get some other nonsensical belief into the head of George Gradgrind, or Augustus Gradgrind, or John Gradgrind, or Joseph Gradgrind (all supposititious, non-existent persons), but into the head of Thomas Gradgrind—no, Sir!

In such terms Mr. Gradgrind always mentally introduced himself, whether to his private circle of acquaintance, or to the public in general. In such terms, no doubt, substituting the words "boys and girls," for "Sir," Thomas Gradgrind now presented Thomas Gradgrind to the little pitchers before him, who were to be filled so full of facts.

Indeed, as he eagerly sparkled at them from the cellerage before mentioned, he seemed a kind of cannon loaded to the muzzle with facts, and prepared to blow them clean out of the regions of childhood at one discharge. He seemed a galvanizing apparatus, too, charged with a grim mechanical substitute for the tender young imaginations that were to be stormed away.

"Girl number twenty," said Mr. Gradgrind, squarely pointing with his square forefinger, "I don't know that girl. Who is that girl?"

"Sissy Jupe, Sir," explained number twenty, blushing, standing up, and curtseying.

"Sissy is not a name," said Mr. Gradgrind. "Don't call yourself Sissy. Call yourself Cecilia."

"It's father as calls me Sissy, Sir," returned the young girl in a trembling voice, and with another curtsey.

"Then he has no business to do it," said Mr. Gradgrind. "Tell him he mustn't. Cecilia Jupe. Let me see. What is your father?"

"He belongs to the horse-riding, if you please, Sir."

Mr. Gradgrind frowned, and waved off the objectionable calling with his hand.

"We don't want to know anything about that, here. You mustn't tell us about that, here. Your father breaks horses, don't he?"

"If you please, Sir, when they can get any to break, they do break horses in the ring, Sir."

"You 'mustn't tell us about the ring, here. Very well, then. Describe your father as a horsebreaker. He doctors sick horses, I dare say?"

"Oh yes, Sir."

"Very well, then. He is a veterinary surgeon, a farrier, and horsebreaker. Give me your definition of a horse."

(Sissy Jupe thrown into the greatest alarm by this demand.)

"Girl number twenty unable to define a horse!" said Mr. Gradgrind, for the general behoof of all the little pitchers. "Girl number twenty possessed of no facts, in reference to one of the commonest of animals! Some boy's definition of a horse. Bitzer, yours."

The square finger, moving here and there, lighted suddenly on Bitzer, perhaps because he chanced to sit in the same ray of sunlight which, darting in at one of the bare windows of the intensely whitewashed room, irradiated Sissy. For, the boys and girls sat on the face of the inclined plane in two compact bodies, divided up the centre by a narrow interval; and Sissy, being at the corner of a row on the sunny side, came in for the beginning of a sunbeam, of which Bitzer, being at the corner of a row on the other side, a few rows in advance, caught the end. But, whereas the girl was so dark-eyed and dark-haired, that she seemed to receive a deeper and more lustrous colour from the sun, when it shone upon her, the boy was so light-eyed and lighted-haired that the self-same rays appeared to draw out of him what little colour he ever possessed. His cold eyes would hardly have been eyes, but for the short ends of lashes which, by bringing them into immediate contrast with something paler than themselves, expressed their form. His short-cropped hair might have been a mere continuation of the sandy freckles on his forehead and face. His skin was so unwholesomely deficient in the natural tinge, that he looked as though, if he were cut, he would bleed white.

"Bitzer," said Thomas Gradgrind. "Your definition of a horse."

"Quadruped. Graminivorous. Forty teeth, namely, twenty-four grinders, four eye-teeth, and twelve incisive. Sheds coat in the spring; in marshy countries, sheds hoofs, too. Hoofs hard, but requiring to be shod with iron. Age known by marks in mouth." Thus (and much more) Bitzer.

"Now girl number twenty," said Mr. Gradgrind. "You know what a horse is."

She curtseyed again, and would have blushed deeper, if she could have blushed deeper than she had blushed all this time. Bitzer, after rapidly blinking at Thomas Gradgrind with both eyes at once, and so catching the light upon his quivering ends of lashes that they looked like the antennae of busy insects, put his knuckles to his freckled forehead, and sat down again.

The third gentleman now stepped forth. A mighty man at cutting and drying, he was; a government officer; in his way (and in most other people's too), a professed pugilist; always in training, always with a system to force down the general throat like a bolus, always to be heard of at the bar of his little Public-office, ready to fight all England. To continue in fistic phraseology, he had a genius for coming up to the scratch, wherever and whatever it was, and proving himself an ugly customer. He would go in and damage any subject whatever with his right, follow up with his left, stop, exchange, counter, bore his opponent (he always fought All England) to the ropes, and fall upon him neatly. He was certain to knock the wind out of common sense, and render that unlucky adversary deaf to the call of time. And he had it in charge from high authority to bring about the great public-office Millennium, when Commissioners should reign upon earth.

"Very well," said this gentleman, briskly smiling, and folding his arms. "What's a horse. Now let me ask you girls and boys, Would you paper a room with representations of horses?"

After a pause, one half of the children cried in chorus, "Yes, Sir!" Upon which the other half, seeing in the gentleman's face that Yes was wrong, cried out in chorus, "No, Sir!"—as the custom is, in these examinations.

"Of course, No. Why wouldn't you?"

A pause. One corpulent slow boy, with a wheezy manner of breathing, ventured the answer, Because he wouldn't paper a room at all, but would paint it.

"You *must* paper it," said the gentleman, rather warmly.

"You must paper it," said Thomas Gradgrind, "whether you like it or not. Don't tell *us* you wouldn't paper it. What do you mean, boy?"

"I'll explain to you, then," said the gentleman, after another and a dismal pause, "why you wouldn't paper a room with representations of horses. Do you ever see horses walking up and down the sides of rooms in reality—in fact? Do you?"

"Yes, Sir!" from one half. "No, Sir!" from the other.

"Of course, No," said the gentleman, with an indignant look at the wrong half. "Why, then, you are not to see anywhere, what you don't see in fact; you are not to have anywhere, what you don't have in fact. What is called Taste, is only another name for Fact."

Thomas Gradgrind nodded his approbation.

"This is a new principle, a discovery, a great discovery," said the gentleman. "Now, I'll try you again. Suppose you were going to carpet a room. Would you use a carpet having a representation of flowers upon it?"

There being a general conviction by this time that "No, Sir!" was always the right answer to this gentleman, the chorus of No was very strong. Only a few feeble stragglers said Yes: among them Sissy Jupe.

"Girl number twenty," said the gentleman, smiling in the calm strength of knowledge.

Sissy blushed, and stood up.

"So you would carpet your room—or your husband's room, if you were a grown woman, and had a husband—with representations of flowers, would you?" Said the gentleman. "Why would you?"

"If you please, Sir, I am very fond of flowers," returned the girl.

"And is that why you would put tables and chairs upon them, and have people walking over them with heavy boots?"

"It wouldn't hurt them, Sir. They wouldn't crush and wither, if you please, Sir. They would be the pictures of what was very pretty and pleasant, and I would fancy—"

"Ay, ay, ay! But you mustn't fancy," cried the gentleman, quite elated by coming so happily to his point. "That's it! You are never to fancy."

"You are not, Cecilia Jupe," Thomas Gradgrind solemnly repeated, "to do anything of that kind."

"Fact, fact, fact!" said the gentleman. And "Fact, fact, fact!" repeated Thomas Gradgrind.

"You are to be in all things regulated and governed," said the gentleman, "by fact. We hope to have, before long, a board of fact, composed of commissioners of fact, who will force the people to be a people of fact, and of nothing but fact. You must discard the word Fancy altogether. You have nothing to do with it. You are not to have, in any object of use or ornament, what would be a contradiction in fact. You don't walk upon flowers in fact; you cannot be allowed to walk upon flowers in carpets. You don't find that foreign birds and butterflies come and perch upon your crockery; you cannot be permitted to paint foreign birds and butterflies upon your crockery. You never meet with quadrupeds going up and down walls; you must not have quadrupeds represented upon walls. You must use," said the gentleman, "for all these purposes, combinations and modification (in primary colors) of mathematical figures which are susceptible of proof and demonstration. This is the new discovery. This is fact. This is taste."

The girl curtseyed, and sat down. She was very young, and she looked as if she were frightened by the matter-of-fact prospect the world afforded.

"Now, if Mr. M'Choakumchild," said the gentleman, "will proceed to give his first lesson here, Mr. Gradgrind, I shall be happy, at your request, to observe his mode of procedure."

Mr. Gradgrind was much obliged. "Mr. M'Choakumchild, we only wait for you."

So, Mr. M'Choakumchild began in his best manner. He and some one hundred and forty other schoolmasters, had been lately turned at the same time, in the same factory, on the same principles, like so many pianoforte legs. He had been put through an immense variety of paces, and had answered volumes of head-breaking questions. Orthography, etymology, syntax, and prosody, biography, astronomy, geography, and general cosmography, the sciences of compound proportion, algebra, land-surveying and levelling, vocal music, and drawing from models, were all at the ends of his ten chilled fingers. He had worked his stony way into Her Majesty's most Honourable Privy Council's Schedule B, and had taken the bloom off the higher branches of mathematics and physical science, French, German, Latin, and Greek. He knew all about all the Water Sheds of all the world (whatever they are), and all the histories of all the peoples, and all the names of all the rivers and mountains, and all the productions, manners, and customs of all the countries, and all their boundaries and bearings on the two-and-thirty points of the compass. Ah, rather overdone, M'Choakumchild. If he had only learnt a little less, how infinitely better he might have taught much more!

He went to work in this preparatory lesson, not unlike Morgiana in the Forty Thieves: looking into all the vessels ranged before him, one after another, to see what they contained. Say, good M'Choakumchild. When from thy boiling store, thou shalt fill each jar brim full by-and-by, dost thou think that thou wilt always kill outright the robber Fancy lurking within—or sometimes only maim him and distort him!

## QUESTIONS

Are you prepared to agree with Trilling that Dickens did not exaggerate? Compare the reasoning of the instructors in that passage with the reasoning criticized by Bradley just above? Pay special attention to the injunctions against papering and carpeting with representations of flowers and horses.

To what extent can Dickens be justified under the theory of the real toad in the imaginary garden?

## JOHN STUART MILL

### ON LIBERTY *

There is something both contemptible and frightful in the sort of evidence on which, of late years, any person can be judicially declared unfit for the management of his affairs; and after his death, his disposal of his property can be set aside if there is enough of it to pay the expenses of litigation—which are charged on the property itself. All the minute details of his daily life are pried into, and whatever is found which, seen through the medium of the perceiving and describing faculties of the lowest of the low, bears an appearance unlike absolute commonplace, is laid before the jury as evidence of insanity, and often with success; the jurors being little, if at all, less vulgar and ignorant than the witnesses, while the judges, with that extraordinary want of knowledge of human nature and life which continually astonishes us in English lawyers, often help to mislead them. These trials speak volumes as to the state of feeling and opinion among the vulgar with regard to human liberty. So far from setting any value on individuality—so far from respecting the right of each individual to act, in things indifferent, as seems good to his own judgment and inclinations, judges and juries cannot even conceive that a person in a state of sanity can desire such freedom. In former days, when it was proposed to burn atheists, charitable people used to suggest putting them in a madhouse instead; it would be nothing surprising nowadays were we to see this done, and the doers applauding themselves because, instead of persecuting for religion, they

---

* From 83–84 n. 3 (Liberal Arts Press ed. 1956).

had adopted so humane and Christian a mode of treating these unfortunates, not without a silent satisfaction at their having thereby obtained their deserts.

## Questions

In what terms might the other writers quoted above have criticized the practice which Mill describes? Does Mill provoke in you any thoughts about the relation of reality to liberty?

*

## PART FIVE

# A MEANINGFUL LIFE
# AND THE SOCIAL ORDER

### INTRODUCTORY NOTE

The problem of working out a viable form of social organization is one that people have been facing ever since men first bonded into groups. But the group that must be brought together is getting larger and more unruly; the technological problems more desperate than promising; and the risks, should the social organization fail, higher—perhaps final.

Force and the threat of force can contribute to a social order of sorts. But force by itself—unmitigated by principle—has never worked as a way of organizing people, whether it were the force of "each man for himself" or the crushing force that the state can monopolize. Indeed, what is more striking, there probably never has been a society in which it was even *tried*, in which people did not arbitrate their capacities for violence with some rituals and customs and senses of value. As Lorenz points out, the "law of the jungle" apparently does not prevail even in the jungle. Nor have internalized unconscious controls—senses of guilt, shame, etc.—ever been adequate, by themselves, to hold a society together. We have always had, between force and the unconscious, a margin for reasoning— for questioning whether a rule of conduct be "just" and "right," for consciously debating whether we ought to do some act or not, for allowing ourselves the sense of a freedom "to be or not to be" what we choose.

One of the critical problems of the age we are entering, however, is that both extremes—control by sheer threat and control by manipulation of the unconscious—are now possibilities as never before. Not long ago they were both but visions of fiction—George Orwell's *1984*, and Aldous Huxley's *Brave New World*. But the technology of genetic engineering, drugs, brain stimulators, and super-sensitive eavesdropping equipment is bringing either of them—and certainly both of them jointly—well within reach. What room will there be, in the new era we are entering, for reason and the margin of freedom that it seems to allow? What room should there be? Reason involves patience, trust, the obtaining of consent, the willingness to tolerate and even to promote differences as a way of working out solutions. But the difficulties the world is facing—the urgency of the "ends"—is going to cause impatience and rising demands for order of any sort, whatever the "means". And people will certainly ask, What is reason, anyway? Is not the freedom that we feel it to allow us but an illusion, born of our ignorance of the real springs of our actions? Why, if we have the technology to do otherwise, and given the rising crises of our civilization, should we allow people the luxury of the illusion, to let them argue about whether it is "right" to obey some law or other social rule?

## CHAPTER SIXTEEN

# One's Obligation to One's Self—And Others

APPLICATION OF THE PRESIDENT AND DIRECTORS OF
GEORGETOWN COLLEGE, INC.

331 F.2d 1000 (D.C.Cir. 1964)

### J. SKELLY WRIGHT, Circuit Judge.

Attorneys for Georgetown Hospital applied for an emergency writ at 4:00 P.M., September 17, 1963, seeking relief from the action of the United States District Court for the District of Columbia denying the hospital's application for permission to administer blood transfusions to an emergency patient. The application recited that "Mrs. Jesse E. Jones is presently a patient at Georgetown University Hospital," "she is in extremis," according to the attending physician "blood transfusions are necessary immediately in order to save her life," and "consent to the administration thereof can be obtained neither from the patient nor her husband." The patient and her husband based their refusal on their religious beliefs as Jehovah's Witnesses. The order sought provided that the attending physicians "may" administer such transfusions to Mrs. Jones as might be "necessary to save her life." After the proceedings detailed in Part IV of this opinion, I signed the order at 5:20 P.M.

## I

Initially, it may be well to put this matter into fuller legal context, including "the nature of the controversy, the relation and interests of the parties, and the relief sought in the instant case." The application was in the nature of a petition in equity to the United States District Court for the District of Columbia, a court of general jurisdiction. Though not fully articulated therein, the application sought a decree in the nature of an injunction and declaratory judgment to determine the legal rights and liabilities between the hospital and its agents on the one hand, and Mrs. Jones and her husband on the other. Mrs. Jones subsequently appeared in the cause, in this court, as respondent to the application. The treatment proposed by the hospital in its application was not a single transfusion, but a series of transfusions. The hospital doctors sought a court determination before undertaking either this course of action or some alternative. The temporary order issued was more limited than the order proposed in the original application, in that the phrase "to save her life" was added, thus limiting the transfusions in both time and number. Such a temporary order to preserve the life of the patient was necessary if the cause were not to be mooted by the death of the patient.

. . . .

Clearly the "case or controversy" raised here is "justiciable," that is, of the type that courts may be called upon to decide. See Baker v. Carr, *supra* Note 2, 369 U.S. at 198.

. . . .

## IV

Let us now reconstruct the narrative of events through the medium of the contemporaneous Memorandum of Facts filed in this cause, the substance of which is as follows:

Mrs. Jones was brought to the hospital by her husband for emergency care, having lost two thirds of her body's blood supply from a ruptured ulcer. She had no personal physician, and relied solely on the hospital staff. She was a total hospital responsibility. It appeared that the patient, age 25, mother of a seven-month-old child, and her husband were both Jehovah's Witnesses, the teachings of which sect, according to their interpretation, prohibited the injection of blood into the body. When death without blood became imminent, the hospital sought the advice of counsel, who applied to the District Court in the name of the hospital for permission to administer blood. Judge Tamm of the District Court denied the application, and counsel immediately applied to me, as a member of the Court of Appeals, for an appropriate writ.

I called the hospital by telephone and spoke with Dr. Westura, Chief Medical Resident, who confirmed the representations made by counsel. I thereupon proceeded with counsel to the hospital, where I spoke to Mr. Jones, the husband of the patient. He advised me that, on religious grounds, he would not approve a blood transfusion for his wife. He said, however, that if the court ordered the transfusion, the responsibility was not his. I advised Mr. Jones to obtain counsel immediately. He thereupon went to the telephone and returned in 10 or 15 minutes to advise that he had taken the matter up with his church and that he had decided that he did not want counsel.

I asked permission of Mr. Jones to see his wife. This he readily granted. Prior to going into the patient's room, I again conferred with Dr. Westura and several other doctors assigned to the case. All confirmed that the patient would die without blood and that there was a better than 50 per cent chance of saving her life with it. Unanimously they strongly recommended it. I then went inside the patient's room. Her appearance confirmed the urgency which had been represented to me. I tried to communicate with her, advising her again as to what the doctors had said. The only audible reply I could hear was "Against my will." It was obvious that the woman was not in a mental condition to make a decision. I was reluctant to press her because of the seriousness of her condition and because I felt that to suggest repeatedly the imminence of death without blood might place a strain on her religious convictions. I asked her whether she would oppose the blood transfusion if the court allowed it. She indicated as best I could make out, that it would not then be her responsibility.

I returned to the doctors' room where some 10 to 12 doctors were congregated, along with the husband and counsel for the hospital. The President of Georgetown University, Father Bunn, appeared and pleaded with Mr. Jones to authorize the hospital to save his wife's life with blood transfusion. Mr. Jones replied that the Scriptures say that we should not drink blood, and consequently his religion prohibited transfusions. The doctors explained to Mr. Jones that a blood transfusion is totally different from drinking blood in that the blood physically goes into a different part and through a different process in the body. Mr. Jones was unmoved. I thereupon signed the order allowing the hospital to administer such transfusions as the doctors should determine were necessary to save her life.

V

This opinion is being written solely in connection with the emergency order authorizing the blood transfusions "to save her life." It should be made clear that no attempt is being made here to determine the merits of the underlying controversy. Actually, the issue on the merits is *res nova*. Because of the demonstrated imminence of death from loss of blood, signing the order was necessary to maintain the *status quo* and prevent the issue respecting the rights of the parties in the premises from becoming moot before full consideration was possible. But maintaining the *status quo* is not the only consideration in determining whether an emergency writ should issue. The likelihood of eventual success on appeal is of primary importance, and thus must be here considered.

Before proceeding with this inquiry, it may be useful to state what this case does not involve. This case does not involve a person who, for religious or other reasons, has refused to seek medical attention. It does not involve a disputed medical judgment or a dangerous or crippling operation. Nor does it involve the delicate question of saving the newborn in preference to the mother. Mrs. Jones sought medical attention and placed on the hospital the legal responsibility for her proper care. In its dilemma, not of its own making, the hospital sought judicial direction.

It has been firmly established that the courts can order compulsory medical treatment of children for any serious illness or injury. . . .

 . . . And if, as shown above, a parent has no power to forbid the saving of his child's life, *a fortiori* the husband of the patient here had no right to order the doctors to treat his wife in a way so that she would die.

The child cases point up another consideration. The patient, 25 years old, was the mother of a seven-month-old child. The state, as *parens patriae*, will not allow a parent to abandon a child, and so it should not allow this most ultimate of voluntary abandonments. The patient had a responsibility to the community to care for her infant. Thus the people had an interest in preserving the life of this mother.

Apart from the child cases, a second range of factors may be considered. It is suggested that an individual's liberty to control himself and his life extends even to the liberty to end his life. Thus, "in those states where attempted suicide has been made lawful by statute (or the lack of one), the refusal of necessary medical aid [to one's self], whether equal to or less than attempted suicide, must be conceded to be lawful." Cawley, Criminal Liability in Faith Healing, 39 Minn.L.Rev. 48, 68 (1954). And, conversely, it would follow that where attempted suicide is illegal by the common law or by statute, a person may not be allowed to refuse necessary medical assistance when death is likely to ensue without it.  Only quibbles about the distinction between misfeasance and non-feasance, or the specific intent necessary to be guilty of attempted suicide, could be raised against this latter conclusion.

If self-homicide is a crime, there is no exception to the law's command for those who believe the crime to be divinely ordained  .  .  . But whether attempted suicide is a crime is in doubt in some jurisdictions, including the District of Columbia.

The Gordian knot of this suicide question may be cut by the simple fact that Mrs. Jones did not want to die.  Her voluntary presence in the hospital as a patient seeking medical help testified to this. Death, to Mrs. Jones, was not a religiously-commanded goal, but an unwanted side effect of a religious scruple.  There is no question here of interfering with one whose religious convictions counsel his death, like the Buddhist monks who set themselves afire.  Nor are we faced with the question of whether the state should intervene to reweigh the relative values of life and death, after the individual has weighed them for himself and found life wanting.  Mrs. Jones wanted to live.

A third set of considerations involved the position of the doctors and the hospital.  Mrs. Jones was their responsibility to treat.  The hospital doctors had the choice of administering the proper treatment or letting Mrs. Jones die in the hospital bed, thus exposing themselves, and the hospital, to the risk of civil and criminal liability in either case.  It is not certain that Mrs. Jones had any authority to put the hospital and its doctors to this impossible choice.  The normal principle that an adult patient directs her doctors is based on notions of commercial contract which may have less relevance to life-or-death emergencies.  It is not clear just where a patient would derive her authority to command her doctor to treat her under limitations which would produce death.  The patient's counsel suggests that this authority is part of constitutionally protected liberty.  But neither the principle that life and liberty are inalienable rights, nor the principle of liberty of religion, provides an easy answer to the question whether the state can prevent martyrdom.  Moreover, Mrs. Jones had no wish to be a martyr.  And her religion merely prevented her consent to a transfusion.  If the law undertook the responsibility of authorizing the transfusion without her consent, no problem would be raised with respect to her religious practice.  Thus, the effect of the order was to preserve for Mrs. Jones the life she wanted without sacrifice of her religious beliefs.

The final, and compelling, reason for granting the emergency writ was that a life hung in the balance.  There was no time for research and reflection.  Death could have mooted the cause in a matter of minutes, if action were not taken to preserve the *status quo*.  To refuse to act, only to find later that the law required action, was a risk I was unwilling to accept.  I determined to act on the side of life.

BURGER, Circuit Judge.  (331 F.2d at 1015)

I believe we should dismiss the petition for rehearing en banc for want of a justiciable controversy, as Judge Danaher does, rather than merely deny it.

This episode presents on the one hand an example of a grave dilemma which confronts those who engage in the healing arts and on the other hand some very basic and fundamental issues on the nature and scope of judicial power. We can sympathize with the one but we cannot safely or appropriately temporize with the other; we have an obligation to deal with the basic question whether any judicially cognizable issue is presented when a legally competent adult refuses, on grounds of conscience, to consent to a medical treatment essential to preserve life. At the outset I would assume that we cannot make a judicial appraisal of justiciability on the basis of any consequences attributable to the order issued in the name of this court. The end, desirable as it obviously developed, cannot establish the existence of a case or controversy if such did not exist independent of the sequel to the enforced medical treatment.

"The touchstone to justiciability is injury to a legally protected right * *." . . . The threshold issue, therefore, is whether the hospital had a right which it was entitled to require the court to enforce. It is not always easy to separate the concepts of standing of a party and justiciability of an issue; the two tend to blend and merge at times. But it would seem beyond challenge that the party seeking relief has the burden of showing affirmatively a legally protected right which is invaded or is about to be invaded by an opposing party.

What, then, is the legally enforceable "right" of the hospital in this context?

We can assume first that a hospital, like a doctor, has certain responsibilities and duties toward a person who, by choice or emergency, comes under its care. No affirmative act of the patient is suggested as invading or threatening any right of the hospital. So we must decide whether an "invasion" of legal right can be spelled out of a relationship between the patient's refusal to accept a standard medical treatment thought necessary to preserve life and the possible consequences to the hospital if, relying on her refusal to consent, it fails to give a transfusion and death or injury follows. The possible economic impact, apart from the moral implications inherent in its responsibilities, perhaps presented an arguable basis for the hospital's claim of protected economic right. It stood in an unenviable "Good Samaritan" posture when the patient categorically refused to consent to a blood transfusion called for by a medical emergency. The choice between violating the patient's convictions of conscience and accepting her decision was hardly an easy one.

However, since it is not disputed that the patient and her husband volunteered to sign a waiver to relieve the hospital of any liability for the consequences of failure to effect the transfusion, any claim to a protected right in the economic damage sphere would appear unsupported.

Can a legally protected right arise out of some other duty-right of the hospital toward a patient, such as a moral obligation to preserve life at all costs?

For me it is difficult to construct an actionable or legally protected right out of this relationship. The affirmative enforcement of a right growing out of a possible moral duty of the hospital toward a patient does not seem to meet the standards of justiciability especially when the only remedy is judicial compulsion touching the sensitive area of conscience and religious belief.

. . . .

Mr. Justice Brandeis, whose views have inspired much of the "right to be let alone" philosophy, said in Olmstead v. United States, 277 U.S. 438, 478, 48 S.Ct. 564, 572, 72 L.Ed. 944 (1928), (dissenting opinion):

> "The makers of our Constitution * * * sought to protect Americans in their beliefs, their thoughts, their emotions and their sensations. They conferred, as against the Government, the right to be let alone—the most comprehensive of rights and the right most valued by civilized man."

Nothing in this utterance suggests that Justice Brandeis thought an individual possessed these rights only as to *sensible* beliefs, *valid* thoughts, *reasonable* emotions, or *well-founded* sensations. I suggest he intended to include a great many foolish, unreasonable and even absurd ideas which do not conform, such as refusing medical treatment even at great risk.

That judicial power is narrow and limited is a concept deeply embedded in our System. Thus the need for external restraints on the powers of Federal Judges was plainly an important corollary to their constitutionally secured tenure. It was quite as clear in the 1780's as it is today that men are not notorious for exercising self-restraint when they possess both permanent tenure *and* plenary power. Under our System no single Branch of Government has both, and no single Branch of Government could safely be entrusted with both.

Confronted by a unique episode such as this, it seems to me we must inquire where an assumption of jurisdiction over such matters could lead us. Physicians, surgeons and hospitals—and others as well—are often confronted with seemingly irreconcilable demands and conflicting pressures. Philosophers and theologians have pondered these problems and different religious groups have evolved different solutions; the solutions and doctrines of one group are sometimes not acceptable to other groups or sects. Various examples readily come to mind: a crisis in childbirth may require someone to decide whether the life of the mother or the child shall be sacrificed; absent a timely and decisive choice both may die. May the physician or hospital require the courts to decide? A patient may be in a critical condition requiring, in the minds of experts, a certain medical or surgical procedure. If the patient has objections to that treatment based on religious conviction, or if he rejects the medical opinion, are the courts empowered to decide for him?

Some of our greatest jurists have emphasized the need for judicial awareness of the limits on judicial power which is simply an acknowledgement of human fallibility.

. . . .

. . . [T]here are myriads of problems and troubles which judges are powerless to solve; and this is as it should be. Some matters of essentially private concern and others of enormous public concern, are beyond the reach of judges. Cf. Pauling v. McNamara, supra.

I am authorized to state that WILBUR K. MILLER and BASTIAN, Circuit Judges, join in the above views.

### NOTES AND QUESTIONS

1. Why, basically, do you suppose Judge Wright decided the way he did? How influenced do you suppose he was by his estimate that the Joneses' allowing her to die would be "immoral"? How far ought the law to go in shaping individual choice on the basis of society's collective—or some judge's individual—ideas of what is moral?

2. Do you think Mrs. Jones was morally wrong in not asking for a transfusion? If so, why? What features of the situation militate for and against the "immorality" of her act, (*e. g.*, that she had a child, that most people in our society look disapprovingly on suicide)? What theories of morality support and condemn her actions? How in these terms would you weigh the actions of (a) her husband; (b) the hospital officials; (c) Judge Wright?

3. Is the legal system, in this case, taking away Mrs. Jones' freedom—or securing her freedom? Did the law allow her to decide for herself what reasons are worth living for and what reasons are worth dying for? Ought the law to have allowed her this choice?

4. How significant would it be to you, in deciding the case, that apparently Mrs. Jones's position arose out of religious convictions? Would your analysis change if she had refused a transfusion because she was "tired of living"? Would your analysis change if you were convinced that Mrs. Jones had been in shape well enough to discuss her choice rationally with Judge Wright? If so, why, and in what way? How would you have decided whether she was or was not being "rational"?

5. Why does Judge Wright take the position that Mrs. Jones did not want to die? What evidence did he have—each way?

According to Karen, *Suicidal Tendency as the Wish to Hurt Someone Else*, 20 Jour. of Individual Psychology 206 (1964), studies of attempted suicide patients show their actions can best be understood as attempts to carry out an aggressive retaliatory act toward significant figures in their present life or towards fantasies of significant figures in their past. The typical patient's primary fantasy was to make others feel guilty or sorry. Might such an intent have been the "real" aim of Mrs. Jones? See the July 1968 Bulletin of Suicidology (Washington: Government Printing Office). What might the "real" intentions of her husband have been? What difference should different intentions make—in morals? In the way in which the law responds?

In John F. Kennedy Memorial Hospital v. Heston, 40 L.W. 2050 (N.J.Sup.Ct. August 13, 1971), the court held that a Jehovah's Witness, injured in an automobile accident, could be compelled to submit to blood transfusions necessary to save her life. Chief Judge Weintraub wrote:

> Complicating the subject of suicide is the difficulty of knowing whether a decision to die is firmly held. Psychiatrists may find that beneath it all a person bent on self-destruction is hoping to be rescued, and most who are rescued do not repeat the attempt, at least not at once. Then, too, there is the question whether in any event the person was and continues to be competent (a difficult concept in this area) to choose to die. And of course there is no opportunity for a trial of these questions in advance of intervention by the State or a citizen.
>
> [The patient] suggests there is a difference between passively submitting to death and actively seeking it. * * If the State may interrupt one mode of self-destruction, it may with equal authority interfere with the other. It is arguably different when an individual, overtaken by illness, decides to let it run a fatal course. But unless the medical option itself is laden with the risk of death or of serious infirmity, the State's interest in sustaining life in such circumstances is hardly distinguishable from its interest in the case of suicide.

6. Compare the situation in this case with a situation in which a doctor with highly developed skills decides to "drop out" of his practice and live on hallucinogenic drugs. In which case can the stronger argument be made that a man ought to subordinate his view of how he ought to live for the needs of the community and its view of how he ought to live? In which case can the stronger argument be made for legal sanction as a "back-up" for moral persuasion?

7. Do you think Judge (now Chief Justice) Burger would have come out differently had the patient been a skilled surgeon? a high government official? Does Judge Burger's reading of Olmstead's "right to be let alone" entail the law's staying clear of homosexual acts among consenting partners? the smoking of marijuana? reading pornography in one's own home? How can the various situations be distinguished?

8. In a case decided a year after Georgetown, the Illinois Supreme Court refused to appoint a conservator for a Jehovah's Witness who refused transfusions; one distinction the Illinois court raised was that the lady involved there had no children. In re Estate of Brooks, 32 Ill.2d 361, 205 N.E.2d 435 (1965). Why should the presence or absence of children make a difference?

*IMMANUAL KANT*

## DUTIES TO ONESELF *

We have dealt at length with questions appertaining to natural religion, and we now proceed to deal similarly with essential morality and with our proper duties towards everything in the world. First amongst these duties is the duty we owe to our own selves.

My duty towards myself cannot be treated juridically; the law touches only our relations with other men; I have no legal obligations towards myself; and whatever I do to myself I do to a consenting party; I cannot commit an act of injustice against myself. What we have to discuss is the use we make of liberty in respect of ourselves. By way of introduction it is to be noted that there is no question in moral philosophy which has received more defective treatment than that of the individual's duty towards himself. No one has framed a proper concept of self-regarding duty. It has been regarded as a detail and considered by way of an afterthought, as an appendix to moral philosophy, on the view that man should give a thought to himself only after he has completely fulfilled his duty towards others. All moral philosophies err in this respect. . . . The reason for all this is the want of a pure concept, which should form the basis of a self-regarding duty. It was taken for granted that a man's duty towards himself consisted . . . in promoting his own happiness. In that case everything would depend on how an individual determined his own happiness; for our self-regarding duties would consist in the universal rule to satisfy all our inclinations in order to further our happiness. This would, however, militate seriously against doing our duty towards others. In fact, the principle of self-regarding duties is a very different one, which has no connexion with our well-being or earthly happiness. Far from ranking lowest in the scale of precedence, our duties towards ourselves are of primary importance and should have pride of place; for (deferring for the moment the definition of what constitutes this duty) it is obvious that nothing can be expected from a man who dishonours his own person. He who transgresses against himself loses his manliness and becomes incapable of doing his duty towards his fellows. A man who performs his duty to others badly, who lacked generosity, kindness and sympathy, but who nevertheless did his duty to himself by leading a proper life, might yet possess a certain inner worth; but he who has transgressed his duty towards himself, can have no inner worth whatever. Thus a man who fails in his duty to himself loses worth absolutely; while a man who fails in his duty to others loses worth only relatively. It follows that the prior condition of our duty to others is our duty to ourselves; we can fulfil the former only in so far as we first fulfil the latter. . . . The most serious offence against the duty one owes to oneself is suicide. But why should suicide be so abominable? It is no answer to say "because God forbids it". Suicide is not an

---

* From Lectures on Ethics 116–20 (L. Infield transl. Century Co. undated).

abomination because God has forbidden it; it is forbidden by God because it is abominable. If it were the other way about, suicide would not be abominable if it were not forbidden; and I should not know why God had forbidden it, if it were not abominable in itself. The ground, therefore, for regarding suicide and other transgressions as abominable and punishable must not be found in the divine will, but in their inherent heinousness. Suicide is an abomination because it implies the abuse of man's freedom of action: he uses his freedom to destroy himself. His freedom should be employed to enable him to live as a man. He is free to dispose as he pleases of things appertaining to his person, but not of his person; he may not use his freedom against himself. For a man to recognize what his duty is towards himself in this respect is far from easy: because although man has indeed a natural horror of suicide, yet we can argue and quibble ourselves into believing that, in order to rid himself of trouble and misery, a man may destroy himself. The argument makes a strong appeal; and in terms of the rule of prudence suicide may often be the surest and best course; none the less suicide is in itself revolting. The rule of morality, which takes precedence of all rules of reflective prudence, commands apodeictically and categorically that we must observe our duties to ourselves; and in committing suicide and reducing himself to a carcase, man uses his powers and his liberty against himself. Man is free to dispose of his condition but not of his person; he himself is an end and not a means; all else in the world is of value only as a means, but man is a person and not a thing and therefore not a means. It is absurd that a reasonable being, an end for the sake of which all else is means, should use himself as a means. It is true that a person can serve as a means for others (e. g. by his work), but only in a way whereby he does not cease to be a person and an end. Whoever acts in such a way that he cannot be an end, uses himself as a means and treats his person as a thing.

## QUESTIONS

1.   In what way can people have duties to themselves as distinct from duties to others? Can we each think of his self as a phenomenon distinct from the way in which we interact with others?

2.   What sort of behaviour is Kant arguing against when he argues against suicide? Would Mrs. Jones be an attempted suicide? Someone who gives up his life for others? Someone who engages in a dangerous activity, like war? How persuaded are you by Kant's argument against any of these acts?

3.   Aside from whether suicide is immoral, what do you suppose Kant would say about a legal sanction making attempted suicide *illegal*? What relationship is there between holding the two views?

4.   Kant says that one's duty to himself "cannot be treated juridically". What does he mean? Are not the laws against suicide, where they exist, an attempt to do just that? Are not even the laws against speeding involved with our duties to ourselves—not to be speeders?

*Albert Camus*

## Absurdity and Suicide *

There is but one truly serious philosophical problem, and that is suicide. Judging whether life is or is not worth living amounts to answering the fundamental question of philosophy. All the rest—whether or not the world has three dimensions, whether the mind has nine or twelve categories—comes afterwards. These are games; one must first answer. And if it is true, as Nietzsche claims, that a philosopher, to deserve our respect, must preach by example, you can appreciate the importance of that reply, for it will precede the definitive act. These are facts the heart can feel; yet they call for careful study before they become clear to the intellect.

If I ask myself how to judge that this question is more urgent than that, I reply that one judges by the actions it entails. I have never seen anyone die for the ontological argument. Galileo, who held a scientific truth of great importance, abjured it with the greatest ease as soon as it endangered his life. In a certain sense, he did right. That truth was not worth the stake. Whether the earth or the sun revolved around the other is a matter of profound indifference. To tell the truth, it is a futile question. On the other hand, I see many people die because they judge that life is not worth living. I see others paradoxically getting killed for the ideas or illusions that give them a reason for living (what is called a reason for living is also an excellent reason for dying). I therefore conclude that the meaning of life is the most urgent of questions. How to answer it? On all essential problems (I mean thereby those that run the risk of leading to death or those that intensify the passion of living) there are probably but two methods of thought: the method of La Palisse and the method of Don Quioxte. Solely the balance between evidence and lyricism can allow us to achieve simultaneously emotion and lucidity. In a subject at once so humble and so heavy with emotion, the learned and the classical dialectic must yield, one can see, to a more modest attitude of mind deriving at one and the same time from common sense and understanding.

Suicide has never been dealt with except as a social phenomenon. On the contrary, we are concerned here, at the outset, with the relationship between individual thought and suicide. An act like this is prepared within the silence of the heart, as is a great work of art.

* From An Absurd Reasoning in The Myth of Sisyphus and Other Essays 3–     4 (Vintage Books ed. 1955). With the permission of Alfred A. Knopf.

EDWARD WESTERMARCK

SUICIDE *

In previous chapters we have discussed the moral valuation of acts, forbearances, and omissions, which directly concern the interests of other men; we shall now proceed to consider moral ideas regarding such modes of conduct as chiefly concern a man's own welfare. Among these we notice, in the first place, acts affecting his existence.

Suicide, or intentional self-destruction, has often been represented as a fruit of higher civilisation; Dr. Steinmetz, on the other hand, in his essay on 'Suicide among Primitive Peoples,' thinks it probable that "there is a greater propensity to suicide among savage than among civilised peoples." The former view is obviously erroneous; the latter probably holds good of certain savages as compared with certain peoples of culture, but cannot claim general validity.

.  .  .  .

Among many savages and barbarians suicide is stated to be very rare, or to occur only occasionally; whereas among others it is represented as either common or extremely prevalent. Of the Kamchadales we are told that the least apprehension of danger drives them to despair, and that they fly to suicide as a relief, not only from present, but even from imaginary evil; "not only those who are confined for some offence, but such as are discontented with their lot, prefer a voluntary death to an uneasy life, and the pains of disease." Among the Hos, an Indian hill tribe, suicide is reported to be so frightfully prevalent as to afford no parallel in any known country:—"If a girl appears mortified by anything that has been said, it is not safe to let her go away till she is soothed. A reflection on a man's honesty or veracity may be sufficient to send him to self-destruction. In a recent case, a young woman attempted to poison herself because her uncle would not partake of the food she had cooked for him."  .  .  .

.  .  .  .

From the opinions on suicide held by uncivilised races we shall pass to those prevalent among peoples of a higher culture. In China suicide is extremely common among all classes and among persons of all ages. For those who have been impelled to this course by a sense of honour the gates of heaven open wide, and tablets bearing their names are erected in the temples in honour of virtuous men or women. As honourable self-murderers are regarded servants or officers of state who choose not to survive a defeat in battle or an insult offered to the sovereign of their country; young men who, when an insult has been paid to their parents which they are unable to avenge, prefer not to survive it; and women who kill themselves on the death of their husbands or fiances.  .  .  .

.  .  .  .

Ancient Greece had its honourable suicides. The Milesian and Corinthian women, who by a voluntary death escaped from falling in-

* From 2 The Origin and Development of the Moral Ideas 229–31, 241–42, 247–52 (MacMillan 1917). With the permission of MacMillan & Co.

to the hands of the enemy, were praised in epigrams.  The story that Themistocles preferred death to bearing arms against his native country was circulated with a view to doing honour to his memory. The tragedians frequently gave expression to the idea that suicide is in certain circumstances becoming to a noble mind.  Hecuba blames Helena for not putting an end to her life by a rope or a sword.  Phae-dra and Leda kill themselves out of shame, Haemon from violent re-morse.  Ajax decides to die after having in vain attempted to kill the Atreidae, maintaining that "one of generous strain should nobly live, or forthwith nobly die."  Instances are, moreover, mentioned of women killing themselves on the death of their husbands; and in Cheos it was the custom to prevent the decrepitude of old age by a voluntary death.  At Athens the right hand of a person who had taken his own life was struck off and buried apart from the rest of the body, evidently in order to make him harmless after death.  Plato says in his *Laws*, probably in agreement with Attic custom, that those who inflict death upon themselves "from sloth or want of manliness," shall be buried alone in such places as are uncultivated and nameless, and that no column or inscription shall mark the spot where they are interred.  At Thebes self-murderers were deprived of the accustomed funeral ceremonies, and in Cyprus they were left unburied.  The ob-jections which philosophers raised against the commission of suicide were no doubt to some extent shared by popular sentiments.  Pytha-goras is represented as saying that we should not abandon our station in life without the orders of our commander, that is, God.  Accord-ing to the Platonic Socrates, the gods are our guardians and we are a possession of theirs, hence "there may be reason in saying that a man should wait, and not take his own life until God summons him."  Aris-totle, again, maintains that he who from rage kills himself commits a wrong against the State, and that therefore the State punishes him and civil infamy is attached to him.  The religious argument could not be foreign to a people who regarded it as impious interference in the order of nature to make a bridge over the Hellespont and to sepa-rate a landscape from the continent; and the idea that suicide is a matter of public concern evidently prevailed in Massilia, where no man was allowed to make away with himself unless the magistrates had given him permission to do so.  But the opinions of the philoso-phers were anything but unanimous.  Plato himself, in his *Laws*, has no word of censure for him who deprives himself by violence of his appointed share of life under the compulsion of some painful and in-evitable misfortune, or out of irremediable and intolerable shame. Hegesias, surnamed the "death-persuader," who belonged to the Cyre-naic school, tried to prove the utter worthlessness and unprofitable-ness of life.  According to Epicurus we ought to consider "whether it be better that death should come to us, or we go to him."  The Stoics, especially, advocated suicide as a relief from all kinds of misery.  Se-neca remarks that it is a man's own fault if he suffers, as, by putting and end to himself, he can put an end to his misery:—"As I would choose a ship to sail in, or a house to live in, so would I choose the most tolerable death when about to die.  .  .  .  Human affairs are in such a happy situation, that no one need be wretched but by choice.

Do you like to be wretched? Live. Do you like it not? It is in your power to return from whence you came." The Stoics did not deny that it is wrong to commit suicide in cases where the act would be an injury to society; Seneca himself points out that Socrates lived thirty days in prison in expectation of death, so as to submit to the laws of his country, and to give his friends the enjoyment of his conversation to the last. Epictetus opposes indiscriminate suicide on religious grounds:—"Friends, wait for God; when he shall give the signal and release you from this service, then go to him; but for the present endure to dwell in the place where he has put you." Such a signal, however, is given often enough: it may consist in incurable disease, intolerable pain, or misery of any kind. "Remember this: the door is open; be not more timid than little children, but as they say, when the thing does not please them, 'I will play no longer,' so do you, when things seem to you of such a kind, say I will no longer play, and be gone: but if you stay, do not complain." Pliny says that the power of dying when you please is the best thing that God has given to man amidst all the sufferings of life.

It seems that the Roman people, before the influence of Christianity made itself felt, regarded suicide with considerable moral indifference. According to Servius, it was provided by the Pontifical laws that whoever hanged himself should be cast out unburied; but from what has been said before it is probable that this practice only owed its origin to fear of the dead man's ghost. Vergil enumerates self-murderers not among the guilty, but among the unfortunate, confounding them with infants who have died prematurely and persons who have been condemned to die on a false charge. Throughout the whole history of pagan Rome there was no statute declaring it to be a crime for an ordinary citizen to take his own life. The self-murderer's rights were in no way affected by his deed, his memory was no less honoured than if he had died a natural death, his will was recognised by law, and the regular order of succession was not interfered with. In Roman law there are only two noteworthy exceptions to the rule that suicide is a matter with which the State has nothing to do: it was prohibited in the case of soldiers, and the enactment was made that the suicide of an accused person should entail the same consequences as his condemnation; but in the latter instance the deed was admitted as a confession of guilt. On the other hand, it seems to have been the general opinion in Rome that suicide under certain circumstances is an heroic and praiseworthy act. Even Cicero, who professed the doctrine of Pythagoras, approved of the death of Cato.

In no question and morality was there a greater difference between classical and Christian doctrines than in regard to suicide. The earlier Fathers of the Church still allowed, or even approved of, suicide in certain cases, namely, when committed in order to procure martyrdom, or to avoid apostacy, or to retain the crown of virginity. To bring death upon ourselves voluntarily, says Lactantius, is a wicked and impious deed; "but when urged to the alternative, either of forsaking of God and relinquishing faith, or of expecting all torture and death, then it is that undaunted in spirit we defy that death with all its previous threats and terrors which others fear." Eusebius and other ecclesiastical writers mention several instances of Christian women putting an end to their lives when their chastity was in danger, and their acts are spoken of with tenderness, if not approbation, indeed some of them were admitted into the calendar of saints. This admission was due to the extreme honour in which virginity was held by the Fathers; St. Jerome, who denied that it was lawful in times of persecution to die by one's own hands, made an exception for cases in which a person's chastity was at stake. But even this exception was abolished by St. Augustine. He allows that the virgins who laid violent hands upon themselves are worthy of compassion, but declares that there was no necessity for their doing so, since chastity is a virtue of the mind which is not lost by the body being in captivity to the will and superior force of another. He argues that there is no passage in the canonical Scriptures which permits us to destroy ourselves either with a view to obtaining immortality or to avoiding calamity. On the contrary, suicide is prohibited in the commandment, "Thou shalt not kill," namely, "neither thyself nor another", for he who kills himself kills no other but a man. This doctrine, which assimilates suicide with murder, was adopted by the Church. Nay, self-murder was declared to be the worse form of murder, "the most grievous thing of all", already St. Chrysostom had declared that "if it is base to destroy others, much more is it to destroy one's self." The self-murderer was deprived of rights which were granted to all other criminals. In the sixth century a Council at Orleans enjoined that "the oblations of those who were killed in the commission of any crime may be received, except of such as laid violent hands on themselves"; and a subsequent Council denied self-murderers the usual rites of Christian burial. It was even said that Judas committed a greater sin in killing himself than in betraying his master Christ to a certain death.

### QUESTIONS

What are the moral and legal significances of the broad variety of attitudes towards taking one's life? What conditions in a society influence the group's attitude towards suicide, e. g., belief in the afterlife, food supply, overpopulation, life expectancy? Is it a good *moral* argument for suicide that *other* societies have condoned it? Does the fact that suicide runs against the grain of our own social standards— if it does—justify invoking official sanctions against the practice?

### JOHN STUART MILL

### ON LIBERTY *

The object of this Essay is to assert one very simple principle, as entitled to govern absolutely the dealings of society with the individual in the way of compulsion and control, whether the means used be physical force in the form of legal penalties, or the moral coercion of public opinion. That principle is, that the sole end for which man-

* From 13–14, 15–18 (George Routledge & Sons 1905).

kind are warranted, individually or collectively, in interfering with the liberty of action of any of their number, is self-protection. That the only purpose for which power can be rightfully exercised over any member of a civilized community, against his will, is to prevent harm to others. His own good, either physical or moral, is not a sufficient warrant. He cannot rightfully be compelled to do or forbear because it will be better for him to do so, because it will make him happier, because, in the opinions of others, to do so would be wise, or even right. These are good reasons for remonstrating with him, or reasoning with him, or persuading him, or entreating him, but not for compelling him, or visiting him with any evil in case he do otherwise. To justify that, the conduct from which it is desired to deter him, must be calculated to produce evil to some one else. The only part of the conduct of any one, for which he is amenable to society, is that which concerns others. In the part which merely concerns himself, his independence is, of right, absolute. Over himself, over his own body and mind, the individual is sovereign.  . . .

It is proper to state that I forego any advantage which could be derived to my argument from the idea of abstract right, as a thing independent of utility. I regard utility as the ultimate appeal on all ethical questions; but it must be utility in the largest sense, grounded on the permanent interest of man as a progressive being. Those interests, I contend, authorized the subjection of individual spontaneity to external control, only in respect to those actions of each, which concern the interest of other people. If anyone does an act hurtful to others, there is a *prima facie* case for punishing him, by law, or, where legal penalties are not safely applicable, by general disapprobation. There are also many positive acts for the benefit of others, which he may rightfully be compelled to perform; such as, to give evidence in a court of justice; to bear his fair share in the common defense, or in any other joint work necessary to the interest of the society of which he enjoys the protections; and to perform certain acts of individual beneficence, such as saving a fellow creature's life, or interposing to protect the defenseless against ill-usage, things which whenever it is obviously a man's duty to do, he may rightfully be made responsible to society for not doing. A person may cause evil to others not only by his actions but by his inaction, and in either case he is justly accountable to them for the injury. The latter case, it is true, requires a much more cautious exercise of compulsion than the former. To make anyone answerable for doing evil to others, is the rule; to make him answerable for not preventing evil is, comparatively speaking, the exception. Yet there are many cases clear enough and grave enough to justify that exception. In all things which regard the external relations of the individual, he is *de jure* amenable to those whose interests are concerned, and, if need be, to society as their protector. There are often good reasons for not holding him to the responsibility; but these reasons must arise from the special expediencies of the case: either because it is a kind of case in which he is on the whole likely to act better, when left to his own discretion, than when controlled in any way in which society have it in their power to control him; or because the attempt to exercise control would produce other evils, greater than those which it would prevent. When such reasons as these preclude the enforcement of responsibility, the conscience of the agent himself should step into the vacant judgment seat, and protect those interests of others which have no external protection; judging himself all the more rigidly, because the case does not admit of his being made accountable to the judgment of his fellow-creatures.

But there is a sphere of action in which society, as distinguished from the individual, has, if any, only an indirect interest; comprehending all that portion of a person's life and conduct which affects only himself, or if it also affects others, only with their free, voluntary, and undeceived consent and participation. When I say only himself, I mean directly, and in the first instance; for whatever affects himself, may affect others *through* himself; and the objection which may be grounded on this contingency, will receive consideration in the sequel. This, then, is the appropriate region of human liberty. It comprises, first, the inward domain of consciousness; demanding liberty of conscience, in the most comprehensive sense; liberty of thought and feeling; absolute freedom of opinion and sentiment on all subjects, practical or speculative, scientific, moral, or theological. The liberty of expressing and publishing opinions may seem to fall under a different principle, since it belongs to that part of the conduct of an individual which concerns other people; but, being almost of as much importance as the liberty of thought itself, and resting in great part on the same reasons, is practically inseparable from it. Secondly, the principle requires liberty of tastes and pursuits; of framing the plan of our life to suit our own character; of doing as we like, subject to such consequences as may follow: without impediment from our fellow-creatures, so long as what we do does not harm them, even though they should think our conduct foolish, perverse, or wrong. Thirdly, from this liberty of each individual, follows the liberty, within the same limits, of combination among individuals; freedom to unite, for any purpose not involving harm to others: the persons combining being supposed to be of full age, and not forced or deceived.

No society in which these liberties are not, on the whole, respected, is free, whatever may be its form of government; and none is completely free in which they do not exist absolute and unqualified. The only freedom which deserves the name, is that of pursuing our own good in our own way, so long as we do not attempt to deprive others of theirs, or impede their efforts to obtain it. Each is the proper guardian of his own health, whether bodily, or mental and spiritual. Mankind are greater gainers by suffering each other to live as seems good to themselves, than by compelling each to live as seems good to the rest.

## QUESTIONS

1. Of how much guidance is Mill's thesis in the solution of any concrete case? In what sense is Mill using the word "harm"? Would Mill, for example, have supported Judge Wright's opinion in *Georgetown* because her death would be a harm to her children? How about the "harm?" of the upset that suicide causes others? Is

"harm" measured by a type of bodily sensation, or will one's definition of harm itself depend upon one's views of the relationships that *should* obtain in a just society?

2.  What are in the general suppositions about human beings that are implicit in Mill's thesis? See the selection from Robert P. Wolff, *infra,* p. 1164.

LORD PATRICK DEVLIN

MORALS AND THE CRIMINAL LAW *

. . . What is the connexion between crime and sin and to what extent, if at all, should the criminal law of England concern itself with the enforcement of morals and punish sin or immorality as such?

The statements of principle in the Wolfenden Report [on homosexual offences and prostitution] provide an admirable and modern starting-point for such an inquiry. . . .

Early in the Report the Committee put forward:

our own formulation of the function of the criminal law so far as it concerns the subjects of this enquiry. In this field, its function, as we see it, is to preserve public order and decency, to protect the citizen from what is offensive or injurious, and to provide sufficient safeguards against exploitation and corruption of others, particularly those who are specially vulnerable because they are young, weak in body or mind, inexperienced, or in a state of special physical, official or economic dependence.

It is not, in our view, the function of the law to intervene in the private lives of citizens, or to seek to enforce any particular pattern of behaviour, further than is necessary to carry out the purposes we have outlined.

The Committee preface their most important recommendation

that the homosexual behavior between consenting adults in private should no longer be a criminal offence, [by stating the argument] which we believe to be decisive, namely, the importance which society and the law ought to give to individual freedom of choice and action in matters of private morality. Unless a deliberate attempt is to be made by society, acting through the agency of the law, to equate the sphere of crime with that of sin, there must remain a realm of private morality and immorality which is in brief and crude terms, not the law's business. To say this is not to condone or encourage private immorality.

Similar statements of principle are set out in the chapters of the Report which deal with prostitution. . . .

* From The Enforcement of Morals 2–17, 24–25 (Oxford Univ. Press 1965).  With the permission of Oxford University Press.

These statements of principle are naturally restricted to the subject-matter of the Report. But they are made in general terms and there seems to be no reason why, if they are valid, they should not be applied to the criminal law in general. They separate very decisively crime from sin, the divine law from the secular, and the moral from the criminal. They do not signify any lack of support for the law, moral or criminal, and they do not represent an attitude that can be called either religious or irreligious. There are many schools of thought among those who may think that morals are not the law's business. There is first of all the agnostic or free-thinker. . . . He cannot accept the divine law; that does not mean that he might not view with suspicion any departure from moral principles that have for generations been accepted by the society in which he lives; but in the end he judges for himself. Then there is the deeply religious person who feels that the criminal law is sometimes more of a hindrance than a help in the sphere of morality, and that the reform of the sinner—at any rate when he injures only himself—should be a spiritual rather than a temporal work. Then there is the man who without any strong feeling cannot see why, where there is freedom in religious belief, there should not logically be freedom in morality as well. All these are powerfully allied against the equating of crime with sin.

I must disclose at the outset that I have as a judge an interest in the result of the inquiry which I am seeking to make as a jurisprudent. As a judge who administers the criminal law and who has often to pass sentence in a criminal court, I should feel handicapped in my task if I thought that I was addressing an audience which had no sense of sin or which thought of crime as something quite different. Ought one, for example, in passing sentence upon a female abortionist to treat her simply as if she were an unlicensed midwife? If not, why not? But if so, is all the panoply of the law erected over a set of social regulations? I must admit that I begin with a feeling that a complete separation of crime from sin (I use the term throughout this lecture in the wider meaning) would not be good for the moral law and might be disastrous for the criminal. But can this sort of feeling be justified as a matter of jurisprudence? And if it be a right feeling, how should the relationship between the criminal and the moral law be stated? Is there a good theoretical basis for it, or is it just a practical working alliance, or is it a bit of both? That is the problem which I want to examine, and I shall begin by considering the standpoint of the strict logician. It can be supported by cogent arguments, some of which I believe to be unanswerable and which I put as follows.

Morals and religion are inextricably joined—the moral standards generally accepted in Western civilization being those belonging to Christianity. Outside Christendom other standards derive from other religions. . . . It may or may not be right for the State to adopt one of these religions as the truth, to found itself upon its doctrines, and to deny to any of its citizens the liberty to practice any other. If it does, it is logical that it should use the secular law wherever it thinks it necessary to enforce the divine. If it does not, it is illogical that it should concern itself with morals as such. But if it leaves matters of religion to private judgment, it should logically leave matters of morals also. A State which refuses to enforce Christian beliefs has lost the right to enforce Christian morals.

If this view is sound, it means that the criminal law cannot justify any of its provisions by reference to the moral law. It cannot say, for example, that murder and theft are prohibited because they are immoral or sinful.  .   .   .

.   .   .   .

.   .   .   There is only one explanation of what has hitherto been accepted as the basis of the criminal law and that is that there are certain standards of behaviour or moral principles which society requires to be observed; and the breach of them is an offence not merely against the person who is injured but against society as a whole.

Thus, if the criminal law were to be reformed so as to eliminate from it everything that was not designed to preserve order and decency or to protect citizens (including the protection of youth from corruption), it would overturn a fundamental principle. It would also end a number of specific crimes. Euthanasia or the killing of another at his own request, suicide, attempted suicide and suicide pacts, duelling, abortion, incest between brother and sister, are all acts which can be done in private and without offence to others and need not involve the corruption or exploitation of others. Many people think that the law on some of these subjects is in need of reform, but no one hitherto has gone so far as to suggest that they should all be left outside the criminal law as matters of private morality. They can be brought within it only as a matter of moral principle. It must be remembered also that although there is much immorality that is not punished by the law, there is none that is condoned by the law. The law will not allow its processes to be used by those engaged in immorality of any sort. For example, a house may not be let for immoral purposes; the lease is invalid and would not be enforced. But if what goes on inside there is a matter of private morality and not the law's business, why does the law inquire into it at all?

.   .   .   .

In jurisprudence, as I have said, everything is thrown open to discussion and, in the belief that they cover the whole field, I have framed three interrogatories addressed to myself to answer:

1.  Has society the right to pass judgment at all on matters of morals? Ought there, in other words, to be a public morality, or are morals always a matter for private judgment?

2.  If society has the right to pass judgment, has it also the right to use the weapon of the law to enforce it?

3.  If so, ought it to use that weapon in all cases or only in some; and if only in some, on what principles should it distinguish.

I shall begin with the first interrogatory and consider what is meant by the right of society to pass a moral judgment, that is, a judgement about what is good and what is evil.   .   .   .

.   .   .   .

.   .   .   What makes a society of any sort is community of ideas, not only political ideas but also ideas about the way its members should behave and govern their lives; these latter ideas are its morals. Every society has a moral structure as well as a political one: or rather, since that might suggest two independent systems, I should say that the structure of every society is made up both of politics and morals. Take, for example, the institution of marriage. Whether a man should be allowed to take more than one wife is something about which every society has to make up its mind one way or the other. In England we believe in the Christian idea of marriage and therefore adopt monogamy as a moral principle. Consequently the Christian institution of marriage has become the basis of family life and so part of the structure of our society. It is there not because it is Christian. It has got there because it is Christian, but it remains there because it is built into the house in which we live and could not be removed without bringing it down. The great majority of those who live in this country accept it because it is the Christian idea of marriage and for them the only true one. But a non-Christian is bound by it, not because it is part of Christianity but because, rightly or wrongly, it has been adopted by the society in which he lives. It would be useless for him to stage a debate designed to prove that polygamy was theologically more correct and socially preferable; if he wants to live in the house, he must accept it as built in the way in which it is.

We see this more clearly if we think of ideas or institutions that are purely political. Society cannot tolerate rebellion; it will not allow argument about the rightness of the cause. Historians a century later may say that the rebels were right and the Government was wrong and a percipient and conscientious subject of the State may think so at the time. But it is not a matter which can be left to individual judgement.

The institution of marriage is a good example for my purpose because it bridges the division, if there is one, between politics and morals. Marriage is part of the structure of our society and it is also the basis of a moral code which condemns fornication and adultery. The institution of marriage would be gravely threatened if individual judgements were permitted about the morality of adultery; on these points there must be a public morality. But public morality is not to be confined to those moral principles which support institutions such as marriage. People do not think of monogamy as something which has to be supported because our society has chosen to organize itself upon it; they think of it as something that is good in itself and offering a good way of life and that it is for that reason that our society has adopted it. I return to the statement that I have already made, that society means a community of ideas; without shared ideas on politics, morals, and ethics no society can exist. Each one of us has ideas about what is good and what is evil; they cannot be kept private from the society in which we live. If men and women try to create a society in which there is no fundamental agreement about good and evil they will fail; if, having based it on common agreement, the agreement goes, the society will disintegrate. For society is not something that is kept together physically; it is held by the invisible bonds of common thought. If the bonds were too far relaxed the members would drift apart. A common morality is part of the bondage. The bondage is part of the price of society; and mankind, which needs society, must pay its price.

. . . . .

You may think that I have taken far too long in contending that there is such a thing as public morality, a proposition which most people would readily accept, and may have left myself too little time to discuss the next question which to many minds may cause greater difficulty: to what extent should society use the law to enforce its moral judgements? But I believe that the answer to the first question determines the way in which the second should be approached and may indeed very nearly dictate the answer to the second question. If society has no right to make judgements on morals, the law must find some special justification for entering the field of morality: if homosexuality and prostitution are not in themselves wrong, then the onus is very clearly on the lawgiver who wants to frame a law against certain aspects of them to justify the exceptional treatment. But if society has the right to make a judgement and has it on the basis that a recognized morality is as necessary to society as, say, a recognized government, then society may use the law to preserve morality in the same way as it uses it to safeguard anything else that is essential to its existence. If therefore the first proposition is securely established with all its implications, society has a prima facie right to legislate against immorality as such.

The Wolfenden Report, notwithstanding that it seems to admit the right of society to condemn homosexuality and prostitution as immoral, requires special circumstances to be shown to justify the intervention of the law. I think that this is wrong in principle and that any attempt to approach my second interrogatory on these lines is bound to break down. I think that the attempt by the Committee does break down and that this is shown by the fact that it has to define or describe its special circumstances so widely that they can be supported only if it is accepted that the law *is* concerned with immorality as such.

The widest of the special circumstances are described as the provision of "sufficient safeguards against exploitation and corruption of others, particularly those who are specially vulnerable because they are young, weak in body or mind, inexperienced, or in a state of special physical, official or economic dependence". The corruption of youth is a well-recognized ground for intervention by the State and for the purpose of any legislation the young can easily be defined. But if similar protection were to be extended to every other citizen, there would be no limit to the reach of the law. The "corruption and exploitation of others" is so wide that it could be used to cover any sort of immorality which involves, as most do, the co-operation of another person. . . .

.  .  .  .

I think, therefore, that it is not possible to set theoretical limits to the power of the State to legislate against immorality. It is not possible to settle in advance exceptions to the general rule or to define inflexibly areas of morality into which the law is in no circumstances to be allowed to enter. Society is entitled by means of its laws to protect itself from dangers, whether from within or without. Here again I think that the political parallel is legitimate. The law of treason is directed against aiding the king's enemies and against sedition from within. The justification for this is that established government is necessary for the existence of society and therefore its safety against violent overthrow must be secured. But an established morality is as necessary as good government to the welfare of society. Societies disintegrate from within more frequently than they are broken up by external pressures. There is disintegration when no common morality is observed and history shows that the loosening of moral bonds is often the first stage of disintegration, so that society is justified in taking the same steps to preserve its moral code as it does to preserve its government and other essential institutions. The suppression of vice is as much the law's business as the suppression of subversive activities; it is no more possible to define a sphere of private morality than it is to define one of private subversive activity. It is wrong to talk of private morality or of the law not being concerned with immorality as such or to try to set rigid bounds to the part which the law may play in the suppression of vice. There are no theoretical limits to the power of the State to legislate against treason and sedition, and likewise I think there can be no theoretical limits to legislation against immorality. You may argue that if a man's sins affect only himself it cannot be the concern of society. If he chooses to get drunk every night in the privacy of his own home, is any one except himself the worse for it? But suppose a quarter or a half of the population got drunk every night, what sort of society would it be? You cannot set a theoretical limit to the number of people who can get drunk before society is entitled to legislate against drunkenness. . . .

In what circumstances the State should exercise its power is the third of the interrogatories I have framed. But before I get to it I must raise a point which might have been brought up in any one of the three. How are the moral judgements of society to be ascertained? By leaving it until now, I can ask it in the more limited form that is now sufficient for my purpose. How is the lawmaker to ascertain the moral judgements of society? It is surely not enough that they should be reached by the opinion of the majority; it would be too much to require the individual assent of every citizen. English law has evolved and regularly uses a standard which does not depend on the counting of heads. It is that of the reasonable man. He is not to be confused with the rational man. He is not

expected to reason about anything and his judgement may be largely
a matter of feeling. It is the viewpoint of the man in the street—or
to use an archaism familiar to all lawyers—the man in the Clapham
omnibus. He might also be called the right-minded man. For my
purpose I should like to call him the man in the jury box, for the moral
judgement of society must be something about which any twelve
men or women drawn at random might after discussion be expected
to be unanimous.   .   .   .

Immorality then, for the purpose of the law, is what every right-
minded person is presumed to consider to be immoral. Any immorality is capable of affecting society injuriously and in effect to a greater or lesser extent it usually does; this is what gives the law its
*locus standi.*   .   .   .

I do not think that one can talk sensibly of a public and private
morality any more than one can of a public or private highway.
Morality is a sphere in which there is a public interest and a private
interest, often in conflict, and the problem is to reconcile the two.
.   .   .

.   .   . Nothing should be punished by the law that does not
lie beyond the limits of tolerance. It is not nearly enough to say
that a majority dislike a practice; there must be a real feeling of
reprobation.   .   .   . It would be possible no doubt to point out
that until a comparatively short while ago nobody thought very
much of cruelty to animals and also that pity and kindliness and
the unwillingness to inflict pain are virtues more generally esteemed
now than they have ever been in the past. But matters of this sort
are not determined by rational argument. Every moral judgement,
unless it claims a divine source, is simply a feeling that no right-
minded man could behave in any other way without admitting that
he was doing wrong. It is the power of a common sense and not
the power of reason that is behind the judgements of society. But
before a society can put a practice beyond the limits of tolerance
there must be a deliberate judgement that the practice is injurious
to society.   .   .   .
.   .   .   .   .

I return now to the main thread of my argument and summarize
it. Society cannot live without morals. Its morals are those standards of conduct which the reasonable man approves. A rational
man, who is also a good man, may have other standards. If he has
no standards at all he is not a good man and need not be further
considered. If he has standards, they may be very different; he
may, for example, not disapprove of homosexuality or abortion. In
that case he will not share in the common morality; but that should
not make him deny that it is a social necessity. A rebel may be
rational in thinking that he is right but he is irrational if he thinks
that society can leave him free to rebel.

A man who concedes that morality is necessary to society must
support the use of those instruments without which morality cannot
be maintained. The two instruments are those of teaching, which
is doctrine, and of enforcement, which is the law. If morals could

be taught simply on the basis that they are necessary to society, there would be no social need for religion; it could be left as a purely personal affair.  But morality cannot be taught in that way. Loyalty is not taught in that way either.  No society has yet solved the problem of how to teach morality without religion.  So the law must base itself on Christian morals and to the limit of its ability enforce them, not simply because they are the morals of most of us, nor simply because they are the morals which are taught by the established Church—on these points the law recognizes the right to dissent—but for the compelling reason that without the help of Christian teaching the law will fail.

*H. L. A. HART*

## LAW, LIBERTY AND MORALITY *

.  .  .  Is the fact that certain conduct is by common standards immoral sufficient to justify making that conduct punishable by law? Is it morally permissible to enforce morality as such?  Ought immorality as such to be a crime?

To this question John Stuart Mill gave an emphatic negative answer in his essay *On Liberty* one hundred years ago, and the famous sentence in which he frames this answer expresses the central doctrine of his essay.  He said, "The only purpose for which power can rightfully be exercised over any member of a civilised community against his will is to prevent harm to others."  And to identify the many different things which he intended to exclude, he added, "His own good either physical or moral is not a sufficient warrant.  He cannot rightfully be compelled to do or forbear because it will be better for him to do so, because it will make him happier, because in the opinions of others, to do so would be wise or even right."

.   .   .   .

.   .   .   Mill's principles are still very much alive in the criticism of law, whatever their theoretical deficiencies may be.  But twice in one hundred years they have been challenged by two masters of the Common Law.  The first of these was the great Victorian judge and historian of the Criminal Law, James Fitzjames Stephen.  His criticism of Mill is to be found in the sombre and impressive book *Liberty, Equality, Fraternity*, which he wrote as a direct reply to Mill's essay.  .  .  .  It is evident from the tone of this book that Stephen thought he had found crushing arguments against Mill and had demonstrated that the law might justifiably enforce morality as such or, as he said, that the law should be "a persecution of the grosser forms of vice."  Nearly a century later, on the publication of the Wolfenden Committee's report, Lord Devlin, now a member of the House of Lords and a most distinguished writer on the criminal law, in his essay on *The Enforcement of Morals* took as his target the Re-

* From 4, 15–16, 48–52, 54, 75–77 (Stanford Univ. Press 1963).  With the permission of the publishers, Stanford University Press.  © 1963 by the Board of Trustees of the Leland Stanford Junior University.

port's contention "that there must be a realm of morality and immorality which is not the law's business" and argued in opposition to it that "the suppression of vice is as much the law's business as the suppression of subversive activities."

.    .    .    .

## THE MODERATE AND THE EXTREME THESIS

When we turn   .   .   .   to the positive grounds held to justify the legal enforcement of morality it is important to distinguish a moderate and an extreme thesis, though critics of Mill have sometimes moved from one to the other without marking the transition. Lord Devlin seems to me to maintain, for most of his essay, the moderate thesis and Stephen the extreme.

According to the moderate thesis, a shared morality is the cement of society; without it there would be aggregates of individuals but no society. "A recognized morality" is, in Lord Devlin's words, "as necessary to society's existence as a recognized government," and though a particular act of immorality may not harm or endanger or corrupt others nor, when done in private, either shock or give offence to others, this does not conclude the matter. For we must not view conduct in isolation from its effect on the moral code: if we remember this, we can see that one who is "no menace to others" nonetheless may by his immoral conduct "threaten one of the great moral principles on which society is based." In this sense the breach of moral principle is an offence "against society as a whole," and society may use the law to preserve its morality as it uses it to safeguard anything else essential to its existence. This is why "the suppression of vice is as much the law's business as the suppression of subversive activities."

By contrast, the extreme thesis does not look upon a shared morality as of merely instrumental value analogous to ordered government, and it does not justify the punishment of immorality as a step taken, like the punishment of treason, to preserve society from dissolution or collapse. Instead, the enforcement of morality is regarded as a thing of value, even if immoral acts harm no one directly, or indirectly by weakening the moral cement of society. I do not say it is possible to allot to one or other of these two theses every argument used, but they do, I think, characterise the main critical positions at the root of most arguments, and they incidentally exhibit an ambiguity in the expression "enforcing morality as such." Perhaps the clearest way of distinguishing the two theses is to see that there are always two levels at which we may ask whether some breach of positive morality is harmful. We may ask first, Does this act harm anyone independently of its repercussion on the shared morality of society? And secondly we may ask, Does this act affect the shared morality and thereby weaken society? The moderate thesis requires, if the punishment of the act is to be justified, an affirmative answer at least at the second level. The extreme thesis does not require an affirmative answer at either level.

Lord Devlin appears to defend the moderate thesis. I say "appears" because, though he says that society has the right to enforce a morality as such on the ground that a shared morality is essential to society's existence, it is not at all clear that for him the statement that immorality jeopardizes or weakens society is a statement of empirical fact. It seems sometimes to be an *a priori* assumption, and sometimes a necessary truth and a very odd one. The most important indication that this is so is that, apart from one vague reference to "history" showing that "the loosening of moral bonds is often the first stage of disintegration," no evidence is produced to show that deviation from accepted sexual morality, even by adults in private, is something which, like treason, threatens the existence of society. No reputable historian has maintained this thesis, and there is indeed much evidence against it. As a proposition of fact it is entitled to no more respect than the Emperor Justinian's statement that homosexuality was the cause of earthquakes. Lord Devlin's belief in it, and his apparent indifference to the question of evidence, are at points traceable to an undiscussed assumption. This is that all morality-sexual morality together with the morality that forbids acts injurious to others such as killing, stealing, and dishonesty—forms a single seamless web, so that those who deviate from any part are likely or perhaps bound to deviate from the whole. It is of course clear (and one of the oldest insights of political theory) that society could not exist without a morality which mirrored and supplemented the law's proscription of conduct injurious to others. But there is again no evidence to support, and much to refute, the theory that those who deviate from conventional sexual morality are in other ways hostile to society.

There seems, however, to be central to Lord Devlin's thought something more interesting, though no more convincing, than the conception of social morality as a seamless web. For he appears to move from the acceptable proposition that *some* shared morality is essential to the existence of any society to the unacceptable proposition that a society is identical with its morality as that is at any given moment of its history, so that a change in its morality is tantamount to the destruction of a society. The former proposition might be even accepted as a necessary rather than an empirical truth depending on a quite plausible definition of society as a body of men who hold certain moral views in common. But the latter proposition is absurd. Taken strictly, it would prevent us saying that the morality of a given society had changed, and would compel us instead to say that one society had disappeared and another one taken its place. But it is only on this absurd criterion of what it is for the same society to continue to exist that it could be asserted without evidence that any deviation from a society's shared morality threatens its existence.

. . . .

The extreme thesis has many variants, and it is not always clear which of them its advocates are concerned to urge. According to some variants, the legal enforcement of morality is only of instrumental value: it is merely a means, though an indispensable one, for preserving morality, whereas the preservation of morality is the end, valuable in itself, which justifies its legal enforcement. According to other variants, there is something intrinsically valuable in the legal enforcement of morality.  What is common to all varieties of the extreme thesis is that, unlike the moderate thesis, they do not hold the enforcement of morality or its preservation to be valuable merely because of their beneficial consequences in securing the existence of society.

. . . .

. . . .  To use coercion to maintain the moral *status quo* at any point in a society's history would be artificially to arrest the process which gives social institutions their value.

This distinction between the use of coercion to enforce morality and other methods which we in fact use to preserve it, such as argument, advice, and exhortation, is both very important and much neglected in discussions of the present topic.  Stephen, in his arguments against Mill, seems most of the time to forget or to ignore these other methods and the great importance which Mill attached to them. For he frequently argues as if Mill's doctrine of liberty meant that men must never express any convictions concerning the conduct of their fellow citizens if that conduct is not harmful to others.  It is true that Mill believed that "the state or the public" is not warranted *"for the purposes of repression or punishment"* in deciding that such conduct is good or bad.  But it is not true that he thought that concerning such conduct or "the experiments in living" which it represents "no one else has anything to say to it."  Nor did he think that society could "draw a line where education ends and perfect moral indifference begins."  In making these ill-founded criticisms Stephen not only misunderstood and so misrepresented Mill, but he showed how narrowly he himself conceived of morality and the processes by which it is sustained.  For Mill's concern throughout his essay is to restrict the use of coercion, not to promote moral indifference.  It is true he includes in the coercion or "constraint" of which he disapproves not only legal enforcement of morality but also other peremptory forms of social pressure such as moral blame and demands for conformity. But it is a disastrous misunderstanding of morality to think that where we cannot use coercion in its support we must be silent and indifferent. In Chapter 4 of his essay Mill takes great pains to show the other resources which we have and should use:

> It would be a great misunderstanding of this doctrine to suppose that it is one of selfish indifference which pretends that human beings have no business with each others conduct in life and that they should not concern themselves about the well-doing or well-being of one another unless their own interest is involved.  . . .  Human beings owe to each other help to distinguish the better from the worse and encouragement to choose the former and avoid the latter.

Discussion, advice, argument—all these, since they leave the individual "the final judge," may according to Mill be used in a society where freedom is properly respected.  We may even "obtrude" on another "considerations to aid his judgment and exhortations to strengthen his will."  We may in extreme cases "warn" him of our adverse judgment or feelings of distaste and contempt.  We may avoid his company and caution others against it. Many might think that Mill here comes perilously near to sanctioning coercion even though he regards these things as "strictly inseparable from the unfavorable judgments of others" and never to be inflicted for the sake of punishment. But if he erred in that direction, it is certainly clear that he recognised the important truth that in morality we are not forced to choose between deliberate coercion and indifference.

LORD PATRICK DEVLIN

## THE ENFORCEMENT OF MORALS *

It is somewhere about this point in the argument that Professor Hart in *Law, Liberty and Morality* discerns a proposition which he describes as central to my thought. He states the proposition and his objection to it as follows. "He appears to move from the acceptable proposition that *some* shared morality is essential to the existence of any society . . . to the unacceptable proposition that a society is identical with its morality as that is at any given moment of its history, so that a change in its morality is tantamount to the destruction of a society . . ." [etc., see *supra* pp. 1143 *ff.* —ed.] In conclusion Professor Hart condemns the whole thesis in the lecture as based on "a confused definition of what a society is".

I do not assert that *any* deviation from a society's shared morality threatens its existence any more than I assert that *any* subversive activity threatens its existence. I assert that they are both activities which are capable in their nature of threatening the existence of society so that neither can be put beyond the law.

For the rest, the objection appears to me to be all a matter of words. I would venture to assert, for example, that you cannot have a game without rules and that if there were no rules there would be no game. If I am asked whether that means that the game is "identical" with the rules, I would be willing for the question to be answered either way in the belief that the answer would lead to nowhere. If I am asked whether a change in the rules means that one game has disappeared and another has taken its place, I would reply probably not, but that it would depend on the extent of the change.

Likewise I should venture to assert that there cannot be a contract without terms. Does this mean that an "amended" contract is a "new" contract in the eyes of the law? I once listened to an argument by an ingenious counsel that a contract, because of the substitution of one clause for another, had "ceased to have affect" within the meaning of a statutory provision. The judge did not accept the argument; but if most of the fundamental terms had been changed, I daresay he would have done.

The proposition that I make in the text is that if (as I understand Professor Hart to agree, at any rate for the purposes of the

* From *op. cit.*, *supra*, 13–14 n.1. With the permission of Oxford University Press.

argument) you cannot have a society without morality, the law can be used to enforce morality as something that is essential to a society. I cannot see why this proposition (whether it is right or wrong) should mean that morality can never be changed without the destruction of society. If morality is changed, the law can be changed. Professor Hart refers to the proposition as "the use of legal punishment to freeze into immobility the morality dominant at a particular time in a society's existence". One might as well say that the inclusion of a penal section into a statute prohibiting certain acts freezes the whole statute into immobility and prevents the prohibitions from ever being modified.

These points are elaborated in the sixth lecture at pp. 115–16 [in The Enforcement of Morals].

QUESTIONS

1.   What empirical and historical judgments does Lord Devlin's argument call for? Even if a society needs some shared values, does it follow that the criminal law ought to be invoked to bring them about, rather than persuasion? What are the effects on the society of relying on the criminal law?

2.   How does Devlin suggest that morality be determined? Why does he rely on "the reasonable man" who is "not expected to reason about anything" and whose judgment "may be largely a matter of feeling"? Is that because Devlin feels that morality is something not amenable to rational debate, or because he is not talking about *moral judgments* being enacted into law so much as *popular sentiments*?

For a criticism of Lord Devlin's views, see Dworkin, *Lord Devlin and the Enforcement of Morals*, 75 Yale L.J. 986 (1966).

## CHAPTER SEVENTEEN

# Obligations to the Symbols of the Social Grouping: Cohesion and Individualism

WEST VIRGINIA STATE BOARD OF EDUCATION v. BARNETTE

319 U.S. 624 (1943)

Mr. Justice JACKSON delivered the opinion of the Court.

. . . .

The Board of Education on January 9, 1942, adopted a resolution containing recitals taken largely from the Court's *Gobitis* [1] opinion and ordering that the salute to the flag become "a regular part of the program of activities in the public schools," that all teachers and pupils "shall be required to participate in the salute honoring the Nation represented by the Flag; provided, however, that refusal to salute the Flag be regarded as an act of insubordination, and shall be dealt with accordingly."

The resolution originally required the "commonly accepted salute to the Flag" which it defined. Objections to the salute as "being too much like Hitler's" were raised by the Parent and Teachers Association, the Boy and Girl Scouts, the Red Cross, and the Federation of Women's Clubs. Some modification appears to have been made in deference to these objections, but no concession was made to Jehovah's Witnesses. What is now required is the "stiff-arm" salute, the saluter to keep the right hand raised with palm turned up while the following is repeated: "I pledge allegiance to the Flag of the United States of America and to the Republic for which it stands; one Nation, indivisible with liberty and justice for all."

Failure to conform is "insubordination" dealt with by expulsion. Readmission is denied by statute until compliance. Meanwhile the expelled child is "unlawfully absent" and may be proceeded against as a delinquent. His parents or guardians are liable to prosecution, and if convicted are subject to fine not exceeding $50 and jail term not exceeding thirty days.

Appellees, citizens of the United States and of West Virginia, brought suit in the United States District Court for themselves and others similarly situated asking its injunction to restrain enforcement of these laws and regulations against Jehovah's Witnesses. The Witnesses are an unincorporated body teaching that the obligation imposed by law of God is superior to that of laws enacted by temporal government. Their religious beliefs include a literal version of Exodus, Chapter 20, verses 4 and 5, which says: "Thou shalt not make unto thee any graven image, or any likeness of anything that is in heaven above, or that is in the earth beneath, or that is in the water under the earth; thou shalt not bow down thyself to them nor serve

1. Minersville School District v. Gobitis,
310 U.S. 586 (1940).

them." They consider that the flag is an "image" within this command. For this reason they refuse to salute it.

Children of this faith have been expelled from school and are threatened with exclusion for no other cause. Officials threaten to send them to reformatories maintained for criminally inclined juveniles. Parents of such children have been prosecuted and are threatened with prosecutions for causing delinquency.

The Board of Education moved to dismiss the complaint setting forth these facts and alleging that the law and regulations are an unconstitutional denial of religious freedom, and of freedom of speech, and are invalid under the "due process" and "equal protection" clauses of the Fourteenth Amendment to the Federal Constitution. The cause was submitted on the pleadings to a District Court of three judges. It restrained enforcement as to the plaintiffs and those of that class. The Board of Education brought the case here by direct appeal.

.  .  .  .

There is no doubt that, in connection with the pledges, the flag salute is a form of utterance. Symbolism is a primitive but effective way of communicating ideas. The use of an emblem or flag to symbolize some system, idea, institution, or personality, is a short cut from mind to mind. Causes and nations, political parties, lodges and ecclesiastical groups seek to knit the loyalty of their followings to a flag or banner, a color or design. The State announces rank, function, and authority through crowns and maces, uniforms and black robes; the church speaks through the Cross, the Crucifix, the altar and shrine, and clerical raiment. Symbols of State often convey political ideas just as religious symbols come to convey theological ones. Associated with many of these symbols are appropriate gestures of acceptance or respect: a salute, a bowed or bared head, a bended knee. A person gets from a symbol the meaning he puts into it, and what is one man's comfort and inspiration is another's jest and scorn.

Over a decade ago Chief Justice Hughes led this Court in holding that the display of a red flag as a symbol of opposition by peaceful and legal means to organized government was protected by the free speech guaranties of the Constitution. Stromberg v. California, 283 U.S. 359. Here it is the State that employs a flag as a symbol of adherence to government as presently organized. It requires the individual to communicate by word and sign his acceptance of the political ideas it thus bespeaks. Objection to this form of communication when coerced is an old one, well known to the framers of the Bill of Rights.

It is also to be noted that the compulsory flag salute and pledge requires affirmation of a belief and an attitude of mind. It is not clear whether the regulation contemplates that pupils forego any contrary convictions of their own and become unwilling converts to the prescribed ceremony or whether it will be acceptable if they simulate assent by words without belief and by a gesture barren of meaning. It is now a commonplace that censorship or suppression of expression of opinion is tolerated by our Constitution only when the expression presents a clear and present danger of action of a kind the State is empowered to prevent and punish. It would seem that involuntary affirmation could be commanded only on even more immediate and urgent grounds than silence. But here the power of compulsion is invoked without any allegation that remaining passive during a flag salute ritual creates a clear and present danger that would justify an effort even to muffle expression. To sustain the compulsory flag salute we are required to say that a Bill of Rights which guards the individual's right to speak his own mind, left it open to public authorities to compel him to utter what is not in his mind.

Whether the First Amendment to the Constitution will permit officials to order observance of ritual of this nature does not depend upon whether as a voluntary exercise we would think it to be good, bad or merely innocuous. Any credo of nationalism is likely to include what some disapprove or to omit what others think essential, and to give off different overtones as it takes on different accents or interpretations. If official power exists to coerce acceptance of any patriotic creed, what it shall contain cannot be decided by courts, but must be largely discretionary with the ordaining authority, whose power to prescribe would no doubt include power to amend. Hence validity of the asserted power to force an American citizen publicly to profess any statement of belief or to engage in any ceremony of assent to one, presents questions of power that must be considered independently of any idea we may have as to the utility of the ceremony in question.

. . . .

National unity as an end which officials may foster by persuasion and example is not in question. The problem is whether under our Constitution compulsion as here employed is a permissible means for its achievement.

Struggle to coerce uniformity of sentiment in support of some end thought essential to their time and country have been waged by many good as well as by evil men. Nationalism is a relatively recent phenomenon but at other times and places the ends have been racial or territorial security, support of a dynasty or regime, and particular plans for saving souls. As first and moderate methods to attain unity have failed, those bent on its accomplishment must resort to an ever-increasing severity. As governmental pressure toward unity becomes greater, so strife becomes more bitter as to whose unity it shall be. Probably no deeper division of our people could proceed from any provocation than from finding it necessary to choose what doctrine and whose program public educational officials shall compel youth to unite in embracing. Ultimate futility of such attempts to compel coherence is the lesson of every such effort from the Roman drive to stamp out Christianity as a disturber of its pagan unity, the Inquisition, as a means to religious and dynastic unity, the Siberian exiles as a means to Russian unity, down to the fast failing efforts of our present totalitarian enemies. Those who begin coercive elimination of dissent soon find themselves exterminating dissenters. Compulsory unification of opinion achieves only the unanimity of the graveyard.

It seems trite but necessary to say that the First Amendment to our Constitution was designed to avoid these ends by avoiding these beginnings. There is no mysticism in the American concept of the State or of the nature or origin of its authority. We set up government by consent of the governed, and the Bill of Rights denies those in power any legal opportunity to coerce the consent. Authority here is to be controlled by public opinion, not public opinion by authority.

The case is made difficult not because the principles of its decision are obscure but because the flag involved is our own. Nevertheless, we apply the limitations of the Constitution with no fear that freedom to be intellectually and spiritually diverse or even contrary will disintegrate the social organization. To believe that patriotism will not flourish if patriotic ceremonies are voluntary and spontaneous instead of a compulsory routine is to make an unflattering estimate of the appeal of our institutions to free minds. We can have intellectual individualism and the rich cultural diversities that we owe to exceptional minds only at the price of occasional eccentricity and abnormal attitudes. When they are so harmless to others or to the State as those we deal with here, the price is not too great. But freedom to differ is not limited to things that do not matter much. That would be a mere shadow of freedom. The test of its substance is the right to differ as to things that touch the heart of the existing order.

If there is any fixed star in our constitutional constellation, it is that no official, high or petty, can prescribe what shall be orthodox in politics, nationalism, religion, or other matters of opinion or force citizens to confess by word or act their faith therein. If there are any circumstances which permit an exception, they do not now occur to us.

We think the action of the local authorities in compelling the flag salute and pledge transcends constitutional limitations on their power and invades the sphere of intellect and spirit which it is the purpose of the First Amendment to our Constitution to reserve from all official control.

The decision of this Court in Minersville School District v. Gobitis and the holdings of those few *per curiam* decisions which preceded and foreshadowed it are overruled, and the judgment enjoining enforcement of the West Virginia Regulation is

*Affirmed.*

.  .  .  .

Mr. Justice FRANKFURTER, dissenting: [2]

One who belongs to the most vilified and persecuted minority in history is not likely to be insensible to the freedoms guaranteed by our Constitution. Were my purely personal attitude relevant I should wholeheartedly associate myself with the general libertarian views in the Court's opinion, representing as they do the thought and action of a lifetime. But as judges we are neither Jew nor Gentile, neither Catholic nor agnostic. We owe equal attachment to the Constitution and are equally bound by our judicial obligations whether we derive our citizenship from the earliest or the latest immigrants to these shores. As a member of this Court I am not justified in writing my

2.   319 U.S. at 646 ff.

private notions of policy into the Constitution, no matter how deeply I may cherish them or how mischievous I may deem their disregard. The duty of a judge who must decide which of two claims before the Court shall prevail, that of a State to enact and enforce laws within its general competence or that of an individual to refuse obedience because of the demands of his conscience, is not that of the ordinary person. It can never be emphasized too much that one's own opinion about the wisdom or evil of a law should be excluded altogether when one is doing one's duty on the bench. The only opinion of our own even looking in that direction that is material is our opinion whether legislators could in reason have enacted such a law. In the light of all the circumstances, including the history of this question in this Court, it would require more daring than I possess to deny that reasonable legislators could have taken the action which is before us for review. Most unwillingly, therefore, I must differ from my brethren with regard to legislation like this. I cannot bring my mind to believe that the "liberty" secured by the Due Process Clause gives this Court authority to deny to the State of West Virginia the attainment of that which we all recognize as a legitimate legislative end, namely, the promotion of good citizenship, by employment of the means here chosen.

. . . .

That which to the majority may seem essential for the welfare of the state may offend the consciences of a minority. But, so long as no inroads are made upon the actual exercise of religion by the minority, to deny the political power of the majority to enact laws concerned with civil matters, simply because they may offend the consciences of a minority, really means that the consciences of a minority are more sacred and more enshrined in the Constitution than the consciences of a majority.

We are told that symbolism is a dramatic but primitive way of communicating ideas. Symbolism is inescapable. Even the most sophisticated live by symbols. But it is not for this Court to make psychological judgments as to the effectiveness of a particular symbol in inculcating concededly indispensable feelings, particularly if the state happens to see fit to utilize the symbol that represents our heritage and our hopes. And surely only flippancy could be responsible for the suggestion that constitutional validity of a requirement to salute our flag implies equal validity of a requirement to salute a dictator. The significance of a symbol lies in what it represents. To reject the swastika does not imply rejection of the Cross. And so it bears repetition to say that it mocks reason and denies our whole history to find in the allowance of a requirement to salute our flag on fitting occasions the seeds of sanction for obeisance to a leader. To deny the power to employ educational symbols is to say that the state's educational system may not stimulate the imagination because this may lead to unwise stimulation.

. . . .

The flag salute exercise has no kinship whatever to the oath tests so odious in history. For the oath test was one of the instruments for suppressing heretical beliefs. Saluting the flag suppresses no belief nor curbs it.  Children and their parents may believe what they please, avow their belief and practice it.  It is not even remotely suggested that the requirement for saluting the flag involves the slightest restriction against the fullest opportunity on the part both of the children and of their parents to disavow as publicly as they choose to do so the meaning that others attach to the gesture of salute.  All channels of affirmative free expression are open to both children and parents.  Had we before us any act of the state putting the slightest curbs upon such free expression, I should not lag behind any member of this Court in striking down such an invasion of the right to freedom of thought and freedom of speech protected by the Constitution.

## NOTES AND QUESTIONS

1.  What are the interests the powers of government are being invoked to protect here?  How do they compare with the interests of "the state" in the *Georgetown* case?

2.  What are the interests being advanced by the refusal of the Appellees to salute the flag—to each of them individually, to their co-religionists, to the broader society, etc.?

3.  Are the Appellees' claims more strongly expressed as a "right" (of each of them as individual citizens) or as an "obligation" (to God and their co-religionists)?  Consider, for example, whether the outcome would have been different if an individual professing obligations to no one other than himself had refused to salute the flag?  Can you justify different results?

Walzer, *The Obligation to Disobey*, 77 Ethics 163 (1967) points out that the right of individual citizens to disobey their government, so championed in liberal political theory, has been an historical rarity.  "Throughout history, when men have disobeyed or rebelled, they have done so, by and large, as representatives of groups, and they have claimed, not merely that they are free to disobey, but that they have an obligation to do so.  Locke says nothing about such obligations, and despite the fact that Thomas Jefferson claimed on behalf of the American colonists that 'it is their right, it is their duty to throw off [despotism]' the idea that men can be obligated to disobey had not played much part in liberal political theory."

Why do you suppose this has been true?  What different moral and legal judgments does it suggest?

4.  As in the *Georgetown* case, *supra*, the actions of those refusing to abide by the law were based upon an interpretation of scripture, *i. e.*, that the flag was an "image" within the meaning of Exodus, Ch. 20.  Should it matter whether this was a good interpretation?  Should the state have an obligation to try to convince the Witnesses that the interpretation was uncalled for?  Do the obligations of the Witnesses depend upon their making a "case" for the appropriateness of the interpretation?

5.  What sort of moral and legal standards run through Justice Frankfurter's dissent?  Notice that he focuses on whether he could "deny that reasonable legislators could have" made the enactment.  Comment on his interpretation of the majority's opinion as meaning

"that the consciences of a minority are more sacred and more enshrined in the Constitution than the consciences of a majority." Can
one judge what Lord Devlin's position would be?—H. L. A. Hart's
(Chapter 16)?

6.  What are the implicit theories pro and con the toleration—
or promotion—of dissident groups?  Are there any sort of empirical
investigations that might be relevant to resolving the issues that divide the Court—and Hart and Devlin?  What is the significance of
the strength of a society's needs for cohesion?  Consider, in this regard, the selections from Linton and Wolff that follow.  Do they
suggest considerations that might shift your evaluation of the outcome of the case?

RALPH LINTON

TOTEMISM AND THE A. E. F. *

Many modern anthropologists discount the supposed differences
in the mental processes of civilized and uncivilized peoples and hold
that the psychological factors which have controlled the growth of
the so-called primitive cultures are still at work in modern society.
It is difficult to obtain evidence on this point, and a record of the development in the American army of a series of beliefs and practises
which show a considerable resemblance to the totemic complexes existing among some primitive peoples may, therefore, be of interest.
The growth of one of these pseudo-totemic complexes can be fully
traced in the case of the 42nd or Rainbow Division.  The name was
arbitrarily chosen by the higher officials and is said to have been selected because the organization was made up of units from many states
whose regimental colors were of every hue in the rainbow.  Little
importance was attached to the name while the division was in America and it was rarely used by enlisted men.  After the organization
arrived in France, its use became increasingly common, and the
growth of a feeling of divisional solidarity finally resulted in its
regular employment as a personal appellation.  Outsiders usually addressed division members as "Rainbow," and to the question "What
are you?" nine out of ten enlisted men would reply "I'm a Rainbow."
This personal use of the name became general before any attitude toward the actual rainbow was developed.  A feeling of connection between the organization and its namesake was first noted in February,
1918, five to six months after the assignment of the name.  At this
time it was first suggested and then believed that the appearance of a
rainbow was a good omen for the division.  Three months later it had
become an article of faith in the organization that there was always
a rainbow in the sky when the division went into action.  A rainbow
over the enemy's lines was considered especially auspicious, and after
a victory men would often insist that they had seen one in this position even when the weather conditions or direction of advance made
it impossible.  This belief was held by most of the officers and en-

* From 26 Am.Anthropologist (N.S.) 296    The American Anthropological Asso-
   (1924).  Reprinted by permission of    ciation.

listed men, and anyone who expressed doubts was considered a heretic and overwhelmed with arguments.

The personal use of the divisional name and the attitude toward the rainbow had both become thoroughly established before it began to be used as an emblem. In the author's regiment this phase first appeared in May, when the organization came in contact with the 77th Division which had its namesake, the Goddess of Liberty, painted on its carts and other divisional property. The idea was taken up at once, and many of the men decorated the carts and limbers in their charge with rainbows without waiting for official permission. As no two of the painted rainbows were alike, the effect was grotesque and the practice was soon forbidden. Nevertheless it continued, more or less surreptitiously, until after the armistice, when it was finally permitted with a standardized rainbow.

The use of rainbows as personal insignia appeared still later, in August or September. The history of the development of shoulder insignia in the American army is well known and need not be given here. The idea apparently originated with the Canadian forces, but the A. E. F. received it indirectly through one of the later American organizations which had adopted it before their arrival in France. The use of such insignia became general in the rear areas before it reached the divisions at the front. The first shoulder insignia seen by the author's regiment were worn by a salvage corps and by one of the newer divisions. This division was rumored to have been routed in its first battle, and it was believed that its members were forced to wear the insignia as punishment. The idea thus reached the 42nd Division under unfavorable auspices, but it was immediately taken up and passed through nearly the same phases as the use of painted insignia on divisional property. The wearing of shoulder insignia was at first forbidden by some of the regimental commanders, but even while it was proscribed many of the men carried insignia with them and pinned them on whenever they were out of reach of their officers. They were worn by practically all members of the division when in the rear areas, and their use by outsiders, or even by the men sent to the division as replacements, was resented and punished. In the case of replacements, the structure was relaxed as they became recognized members of the group.

All the other army organizations which were in existence long enough to develop a feeling of group solidarity seem to have built up similar complexes centering about their group names. The nature of some of these names precluded the development of the ideas of the namesake's guardianship or omen giving, but in such cases the beliefs which were associated with the rainbow by the 42nd Division were usually developed in connection with something other than the group namesake. In some organizations the behavior of an animal mascot, or even of an abnormal person, was considered ominous. In one instance a subnormal hysteric acquired a reputation as a soothsayer and was relieved of regular duty by the other enlisted men on condition that he foretell the outcome of an expected attack. The successive stages in the development of these complexes were not always the same as in the case of the 42nd Division. Many of the later organizations seem to have taken over such complexes with little change except the substitution of their namesake for that of the group from which they borrowed.

By the end of the war, the A. E. F. had become organized into a series of well defined, and often mutually jealous, groups each of which had its individual complex of ideas and observances. These complexes all conformed to the same general pattern but differed in content. The individual complexes bound the members of each group together and enabled them to present a united front against other groups. In the same way the uniformity of pattern gave a basis for mutual understanding and tolerance and united all the groups against persons or organizations outside the system.

The conditions in the American army after these group complexes had become fully developed may be summarized as follows:

(1) A division of the personnel into a number of groups conscious of their individuality;

(2) the possession by each of these groups of a distinctive name derived from some animal, object or natural phenomenon;

(3) the use of this name as a personal appellation in conversation with outsiders;

(4) the use of representations of the group namesake for the decoration of group property and for personal adornment, with a taboo against its use by members of other groups;

(5) a reverential attitude toward the group namesake and its representations;

(6) in many cases, an unformulated belief that the group namesake was also a group guardian capable of giving omens.

Almost any investigator who found such a condition existing among an uncivilized people would class these associated beliefs and practices as a totemic complex. It shows a poverty of content when contrasted with the highly developed totemism of the Australians or Melanesians, but is fully as rich as the totemic complexes of some of the North American Indian tribes.

*Robert Paul Wolff*

## Beyond Tolerance *

Like all political philosophies, the liberal theory of the state bases itself upon a conception of human nature. In its most primitive form —and it is thus that a philosophy often reveals itself best—liberalism views man as a rationally calculating maximizer of pleasure and minimizer of pain. The term "good," says Bentham, means "pleasant," and the term "bad" means "painful." In all our actions, we seek the first and avoid the second. Rationality thus reduces to a calculating prudence; its highest point is reached when we deliberately shun the present pleasure for fear of the future pain. It is of course a com-

* From A Critique of Pure Tolerance 27– 33 (Beacon Press 1965). With per- mission of Beacon Press and Professor Wolff.

monplace that this bookkeeping attitude toward sensation is the direct reflection of the bourgeois merchant's attitude toward profit and loss. Equally important, however, is the implication of the theory for the relations between one man and another. If the simple psychological egoism of liberal theory is correct, then each individual must view others as mere instruments in the pursuit of his private ends. As I formulate my desires and weigh the most prudent means for satisfying them, I discover that the actions of other persons, bent upon similar lonely quests, may affect the outcome of my enterprise. In some cases, they threaten me; in others, the possibility exists of a mutually beneficial cooperation. I adjust my plans accordingly, perhaps even entering into quite intricate and enduring alliances with other individuals. But always I seek my own pleasure (or happiness—the shift from one to the other is not of very great significance in liberal theory, although Mill makes much of it). For me, other persons are obstacles to be overcome or resources to be exploited—always means, that is to say, and never ends in themselves. To speak fancifully, it is as though society were an enclosed space in which float a number of spherical balloons filled with an expanding gas. Each balloon increases in size until its surface meets the surface of the other balloons; then it stops growing and adjusts to its surroundings. Justice in such a society could only mean the protection of each balloon's interior (Mill's private sphere) and the equal apportionment of space to all. What took place within an individual would be no business of the others.

In the more sophisticated versions of liberal philosophy, the crude picture of man as a pleasure maximizer is softened somewhat. Mill recognizes that men may pursue higher ends than pleasure, at least as that feeling or sensation is usually understood, and he even recognizes the possibility of altruistic or other-regarding feelings of sympathy and compassion. Nevertheless, society continues to be viewed as a system of independent centers of consciousness, each pursuing its own gratification and confronting the others as beings standing-over-against the self, which is to say, as *objects*. The condition of the individual in such a state of affairs is what a different tradition of social philosophy would call "alienation."

Dialectically opposed to the liberal philosophy and speaking for the values of an earlier, pre-industrial, age is the conservative philosophy of community. The involvement of each with all, which to Mill was a threat and an imposition, is to such critics of liberalism as Burke or Durkheim a strength and an opportunity. It is indeed the greatest virtue of society, which supports and enfolds the individual in a warm, effective community stretching backwards and forwards in time and bearing within itself the accumulated wisdom and values of generations of human experience.

The fundamental insight of the conservative philosophy is that man is by nature a social being. This is not simply to say that he is gregarious, that he enjoys the company of his fellows, although that is true of man, as it is also of monkeys and otters. Rather, man is social in the sense that his essence, his true being, lies in his involvement in a human community. Aristotle, in the opening pages of the

*Politics*, says that man is by nature a being intended to live in a political community. Those men who, by choice, live outside such a community are, he says, either lower or higher than other men—that is, either animals or angels. Now man is like the animals in respect to his bodily desires, and he is like the angels in respect of his reason. In a sense, therefore, liberalism has made the mistake of supposing that man is no more than a combination of the bestial and the angelic, the passionate and the rational. From such an assumption it follows naturally that man, like both beasts and angels, is essentially a lonely creature.

But, Aristotle tells us, man has a mode of existence peculiar to his species, based on the specifically human faculty for communication. That mode of existence is society, which is a human community bound together by rational discourse and shared values. Prudence and passion combine to make a rational pleasure calculator, but they do not make a man.

The conservative figure whose work contrasts most sharply with Mill's is the French sociologist Emile Durkheim. In a seminal study of social integration entitled *Suicide*, Durkheim undertook to expose the foundations of the individual's involvement with his society by examining the conditions under which that involvement broke down in the most dramatic way. Durkheim discovered that proneness to suicide was associated, in contemporary western society, with one of two sorts of conditions, both of which are parts of what Mill calls "liberty." The loosening of the constraints of traditional and group values creates in some individuals a condition of lawlessness, an absence of limits on desire and ambition. Since there is no intrinsic limit to the quantity of satisfaction which the self can seek, it finds itself drawn into an endless and frustrating pursuit of pleasure. The infinitude of the objective universe if unconstrained for the individual within social or subjective limits, and the self is simply dissipated in the vacuum which it strives to fill. When this lack of internal limitation saps the strength and organization of the personality beyond bearable limits, suicide is liable to result; Durkheim labels this form of suicide "anomic" in order to indicate the lawlessness which causes it.

Freedom from the constraint of traditional and social values brings with it a loss of limits and the abyss of anomie, according to Durkheim. (Note that the term "anomie," as originally defined by Durkheim, does *not* mean loneliness, loss of a sense of identity, or anonymity in a mass. It means quite precisely a-nomie, or lack of law.) Freedom from the constricting bonds of an intimate social involvement brings with it a second form of psychic derangement, called by Durkheim "egoism," which also leads in extreme cases to suicide. Durkheim sees the human condition as inherently tragic. The individual is launched upon an infinite expanse, condemned to seek a security which must always pass away in death and to project meaning into a valueless void. The only hope is for men to huddle together and collectively create the warm world of meaning and coherence which impersonal nature cannot offer. Each of us sees himself reflected in the other selves of his society, and together we manage to forget for a time the reality beyond the walls.

.   .   .

Durkheim marshalls statistics to show that where the intensity of the collective life of a community diminishes—as their "freedom," in Mill's sense, increases, therefore—the rate of suicide rises.  Thus Protestant communities exhibit higher rates than Catholic communities, which in turn surpass the inward-turning Jewish communities. So too, education is "positively" correlated with suicide, for although knowledge in itself is not harmful to the human personality, the independence of group norms and isolation which higher education carries with it quite definitely is inimical.  One might almost see in the varying suicide rates a warning which society issues to those of its number who foolishly venture through the walls of the town into the limitless and lonely wastes beyond.

It seems, if Durkheim is correct, that the very liberty and individuality which Mill celebrates are deadly threats to the integrity and health of the personality.  So far from being superfluous constraints which thwart the free development of the self, social norms protect us from the dangers of anomie; and that invasive intimacy of each with each which Mill felt as suffocating is actually our principal protection against the soul-destroying evil of isolation.

Ex parte Starr

263 F. 145 (D.Mont.1920)

BOURQUIN, District Judge.  In this habeas corpus it appears that in February, 1918, the Montana Legislature enacted a statute "defining the crime of sedition," which, in so far as it relates to the flag, is like the federal Espionage Law of May, 1918.  In August, 1918, an information was filed in the state court, charging that in March, 1918, this petitioner had "committed the crime of sedition," by uttering and publishing contemptuous and slurring language about the flag and language calculated to bring the flag into contempt and disrepute, as follows:

"What is this thing anyway?  Nothing but a piece of cotton with a little paint on it and some other marks in the corner there.  I will not kiss that thing.  It might be covered with microbes."

Tried and convicted, he was sentenced to the state penitentiary for not less than 10 years nor more than 20 years at hard labor, and to pay a fine of $500 and costs.  Not apparent whether he appealed; in November, 1919, he applied to the State Supreme Court for habeas corpus, was denied, and thereupon made this application.

His principal contention is that the state law is repugnant to the federal Constitution, in that it assumes powers vested in the United States alone and by it exercised, and hence that he is imprisoned in violation of the Thirteenth and Fourteenth Amendments.  Despite Urquhart v. Brown, 205 U.S. 179, 181, 27 S.Ct. 459, 51 L.Ed. 760, Frank's Case, 237 U.S. 309, 328, 35 S.Ct. 582, 59 L.Ed. 969, warrants consideration of the merits of petitioner's application. That the state may legislate in protection of the flag is settled by Halter v. Nebraska, 205 U.S. 34, 41, 27 S.Ct. 419, 51 L.Ed. 696, 10 Ann.Cas. 525. Although that case leaves open whether such state legislation will be superseded by later like federal legislation, the issue is not involved herein, for that petitioner's offense against the state is prior to the federal law, which latter neither pardons the offense nor draws it within federal jurisdiction.

In the matter of his offense and sentence, obviously petitioner was more sinned against than sinning. It is clear that he was in the hands of one of those too common mobs, bent upon vindicating its peculiar standard of patriotism and its odd concept of respect for the flag by compelling him to kiss the latter—a spectacle for the pity as well as the laughter of gods and men! Its unlawful and disorderly conduct, not his just resistance, nor the trivial and innocuous retort into which they goaded him, was calculated to degrade the sacred banner and to bring it into contempt. Its members, not he, should have been punished.

Patriotism is the cement that binds the foundation and the superstructure of the state. The safety of the latter depends upon the integrity of the former. Like religion, patriotism is a virtue so indispensable and exalted, its excesses pass with little censure. But when, as here, it descends to fanaticism, it is of the reprehensible quality of the religion that incited the massacre of St. Bartholomew, the tortures of the Inquisition, the fires of Smithfield, the scaffolds of Salem and is equally cruel and murderous. In its name, as in that of Liberty, what crimes have been committed! In every age it, too, furnishes its heresy hunters and its witch burners, and, it, too, is a favorite mask for hypocrisy, assuming a virtue which it haveth not. So the mobs mentioned were generally the chosen and last resort of the slacker, military and civil, the profiteer, and the enemy sympathizer, masquerading as superpatriots to divert attention from their real character. Incidentally, it is deserving of mention here that in the records of this court is a report of its grand jury that before it attempts had been made to prostitute the federal Espionage Law to wreak private vengeance and to work private ends.

As for the horrifying sentence itself, it is of those criticized by Mr. Justice Holmes in Abrams' Case, 250 U.S. 616, 40 S.Ct. 17, 63 L.Ed. 1173, in that, if it be conceded trial and conviction are warranted, so frivolous is the charge that a nominal fine would serve every end of justice. And it, with too many like, goes far to give color, if not justification, to the bitter comment of George Bernard Shaw, satirist and cynic, that during the war the courts in France, bleeding under German guns, were very severe; the courts in England, hearing but the echoes of those guns, were grossly unjust; but the courts of the United States, knowing naught save censored news of those guns, were stark, staring, raving mad. All this, however, cannot affect habeas corpus. It can appeal to the pardoning power alone.

The state law is valid, petitioner's imprisonment is not repugnant to the federal Constitution, this court cannot relieve him, and the writ is denied.

## CREWS v. CLONCS

303 F.Supp. 1370 (S.D.Ind.1969)

NOLAND, District Judge.

The plaintiff, Tyler Crews, age 16 years, brings this action by his father and next friend, Borden Crews. The defendants are Eugene Cloncs, Principal of North Central High School; Dr. J. Everett Light, Superintendent of the Metropolitan School District of Washington Township; Billy Walker, Vice-Principal of North Central High School; Dr. H. Dean Evans, Assistant-Superintendent of said School District, and the following named elected members of the Board of Education, Metropolitan School District of Washington Township: John R. Mote, William T. Ray, Dr. Ray H. Behnke, William L. Smart, and Ted B. Lewis. . . .

The plaintiff contends that the defendants have violated his Constitutional rights by suspending him from attendance at North Central High School until he cuts his hair to a length specified by the defendants.

The length of plaintiff's hair on various dates was stipulated for the record and a picture of plaintiff was introduced in evidence showing his appearance in the fall of 1967, after he had cut his hair as required by Vice-Principal Billy Walker. At the various times complained of, and at the time of suspension, it is admitted that plaintiff's hair was over his ears and below his collar, contrary to the school's requirement of hair length "above the collar, above the ears and out of the eyes".

The Court would note that at the time of the pre-trial conference, the plaintiff's hair was parted in the middle and hung several inches below the shoulders in back and on the chest in front, in what would normally be described as feminine in style. Nine days later, at the trial, the plaintiff had cut his hair; however his hair, parted in the middle, still extended over the ears, over the collar, and reached to shoulder length. After this haircut and before the trial, plaintiff again requested that he be admitted to North Central High School, but was denied by the school principal since this haircut still did not meet the announced hair style requirement.

. . . .

Thereafter, plaintiff commenced this action.

. . . .

The authority of school boards and school administrators to use their discretion in enforcing rules and regulations, including the right to exclude or suspend students violating such rules and regulations is summarized in 11 Ind. Legal Encyclopedia, Education, Sec. 192, pp. 295, 296 and 297, as follows:

"School authorities have a reasonable discretion in determining what is necessary to maintain discipline in the schools under their control, and they adopt reasonable rules and regulations for the discipline and government of such schools. * *

"School authorities not only have the power to promulgate

reasonable rules and regulations for the discipline and government of the schools under their control, but they also have the powers to enforce such rules by the proper means. * *

"School authorities have the power to suspend, expel, or exclude pupils from school for infractions of their rules or where the welfare of the school system requires such action on their part."

This Court has no desire to interfere with the duly constituted authority of school boards and school administrators to adopt and to enforce reasonable rules and regulations. Neither does the Court propose to substitute its judgment for that of the school boards and school administrators absent a clearly defined violation of Constitutional rights. As recently stated by the Supreme Court:

"Judicial interposition in the operation of the public school system of the Nation raises problems requiring care and restraint. * * * By and large, public education in our Nation is committed to the control of state and local authorities. Courts do not and cannot intervene in the resolution of conflicts which arise in the daily operation of school systems and which do not directly and sharply implicate basic constitutional values." Epperson v. Arkansas, 393 U.S. 97, 104, 89 S.Ct. 266, 21 L.Ed.2d 228 (1968).

The long hair case of today may be a shaven head case tomorrow, or a brilliantly dyed hair case of some other time. The possible extremes of dress and attire are nearly unlimited.

. . . .

Plaintiff alleges that the action of the school authorities constitutes an unjustifiable infringement of his substantive due process rights under the First and the Fourteenth Amendments, asserting that the wearing of long hair constitutes symbolic speech. In Tinker v. Des Moines Independent Community School Dist., 393 U.S. 503, 89 S.Ct. 733, 21 L.Ed.2d 731 (1969), the Supreme Court held that the wearing of black arm bands by secondary school pupils protesting the Vietnam war constituted symbolic speech protected by the First Amendment; however, it is not so clear a question whether wearing long hair in this case is also First Amendment protected speech.

In view of the vagueness of plaintiff's answer to the question why he wears long hair, set out above,[3] this Court assumes without deciding that plaintiff's choice of hair styles is an expression of opinion which constitutes symbolic speech protected by the First Amendment. However, it is clear that the right to free expression is not absolute, and that it may be infringed by state authority upon a showing of a compelling reason; particularly is this the case when "pure speech" is not involved but rather conduct which reflects or is imbued

---

3. The plaintiff's statement why he wore his hair long was as follows:

"I think it looks better for one reason, and for another reason, I don't associate with a group, but I try to disassociate with general so-ciety, you know, people that look normal, because I am not entirely satisfied with things that are happening like this."

303 F.Supp. at 1373.

with speech or opinion.  Cox v. State of Louisiana, 379 U.S. 536, 555, 85 S.Ct. 453, 13 L.Ed.2d 471 (1965).

Here the interest of the state is in maintaining an orderly and efficient school system, an academic atmosphere in which knowledge can be peacefully transmitted to the pupils.  The importance of this state interest cannot be overstated.

.  .  .  .

In the case at bar, evidence was presented, and this Court finds, that plaintiff's appearance directly caused disturbances and disruption of the educational process, both in the academic classroom and during physical education classes.  Plaintiff's conduct "materially and substantially interfere[d] with the requirements of appropriate discipline in the operation of the school."  Burnside v. Byars, 363 F.2d 744, 749 (5th Cir. 1966).

It is important to note that the disruption found here resulted not from the very fact that a student had violated a rule; rather, it resulted directly from plaintiff's wearing long hair.  Had disruption resulted indirectly merely because a pupil chose to flaunt the school's authority by violating a rule, it would lend absolutely no constitutional support to the rule itself.  Breen v. Kahl, 296 F.Supp. 702 (W.D.Wis.1969).

.  .  .  .

Finally, plaintiff argues that under the case of Griswold v. State of Connecticut, 381 U.S. 479, 85 S.Ct. 1678, 14 L.Ed.2d 510 (1965), there is a right of privacy, indeed a right of personality or of individuality, which is within penumbras of particular provisions of the Bill of Rights, formed by emanations which help give life and substance to the explicit constitutional guarantees, and with which the state may not interfere.  In *Griswold* the Court held that a statute making use of contraceptives illegal was unconstitutional as violative of such an individual right of privacy.

In effect, plaintiff urges that a secondary school pupil has a fundamental personal right of free choice of grooming.  In the circumstances of this case, the Court disagrees.  While the right of privacy of a husband and wife may well be a fundamental right within the philosophy and framework of the Bill of Rights, a choice of grooming in the public schools is not such a fundamental right.  Davis v. Firment, 269 F.Supp. 524 (E.D.La.1967).  A real and substantial constitutional difference exists between the two courses of conduct— to ignore it would be myoptic [sic].  As stated by Justice Goldberg, concurring in *Griswold*, supra, in determining which rights are fundamental, judges must look to the " 'traditions and [collective] conscience of our people' to determine whether a principle is 'so rooted [there] * * * as to be ranked as fundamental.'  The inquiry is whether a right involved 'is of such a character that it cannot be denied without violating those fundamental principles of liberty and justice which lie at the base of all our civil and political institutions'."  (Citations omitted.)

Even should it be felt that choice of hair style is included within the right of privacy, no one suggests that it is an unrestricted right.

It appears to the Court that the state has met its "substantial burden of justification", (Justice White, concurring in *Griswold*, supra,) of the regulation by a showing of the classwork disruption which resulted directly from plaintiff's conduct. Little harm will result to plaintiff from trimming his hair—his opinions and beliefs, personality and individuality, will still be his own; contrasted to this result, if plaintiff is permitted to attend school with long hair, uninvolved pupils, who are completely indifferent to plaintiff's hair style, will be impeded in attaining the education they need and deserve.

## RICHARDS v. THURSTON

### 304 F.Supp. 449 (D.Mass.1969)

Plaintiff, who was suspended from general high school for refusal to have his hair cut, filed complaint seeking restoration to his status as member of senior class. The District Court, Wyzanski, Chief Judge, held that plaintiff could not properly be suspended from general high school for refusal to have his hair cut to extent approved by principal.

Judgment for plaintiff.

. . . .

WYZANSKI, Chief Judge.

. . . .

## SECOND SUPPLEMENTARY OPINION

My attention has been called to Crews v. Cloncs, (S.D.Ind.) 303 F.Supp. 1370, as reported in 38 U.S. Law Week 2187. There a student sought to have a principal enjoined from suspending him for having violated a regulation against wearing long hair. Chiefly on the ground that "The school authorities unequivocally state that long hair disrupts classroom atmosphere, impedes classroom decorum, disturbs other students, creates class disruption, and involves health and safety standards in physical education classes", the court denied relief. It seems that the court concluded that plaintiff was barred principally because his long hair caused others to be disorderly. This Court takes the position that that is not a valid ground for denying plaintiff's liberty to wear his hair as he pleases. A man may not be restrained "from doing a lawful act merely because he knows that his doing it may cause another to do an unlawful act." Beatty v. Gillbanks, 9 Q.B.D. 308, 314 (1882) (where it was held that the Salvation Army could not be forbidden to parade merely because hostile groups choose to start a disturbance). As Professor Zechariah Chafee, Jr. observed in Free Speech In The United States (1941) pp. 151–152, 160–161, it is absurd to punish a person "because his neighbors have no self-control and cannot refrain from violence." And as an illustration of such absurdity Professor Chafee referred to the imprisonment of Joseph Palmer because he persisted in wearing such a long beard that people kept mobbing him.

NOTES AND QUESTIONS

1. Compare the hair-length cases with the flag cases. What values are more intruded upon in the instance of enforced flag-saluting (with the threat of expulsion from secondary school) than in enforced hair-cutting (with the same threat)? See ROSZAK, THE MAKING OF A COUNTER CULTURE (1969); C. REICH, THE GREENING OF AMERICA (1970).

2. Is the society's interest in political nonconformity more acute than its interest in "life-style" non-conformity? Should courts be more inclined to protect "political" rights than "life-style" rights? On what bases can such a distinction be made? And how far might life-style rights extend? Consider in both regards Eldridge Cleaver's claim that

> "I became a rapist . . . . Rape was an insurrectionary act. It delighted me that I was defying and trampling upon the white man's law, upon his system of values . . . ."

SOUL ON ICE 14 (1968).

3. Carlson, "Strife Over Hair: The Historical Roots", Wall Street Journal, April 23, 1970, points out that there is a long tradition of hair length and style being a matter of social concern "and most of all during revolutions and times of political turmoil. Historically, political outs have displayed unhappiness with ruling orders by departing from approved hair styles." In England's Seventeenth century civil war, the opposing parties were quite literally identified in terms of their haircuts. The Cavaliers, supporting Charles I, "wore ringlets that cascaded down the back. One ringlet, known as a lovelock, was worn carelessly over one shoulder and tied with a ribbon bow." Cromwell's supporters became known as Roundheads, owing to the "pudding-basin" cut they affected. The unsuccessful Taipeng revolt against the Manchus became known as the Long-Haired Rebellion, the rebels refusing to shave the front of their heads as the Manchus prescribed. Jean-Paul Marat, the French revolutionist, set something of a revolutionary style by going untrimmed and unshaven —as well as unwashed.

"Priests", Carlson observes, "have regularly declaimed against the evils of long hair; towards the end of the 11th Century, the Pope decreed that persons wearing long hair should be excommunicated, and not prayed for when dead."

Why should hair become such a focal point of rally and concern? What significance does your answer have for judging how the legal system ought to greet "the long hair case of today . . . the shaven head case tomorrow, or a brilliantly dyed hair case of some other time"?

NOTE: PROTEAN MAN

Writing in the Winter, 1968, Partisan Review, Yale Psychologist Robert Jay Lifton stated that in the course of studying young Chinese, Japanese, and Americans, he became convinced that a new kind of man was emerging throughout the world, one he calls "Protean Man". The name derives from Proteus of Greek mythology, who continually changed his shape, as from one animal to another. "The protean style of self-process" is characterized by an interminable series of experiments and explorations—some shallow, some profound—each of which may be readily abandoned in favor of still new psychological quests." This behavior—which can be seen in psychoanalytic terms as freedom from super-ego and strongly internalized attitudes towards right and wrong—is claimed by Lifton to extend to all areas of human experience. He cites two historical developments in particular which have contributed to what he calls "a totally new 'world-self' ". The first he calls "historical" (or psycho-historical) dislocation, by which he refers to a break in the sense of connection people have traditionally felt with strong cultural symbols. The second is what he calls the "flooding of imagery produced by the extraordinary flow of post-modern cultural influences over the mass communication networks." What has emerged is a rapid shift from one life style to another.

> Underlying his flux in emotions and beliefs is a profound inner sense of absurdity which most often finds expression in a tone of mockery. The feeling of absurdity, of course, has a considerable modern tradition, and has been discussed by writers like Camus as a function of man's spiritual homelessness and inability to find meaning in traditional belief systems. But absurdity and mockery have taken much more extreme form in the post World War II world, and have in fact become a prominent part of a universal life style.

*PLATO*

THE LAWS *

 .   .   . I say that in states generally no one has observed that the plays of childhood have a great deal to do with the permanence or want of permanence in legislation. For when plays are ordered with a view to children having always the same games, and amusing themselves after the same manner, and finding delight in the same playthings, the more solemn institutions of the state are allowed to remain undisturbed. Whereas if sports are disturbed, and innovations are made in them, and they constantly change, and the young never speak of their having the same likings, or the same established notions of good and bad taste, either in the bearing of their bodies or in their dress, but he who devises something new and out of the way in figures and colours and the like is held in special honour, we may truly say that no greater evil can happen in a state; for he who changes the sports is secretly changing the manners of the young, and making the old to be dishonoured among them and the new to be

---

* From 4 The Dialogues of Plato 363–65, 368, 369–70, 376, 269–70 (797–99, 801, 802–03, 809, 700–01 of the Stephanus pagination) (B. Jowett transl. 4th ed. Oxford 1953).

honoured.  And I affirm that there is nothing which is a greater injury to all states than saying or thinking thus.

. . . .

. . .   The argument affirms that any change whatever except from evil is the most dangerous of all things;  this is true in the case of the seasons and of the winds, in the management of our bodies and the habits of our minds—true of all things except, as I said before, of the bad.  He who looks at the constitution of individuals accustomed to eat any sort of meat, or drink any drink, or to do any work which they can get, may see that they are at first disordered by them, but afterwards, as time goes on, their bodies grow adapted to them, and they learn to know and like variety, and have good health and enjoyment of life;  and if ever afterwards they are confined again to a superior diet, at first they are troubled with disorders, and with difficulty become habituated to their new food.  A similar principle we may imagine to hold good about the minds of men and the natures of their souls.  For when they have been brought up in certain laws, which by some Divine Providence have remained unchanged during long ages, so that no one has any memory or tradition of their ever having been otherwise than they are, then everyone is afraid and ashamed to change that which is established.  The legislator must somehow find a way of implanting this reverence for antiquity, and I would propose the following way :—People are apt to fancy, as I was saying before, that when the plays of children are altered they are merely plays, not seeing that the most serious and detrimental consequences arise out of the change;  and they readily comply with the child's wishes instead of deterring him, not considering that these children who make innovations in their games, when they grow up to be men, will be different from the last generation of children, and, being different, will desire a different sort of life, and under the influence of this desire will want other institutions and laws;  and no one of them reflects that there will follow what I just now called the greatest of evils to states.  Changes in bodily fashions are no such serious evils, but frequent changes in the praise and censure of manners are the most influential of all, and require the utmost prevision.

. . . .

. . .   [We shall] make a law that the poet shall compose nothing contrary to the ideas of the lawful, or just, or beautiful, or good, which are allowed in the state  . . .   nor shall he be permitted to communicate his compositions to any private individuals, until he shall have shown them to the appointed judges and the guardians of the law, and they are satisfied with them.

. . . .

. . . .   The order of songs and dances shall be as follows:—There are many ancient musical compositions and dances which are excellent, and from these it is fair to select what is proper and suitable to the newly-founded city;  and they shall choose judges of not less than fifty years of age, who shall make the selection, and any of the old poems which they deem sufficient they shall include;  any that are deficient or altogether unsuitable, they shall either utterly throw aside, or examine and amend, taking into their counsel poets and musicians, and making use of their poetical genius; but explaining to them the wishes of the legislator in order that they may regulate dancing, music, and all choral strains, according to the mind of the judges; and not allowing them to indulge, except in some few matters, their individual pleasures and fancies. Now the irregular strain of music is always made ten thousand times better by attaining to law and order, and rejecting the honeyed Muse—not however that we mean wholly to exclude pleasure, which is the characteristic of all music. And if a man be brought up from childhood to the age of discretion and maturity in the use of the orderly and severe music, when he hears the opposite he detests it, and calls it illiberal; but if trained in the sweet and vulgar music, he deems the severer kind cold and displeasing.

. . . .

. . . Now neither sheep nor any other animals can live without a shepherd, nor can children be left without tutors, or slaves without masters. And of all animals the boy is the most unmanageable; inasmuch as he has the fountain of reason in him not yet regulated, he is an insidious and sharp-witted animal, and the most insubordinate of them all. Wherefore he must be bound with many bridles; in the first place, when he gets away from mothers and nurses, he must be under the management of tutors on account of his childishness and foolishness; then, again, being a freeman, he must be controlled by teachers, no matter what they teach, and by studies; but he is also a slave, and in that regard any freeman who comes in his way may punish him and his tutor and his instructor, if any of them does anything wrong; and he who comes across him and does not inflict upon him the punishment which he deserves, shall incur the greatest disgrace; and let the guardian of the law, who is the director of education, see to him who coming in the way of the offences which we have mentioned, does not chastise them when he ought, or chastises them in a way which he ought not; let him keep a sharp look-out, and take especial care of the training of our children, directing their natures, and always turning them to good according to the law.

. . . .

. . . [L]et us speak of the laws about music,—that is to say, such music as then existed,—in order that we may trace the growth of the excess of freedom from the beginning. Now music was early divided among us into certain kinds and manners. One sort consisted of prayers to the Gods, which were called hymns; and there was another and opposite sort called lamentations, and another termed paeans, and another, celebrating (I believe) the birth of Dionysus, called "dithyrambs". And they used the actual word "laws", or γόμοι, for another kind of song; and to this they added the term "citharoedic". All these and others were duly distinguished, nor were the performers allowed to confuse one style of music with another. And the authority which determined and gave judgment, and punished the disobedient, was not expressed in a hiss, nor in the most unmusical shouts of the multitude, as in our days, nor in applause and clapping of hands. But the directors of public instruction insisted that the spectators should listen in silence to the end; and boys and their tutors, and the multitude in general, were kept quiet by a hint from a stick.  Such was the good order which the multitude were willing to observe; they would never have dared to give judgment by noisy cries.  And then, as time went on, the poets themselves introduced the reign of vulgar and lawless innovation.  They were men of genius, but they had no perception of what is just and lawful in music; raging like bacchanals and possessed with inordinate delights —mingling lamentations with hymns, and paeans with dithyrambs; imitating the sounds of the flute on the lyre, and making one general confusion; ignorantly affirming that music has no truth, and, whether good or bad, can only be judged of rightly by the pleasure of the hearer.  And by composing such licentious works, and adding to them words as licentious, they have inspired the multitude with lawlessness and boldness, and made them fancy that they can judge for themselves about melody and song.  And in this way the theatres from being mute have become vocal, as though they had understanding of good and bad in music and poetry; and instead of an aristocracy, an evil sort of theatrocracy has grown up.  For if there had been a democracy in music alone, consisting of free men, no fatal harm would have been done; but in music there first arose the universal conceit of omniscience and general lawlessness;—freedom came following afterwards, and men, fancying that they knew what they did not know, had no longer any fear, and the absence of fear begets shamelessness.  For what is this shamelessness, which is so evil a thing, but the insolent refusal to regard the opinion of the better by reason of an over-daring sort of liberty?

QUESTIONS

1.   Plato seems to have taken the position, especially in his later works (of which The Laws is one) that all change was bad per se.  See K. POPPER, THE OPEN SOCIETY AND ITS ENEMIES, Vol. 1 (1962), which is highly critical of the threat of totalitarianism that Professor Popper finds to run through Plato's works.

2.   Is there empirical support for Plato's fears?  What normative values militate for and against the actions he would take?  How far, for example, do the observations of Wolff and Durkheim (discussed in Wolff) go towards supporting Plato?  Lord Devlin?  What position might each of them have taken on the phenomena of "rock festivals"?  See Town of Preble v. Song Mountain, Inc., 308 N.Y.S.2d 1001 (1970), enjoining a rock festival on the grounds that "The potential for harm to the community, the public, far outweighs any good which might be derived from such an event."  308 N.Y.S.2d at 1014.  What "harms" and what "goods" do you suppose were put in the balance?

3.   Are the arguments from anomie—the need for rules in human life—inconsistent with Mill's libertarianism, as Wolff seems to suggest, above?  Does the fact that there may be biological and psychological needs for social stability entail enforcing stability through the force of government?

4.   So far as biological and sociological needs are relevant to the regulation of social disruptions, is it clear that homeostasis—tension

reduction—is an unqualified need? Are there values, to the society and to the individual character structures, of conflict? See L. COSER, THE FUNCTION OF SOCIAL CONFLICT (1956). B. Fere, in *The Therapeutic Value of Crisis*, 13 Psychological Rep. 275 (1963), maintains that crises for both individuals and groups are "inevitable and . . . a prerequisite to growth" and "an important impetus to the development of thinking and learning processes." See also the discussions of the need for stimulation in R. ARDREY, THE TERRITORIAL IMPERATIVE (1966).

## CHAPTER EIGHTEEN

# Obligations to Institutional Processes of Decision: The Problem of "Civil Disobedience"

INTRODUCTORY NOTE

Why should anyone consider himself *morally obligated* to obey the law *as such* (rather than to obey it only if, and to the extent that, it coincides with what we would do anyway, or if he cannot get away with violating it)? If someone thinks that it is moral to do act *X*, and the law prohibits *X*, what moral (as opposed to practical) considerations does the unlawfulness of *X* add? On what obligation-creating bases do such considerations rest, *e. g.*, promise, consent, reliance, reciprocity? If the law adds a moral consideration, is the consideration absolute or prima facie only? And if prima facie, what sorts of considerations—factual and theoretical—override the presumptive moral obligation to obey? What distinctions can be made in terms of the aims of the law-breakers? Of the numbers who support them? Of the damage that their violations cause? Of the alternative courses of law-making open to them? What broad ethical frameworks are presupposed by the various answers that have been given to these questions?

---

UNITED STATES DISTRICT COURT FOR THE
CENTRAL DISTRICT OF CALIFORNIA

March 1971 Grand Jury

| | |
|---|---|
| UNITED STATES OF AMERICA,<br>Plaintiff,<br><br>v.<br><br>DANIEL ELLSBERG,<br>Defendant. | No. 8354 CD<br>INDICTMENT<br>[18 U.S.C. § 793(e): Unauthorized Possession of Defense Information]<br>[18 U.S.C. § 641: Conversion of Government Property] |

The Grand Jury Charges:

Count One

[18 U.S.C. § 793(e)]

That on various dates within the period from in or about September, 1969, to in or about October, 1969, the exact dates being to the Grand Jury unknown, within the Central District of California, DANIEL ELLSBERG having unauthorized possession of, access to, and control over copies of certain documents and writings relating to the national defense, which documents and writings were originally contained in separately bound volumes of sets consisting of forty-seven (47) and eighteen (18) volumes respectively, of xerox copies of a study entitled "United States—Vietnam Relations, 1945–1967" consisting of descriptive text, cablegrams, memoranda, decision papers and other internal Executive Branch documents, all but one of which documents were classified Top Secret, the remaining document being classified Confidential; did willfully, knowingly and unlawfully retain the same and fail to deliver them to the officer or employee of the United States entitled to receive them.

### Count Two

### [18 U.S.C. § 641]

That on various dates within the period from in or about September, 1969, to in or about October, 1969, the exact dates being to the Grand Jury unknown, within the Central District of California, DANIEL ELLSBERG did willfully, knowingly and unlawfully convert to his own use copies of certain documents and writings, which documents and writings were originally contained in separately bound volumes of sets consisting of forty-seven (47) and eighteen (18) volumes respectively, of xerox copies of a study entitled "United States—Vietnam Relations, 1945–1967", consisting of descriptive text, cablegrams, memoranda, decision papers and other internal Executive Branch documents, the aforesaid documents and writings being things of value of the United States having a value in excess of one hundred dollars ($100.00).

A TRUE BILL

s/ Patricia L. Jones

---

Foreman

s/ PAUL C. VINCENT

---

PAUL C. VINCENT
Attorney for the Government

---

## WALKER v. CITY OF BIRMINGHAM

388 U.S. 307 (1966)

Mr. Justice STEWART delivered the opinion of the Court.

On Wednesday, April 10, 1963, officials of Birmingham, Alabama, filed a bill of complaint in a state circuit court asking for injunctive relief against 139 individuals and two organizations. The bill and accompanying affidavits stated that during the preceding seven days:

> "[R]espondents [had] sponsored and/or participated in and/or conspired to commit and/or to encourage and/or to participate in certain movements, plans or projects commonly called 'sit-in' demonstrations, 'kneel-in' demonstrations, mass street parades, trespasses on private property after being warned to leave the premises by the owners of said property, congregating in mobs upon the public streets

and other public places, unlawfully picketing private places
of business in the City of Birmingham, Alabama; violation
of numerous ordinances and statutes of the City of Birmingham and State of Alabama . . . ."

It was alleged that this conduct was "calculated to provoke breaches
of the peace," "threaten[ed] the safety, peace and tranquility of the
City," and placed "an undue burden and strain upon the manpower of
the Police Department."

The bill stated that these infractions of the law were expected
to continue and would "lead to further imminent danger to the lives,
safety, peace, tranquility and general welfare of the people of the
City of Birmingham," and that the "remedy by law [was] inadequate." The circuit judge granted a temporary injunction as prayed
in the bill, enjoining the petitioners from, among other things, participating in or encouraging mass street parades or mass processions
without a permit as required by a Birmingham ordinance.

Five of the eight petitioners were served with copies of the writ
early the next morning. Several hours later four of them held a press
conference. There a statement was distributed, declaring their intention to disobey the injunction because it was "raw tyranny under
the guise of maintaining law and order."[1] At this press conference
one of the petitioners stated: "That they had respect for the Federal
Courts, or Federal Injunctions, but in the past the State Courts had
favored local law enforcement, and if the police couldn't handle it,
the mob would."

---

1. The Statement distributed by petitioners read:

"In our struggle for freedom we
have anchored our faith and hope
in the rightness of the Constitution
and the moral laws of the universe.

"Again and again the Federal judiciary has made it clear that the
priviledges [sic] guaranteed under the
First and the Fourteenth Amendments
are to [sic] sacred to be trampled upon by the machinery of state government and police power. In the past
we have abided by Federal injunctions
out of respect for the forthright and
consistent leadership that the Federal
judiciary has given in establishing the
principle of integration as the law
of the land.

"However we are now confronted
with recalcitrant forces in the Deep
South that will use the courts to
perpetuate the unjust and illegal system of racial separation.

"Alabama has made clear its determination to defy the law of the
land. Most of its public officials, its
legislative body and many of its law
enforcement agents have openly de-
fied the desegration decision of the
Supreme Court. We would feel
morally and legal [sic] responsible to
obey the injunction if the courts of
Alabama applied equal justice to all
of its citizens. This would be sameness made legal. However the
ussuance [sic] of this injunction is a
blatant of *difference* made *legal*.

"Southern law enforcement agencies have demonstrated now and
again that they will utilize the force
of law to misuse the judicial process.

"This is raw tyranny under the
guise of maintaining law and order.
We cannot in all good conscience obey
such an injunction which is an unjust, undemocratic and unconstitutional misuse of the legal process.

"We do this not out of any desre-
spect [sic] for the law but out of the
highest respect for *the* law. This is
not an attempt to evade or defy the
law or engage in chaotic anarchy.
Just as in all good conscience we cannot obey unjust laws, neither can we
respect the unjust use of the courts.

"We believe in a system of law
based on justice and morality. Out
of our great love for the Constitution
of the U. S. and our desire to purify
the judicial system of the state of
Alabama, we risk this critical move
with an awareness of the possible
consequences involved."

Appendix B to Opinion of the Court,
388 U.S. at 323–24.

That night a meeting took place at which one of the petitioners announced that "[i]njunction or no injunction we are going to march tomorrow." The next afternoon, Good Friday, a large crowd gathered in the vicinity of Sixteenth Street and Sixth Avenue North in Birmingham. A group of about 50 or 60 proceeded to parade along the sidewalk while a crowd of 1,000 to 1,500 onlookers stood by, "clapping, and hollering, and [w]hooping." Some of the crowd followed the marchers and spilled out into the street. At least three of the petitioners participated in this march.

Meetings sponsored by some of the petitioners were held that night and the following night, where calls for volunteers to "walk" and go to jail were made. On Easter Sunday, April 14, a crowd of between 1,500 and 2,000 people congregated in the midafternoon in the vicinity of Seventh Avenue and Eleventh Street North in Birmingham. One of the petitioners was seen organizing members of the crowd in formation. A group of about 50, headed by three other petitioners, started down the sidewalk two abreast. At least one other petitioner was among the marchers. Some 300 or 400 people from among the onlookers followed in a crowd that occupied the entire width of the street and overflowed onto the sidewalks. Violence occurred. Members of the crowd threw rocks that injured a newspaperman and damaged a police motorcycle.

The next day the city officials who had requested the injunction applied to the state circuit court for an order to show cause why the petitioners should not be held in contempt for violating it. At the ensuing hearing the petitioners sought to attack the constitutionality of the injunction on the ground that it was vague and overbroad, and restrained free speech. They also sought to attack the Birmingham parade ordinance upon similar grounds, and upon the further ground that the ordinance had previously been administered in an arbitrary and discriminatory manner.

The circuit judge refused to consider any of these contentions, pointing out that there had been neither a motion to dissolve the injunction, or an effort to comply with it by applying for a permit from the city commission before engaging in the Good Friday and Easter Sunday parades. Consequently, the court held that the only issues before it were whether it had jurisdiction to issue the temporary injunction, and whether thereafter the petitioners had knowingly violated it. Upon these issues the court found against the petitioners, and imposed upon each of them a sentence of five days in jail and a $50 fine, in accord with an Alabama statute.

The Supreme Court of Alabama affirmed. That court, too, declined to consider the petitioners' constitutional attacks upon the injunction and the underlying Birmingham parade ordinance:

> "It is to be remembered that petitioners are charged with violating a temporary injunction. We are not reviewing a denial of a motion to dissolve or discharge a temporary injunction. Petitioners did not file any motion to vacate the temporary injunction until after the Friday and Sunday parades. Instead, petitioners deliberately defied the order

of the court and did engage in and incite others to engage in mass street parades without a permit.

. . . . . . . . . .

"We hold that the circuit court had the duty and authority, in the first instance, to determine the validity of the ordinance, and, until the decision of the circuit court is reversed for error by orderly review, either by the circuit court or a higher court, the orders of the circuit court based on its decision are to be respected and disobedience of them is contempt of its lawful authority, to be punished. Howat v. State of Kansas, 258 U.S. 181." 279 Ala. 53, 60, 62–63, 181 So.2d 493, 500, 502.

Howat v. Kansas, 258 U.S. 181, was decided by this Court almost 50 years ago. That was a case in which people had been punished by a Kansas trial court for refusing to obey an antistrike injunction issued under the state industrial relations act. They had claimed a right to disobey the court's order upon the ground that the state statute and the injunction based upon it were invalid under the Federal Constitution. The Supreme Court of Kansas had affirmed the judgment, holding that the trial court "had general power to issue injunctions in equity and that, even if its exercise of the power was erroneous, the injunction was not void, and the defendants were precluded from attacking it in this collateral proceeding . . . that, if the injunction was erroneous, jurisdiction was not thereby forfeited, that the error was subject to correction only by the ordinary method of appeal, and disobedience to the order constituted contempt." 258 U.S., at 189.

This Court, in dismissing the writ of error, not only unanimously accepted but fully approved the validity of the rule of state law upon which the judgment of the Kansas Court was grounded:

"An injunction duly issuing out of a court of general jurisdiction with equity powers upon pleadings properly invoking its action, and served upon persons made parties therein and within the jurisdiction, must be obeyed by them however erroneous the action of the court may be, even if the error be in the assumption of the validity of a seeming but void law going to the merits of the case. It is for the court of first instance to determine the question of the validity of the law, and until its decision is reversed for error by orderly review, either by itself or by a higher court, its orders based on its decision are to be respected, and disobedience of them is contempt of its lawful authority, to be punished." 258 U.S., at 189–190.

The rule of state law accepted and approved in Howat v. Kansas is consistent with the rule of law followed by the federal courts.

In the present case, however, we are asked to hold that this rule of law, upon which the Alabama courts relied, was constitutionally impermissible. We are asked to say that the Constitution compelled Alabama to allow the petitioners to violate this injunction, to organize and engage in these mass street parades and demonstrations, without any previous effort on their part to have the injunction dissolved or modified, or any attempt to secure a parade permit in accordance with its terms. Whatever the limits of Howat v. Kansas, we cannot accept the petitioner's contentions in the circumstances of this case.

Without question the state court that issued the injunction had, as a court of equity, jurisdiction over the petitioners and over the subject matter of the controversy. And this is not a case where the injunction was transparently invalid or had only a frivolous pretense to validity. We have consistently recognized the strong interest of state and local governments in regulating the use of their streets and other public places. . . .

The generality of the language contained in the Birmingham parade ordinance upon which the injunction was based would unquestionably raise substantial constitutional issues concerning some of its provisions. . . . The petitioners, however, did not even attempt to apply to the Alabama courts for an authoritative construction of the ordinance. Had they done so, those courts might have given the licensing authority granted in the ordinance a narrow and precise scope, as did the New Hampshire courts in Cox v. New Hampshire and Poulos v. New Hampshire . . . .. Here, just as in *Cox* and *Poulos*, it could not be assumed that this ordinance was void on its face.

The breadth and vagueness of the injunction itself would also unquestionably be subject to substantial constitutional question. But the way to raise that question was to apply to the Alabama courts to have the injunction modified or dissolved. The injunction in all events clearly prohibited mass parading without a permit, and the evidence shows that the petitioners fully understood that prohibition when they violated it.

. . . . .

This case would arise in quite a different constitutional posture if the petitioners, before disobeying the injunction, had challenged it in the Alabama courts, and had been met with delay or frustration of their constitutional claims. But there is no showing that such would have been the fate of a timely motion to modify or dissolve the injunction. . . .

. . . . . [T]he petitioners [were] on notice that they could not bypass orderly judicial review of the injunction before disobeying it. Any claim that they were entrapped or misled is wholly unfounded, a conclusion confirmed by evidence in the record showing that when the petitioners deliberately violated the injunction they expected to go to jail.

The rule of law that Alabama followed in this case reflects a belief that in the fair administration of justice no man can be judge in his own case, however exalted his station, however righteous his motives, and irrespective of his race, color, politics, or religion. This Court cannot hold that the petitioners were constitutionally free to ignore all the procedures of the law and carry their battle to the streets. One may sympathize with the petitioners' impatient commitment to their cause. But respect for judicial process is a small price to pay for the civilizing hand of law, which alone can give abiding meaning to constitutional freedom.

Affirmed.

Mr. Chief Justice WARREN, whom Mr. Justice BRENNAN and Mr. Justice FORTAS join, dissenting.[2]

.  .  .  .

These facts lend no support to the court's charges that petitioners were presuming to act as judges in their own case, or that they had a disregard for the judicial process. They did not flee the jurisdiction or refuse to appear in the Alabama courts. Having violated the injunction, they promptly submitted themselves to the courts to test the constitutionality of the injunction and the ordinance it parroted. They were in essentially the same position as persons who challenge the constitutionality of a statute by violating it, and then defend the ensuing criminal prosecution on constitutional grounds. It has never been thought that violation of a statute indicated such a disrespect for the legislature that the violator always must be punished even if the statute was unconstitutional. On the contrary, some cases have required that persons seeking to challenge the constitutionality of a statute first violate it to establish their standing to sue. Indeed, it shows no disrespect for law to violate a statute on the ground that it is unconstitutional and then to submit one's case to the courts with the willingness to accept the penalty if the statute is held to be valid.

.  .  .  .

Mr. Justice BRENNAN, with whom THE CHIEF JUSTICE, Mr. Justice DOUGLAS, and Mr. Justice FORTAS, join, dissenting.

.  .  .  .

It is said that petitioners should have sought to dissolve the injunction before conducting their processions. That argument is plainly repugnant to the principle that First Amendment freedoms may be exercised in the face of legislative prior restraints, and *a fortiori* of *ex parte* restraints broader than such legislative restraints, which may be challenged in any subsequent proceeding for their violation. But at all events, prior resort to a motion to dissolve this injunction could not be required because of the complete absence of any time limits on the duration of the *ex parte* order. . . . Even the Alabama Supreme Court's Rule 47 leaves the timing of full judicial consideration of the validity of the restraint to that court's untrammeled discretion.

The shifting of the burden to petitioners to show the lawfulness of their conduct prior to engaging in enjoined activity also is contrary to the principle, settled by Speiser v. Randall, 357 U.S. 513, 526, that

> "The man who knows that he must bring forth proof and persuade another of the lawfulness of his conduct necessarily must steer far wider of the unlawful zone than if the

<hr/>

**2.** 388 U.S. at 327.

State must bear these burdens  . . . .  In practical operation, therefore, this procedural device must necessarily produce a result which the State could not command directly.  It
can only result in a deterrence of speech which the Constitution makes free."

NOTES AND QUESTIONS

1.  What reasons are there for the court's refusal to inspect the
underlying constitutional grievances of the marchers?  Why should
the violation of a state court order, under claim of constitutional
right, be treated differently than the violation of a state legislative
enactment, under claim of constitutional rights?  Are there not in
both cases, alternative methods for testing constitutionality?  Is
the integrity of the judicial processes any less diminished in the one
case than in the other?

2.  Are the demonstrators claiming they are both morally right
and legally right?  What obligations to the legal system were the
demonstrators acknowledging?  What sorts of moral principles can
they rely on?  On what assumptions can one say that they were
"right" morally and yet the court "right" legally?  Would the arguments of the demonstrators have supported, say, their not submitting
to arrest?  their use of violence to resist arrest?  their refusal, in
the courtroom, to observe decorum?  What different values are involved in each of these possible reactions?  Why should the demonstrators claim only a right to disobey the law—why do their arguments not entail their being under a "duty" *to disobey*?  See Walzer, *The Obligation to Disobey*, 77 Ethics 163 (1967).  What differences—practical and theoretical, would such a shift in terminology involve?

3.  What characteristics of the disobedients' actions inure to
their moral force, and which detract from it?  How are there claims
different from those of burglars?  Does it matter, for example,
whether the majority of the people of Alabama thought that the demonstrations were illegal—or immoral?  Does it matter whether the
demonstrators had available other means of publicizing their grievances?

4.  Consider the following remarks of Dean Rostow,

. . .  [T]he law cannot and should not distinguish
between the rights of protest of those who do and those who
do not generally accept the rightness of our constitutional
system.  The history of attempts to condemn or to restrict
the civil rights of those deemed "disloyal" or "un-American"
is not a happy one, and I cannot believe it is wise or practicable for this purpose to distinguish between appeals to the
conscience of the nation made by those who in their hearts
are attached to the fundamental principles of the Constitution, and those who would gladly destroy it.  The distinction
is subjective.  Ample and depressing experience attests to
the difficulties of applying such a test.  Our legal order has
generally—and, in my view, rightly—addressed itself in

large part to actions, and sought to avoid distinctions as to legal rights based on distinctions of attitude. Good men and bad men, anarchists and conservatives, men of all faiths and of no faith, are equally protected by the Constitution and its Bill of Rights, and equally bound by valid laws enacted through constitutional procedures. All are equally free to appeal to the conscience of the nation, and to its traditional values, whether their appeal is made in good faith or in bad.

*The Rightful Limits of Freedom in a Liberal State: Of Civil Disobedience* in Is LAW DEAD? 83–84 (1971).

5. Is the violation of law from considerations of conscience a monopoly of college students and minority group protesters? Consider in this regard the selections that follow.

*Abraham Lincoln*

## First Inaugural Address (March 4, 1861).*

I do not forget the position assumed by some that constitutional questions are to be decided by the Supreme Court, nor do I deny that such decisions must be binding in any case upon the parties to a suit as to the object of that suit, while they are also entitled to very high respect and consideration in all parallel cases by all other departments of the Government. And while it is obviously possible that such decision may be erroneous in any given case, still the evil effect following it, being limited to that particular case, with the chance that it may be overruled and never become a precedent for other cases, can better be borne than could the evils of a different practice. At the same time, the candid citizen must confess that if the policy of the Government upon vital questions affecting the whole people is to be irrevocably fixed by decisions of the Supreme Court, the instant they are made in ordinary litigation between parties in personal actions the people will have ceased to be their own rulers, having to that extent practically resigned their Government into the hands of that eminent tribunal. . . .

*Evelle J. Younger* †

## Public Statement of Wednesday, December 17, 1969

For some time, my staff and I have been of the opinion that the court-imposed restrictions on the dissemination of proper public information by public officials in criminal cases is unwarranted and beyond the inherent power of the court.

---

* From 6 Messages and Papers of the Presidents 9–10 (Richardson ed. 1897). The remarks were made in apparent reference to Dred Scott v. Sandford, 19 How. 395 (1857).

† District Attorney for Los Angeles County.

In the case of People vs. Sirhan Bishara Sirhan, we sought to attack such orders through judicial review without violating the orders themselves.

I recently took the position that in the matter of the Sharon Tate-La Bianca murder case, that the court order restricting public announcements would be honored by my office, although it was our opinion that it, too, was unwarranted and beyond the inherent power of the court.

On December 9, 1969, in the Pasadena Municipal Court, at the end of a preliminary hearing that involved Judge Lloyd Davis, another muzzling order was made. Knowing that our attack through judicial review has been unsuccessful, it is the express purpose of this meeting to violate the order of Judge John F. Hassler.

At the end of the preliminary hearing, Judge Hassler ordered that the prosecuting attorney and his staff, defense counsel and his staff, court attaches and any other persons connected with the case shall not, at any time, unless relieved by order of another court, discuss the subject action or offer any opinion on the merits, either in favor of or against the People or the defendant. This is only a portion of that order.

As you can see, when my staff and I discussed this case at a staff meeting, we were technically in violation of the "gag" rule imposed by the court.

Under California law, any defendant, upon motion, is entitled to a closed preliminary examination. In the instant case involving Judge Davis, counsel for the defendant asked and was granted a closed hearing, pursuant to Section 868 of the Penal Code. The judge is required, under this section, to invoke a closed session regardless of opposition by the prosecution.

This resulted in the exclusion of the press as well as the public. This closed session was further accentuated by Judge Hassler's issuing of a "gag" order. Taken together, the closed session and the "gag" order effectively prevents public review of this case or the activity of this office.

Judge Davis was held to answer in the preliminary examination and the case will now proceed to the Superior Court with the charge of Assault With A Deadly Weapon. I feel that the people of the community are entitled to know what transpired at the time of the preliminary examination.

Mrs. Mary Davis, the alleged victim, was called as a witness. Without asserting any constitutional privilege, but by asserting what she called personal privilege, she refused to testify as to any events concerning a stab wound which she received in her back. At the conclusion of the hearing, the judge held her in contempt for her failure to testify and then purged her of the contempt.

The People proceeded to call expert medical testimony to establish the nature of the wound and that in the opinion of the expert, it could not have been self-inflicted. Other evidence was introduced from additional witnesses which satisfied the magistrate that the defendant should be held for trial for the crime of Assault With A Deadly Weapon in the Superior Court.

It is my feeling that the community is entitled to know what transpired at the time of that hearing once the defendant is held to answer in the Superior Court, and to deny this information to the public is to deny the First Amendment right to the freedom of fair expression.

I am not intending to convey by this statement a comment in any way as to the guilt or innocence of the accused, but to disclose what occurred at a duly constituted judicial proceeding.

A copy of this statement is being mailed to Judge Hassler for whatever action he may desire to take.

## An Ordinance, to Nullify Certain Acts of the Congress of the United States, Purporting to be Laws, Laying Duties and Imposts on the Importation of Foreign Commodities.

1 So.Car.Stats. 329 (1832)

*Whereas,* the Congress of the United States, by various acts, purporting to be acts laying duties and imposts on foreign imports, but in reality intended for the protection of domestic manufactures, and the giving of bounties to classes and individuals engaged in particular employments, at the expense and to the injury and oppression of other classes and individuals, and by wholly exempting from taxation certain foreign commodities, such as are not produced or manufactured in the United States, to afford a pretext for imposing higher and excessive duties on articles similar to those intended to be protected, hath exceeded its just powers under the Constitution, which confers on it no authority to afford such protection, and hath violated the true meaning and intent of the Constitution, which provides for equality in imposing the burdens of taxation upon the several States and portions of the Confederacy. *And whereas,* the said Congress, exceeding its just power to impose taxes and collect revenue for the purpose of effecting and accomplishing the specific objects and purposes which the Constitution of the United States authorizes it to effect and accomplish, hath raised and collected unnecessary revenue, for objects unauthorized by the Constitution—

*We, therefore, the People of the State of South Carolina, in Convention assembled, do Declare and Ordain, and it is hereby Declared and Ordained,* That the several acts and parts of acts of the Congress of the United States, purporting to be laws for the imposing of duties and imposts on the importation of foreign commodities, and now having actual operation and effect within the United States, and more especially an act entitled "an act in alteration of the several acts imposing duties on imports," approved on the nineteenth day of May, one thousand eight hundred and twenty-eight, and also, an act entitled "an act to alter and amend the several acts imposing duties on imports," approved on the fourteenth day of July, one thousand eight hundred and thirty-two, are unauthorized by the Constitution of the United States, and violate the true meaning and intent thereof, and are null, void, and no law, nor binding upon this State, its officers, or citizens; and all promises, contracts and obligations, made or entered into, or to be made or entered into, with purpose to secure the duties imposed by said acts, and all judicial proceedings which shall be hereafter had in affirmance thereof, are, and shall be held, utterly null and void.

*And it is further Ordained,* That it shall not be lawful for any of the constituted authorities, whether of this State, or of the United States, to enforce the payment of duties imposed by the said acts, within the limits of this State; but it shall be the duty of the Legislature to adopt such measures and pass such acts as may be necessary to give full effect to this Ordinance, and to prevent the enforcement and arrest the operation of the said acts and parts of acts of the Congress of the United States, within the limits of this State, from and after the first day of February next; and the duty of all other constituted authorities, and of all persons residing or being within the limits of this State, and they are hereby required and enjoined, to obey and give effect to this Ordinance, and such acts and measures of the Legislature as may be passed or adopted in obedience thereto.

*And it is further Ordained,* That in no case of law or equity, decided in the Courts of this State, wherein shall be drawn in question the authority of this Ordinance, or the validity of such acts or acts of the Legislature as may be passed for the purpose of giving effect thereto, or the validity of the aforesaid acts of Congress, imposing duties, shall any appeal be taken or allowed to the Supreme Court of the United States; nor shall any copy of the record be permitted or allowed for that purpose; and if any such appeal shall be attempted to be taken, the Courts of this State shall proceed to execute and enforce their judgments, according to the laws and usages of the State, without reference to such attempted appeal, and the person or persons attempting to take such appeal may be dealt with as for a contempt of the Court.

*And it is further Ordained,* That all persons now holding any office of honor, profit or trust, civil or military, under this State, (members of the Legislature excepted) shall, within such time, and in such manner as the Legislature shall prescribe, take an oath, well and truly to obey, execute and enforce this Ordinance, and such act or acts of the Legislature as may be passed in pursuance thereof, according to the true intent and meaning of the same; . . . .

And we, the People of South Carolina, to the end that it may be fully understood by the Government of the United States, and the People of the co-States, that we are determined to maintain this, our Ordinance and Declaration, at every hazard, *Do further Declare,* that we will not submit to the application of force, on the part of the Federal Government, to reduce this State to obedience; but that we will consider the passage, by Congress, of any act authorizing the employment of a military or naval force against the State of South Carolina, her constituted authorities or citizens, or any act abolishing

or closing the ports of this State, or any of them, or otherwise obstructing the free ingress and egress of vessels to and from the said
ports, or any other act, on the part of the Federal Government, to coerce the State, shut up her ports, destroy or harass her commerce, or
to enforce the acts hereby declared to be null and void, otherwise than
through the civil tribunals of the country, as inconsistent with the
longer continuance of South Carolina in the Union: and that the
People of this State will thenceforth hold themselves absolved from
all further obligation to maintain or preserve their political connexion
with the people of the other States, and will forthwith proceed to
organize a separate Government, and to do all other acts and things
which sovereign and independent States may of right do.

*Done in Convention, at Columbia, the twenty-fourth day of
November, in the year of our Lord one thousand eight hundred and
thirty-two, and in the fifty-seventh year of the Declaration of the Independence of the United States of America.*

QUESTIONS

How do the respective actions of Lincoln, District Attorney
Younger, and South Carolina compare to those of the demonstrators
in *Walker*? Which case of "disobedience" can claim the higher
legitimacy? Why?

*THOMAS JEFFERSON*

LETTER TO JAMES MADISON *

Dear Sir

. . . . I hold it that a little rebellion now and then is a good
thing, and as necessary in the political world as storms in the physical.
Unsuccessful rebellions indeed generally establish the incroachments
on the rights of the people which have produced them. An observation of this truth should render honest republican governors so mild
in their punishment of rebellions, as not to discourage them too much.
It is a medecine necessary for the sound health of government.

*THOMAS JEFFERSON*

LETTER TO WILLIAM STEPHENS SMITH †

Dear Sir

. . . . The British ministry have so long hired their
gazetteers to repeat and model into every form lies about our being
in anarchy, that the world has at length believed them, the English
nation has believed them, the ministers themselves have come to believe them, and what is more wonderful, we have believed them ourselves. Yet where does this anarchy exist? Where did it ever exist,
except in the single instance of Massachusets? And can history pro-

* From 2 The Papers of Thomas Jeffer-       † From 12 *Id.,* 355–57.
son 92–93 (Princeton Univ. Press
1955).

duce an instance of a rebellion so honourably conducted? I say nothing of it's motives. They were founded in ignorance, not wickedness. God forbid we should every be 20. years without such a rebellion. The people can not be all, and always, well informed. The part which is wrong will be discontented in proportion to the importance of the facts they misconceive. If they remain quiet under such misconceptions it is a lethargy, the forerunner of death to the public liberty. We have had 13. states independent 11. years. There has been one rebellion. That comes to one rebellion in a century and a half for each state. What country before ever existed a century and half without a rebellion? And what country can preserve it's liberties if their rulers are not warned from time to time that their people preserve the spirit of resistance? Let them take arms. The remedy is to set them right as to facts, pardon and pacify them. What signify a few lives lost in a century or two? The tree of liberty must be refreshed from time to time with the blood of patriots and tyrants. It is it's natural manure.

CHARLES L. BLACK, JR.

## THE PROBLEM OF THE COMPATIBILITY OF CIVIL DISOBEDIENCE WITH AMERICAN INSTITUTIONS OF GOVERNMENT *

During the past few years, we have often heard the term "civil disobedience" used to describe the actions of persons who actively disobey local or state laws commanding racial segregation or who peacefully demonstrate to make plain and public their disapproval of this or some other racial discrimination. These people do, indeed, act in conscious violation of what is asserted to be legal authority, and they do offer themselves for arrest by the constituted authorities. But they do so in the belief, more or less clearly held and more or less clearly warranted, that the law itself is on their side and that the law's processes, in the end, will uphold them or will fail to do so only through an error in law. They appeal, in our federal system, over the head of the law and authority of the state, to the law and authority of the nation.

A first instance may be the case of the Freedom Riders of the summer of 1961. Most of these people were guilty of the offenses of riding unsegregated on interstate journeys, of standing about together unsegregated in waiting rooms, and of seeking unsegregated service in the station restaurants of interstate bus lines and railroads. There was a flavor of disobedience to law about all this, both because state and local statutes and ordinances forbade it and because local authorities—sometimes applying a legal epithet, such as breach of the peace, that confused only if one desired to be confused—sought to punish it by legal processes. But there was not the faintest real doubt that the ordinances were void under federal law and that punishment of conduct protected by federal law cannot be justified in law by calling that

* From 43 Texas L.Rev. 492, 496–98 (1965). Reprinted by permission of    the Texas Law Review and Professor Rothman.

conduct by some name that hopefully carries the inference of punishability. By and large, the Freedom Rides were instances of conduct clearly lawful, and the defiance of law was all on the other side.

The sit-in cases in establishments not directly in the stream of interstate commerce and not at the time subjected to federal statutory regulation present a different picture. Whether the federal constitution protects the right peaceably to remain on one's stool at a public lunchcounter after one has been refused service and asked to leave in obedience to a custom of segregation is a question of real difficulty. The point of law at issue, I remind you, is in that most storm-vexed field of law, the field of "state action." The guarantees of the fourteenth amendment, run only against actions of the states, and in the sit-in cases the immediate decision to discriminate was that of the proprietor. On the other hand, what the fourteenth amendment forbids a state to do is to "deny" equal protection of the laws, a form of words which surely imports some affirmative obligation, though its contours are not yet worked out. It can be contended that the custom of segregation to which the segregating proprietor conforms has for so many decades been supported by state law and policy that state power must be held a part of the causation behind individual acts taken in conformance to the custom. It would perhaps have surprised the sit-inners, in the total ambient, to learn that state power was to no significant extent involved in the segregation pattern to which they were being subjected; indeed, as a personal opinion, I am inclined to think it will surprise historians of the period to learn that this contention was so seriously urged and taken so seriously.

But the ultimate legal question is by all objective indices genuinely doubtful. The Supreme Court has split on it, three to three to three. The scholarly community is split on it. And we may never have an authoritative settlement from the Court because the Civil Rights Act of 1964 would seem now to furnish a complete statutory defense to the sit-inner and so to make moot the question of the impact of the fourteenth amendment considered alone.

The point, when we come to evaluate the act of the sit-inner, is that he usually acted under a claim of legal right, a claim not virtually certain of validity, as with the Freedom Riders, but tenable at the least and put forward in good faith. This is not to say that the children who marched into town to put their courage up against three centuries of prejudice did so while holding in their minds a clear legal theory, or several clear legal theories, on the "state action" problem; but they did, by and large, come in with the belief that they were in the right—in the legal as well as in the moral right.

The point may be made clear by a contrast between the respective acts of John Hampden and Henry Thoreau. The disobedience of each consisted in a refusal to pay taxes, one of the most purely passive but at the same time one of the most radically subversive of civil disobediences. But Thoreau took his stand, not on the ground that under law the tax was not owing, but on the ground that as a matter of moral choice quite outside the realm of legality he preferred and indeed felt bound to withhold his support from a government that enforced slavery. Hampden, on the other hand, withheld payment on the ground that the ship-money as a matter of law was not owing. The sit-inners, in the main, are with Hampden.

In all such cases, great or small, there is an element of claimed legal right and hence of an implied submission to rather than defiance of the order of law. There is, usually, a strong admixture of a moral in addition to a legal claim; the thing combatted, as in Montgomery, is felt to be wrong as well as unlawful. Nor is the legal claim always clear or even explicit; it is likely, for example, that the lady whose refusal to move back in the bus set the Montgomery movement going was consciously motivated rather by a realization that the request was an affront to her humanity than by an apprehension that her legal rights were being violated. But even this, the extremest case, the case of the person protesting injustice without thought to law, but under circumstances which do in fact found a tenable (and in her case a valid) legal claim, is very far indeed from the case of pure civil disobedience, of considered disobedience to what is known to be valid law under the applicable legal system.

## GROSSNER v. TRUSTEES OF COLUMBIA UNIVERSITY

287 F.Supp. 535 (S.D.N.Y. 1968)

FRANKEL, District Judge.

In this lawsuit, which grows out of grave troubles recently experienced at Columbia University, nine assorted plaintiffs—five students, the pastor of a church near the University, a chapter president of the Congress of Racial Equality, an alumnus, and a lecturer in the College and Graduate Faculties—assert for "themselves and all persons similarly situated" various "causes of action" and demands for injunctive relief. They have moved for an injunction *pendente lite.* The application for such extraordinary relief is without merit, and will be denied. A cross-motion for summary judgment will be held in abeyance.

### I.

The plaintiffs complain broadly that they and members of their "classes" have for some time been protesting against the "policy-making structure of the University," the President's "unlimited and undefined" disciplinary powers, the planned construction of a University gymnasium in a public recreational area, and the University's involvement in the "Institute for Defense Analysis [*sic*] * * *, a consortium of twelve American universities conduction [*sic*] research for the Department of Defense." Before April 23, 1968, it is alleged, plaintiffs attempted to communicate such protests "to the appropriate officials of the University without any serious consideration or response thereto being given." . . . Moreover, they charge, on September 25, 1967, defendant Kirk, the University President, "issued an edict prohibiting further protest demonstrations within the buildings of the University, no matter how peaceful or non-violent." . . . On April 23, plaintiffs and others assembled and went to the offices of the President in Low Memorial Library. When they learned that the President was refusing to meet with them, they proceeded to the site of the disputed gymnasium, but they were soon dispersed by the police. The plaintiffs then "returned to the campus to begin a peaceful demonstration in Hamilton Hall to protest the refusals of the University to give reasonable consideration to the structural and policy changes hereinabove referred to." . . . "In addition to the said demonstration in Hamilton Hall, from April 23 to April 30, 1968, plaintiffs, in their attempt to bring about a discussion and negotiations of the said structural and policy changes with the appropriate University officials, assembled" in three other University buildings and in "the offices of the defendant KIRK, where they remained until their arrests on the latter date * * *."

. . . .

Notwithstanding that their occupation of the buildings was "peaceful and orderly," plaintiffs charge, defendant President called in the police, who, at about two a. m. on April 30, 1968, "without any provocation by plaintiffs and members of their classes, * * * utilizing excessive and unnecessary force and in a brutal and inhuman manner physically assaulted and beat plaintiffs and the members of their classes and arrested more than 700 thereof." Then, it is asserted "upon information and belief," various charges of criminal trespass, resisting arrest, disorderly conduct, loitering, inciting to riot, and possession of weapons and dangerous instruments and appliances were filed against those so arrested.

The complaint goes on to allege that defendant University officials have brought or are threatening disciplinary proceedings arising from the foregoing events under University statutes which are vague, devoid of standards, offensive to principles of due process, and contrary to the protections of the First and Fourteenth Amendments. The threats of discipline "and/or arrest" are allegedly "being made * * * in bad faith without any hope of ultimate success and with the basic purpose and effect of intimidating and harassing * * * and punishing [plaintiffs] for, and deterring them from," exercising their First Amendment rights.

In order to avoid the "chilling effect" of such action by defendants, plaintiffs' first "cause of action" is to enjoin the University disciplinary proceedings and declare void a general statute of the University announcing its disciplinary powers.

. . . .

The sixth and final "cause of action" charges that the University structure, "essentially unchanged since 1754, affords no participatory power in the faculty or student body in the determination of policies and programs of the University." . . . Plaintiffs say this "structure" violates unspecified "constitutional rights of faculty and students as well as the rights of members of the community affected by the actions of the University, in that it provides for a self-perpetuating body" of irresponsible trustees, "all in violation of the fundamental tenets of a democratic society as outlined in the Constitution of the

United States." The court is asked to order a restructuring of the University under a "program to be submitted to this Court for its approval."

## II.

. . . .

From the several affidavits on both sides, the undisputed facts and the unresolved disputes become sufficiently apparent for present purposes. It is clear that some hundreds of students and others conducted round-the-clock sit-ins occupying University buildings and the President's office for the week or so beginning April 23, and that they left on April 30 only because they were forcibly removed. At the outset of this "peaceful" protest, the Acting Dean of Columbia College was held captive in his office in Hamilton Hall for some 24 hours. During the occupancy of President Kirk's office, his files were rifled, documents were removed, and copies were made of correspondence, memoranda, diaries and other records. Since that time, copies of such records have been widely circulated on the campus and to public communications media.

It is undisputed, despite some equivalent legalisms for plaintiffs, that those participating in the sit-ins denied access to the buildings to faculty members, students and University personnel, among others. Through the week of sit-ins, faculty members and others sought to persuade the occupants to leave peaceably. When these negotiations failed, the police moved in on the night of April 29-30 to force the departures and make the arrests which are central in plaintiffs' complaint. Plaintiff Morris Grossner was among those arrested on that night.

. . . .

## III.

Our highest Court has made clear in the labors of a long generation that the First Amendment's mandate protecting free expression "must be taken as a command of the broadest scope that explicit language, read in the context of a liberty-loving society, will allow." Bridges v. State of California, 314 U.S. 252, 263, 62 S.Ct. 190, 194, 86 L.Ed. 192 (1941). The Court has insisted steadily on the "principle that debate on public issues should be uninhibited, robust, and wide-open * * *." New York Times Co. v. Sullivan, 376 U.S. 254, 270, 84 S.Ct. 710, 721, 11 L.Ed.2d 686 (1964). It has also made clear, however, the gross error of believing that every kind of conduct (however non-verbal and physically destructive or obstructive) must be treated simply as protected "speech" because those engaged in it intend to express some view or position . . . .. Similarly, the Court has rejected the notion that "everyone with opinions or beliefs to express may do so at any time and at any place." Cox v. State of Louisiana, 379 U.S. 559, 574, 85 S.Ct. 476, 486, 13 L.Ed.2d 487 (1965); . . . . Without such inescapably necessary limits, the First Amendment would be a self-destroying license for "peaceful" "expression" by the seizure of streets, buildings and offices by mobs, large or small, driven by motives (and toward objectives) that different viewers might deem "good or bad." . . . It is such a license plaintiffs claim when they state the basic premise of their lawsuit as follows:

> "Plaintiffs maintain, consistent with the American tradition of democratic and legal confrontation, that the non-violent occupation of five buildings of Columbia University for less than one week in the circumstances of this case is fully protected by the First Amendment guarantees of the right to petition government for the redress of grievances, * * * to assemble and to speak. Plaintiffs maintain that the non-violent occupation of the buildings was absolutely necessary to breathe life into the First Amendment principle that government institutions should reflect the will of the people and that this interest must prevail under any balancing test against the inconvenience to defendant Columbia University in having five of its buildings occupied by students for approximately one week."

Embellishing such untenable propositions, plaintiffs (or, more fairly, the sixteen attorneys who sign their brief) proceed to argue that the rhetoric and the tactics of the American Revolution are the guides by which judges are to construe the First Amendment. The "rule of law," they explain, must not be overrated: "Had the Americans agreed that the rule of law, however, despotic, must always prevail; had the Americans felt that dropping the tea in the harbor was going too far; had the Americans not focused on fundamental principles, this country might still be a colony to-day." The message, insofar as it is intelligible, possibly means that a tea party today, if nothing else could achieve repeal of a hated tax, would be protected by the First Amendment. Or possibly it means something else. Whatever it is meant to mean, and whatever virtues somebody might think such ideas might have in other forums, arguments like this are at best useless (at worse deeply pernicious) nonsense in courts of law. See Fortas, Concerning Dissent and Civil Disobedience 34 (1968) . . . .

It is surely non-sense of the most literal kind to argue that a court of law should subordinate the "rule of law" in favor of more "fundamental principles" of revolutionary action designed forcibly to oust governments, courts and all. But this self-contradictory sort of theory—all decked out in the forms of law with thick papers, strings of precedent, and the rest—is ultimately at the heart of plaintiffs' case. And so it is not surprising that plaintiffs' efforts to implement the theory have led them to champion a series of propositions of unsound constitutional law.

### NOTES AND QUESTIONS

1. What moral and legal grounds are available to the students and other University-affiliated protestors in the *Grossner* case that are not available to the protestors in *Walker*? In which case is the moral claim stronger? In which case is the legal position stronger? What difference does it make whether the practices of traditionally

"private" or traditionally "public" institutions are being challenged?
Note, too, the relief that the plaintiffs in *Grossner* are seeking.  To
what extent do the arguments of the *Grossner* plaintiffs presuppose
the validity of the legal structure, and to what extent do their arguments argue "around" the system?  How do the actions of the *Grossner* plaintiffs compare with those of the governing officials of South
Carolina in 1832?  of Lincoln?

2.  In Scoggin v. Lincoln University, 291 F.Supp. 161 (W.D.Mo.
1968), the court observed:

"We who live today tend to view the current scene of student unrest and violence as a totally new historical phenomenon.  Professor
Lewis B. Mayhew of Stanford University recently suggested that there
may be "good reason to believe that the present wave of student unrest may be qualitatively different from those [of] earlier times,"
Saturday Review, August 17, 1968, p. 57.  But he also made clear that
the problem of restless students was indeed an old one.  In order "to
put the problem in some kind of historical perspective" he stated that:

> Students have always been difficult to live with and have
> frequently assumed postures which bothered adults and dis-
> turbed institutions.  Medieval students rioted, dumped gar-
> bage on passersby, wrote erotic or ribald poems and read
> them on church steps and in other sanctuaries of the Estab-
> lishment, coerced their professors and occasionally killed
> one.  Colonial college students rioted about food, stole, took
> pot shots at university presidents, protested infringement of
> their private lives, and gradually forced colleges to modify
> stringent rules regarding personal conduct.  Nineteenth-cen-
> tury college students took sides over the Civil War and de-
> manded a voice in academic governance.  Twentieth-century
> signed the Oxford Peace Pledge, joined in the Spanish Civil
> War, rioted over food, violated the Eighteenth Amendment,
> and experimented with sex.  * * *.  [A]t least an impor-
> tant portion of student protest replicates those of the past
> simply because the process of growing up is, after all, a hu-
> man process that has not changed much in quite a few years.

"Full credit may be given for the teaching of history that student
protests have, on not infrequent occasions, been, to again borrow Professor Mayhew's words, in 'real responses to bad conditions.'  He
stated, for example, that:

> A confrontation between Princeton students of different per-
> suasions, a hundred years ago, dramatized the serious moral
> questions as to whether justice lay with the North or the
> South.  Student agitation over strict rules of conduct was
> sparked by an overzealous desire on the part of faculty to im-
> pose a Puritan ideal of conduct which was inappropriate in
> a changing society.  Perhaps historical reflection might sug-
> gest that old standards can be changed and the world still
> turn.

"But students from medieval times to the present have been required to learn that a riot is no less a riot simply because those who

constitute the mob happen to be students.  Acceptance of the time-tested techniques of demagogy and glorification of the violence of the mob by a student to support what he may believe to be an ideal does not alter the nature of his conduct nor does his youth give him immunity from disciplinary action based on conduct that may violate a valid rule of a particular educational institution, to say nothing of violations of the civil and criminal laws that govern the society of which, whether he likes it or not, he is a part.

"The necessity that we learn from the past is not confined to the students.  Professor Mayhew stated that:

> In virtually every major campus upset since 1964, there was a lack of procedures and procedural rights which could have kept grievances within legitimate bounds.  The technique of direct administrative handling of disciplinary matters has lost its legitimacy in the eyes of students and many faculty, and this fact should be recognized.  The nature of needed changes seems reasonably clear.

"The glory of education in a democratic society is that all who must learn can and do learn so that appropriate changes are made in a peaceful manner.  It is by this process, which sometimes operates more slowly than many desire, that the occasion for violence and its lure to the immature is removed."  291 F.Supp. at 173–74

Compare the views of Professor Mayhew, quoted in *Scoggin*, with those of Robert Nisbet, "The Restoration of Academic Authority", *Wall Street Journal*, August 19, 1970.  Professor Nisbet takes the position that the student (what he calls) "insurrections" did not break down academic authority, but that it was the other way around: the prior breakdown of authority through substantial increase in "participatory democracy" caused the uprisings.  "Over and over one finds that the worst and most prolonged of insurrections occur precisely where grants of governing authority to students and faculty have been greatest."  Nisbet claims that no other major institution has existed in modern times "with the minimum of formal regulation and of contractual detail".  "Potent though this structure of authority was, it was yet so finely drawn, and so much a part of the very atmosphere, as to be nearly invisible."  In Nisbet's view, such a system of authority could not withstand the challenges of a militant minority.  He adds

> It seems extremely unlikely therefore that present circumstances are likely to produce anything but new forms of *power* on the campus.  Power, unlike the kind of authority I described just above, is at once more personal, more direct, more detailed and more formal.  Although most persons tend to think of *freedom* as the consequence of eroding authority in a culture, this is not the case, for freedom cannot exist save in circumstances of accepted authority.  *Power*, not freedom is the invariable response in history to conditions of shattered authority.  The history of the modern national state can be written in terms of the declining authorities of other, older, traditional forms of authority in society.

JOHN LOCKE

## OF THE BEGINNING OF POLITICAL SOCIETIES *

95.   Men being, as has been said, by nature all free, equal, and independent, no one can be put out of this estate, and subjected to the political power of another, without his own consent.  The only way whereby any one divests himself of his natural liberty and puts on the bonds of civil society is by agreeing with other men to join and unite into a community for their comfortable, safe, and peaceable living one amongst another, in a secure enjoyment of their properties, and a greater security against any that are not of it.  This any number of men may do, because it injures not the freedom of the rest; they are left as they were in the liberty of the state of nature.  When any number of men have so consented to make one community or government, they are thereby presently incorporated, and make one body politic, wherein the majority have a right to act and conclude the rest.

96.   For when any number of men have, by the consent of every individual, made a community, they have thereby made that community one body, with a power to act as one body, which is only by the will and determination of the majority.  For that which acts any community being only the consent of the individuals of it, and it being necessary to that which is one body to move one way, it is necessary the body should move that way whether the greater force carries it, which is the consent of the majority;  or else it is impossible it should act or continue one body, one community, which the consent of every individual that united into it agreed that it should;  and so every one is bound by that consent to be concluded by the majority.  And therefore we see that in assemblies empowered to act by positive laws, where no number is set by that positive law which empowers them, the act of the majority passes for the act of the whole, and of course determines, as having by the law of nature and reason the power of the whole.

97.   And thus every man, by consenting with others to make one body politic under one government, puts himself under an obligation to every one of that society, to submit to the determination of the majority, and to be concluded by it;  or else this original compact whereby he with others incorporates into one society, would signify nothing, and be no compact, if he be left free and under no other ties than he was in before in the state of nature.  For what appearance would there be of any compact?  What new engagement if he were no farther tied by any decrees of the society, than he himself thought fit, and did actually consent to?  This would be still as great a liberty as he himself had before his compact, or any one else in the state of nature hath, who may submit himself and consent to any acts of it if he thinks fit.

98.   For if the consent of the majority shall not in reason be received as the act of the whole, and conclude every individual, nothing

* From An Essay Concerning the True
Original Extent and End of Civil Government (MacMillan Co. rev. ed. 1956).

but the consent of every individual can make anything to be the act of the whole, but such a consent is next to impossible ever to be had, if we consider the infirmities of health and avocations of business, which in a number, though much less than that of a commonwealth, will necessarily keep many away from the public assembly. To which if we add the variety of opinions, and contrariety of interests, which unavoidably happen in all collections of men, the coming into society upon such terms would be only like Cato's coming into the theatre, *tantum et exiret.* Such a constitution as this would make the mighty Leviathan of a shorter duration than the feeblest creatures, and not let it outlast the day it was born in; which cannot be supposed, till we can think that rational creatures should desire and constitute societies only to be dissolved. For where the majority cannot conclude the rest, there they cannot act as one body, and consequently will be immediately dissolved again.

99.   Whosoever therefore out of a state of nature unite into a community must be understood to give up all the power necessary to the ends for which they unite into society, to the majority of the community, unless they expressly agreed in any number greater than the majority. And this is done by barely agreeing to unite into one political society, which is all the compact that is, or needs be, between the individuals that enter into or make up a commonwealth. And thus that which begins and actually constitutes any political society is nothing but the consent of any number of freemen capable of a majority to unite and incorporate into such a society. And this is that, and that only, which did or could give beginning to any lawful government in the world.

*PLATO*

## Crito *

*Crito.* Fear not [3]—there are persons who are willing to get you out of prison at no great cost; and as for the informers, you know that they are far from being exorbitant in their demands—a little money will satisfy them. My means, which are certainly ample, are at your service, and if out of regard for my interests you have a scruple about spending my money, there are strangers who will give you the use of theirs; and one of them, Simmias the Theban, has brought a large sum for this very purpose; and Cebes and many others are prepared to spend their money in helping you to escape. I say, therefore, do not shirk the effort on our account, and do not say, as you did in the court, that you will have a difficulty in knowing what to do with yourself anywhere else. For men will love you

---

* From 1 The Dialogues of Plato 373–75, 379–84 (45–47, 50–54 of the Stephanus pagination). (B. Jowett transl. 4th ed. Oxford 1953).

3.   Socrates had been sentenced to death by the Athenians under an indictment for being "an evil doer and corrupter of the youth, who does not receive the gods whom the state receives, but introduces new divinities". 1 The Dialogues of Plato, *op. cit.*, 331. Crito, a friend, is in this passage paying a visit to Socrates's prison cell on the scheduled execution date, offering a possibility of escape.

in other places to which you may go, and not in Athens only; there are friends of mine in Thessaly, if you like to go to them, who will value and protect you, and no Thessalian will give you any trouble. Nor can I think that you are at all justified, Socrates, in betraying your own life when you might be saved; in acting thus you are working to bring on yourself the very fate, which your enemies would and did work to bring on you, your own destruction. And further I should say that you are deserting your own children; for you might bring them up and educate them; instead of which you go away and leave them, and they will have to take their chance; and if they do not meet with the usual fate of orphans, there will be small thanks to you. No man should bring children into the world who is unwilling to persevere to the end in their nurture and education. But you appear to be choosing the easier part, not the better and manlier, which would have been more becoming in one who professes to care for virtue in all his life, like yourself. And indeed, I am ashamed not only of you, but of us who are your friends, when I reflect that the whole business may be attributed entirely to our want of courage. The trial need never have come on, or might have been managed differently; and this last opportunity will seem (crowning futility of it all) to have escaped us through our own incompetence and cowardice, who might have saved you if we had been good for anything, and you might have saved yourself; for there was no difficulty at all. See now, Socrates, how discreditable as well as disastrous are the consequences, both to us and you. Make up your mind then, or rather have your mind already made up, for the time of deliberation is over, and there is only one thing to be done, which must be done this very night, and if we delay at all will be no longer practicable or possible; I beseech you therefore, Socrates, be persuaded by me, and do not say me nay.

*Socrates.* Dear Crito, your zeal is invaluable, if a right one; but if wrong, the greater the zeal the greater the danger; and therefore we ought to consider whether I shall or shall not do as you say. For I am and always have been one of those natures who must be guided by reason, whatever the reason may be which upon reflection appears to me to be the best; and now that this chance has befallen me, I cannot repudiate my own doctrines, which seem to me as sound as ever: the principles which I have hitherto honoured and revered I still honour, and unless we can at once find other and better principles, I am certain not to agree with you; no, not even if the power of the multitude could let loose upon us many more imprisonments, confiscations, deaths, frightening us like children with hobgoblin terrors. What will be the fairest way of considering the question? Shall I return to your old argument about the opinions of men?—we were saying that some of them are to be regarded, and others not. Now were we right in maintaining this before I was condemned? And has the argument which was once good now proved to be talk for the sake of talking—mere childish nonsense? That is what I want to consider with your help, Crito:—whether, under my present circumstances, the argument will appear to me in any way different or not; and whether we shall dismiss or accept it. That argument, which, as I believe, is maintained by many persons of authority, was to the effect, as I was saying, that the opinions of some men are to be regarded, and of other men not to be regarded.  Now you, Crito, are not going to die tomorrow—at least, there is no human probability of this—and therefore you are disinterested and not liable to be deceived by the circumstances in which you are placed.  Tell me then, I beg you, whether I am right in saying that some opinions, and the opinions of some men only, are to be valued, and that others are to be disregarded.  Is not this true?

.  .  .  .

*Cr.*  You may proceed, for I have not changed my mind.

*Soc.*  Then I will go on to the next point, which may be put in the form of a question:—Ought a man to do what he admits to be right, or ought he to betray the right?  .  .  .

But if this is true, what is the application?  In leaving the prison against the will of the Athenians, do I wrong any?  or rather do I not wrong those whom I ought least to wrong?  Do I not desert the principles which were acknowledged by us to be just—what do you say?

*Cr.*  I cannot answer your question, Socrates; for I do not understand it.

*Soc.*  Then consider the matter in this way:—Imagine that I am about to run away (you may call the proceeding by any name which you like), and the laws and the state appear to me and interrogate me: "Tell us, Socrates," they say; "what are you about? are you not going by an act of yours to bring us to ruin—the laws, and the whole state, as far as in you lies?  Do you imagine that a state can subsist and not be overthrown, in which the decisions of law have no power, but are set aside and trampled upon by individuals?"  What will be our answer, Crito, to these and the like words?  Any one, and especially a rhetorician, will have a good deal to say against the subversion of the law which requires a sentence to be carried out.  Shall we reply, "Yes; but the state has injured us and given an unjust sentence."  Suppose we say that?

*Cr.*  Very good, Socrates.

*Soc.*  "And was that our agreement with you?" the law would answer; "or were you to abide by the sentence of the state?"  And if we were to express our astonishment at their words, the law would probably add: "Answer, Socrates, instead of opening your eyes—you are in the habit of asking and answering questions.  Tell us,—What complaint have you to make against us which justifies you in attempting to ruin us and the state?  In the first place did we not bring you into existence?  Your father married your mother by our aid and begat you.  Say whether you have any objection to urge against those of us who regulate marriage?"  None, I should reply.  "Or against those of us who after birth regulate the nurture and education of children, in which you also were trained?  Were not the laws, which have the charge of education, right in commanding your father to train you in music and gymnastic?"  Right, I should reply.  "Well then, since you were brought into the world and nurtured and educated by us, can you deny in the first place that you are our child and slave, as your fathers were before you? And if this is true you cannot suppose that you are on equal terms with us in matters of right and wrong, or think that you have a right to do to us what we are doing to you. Would you have any right to strike or revile or do any other evil to your father or your master, if you had one, because you have been struck or reviled by him, or received some other evil at his hands?—you would not say this? And because we think right to destroy you, do you think that you have any right to destroy us in return, and your country as far as in you lies? Will you, O professor of true virtue, pretend that you are justified in this? Has a philosopher like you failed to discover that our country is more precious and higher and holier far than mother or father or any ancestor, and more to be regarded in the eyes of the gods and of men of understanding? also to be soothed, and gently and reverently entreated when angry, even more than a father, and either to be persuaded, or if not persuaded, to be obeyed? And when we are punished by her, whether with imprisonment or stripes, the punishment is to be endured in silence; and if she leads us to wounds or death in battle, thither we follow as is right; neither may any one yield or retreat or leave his rank, but whether in battle or in a court of law, or in any other place, he must do what his city and his country order him; or he must change their view of what is just: and if he may do no violence to his father or mother, much less may he do violence to his country." What answer shall we make to this, Crito? Do the laws speak truly, or do they not?

*Cr.* I think that they do.

*Soc.* Then the laws will say: "Consider, Socrates, if we are speaking truly that in your present attempt you are going to do us a wrong. For, having brought you into the world, and nurtured and educated you, and given you and every other citizen a share in every good which we had to give, we further proclaim to any Athenian by the liberty which we allow him, that if he does not like us, the laws, when he has become of age and has seen the ways of the city, and made our acquaintance, he may go where he pleases and take his goods with him. None of us laws will forbid him or interfere with anyone who does not like us and the city, and who wants to emigrate to a colony or to any other city; he may go where he likes, with his property. But he who has experience of the manner in which we order justice and administer the state, and still remains, has by so doing entered into an implied contract that he will do as we command him. And he who disobeys us is, as we maintain, thrice wrong; first, because in disobeying us he is disobeying his parents; secondly, because we are the authors of his education; thirdly, because having made an agreement with us that he will duly obey our commands, he neither obeys them nor convinces us that our commands are unjust; although we do not roughly require unquestioning obedience, but give him the alternative of obeying or convincing us;—that is what we offer, and he does neither.

"These are the sort of accusations to which, as we were saying, you, Socrates, will be exposed if you accomplish your intentions; you, above all other Athenians." Suppose now I ask, why I rather than anybody else? No doubt they will justly retort upon me that I above all other Athenians have acknowledged the agreement. "There is clear proof," they will say, "Socrates, that we and the city were not displeasing to you. Of all Athenians you have been the most constant resident in the city, which, as you never leave, you may be supposed to love. For you never went out of the city either to see the games, except once when you went to the Isthmus, or to any other place unless when you were on military service; nor did you travel as other men do. Nor had you any curiosity to know other states or their laws: your affections did not go beyond us and our state; we were your special favourites, and you acquiesced in our government of you; and here in this city you begat your children, which is a proof of your satisfaction. Moreover, you might in the course of the trial, if you had liked, have fixed the penalty at banishment; you might then have done with the state's assent what you are now setting out to do without it. But you pretended that you preferred death to exile, and that you were not unwilling to die. And now you have forgotten these fine sentiments, and pay no respect to us the laws, of whom you are the destroyer; and are doing what only a miserable slave would do, running away and turning your back upon the compacts and agreements of your citizenship which you made with us. And first of all answer this very question: Are we right in saying that you agreed to live under our government in deed, and not in word only? Is that true or not?" How shall we answer, Crito? Must we not assent?

*Cr.*   We cannot help it, Socrates.

*Soc.*   Then will they not say: "You, Socrates, are breaking the covenants and agreements which you made with us at your leisure, not under any compulsion or deception, or in enforced haste, but after you have had seventy years to think of them, during which time you were at liberty to leave the city, if we were not to your mind or if our covenants appeared to you to be unfair. You had your choice, and might have gone either to Lacedaemon or Crete, both which states are often praised by you for their good government, or to some other Hellenic or foreign state. Whereas you, above all other Athenians, seemed to be so fond of the state, and obviously thus of us, her laws (for who would care about a state without its laws?) that you never stirred out of her; the halt, the blind, the maimed were not more stationary in her than you were. And now you refuse to abide by your agreements. Not so, Socrates, if you will take our advice; do not make yourself ridiculous by leaving the city.

"For just consider, if you transgress and err in this sort of way, what good will you do either to yourself or to your friends? That your friends will be in danger of being driven into exile and deprived of citizenship, or of losing their property, is tolerably certain; and you yourself, if you fly to one of the neighbouring cities, as, for example, Thebes or Megara, both of which are well governed, will come to them as an enemy of their government and all patriotic citizens will look askance at you as a subverter of the laws, and you will confirm in the minds of the judges the justice of their own condemnation of you.  For he who is a corrupter of the laws is more than likely to be a corrupter of the young and foolish portion of mankind. Will you then flee from well-ordered cities and virtuous men? and is existence worth having on these terms?  Or will you go to them without shame, and talk to them, saying—what will you say to them? What you say here about virtue and justice and institutions and laws being the best things among men?  Would that be decent of Socrates? Surely not.  But if you go away from well-governed states to Crito's friends in Thessaly, where there is great disorder and licence, they will be charmed to hear the tale of your escape from prison, set off with ludicrous particulars of the manner in which you were wrapped in a goatskin or some other disguise, and metamorphosed as the manner is of runaways; but will there be no one to remind you that in your old age, when little time was left to you, you were not ashamed to violate the most sacred laws from a greedy desire of life? Perhaps not, if you keep them in a good temper; but if they are out of temper you will hear many degrading things.  You will live, but how?—fawning upon all men, and the servant of all men; and doing what?—faring sumptuously in Thessaly, having gone abroad in order that you may get a dinner.  And where will be your fine sentiments about justice and virtue?  Say that you wish to live for the sake of your children—you want to bring them up and educate them—will you take them into Thessaly and deprive them of Athenian citizenship?  Is this the benefit which you will confer upon them?  Or are you under the impression that they will be better cared for and educated here if you are still alive, although absent from them;  for your friends will take care of them?  Do you fancy that if you have left Athens for Thessaly they will take care of them, but if you have left it for the other world that they will not take care of them?  Nay; but if they who call themselves friends are good for anything, they will—to be sure they will.

"Listen, then, Socrates, to us who have brought you up.  Think not of life and children first, and of justice afterwards, but of justice first, that you may so vindicate yourself before the princes of the world below.  For neither will you nor any that belong to you be happier or holier or juster in this life, or happier in another, if you do as Crito bids.  Now you depart, if it must be so, in innocence, a sufferer and not a doer of evil; a victim, not of the laws but of men. But if you leave the city, basely returning evil for evil, and injury for injury, breaking the covenants and agreements which you have made with us, and wronging those whom you ought least of all to wrong, that is to say, yourself, your friends, your country, and us, we shall be angry with you while you live, and our brethren, the laws in the world below, will give you no friendly welcome; for they will know that you have done your best to destroy us.  Listen, then, to us and not to Crito."

This, dear Crito, is the voice which I seem to hear murmuring in my ears, like the sound of the flute in the ears of the mystic; that voice, I say, is humming in my ears, and prevents me from hearing any other.  Be assured, then, that anything more which you may say to shake this my faith will be said in vain. Yet speak, if you have anything to say.

*Cr.*  I have nothing to say.

*Soc.*  It is enough then, Crito. Let us fulfil the will of God, and follow whither He leads.

## QUESTIONS

If Socrates believed that his sentence was unjust (see his defense in the *Apology*), why was it just to submit to it? What strains run through his arguments to Crito? Is Socrates's basic concern that he will lose face, be unhappy and pursued if he does not submit (an argument, apparently, based on hedonism)? Or that he *agreed* (an argument, apparently, based on an obligation to keep promises)? How far can the reasoning from promises go? Does one ever impliedly promise to be treated unjustly? Might he not have argued that the state, in accusing him unjustly, breached its promise to him? Had Socrates, through his teachings, not already "repaid in full" his "debt" to the state for his having educated and nurtured him? What were the real evils that Socrates might have been contemplating that his fleeing would cause?

### HENRY DAVID THOREAU

## CIVIL DISOBEDIENCE *

I heartily accept the motto, "That government is best which governs least"; and I should like to see it acted up to more rapidly and systematically. Carried out, it finally amounts to this, which also I believe—"That government is best which governs not at all"; and when men are prepared for it, that will be the kind of government which they will have. Government is at best but an expedient; but most governments are usually, and all governments are sometimes, inexpedient. The objections which have been brought against a standing army, and they are many and weighty, and deserve to prevail, may also at last be brought against a standing government. The standing army is only an arm of the standing government. The government itself, which is only the mode which the people have chosen to execute their will, is equally liable to be abused and perverted before the people can act through it. Witness the present Mexican war, the work of comparatively a few individuals using the standing government as their tool; for, in the outset, the people would not have consented to this measure.

This American government—what is it but a tradition, though a recent one, endeavoring to transmit itself unimpaired to posterity, but each instant losing some of its integrity? It has not the vitality and force of a single living man; for a single man can bend it to his will. It is a sort of wooden gun to the people themselves. But it

* From The Portable Thoreau 109–15,
117–20, 126–27, 130–33, 136–37 (C.
Bode ed. Viking Press 1947).

is not the less necessary for this; for the people must have some complicated machinery or other, and hear its din, to satisfy that idea of government which they have. Governments show thus how successfully men can be imposed on, even impose on themselves, for their own advantage. It is excellent, we must all allow. Yet this government never of itself furthered any enterprise, but by the alacrity with which it got out of its way. *It* does not keep the country free. *It* does not settle the West. *It* does not educate. The character inherent in the American people has done all that has been accomplished; and it would have done somewhat more, if the government had not sometimes got in its way. For government is an expedient by which men would fain succeed in letting one another alone; and, as has been said, when it is most expedient, the governed are most let alone by it. . . .

But, to speak practically and as a citizen, unlike those who call themselves no-government men, I ask for, not at once no government, but *at once* a better government. Let every man make known what kind of government would command his respect, and that will be one step toward obtaining it.

After all, the practical reason why, when the power is once in the hands of the people, a majority are permitted, and for a long period continue, to rule is not because they are most likely to be in the right, nor because this seems fairest to the minority, but because they are physically the strongest. But a government in which the majority rule in all cases cannot be based on justice, even as far as men understand it. Can there not be a government in which majorities do not virtually decide right and wrong, but conscience?— in which majorities decide only those questions to which the rule of expediency is applicable? Must the citizen ever for a moment, or in the least degree, resign his conscience to the legislator? Why has every man a conscience, then? I think that we should be men first, and subjects afterward. It is not desirable to cultivate a respect for the law, so much as for the right. The only obligation which I have a right to assume is to do at any time what I think right. It is truly enough said that a corporation has no conscience; but a corporation of conscientious men is a corporation *with* a conscience. Law never made men a whit more just; and, by means of their respect for it, even the well-disposed are daily made the agents of injustice. A common and natural result of an undue respect for law is, that you may see a file of soldiers, colonel, captain, corporal, privates, powder-monkeys, and all, marching in admirable order over hill and dale to the wars, against their wills, ay, against their common sense and consciences, which makes it very steep marching indeed, and produces a palpitation of the heart. They have no doubt that it is a damnable business in which they are concerned; they are all peaceably inclined. Now, what are they? Men at all? or small movable forts and magazines, at the service of some unscrupulous man in power? Visit the Navy Yard, and behold a marine, such a man as an American government can make, or such as it can make a man with its black arts—a mere shadow and reminiscence of humanity, a man laid out alive and standing, and already, as one may say, buried under arms with funeral accompaniments, though it may be,

> "Not a drum was heard, not a funeral note,
>     As his corse to the rampart we hurried;
> Not a soldier discharged his farewell shot
>     O'er the grave where our hero we buried."

The mass of men serve the state thus, not as men mainly, but as machines, with their bodies. They are the standing army, and the militia, jailers, constables, posse comitatus, etc. In most cases there is no free exercise whatever of the judgment or of the moral sense; but they put themselves on a level with wood and earth and stones; and wooden men can perhaps be manufactured that will serve the purpose as well. Such command no more respect than men of straw or a lump of dirt. They have the same sort of worth only as horses and dogs. Yet such as these even are commonly esteemed good citizens . . . [M]ost legislators, politicians, lawyers, ministers, and office-holders serve the state chiefly with their heads; and, as they rarely make any moral distinctions, they are as likely to serve the devil, without *intending* it, as God. A very few—as heroes, patriots, martyrs, reformers in the great sense, and *men*—serve the state with their consciences also, and so necessarily resist it for the most part; and they are commonly treated as enemies by it. A wise man will only be useful as a man, and will not submit to be "clay," and "stop a hole to keep the wind away," but leave that office to his dust at least:

> "I am too high-born to be propertied,
> To be a secondary at control,
> Or useful serving-man and instrument
> To any sovereign state throughout the world."

He who gives himself entirely to his fellow men appears to them useless and selfish; but he who gives himself partially to them is pronounced a benefactor and philanthropist.

How does it become a man to behave toward this American government today? I answer, that he cannot without disgrace be associated with it. I cannot for an instant recognize that political organization as *my* government which is the *slave's* government also.

All men recognize the right of revolution; that is, the right to refuse allegiance to, and to resist, the government, when its tyranny or its inefficiency are great and unendurable. But almost all say that such is not the case now. But such was the case, they think, in the Revolution of '75. If one were to tell me that this was a bad government because it taxed certain foreign commodities brought to its ports, it is most probable that I should not make an ado about it, for I can do without them. All machines have their friction; and possibly this does enough good to counterbalance the evil. At any rate, it is a great evil to make a stir about it. But when the friction comes to have its machine, and oppression and robbery are organized, I say, let us not have such a machine any longer. In other words, when a sixth of the population of a nation which has undertaken to be the refuge of liberty are slaves, and a whole country is unjustly overrun and conquered by a foreign army, and subjected to military law, I think that it is not too soon for honest men to rebel and revolutionize. What makes this duty the more urgent is the fact that the country so overrun is not our own, but ours is the invading army.

Paley, a common authority with many on moral questions, in his chapter on the "Duty of Submission to Civil Government," resolves all civil obligation into expediency; and he proceeds to say that "so long as the interest of the whole society requires it, that is, so long as the established government cannot be resisted or changed without public inconveniency, it is the will of God . . . that the established government be obeyed—and no longer. This principle being admitted, the justice of every particular case of resistance is reduced to a computation of the quantity of the danger and grievance on the one side, and of the probability and expense of redressing it on the other." Of this, he says, every man shall judge for himself. But Paley appears never to have contemplated those cases to which the rule of expediency does not apply, in which a people, as well as an individual, must do justice, cost what it may. If I have unjustly wrested a plank from a drowning man, I must restore it to him though I drown myself. This, according to Paley, would be inconvenient. But he that would save his life, in such a case, shall lose it. This people must cease to hold slaves, and to make war on Mexico, though it cost them their existence as a people.

In their practice, nations agree with Paley; but does anyone think that Massachusetts does exactly what is right at the present crisis?

"A drab of state, a cloth-o'silver slut,
To have her train borne up, and her soul trail in
the dirt."

Practically speaking, the opponents to a reform in Massachusetts are not a hundred thousand politicians at the South, but a hundred thousand merchants and farmers here, who are more interested in commerce and agriculture than they are in humanity, and are not prepared to do justice to the slave and to Mexico, *cost what it may*. I quarrel not with far-off foes, but with those who, near at home, co-operate with, and do the bidding of, those far away, and without whom the latter would be harmless. We are accustomed to say, that the mass of men are unprepared; but improvement is slow, because the few are not materially wiser or better than the many. It is not so important that many should be as good as you, as that there be some absolute goodness somewhere; for that will leaven the whole lump. There are thousands who are *in opinion* opposed to slavery and to the war, who yet in effect do nothing to put an end to them; who, esteeming themselves children of Washington and Franklin, sit down with their hands in their pockets, and say that they know not what to do, and do nothing; who even postpone the question of freedom to the question of free trade, and quietly read the prices-current along with the latest advices from Mexico, after dinner, and, it may be, fall asleep over them both. What is the price-current of an honest man and patriot today? They hesitate, and they regret, and sometimes they petition; but they do nothing in earnest and with effect. They will wait, well disposed, for others to remedy the evil, that they may no longer have it to regret. At most, they give only a cheap vote, and a feeble countenance and Godspeed, to the right, as it goes by them. There are nine hundred and ninety-nine patrons of virtue to one virtuous man. But it is easier to deal with the real possessor of a thing than with the temporary guardian of it.

.   .   .   .

It is not a man's duty, as a matter of course, to devote himself to the eradication of any, even the most enormous, wrong; he may still properly have other concerns to engage him; but it is his duty, at least, to wash his hands of it, and, if he gives it no thought longer, not to give it practically his support. If I devote myself to other pursuits and contemplations, I must first see, at least, that I do not pursue them sitting upon another man's shoulders. I must get off him first, that he may pursue his contemplations too. See what gross inconsistency is tolerated. I have heard some of my townsmen say, "I should like to have them order me out to help put down an insurrection of the slaves, or to march to Mexico—see if I would go"; and yet these very men have each, directly by their allegiance, and so indirectly, at least, by their money, furnished a substitute. The soldier is applauded who refuses to serve in an unjust war by those who do not refuse to sustain the unjust government which makes the war; is applauded by those whose own act and authority he disregards and sets at naught;   .   .   .   After the first blush of sin comes its indifference; and from immoral it becomes, as it were, *un*moral, and not quite unnecessary to that life which we have made.

The broadest and most prevalent error requires the most disinterested virtue to sustain it. The slight reproach to which the virtue of patriotism is commonly liable, the noble are most likely to incur. Those who, while they disapprove of the character and measures of a government, yield to it their allegiance and support are undoubtly its most conscientious supporters, and so frequently the most serious obstacles to reform. Some are petitioning the State to dissolve the Union, to disregard the requisitions of the President. Why do they not dissolve it themselves—the union between themselves and the State—and refuse to pay their quota into its treasury? Do not they stand in the same relation to the State that the State does to the Union? And have not the same reasons prevented the State from resisting the Union which have prevented them from resisting the State?

How can a man be satisfied to entertain an opinion merely, and to enjoy *it*?   .   .   .   [I]t divides the *individual*, separating the diabolical in him from the devine.

Unjust laws exist: shall we be content to obey them, or shall we endeavor to amend them, and obey them until we have succeeded, or shall we transgress them at once? Men generally, under such a government as this, think that they ought to wait until they have persuaded the majority to alter them. They think that, if they should resist, the remedy would be worse than the evil. But it is the fault of the government itself that the remedy *is* worse than the evil. *It* makes it worse. Why is it not more apt to anticipate and provide for reform? Why does it not cherish its wise minority? Why does it cry and resist before it is hurt? Why does it not encourage its citizens to be on the alert to point out its faults, and *do* better than it would have them? Why does it always crucify Christ, and excommunicate Copernicus and Luther, and pronounce Washington and Franklin rebels?

. . . .

If the injustice is part of the necessary friction of the machine of government, let it go, let it go: perchance it will wear smooth—certainly the machine will wear out. If the injustice has a spring, or a pulley, or a rope, or a crank, exclusively for itself, then perhaps you may consider whether the remedy will not be worse than the evil; but if it is of such a nature that it requires you to be the agent of injustice to another, then, I say, break the law. Let your life be a counter-friction to stop the machine. What I have to do is to see, at any rate, that I do not lend myself to the wrong which I condemn.

As for adopting the ways which the State has provided for remedying the evil, I know not of such ways. They take too much time, and a man's life will be gone. I have other affairs to attend to. I came into this world, not chiefly to make this a good place to live in, but to live in it, be it good or bad. A man has not everything to do, but something; and because he cannot do *everything*, it is not necessary that he should do *something* wrong. It is not my business to be petitioning the Governor or the Legislature any more than it is theirs to petition me; and if they should not hear my petition, what should I do then? But in this case the State has provided no way: its very Constitution is the evil. This may seem to be harsh and stubborn and unconciliatory; but it is to treat with the utmost kindness and consideration the only spirit that can appreciate or deserves it. So is all change for the better, like birth and death, which convulse the body.

I do not hesitate to say, that those who call themselves Abolitionists should at once effectually withdraw their support, both in person and property, from the government of Massachusetts, and not wait till they constitute a majority of one, before they suffer the right to prevail through them. . . .

. . . .

I have paid no poll-tax for six years. I was put into a jail once on this account, for one night; and, as I stood considering the walls of solid stone, two or three feet thick, the door of wood and iron, a foot thick, and the iron grating which strained the light, I could not help being struck with the foolishness of that institution which treated me as if I were mere flesh and blood and bones, to be locked up. I wondered that it should have concluded at length that this was the best use it could put me to, and had never thought to avail itself of my services in some way. I saw that, if there was a wall of stone between me and my townsmen, there was a still more difficult one to climb or break through before they could get to be as free as I was. I did not for a moment feel confined, and the walls seemed a great waste of stone and mortar. I felt as if I alone of all my townsmen had paid my tax. They plainly did not know how to treat me, but behaved like persons who are underbred. In every threat and in every compliment there was a blunder; for they thought that my chief desire was to stand the other side of that stone wall. I could not but smile to see how industriously they locked the door on my meditations, which followed them out again without let or hindrance, and *they* were really all that was dangerous. As they could not reach me, they had resolved to punish my body; just as boys, if they cannot come at some person against whom they have a spite, will abuse his dog. I saw that the State was half-witted, that it was timid as a lone woman with her silver spoons, and that it did not know its friends from its foes, and I lost all my remaining respect for it, and pitied it.

Thus the State never intentionally confronts a man's sense, intellectual or moral, but only his body, his senses. It is not armed with superior wit or honesty, but with superior physical strength. I was not born to be forced. I will breathe after my own fashion. Let us see who is the strongest. What force has a multitude? They only can force me who obey a higher law than I. They force me to become like themselves. I do not hear of *men* being forced to live this way or that by masses of men. . . . If a plant cannot live according to its nature, it dies; and so a man.

. . . . .

I have never declined paying the highway tax, because I am as desirous of being a good neighbor as I am of being a bad subject; and as for supporting schools, I am doing my part to educate my fellow-countrymen now. It is for no particular item in the tax bill that I refuse to pay it. I simply wish to refuse allegiance to the State, to withdraw and stand aloof from it effectually. I do not care to trace the course of my dollar, if I could, till it buys a man or a musket to shoot one with—the dollar is innocent—but I am concerned to trace the effects of my allegiance. In fact, I quietly declare war with the State, after my fashion, though I will still make what use and get what advantage of her I can, as is usual in such cases.

. . . . .

I do not wish to quarrel with any man or nation. I do not wish to split hairs, to make fine distinctions, or set myself up as better than my neighbors. I seek rather, I may say, even an excuse for conforming to the laws of the land. I am but too ready to conform to them. Indeed, I have reason to suspect myself on this head; and each year, as the tax-gatherer comes round, I find myself disposed to review the acts and position of the general and State governments, and the spirit of the people, to discover a pretext for conformity.

"We must affect our country as our parents,
    And if at any time we alienate

Our love or industry from doing it honor,
We must respect effects and teach the soul
Matter of conscience and religion,
And not desire of rule or benefit."

I believe that the State will soon be able to take all my work of this sort out of my hands, and then I shall be no better a patriot than my fellow-countrymen. Seen from a lower point of view, the Constitution, with all its faults, is very good; the law and the courts are very respectable; even this State and this American government are, in many respects, very admirable, and rare things, to be thankful for, such as a great many have described them; but seen from a point of view a little higher, they are what I have described them; seen from a higher still, and the highest, who shall say what they are, or that they are worth looking at or thinking of at all?

. . . .

. . . Is a democracy, such as we know it, the last improvement possible in government? Is it not possible to take a step further towards recognizing and organizing the rights of man? There will never be a really free and enlightened State until the State comes to recognize the individual as a higher and independent power, from which all its own power and authority are derived, and treats him accordingly. I please myself with imagining a State at last which can afford to be just to all men, and to treat the individual with respect as a neighbor; which even would not think it inconsistent with its own repose if a few were to live aloof from it, not meddling with it, nor embraced by it, who fulfilled all the duties of neighbors and fellow men. A State which bore this kind of fruit, and suffered it to drop off as fast as it ripened, would prepare the way for a still more perfect and glorious State, which also I have imagined, but not yet anywhere seen.

*RICHARD A. WASSERSTROM*

## THE OBLIGATION TO OBEY THE LAW *

The question of what is the nature and extent of one's obligation to obey the law is one of those relatively rare philosophic questions which can never produce doubts about the importance of theory for practice. To ask under what circumstances, if any, one is justified in disobeying the law, is to direct attention to problems which all would acknowledge to be substantial. Concrete, truly problematic situations are as old as civil society.

The general question was posed—though surely not for the first time—well over two thousand years ago in Athens when Crito revealed to Socrates that Socrates' escape from prison could be easily and successfully accomplished. The issue was made a compelling one—though once again surely not for the first time—by Crito's insistence that escape was not only possible but also *desirable*, and that disobedience to

* From 10 U.C.L.A.L.Rev. 780, 780–85, 790–92, 797–801, 805–07 (1963). With    permission of the Regents of the University of California and the author.

law was in *this* case at least, surely justified. And the problem received at the hand of Socrates—here perhaps for the first time—a sustained theoretical analysis and resolution.

Just as the question of what is the nature and extent of one's obligation to obey the law demanded attention then—as it has throughout man's life in the body politic—it is no less with us today in equally vexing and perplexing forms. Freedom rides and sit-ins have raised the question of whether the immorality of segregation may justify disobeying the law. The all too awesome horrors of a nuclear war have seemed to some to require responsive action, including, if need be, deliberate but peaceful trespasses upon government-owned atomic testing grounds. And the rightness of disobedience to law in the face of court-ordered school integration has been insisted upon by the citizens of several states and acted upon by the governor of at least one.

.   .   .   .

More important is the fact that historically the topic has generally been examined from only one very special aspect of the problem. Those philosophers who have seriously considered questions relating to one's obligation to obey the law have considered them only in the context of revolution. They have identified the conditions under which one would, if ever, be justified in disobeying the law with the conditions under which revolution would, if ever, be justified; and they have, perhaps not surprisingly, tended thereby to conclude that one would be justified in disobeying the law if, and only if, revolution itself would in that case be justified.

To view the problem in a setting of obedience or revolution is surely to misconstrue it. It is to neglect, among other things, something that is obviously true—that most people who disobey the law are not revolutionaries and that most acts of disobedience of the law are not acts of revolution. Many who disobey the law are, of course, ordinary criminals: burglars, kidnappers, embezzlers, and the like. But even of those who disobey the law under a claim of justification, most are neither advocates nor practitioners of revolution.

.   .   .   .

There are several different views which could be held concerning the nature of the stringency of one's obligation to obey the law. One such view, and the one which I shall be more concerned to show to be false, can be characterized as holding that one has an *absolute* obligation to obey the law. I take this to mean that a person is never justified in disobeying the law; to know that a proposed action is illegal is to know all one needs to know in order to conclude that the action ought not to be done; to cite the illegality of an action is to give a sufficient reason for not having done it. A view such as this is far from uncommon. President Kennedy expressed the thoughts of many quite reflective people when he said not too long ago:

>   .   .   .   [O]ur nation is founded on the principle that observance of the law is the eternal safeguard of liberty and defiance of the law is the surest road to tyranny.

The law which we obey includes the final rulings of the courts as well as the enactments of our legislative bodies. Even among law-abiding men few laws are universally loved.

But they are universally respected and not resisted.

Americans are free, in short, to disagree with the law, but not to disobey it. For in a government of laws and not of men, no man, however prominent or powerful, and no mob, however unruly or boisterous, is entitled to defy a court of law.

If this country should ever reach the point where any man or group of men, by force or threat of force, could long deny the commands of our court and our Constitution, then no law would stand free from doubt, no judge would be sure of his writ and no citizen would be safe from his neighbors.

A more moderate or weaker view would be that which holds that, while one does have an obligation to obey the law, the obligation is a prima facie rather than absolute one. If one knows that a proposed course of conduct is illegal then one has a good—but not necessarily a sufficient—reason for refraining from engaging in that course of conduct. Under this view, a person may be justified in disobeying the law, but an act which is in disobedience of the law does have to be justified, whereas an act in obedience of the law does not have to be justified.

It is important to observe that there is an ambiguity in this notion of a prima facie obligation. For the claim that one has a prima facie obligation to obey the law can come to one of two different things. On the one hand, the claim can be this: the fact that an action is an act of disobedience is something which always does count against the performance of the action. If one has a prima facie obligation to obey the law, one always has that obligation—although, of course, it may be overridden by other obligations in any particular case. Thus the fact that an action is illegal is a relevant consideration in every case and it is a consideration which must be outweighed by other considerations before the performance of an illegal action can be justified.

On the other hand, the claim can be weaker still. The assertion of a prima facie obligation to obey the law can be nothing more than the claim that as a matter of fact it is *generally* right or obligatory to obey the law. As a rule the fact that an action is illegal is a relevant circumstance. But in any particular case, after deliberation, it might very well turn out that the illegality of the action was not truly relevant. For in any particular case the circumstances might be such that there simply was nothing in the fact of illegality which required overriding—e. g., there were no bad consequences at all which would flow from disobeying the law in this case.

The distinction can be made more vivid in the following fashion. One person, A, might hold the view that any action in disobedience of the law is intrinsically bad. Some other person, B, might hold the view that no action is intrinsically bad unless it has the property, P, and that not all actions in disobedience of the law have that property.

Now for *A*, the fact of disobedience is *always* a relevant consideration, for *B*, the fact of disobedience may always be initially relevant because of the existence of some well-established hypothesis which asserts that the occurrence of any action of disobedience is correlated highly with the occurrence of *P*. But if in any particular case disobedience does not turn out to have the property, *P*, then, upon reflection, it can be concluded by *B* that the fact that disobedience is involved is not a reason which weighs against the performance of the act in question. To understand *B*'s position it is necessary to distinguish the relevance of *considering* the fact of disobedience from the relevance of the fact of disobedience. The former must always be relevant, the latter is not.

Thus there are at least three different positions which might be taken concerning the character of the obligation to obey the law or the rightness of disobedience to the law. They are: (1) One has an absolute obligation to obey the law; disobedience is never justified. (2) One has an obligation to obey the law but this obligation can be overridden by conflicting obligations; disobedience can be justified, but only by the presence of outweighing circumstances. (3) One does not have a special obligation to obey the law, but it is in fact usually obligatory, on other grounds, to do so; disobedience to law often does turn out to be unjustified.

. . . .

. . . . [I]t is clear that if the case against ever acting illegally is to be made out, conceptual analysis alone cannot do it. Indeed, arguments of quite another sort must be forthcoming. And it is to these that I now turn.

One such argument, and the most common argument advanced, goes something like this: The reason why one ought never to disobey the law is simply that the consequences would be disastrous if everybody disobeyed the law. The reason why disobedience is never right becomes apparent once we ask the question "But what if everyone did that?"

Consider again the case of the doctor who has to decide whether he is justified in performing an illegal abortion. If he only has a prima facie duty to obey the law it looks as though he might justifiably decide that in this case his prima facie obligation is overridden by more stringent conflicting obligations. Or, if he is simply a utilitarian, it appears that he might rightly conclude that the consequences of disobeying the abortion law would be on the whole and in the long run less deleterious than those of obeying. But this is simply a mistake. The doctor would inevitably be neglecting the most crucial factor of all, namely, that in performing the abortion he was disobeying the law. And imagine what would happen if everyone went around disobeying the law. The alternatives are obeying the law and general disobedience. The choice is between any social order and chaos. As President Kennedy correctly observed, if any law is disobeyed, then no law can be free from doubt, no citizen safe from his neighbor.

Such an argument, while perhaps overdrawn, is by no means uncommon. Yet, as it stands, it is an essentially confused one. Its respective claims, if they are to be fairly evaluated, must be delineated with some care.

At a minimum, the foregoing attack upon the possibility of justified disobedience might be either one or both of two radically different kinds of objection. The first, which relates to the consequences of an act of disobedience, is essentially a *causal* argument. The second questions the *principle* that any proponent of justified disobedience invokes. As to the causal argument, it is always relevant to point out that any act of disobedience may have certain consequences simply because it is an act of disobedience. Once the occurrence of the act is known, for example, expenditure of the state's resources may become necessary. The time and energy of the police will probably be turned to the task of discovering who it was who did the illegal act and of gathering evidence relevant to the offense. And other resources might be expended in the prosecution and adjudication of the case against the perpetrator of the illegal act. Illustrations of this sort could be multiplied, no doubt, but I do not think either that considerations of this sort are very persuasive or that they have been uppermost in the minds of those who make the argument now under examination. Indeed, if the argument is a causal one at all, it consists largely of the claim that any act of disobedience will itself cause, to some degree or other, general disobedience of all laws; it will cause or help to cause the overthrow or dissolution of the state. And while it is possible to assert that any act of disobedience will tend to further social disintegration or revolution, it is much more difficult to see why this must be so.

The most plausible argument would locate this causal efficacy in the kind of example set by any act of disobedience. But how plausible is this argument? It is undeniable, of course, that the kind of example that will be set is surely a relevant factor. Yet, there is nothing that precludes any proponent of justified disobedience from taking this into account. If, for example, others will somehow infer from the doctor's disobedience of the abortion law that they are justified in disobeying *any* law under *any* circumstances, then the doctor ought to consider this fact. This is a consequence—albeit a lamentable one—of his act of disobedience. Similarly, if others will extract the proper criterion from the act of disobedience, but will be apt to misapply it in practice, then this too ought to give the doctor pause. It, too, is a consequence of acting. But if the argument is that disobedience would be wrong even if no bad example were set and no other deleterious consequences likely then the argument must be directed against the principle the doctor appeals to in disobeying the law, and not against the consequences of his disobedience at all.

As to the attack upon a principle of justified disobedience, as a principle, the response "But what if everyone disobeyed the law?" does appear to be a good way to point up both the inherent inconsistency of almost any principle of justified disobedience and the manifest undesirability of adopting such a principle. Even if one need not worry about what others will be led to do by one's disobedience, there is surely something amiss if one cannot consistently defend his right to do what one is claiming he is right in doing.

In large measure, such an objection is unreal.  The appeal to "But what if everyone did that?" loses much, if not all, of its persuasiveness once we become clearer about what precisely the "did that" refers to.  If the question "But what if everyone did that?" is simply another way of asking "But what if everybody disobeyed the law?" or "But what if people generally disobeyed the laws?" then the question is surely quasi-rhetorical.  To urge general or indiscriminate disobedience to laws is to invoke a principle that, if coherent, is manifestly indefensible.  It is equally plain, however, that with few exceptions such a principle has never been seriously espoused.

.   .   .   .

What then are the arguments which might plausibly be advanced?  One very common argument goes like this:  It is, of course, true that even democratically selected and democratically constituted legislatures can and do make mistakes.  Nevertheless, a person is never justified in disobeying the law as long as there exist alternative, "peaceful" procedures by which to bring about the amendment or repeal of undesirable or oppressive laws.  The genuine possibility that rational persuasion and argument can bring a majority to favor any one of a variety of competing views, both requires that disapproval always be permitted and forbids that disobedience ever be allowed.  This is so for several reasons.

First, it is clearly unfair and obviously inequitable to accept the results of any social decision-procedure only in those cases in which the decision reached was one of which one approves, and to refuse to accept those decisions which are not personally satisfying.  If there is one thing which participation, and especially voluntary participation, in a decision-procedure entails, it is that all of the participants must abide by the decision regardless of what it happens to be.  If the decision-procedure is that of majority rule, then this means that any person must abide by those decisions in which he was in a minority just as much as it means that he can insist that members of the minority abide when he is a member of the majority.

As familiar as the argument is, its plausibility is far from assured.  On one reading, at least, it appears to be one version of the universalization argument.  As such, it goes like this.  Imagine any person, *A*, who has voted with the majority to pass a law making a particular kind of conduct illegal.  *A* surely would not and could not acknowledge the right of any person voting with the minority justifiably to disobey that law.  But, if *A* will not and cannot recognize a right of justified disobedience here, then *A* certainly cannot consistently or fairly claim any right of justified disobedience on his part in those cases in which he, *A*, happened to end up being in a minority.  Thus, justified disobedience can never be defensible.

This argument is fallacious.  For a person who would insist that justified disobedience was possible even after majoritarian decision-making could very plausibly and consistently acknowledge the right of any person to disobey the law under appropriate circumstances regardless of how that person had voted on any particular law.  Consider, once again, the case already put of the doctor and the pregnant girl. The doctor can surely be consistent in claiming both that circumstances make the performance of the illegal abortion justified and that any comparable action would also be right irrespective of how the actor, or the doctor, or anyone else, happened to have voted on the abortion law, or any other law. The point is simply that there is no reason why any person cannot consistently: (1) hold the view that majority decision-making is the best of all forms of decision-making; (2) participate voluntarily in the decision-making process; and (3) believe that it is right for *anyone* to disobey majority decisions whenever the relevant moral circumstances obtain, *e. g.*, whenever the consequence of obedience to that law at that time would on the whole be more deleterious than those of obedience.

But this may be deemed too facile an answer; it also may be thought to miss the point. For it might be argued that there is a serious logical inconsistency of a different sort which must arise whenever a voluntary participant in a social decision-procedure claims that not all the decisions reached in accordance with that procedure need be obeyed. Take the case of majority rule. It is inconsistent for anyone voluntarily to participate in the decision-process and yet at the same time to reserve the right to refuse to abide by the decision reached in any particular case. The problem is not an inability to universalize a principal of action. The problem is rather that of making any sense at all out of the notion of having a majority decide anything— of having a procedure by which to make group decisions. The problem is, in addition, that of making any sense at all out of the fact of voluntary participation in the decision-procedure—in knowing what this participation can come to if it does not mean that every participant is bound by all of the decisions which are reached. What can their participation mean if it is not an implicit promise to abide by all decisions reached? And even if the point is not a logical one, it is surely a practical one. What good could there possibly be to a scheme, an institutional means for making social decisions, which did not bind even the participants to anything?

The answer to this argument—or set of arguments—is wholly analogous to that which has been given earlier. But because of the importance and prevalence of the argument some repetition is in order.

One can simply assert that the notion of any social decision-making procedure is intelligible only if it entails that all participants always abide by all of the decisions which are made, no matter what those decisions are. Concomitantly, one can simply insist that any voluntary participant in the decision-process must be consenting or promising to abide by all decisions which are reached. But one cannot give as a plausible reason for this assertion the fact that the notion of group decision-making becomes incoherent if anything less in the way of adherence is required of all participants. And one cannot cite as a plausible reason for this assertion the fact that the notion of voluntary participation loses all meaning if anything less than a promise of absolute obedience is inferred.

It is true that the notion of a group decision-making procedure would be a meaningless notion if there were no respects in which a group decision was in any way binding upon each of the participants. Decisions which in no way bind anyone to do anything are simply not decisions. And it is also true that voluntary participation is an idle, if not a vicious, act if it does not commit each participant to something. If any voluntary participant properly can wholly ignore the decisions which are reached, then something is surely amiss.

But to say all this is not to say very much. Group decision-making can have a point just because it does preclude any participant from taking some actions which in the absence of the decision, he might have been justified in performing. And voluntary participation can still constitute a promise of sorts that one will not perform actions which, in the absence of voluntary participation, might have been justifiable. If the fact of participation in a set of liberal political institutions does constitute a promise of sorts, it can surely be a promise that the participant will not disobey a law just because obedience would be inconvenient or deleterious to him. And if this is the scope of the promise, then the fact of voluntary participation does make a difference. For in the absence of the participation in the decision to make this conduct illegal, inconvenience to the actor might well have been a good reason for acting in a certain way. Thus, participation can create new obligations to behave in certain ways without constituting a promise not to disobey the law under any circumstances. And if this is the case, adherence to a principle of justified disobedience is not inconsistent with voluntary participation in the decision-making process.

Indeed, a strong point can be made. The notion of making laws through voluntary participation in democratic institutions is not even inconsistent with the insistence that disobedience is justified whenever the consequences of disobedience are on the whole more beneficial than those of obedience. This is so because a promise can be a meaningful promise even if an appeal to the consequences of performing the promise can count as a sufficient reason for not performing the promise. And if this is the case for promises generally, it can be no less the case for the supposed promise to obey the law.

Finally, even if it were correct that voluntary participation implied a promise to obey, and even if it were the case that the promise must be a promise not to disobey on consequential grounds, all of this would still not justify the conclusion that one ought never to disobey the law. It would, instead, only demonstrate that disobeying the law must be prima facie wrong, that everyone has a prima facie obligation to obey the law. This is so just because it is sometimes right even to break one's own promises. And if this, too, is a characteristic of promises generally, it is, again, no less a characteristic of the promise to obey the law.

There is one final argument which requires brief elucidation and analysis. It is in certain respects a peculiarly instructive one both in its own right and in respect to the thesis of this article.

.   .   .   .

It may be true that on some particular occasions the consequences of disobeying a law will in fact be less deleterious on the whole than those of obeying it—even in a democracy. It may even be true that on some particular occasions disobeying a law will be just whereas obeying it would be unjust. Nevertheless, the reason why a person is never justified in disobeying a law—in a democracy—is simply this: The chances are so slight that he will disobey only those laws in only those cases in which he is in fact justified in doing so, that the consequences will on the whole be less deleterious if he never disobeys any law. Furthermore, since anyone must concede the right to everyone to disobey the law when the circumstances so demand it, the situation is made still worse. For once we entrust this right to everyone we can be sure that many laws will be disobeyed in a multitude of cases in which there was no real justification for disobedience. Thus, given what we know of the possibilities of human error and the actualities of human frailty, and given the tendency of democratic societies to make illegal only those actions which would, even in the absence of a law, be unjustified, we can confidently conclude that the consequences will on the whole and in the long run be best if no one ever takes it upon himself to "second-guess" the laws and to conclude that in his case his disobedience is justified.

The argument is, in part, not very different from those previously considered. And thus, what is to be said about it is not very different either. Nonetheless, upon pain of being overly repetitive, I would insist that there is a weak sense in which the argument is quite persuasive and a strong sense in which it is not. For the argument makes, on one reading, too strong an empirical claim—the claim that the consequences will in the long run always in fact be better if no one in a democracy ever tries to decide when he is justified in disobeying the law. As it stands, there is no reason to believe that the claim is or must be true, that the consequences will always be better. Indeed, it is very hard to see why, despite the hypothesis, someone might still not be justified in some particular case in disobeying a law. Yet, viewed as a weaker claim, as a summary rule, it does embody a good deal that is worth remembering. It can, on this level, be understood to be a persuasive reminder of much that is relevant to disobedience: that in a democracy the chances of having to live under bad laws are reduced; that in a democracy there are typically less costly means available by which to bring about changes in the law; that in a democracy—as in life in general—a justified action may always be both inaptly and ineptly emulated; and that in a democracy—as in life in general—people often do make mistakes as to which of their own actions are truly justified. These are some of the lessons of human experience which are easy to forget and painful to relearn.

But there are other lessons, and they are worth remembering too. What is especially troubling about the claim that disobedience of the law is never justified, what is even disturbing about the claim that disobedience of the law is never justified in a democratic or liberal society, is the facility with which its acceptance can lead to the neglect of important moral issues. If no one is justified in disobeying the Supreme Court's decision in Brown v. Board of Educ. this is so because, among other things, there is much that is wrong with segregation. If there was much that was peculiarly wrong in Mississippi this fall, this was due to the fact, among other facts, that a mob howled and a governor raged when a court held that a person whose skin was black could go to a white university. Disobeying the law is often—even usually—wrong; but this is so largely because the illegal is usually restricted to the immoral and because morally right conduct is still less often illegal. But we must always be sensitive to the fact that this has not always been the case, is not now always the case and need not always be the case in the future. And undue concentration upon what is wrong with disobeying the law rather than upon the wrong which the law seeks to prevent can seriously weaken and misdirect that awareness.

CHRISTOPHER D. STONE

## COMMENTS ON EUGENE ROSTOW'S "THE RIGHTFUL LIMITS OF FREEDOM" *

One should keep firmly in mind what [Dean] Rostow is *not* saying.[4] He is not saying, merely, that there is a presumptive moral quality to the law, which anyone who is contemplating a violation of the law is under an obligation to take into account before he goes ahead with his actions. Nor do I understand him to be saying merely that the morality of the law should prima facie dominate over other moral tugs that the actor might feel, so that only the very strongest countervailing moral consideration can make a violation of a democracy's laws "right." He is saying, beyond this, that in *no case* has a citizen in a "society of consent" a right to violate the law, no matter how nonviolent he may be, and no matter how earnestly he may feel that his actions are destined to further the common good, moral or otherwise.

Now, it should be obvious that Rostow has carved out for himself the hardest of these positions to maintain. It is not, I think, because he feels that the social compact leaves him, as a matter of abstract logic, no choice but to defend that particular interpretation. His is distinctly an interpretation of the social compact read (as it must be) against the author's views—of life, of history, of the capacities and limitations of competing ways of organizing our lives. Much of his paper speaks from this level, and what it comes down to, in sum, is the strong doubt that a society can hold together upon a citizenry of Thoreaus, each opting to follow or disregard the society's commands as he chooses.

There are thus two separate problems to explore and then tie together: First, how far can the argument from social compact go, on its own terms, in convincing the potential dissident that he has a moral duty to obey all laws? Second, when we have those limits in better perspective, what additional empirical and historical judgments does one have to agree with to sustain Rostow's position?

* From Comments on Eugene Rostow's "The Rightful Limits of Freedom in a Liberal Democratic State: Of Civil Disobedience" in Is Law Dead? 94–102 (Simon & Schuster 1971).

4. Is Law Dead?, *op. cit.*, 39 ff.

In answering the first question, one ought to recognize that Rostow's argument from social compact does not have to stand or fall depending on whether it can persuade everybody to obey the law in every situation. Some people—cultists, madmen, extreme dissidents—are going to disobey some laws, and perhaps the law in general, no matter what moral arguments we present to them; just as others, through their unquestioningly positive attitudes towards authority, are going sheepishly to obey the law no matter what it tells them to do and what sort of government has issued it. Neither of these two extremes is within the reach of moral suasion, and we cannot expect Rostow's efforts to apply to either of them.

What we have got to test Rostow's position against involves the vast majority of others, those who lie somewhere between these extremes, who find themselves in situations where they (a) more or less consciously feel a dilemma of whether to obey the law; (b) perceive, or can be made to perceive their dilemma as a moral one (that is, one the solution of which can be advanced by the application of moral terms); and (c) are genuinely willing to apply the intellectual energy that the working out of a moral conclusion demands.

These people can be divided into three groups so far as they help us isolate the problems that Rostow's position faces. First, there will be a group which (a) thinks that the compact model, with its constellation of contract terminology, is the best possible guide to determining political obligation, and (b) also feels that it is applicable to our present society; second, a group which, like the first group, believes in the compact analysis as a way of ordering people's choices in the best of all possible worlds, but is not convinced that it is appropriate to our present circumstances; and, third, a group of people who are principled, in the sense that they genuinely want to orient their impulses in accordance with some moral principles, but for whom the compact model and its elaborate metaphors hold no attraction.

The first group, composed of persons who by definition both subscribe to the compact metaphor as an ideal guide *and* feel it is presently applicable, are those to whom Rostow's argument is going to have the most success. They are committed to accept the relevance of the questions that the model brings with it: Have you not made a *promise* to do such and such? Has not someone else, or the entire society, *relied* on your *implied agreement*? Have you not signified *consent* by *accepting* such and such *benefits*? What Rostow is able to do for these people is to clarify the nature of their commitment by dispelling a number of misconceptions about what the model entails and what it does not. He explains, for example, that when one agrees to a contract, one is accepting a total package, and has not retained the "right" to breach without liability because he would prefer not to have had one or two of the clauses that went along with the whole bargain—or because some of the terms are turning out badly for him.

But ultimately, is there anything in the principles of these people's commitment that entails what Rostow wants finally to convince them of: that they have no "right" to disobey *any* law that has been enacted and sanctioned by the processes "agreed upon," that is, has been passed by a constitutionally apportioned Congress, signed by the President, upheld by the judges and so on? Rostow can show them—and does show them—that when they violate the law, they are breaching "a covenant with moral dimensions, and . . . not committing a purely technical offense" because their obligation to the law is "rooted in [their] own promises." But even supposing this, and supposing that we are now addressing people who give large moral weight to promise-keeping, where does that leave us? Do we not sometimes think it "moral" that we break some promises, "promises" usually of a more specific and considered kind than our "promise" to the state? This is an especially telling point when we observe that our lives are full of countervailing promises, some to the state (say) and some to our family, friends, and colleagues. Even if we accept an obligation to keep promises, and agree to regard our obligations to the state as rooted in a very important promise, it is not to tell us which of the promises is to prevail in any concrete case.

Take, for example, the case Rostow cites of the internment, during the war, of the Japanese Americans. Rostow says that the nation's act was wrong but that it "was not a complete breach of the social contract, which would justify revolution, or tactics of violence that represent the same idea." Maybe. But Rostow has cut out for himself a much harder task than to argue against *revolution* or even *violence*; he wants to argue against even nonviolent disobedience to law. The real case to test Rostow's position demands we suppose a citizen of Japanese descent who is faced with the choice of turning himself and his family in to a "relocation center," as per the law, or hiding out. Has he not made "promises" to his family? Have they not "relied" on him? The set of obligations to his children and to his nation came about in much the same way—in a hospital room. What is there about keeping promises, per se, which tells him that his violating the law by hiding out and protecting his family is immoral, rather than the contrary? There are arguments both ways; but the further one tracks them, the less he finds himself arguing about simple promise-keeping.

Rostow evidently bases his compact argument not merely on the obligation to keep promises, but on the supportive position that, in conditions of democracy, we are bound to assume that the machinery of state—not the various conjectures of various dissidents—expresses the will of the majority and the community's sense of justice. Here, too, however, we are not apt to dissuade from civil disobedience even those who agree with the premise. Most civil disobedients do not doubt to start with that the laws are expressive of the community's will. They may think, however, that the community's sense of justice is both *wrong* (its increasing discredit is a factor that compact theorists will have to contend with) and intruding into areas in which they never "agreed" that the larger community's sense of justice ought to prevail; *e. g.*, in tolerating segregation. If the disobedient feels strongly, then he is not apt to find anything in the assumption that the majority's will is prevailing to dissuade him from committing some technically illegal but non-violent protest to stir the majority to reconsider its views more rapidly than could be accomplished through lawful channels. There are arguments to be made, of course, for his exercising restraint. The point is that the social compact, so far as it is predicated on either the obligation to keep promises or on the presumption that the majority's sense of justice will be effectuated in a democracy, stops far short of—indeed, is quite indecisive with respect to—convincing anyone in a real dilemma.

The problem is, in more general terms, that there is simply nothing odd or striking about people believing in the compact metaphor, but only insofar as they are deemed bound by decisions which affect all parties in a pretty much nondiscriminatory way (say, when Congress decides how much money is to go to the highway trust fund and how much to foreign aid). But it is far harder to convince anyone that he has so "promised" to abide by the laws that he is morally bound not to disobey an order which singles him out for concentration camp because of his race. Certainly no judge, in interpreting the humdrum contracts that are his daily fare, would impute such unlikely intentions to the parties before him.

Rostow acknowledges the difficulty that countervailing moral tugs pose for the compact analysis, but seems to suggest, as a way around them, what appears at first blush a compromise position: that the actor who feels overwhelmed by his other moral commitments and breaks the law "should at least respect his duty to the law he has helped make by accepting its penalties." This is, however, considerably less than the solution one wanted. The whole aim of a moral model is to offer a framework people can use to resolve their obligations by moral analysis and suasion—that is, before force (the individual's or the state's) is the only recourse that remains. Thus, what the potential disobedient wants from the moral model is guidance as to whether it is "right" to break the law in the first place. Once he has chosen to do so, whether he "accepts" the law's penalties is beside the point of the social compact as a moral model, because he has made the basic *moral choice* we were concerned with, and it is only in limited cases that he still is the object of a *moral argument*. Once he is in the hands of the state, the choices are those of the state, and whether he "accepts" what the state does to him is more a matter of psychological interest than a moral dilemma on the same order as that which the disobedient faced originally.

The second group of people present to Rostow's position all these problems and an additional one. While they are (unlike the next group) attracted by the compact metaphor as a guide for ordering one's obligations, they feel that given the structure of our present society, with, for example, the present maldistribution of effective participation, the compact simply is not applicable *now*. Their position might be likened to that of the industrial workers in the early part of the century, who wanted to organize their relations with their employers on the basis of contract, but who felt that until bargaining power was equalized by changes in the negotiating structure, contract negotiations should not bind—or even be entered into. Rostow is, I take it, acknowledging argument of this sort in his special efforts to respond to the Negroes and students. But throughout his paper as a whole, there is not the sort of support that many readers will demand of his repeated assertions that ours is "a society of consent," that our government's powers are legitimate "because authorized and renewed by procedure all must respect," and that ours is "a society of liberty and equality." These are grand claims, but nonetheless they are very much in question today by people who are not in bad faith, and whose attitude towards the arguments from compact are influenced accordingly.

The third group is the most difficult of all to deal with, and, again, I do not think that its members can be dismissed as of bad faith. Many people want keenly to keep some set of obligations to the state and to their fellow citizens, but simply find the compact unacceptable as a strategy of argument for anyone who is not already convinced.

Rostow, anticipating them, speaks of Locke's social-compact model as "the only modern rival to the doctrine that power proceeds from the barrel of a gun," and the truth of this negative, alone, may be seen as shifting the burden back on his critics. Certainly no one can have much taste for positivism after what we saw in Europe in the thirties—and since—and arguments, like Plato's, from the healthy body, or like Filmer's, from the divine right of kings, are no less unsupportably fictive than the compact. These objectors ought to recognize, too, how hard it is to think of a model that promises to fulfill as many goals as does the compact. Its terms encompass in one set of shared symbols reminders (a) to the governors as to their obligations to the governed; (b) to the governed, as to their duty to obey laws; and (c) to the governed, as to their duty when not to obey, or perhaps even affirmatively to disobey, the laws. Further, on a less tangible but at least equally important level, it develops and reinforces a broad range of attitudes towards life that we attach high importance to—senses of our freedom, dignity, autonomy and choice.

These are all, I feel, strong arguments. But we have to recognize, as a fact, that notwithstanding them the compact model does not seem to have a great deal of attraction as a model. And the real *sine qua non* of a model of political obligation is not its abstract intellectual appeal (as a matter of its coherence with other beliefs the society deems acceptable) but its capacity to exercise influence over real people.

What is the reason for the compact model's lack of drawing power?

For one thing, as observed already, even on its premises it does not seem to give much guidance in most of the very cases one feels strongly enough about to want to think through morally. An argument that is based on promise, reliance, and so forth, is always going to turn up counter-promises and counter-reliances, usually of a more immediate and tangible sort than those to the state.

Secondly, I think we ought to recognize too that people today have associations towards contractual obligation different than they had in Locke's time. In Locke's time, for example, the prevalent epistemology and psychology were of a much simpler sort—everyone was assumed to know the world, and know his wants, by simply inspecting and inventorying basic concepts and perceptions. A neo-Kantian, neo-Freudian era in theories of knowledge lends itself to increased doubts that "the facts" people have to go on are really so simple, or that people "really" know what they want. Many of the avante-garde skeptics of compact obligations can be read as saying, from this perspective, that our knowledge and wants are so inadequate and manipulable, that we do not have, in contract terminology, contractual capacity in our political lives; in all events, the fictions seem just that much more fictive.

The political model cannot but suffer, too, from the fact that the contracts people today really know of—those with their insurance agent and telephone company—seem so imposed on them and so unwilled. The bills are paid, but the feeling of moral commitment to one's contracts must be minimal.

There is a deeper level of problem, as well. In Locke's day the contract had the attractiveness of an instrument that liberated people (from status) and was (like promise-keeping) fundamental to long-term, orderly planning; an age that is putting more and more emphasis on spontaneity and the present is apt to regard a contract as less desirable and understandable, as "binding." This lost luster carries down to the very level of promise-keeping, on which the contract's obligatoriness is rested. In the age into which we are entering, the keeping of a promise tends to seem more and more *immoral*. It is viewed as if the speaker said "I will carry out some action because of the person that I was when I made the promise." New senses of change and speed are tending to replace that thinking with a morality which demands that appeals for moral support be addressed to one's present commitments; that is, "I love you," not "I promised to love you." In such times the compact model, along with promises, contracts, and loyalty oaths, is going to have lessened moral appeal.

None of this is to say that Rostow is wrong in his basic position. But the objections that these three groups of people present place for us in clearer perspective the difficulties that the compact model faces in arresting the centrifugal forces that are pulling us apart.

My sense is that we will not resolve these problems until we have a deeper understanding than we now have of how important it is for a society to have *any single shared model of obligation at all*. The persuasiveness of all the steps of Rostow's argument—the defense of the social compact as an ideal model of obligation, the judgment that the model is applicable to our present society, the interpretation that it admits of no exceptions by appeal to "higher" moral claims—are all in some ways responsive to that one problem.

I say this because, when we get right down to it, whether we deem the compact model applicable to our society is not a pure empirical question about "the facts" of our daily lives—for example, whether the distribution of effective voting power is "really" equal—but a decision of degree that is very much influenced by theoretical and pragmatic considerations about what will happen to us if we act *as though* there is no compact. People who feel that there are large values in having *some* shared model of obligation to guide us will be that much less hasty to throw over whatever we do have because they spot (who could not spot?) some structural inequities. And similarly with respect to whether we should admit of exceptions. We cannot answer that without having a good sense of what it is, exactly, we can hope a firm set of guidelines to do for us. For the higher our expectations of what unyielding fidelity to law can bring, the less prone we will be to undermine it with special allowances for "good faith" lawbreakers.

### UNITED STATES v. SISSON

297 F.Supp. 902, 904–5, 908, 909 (1969)

Prosecution for violation of Military Selective Service Act of 1967, in which the District Court, Wyzanski, Chief Judge, held, inter alia, that requiring combat duty in Vietnam war of a selective service registrant who was conscientiously opposed to American military activities in Vietnam but who was not in a formal sense a religious conscientious objector the Military Selective Service Act of 1967, as applied to registrant, violated the free exercise clause and the establishment of religion clause of the First Amendment, and the due process clause of the Fifth Amendment.

WYZANSKI, Chief Judge

. . . .

Sisson does not now and never did claim that he is or was in the narrow statutory sense a religious conscientious objector.

Sisson graduated in 1963 from the Phillips Exeter Academy and in 1967 from Harvard College. He enlisted in the Peace Corps in July 1967, but after training he was, for reasons that have no moral connotations, "deselected" in September 1967. In January 1968 he went to work as a reporter for The Southern Courier, published in Montgomery, Alabama. That paper assigned him to work in Mississippi, where he was when he received the induction order.

The first formal indication in the record that Sisson had conscientious scruples is a letter of February 29, 1968 in which he notified Local Board No. 114 that "I find myself to be conscientiously opposed to service in the Armed Forces. Would you please send me SSS Form No. 150 so that I might make my claim as a conscientious objector." On receiving the form, Sisson concluded that his objection not being religious, within the administrative and statutory definitions incorporated in that form, he was not entitled to have the benefit of the form. He, therefore, did not execute it.

But, although the record shows no earlier formal indication of conscientious objection, Sisson's attitude as a non-religious conscientious objector has had a long history. Sisson himself referred to his moral development, his educational training, his extensive reading of reports about and comments on the Vietnam situation, and the degree to which he had familiarized himself with the U. N. Charter, the charter and judgments of the Nuremberg Tribunal, and other domestic and international matters bearing upon the American involvement in Vietnam.

On the stand Sisson was diffident, perhaps beyond the requirements of modesty. But he revealed sensitiveness, not arrogance or obstinacy. His answers lacked the sharpness that sometimes reflects a prepared mind. He was entirely without eloquence. No line he spoke remains etched in memory. But he fearlessly used his own words, not mouthing formulae from court cases or manuals for draft avoidance.

There is not the slightest basis for impugning Sisson's courage. His attempt to serve in the Peace Corps, and the assignment he took on a Southern newspaper were not acts of cowardice or evasion. Those actions were assumptions of social obligations. They were in the pattern of many conscientious young men who have recently come of age. From his education Sisson knows that his claim of conscientious objection may cost him dearly. Some will misunderstand his motives. Some will be reluctant to employ him.

Nor was Sisson motivated by purely political considerations. Of course if "political" means that the area of decision involves a judgment as to the conduct of a state, then any decision as to any war is not without some political aspects. But Sisson's table of ultimate values is moral and ethical. It reflects quite as real, pervasive, durable, and commendable a marshalling of priorities as a formal religion. It is just as much a residue of culture, early training, and beliefs shared by companions and family. What another derives from the discipline of a church, Sisson derives from the discipline of conscience.

Thus, Sisson bore the burden of proving by objective evidence that he was sincere. He was as genuinely and profoundly governed by his conscience as would have been a martyr obedient to an orthodox religion.

. . . . .

There are two main categories of conflicting claims. First, there are both public and private interests in the common defense. Second there are both public and private interests in individual liberty.

Every man, not least the conscientious objector, has an interest in the security of the nation. Dissent is possible only in a society strong enough to repel attack. The conscientious will to resist springs from moral principles. It is likely to seek a new order in the same society, not anarchy or submission to a hostile power. Thus conscience rarely wholly disassociates itself from the defense of the ordered society within which it functions and which it seeks to reform not to reduce to rubble.

In parallel fashion, every man shares and society as a whole shares an interest in the liberty of the conscientious objector, religious or not. The freedom of all depends on the freedom of each. Free men exist only in free societies. Society's own stability and growth, its physical and spiritual prosperity are responsive to the liberties of its citizens, to their deepest insights, to their free choices —"That which opposes, also fits."

Those rival categories of claims cannot be mathematically graded. There is no table of weights and measures. Yet there is no insuperable difficulty in distinguishing orders of magnitude.

The sincerely conscientious man, whose principles flow from reflection, education, practice, sensitivity to competing claims, and a search for a meaningful life, always brings impressive credentials. When he honestly believes that he will act wrongly if he kills, his claim obviously has great magnitude. That magnitude is not appreciably lessened if his belief relates not to war in general, but to a particular war or to a particular type of war. Indeed a selective conscientious objector might reflect a more discriminating study of the problem, a more sensitive conscience, and a deeper spiritual understanding.

. . . .

The suggestion that courts cannot tell a sincere from an insincere conscientious objector underestimates what the judicial process performs every day. Ever since, in Edginton v. Fitzmaurice (188[5]) L.R. 29 Ch.Div. [4]59, Bowen L. J. quipped that "the state of a man's mind is as much a fact as the state of his digestion", each day courts have applied laws, criminal and civil, which make sincerity the test of liability.

. . . .

Sisson's case being limited to a claim of conscientious objection to combat service in a foreign campaign, this court holds that the free exercise of religion clause in the First Amendment and the due process clause of the Fifth Amendment prohibit the application of the 1967 draft act of Sisson to require him to render combat service in Vietnam.

The chief reason for reaching this conclusion after examining the competing interests is the magnitude of Sisson's interest in not killing in the Vietnam conflict as against the want of magnitude in the country's present need for him to be so employed.

The statute as here applied creates a clash between law and morality for which no exigency exists, and before, in Justice Sutherland's words, "the last extremity" or anything close to that dire predicament has been glimpsed, or even predicted, or reasonably feared.

When the state through its laws seeks to override reasonable moral commitments it makes a dangerously uncharacteristic choice. The law grows from the deposits or morality. Law and morality are, in turn, debtors and creditors of each other. The law cannot be adequately enforced by the courts alone, or by courts supported merely by the police and the military. The true secret of legal might lies in the habits of conscientious men disciplining themselves to obey the law they respect without the necessity of judicial and administrative orders. When the law treats a reasonable, conscientious act as a crime it subverts its own power. It invites civil disobedience. It impairs the very habits which nourish and preserve the law.

[The discussions of the Establishment of Religion and Due Process violations are omitted—Ed.] [5]

## QUESTIONS

1. Was Sisson a civil disobedient? How did his aims and motives differ from those of the demonstrators in *Walker* and *Grossner*? What other significant differences can you find? Would the *Walker* demonstrators have wanted a result such as in *Sisson*?

2. What values is Wyzanski's opinion fostering? Does it discriminate against the uneducated and unreflective?

3. Do we need law? And if so, for what? Can a society maintain a posture in which a range of important issues are decided not by a congress—for all men as a corporate group, but by the individual himself? To what other areas of life could and should Judge Wyzanski's reasoning extend?

Consider in these regards the selections in the chapter that follows.

5. The United States Supreme Court dismissed the government's appeal from *Sisson* without reaching the merits of his claim, 399 U.S. 267 (1970), thus leaving Wyzanski's opinion to stand, yet stopping short of endorsing it. Subsequently, the Supreme Court decided expressly to rule on the matter and held 8–1 that there need be no exemption for conscientious objectors whose objection was to a specific war. Gillette v. United States, 401 U.S. 437 (1971). "Sincerity," Justice Marshall wrote for the majority, "is a concept that can bear only so much weight."

## CHAPTER NINETEEN

# The Future of Trust

## INTRODUCTORY NOTE

We have seen, throughout this book, the many levels of difficulty that are involved in organizing a society through legal edicts—or even by some combination of legal and other social sanction. What are the prospects for our moving towards the other, utopian extreme: a regime in which the reins of law, rule, order, and even superego, are relaxed to allow increasing experimentation and autonomy? Can we come to trust one another (and one's own self) to wear our hair whatever length; to view whatever literature; to fight, if at all, only in conflicts that one himself supports; to let one another live as one chooses and die as one chooses?

Obviously, the problems that such a transition involves are too enormous and complex for full treatment here. What are presented, instead, are a short series of selections under three headings, (a) the Possibility, (b) the Fears, and (c) the Prospects of Trust.

The first section is designed to give glimpses of societies—real and fictitious—in which the need for rigid, authoritarian guidance is not so acute as we know it. *E. g.*, in Swift's land of the completely rational Houyhnhnms, Gulliver finds a people whose language apparently does not even contain a word for edict or law; among the Tiv of Africa, our concept of a jury's *telling* the accused the verdict—rather than discussing and working it out with him—would be a travesty of the social ideals.

The second section, regarding the fears of trust, concerns itself with the estimates of human and social capacities that underlie the view that mankind needs to be bound by a host of clearly spelled-out laws.

The final section, that concerned with the prospects for moving in the direction of increasing trust, regards our present from an historical distance. It questions how warranted are the fears that, without strong control mechanisms, we would fall into a "war of everyone against every one". What new feelings of, *e. g.*, personal and social abundance, might allow these fears to yield? What forms of societal organization might unfold? What are the chances that such forms will evolve?

---

## A.  The Possibility  .  .  .

CHRISTOPHER D. STONE

### EXISTENTIAL HUMANISM AND THE LAW *

.  .  .  [B]oth the lawmaker and the existential psychologist recognize that each human being carries, deep within the rhythm of his body, unfulfilled needs so basic that not even language can surface them intact.  .  .  .

The existential humanist represents the capacity of the human being for trust.  He expects to find, in the drowned-out inner noises, the finest of which man is capable.  He speaks for the forces that would open up the body, let the noises vent, and celebrate and build upon what we have got.

The lawmaker represents, if not the capacity of the human being for distrust, at least his capacity for skepticism.  The lawmaker, too, wants to allow "the pursuit of happiness."  But he is fearful of the potential of the inner noises to drum up in violence, anarchy, and disorder.  His mood is to keep them contained, hushing them with "reason" or shouting them down with threat.

Now, the truth is that both are right.  What is sealed up inside a man undoubtedly includes some of his best *and* some of his worst potential.  But it does not follow that at any stage of history, the particular balance that is struck between the expressible and the inexpressible, or the particular modes of enforcing that balance, is defensible.  Societies, like individuals, are dynamic.  The basic attitudes people enmesh themselves with are subject to change.  Some of these changes arise from new levels of technological, economic, and military strengths and threats, which bring with them shifts in our capacities to trust and to tolerate.  Other changes seem less immediately rooted in identifiable conditions of life.  There is evidence, for example, that societies alternate faith in the rational and the irrational, so that first one dominates, then the other, not so much on account of anything else that is happening as because each phase is simply a working out of its own inner social logic.[1]  In all events, whatever causes these shifts, they involve attitudinal changes so fundamental as to entail, or at least to allow for, new phases in the constraints and methods of law.

The aim must be for the lawmaker, as symbolic custodian of the repressive, or skeptical, forces, to acquaint himself with the human stuff with which the existential humanist deals, and to be prepared continuously to revise his estimates of legal needs in the light of these shifting social and human possibilities.

.  .  .  .

What we must come to grips with is this.  From the point of each individual, considered separately, an ideal society would be geared

---

* From Existential Humanistic Psychology 152–56, 159–69 (Tom Greening ed. Brooks/Cole 1971).

1. See E. Dodds, The Greeks and the Irrational (1951), *infra* at 1277.

toward his fulfillment at two levels. First, it would be so structured (or unstructured) as to enable him to test his potentialities to the fullest, enabling him to decide what actions would fulfill him at any stage of his life. Second, it would be so structured as to enable him to carry out those actions that he finds he truly desires. The first stage is thus concerned with permitting and perhaps promoting discovery and knowledge; the second is concerned with increasing possible courses of action.[2]

The dilemma these ideals involve us in is pointed up by Dostoevsky's Raskolnikov[3] and Camus' Meursault: in the course of "self-discovery" any individual might, in fathoming his capacities for anger or aimlessness, test what it feels like to kill. The group response to this situation is many-sided and complex: social forces simultaneously act to prevent one from wanting to know what it is like to kill (internalized morality); control access to the instruments of killing (to some extent, administrative law); channelize the urge to kill to socially permissible expressions (war, contact sports, business); and the volition that, for one reason or another, cannot be dammed up or rechanneled is met with by threat and physical restraint (mob retribution and the criminal law).

The question of government is, which if any of these group responses is one prepared to accept as a counter to what sorts of threats. For the man who places the highest premium on allowing individual self-discovery, the answer might be: no sorts of social controls, no matter how ominous the threat to other values. Here we ought to note that if what the existentialist wants to optimize is *autonomy*[4] then, at least on the face of the word, there is a suggestion that no compromise with social control is possible: "auto" is from the Greek *autos*, meaning "self," and *nomous* means "word" or "law." To be autonomous therefore means to be a giver of one's own law—to be one's own legislator and judge. As an ideal, such a pure and uncompromising existentialism can be extolled romantically, as perhaps in Nietzsche, but not so when it leaves the pages of literature and brings down on us the sporadic "senseless" murders that always command such public horror and interest.

The existential humanist, if I understand him aright, is not so dogged by some of these anarchistic threats that the "pure" existentialist may have to confront. He recognizes the need for, and even sees dignity in, some forms of compromise with demands for group well-being, although he may be opposed to the propriety of any given control measure (capital punishment, for example). Moreover, he certainly looks forward to these controls gradually coming more and more from within the individual as society progresses. For he sees, or ought to see, that at least while that stage is, hopefully, unfolding,

---

2. This dichotomy between knowledge and action is useful but misleading. The more closely a society approached a self-actualizing ideal, the more archaic and strange the suggestion of separating the stages—knowledge from action—would become.

3. In Crime and Punishment, *infra* at 1252.

4. Or, if one prefers, *authenticity*, which is not far removed: *authentikos* (original, primary, first hand) is equivalent to authent(es): one who does things himself.

some controls to avert mutual self-annihilation are the *sine qua non* of everybody's autonomy and thus should pass the existential-humanist muster if only on those grounds.

But the existential humanist, as I understand him, is concerned to discover how much social control does not spring from a desire to preserve life or even to advance the greatest good of the greatest number.[5] Much of it (whatever rationalizations we lawyers and our ilk may introduce after the fact) is born of no sober second thought whatsoever. It weighs on each individual as a heavy legacy from the dead. It springs from guilt, shame, and anxiety, and often from a guilt, shame, and anxiety that, if it ever was "appropriate" arguendo, is no longer appropriate save as a sort of common ritual that serves to glue the society together. And a defense that must rest on these terms places the society above the individual in a way unacceptable to the existential humanist.

What the existential humanist wants need not be an anarchy of boundless self-discovery. Indeed, he may be aware that sheer unrestrainedness, sheer disorder, would be inconsistent with freedom, for a systematic inventorying and implementation of our desires could not be achieved without some areas of fixed expectations, some order, and some rules. . . . His program is to bring the society to a greater and greater awareness of the limits that past and present forces impose on our autonomy (or authenticity), to call those limits to question—a project that necessarily involves each man's calling to question what he wants to make of himself—and to peel away gradually the repression that, at each level of social possibility, appears as what Marcuse would term "surplus".

. . . .

What I think this discussion shows us is the need to . . . come to grips ultimately with the entire vocabulary of concepts underlying a legal system: rights, privileges, ownership, duty, and so on. These basic terms are so woven into the fabric of our thought that a special effort is necessary to make visible the role they play in defining our senses of self, and in adjusting the boundaries that we feel between the self and others.

Perhaps the significance of these terms becomes more apparent if we turn to other societies, where we find different attitudes toward, say, the assertion of one's "right" and find those attitudes, in turn, part of the expression of significantly different attitudes toward life. Among the Chinese, for example, Escarra writes,

> . . . there is no place for law in the Latin sense of the term. Not even rights of individuals are guaranteed by law. There are only duties and mutual compromises governed by the idea of order, responsibility, hierarchy and harmony. . . . To take advantage of one's position, to

---

5. I am not clear in my own mind how a man who associates himself with existential humanism stands on utilitarianism: if he feels that an act he contemplates will advance his self-realization but that it will cause more suffering than pleasure to others, will he go ahead and do it anyway? I assume that the pure existentialist is inclined wholly to discount the utilitarian calculus in deciding what to do.

invoke one's "rights", has always been looked at askance in China. The great art is to give way (*jang*) on certain points, and thus accumulate an invisible fund of merit whereby one can later obtain advantages in other directions.[6]

What Escarra points up, and what is confirmed by other commentators, is the relationship between the sense of having a "right" and a broader view of life that comprehends attitudes of trust in the harmony and primacy of nature, and an emphasis on the unity rather than the separateness of each individual.

Indeed, if we contrast the Chinese view with the view of the great nineteenth-century German legal scholar, Von Jhering, we see the possibility of still other planes of internal sensation that must be involved in the invocation of rights. Von Jhering took the position that the citizen had a strong moral duty not to turn the other cheek but always to seek redress in the courts. The timbre of his phrasing is, I think, instructive:

> The man who does not feel that when his rights are despised and trampled under foot, not only the object of those rights, but his own person is at stake; the man who, placed in such a condition, does not feel impelled to assert himself and his right cannot be helped. . . . Egotism, without any redeeming quality, and materialism are the traits which distinguish him. . . . To him I have nothing to say but these words of Kant. . . . "When a man has made a worm of himself, he cannot complain if he is trampled under foot. . . ." And from "duty in relation to the dignity of humanity in us," he draws the maxim, "let not your rights be trampled under foot by others unpunished."[7]

What I am suggesting is, of course, that the job of the existential humanist might well be to study different attitudes regarding the invoking of rights and duties in legal and legalistic contexts and explore both the different feelings that back them up and the social conditions that make those feelings urgent. What, along these lines, have our concepts of ownership done in the development of personality; in terms of our preoccupation with things outside the self; in terms of a division among people and between people and nature?

It is for insights on these levels that one ought to be searching in a review of the criminal law. What does the criminal law *do*? One is tempted to respond that it controls deviancy, which is obvious. What is not so obvious is that when we conceive of the criminal law in its fullest ambit, as includng arraignments, trials, prisons, paroles, and so forth, we see that it controls deviancy not only in the negative sense of the word (as *limiting* it) but it controls in the sense of *regulating* as well, letting some crime and criminality work their way through and be put on public display. . . . From one point of view, this agreement to live with crime reflects a social judgment that the measures necessary to eliminate it entirely would be too harsh and costly to pay. But there is also a suggestion of an ambivalence in the

---

6.   J. Escarra, Le Droit Chinois 17    7.   The Struggle For Law x–xi (5th ed. (Paris 1936).                 1879).

public mind toward allowing a broad range of experiments in criminality, some for the sake of what the crimes accomplish and some for the sake of the counterauthoritarianism they implicitly assert and kindle.

This suggestion is especially strong when one considers how many devices the society would have at its command if it wanted to limit deviancy completely. One should not think merely of the ultramodern gadgetry of suppression and surveillance but, at the other end of the spectrum, of the subtler enculturating processes the society calls on to restrain deviancy long before the threat of criminal punishment needs to be raised. The very fact that a culture shares the same vocabulary and language structure makes it likely that people will perceive and organize their experiences in somewhat the same ways. These cognitive restraints may afford, in themselves, only a weak bond, but they are reinforced by the internalizing mechanisms of family, church, school, and peer group. Original objects of sexuality and aggression are lost sight of in an enormous social labyrinth of threats and promises.

Some potential "deviancy" slips through (and some more is undoubtedly provoked by) the enculturation process. But even then legal devices for smoothing out the problems short of criminal punishment are available: in many instances private civil litigation, for example, can enable an injured man to recover damages from his assailant, and quite likely dissuade the assailant from such conduct in the future, without his having to be clapped in jail.

When we set the threat of criminal sanction in the context of these other sources of socially legislated *nomous*, a whole series of issues is underscored that might otherwise be overlooked.

For one thing, as already indicated, the fact that so much crime and criminality surface in spite of society's alternate, and potentially quite effective, control devices raises a suggestion that the human and social functions of letting people act out "criminal" tendencies may be larger, and may reflect the working of more powerful forces, than one is first inclined to suspect.

But beyond this, the availability of so many alternative ways of social regulation suggests the possibility of gradually lifting away the use of the criminal sanction without plunging the society into more anarchy and chaos than it wants and needs. This possibility would seem to promise a gradual investing of more autonomy in the individual: in removing more and more areas of activity from the institutionalized threat of the criminal law, we could place correspondingly greater weight on the more loosely organized threats and promises of organized groups, such as self-selected peers. From there (this hope would be), we could move to a realm, apparently more consistent with the concept of autonomy, in which people chose their behavior on the basis of internalized controls only.

The problem with this line of development is that the mechanisms that internalize social control are more effective restraints, and in many ways more *dehumanizing*, than putting a man in prison. The man who is threatened with prison is at least accorded the choice: to obey the law or take the consequences. In important ways, that is a better state of affairs than a society that so structured its citizens' values that they were not even able to *think about* such a choice. Thus it would be a step backward to substitute internalized sanctions for criminal sanctions, if that process came to nothing more than substituting more internalized threats and promises, which can only be dimly seen and considered, for those that are externally and flagrantly imposed. Indeed, if the aim of existential humanism, like psychotherapy, is to achieve a realm in which neither threat nor promise shall have nor need have any dominion . . . , we might prefer to see an at least temporary movement that diminished the force and effectiveness of the mechanisms of internalized control by placing *more* matters under the law of crimes.

. . . .

### The Path of the Law

What direction is the law now taking; that is, what direction is it now allowing us—perhaps leading us—to take?

. . . .

Certainly it is fair to say that, at least in the courts, the overwhelming evidence points in the direction of further trust; that is, toward more willingness to allow individuals to test their own limits and explore individual paths of self-discovery and fulfillment. (There are, we know, reactions elsewhere in the society, often with the Supreme Court as a focus of the anger; this is, on one level, a heavy burden for the law, but history may reveal that one of the most important functions of the courts was to bring these reactions to the surface, as part of a process of their passing away.)

Of course, when most of us think about trends toward liberation and trust, what comes to mind most readily is the increased availability of pornography. Perhaps the reason is that, of all that the courts are being held responsible for, this development is the least subtly evident to the opponents of instinctual exploration; and they have fastened on the matter so tenaciously in their denunciation of the courts that pornography has achieved at least a symbolic importance that keeps it continually, and perhaps too exclusively, before the public.

. . . .

Interestingly enough, some of the most important humanistic developments in the law do not deal directly with individual choice so much as with the development of *group* identity. The reason is not so strange. The fathoming of one's feelings as part of a group may be a necessary way station on the road to individual autonomy, and here developments both in the law and toward the law are playing an important role.

This situation has been most obviously true in the struggles of Blacks and Whites to measure the distances they want to keep between themselves. The law has served not only as a vehicle for regulating that distance, but the availability of the law as a focal point of discussions and agitation *about* the law has pointed up the importance of a whole complex of processes the law is involved in, beyond the level of issuing commands.

The problem of group identity among the blacks is now being paralleled by the demands of youth for increased dignity and responsibility. This situation can be seen as part of a significant shift in sources of authority, away from the traditional gerontocracy and toward a sort of "juvenocracy." On the most surface levels, it has expressed itself in the law in terms of legislation to lower the voting age and the various reforms of the military draft system. At other levels it shows up in the far-reaching reforms the courts are instituting in juvenile proceedings, belatedly according the alleged youth offender many of the protections and dignities accorded adult defendants in criminal trials, such as they are. I think, however, that in order to understand how pervasively involved the law is with the youth movement, we have to see how developments in the law, not expressly related to youth on the surface, are significantly perceived as part of their movement by the young. Marijuana laws are an obvious case in point. A less obvious example came to my attention in a classroom discussion of Brown v. Board of Education (the school integration case), which most of us have come to think of as a landmark in the Black struggle. One of my students, however, saw it quite differently: as a case involving the rights of the young to meet people from other races and decide for themselves whom they want to hate, rather than to have that hatred "legislated" by their elders.

The law is being deeply involved, too, in the historical struggle of the woman to find in herself the capacity to ask to be considered a person, and the continuing struggle in the man to find in himself the capacity to grant that recognition. Historically, the law has denied the woman on levels too numerous to recount (denials that are no less distorting because of what they implicitly affirm—of the existence in the woman of strange and mysterious and subversive powers.[8]) In ancient legal systems the woman was typically a jural nonentity, incapable of ownership, testimony, and civic privilege, and disregarded in determining descent. In fact, where the law did recognize and bestow some benefit on women, it was often in a way that reinforced the dominance-submission male ideal, as by "liberal" legislation creating shorter working hours for women, or guaranteeing a favorable balance of settlement in a divorce action.

In the law as elsewhere, there is a new tone. Most recently, we have had the courts interpret the 1963 Equal Pay Act in such way as to make it difficult for employers under the act to rationalize lesser salaries for women engaged in substantially the same work as men.[9] When we remember that only a half century ago a "radical" Supreme Court was giving in to demands on behalf of women to give legal recognition to the inferiority of women as workers,[10] we are made aware of

---

8. "Nature has given women so much power that the law has very wisely given them little." [Samuel Johnson].

9. Wheaton Glass Co. v. Schultz, 421 F.2d 259 (3rd Cir. 1970), cert. denied.

10. Muller v. Oregon, 208 U.S. 412 (1908). There, speaking for a unani-

mous Court, Justice Brewer upheld the constitutionality of Oregon's limiting to ten the number of hours a woman could work in a factory each day. "History discloses," the Court observed at the urging of then lawyer Louis Brandeis, "that woman has always been dependent on man. . . . The two sexes differ in structure of

how much one's view of his "rights" is subject to change with new levels of self-image and self-awareness.

. . . .

The final area of individual self-realization I want to consider is the draft. As with suicide, the draft involves the law in setting a tone of how much people are prepared to substitute trust and persuasion in place of force and threat. On the legislative front, the movement toward a volunteer army is partly a reflection of such sentiments, although it is an expression of many other factors as well. In courts, there have been less ambiguous responses with pronounced existential-humanist implication. Of particular interest here is the *Sisson* case.[11]

. . . Technically, the grounds for [Judge Wyzanski's] decision were that to apply the Selective Service Act so as to deny Sisson conscientious-objector status would constitute an establishment of religion in violation of the First Amendment, or, in the alternative, a violation of Sisson's rights either to free exercise of religion or of due process of law. But underneath the technical rubric, what Judge Wyzanski was really seeking to protect was what the existential humanist would call Sisson's right to become. And without reaching, I think it fair to say that what impressed him about Sisson's case was, again, what the existential humanist would call Sisson's authenticity. The opinion was careful to note that

> Sisson himself referred to his moral development, his educational training, his extensive reading of reports about and comments on the Vietnam situation, and the degree to which he had familiarized himself with the U.N. Charter, the charter and judgments of the Nuremberg Tribunal. . . .
> On the stand Sisson was diffident perhaps beyond the requirements of modesty. But he revealed sensitiveness, not arrogance or obstinacy. His answer lacked the sharpness that sometimes reflects a prepared mind. . . . He fearlessly used his own words, not mouthing formulae from court cases or manuals for draft avoidance.

Judge Wyzanski is not regarded as weighing lightly the needs of national unity and defense. But he was unprepared to pose a choice of war or jail to a young man who was so genuinely trying to find himself:

> whose principles flow from reflection, education, practice, sensitivity to competing claims, and a search for a meaningful life . . . . When he honestly believes he will act wrongly if he kills, his claim obviously has great magnitude. That magnitude is not appreciably lessened if his belief re-

body, in the functions to be performed by each, in the amount of physical strength, in the capacity for long-continued labor, particularly when done standing . . . ." In the *Shultz* case, the U. S. Court of Appeals for the Third Circuit, without even referring to Brewer's opinion, said simply that the Equal Pay Act "was intended to overcome the age-old belief in women's inferiority and to eliminate the depressing effects on living standards of reduced wages for female workers and the economic and social consequences which flow from it."

11. United States v. Sisson, 297 F.Supp. 902 (1969), *supra* at 1229.

lates not to war in general, but to a particular war or to a particular type of war. Indeed a selective conscientious objector might reflect a more discriminating study of the problem, a more sensitive conscience, and a deeper spiritual understanding.

This is an extraordinary sensitivity to find in the law, especially expressed in such terms. From the point of view of autonomy, what it suggests is that, at least as to a matter as critical as going to war, some day each man may come to be recognized as his own Congress, with power to decide legitimacy for himself. Only a strong and morally confident nation can afford to trust such separate responsibility to each of its citizens. But as Judge Wyzanski noted, to do so reinforces the individual freedom, which makes for "society's own stability and growth, its physical and spiritual prosperity."

Note

Consider the following from a chapter entitled "Anonymity as Deliverance from the Law".

.   .   .   Law means anything that binds us uncritically to inherited conventions.   .   .   .

.   .   .   When Law rather than Gospel becomes the basis for our lives, it militates against choice and freedom. It decides for us, thus sapping our powers of responsibility. Similarly, Gospel in a broader sense means a summons to choice and answerability.   .   .   In the anonymity of urban culture, far from the fishbowl of town life, modern man experiences both the terror and the delight of human freedom more acutely. The biblical God is present for man today in the world of social reality, and Law and Gospel provide us an angle of vision by which to understand secular events, including urbanization. The God of the Gospel is the One who wills freedom and responsibility, who points toward the future in hope. The Law, on the other hand, includes any cultural phenomenon which holds men in immaturity, in captivity to convention and tradition. The Law is enforced by the weight of human opinion; the Gospel is the activity of God creating new possibilities in history. Law signifies the fact that man does live in society; Gospel points to the equally important fact that he is more than the intersection of social forces. He feels himself summoned to choose, to actualize a potential selfhood which is more than the sum of genes plus glands plus class.   .   .   .

H. Cox, The Secular City 40–41 (1966).

*Roscoe Pound*

## The Limits of Effective Legal Action *

The Puritan conceived of laws simply as guides to the individual conscience. The individual will was not to be coerced . . . . But as all men's consciences were not enlightened, laws were proper to set men to thinking, to declare to them what their fellows thought on this point and that, and to afford guides to those whose consciences did not speak with assurance. . . . (M)any still think of law after the Puritan fashion.

*Jonathan Swift*

## A Voyage to the Country of the Houyhnhnms †

In the midst of all this happiness, and when I looked upon myself to be fully settled for life, my master sent for me one morning a little earlier than his usual hour. I observed by his countenance that he was in some perplexity, and at a loss how to begin what he had to speak. After a short silence, he told me, he did not know how I would take what he was going to say; that in the last general assembly, when the affair of the *Yahoos* was entered upon, the representative had taken offence at his keeping a *Yahoo* (meaning myself) in his family more like a *Houyhnhnm* than a brute animal. That he was known frequently to converse with me, as if he could receive some advantage or pleasure in my company; that such a practice was not agreeable to reason or nature, or a thing ever heard of before among them. The assembly did therefore exhort him . . . to . . . command me to swim back to the place, whence I came. . . .

My master added, that he was daily pressed by the *Houyhnhnms* of the neighbourhood to have the assembly's exhortation executed, which he could not put off much longer. . . .

I should here observe to the reader, that a decree of the general assembly in this country, is expressed by the word *hnhloayn*, which signifies an exhortation, as near as I can render it; for they have no conception how a rational creature can be compelled, but only advised, or exhorted; because no person can disobey reason, without giving up his claim to be a rational creature.

---

* From 3 A.B.J.A. 55 (1917). With permission of the American Bar Association.

† From Gulliver's Travels 110–12 (W. C. Taylor ed. 1878).

*Paul Bohannan*

## Justice and Judgment Among the Tiv *

In the preceding sections we have examined the actions of the principal litigants and of the witnesses during the course of a *jir*. This section concerns the activities of the *mbatarev* as judges. The actions of the judges are directed towards examining or investigating (*tov*) the *jir*.[12] To 'investigate' a *jir* involves listening, asking questions, discussing with other *mbatarev* and elders, making suggestions for settlement. After the *jir* has been 'investigated' it is 'ended', which will form the subject of the next section. . . .

The final question which must be investigated in this section is that of the authority of the *mbatarev*. Most litigants look upon the *mbatarev* as arbitrators to whom they may or may not bring a *jir*, as they are inclined. It is my opinion that in the eyes of most people no *ortaregh* has any authority whatever; or, at least, no *ortaregh* or anyone else ought to have any authority. This does not mean that people do not yield them a great deal of power in virtue of their influence, derived from their personalities and social positions, and a great deal of power in jural matters. It means rather that Tiv are, ideologically, fierce egalitarians in the matter of authority, even while they are realists in the matter of personal power. Most *imbatarev* are respected and, to some extent, feared. The fact that the power of the British Administration lies behind them is known to all and is, I think, greatly over-estimated. The Government would probably not back up the *mbatarev* to the point that most Tiv think.

Cases of contempt of court in Tivland always arise from contumacy—the expression of personal contempt for the judges—and seldom or never from failure to carry out court orders. . . . . .

. . . .

## V.  ENDING (KURE) THE JIR

The task of the *mbatarev* in 'ending' a *jir* is not to make a decision but to make suggestions for settlement. In a properly run *jir* the principal litigants must also play their parts: they must both concur (*lumun*) in the judgment.

Tiv litigants would seem to believe that the proper and correct solution of a dispute 'exists'. It 'is'. The task of the judge is to find it. In the old days the principal litigants would go from one elder of the community to another until they discovered one who could penetrate the details of the case and emerge with this 'correct' solution. To a lesser extent, they still do so today. It is obvious to Tiv that when a right decision has been reached, both litigants will concur in it, even though the particular judgment may not be wholly in favour of either. The importance of such concurrence by the litigants can-

* From 51, 59, 64–66 (Oxford U. Press 1955). With permission of the International African Institute and Professor Bohannan.

12.  The author translates *jir* as "court case or moot."

not be over-emphasized. It is to misunderstand the Tiv view to say
that Tiv courts have or have not the 'authority' to 'enforce' a 'decision'. 'Authority', 'enforcement', and 'decision' are all Western
legal concepts which spring from our notions and ideas of authority
hierarchies. They are part of the Western folk system concerning
our jural and governmental institutions. If Tiv judges make a settlement in which both parties can concur, there is no problem of 'enforcing a decision'. If they do not, they have not, by Tiv definition,
'ended the *jir*' satisfactorily. The correct solution is known to have
been found when all the judges and the litigants concur.

Tiv *jir*, then, discovers a solution to a dispute which is in accordance with the *inja* of the Tiv, and in which all other persons concerned in the *jir* concur. This is comparable to, but vastly different
from, the fact that Western courts make a decision in accordance with
the facts of the case and with the 'law', and have the authority to
enforce that decision. It is very difficult to discuss the acts and
values of either system in the words and concepts and language of
the other.

Concurrence of the litigants never occurs without concurrence of
the entire community; no one is ready to make concessions while any
portion of public opinion still supports him. It is the opinion of the
community which forces concurrence. Judging, like all other activities of Tiv leaders, consists largely in the timely suggestion of
what the majority thinks is right or desirable.

The 'correct solution' changes as the situation of both litigants
changes. Tiv, therefore, tend to deplore 'final decisions', which their
European administrators, of course, prefer. Tiv feel that making a
final decision, in the English sense, often perpetuates conditions
which will eventually become unjust. It sometimes appears to foreigners that Tiv do not want their courts to make decisions at all,
but it seems more accurate to say that they want the judges to point
out a *modus vivendi*, which will endure while the situation endures.

For Tiv judges to settle a *jir* by any standards other than the
concurrence of the litigants, and eventually of the community, is to
settle it 'by force' (*sa apela*). This literal translation might be
more meaningfully rendered 'settled by despotic action'. If a Tiv
Native Authority court uses its government-backed authority to enforce a decision in which the litigants do not concur, and in which
community opinion does not insist that they concur, that said court
is to have 'heard the *jir* by force'. This is the worst thing that can
be said for any *jir*. It is much worse, in the Tiv view, than the
acceptance of bribes. Bribery is at least not capricious.

QUESTIONS

What different concepts of self prevail in these different societies? What sorts of different attitudes towards one's self underlie these different attitudes towards "rights" and "responsibility"?
What emotional feelings are involved in different concepts of self?
How is each society's view of man reinforced by the way in which
the law is apt to treat him? Why does Von Ihering, quoted *supra*

at 1237, feel so strongly about the moral need not to turn the other cheek? Why might the Houyhnhnms—Swift's paragon of the rational creature—have no concept for command or edict among themselves (although the Yahoo could apparently be commanded)?

JOSEPH NEEDHAM

THE UNITY OF THE ETHICAL AND COSMIC ORDER *

This rapid survey of the history of Chinese law has confirmed the conclusion already suggested at the end of the Section on the ancient school of Legalists [13] and at the beginning of the present Section. The struggle between systematic law and law administered by men paternalistically judging every new case on its own merits and in accordance with *li* . . . was settled decisively in favour of the latter. But one would not appreciate the full force of the word *li* if one failed to recognise that the customs, usages and ceremonials which it summed up were not simply those which had empirically been found to agree with the instinctive feelings of rightness experienced by the Chinese people "everywhere under Heaven"; they were those which, it was believed, accorded with the "will" of Heaven, indeed with the structure of the universe. Hence the basic disquiet aroused in the Chinese mind by crimes, or even disputes, because they were felt to be disturbances in the Order of Nature. Already the Hung Fan chapter of the *Shu Ching* (Historical Classic), which if not written in the early Chou time is quite old enough for our purpose, indicates that excessive rain is a sign of the emperor's injustice, prolonged drought indicates that he is making serious mistakes, intense heat accuses him of negligence, extreme cold of lack of consideration, and strong winds (curiously enough) show that he is being apathetic. In the *Chou Li* (Record of the Rites of Chou) and in many other ancient texts there is upheld the idea that punishments can only be carried out in autumn, when all things are dying; to execute criminals in the spring would have a deleterious effect on the growing crops. In trying to visualise what this "phenomenalism" meant to the ancient Chinese, Eberhard has made the interesting suggestion that they thought of Heaven and Earth as if the sequences of their phenomena proceeded along two parallel strands in time, as if in two parallel wires, and that perturbations in one sequence affected the other as if by a kind of inductance.

. . . .

We are thus in presence of a thorough parallelism at the three levels of cosmos, human society and individual body. But it seems that the Western conception was deeply different from the Chinese. The former saw justice and law at all levels, closely associated with personalised beings, enacting laws or administering them. The latter

* From 2 Science and Civilisation in China 526–29, 531–32 (Cambridge U. Press 1962). With permission of the Syndics of the Cambridge University Press.

13. See *infra* at 1255.

saw only that righteousness embodied in good custom represented the harmony necessary for the existence and function of the social organism. It recognised also a harmony in the function of the heavens, and, if pressed, would have admitted one in the functions of the individual body also, but these harmonies were spontaneous, not decreed. Discord in one was echoed by dysharmony in the others.

.  .  .

If, then, all crimes and disputes were looked upon in ancient China, not primarily as infractions of a purely human, though imperial, legal code, but rather as ominous disturbances in the complex network of causal filaments by which mankind was connected on all sides with surrounding Nature, it was perhaps the very subtlety of these which made positive law seem so unsatisfactory. The preface of the +7th-century Thang code suggests that it is dangerous and ominous to "leave *li* and engage in legally fixed punishments (*chhu li ju hsing*)".

> In this conception [Escarra well writes], there is no place for law in the Latin sense of the term. Not even rights of individuals are guaranteed by law. There are only duties and mutual compromises governed by the ideas of order, responsibility, hierarchy and harmony. The prince, assisted by the sages, ensures the dominance of these throughout the realm. The supreme ideal of the *chün tzu* is to demonstrate in all circumstances a just measure, a ritual moderation; as is shown in the Chinese taste for arbitration and reciprocal concessions. To take advantage of one's position, to invoke one's "rights", has always been looked at askance in China. The great art is to give way (*jang*) on certain points, and thus accumulate an invisible fund of merit whereby one can later obtain advantages in other directions.[14]

Hence the lack of "positivisation" (Gernet) of primitive customary law in China, and the failure of the Legalists. As Granet says, "The Sophists did not succeed in persuading the Chinese that there could exist necessarily contradictory terms. Nor did the Legalists succeed in getting them to accept the idea of unvarying regulations and sovereign Law."

The truth of what has just been said will certainly be appreciated by everyone who has lived in China. To this day "the Chinese method is, in practice, to fix responsibility in terms, not of 'who has done something' but of 'what has happened'. . . . "

.  .  .  .

As has been pointed out by [Jerome] Frank, ancient Greek, as opposed to ancient Roman law, shared to a considerable extent the characteristic Indian and Chinese preference for equity and arbitration as opposed to abstract formulae. This he calls the "individualisation of cases." In an earlier work he had made the interesting suggestion that one may see in the Roman "quest for a practically unrealisable legal certainty" a certain masculine element, while in

14.  *Supra* p. 1237 at n. 6.

the milder Asian dominance of equity and the flexible determination of all cases on their individual merits a certain feminine element manifested itself. It is certainly notable that the Roman legal system arose in a society in which the power of the father (*patria potestas*) was carried to the extreme. Certainly in most cultures the father stands for the strict rules which the child is supposed to obey, while the mother stands for lenience and the principle that "circumstances alter cases". On the one hand there is the ideal of the closed, static and consistent system of law, on the other, the "feminine" attitudes of flexibility, tact, understanding and intuition. How striking is this suggestion in the light of what we have seen in Section 10*d, i* on the Taoists, the whole of whose philosophy and symbolism was permeated by an emphasis on the feminine. We saw, too, that in the realm of nature-philosophy, Han Confucianism adopted a great deal of the Taoist thought of the Warring States period, just as, later on, Neo-Confucianism was deeply affected by the Taoism of the Thang. Could we not go so far as to say that when Han Confucianism triumphed over the excessive maleness of the Chhin Legalists, it did so partly by accepting from Taoism an attitude to law which rejected the search for a "code fixed beforehand", and granted to magistrates the widest freedom to follow principles of equity, arbitration and "natural law"?

*HACKWORTH*

## Digest of International Law *

Whether the answer to the question as to how international law is made effective is to be found in the will of the state, in the state's ultimate responsibility for its own action or failure to act, in its fear of war or reprisals, in the effect of world opinion, or in a combination of any two or more of these, it is certain that states, sovereigns, parliaments, and public officials usually feel either bound by the commonly accepted precepts of international law or under the necessity of explaining their departure from those precepts. Whatever be the sanction upon which the enforcement of international law rests, its effectiveness increases as the nations of the world find it not only to their benefit but also to the benefit of the community of nation to conduct their relations according to certain generally accepted standards possible of performance and at the same time fair and reasonable.

Note

See M. Barkun, Law Without Sanction (1968) (subtitled *Order in Primitive Societies and the World Community*) and L. Fallers, Law Without Precedent (1969).

* From Volume 1 at 12 (1940).

## B.   .   .   .   *The Fears*   .   .   .

MARTIN BIRNBACH

### NEO-FREUDIAN SOCIAL PHILOSOPHY *

.   .   .   .

Unmitigated hedonism cannot persist in a world of limited resources. The grim force of economic need requires some renunciation of pleasure-seeking activities in the interest of survival of the species and the diversion, by sublimation, of sexual energies to goals of social value. In the name of society, education takes up the task of restraint by teaching avoidance of the pleasures attendant on purely and persistently hedonic activity. Society depends on the supremacy of the ego-instinct; the individual pays the price of renunciation in terms of neurosis.

THOMAS HOBBES

### OF THE NATURAL CONDITION OF MANKIND AS CONCERNING THEIR FELICITY, AND MISERY †

Nature hath made men so equal, in the faculties of the body, and mind; as that though there be found one man sometimes manifestly stronger in body, or of quicker mind than another; yet when all is reckoned together, the difference between man, and man, is not so considerable, as that one man can thereupon claim to himself any benefit, to which another may not pretend, as well as he. For as to the strength of body, the weakest has strength enough to kill the strongest, either by secret manchination, or by confederacy with others, that are in the same danger with himself.

And as to the faculties of the mind, setting aside the arts grounded upon words, and especially that skill of proceeding upon general, and infallible rules, called science; which very few have, and but in few things; as being not a native faculty, born with us; nor attained, as prudence, while we look after somewhat else, I find yet a greater equality amongst men, than that of strength. For prudence, is but experience; which equal time, equally bestows on all men, in those things they equally apply themselves unto. That which may perhaps make such equality incredible, is but a vain conceit of one's own wisdom, which almost all men think they have in a greater degree, than the vulgar; that is, than all men but themselves, and a few others, whom by fame, or for concurring with themselves, they approve. For such is the nature of men, that howsoever they may acknowledge many others to be more witty, or more eloquent, or more learned; yet they will hardly believe there be many so wise as them-

---

* From 11. With permission of Stanford University Press.

† From Leviathan, chs. 13–14 in 3 The English Works of Thomas Hobbes 110–17 (W. Molesworth ed. London 1839).

selves; for they see their own wit at hand, and other men's at a distance. But this proveth rather that men are in that point equal, than unequal. For there is not ordinarily a greater sign of the equal distribution of any thing, than that every man is contented with his share.

From this equality of ability, ariseth equality of hope in the attaining of our ends. And therefore if any two men desire the same thing, which nevertheless they cannot both enjoy, they become enemies; and in the way to their end, which is principally their own conservation, and sometimes their delectation only, endeavour to destroy, or subdue one another. And from hence it comes to pass, that where an invader hath no more to fear, than another man's single power; if one plant, sow, build, or possess a convenient seat, others may probably be expected to come prepared with forces united, to dispossess, and deprive him, not only of the fruit of his labour, but also of his life, or liberty. And the invader again is in the like danger of another.

And from this diffidence of one another, there is no way for any man to secure himself, so reasonable, as anticipation; that is, by force, or wiles, to master the persons of all men he can, so long, till he see no other power great enough to endanger him: and this is no more than his own conservation requireth, and is generally allowed. Also because there be some, that taking pleasure in contemplating their own power in the acts of conquest, which they pursue farther than their security requires; if others, that otherwise would be glad to be at ease within modest bounds, should not by invasion increase their power, they would not be able, long time, by standing only on their defence, to subsist. And by consequence, such augmentation of dominion over men being necessary to a man's conservation, it ought to be allowed him.

Again, men have no pleasure, but on the contrary a great deal of grief, in keeping company, where there is no power able to overawe them all. For every man looketh that his companion should value him, at the same rate he sets upon himself: and upon all signs of contempt, or undervaluing, naturally endeavours, as far as he dares, (which amongst them that have no common power to keep them in quiet, is far enough to make them destroy each other), to extort a greater value from his contemners, by damage; and from others, by the example.

So that in the nature of man, we find three principal causes of quarrel. First, competition; secondly, diffidence; thirdly, glory.

The first, maketh men invade for gain; the second, for safety; and the third, for reputation. The first use violence, to make themselves masters of other men's persons, wives, children, and cattle; the second, to defend them; the third, for trifles, as a word, a smile, a different opinion, and any other sign of undervalue, either direct in their persons, or by reflection in their kindred, their friends, their nation, their profession, or their name.

Hereby it is manifest, that during the time men live without a common power to keep them all in awe, they are in that condition which is called war; and such a war, as is of every man, against every man. For WAR, consisteth not in battle only, or the act of fighting; but in a tract of time, wherein the will to contend by battle is sufficiently known: and therefore the notion of *time*, is to be considered in the nature of war; as it is in the nature of weather. For as the nature of foul weather, lieth not in a shower or two of rain; but in an inclination thereto of many days together: so the nature of war, consisteth not in actual fighting; but in the known disposition thereto, during all the time there is no assurance to the contrary. All other time is PEACE.

Whatsoever therefore is consequent to a time of war, where every man is enemy to every man; the same is consequent to the time, wherein men live without other security, than what their own strength, and their own invention shall furnish them withal. In such condition, there is no place for industry; because the fruit thereof is uncertain: and consequently no culture of the earth; no navigation, nor use of the commodities that may be imported by sea; no commodious building; no instruments of moving, and removing, such things as require much force; no knowledge of the face of the earth; no account of time; no arts; no letters; no society; and which is worst of all, continual fear, and danger of violent death; and the life of man, solitary, poor, nasty, brutish, and short.

It may seem strange to some man, that has not well weighed these things; that nature should thus dissociate, and render men apt to invade, and destroy one another: and he may therefore, not trusting to this inference, made from the passions, desire perhaps to have the same confirmed by experience. Let him therefore consider with himself, when taking a journey, he arms himself, and seeks to go well accompanied; when going to sleep, he locks his doors; when even in his house he locks his chests; and this when he knows there be laws, and public officers, armed, to revenge all injuries shall be done him; what opinion he has of his fellow-subjects, when he rides armed; of his fellow citizens, when he locks his doors; and of his children, and servants, when he locks his chests. Does he not there as much accuse mankind by his actions, as I do by my words? But neither of us accuse man's nature in it. The desires, and other passions of man, are in themselves no sin. No more are the actions, that proceed from those passions, till they know a law that forbids them: which till laws be made they cannot know: nor can any law be made, till they have agreed upon the person that shall make it.

It may peradventure be thought, there was never such a time, nor condition of war as this; and I believe it was never generally so, over all the world: but there are many places, where they live so now. For the savage people in many places of America, except the government of small families, the concord whereof dependeth on natural lust, have no government at all; and live at this day in that brutish manner, as I said before. Howsoever, it may be perceived what manner of life there would be, where there were no common power to fear, by the manner of life, which men that have formerly livered under a peaceful government, use to degenerate into, in a civil war.

But though there had never been any time, wherein particular men were in a condition of war one against another; yet in all times, kings, and persons of sovereign authority, because of their independency, are in continual jealousies, and in the state and posture of gladiators; having their weapons pointing, and their eyes fixed on one another; that is, their forts, garrisons, and guns upon the frontiers of their kingdoms; and continual spies upon their neighbours; which is a posture of war. But because they uphold thereby, the industry of their subjects; there does not follow from it, that misery, which accompanies the liberty of particular men.

To this war of every man, against every man, this also is consequent; that nothing can be unjust. The notions of right and wrong, justice and injustice have there no place. Where there is no common power, there is no law: where no law, no injustice. . . .

## OF THE FIRST AND SECOND NATURAL LAWS, AND OF CONTRACTS.

The right of nature, which writers commonly call *jus naturale*, is the liberty each man hath, to use his own power, as he will himself, for the preservation of his own nature; that is to say, of his own life; and consequently, of doing any thing, which in his own judgment, and reason, he shall conceive to be the aptest means thereunto . . . .

And because the condition of man, as hath been declared in the precedent chapter, is a condition of "war of everyone against every one: in which case every one is governed by his own reason; and there is nothing he can make use of, that may not be a help unto him, in preserving his life against his enemies; it followeth, that in such a condition, every man has a right to every thing; even to one another's body. And therefore, as long as this natural right of every man to every thing endureth, there can be no security to any man, how strong or wise soever he be, of living out the time, which nature ordinarily alloweth men to live." And consequently it is a precept, or general rule of reason, *that every man, ought to endeavour peace, as far as he has hope of obtaining it; and when he cannot obtain it, that he may seek, and use, all helps, and advantages of war.* The first branch of which rule, containeth the first, and fundamental law of nature; which is, *to seek peace, and follow it.* The second, the sum of the right of nature; which is, *by all means we can, to defend ourselves.*

*FYODOR DOSTOEVSKY*

### CRIME AND PUNISHMENT *

. . . . [Raskolnikov] began simply and modestly. ". . . I don't contend that extraordinary people are always bound to commit breaches of morals, as you call it. In fact, I doubt whether such an argument could be published. I simply hinted that an 'extraordinary'

---

*From 234–37 of the Heritage Press ed. 1938.

man has the right  .  .  .  that is not an official right, but an inner right to decide in his own conscience to overstep  .  .  .  certain obstacles, and only in case it is essential for the practical fulfilment of his idea (sometimes, perhaps, of benefit to the whole of
humanity).  .  .  .  I maintain that if the discoveries of Kepler
and Newton could not have been made known except by sacrificing
the lives of one, a dozen, a hundred, or more men, Newton would
have had the right, would indeed have been in duty bound  .  .  .
to *eliminate* the dozen or the hundred men for the sake of making
his discoveries known to the whole of humanity. But it does not
follow from that that Newton had a right to murder people right
and left and to steal every day in the market. Then, I remember, I
maintain in my article that all  .  .  .  well, legislators and leaders
of men, such as Lycurgus, Solon, Mahomet, Napoleon, and so on, were
all without exception criminals, from the very fact that, making a
new law, they transgressed the ancient one, handed down from their
ancestors and held sacred by the people, and they did not stop short
at bloodshed either, if that bloodshed—often of innocent persons
fighting bravely in defence of ancient law—were of use to their cause.
It's remarkable, in fact, that the majority, indeed, of these bene-
factors and leaders of humanity were guilty of terrible carnage. In
short, I maintain that all great men or even men a little out of the
common, that is to say capable of giving some new word, must from
their very nature be criminals—more or less, of course. Otherwise
it's hard for them to get out of the common rut; and to remain in the
common rut is what they can't submit to, from their very nature
again, and to my mind they ought not, indeed, to submit to it. You
see that there is nothing particularly new in all that. The same thing
has been printed and read a thousand times before. As for my division of people into ordinary and extraordinary, I acknowledge that
it's somewhat arbitrary, but I don't insist upon exact numbers. I
only believe in my leading idea that men are *in general* divided by a
law of nature into two categories, inferior (ordinary), that is, so to
say, material that serves only to reproduce its kind, and men who
have the gift or the talent to utter *a new word*. There are, of course,
innumerable subdivisions, but the distinguishing features of both
categories are fairly well marked. The first category, generally
speaking, are men conservative in temperament and law-abiding;
they live under control and love to be controlled. To my thinking it
is their duty to be controlled, because that's their vocation, and there
is nothing humiliating in it for them. The second category all transgress the law; they are destroyers or disposed to destruction according to their capacities. The crimes of these men are of course relative and varied; for the most part they seek in very varied ways the
destruction of the present for the sake of the better. But if such a
one is forced for the sake of his idea to step over a corpse or wade
through blood, he can, I maintain, find within himself, in his conscience, a sanction for wading through blood—that depends on the
idea and its dimensions, note that. It's only in that sense I speak
of their right to crime in my article (you remember it began with the
legal question). There's no need for much anxiety, however; the

masses will scarcely ever admit this right, they punish them or hang them (more or less), and in doing so fulfill quite justly their conservative vocation. But the same masses set these criminals on a pedestal in the next generation and worship them (more or less). The first category is always the man of the present, the second the man of the future. The first preserve the world and people it, the second move the world and lead it to its goal. Each class has an equal right to exist. In fact, all have equal rights with me—and *vive la guerre eternelle*—till the New Jerusalem, of course!" . . .

*JAMES BRYCE*

### THE CHARACTERISTIC NOTES OF THE COMMON LAW. *

Now, what is it that a skilled observer would select as being the peculiar and characteristic notes of the Common Law? I think he would begin by saying that the most characteristic of them was the firm grasp which it has of the rights of the individual citizen. The citizen is conceived of, he is dealt with, as being a centre of force, an active atom, a person in whom there inhere certain powers and capacities which he is entitled to assert and make effective, not only against other citizens, but against all citizens taken together, that is to say, against the community and the State itself and its organ, the Executive Government.

Secondly, our observer would note as another characteristic feature, the recognition by the Common Law of the State and the Executive as clothed with the authority of the whole community, as being an effective power, entitled to require and compel the obedience of the community wherever and whenever the State does not trespass on the rights which are legally secured to an individual. . . .

From the equal recognition of these two principles there follows a third characteristic. If principles apparently antagonistic are to be reconciled, there must be a precise delimitation of their respective bounds and limits. The law must be definite and exact. Now, precision, definiteness, exactitude, are features of the Common Law so conspicuous that the unlearned laity—of whom there are perhaps some present to-day—have often thought that they have been developed to an inordinate degree. They have made the law, not only very minute, but very technical.

With the love of precision there naturally goes a love of certainty and fixity. The spirit of the Common Law is a conservative spirit, which stands upon what exists, distrusting change, and refusing change until change has obviously become necessary. There is a dictum familiar to the profession in England which says: 'It is better that the law should be certain than that the law should be just.' That is a dictum which cannot expect the laity to appreciate as lawyers may. But there is a truth in it.

. . . .

* From The Influence of National Character and Historical Environment on the Development of the Common Law 24 L.Q.Rev. 9, 11–13 (1908).

With the love of certainty and definiteness there naturally goes a respect for the forms of legal proceedings and for the precise verbal expression that has been given to legal rules. This is a quality which belongs to most legal systems in their earlier stages. In the Common Law it held its ground with great pertinacity until very recently, both in England and here. . . .

JOSEPH NEEDHAM

## THE *Fa Chia* (LEGALISTS) *

It has often been said that the peculiar glory of Chinese law lay in the fact that throughout its history (after the failure of the Legalists) it remained indissolubly connected with custom based on what were considered easily demonstrable ethical principles, and that enactments of positive law, with their codifications, were reduced to the absolute minimum. Yet perhaps this very aversion from codification and positive law, that is to say, the willed legislation of human rulers, was one of the factors which made the Chinese intellectual climate uncongenial to the development of systematised scientific thought. How this could be is the tale which we have to unfold.

Although the elaboration of China's first criminal codes goes back, as we shall see later . . . . to the —6th century, the rise of the school of the Legalists as such did not take place till the —4th. They flourished first in the north-eastern State of Chhi, and in the three succession States of Han, Wei and Chao (into which the former State of Chin had been divided after —403), but they reached their position of real dominance in Chhin during the —3rd century, where their policies helped to bring about that rise to power which enabled the last prince of Chhin to become the first emperor of a unified China . . . . .

The fundamental idea of the Legalists was that *li*, the complex of customs, usages, ceremonies and compromises, paternalistically administered according to Confucian ideals, was inadequate for forceful and authoritarian government. Their watchword, therefore, was *fa*, positive law, particularly *hsien ting·fa*, "laws fixed beforehand", to which everyone in the State, from the ruler himself down to the lowest public slave, was bound to submit, subject to sanctions of the severest and cruellest kind. The lawgiving prince must surround himself with an aura of *wei* (majesty) and *shih* (authority, power, influence). . . .

. . . . The central conception of *fa*, or positive law, enacted by the lawgiving prince without regard to considerations of accepted morality, or the goodwill of the people, appears everywhere in Shang Yang . . . . and Han Fei Tzu. Rules for rewards and punishments being made perfectly clear and definite, and published in every locality, the people will know how to behave. The law should, so to speak, ap-

* From 2 Science and Civilisation in        With permission of the Syndics of the
  China 204–11 (Cambridge U. Press).       Cambridge University Press.

ply itself, and not require the constant interference of the ruler. "Law is the authoritative principle for the people, and is the basis of government  .  .  .  it is what shapes the people" says Shang Yang. If law is strong the country is strong, says Han Fei Tzu, if it is weak the country will be weak  .  .  .  Punishments were to be deterrent in the highest degree. "Punish severely the lightest crimes, such was the law of Kungsun Yang", says Han Fei Tzu in his chapter 30, continuing, "If small offences do not occur, great crimes will not follow, and thus people will commit no crimes and disorder will not arise." This idea  .  .  .  was the Legalist version of the famous phrase in the *Shu Ching* (Historical Classic), *phi i chih phi*— punishment to end punishment—a phrase perhaps almost as devoid of justification as the "war to end war" of our own time.

Much is said of the draconic nature of the punishments recommended by the Fa Chia. It should be made worse for the people to fall into the hands of the police of their own State than to fight the forces of an enemy State in battle. The timorous should be put to death in the manner they most hate. Strictness in application of penalties should have no exceptions. A principle similar to the later *pao chia* system was employed; men serving in the army were divided into squads of five men each, and if one of these were killed, the other four were beheaded for allowing it to happen.  .  .  .

The Legalists were conscious of this conflict between theoretically constructed positive law on the one hand, and ethics and equity, and even what one might call human common sense, on the other. Han Fei says:

> Severe penalties are what the people fear, heavy punishments are what the people hate. Accordingly the sage promulgates what they wear in order to forbid the practice of wickedness, and establishes what they hate in order to prevent villainous acts. Thus the State is safe and no outrage can occur. From this I know well that benevolence, righteousness, love and favour are not worth adopting, while severe punishment and heavy penalties can maintain the State in order.

Shang Yang, says Duyvendak, is completely and consciously *amoral*. His great fear is that the people should become interested in the traditional virtues, and thereby set up other standards of conduct than those established by law. Virtue is not "goodness" or "benevolence" but obedience to the law as fixed by the State, whatever it may seem good to the ruler that it should be. Hence the Legalist doctrine of the Six Parasitic Functions (*liu shih kuan*; lit. "Six Lice"). In its oldest formulation these are named as care for old age, living on others (without employment), beauty, love, ambition and virtuous conduct. The things which sap the authoritarian State are extended in other lists to include further—the study of the Odes and History Classics, the Rites, Music, filial piety, brotherly duty, moral culture, sincerity and faith, chastity and integrity, benevolence and righteousness, criticism of the army, and being ashamed to fight—all, except the last two perhaps, implying direct hits at the Confucian system or morality.[15] Han Fei Tzu, for his part, comes forward with a parallel list, that of the Five Gnawing Worms (*wu tou*) which destroys the State: (1) the Confucian scholar praising the ancient sage-kings and discussing benevolence and righteousness; (2) the clever talker (or sophist; a hit at the Ming Chia?) using events to his private advantage and falsifying words; (3) the soldier of fortune collecting troops of adherents; (4) the merchant and artisan accumulating wealth; and (5) the official thinking only of personal interest.

The open conflict between Legalist law and Confucian ethics illustrates itself in concrete form in the debate as to whether a son should conceal his father's crime, or denounce it and give evidence against him. It had started already in the 16th century, for Confucius had decisively given his opinion that filial piety should prevail against State law. Han Fei Tzu, however, argued with great insistence in the opposite sense, as a Legalist was bound to do. . . .

The complete rupture with traditional ethical concepts shows itself also in the positive recommendation of Shang Yang that officials should be chosen for their ruthlessness: "If virtuous officials are employed by the prince, the people will love their own relations; but if wicked officials are employed, the people will love the statutes. . . . In the former case the people will be stronger than the law; in the latter, the law will be stronger than the people."

It was quite in accordance with the general outlook of the Legalists that all their writings glorify first war and then to a lesser extent agriculture; they had no use either for scholars or for merchants and traders. . . .

There is one feature in Legalism which is of particular interest for the historian of science, namely, its tendency towards the quantitative. The word *shu*, which often appears, means not only number but quantitative degree, and even statistical method. Already in the oldest parts of the *Shang Chun Shu*, says Duyvendak, there is a preference for expressing everything in numerical figures, points, units, degrees of penalties, numbers of granaries, amounts of available fodder, etc. . . .

. . . [C]hapter 14 condemns what it calls "reliance on private appraisal" and speaks of the folly of trying to weigh things without standard scales, or forming an opinion about lengths in the absence of accepted units such as feet and inches. Other schools, such as the Mohists, had made a good deal of rhetorical play with "models" and "measures", but this quantitative element in the Legalists was connected, I would suggest, with the discovery which they made that positive law, divorced from all ethical considerations, enabled them, and the rulers whom they advised, to achieve enhanced efficiency by strict regulation of weights, measures and dimensions. Hu Shih, indeed, points out that perhaps "standard" was the oldest meaning of

15. Compare the views of the Legalists with those of Plato in Laws, excerpted *supra* at 1174.

the word *fa*, since in *Kuan Tzu*, chapter 6, it is defined as including measures of lengths, weights, volumes of solids and liquids, T-squares and compasses. . . .

The *Shang Chün Shu* elaborates:

The former kings hung up balances with standard weights and fixed the lengths of the foot and the inch. Still today these are followed as models (*fa*) because the divisions are clear. No (practical) merchant would proceed by dismissing standard scales and then deciding about the weights (of things), nor would be abolish feet and inches and then form opinions about the lengths (of things). Such (conclusions) would have no force (*wei chhi pu pi yeh*). Turning one's back on models and measures (*fa tu*), depending upon private conviction (*ssu i*), takes away all force and certainty. Without a model, only a Yao could judge knowledge and ability, worth or its opposite. But the world does not consist exclusively of men like Yao. This was why the former kings understood that no reliance could be placed on individual opinions or biased approval; this is why they set up models and made distinctions clear. Those who fulfill the standard were rewarded; those who harmed the public interest were put to death.

The whole argument, of course, used though it was again and again, depended on a false analogy, namely, that human conduct and human emotions could be measured as quantitatively as a picul of salt or an ell of cloth. Liang Chhi-Chhao, in his discussion of the Legalists, saw this extremely clearly. The certainty and predictability of low-level phenomena cannot be found in the realms of "free-will" at the higher levels. And he characterised the Legalist school as mechanistic (*chi hsieh chu-i*), while the Confucians instinctively made allowance for the true organic (*seng chi thi*) character of man and of society.

*LON FULLER*

## THE MORAL AND EMOTIONAL FOUNDATIONS OF POSITIVISM *

If we ignore the specific theories of law associated with the positivistic philosophy, I believe we can say that the dominant tone of positivism is set by a fear of a purposive interpretation of law and legal institutions, or at least by a fear that such an interpretation may be pushed too far. I think one can find confirmatory traces of this fear in all of those classified as "positivists" by Professor Hart, with the outstanding exception of Bentham, who is in all things a case apart and who was worlds removed from anything that could be called *ethical* positivism.

* From Positivism and Fidelity to Law— Reply to Professor Hart 71 Harv.L. Rev. 630, 669–72 (1958). With permission of Harvard Law Review Association.

Now the belief that many of us hold, that this fear of purpose takes a morbid turn in positivism, should not mislead us into thinking that the fear is wholly without justification, or that it reflects no significant problem in the organization of society.

Fidelity to law *can* become impossible if we do not accept the broader responsibilities (themselves purposive, as all responsibilities are and must be) that go with a purposive interpretation of law. One can imagine a course of reasoning that might run as follows: This statute says absinthe shall not be sold. What is its purpose? To promote health. Now, as everyone knows, absinthe is a sound, wholesome, and beneficial beverage. Therefore, interpreting the statute in the light of its purpose, I construe it to direct a general sale and consumption of that most healthful of beverages, absinthe.

. . . .

It is one of the great virtues of Professor Hart's essay that it makes explicit positivism's concern for the ideal of fidelity to law. Yet I believe, though I cannot prove, that the basic reason why positivism fears a purposive interpretation is not that it may lead to anarchy, but that it may push us too far in the opposite direction. It sees in a purposive interpretation, carried too far, a threat to human freedom and human dignity.

Let me illustrate what I mean by supposing that I am a man without religious beliefs living in a community of ardent Protestant Christian faith. A statute in this community makes it unlawful for me to play golf on Sunday. I find this statute an annoyance and accept its restraints reluctantly. But the annoyance I feel is not greatly different from that I might experience if, though it were lawful to play on Sunday, a power failure prevented me from taking the streetcar I would normally use in reaching the course. In the vernacular, "it is just one of those things."

What a different complexion the whole matter assumes if a statute compels me to attend church, or, worse still, to kneel and recite prayers! Here I may feel a direct affront to my integrity as a human being. Yet the purpose of both statutes may well be to increase church attendance. The difference may even seem to be that the first statute seeks its end slyly and by indirection, the second honestly and openly. Yet surely this is a case in which indirection has its virtues and honesty its heavy price in human dignity.

Now I believe that positivism fears that a too explicit and uninhibited interpretation in terms of purpose may well push the first kind of statute in the direction of the second. If this is a basic concern underlying the positivistic philosophy, that philosophy is dealing with a real problem, however inept its response to the problem may seem to be. For this problem of the impressed purpose is a crucial one in our society. One thinks of the obligation to bargain "in good faith" imposed by the National Labor Relations Act. One recalls the remark that to punish a criminal is less of an affront to his dignity than to reform and improve him. The statutory preamble comes to mind: the increasing use made of it, its legislative wisdom, the significance that should be accorded to it in judicial interpretation. The flag salute cases will, of course, occur to everyone. I myself recall the splendid analysis by Professor von Hippel of the things that were fundamentally wrong about Nazism, and his conclusion that the grossest of all Nazi perversities was that of coercing acts, like the putting out of flags and saying, "Heil Hitler!" that have meaning only when done voluntarily, or, more accurately, have a meaning when coerced that is wholly parasitic on an association of them with past voluntary expressions.

Questions of this sort are undoubtedly becoming more acute as the state assumes a more active role with respect to economic activity. No significant economic activity can be organized exclusively by "don'ts." By its nature economic production requires a co-operative effort. In the economic field there is special reason, therefore, to fear that "This you may not do" will be transformed into "This you must do—but willingly." As we all know, the most tempting opportunity for effecting this transformation is presented by what is called in administrative practice "the prehearing conference," in which the negative threat of a statute's sanctions may be used by its administrators to induce what they regard, in all good conscience, as "the proper attitude."

JOHN STUART MILL

## AUGUSTE COMTE AND POSITIVISM *

. . . [W]e often, as already intimated, find [Comte] using the name metaphysical to denote certain practical conclusions, instead of a particular kind of theoretical premises [sic]. Whatever goes by the different names of the revolutionary, the radical, the democratic, the liberal, the free-thinking, the sceptical, or the negative and critical school or party in religion, politics, or philosophy, all passes with him under the designation of metaphysical, and whatever he has to say about it forms part of his description of the metaphysical school of social science. He passes in review, one after another, what he deems the leading doctrines of the revolutionary school of politics, and dismisses them all as mere instruments of attack upon the old social system, with no permanent validity as social truth.

He assigns only this humble rank to the first of all the articles of the liberal creed, "the absolute right of free examination, or the dogma of unlimited liberty of conscience." As far as this doctrine only means that opinions, and their expression, should be exempt from *legal* restraint, either in the form of prevention or of penalty, M. Comte is a firm adherent of it: but the *moral* right of every human being, however ill-prepared by the necessary instruction and discipline, to erect himself into a judge of the most intricate as well as the most important questions that can occupy the human intellect, he resolutely denies. "There is no liberty of conscience," he said in an early work, "in astronomy, in physics, in chemistry, even in physiology, in the sense that every one would think it absurd not to accept in confidence

---

* From 73–74 (U. of Michigan Press 1961).

the principles established in those sciences by the competent persons. If it is otherwise in politics, the reason is merely because, the old doctrines having gone by and the new ones not being yet formed, there are not properly, during the interval, any established opinions." When first mankind outgrew the old doctrines, an appeal from doctors and teachers to the outside public was inevitable and indispensable, since without the toleration and encouragement of discussion and criticism from all quarters, it would have been impossible for any new doctrines to grow up. But in itself, the practice of carrying the questions which more than all others require special knowledge and preparation, before the incompetent tribunal of common opinion, is, he contends, radically irrational, and will and ought to cease when once mankind have again made up their minds to a system of doctrine. The prolongation of this provisional state, producing an ever-increasing divergence of opinions, is already, according to him, extremely dangerous, since it is only when there is a tolerable unanimity respecting the rule of life, that a real moral control can be established over the self-interest and passions of individuals. Besides which, when every man is encouraged to believe himself a competent judge of the most difficult social questions, he cannot be prevented from thinking himself competent also to the most important public duties, and the baneful competition for power and official functions spreads constantly downwards to a lower and lower grade of intelligence. In M. Comte's opinion, the peculiarly complicated nature of sociological studies, and the great amount of previous knowledge and intellectual discipline requisite for them, together with the serious consequences that may be produced by even temporary errors on such subjects, render it necessary in the case of ethics and politics, still more than of mathematics and physics, that whatever legal liberty may exist of questioning and discussing, the opinions of mankind should really be formed for them by an exceedingly small number of minds of the highest class, trained to the task by the most thorough and laborious mental preparation: and that the questioning of their conclusions by any one, not of an equivalent grade of intellect and instruction, should be accounted equally presumptuous, and more blamable, than the attempts occasionally made by sciolists to refute the Newtonian astronomy.

*ERICH FROMM*

### ESCAPE FROM FREEDOM *

The social history of man started with his emerging from a state of oneness with the natural world to an awareness of himself as an entity separate from surrounding nature and men. Yet this awareness remained very dim over long periods of history. The individual continued to be closely tied to the natural and social world from which he emerged; while being partly aware of himself as a separate entity, he felt also part of the world around him. The grow-

* From 24–25, 28–30, 35–37 (Rhinehart & Co. 1941). Copyright 1941, 1969 by Erich Fromm. Reprinted by permission of Holt, Rhinehart and Winston, Inc.

ing process of the emergence of the individual from his original ties, a process which we may call "individuation," seems to have reached its peak in modern history in the centuries between the Reformation and the present.

In the life history of an individual we find the same process. A child is born when it is no longer one with its mother and becomes a biological entity separate from her. Yet, while this biological separation is the beginning of individual human existence, the child remains functionally one with its mother for a considerable period.

To the degree to which the individual, figuratively speaking, has not yet completely severed the umbilical cord which fastens him to the outside world, he lacks freedom; but these ties give him security and a feeling of belonging and of being rooted somewhere. I wish to call these ties that exist before the process of individuation has resulted in the complete emergence of an individual "primary ties." They are organic in the sense that they are a part of normal human development; they imply a lack of individuality, but they also give security and orientation to the individual. They are the ties that connect the child with its mother, the member of a primitive community with his clan and nature, or the medieval man with the Church and his social caste. Once the stage of complete individuation is reached and the individual is free from these primary ties, he is confronted with a new task: to orient and root himself in the world and to find security in other ways than those which were characteristic of his preindividualistic existence.

. . . .

The more the child grows and to the extent to which primary ties are cut off, the more it develops a quest for freedom and independence. But the fate of this quest can only be fully understood if we realize the dialectic quality in this process of growing individuation.

This process has two aspects: one is that the child grows stronger physically, emotionally, and mentally. In each of these spheres intensity and activity grow. At the same time, these spheres become more and more integrated. An organized structure guided by the individual's will and reason develops. If we call this organized and integrated whole of the personality the self, we can also say that the *one side of the growing process of individuation is the growth of self-strength.* The limits of the growth of individuation and the self are set, partly by individual conditions, but essentially by social conditions. For although the differences between individuals in this respect appear to be great, every society is characterized by a certain level of individuation beyond which the normal individual cannot go.

The other aspect of the process of individuation is *growing aloneness.* The primary ties offer security and basic unity with the world outside of oneself. To the extent to which the child emerges from that world it becomes aware of being alone, of being an entity separate from all others. This separation from a world, which in comparison with one's own individual existence is overwhelmingly strong and powerful, and often threatening and dangerous, creates a feeling of powerlessness and anxiety. As long as one was an integral part of that world, unaware of the possibilities and responsibilities of individual action, one did not need to be afraid of it. When one has become an individual, one stands alone and faces the world in all its perilous and overpowering aspects.

Impulses arise to give up one's individuality, to overcome the feeling of aloneness and powerlessness by completely submerging oneself in the world outside. These impulses, however, and the new ties arising from them, are not identical with the primary ties which have been cut off in the process of growth itself. Just as a child can never return to the mother's womb physically, so it can never reverse, physically, the process of individuation. Attempts to do so necessarily assume the character of submission, in which the basic contradiction between the authority and the child who submits to it is never eliminated. Consciously the child may feel secure and satisfied, but unconsciously it realizes that the price it pays is giving up strength and the integrity of its self. Thus the result of submission is the very opposite of what it was to be: submission increases the child's insecurity and at the same time creates hostility and rebelliousness, which is the more frightening since it is directed against the very persons on whom the child has remained—or become—dependent.

. . . .

"Freedom from" is not identical with positive freedom, with "freedom to." The emergence of man from nature is a long-drawn-out process; to a large extent he remains tied to the world from which he emerged; he remains part of nature—the soil he lives on, the sun and moon and stars, the trees and flowers, the animals, and the group of people with whom he is connected by the ties of blood. Primitive religions bear testimony to man's feeling of oneness with nature. Animate and inanimate nature are part of his human world or, as one may also put it, he is still part of the natural world.

These primary ties block his full human development; they stand in the way of the development of his reason and his critical capacities; they let him recognize himself and others only through the medium of his, or their, participation in a clan, a social or religious community, and not as human beings; in other words, they block his development as a free, self-determining, productive individual. But although this is one aspect, there is another one. This identity with nature, clan, religion, gives the individual security. He belongs to, he is rooted in, a structuralized whole in which he has an unquestionable place. He may suffer from hunger or suppression, but he does not suffer from the worst of all pains—complete aloneness and doubt.

We see that the process of growing human freedom has the same dialectic character that we have noticed in the process of individual growth. On the one hand it is a process of growing strength and integration, mastery of nature, growing power of human reason, and growing solidarity with other human beings. But on the other hand this growing individuation means growing isolation, insecurity, and thereby growing doubt concerning one's own role in the universe, the meaning of one's life, and with all that a growing feeling of one's own powerlessness and insignificance as an individual.

If the process of the development of mankind had been harmonious, if it had followed a certain plan, then both sides of the development—the growing strength and the growing individuation—would have been exactly balanced. As it is, the history of mankind is one of conflict and strife. Each step in the direction of growing individuation threatened people with new insecurities. Primary bonds once severed cannot be mended; once paradise is lost, man cannot return to it. There is only one possible, productive solution for the relationship of individualized man with the world: his active solidarity with all men and his spontaneous activity, love and work, which unite him again with the world, not by primary ties but as a free and independent individual.

However, if the economic, social and political conditions on which the whole process of human individuation depends, do not offer a basis for the realization of individuality in the sense just mentioned, while at the same time people have lost those ties which gave them security, this lag makes freedom an unbearable burden. It then becomes identical with doubt, with a kind of life which lacks meaning and direction. Powerful tendencies arise to escape from this kind of freedom into submission or some kind of relationship to man and the world which promises relief from uncertainty, even if it deprives the individual of his freedom.

## C. . . . *The Prospects of Trust.*

Robert Paul Wolff

### In Defense of Anarchism *

. . . When a boy is asked what he wants to be, he is really being asked which already existing social role he wishes to adopt as an adult. His answer—that he wants to be a fireman, or an engineer, or an explorer—indicates that he understands perfectly well the nature of the question. He may see himself, at least in a society like ours, as exercising some control over the roles which he shall adopt; but neither the questioner nor the boy would suppose that either of them has any control over the existence and nature of the roles themselves! Even the social rebel characteristically opts for an existing role, that of bohemian, or beatnik, or revolutionary. Like all role-players, such rebels wear the clothes, live in the quarters, and use the language appropriate to the role which they have chosen.

In any reasonably complex society, social roles are in turn organized into even more extensive patterns of behavior and belief, to

* From 74–75, 65, 78–82 (Harper Trochbooks ed. 1970). With permission of Harper & Row and Professor Wolff.

which we apply the term "institutions." The church, the state, the army, the market are all such systems of roles. The characteristic interactions of the constituent roles of an institution are determined independently of particular individuals, just as the roles themselves are. At this level of complexity of organization, however, a new phenomenon appears which vastly increases the apparent objectivity of social reality, namely what has come to be known as the "paradox of unintended consequences." Each person in an institutional structure pursues goals and follows patterns at least partially laid down for him by the society—that is, already existing when he takes on the role and hence *given* to him. In his roles, however, he should be able to see the relationship between what he does and what results, even though he may not feel free to alter his goals or try new means. In the process of interaction with other individual role-players, more far-reaching results will be produced which may be neither anticipated nor particularly desired by any person in the system. These unintended consequences will therefore appear to the role-players as somehow not their doing, and hence objective in just the way that natural occurrences are objective. . . .

. . . [M]en come to imagine themselves more completely enslaved by society than they ever were by nature. Yet their conviction is fundamentally wrong, for while the natural world really does exist independently of man's beliefs or desires, and therefore exercises a constraint on his will which can at best be mitigated or combatted, the social world is nothing in itself, and consists merely of the totality of the habits, expectations, beliefs, and behavior patterns of all the individuals who live in it. To be sure, insofar as men are ignorant of the total structures of the institutions within which they play their several roles, they will be the victims of consequences unintended by anyone; and, of course, to the extent that men are set against one another by conflicting interests, those whose institutional roles give them advantages of power or knowledge in the social struggle will prevail over those who are relatively disadvantaged. But since each man's unfreedom is entirely a result either of ignorance or of a conflict of interests, it ought to be in principle possible for a society of rational men of good will to eliminate the domination of society and subdue it to their wills in a manner that is impossible in the case of nature.

. . . . .

It should now be clear why I am unwilling to accept as final the negative results of our search for a political order which harmonizes authority and autonomy. The state is a social institution, and therefore no more than the totality of the beliefs, expectations, habits, and interacting roles of its members and subjects. When rational men, in full knowledge of the proximate and distant consequences of their actions, determine to set private interest aside and pursue the general good, it *must* be possible for them to create a form of association which accomplishes that end without depriving some of them of their moral autonomy. The state, in contrast to nature, cannot be ineradicably *other*.

## UTOPIAN GLIMPSES OF A WORLD WITHOUT STATES

Through the exercise of *de facto* legitimate authority, states achieve what Max Weber calls the imperative coordination of masses of men and women. To some extent, of course, this coordination consists in the more-or-less voluntary submission by large numbers of people to institutional arrangements which are directly contrary to their interests. Threats of violence or economic sanction play a central role in holding the people in line, although as Weber very persuasively argues, the myth of legitimacy is also an important instrument of domination.

But even if there were no exploitation or domination in society, it would still be in men's interest to achieve a very high level of social coordination, for reasons both of economic efficiency and of public order. At our present extremely advanced stage of division of labor, relatively minor disruptions of social coordination can produce a breakdown of the flow of goods and services necessary to sustain life.

Consequently, it is worth asking whether a society of men who have been persuaded of the truth of anarchism—a society in which no one claims legitimate authority or would believe such a claim if it were made—could through alternative methods achieve an adequate level of social coordination.

There are, so far as I can see, three general sorts of purposes, other than the domination and exploitation of one segment of society by another, for which men might wish to achieve a high order of social coordination. First, there is the collective pursuit of some *external* national goal such as national defense, territorial expansion, or economic imperialism. Second, there is the collective pursuit of some *internal* goal which requires the organization and coordination of the activities of large numbers of people, such as traffic safety, to cite a trivial example, or the reconstruction of our cities, to cite an example not so trivial. Finally, there is the maintenance of our industrial economy whose functional differentiation and integration— to use the sociologist's jargon—are advanced enough to sustain an adequately high level of production. Is there any way in which these ends could be served other than by commands enforced by coercion and by the myth of legitimacy?

I do not now have a complete and coherent answer to this question, which is in a way the truest test of the political philosophy of anarchism, but I shall make a few suggestions which may open up fruitful avenues of investigation.

With regard to matters of national defense and foreign adventure, it seems to me that there is much to be said for the adoption of a system of voluntary compliance with governmental directives. If we assume a society of anarchists—a society, that is to say, which has achieved a level of moral and intellectual development at which superstitious beliefs in legitimacy of authority have evaporated—then the citizenry would be perfectly capable of choosing freely whether to defend the nation and carry its purpose beyond the national borders. The army itself could be run on the basis of voluntary commitments and submission to orders. To be sure, the day might arrive when there were not enough volunteers to protect the freedom and security of the society. But if that were the case, then it would clearly be illegitimate to command the citizens to fight. Why should a nation continue to exist if its populace does not wish to defend it? One thinks here of the contrast between the Yugoslav partisans or Israeli soldiers, on the one hand, and the American forces in Vietnam on the other.

The idea of voluntary compliance with governmental directives is hardly new, but it inevitably provokes the shocked reaction that social chaos would result from any such procedure. My own opinion is that superstition rather than reason lies behind this reaction. I personally would feel quite safe in an America whose soldiers were free to choose when and for what they would fight.

Voluntary compliance would go far toward generating sufficient social coordination to permit collective pursuit of domestic goals as well. In addition, I believe that much could be done through the local, community-based development of a consensual or general will with regard to matters of collective rather than particular interest. In the concluding chapter of my book, *The Poverty of Liberalism,* I have offered a conceptual analysis of the several modes of community. I will simply add that achievement of the sorts of community I analyzed there would require a far-reaching decentralization of the American economy.

This last point brings me to the most difficult problem of all—namely, the maintenance of a level of social coordination sufficient for an advanced industrial economy. As Friedrich Hayek and a number of other classical liberal political economists have pointed out, the natural operation of the market is an extremely efficient way of coordinating human behavior on a large scale without coercion or appeal to authority. Nevertheless, reliance on the market is fundamentally irrational once men know how to control it in order to avoid its undesired consequences. The original laissez-faire liberals viewed the laws of the market as objective laws of a benevolent nature; modern laissez-faire liberals propose that we go on confusing nature and society, even though we have the knowledge to subordinate the market to our collective will and decision.

Only extreme economic decentralization could permit the sort of voluntary economic coordination consistent with the ideals of anarchism and affluence. At the present time, of course, such decentralization would produce economic chaos, but if we possessed a cheap, local source of power and an advanced technology of small-scale production, and if we were in addition willing to accept a high level of economic waste, we might be able to break the American economy down into regional and subregional units of manageable size. The exchanges between the units would be inefficient and costly—very large inventory levels, inelasticities of supply and demand, considerable waste, and so forth. But in return for this price, men would have increasing freedom to act autonomously. In effect, such a society would enable all men to be autonomous agents, whereas in our present society, the relatively few autonomous men are—as it were—parasitic upon the obedient, authority-respecting masses.

These remarks fall far short of a coherent projection of an anarchist society, but they may serve to make the ideal seem a bit less like a mere fantasy of utopian political philosophy.

## QUESTIONS

1. What does Wolff mean, "the social world is nothing in itself", and the state is "no more than the totality of the beliefs, expectations, habits, and interacting roles of its members and subjects." Is a corporation, state or other group no more than the sum of its members? How strong are the forces that the structure—itself—exerts? Cf. M. WEBER, THE THEORY OF SOCIAL AND ECONOMIC ORGANIZATION (1947).

2. How convincing is Wolff's dichotomy between the natural and social world? In what sense does the one "really  .  .  . exist independently of man's beliefs or desires" and the other not?

*DANE RUDHYAR*

## THE PLENARY SOCIETY *

. . . At the tribal stage of human evolution the tribe is a most effective and binding matrix; and so is the land on which the tribesmen work and which feeds them. A tribesman actually has only the rudiment or rather the potentiality, of individual selfhood. Selfhood for him has a generic character defined by race, land and rigid traditions and rituals.

The rudimentary individuality of primitive man did not develop for long ages, but this is not the place to study in historical-cultural detail various phases of the development of man's consciousness of himself as an individual. All that it is necessary to say is that in the archaic tribal state matricial relationships have an overwhelming power. The human being is in a prenatal state so far as his sense of individuality is concerned. The tribal "we" does not allow much freedom of development to the individual "I." This development can only come through relationships of an associative type. But the tribesman's associative relationships operate exclusively at first within a matricial frame of reference, i. e. within the tribal whole of activities.

Through intertribal exchanges of needed goods and through marriage, through wars of conquest and the making of slaves who are incorporated into the tribe, new associative relationships are made. The tribe grows into a kingdom, and in cities men can relate to each other in freer ways, while trading and the ambition for power on an individualistic basis develop mental cunning and intellectual capacities. All these new factors tend to isolate man from the matrices which had so closely bound him; and the process of individualization proceeds.

Man, by then, has developed an ego which is based no longer on the particular function he fulfills in the tribal organism but on a new

* From The Planetarization of Consciousness 97–99, 287–88, 297–303, 304–07 (Servire/Vassenaar The Netherlands 1970 [Harper & Row 1972]). With permission of Dane Rudhyar.

ability to take a stand, exclusively his own. It is on that basis—also on the basis of what he possesses and of his social station in the city or kingdom—that he enters into relationship with other men, in terms of strictly associative relationships. The original "we" has changed into a possessive, and perhaps blatantly expressed "I." This ego— "I" in many cases no longer feels a relationship of identification with Nature in general. His relationship to a house or a field is more likely to be a possessive one: they belong to him. The matricial power of the land loses its intensity, though it remains as a sometimes unconscious compulsion, a kind of instinctual and even irrational biopsychic bondage; and today we still see such a bond very widespread all over the world.

The glorification of individualism came in the Mosaic revelation of the greatest Name of God: "I am that I am"—which I believe really means: I am the absolute fact of being "I"—"I" without my attribute —just "I." For Western man individuality is God's signature within him. He is an individual "by divine right"; a king in his own kingdom. But it soon becomes a lonely kingdom disturbed by constant feudal conflicts. Moses was perhaps the first "rugged individualist"; he also spoke with God "face to face as a man speaketh unto his friend." Then began what became known as a "dialogue" between God and man, between the personal I and the absolute Thou (cf. Buber's writings). Indeed the individual must be able to communicate with a divine absolutely and always reliable Thou, because he is no longer able to enter into relationship in the depths of his existence with other individuals—so alone and alienated from his fellowman has he become. Today LSD is taken by even more alienated young people in order to exercise their sense of ego, and to re-enter the lost Edenic state of unity with all—a return to Paradise, but alas artificial and dangerous paradises that present only relief perhaps, but no lasting ultimate solution to the tragic tensions of individual existence.

If the communal, unconscious and compulsive identification of tribesmen with the living and psychic wholeness of the tribe constituted the thesis of a dialectical process, and the pure, quasi-absolute individualism which has been an abstract ideal for many men in our theoretically "democratic" Western world is the antithesis, what kind of a synthesis can we then expect will emerge from our historical "Age of conflicts" when, or if, a New Age begins?

The phrase "unity in diversity" has been used by a number of thinkers working toward the ushering in of such a New Age whose motto would indeed be "synthesis." But such a phrase, however beautiful and hopeful it sounds, needs explanation; above all, it fails to take into consideration the most essential element in the situation. What is needed is a clear realization of the fact that unless men participating in this postulated New Age enter it as conscious "selves" and not only as "egos," there will be no New Age. The final WE-realization which represents the state of synthesis cannot emerge from human minds whose consciousness is structured by a rigid and closed ego, but only from human persons who have clearly realized that the very source and sustaining power of their total "field of existence" is the self, and whose egos have become utterly dedicated servants of the self—and therefore of humanity as a whole.[16]

. . . .

16.  On the distinction between ego and self, Rudhyar had written:

> The ego is that which structures the operation of the mind and, through the mind at its most instinctual level, the conscious feeling-responses of the person. . . . The formation and development of the ego have been conditioned and often almost entirely determined by family and social pressures, by school education, by imitative behavior often strengthened by a sense of dependence upon exemplars—the parents, friends, etc.— and a feeling of social or personal inferiority. Thus the ego has been called a "social construct." It remains bound to local factors of race, climate, culture, as long as mankind has not reached a global state of operation. . . .

When most people today speak of self—of myself and yourself, of "the self in transformation" (title of a book by Dr. Fingarette)—they are referring to the individual person whose consciousness is structured, i.e. defined and limited by an ego. When a person says "I was beside myself" he implies that whatever acted as "I" was really alien to the conscious field within which his ego normally rules, rejecting into the abyss of the subconscious (or personal unconscious, according to Carl Jung) feelings, thoughts and motivations that do not fit into this ego-controlled field of consciousness. The "I" of the normal human being speaks from the throne of the ego.

What I call self is something entirely different; though without the presence of the self vibrating through the total field of activity which constitutes the person-as-a-whole there could be no ego— simply because there would be no living organism. The self is the center of power in the whole organism; the ego is a structure of consciousness which is made possible by the integrating power of the self. But the ego is not the self.

. . .

Perhaps a more "subjective" approach will help us to see more clearly what these two levels represent.

. . . .

The basic problem here is not the emptying of what the normal ego-consciousness holds—its emotional and mental contents—but the transformation and indeed the dissolution of the container itself, viz. the consciousness in its formed, ego-structured condition as "mind." What should start the quest is not the will or desire to "reach" the pure condition of "I," but a readiness to do what Jung graphically called "relaxing the cramp in the conscious"—a readiness without expectation, and especially without the expectation of remaining conscious, at least not in the sense in which the ego has been conscious until then. The true inward quest should begin not only with the willingness to surrender the contents of the normal everyday ego-consciousness but in an attitude of non-attachment to the container of these contents.

. . . .

Let us try to indicate what such an inward quest might mean and lead to, if undertaken in such a spirit of total surrender—of container as well as of contents.

I am the adventurer. I close my eyes. I try to quiet down and still the surface-waves of sense-impressions, the emotional eddies and the currents of thought which affect my consciousness. Then I try to let go entirely, to forget that "I" exist, that anything exists. All is void. And yet . . . a heart beats, lungs expand and contract, motions are dimly felt. Through whatever is now sensed, there is a great peace—the silence of a calm ocean unmoved by winds. Within this silence, as it deepens, an awareness of quiet, rhythmic activity seems to arise. It may best be spoken of as a soundless "tone," a vibration of definite pitch, though it seems also to contain a myriad of overtones. What is this "tone"? It is so pure, so simple. It is; it so definitely, irrevocably "is"! It seems to spread through that great peace of which I am aware; but is there an "I" that is aware? Whatever is aware is implied in this "is-ness," in that undeniable fact—that tone, that peace, that no-whereness and nothingness that spreads everywhere. Yet it is centered. It is rhythmic, unperturbable movement; but so still, so pure!

A third phase (synthesis) is slowly emerging beyond the individualism of our theoretically "democratic" society. As the true character of this phase becomes clearer and more widely accepted—first within small groups, then more generally—a new basis for ethical valuation will be formulated; and it is even now gradually and tentatively taking form. I speak here of the ethics of wholeness; but the character of this future "wholeness" will be very different from that of the primitive wholes, i. e. the tribal communities. It will be essentially different because these new social wholes will be constituted by groups of individuals who, theoretically at least, will be conscious and self-determined individual persons operating at the level of Ideity (that is, of the conscious and creative individualized mind). These persons will have chosen as individuals to come together and to become integrated into a super-personal whole. We see today very interesting and promising attempts by young people gathering into "communes" in more or less remote places away from the anarchistic jungles of our cities; and this may be a small and uncertain beginning.

We shall presently discuss what is implied in this kind of group integration and show that it can only operate successfully if the Presence of the Principle of Wholeness, ONE, is not only recognized but made an essential, determining factor in the "commune"—and eventually in the entire planetary human society. Let me say at once that what this means is that the most central factor in the situation is the motivation of the individual to consciously and deliberately join such a communal whole. It is this motivation which must always make the essential difference between what we today call "democracy" and what I envision as the "holarchic" approach to the new type of social organization—the plenary society.

. . . .

. . . . The essential need in societies of individualized persons is to neutralize the centrifugal and aggressive tendency of the ego. In tribal societies whatever there was of centrifugal tendency in tribesmen could be neutralized by rituals which revivified the power of the common Root (the tribal god, the Great Ancestor) and made more evident the basic and factual participation of men, women and children in life-processes essential to the strength of the community —and these included sexual activities as well as agricultural festivals, dances for rain, etc.

While some of these ritualistic celebrations and festivals are still operative in societies of relatively individualized or individualizing

It is perhaps what men call "existence." Whose existence?

If the thought of such a question enters the consciousness, something changes. The feeling-experience is no longer the same. It becomes somehow limited, a little awkward, indeed "self-conscious" in the colloquial sense of this term. The conscious "I" has taken hold of the feeling and made it a conscious fact; it is then almost impossible to avoid comparing it with other experiences, formulating it in words—thus mentalizing it according to the language and the traditional concepts of my culture (or in terms of my revolt against these concepts and of my search for a more satisfying culture).

(*op. cit.*, 71–72, 77, 78–79).

ego-minds, the more essential purpose now is to present, as vividly as possible, to the feelings and the minds of individuals and of social groups of individuals the ideal of union—an ideal even more than a fact; a goal to be striven for with a feeling of more or less individual dedication. Such dedication is considered to be the responsibility —the free choice—of individuals, even if the contagious power of group interplay is also seen and used as a potent incentive to the "conversion" of the individual and as a strongly contributing factor in the steady operation of the spirit of dedication.

Such a spirit requires "faith." At the tribal pre-individual level there is, strictly speaking, no need of faith for the determining bio-psychic facts are evident to all. All that is necessary is to emphasize repeatedly this evidence through ceremonials in which the whole tribe participates at two levels, the outer group-level and the more occult field controlled by initiation. But in the societies where ego-differentiation and ego-conflicts are the evident facts of social life, where class fights against class and often ethnic group against ethnic group, what is needed is faith in the possibility of a future condition of unity. It is, in Christianity, faith in the "one God" and His factual incarnation in a divine-human personage whose life is a universal example to be "imitated" by all men, however diverse their racial origins and their egocentric propensities; and, in Buddhism, faith in the possibility of attaining a "state of consciousness" in which all individual differences cease or are absorbed—a possibility also demonstrated by one great Exemplar, Gautama, the Buddha.

In these societies in which the central preoccupation is how to deal with individual egos bent upon asserting their rights for independent action and minds increasingly eager to have their own opinions, morality has to be enforced by law, and rationality by strict practice and training or education. They must be enforced if the realization of the "collective interest" and of what is required for "collective survival," at the community or the national level, is not sufficient to produce social cohesion and wholesome group-operation in government, in business, in education and in sports. The basic and subtler aspect of enforcement is moral indoctrination; and at the more material level, propaganda and overt or hidden persuasion. All forms of persuasion appear legitimate. The individual has to be made to believe that his self-interest is to be seemingly unselfish in all interpersonal relationships.

What is called the Golden Rule as usually formulated: "Do not do to others what you do not want done to you," is a typical case of the kind of morality which is based on self-interest and is directed toward human beings who think and feel egocentrically as "individuals." It is indeed a sad reflection on the nature of a historical phase of the evolution of mankind and of human consciousness, because it implies that a man cannot base his action upon any broader and more inclusive concern than his own person, a concern for his own personal welfare. It implies that the realization that every human being is part of a "greater whole," humanity, is simply not any match for the selfcentered drives of ego-controlled individuals. Relationships are limited to the individual-to-individual type, actually ignoring the even more fundamental relationship of the individual to the whole—the whole of humanity. In the place of the individual-to-whole relationship religion pictures a purely ideal and transcendent relationship between a man and God—a mystical I-Thou relationship.

At the tribal stage of evolution (thesis) what happens to a particular person is entirely secondary to the effect the action may have on the tribe as a whole. We are now in the stage of antithesis at which individuals are the main concern in the ethical sphere—at least theoretically and excluding cases of so-called "national interest" or even of community welfare and health. The characteristic feature of such an evolutionary stage and of our modern more or less "democratic" societies is that, in fact, values relevant to the welfare of the collectivity are constantly in conflict with values referring to the "rights" of the individual. Such societies indeed represent transition stages of human development, and their existence characterizes what I have elsewhere called "the Age of Conflicts." The type of morality they believe in is a "morality of conflict." It is a morality which seeks constantly to effect a compromise between a concern for the individual and a concern, not really for the community, but for a particular condition of existence in the community, that is, for a traditional and institutionalized collective way of life. It is a morality based on the danger that would-be individuals still driven by life-urges cause to an unsteady type of society, always on the brink of possible chaos.

## FREEDOM OF CHOICE

The usual concept of morality in such societies of individuals in more or less constant conflict with each other—conflicts of personalities, conflicts of interest, conflicts of religions or ideological beliefs—rests on the belief that these individuals are free to choose between alternatives of conduct. Each individual it is said can make "free decisions," just because he is an individual in whom a God-created Soul or an essentially spiritual principle operates. He is free to choose between "right" and "wrong," "good" and "evil"—between moral and immoral ways of behavior. The moral issue may not refer to a particular act but rather to a generalized attitude from which a series of acts inevitably flows; but in any case man as an individual can choose; he has moral freedom and thus responsibility.

Thus stated, the issue seems fairly clear. Even an irreligious thinker like the French existentialist, Jean-Paul Sartre believes that "The human situation is to be defined as one of free choice without excuse and without assistance" (cf. L'EXISTENTIALISME EST UN HUMANISME). However when one looks at the actual facts of the social situation without emotionalism or traditional bias, and with a sense of historical objectivity, one should realize that the concept of freedom of choice and moral responsibility is a very ambiguous one. It is ambiguous because it simply does not question its most basic implication; that is, that every man is an "individual." It does not try to ascertain what it is that is supposedly able to make the choice —what it is that is "free."

We came upon such a situation when we discussed the real meaning of the little word, "I"; also with reference to the problem of reincarnation—the reincarnation of this mysterious "I." If there is no well-defined or at least relatively stable realization of being "I" there can be no moral choice, as we usually understand the term; and this fact has been accepted in our present-day legal system which absolves from moral responsibility and guilt a person judged insane or even temporarily insane, and at the time unable to distinguish between the moral value of his or her actions. The social community may protect itself from the danger of repetition of such a type of behavior and therefore can lock up the person or try to restore him to a "normal" condition of sanity; but this theoretically has nothing to do with moral guilt. The same type of protective behavior would apply to a person who has an incurable but highly contagious disease or who is a carrier of such a disease.

It is obviously very difficult to determine exactly where moral responsibility ceases in a person; and this is reflected in many famous criminal cases, like that of Sirhan Sirhan, who assassinated Robert Kennedy. What our society as a whole does not yet fully recognize is that the very concept of "being an individual" is a very relative and ambiguous one. It does not do so because it is still dominated by the Christian belief that every man has, or is, a God-created soul, and that this soul has the power to make free choices, except in cases of total insanity—which then implies that the soul has withdrawn from the body.

According to the holistic philosophy of evolution presented in this book, man at the first level of his evolution, what I call the "tribal" level, and also in his early years as a very young child cannot be considered an "individual"; he has only the potentiality of becoming an individual. He functions in the realm of "Life" where there is no individual freedom and instincts are compulsive forces. Intelligence, as the capacity to see that there are alternative possibilities of action, is not yet developed or only in a most rudimentary state completely dominated by the instinct for survival, a survival which usually tends to imply the need for aggressive acts. One can therefore not significantly speak of moral choice at that biological and generic level.

It is only when a human being is sufficiently individualized to pit his desires for power and for the possession of what he wants against the traditional ways of thinking and acting of his community that the possibility for that man to really "choose" begins. His moral choice is based on the co-existence of two opposite motives for action, and on the conflict between these motives. Morality, as the term is usually understood, therefore implies a situation of conflicts: individual against community.

In a sense of course the two principles, "individual" and "collective," always co-exist; again we have here a situation which can be symbolized by the cyclic interplay of the Chinese Yang and Yin. We stated that the principle of individuality is latent in the realm of Life; and that mind exists in a primitive condition in all living beings. But until the relationship between the two principles has reached a point of near-balance, the principle of individuality cannot assert itself with the character of moral responsibility because the human being is not sufficiently individualized to make really free choices.

In other words there can be no absolute state of moral responsibility any more than there can be absolute states of unity or multiplicity, and no absolute value to individualism or collectivism. It is always a question of more or less. And this "more or less" depends on the phase of cyclic development which has been reached by the individual and also by his society. There are periods in the cyclic interplay of the two polarities of existence (Yang and Yin) in which one of the two poles gains a definite and outwardly effectual domination over the other. There are periods of crisis in which a basic change occurs. There was one such period in the development of man's consciousness and man's social behavior when the old and long-lasting early tribal state was challenged by the self-assertive power of individuals. We are still living in such a period of evolutionary crisis. And the most actue phase of such a crisis is no doubt represented by the Hebraic-Christian tradition which has emphasized the sense of sin and guilt, and as a result the need for "atonement," divine or human.

. . . .

. . . . [S]elf is superseded by ego; and it is the ego that makes choices. It is the ego that seeks to assert itself, to protest against social regulations or religious ideals which seem to curtail its "freedom," i. e. which run counter to the ego's desires and fears. It is the ego that commits crimes or sins. Then also the ideal of a free society, "democracy," becomes perverted; it cannot work out, nor does it really make sense in a society of egos, by egos, and for the greatest glory of predatory and competitive egos.

In the mean time history has shown us various ways in which the power of the collectivity has sought to control, to minimize and also to guide, with the help of religious and moral exemplars, the growing challenge of individual egos to society. On the one hand society has imposed a system of laws and harsh punishments to try to force egocentric individuals to "choose" the traditional ways of behavior, and of thinking and feeling (family feelings, national feelings, etc.); on the other hand organized religion, as the "spiritual" side of the coin establishing a system of collective values, has sought to compel individuals "to be good" by evoking the imagery of after-death sanctions and speaking to the deepest feeling-needs of the faithful—the threat of excommunication as well as the dramatization of the great Exemplar, Jesus, stirring collective mass-emotions.

Now these social and religious means to impel and, if possible, to subtly compel individuals to make the correct choices are losing their efficacy. The "rugged individualism" of frontier days has given way to a strange combination of (1) intense eagerness to make "authentic" decisions which challenge the Establishment in all its forms: social, educational and religious; and (2) subservience to patterns of comfortable living imposed from the outside by "hidden persuaders," but also from the inside by the even more subtle pressures of psychological insecurity, neurotic reactions, and fear of losing all the "good things of life."

A tremendously complex industrial society and life in huge, monstrous cities make the choice between alternatives increasingly difficult and therefore the concepts of moral decisions more ambiguous or meaningless. It is for this reason that, on the one hand, society is developing the fantastic paraphernalia of research teams and projections into the future made by trained and supposedly objective specialists aided by computers; while on the other hand masses of distraught and uprooted individuals rush to clairvoyants, astrologers, and mediums, i. e. to anyone who might help make choices on the basis of some presumably transcendent kind of knowledge.

What else can the individual do? Only one thing: that is, to reach beyond egocentric and emotional or strictly intellectual "reasons" on which to base his moral decisions and in a state of ego-less attention and inner quietude and faith to "resonate" to the inner images and the promptings which arise in the Ideity-field of which this individual occupies the negative-receptive pole, while the Soul is the positive-active pole. This is what would provide a truly "individual" foundation for "moral" decisions. This is what, in terms of Hindu philosophy, would be to fulfill one's dharma, one's "truth of being." And evidently it is to such a possibility that European existentialists meant to refer when speaking of "authentic" acts; what Dr. Jacob Moreno, founder of Psychodrama and Group-therapy meant when he spoke long ago, with a kind of religious fervor, of "spontaneity and creativity," stressing that he meant by these terms more than they usually convey to our modern individuals so eager to express themselves.

But all these beautiful words—dharma-fulfillment, authenticity, spontaneity, creativity, self-actualization (Abraham Maslow), etc.— become not only empty, but masks for egocentricity and in some cases licence, if not chaos, when the actor is the ego instead of the true individual in whose person the power of the individualized "self" (as I defined this term) has been raised to consciousness and to the heart-center. Likewise the very concept of democracy can only be a rather sad and often bitter joke when the citizen, who is theoretically free, independent and "equal," is in fact an egocentric person unable to resist the pressures of "special interests" and indeed to make decisions arrived at in terms of their adequacy to the basic "truth" of the Soul-Image which seeks to find in him, the individual person, an agent for its embodiment.

What then is the next step ahead—the "synthesis" that would provide valid effective answers to the plight of a society which retains from the early archaic state of "thesis" only a materialized concept of collective power over individuals who, in turn, are led by the appetites of ever more brittle, more sadistic and above all more "alienated" egos, substituting for their true individual selves?

What is needed, fairly obviously, are two simultaneous approaches which in fact represent the two aspects of the same process of human evolution: the individual approach and the social approach. The first refers to the overcoming of the ego and a radical repolarization and transmutation of the energies of the Life-field in man; the second, to the formulation of new ideals, new archetypal Images of society. As society is simply the result of a process of organization of interpersonal and intergroup relationships, this second approach implies the acceptance and demonstration, even against the pressures of our transitional and cathartic era, of a new type of relationship, and especially of a new quality of relatedness.

The term "new" is of course not strictly accurate for, as we have already seen, this quality of relatedness has been extolled by the "Great Religions" of past millennia and demonstrated by a number of individual men and women seeking to attune their consciousness, their feelings and their actions to the great examples of the Buddha, Christ, St. Francis and numerous others. But as a Hindu proverb states: "A few drops of rain do not constitute the monsoon." The beautiful agape-love of a relatively few true Christian saints and their humble followers, and the "compassion" enshrined in the Bodhisattva ideals of Northern Buddhism, at best only herald the future and much longed-for New Age. Something more is needed: a vision of social living in which a totally new concept of society would call for and indeed make possible the world-wide spread of a new type of interpersonal relationships—relationships based on unpossessive love and the freedom to perform authentic acts in and through which the Soul-Images of the acting individuals would radiate and fulfill their planetary function, i. e. the individuals' dharma.

## E. R. DODDS

### THE GREEKS AND THE IRRATIONAL *

If future historians are to reach a more complete explanation [of the irrationalism which emerged in the Hellenistic period] . . . I think that, without ignoring either the intellectual or the economic factor, they will have to take account of another sort of motive, less conscious and less tidily rational. I have already suggested that behind the acceptance of astral determinism there lay, among other things, the fear of freedom—the unconscious flight from the heavy burden of individual choice which an open society lays upon its members. If such a motive is accepted as a *vera causa* (and there is pretty strong evidence that it is a *vera causa* to-day), we may suspect its operation in a good many places. We may suspect it in the hardening of philosophical speculation into quasi-religious dogma which provided the individual with an unchanging rule of life; in the dread of inconvenient research expressed even by a Cleanthes or an Epicurus; later, and on a more popular level, in the demand for a prophet or a scripture; and more generally, in the pathetic reverence for the written word characteristic of late Roman and mediaeval times—a readiness, as Nock puts it, "to accept statements because they were in books, or even because they were said to be in books."

* From 252–55 (U. of California Press 1951). With permission of The Regents of the University of California.

When a people has travelled as far towards the open society as the Greeks had by the third century B.C., such a retreat does not happen quickly or uniformly. Nor is it painless for the individual. For the refusal of responsibility in any sphere there is always a price to be paid, usually in the form of neurosis. And we may find collateral evidence that the fear of freedom is not a mere phrase in the increase of irrational anxieties and the striking manifestations of neurotic guilt-feeling observable in the later stages of the retreat. These things were not new in the religious experience of the Greeks: we encountered them in studying the Archaic Age. But the centuries of rationalism had weakened their social influence and thus, indirectly, their power over the individual. Now they show themselves in new forms and with a new intensity. I cannot here go into the evidence; but we can get some measure of the change by comparing the "Superstitious Man" of Theophrastus, who is hardly more than an old-fashioned observer of traditional taboos, with Plutarch's idea of a superstitious man as one who "sits in a public place clad in sackcloth or filthy rags, or wallows naked in the mire, proclaiming what he calls his sins." Plutarch's picture of religious neurosis can be amplified from a good many other sources: striking individual documents are Lucian's portrait of Peregrinus, who turned from his sins first to Christianity, then to pagan philosophy, and after a spectacular suicide became a miracle-working pagan saint; and the self-portrait of another interesting neurotic, Aelius Aristides. Again, the presence of a diffused anxiety among the masses shows itself clearly, not only in the reviving dread of portmortem punishments but in the more immediate terrors revealed by extant prayers and amulets. Pagan and Christian alike prayed in the later Imperial Age for protection against invisible perils—against the evil eye and daemonic possession, against "the deceiving demon" or "the headless dog." One emulet promises protection "against every malice of a frightening dream or of beings in the air"; a second, "against enemies, accusers, robbers, terrors, and apparitions in dreams"; a third—a Christian one—against "unclean spirits" hiding under your bed or in the rafters or even in the rubbish-pit. The Return of the Irrational was, as may be seen from these few examples, pretty complete.

There I must leave the problem. But I will not end this book without making a further confession. I have purposely been sparing in the use of modern parallels, for I know that such parallels mislead quite as often as they illuminate. But as a man cannot escape from his own shadow, so no generation can pass judgment on the problems of history without reference, conscious or unconscious, to its own problems. And I will not pretend to hide from the reader that in writing these chapters, and especially this last one, I have had our own situation constantly in mind. We too have witnessed the slow disintegration of an inherited conglomerate, starting among the educated class but now affecting the masses almost everywhere, yet still very far from complete. We too have experienced a great age of rationalism, marked by scientific advances beyond anything that earlier times had thought possible, and confronting mankind with the prospect of a society more open than any it has ever known.

And in the last forty years we have also experienced something else—
the unmistakeable symptoms of a recoil from that prospect. It would
appear that, in the words used recently by Andre Malraux, "Western
civilisation has begun to doubt its own credentials."

What is the meaning of this recoil, this doubt? Is it the hesitation before the jump, or the beginning of a panic flight? I do not
know. On such a matter a simple professor of Greek is in no position to offer an opinion. But he can do one thing. He can remind
his readers that once before a civilised people rode to this jump—
rode to it and refused it. And he can beg them to examine all the
circumstances of that refusal.

Was it the horse that refused, or the rider? That is really the
crucial question. Personally, I believe it was the horse—in other
words, those irrational elements in human nature which govern without our knowledge so much of our behaviour and so much of what
we think is our thinking. And if I am right about this, I can see
in it grounds for hope. As these chapters have, I trust, shown, the
men who created the first European rationalism were never—until
the Hellenistic Age—"mere" rationalists: that is to say, they were
deeply and imaginatively aware of the power, the wonder, and the
peril of the Irrational. But they could describe what went on below
the threshold of consciousness only in mythological or symbolic language; they had no instrument for understanding it, still less for
controlling it; and in the Hellenistic Age too many of them made
the fatal mistake of thinking they could ignore it. Modern man, on
the other hand, is beginning to acquire such an instrument. It is
still very far from perfect, nor is it always skilfully handled; in
many fields, including that of history, its possibilities and its limitations have still to be tested. Yet it seems to offer the hope that if
we use it wisely we shall eventually understand our horse better;
that, understanding him better, we shall be able by better training
to overcome his fears; and that through the overcoming of fear
horse and rider will one day take that decisive jump, and take it
successfully.

RICHARD E. SULLIVAN

## THE END OF THE "LONG RUN" *

### I

If, a thousand years from now, there still remains a civilized society interested in its past, the historians of that distant era will undoubtedly seek some explanation of the role and significance of the
20th century in the total stream of human history. Their evaluations
of this troubled era will probably be numerous. Already the analysts
of human behavior have begun to diverge in their generalizations concerning the fundamental nature of the 20th century. They speak in

* From 4 The Centennial Review of Arts     permission of Richard E. Sullivan and
and Sciences 391–408 (1960). With     The Centennial Review.

terms of the ethic of the "organization man," of the victory of "the rebel," of the plight of "the lonely crowd," and of "the revolt of the masses." Their estimates of the trends of this century suggest strongly that there is emerging a radical change in human outlook, capable of causing those looking back from the vantage point of a thousand years hence to conclude that the 20th century was the point of departure for a fundamental adjustment of human values.

However, after all manner of historians of the year 3000 A.D. have picked over the bones of the 20th century and pronounced their judgment of its place in the historical continuum, the consumate historian and artist—the Toynbee of the 31st century—will have his say. I suspect that he will disregard most of the trends that seem so world-shaking to us in the 1960's in favor of a very simple characterization of our century. He will say that this was the first century in world history when man ceased believing that time was working in favor of his deliverance. He will point out that during the 20th century all men were faced with the possibility that one twist of fate, one gesture, one ill-chosen word, one ill-conceived act could result in the annihilation of civilization and humanity. Once that fact had sunk into the mass consciousness, our 31st century Toynbee will say, then man could no longer explain his disposition to suffer evils on the ground that developments "in the long run" would remove them. Humanity could not longer depend on its ancient and respectable rationale for delaying the solution of problems, for condoning wickedness, for suffering tyranny, and for fending off danger-dependence on "the long run" developments which would remove the present source of discomfort.

Perhaps as an historian I am too sensitive about the phrase "the long run." I have heard my fellow historians use it to explain nearly everything across the whole spectrum of history. I have read repeatedly the works of scholars who went to the utmost pains to describe a problem that bedeviled a past generation and who then proceeded to say that "in the long run" this difficulty resolved itself because of the emergence of new factors and forces. One cannot be subjected to this experience hundreds of times without being seduced into the assumption that "the long run" is some kind of fourth dimensional force which intervenes in human affairs to resolve all problems automatically and painlessly, irrespective of how wisely or foolishly men may act at any given moment. Probably one could best define the historian as a disciple of the gospel of "the long run," meaning that his function is and has always been to assure people that time works in favor of the welfare of men. However, if the historian is the high priest of this cult, around him are legions of worshippers whose acts prove that they are the true believers. They go penniless to buy a car or a house with complete trust that in the long run they will find the wherewithall to pay for it. They sire children with genuine faith that the long run course of development will provide happiness for their offspring. They pour their best energies into the creation of some seemingly fantastic machine or organization that promises in the long run to benefit someone. With charming innocence they console the heartbroken with the advice that time has a way of solving everything. They even sacrifice their lives for a cause on the completely unprovable assumption that their immolation will benefit the future. Faith in the magic of "the long run" is seemingly as much a part of the human make-up as the brain or the liver.

So it has been since the beginning of human endeavor. A history of the world could be written around the theme of human reliance on the long run solution. It would leave little unaccounted for. Men have always been more content to wait for things to develop than to grapple with issues actively and immediately. They have been satisfied to suffer unspeakable indignities in the simple faith that eventually, "in the long run," their situation would be alleviated. The revolutionist, intent on acting *immediately* to relieve human misery, is actually a rare figure in human history, although in the past he sometimes has been presented as the prime mover in the historical process. He attracts so much attention, I believe, simply because he represents such a unique specimen in the totality of mankind, such an unusual departure from the norm. The real moving force in human history has been the trusting, essentially lazy, somewhat frightened, yet always optimistic man who was sure that, if he waited, cosmic justice would be done in his favor. So numerous has been his breed that "waiting for the long run developments" has always been a decisive factor in shaping human affairs.

## II

Skimming back across the ages will supply numerous examples to demonstrate the antiquity of the "long-run" interpretation of the working of destiny. Although he left posterity poorly informed about his mental processes, the most primitive Old Stone Age hunter probably found his greatest consolation during the lean season in the conviction that by waiting he would take his game; indeed the very method of his hunting emphasized the wisdom of waiting for nature to thrust her fruits on him in the form of an unsuspecting animal that wandered across his path by accident. Certainly by the time the great civilizations of the ancient Near East had emerged, men had surrendered to the long run point of view. Both Egyptian and Babylonian religious literature is replete with the spirit of calm resignation to the fact that the divinely ordained and controlled universe contained a safe refuge for puny man. . . .

Much more explicit were the Hebrew exponents of the idea that "in the fulness of time"—i. e., in the long run—all things would evolve toward perfection. The idea saturates the prophetic writings of the Old Testament. These writings were produced at a period in Hebrew history when, judged by the expectation of the chosen children of Yahweh, the future looked hopeless. The Hebrews had suffered division of their hard-won national kingdom, conquest at the hands of the vicious Assyrians and sinful Chaldeans, and mass deportation from their native soil and sacred temple to whorish Babylon. These tragedies were accompanied by a paralyzing religious confusion which took the form of extensive apostasy from Yahweh-worship. Yet listen to what the prophets cried in the midst of misery: "Come, my people, enter thou into thy chambers, and shut thy doors about thee: hide thyself as it were for a little moment, until the indignation is overpast." (Isaiah 26:20). How must the "little moment" be spent? "And the people shall be oppressed, everyone by another, and everyone by his neighbor: the child shall behave himself proudly against the ancient, and the base against the honourable." (Isaiah 3:5). "And they shall look unto the earth; and behold trouble and darkness, dimness of anguish; and they shall be driven to darkness." (Isaiah 8:22). But all that would pass. "Behold, the Lord God will come with strong hand . . . . He shall feed his flock like a shepherd." (Isaiah 40:10–11). "The ransomed of the Lord shall return, and come to Zion with songs and everlasting joy upon their heads: they shall obtain joy and gladness, and sorrow and sighing shall flee away." (Isaiah 35:10). How long Zion must wait and suffer the prophets never say. Yet waiting is the solution to the problem. In the fulness of time today's ills will be resolved by a cosmic force beyond man's control, yet working for his ultimate deliverance.

Greek thought reflected a similar easy confidence that things would unfold themselves for the good, no matter how dreadful the present might be. Who can forget the patiently waiting Penelope engaged in her senseless spinning amidst her greedy, too anxious suitors? Why did she not act to resolve her quandary? Because the operation of the universal order would bring back Ulysses. . . Socrates concludes on what is almost a triumphant note: "But we have sufficiently shown, in what has preceded, that all this, if only possible, is assuredly for the best." (*Republic*, VI, 502).

Christian thinkers caught up these many threads out of the ancient past to reassert a philosophy of history that assured all believers of the inevitable working out of things for the salvation of humanity. Their confident affirmations, made amid the disheartening spectacle of the collapse of the Roman Empire, the degeneration of Graeco-Roman moral values, and the onslaught of the barbarians, were unquestionably of major significance in unloosing the energy needed to establish a Christian civilization over much of Europe, western Asia, and northern Africa. St. Paul catalogued enough evidence of human iniquity to force a man with any sense of justice to the conclusion that humanity was damned. Yet he did not reach that conclusion. "For I reckon that the sufferings of this present time are not worthy to be compared to the glory which shall be revealed in us." (Romans 8:18) . . . .

### III

The passage of centuries and the flow of intellectual pursuits into new channels gradually eroded the basis of the old faith that in the long run all things work out for the best. Most of the hope of the ancients rested in their conviction that superhuman powers had ordained the ultimate perfection of man and the world. This premise eventually came under attack. The humanists of the Renaissance period doubted that man needed to depend on divinity for anything. Rationalists concluded to their own satisfaction that man possessed in his intellect a tool capable of elevating him to divine heights. Scientists discovered a method by which rational powers could be harnessed to the performance of feats surpassing the deeds of the gods. Slowly the proponents of these new schools of thought hacked to pieces the foundations of the old cosmic optimism upon which men found assurance that an almighty power would save everything if one would wait for that power to unfold its plans through time.

However, the revolt against God which, during the last four or five centuries, has rocked the foundations of the value system of western society has hardly disturbed the superstructure, man's happy confidence that things will work out for the best. If anything, faith in "the long run" grew as faith in the Almighty declined. New reasons have been discovered to assure men that *time* would advance all things toward perfection and resolve all the evils that press in upon humanity. God can now be neutral or even non-existent. For the rationalists of the Enlightenment, the key to perfection was education, that is, the process of unshackling man's innate rational powers. Education was a process requiring time, a leading out that occurred step by step. John Locke and his disciples assured the world that the ideal polity could be created by reasonable men entering a compact for that purpose; they need only discover the right moment "in the course of human events" to end forever the tyranny that had plagued unenlightened men. It remained for the scientists of the 19th century with their theory of evolution to formulate a surer guarantee of ultimate perfection than did all the powers of Osiris, Yahweh, or Zeus. Evolutionism was the doctrine of "the long run" *par excellence.* It applied not only to flowers, bugs, planets, and man the physical being; evolutionism became the basic premise for a whole new science: social science. Herbert Spencer defined the new creed in these words: "Whether it be in the development of the Earth, in the development of Life upon its surface, in the development of Society, of Government, of Manufactures, of Commerce, of Language, Literature, Science, Art, this same evolution of the simple into the complex, through successive differentiations, holds throughout. . . . Progress is not an accident but a necessity. What we call evil and immorality must disappear. It is certain that man must become perfect." . . .
. . . .

Now, at mid-20th century, we are face to face with an awesome fact. We no longer have the least assurance that the passage of time will resolve our difficulties, that either the plans of benign gods or the inexorable processes of nature or the wisdom of man are working for the perfection of the unwise and the imperfect. Anyone viewing the present objectively must conclude that man's ancient consoling faith in "the long run" is only an opiate, suspending its users in a fantastic world. Already some have put aside the pipe and, after the initial shock of abstinence, are beginning to discern the realities of the moment. The dimensions of the real situation are indeed monstrous and terrifying. For it is clear that nothing assures that civilization or even life itself will exist a millennium or a year or a minute hence. No one can live as if some force beyond human control assures a happy future unless he is willing to live in a dream world. All must eliminate any considerations of "the long run" from their calculations. For the first time in history, men must face the implications of living within a framework in which the future is a dubious quantity.

# TABLE OF CASES

The principal cases are in italic type. Cases cited or discussed are in roman type. References are to pages.

# TABLE OF BOOKS, ARTICLES AND OTHER SOURCES

References are to Pages

# INDEX

---

---

# University Casebook Series

January, 1979

---

**BUSINESS TORTS (1972)**

Milton Handler, Professor of Law Emeritus, Columbia University.

**CIVIL PROCEDURE, see Procedure**

**CLINIC, see also Lawyering Process**

**COMMERCIAL AND CONSUMER TRANSACTIONS, Second Edition (1978)**

William D. Warren, Dean of the School of Law, University of California, Los Angeles.
William E. Hogan, Professor of Law, Cornell University.
Robert L. Jordan, Professor of Law, University of California, Los Angeles.

**COMMERCIAL AND INVESTMENT PAPER, Third Edition (1964) with Statutory Materials**

The late Roscoe T. Steffen, Professor of Law, University of California, Hastings College of the Law.

**COMMERCIAL LAW, CASES & MATERIALS ON, Third Edition (1976)**

E. Allan Farnsworth, Professor of Law, Columbia University.
John Honnold, Professor of Law, University of Pennsylvania.

**COMMERCIAL PAPER, Second Edition (1976)**

E. Allan Farnsworth, Professor of Law, Columbia University.

**COMMERCIAL PAPER AND BANK DEPOSITS AND COLLECTIONS (1967) with Statutory Supplement**

William D. Hawkland, Professor of Law, University of Illinois.

**COMMERCIAL TRANSACTIONS—Text, Cases and Problems, Fourth Edition (1968)**

Robert Braucher, Professor of Law Emeritus, Harvard University, and
The late Arthur E. Sutherland, Jr., Professor of Law, Harvard University.

**COMPARATIVE LAW, Third Edition (1970)**

Rudolf B. Schlesinger, Professor of Law, Hastings College of the Law.

**COMPETITIVE PROCESS, LEGAL REGULATION OF THE, Second Edition (1979) with Statutory Supplement**

Edmund W. Kitch, Professor of Law, University of Chicago.
Harvey S. Perlman, Professor of Law, University of Virginia.

**CONFLICT OF LAWS, Seventh Edition (1978)**

Willis L. M. Reese, Professor of Law, Columbia University, and
Maurice Rosenberg, Professor of Law, Columbia University.

**CONSTITUTIONAL LAW, Fifth Edition (1977), with 1978 Supplement**

Edward L. Barrett, Jr., Professor of Law, University of California, Davis.

**CONSTITUTIONAL LAW, Ninth Edition (1975), with 1978 Supplement**

Gerald Gunther, Professor of Law, Stanford University.

**CONSTITUTIONAL LAW, INDIVIDUAL RIGHTS IN, Second Edition (1976), with 1978 Supplement**

Gerald Gunther, Professor of Law, Stanford University.

**CONTRACT LAW AND ITS APPLICATION, Second Edition (1977)**
> Addison Mueller, Professor of Law Emeritus, University of California, Los Angeles.
> Arthur I. Rosett, Professor of Law, University of California, Los Angeles.

**CONTRACT LAW, STUDIES IN, Second Edition (1977)**
> Edward J. Murphy, Professor of Law, University of Notre Dame.
> Richard E. Speidel, Professor of Law, University of Virginia.

**CONTRACTS, Third Edition (1977)**
> John P. Dawson, Professor of Law Emeritus, Harvard University, and
> William Burnett Harvey, Professor of Law and Political Science, Boston University.

**CONTRACTS, Second Edition (1972) with Statutory Supplement**
> E. Allan Farnsworth, Professor of Law, Columbia University.
> William F. Young, Jr., Professor of Law, Columbia University.
> Harry W. Jones, Professor of Law, Columbia University.

**CONTRACTS, Second Edition (1978) with Statutory and Administrative Law Supplement (1978)**
> Ian R. Macneil, Professor of Law, Cornell University.

**COPYRIGHT, Unfair Competition, and Other Topics Bearing on the Protection of Literary, Musical, and Artistic Works, Third Edition (1978)**
> Benjamin Kaplan, Professor of Law Emeritus, Harvard University, and
> Ralph S. Brown, Jr., Professor of Law, Yale University.

**CORPORATE FINANCE, Second Edition (1979)**
> Victor Brudney, Professor of Law, Harvard University.
> Marvin A. Chirelstein, Professor of Law, Yale University.

**CORPORATE READJUSTMENTS AND REORGANIZATIONS (1976)**
> Walter J. Blum, Professor of Law, University of Chicago.
> Stanley A. Kaplan, Professor of Law, University of Chicago.

**CORPORATION LAW, BASIC, Second Edition (1979) with Documentary Supplement**
> Detlev F. Vagts, Professor of Law, Harvard University.

**CORPORATIONS, Fourth Edition—Unabridged (1969) with 1977 Supplement and 1978 Special Supplement**
> William L. Cary, Professor of Law, Columbia University.

**CORPORATIONS, Fourth Edition—Abridged (1970) with 1977 Supplement and 1978 Special Supplement**
> William L. Cary, Professor of Law, Columbia University.

**CORPORATIONS, THE LAW OF:  WHAT CORPORATE LAWYERS DO (1976)**
> Jan G. Deutsch, Professor of Law, Yale University.
> Joseph J. Bianco, Professor of Law, Yeshiva University.

**CORPORATIONS COURSE GAME PLAN (1975)**
> David R. Herwitz, Professor of Law, Harvard University.

**CORPORATIONS, see also Enterprise Organization**

**CREDIT TRANSACTIONS AND CONSUMER PROTECTION (1976)**
> John Honnold, Professor of Law, University of Pennsylvania.

**CREDITORS' RIGHTS, Fifth Edition (1957)**

> The late John Hanna, Professor of Law Emeritus, Columbia University, and
> The late James Angell MacLachlan, Professor of Law Emeritus, Harvard
> University.

**CREDITORS' RIGHTS AND CORPORATE REORGANIZATION, Fifth Edition (1957)**

> The late John Hanna, Professor of Law Emeritus, Columbia University, and
> The late James Angell MacLachlan, Professor of Law Emeritus, Harvard
> University.

**CREDITORS' RIGHTS, see also Debtor-Creditor Law**

**CRIMINAL LAW (1973)**

> Fred E. Inbau, Professor of Law Emeritus, Northwestern University.
> James R. Thompson, Professor of Law Emeritus, Northwestern University.
> Andre A. Moenssens, Professor of Law, University of Richmond.

**CONSTITUTIONAL CRIMINAL PROCEDURE (1977)**

> James E. Scarboro, Professor of Law, University of Colorado.
> James B. White, Professor of Law, University of Chicago.

**CRIMINAL PROCEDURE (1974) with 1977 Supplement**

> Fred E. Inbau, Professor of Law Emeritus, Northwestern University.
> James R. Thompson, Professor of Law Emeritus, Northwestern University.
> James B. Haddad, Professor of Law, Northwestern University.
> James B. Zagel, Chief, Criminal Justice Division, Office of Attorney
> General of Illinois.
> Gary L. Starkman, Assistant U. S. Attorney, Northern District of Illinois.

**CRIMINAL JUSTICE, THE ADMINISTRATION OF, CASES AND MATERIALS ON, Second Edition (1969)**

> Francis C. Sullivan, Professor of Law, Louisiana State University.
> Paul Hardin III, Professor of Law, Duke University.
> John Huston, Professor of Law, University of Washington.
> Frank R. Lacy, Professor of Law, University of Oregon.
> Daniel E. Murray, Professor of Law, University of Miami.
> George W. Pugh, Professor of Law, Louisiana State University.

**CRIMINAL JUSTICE ADMINISTRATION AND RELATED PROCESSES, Successor Edition (1976), with 1978 Supplement**

> Frank W. Miller, Professor of Law, Washington University.
> Robert O. Dawson, Professor of Law, University of Texas.
> George E. Dix, Professor of Law, University of Texas.
> Raymond I. Parnas, Professor of Law, University of California, Davis.

**CRIMINAL LAW, Second Edition (1975)**

> Lloyd L. Weinreb, Professor of Law, Harvard University.

**CRIMINAL LAW AND ITS ADMINISTRATION (1940), with 1956 Supplement**

> The late Jerome Michael, Professor of Law, Columbia University, and
> Herbert Wechsler, Professor of Law, Columbia University.

**CRIMINAL LAW AND PROCEDURE, Fifth Edition (1977)**

> Rollin M. Perkins, Professor of Law Emeritus, University of California,
> Hastings College of the Law.
> Ronald N. Boyce, Professor of Law, University of Utah.

**CRIMINAL PROCESS, Third Edition (1978)**

> Lloyd L. Weinreb, Professor of Law, Harvard University.

**DAMAGES, Second Edition (1952)**

> The late Charles T. McCormick, Professor of Law, University of Texas, and
> The late William F. Fritz, Professor of Law, University of Texas.

**DEBTOR–CREDITOR LAW (1974) with 1978 (Case-Statutory Supplement**

> William D. Warren, Dean of the School of Law, University of California,
> Los Angeles.
> William E. Hogan, Professor of Law, Cornell University.

**DECEDENTS' ESTATES (1971)**

> The late Max Rheinstein, Professor of Law Emeritus, University of Chicago.
> Mary Ann Glendon, Professor of Law, Boston College Law School.

**DECEDENTS' ESTATES AND TRUSTS, Fifth Edition (1977)**

> John Ritchie III, Professor of Law Emeritus, University of Virginia.
> Neill H. Alford, Jr., Professor of Law, University of Virginia.
> Richard W. Effland, Professor of Law, Arizona State University.

**DECEDENTS' ESTATES AND TRUSTS (1968)**

> Howard R. Williams, Professor of Law, Stanford University.

**DOMESTIC RELATIONS, Third Edition (1978)**

> Walter Wadlington, Professor of Law, University of Virginia.
> Monrad G. Paulsen, Dean of the Law School, Yeshiva University.

**DOMESTIC RELATIONS, see also Family Law**

**DYNAMICS OF AMERICAN LAW, THE: Courts, the Legal Process and Freedom of Expression (1968)**

> Marc A. Franklin, Professor of Law, Stanford University.

**ELECTRONIC MASS MEDIA (1976) (paper back), with 1977 Supplement**

> William K. Jones, Professor of Law, Columbia University.

**ENTERPRISE ORGANIZATION, Second Edition (1977), with Statutory and Formulary Supplement (1979)**

> Alfred F. Conard, Professor of Law, University of Michigan.
> Robert L. Knauss, Dean of the School of Law, Vanderbilt University.
> Stanley Siegel, Professor of Law, University of California, Los Angeles.

**ENVIRONMENTAL PROTECTION, SELECTED LEGAL AND ECONOMIC ASPECTS OF (1971)**

> Charles J. Meyers, Dean of the Law School, Stanford University.
> A. Dan Tarlock, Professor of Law, Indiana University.

**EQUITY AND EQUITABLE REMEDIES (1975)**

> Edward D. Re, Adjunct Professor of Law, St. John's University.

**EQUITY, RESTITUTION AND DAMAGES, Second Edition (1974)**

> The late Robert Childres, Professor of Law, Northwestern University.
> William F. Johnson, Jr., Adjunct Professor of Law, New York University.

**ESTATE PLANNING PROBLEMS (1973) with 1977 Supplement**

> David Westfall, Professor of Law, Harvard University.

**ETHICS, see Legal Profession, also Professional Responsibility**

**EVIDENCE, Third Edition (1976)**

The late David W. Louisell, Professor of Law, University of California, Berkeley.

John Kaplan, Professor of Law, Stanford University.

Jon R. Waltz, Professor of Law, Northwestern University.

**EVIDENCE, Sixth Edition (1973) with 1976 Supplement**

The late John M. Maguire, Professor of Law Emeritus, Harvard University.

Jack B. Weinstein, Professor of Law, Columbia University.

James H. Chadbourn, Professor of Law, Harvard University.

John H. Mansfield, Professor of Law, Harvard University.

**EVIDENCE (1968)**

Francis C. Sullivan, Professor of Law, Louisiana State University.

Paul Hardin, III, Professor of Law, Duke University.

**FAMILY LAW, see also Domestic Relations**

**FAMILY LAW (1978)**

Judith C. Areen, Professor of Law, Georgetown University.

**FAMILY LAW: STATUTORY MATERIALS, Second Edition**

Monrad G. Paulsen, Dean of the Law School, Yeshiva University.

Walter Wadlington, Professor of Law, University of Virginia.

**FEDERAL COURTS, Sixth Edition (1976), with 1978 Supplement**

The late Charles T. McCormick, Professor of Law, University of Texas.

James H. Chadbourn, Professor of Law, Harvard University, and

Charles Alan Wright, Professor of Law, University of Texas.

**FEDERAL COURTS AND THE FEDERAL SYSTEM, Second Edition (1973) with 1977 Supplement**

The late Henry M. Hart, Jr., Professor of Law, Harvard University.

Herbert Wechsler, Professor of Law, Columbia University.

Paul M. Bator, Professor of Law, Harvard University.

Paul J. Mishkin, Professor of Law, University of California, Berkeley.

David L. Shapiro, Professor of Law, Harvard University.

**FEDERAL RULES OF CIVIL PROCEDURE, 1978 Edition**

**FEDERAL TAXATION, see Taxation**

**FUTURE INTERESTS AND ESTATE PLANNING (1961) with 1962 Supplement**

The late W. Barton Leach, Professor of Law, Harvard University, and

James K. Logan, formerly Dean of the Law School, University of Kansas.

**FUTURE INTERESTS (1958)**

The late Philip Mechem, Professor of Law Emeritus, University of Pennsylvania.

**FUTURE INTERESTS (1970)**

Howard R. Williams, Professor of Law, Stanford University.

**GOVERNMENT CONTRACTS, FEDERAL (1975)**

John W. Whelan, Professor of Law, Hastings College of the Law.

Robert S. Pasley, Professor of Law Emeritus, Cornell University.

**HOUSING (THE ILL-HOUSED) (1971)**

Peter W. Martin, Professor of Law, Cornell University.

**INJUNCTIONS (1972)**

Owen M. Fiss, Professor of Law, Yale University.

**INSTITUTIONAL INVESTORS, 1978**

David L. Ratner, Professor of Law, Cornell University.

**INSURANCE (1971)**

William F. Young, Professor of Law, Columbia University.

**INTERNATIONAL LAW, See also Transnational Legal Problems and United Nations Law**

**INTERNATIONAL LEGAL SYSTEM (1973) with Documentary Supplement**

Noyes E. Leech, Professor of Law, University of Pennsylvania.
Covey T. Oliver, Professor of Law, University of Pennsylvania.
Joseph Modeste Sweeney, Professor of Law, Tulane University.

**INTERNATIONAL TRADE AND INVESTMENT, REGULATION OF (1970)**

The late Carl H. Fulda, Professor of Law, University of Texas.
Warren F. Schwartz, Professor of Law, University of Virginia.

**INTERNATIONAL TRANSACTIONS AND RELATIONS (1960)**

Milton Katz, Professor of Law, Harvard University, and
Kingman Brewster, Jr., formerly President, Yale University.

**INTRODUCTION TO THE STUDY OF LAW (1970)**

E. Wayne Thode, Professor of Law, University of Utah.
J. Leon Lebowitz, Professor of Law, University of Texas.
Lester J. Mazor, Professor of Law, Hampshire College.

**INTRODUCTION TO LAW, see also Legal Method, also On Law in Courts, also Dynamics of American Law**

**JUDICIAL CODE: Rules of Procedure in the Federal Courts with Excerpts from the Criminal Code, 1978 Edition**

The late Henry M. Hart, Jr., Professor of Law, Harvard University, and
Herbert Wechsler, Professor of Law, Columbia University.

**JURISPRUDENCE (Temporary Edition Hard Bound) (1949)**

Lon L. Fuller, Professor of Law Emeritus, Harvard University.

**JUVENILE COURTS (1967)**

Hon. Orman W. Ketcham, Juvenile Court of the District of Columbia.
Monrad G. Paulsen, Dean of the Law School, Yeshiva University.

**JUVENILE JUSTICE PROCESS, Second Edition (1976)**

Frank W. Miller, Professor of Law, Washington University.
Robert O. Dawson, Professor of Law, University of Texas.
George E. Dix, Professor of Law, University of Texas.
Raymond I. Parnas, Professor of Law, University of California, Davis.

**LABOR LAW, Eighth Edition (1977) with Case and Statutory Supplements**

Archibald Cox, Professor of Law, Harvard University, and
Derek C. Bok, President, Harvard University.
Robert A. Gorman, Professor of Law, University of Pennsylvania.

**LABOR LAW (1968) with Statutory Supplement and 1974 Case Supplement**

Clyde W. Summers, Professor of Law, University of Pennsylvania.

Harry H. Wellington, Dean of the Law School, Yale University.

**LAND FINANCING, Second Edition (1977)**

Norman Penney, Professor of Law, Cornell University.

Richard F. Broude, of the California Bar.

**LAW, LANGUAGE AND ETHICS (1972)**

William R. Bishin, Professor of Law, University of Southern California.

Christopher D. Stone, Professor of Law, University of Southern California.

**LAWYERING PROCESS (1978) with Civil Problem Supplement and Criminal Problem Supplement**

Gary Bellow, Professor of Law, Harvard University.

Bea Moulton, Professor of Law, Arizona State University.

**LEGAL METHOD, Second Edition (1952)**

Noel T. Dowling, late Professor of Law, Columbia University,

The late Edwin W. Patterson, Professor of Law, Columbia University, and

Richard R. B. Powell, Professor of Law, University of California, Hastings College of the Law.

Second Edition by Harry W. Jones, Professor of Law, Columbia University.

**LEGAL METHODS (1969)**

Robert N. Covington, Professor of Law, Vanderbilt University.

The late E. Blythe Stason, Professor of Law, Vanderbilt University.

John W. Wade, Professor of Law, Vanderbilt University.

The late Elliott E. Cheatham, Professor of Law, Vanderbilt University.

Theodore A. Smedley, Professor of Law, Vanderbilt University.

**LEGAL PROFESSION (1970)**

Samuel D. Thurman, Dean of the College of Law, University of Utah.

Ellis L. Phillips, Jr., Member of the New York Bar.

The late Elliott E. Cheatham, Professor of Law, Vanderbilt University.

**LEGISLATIVE AND ADMINISTRATIVE PROCESSES (1976)**

Hans A. Linde, Professor of Law, University of Oregon.

George Bunn, Professor of Law, University of Wisconsin.

**LEGISLATION, Third Edition (1973)**

The late Horace E. Read, Vice President, Dalhousie University.

John W. MacDonald, Professor of Law Emeritus, Cornell Law School.

Jefferson B. Fordham, Professor of Law, University of Utah, and

William J. Pierce, Professor of Law, University of Michigan.

**LOCAL GOVERNMENT LAW, Revised Edition (1975)**

Jefferson B. Fordham, Professor of Law, University of Utah.

**MASS MEDIA LAW (1976)**

Marc A. Franklin, Professor of Law, Stanford University.

**MENTAL HEALTH PROCESS, Second Edition (1976)**

Frank W. Miller, Professor of Law, Washington University.

Robert O. Dawson, Professor of Law, University of Texas.

George E. Dix, Professor of Law, University of Texas.

Raymond I. Parnas, Professor of Law, University of California, Davis.

**MODERN REAL ESTATE TRANSACTIONS, Second Edition (1958)**

Allison Dunham, Professor of Law, University of Chicago.

**MUNICIPAL CORPORATIONS, see Local Government Law**

**NEGOTIABLE INSTRUMENTS, see Commercial Paper**

**NEW YORK PRACTICE, Fourth Edition (1978)**

Herbert Peterfreund, Professor of Law, New York University.
Joseph M. McLaughlin, Dean of the Law School, Fordham University.

**OIL AND GAS, Fourth Edition (1979)**

Howard R. Williams, Professor of Law, Stanford University,
Richard C. Maxwell, Professor of Law, University of California, Los Angeles, and
Charles J. Meyers, Dean of the Law School, Stanford University.

**ON LAW IN COURTS (1965)**

Paul J. Mishkin, Professor of Law, University of California, Berkeley.
Clarence Morris, Professor of Law Emeritus, University of Pennsylvania.

**OWNERSHIP AND DEVELOPMENT OF LAND (1965)**

Jan Krasnowiecki, Professor of Law, University of Pennsylvania.

**PARTNERSHIP PLANNING (1970) (Pamphlet)**

William L. Cary, Professor of Law, Columbia University.

**PATENT, TRADEMARK AND COPYRIGHT LAW (1959)**

E. Ernest Goldstein, Professor of Law, University of Texas.

**PERSPECTIVES ON THE LAWYER AS PLANNER (Reprint of Chapters One through Five of Planning by Lawyers) (1978)**

Louis M. Brown, Professor of Law, University of Southern California.
Edward A. Dauer, Professor of Law, Yale University.

**PLANNING BY LAWYERS, MATERIALS ON A NONADVERSARIAL LEGAL PROCESS (1978)**

Louis M. Brown, Professor of Law, University of Southern California.
Edward A. Dauer, Professor of Law, Yale University.

**PLEADING AND PROCEDURE, see Procedure, Civil**

**POLICE FUNCTION (1976) (Pamphlet)**

Chapters 1–11 of Miller, Dawson, Dix & Parnas' Criminal Justice Administration, Second Edition.

**PREVENTIVE LAW, see also Planning by Lawyers**

**PROCEDURE—Biography of a Legal Dispute (1968)**

Marc A. Franklin, Professor of Law, Stanford University.

**PROCEDURE—CIVIL PROCEDURE, Second Edition (1974)**

James H. Chadbourn, Professor of Law, Harvard University.
A. Leo Levin, Professor of Law, University of Pennsylvania.
Philip Shuchman, Professor of Law, University of Connecticut.

**PROCEDURE—CIVIL PROCEDURE, Fourth Edition (1978)**

The late Richard H. Field, Professor of Law, Harvard University.
Benjamin Kaplan, Professor of Law Emeritus, Harvard University.
Kevin M. Clermont, Professor of Law, Cornell University.

**PROCEDURE—CIVIL PROCEDURE, Third Edition (1976) with 1978 Supplement**

Maurice Rosenberg, Professor of Law, Columbia University.
Jack B. Weinstein, Professor, of Law, Columbia University.
Hans Smit, Professor of Law, Columbia University.
Harold L. Korn, Professor of Law, Columbia University.

**PROCEDURE—PLEADING AND PROCEDURE: State and Federal, Fourth Edition (1979)**

The late David W. Louisell, Professor of Law, University of California, Berkeley.
Geoffrey C. Hazard, Jr., Professor of Law, Yale University.

**PROCEDURE—FEDERAL RULES OF CIVIL PROCEDURE, 1978 Edition**

**PROCEDURE PORTFOLIO (1962)**

James H. Chadbourn, Professor of Law, Harvard University, and
A. Leo Levin, Professor of Law, University of Pennsylvania.

**PRODUCTS AND THE CONSUMER: DECEPTIVE PRACTICES (1972)**

W. Page Keeton, Professor of Law, University of Texas.
Marshall S. Shapo, Professor of Law, University of Virginia.

**PRODUCTS AND THE CONSUMER: DEFECTIVE AND DANGEROUS PRODUCTS (1970)**

W. Page Keeton, Professor of Law, University of Texas.
Marshall S. Shapo, Professor of Law, University of Virginia.

**PROFESSIONAL RESPONSIBILITY (1976) with 1978 Supplement and Special California Supplement**

Thomas D. Morgan, Professor of Law, University of Illinois.
Ronald D. Rotunda, Professor of Law, University of Illinois.

**PROPERTY, Fourth Edition (1978)**

John E. Cribbet, Dean of the Law School, University of Illinois.
Corwin W. Johnson, Professor of Law, University of Texas.

**PROPERTY—PERSONAL (1953)**

The late S. Kenneth Skolfield, Professor of Law Emeritus, Boston University.

**PROPERTY—PERSONAL, Third Edition (1954)**

The late Everett Fraser, Dean of the Law School Emeritus, University of Minnesota—Third Edition by
Charles W. Taintor II, late Professor of Law, University of Pittsburgh.

**PROPERTY—REAL—INTRODUCTION, Third Edition (1954)**

The late Everett Fraser, Dean of the Law School Emeritus, University of Minnesota.

**PROPERTY—REAL PROPERTY AND CONVEYANCING (1954)**

Edward E. Bade, late Professor of Law, University of Minnesota.

**PROPERTY, MODERN REAL, FUNDAMENTALS OF (1974) with 1978 Supplement**

Edward H. Rabin, Professor of Law, University of California, Davis.

**PROPERTY, REAL, PROBLEMS IN (Pamphlet) (1969)**

Edward H. Rabin, Professor of Law, University of California, Davis.

**PROSECUTION AND ADJUDICATION (1976) (Pamphlet)**

Chapters 12–16 of Miller, Dawson, Dix & Parnas' Criminal Justice Administration, Second Edition.

**PUBLIC UTILITY LAW, see Free Enterprise, also Regulated Industries**

**REAL ESTATE PLANNING (1974) with 1976 Problems and Statutory Supplement**
Norton L. Steuben, Professor of Law, University of Colorado.

**RECEIVERSHIP AND CORPORATE REORGANIZATION, see Creditors' Rights**

**REGULATED INDUSTRIES, Second Edition, 1976**
William K. Jones, Professor of Law, Columbia University.

**RESTITUTION, Second Edition (1966)**
John W. Wade, Professor of Law, Vanderbilt University.

**SALES AND SALES FINANCING, Fourth Edition (1976)**
John Honnold, Professor of Law, University of Pennsylvania.

**SECURITY, Third Edition (1959)**
The late John Hanna, Professor of Law Emeritus, Columbia University.

**SECURITIES REGULATION, Fourth Edition (1977) with 1978 Selected Statutes Supplement and 1978 Cases and Releases Supplement**
Richard W. Jennings, Professor of Law, University of California, Berkeley.
Harold Marsh, Jr., Member of the California Bar.

**SENTENCING AND THE CORRECTIONAL PROCESS, Second Edition (1976)**
Frank W. Miller, Professor of Law, Washington University.
Robert O. Dawson, Professor of Law, University of Texas.
George E. Dix, Professor of Law, University of Texas.
Raymond I. Parnas, Professor of Law, University of California, Davis.

**SOCIAL WELFARE AND THE INDIVIDUAL (1971)**
Robert J. Levy, Professor of Law, University of Minnesota.
Thomas P. Lewis, Dean of the College of Law, University of Kentucky.
Peter W. Martin, Professor of Law, Cornell University.

**TAX, POLICY ANALYSIS OF THE FEDERAL INCOME (1976)**
William A. Klein, Professor of Law, University of California, Los Angeles.

**TAXATION, FEDERAL INCOME (1976) with 1977 Supplement**
Erwin N. Griswold, Dean Emeritus, Harvard Law School.
Michael J. Graetz, Professor of Law, University of Virginia.

**TAXATION, FEDERAL INCOME, Second Edition (1977)**
James J. Freeland, Professor of Law, University of Florida.
Stephen A. Lind, Professor of Law, University of Florida.
Richard B. Stephens, Professor of Law Emeritus, University of Florida.

**TAXATION, FEDERAL INCOME, Volume I, Personal Tax (1972) with 1979 Supplement; Volume II, Corporate and Partnership Taxation (1973)**
Stanley S. Surrey, Professor of Law, Harvard University.
William C. Warren, Professor of Law Emeritus, Columbia University.
Paul R. McDaniel, Professor of Law, Boston College Law School.
Hugh J. Ault, Professor of Law, Boston College Law School.

**TAXATION, FEDERAL WEALTH TRANSFER (1977)**

Stanley S. Surrey, Professor of Law, Harvard University.
William C. Warren, Professor of Law Emeritus, Columbia University, and
Paul R. McDaniel, Professor of Law, Boston College Law School.
Harry L. Gutman, Instructor, Harvard Law School and Boston College Law
School.

**TAXES AND FINANCE—STATE AND LOCAL (1974)**

Oliver Oldman, Professor of Law, Harvard University.
Ferdinand P. Schoettle, Professor of Law, University of Minnesota.

**TORT LAW AND ALTERNATIVES: INJURIES AND REMEDIES, Second Edition (1979)**

Marc A. Franklin, Professor of Law, Stanford University.

**TORTS, Third Edition (1976)**

The late Harry Shulman, Dean of the Law School, Yale University.
Fleming James, Jr., Professor of Law Emeritus, Yale University.
Oscar S. Gray, Professor of Law, University of Maryland.

**TORTS, Sixth Edition (1976)**

The late William L. Prosser, Professor of Law, University of California,
Hastings College of the Law.
John W. Wade, Professor of Law, Vanderbilt University.
Victor E. Schwartz, Professor of Law, University of Cincinnati.

**TRADE REGULATION (1975) with 1977 Supplement**

Milton Handler, Professor of Law Emeritus, Columbia University.
Harlan M. Blake, Professor of Law, Columbia University.
Robert Pitofsky, Professor of Law, Georgetown University.
Harvey J. Goldschmid, Professor of Law, Columbia University.

**TRADE REGULATION, see Antitrust**

**TRANSNATIONAL LEGAL PROBLEMS, Second Edition (1976) with Documentary Supplement**

Henry J. Steiner, Professor of Law, Harvard University.
Detlev F. Vagts, Professor of Law, Harvard University.

**TRIAL, see also Lawyering Process**

**TRIAL ADVOCACY (1968)**

A. Leo Levin, Professor of Law, University of Pennsylvania.
Harold Cramer, Esq., Member of the Philadelphia Bar, (Maurice Rosenberg, Professor of Law, Columbia University, as consultant).

**TRUSTS, Fifth Edition (1978)**

The late George G. Bogert, James Parker Hall, Professor of Law Emeritus,
University of Chicago.
Dallin H. Oaks, President, Brigham Young University.

**TRUSTS AND SUCCESSION (Palmer's), Third Edition (1978)**

Richard V. Wellman, Professor of Law, University of Georgia.
Lawrence W. Waggoner, Professor of Law, University of Michigan.
Olin L. Browder, Jr., Professor of Law, University of Michigan.

**UNFAIR COMPETITION, see Competitive Process and Business Torts**

**UNITED NATIONS IN ACTION (1968)**

Louis B. Sohn, Professor of Law, Harvard University.

**UNITED NATIONS LAW, Second Edition (1967) with Documentary Supplement (1968)**

Louis B. Sohn, Professor of Law, Harvard University.

**WATER RESOURCE MANAGEMENT (1971) with 1973 Supplement**

Charles J. Meyers, Dean of the Law School, Stanford University.
A. Dan Tarlock, Professor of Law, Indiana University.

**WILLS AND ADMINISTRATION, 5th Edition (1961)**

The late Philip Mechem, Professor of Law, University of Pennsylvania, and
The late Thomas E. Atkinson, Professor of Law, New York University.

**WORLD LAW, see United Nations Law**

END OF VOLUME